Applications of Sociology's Major Theoretical Approaches

Sociology provides comprehensive coverage of the major sociological perspectives. The summary table below includes a sample of the topics in this text that have been explored using these approaches. The numbers in parentheses indicate the pertinent chapters.

FUNCTIONALIST PERSPECTIVE

Defined and explained (1)
Adoption (12)
AIDS and social networks (5)
Anomie theory of deviance (8)
Bilingualism (3)
Bureaucratization of schools (13)
Culture (3, 13)
Davis and Moore's view of stratification (9)
Disengagement theory of aging (11)
Dominant ideology (3)
Durkheim's view of deviance (8)
Dysfunctions of racism (10)
Electronic surveillance (16)
Ethnocentrism (3)
Family (12)
Formal organizations (6)
Gans's functions of poverty (9)
Gay marriage (12)
Gender stratification (11)
Health and illness (15)
Human ecology (14)
Immigration (10)
In-groups and out-groups (6)
Integrative function of religion (13)
Internet (16)
Media and social norms (7)
Media and socialization (7)
Media and status conferral (7)
Media promotion of consumption (7)
Multinational corporations (9)
Narcotizing effect of the media (7)
Racial prejudice and discrimination (10)
Social change (13, 16)
Social control (8, 13)
Social institutions (5)
Social networks (5)
Socialization in schools (4, 13)
Sports (1)
Subcultures (3)
Urban ecology (15)
Value neutrality (2)

CONFLICT PERSPECTIVE

Defined and explained (1)
Abortion (11)
Access to health care (15)
Access to technology (16)
Adoption (12)
Affirmative action (14)
Age stratification (11)
AIDS crisis (5)
Bilingualism (3)
Bureaucratization of schools (13)
Capitalism (13, 14)
Corporate welfare (9)
Correspondence principle (13)
Credentialism (13)
Culture (3)
Day care funding (4)
Deviance (8)
Disability as a master status (5)
Domestic violence (12)
Dominant ideology (3, 7, 9)
Downsizing (14)
Elite model of the U.S. power structure (14)
Environmental issues (14)
Ethnocentrism (3)
Exploitation theory of racial subordination (10)
Family (12)
Gay marriage (12)
Gender stratification (11)
Gender equity in education (13)
Gun control (8)
Hidden curriculum (13)
Immigration (10)
Iron Law of Oligarchy (6)
Labor unions (6)
Marx's view of stratification (9)
Media gatekeeping (7)
Media stereotypes (7)
Media violence (7)
Medicalization of society (15)
Model minority (10)
Multinational corporations (9)
New urban sociology (15)
Poverty (9)
Privacy and technology (16)
Racial profiling (10)
Racism and health (15)
Religion and social control (13)
Social change (16)
Social control (8)
Social institutions (5)
Sports (1)
Subcultures (3)
Tracking (13)
Victimless crimes (8)
White-collar crime (8)
World systems analysis (9, 15)

INTERACTIONIST PERSPECTIVE

Defined and explained (1)
Activity theory of aging (11)
Affirmative action (14)
AIDS and its impact (5)
Charismatic authority (14)
Conspicuous consumption (9)
Contact hypothesis (10)
Differential association (8)
Dramaturgical approach (4, 14)
Electronic communication (7, 16)
Family (12)
Gay marriage (12)
Gender stratification (11)
Health and illness (15)
Human relations approach (6)
Media violence (7)
Negotiated order (5)
Privacy and technology (7, 16)
Racial stereotyping (10)
Routine activities theory (8)
School prayer (13)
Small groups (6)
Social institutions (5)
Sports (1)
Tattoo symbols of 9/11 (1)
Teacher-expectancy effect (13)
Teenage pregnancy (12)
Unions (6)

FEMINIST PERSPECTIVE

Defined and explained (1)
Day care funding (4)
Domestic violence (12)
Dominant ideology (3)
Ethnographic research (2)
Family (12)
Gender stratification (11)
Language (3)
Media stereotypes (7)
Media violence (7)
Pornography (7)
Rape (8)
Sports (1)
Victimless crimes (8)
Women in public (1)

LABELING THEORY

Defined and explained (8)
AIDS and labeling (5, 15)
Disabilities and labeling (5)
Health and illness (15)
Presentation of the self (4)
Racial profiling (10)
Societal reaction approach (8)
Teacher-expectancy effect (13)
Victimless crimes (8)

B9LT-6LAK-7DFO-PPWE-3Z8U

REGISTRATION CODE
REGISTRATION CODE
REGISTRATION CODE

The McGraw-Hill Companies

Mc
Graw
Hill
Higher Education

IMPORTANT

HERE IS YOUR REGISTRATION CODE TO ACCESS MCGRAW-HILL PREMIUM CONTENT AND MCGRAW-HILL ONLINE RESOURCES

For key premium online resources you need THIS CODE to gain access. Once the code is entered, you will be able to use the web resources for the length of your course.

Access is provided only if you have purchased a new book.

If the registration code is missing from this book, the registration screen on our website, and within your WebCT or Blackboard course will tell you how to obtain your new code. Your registration code can be used only once to establish access. It is not transferable.

To gain access to these online resources

1. **USE** your web browser to go to: www.mhhe.com/schaefer6

2. **CLICK** on "First Time User"

3. **ENTER** the Registration Code printed on the tear-off bookmark on the left

4. After you have entered your registration code, click on "Register"

5. **FOLLOW** the instructions to setup your personal UserID and Password

6. **WRITE** your UserID and Password down for future reference. Keep it in a safe place.

If your course is using WebCT or Blackboard, you'll be able to use this code to access the McGraw-Hill content within your instructor's online course.

To gain access to the McGraw-Hill content in your instructor's WebCT or Blackboard course simply log into the course with the user ID and Password provided by your instructor. Enter the registration code exactly as it appears to the right when prompted by the system. You will only need to use this code the first time you click on McGraw-Hill content.

These instructions are specifically for student access. Instructors are not required to register via the above instructions.

The McGraw-Hill Companies

Mc Graw Hill **Higher Education**

Thank you, and welcome to your McGraw-Hill Online Resources.

ISBN 0-07-296169-4 SCHAEFER: SOCIOLOGY: A BRIEF INTRODUCTION, 6/E

Enjoy your complimentary copy of *Contexts*, the American Sociological Association's groundbreaking magazine, free with new copies of *Sociology: A Brief Introduction, Sixth Edition* by Richard Schaefer

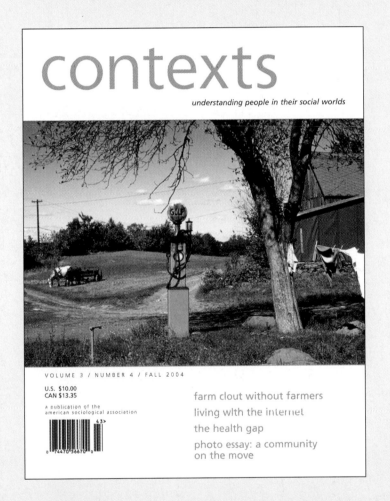

contexts

understanding people in their social worlds

VOLUME 3 / NUMBER 4 / FALL 2004

U.S. $10.00
CAN $13.35

a publication of the
american sociological association

farm clout without farmers

living with the internet

the health gap

photo essay: a community
on the move

Contexts: Understanding People in Their Social Worlds

Sociology Around the World

The countries that are identified on this map are cited in the book, either in the context of research studies or in relevant statistical data. Refer to the subject index for specific page references.

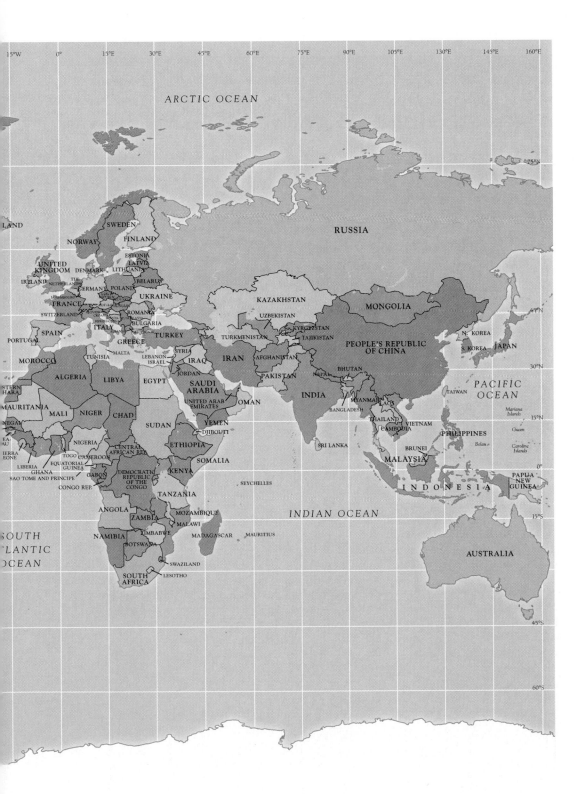

ARCTIC OCEAN

RUSSIA

SWEDEN

NORWAY   FINLAND

                ESTONIA
UNITED   LATVIA
KINGDOM   DENMARK   LITHUANIA
IRELAND   NETHERLANDS   BELARUS
          GERMANY   POLAND
FRANCE   UKRAINE   KAZAKHSTAN   MONGOLIA
SWITZERLAND   ROMANIA   N. KOREA
                          BULGARIA   UZBEKISTAN   KYRGYZSTAN   S. KOREA JAPAN
SPAIN   ITALY   TAJIKISTAN   PEOPLE'S REPUBLIC
PORTUGAL   GREECE   TURKEY   TURKMENISTAN   OF CHINA
                    MALTA   SYRIA   TAIWAN
MOROCCO   TUNISIA   LEBANON IRAQ   IRAN   AFGHANISTAN   BHUTAN   PACIFIC
                        ISRAEL   OCEAN
          ALGERIA   LIBYA   JORDAN   PAKISTAN   NEPAL   30°N
WESTERN   EGYPT   SAUDI   MYANMAR LAOS
HARA   ARABIA   INDIA   Mariana
MAURITANIA   UNITED ARAB OMAN   BANGLADESH   THAILAND   Islands   15°N
          MALI   NIGER   CHAD   EMIRATES   Guam
NEGAL   YEMEN   SRI LANKA   CAMBODIA VIETNAM   PHILIPPINES
EA   SUDAN   DJIBOUTI   Belau   Caroline
AU   NIGERIA   BRUNEI   Islands
SIERRA   TOGO CAMEROON   CENTRAL   ETHIOPIA   MALAYSIA   0°
LEONE   EQUATORIAL   AFRICAN REB.   PAPUA
LIBERIA   GUINEA   GABON   SOMALIA   INDONESIA   NEW
GHANA   DEMOCRATIC   KENYA   GUINEA
SAO TOME AND PRINCIPE   REPUBLIC
          CONGO REP.   OF THE
                          CONGO   TANZANIA   SEYCHELLES
                                                                    INDIAN OCEAN   AUSTRALIA
          ANGOLA   MOZAMBIQUE
                ZAMBIA   MALAWI
SOUTH   ZIMBABWE
ATLANTIC   NAMIBIA   MADAGASCAR   MAURITIUS
OCEAN   BOTSWANA
                          SWAZILAND
          SOUTH   LESOTHO
          AFRICA

15°N 75°N 45°N 30°N 15°N 0° 15°S 45°S 60°S

15°W 0° 15°E 30°E 45°E 60°E 75°E 90°E 105°E 130°E 145°E 160°E

About the Author

Taking Sociology To Work

www.
mhhe.com
/schaefer6

RICHARD T. SCHAEFER: Professor, DePaul University
B.A. Northwestern University
M.A., Ph.D. University of Chicago

Growing up in Chicago at a time when neighborhoods were going through transitions in ethnic and racial composition, Richard T. Schaefer found himself increasingly intrigued by what was happening, how people were reacting, and how these changes were affecting neighborhoods and people's jobs. His interest in social issues caused him to gravitate to sociology courses at Northwestern University, where he eventually received a B.A. in sociology.

"Originally as an undergraduate I thought I would go on to law school and become a lawyer. But after taking a few sociology courses, I found myself wanting to learn more about what sociologists studied, and fascinated by the kinds of questions they raised." This fascination led him to obtain his M.A. and Ph.D. in sociology from the University of Chicago. Dr. Schaefer's continuing interest in race relations led him to write his master's thesis on the membership of the Ku Klux Klan and his doctoral thesis on racial prejudice and race relations in Great Britain.

Dr. Schaefer went on to become a professor of sociology, and now teaches at DePaul University in Chicago. In 2004 he was named to the Vincent DePaul professorship in recognition of his undergraduate teaching and scholarship. He has taught introductory sociology for over 30 years to students in colleges, adult education programs, nursing programs, and even a maximum-security prison. Dr. Schaefer's love of teaching is apparent in his interaction with his students. "I find myself constantly learning from the students who are in my classes and from reading what they write. Their insights into the material we read or current events that we discuss often become part of future course material and sometimes even find their way into my writing."

Dr. Schaefer is author of the ninth edition of *Sociology* (McGraw-Hill, 2005) and of *Sociology Matters* (McGraw-Hill, 2004). Dr. Schaefer is also the author of *Racial and Ethnic Groups*, now in its tenth edition, and *Race and Ethnicity in the United States*, third edition. His articles and book reviews have appeared in many journals, including *American Journal of Sociology; Phylon: A Review of Race and Culture; Contemporary Sociology; Sociology and Social Research; Sociological Quarterly*; and *Teaching Sociology*. He served as president of the Midwest Sociological Society in 1994–1995.

Dr. Schaefer's advice to students is to "look at the material and make connections to your own life and experiences. Sociology will make you a more attentive observer of how people in groups interact and function. It will also make you more aware of people's different needs and interests—and perhaps more ready to work for the common good, while still recognizing the individuality of each person."

SIXTH EDITION

SOCIOLOGY
A Brief Introduction

Richard T. Schaefer
DePaul University

Boston   Burr Ridge, IL   Dubuque, IA   Madison, WI   New York   San Francisco   St. Louis
Bangkok   Bogotá   Caracas   Kuala Lumpur   Lisbon   London   Madrid   Mexico City
Milan   Montreal   New Delhi   Santiago   Seoul   Singapore   Sydney   Taipei   Toronto

Dedication

To my son, Peter

 Higher Education

SOCIOLOGY: A BRIEF INTRODUCTION, SIXTH EDITION
Published by McGraw-Hill, a business unit of The McGraw-Hill Companies, Inc., 1221 Avenue of the Americas, New York, NY, 10020. Copyright © 2006, 2004, 2002, 2000, 1997, 1994 by The McGraw-Hill Companies, Inc. All rights reserved. No part of this publication may be reproduced or distributed in any form or by any means, or stored in a database or retrieval system, without the prior written consent of The McGraw-Hill Companies, Inc., including, but not limited to, in any network or other electronic storage or transmission, or broadcast for distance learning.
Some ancillaries, including electronic and print components, may not be available to customers outside the United States.

This book is printed on acid-free paper.

1 2 3 4 5 6 7 8 9 0 DOW/DOW 0 9 8 7 6 5 4

ISBN   0-07-296158-9 (student edition)
ISBN   0-07-296161-9 (annotated instructor's edition)

Publisher: *Phillip A. Butcher*
Sponsoring editor: *Sherith H. Pankratz*
Director of development and media technology: *Rhona Robbin*
Senior marketing manager: *Daniel M. Loch*
Producer, media technology: *Jessica Bodie Richards*
Senior project manager: *Diane M. Folliard*
Senior production supervisor: *Carol A. Bielski*
Design manager: *Laurie J. Entringer*
Lead media project manager: *Marc Mattson*
Photo research coordinator: *Nora Agbayani*
Art editor: *Emma C. Ghiselli*
Photo researchers: *PhotoSearch, Inc.*
Cover and interior design: *Kiera Pohl*
Cover credit: *Diana Ong/SuperStock*
Typeface: *10/12 Minion*
Compositor: *Prographics*
Printer: *Quebecor World Versailles*

Library of Congress Cataloging-in-Publication Data

Schaefer, Richard T.
    Sociology: a brief introduction/Richard T. Schaefer.— 6th, annotated instructor's ed.
        p. cm
    Includes bibliographical references and index.
        ISBN 0-07-296158-9 (softcover : alk. paper) — ISBN 0-07-296161-9 (AIE : alk. paper)
        1. Sociology. 2. United States—Social conditions—1980- I. Title. I.
HM585.S324 2006
301—dc22
2004055973

www.mhhe.com

Contents in Brief

Contents

1
UNDERSTANDING SOCIOLOGY   1

2
SOCIOLOGICAL RESEARCH   27

x Contents

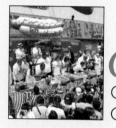

6 GROUPS AND ORGANIZATIONS 128

7 THE MASS MEDIA 150

8 DEVIANCE AND SOCIAL CONTROL 172

14
GOVERNMENT, THE
ECONOMY, AND THE
ENVIRONMENT   359

15
POPULATION,
COMMUNITIES, AND
HEALTH   388

16
SOCIAL MOVEMENTS, SOCIAL CHANGE, AND TECHNOLOGY   423

Chapter-Opening Excerpts

Every chapter in this textbook begins with an excerpt from one of the works listed below. These excerpts convey the excitement and relevance of sociological inquiry and draw readers into the subject matter for each chapter.

Boxed Features and Photo Essays

Taking Sociology To Work

Photo Essays

Social Policy Sections

Maps and Summing Up Tables

Mapping Life Nationwide

Mapping Life Worldwide

summingUP Tables

Preface

Without a doubt, you have thought about sociological issues before opening this book. Have you or a childhood friend ever spent time in day care? Are your parents or a friend's parents divorced? Do you know someone who owns a gun? Is plagiarism a problem on your campus? Have you participated in an antiwar protest? Chances are you have been touched by most or all of these issues. If you are like most students, you've also spent a great deal of time thinking about your future career. If you major in sociology, what occupations can you choose from?

These are just some of the topics of immediate personal interest that are dealt with in this book. Sociologists also address broader issues, from bilingual education to the existence of slavery in the 21st century. Sociology includes the study of immigration, homelessness, overpopulation, and the process and problems of growing old in different cultures. In the aftermath of September 11, 2001, sociology has been called on to explain the social consequences of the attacks—how people coped following the disasters, how they reacted to minority group members. These issues, along with many others, are of great interest to me, but it is the sociological explanations for them that I find especially compelling. The introductory sociology class provides the ideal laboratory in which to study our own society and those of our global neighbors.

After more than 30 years of teaching sociology to students in colleges, adult education programs, nursing programs, an overseas program based in London, and even a maximum-security prison, I am firmly convinced that the discipline can play a valuable role in teaching critical thinking skills. Sociology can help students to better understand the workings of their own lives as well as of their society and other cultures. The distinctive emphasis on social policy found in this text shows students how to use the sociological imagination in examining such public policy issues as sexual harassment, the AIDS crisis, welfare reform, the death penalty, and privacy and censorship in an electronic age.

My hope is that through their reading of this book, students will begin to think like sociologists and will be able to use sociological theories and concepts in evaluating human interactions and institutions. From the introduction of the concept of sociological imagination in Chapter 1—which draws on C. Wright Mills's analysis of divorce as a societal concern—this text stresses the distinctive way in which sociologists examine and question even the most familiar patterns of social behavior.

The first nine editions of *Sociology* have been well received; the book is currently used in more than 500 colleges and universities. But some instructors have sought a more concise view of the discipline that would permit them to assign additional material or projects. This brief introduction to sociology was developed to meet that need. *Sociology: A Brief Introduction,* Sixth Edition, brings the research into the 21st century and introduces a number of features designed to appeal to today's students. One thing that remains unchanged, however, is the steady focus on three especially important points:

- **Comprehensive and balanced coverage of theoretical perspectives throughout the text.** Chapter 1 introduces, defines, and contrasts the functionalist, conflict, and interactionist perspectives. We explore these distinctive views of such topics as social institutions (Chapter 5), deviance (Chapter 8), the family (Chapter 12), education (Chapter 13), and health (Chapter 15). In addition, the feminist perspective is introduced in Chapter 1. Other theoretical approaches particular to certain topics are presented in later chapters.
- **Strong coverage of issues pertaining to gender, age, race, ethnicity, and class in all chapters.** Examples of such coverage include social policy sections on bilingualism (Chapter 3), welfare (Chapter 9), immigration (Chapter 10), and affirmative action (Chapter 14); a chapter opener on the "beauty myth" (Chapter 11); boxes on urban

poverty and joblessness (Chapter 9), prejudice against Arab Americans and Muslim Americans (Chapter 10), and domestic violence (Chapter 12); and sections on the social construction of race (Chapter 10) and gender equity in education (Chapter 13).

- **Integrated coverage of cross-cultural and global material throughout the text.** Chapter 9 treats the topic of stratification from a global perspective. This chapter introduces world systems analysis and dependency theory, and examines multinational corporations and the global economy. Every chapter presents global material and makes use of cross-cultural examples. Among the topics examined are:

  The controversy over the ban on Muslim headscarves in French public schools (Chapter 4)

  The global "McDonaldization of society" (Chapter 6)

  The status of women around the world (Chapter 11)

  Issues of aging around the world (Chapter 11)

  Transmission of cultural values through education (Chapter 13)

  Affirmative action in Malaysia and Brazil (Chapter 14)

  Population policy in China (Chapter 15)

  Global social change (Chapter 16)

I take great care to introduce the basic concepts and research methods of sociology and to reinforce this material in all chapters. The most recent data are included, making this book more current than all previous editions.

SPECIAL FEATURES

Integrated Learning System

The text, its accompanying CD-ROM, *Reel Society* 2.0, and the Online Learning Center website work together as an integrated learning system to bring the theories, research findings, and basic concepts of sociology to life for students. Offering a combination of print, multimedia, and web-based materials, this comprehensive system meets the needs of instructors and students with a variety of teaching and learning styles. The material that follows describes the many features of the text, CD-ROM, and Online Learning Center, as well as the supplementary materials that support those resources.

Poster Art

Each chapter opens with a reproduction of a poster or piece of graphic art that illustrates a key theme or concept of the chapter. Accompanying captions help readers to grasp the relevance of the artwork to the chapter.

Chapter-Opening Excerpts

The chapter-opening passages convey the excitement and relevance of sociological inquiry by means of lively excerpts from writings of sociologists and others who explore sociological topics. These openers are designed to expose students to vivid writing on a broad range of topics and to stimulate their sociological imaginations. For example, Chapter 1 opens with Barbara Ehrenreich's account of her experiment in survival as a low-wage worker, drawn from her best-selling book *Nickel and Dimed*. Chapter 3 begins with J. A. English-Lueck's sketch of a typical morning for an immigrant software engineer in California's multicultural Silicon Valley. Chapter 5 opens with a description of Philip Zimbardo's now-classic mock prison study. And in the opening to Chapter 16, Howard Rheingold connects the fall of President Joseph Estrada of the Philippines to the invention of text messaging.

Chapter Overview

The chapter-opening excerpt is followed by a chapter overview that provides a bridge between the excerpt and the chapter content. In addition, the overview poses questions and describes the content of the chapter in narrative form.

Key Terms

I have given careful attention to presenting understandable and accurate definitions of each key term. These terms are highlighted in bold italics when they are introduced. A list of key terms and definitions—with page references—follows the end of each chapter. In addition, the glossary at the end of the book includes the definitions of the textbook's key terms and the page references for each term.

Research in Action

These sections present sociological findings on topics such as divorce, political apathy among young people, and prejudice against Arab Americans and Muslim Americans.

Sociology in the Global Community

These sections provide a global perspective on topics such as aging, domestic violence, and the "offshoring" of service jobs.

Social Inequality

These sections illustrate various types of social stratification. Featured topics include discretionary justice, the Latino middle class, and the "stained glass ceiling" that hovers over female clergy.

Taking Sociology to Work

These sections profile individuals who majored in sociology and use its principles in their work. While these people are employed in a variety of occupations and professions, they share a conviction that their background in sociology has been valuable in their careers.

Sociology on Campus

New to this edition, these sections apply the sociological perspective to issues of immediate interest to today's students. Title IX, plagiarism, and antiwar protests are among the featured topics.

Use Your Sociological Imagination

In the spirit of C. Wright Mills, these short, thought-provoking sections encourage students to apply the sociological concepts they have learned to the world around them. Through open-ended "what-if" questions, students step into the shoes of researchers, famous sociologists, and people of other cultures and generations.

Illustrations

The photographs, cartoons, figures, and tables are closely linked to the themes of the chapters. The maps, titled Mapping Life Nationwide and Mapping Life Worldwide, show the prevalence of social trends. A world map highlighting those countries used as examples in the text appears on pages ii–iii.

Think About It

Selected tables and figures include stimulating questions that prompt students to interpret the data and think about their deeper meaning. Students search for trends in the data, wonder about the underlying reasons for the trends, and apply the implications to their own lives.

Photo Essays

Six photo essays—three of them new—enliven the text. Each begins with a question that is intended to prompt students to see some part of everyday life with new eyes—those of a sociologist. For instance, the essay in Chapter 1 asks "Are You What You Own?" and the essay in Chapter 8 asks "Who Is Deviant?" The photos and captions that follow suggest the answer to the question.

Social Policy Sections

The social policy sections that close all but one of the chapters play a critical role in helping students to think like sociologists. They apply sociological principles and theories to important social and political issues being debated by policymakers and the general public. New to this edition are sections on gun control (Chapter 8), gay marriage (Chapter 12), and financing health care (Chapter 15). All the social policy sections now present a global perspective. All close with a postscript called "Getting Involved," which directs students who are interested in the issue to the Online Learning Center. There they will find a list of relevant websites, as well as survey data on U.S. public opinion regarding the issue.

Cross Reference Icons

When the text discussion refers to a concept introduced earlier in the book, an icon in the margin points the reader to the exact page.

Chapter Summaries

Each chapter includes a brief numbered summary to aid students in reviewing the important themes.

Critical Thinking Questions

After the summary, each chapter includes critical thinking questions that will help students analyze the social world in which they participate. Critical thinking is an essential element in the sociological imagination.

Key Terms

Each chapter includes a list of key terms and their definitions. For ease of use, the definitions are followed by cross-references to the text discussions where the terms are first mentioned.

Internet Connection Exercises

Exercises in each chapter take students online to analyze social issues relevant to chapter topics. Throughout the text an icon signals where more information and/or updates are available on the book's website.

Online Learning Center with PowerWeb

These sections give students and instructors an overview of the wide array of resources available on the website that accompanies this book.

Reel Society Interactive Movie CD-ROM 2.0

These sections identify scenes on the CD that pertain to relevant topics in each chapter.

Inside Covers

The inside front cover showcases several components of the Online Learning Center. The page facing the inside front cover presents a table that summarizes the book's applications of sociology's major theoretical perspectives. The inside back cover features a visual guide to the *Reel Society* Interactive Movie CD-ROM 2.0. The page facing the inside back cover highlights the book's coverage of race and ethnicity, gender, and social class.

WHAT'S NEW IN THE SIXTH EDITION?

The most important changes in this edition include the following (refer as well to the chapter-by-chapter list of changes on pages xxiv–xxvii and to the *Visual Preview* on pages xxxi–xxxvi):

Content

- Three new case studies provide a closer look at the social worlds of three different countries, illustrating the impact of globalization on each. In Chapter 9, "Stratification in Mexico" discusses the economic importance of the "migradollars" Mexican immigrants to the United States send home to their families. In Chapter 13, "Religion in India" takes a closer look at several religions and their role in Indian politics. In Chapter 14, "Capitalism in China" describes China's transition from managed socialism to a more open system that embraces free enterprise and investment by multinational corporations. Another short case study, "Bureaucracy and

the Space Shuttle *Columbia,*" illustrates the dangers of bureaucratic decision making in Chapter 6.
- "Sociology on Campus" boxes apply the sociological perspective to several issues of immediate interest to today's students.
- A new section in Chapter 14, "War and Peace," examines war and terrorism as means of resolving international conflicts through the exertion of power. The section describes the governmental decision-making process that precedes a declaration of war in the United States, and traces the evolution of U.S. public opinion on war and the changing composition of the U.S. military. It also considers potential deterrents to war, including international trade and the activities of nongovernmental organizations (NGOs).
- Three new chapter-opening excerpts, drawn from sociological writings, convey the excitement and relevance of sociological inquiry: *Cultures@silicon valley* by J. A. English-Lueck (Chapter 3), *No Shame in My Game* by Katherine S. Newman (Chapter 9), and *Smart Mobs* by Howard Rheingold (Chapter 16).
- Material in several chapters provides a sociological analysis of the aftermath of September 11, 2001. Topics covered include the impact of regime change in Iraq and other countries, continuing distrust of Muslim and Arab Americans, and the issue of the individual's right to privacy versus government's need for intelligence on terrorist activities.

Pedagogy

- Twenty Summing Up tables help to pull together coverage of the major theoretical perspectives.
- Seven new U.S. maps illustrate important sociological trends and developments.
- At the end of every social policy section, a new feature, "Getting Involved," directs interested students to the Online Learning Center, where they will find a list of relevant websites and survey data on U.S. public opinion regarding the featured issue.

Supplements

- *Reel Society* Interactive Movie CD-ROM 2.0 Available on request as a separate package option with *Sociology: A Brief Introduction*, Sixth Edition, *Reel Society* 2.0 is a two-CD-ROM video set designed to demonstrate key topics in sociology through episodes typical of campus life. Featuring almost two hours of video, *Reel Society* 2.0 includes all the footage from *Reel Society* 1.0 plus new video involving additional characters and episodes. These movie scenes are augmented by a robust array of review, assessment, and reporting features.

Students can follow the storyline from start to finish using "Story Mode" or choose only those scenes that apply to a given chapter or topic with "Study Mode." In either case, they can take advantage of several review and assessment features, including explanatory screens, a glossary, self-quizzes, and homework assignments. The "Scorecard" feature tracks a student's completion of CD-ROM assignments and reports it to the instructor using e-mail and print features. Additional activities and assignments are found on the *Reel Society* website (**www.mhhe.com/reelsociety**).

Instructors receive their own version of the CD, which allows them to set the viewing options and choose the displayed assignments. A detailed 75-page Instructor's Manual (available on the Instructor's Resource CD-ROM) helps instructors to integrate *Reel Society* 2.0 into their courses. Test questions related to the movie can also be found on the Instructor's Resource CD.

- **New Online Learning Center** This website features interactive quizzes; video clips with accompanying essay questions; interactive maps; three interactive games (Name That Sociologist, What Perspective Am I? and What Concept Am I?); diagnostic midterm and final exams; Getting Involved: annotated links to sites of organizations that study or take a position on policy issues discussed in the text; links to additional information about the chapter-opening excerpts and their authors; and SurveyTutor, software that allows students to construct and electronically disseminate their own polls for class research projects.
- **New NBC Lecture Launcher Videotape, Vol. 3** This 60-minute VHS videotape features brief clips (3–8 minutes each) from *NBC News* and the *Today Show* that dramatize sociological concepts, serve as lecture launchers, and generate class discussion. This videotape is accompanied by a guide that is available on the Online Learning Center website (**www.mhhe.com/schaefer6**).

This edition has been thoroughly updated. It includes the most recent data and research findings from the Census Bureau, Bureau of Labor Statistics, Current Population Reports, the Population Reference Bureau, the World Bank, the United Nations Development Programme, and the Centers for Disease Control. A more complete, chapter-by-chapter listing of the most significant new material in this edition follows.

WHAT'S NEW IN EACH CHAPTER?

Chapter 1: Understanding Sociology

- Expanded, reader-friendly introduction to the definition of sociology
- New examples of the sociological imagination
- Discussion of approaches to the death penalty in different social sciences
- Discussion (in the interactionist section) of tattoo symbols of the terrorist attacks of September 11, 2001
- Discussion of how sociologists' research can influence public policy decisions

Chapter 2: Sociological Research

- Chapter-opening poster: "There Are Still Traditional Families"
- Research in Action box: "Polling in Baghdad," with photo
- Sociology on Campus box: "Does Hard Work Lead to Better Grades?"
- Taking Sociology to Work box: "Dave Eberbach, Research Coordinator, United Way of Central Iowa"
- Section on the ethics of research funding
- Discussion of experimental research on the effectiveness of treatment programs for men charged repeatedly with domestic assault
- Two-part Mapping Life Nationwide map: "Educational Levels and Household Income in the United States"
- Summing Up table: "Major Research Designs"
- Updated social policy section on the study of human sexuality, with discussions of (*a*) recent attempts to deny funding for NIH research on sexuality and (*b*) changing sexual behavior in China

Chapter 3: Culture

- Chapter-opening excerpt from *Cultures@Silicon Valley* by J. A. English-Lueck
- Photo essay: "Are You What You Eat?"
- Sociology on Campus box: "A Culture of Cheating?"
- Discussion of the trend toward observance of Christmas in non-Christian societies as an example of globalization
- Expanded section on nonverbal communication, with examples of cultural differences in touching and hand signals

- Expanded section on acceptance of norms, with discussion of security searches in postwar Iraq as a violation of norms governing touching
- Discussion of the Phishhead subculture
- Expanded section on ethnocentrism, with discussion of how cultural differences between Americans and Iraqis have complicated U.S. efforts at democratic reform
- Summing Up table: "Major Theoretical Perspectives on Culture"

Chapter 4: Socialization

- Discussion of the controversy over Muslim headscarves in French schools as an example of children's use of symbolic communication, with photo
- Summing Up table: "Theoretical Approaches to Development of the Self"
- Expanded discussion of the life course approach, including table, "Milestones in the Transition to Adulthood"
- Discussion of the gender gap in technological training
- Discussion of gender differences in high school students' paths to popularity
- Updated discussion of children's exposure to television and the Internet

Chapter 5: Social Interaction and Social Structure

- Photo essay: "Why Do We Gather Together?"
- Revised Research in Action box: "Social Networks among Low-Income Women"
- Discussion of *diwaniyas*, traditional Kuwaiti men's groups
- Updated discussion of electronic networking among U.S. soldiers and their families
- Section on Durkheim's concepts of mechanical and organic solidarity
- Thoroughly updated social policy section on the AIDS crisis, including discussion of the claim that medical regimens "wouldn't work" in Africa

Chapter 6: Groups and Organizations

- Chapter-opening excerpt from the Revised New Century Edition of George Ritzer's *McDonaldization of Society*
- Section on focus groups
- Sociology in the Global Community box: "Amway the Chinese Way"

- Figure: "Membership in Voluntary Associations in the United States" (pie graph)
- Section on organizational restructuring, with photo
- Case study: "Bureaucracy and the Space Shuttle *Columbia*," with photo
- Revised social policy section, "The State of the Unions," including discussion of the establishment of the Department of Homeland Security, with attendant restrictions on unionization and collective bargaining

Chapter 7: The Mass Media

- Figure showing recent changes in media usage
- Discussion of the controversial role of the media as an agent of religious socialization in India
- Discussion of the status conferral function of Internet searches
- Section on the promotion of consumption as a media function
- Discussion of the increase in local TV programming in other nations
- Discussion of the feminist perspective on pornography
- Updated Sociology in the Global Community box: "Al Jazeera Is on the Air," with discussion of new U.S. government-sponsored satellite network, Al Hurra
- Updated Social Policy section: "Media Violence"

Chapter 8: Deviance and Social Control

- Figure: "Catching Music Thieves"
- Mapping Life Nationwide map: "The Status of Medical Marijuana"
- Sociology on Campus box: "Binge Drinking"
- Figure: "Race and the Death Penalty," in Social Inequality box on discretionary justice
- Summing Up table: "Approaches to Deviance"
- Social Policy section: "Gun Control"

Chapter 9: Stratification in the United States and Worldwide

- Chapter-opening excerpt from Katherine S. Newman, *No Shame in My Game*
- Sociology in the Global Community box: "Under Pressure: The Caste System in India"
- Section on the estate system

- Section on the interactionist view of stratification (Thorstein Veblen, conspicuous consumption and conspicuous leisure)
- Summing Up table: "Major Perspectives on Social Stratification"
- Case study on stratification in Mexico
- Updated social policy section on welfare in North America and Europe

Chapter 10: Racial and Ethnic Inequality

- Updated discussion of hate crimes
- Updated Research in Action box, "Prejudice against Arab Americans and Muslim Americans"
- Discussion of new experiment on racial discrimination by prospective employers
- Section on the privileges of the dominant
- Discussion of discriminatory effects of the Aviation and Transportation Security Act
- New Taking Sociology to Work box: "Prudence Hannis, Researcher and Community Activist, Quebec Native Women"
- Discussion of racial profiling
- Updated Social Policy section, "Global Immigration"

Chapter 11: Stratification by Gender and Age

- Sociology in the Global Community box: Aging Worldwide: Issues and Consequences
- Discussion of stay-at-home fathers
- Discussion of men who pursue nontraditional occupations (preschool teacher, nurse)
- Discussion of males' underperformance in school
- Research in Action box: "Gender Differences in Physicians' Communication with Patients"
- Discussion of the *glass escalator* (rapid promotion of men in female-dominated occupations)
- Discussion of Senate Subcommittee on Aging's panel on media portrayal of older people
- Discussion of apparent countertrend in age discrimination
- Revised social policy section on abortion

Chapter 12: The Family and Intimate Relationships

- Additional examples of families around the globe
- Discussion of households in which women earn more money than their husbands

- Summing Up table: "Sociological Perspectives on the Family"
- Discussion of Navajo families
- Photo essay: "What Is a Family?"
- Discussion of foster children
- Discussion of recent increase in the divorce rate in South Korea
- Discussion of frequency of cohabitation among racial and ethnic groups
- Discussion of the Healthy Marriage Initiative
- Social Policy section: "Gay Marriage"

Chapter 13: Religion and Education

- Photo essay: "Why Do Sociologists Study Religion?"
- Summing Up table: "Major World Religions"
- Social Inequality box: "The Stained Glass Ceiling"
- Summing Up table: "Sociological Perspectives on Religion"
- Case study: "Religion in India"
- Discussion of the legacy of *Brown v. Board of Education*
- Discussion of the importance of educating girls in developing nations
- Sociology on Campus box: "The Debate over Title IX"
- Summing Up table: "Sociological Perspectives on Education"
- Section on homeschooling
- Updated social policy section, "Religion in the Schools"

Chapter 14: Government, the Economy, and the Environment

- Discussion of the destabilizing effect of increased demand for the metal coltan on the Democratic Republic of the Congo
- Section: "The Informal Economy"
- Case study: "Capitalism in China"
- Extension of Weber's conceptualization of power to globalization and the rise of multinational corporations
- Discussion of the interlocking membership of the boards of directors, Fortune 1,000 corporations
- Research in Action box: "Why Don't Young People Vote?"
- Section: "War, Peace, and Terrorism," with figure and photo
- Taking Sociology to Work box: "Richard J. Hawk, Vice President and Financial Consultant, Smith Barney"

- Sociology in the Global Community box: "Off-shoring Service Jobs"
- Updated discussion of the environmental implications of consumerism in North America and Europe
- Discussion of new study on the relationship between siting of environmental hazards and segregation in nearby schools
- Updated social policy section on affirmative action, including discussions of (a) the Supreme Court decision on the University of Michigan programs and (b) affirmative action programs in other countries, including Malaysia and Brazil

Chapter 15: Population, Communities, and Health

- Taking Sociology to Work box: "Kelsie Lenor Wilson-Dorsett, Deputy Director, Department of Statistics, Government of Bahamas"
- Sociology in the Global Community box: "Population Policy in China"
- Section on asset-based community development (ABCD)
- Discussion of the arrival of big-city problems in rural communities
- Discussion of the interactionist perspective on how medical students learn to play the role of physician

Chapter 16: Social Movements, Social Change, and Technology

- Chapter-opening poster: "Eternal life can be reached through cloning technology!"
- Chapter-opening excerpt from Howard Rheingold, *Smart Mobs*
- Sociology on Campus box: "Antiwar Protests"
- Summing Up table: "Contributions to Social Movement Theory"
- Discussion of biotechnology as a manifestation of the medicalization of society
- Discussion of sex selection in connection with in vitro fertilization
- Research in Action box: "The Human Genome Project"
- Condensed and updated social policy section on privacy and censorship, including (a) new opening on electronic surveillance, (b) discussion of the habituation of young people to online surveillance, and (c) discussion of the Patriot Act.

SUPPORT FOR INSTRUCTORS AND STUDENTS

PRINT RESOURCES

Annotated Instructor's Edition

An annotated instructor's edition (AIE) of the text, prepared by Rebecca Matthews of the University of Iowa, offers page-by-page annotations to assist instructors in using textbook material.

Study Guide

The study guide, prepared by Rebecca Matthews, includes standard features such as detailed key points, definitions of key terms, multiple-choice questions, fill-in questions, and true–false questions. All study guide questions are keyed to specific pages in the textbook, and page references are provided for key points and definitions of key terms.

In addition to the questions in the study guide, students can test their mastery of the subject matter by taking the quizzes on the *Reel Society* CD-ROM and on the Online Learning Center website. Students therefore have three different sets of questions to draw on for review.

Primis Customized Readers

An array of first-rate readings are available to adopters in a customized electronic database. Some are classic articles from the sociological literature; others are provocative pieces written especially for McGraw-Hill by leading sociologists.

McGraw-Hill Dushkin

Any of the Dushkin publications can be packaged with this text at a discount: Annual Editions, Taking Sides, Sources, Global Studies. For more information, please visit the website at **www.dushkin.com**.

Digital and Video Resources

VHS Videotapes

Three VHS videotapes (one 90 minutes and two 60 minutes long) feature brief clips (3–8 minutes each) from *NBC News* and the *Today Show* that dramatize sociological concepts, serve as lecture launchers, and generate class discussion. Each is accompanied by a guide that is available on the Online Learning Center website (**www.mhhe.com/schaefer6**).

eInstruction: The Classroom Performance System

The Classroom Performance System (CPS) is a wireless response system that allows instructors to receive immediate feedback from students. CPS units include easy-to-use software for instructors' use in creating questions and assessments and delivering them to students. The units also include individual wireless response pads for students' use in responding. Suggested questions, prepared by Rebecca Matthews of the University of Iowa, appear on the Instructor's Edition of the Schaefer website, **www.mhhe. com/schaefer6**. CPS also runs alongside the PowerPoint slides that supplement Schaefer's *Sociology*. For further details, go to **www.mhhe.com/einstruction.**

PageOut: The Course Website Development Center

All online content for *Sociology,* Sixth Edition, is supported by WebCT, eCollege.com, Blackboard, and other course management systems. Additionally, McGraw-Hill's PageOut service is available to get you and your course up and running online in a matter of hours, at no cost. PageOut was designed for instructors just beginning to explore web options. Even the novice computer user can create a course website with a template provided by McGraw-Hill (no programming knowledge necessary). To learn more, ask your McGraw-Hill representative for details, or visit **www.mhhe.com/pageout.**

Reel Society *Interactive Movie CD-ROM 2.0*

 Available on request as a separate package option with *Sociology: A Brief Introduction,* Sixth Edition, *Reel Society* 2.0 is a two-CD-ROM video set (with an accompanying guidebook) designed to demonstrate key topics in sociology through episodes typical of campus life. Featuring two hours of video, *Reel Society* 2.0 includes all the footage from *Reel Society* 1.0 plus new video involving additional characters and episodes. These movie scenes are augmented by a robust array of review, assessment, and reporting features.

Reel Society 2.0 is built around the learning objectives of a typical introductory sociology course. Students explore a variety of key sociological concepts and perspectives firsthand, including the conflict, functionalist, and interactionist perspectives, stratification, social mobility, the family, education, religion, and politics.

Students can follow the storyline from start to finish using "Story Mode" or choose only those scenes that apply to a given chapter or topic with "Study Mode." In either case, they can take advantage of several review and assessment features, including explanatory screens, a glossary, self-quizzes, and homework assignments. The "Scorecard" feature tracks a student's completion of CD-ROM assignments and reports it to the instructor using e-mail and print features. Additional activities and assignments are found on the *Reel Society* website (**www. mhhe.com/reelsociety**).

Instructors receive their own version of the CD, which allows them to set the viewing options and choose the displayed assignments. A detailed 75-page Instructor's Manual (available on the Instructor's Resource CD-ROM) helps instructors to integrate *Reel Society* 2.0 into their courses. Test questions related to the movie can also be found on the Instructor's Resource CD.

John Tenuto of College of Lake County (in Illinois) served as the academic consultant throughout the development of *Reel Society* 1.0. The script for *Reel Society* 1.0 was reviewed by the following instructors: Jan Abu Shakrah, Portland Community College; Grant Farr, Portland State University; Rebecca Matthews, University of Iowa; Kenneth L. Stewart, Angelo State University (in Texas); and Cheryl Tieman, Radford University (in Virginia). In addition, students from George Mason University in Virginia offered their reactions to the script during a focus group.

Gene Bryan Johnson served as executive producer of *Reel Society* 2.0, working closely with media producer Jessica Bodie and senior development editor Thom Holmes of McGraw-Hill, the staff at Will Interactive, Inc., and academic adviser Rebecca Matthews, who reviewed the script for the new video footage and created the content for the quizzes, discussion questions, and Instructor's Manual. The following instructors also reviewed the script for the new video: Tom Brignall, Tennessee Technological University; Barbara Karcher, Kennesaw State University; Jerome Krase, Brooklyn College; and Sybil Dione Rosado, Benedict College.

Online Learning Center Website

 The Online Learning Center website that accompanies this text (**www.mhhe.com/ schaefer6**) offers a rich array of resources for instructors and students, most of which were developed by Lynn Newhart of Rockford College in Illinois. Here you will find the author's audio introductions to each chapter, as well as interactive quizzes and maps, social policy exercises, Getting Involved (annotated links to sites of organizations that study or take a position on policy issues discussed in the text), PowerPoint slides, Census 2000 updates, chapter glossaries, vocabulary flash cards, PowerWeb, video clips, additional information about the chapter-opening excerpts and their authors, news updates, and other resources. New Online Learning Center website features include interactive quizzes, video clips with accompanying essay questions, interactive maps, three interactive games (Name That Sociologist, What Concept Am I? and What Perspective Am I?), diagnostic midterm and final exams, links to additional information about the chapter-opening excerpts and their authors, and SurveyTutor, software that allows students to construct and electronically disseminate their own polls for class research projects. It's also possible to link directly to Internet sites from the Online Learning Center. And you can use any of the material from the Online Learning Center in a course website that you create using PageOut.

PowerWeb

 PowerWeb is a resource for the introductory course that is fully integrated with the Online Learning Center website. PowerWeb content is password-protected on the Online Learning Center and includes referenced course-specific web links and articles, student study tools, weekly updates, and additional resources.

In addition to the PowerWeb site for sociology, a special PowerWeb site on violence and terrorism is available from a link on the Online Learning Center. Created in response to the events of September 11, 2001, and their aftermath, this unique website helps instructors and students to integrate coverage of terrorism into their courses. Not just another long list of URLs, the site includes the full texts of thought-provoking articles on terrorism from the scholarly and popular press, as well as weekly updates and a 24-hour newsfeed.

Accompanying both the PowerWeb site for sociology and the site for violence and terrorism are correlation guides that link relevant articles to specific chapters in the textbook, and provide suggested questions and activities. These correlation guides can be found on the Online Learning Center website. For further information about PowerWeb, visit the following site: **www.dushkin.com/ powerweb/pwwl.mhtml.**

PowerPoint Slides

Adopters of *Sociology* can also receive a set of PowerPoint slides developed especially for this edition by Richard T. Schaefer and Gerry Williams. The slides are included on the Instructor's Resource CD-ROM (described below) and in the Instructor's Edition of the Online Learning Center website. The set includes bulleted lecture points, graphs, and maps. The PowerPoints on the Instructor's Resource CD-ROM include video clips from *NBC News* and *The Today Show*. Instructors are welcome to generate overhead transparencies from the slides.

Instructor's Resource CD-ROM with Computerized Test Bank

This CD-ROM includes the contents of the Instructor's Resource Manual; a Test Bank in computerized and Word formats; the instructor's guides to the *Reel Society* 2.0 CD and NBC News Lecture Launcher Videotape, Vol. 3; and PowerPoint slides for instructors' convenience in customizing multimedia lectures. The Instructor's Resource Manual, prepared by Richard T. Schaefer and Rebecca Matthews of the University of Iowa, provides sociology instructors with detailed chapter outlines, learning objectives, additional lecture ideas (16 of which are new to this edition), class discussion topics, essay questions, topics for student research (along with suggested research materials for each topic), and suggested additional readings. Media materials are suggested for each chapter, including videotapes and films. New to this edition is a chapter-by-chapter "Resource Integrator" guide that is designed to help instructors incorporate into the classroom the resources found in the instructor's manual, *Reel Society* 2.0, and the Online Learning Center website. The test bank was written by Clayton Steenberg of Arkansas State University. Multiple-choice and true–false questions are included for each chapter; they will be useful in testing students on basic sociological concepts, application of theoretical perspectives, and recall of important factual information. Correct answers and page references are provided for all questions.

Primis Online

Professors can customize this book by selecting from it only those chapters they want to use in their courses. Primis Online allows users to choose and change the order of chapters, as well as to add readings from McGraw-Hill's vast database of content. Both custom-printed textbooks and electronic eBooks are available. To learn more, contact your McGraw-Hill sales representative, or visit our website at **www.mhhe.com/primis/online.**

ACKNOWLEDGMENTS

Betty Morgan played an integral role in the preparation of the Sixth Edition, and collaborated with me on several earlier editions. Her efforts have greatly enhanced my presentation of the sociological imagination.

I deeply appreciate the contributions to this book made by my editors. Rhona Robbin, director of development and media technology at McGraw-Hill, has continually and successfully challenged me to make each edition better than its predecessor.

I have received strong support and encouragement from Phillip Butcher, publisher; Sherith Pankratz, sponsoring editor; and Dan Loch, senior marketing manager. Additional guidance and support were provided by Amy Shaffer, editorial coordinator, and Trish Starner, editorial assistant; Diane Folliard, senior project manager; Laurie Entringer, designer; Jessica Bodie, media producer; Nora Agbayani, Deborah Bull, and Jen Sanfilippo, photo editors; Emma Ghiselli, art editor; and Judy Brody, permissions editor.

I would also like to acknowledge the contributions of the following individuals: Rebecca Matthews of the University of Iowa for her work on the annotated instructor's edition, the Instructor's Resource Manual, the study guide, and the CPS questions, as well as her contributions to *Reel Society* 2.0; Gene Bryan Johnson, executive producer for *Reel Society* 2.0; Thom Holmes and Jessica Bodie of McGraw-Hill for their work on both versions of *Reel Society*; John Tenuto of Lake County College in Illinois for his work on *Reel Society* 1.0; Clayton Steenberg of Arkansas State University for his work on the test bank; Lynn Newhart of Rockford College for her work on the Online Learning Center; and Gerry Williams for his contributions of the PowerPoint slides.

As is evident from these acknowledgments, the preparation of a textbook is truly a team effort. The most valuable member of this effort continues to be my wife, Sandy. She provides the support so necessary in my creative and scholarly activities.

I have had the good fortune to be able to introduce students to sociology for many years. These students have been enormously helpful in spurring on my own sociological imagination. In ways I can fully appreciate but cannot fully acknowledge, their questions in class and queries in the hallway have found their way into this textbook.

Richard T. Schaefer
www.schaefersociology.net
schaeferrt@aol.com

As a full-service publisher of quality educational products, McGraw-Hill does much more than just sell textbooks to your students. We create and publish an extensive array of print, video, and digital supplements to support instruction on your campus. Orders of new (versus used) textbooks help us to defray the cost of developing such supplements, which is substantial. Please consult your local McGraw-Hill representative to learn about the availability of the supplements that accompany Sociology. If you are not sure who your representative is, you can find him or her by using the Rep Locator at www.mhhe.com.

ACADEMIC REVIEWERS

This edition continues to reflect many insightful suggestions made by reviewers of the first nine hardcover editions and the five paperback brief editions. The current edition has benefited from constructive and thorough evaluations provided by sociologists from both two-year and four-year institutions.

Robert Boyd
Mississippi State University

Andrew Cho
Shoreline Community College

Jack Estes
Borough of Manhattan Community College

Kathleen French
Windward Community College

Kathryn Hadley
California State University, Sacramento

Mark Hardt
Montana State University, Billings

Norma Hendrix
East Arkansas Community College

Louis Hicks
St. Mary's College of Maryland

Xuemei Hu
Union County College

David Kyle
University of California, Berkeley

Diane Levy
University of North Carolina, Wilmington

John S. Mahoney
Virginia Commonwealth University

Frank Phillips
Cumberland County College

Ralph Pyle
Michigan State University

Kristin Sajadi
University of Memphis

Lenny Steverson
South Georgia College

Linda Treiber
North Carolina State University

Chaim Waxman
Rutgers University

Keith Whitworth
Texas Christian University

Dale Yeatts
University of North Texas

Teaching Students to Think Sociologically

The sixth edition of *Sociology: A Brief Introduction* continues its tradition of teaching students how to think critically about society and their own lives from a wide range of classical and contemporary sociological perspectives.

Ray Kroc (1902–1984), the genius behind the franchising of McDonald's restaurants, was a man with big ideas and grand ambitions. But even Kroc could not have anticipated the astounding impact of his creation. McDonald's is the basis of one of the most influential developments in contemporary society. Its reverberations extend far beyond its point of origin in the United States and in the fast-food business. It has influenced a wide range of undertakings, indeed the way of life, of a significant portion of the world. And in spite of McDonald's recent and well-publicized economic difficulties, that impact is likely to expand at an accelerating rate.

However, this is *not* a book about McDonald's, or even about the fast-food business. . . . I devote all this attention to McDonald's . . . because it serves here as the major example of, and the paradigm for, a wide-ranging process I call *McDonaldization*. . . . As you will see, McDonaldization affects not only the restaurant business but also education, work, the criminal justice system, health care, travel, leisure, dieting, politics, the family, religion, and virtually every other aspect of society. McDonaldization has shown every sign of being an inexorable process, sweeping through seemingly impervious institutions and regions of the world.

Other types of business are increasingly adapting the principles of the fast-food industry to their needs. Said the vice chairman of Toys "R" Us, "We want to be thought of as a sort of McDonald's of toys." . . . Other chains with similar ambitions include Gap, Jiffy Lube, AAMCO Transmissions, Midas Muffler & Brake Shops, Great Clips, H&R Block, Pearle Vision, Bally's. . . .

Other nations have developed their own variants of this American institution. . . . Paris, a city whose love for fine cuisine might lead you to think it would prove immune to fast food, has a large number of fast-food croissanteries; the revered French bread has also been McDonaldized. India has a chain of fast-food restaurants, Nirula's, that sells mutton burgers (about 80% of Indians are Hindus, who eat no beef) as well as local Indian cuisine. Mos Burger is a Japanese chain with over fifteen hundred restaurants that in addition to the usual fare, sells Teriyaki chicken burgers, rice burgers, and "Oshiruko with brown rice cake." . . .

McDonald's is such a powerful model that many businesses have acquired nicknames beginning with Mc. Examples include "McDentists" and "McDoctors," meaning drive-in clinics designed to deal quickly and efficiently with minor dental and medical problems; "McChild" care centers, meaning child care centers such as KinderCare; "McStables," designating the nationwide race horse-training operation of Wayne Lucas; and "McPaper," describing the newspaper *USA TODAY*. (Ritzer 2004a:1–4, 10–11)

Additional information about this excerpt can be found on the Online Learning Center at **www.mhhe.com/schaefer6**.

129

---

130 Chapter 6

In this excerpt from *The McDonaldization of Society*, sociologist George Ritzer contemplates the enormous influence of a well-known fast-food organization on modern-day culture and social life. Ritzer defines *McDonaldization* as "the process by which the principles of the fast-food restaurant are coming to dominate more and more sectors of American society as well as of the rest of the world" (Ritzer 2004a:1). In his book, he shows how the business principles on which the fast-food industry is founded—efficiency, calculability, predictability, and control—have changed not only the way Americans do business and run their organizations, but the way they live their lives. Today, busy families rely on the takeout meals served up by fast-food establishments, and McDonald's has become a regular meeting place for social groups from adolescents to senior citizens.

Despite the runaway success of McDonald's and its imitators, and the advantages these enterprises bring to millions of people around the world, Ritzer is critical of their effect on society. The waste and environmental degradation created by billions of disposable containers and the dehumanized work routines of fast-food crews are two of the disadvantages he cites in his critique. Would the modern world be a better one, Ritzer asks, if it were less McDonaldized?

This chapter considers the impact of groups and organizations on social interaction. Do we behave differently in large groups than in small ones? How do we make large organizations manageable? What effect are current social changes having on the structure of groups? We'll begin by noting the distinctions between various types of groups, with particular attention to the dynamics of small groups. We'll examine how and why formal organizations came into existence and describe Max Weber's model of the modern bureaucracy. In a case study of the loss of the space shuttle *Columbia*, we'll see how NASA's bureaucratic culture contributed to the ship's disastrous accident. Finally, we'll look at recent changes in the workplace, some of which are designed to counteract the failures of bureaucracies. The social policy section at the end of the chapter focuses on the status of organized labor today.

UNDERSTANDING GROUPS

Most of us use the term *group* loosely to describe any collection of individuals, whether three strangers sharing an elevator or hundreds attending a rock concert. However, in sociological terms a *group* is any number of people with similar norms, values, and expectations who interact with one another on a regular basis. College sororities and fraternities, dance companies, tenants' associations, and chess clubs are all considered examples of groups. The important point is that members of a group share some sense of belonging. This characteristic distinguishes groups from mere *aggregates* of people, such as passengers who happen to be together on an airplane flight, or from *categories* of people—those who share a common feature (such as being retired) but otherwise do not act together.

Consider the case of a college a cappella singing group. It has agreed-on values and social norms. All members want to improve their singing skills and schedule lots of performances. In addition, like many groups, the singing ensemble has both a formal and an informal structure. The members meet regularly to rehearse; they choose leaders to run the rehearsals and manage their affairs. At the same time, some group members may take on unofficial leadership roles by coaching new members in singing techniques and performing skills.

The study of groups has become an important part of sociological investigation because they play such a key role in the transmission of culture. As we interact with others, we pass on our ways of thinking and acting—from language and values to ways of dressing and leisure activities.

Types of Groups

Sociologists have made a number of useful distinctions between types of groups—primary and secondary groups, in-groups and out-groups, and reference groups.

Primary and Secondary Groups

Charles Horton Cooley (1902) coined the term *primary group* to refer to a small group characterized by intimate, face-to-face association and cooperation. The members of a street gang constitute a primary group; so do mem-

---

Intriguing Book Excerpts

Chapter openers convey the excitement and relevance of sociological inquiry by means of lively excerpts from writings of sociologists and others who explore sociological topics.

Book Excerpt Links to Chapters

Chapter overviews provide a bridge between the chapter-opening excerpt and the content of the chapter.

White."

The one-drop rule was a vivid example of the *social construction of race*—the process by which people come to define a group as a race based in part on physical characteristics, but also on historical, cultural, and economic factors. For example, in the 1800s, immigrant groups such as Italian and Irish Americans were not at first seen as being "White," but as foreigners who were not necessarily trustworthy. The social construction of race is an ongoing process that is subject to debate, especially in a diverse society such as the United States, where each year increasing numbers of children are born to parents of different racial backgrounds.

In the 2000 census, nearly 7 million people in the United States (or about 2 percent of the population) reported that they were of two or more races. Half the people classified as multiracial were under age 18, suggesting that this segment of the population will grow in the years to come. People who claimed both White and American Indian ancestry were the largest group of multiracial residents (Grieco and Cassidy 2001).

This statistical finding of millions of multiracial people obscures how individuals handle their identity, however. The prevailing social construction of race pushes people to choose just one race, even if they acknowledge a broader cultural background. For example, the enrollment forms for government programs typically include only a few broad racial-ethnic categories. This approach to racial categorization is part of a long history that dictates single-race identities. Still, many individuals, especially young adults, struggle against social pressure to choose a single identity, and instead openly embrace multiple heritages. Tiger Woods, the world's best-known professional golfer,

Not long ago, these children of a White mother and an African American father would automatically have assumed their father's racial identity. Today, however, some children of mixed-race families identify themselves as biracial.

respond not only to the objective features of a situation or person but also to the *meaning* that situation or person has for them. Thus, we can create false images or stereotypes that become real in their consequences. *Stereotypes* are unreliable generalizations about all members of a group that do not recognize individual differences within the group.

In the last 30 years, critics have pointed out the power of the mass media to perpetuate false racial and ethnic stereotypes. Television is a prime example: Almost all the leading dramatic roles are cast as Whites, even in urban-based programs like *Friends* (see Chapter 7). Blacks tend to be featured mainly in crime-based dramas.

Use Your Sociological Imagination WWW.

Using a TV remote control, how quickly do you think you could find a television show in which all the characters share your own racial or ethnic background? What about a show in which all the characters share a different background from your own—how quickly could you find one?

"Use Your Sociological Imagination" Sections

These sections within each chapter pose questions designed to stimulate students' sociological imagination to help them figure out how major concepts and issues apply to their own lives. Students can respond to the questions in these sections on the Online Learning Center and e-mail their answers to their instructors.

Analyzing a Broad Range of Contemporary Issues

Hallmark Social Policy Sections

These discussions provide a sociological perspective on contemporary social issues such as gun control, global immigration, and gay marriage. Providing a global view of the issues, these sections are organized around a consistent heading structure and include questions designed to stimulate critical thinking about the issues being explored.

320 Chapter 12

SOCIAL POLICY and THE FAMILY — Gay Marriage

The Issue

In the United States, attitudes toward marriage are complex. As always, society and popular culture suggest that a young man or woman should find the perfect mate, settle down and marry, and live "happily ever after." But young people are also bombarded by messages implying the frequency of adultery and the acceptability of divorce. In this atmosphere, the idea of same-sex marriage strikes some people as only the latest of many attacks on traditional marriage. To others, it seems an overdue acknowledgment of the formal relationships that faithful, monogamous gay couples have long maintained.

Sin or civil right? Protesters both for and against gay marriage clashed in this demonstration outside the Massachusetts State House in Boston.

The Setting

In 2004, in his State of the Union message, President George W. Bush warned "activist judges" against attempts to broaden the definition of marriage to include same-sex couples. The only recourse to such measures, he said, would be a constitutional amendment banning same-sex unions.

What made gay marriage the focus of national attention? Events in two states brought the issue to the forefront. In 1999, Vermont gave gay couples the legal benefits of marriage through civil union, but stopped short of calling the arrangement a marriage. Then, in 2003, the Massachusetts Supreme Court ruled 4–3 that under the state's constitution, gay couples have the right to marry.

Sociological Insights

Functionalists have traditionally seen marriage as a social institution that is closely tied to human reproduction. Same-sex marriage would at first appear not to fit that arrangement. But many same-sex couples are entrusted with the socialization of young children, whether or not their relationship is recognized by the state. Functionalists also wonder whether religious views toward marriage can be ignored. The courts have focused on civil marriage, but religious views are hardly irrelevant, even in a country like the United States, which observes a separation between religion and the state. Indeed, religious teachings have led even some staunch supporters of gay rights to oppose same-sex marriage on spiritual grounds.

Conflict theorists have charged that denial of the right to marry reinforces the second-class status of gays and lesbians. Some have compared the ban against gay marriage to past policies that banned interracial marriage in 32 states (Liptak 2004b).

Interactionists generally avoid the policy question and focus instead on the nature of same-sex households. They ask many of the same questions about gay partner relations and child rearing that they raise about conventional couples. Of course, much less research has been done on same-sex households than on other families, but the studies published to date raise the same issues as those that apply to conventional married couples, plus a few more. For gay couples, the support or opposition of family, co-workers, and friends looms large (Dundas and Kaufman 2000; G. Dunne 2000).

Recently, national surveys of attitudes toward gay marriage have been showing volatile shifts in public opinion. Typically, people are more opposed to gay

---

Social Inequality Boxes

These boxes on social issues such as discretionary justice, disability as a master status, and the stained glass ceiling that limits career opportunities for clergy women, highlight an important area of analysis for sociologists today.

Social Inequality 8-2 DISCRETIONARY JUSTICE

Race matters in the criminal justice system. Conflict theorists remind us that while the basic purpose of law is to maintain stability and order, it can actually perpetuate inequality. In many cases, criminal justice officials use their *discretionary powers*—decisions made on their own discretion about whether to press charges or drop them, whether to set bail and how much, whether to offer parole or deny it—in biased ways. Researchers have found that discretionary differences in the way social control is exercised put African Americans and Latinos at a disadvantage in the justice system, both as juveniles and as adults. In this way, Richard Quinney and other conflict theorists argue, the criminal justice system keeps the poor and oppressed in their deprived positions.

How do sociologists determine whether suspects and offenders are treated dif-

On average, White offenders receive shorter sentences than comparable Latino and African American offenders.

ferently based on racial, ethnic, and social class backgrounds? One way is to look at convicted criminals and compare the sentences they receive for equivalent crimes. The task can be complicated, because researchers must take into consideration a number of factors that affect sentencing. For example, in their study of federal court data, sociologists Darrell Steffensmeier and Stephen Demuth examined the severity of the crime and the convict's prior arrest record. Even after taking these and other factors into consideration, they found that on average, White offenders re...

up 71 percent of the U.S. population, they constitute only 45 percent of criminals sentenced to death. Conflict theorists point out that the overwhelming majority of prosecutors in death penalty cases are White and non-Hispanic. The victim's race matters a great deal in these cases, as well. Studies have consistently shown that a convicted criminal is much more likely to be sentenced to death if the victim is White and non-Hispanic than if the victim is non-White or Hispanic.

Race and the Death Penalty

Let's Discuss

1. Do you know anyone who was treated leniently by the criminal justice system? If so, was the person White and non-Hispanic? Why do you think police and/or other officials used their discretionary powers to excuse the person's offense or reduce the penalties?
2. Besides race, what other factors might contribute to the disproportionately severe sentencing of Black and Hispanic defendants? Explain.

U.S. Population: White Non-Hispanic 71%, All others 29%
Death Penalty Prosecutors: White Non-Hispanic 97%, All others 3%
Death Row Inmates: White Non-Hispanic 45%, All others 55%
Race of Victim in Death Penalty Cases: White Non-Hispanic 81%, All others 19%

New Section on War and Peace

A new section in Chapter 14 examines war and terrorism as means of resolving international conflicts through the exertion of power. It also considers potential deterrents to war, including international trade and nongovernmental organizations (NGOs).

xxxii

A representative of the International Red Crescent Society delivers an aid parcel in the southern Iraqi town of Safwan. The Red Crescent delivers emergency aid to victims of war and disaster in Muslim communities. Such nongovernmental organizations (NGOs) help to bind countries together, promoting peaceful relations.

Peace, they contend, can best be maintained by developing strong mutual security agreements between potential adversaries (Etzioni 1965; Shostak 2002).

In recent years, the United States has begun to recognize that its security can be threatened not just by nation states, but by political groups that operate outside the bounds of legitimate authority. Indeed, terrorism is now considered the foremost threat to U.S. security—one the U.S. military is unaccustomed to fighting.

Terrorism

Acts of terror, whether perpetrated by a few or by many people, can be a powerful political force. Formally defined, *terrorism* is the use or

Exploring Diverse Cultures in Our Global World

CASE STUDY: CAPITALISM IN CHINA

Today's China is not the China of past generations. In a country where the Communist Party once dominated people's lives, few now bother to follow party proceedings. Instead, after a decade of rapid economic growth, most Chinese are more interested in acquiring the latest consumer goods. Ironically, it was party officials' decision to transform China's economy by opening it up to capitalism that reduced the once omnipotent institution's influence.

THE ROAD TO CAPITALISM

When the communists assumed leadership of China in 1949, they cast themselves as the champions of workers and peasants and the enemies of those who exploited workers, namely landlords and capitalists. Profit making was outlawed, and those who engaged in it were arrested. By the 1960s, China's economy was dominated by huge state-controlled enterprises, such as factories. Even private farms were transformed into community-owned organizations. Peasants essentially worked for the government, receiving payment in goods based on their contribution to the collective. In addition, they could receive a small plot of land on which to produce food for their families or for exchange with others. But while the centralization of production for the benefit of all seemed to make sense ideologically, it did not work well economically.

In the 1980s, the government eased restrictions against private enterprise somewhat, permitting small businesses with no more than seven employees. But business owners could not hold policymaking positions in the party, at any level. Late in the decade, party leaders began to make market-oriented reforms, revising the nation's legal structure to promote private business. For the first time, private entrepreneurs were allowed to compete with some state-controlled businesses. By the mid-1990s, impressed with the results of the experiment, party officials had begun to hand some ailing state-controlled businesses over to private entrepreneurs, in hopes they could be turned around (Lynch 2002; Pan 2002).

THE CHINESE ECONOMY TODAY

Today, the entrepreneurs who weathered government harassment during the Communist Party's early years are among the nation's wealthiest capitalists. Some even hold positions on government advisory boards. The growing free-market economy they spawned has brought significant inequality to Chinese workers, however. While wages are up for millions, the average wage bought less in 2004 than it did 10 years before, given price increases. Marxist critics have condemned China's leaders for reducing Chinese work... omy (Kal...

New Country Case Studies

Three new case studies provide a closer look at the social worlds of three countries, illustrating the impact of globalization on each. These cases explore stratification in Mexico (Chapter 9), religion in India (Chapter 13), and capitalism in China (Chapter 14).

Revealing Photo Essays

Six photo essays (three of them new to this edition) provide glimpses of ways of life in different cultures. Each begins with a question that is intended to prompt students to see some part of everyday life with new eyes—those of a sociologist. The accompanying photos and captions suggest the answer to the question. This photo essay invites students to analyze the social factors that influence individuals to adopt religious beliefs.

Sociology in the Global Community Boxes

These boxes provide a global perspective on topics such as the offshoring of service jobs, life in the global village, and the impact of global media such as Al Jazeera network.

Relating Sociology to Students' Lives

New "Sociology on Campus" Boxes

These boxes on topics such as cheating, binge drinking, the debate over Title IX, and anti-war protests apply a sociological perspective to several issues of immediate interest to students.

"Taking Sociology To Work" Boxes

"Taking Sociology To Work" boxes underscore the value of an undergraduate degree in sociology through the use of profiles of individuals who majored in sociology and use its principles in their work.

"Research in Action" Boxes

These boxes present sociological findings on relevant topics such as the lingering impact of divorce, the challenge of doing survey research in Baghdad, and the impact of Wal-Mart on communities.

Sociology on Campus

3-2 A CULTURE OF CHEATING?

On November 21, 2002, after issuing several warnings, officials at the U.S. Naval Academy seized the computers of almost 100 midshipmen suspected of downloading movies and music illegally from the Internet. Officers at the school may have taken the unusually strong action to avoid liability on the part of the U.S. government, which owns the computers students were using. But across the nation, college administrators have been trying to restrain students from downloading pirated entertainment for free. The practice is so widespread, it has been slowing down the high-powered computer networks colleges and universities depend on for research and admissions.

Illegal downloading is just one aspect of the growing problem of copyright violation, both on campus and off. Now that college students can use personal computers to surf the Internet, most do their research online. Apparently, the temptation to cut and paste passages from website postings and pass them off as one's own is irresistible to many. Surveys done

Integrity estimates that at most schools, more than three quarters of the students engage in some form of cheating. Students not only cut passages from the Internet and paste them into their papers without citing the source; they share questions and answers on exams, collaborate on assignments they are supposed to do independently, and even falsify the results of their laboratory experiments. Worse, many professors have become inured to the problem and have ceased to report it.

To address what they consider an alarming trend, many schools are rewrit-

Cheating is considerably less common at schools with honor codes than at schools without honor codes.

ing or adopting new academic honor codes. According to the Center for Academic Integrity, cheating on tests and papers is considerably less common at

dent cheating reflects widely publicized instances of cheating in public life, which have served to create an alternative set of values in which the means justify the end. When young people see sports heroes, authors, entertainers, and corporate executives exposed for cheating in one form or another, the message seems to be "Cheating is OK, as long as you don't get caught." More than proctoring of exams or reliance on search engines to identify plagiarism, then, educating students about the need for academic honesty seems to reduce the incidence of cheating. "The feeling of being treated as an adult and responding in kind," says Professor Donald McCabe of Rutgers University, "it's clearly there for many students. They don't want to violate that trust."

Let's Discuss

1. Do you know anyone who has engaged in Internet plagiarism? What about cheating on tests or falsifying laboratory results? If so, how did

---

Taking Sociology To Work

www.mhhe.com/schaefer6

RICHARD J. HAWK **Vice President and Financial Consultant, Smith Barney**

Richard Hawk had no idea what he wanted to do with his life when he entered DePauw University in Indiana, and no idea what sociology was about when he registered for his first course. But he soon realized that he liked the faculty in the sociology department, and he liked the perspective the subject gave him on other subjects he was studying—economics, history, and communications. In his junior year, Hawk took a course on marriage and the family that helped him to see the "trickle-down effect" of major economic decisions on individuals and communities.

Today, Hawk credits sociology with giving him "a better overall understanding of things," one he uses daily. Asked to elaborate, he replies, "You have to realize that everyone is affected one way or another" by economic and political decisions. He points to the war in Iraq: "Half of the forces are reservists. Look at the social and financial effect on the family, the economic effect on the companies these people work for domestically, not to mention the obvious effects on the Iraqi people." Hawk sees these effects play themselves out in his clients' lives, whether they are physicians or blue-collar workers facing an early retirement. In developing their financial plans, he keeps the big picture in mind.

As a financial consultant, Hawk meets with clients, confers with money managers and financial analysts, and prepares proposals for prospective clients. He applies the same analytical perspective that he uses with clients to the economy and current business issues. "The past few years have not been particularly kind to the equity markets," he observes. "We were in a technology bubble, and as a result, we have been experiencing dramatic changes in accounting methods, compensation issues, and ethics in general."

Hawk advises first-time sociology students to approach the subject with an open mind, to "be willing to look at issues from a different perspective." Doing so, he thinks, will pay off in some valuable insights.

Let's Discuss

1. Pick an economic issue or decision that has been in the news recently and show how it could affect your family.
2. Take the same issue or decision and imagine how it might affect the people you will deal with in your future career.

Research in Action

15-2 STORE WARS

No organization exists in a vacuum, especially not a corporate giant. Executives of Wal-Mart know that. The epitome of the superstore, Wal-Mart has become the center of controversy in towns and cities across the United States, despite the familiar smiley-face logo and its red, white, and blue corporate image. The reason: A new Wal-Mart can have powerfully negative effects on the surrounding community.

Wal-Mart was founded in 1962 by Sam Walton, whose strategy was to locate new stores in rural communities, where competition from other retailers was weak and unions were not organized. Over the years, as the enormously successful discount chain expanded to become the world's largest corporation, Wal-Mart began to move into the fringes of metropolitan areas as well. But the residents of the communities Wal-Mart moved into did not always welcome their new neighbor.

In Ashland, Virginia, a community of 7,200 people, residents worried that

documentary *Store Wars*, ultimately lost its battle because of Wal-Mart's promised low prices and increased tax revenues. But citizens in many other communities have won, at least temporarily.

On the urban fringes, too, residents have mobilized to stop new superstores. In Bangor, Maine, environmentalists raised an alarm over a proposed Wal-Mart superstore, to be located next to a marsh that sheltered endangered wildlife. Activists in Riverside, California, also challenged Wal-Mart, again on environmental grounds.

In Ashland, Virginia, residents worried that Wal-Mart would destroy the small-town atmosphere they treasured.

But the issue is more complicated in these areas, because communities on the urban fringe are hardly untouched by economic development. Wal-Mart's pro-

of urban sprawl, some planners are beginning to advocate "smart growth"—restoring the central city and its older suburbs rather than abandoning them for the outer rings.

Not all communities reject superstores. In countries like Mexico, where the economic outlook has been poor recently, people welcomed Wal-Mart. From Tijuana to Cancún, in fact, public reaction to the U.S. chain's arrival has been almost universally positive. Mexican shoppers appreciate Wal-Mart's wide selection and low prices.

Wal-Mart executives are unapologetic about the chain's rapid expansion. They argue that their aggressive competition has lowered prices and raised working people's standard of living. And they say they have given back to the communities where their stores are located by donating money to educational institutions and local agencies.

Let's Discuss

1. Is there a Wal-Mart, Home Depot,

Offering Distinctive Pedagogy and Illustrations that Reinforce Content

summingUP

Table 3-2	Major Theoretical Perspectives on Culture		
	Functionalist Perspective	**Conflict Perspective**	**Interactionist Perspective**
Norms	Norms reinforce societal standards	Norms reinforce patterns of dominance	Norms are maintained through face-to-face interaction
Values	Values are collective conceptions of what is good	Values may perpetuate social inequality	Values are defined and redefined through social interaction
Culture and society	Culture reflects a society's strong central values	Culture reflects a society's dominant ideology	A society's core culture is perpetuated through daily social interactions
Cultural variation	Subcultures serve the interests of subgroups; ethnocentrism reinforces group solidarity	Countercultures question the dominant social order; ethnocentrism devalues groups	Customs and traditions are transmitted through intergroup contact and through the media

government. Before the 2003 war in Iraq, U.S. planners had assumed that Iraqis would adapt to a new form of government in the same way the Germans and Japanese did following World War II. But in the Iraqi culture, unlike the German and Japanese cultures, loyalty to the family and the extended clan comes before patriotism and the common good. In a country in which almost half of all people, even those in the cities, marry a first or second cousin, citizens are predisposed to favor

Cultural Relativism

While ethnocentrism evaluates foreign cultures using the familiar culture of the observer as a standard of correct behavior, **cultural relativism** views people's behavior from the perspective of their own culture. It places a priority on understanding other cultures, rather than dismissing them as "strange" or "exotic." Unlike ethnocentrism, cultural relativism employs the kind of value neutrality in scientific study that Max Weber saw

New "Summing Up" Tables

Twenty "Summing Up" tables pull together coverage of the major theoretical perspectives.

Demographic Map Program

Two kinds of maps— "Mapping Life Nationwide" and "Mapping Life Worldwide"—are featured throughout the text. Interactive versions of many of these maps with accompanying questions appear on the book's Online Learning Center website.

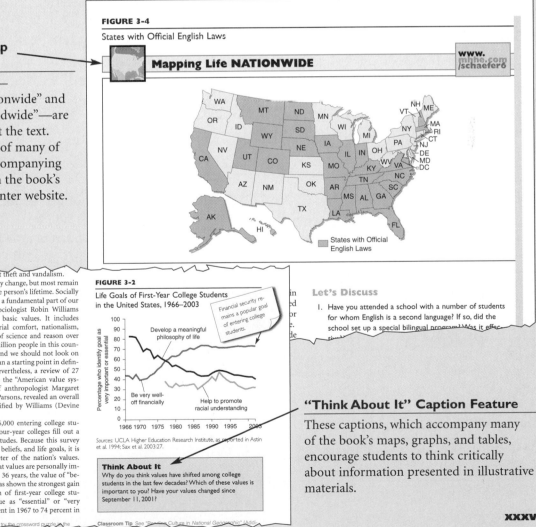

FIGURE 3-4

States with Official English Laws

Mapping Life NATIONWIDE

www.mhhe.com/schaefer6

States with Official English Laws

probably have stiff laws against theft and vandalism.

The values of a culture may change, but most remain relatively stable during any one person's lifetime. Socially shared, intensely felt values are a fundamental part of our lives in the United States. Sociologist Robin Williams (1970) has offered a list of basic values. It includes achievement, efficiency, material comfort, nationalism, equality, and the supremacy of science and reason over faith. Obviously, not all 290 million people in this country agree on all these values, and we should not look on such a list as anything more than a starting point in defining the national character. Nevertheless, a review of 27 different attempts to describe the "American value system," including the works of anthropologist Margaret Mead and sociologist Talcott Parsons, revealed an overall similarity to the values identified by Williams (Devine 1972).

Each year more than 276,000 entering college students at 413 of the nation's four-year colleges fill out a questionnaire about their attitudes. Because this survey focuses on an array of issues, beliefs, and life goals, it is commonly cited as a barometer of the nation's values. The respondents are asked what values are personally important to them. Over the last 36 years, the value of "being very well-off financially" has shown the strongest gain in popularity; the proportion of first-year college students who endorse this value as "essential" or "very important" rose from 44 percent in 1967 to 74 percent in

FIGURE 3-2

Life Goals of First-Year College Students in the United States, 1966–2003

Financial security remains a popular goal of entering college students.

- Develop a meaningful philosophy of life
- Be very well-off financially
- Help to promote racial understanding

Percentage who identify goal as very important or essential

1966 1970 1975 1980 1985 1990 1995 2000

Sources: UCLA Higher Education Research Institute, as reported in Astin et al. 1994; Sax et al. 2003:27.

Think About It
Why do you think values have shifted among college students in the last few decades? Which of these values is important to you? Have your values changed since September 11, 2001?

Let's Discuss

1. Have you attended a school with a number of students for whom English is a second language? If so, did the school set up a special bilingual program? Was it effective...

"Think About It" Caption Feature

These captions, which accompany many of the book's maps, graphs, and tables, encourage students to think critically about information presented in illustrative materials.

Web Resource Encourage students to try the crossword puzzle in the

Classroom Tip See "Reading Culture in *National Geographic*" (Addi...

Featuring Meaningful Resources that Promote Active Learning

New "Getting Involved" Sections

Included at the end of each social policy section, "Getting Involved" sections direct students who are interested in the issue to the Online Learning Center, where they will find websites, as well as survey data on U.S. public opinion regarding the issue.

they suggest that children will face enormous social pressure to conform to the beliefs and practices of a religious majority.

Policy Initiatives

School education is fundamentally a local issue, so most initiatives and lobbying have taken place at the local or state level. A significant departure from the local nature of this issue came in 2003, when President George W. Bush declared that schools whose policies prevent constitutionally protected school prayer risk losing their federal education funds. At the same time, federal courts were taking a hard line on religion in the schools. In a decision that is unlikely to be upheld, a federal appeals court ruled that reciting the phrase "under God" during the Pledge of Allegiance that opens each school day violates the U.S. Constitution (Religion News Service 2003).

sectarian religious control of public education. They worry that at some point in the future, teachers may not be able to use books or make statements that conflict with fundamentalist interpretations of the Bible. For advocates of a liberal education who are deeply committed to intellectual (and religious) diversity, this is a genuinely frightening prospect.

Let's Discuss

1. Was there any organized prayer in the school you attended? Was creationism part of the curriculum?
2. Do you think that promoting religious observance is a legitimate function of education?
3. How might a conflict theorist view the issue of organized school prayer?

GETTING INVOLVED

To get involved in the debate over religion in the schools, visit this text's Online Learning Center, which offers links to relevant websites. Check out the Social

Policy section on the Online Learning Center as well; it provides survey data on U.S. public opinion regarding this issue.

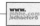

www. mhhe.com /schaefer6

TECHNOLOGY RESOURCES

Internet Connection

www. mhhe.com /schaefer6

Note: While all the URLs listed were current as of the printing of this book, these sites often change. Please check our website (www.mhhe.com/schaefer6) for updates, hyperlinks, and exercises related to these sites.

1. The National Science Foundation (NSF) is a major source of funding for sociologists. Explore the Sociology Program page at the NSF's website (www.nsf.gov/sbe/ses/social/start.htm). To get some idea of contemporary sociologists' research interests, click on the link to "Sociology Program

Awards Search" in the middle of the page, under "Grant/Award Administration and Information."

2. The website of the Hull House Museum (www.uic.edu/jaddams/hull/hull_house.html) provides a wealth of information on Jane Addams and her life work. To view historical photographs of Hull House and the people Addams served, click on "Urban Experience in Chicago."

Online Learning Center with PowerWeb

Visit the Online Learning Center, this textbook's specific website, at www.mhhe.com/schaefer6. The student center in the Online Learning Center offers a variety of helpful and interesting resources and activities for each chapter. The resources include chapter outlines and summaries, quizzes with feedback, video clips about current issues, direct links to Internet sites, including those found in the Internet Connection sections at the end of

each chapter in your text, relevant news updates, and audio clips by the author. The activities include flashcards, crossword puzzles, interactive maps, and interactive exercises. Don't pass up this opportunity to learn more about sociology and to take advantage of resources that will help you master the material in your text and get a better grade in the course!

Reel Society Interactive Movie CD-ROM 2.0

Exercise your imagination and step into the world of *Reel Society*, a professionally produced movie on CD-ROM that demonstrates the sociological imagination through typical scenarios drawn from campus life. In this movie you will become part of the exploits of several college students, and will influence the plot by making key choices for them. Through it all, you'll learn to relate sociological thought to real life through a variety of issues and perspectives. In addition to the interactive movie, *Reel Society* includes explanatory text screens and a glossary, as well as quizzes and discussion questions to test your knowledge of sociology. The CD also includes a link to the Online Learning Center website for *Reel Society*.

Reel Society 2.0 can be used to spark discussion about the following topics from this chapter:

- The Sociological Imagination
- Major Theoretical Perspectives
- Speaking Across Race, Gender, and National Boundaries

Web Resource Encourage students to visit the student center in the Online Learning Center (www.mhhe.com/schaefer6) and take either the Multiple Choice Quiz or the True/False Quiz to see how well they understand the concepts presented in the chapter. Remind them that these quizzes provide immediate feedback for incorrect answers.

Web Resource Alert students to the "Social Policy" component in the student center of the Online Learning Center (www.mhhe.com/schaefer6). "Social Policy" presents overviews of current, and sometimes controversial, social policies, as well as graphs and charts.

Integrated Technology Resources

These resources include Internet exercises, brief descriptions of specific content on the Online Learning Center website, and a listing of relevant topics that are explored on the *Reel Society* Interactive Movie CD-ROM 2.0. (The inside covers of the text feature screen shots from these resources.)

chapter

UNDERSTANDING SOCIOLOGY

1

Sociology encompasses a wide range of subjects, from global social issues to the popular culture of a particular society. The comic books shown here fill the stalls of street vendors just outside the railroad station in Bombay, India. Sociologists can learn a great deal about people's values and customs by studying the print media and other forms of entertainment they enjoy.

I am, of course, very different from the people who normally fill America's least attractive jobs, and in ways that both helped and limited me. Most obviously, I was only visiting a world that others inhabit full-time, often for most of their lives. With all the real-life assets I've built up in middle age—bank account, IRA, health insurance, multi-room home—waiting indulgently in the background, there was no way I was going to "experience poverty" or find out how it "really feels" to be a long-term low-wage worker. My aim here was much more straightforward and objective—just to see whether I could match income to expenses, as the truly poor attempt to do every day....

In Portland, Maine, I came closest to achieving a decent fit between income and expenses, but only because I worked seven days a week. Between my two jobs, I was earning approximately $300 a week after taxes and paying $480 a month in rent, or a manageable 40 percent of my earnings. It helped, too, that gas and electricity were included in my rent and that I got two or three free meals each weekend at the nursing home. But I was there at the beginning of the off-season. If I had stayed until June 2000 I would have faced the Blue Haven's summer rent of $390 a week, which would of course have been out of the question. So to survive year-round, I would have had to save enough, in the months between August 1999 and May 2000, to accumulate the first month's rent and deposit on an actual apartment. I think I could have done this—saved $800 to $1,000—at least if no car trouble or illness interfered with my budget. I am not sure, however, that I could have maintained the seven-day-a-week regimen month after month or eluded the kinds of injuries that afflicted my fellow workers in the housecleaning business.

In Minneapolis—well, here we are left with a lot of speculation. If I had been able to find an apartment for $400 a month or less, my pay at Wal-Mart—$1,120 a month before taxes—might have been sufficient, although the cost of living in a motel while I searched for such an apartment might have made it impossible for me to save enough for the first month's rent and deposit. A weekend job, such as the one I almost landed at a supermarket for about $7.75 an hour, would have helped, but I had no guarantee that I could arrange my schedule at Wal-Mart to reliably exclude weekends. If I had taken the job at Menards and the pay was in fact $10 an hour for eleven hours a day, I would have made about $440 a week after taxes—enough to pay for a motel room and still have something left over to save up for the initial costs of an apartment. But were they really offering $10 an hour? And could I have stayed on my feet eleven hours a day, five days a week? So yes, with some different choices, I probably could have survived in Minneapolis. But I'm not going back for a rematch. *(Ehrenreich 2001:6, 197–198)* ■ ◉

Additional information about this excerpt can be found on the Online Learning Center at **www.mhhe.com/schaefer6**.

Nickel *and* **Dimed**

On (Not) Getting By in America

BARBARA EHRENREICH

In her undercover attempts to survive as a low-wage worker in different cities in the United States, journalist Barbara Ehrenreich revealed patterns of human interaction and used methods of study that foster sociological investigation. This excerpt from her book *Nickel and Dimed: On (Not) Getting By in America* describes how she left a comfortable home and assumed the identity of a divorced, middle-aged housewife with no college degree and little working experience. She set out to get the best-paying job and the cheapest living quarters she could find, to see whether she could make ends meet. Months later, physically exhausted and demoralized by demeaning work rules, Ehrenreich confirmed what she had suspected before she began: getting by in this country as a low-wage worker is a losing proposition.

Ehrenreich's study focused on an unequal society, which is a central topic in sociology. Social inequality has a pervasive influence on human interactions and institutions. Certain groups of people control scarce resources, wield power, and receive special treatment. The poster that opens this chapter illustrates another common focus of sociologists, the elements of culture that define a society. In India, comic books are a very popular form of media that reflect central cultural values.

While it might be interesting to know how one individual is affected by the need to make ends meet, or even by the contents of an adventure comic, sociologists consider how entire groups of people are affected by these kinds of factors, and how society itself might be altered by them. Sociologists, then, are not concerned with what one individual does or does not do, but with what people do as members of a group or in interaction with one another, and what that means for individuals and for society as a whole.

As a field of study, sociology is extremely broad in scope. You will see throughout this book the range of topics sociologists investigate—from suicide to TV viewing habits, from Amish society to global economic patterns, from peer pressure to pickpocketing techniques. Sociology looks at how others influence our behavior; how major social institutions like the government, religion, and the economy affect us; and how we ourselves affect other individuals, groups, and even organizations.

How did sociology develop? In what ways does it differ from other social sciences? This chapter will explore the nature of sociology as both a field of inquiry and an exercise of the "sociological imagination." We'll look at the discipline as a science and consider its relationship to other social sciences. We'll meet three pioneering thinkers—Émile Durkheim, Max Weber, and Karl Marx—and examine the theoretical perspectives that grew out of their work. Finally, we'll consider the ways sociology helps us to develop a sociological imagination. ■

WHAT IS SOCIOLOGY?

"What has sociology got to do with me or with my life?" As a student, you might well have asked this question when you signed up for your introductory sociology course. To answer it, consider these points: Are you influenced by what you see on television? Do you use the Internet? Did you vote in the last election? Are you familiar with binge drinking on campus? Do you use alternative medicine? These are just a few of the everyday life situations described in this book that sociology can shed light on. But as the opening excerpt indicates, sociology also looks at large social issues. We use sociology to investigate why thousands of jobs have moved from the United States to developing nations, what social forces promote prejudice, what leads someone to join a social movement and work for social change, how access to computer technology can reduce social inequality, and why relationships between men and women in Seattle differ from those in Singapore.

Sociology is, very simply, the systematic study of social behavior and human groups. It focuses on social relationships; how those relationships influence people's behavior; and how societies, the sum total of those relationships, develop and change.

The Sociological Imagination

In attempting to understand social behavior, sociologists rely on an unusual type of creative thinking. A leading sociologist, C. Wright Mills, described such thinking as the *sociological imagination*—an awareness of the relationship between an individual and the wider society. This

Classroom Tip See "Stimulating Classroom Discussions about *Nickel and Dimed*" (Class Discussion Topics).
Web Resource Encourage students to visit the Online Learning Center at **www.mhhe.com/schaefer6** and explore the student center. Note that there are several kinds of valuable learning aids, including quizzes, puzzles, audio clips, and activities.

Classroom Tip Tell students when your department was founded, how many sociology majors you have, and how many degrees were presented last year.
Classroom Tip Share with students how you came to be interested in sociology.
Key Person C. Wright Mills (Mills's power elite model of the United States is analyzed in Chapter 14.)

Are You What You Own?

Use your sociological imagination to analyze the "material world" of three different societies. These photos come from the book *Material World: A Global Family Portrait*. The photographers selected a "statistically average" family in each country they visited and took pictures of that family with all the possessions in the household. Shown here are families in the United States (Texas), in Mali, and in Iceland.

What do the material goods tell you about the kind of transport, food, shelter, and lifestyle in each culture? How does climate affect the goods they own? What effect would family size have on a family's economic position? Which possessions are geared to recreation, which to subsistence? How do these families make use of natural resources? What means of communication are available to each of them? Why do you think the Mali family owns so many pots, baskets, and serving utensils? Why might the family in Iceland be so musical? What do the books and the family Bible tell us about the background and interests of the Texas family? How do you think each family would react if they lived with the belongings of the other two households?

These photos make us aware that when we look at people's material possessions, we learn something about the social, economic, and geographic factors that influence their way of life. The photos may also prompt us to think sociologically about our own material possessions, and what they say about us and about our society (Menzel 1994).

The Skeen family in Pearland, Texas, United States

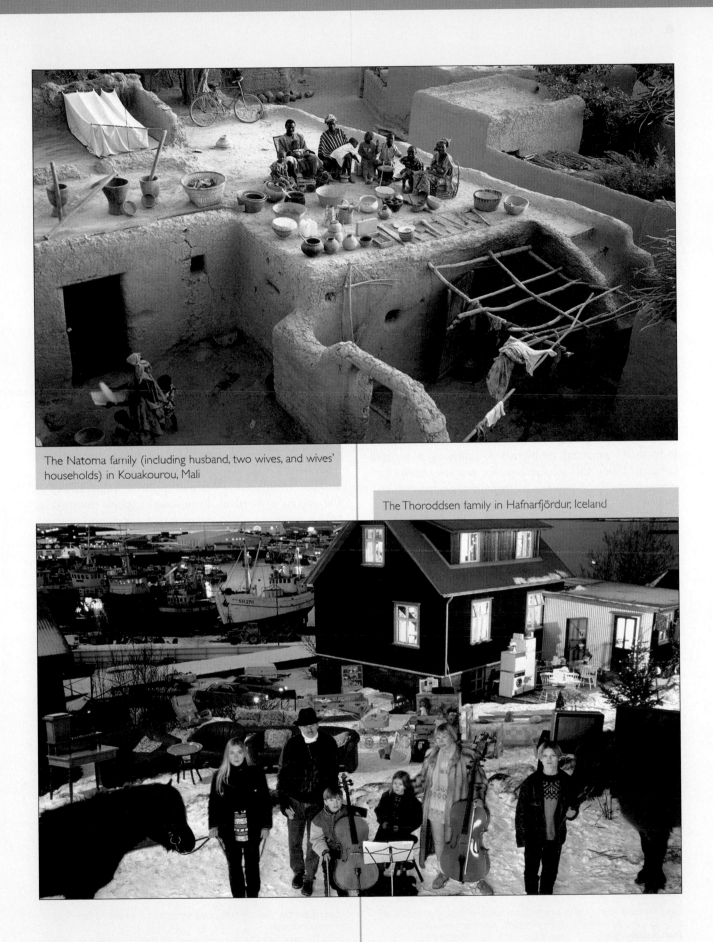

The Natoma family (including husband, two wives, and wives' households) in Kouakourou, Mali

The Thoroddsen family in Hafnarfjördur, Iceland

awareness allows all of us (not just sociologists) to comprehend the links between our immediate, personal social settings and the remote, impersonal social world that surrounds and helps to shape us. Barbara Ehrenreich certainly used a sociological imagination when she studied low-wage workers (Mills [1959] 2000a).

A key element in the sociological imagination is the ability to view one's own society as an outsider would, rather than only from the perspective of personal experiences and cultural biases. Consider something as simple as sporting events. On college campuses in the United States, thousands of students cheer well-trained football players. In Bali, Indonesia, dozens of spectators gather around a ring to cheer on well-trained roosters engaged in cockfights. In both instances, the spectators debate the merits of their favorites and bet on the outcome of the events. Yet what is considered a normal sporting event in one part of the world is considered unusual in another part.

The sociological imagination allows us to go beyond personal experiences and observations to understand broader public issues. Divorce, for example, is unquestionably a personal hardship for a husband and wife who split apart. However, C. Wright Mills advocated using the sociological imagination to view divorce not simply as an individual's personal problem but rather as a societal concern. Using this perspective, we can see that an increase in the divorce rate actually redefines a major social institution—the family. Today's households frequently include stepparents and half-siblings whose parents have divorced and remarried.

The sociological imagination is an empowering tool. It allows us to look beyond a limited understanding of human behavior to see the world and its people in a new way and through a broader lens than we might otherwise use. It may be as simple as understanding why a roommate prefers country music to hip-hop, or it may open up a whole different way of understanding other populations in the world. For example, in the aftermath of the terrorist attacks on the United States on September 11, 2001, many citizens wanted to understand how Muslims throughout the world perceived their country, and why. From time to time this textbook will offer you the chance to exercise your own sociological imagination in a variety of situations. We'll begin with one that may be close to home for you.

Use Your Sociological Imagination
www.mhhe.com/schaefer6

You are walking down the street in your city or hometown. In looking around you, you can't help noticing that half or more of the people you see are overweight. How do you explain your observation? If you were C. Wright Mills, how do you think you would explain it?

Let's Discuss Ask students why they are taking a sociology class. Did they take any sociology or social problems courses in high school?
Reel Society See Sociological Imagination in the Topic Index.
Classroom Tip/Contemporary Culture See "Personal Experiences and the Sociological Imagination" (Class Discussion Topics).

Sociology and the Social Sciences

Is sociology a science? The term *science* refers to the body of knowledge obtained by methods based on systematic observation. Just like other scientific disciplines, sociology involves the organized, systematic study of phenomena (in this case, human behavior) in order to enhance understanding. All scientists, whether studying mushrooms or murderers, attempt to collect precise information through methods of study that are as objective as possible. They rely on careful recording of observations and accumulation of data.

Of course, there is a great difference between sociology and physics, between psychology and astronomy. For this reason, the sciences are commonly divided into natural and social sciences. *Natural science* is the study of the physical features of nature and the ways in which they interact and change. Astronomy, biology, chemistry, geology, and physics are all natural sciences. *Social science* is the study of the social features of humans and the ways in which they interact and change. The social sciences include sociology, anthropology, economics, history, psychology, and political science.

These social science disciplines have a common focus on the social behavior of people, yet each has a particular orientation. Anthropologists usually study past cultures and preindustrial societies that continue today, as well as the origins of humans. Economists explore the ways in which people produce and exchange goods and services, along with money and other resources. Historians are concerned with the peoples and events of the past and their significance for us today. Political scientists study international relations, the workings of government, and the exercise of power and authority. Psychologists investigate personality and individual behavior. So what do *sociologists* focus on? They study the influence that society has on people's attitudes and behavior and the ways in which people interact and shape society. Because humans are social animals, sociologists scientifically examine our social relationships with others.

Let's consider how the different social sciences might approach the hotly debated issue of the death penalty. Historians would be interested in the development of the use of capital punishment from colonial days to the present. Economists might conduct research that compares the costs of incarcerating a person for life to the expense of conducting the appeals that come with death penalty cases. Psychologists would look at individual cases and assess the impact of the death penalty on the families of both the victim and the death row inmate. Political scientists would study the different stances taken by elected officials and the implications of their stands for their reelection campaigns.

Classroom Tip See Class Discussion Topics for exercises on the sociological imagination.
Let's Discuss Ask students for a show of hands: How many students are majoring in a natural science? In a social science?
Classroom Tip Take a topic (e.g., suicide, religion, crime) and demonstrate how each social science examines that topic.

And what approach would sociologists take? They might look at how race and ethnicity affect the outcome of death penalty cases. According to a study released in 2003, 80 percent of death penalty cases in the United States involve White victims, even though only 50 percent of all murder victims are White (see Figure 1-1). It appears that the race of the victim influences whether a defendant will be charged with capital murder (that is, murder punishable by death) and whether he or she will eventually receive the death penalty. Thus, the criminal justice system seems more intent on handing down harsh punishments when the victims are White than when they are minorities.

Sociologists put their sociological imaginations to work in a variety of areas—including aging, the family, human ecology, and religion. Throughout this textbook, you will see how sociologists develop theories and conduct research to study and better understand societies. And you will be encouraged to use your own sociological imagination to examine the United States (and other societies) from the viewpoint of a respectful but questioning outsider.

Sociology and Common Sense

Sociology focuses on the study of human behavior. Yet we all have experience with human behavior and at least some knowledge of it. All of us might well have theories about why people become homeless, for example. Our theories and opinions typically come from "common sense"—that is, from our experiences and conversations, from what we read, from what we see on television, and so forth.

In our daily lives, we rely on common sense to get us through many unfamiliar situations. However, this commonsense knowledge, while sometimes accurate, is not always reliable, because it rests on commonly held beliefs rather than on systematic analysis of facts. It was once considered common sense to accept that the earth was flat—a view rightly questioned by Pythagoras and Aristotle. Incorrect commonsense notions are not just a part of the distant past; they remain with us today.

In the United States today, "common sense" tells us that young people flock to movie theaters showing *The Passion of The Christ* or to concerts featuring Christian rock because religion is becoming more important to them. However, this particular "commonsense" notion—like the notion that the earth is flat—is untrue, and is not supported by sociological research. Through 2003, annual surveys of first-year college students show a decline in the percentage who attend religious services even occasionally. Increasing numbers of college students claim to have no religious preference. The trend encompasses not just organized religion, but other forms of spirituality. Fewer students pray or meditate today than in the past, and fewer consider their level of spirituality to be very high (Sax et al. 2003).

Similarly, disasters do not generally produce panic. In the aftermath of disasters such as explosions, greater social organization and structure emerge to deal with a community's problems. In the United States, for example, an emergency operations group often coordinates public services and even certain services normally performed by the private sector, such as food distribution. Decision making becomes more centralized in times of disaster.

Like other social scientists, sociologists do not accept something as a fact because "everyone knows it." Instead, each piece of information must be tested and recorded, then analyzed in relationship to other data. Sociologists rely on scientific studies in order to describe and understand a social environment. At times, the findings of sociologists may seem like common sense, because they deal with familiar facets of everyday life. The difference is that such findings have been *tested* by researchers. Common sense now tells us that the earth is round. But this particular commonsense notion is based on centuries of scientific work that began with the breakthroughs made by Pythagoras and Aristotle.

FIGURE 1-1

Race of Victims in Death Penalty Cases

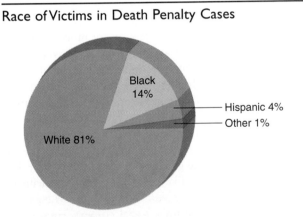

Note: Data are for all death penalty cases from 1976 through January 30, 2004.

Source: Death Penalty Information Center 2004.

The death penalty is more likely to be imposed when the victim is White. Nationally, 50 percent of all murder victims are White, but in cases tried under the death penalty, the percentage of White victims is more than 80 percent.

Contemporary Culture Discuss the differences between common-sense and sociological interpretations of affirmative action.

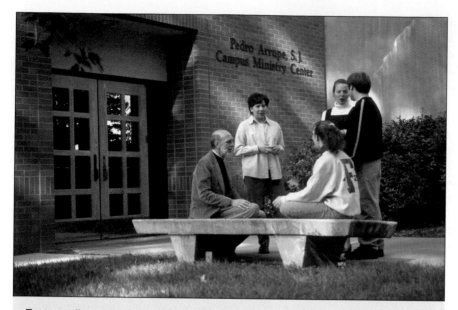

Fewer college students attend religious services today than in the past, despite the presence of on-campus ministries such as this Jesuit center at Fairfield University, Connecticut. Sociological research confirms the downward trend in religious observance.

WHAT IS SOCIOLOGICAL THEORY?

Why do people commit suicide? One traditional commonsense answer is that people inherit the desire to kill themselves. Another view is that sunspots drive people to take their own lives. These explanations may not seem especially convincing to contemporary researchers, but they represent beliefs widely held as recently as 1900.

Sociologists are not particularly interested in why any one individual commits suicide; they are more concerned with identifying the social forces that systematically cause some people to take their own lives. In order to undertake this research, sociologists develop a *theory* that offers a general explanation of suicidal behavior.

We can think of theories as attempts to explain events, forces, materials, ideas, or behavior in a comprehensive manner. In sociology, a *theory* is a set of statements that seeks to explain problems, actions, or behavior. An effective theory may have both explanatory and predictive power. That is, it can help us to see the relationships among seemingly isolated phenomena, as well as to understand how one type of change in an environment leads to other changes.

The World Health Organization (2002) estimated that a total of 815,000 people committed suicide in 2000. More than a hundred years earlier, a sociologist tried to look at suicide data scientifically. Émile Durkheim

([1897] 1951) developed a highly original theory about the relationship between suicide and social factors. He was primarily concerned not with the personalities of individual suicide victims, but rather with suicide rates and how they varied from country to country. As a result, when he looked at the number of reported suicides in France, England, and Denmark in 1869, he also noted the total population of each country in order to determine the rate of suicide in each nation. He found that whereas England had only 67 reported suicides per million inhabitants, France had 135 per million and Denmark had 277 per million. The question then became: "Why did Denmark have a comparatively high rate of reported suicides?"

Durkheim went much deeper into his investigation of suicide rates. The result was his landmark work *Suicide,* published in 1897. Durkheim refused to accept unproved explanations regarding suicide, including the beliefs that cosmic forces or inherited tendencies caused such deaths. Instead, he focused on social factors, such as the cohesiveness or lack of cohesiveness of religious, social, and occupational groups.

Durkheim's research suggested that suicide, while a solitary act, is related to group life. Protestants had much higher suicide rates than Catholics; the unmarried had much higher rates than married people; and soldiers were more likely to take their lives than civilians. In addition, there seemed to be higher rates of suicide in times of peace than in times of war and revolution, and in times of economic instability and recession rather than in times of prosperity. Durkheim concluded that the suicide rates of a society reflected the extent to which people were or were not integrated into the group life of the society.

Émile Durkheim, like many other social scientists, developed a *theory* to explain how individual behavior can be understood within a social context. He pointed out the influence of groups and societal forces on what had always been viewed as a highly personal act. Clearly, Durkheim offered a more *scientific* explanation for the causes of suicide than that of sunspots or inherited tendencies. His theory has predictive power, since it suggests that suicide rates will rise or fall in conjunction with certain social and economic changes.

Key Person Émile Durkheim
Classroom Tip Do a debunking exercise: Ask students who is more likely to commit suicide, Protestants or Catholics. What is the poverty level for a family of four? Are the divorce rate and birthrate going up or down? Indicate how Émile Durkheim utilized the sociological imagination in his study of suicide.

Let's Discuss Introduce the topic of suicide by asking what types of people are more likely to commit suicide (common sense) and note Durkheim's findings.
Classroom Tip See "Émile Durkheim's Analysis of Suicide" (Additional Lecture Ideas).

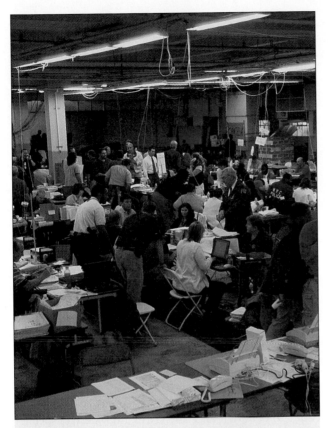

Do disasters produce panic or an organized, structured response? Common sense might tell us the former, but, in fact, disasters bring out a great deal of structure and organization to deal with their aftermath. When the September 11, 2001, terrorist attack destroyed New York City's emergency command center, officials quickly set up this one to direct the search and recovery effort.

Of course, a theory—even the best of theories—is not a final statement about human behavior. Durkheim's theory of suicide is no exception. Sociologists continue to examine factors that contribute to differences in suicide rates around the world and to a particular society's rate of suicide. For example, although the overall rate of suicide in New Zealand is only marginally higher than the rate in the United States, the suicide rate among young people is 41 percent higher in New Zealand. Sociologists and psychiatrists from that country suggest that their remote, sparsely populated society maintains exaggerated standards of masculinity that are especially difficult for young males. Gay adolescents who fail to conform to their peers' preference for sports are particularly vulnerable to suicide (Shenon 1995).

Global View Durkheim's landmark study of suicide rates examines variations in suicide rates in several European countries.
Classroom Tip See "Using Maps to Understand Sociological Theory" (Class Discussion Topics).
Classroom Tip See "Founders of Sociology" (Class Discussion Topics).

Use Your Sociological Imagination www. mhhe.com /schaefer6

If you were Durkheim's successor in his research on suicide, how would you investigate the factors that may explain the increase in suicide rates among young people in the United States today?

THE DEVELOPMENT OF SOCIOLOGY

People have always been curious about sociological matters—how we get along with others, what we do for a living, whom we select as our leaders. Philosophers and religious authorities of ancient and medieval societies made countless observations about human behavior. They did not test or verify those observations scientifically; nevertheless, their observations often became the foundation for moral codes. Several of the early social philosophers predicted that a systematic study of human behavior would emerge one day. Beginning in the 19th century, European theorists made pioneering contributions to the development of a science of human behavior.

Early Thinkers

Auguste Comte

The 19th century was an unsettling time in France. The French monarchy had been deposed in the revolution of 1789, and Napoleon had suffered defeat in his effort to conquer Europe. Amid this chaos, philosophers considered how society might be improved. Auguste Comte (1798–1857), credited with being the most influential of the philosophers of the early 1800s, believed that a theoretical science of society and a systematic investigation of behavior were needed to improve society. He coined the term *sociology* to apply to the science of human behavior.

Writing in the 1800s, Comte feared that the excesses of the French Revolution had permanently impaired France's stability. Yet he hoped that the systematic study of social behavior would eventually lead to more rational human interactions. In Comte's hierarchy of the sciences, sociology was at the top. He called it the "queen," and its practitioners "scientist-priests." This French theorist did not simply give sociology its name; he presented a rather ambitious challenge to the fledgling discipline.

Harriet Martineau

Scholars learned of Comte's works largely through translations by the English sociologist Harriet Martineau (1802–1876). But Martineau was a pathbreaker in her own right. She offered insightful observations of the customs and social practices of both her native Britain and

Key Person Auguste Comte
Key Person Harriet Martineau
Classroom Tip See "Women Sociologists in the 20th and 21st Centuries" (Additional Lecture Ideas).
Gender Harriet Martineau was an early female pioneer of sociology.

Harriet Martineau, an early pioneer of sociology, studied social behavior both in her native England and in the United States.

the United States. Martineau's book *Society in America* ([1837] 1962) examined religion, politics, child rearing, and immigration in the young nation. It gives special attention to social class distinctions and to such factors as gender and race. Martineau ([1838] 1989) also wrote the first book on sociological methods.

Martineau's writings emphasized the impact that the economy, law, trade, health, and population could have on social problems. She spoke out in favor of the rights of women, the emancipation of slaves, and religious tolerance. Later in life, deafness did not keep her from being an activist. In Martineau's (1877) view, intellectuals and scholars should not simply offer observations of social conditions; they should *act* on their convictions in a manner that will benefit society. That is why Martineau conducted research on the nature of female employment and pointed to the need for further investigation of the issue (Deegan 2003; Hill and Hoecker-Drysdale 2001).

Herbert Spencer

Another important early contributor to the discipline of sociology was Herbert Spencer (1820–1903). A relatively

prosperous Victorian Englishman, Spencer (unlike Martineau) did not feel compelled to correct or improve society; instead, he merely hoped to understand it better. Drawing on Charles Darwin's study *On the Origin of Species,* Spencer applied the concept of evolution of the species to societies in order to explain how they change, or evolve, over time. Similarly, he adapted Darwin's evolutionary view of the "survival of the fittest" by arguing that it is "natural" that some people are rich while others are poor.

Spencer's approach to societal change was extremely popular in his own lifetime. Unlike Comte, Spencer suggested that since societies are bound to change eventually, one need not be highly critical of present social arrangements or work actively for social change. This viewpoint appealed to many influential people in England and the United States who had a vested interest in the status quo and were suspicious of social thinkers who endorsed change.

Émile Durkheim

Émile Durkheim made many pioneering contributions to sociology, including his important theoretical work on suicide. The son of a rabbi, Durkheim (1858–1917) was educated in both France and Germany. He established an impressive academic reputation and was appointed one of the first professors of sociology in France. Above all, Durkheim will be remembered for his insistence that behavior must be understood within a larger social context, not just in individualistic terms.

As one example of this emphasis, Durkheim ([1912] 2001) developed a fundamental thesis to help explain all forms of society. Through intensive study of the Arunta, an Australian tribe, he focused on the functions that religion performed and underscored the role of group life in defining what we consider to be religious. Durkheim concluded that like other forms of group behavior, religion reinforces a group's solidarity.

Another of Durkheim's main interests was the consequences of work in modern societies. In his view, the growing division of labor in industrial societies, as workers became much more specialized in their tasks, led to what he called anomie. **Anomie** refers to the loss of direction felt in a society when social control of individual behavior has become ineffective. The state of anomie occurs when people have lost their sense of purpose or direction, often during a time of profound social change. In a period of anomie, people are so confused and unable to cope with the new social environment that they may resort to taking their own lives.

Global View Martineau studied social practices of both her native Britain and the United States.

Key Persons Herbert Spencer, Charles Darwin, Émile Durkheim
Theory Émile Durkheim's functional analysis of religion is examined in more detail in Chapter 13.

FIGURE 1-2

Early Social Thinkers

	Émile Durkheim 1858–1917	**Max Weber 1864–1920**	**Karl Marx 1818–1883**
Academic training	Philosophy	Law, economics, history, philosophy	Philosophy, law
Key works	1893—*The Division of Labor in Society*	1904–1905—*The Protestant Ethic and the Spirit of Capitalism*	1848—*The Communist Manifesto*
	1897—*Suicide: A Study in Sociology*	1922—*Wirtschaft und Gesellschaft*	1867—*Das Kapital*
	1912—*Elementary Forms of Religious Life*		

Durkheim was concerned about the dangers that alienation, loneliness, and isolation might pose for modern industrial societies. He shared Comte's belief that sociology should provide direction for social change. As a result, he advocated the creation of new social groups—mediators between the individual's family and the state—which would provide a sense of belonging for members of huge, impersonal societies. Unions would be an example of such groups.

Like many other sociologists, Durkheim did not limit his interests to one aspect of social behavior. Later in this book we will consider his thinking on crime and punishment, religion, and the workplace. Few sociologists have had such a dramatic impact on so many different areas within the discipline.

Max Weber

Another important early theorist was Max Weber (pronounced "VAY-ber"). Born in Germany, Weber (1864–1920) studied legal and economic history, but gradually developed an interest in sociology. Eventually, he became a professor at various German universities. Weber taught his students that they should employ ***Verstehen,*** the German word for "understanding" or "insight," in their intellectual work. He pointed out that we cannot analyze our social behavior by the same type of objective criteria we use to measure weight or tempera-

ture. To fully comprehend behavior, we must learn the subjective meanings people attach to their actions—how they themselves view and explain their behavior.

For example, suppose that a sociologist was studying the social ranking of individuals in a fraternity. Weber would expect the researcher to employ *Verstehen* to determine the significance of the fraternity's social hierarchy for its members. The researcher might examine the effects of athleticism or grades or social skills or seniority on standing within the fraternity. He or she would seek to learn how the fraternity members relate to other members of higher or lower status. While investigating these questions, the researcher would take into account people's emotions, thoughts, beliefs, and attitudes (L. Coser 1977).

We also owe credit to Weber for a key conceptual tool: the ideal type. An ***ideal type*** is a construct or model for evaluating specific cases. In his own works, Weber identified various characteristics of bureaucracy as an ideal type (discussed in detail in Chapter 6). In presenting this model of bureaucracy, Weber was not describing any particular business, nor was he using the term *ideal* in a way that suggested a positive evaluation. Instead, his purpose was to provide a useful standard for measuring how bureaucratic an actual organization is (Gerth and Mills 1958). Later in this textbook, we will use the concept of *ideal type* to study the family, religion, authority, and economic systems, as well as to analyze bureaucracy.

Let's Discuss Does Weber's view of Verstehen mean that sociologists can never "take sides"? The issue of neutrality and politics in research is discussed in Chapter 2.

Student Alert Ideal types are valuable in studying human behavior. But point out that *ideal,* as used here, means "typical of a genre" (not "best").

Although their professional careers coincided, Émile Durkheim and Max Weber never met and probably were unaware of each other's existence, let alone ideas. Such was not true of the work of Karl Marx. Durkheim's thinking about the impact of the division of labor in industrial societies was related to Marx's writings, while Weber's concern for a value-free, objective sociology was a direct response to Marx's deeply held convictions. Thus, it is not surprising that Karl Marx is viewed as a major figure in the development of sociology, as well as several other social sciences (see Figure 1-2 on page 11).

Karl Marx

Karl Marx (1818–1883) shared with Durkheim and Weber a dual interest in abstract philosophical issues and the concrete reality of everyday life. Unlike the others, Marx was so critical of existing institutions that a conventional academic career was impossible. He spent most of his life in exile from his native Germany.

Marx's personal life was a difficult struggle. When a paper he had written was suppressed, he fled to France. In Paris, he met Friedrich Engels (1820–1895), with whom he formed a lifelong friendship. They lived at a time when European and North American economic life was increasingly dominated by the factory rather than the farm.

While in London in 1847, Marx and Engels attended secret meetings of an illegal coalition of labor unions known as the Communist League. The following year they prepared a platform called *The Communist Manifesto,* in which they argued that the masses of people with no resources other than their labor (whom they referred to as the *proletariat*) should unite to fight for the overthrow of capitalist societies. In the words of Marx and Engels:

> The history of all hitherto existing society is the history of class struggles. . . . The proletarians have nothing to lose but their chains. They have a world to win. WORKING MEN OF ALL COUNTRIES UNITE! (Feuer 1989:7, 41)

After completing *The Communist Manifesto,* Marx returned to Germany, only to be expelled. He then moved to England, where he continued to write books and essays. Marx lived there in extreme poverty. He pawned most of his possessions, and several of his children died of malnutrition and disease. Marx clearly was an outsider in British society, a fact that may well have colored his view of Western cultures.

In Marx's analysis, society was fundamentally divided between two classes that clashed in pursuit of their own interests. When he examined the industrial societies of his time, such as Germany, England, and the United

States, he saw the factory as the center of conflict between the exploiters (the owners of the means of production) and the exploited (the workers). Marx viewed these relationships in systematic terms; that is, he believed that a system of economic, social, and political relationships maintained the power and dominance of the owners over the workers. Consequently, Marx and Engels argued that the working class should *overthrow* the existing class system. Marx's influence on contemporary thinking has been dramatic. His writings inspired those who would later lead communist revolutions in Russia, China, Cuba, Vietnam, and elsewhere.

Even apart from the political revolutions that his work fostered, Marx's significance is profound. Marx emphasized the *group* identifications and associations that influence an individual's place in society. This area of study is the major focus of contemporary sociology. Throughout this textbook, we will consider how membership in a particular gender classification, age group, racial group, or economic class affects a person's attitudes and behavior. In an important sense, we can trace this way of understanding society back to the pioneering work of Karl Marx.

Modern Developments

Sociology today builds on the firm foundation developed by Émile Durkheim, Max Weber, and Karl Marx. However, the field certainly has not remained stagnant over the last hundred years. While Europeans have continued to make contributions to the discipline, sociologists from throughout the world and especially the United States have advanced sociological theory and research. Their new insights have helped us to better understand the workings of society.

Charles Horton Cooley

Charles Horton Cooley (1864–1929) was typical of the sociologists who came to prominence in the early 1900s. Born in Ann Arbor, Michigan, Cooley received his graduate training in economics but later became a sociology professor at the University of Michigan. Like other early sociologists, he had become interested in this "new" discipline while pursuing a related area of study.

Cooley shared the desire of Durkheim, Weber, and Marx to learn more about society. But to do so effectively, he preferred to use the sociological perspective to look first at smaller units—intimate, face-to-face groups such as families, gangs, and friendship networks. He saw these groups as the seedbeds of society, in the sense that they shape people's ideals, beliefs, values, and social nature. Cooley's work increased our understanding of groups of relatively small size.

Key Persons Karl Marx, Friedrich Engels
Theory Marx's analysis formed the basis for contemporary conflict theory.
Global View Marx's theories, while drawing on his observations in Europe, have been applied on every continent.
Classroom Tip Marx's view of class consciousness is discussed in Chapter 9.

Student Alert Remind students that the importance of Marx's work for sociology is not negated by the overthrow of Communist states.
Global View After students have learned Marxist theory, note how his theory differs from practices in the so-called Marxist states.
Key Persons Charles Horton Cooley

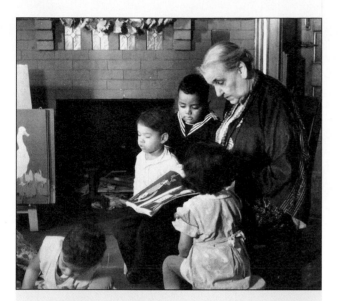

In a photograph taken around 1930, social reformer Jane Addams reads to children at the Mary Crane Nursery. Addams was an early pioneer both in sociology and in the settlement house movement.

Jane Addams

In the early 1900s, many leading sociologists in the United States saw themselves as social reformers dedicated to systematically studying and then improving a corrupt society. They were genuinely concerned about the lives of immigrants in the nation's growing cities, whether those immigrants came from Europe or from the rural American South. Early female sociologists, in particular, often took active roles in poor urban areas as leaders of community centers known as *settlement houses*. For example, Jane Addams (1860–1935), a member of the American Sociological Society, cofounded the famous Chicago settlement, Hull House.

Addams and other pioneering female sociologists commonly combined intellectual inquiry, social service work, and political activism—all with the goal of assisting the underprivileged and creating a more egalitarian society. For example, working with the Black journalist and educator Ida Wells-Barnett, Addams successfully prevented racial segregation in the Chicago public schools. Addams's efforts to establish a juvenile court system and a women's trade union reveal the practical focus of her work (Addams 1910, 1930; Deegan 1991; Lengermann and Niebrugge-Brantley 1998).

By the middle of the 20th century, however, the focus of the discipline had shifted. Sociologists for the most part restricted themselves to theorizing and gathering information; the aim of transforming society was left to social workers and activists. This shift away from social reform was accompanied by a growing commitment to scientific methods of research and to value-free interpretation of data. Not all sociologists were happy with this emphasis. A new organization, the Society for the Study of Social Problems, was created in 1950 to deal more directly with social inequality and other social problems.

Robert Merton

Sociologist Robert Merton (1910–2003) made an important contribution to the discipline by successfully combining theory and research. Born to Slavic immigrant parents in Philadelphia, Merton subsequently won a scholarship to Temple University. He continued his studies at Harvard, where he acquired his lifelong interest in sociology. Merton's teaching career was based at Columbia University.

Merton (1968) produced a theory that is one of the most frequently cited explanations of deviant behavior. He noted different ways in which people attempt to achieve success in life. In his view, some may deviate from the socially approved goal of accumulating material goods or the socially accepted means of achieving that goal. For example, in Merton's classification scheme, "innovators" are people who accept the goal of pursuing material wealth but use illegal means to do so, including robbery, burglary, and extortion. Merton based his explanation of crime on individual behavior that has been influenced by society's approved goals and means, yet it has wider applications. It helps to account for the high crime rates among the nation's poor, who may see no hope of advancing themselves through traditional roads to success. Chapter 8 discusses Merton's theory in greater detail.

Merton also emphasized that sociology should strive to bring together the "macro-level" and "micro-level" approaches to the study of society. *Macrosociology* concentrates on large-scale phenomena or entire civilizations. Émile Durkheim's cross-cultural study of suicide is an example of macro-level research. More recently, macrosociologists have examined international crime rates (see Chapter 8), the stereotype of Asian Americans as a "model minority" (see Chapter 10), and the population patterns of developing countries (see Chapter 15). In contrast, *microsociology* stresses the study of small groups, often through experimental means. Sociological research on the micro level has included studies of how divorced men and women disengage from significant social roles (see Chapter 5); of how conformity can influence the expression of prejudiced attitudes (see Chapter 8); and of how a teacher's expectations can affect a student's academic performance (see Chapter 13).

Today sociology reflects the diverse contributions of earlier theorists. As sociologists approach such topics as divorce, drug addiction, and religious cults, they can draw on the theoretical insights of the discipline's pioneers. A careful reader can hear Comte, Durkheim, Weber, Marx, Cooley, Addams, and many others speaking through the pages of current research. Sociology has also broadened beyond the intellectual confines of North America and Europe. Contributions to the discipline now come from sociologists studying and researching human behavior in other parts of the world. In describing the work of these sociologists, it is helpful to examine a number of influential theoretical approaches (also known as *perspectives*).

MAJOR THEORETICAL PERSPECTIVES

Sociologists view society in different ways. Some see the world basically as a stable and ongoing entity. They are impressed with the endurance of the family, organized religion, and other social institutions. Other sociologists see society as composed of many groups in conflict, competing for scarce resources. To still other sociologists, the most fascinating aspects of the social world are the everyday, routine interactions among individuals that we sometimes take for granted. These three views, the ones most widely used by sociologists, are the functionalist, conflict, and interactionist perspectives. Together, these approaches will provide an introductory look at the discipline.

Functionalist Perspective

Think of society as a living organism in which each part of the organism contributes to its survival. This view is the *functionalist perspective,* which emphasizes the way in which the parts of a society are structured to maintain its stability.

Talcott Parsons (1902–1979), a Harvard University sociologist, was a key figure in the development of functionalist theory. Parsons was greatly influenced by the work of Émile Durkheim, Max Weber, and other European sociologists. For over four decades, he dominated sociology in the United States with his advocacy of functionalism. Parsons saw any society as a vast network of connected parts, each of which helps to maintain the system as a whole. His functionalist approach holds that if an aspect of social life does not contribute to a society's stability or survival—if it does not serve some identifiably useful function or promote value consensus among members of a society—it will not be passed on from one generation to the next.

Let's examine prostitution as an example of the functionalist perspective. Why is it that a practice so widely condemned continues to display such persistence and vitality? Functionalists suggest that prostitution satisfies needs that may not be readily met through more socially acceptable forms of sexual expression, such as courtship or marriage. The "buyer" receives sex without any responsibility for procreation or sentimental attachment; at the same time, the "seller" makes a living through the exchange.

Such an examination leads us to conclude that prostitution does perform certain functions that society seems to need. However, that is not to suggest that prostitution is a desirable or legitimate form of social behavior. Functionalists do not make such judgments. Rather, advocates of the functionalist perspective hope to explain how an aspect of society that is so frequently attacked can nevertheless manage to survive (K. Davis 1937).

Manifest and Latent Functions

A college catalog typically states various functions of the institution. It may inform you, for example, that the university intends to "offer each student a broad education in classical and contemporary thought, in the humanities, in the sciences, and in the arts." However, it would be quite a surprise to find a catalog that declared, "This university was founded in 1895 to keep people between the ages of 18 and 22 out of the job market, thus reducing unemployment." No college catalog will declare this as the purpose of the university. Yet societal institutions serve many functions, some of them quite subtle. The university, in fact, *does* delay people's entry into the job market.

Robert Merton (1968) made an important distinction between manifest and latent functions. *Manifest functions* of institutions are open, stated, conscious functions. They involve the intended, recognized consequences of an aspect of society, such as the university's role in certifying academic competence and excellence. In contrast, **latent functions** are unconscious or unintended functions that may reflect hidden purposes of an institution. One latent function of universities is to hold down unemployment. Another is to serve as a meeting ground for people seeking marital partners.

Dysfunctions

Functionalists acknowledge that not all parts of a society contribute to its stability all the time. A *dysfunction* refers to an element or process of a society that may actually disrupt the social system or reduce its stability.

We view many dysfunctional behavior patterns, such as homicide, as undesirable. Yet we should not automatically interpret them in this way. The evaluation of a dysfunction depends on one's own values or, as the saying

This postage stamp honors W. E. B. Du Bois, who challenged the status quo in both academic and political circles. The first Black person to receive a doctorate from Harvard University, Du Bois later helped organize the National Association for the Advancement of Colored People (NAACP).

goes, on "where you sit." For example, the official view in prisons in the United States is that inmate gangs should be eradicated because they are dysfunctional to smooth operations. Yet some guards have actually come to view prison gangs as a functional part of their jobs. The danger posed by gangs creates a "threat to security," requiring increased surveillance and more overtime work for guards, as well as requests for special staffing to address gang problems (G. Scott 2001).

Conflict Perspective

Where functionalists see stability and consensus, conflict sociologists see a social world in continual struggle. The *conflict perspective* assumes that social behavior is best understood in terms of conflict or tension between competing groups. Such conflict need not be violent; it can take the form of labor negotiations, party politics, competition between religious groups for new members, or disputes over the federal budget.

Throughout most of the 1900s, the functionalist perspective had the upper hand in sociology in the United States. However, the conflict approach has be-

come increasingly persuasive since the late 1960s. The widespread social unrest resulting from battles over civil rights, bitter divisions over the war in Vietnam, the rise of the feminist and gay liberation movements, the Watergate political scandal, urban riots, and confrontations at abortion clinics have offered support for the conflict approach—the view that our social world is characterized by continual struggle between competing groups. Currently, the discipline of sociology accepts conflict theory as one valid way to gain insight into a society.

The Marxist View

As we saw earlier, Karl Marx viewed struggle between social classes as inevitable, given the exploitation of workers under capitalism. Expanding on Marx's work, sociologists and other social scientists have come to see conflict not merely as a class phenomenon but as a part of everyday life in all societies. In studying any culture, organization, or social group, sociologists want to know who benefits, who suffers, and who dominates at the expense of others. They are concerned with the conflicts between women and men, parents and children, cities and suburbs, Whites and Blacks, to name only a few. Conflict theorists are interested in how society's institutions—including the family, government, religion, education, and the media—may help to maintain the privileges of some groups and keep others in a subservient position. Their emphasis on social change and the redistribution of resources makes conflict theorists more "radical" and "activist" than functionalists (Dahrendorf 1959).

An African American View: W. E. B. Du Bois

One important contribution of conflict theory is that it has encouraged sociologists to view society through the eyes of those segments of the population that rarely influence decision making. Some early Black sociologists, including W. E. B. Du Bois (1868–1963), conducted research that they hoped would assist the struggle for a racially egalitarian society. Du Bois believed that knowledge was essential in combating prejudice and achieving tolerance and justice. Sociology, he contended, had to draw on scientific principles to study social problems such as those experienced by Blacks in the United States. Du Bois made a major contribution to sociology through his in-depth studies of urban life, both White and Black.

Du Bois had little patience with theorists such as Herbert Spencer, who seemed content with the status quo. He advocated basic research on the lives of Blacks, to separate opinion from fact. In this way he documented their relatively low status in Philadelphia and Atlanta. Du Bois believed that the granting of full political rights

Theory Conflict perspective introduced
Classroom Tip See "Revisiting Functionalism" (Class Discussion Topics).
Classroom Tip See "Functionalist and Conflict Views of Popular Music" (Additional Lecture Ideas).
Classroom Tip Distinguish between Marxist theory and conflict theory.

Key Person W. E. B. Du Bois
Race/Ethnicity W. E. B. Du Bois was the first major African American sociologist. He examined urban communities, social networks, formal organizations, and health care delivery.
Classroom Tip See "W. E. B. Du Bois—The Sociologist" (Additional Lecture Ideas).

to Blacks was essential to their social and economic progress in the United States. Because many of his ideas challenged the status quo, he did not find a receptive audience within either the government or the academic world. As a result, Du Bois became increasingly involved with organizations whose members questioned the established social order. He helped to found the National Association for the Advancement of Colored People, better known as the NAACP (D. Lewis 1994, 2000).

The addition of diverse views within sociology in recent years has led to some valuable research, especially on African Americans. For many years, African Americans were understandably wary of participating in medical research studies, because those studies had been used for such purposes as justifying slavery or determining the impact of untreated syphilis. Now, however, African American sociologists and other social scientists are working to involve Blacks in useful ethnic medical research on diabetes and sickle cell anemia, two disorders that strike Black populations especially hard (A. Young, Jr. and Deskins, Jr. 2001).

The Feminist View

Sociologists began embracing the feminist perspective only in the 1970s, although it has a long tradition in many other disciplines. The *feminist view* sees inequity in gender as central to all behavior and organization. Because it

Ida Wells-Barnett explored what it meant to be female and Black living in the United States. Her work established her as one of the earliest feminist theorists.

clearly focuses on one aspect of inequality, it is often allied with the conflict perspective. Proponents of the feminist perspective tend to focus on the macro level, just as conflict theorists do. Drawing on the work of Marx and Engels, contemporary feminist theorists often view women's subordination as inherent to capitalist societies. Some radical feminist theorists, however, view the oppression of women as inevitable in *all* male-dominated societies, whether *capitalist, socialist,* or *communist.*

An early example of this perspective (long before the label came into use by sociologists) can be seen in the life and writings of Ida Wells-Barnett (1862–1931). Following her groundbreaking publications in the 1890s on the practice of lynching Black Americans, she became an advocate in the women's rights campaign, especially the struggle to win the vote for women. Like feminist theorists who succeeded her, Wells-Barnett used her analysis of society as a means of resisting oppression. In her case, she researched what it meant to be African American, a woman in the United States, and a Black woman in the United States (Wells-Barnett 1970).

Feminist scholarship in sociology has broadened our understanding of social behavior by taking it beyond the White male point of view. For example, a family's social standing is no longer defined solely by the husband's position and income. Feminist scholars have not only challenged stereotyping of women and men; they have argued for a gender-balanced study of society in which women's experiences and contributions are as visible as those of men (England 1999; Komarovsky 1991; Tuchman 1992).

The feminist perspective has given sociologists new views of familiar social behavior. For example, past research on crime rarely considered women, and when it did, tended to focus on "traditional" crimes by women, like shoplifting. Such a view tended to ignore the role women play in all types of crime, as well as the disproportionate role they play as *victims* of crime. Research conducted by Meda Chesney-Lind and Noelie Rodriguez (1993) showed that nearly all women in prison had suffered physical and/or sexual abuse when they were young; half had been raped. Contributions by both feminist and minority scholars have enriched all the sociological perspectives.

Use Your Sociological Imagination www.mhhe.com/schaefer6

You are a sociologist who uses the conflict perspective to study various aspects of our society. How do you think you would interpret the practice of prostitution? Contrast this view with the functionalist perspective. Do you think your comments would differ if you took the feminist view, and if so, how?

Gender Note the preponderance of White male sociologists as opposed to female and non-White sociologists in the history of sociology.
Key Person Ida Wells-Barnett
Gender Stress the relevance of conflict theory to feminist scholarship.
Gender Feminist scholarship offers insights into the behavior of both women and men.

Classroom Tip Distinguish between the Marxist, the racial, and the feminist versions of conflict theory.
Classroom Tip See "The Perspectives: A College Education" (Class Discussion Topics).

Interactionist Perspective

Workers interacting on the job, encounters in public places like bus stops and parks, behavior in small groups—all these aspects of microsociology catch the attention of interactionists. Whereas functionalist and conflict theorists both analyze large-scale, societywide patterns of behavior, theorists who take the *interactionist perspective* generalize about everyday forms of social interaction in order to explain society as a whole. In the 1990s, for example, the workings of juries became a subject of public scrutiny. High-profile trials ended in verdicts that left some people shaking their heads. Long before jury members were being interviewed on their front lawns following a trial, interactionists tried to better understand behavior in the small-group setting of a jury deliberation room.

Interactionism is a sociological framework for viewing human beings as living in a world of meaningful objects. Those "objects" may include material things, actions, other people, relationships, and even symbols. Because interactionists see symbols as an especially important part of human communication, the interactionist perspective is sometimes referred to as the *symbolic interactionist perspective.* Members of a society share the social meanings of symbols. In the United States, for example, a salute symbolizes respect, while a clenched fist signifies defiance. Another culture might use different gestures to convey a feeling of respect or defiance. These types of symbolic interaction are classified as forms of *nonverbal communication,* which can include many other gestures, facial expressions, and postures.

Symbols in the form of tattoos took on special importance in the aftermath of September 11, 2001. Tattoo parlors in lower Manhattan were overwhelmed with requests from various groups for designs that carried symbolic significance for them. New York City firefighters asked for tattoos with the names of their fallen colleagues; police officers requested designs incorporating their distinctive NYPD shield; recovery workers at Ground Zero sought tattoos that incorporated the image of the giant steel cross, the remnant of a massive cross-beam in a World Trade Center building. Through symbols such as these tattoos, people communicate their values and beliefs to those around them (Scharnberg 2002).

While the functionalist and conflict approaches were initiated in Europe, interactionism developed first in the United States. George Herbert Mead (1863–1931) is widely regarded as the founder of the interactionist perspective. Mead taught at the University of Chicago from 1893 until his death. His sociological analysis, like that of Charles Horton Cooley, often focused on human interactions in one-to-one situations and small groups. Mead was interested in observing the most minute forms of communication—smiles, frowns, nods—and in understanding how such individual behaviors were influenced by the larger context of a group or society. Despite his innovative views, Mead only occasionally wrote articles, and never a book. He was an extremely popular teacher; in fact, most of his insights have come to us through edited volumes of lectures that his students published after his death.

As Mead's teachings have become better known, sociologists have expressed greater interest in the interactionist

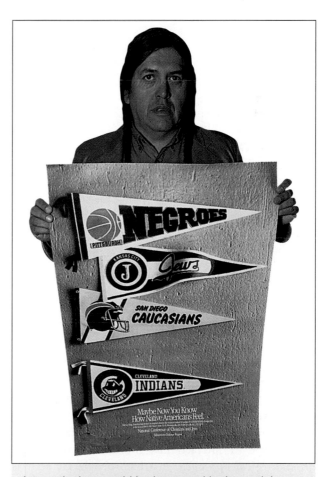

Interactionists would be interested in the social significance of team mascots and symbols. This Native American is protesting the use of the word *Indians* by a major league baseball team. By making up other team names that other groups might find offensive, he invites you to put yourself in his shoes.

Theory Interactionist theory introduced.
Key Person George Herbert Mead
Classroom Tip For more on the interactionist approach, see "Breaching Experiments" (Additional Lecture Ideas).

Table 1-1	Comparing Major Theoretical Perspectives		
	Functionalist	**Conflict**	**Interactionist**
View of society	Stable, well integrated	Characterized by tension and struggle between groups	Active in influencing and affecting everyday social interaction
Level of analysis emphasized	Macro	Macro	Micro, as a way of understanding the larger macro phenomena
Key concepts	Manifest functions Latent functions Dysfunctions	Inequality Capitalism Stratification	Symbols Nonverbal communication Face-to-face interaction
View of the individual	People are socialized to perform societal functions	People are shaped by power, coercion, and authority	People manipulate symbols and create their social worlds through interaction
View of the social order	Maintained through cooperation and consensus	Maintained through force and coercion	Maintained by shared understanding of everyday behavior
View of social change	Predictable, reinforcing	Change takes place all the time and may have positive consequences	Reflected in people's social positions and their communications with others
Example	Public punishments reinforce the social order	Laws reinforce the positions of those in power	People respect laws or disobey them based on their own past experience
Proponents	Émile Durkheim Talcott Parsons Robert Merton	Karl Marx W. E. B. Du Bois Ida Wells-Barnett	George Herbert Mead Charles Horton Cooley Erving Goffman

perspective. Many have moved away from what may have been an excessive preoccupation with the large-scale (macro) level of social behavior and have redirected their attention toward behavior that occurs in small groups (micro level).

Erving Goffman (1922–1982) popularized a particular type of interactionist method known as the **dramaturgical approach,** in which people are seen as theatrical performers. The dramaturgist compares everyday life to the setting of the theater and stage. Just as actors project certain images, all of us seek to present particular features of our personalities while we hide other qualities. Thus, in a class, we may feel the need to project a serious image; at a party, we want to look relaxed and friendly.

Student Alert The list of "proponents" in Table 1-1 is only illustrative; hundreds of names could be used.
Key Person Erving Goffman

The Sociological Approach

Which perspective should a sociologist use in studying human behavior? Functionalist? Conflict? Interactionist? In fact, sociologists make use of all the perspectives summarized in Table 1-1, since each offers unique insights into the same issue. We gain the broadest understanding of our society, then, by drawing on all the major perspectives, noting where they overlap and where they diverge.

Although no one approach is correct by itself, and sociologists draw on all of them for various purposes, many sociologists tend to favor one particular perspective over others. A sociologist's theoretical orientation influences his or her approach to a research problem in important ways—including the choice of what to study, how to study it, and what questions to pose (or not to pose).

Classroom Tip For more on Goffman's work and the dramaturgical approach, see "An Interactionist View of Sidewalk Etiquette" (Additional Lecture Ideas).

1-1 LOOKING AT SPORTS FROM THREE THEORETICAL PERSPECTIVES

We watch sports. Talk sports. Spend money on sports. Some of us live and breathe sports. Because sports occupy much of our time and directly or indirectly consume and generate a great deal of money, it should not be surprising that sports have sociological components that can be analyzed by the various theoretical perspectives.

Functionalist View

In examining any aspect of society, functionalists emphasize the contribution it makes to overall social stability. Functionalists regard sports as an almost religious institution that uses ritual and ceremony to reinforce the common values of a society:

- Sports socialize young people into such values as competition and patriotism.
- Sports help to maintain people's physical well-being.
- Sports serve as a safety valve for both participants and spectators, who are allowed to shed tension and aggressive energy in a socially acceptable way.
- Sports "bring together" members of a community (supporting local athletes and teams) or even a nation (as seen during World Cup matches and the Olympics) and promote an overall feeling of unity and social solidarity.

Conflict View

Conflict theorists argue that the social order is based on coercion and exploitation. They emphasize that sports reflect and even exacerbate many of the divisions of society:

- Sports are a form of big business in which profits are more important than the health and safety of the workers (athletes).
- Sports perpetuate the false idea that success can be achieved simply through hard work, while failure should be blamed on the individual alone (rather than on injustices in the larger social system). Sports also serve as an "opiate" that encourages people to seek a "fix" or temporary "high" rather than focus on personal problems and social issues.

Despite their differences, functionalists, conflict theorists, and interactionists would all agree that there is much more to sports than exercise or recreation.

- Sports maintain the subordinate role of Blacks and Latinos, who toil as athletes but are less visible in supervisory positions as coaches, managers, and owners.
- Gender expectations encourage female athletes to be passive and gentle, qualities that do not support the emphasis on competitiveness in sports.

Interactionist View

In studying the social order, interactionists are especially interested in shared understandings of everyday behavior. Interactionists examine sports on the micro level by focusing on how day-to-day social behavior is shaped by the distinctive norms, values, and demands of the world of sports:

- Sports often heighten parent–child involvement; they may lead to parental expectations for participation and (sometimes unrealistically) for success.
- Participation in sports provides friendship networks that can permeate everyday life.
- Despite class, racial, and religious differences, teammates may work together harmoniously and may even abandon previous stereotypes and prejudices.
- Relationships in the sports world are defined by people's social positions as players, coaches, and referees—as well as by the high or low status that individuals hold as a result of their performances and reputations.

Despite their differences, functionalists, conflict theorists, and interactionists would all agree that there is much more to sports than exercise or recreation. They would also agree that sports and other popular forms of culture are worthy subjects of serious study by sociologists.

Let's Discuss

1. Have you experienced or witnessed discrimination in sports based on gender or race? How did you react? Has the representation of Blacks or women on teams been controversial on your campus? In what ways?
2. Which perspective do you think is most useful in looking at the sociology of sports? Why?

Sources: Acosta and Carpenter 2001; H. Edwards 1973; Eitzen 2003; Fine 1987.

Classroom Tip See "Sociologists and Their Theoretical Preferences" (Additional Lecture Ideas).

(See Box 1-1 on page 19 for an example of how a researcher would study sports from different perspectives.) Whatever the purpose of sociologists' work, their research will always be guided by their theoretical viewpoints. Research results, like theories, shine a spotlight on one part of the stage, leaving others in relative darkness.

DEVELOPING A SOCIOLOGICAL IMAGINATION

In this book, we will be illustrating the sociological imagination in several different ways—by showing theory in practice and research in action; by exploring the significance of social inequality; by speaking across race, gender, and national boundaries; and by highlighting social policy throughout the world.

Theory in Practice

We will illustrate how the major sociological perspectives are helpful in understanding today's issues, from capital punishment to the AIDS crisis. Sociologists do not necessarily declare "Here I am using functionalism," but their research and approaches do tend to draw on one or more theoretical frameworks, as will become clear in the pages to follow.

Research in Action

Sociologists actively investigate a variety of issues and social behavior. We have already seen that research can shed light on the social factors that affect suicide rates and decision making in the jury box. Sociological research often has direct applications to improving people's lives, as in the case of increasing the participation of African Americans in diabetes testing. Throughout the rest of the book, the research performed by sociologists and other social scientists will shed light on group behavior of all types.

The Significance of Social Inequality

Who holds power? Who doesn't? Who has prestige? Who lacks it? Perhaps the major theme of analysis in sociology today is *social inequality,* a condition in which members of society have differing amounts of wealth, prestige, or power. Barbara Ehrenreich's research among low-wage workers uncovered some aspects of social inequality. Whether using the functionalist or feminist perspective, focusing on Arizona or Afghanistan, considering a garden club or the global marketplace, sociologists often see behavior as shaped by social inequality.

Some sociologists, in seeking to understand the effect of inequality, have made the case for social justice. W. E. B. Du Bois ([1940] 1968:418) noted that the greatest power in the land is not "thought or ethics, but wealth." As we have seen, the contributions of Karl Marx, Jane Addams, and Ida Wells-Barnett also focused on social inequality and social justice. Joe Feagin (2001) echoed this sentiment for the overarching importance of social inequality in a presidential address to the American Sociological Association.

Throughout, this book will highlight the work of sociologists on social inequality. Many chapters also feature a box with this theme.

Speaking across Race, Gender, and National Boundaries

Sociologists include both men and women, people from a variety of ethnic, national, and religious origins. In their work, sociologists seek to draw conclusions that speak to all people—not just the affluent or powerful. Doing so is not always easy. Insights into how a corporation can increase its profits tend to attract more attention and financial support than do, say, the merits of a needle exchange program for low-income inner-city residents. Yet sociology today, more than ever, seeks to better understand the experiences of all people. In Box 1-2 we look at how a woman's role in public places is defined differently from that of a man in different parts of the world.

Social Policy throughout the World

One important way we can use a sociological imagination is to enhance our understanding of current social issues throughout the world. Beginning with Chapter 2, each chapter will conclude with a discussion of a contemporary social policy issue. In some cases, we will examine a specific issue facing national governments. For example, government funding of child care centers will be discussed in Chapter 4, Socialization; immigration policies in Chapter 10, Racial and Ethnic Inequality; and religion in schools in Chapter 13, Religion and Education. These social policy sections will demonstrate how fundamental sociological concepts can enhance our critical thinking skills and help us to better understand current public policy debates taking place around the world.

In addition, sociology has been used to evaluate the success of programs or the impact of changes brought about by policymakers and political activists. For example, Chapter 9, Stratification in the United States and

Classroom Tip See "Theory Triumvirate" (Class Discussion Topics).
Policy Pointer The issue of social inequality is explored in Chapter 9.
Student Alert Explain the relationship between the sociological imagination and "theory in practice," "research in action," "social inequality," "speaking across race, gender, and national boundaries," and "social policy."

Policy Pointer Underscore the textbook's social policy focus. Other social policy sections include such topics as human sexuality, bilingualism, and the AIDS crisis.
Global View Have students note the global aspects of the social policy sections.

By definition, a public place, such as a sidewalk or a park, is open to all persons. Even some private establishments, such as restaurants, are intended to be open to people as a whole. Yet sociologists and other social scientists have found that societies define access to these places differently for women and for men.

In many Middle Eastern societies, women are prohibited from public places and are restricted to certain places in the house. In such societies, the coffeehouse and the market are considered male domains. Some other societies, such as Malagasy, strictly limit the presence of women in public places, yet allow women to conduct the haggling that is a part of shopping in open-air markets. In some West African societies, women actually control the marketplace. In various eastern European countries and Turkey, women appear to be free to move about in public places, but the coffeehouse remains the exclusive preserve of males. Contrast this with coffeehouses in North America, where women and men mingle freely and even engage each other in conversation as total strangers.

While casual observers may view both private and public space in the United States as gender-neutral, private all-male clubs do persist, and even in public

spaces women experience some inequality. Erving Goffman, an interactionist, conducted some classic studies of public spaces. He found them to be settings for routine interactions, such as the "helping" encounters that occur when a person is lost and asks for directions. But sociologist Carol Brooks Gardner has offered a feminist critique of Goffman's work: "Rarely does Goffman emphasize the habitual disproportionate fear that women

---

> *Women are well aware that a casual helping encounter with a man in a public place can too easily lead to undesired sexual queries or advances.*

---

can come to feel in public toward men, much less the routine trepidation that ethnic and racial minorities and the disabled can experience" (1989:45). Women are well aware that a casual helping encounter with a man in a public place can too easily lead to undesired sexual queries or advances.

Whereas Goffman suggests that street remarks about women occur rarely—and that they generally hold no unpleasant

or threatening implications—Gardner (1989:49) counters that "for young women especially, . . . appearing in public places carries with it the constant possibility of evaluation, compliments that are not really so complimentary after all, and harsh or vulgar insults if the woman is found wanting." She adds that these remarks are sometimes accompanied by tweaks, pinches, or even blows, unmasking the latent hostility of many male-to-female street remarks.

According to Gardner, many women have a well-founded fear of the sexual harassment, assault, and rape that can occur in public places. She concludes that "public places are arenas for the enactment of inequality in everyday life for women and for many others" (1989:56).

Let's Discuss

1. How would a coffeehouse in Turkey differ from one in Seattle, Washington? What might account for these differences?

2. Do you know a woman who has encountered sexual harassment in a public place? How did she react? Has her social behavior changed as a result of the experience?

Sources: Cheng and Liao 1994; C. Gardner 1989, 1990, 1995; Goffman 1963b, 1971; Rosman and Rubel 1994.

Worldwide, includes a discussion of research on the effectiveness of welfare reform experiments. Such discussions underscore the many practical applications of sociological theory and research.

Sociologists expect the next quarter of a century to be perhaps the most exciting and critical period in the history of the discipline. That is because of a growing recognition—both in the United States and around

the world—that current social problems *must* be addressed before their magnitude overwhelms human societies. We can expect sociologists to play an increasing role in government by researching and developing public policy alternatives. It seems only natural for this textbook to focus on the connection between the work of sociologists and the difficult questions confronting policymakers and people in the United States and around the world.

Global View   Note and have students cite other cross-cultural illustrations of gender differences in public behavior.

Theory   Gardner's study included observation research and interviews.
Gender   Gardner applied her sociological imagination in studying the experiences of women in public places.

CHAPTER RESOURCES

Summary

Sociology is the systematic study of social behavior and human groups. In this chapter, we examine the nature of sociological theory, the founders of the discipline, theoretical perspectives in contemporary sociology, and ways to exercise the "sociological imagination."

1. The *sociological imagination* is an awareness of the relationship between an individual and the wider society. It is based on the ability to view our own society as an outsider might, rather than from the perspective of our limited experiences and cultural biases.

2. In contrast to other *social sciences,* sociology emphasizes the influence that groups can have on people's behavior and attitudes and the ways in which people shape society.

3. Knowledge that relies on "common sense" is not always reliable. Sociologists must test and analyze each piece of information they use.

4. Sociologists employ *theories* to examine the relationships between observations or data that may seem completely unrelated.

5. Nineteenth-century thinkers who contributed sociological insights included Auguste Comte, a French philosopher; Harriet Martineau, an English sociologist; and Herbert Spencer, an English scholar.

6. Other important figures in the development of sociology were Émile Durkheim, who pioneered work on suicide; Max Weber, who taught the need for "in-

sight" in intellectual work; and Karl Marx, who emphasized the importance of the economy and social conflict.

7. In the 20th century, the discipline of sociology was indebted to the U.S. sociologists Charles Horton Cooley and Robert Merton.

8. *Macrosociology* concentrates on large-scale phenomena or entire civilizations, whereas *microsociology* stresses the study of small groups.

9. The *functionalist perspective* emphasizes the way in which the parts of a society are structured to maintain its stability.

10. The *conflict perspective* assumes that social behavior is best understood in terms of conflict or tension between competing groups.

11. The *interactionist perspective* is primarily concerned with fundamental or everyday forms of interaction, including symbols and other types of nonverbal communication.

12. Sociologists make use of all three perspectives, since each offers unique insights into the same issue.

13. This textbook makes use of the sociological imagination by showing theory in practice and research in action; by focusing on the significance of social inequality; by speaking across race, gender, and national boundaries; and by highlighting social policy around the world.

Critical Thinking Questions

1. What aspects of the social and work environment in a fast-food restaurant would be of particular interest to a sociologist because of his or her "sociological imagination"?

2. What are the manifest and latent functions of a health club?

3. How might an interactionist study a place where you have been employed or an organization in which you are a member?

Student Alert Reading the chapter summaries is a good review; it does not replace the entire chapter.
Classroom Tip Discuss how to use the Summary, Critical Thinking Questions, and Key Terms sections at the end of each chapter.
Classroom Tip Use the Critical Thinking Questions as the basis for classroom discussions, written homework assignments, or essays on tests.

Key Terms

Anomie   The loss of direction felt in a society when social control of individual behavior has become ineffective. (page 10)

Conflict perspective   A sociological approach that assumes that social behavior is best understood in terms of conflict or tension between competing groups. (15)

Dramaturgical approach   A view of social interaction in which people are seen as theatrical performers. (18)

Dysfunction   An element or process of a society that may disrupt the social system or reduce its stability. (14)

Feminist view   A sociological approach that views inequity in gender as central to all behavior and organization. (16)

Functionalist perspective   A sociological approach that emphasizes the way in which the parts of a society are structured to maintain its stability. (14)

Ideal type   A construct or model for evaluating specific cases. (11)

Interactionist perspective   A sociological approach that generalizes about everyday forms of social interaction in order to explain society as a whole. (17)

Latent function   An unconscious or unintended function that may reflect hidden purposes. (14)

Macrosociology   Sociological investigation that concentrates on large-scale phenomena or entire civilizations. (13)

Manifest function   An open, stated, and conscious function. (14)

Microsociology   Sociological investigation that stresses the study of small groups, often through experimental means. (13)

Natural science   The study of the physical features of nature and the ways in which they interact and change. (6)

Nonverbal communication   The sending of messages through the use of gestures, facial expressions, and postures. (17)

Science   The body of knowledge obtained by methods based on systematic observation. (6)

Social inequality   A condition in which members of society have differing amounts of wealth, prestige, or power. (20)

Social science   The study of the social features of humans and the ways in which they interact and change. (6)

Sociological imagination   An awareness of the relationship between an individual and the wider society. (3)

Sociology   The systematic study of social behavior and human groups. (3)

Theory   In sociology, a set of statements that seeks to explain problems, actions, or behavior. (8)

Verstehen   The German word for "understanding" or "insight"; used to stress the need for sociologists to take into account the subjective meanings people attach to their actions. (11)

TECHNOLOGY RESOURCES

Internet Connection

Note: While all the URLs listed were current as of the printing of this book, these sites often change. Please check our website (www.mhhe.com/schaefer6) for updates, hyperlinks, and exercises related to these sites.

1. The National Science Foundation (NSF) is a major source of funding for sociologists. Explore the Sociology Program page at the NSF's website (**www.nsf.gov/sbe/ses/sociol/start.htm**). To get some idea of contemporary sociologists' research interests, click on the link to "Sociology Program

Awards Search" in the middle of the page, under "Grant/Award Administration and Information."

2. The website of the Hull House Museum (**www.uic.edu/jaddams/hull/hull_house.html**) provides a wealth of information on Jane Addams and her life work. To view historical photographs of Hull House and the people Addams served, click on "Urban Experience in Chicago."

Online Learning Center with PowerWeb

Visit the Online Learning Center, this textbook's specific website, at **www.mhhe.com/schaefer6**. The student center in the Online Learning Center offers a variety of helpful and interesting resources and activities for each chapter. The resources include chapter outlines and summaries, quizzes with feedback, video clips about current issues, direct links to Internet sites, including those found in the Internet Connection sections at the end of

each chapter in your text, relevant news updates, and audio clips by the author. The activities include flashcards, crossword puzzles, interactive maps, and interactive exercises. Don't pass up this opportunity to learn more about sociology and to take advantage of resources that will help you master the material in your text and get a better grade in the course!

Reel Society Interactive Movie CD-ROM 2.0

Exercise your imagination and step into the world of *Reel Society,* a professionally produced movie on CD-ROM that demonstrates the sociological imagination through typical scenarios drawn from campus life. In this movie you will become part of the exploits of several college students, and will influence the plot by making key choices for them. Through it all, you'll learn to relate sociological thought to real life through a variety of issues and perspectives. In addition to the interactive movie, *Reel Society* includes explanatory text screens and a glossary, as well as quizzes and discussion questions to test your knowledge of sociology. The CD also includes a link to the Online Learning Center website for *Reel Society.*

Reel Society 2.0 can be used to spark discussion about the following topics from this chapter:

- The Sociological Imagination
- Major Theoretical Perspectives
- Speaking Across Race, Gender, and National Boundaries

CAREERS
IN SOCIOLOGY

An undergraduate degree in sociology doesn't just serve as excellent preparation for future graduate work in sociology. It also provides a strong liberal arts background for entry-level positions in business, social services, foundations, community organizations, not-for-profit groups, law enforcement, and many types of governmental jobs. A number of fields—among them marketing, public relations, and broadcasting—now require investigative skills and an understanding of the diverse groups found in today's multiethnic and multinational environment. Moreover, a sociology degree requires accomplishment in oral and written communication, interpersonal skills, problem solving, and critical thinking—all job-related skills that may give sociology graduates an advantage over those who pursue more technical degrees (Benner and Hitchcock 1986; Billson and Huber 1993).

Consequently, while few occupations specifically require an undergraduate degree in sociology, such academic training can be an important asset in entering a wide range of occupations (American Sociological Association 1993, 2002). To emphasize this point, a number of chapters in this book highlight a real-life professional who describes how the study of sociology has helped in his or her career. Look for the "Taking Sociology to Work" boxes.

The accompanying figure summarizes the sources of employment for those with BA or BS degrees in sociology. It shows that the areas of social services, education, business, and government offer major career opportunities for sociology graduates. Undergraduates who know where their career interests lie are well advised to enroll in sociology courses and specialties best suited to those interests. For example, students hoping to become health planners would take a class in medical sociology; students seeking employment as social science research assistants would focus on courses in statistics and methods. Internships, such as placements at city planning agencies and survey research organizations, afford another way for sociology students to prepare for careers. Studies show that students who choose an internship placement have less trouble finding jobs, obtain better jobs, and enjoy greater

Occupational Fields of Sociology BA/MA Graduates

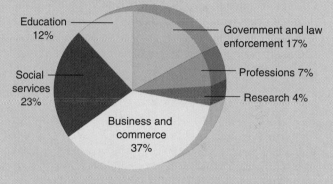

Source: Schaefer 1998b.

job satisfaction than students without internship placements (Salem and Grabarek 1986).

Many college students view social work as the field most closely associated with sociology. Traditionally, social workers received their undergraduate training in sociology and allied fields such as psychology and counseling. After some practical experience, social workers would generally seek a master's degree in social work (MSW) to be considered for supervisory or administrative positions. Today, however, some students choose (where it is available) to pursue a bachelor's degree in social work (BSW). This degree prepares graduates for direct service positions such as caseworker or group worker.

Many students continue their sociological training beyond the bachelor's degree. More than 250 universities in the United States have graduate programs in sociology that offer PhD and/or master's degrees. These programs differ greatly in their areas of specialization, course requirements, costs, and the research and teaching opportunities available to graduate students. About 55 percent of the graduates are women (American Sociological Association 2004; Spalter-Roth and Lee 2000).

Higher education is an important source of employment for sociologists with graduate degrees. About 83 percent of recent PhD recipients in sociology seek employment in colleges and universities. These sociologists teach not only majors committed to the discipline but also students hoping to become doctors, nurses, lawyers, police officers, and so forth (Spalter-Roth et al. 2000).

Sociologists who teach in colleges and universities may use their knowledge and training to influence public policy. For example, sociologist Andrew Cherlin (2003) recently commented on the debate over proposed federal funding to promote marriage among welfare recipients. Citing the results of two of his studies, Cherlin questioned the potential effectiveness of such a policy in strengthening low-income families. Because many single mothers choose to marry someone other than the father of their children—sometimes for good reason—their children often grow up in stepfamilies. Cherlin's research shows that children who are raised in stepfamilies are no better off than those in single-parent families. He sees government efforts to promote marriage as a politically motivated attempt to foster traditional social values in a society that has become increasingly diverse.

For sociology graduates interested in academic careers, the road to a PhD (or doctorate) can be long and difficult. This degree symbolizes competence in original research; each candidate must prepare a book-length study known as a dissertation. Typically, a doctoral student in sociology will engage in four to seven years of intensive work, including the time required to complete the dissertation. Yet even this effort is no guarantee of a job as a sociology professor.

The good news is that over the next 10 years, the demand for instructors is expected to increase because of high rates of retirement among faculty from the baby-boom generation, as well as the anticipated slow but steady growth in the college student population in the United States. Nonetheless, anyone who launches an academic career must be prepared for considerable uncertainty and competition in the college job market (American Sociological Association 2002; Huber 1985).

Of course, not all people working as sociologists teach or hold doctoral degrees. Take government, for example. The Census Bureau relies on people with sociological training to interpret data for other government agencies and the general public. Virtually every agency depends on survey research—a field in which sociology students can specialize—in order to assess everything from community needs to the morale of the agency's own workers. In addition, people with sociological training can put their academic knowledge to effective use in probation and parole, health sciences, community development, and recreational services. Some people working in government or private industry have a master's degree (MA or MS) in sociology; others have a bachelor's degree (BA or BS).

Currently, about 22 percent of the members of the American Sociological Association use their sociological skills outside the academic world, whether in social service agencies or in marketing positions for business firms. Increasing numbers of sociologists with graduate degrees are employed by businesses, industry, hospitals, and nonprofit organizations. Studies show that many sociology graduates are making career changes from social service areas to business and commerce. As an undergraduate major, sociology is excellent preparation for employment in many parts of the business world (American Sociological Association 2001).

Whether you take a few courses in sociology or actually complete a degree, you will benefit from the critical thinking skills developed in this discipline. Sociologists emphasize the value of being able to analyze, interpret, and function within a variety of working situations; this is an asset in virtually any career. Moreover, given rapid technological change and the expanding global economy, all of us will need to adapt to substantial social change, even in our own careers. Sociology provides a rich conceptual framework that can serve as a foundation for flexible career development and can assist you in taking advantage of new employment opportunities (American Sociological Association 1995, 2002).

 For more information on career opportunities for individuals with a background in sociology, visit the Online Learning Center at **www.mhhe.com/schaefer6**. Go to "Student Edition," and in the section titled "Course-wide Content," click on "Web Resources." Then click on "Career Opportunities," which will provide you with numerous links to sites offering career advice and information.

chapter

2

SOCIOLOGICAL RESEARCH

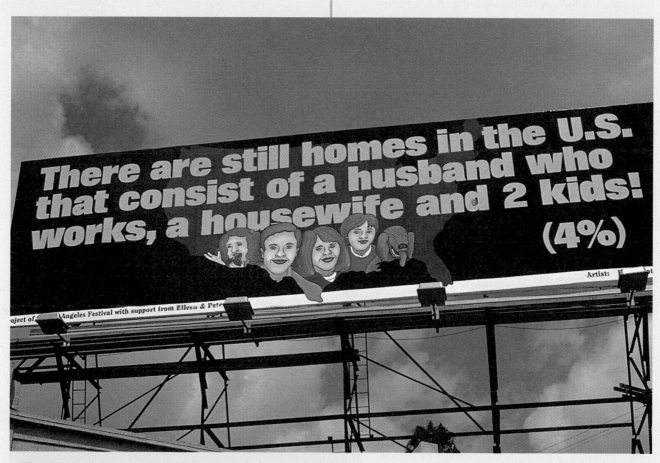

The data social scientists collect often confirm what people think, but sometimes—as this 1992 billboard suggests—they surprise us. Today, the percentage of homes in the United States with two children, a working father, and a homemaker mother remains relatively unchanged.

What Is the Scientific Method?

Major Research Designs

Ethics of Research

Technology and Sociological Research

Social Policy and Sociological Research: Studying Human Sexuality

Boxes

RESEARCH IN ACTION: Polling in Baghdad

SOCIOLOGY ON CAMPUS: Does Hard Work Lead to Better Grades?

TAKING SOCIOLOGY TO WORK: Dave Eberbach, Research Coordinator, United Way of Central Iowa

27

Because public interactions generally matter for only a few crucial seconds, people are conditioned to rapid scrutiny of the looks, speech, public behavior, gender, and color of those sharing the environment.... [T]he central strategy in maintaining safety on the streets is to avoid strange black males....

Many blacks perceive whites as tense or hostile to them in public. They pay attention to the amount of eye contact given. In general, black males get far less time in this regard than do white males. Whites tend not to "hold" the eyes of a black person. It is more common for black and white strangers to meet each other's eyes for only a few seconds, and then to avert their gaze abruptly. Such behavior seems to say, "I am aware of your presence," and no more. Women especially feel that eye contact invites unwanted advances, but some white men feel the same and want to be clear about what they intend. This eye work is a way to maintain distance, mainly for safety and social purposes. Consistent with this, some blacks are very surprised to find a white person who holds their eyes longer than is normal according to the rules of the public sphere. As one middle-aged white female resident commented:

Just this morning, I saw a [black] guy when I went over to Mr. Chow's to get some milk at 7:15. You always greet people you see at 7:15, and I looked at him and smiled. And he said "Hello" or "Good morning" or something. I smiled again. It was clear that he saw this as surprising....

Many people, particularly those who see themselves as more economically privileged than others in the community, are careful not to let their eyes stray, in order to avoid an uncomfortable situation. As they walk down the street they pretend not to see other pedestrians, or they look right at them without speaking, a behavior many blacks find offensive....

Moreover, whites of the Village often scowl to keep young blacks at a social and physical distance. As they venture out on the streets of the Village and, to a lesser extent, of Northton, they may plant this look on their faces to ward off others who might mean them harm. Scowling by whites may be compared to gritting [looking "tough"] by blacks as a coping strategy. At times members of either group make such faces with little regard for circumstances, as if they were dressing for inclement weather. But on the Village streets it does not always storm, and such overcoats repel the sunshine as well as the rain, frustrating many attempts at spontaneous human communication. *(Anderson 1990:208, 220–221)* ■ ◎

Additional information about this excerpt can be found on the Online Learning Center at **www.mhhe.com/schaefer6**.

ELIJAH ANDERSON

STREETWISE

Race, Class, and Change in an Urban Community

his study of "eye work" was part of extensive research into life on the street that sociologist Elijah Anderson conducted in two adjacent neighborhoods of Philadelphia— "the Village," a racially mixed area with mixed incomes, and "Northton," mostly Black and low-income. Anderson became intrigued with the nature of social interaction between strangers on the street shortly after moving into the Village community in 1975. Over the next 14 years he undertook a formal study. Using the interactionist perspective, he focused on how such a diverse group of people related to one another in everyday life. In particular, he was interested in their "public behavior," including the way they used eye contact in their daily encounters.

Like any good scientist, Anderson was thorough in his research. He interviewed residents, videotaped street scenes, took extensive notes, photographed settings, and hung out for hours at a time in the local bars, Laundromats, and corner stores in the course of his observations. As a Black man, he was also able to draw on his own experiences with the Whites in his neighborhood. Anderson systematically traced how social changes—including gentrification of previously low-income areas, increasing drug use and crime, and declining city services—affected social relations and the ways people negotiated public spaces. Three of his books, *A Place on the Corner* (1978), *Streetwise* (1990), and *Code of the Streets* (1999), came out of this research, and he hopes other researchers will make use of his database for their own studies.

Effective sociological research can be quite thought-provoking. It may suggest many new questions about social interactions that require further study, such as why we make assumptions about people's intentions based merely on their gender or age or race. In some cases, rather than raising additional questions, a study will simply confirm previous beliefs and findings. Sociological research can also have practical applications. For instance, research results that disconfirm accepted beliefs about marriage and the family may lead to changes in public policy.

This chapter will examine the research process used in conducting sociological studies. How do sociologists go about setting up a research project? And how do they ensure that the results of the research are reliable and accurate? Can they carry out their research without violating the rights of those they study?

We will first look at the steps that make up the scientific method used in research. Then we will take a look at various techniques commonly used in sociological research, such as experiments, observations, and surveys. We will pay particular attention to the ethical challenges sociologists face in studying human behavior, and to the debate raised by Max Weber's call for "value neutrality" in social science research. We will also examine the role technology plays in research today. The social policy section considers the difficulties in researching the controversial subject of human sexuality.

Whatever the area of sociological inquiry and whatever the perspective of the sociologist—whether functionalist, conflict, interactionist, or any other— there is one crucial requirement: imaginative, responsible research that meets the highest scientific and ethical standards. ■

WHAT IS THE SCIENTIFIC METHOD?

Like all of us, sociologists are interested in the central questions of our time. Is the family falling apart? Why is there so much crime in the United States? Is the world lagging behind in its ability to feed a growing population? Such issues concern most people, whether or not they have academic training. However, unlike the typical citizen, the sociologist has a commitment to use the *scientific method* in studying society. The scientific method is a systematic, organized series of steps that ensures maximum objectivity and consistency in researching a problem.

Many of us will never actually conduct scientific research. Why, then, is it important that we understand the scientific method? The answer is that it plays a major role in the workings of our society. Residents of the United States are constantly bombarded with "facts" or "data." A television news report informs us that "one in every two marriages in this country now ends in divorce,"

Classroom Tip See "Stimulating Classroom Discussions about *Streetwise*" (Class Discussion Topics).
Theory Anderson's analysis is an example of the interactionist perspective.
Classroom Tip Return to Anderson's study throughout the unit as an example of various research methodologies.
Key Person Elijah Anderson

Methods Explain the significance of the race of the researcher in observation research. See Elliot Liebow's *Tally's Corner*.
Student Alert Be sure that students understand the difference between rigorous sociological studies and the "studies" that are often presented in popular magazines or in political advertisements.

FIGURE 2-I

The Scientific Method

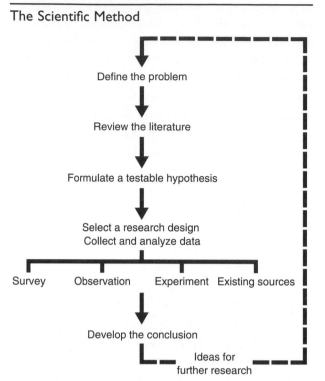

The scientific method allows sociologists to objectively and logically evaluate the data they collect. Their findings can suggest ideas for further sociological research.

sis, (4) selecting the research design and then collecting and analyzing data, and (5) developing the conclusion (see Figure 2-1). We'll use an actual example to illustrate the workings of the scientific method.

Defining the Problem

Does it "pay" to go to college? Some people make great sacrifices and work hard to get a college education. Parents borrow money for their children's tuition. Students work part-time jobs or even take full-time positions while attending evening or weekend classes. Does it pay off? Are there monetary returns for getting that degree?

The first step in any research project is to state as clearly as possible what you hope to investigate—that is, *define the problem*. In this instance, we are interested in knowing how schooling relates to income. We want to find out the earnings of people with different levels of formal schooling. Early on, any social science researcher must develop an operational definition of each concept being studied. An ***operational definition*** is an explanation of an abstract concept that is specific enough to allow a researcher to assess the concept. For example, a sociologist interested in status might use membership in exclusive social clubs as an operational definition of status. Someone studying prejudice might consider a person's unwillingness to hire or work with members of minority groups as an operational definition of prejudice.

yet Chapter 12 will show that this assertion is based on misleading statistics. Almost daily, advertisers cite supposedly scientific studies to prove that their products are superior. Such claims may be accurate or exaggerated. We can better evaluate such information—and will not be fooled so easily—if we are familiar with the standards of scientific research. These standards are quite stringent, and they demand as strict adherence as possible.

The scientific method requires precise preparation in developing useful research. Otherwise, the research data collected may not prove accurate. Sociologists and other researchers follow five basic steps in the scientific method: (1) defining the problem, (2) reviewing the literature, (3) formulating the hypothe-

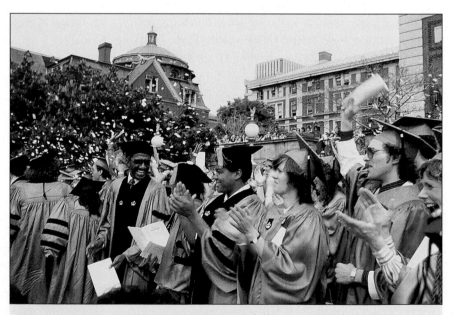

It seems reasonable to assume that these Columbia University graduates will earn more income than high school graduates. But how would you go about testing that hypothesis?

Classroom Tip See "Useful Statistics" (Additional Lecture Ideas).
Let's Discuss Why is it important that sociology be held to the same rigorous standards of the scientific method as the physical sciences are?
Classroom Tip See "Theory and Research" (Class Discussion Topics).

Methods Explain the difficulty of creating operational definitions for abstract concepts such as status and prejudice.
Theory Detail the relationship between education and income from each of the theoretical perspectives.

In our example, we need to develop two operational definitions—education and earnings—in order to study whether it pays to get an advanced educational degree. We'll define education as the number of years of schooling a person has achieved, and earnings as the income a person reports having received in the last year.

Initially, we will take a functionalist perspective (although we may end up incorporating other approaches). We will argue that opportunities for more earning power are related to level of schooling and that schools prepare students for employment.

Reviewing the Literature

By conducting a *review of the literature*—relevant scholarly studies and information—researchers refine the problem under study, clarify possible techniques to be used in collecting data, and eliminate or reduce avoidable mistakes. In our example, we would examine information about the salaries for different occupations. We would see if jobs that require more academic training are better rewarded. It would also be appropriate to review other studies on the relationship between education and income.

The review of the literature would soon tell us that many other factors besides years of schooling influence earning potential. For example, we would learn that the children of rich parents are more likely to go to college than those from modest backgrounds, so we might consider the possibility that the same parents may later help their children secure better-paying jobs.

We might also look at macro-level data, such as state-by-state comparisons of income and educational levels. In one macro-level study based on census data, researchers found that in states whose residents have a relatively high level of education, household income levels are high as well (see Figure 2-2, page 32). This finding suggests that schooling may well be related to income, though it does not speak to the micro-level relationship we are interested in. That is, we want to know whether *individuals* who are well educated are also well paid.

Formulating the Hypothesis

After reviewing earlier research and drawing on the contributions of sociological theorists, the researchers may then *formulate the hypothesis*. A **hypothesis** is a speculative statement about the relationship between two or more factors known as variables. Income, religion, occupation, and gender can all serve as variables in a study. We can define a **variable** as a measurable trait or characteristic that is subject to change under different conditions.

Researchers who formulate a hypothesis generally must suggest how one aspect of human behavior influences or affects another. The variable hypothesized to cause or influence another is called the **independent variable.** The second variable is termed the **dependent variable** because its action "depends" on the influence of the independent variable.

Our hypothesis is that the higher one's educational degree, the more money one will earn. The independent variable that is to be measured is the level of education. The variable that is thought to "depend" on it—income—must also be measured.

Identifying independent and dependent variables is a critical step in clarifying cause-and-effect relationships. As shown in Figure 2-3 (page 33), **causal logic** involves the relationship between a condition or variable and a particular consequence, with one event leading to the other. For instance, being less integrated into society may be directly related to, or produce a greater likelihood of, suicide. Similarly, the time students spend reviewing material for a quiz may be directly related to, or produce a greater likelihood of, getting a high score on the quiz.

A **correlation** exists when a change in one variable coincides with a change in the other. Correlations are an indication that causality *may* be present; they do not necessarily indicate causation. For example, data indicate that working mothers are more likely to have delinquent children than are mothers who do not work outside the home. But this correlation is actually caused by a third variable: family income. Lower-class households are more likely to have a full-time working mother; at the same time, reported rates of delinquency are higher in this class than at other economic levels. Consequently, while having a mother who works outside the home is correlated with delinquency, it does not *cause* delinquency. Sociologists seek to identify the *causal* link between variables; this causal link is generally described in the hypothesis.

Collecting and Analyzing Data

How do you test a hypothesis to determine if it is supported or refuted? You need to collect information, using one of the research designs described later in the chapter. The research design guides the researcher in collecting and analyzing data.

Selecting the Sample

In most studies, social scientists must carefully select what is known as a sample. A **sample** is a selection from a larger population that is statistically representative of that population. There are many kinds of samples, but the one

---

Student Alert Note that an early step in the scientific method is reviewing scientific studies, not simply drawing on commonsense beliefs.
Student Alert A hypothesis is not the same as a guess or hunch, because a hypothesis is based on a review of scientific studies.
Classroom Tip Make sure that students understand the differences between independent and dependent variables. This is often a problem!

Let's Discuss What other independent variables could be used in a study of income?
Classroom Tip The discussion of correlation, family income, and delinquency shows how a misguided commonsense belief can be clarified through scientific research.

FIGURE 2-2

Educational Level and Household Income in the United States

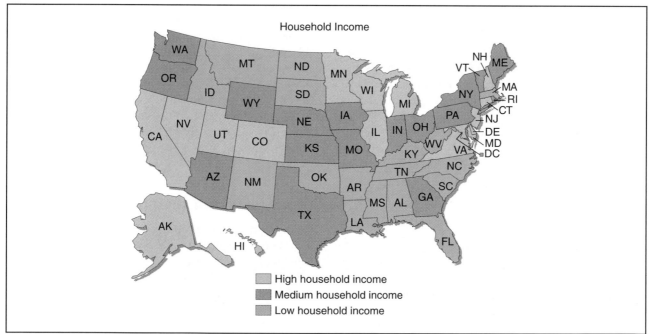

In general, states with high educational levels (top) also have high household incomes (bottom).

Notes: Education data are for 2000. Cutoffs for high/medium and medium/low educational levels were 27 percent and 23 percent of the population with a college degree, respectively; median for the entire nation was 25.6 percent. Income data are 2000–2001 two-year average medians. Cutoffs for high/medium and medium/low household income levels were $44,000 and $39,000, respectively; national median household income was $42,695.

Sources: Bureau of the Census 2002a:141; DeNavas-Walt and Cleveland 2002:11.

FIGURE 2-3

Causal Logic

In *causal logic* an independent variable (often designated by the symbol *x*) influences a dependent variable (generally designated as *y*); thus, *x* leads to *y*. For example, parents who attend church regularly (*x*) are more likely to have children who are churchgoers (*y*). Notice that the first two pairs of variables are taken from studies already described in this textbook.

Think About It
Identify two or three dependent variables that might be influenced by this independent variable: number of alcoholic drinks ingested.

social scientists use most frequently is the random sample. In a **random sample,** every member of an entire population being studied has the same chance of being selected. Thus, if researchers want to examine the opinions of people listed in a city directory (a book that, unlike the telephone directory, lists all households), they might use a computer to randomly select names from the directory. The results would constitute a random sample. The advantage of using specialized sampling techniques is that sociologists do not need to question everyone in a population.

It is all too easy to confuse the careful scientific techniques used in representative sampling with the many *nonscientific* polls that receive much more media attention. For example, television viewers and radio listeners are often encouraged to e-mail their views on headline news or political contests. Such polls reflect nothing more than the views of those who happened to see the televi-

sion program (or hear the radio broadcast) and took the time, perhaps at some cost, to register their opinions. These data do not necessarily reflect (and indeed may distort) the views of the broader population. Not everyone has access to a television or radio, time to watch or listen to a program, or the means and/or inclination to send e-mail. Similar problems are raised by the "mail-back" questionnaires found in many magazines and by "mall intercepts," in which shoppers are asked about some issue. Even when these techniques include answers from tens of thousands of people, they will be far less accurate than a carefully selected representative sample of 1,500 respondents.

For the purposes of our research example, we will use information collected in the General Social Survey (GSS). Since 1972, the National Opinion Research Center (NORC) has conducted this national survey 23 times, most recently in 2002. In this survey, a representative sample of the adult population is interviewed on a variety of topics for about one and a half hours. The author of this book examined the responses of the 1,875 people interviewed in 2002 concerning their level of education and income.

"And don't waste your time canvassing the whole building, young man. We think alike."

When conducting a study, researchers must draw their sample carefully so that it is representative of the general population.

Table 2-1	Education and Income				
	Income by Education (Percentage of Graduates in Each Income Group)				
Income Group	**Less Than High School Education**	**High School Diploma**	**Associate's Degree**	**BA/BS**	**Graduate Degree**
Under $15,000	50%	31%	11%	17%	11%
$15,000–$24,999	25	22	18	12	8
$25,000–$34,999	14	26	32	22	17
$35,000–$59,999	7	15	18	23	25
$60,000 and over	4	6	21	26	39
Total	100%	100%	100%	100%	100%

Note: N = 1,875.

Source: Author's analysis of General Social Survey 2002 in J. A. Davis et al. 2003.

Ensuring Validity and Reliability

The scientific method requires that research results be both valid and reliable. *Validity* refers to the degree to which a measure or scale truly reflects the phenomenon under study. A valid measure of income depends on the gathering of accurate data. Various studies show that people are reasonably accurate in reporting how much money they earned in the most recent year. *Reliability* refers to the extent to which a measure produces consistent results. One problem of reliability is that some people may not *disclose* accurate information, but most do. In the General Social Survey, only 5 percent of the respondents refused to give their income or indicated they did not know what their income was. That means 95 percent of the respondents gave their income, which we can assume is reasonably accurate (given their other responses about occupation and years in the labor force).

Developing the Conclusion

Scientific studies, including those conducted by sociologists, do not aim to answer all the questions that can be raised about a particular subject. Therefore, the conclusion of a research study represents both an end and a beginning. It terminates a specific phase of the investigation but should also generate ideas for future study.

Supporting Hypotheses

In our example, we find that the data support our hypothesis: People with more formal schooling *do* earn more

money than others. Those with a high school diploma earn more than those who failed to complete high school, but those with an associate's degree earn more than high school graduates. The relationship continues through more advanced levels of schooling, so that those with graduate degrees earn the most (see Table 2-1).

The relationship is not perfect. Some people who drop out of high school end up with high incomes, whereas some with advanced degrees earn modest incomes, as shown in Figure 2-4. A successful entrepreneur, for example, might not have much formal schooling, while a holder of a doctorate degree may choose to work for a low-paying nonprofit institution. Sociologists are interested in both the general pattern that emerges from their data and exceptions to the pattern.

Sociological studies do not always generate data that support the original hypothesis. In many instances, a hypothesis is refuted, and researchers must reformulate their conclusions. Unexpected results may also lead sociologists to reexamine their methodology and make changes in the research design.

Controlling for Other Factors

A *control variable* is a factor that is held constant to test the relative impact of the independent variable. For example, if researchers wanted to know how adults in the United States feel about restrictions on smoking in public places, they would probably attempt to use a respondent's smoking behavior as a control variable. That is, how do smokers versus nonsmokers feel about smoking

Student Alert Note the value of discovering that a hypothesis is proven incorrect by research.

Theory Discuss the relationship between race and income and between gender and income from a conflict perspective.

Doonesbury

Think About It
What would constitute a less biased question for a survey on smoking?

---

in public places? The researchers would compile separate statistics on how smokers and nonsmokers feel about antismoking regulations.

Our study of the influence of education on income suggests that not everyone enjoys equal educational opportunities, a disparity that is one of the causes of p. 20 social inequality. Since education affects a person's income, we may wish to call on the conflict perspective to explore this topic further. What impact does a person's race or gender have? Is a woman with a college degree likely to earn as much as a man with similar schooling? Later in this textbook we will consider these other factors and variables. That is, we will examine the impact that education has on income while controlling for variables such as gender and race.

FIGURE 2-4

Impact of a College Education on Income

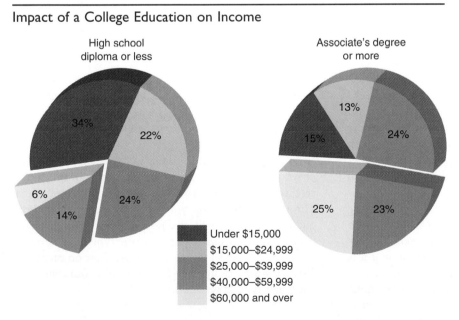

Source: Author's analysis of General Social Survey 2002 in J. A. Davis et al. 2003.

Fifty-six percent of people with a high school diploma or less (left) earn under $25,000 a year, while only 20 percent earn $40,000 or more. In contrast, 48 percent of those with an associate's degree or higher (right) earn $40,000 or more, while only 28 percent earn less than $25,000.

In Summary: The Scientific Method

Let us briefly summarize the process of the scientific method through a review of the example. We *defined a problem* (the question of whether it pays to get a higher educational degree). We *reviewed the literature* (other studies of the relationship between education and income) and *formulated a hypothesis* (the higher one's educational degree, the more money one will earn). We *collected and analyzed the data,* making sure the sample was representative and the data were valid and reliable. Finally, we *developed the conclusion:* The data do support our hypothesis about the influence of education on income.

MAJOR RESEARCH DESIGNS

An important aspect of sociological research is deciding *how* to collect the data. A **research design** is a detailed plan or method for obtaining data scientifically. Selection of a research design is often based on the theories and hypotheses the researcher starts with (Merton 1948). The choice requires creativity and ingenuity, because it directly influences both the cost of the project and the amount of time needed to collect the data. Research designs that sociologists regularly use to generate data include surveys, observation, experiments, and existing sources.

Surveys

Almost all of us have responded to surveys of one kind or another. We may have been asked what kind of detergent we use, which presidential candidate we intend to vote for, or what our favorite television program is. A **survey** is a study, generally in the form of an interview or questionnaire, that provides researchers with information about how people think and act. Among the United States' best-known surveys of opinion are the Gallup poll and the Harris poll. As anyone who watches the news during presidential campaigns knows, these polls have become a staple of political life.

When you think of surveys, you may recall seeing many "person on the street" interviews on local television news shows. Although such interviews can be highly entertaining, they are not necessarily an accurate indication of public opinion. First, they reflect the opinions of only those people who happen to be at a certain location. Such a sample can be biased in favor of commuters, middle-class shoppers, or factory workers, depending on which street or area the newspeople select. Second, television interviews tend to attract outgoing people who are willing to appear on the air, while they frighten away others who may feel intimidated by a camera. As we've seen, a survey must be based on precise, representative sampling if it is to genuinely reflect a broad range of the population.

In preparing to conduct a survey, sociologists must not only develop representative samples; they must exercise great care in the wording of questions. An effective survey question must be simple and clear enough for people to understand. It also must be specific enough so that there are no problems in interpreting the results. Open-ended questions ("What do you think of the program-

ming on educational television?") must be carefully phrased to solicit the type of information desired. Surveys can be indispensable sources of information, but only if the sampling is done properly and the questions are worded accurately and without bias. Box 2-1 describes the special challenges of conducting a public opinion poll in Iraq after the defeat of Saddam Hussein's regime in 2003.

There are two main forms of the survey: the **interview,** in which a researcher obtains information through face-to-face or telephone questioning, and the **questionnaire,** in which the researcher uses a printed or written form to obtain information from a respondent. Each of these has its own advantages. An interviewer can obtain a higher response rate because people find it more difficult to turn down a personal request for an interview than to throw away a written questionnaire. In addition, a skillful interviewer can go beyond written questions and probe for a subject's underlying feelings and reasons. On the other hand, questionnaires have the advantage of being cheaper, especially in large samples.

Studies have shown that the characteristics of the interviewer have an impact on survey data. For example, women interviewers tend to receive more feminist responses from female subjects than do male researchers, and African American interviewers tend to receive more detailed responses about race-related issues from Black subjects than do White interviewers. The possible impact of gender and race indicates again how much care social research requires (D. W. Davis 1997; Huddy et al. 1997).

The survey is an example of **quantitative research,** which collects and reports data primarily in numerical form. Most of the survey research discussed so far in this book has been quantitative. While this type of research can make use of large samples, it can't offer great depth and detail on a topic. That is why researchers also make use of **qualitative research,** which relies on what is seen in field and naturalistic settings, and often focuses on small groups and communities rather than large groups or whole nations. The most common form of qualitative research is observation, which we consider next. Throughout this book you will find examples of both quantitative and qualitative research, since both are used widely. Some sociologists prefer one type of research to the other, but we learn most when we draw on many different research designs and do not limit ourselves to a particular type of research.

Observation

As we saw in the chapter opening, Elijah Anderson gathered his information on street life in Philadelphia by *observing* the everyday interactions among residents.

Classroom Tip See "Defending Surveys" (Class Discussion Topics).
Classroom Tip See "Coding" (Class Discussion Topics).
Methods The Gallup poll is an example of a survey.
Classroom Tip See "Asking the Correct Questions," "Framing Survey Questions about Interracial Friendships" (Additional Lecture Ideas).

Contemporary Culture Discuss preelection polls.
Gender/Race/Ethnicity Impact of the race/ethnicity of the interviewer
Web Resource Encourage students to visit the student center in the Online Learning Center (**www.mhhe.com/schaefer6**) and listen to the audio clip. Richard Schaefer, the author of this textbook, discusses how poverty could be studied from both a qualitative and a quantitative perspective.

2-1 POLLING IN BAGHDAD

In 2003, as the U.S. Army launched the war in Iraq, pollsters watched President George W. Bush's approval rating carefully. Such periodic measures of the public pulse have become routine in the United States, an accepted part of presidential politics. But in Iraq, a totalitarian state ruled for 24 years by dictator Saddam Hussein, polling of public opinion on political and social issues was unknown until August 2003, when representatives of the Gallup Organization began regular surveys of the residents of Baghdad. Later in the occupation, Gallup extended its survey to other areas in Iraq.

Needless to say, conducting a scientific survey in the war-torn city presented unusual challenges. Planners began by assuming that no census statistics would be available, so they used satellite imagery to estimate the population in each of Baghdad's neighborhoods. They later located detailed statistics for much of Baghdad, which they updated for use in their sampling procedure. Gallup's planners also expected that they would need to hire trained interviewers from outside Iraq, but were fortunate to find some government employees who had become familiar with Baghdad's neighborhoods while conducting consumer surveys. To train and supervise these interviewers, Gallup hired two seasoned executives from the Pan Arab Research Center in Dubai.

To administer the survey, Gallup chose the time-tested method of private, face-to-face interviews in people's homes. This method not only put respondents at ease; it allowed women to participate in the survey at a time when venturing out in public may have been dangerous for them. In all, Gallup employees conducted over 3,400 person-to-person interviews in the privacy of Iraqis' homes. Respondents, they found, were eager to offer opinions, and would talk with them at length. Only 3 percent of those who were sampled declined to be interviewed.

Needless to say, conducting a scientific survey in the war-torn city presented unusual challenges.

The survey's results are significant, since the more than 6 million people who live in Baghdad constitute a quarter of Iraq's population. Asked which of several forms of government would be acceptable to them, equal numbers of respondents chose (1) a multiparty parliamentary democracy and (2) a system of governance that includes consultations with Islamic leaders. Fewer respondents endorsed a constitutional democracy or an Islamic kingdom. At a time when representatives of the Iraqi people had convened to establish a new form of government for the nation, this kind of information would prove invaluable.

Let's Discuss

1. The 97 percent response rate interviewers obtained in this survey was extremely high. Why do you think the response rate was so high, and what do you think it tells political analysts about the residents of Baghdad?
2. What might be some limitations of this survey?

A Gallup employee interviews an Iraqi army veteran at his home in Baghdad. Pollsters had to carefully estimate the population of Baghdad's many districts, subdistricts, and neighborhoods to obtain a statistically representative sample of respondents.

Sources: Gallup 2003; Gallup 2004; Saad 2003.

Contemporary Culture Discuss the questions that students would add to a survey of Iraqi public opinion.
Gender How might men and women respond differently to questions in the Baghdad poll?

Methods Discuss other research methods through which social scientists could or could not assess Iraqi public opinion.
Let's Discuss Why is it important to gauge Iraqi public opinion?

Investigators who collect information through direct participation and/or by closely watching a group or community are engaged in *observation.* This method allows sociologists to examine certain behaviors and communities that could not be investigated through other research techniques.

An increasingly popular form of qualitative research in sociology today is ethnography. *Ethnography* refers to efforts to describe an entire social setting through extended systematic observation. Typically, the description emphasizes how the subjects themselves view their social setting. Anthropologists rely heavily on ethnography. Much as an anthropologist seeks to understand the people of some Polynesian island, the sociologist as ethnographer seeks to understand and present an entire way of life in some setting. Anderson's study involved understanding not just the behavior of pedestrians, but all facets of life in two urban neighborhoods (P. Adler and Adler 2003).

In some cases, the sociologist actually joins a group ◀ **p. 3** for a period to get an accurate sense of how it operates. This approach is called *participant observation.* In the study of low-wage workers described in Chapter 1, as well as in Anderson's study of "eye work," the researcher was a participant observer.

During the late 1930s, in a classic example of participant-observation research, William F. Whyte moved into a low-income Italian neighborhood in Boston. For nearly four years he was a member of the social circle of "corner boys" that he describes in *Street Corner Society.* Whyte revealed his identity to these men and joined in their conversations, bowling, and other leisure-time activities. His goal was to gain greater insight into the community that these men had established. As Whyte (1981:303) listened to Doc, the leader of the group, he "learned the answers to questions I would not even have had the sense to ask if I had been getting my information solely on an interviewing basis." Whyte's work was especially valuable, since at the time the academic world had little direct knowledge of the poor, and tended to rely for information on the records of social service agencies, hospitals, and courts (P. Adler et al. 1992).

The initial challenge that Whyte faced—and that every participant observer encounters—was to gain acceptance into an unfamiliar group. It is no simple matter for a college-trained sociologist to win the trust of a religious cult, a youth gang, a poor Appalachian community, or a circle of skid row residents. It requires a great deal of patience and an accepting, nonthreatening type of personality on the part of the observer.

Observation research poses other complex challenges for the investigator. Sociologists must be able to fully understand what they are observing. In a sense, then, researchers must learn to see the world as the group sees it in order to fully comprehend the events taking place around them.

This raises a delicate issue. If the research is to be successful, the observer cannot allow the close associations or even friendships that inevitably develop to influence the subjects' behavior or the conclusions of the study. Anson Shupe and David Bromley (1980), two sociologists who have used participant observation, have likened this challenge to that of walking a tightrope. Even while working hard to gain acceptance from the group being studied, the participant observer *must* maintain some degree of detachment.

The feminist perspective in sociology has drawn attention to a shortcoming in ethnographic research. For most of the history of sociology, studies were conducted

How do people respond to being observed? Evidently these employees at the Hawthorne plant enjoyed the attention paid them when researchers observed them at work. No matter what variables were changed, the workers increased their productivity, even when the level of lighting was *reduced.*

Classroom Tip See "Ethnographies" (Class Discussion Topics).
Student Alert Be sure that students understand how participant observation differs from observation research.
Key Person William F. Whyte
Methods Whyte's study of "corner boys" is an example of participant observation research.

Classroom Tip See "The Personal Implications of Ethnographic Research" (Added Lecture Ideas).
Classroom Tip See "Role Conflict and Observation Research" (Class Discussion Topics).

on male subjects or about male-led groups and organizations, and the findings were generalized to all people. For example, for many decades studies of urban life focused on street corners, neighborhood taverns, and bowling alleys—places where men typically congregated. Although the insights gained were valuable, they did not give a true impression of city life because they overlooked the areas where women were likely to gather, such as playgrounds, grocery stores, and front stoops. The feminist perspective focuses on these arenas. Feminist researchers also tend to involve and consult their subjects more than other researchers, and they are more oriented to seeking change, raising consciousness, and trying to affect policy. In addition, feminist researchers are particularly open to a multidisciplinary approach, such as making use of historical evidence or legal studies as well as feminist theory (Baker 1999; L. Lofland 1975; Reinharz 1992).

Experiments

When sociologists want to study a possible cause-and-effect relationship, they may conduct experiments. An *experiment* is an artificially created situation that allows a researcher to manipulate variables.

In the classic method of conducting an experiment, two groups of people are selected and matched for similar characteristics, such as age or education. The researchers then assign the subjects to one of two groups: the experimental or the control group. The *experimental group* is exposed to an independent variable; the *control group* is not. Thus, if scientists were testing a new type of antibiotic, they would administer the drug to an experimental group but not to a control group.

Sociologists don't often rely on this classic form of experiment, because it generally involves manipulating human behavior in an inappropriate manner, especially in a laboratory setting. However, they do try to re-create experimental conditions in the field. For example, they may compare children's academic performance in two schools with different curricula. Another area of investigation that has led to several experimental studies in the field is the relative effectiveness of treatment programs for men charged repeatedly with domestic assault. In Broward County, Florida, and Brooklyn, New York, researchers compared the reoffense rates of control subjects who received no treatment with those of subjects who had completed either a short-term (8-week) program or a long-term (26-week) program. They found that while neither program entirely prevented repeat offenses, subjects who completed a long-term program had lower reoffense rates than the others. Researchers

also discovered that the completion rate was higher in the short-term programs than in the long-term programs, though not high enough to recommend them over long-term programs. They suggested the development of more long-term treatment programs, along with methods of improving participation rates (S. Jackson et al. 2003).

In some experiments, just as in observation research, the presence of a social scientist or other observer may affect the behavior of the people being studied. The recognition of this phenomenon grew out of an experiment conducted during the 1920s and 1930s at the Hawthorne plant of the Western Electric Company. A group of researchers set out to determine how to improve the productivity of workers at the plant. The investigators manipulated such variables as the lighting and working hours to see what impact the changes had on productivity. To their surprise, they found that *every* step they took seemed to increase productivity. Even measures that seemed likely to have the opposite effect, such as reducing the amount of lighting in the plant, led to higher productivity.

Why did the plant's employees work harder even under less favorable conditions? Their behavior apparently was influenced by the greater attention being paid to them in the course of the research, and by the novelty of being subjects in an experiment. Since that time, sociologists have used the term *Hawthorne effect* in referring to the unintended influence that observers of experiments can have on their subjects (S. Jones 1992; Lang 1992; Pelton 1994).

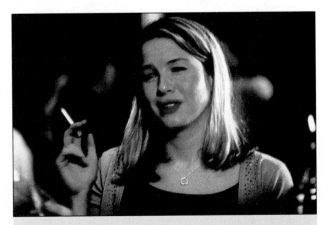

Content analysis of recent films finds this unstated message: smoking is cool. In this still from the 2001 movie *Bridget Jones's Diary,* Renee Zellweger enjoys a cigarette. If the movie industry is made aware of the frequency of such scenes and the message they send to young viewers, perhaps executives will try to alter the message.

Gender Sexism sometimes restricts female sociologists from conducting effective observation research in predominantly male environments. Is the opposite true, too?
Contemporary Culture Ask students how they would study racial profiling.

Methods The research on the Hawthorne plant is an example of an experiment.
Methods Was the Hawthorne study valid? Was it reliable?

Table 2-2	Existing Sources Used in Sociological Research

Most Frequently Used Sources
Census data

Crime statistics

Birth, death, marriage, divorce, and health statistics

Other Sources
Newspapers and periodicals

Personal journals, diaries, e-mail, and letters

Records and archival material of religious organizations, corporations, and other organizations

Transcripts of radio programs

Videotapes of motion pictures and television programs

Webpages, weblogs, and chatrooms

Song lyrics

Scientific records (such as patent applications)

Speeches of public figures (such as politicians)

Votes cast in elections or by elected officials on specific legislative proposals

Attendance records for public events

Videotapes of social protests and rallies

Literature, including folklore

Use Your Sociological Imagination www.mhhe.com/schaefer6

You are a researcher interested in the effect of TV watching on schoolchildren's grades. How would you go about setting up an experiment to measure this effect?

Use of Existing Sources

Sociologists do not necessarily need to collect new data in order to conduct research and test hypotheses. The term *secondary analysis* refers to a variety of research techniques that make use of previously collected and publicly accessible information and data. Generally, in conducting secondary analysis, researchers utilize data in ways that were unintended by the initial collectors of information. For example, census data are compiled for specific uses by the federal government but are also valuable to marketing specialists in locating everything from bicycle stores to nursing homes.

Sociologists consider secondary analysis to be *nonreactive,* since it does not influence people's behavior. As an example, Émile Durkheim's statistical analysis of suicide neither increased nor decreased human self-destruction. Researchers, then, can avoid the Hawthorne effect by using secondary analysis.

There is one inherent problem, however: the researcher who relies on data collected by someone else may not find exactly what is needed. Social scientists studying family violence can use statistics from police and social service agencies on *reported* cases of spouse abuse and child abuse. But how many cases are not reported? Government bodies have no precise data on *all* cases of abuse.

Many social scientists find it useful to study cultural, economic, and political documents, including newspapers, periodicals, radio and television tapes, the Internet, scripts, diaries, songs, folklore, and legal papers, to name some examples (see Table 2-2). In examining these sources, researchers employ a technique known as *content analysis,* which is the systematic coding and objective recording of data, guided by some rationale.

Using content analysis, Erving Goffman (1979) conducted a pioneering exploration of how advertisements

Methods Sociologists' use of existing sources and secondary analysis is introduced.
Classroom Tip See "Content Analysis of the Rodney King Beating" (Additional Lecture Ideas).

Key Person Erving Goffman
Theory Goffman's study is an example of microsociology and the interactionist perspective.

Table 2-3	Major Research Designs			
Method	**Examples**	**Advantages**	**Limitations**
Survey	Questionnaires Interviews	Yields information about specific issues	Can be expensive and time-consuming
Observation	Ethnography	Yields detailed information about specific groups or organizations	Involves months if not years of labor-intensive data gathering
Experiment	Deliberate manipulation of people's social behavior	Yields direct measures of people's behavior	Ethical limitations on the degree to which subjects' behavior can be manipulated
Existing sources/ Secondary analysis	Analysis of census or health data Analysis of films or TV commercials	Cost-efficiency	Limited to data collected for some other purpose

summingUP

portrayed women. The ads typically showed women as being subordinate to or dependent on others, or as being instructed by men. They engaged in caressing and touching gestures more than men. Even when presented in leadership roles, women were likely to be shown striking seductive poses or gazing out into space.

Today, researchers who analyze film content are finding an increase in smoking in motion pictures, despite heightened public health concerns. For example, a 2003 analysis showed significant tobacco use in 54 percent of the top-grossing motion pictures. One out of five of those movies showed either minors or pregnant women smoking. This type of content analysis can have clear social policy implications if it draws the motion picture industry's attention to the message films may be delivering, especially to young people: that smoking is acceptable, even desirable (American Lung Association 2003).

Table 2-3 summarizes the major research designs. Often, research designs mix different techniques. In the study described in Box 2-2 (page 42), the researchers combined survey research with existing sources to investigate the relationship between college students' behavior and their academic achievement.

ETHICS OF RESEARCH

A biochemist cannot inject a drug into a human being unless it has been thoroughly tested and the subject agrees to the shot. To do otherwise would be both unethical and illegal. Sociologists, too, must abide by certain specific standards in conducting research, called a *code of ethics.* The professional society of the discipline, the American Sociological Association (ASA), first published the society's *Code of Ethics* in 1971 and revised it most recently in 1997. It puts forth the following basic principles:

1. Maintain objectivity and integrity in research.
2. Respect the subject's right to privacy and dignity.
3. Protect subjects from personal harm.
4. Preserve confidentiality.
5. Seek informed consent when data are collected from research participants or when behavior occurs in a private context.
6. Acknowledge research collaboration and assistance.
7. Disclose all sources of financial support (American Sociological Association 1997).

These basic principles probably seem clear-cut. How could they lead to any disagreement or controversy? Yet many delicate ethical questions cannot be resolved simply by reading these seven principles. For example, should a sociologist who is engaged in participant-observation research always protect the confidentiality of subjects? What if the subjects are members of a religious cult allegedly engaged in unethical and possibly illegal activities? What if the sociologist is interviewing political activists and is questioned by government authorities about the research?

Classroom Tip See Class Discussion Topics for several activities about content analysis.
Contemporary Culture Have students illustrate content analysis by examining music videos.

Classroom Tip See "Teaching the Ethics of Sociological Research" (Class Discussion Topics).

Does a serious work ethic pay off in better grades? Sociologist William Rau wanted to answer that question. Working with Ann Durand, a former student who is now employed in the research department of State Farm Insurance Companies, Rau devised a research study. The dependent variable was easy to measure—the two could use an already existing data source, students' grade point averages (GPAs). But how could they measure the independent variable, a student's work ethic?

After considering many possibilities, the two researchers decided to focus on students' drinking behavior and study habits. They developed a scale comprised of a series of items on which students rated their drinking and studying behavior. At one extreme were many hours of daily studying and abstention from drinking. At the other extreme were frequent drinking—even on weekdays—and infrequent studying, usually cramming just before tests. The operational definition of students' work ethic became students' self-reports of their drinking and studying behavior in response to a series of questions.

Rau and Durand administered their behavior scale to 255 students and then

Generally, students who drank less and studied more performed better.

compared the scores on the scale to students' GPAs. The results were fairly striking. Generally, those students who drank less and studied more than others performed better academically, as measured by their GPAs. The researchers had been careful to control for students' ability levels using two more existing sources of data, students' class ranks in high school and their scores on college entrance exams. These sources indicated that the abstainers had not arrived at college better prepared than other students. Hard work really *does* pay off in better grades.

Let's Discuss

1. Where does your own drinking and studying behavior fall on Rau and Durand's behavior scale? What is your GPA? Is your academic achievement consistent with your drinking and studying behavior?

2. What other ways of measuring a student's work ethic could the researchers have considered? Can you think of any other variable besides a student's ability level that might have distorted the study's results?

Source: Rau and Durand 2000.

Because most sociological research uses *people* as sources of information—as respondents to survey questions, subjects of observation, or participants in experiments—these sorts of questions are important. In all cases, sociologists need to be certain they are not invading their subjects' privacy. Generally, they do so by assuring subjects of anonymity and by guaranteeing the confidentiality of their personal information. In addition, research proposals that involve human subjects must now be overseen by a review board, whose members seek to ensure that subjects are not placed at an unreasonable level of risk. If necessary, the board may ask researchers to revise their research designs to conform to the code of ethics.

Classroom Tip Analyze the ethical problems of having a researcher conduct observation research in your classroom.

We can appreciate the seriousness of the ethical problems researchers confront by considering the experience of sociologist Rik Scarce, described in the next section. Scarce's vow to protect his subjects' confidentiality got him into considerable trouble with the law.

Confidentiality

Like journalists, sociologists occasionally find themselves subject to questions from law enforcement authorities because of knowledge they have gained in the course of their work. This uncomfortable situation raises profound ethical questions.

In May 1993, Rik Scarce, a doctoral candidate in sociology at Washington State University, was jailed for contempt of court. Scarce had declined to tell a federal grand jury what he knew—or even whether he knew anything—about a 1991 raid on a university research laboratory by animal rights activists. At the time, Scarce was conducting research for a book about environmental protestors and knew at least one suspect in the break-in. Curiously, although he was chastised by a federal judge, Scarce won respect from fellow prison inmates, who regarded him as a man who "wouldn't snitch" (Monaghan 1993:A8).

The American Sociological Association supported Scarce's position when he appealed his sentence. Scarce maintained his silence. Ultimately the judge ruled that nothing would be gained by further incarceration, and Scarce was released after serving 159 days in jail. In January 1994, the U.S. Supreme Court declined to hear Scarce's case on appeal. The Court's failure to consider his case led Scarce (1994, 1995) to argue that federal legislation is needed to clarify the rights of scholars and members of the press to preserve the confidentiality of those they interview.

Research Funding

Sometimes disclosing all the sources of funding for a study, as required in principle 7 of the ASA's *Code of Ethics,* is not a sufficient guarantee of ethical conduct. Especially in the case of both corporate and government funding, money given ostensibly for the support of basic research may come with strings attached. Accepting funds from a private organization or even a government agency that stands to benefit from a study's results can call into question a researcher's objectivity and integrity (principle 1).

The Exxon Corporation's support for research on jury verdicts is a good example of this kind of conflict of interest. On March 24, 1989, the Exxon oil tanker *Valdez* hit a reef off the coast of Alaska, spilling over 11 million gallons of oil into Prince William Sound. A decade and

A floating containment barrier encircles the Exxon oil tanker *Valdez* after its grounding on a reef off the coast of Alaska. Exxon executives spent a million dollars to fund academic research that they hoped would support lawyers' efforts to reduce the $5.3 billion judgment against the corporation for negligence in the environmental disaster.

a half later, the *Valdez* disaster is still regarded as the world's worst oil spill in terms of its environmental impact. In 1994 a federal court ordered Exxon to pay $5.3 billion in damages for the accident. Exxon appealed the verdict, and began approaching legal scholars, sociologists, and psychologists who might be willing to study jury deliberations. The corporation's objective was to develop academic support for its lawyers' contention that the punitive judgments in such cases result from faulty deliberations and do not have a deterrent effect.

Some scholars have questioned the propriety of accepting funds under these circumstances, even if the source is disclosed. In at least one case, an Exxon employee explicitly told a sociologist that the corporation offers financial support to scholars who have shown the tendency to express views similar to its own. An argument also can be made that Exxon was attempting to set scholars' research agendas with its huge war chest. Rather than funding studies on the improvement of cleanup technologies or the assignment of long-term environmental costs, Exxon chose to shift

Key Person Rik Scarce
Let's Discuss Should there be limits on scholars' control over their research notes? If so, under what circumstances should researchers be forced to violate confidentiality? Was Scarce correct in declining to testify before the grand jury? Was the court correct in sending him to jail?

Contemporary Culture How do students feel about corporate sponsorship of social science research?
Let's Discuss Discuss Exxon sponsorship of social science research from a conflict perspective.

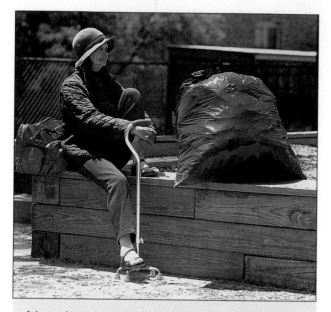

A homeless woman living in Chicago. Sociologist Peter Rossi came under attack by the Chicago Coalition for the Homeless for finding in a carefully researched study that the city's homeless population was far below the Coalition's estimate. The Coalition accused Rossi of hampering their efforts at social reform.

scientists' attention to the validity of the legal awards in environmental cases.

The scholars who accepted Exxon's support deny that it influenced their work or changed their conclusions. Some received support from other sources as well, such as the National Science Foundation and Harvard University's Olin Center for Law, Economics, and Business. Many of their findings were published in respected academic journals after review by a jury of peers. Still, at least one researcher who participated in the studies refused monetary support from Exxon to avoid even the suggestion of a conflict of interest.

To date, Exxon has spent roughly $1 million on the research, and at least one compilation of studies congenial to Exxon's point of view has been published. As ethical considerations require, the academics who conducted the studies disclosed Exxon's role in funding the research. In 2001, drawing on their studies, Exxon's lawyers succeeded in persuading an appeals court to reduce the corporation's legal damages from $5.3 to $4 billion. The case is now under appeal by Exxon in an attempt to further reduce the damages (Sunstein et al. 2003; Zarembo 2003).

Value Neutrality

The ethical considerations of sociologists lie not only in the methods they use and the funding they accept, but in the way they interpret their results. Max Weber ([1904] 1949) recognized that personal values would influence the questions that sociologists select for research. In his view, that was perfectly acceptable, but under no conditions could a researcher allow his or her personal feelings to influence the *interpretation* of data. In Weber's phrase, sociologists must practice **value neutrality** in their research.

As part of this neutrality, investigators have an ethical obligation to accept research findings even when the data run counter to their own personal views, to theoretically based explanations, or to widely accepted beliefs. For example, Émile Durkheim challenged popular conceptions **pp. 8–9** when he reported that social (rather than supernatural) forces were an important factor in suicide.

Some sociologists believe that neutrality is impossible. They worry that Weber's insistence on value-free sociology may lead the public to accept sociological conclusions without exploring researchers' biases. Others, drawing on the conflict perspective as Alvin Gouldner (1970) does, have suggested that sociologists may use objectivity as a justification for remaining uncritical of existing institutions and centers of power. These arguments are attacks not so much on Weber himself as on the way his goals have been misinterpreted. As we have seen, Weber was quite clear that sociologists may bring values to their subject matter. In his view, however, they must not confuse their own values with the social reality under study (Bendix 1968).

Let's consider what might happen when researchers bring their own biases to the investigation. A person investigating the impact of intercollegiate sports on alumni contributions, for example, may focus only on the highly visible revenue-generating sports of football and basketball and neglect the so-called minor sports, such as tennis or soccer, which are more likely to involve women athletes. Despite the early work of W. E. B. Du Bois and Jane Addams, sociologists still need to be reminded that the discipline often fails to adequately consider all people's social behavior.

In her book *The Death of White Sociology* (1973) Joyce Ladner called attention to the tendency of mainstream sociology to treat the lives of African Americans as a social problem. More recently, feminist sociologist Shulamit Reinharz (1992) has argued that sociological research should be not only inclusive but open to bringing about social change and to drawing on relevant research by nonsociologists. Both Reinharz and Ladner maintain that researchers should always analyze whether women's

Key Person Max Weber
Student Alert Relate Weber's concept of value neutrality to the discussion of *Verstehen* in Chapter 1.

Classroom Tip Relate Weber's concept of value neutrality to the concept of cultural relativism that is introduced in Chapter 3.
Key Persons Alvin Gouldner, Joyce Ladner, Shulamit Reinharz

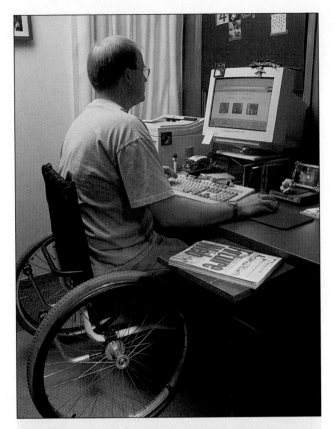

Computers have vastly extended the range and capability of sociological research, both by allowing large amounts of data to be stored and analyzed and by facilitating communication with other researchers via websites, newsgroups, and e-mail.

unequal social status has affected their studies in any way. For example, one might broaden the study of the impact of education on income to consider the implications of the unequal pay status of men and women. The issue of value neutrality does not mean that sociologists can't have opinions, but it does mean that they must work to overcome any biases, however unintentional, that they may bring to their analysis of research.

Peter Rossi (1987) admits to having liberal inclinations that direct him to fields of study. Yet in line with Weber's view of value neutrality, Rossi's commitment to rigorous research methods and objective interpretation of data has sometimes led him to controversial findings that are not necessarily supportive of his own liberal values. For example, his measure of the extent of homelessness in Chicago in the mid-1980s fell far below the estimates of the Chicago Coalition for the Homeless. Coalition members bitterly attacked Rossi for hampering their social reform efforts by minimizing the extent of home-

lessness. Rossi (1987:79) concluded that "in the short term, good social research will often be greeted as a betrayal of one or another side to a particular controversy."

TECHNOLOGY AND SOCIOLOGICAL RESEARCH

Advances in technology have affected all aspects of our lives, and sociological research is no exception. The increased speed and capacity of computers are enabling sociologists to handle larger and larger sets of data. In the recent past, only people with grants or major institutional support could easily work with census data. Now anyone with a desktop computer and modem can access census information and learn more about social behavior. Moreover, data from foreign countries concerning crime statistics and health care are sometimes as available as information from the United States.

Researchers usually rely on computers to deal with quantitative data—that is, numerical measures—but electronic technology is also assisting them with qualitative data, such as information obtained in observational research. Numerous software programs, such as Ethnograph and NUD*IST, allow the researcher not only to record observations but also to identify common behavioral patterns or similar concerns expressed in interviews. For example, after observing students in a college cafeteria over several weeks and putting her observations into the computer, a researcher could group all the observations according to certain variables, such as "sorority" or "study group."

The Internet affords an excellent opportunity to communicate with fellow researchers, as well as to locate useful information on social issues that has been posted on websites. It would be impossible to calculate all the sociological postings on websites or Internet mailing lists. Of course, researchers need to apply the same critical scrutiny to Internet material that they would to any printed resource.

How useful is the Internet for conducting survey research? That is still unclear. It is relatively easy to send out a questionnaire or post one on an electronic bulletin board. This is an inexpensive way to reach large numbers of potential respondents and get a quick response. However, there are some obvious dilemmas. How do you protect a respondent's anonymity? How do you define the potential audience? Even if you know to whom you sent the questionnaire, the respondents may forward it to others.

Web-based surveys are still in their early stages. Even so, the initial results are promising. For example,

DAVE EBERBACH   Research Coordinator, United Way of Central Iowa

As a research specialist, Dave Eberbach uses his training in sociology to work for social change. Eberbach looks for small pockets of poverty that are generally hidden in state and county statistics. By zeroing in on conditions in specific neighborhoods, he empowers state and local agencies that work on behalf of the disadvantaged.

Eberbach, who is based in Des Moines, Iowa, was hired to establish a "data warehouse" of social statistics for the local United Way. Part of his job has been to demonstrate to agencies how the information in the database can be of use to them. "We have moved most of our data presentations away from charts and graphs, and on to maps of the county, the city and the neighborhood," he explains. "This allows people to truly 'see' the big picture."

When Eberbach entered Grinnell College in 1985, he had already taken a sociology course and knew that the subject interested him. Still, he could not have foreseen all the practical uses he might have had for what he learned. "Never assume that you'll never need to know something (including statistics)," he advises. "Life has a funny way of bringing things around again."

At Grinnell, Eberbach benefited from the presence of several visiting professors who exposed him to a variety of cultural and racial perspectives. His personal acquaintance with them complemented the concepts he was learning in his sociology classes.

Today, Eberbach draws on his college experiences at the United Way, where his work brings him into contact with a diverse group of people.

Sociology has also helped Eberbach in his chosen specialty, research. "I believe that I am a better 'data person' because of my sociology background," he claims. "The human context for data is as important and can get lost or misdirected by pure statistics," he explains. "My sociology background has helped me ask the appropriate questions to make effective change in our community."

Let's Discuss

1. Do you know what you want to be doing 10 years from now? If so, how might a knowledge of statistics help you in your future occupation?
2. What kinds of statistics, specifically, might you find in the United Way's data warehouse? Where would they come from?

InterSurvey has created a pool of Internet respondents, initially selected by telephone, to serve as a diverse and representative sample. Using similar methods to locate 50,000 adult respondents in 33 nations, the National Geographic Society conducted an online survey that focused on migration and regional culture. Social scientists are closely monitoring these new approaches to gauge how they might revolutionize one type of research design (Bainbridge 1999; Morin 2000).

This new technology is exciting, but there is one basic limitation to the methodology: Internet surveying works only with those who have access to the Internet and are online. For some market researchers, such a limitation is acceptable. For example, if you were interested in the willingness of Internet users to order books or make travel reservations online, limiting the sample population to those who are already online makes sense. However, if you were surveying the general public about their plans to buy a computer in the coming year or their views on a particular candidate, your online research would need to be supplemented by more traditional sampling procedures, such as mailed questionnaires.

We have seen that researchers rely on a number of tools, from time-tested observational research and use of existing sources to the latest in computer technologies. The social policy section that follows will describe researchers' efforts to survey the general population about a controversial aspect of social behavior: human sexuality. This investigation was complicated by its potential social policy implications. Because in the real world, sociological research can have far-reaching consequences for public policy and public welfare, each of the following chapters in this book will close with a social policy section.

SOCIAL POLICY and SOCIOLOGICAL RESEARCH | Studying Human Sexuality

The Issue

Reality TV shows often feature an attempt to create a relationship or even a marriage between two strangers. In a picturesque setting, an eligible bachelor or bachelorette interviews potential partners—all of them good-looking—and gradually eliminates those who seem less promising. The questions that are posed on camera can be explicit. "How many sexual partners have you had?" "How often would you be willing to have sex?"

The Kaiser Family Foundation conducts a study of sexual content on television every two years. The latest report, released in 2003, shows that more than two-thirds of all shows on TV include some sexual content, up from about half of all shows four years earlier (Figure 2-5). Media representations of sexual behavior are important because surveys of teens and young adults tell us that television is a top source of information and ideas about sex for them; it has more influence than schools, parents, or peers.

In this age of devastating sexually transmitted diseases, there is no time more important to increase our scientific understanding of human sexuality. As we will see, however, this is a difficult topic to research because of all the preconceptions, myths, and beliefs people bring to the subject of sexuality. How does one carry out scientific research on such a controversial and personal topic?

The Setting

Sociologists have little reliable national data on patterns of sexual behavior in the United States. Until recently, the only comprehensive study of sexual behavior was the famous two-volume Kinsey Report prepared in the 1940s (Kinsey et al. 1948, 1953). Although the Kinsey Report is still widely quoted, the volunteers interviewed for the report were not representative of the nation's adult population. Every two years the general public is interviewed as a part of the federally funded General Social Survey, which provides some useful information on sexual attitudes. For instance, Figure 2-6 (page 48) shows how attitudes about premarital sexual behavior have changed since the early 1970s.

In part, we lack reliable data on patterns of sexual behavior because it is difficult for researchers to obtain accurate information about this sensitive subject. Moreover, until AIDS emerged in the 1980s, there was little scientific demand for data on sexual behavior, except for specific concerns such as contraception. Finally, even

FIGURE 2-5

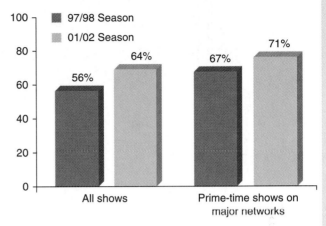

Percent of Television Shows That Contain Sexual Content

Source: Kaiser Family Foundation 2001:2, 2003:38, 40.

though the AIDS crisis has reached dramatic proportions (as will be discussed in the social policy section of Chapter 5), government funding for studies of sexual behavior is controversial. Because the General Social Survey concerns sexual attitudes rather than behavior, its funding has not been jeopardized.

Sociological Insights

The controversy surrounding research on human sexual behavior raises the issue of value neutrality (see pages 44–45), which becomes especially delicate when one considers the relationship of sociology to the government. The federal government has become the major source of funding for sociological research. Yet Max Weber urged that sociology remain an autonomous discipline and not become unduly influenced by any one segment of society. According to Weber's ideal of value neutrality, sociologists must remain free to reveal information that is embarrassing to the government, or for that matter, supportive of government institutions. Thus, researchers who are investigating a prison riot must be ready to examine objectively not only the behavior of inmates but also the conduct of prison officials before and during the outbreak. Maintaining objectivity may be difficult if sociologists fear that findings which are critical of government institutions will jeopardize their chances of obtaining federal support for new research projects.

Classroom Tip Discuss the purpose and value of social policy sections.
Contemporary Culture Have students cite and critically analyze the treatment of human sexuality on television and in popular music.

Classroom Tip Explain to students how innovative the Kinsey reports were at the time they were conducted and published.
Methods The General Social Survey is an example of survey research.

FIGURE 2-6

Views on Sex before Marriage

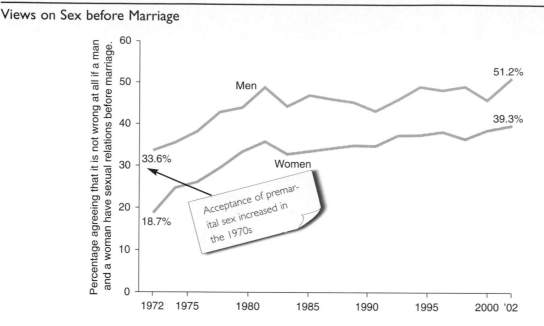

Source: Author's analysis of General Social Surveys, 1972–2002; see J. A. Davis et al. 2003.

Although the American Sociological Association's *Code of Ethics* requires sociologists to disclose all funding sources, it does not address the issue of whether sociologists who accept funding from a particular agency or corporation may also accept the agency's perspective on what needs to be studied. As we saw in our discussion of research funded by the Exxon Corporation (pages 43–44), this question is a knotty one. As the next section will show, applied sociological research on human sexuality has run into barriers constructed by government funding agencies.

Policy Initiatives

In 1987 the National Institute of Child Health and Human Development sought proposals for a national survey of sexual behavior. Sociologists responded with various plans that a review panel of scientists approved for funding. However, in 1991, led by Senator Jesse Helms and other conservatives, the U.S. Senate voted 66–34 to forbid funding any survey on adult sexual practices. Helms appealed to popular fears by arguing that such surveys were intended to "legitimize homosexual lifestyles" and to support "sexual decadence." Two years earlier, a similar debate in Great Britain had led to the denial of government funding for a national sex survey (A. Johnson et al. 1994; Laumann et al. 1994a:36).

Despite the vote by the U.S. Senate, sociologists Edward Laumann, John Gagnon, Stuart Michaels, and Robert Michael developed the National Health and Social Life Survey (NHSLS) to better understand the sexual practices of adults in the United States. The researchers raised $1.6 million of *private* funding to make their study possible (Laumann et al. 1994a, 1994b).

The NHSLS researchers made great efforts to ensure privacy during the interviews, as well as confidentiality and security in maintaining data files. Perhaps because of this careful effort, the interviewers did not typically experience problems getting responses, even though they were asking people about their sexual behavior. All interviews were conducted in person, although a confidential form included questions about sensitive subjects such as family income and masturbation. The researchers used several techniques to test the accuracy of subjects' responses, such as asking redundant questions at different times and in different ways during the 90-minute interview. These careful procedures helped to establish the validity of the NHSLS findings.

Research dealing with human sexuality continues to receive special scrutiny by Congress. In July 2003, by a vote of 212 to 210, the House of Representatives narrowly defeated an effort to block funding for a series of grants approved by the National Institutes of Health. The four grants were earmarked for the collection of data on sexual risk taking, the sexual habits of older men, drug use, and bisexuality. But the battle is far from over. Opponents have placed proposals to investigate

Policy Pointer Note the relevance of the American Sociological Association's *Code of Ethics.*
Let's Discuss Why is government-supported sociological research an ethical issue?

Policy Pointer Note the sometimes critical role of funding in determining which subjects are studied.
Let's Discuss What are the advantages and disadvantages of private funding for researchers?

human sexuality on a "hit list" of projects that would require further justification to Congress, beyond approval by the scientific community (Associated Press 2003; Waxman 2003).

Despite these political battles, the authors of the NHSLS believe that their research is important. They argue that using data from their survey allows us to more easily address public policy issues such as AIDS, sexual harassment, welfare reform, sex discrimination, abortion, teenage pregnancy, and family planning. Moreover, the research findings help to counter some "common-sense" notions. For instance, contrary to the popular beliefs that women regularly use abortion for birth control, and that poor teens are the most likely socioeconomic group to have abortions, researchers found that three-fourths of all abortions are the first for the woman, and that well-educated and affluent women are more likely to have abortions than poor teens (Sweet 2001).

Scholars in China, aware of the NHSLS, have begun to collaborate with sociologists in the United States on a similar study in China. The data are just now being analyzed, but responses thus far indicate dramatic differences in the sexual behavior of people in their 20s, compared to that reported at the same age by people who are now in their 50s. Younger-generation Chinese are more active sexually and have more partners than their parents did. Partly in response to these preliminary results, the Chinese Ministry of Health has sought U.S. assistance on HIV/AIDS prevention and research (Braverman 2002).

Let's Discuss

1. Do you see any merit in the position of those who oppose government funding for research on sexual behavior? Explain your reasoning.
2. Exactly how could the results of research on human sexual behavior be used to control sexually transmitted diseases?

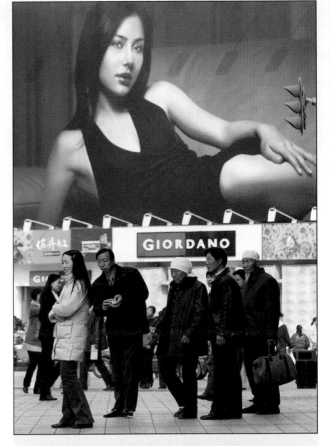

This sexually provocative billboard in Beijing advertises South Korean cell phones. Increasingly, multinational corporations are turning to sex to sell sophisticated consumer products to younger-generation Chinese.

3. Compare the issue of value neutrality in government-funded research to the same issue in corporate-funded research. Are concerns about conflict of interest more or less serious in regard to government funding?

www. mhhe.com /schaefer6

GETTING INVOLVED

To get involved in the debate over research on human sexuality, visit this text's Online Learning Center, which offers links to relevant websites. Check out the Social Policy section on the Online Learning Center as well; it provides survey data on U.S. public opinion regarding this issue.

Gender In research on human sexuality, gender is often a key variable.
Classroom Tip See "Using Humor" (Class Discussion Topics).

CHAPTER RESOURCES

Summary

Sociologists are committed to the use of the scientific method in their research efforts. In this chapter we examined the basic principles of the scientific method and studied various techniques used by sociologists in conducting research.

1. There are five basic steps in the *scientific method:* defining the problem, reviewing the literature, formulating the hypothesis, collecting and analyzing the data, and developing the conclusion.
2. Whenever researchers wish to study abstract concepts, such as intelligence or prejudice, they must develop workable *operational definitions.*
3. A *hypothesis* usually states a possible relationship between two or more variables.
4. By using a *sample,* sociologists avoid having to test everyone in a population.
5. According to the scientific method, research results must possess both *validity* and *reliability.*
6. An important part of scientific research is devising a plan for collecting data, called a *research design.* Sociologists use four major research designs: surveys, observation, experiments, and existing sources.
7. The two principal forms of *survey* research are the *interview* and the *questionnaire.*
8. *Observation* allows sociologists to study certain behaviors and communities that cannot be investigated through other research methods.
9. When sociologists wish to study a cause-and-effect relationship, they may conduct an *experiment.*
10. Sociologists also make use of existing sources in *secondary analysis* and *content analysis.*
11. The *Code of Ethics* of the American Sociological Association calls for objectivity and integrity in research, confidentiality, and disclosure of all sources of financial support.
12. Max Weber urged sociologists to practice *value neutrality* in their research by ensuring that their personal feelings do not influence the interpretation of data.
13. Technology today plays an important role in sociological research, whether it be a computer database or information from the Internet.
14. Despite failure to obtain government funding, researchers developed the National Health and Social Life Survey (NHSLS) to better understand the sexual practices of adults in the United States.

Critical Thinking Questions

1. Suppose your sociology instructor has asked you to do a study of homelessness. Which research technique (survey, observation, experiment, or existing sources) would you find most useful? How would you use that technique to complete your assignment?
2. How can a sociologist genuinely maintain value neutrality while studying a group that he or she finds repugnant (for example, a White supremacist organization, a satanic cult, or a group of convicted rapists)?
3. New technologies have benefited sociological research by facilitating statistical analysis and encouraging communication among scholars. Can you think of any potential drawbacks these new technologies might have for sociological investigation?

Key Terms

Causal logic The relationship between a condition or variable and a particular consequence, with one event leading to the other. (page 31)

Code of ethics The standards of acceptable behavior developed by and for members of a profession. (41)

Content analysis The systematic coding and objective recording of data, guided by some rationale. (40)

Control group The subjects in an experiment who are not introduced to the independent variable by the researcher. (39)

Control variable A factor that is held constant to test the relative impact of an independent variable. (34)

Correlation A relationship between two variables in which a change in one coincides with a change in the other. (31)

Dependent variable The variable in a causal relationship that is subject to the influence of another variable. (31)

Ethnography The study of an entire social setting through extended systematic observation. (38)

Experiment   An artificially created situation that allows a researcher to manipulate variables. (39)

Experimental group   The subjects in an experiment who are exposed to an independent variable introduced by a researcher. (39)

Hawthorne effect   The unintended influence that observers of experiments can have on their subjects. (39)

Hypothesis   A speculative statement about the relationship between two or more variables. (31)

Independent variable   The variable in a causal relationship that causes or influences a change in a second variable. (31)

Interview   A face-to-face or telephone questioning of a respondent to obtain desired information. (36)

Observation   A research technique in which an investigator collects information through direct participation and/or by closely watching a group or community. (38)

Operational definition   An explanation of an abstract concept that is specific enough to allow a researcher to assess the concept. (30)

Qualitative research   Research that relies on what is seen in field or naturalistic settings more than on statistical data. (36)

Quantitative research   Research that collects and reports data primarily in numerical form. (36)

Questionnaire   A printed or written form used to obtain information from a respondent. (36)

Random sample   A sample for which every member of an entire population has the same chance of being selected. (33)

Reliability   The extent to which a measure produces consistent results. (34)

Research design   A detailed plan or method for obtaining data scientifically. (36)

Sample   A selection from a larger population that is statistically representative of that population. (31)

Scientific method   A systematic, organized series of steps that ensures maximum objectivity and consistency in researching a problem. (29)

Secondary analysis   A variety of research techniques that make use of previously collected and publicly accessible information and data. (40)

Survey   A study, generally in the form of an interview or questionnaire, that provides researchers with information about how people think and act. (36)

Validity   The degree to which a measure or scale truly reflects the phenomenon under study. (34)

Value neutrality   Max Weber's term for objectivity of sociologists in the interpretation of data. (44)

Variable   A measurable trait or characteristic that is subject to change under different conditions. (31)

TECHNOLOGY RESOURCES

Internet Connection

www.mhhe.com/schaefer6

Note: While all the URLs listed were current as of the printing of this book, these sites often change. Please check our website (www. mhhe.com/schaefer6) for updates, hyperlinks, and exercises related to these sites.

1. Oral history is a type of qualitative research that is often used in ethnographic studies. Go to the website of the Oral History Society (**www.oral history.org.uk**) and read the section that guides you through the process of recording an oral history.

2. The Substance Abuse and Mental Health Services Administration (SAMHSA) conducts a national household survey on drug abuse. To read about Ecstasy use among adolescents and young adults, link to http://oas.samhsa.gov/2k3/ecstasy/ecstasy.htm.

Online Learning Center with PowerWeb

When you visit the student center of the Online Learning Center, one of the Internet exercises for this chapter will give you an opportunity to become a sociological researcher. In this exercise, you will conduct a content analysis of two popular magazines for women and two popular magazines for men. You will be asked to examine the colors, models, clothing, and topics and analyze them from a sociological viewpoint. After this learning experience, you will never look at magazines the same way again!

Reel Society Interactive Movie CD-ROM 2.0

Reel Society 2.0 can be used to spark discussion about the following topics from this chapter:

- The Scientific Method
- Neutrality and Politics in Research

chapter

CULTURE

3

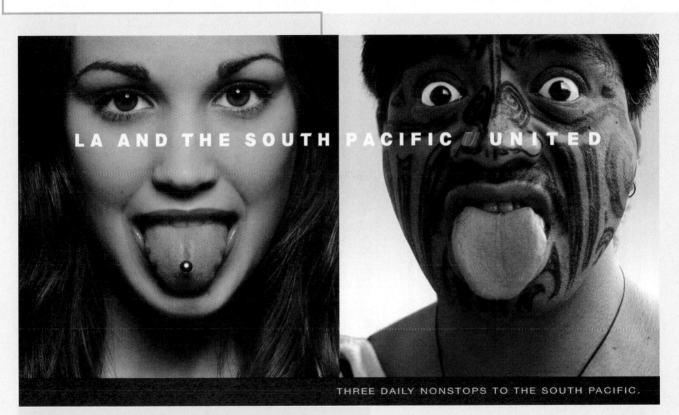

LA AND THE SOUTH PACIFIC / UNITED

THREE DAILY NONSTOPS TO THE SOUTH PACIFIC.

Each culture has its own forms of individual expression, as this billboard for United Airlines illustrates. The young woman from Los Angeles shows off her tongue stud, the South Pacific islander displays a ceremonial tattooed face.

Asok is a software engineer in one of the showcase companies in Silicon Valley, a gleaming edifice of glass and tile. He and his wife were born in India. Like many of his network of friends, he went to Stanford University to pursue a graduate degree and found work in a large company. He stayed in that company for three years, coding, learning American ways, and discovering that political hierarchies in American workplaces are very different from those he had known in India. Eager and enthusiastic, he put his heart and soul into his first project. His teammates were like family. They worked long hours together, eighty to a hundred hours per week in the crunch times. They went to Burgess Park for picnics, and loaned each other money. It was a heady experience. Suddenly, the product on which his project was based was canceled. His group was broken up and his teammates were distributed among a number of other projects. . . .

Priyesh and his wife, Sima, old friends of Asok's, are having breakfast. Sima tells Priyesh that her relatives were asking if they will go back to India soon. They shake their heads, wondering why they would want to go back. She says, "I do not miss India . . . anything Indian I want I have it right here—grocery stores, temples, cultural programs, Hindu magazines. There are three movie theaters in the Bay Area showing Hindi movies seven days a week. I only miss my family." Priyesh reflects that here in Silicon Valley he can have all the good parts of India—the people and culture—without having to put up with a decaying bureaucracy and failing infrastructure. They argue gently about whether they really live in an Indian world. She points out that while many of their friends are Indian, including a recently immigrated cousin, Priyesh still has to work with many non-Indians.

Sima adds that she has to interact with very different cultures in their son's preschool—where they celebrate Chinese New Year and Cinco de Mayo. She pauses and then notes that it isn't really too different from interacting with all the different religions and cultures back in India. Priyesh scoffs at the whole problem. All these cultural differences don't matter to him. When he is at work, it is the technology that matters. . . .

Priyesh goes back into his home office. He makes a practice of telecommuting every day from about six to nine o'clock in the morning. . . . He can, at the very least, spend those hours reviewing his e-mail. He gets from fifty to one hundred e-mails each day. Many are work-related, but others connect him to mailing lists of people who are interested in technology stock investment, or people who like to play Indian music or tennis. They will send each other quick messages to set up meeting times or to announce the arrival of a particular artist. He also stays in touch with his family in India with e-mail, since that is the most convenient way to communicate across time zones. (English-Lueck 2002:1–3) ■ ◉

cultures@siliconvalley

j.a.english-lueck

Additional information about this excerpt can be found on the Online Learning Center at **www.mhhe.com/schaefer6.**

I this excerpt from the book *Cultures@ Silicon Valley* by Jan English-Lueck, an anthropologist describes the daily lives of some typical residents of California's world-famous center for cutting-edge technologies. English-Lueck is a professor and chair of the Department of Anthropology at San Jose State University. Fascinated by the mix of cultures and entrepreneurism that powers her region's high-tech economy, she has spent 10 years doing ethnographic research on the software engineers who immigrate from India and Ireland to work in the corporations that invented the Information Age. She sees the community as a microcosm of globalization, where new technologies intersect with international business interests and a multicultural, transnational workforce.

The Silicon Valley culture revealed by English-Lueck's painstaking research is a many-layered mosaic of ethnic traditions, corporate values, consumerism, and global mass media. The well-educated immigrants who staff Silicon Valley's software development departments maintain close-knit ethnic networks, which provide a sense of stability that is lacking in their high-risk business. They accept the corporate profit motive, which means that their jobs are only as secure as the prospects for the new technologies they develop. They consider the demands of learning to live with people of other nationalities a worthwhile exchange for the comfort and efficiency of life in a developed country. And they allow the high-tech gadgets they create to alter the way they live their lives, changing the ways they work and communicate with others.

Though the high-tech industry has suffered in the recent economic recession, immigrants are still drawn to Silicon Valley, and the corporations that reside there are still developing new technologies with which to integrate diverse cultures. In the future, the United States will continue to rely on talented people from around the world. In our rapidly globalizing culture, then, understanding other cultures is vital to our national well-being. How do cultures differ and how are they the same? How does our culture change as we encounter cultures very different from our own? What accounts for cultural variation between and within societies? And what are the cultural implications of the trend toward globalization?

In this chapter we will study the development of culture around the world, including the cultural effects of the worldwide trend toward globalization. We will see just how basic the study of culture is to sociology. We will examine the meaning of culture and society, as well as the development of culture from its roots in the prehistoric human experience to the technological advances of today. We will define and explore the major aspects of culture, including language, norms, sanctions, and values. We will see how cultures develop a dominant ideology, and how functionalist and conflict theorists view culture. Our discussion will focus both on general cultural practices found in all societies and on the wide variations that can distinguish one society from another. In the social policy section we will look at the conflicts in cultural values that underlie current debates over bilingualism. ■

CULTURE AND SOCIETY

Culture is the totality of learned, socially transmitted customs, knowledge, material objects, and behavior. It includes the ideas, values, and artifacts (for example, DVDs, comic books, and birth control devices) of groups of people. Patriotic attachment to the flag of the United States is an aspect of culture, as is a national passion for the tango in Argentina.

Sometimes people refer to a particular person as "very cultured" or to a city as having "lots of culture." That use of the term *culture* is different from our use in this textbook. In sociological terms, *culture* does not refer solely to the fine arts and refined intellectual taste. It consists of *all* objects and ideas within a society, including ice cream cones, rock music, and slang words. Sociologists consider both a portrait by Rembrandt and the work of graffiti spray painters to be aspects of culture. A tribe that cultivates soil by hand has just as much culture as a people that relies

Are You What You Eat?

The foods people eat, along with the customs they observe in preparing and consuming their meals, say a great deal about their culture. In some cultures, such as that of Papua New Guinea, roast pork is a delicacy reserved for feasts; in others it is forbidden food. In U.S. culture, genetically modified food is accepted without much question, but in Europe it is banned. Because Swedish people put great value on natural, organic foods, 99 percent of mothers in Sweden breast-feed their infants—a rate much higher than that in the United States.

In some cultures, such as France, fine cuisine is a cultural institution. The French prefer fresh local produce lovingly prepared, consumed slowly along with good conversation and a bottle of wine. To the French and to gourmets around the world, great chefs are celebrities.

Given their reverence for food, the French would be most unlikely to participate in a contest designed to see who can gobble down the most hot dogs. In the United States and Japan, these public events are quite popular. But though the Japanese admire American culture, they stop short at copying the American habit of eating fast food on the street while rushing from one place to another. The Japanese will purchase food from a street vendor, but they will not walk around while eating it, because doing so would show disrespect for the preparer.

Hong Kong

Coney Island, New York

Paris

on computer-operated machinery. Each people has a distinctive culture with its own characteristic ways of gathering and preparing food, constructing homes, structuring the family, and promoting standards of right and wrong.

The fact that you share a similar culture with others helps to define the group or society to which you belong. A fairly large number of people are said to constitute a *society* when they live in the same territory, are relatively independent of people outside their area, and participate in a common culture. Metropolitan Los Angeles is more populous than at least 150 nations, yet sociologists do not consider it a society in its own right. Rather, they see it as part of—and dependent on—the larger society of the United States.

A society is the largest form of human group. It consists of people who share a common heritage and culture. Members of the society learn this culture and transmit it from one generation to the next. They even preserve their distinctive culture through literature, art, video recordings, and other means of expression. If it were not for the social transmission of culture, each generation would have to reinvent television, not to mention the wheel.

Having a common culture also simplifies many day-to-day interactions. For example, when you buy an airline ticket, you know you don't have to bring along hundreds of dollars in cash. You can pay with a credit card. When you are part of a society, you take for granted many small (as well as more important) cultural patterns. You assume that theaters will provide seats for the audience, that physicians will not disclose confidential information, and that parents will be careful when crossing the street with young children. All these assumptions reflect basic values, beliefs, and customs of the culture of the United States.

Language is a critical element of culture that sets humans apart from other species. Members of a society generally share a common language, which facilitates day-to-day exchanges with others. When you ask a hardware store clerk for a flashlight, you don't need to draw a picture of the instrument. You share the same cultural term for a small, portable battery-operated light. However, if you were in England and needed this item, you would have to ask for an "electric torch." Of course, even within the same society, a term can have a number of different meanings. In the United States, *grass* signifies both a plant eaten by grazing animals and an intoxicating drug.

DEVELOPMENT OF CULTURE AROUND THE WORLD

We've come a long way from our prehistoric heritage. The human species has produced such achievements as the

ragtime compositions of Scott Joplin, the poetry of V. S. Naipaul, the paintings of Johannes Vermeer, the novels of Jane Austen, and the films of Akira Kurosawa. As we begin a new millennium, we can transmit an entire book around the world via the Internet, clone cells, and prolong lives through organ transplants. We can peer into the outermost reaches of the universe or analyze our innermost feelings. In all these ways, we are remarkably different from other species of the animal kingdom.

Cultural Universals

All societies have developed certain common practices and beliefs, known as *cultural universals.* Many cultural universals are, in fact, adaptations to meet essential human needs, such as people's need for food, shelter, and clothing. Anthropologist George Murdock (1945:124) compiled a list of cultural universals, including athletic sports, cooking, funeral ceremonies, medicine, marriage, and sexual restrictions.

The cultural practices Murdock listed may be universal, but the manner in which they are expressed varies from culture to culture. For example, one society may let its members choose their own marriage partners. Another may encourage marriages arranged by the parents.

Not only does the expression of cultural universals vary from one society to another; it also may change dramatically over time within a society. Each generation, and each year for that matter, most human cultures change and expand through the processes of innovation and diffusion.

Innovation

The process of introducing a new idea or object to a culture is known as *innovation.* Innovation interests sociologists because of the social consequences of introducing something new. There are two forms of innovation: discovery and invention. *Discovery* involves making known or sharing the existence of an aspect of reality. The finding of the DNA molecule and the identification of a new moon of Saturn are both acts of discovery. A significant factor in the process of discovery is the sharing of new-found knowledge with others. By contrast, an *invention* results when existing cultural items are combined into a form that did not exist before. The bow and arrow, the automobile, and the television are all examples of inventions, as are Protestantism and democracy.

Globalization, Diffusion, and Technology

The Christmas season is in full swing, and the city is aglow with evergreen wreaths, snowmen, and silvery

Key Person George Murdock
Classroom Tip Additional examples of Murdock's cultural universals include bodily adornment, calendars, dancing, games, greetings, incest taboos, hairstyles, language, personal names, religion, and weaning.
Let's Discuss Why are dancing, hairstyles, and religion cultural universals? What functions do these examples serve?

In Vietnam, Santa Claus rides a bicycle loaded with gifts. The observance of Western holidays in non-Western countries is one sign of globalization.

not just in the United States, but throughout the world. One example of the massive global impact was the downturn in international tourism, which lasted for at least two years. The effects have been felt by people far removed from the United States, including African game wardens and Asian taxi drivers. Some observers see globalization and its effects as the natural result of advances in communications technology, particularly the Internet and satellite transmission of the mass media. Others view it more critically, as a process that allows multinational corporations to expand unchecked. We will examine this issue more fully in Box 3-1, on page 60 (Chase-Dunn et al. 2000; Feketekuty 2001; Feuer 1989; Pearlstein 2001; Ritzer 2004b).

As the observance of Western holidays shows, more and more cultural expressions and practices are crossing national borders and having an effect on the traditions and customs of the societies exposed to them. Sociologists use the term ***diffusion*** to refer to the process by which a cultural item spreads from group to group or society to society. Diffusion can occur through a variety of means, among them exploration, military conquest, missionary work, the influence of the mass media, tourism, and the Internet.

Sociologist George Ritzer coined the term "McDonaldization of society" to describe how the principles of fast-food restaurants developed in the United States have come to dominate more and more sectors of societies throughout the world. For example, hair salons and medical clinics now take walk-in appointments. In Hong Kong, sex selection clinics offer a menu of items, from fertility enhancement to methods of increasing the likelihood of having a child of the desired sex. Religious groups—from evangelical preachers on local stations or websites to priests at the Vatican Television Center—use marketing techniques similar to those that are used to sell "happy meals."

McDonaldization is associated with the melding of cultures, through which we see more and more similarities in cultural expression. In Japan, for example, African entrepreneurs have found a thriving market for hip-hop fashions popularized by teens in the United States. In Austria, the McDonald's organization itself has drawn on the Austrians' love of coffee, cake, and conversation to create the McCafe, a new part of its fast-food chain. Many

bells. On the street, shoppers hurry past bakery windows stocked with tempting holiday confections. Handel's *Messiah* is being performed tonight at the music hall. No, this isn't New York, London, or Berlin; it's Beijing. China, the country that exports many of the toys that end up under the Christmas tree in the United States, has caught the holiday spirit. But you won't find many manger scenes here, where some people who take the message of Christmas seriously are still persecuted. For the Chinese, Christmas is merely a chic Western custom, a welcome chance to relax with family and friends (Marquand 2002).

Not just in China, but in Vietnam, South Korea, and the Philippines, the observance of Western holidays is one more sign of the rapidly escalating *globalization* of culture. ***Globalization*** is the worldwide integration of government policies, cultures, social movements, and financial markets through trade and the exchange of ideas. While public discussion of globalization is relatively recent, intellectuals have been pondering its social consequences for a long time. Karl Marx and Friedrich Engels warned in *The Communist Manifesto* (written in 1848) of a world market that would lead to production in distant lands, sweeping away existing working relationships.

Today, developments outside a country are as likely to influence people's lives as changes at home. For example, though much of the world was already in recession by September 2001, the terrorist attacks on New York and Washington, D.C., caused an immediate economic decline

Imagine a "borderless world" in which culture, trade, commerce, money, and even people move freely from one place to another. Popular culture is widely shared, whether it be Japanese sushi or U.S. running shoes, and the English speaker who answers questions on the telephone about your credit card account is as likely to be in India or Ireland as in the United States. In this world, even the sovereignty of nations is at risk, challenged by political movements and ideologies that span nations.

There is no need to imagine this world, for we are already living in the age of globalization. African tribal youngsters wear Michael Jordan T-shirts; Thai teens dance to techno music; American children collect Pokémon cards. Ethnic accessories have become a fashion statement in the United States, and Asian martial arts have swept the world.

How did we get to this point? First, sociologists take note of advances in communications technology. Satellite TV, cell phones, the Internet, and the like allow information to flow freely across the world and serve to link global markets. Second, corporations in the industrial nations have become multinational, with both factories and markets in developing countries. Business leaders welcome the opportunity to sell consumer goods in populous countries such as China and India. Finally, these multinational firms have cooperated with global financial institutions, organizations, and governments to promote free trade—unrestricted or lightly restricted commerce across national borders.

Globalization is not universally welcomed. Many critics see the dominance of "businesses without borders" as benefiting the rich, particularly the very wealthy in industrial countries, at the expense of the poor in less developed nations. They consider globalization to be a successor to the imperialism and colonialism that oppressed Third World nations for centuries.

Another criticism of globalization comes from people who feel overwhelmed by global culture. The trend setters are likely to be far removed culturally and spatially from the daily lives of individuals. And when cultural change can come from any part of the global village, no single style can dominate a local community for long. Embedded in the concept of globalization is the notion of the cultural domination of developing nations by more affluent nations. Simply

> *Even James Bond movies and Britney Spears may be seen as threats to native cultures, if they dominate the media at the expense of local art forms.*

put, people lose their traditional values and begin to identify with the culture of dominant nations. They may discard or neglect their native language and dress as they attempt to copy the icons of mass-market entertainment and fashion. Even James Bond movies and Britney Spears may be seen as threats to native cultures, if they dominate the media at the expense of local art forms. As Sembene Ousmane, one of Africa's most prominent writers and filmmakers, noted, "[Today] we are more familiar with European fairy tales than with our own traditional stories" (World Development Forum 1990:4).

Some societies try to protect themselves from the invasion of too much culture from other countries, especially the economically dominant United States. In Brazil, for example, a toy manufacturer has challenged Barbie's popularity by designing a doll named Susi that looks more like Brazilian girls. Susi has a slightly smaller chest, much wider thighs, and darker skin than Barbie. Her wardrobe includes the skimpy bikinis favored on Brazilian beaches as well as a soccer shirt honoring the national team. Brazilians have responded: In Brazil, five Susi dolls are sold for every two Barbies.

Of course, globalization has its positive side too. Many developing nations are taking their place in the world of commerce and bringing in much needed income. The communications revolution helps people to stay connected and gives them access to knowledge that can improve living standards and even save lives. For example, people suffering from illnesses are now accessing treatment programs that were developed outside their own nation's medical establishment. The key seems to be finding a balance between the old ways and the new—becoming modernized without leaving meaningful cultural traditions behind.

Let's Discuss

1. How are you affected by globalization? What items of popular culture do you enjoy that come from other nations? Which aspects of globalization do you find advantageous and which do you find objectionable?

2. How would you feel if the customs and traditions you grew up with were replaced by the culture or values of another country? How might you try to protect your culture?

Sources: Dodds 2000; Downie 2000; Giddens 1991; Hansen 2001; Hirst and Thompson 1996; Legrain 2003; Ritzer 2004b; Sernau 2001.

Let's Discuss Is the United States resistant to the "invasion" of cultural characteristics from other societies?

Global View/Theory The Internet and television enter homes throughout the world, and both are dominated by the English language. Examine from a conflict perspective.

critical observers believe that McDonaldization and globalization serve to dilute the distinctive aspects of a society's culture (Alfino et al. 1998; Ritzer 2002, 2004a).

Technology in its many forms has increased the speed of cultural diffusion and broadened the distribution of cultural elements. Sociologist Gerhard Lenski has defined **technology** as "cultural information about how to use the material resources of the environment to satisfy human needs and desires" (Nolan and Lenski 2004:37). Today's technological developments no longer await publication in journals with limited circulation. Press conferences, often carried simultaneously on the Internet, trumpet the new developments.

Technology not only accelerates the diffusion of scientific innovations but also transmits culture. Later, in Chapter 16, we will discuss the concern in many parts of the world that the English language and North American culture dominate the Internet and World Wide Web. Such control, or at least dominance, of technology influences the direction of diffusion of culture. Websites cover even the most superficial aspects of U.S. culture but offer little information about the pressing issues faced by citizens of other nations. People all over the world find it easier to visit electronic chat rooms about daytime television shows like *All My Children* than to learn about their own governments' policies on day care or infant nutrition.

Sociologist William F. Ogburn (1922) made a useful distinction between the elements of material and nonmaterial culture. **Material culture** refers to the physical or ◄ pp. 4-5 technological aspects of our daily lives, including food, houses, factories, and raw materials. **Nonmaterial culture** refers to ways of using material objects and to customs, beliefs, philosophies, governments, and patterns of communication. Generally, the nonmaterial culture is more resistant to change than the material culture. Consequently, Ogburn introduced the term **culture lag** to refer to the period of maladjustment when the nonmaterial culture is still struggling to adapt to new material conditions. For example, the ethics of using the Internet, particularly issues concerning privacy and censorship, have not yet caught up with the explosion in Internet use and technology (see the social policy section in Chapter 16).

Use Your Sociological Imagination www.mhhe.com/schaefer6

If you grew up in your parents' generation—without computers, e-mail, the Internet, pagers, and cell phones—how would your daily life differ from the one you lead today?

Sociobiology

While sociology emphasizes diversity and change in the expression of culture, another school of thought, sociobiology, stresses the universal aspects of culture. **Sociobiology** is the systematic study of how biology affects human social behavior. Sociobiologists assert that many of the cultural traits humans display, such as the almost universal expectation that women will be nurturers and men will be providers, are not learned but are rooted in our genetic makeup.

Sociobiology is founded on the naturalist Charles Darwin's (1859) theory of evolution. In traveling the world, Darwin had noted small variations in species—in the shape of a bird's beak, for example—from one location to another. He theorized that over hundreds of generations, random variations in genetic makeup had helped certain members of a species to survive in a particular environment. A bird with a differently shaped beak might have been better at gathering seeds than other birds, for instance. In reproducing, these lucky individuals had passed on their advantageous genes to succeeding generations. Eventually, given their advantage in survival, individuals with the variation began to outnumber other members of the species. The species was slowly adapting to its environment. Darwin called this process of adaptation to the environment through random genetic variation *natural selection.*

Sociobiologists apply Darwin's principle of natural selection to the study of social behavior. They assume that particular forms of behavior become genetically linked to a species if they contribute to its fitness to survive (van den Berghe 1978). In its extreme form, sociobiology suggests that *all* behavior is the result of genetic or biological factors and that social interactions play no role in shaping people's conduct.

Sociobiologists do not seek to describe individual behavior on the level of "Why is Fred more aggressive than Jim?" Rather, they focus on how human nature is affected by the genetic composition of a *group* of people who share certain characteristics (such as men or women, or members of isolated tribal bands). In general, sociobiologists have stressed the basic genetic heritage that *all* humans share, and have shown little interest in speculating about alleged differences between racial groups or nationalities (E. Wilson 1975, 1978).

Some researchers insist that intellectual interest in sociobiology will only deflect serious study of the more significant influence on human behavior, the social environment. Yet Lois Wladis Hoffman (1985), in her presidential address to the Society for the Psychological Study of Social Issues, argued that sociobiology poses a valuable challenge to social scientists to better document their own research. Interactionists, for example, could show how social behavior is not programmed by human biology, but instead adjusts continually to the attitudes and responses of others.

Key Persons Gerhard Lenski, William Ogburn

Classroom Tip See "Biological Influences on Human Behavior" (Additional Lecture Ideas).
Theory Note the conflict theorists' concerns about sociobiology.

Certainly most social scientists would agree that there is a biological basis for social behavior. But there is less support for the extreme positions taken by certain advocates of sociobiology. Like interactionists, conflict theorists and functionalists believe that people's behavior rather than their genetic structure defines social reality. Conflict theorists fear that the sociobiological approach could be used as an argument against efforts to assist disadvantaged people, such as schoolchildren who are not competing successfully (Guterman 2000; Segerstråle 2000; E. Wilson 2000).

ELEMENTS OF CULTURE

Each culture considers its own distinctive ways of handling basic societal tasks to be "natural." But in fact, methods of education, marital ceremonies, religious doctrines, and other aspects of culture are learned and transmitted through human interaction within specific societies. Parents in India are accustomed to arranging marriages for their children; parents in the United States leave marital decisions up to their offspring. Lifelong residents of Naples consider it natural to speak Italian; lifelong residents of Buenos Aires feel the same way about Spanish. Let's take a look at the major aspects of culture that shape the way the members of a society live: language, norms, sanctions, and values.

Language

The English language makes extensive use of words dealing with war. We speak of "conquering" space, "fighting" the "battle" of the budget, "waging war" on drugs, making a "killing" on the stock market, and "bombing" an examination; something monumental or great is "the bomb." An observer from an entirely different and warless culture could gauge the importance that war and the military have had in our lives simply by recognizing the prominence that militaristic terms have in our language. On the other hand, in the Old West, words such as *gelding, stallion, mare, piebald,* and *sorrel* were all used to describe one animal—the horse. Even if we knew little of that period in history, we could conclude from the list of terms that horses were important to the culture. Similarly, the Slave Indians of northern Canada, who live in a frigid climate, have 14 terms to describe ice, including 8 for different kinds of "solid ice" and others for "seamed ice," "cracked ice," and "floating ice." Clearly, language reflects the priorities of a culture (Basso 1972; Haviland 2002).

Language is, in fact, the foundation of every culture. **Language** is an abstract system of word meanings and

symbols for all aspects of culture. It includes speech, written characters, numerals, symbols, and nonverbal gestures and expressions. Figure 3-1 shows where the major languages of the world are spoken.

Because language is the foundation of every culture, the ability to speak other languages is crucial to intercultural relations. Throughout the Cold War era, beginning in the 1950s and continuing well into the 1970s, the U.S. government encouraged the study of Russian by developing special language schools for diplomats and military advisors who dealt with the Soviet Union. And following September 11, 2001, the nation recognized how few skilled translators it had for Arabic and other languages spoken in Muslim countries. Language quickly became a key not only to tracking potential terrorists, but to building diplomatic bridges with Muslim countries willing to help in the war against terrorism.

While language is a cultural universal, striking differences in the use of language are evident around the world. Such is the case even when two countries use the same spoken language. For example, an English-speaking person from the United States who is visiting London might be puzzled the first time an English friend says "I'll ring you up." The friend means "I'll call you on the telephone."

Sapir-Whorf Hypothesis

Language does more than simply describe reality; it also serves to *shape* the reality of a culture. For example, most people in the United States cannot easily make the verbal distinctions concerning ice that are possible in the Slave Indian culture. As a result, they are less likely to notice such differences.

The **Sapir-Whorf hypothesis,** named for two linguists, describes the role of language in shaping our interpretation of reality. According to Sapir and Whorf, since people can conceptualize the world only through language, language *precedes* thought. Thus, the word symbols and grammar of a language organize the world for us. The Sapir-Whorf hypothesis also holds that language is not a given. Rather, it is culturally determined and encourages a distinctive interpretation of reality by focusing our attention on certain phenomena.

In a literal sense, language may color how we see the world. Berlin and Kay (1991) have noted that humans possess the physical ability to make millions of color distinctions, yet languages differ in the number of colors they recognize. The English language distinguishes between yellow and orange, but some other languages do not. In the Dugum Dani language of New Guinea's West Highlands, there are only two basic color terms—*modla* for "white" and *mili* for "black." By contrast, there are 11

FIGURE 3–1

Languages of the World

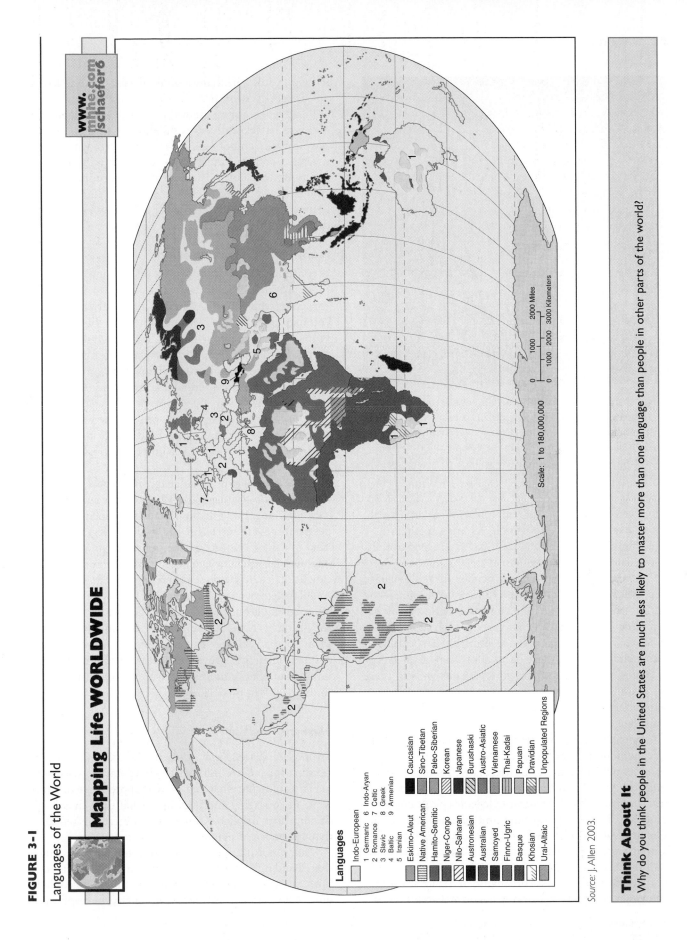

Mapping Life WORLDWIDE

www.
mhhe.com
/schaefer6

Languages

Indo-European

1 Germanic   6 Indo-Aryan
2 Romance   7 Celtic
3 Slavic   8 Greek
4 Baltic   9 Armenian
5 Iranian

Eskimo-Aleut   Caucasian
Native American   Sino-Tibetan
Hamito-Semitic   Paleo-Siberian
Niger-Congo   Korean
Nilo-Saharan   Japanese
Austronesian   Burushaski
Australian   Austro-Asiatic
Samoyed   Vietnamese
Finno-Ugric   Thai-Kadai
Basque   Papuan
Khosian   Dravidian
Ural-Altaic   Unpopulated Regions

Scale: 1 to 180,000,000

0   1000   2000 Miles
0   1000   2000   3000 Kilometers

Source: J. Allen 2003.

Think About It

Why do you think people in the United States are much less likely to master more than one language than people in other parts of the world?

Hand signals have different meanings in different cultures. U.S. film critic Roger Ebert uses the thumbs-up sign to recommend a new movie, but in Australia his gesture would be seen as offensive rather than complimentary.

basic terms in English. Russian and Hungarian, though, have 12 color terms. Russians have terms for light blue and dark blue, while Hungarians have terms for two different shades of red (Roberson et al. 2000).

Feminists have noted that gender-related language can reflect—although in itself it does not determine—the traditional acceptance of men and women in certain occupations. Each time we use a term such as *mailman, policeman,* or *fireman,* we are implying (especially to young children) that these occupations can be filled only by males. Yet many women work as *letter carriers, police officers,* and *firefighters*—a fact that is being increasingly recognized and legitimized through the use of such nonsexist language.

Language can also transmit stereotypes related to race. Look up the meanings of the adjective *black* in dictionaries published in the United States. You will find *dismal, gloomy or forbidding, destitute of moral light or goodness, atrocious, evil, threatening, clouded with anger.* By contrast, dictionaries list *pure* and *innocent* among the meanings of the adjective *white.* Through such patterns of language, our culture reinforces positive associations with the term (and skin color) *white* and negative associations with *black.* Is it surprising, then, that a list meant to prevent people from working in a profession is called a

blacklist, while a lie that we think of as somewhat acceptable is called a *white lie?*

Language can shape how we see, taste, smell, feel, and hear. It also influences the way we think about the people, ideas, and objects around us. Language communicates a culture's most important norms, values, and sanctions to people. That's why the introduction of a new language into a society is such a sensitive issue in many parts of the world (see the social policy section at the end of this chapter).

Nonverbal Communication

If you don't like the way a meeting is going, you might suddenly sit back, fold your arms, and turn down the corners of your mouth. When you see a friend in tears, you may give a quick hug. After winning a big game you probably high-five your teammates. These are all examples of *nonverbal communication,* the use of gestures, facial expressions, and other visual images to communicate.

We are not born with these expressions. We learn them, just as we learn other forms of language, from people who share our same culture. This is as true for the basic expressions of happiness and sadness as it is for more complex emotions such as shame or distress (Fridlund et al. 1987).

Like other forms of language, nonverbal communication is not the same in all cultures. For example, sociological research at the micro level documents that people from various cultures differ in the degree to which they touch others during the course of normal social interactions. Even experienced travelers are sometimes caught off guard by these differences. In Saudi Arabia, a middle-aged man may want to hold hands with a partner after closing a business deal. The gesture, which would shock an American businessman, is considered a compliment in that culture. The meaning of hand signals is another form of nonverbal communication that can differ from one culture to the next. In Australia, the thumbs-up sign is considered rude (Passero 2002).

Norms

"Wash your hands before dinner." "Thou shalt not kill." "Respect your elders." All societies have ways of encouraging and enforcing what they view as appropriate behavior while discouraging and punishing what they consider to be improper behavior. **Norms** are the established standards of behavior maintained by a society.

For a norm to become significant, it must be widely shared and understood. For example, in movie theaters in the United States, we typically expect that people will be quiet while the film is shown. Of course, the application

Race/Ethnicity/Gender Explain how language shapes our thoughts and actions about various ethnic and racial groups and about men and women.
Classroom Tip See "Sexism in Language—English and Japanese" (Additional Lecture Ideas).
Classroom Tip See "Desexing English" (Class Discussion Topics).
Theory Microsociological analysis of communication

Global View Cross-cultural variations in nonverbal communication
Classroom Tip See "Graffiti" (Class Discussion Topics).
Classroom Tip Anthropologist Edward Hall has described "distances" for various social interactions. See "Conversational Distance" (Additional Lecture Ideas).
Let's Discuss Why is "distance" at an ATM important?

of this norm can vary, depending on the particular film and type of audience. People who are viewing a serious artistic film will be more likely to insist on the norm of silence than those who are watching a slapstick comedy or horror movie.

Types of Norms

Sociologists distinguish between norms in two ways. First, norms are classified as either formal or informal. *Formal norms* generally have been written down and specify strict punishments for violators. In the United States, we often formalize norms into laws, which are very precise in defining proper and improper behavior. Sociologist Donald Black (1995) has termed *law* "governmental social control," meaning that laws are formal norms enforced by the state. Laws are just one example of formal norms. The requirements for a college major and the rules of a card game are also considered formal norms.

By contrast, *informal norms* are generally understood but not precisely recorded. Standards of proper dress are a common example of informal norms. Our society has no specific punishment or sanction for a person who comes to school, say, wearing a monkey suit. Making fun of the nonconforming student is usually the most likely response.

Norms are also classified by their relative importance to society. When classified in this way, they are known as *mores* and *folkways*. **Mores** (pronounced "MOR-ays") are norms deemed highly necessary to the welfare of a society, often because they embody the most cherished principles of a people. Each society demands obedience to its mores; violation can lead to severe penalties. Thus, the United States has strong mores against murder, treason, and child abuse, which have been institutionalized into formal norms.

Folkways are norms governing everyday behavior. Folkways play an important role in shaping the daily behavior of members of a culture. Society is less likely to formalize folkways than mores, and their violation raises comparatively little concern. For example, walking up a "down" escalator in a department store challenges our standards of appropriate behavior, but it will not result in a fine or a jail sentence.

In many societies around the world, folkways exist to reinforce patterns of male dominance. Various folkways reveal men's hierarchical position above women within the traditional Buddhist areas of southeast Asia. In the sleeping cars of trains, women do not sleep in upper berths above men. Hospitals that house men on the first floor do not place women patients on the second floor. Even on clotheslines, folkways dictate male dominance: women's attire is hung lower than that of men (Bulle 1987).

Use Your Sociological Imagination www.mhhe.com/schaefer6

You are a high school principal. What norms would you want to govern the students' behavior? How might these norms differ from those appropriate for college students?

Acceptance of Norms

People do not follow norms, whether mores or folkways, in all situations. In some cases, they can evade a norm because they know it is weakly enforced. It is illegal for U.S. teenagers to drink alcoholic beverages, yet drinking by minors is common throughout the nation. (In fact, teenage alcoholism is a serious social problem.)

In some instances, behavior that appears to violate society's norms may actually represent adherence to the norms of a particular group. Teenage drinkers are conforming to the standards of their peer group when they violate norms that condemn underage drinking. Similarly, business executives who use shady accounting techniques may be responding to a corporate culture that demands the maximization of profits at any cost, including the deception of investors and government regulatory agencies.

Norms are violated in some instances because one norm conflicts with another. For example, suppose that you live in an apartment building and one night hear the screams of the woman next door, who is being beaten by her husband. If you decide to intervene by ringing their doorbell or calling the police, you are violating the norm of "minding your own business," while at the same time following the norm of assisting a victim of violence.

Even if norms do not conflict, there are always exceptions to any norm. The same action, under different circumstances, can cause one to be viewed as either a hero or a villain. Secretly taping telephone conversations is normally considered illegal and abhorrent. However, it can be done with a court order to obtain valid evidence for a criminal trial. We would heap praise on a government agent who used such methods to convict an organized crime figure. In our culture, we tolerate killing another human being in self-defense, and we actually reward killing in warfare.

Acceptance of norms is subject to change as the political, economic, and social conditions of a culture are transformed. Until the 1960s, for example, formal norms throughout much of the United States prohibited the marriage of people from different racial groups. Over the last half century, however, such legal prohibitions were cast aside. The process of change can be seen today in the increasing acceptance of single parents and growing support for the legalization of marriage between same-sex couples (see Chapter 12).

Cockfighting, anyone? It's legal only in New Mexico, Louisiana, and Oklahoma (shown here), but practiced behind closed doors elsewhere in the nation. What does this situation tell us about social norms?

Sanctions are penalties and rewards for conduct concerning a social norm. Note that the concept of *reward* is included in this definition. Conformity to a norm can lead to positive sanctions such as a pay raise, a medal, a word of gratitude, or a pat on the back. Negative sanctions include fines, threats, imprisonment, and stares of contempt.

Table 3-1 (opposite) summarizes the relationship between norms and sanctions. As you can see, the sanctions that are associated with formal norms (those that are written down and codified) tend to be formal as well. If a coach sends too many players onto the field, the team will be penalized 15 yards. The driver who fails to put money in the parking meter will receive a ticket and have to pay a fine. But sanctions for violations of informal norms can vary. The college graduate who goes to the bank interview in shorts will probably lose any chance of getting the job; on the other hand, he or she might be so brilliant that bank officials will overlook the unconventional attire.

When circumstances require the sudden violation of long-standing cultural norms, the change can upset an entire population. In Iraq, where Muslim custom strictly forbids touching by strangers for men and especially for women, the war that began in 2003 has brought numerous daily violations of the norm. Outside important mosques, government offices, and other facilities likely to be targeted by terrorists, visitors must now be patted down and have their bags searched by Iraqi security guards. To reduce the discomfort caused by the procedure, women are searched by female guards and men by male guards. Despite that concession, and the fact that many Iraqis admit or even insist on the need for such measures, people still wince at the invasion of their personal privacy. In reaction to the searches, Iraqi women have begun to limit the contents of the bags they carry or simply to leave them at home (Rubin 2003).

The entire fabric of norms and sanctions in a culture reflects that culture's values and priorities. The most cherished values will be most heavily sanctioned; matters regarded as less critical will carry light and informal sanctions.

Values

Though we each have our own personal set of standards—which may include caring or fitness or success in business—we also share a general set of objectives as members of a society. Cultural *values* are these collective conceptions of what is considered good, desirable, and proper—or bad, undesirable, and improper—in a culture. They indicate what people in a given culture prefer as well as what they find important and morally right (or wrong). Values may be specific, such as honoring one's parents and owning a home, or they may be more general, such as health, love, and democracy. Of course, the members of a society do not uniformly share its values. Angry political debates and billboards promoting conflicting causes tell us that much.

Values influence people's behavior and serve as criteria for evaluating the actions of others. The values,

Sanctions

Suppose a football coach sends a 12th player onto the field. Imagine a college graduate showing up in shorts for a job interview at a large bank. Or consider a driver who neglects to put any money into a parking meter. These people have violated widely shared and understood norms. So what happens? In each of these situations, the person will receive sanctions if his or her behavior is detected.

Table 3-1	Norms and Sanctions	
Norms	**Sanctions**	
	Positive	**Negative**
Formal	Salary bonus	Demotion
	Testimonial dinner	Firing from a job
	Medal	Jail sentence
	Diploma	Expulsion
Informal	Smile	Frown
	Compliment	Humiliation
	Cheers	Belittling

norms, and sanctions of a culture are often directly related. For example, if a culture highly values the institution of marriage, it may have norms (and strict sanctions) that prohibit the act of adultery or make divorce difficult. If a culture views private property as a basic value, it will probably have stiff laws against theft and vandalism.

The values of a culture may change, but most remain relatively stable during any one person's lifetime. Socially shared, intensely felt values are a fundamental part of our lives in the United States. Sociologist Robin Williams (1970) has offered a list of basic values. It includes achievement, efficiency, material comfort, nationalism, equality, and the supremacy of science and reason over faith. Obviously, not all 290 million people in this country agree on all these values, and we should not look on such a list as anything more than a starting point in defining the national character. Nevertheless, a review of 27 different attempts to describe the "American value system," including the works of anthropologist Margaret Mead and sociologist Talcott Parsons, revealed an overall similarity to the values identified by Williams (Devine 1972).

Each year more than 276,000 entering college students at 413 of the nation's four-year colleges fill out a questionnaire about their attitudes. Because this survey focuses on an array of issues, beliefs, and life goals, it is commonly cited as a barometer of the nation's values. The respondents are asked what values are personally important to them. Over the last 36 years, the value of "being very well-off financially" has shown the strongest gain in popularity; the proportion of first-year college students who endorse this value as "essential" or "very important" rose from 44 percent in 1967 to 74 percent in

2003 (see Figure 3-2). In contrast, the value that has shown the most striking decline in endorsement by students is "developing a meaningful philosophy of life." While this value was the most popular in the 1967 survey, endorsed by more than 80 percent of the respondents, it had fallen to ninth place on the list by 2003, when it was endorsed by less than 40 percent of students entering college.

During the 1980s and 1990s, support for values having to do with money, power, and status grew. At the same time, support for certain values having to do with social awareness and altruism, such as "helping others," declined. According to the 2003 nationwide survey, only 39 percent of first-year college students stated that "influencing social values" was an "essential" or "very important" goal. The proportion of students for whom "helping to promote racial understanding" was an essential or very important goal reached a record high of 42 percent in 1992, but fell to 31 percent in 2003. Like other aspects of culture, such as language and norms, a nation's values are not necessarily fixed.

Recently, cheating has become a hot issue on college campuses. Professors who take advantage of

FIGURE 3-2

Life Goals of First-Year College Students in the United States, 1966–2003

Sources: UCLA Higher Education Research Institute, as reported in Astin et al. 1994; Sax et al. 2003:27.

> **Think About It**
> Why do you think values have shifted among college students in the last few decades? Which of these values is important to you? Have your values changed since September 11, 2001?

computerized services than can identify plagiarism, such as the search engine Google, have been shocked to learn that many of the papers their students hand in are plagiarized in whole or in part. Box 3-2 examines the shift in values that underlies this decline in academic integrity.

Another value that has begun to change recently, not just among students but among the public in general, is the right to privacy. Americans have always valued their privacy and resented government intrusions into their personal lives. In the aftermath of the terrorist attacks of September 11, 2001, however, many citizens called for greater protection against the threat of terrorism. In response, the U.S. government broadened its surveillance powers and increased its ability to monitor people's behavior without court approval. In 2001, shortly after the attacks, Congress passed the Patriot Act, which empowers the Federal Bureau of Investigation to access individuals' medical, library, student, and phone records without informing them or obtaining a search warrant. We will discuss the ambivalence Americans felt about increased government surveillance and the threat it posed to people's privacy in the social policy section in Chapter 16.

CULTURE AND THE DOMINANT IDEOLOGY

Both functionalist and conflict theorists agree that culture and society reinforce each other, but for different reasons. Functionalists maintain that stability requires a consensus and the support of society's members; thus the need for strong central values and common norms. This view of culture became popular in sociology beginning in the 1950s. It was borrowed from British anthropologists who thought that the function of all cultural traits was to stabilize a culture. From a functionalist perspective, a cultural trait or practice will persist if it fulfills functions that society seems to need or contributes to overall social stability and consensus. This view helps to explain why widely condemned social practices such as prostitution

◀ p. 14 continue to survive.

Conflict theorists agree that a common culture may exist, but they argue that it serves to maintain the privileges of certain groups. Moreover, while protecting their own self-interests, powerful groups may keep others in a subservient position. The term **dominant ideology** describes the set of cultural beliefs and practices that helps to maintain powerful social, economic, and political interests. This concept was first used by Hungarian Marxist Georg Lukacs (1923) and Italian Marxist Antonio

Gramsci (1929), but it did not gain an audience in the United States until the early 1970s. In Karl Marx's view, a capitalist society has a dominant ideology that serves the interests of the ruling class.

From a conflict perspective, the dominant ideology has major social significance. Not only do a society's most powerful groups and institutions control wealth and property; even more important, they control the means of producing beliefs about reality through religion, education, and the media. Feminists would also argue that if all a society's most important institutions tell women that they should be subservient to men, this dominant ideology will help to control women and keep them in a subordinate position.

A growing number of social scientists believe it is not easy to identify a "core culture" in the United States. For support, they point to the lack of consensus on national values, the diffusion of cultural traits, the diversity within our culture, and the changing views of young people (look again at Figure 3-2). Yet there is no way of denying that certain expressions of values have greater influence than others, even in so complex a society as the United States (Abercrombie et al. 1980, 1990; Robertson 1988).

CULTURAL VARIATION

Each culture has a unique character. Inuit tribes in northern Canada, wrapped in furs and dieting on whale blubber, have little in common with farmers in Southeast Asia, who dress for the heat and subsist mainly on the rice they grow in their paddies. Cultures adapt to meet specific sets of circumstances, such as climate, level of technology, population, and geography. This adaptation to different conditions shows up in differences in all elements of culture, including norms, sanctions, values, and language. Thus, despite the presence of cultural universals such as courtship and religion, great diversity exists among the world's many cultures. Moreover, even *within* a single nation, certain segments of the populace develop cultural patterns that differ from the patterns of the dominant society.

Aspects of Cultural Variation

Subcultures

Rodeo cowboys, residents of a retirement community, workers on an offshore oil rig—all are examples of what sociologists refer to as *subcultures*. A **subculture** is a segment of society that shares a distinctive pattern of mores, folkways, and values that differs from the pattern of the larger society. In a sense, a subculture can be thought of as

Theory Functionalist view of culture and why certain cultural traits persist over time

Theory Conflict view of how a common culture maintains the privileges of some groups and keeps others subordinate

Theory Contrast feminist view to functionalist view of cultural traits.

Web Resource Encourage students to listen to the audio clip when they visit the student center in the Online Learning Center at **www.mhhe.com/schaefer6.** They can hear Richard Schaefer, the author of the text, discuss the concept of dominant ideology.

Theory Compare functionalist and conflict views concerning cultural variation.

3-2   A CULTURE OF CHEATING?

On November 21, 2002, after issuing several warnings, officials at the U.S. Naval Academy seized the computers of almost 100 midshipmen suspected of downloading movies and music illegally from the Internet. Officers at the school may have taken the unusually strong action to avoid liability on the part of the U.S. government, which owns the computers students were using. But across the nation, college administrators have been trying to restrain students from downloading pirated entertainment for free. The practice is so widespread, it has been slowing down the high-powered computer networks colleges and universities depend on for research and admissions.

Illegal downloading is just one aspect of the growing problem of copyright violation, both on campus and off. Now that college students can use personal computers to surf the Internet, most do their research online. Apparently, the temptation to cut and paste passages from website postings and pass them off as one's own is irresistible to many. Surveys done by the Center for Academic Integrity show that from 1999 to 2001, the percentage of students who approved of this type of plagiarism rose from 10 percent to 41 percent. At the same time, the percentage who considered cutting and pasting from the Internet to be a serious form of cheating fell from 68 percent to 27 percent.

Other forms of cheating are becoming rampant, as well. The Center for Academic Integrity estimates that at most schools, more than three quarters of the students engage in some form of cheating. Students not only cut passages from the Internet and paste them into their papers without citing the source; they share questions and answers on exams, collaborate on assignments they are supposed to do independently, and even falsify the results of their laboratory experiments. Worse, many professors have become inured to the problem and have ceased to report it.

To address what they consider an alarming trend, many schools are rewrit-

---

Cheating is considerably less common at schools with honor codes than at schools without honor codes.

---

ing or adopting new academic honor codes. According to the Center for Academic Integrity, cheating on tests and papers is considerably less common at schools with honor codes than at schools without honor codes. Cornell, Duke, and Kansas State University are just three of a growing number of schools that are instituting or strengthening their honor codes in an attempt to curb student cheating.

This renewed emphasis on honor and integrity underscores the influence of cultural values on social behavior. Observers contend that the increase in stu-

dent cheating reflects widely publicized instances of cheating in public life, which have served to create an alternative set of values in which the means justify the end. When young people see sports heroes, authors, entertainers, and corporate executives exposed for cheating in one form or another, the message seems to be "Cheating is OK, as long as you don't get caught." More than proctoring of exams or reliance on search engines to identify plagiarism, then, educating students about the need for academic honesty seems to reduce the incidence of cheating. "The feeling of being treated as an adult and responding in kind," says Professor Donald McCabe of Rutgers University, "it's clearly there for many students. They don't want to violate that trust."

Let's Discuss

1. Do you know anyone who has engaged in Internet plagiarism? What about cheating on tests or falsifying laboratory results? If so, how did the person justify these forms of dishonesty?

2. Even if cheaters aren't caught, what negative effects does their academic dishonesty have on them? What effects does it have on students who are honest? Could an entire college or university suffer from students' dishonesty?

Sources: Argetsinger and Krim 2002; Center for Academic Integrity 2004; R. Murray Thomas 2003; Zernike 2002.

---

a culture existing within a larger, dominant culture. The existence of many subcultures is characteristic of complex societies such as the United States.

Members of a subculture participate in the dominant culture while at the same time engaging in unique and distinctive forms of behavior. Frequently, a subculture will develop an ***argot,*** or specialized language, that distinguishes it from the wider society. For example, if you were to join a band of pickpockets you would need to learn what the dip, dish, and tailpipe are expected to do (see Figure 3-3, page 70).

Argot allows insiders—the members of the subculture—to understand words with special meanings. It also establishes patterns of communication that outsiders can't understand. Sociologists associated with the interactionist perspective emphasize that language and symbols offer a powerful way for a subculture to feel cohesive and maintain its identity.

Let's Discuss Have students note cultural variations they have experienced in their travels or upon first visiting the United States, if they are from abroad.

Classroom Tip See "Professional Football Players as a Subculture" (Additional Lecture Ideas).

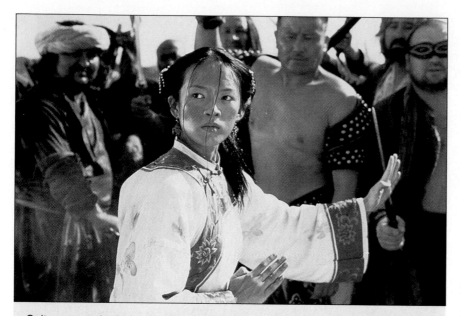

Cultures vary in their taste for films. Europeans and North Americans enjoyed the exotic aspects of *Crouching Tiger, Hidden Dragon* (shown here), but it was not well received in China. Audiences there found it slow-paced, and they were especially annoyed by the clumsy Mandarin spoken by actors more used to Cantonese roles.

Music fans often form subcultures dedicated to a particular type of music or musician. Recently a subculture called Phishheads, after the Vermont jam rock band Phish, has emerged. The group is reminiscent of the Deadheads who devote themselves to the Grateful Dead.

Subcultures develop in a number of ways. Often a subculture emerges because a segment of society faces problems or even privileges unique to its position. Subcultures may be based on common age (teenagers or old people), region (Appalachians), ethnic heritage (Cuban Americans), occupation (firefighters), or beliefs (deaf activists working to preserve deaf culture). Certain subcultures, such as computer hackers, develop because of a shared interest or hobby. In still other subcultures, such as that of prison inmates, members have been excluded from conventional society and are forced to develop alternative ways of living.

Functionalist and conflict theorists agree that variation exists within a culture. Functionalists view subcultures as variations of particular social environments and as evidence that differences can exist within a common culture. However, conflict theorists suggest that variations often reflect the inequality of social arrangements within a society. A conflict perspective would view the challenge to dominant social norms by African American activists, the feminist movement, and the disability rights movement as a reflection of inequity based on race, gender, and disability status. Conflict theorists also argue that subcultures sometimes emerge when the dominant society unsuccessfully tries to suppress a practice, such as the use of illegal drugs.

Countercultures

By the end of the 1960s, an extensive subculture had emerged in the United States, composed of young people turned off by a society they believed was too materialistic and technological. This group included primarily political radicals and "hippies" who had "dropped out" of mainstream social institutions. These young men and women rejected the pressure to accumulate more and more cars, larger and larger homes, and an endless array of material goods. Instead, they expressed a desire to live in a culture based on more humanistic values, such as sharing, love, and coexistence with the environment. As a political force, this subculture opposed the United States' involvement in the war in Vietnam and encouraged draft resistance (Flacks 1971; Roszak 1969).

FIGURE 3-3

The Argot of Pickpockets

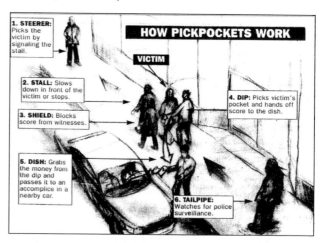

Source: Gearty 1996.

Classroom Tip See "The Skinhead Counterculture" (Additional Lecture Ideas).

Classroom Tip Another example of a counterculture is the "survivalists," who see nuclear war as inevitable and have, in some cases, created armed camps to defend themselves from city dwellers after a nuclear attack.

When a subculture conspicuously and deliberately opposes certain aspects of the larger culture, it is known as a *counterculture*. Countercultures typically thrive among the young, who have the least investment in the existing culture. In most cases, a 20-year-old can adjust to new cultural standards more easily than someone who has spent 60 years following the patterns of the dominant culture (Zellner 1995).

In the wake of the terrorist attacks of September 11, 2001, people around the United States learned of the existence of terrorist groups operating as a counterculture within their country. This was a situation that generations have lived with in Northern Ireland, Israel and the Palestinian territory, and many other parts of the world. But terrorist cells are not necessarily fueled only by outsiders. Frequently people become disenchanted with the policies of their own country, and a few take very violent steps.

Culture Shock

Anyone who feels disoriented, uncertain, out of place, or even fearful when immersed in an unfamiliar culture may be experiencing *culture shock.* For example, a resident of the United States who visits certain areas in China and wants local meat for dinner may be stunned to learn that the specialty is dog meat. Similarly, someone from a strict Islamic culture may be shocked upon first seeing the comparatively provocative dress styles and open displays of affection that are common in the United States and various European cultures.

All of us, to some extent, take for granted the cultural practices of our society. As a result, it can be surprising and even disturbing to realize that other cultures do not follow our way of life. The fact is that customs that seem strange to us are considered normal and proper in other cultures, which may see our own mores and folkways as odd.

Use Your Sociological Imagination www.mhhe.com/schaefer6

You arrive in a developing African country as a Peace Corps volunteer. What aspects of a very different culture do you think would be the hardest to adjust to? What might the citizens of that country find shocking about your culture?

Attitudes toward Cultural Variation

Ethnocentrism

Many everyday statements reflect our attitude that our own culture is best. We use terms such as *underdeveloped,*

Let's Discuss Have our norms changed as a result of the terrorist attacks on the World Trade Center and the Pentagon?
Global View Note cultural variation in the United States, China, Islamic cultures, India, and Africa.
Classroom Tip See "Cross-Cultural Interaction" (Class Discussion Topics).

backward, and *primitive* to refer to other societies. What "we" believe is a religion; what "they" believe is superstition and mythology.

It is tempting to evaluate the practices of other cultures on the basis of our own perspectives. Sociologist William Graham Sumner (1906) coined the term *ethnocentrism* to refer to the tendency to assume that one's own culture and way of life represent the norm or are superior to all others. The ethnocentric person sees his or her own group as the center or defining point of culture and views all other cultures as deviations from what is "normal." Westerners who think cattle are to be used for food might look down on India's Hindu religion and culture, which views the cow as sacred. Or people in one culture may dismiss as unthinkable the mate selection or child-rearing practices of another culture.

Conflict theorists point out that ethnocentric value judgments serve to devalue groups and to deny equal opportunities. Psychologist Walter Stephan notes a typical example of ethnocentrism in New Mexico's schools. Both Hispanic and Native American cultures teach children to look down when they are being criticized by adults, yet many "Anglo" (non-Hispanic White) teachers believe that you should look someone in the eye when you are being criticized. "Anglo teachers can feel that these students are being disrespectful," notes Stephan. "That's the kind of misunderstanding that can evolve into stereotype and prejudice" (Goleman 1991:C8).

Ethnocentric value judgments have also complicated U.S. efforts at democratic reform of the Iraqi

"IT'S ENDLESS. WE JOIN A COUNTER-CULTURE; IT BECOMES THE CULTURE. WE JOIN ANOTHER COUNTER-CULTURE; IT BECOMES THE CULTURE..."

Cultures change. Fashions we once regarded as unacceptable—such as men wearing earrings and people wearing jeans in the workplace—or associated with fringe groups (such as men and women with tattoos) are now widely accepted. These countercultural practices have been absorbed by mainstream culture.

Classroom Tip See "Conflicting Cultures" (Additional Lecture Ideas).
Web Resource Encourage students to take the multiple-choice quiz in the student center of the Online Learning Center (**www.mhhe.com/schaefer6**). Remind them that they will receive instant feedback for incorrect answers.

summingUP

Table 3-2	Major Theoretical Perspectives on Culture		
	Functionalist Perspective	**Conflict Perspective**	**Interactionist Perspective**
Norms	Norms reinforce societal standards	Norms reinforce patterns of dominance	Norms are maintained through face-to-face interaction
Values	Values are collective conceptions of what is good	Values may perpetuate social inequality	Values are defined and redefined through social interaction
Culture and society	Culture reflects a society's strong central values	Culture reflects a society's dominant ideology	A society's core culture is perpetuated through daily social interactions
Cultural variation	Subcultures serve the interests of subgroups; ethnocentrism reinforces group solidarity	Countercultures question the dominant social order; ethnocentrism devalues groups	Customs and traditions are transmitted through intergroup contact and through the media

government. Before the 2003 war in Iraq, U.S. planners had assumed that Iraqis would adapt to a new form of government in the same way the Germans and Japanese did following World War II. But in the Iraqi culture, unlike the German and Japanese cultures, loyalty to the family and the extended clan comes before patriotism and the common good. In a country in which almost half of all people, even those in the cities, marry a first or second cousin, citizens are predisposed to favor their own kin in government and business dealings. Why trust a stranger from outside the family? What Westerners would criticize as nepotism, then, is actually an acceptable, even admirable, practice to Iraqis (J. Tierney 2003).

Functionalists, on the other hand, point out that ethnocentrism serves to maintain a sense of solidarity by promoting group pride. Denigrating other nations and cultures can enhance our own patriotic feelings and belief that our way of life is superior. Yet this type of social stability is established at the expense of other peoples. Of course, ethnocentrism is hardly limited to citizens of the United States. Visitors from many African cultures are surprised at the disrespect that children in the United States show their parents. People from India may be repelled by our practice of living in the same household with dogs and cats. Many Islamic fundamentalists in the Arab world and Asia view the United States as corrupt, decadent, and doomed to destruction. All these people may feel comforted by membership in cultures that in their view are superior to ours.

Cultural Relativism

While ethnocentrism evaluates foreign cultures using the familiar culture of the observer as a standard of correct behavior, ***cultural relativism*** views people's behavior from the perspective of their own culture. It places a priority on understanding other cultures, rather than dismissing them as "strange" or "exotic." Unlike ethnocentrism, cultural relativism employs the kind of value neutrality in scientific study that Max Weber saw as so important.

Cultural relativism stresses that different social contexts give rise to different norms and values. Thus, we must examine practices such as polygamy, bullfighting, and monarchy within the particular contexts of the cultures in which they are found. While cultural relativism does not suggest that we must unquestionably *accept* every cultural variation, it does require a serious and unbiased effort to evaluate norms, values, and customs in light of their distinctive culture.

An interesting extension of cultural relativism is referred to as xenocentrism. ***Xenocentrism*** is the belief that the products, styles, or ideas of one's society are inferior to those that originate elsewhere. In a sense, it is a reverse ethnocentrism. For example, people in the United States often assume that French fashions or Japanese electronic devices are superior to their own. Are they? Or are people unduly charmed by the lure of goods from exotic places? Such fascination with overseas products can be damaging to competitors in the United States. Some U.S. companies have responded by creating products that

p. 44

Key Person William Graham Sumner
Classroom Tip See "Hostages to Tourism" (Additional Lecture Ideas).
Race/Ethnicity Ethnocentrism in New Mexico's schools in treatment of Hispanic and Native American students
Theory Conflict view of ethnocentrism as contributing to denial of equal opportunities

Theory Functionalists argue that ethnocentrism promotes solidarity and group pride.
Classroom Tip See "Teaching Ethnocentrism and Cultural Relativity" (Class Discussion Topics).
Let's Discuss Should our laws be changed to accommodate cultural diversity?

sound European, such as Häagen-Dazs ice cream (made in Teaneck, New Jersey). Conflict theorists are most likely to consider the economic impact of xenocentrism in the developing world. Consumers in developing nations frequently turn their backs on locally produced goods and instead purchase items imported from Europe or North America (Warner Wilson et al. 1976).

Table 3-2 summarizes the major sociological perspectives on culture. How one views a culture—whether from an ethnocentric point of view or through the lens of cultural relativism—has important consequences in the area of social policy. A hot issue today is the extent to which a nation should accommodate nonnative language speakers by sponsoring bilingual programs. We'll take a close look at this issue in the next section.

SOCIAL POLICY and CULTURE

Bilingualism

The Issue

In Sri Lanka, Tamils seek to break away from the Sinhalese-speaking majority. Romanian radio announces that in areas where 20 percent of the people speak Hungarian, bilingual road and government signs will be posted. In schools from Miami to Boston to Chicago, administrators strive to deliver education to their Creole-speaking Haitian students. All over the world, nations face the challenge of how to deal with residential minorities who speak a language different from that of the mainstream culture.

Bilingualism refers to the use of two or more languages in a particular setting, such as the workplace or schoolroom, treating each language as equally legitimate. Thus, a teacher of bilingual education may instruct children in their native language while gradually introducing them to the language of the host society. If the curriculum is also bicultural, it will teach children about the mores and folkways of both the dominant culture and the subculture. To what degree should schools in the United States present the curriculum in a language other than English? This issue has prompted a great deal of debate among educators and policymakers.

The Setting

Languages know no political boundaries. Despite the portrayal of dominant languages in Figure 3-1 (page 63), minority languages are common in many nations. For example, Hindi is the most widely spoken language in India, and English is used widely for official purposes, but 18 other languages are officially recognized in the nation of about 1 billion people. According to the 2000 Census, 47 million residents of the United States over the age of five—that's about 18 percent of the population—speak a language other than English as their primary language. In-deed, 32 different languages are each spoken by at least 200,000 residents of this country (Bureau of the Census 2003d; Shin and Bruno 2003).

Schools throughout the world must deal with incoming students who speak many different languages. Do bilingual programs in the United States help these children to learn English? It is difficult to reach firm conclusions because bilingual programs in general vary so widely in their quality and approach. They differ in the length of the transition to English and in how long they allow students to remain in bilingual classrooms. Moreover, results have been mixed. In the years since California effectively dismantled its bilingual education program, reading and math scores of students with limited English proficiency rose dramatically, especially in the lower grades. Yet a major overview of 17 different studies, done at Johns Hopkins University, found that students who are offered lessons in both English and their home languages make better progress than similar children who are taught only in English (Slavin and Cheung 2003).

Sociological Insights

For a long time, people in the United States demanded conformity to a single language. This demand coincided with the functionalist view that language serves to unify members of a society. Immigrant children from Europe and Asia—including young Italians, Jews, Poles, Chinese, and Japanese—were expected to learn English once they entered school. In some cases, immigrant children were actually forbidden to speak their native languages on school grounds. Little respect was granted to immigrants' cultural traditions; a young person would often be teased about his or her "funny" name, accent, or style of dress.

Race/Ethnicity The debate over bilingualism in the United States grows out of the many languages spoken here.
Theory Bilingualism is examined from a functionalist and conflict view.
Student Alert Indicate the relationship between the social policy topic and concepts presented in the chapter: dominant ideology, ethnocentrism, subcultures, and so on.

Global View Highlight the different ways in which other cultures have responded to language variations.
Web Resource Encourage students to try the interactive activities in the student center of the Online Learning Center (www.mhhe.com/schaefer6). They will be required to complete an assignment in the "foreign" language of Pig Latin.

Recent decades have seen challenges to this pattern of forced obedience to the dominant ideology. Beginning in the 1960s, active movements for Black pride and ethnic pride insisted that people regard the traditions of all racial and ethnic subcultures as legitimate and important. Conflict theorists explain this development as a case of subordinated language minorities seeking opportunities for self-expression. Partly as a result of these challenges, people began to view bilingualism as an asset. It seemed to provide a sensitive way of assisting millions of non-English-speaking people in the United States to *learn* English in order to function more effectively within the society.

The perspective of conflict theory also helps us to understand some of the attacks on bilingual programs. Many of them stem from an ethnocentric point of view, which holds that any deviation from the majority is bad. This attitude tends to be expressed by those who wish to stamp out foreign influence wherever it occurs, especially in our schools. It does not take into account that success in bilingual education may actually have beneficial results, such as decreasing the number of high school dropouts and increasing the number of Hispanics in colleges and universities.

Policy Initiatives

Bilingualism has policy implications largely in two areas: efforts to maintain language purity and programs to enhance bilingual education. Nations vary dramatically in their tolerance for a variety of languages. China continues to tighten its cultural control over Tibet by extending instruction of Mandarin, a Chinese dialect, from high school into the elementary schools, which will now be bilingual along with Tibetan. Even more forceful is Indonesia, which has a large Chinese-speaking minority; public display of Chinese-language signs or books there is totally banned. By contrast, nearby Singapore establishes English as the medium of instruction but allows students to take their mother tongue as a second language, be it Chinese, Malay, or Tamil (Farley 1998).

In many nations, language dominance is a regional issue—for example, in Miami or along the Tex-Mex border, where Spanish speaking is prevalent. A particularly virulent bilingual hot spot is Quebec, the French-speaking province of Canada. The Québécois, as they are known, represent 83 percent of the province's population, but only 25 percent of Canada's total population. A law implemented in 1978 mandated education in French for all Quebec's children except those whose parents or siblings had learned English elsewhere in

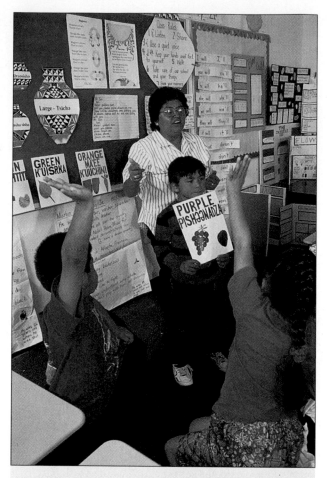

In this Native American school at Acoma Pueblo, New Mexico, children are learning to read and write in their native language as well as in English.

Canada. While special laws like this one have advanced French in the province, dissatisfied Québécois have tried to form their own separate country. In 1995, the people of Quebec voted to remain united with Canada by only the narrowest of margins (50.5 percent). Language and language-related cultural areas both unify and divide this nation of 32 million people (Krauss 2003; Schaefer 2004).

Policymakers in the United States have been somewhat ambivalent in dealing with the issue of bilingualism. In 1965, the Elementary and Secondary Education Act (ESEA) provided for bilingual, bicultural education. In the 1970s, the federal government took an active role in establishing the proper form for bilingual programs. However, more recently, federal policy has been less supportive of bilingualism, and local school districts have been forced to provide an increased share of funding for their bilingual programs. Yet bilingual programs are an expense that many communities and states are unwilling

FIGURE 3-4

States with Official English Laws

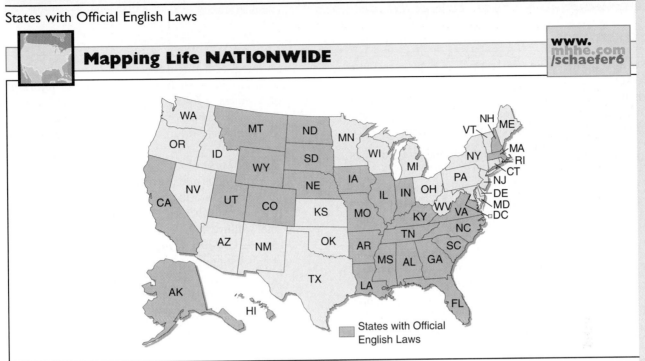

Mapping Life NATIONWIDE

www.mhhe.com/schaefer6

☐ States with Official English Laws

Source: U.S. English 2004.

to pay for and are quick to cut back. In 1998, voters in California approved a proposition that all but eliminated bilingual education: it requires instruction in English for 1.4 million children who are not fluent in the language.

In the United States, repeated efforts have been made to introduce a constitutional amendment declaring English the official language of the nation. A major force behind efforts to restrict bilingualism is U.S. English, a nationwide organization founded in 1983 that now claims to have 1.7 million members. Its adherents say they feel like strangers in their own neighborhoods, aliens in their own country. By contrast, Hispanic leaders see the U.S. English campaign as a veiled expression of racism.

Despite such challenges, U.S. English seems to be making headway in its efforts to oppose bilingualism. By 2004, 27 states had declared English to be their official language (see Figure 3-4). The actual impact of these measures, beyond their symbolism, is unclear.

Let's Discuss

1. Have you attended a school with a number of students for whom English is a second language? If so, did the school set up a special bilingual program? Was it effective? What is your opinion of such programs?

2. The ultimate goal of both English-only and bilingual programs is for foreign-born students to become proficient in English. Why should the type of program students attend matter so much to so many people? List all the reasons you can think of for supporting or opposing such programs. What do you see as the primary reason?

3. Besides bilingualism, can you think of another issue that has become controversial recently because of a clash of cultures? Analyze the issue from a sociological point of view.

GETTING INVOLVED

To get involved in the debate over bilingualism, visit this text's Online Learning Center, which offers links to relevant websites. Check out the Social Policy section on the Online Learning Center as well; it provides survey data on U.S. public opinion regarding this issue.

Let's Discuss Should all states have official English laws?
Classroom Tip See "Using Humor" (Class Discussion Topics).

CHAPTER RESOURCES

Summary

Culture is the totality of learned, socially transmitted customs, knowledge, material objects, and behavior. This chapter examines the basic elements that make up a culture, social practices common to all cultures, and variations that distinguish one culture from another.

1. A shared culture helps to define the group or society to which we belong.
2. Anthropologist George Murdock compiled a list of *cultural universals,* or general practices found in every culture, including marriage, sports, cooking, medicine, and sexual restrictions.
3. Human culture is constantly expanding through the process of *innovation,* which includes both *discovery* and *invention.*
4. *Diffusion*—the spread of cultural items from one place to another—has fostered *globalization.* But people resist ideas that seem too foreign, as well as those they perceive as threatening to their own values and beliefs.
5. *Language,* an important element of culture, includes speech, written characters, numerals, and symbols, as well as gestures and other forms of nonverbal communication. Language both describes culture and shapes it.

6. Sociologists distinguish between *norms* in two ways, classifying them either as *formal* or *informal* or as *mores* or *folkways.*
7. The formal norms of a culture will receive the heaviest *sanctions;* informal norms will carry light sanctions.
8. The *dominant ideology* of a culture is the set of cultural beliefs and practices that help to maintain powerful social, economic, and political interests.
9. In a sense, a *subculture* can be thought of as a small culture that exists within a larger, dominant culture. *Countercultures* are subcultures that deliberately oppose aspects of the larger culture.
10. People who measure other cultures by the standard of their own engage in *ethnocentrism.* By contrast, *cultural relativism* is the practice of viewing people from the perspective of their own culture.
11. The social policy of *bilingualism* calls for the use of two or more languages, treating each as equally legitimate. It is supported by those who want to ease the transition of non-native language speakers into a host society, but opposed by those who adhere to a single cultural tradition and language.

Critical Thinking Questions

1. Select three cultural universals from George Murdock's list (see page 58) and analyze them from a functionalist perspective. Why are these practices found in every culture? What functions do they serve?
2. Drawing on the theories and concepts presented in this chapter, apply sociological analysis to one subculture with which you are familiar. Describe the norms, values, argot, and sanctions evident in that subculture.
3. In what ways is the dominant ideology of the United States evident in the nation's literature, music, movies, theater, television programs, and sporting events?

Key Terms

Argot   Specialized language used by members of a group or subculture. (page 69)
Bilingualism   The use of two or more languages in a particular setting, such as the workplace or schoolroom, treating each language as equally legitimate. (73)
Counterculture   A subculture that deliberately opposes certain aspects of the larger culture. (71)
Cultural relativism   The viewing of people's behavior from the perspective of their own culture. (72)

Cultural universal   A common practice or belief found in every culture. (58)
Culture   The totality of learned, socially transmitted customs, knowledge, material objects, and behavior. (55)
Culture lag   A period of maladjustment when the nonmaterial culture is still struggling to adapt to new material conditions. (61)

Culture shock   The feeling of surprise and disorientation that people experience when they encounter cultural practices that are different from their own. (71)

Diffusion   The process by which a cultural item spreads from group to group or society to society. (59)

Discovery   The process of making known or sharing the existence of an aspect of reality. (58)

Dominant ideology   A set of cultural beliefs and practices that helps to maintain powerful social, economic, and political interests. (68)

Ethnocentrism   The tendency to assume that one's own culture and way of life represent the norm or are superior to all others. (72)

Folkway   A norm governing everyday behavior whose violation raises comparatively little concern. (65)

Formal norm   A norm that has been written down and that specifies strict punishments for violators. (65)

Globalization   The worldwide integration of government policies, cultures, social movements, and financial markets through trade and the exchange of ideas. (59)

Informal norm   A norm that is generally understood but not precisely recorded. (65)

Innovation   The process of introducing a new idea or object to a culture through discovery or invention. (58)

Invention   The combination of existing cultural items into a form that did not exist before. (58)

Language   An abstract system of word meanings and symbols for all aspects of culture; includes gestures and other nonverbal communication. (62)

Law   Governmental social control. (65)

Material culture   The physical or technological aspects of our daily lives. (61)

Mores   Norms deemed highly necessary to the welfare of a society. (65)

Nonmaterial culture   Ways of using material objects, as well as customs, beliefs, philosophies, governments, and patterns of communication. (61)

Norm   An established standard of behavior maintained by a society. (64)

Sanction   A penalty or reward for conduct concerning a social norm. (66)

Sapir-Whorf hypothesis   A hypothesis concerning the role of language in shaping our interpretation of reality. It holds that language is culturally determined. (62)

Society   A fairly large number of people who live in the same territory, are relatively independent of people outside it, and participate in a common culture. (58)

Sociobiology   The systematic study of how biology affects human social behavior. (61)

Subculture   A segment of society that shares a distinctive pattern of mores, folkways, and values that differs from the pattern of the larger society. (68)

Technology   Cultural information about how to use the material resources of the environment to satisfy human needs and desires. (61)

Value   A collective conception of what is considered good, desirable, and proper—or bad, undesirable, and improper—in a culture. (66)

Xenocentrism   The belief that the products, styles, or ideas of one's society are inferior to those that originate elsewhere. (72)

TECHNOLOGY RESOURCES

Internet Connection

Note: While all the URLs listed were current as of the printing of this book, these sites often change. Please check our website (www.mhhe.com/schaefer6) for updates, hyperlinks, and exercises related to these cites.

1. One of the more interesting examples of argot comes from the prison subculture. To see an extensive glossary of terms used by prison inmates, visit the Other Side of the Wall (**www.prisonwall.org**) and select "Prisoner's Dictionary."

2. Our society recently developed a new set of norms to govern behavior on the Internet. Are you familiar with these rules? Test your knowledge of appropriate behavior on the Net by exploring the Netiquette site (**www.albion.com/netiquette/index.html**).

Online Learning Center with PowerWeb

In this chapter you have learned that language is the foundation of every culture. For a long time, people in the United States demanded conformity to a single language. More recently, however, we have seen challenges to this forced obedience to our dominant ideology. One of the interactive exercises in the student center of the On-line Learning Center (**www.mhhe.com/schaefer6**) requires you to use a "foreign" language to do the activity. You will be taught a simple language called Pig Latin. Give it a try and see whether or not you feel competent completing the exercise in this "foreign" language.

Reel Society Interactive Movie CD-ROM 2.0

Reel Society 2.0 can be used to spark discussion about the following topics from this chapter:

- Cultural Universals
- Norms

chapter

SOCIALIZATION

Schools can sometimes be stressful arenas of socialization. The poster shown above informs schoolchildren in Japan that they can call a hotline and receive advice concerning stress, bullying by classmates, and corporal punishment from their teachers.

The Role of Socialization

The Self and Socialization

Socialization and the Life Course

Agents of Socialization

Social Policy and Socialization: Child Care around the World

Boxes

SOCIOLOGY IN THE GLOBAL COMMUNITY: Raising Amish Children

SOCIOLOGY ON CAMPUS: Impression Management by Students

79

Charisse...is sixteen and lives with her mother and younger sister, Deanne, across the street from St. Mary's Catholic Church and School. Charisse's mother is a personnel assistant at a Chicago university, and is taking classes there to get her bachelor's degree. Mr. Baker is a Chicago firefighter. While her father and mother are separated, Charisse sees her father many times a week at the afterschool basketball hour that he supervises at St. Mary's gym. He and Charisse's mother are on very good terms, and Charisse has a loving relationship with both parents. Mr. Baker is as active as any parent could be, attending the father/daughter dances at Charisse's high school, never missing a big performance, and visiting his daughters often.

Charisse and her sister are being raised by the neighborhood family in addition to their biological parents. "We [are] real close. Like all our neighbors know us because my dad grew up over here. Since the '60s." Charisse is a third-generation Grovelandite just like Neisha Morris. Her grandparents moved into Groveland with Charisse's then-teenage father when the neighborhood first opened to African Americans.... Now Charisse is benefiting from the friends her family has made over their years of residence in Groveland, especially the members of St. Mary's church, who play the role of surrogate parents. When Charisse was in elementary school at St. Mary's, her late paternal grandmother was the school secretary, and so the Baker girls were always under the watchful

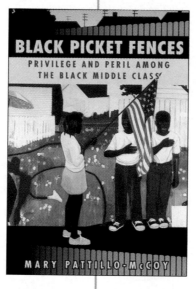

eye of their grandmother as well as the staff, who were their grandmother's friends. And in the evenings Charisse's mother would bring her and her sister to choir practice, where they accumulated an ensemble of mothers and fathers.

After St. Mary's elementary school, Charisse went on to St. Agnes Catholic High School for girls, her father's choice. St. Agnes is located in a suburb of Chicago and is a solid, integrated Catholic school where 100 percent of the girls graduate and over 95 percent go on to college....

Most of Charisse's close friends went to St. Mary's and now go to St. Agnes with her, but her choice of boyfriends shows modest signs of rebellion.... Many of Charisse's male interests are older than she, and irregularly employed—although some are in and out of school. She meets many of them hanging out at the mall. One evening, members of the church's youth choir sat around talking about their relationships. Charisse cooed while talking about her present boyfriend, who had just graduated from high school but did not have a job and was uncertain about his future. But in the middle of that thought, Charisse spontaneously changed her attentions to a new young man that she had just met. "Charisse changes boyfriends like she changes her clothes," her sister joked, indicating the impetuous nature of adolescent relationships. (Pattillo-McCoy 1999:100–102) ■ 🌀

Additional information about this excerpt can be found on the Online Learning Center at **www.mhhe.com/schaefer6.**

his excerpt from *Black Picket Fences: Privilege and Peril among the Black Middle Class* describes the upbringing of a young resident of Groveland, a close-knit African American community in Chicago. The author, sociologist Mary Pattillo-McCoy, became acquainted with Charisse while living in the Groveland neighborhood, where she was doing ethnographic research. Charisse's childhood is similar to that of other youths in many respects. Regardless of race or social class, a young person's development involves a host of influences, from parents, grandparents, and siblings to friends and classmates, teachers and school administrators, neighbors and churchgoers—even youths who frequent the local mall. Yet in some ways, Charisse's development is specifically influenced by her race and social class. Contact with family and community members, for instance, has undoubtedly prepared her to deal with prejudice and the absence of positive images of African Americans in the media.

Sociologists, in general, are interested in the patterns of behavior and attitudes that emerge *throughout* the life course, from infancy to old age. These patterns are part of the lifelong process of **socialization,** in which people learn the attitudes, values, and behaviors appropriate for members of a particular culture. Socialization occurs through human interactions. We learn a great deal from those people most important in our lives—immediate family members, best friends, and teachers. But we also learn from people we see on the street, on television, on the Internet, and in films and magazines. From a microsociological perspective,

socialization helps us to discover how to behave "properly" and what to expect from others if we follow (or challenge) society's norms and values. From a macrosociological perspective, socialization provides for the transmission of a culture from one generation to the next, and thereby for the long-term continuance of a society.

Socialization also shapes our self-images. For example, in the United States, a person who is viewed as "too heavy" or "too short" does not conform to the ideal cultural standard of physical attractiveness. This kind of unfavorable evaluation can significantly influence the person's self-esteem. In this sense, socialization experiences can help to shape our personalities. In everyday speech, the term *personality* is used to refer to a person's typical patterns of attitudes, needs, characteristics, and behavior.

How much of a person's personality is shaped by culture, as opposed to inborn traits? In what ways does socialization continue into adulthood? Who are the most powerful agents of socialization? In this chapter we will examine the role of socialization in human development. We will begin by analyzing the interaction of heredity and environmental factors. We pay particular attention to how people develop perceptions, feelings, and beliefs about themselves. The chapter will also explore the lifelong nature of the socialization process, as well as important agents of socialization, among them the family, schools, peers, and the media. Finally, the social policy section will focus on the socialization experience of group child care for young children. ∎

THE ROLE OF SOCIALIZATION

What makes us who we are? Is it the genes we are born with, or the environment in which we grow up? Researchers have traditionally clashed over the relative importance of biological inheritance and environmental factors in human development—a conflict called the *nature versus nurture* (or *heredity versus environment*) debate. Today, most social scientists have moved beyond this debate, acknowledging instead the *interaction* of

these variables in shaping human development. However, we can better appreciate how heredity and environmental factors interact and influence the socialization process if we first examine situations in which one factor operates almost entirely without the other (Homans 1979).

Social Environment: The Impact of Isolation

In the 1994 movie *Nell*, Jodie Foster played a young woman hidden from birth by her mother in a backwoods cabin. Raised without normal human contact, Nell crouches like an animal, screams wildly, and speaks or sings in a language all her own. This movie was drawn from the actual account of an emaciated 16-year-old boy who appeared mysteriously in 1828 in the town square of Nuremberg, Germany (Lipson 1994).

The Case of Isabelle

Some viewers may have found the story of Nell difficult to believe, but the painful childhood of Isabelle was all too real. For the first six years of her life, Isabelle lived in almost total seclusion in a darkened room. She had little contact with other people, with the exception of her mother, who could neither speak nor hear. Isabelle's mother's parents had been so deeply ashamed of Isabelle's illegitimate birth that they kept her hidden away from the world. Ohio authorities finally discovered the child in 1938, when Isabelle's mother escaped from her parents' home, taking her daughter with her.

When she was discovered at age six, Isabelle could not speak. She could merely make various croaking sounds. Her only communications with her mother were simple gestures. Isabelle had been largely deprived of the typical interactions and socialization experiences of childhood. Since she had seen few people, she initially showed a strong fear of strangers and reacted almost like a wild animal when confronted with an unfamiliar person. As she became accustomed to seeing certain individuals, her reaction changed to one of extreme apathy. At first, observers believed that Isabelle was deaf, but she soon began to react to nearby sounds. On tests of maturity, she scored at the level of an infant rather than a six-year-old.

Specialists developed a systematic training program to help Isabelle adapt to human relationships and socialization. After a few days of training, she made her first attempt to verbalize. Although she started slowly, Isabelle quickly passed through six years of development. In a little over two months she was speaking in complete sentences. Nine months later she could identify both words and sentences. Before Isabelle reached the age of nine, she was ready to attend school with other children. By her 14th year she was in sixth grade, doing well in school, and emotionally well-adjusted.

Yet without an opportunity to experience socialization in her first six years, Isabelle had been hardly human in the social sense when she was first discovered. Her inability to communicate at the time of her discovery—despite her physical and cognitive potential to learn—and her remarkable progress over the next few years underscore the impact of socialization on human development (K. Davis 1940, 1947).

Isabelle's experience is important for researchers because it is one of only a few cases of children reared in total isolation. Unfortunately, however, there are many cases of children raised in extremely neglectful social circumstances. Recently, attention has focused on infants and young children in orphanages in the formerly communist countries of Eastern Europe. For example, in Romanian orphanages, babies lie in their cribs for 18 to 20 hours a day, curled against their feeding bottles and receiving little adult care. Such minimal attention continues for the first five years of their lives. Many of them are fearful of human contact and prone to unpredictable antisocial behavior. This situation came to light as families in North America and Europe began adopting thousands of these children. The adjustment problems for about 20 percent of them were often so dramatic that the adopting families suffered guilty fears of being ill-fit adoptive parents. Many of them have asked for assistance in dealing with the children. Slowly, efforts are being made to introduce the deprived youngsters to feelings of attachment that they have never experienced before (Groza et al. 1999; Talbot 1998).

Increasingly, researchers are emphasizing the importance of early socialization experiences for children who grow up in more normal environments. We now know that it is not enough to care for an infant's physical needs; parents must also concern themselves with children's social development. If, for example, children are discouraged from having friends, they will miss out on social interactions with peers that are critical for emotional growth.

Primate Studies

Studies of animals raised in isolation also support the importance of socialization in development. Harry Harlow (1971), a researcher at the primate laboratory of the University of Wisconsin, conducted tests with rhesus monkeys that had been raised away from their mothers and away from contact with other monkeys. As was the case with Isabelle, the rhesus monkeys raised in isolation were fearful and easily frightened. They did not mate, and the females who were artificially inseminated became abusive mothers. Apparently, isolation had had a damaging effect on the monkeys.

A creative aspect of Harlow's experimentation was his use of "artificial mothers." In one such experiment, Harlow presented monkeys raised in isolation with two substitute mothers—one cloth-covered replica and one covered with wire that had the ability to offer milk. Monkey after monkey went to the wire mother for the life-giving milk, yet spent much more time clinging to the more motherlike cloth model. It appears that the infant monkeys developed greater social attachments from their

---

Gender Researchers who study isolated upbringings note that children who have been isolated are disproportionately female, reflecting the less-valued position of girls and women in many societies.

Classroom Tip See "Early Socialization in Orphanages" (Additional Lecture Ideas).

Let's Discuss Are the studies of children in Romanian orphanages comparable to the case of Isabelle? What type of care do children need to develop normally?

Key Person Harry Harlow

Methods Harlow's research with rhesus monkeys is an example of an experiment.

need for warmth, comfort, and intimacy than from their need for milk.

While the isolation studies just discussed may seem to suggest that heredity can be dismissed as a factor in the social development of humans and animals, studies of twins provide insight into a fascinating interplay between hereditary and environmental factors.

> **Use Your Sociological Imagination** www. mhhe.com /schaefer6
>
> What events in your life have had a strong influence on who you are?

The Influence of Heredity

Identical twins Oskar Stohr and Jack Yufe were separated soon after their birth and raised on different continents, in very different cultural settings. Oskar was reared as a strict

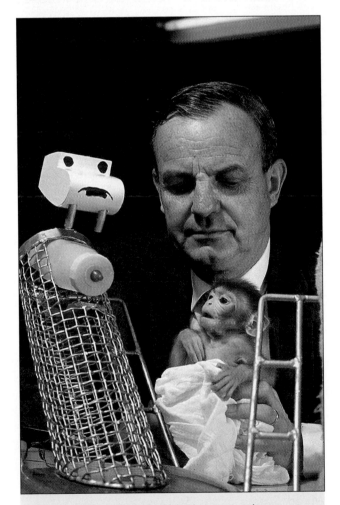

Harry Harlow with one of his rhesus monkeys, gazing at its surrogate wire mother.

Catholic by his maternal grandmother in the Sudetenland of Czechoslovakia. As a member of the Hitler Youth movement in Nazi Germany, he learned to hate Jews. By contrast, his brother Jack was reared in Trinidad by the twins' Jewish father. Jack joined an Israeli kibbutz (a collective settlement) at age 17 and later served in the Israeli army. But when the twins were reunited in middle age, some startling similarities emerged: they both wore wire-rimmed glasses and mustaches. They both liked spicy foods and sweet liqueurs, were absent-minded, flushed the toilet before using it, stored rubber bands on their wrists, and dipped buttered toast in their coffee (Holden 1980).

The twins also differed in many important respects: Jack was a workaholic; Oskar enjoyed leisure-time activities. Whereas Oskar was a traditionalist who was domineering toward women, Jack was a political liberal much more accepting of feminism. Finally, Jack was extremely proud of being Jewish, while Oskar never mentioned his Jewish heritage (Holden 1987).

Oskar and Jack are prime examples of the interplay of heredity and environment. For a number of years, the Minnesota Twin Family Study has been following pairs of identical twins reared apart to determine what similarities, if any, they show in personality traits, behavior, and intelligence. Preliminary results from the available twin studies indicate that *both* genetic factors *and* socialization experiences are influential in human development. Certain characteristics, such as temperaments, voice patterns, and nervous habits, appear to be strikingly similar even in twins reared apart, suggesting that these qualities may be linked to hereditary causes. However, identical twins reared apart differ far more in their attitudes, values, chosen mates, and even drinking habits; these qualities, it would seem, are influenced by environmental factors. In examining clusters of personality traits among such twins, researchers have found marked similarities in their tendency toward leadership or dominance, but significant differences in their need for intimacy, comfort, and assistance.

Researchers have also been impressed with the similar scores on intelligence tests of twins reared apart in *roughly similar* social settings. Most of the identical twins register scores even closer than those that would be expected if the same person took a test twice. At the same time, however, identical twins brought up in *dramatically different* social environments score quite differently on intelligence tests—a finding that supports the impact of socialization on human development (McGue and Bouchard 1998; Minnesota Twin Family Study 2004).

We need to be cautious when reviewing studies of twin pairs and other relevant research. Widely broadcast findings have often been based on extremely small samples and preliminary analysis. For example, one study (not involving twin pairs) was frequently cited as confirming genetic links with behavior. Yet the researchers had to retract their conclusions after they increased the sample and reclassified two of the original cases. After these changes, the initial findings were no longer valid.

Critics add that studies of twin pairs have not provided satisfactory information concerning the extent to which separated identical twins may have had contact with each other, even though they were raised apart. Such interactions—especially if they were extensive—could call into question the validity of the twin studies. As this debate continues, we can certainly anticipate numerous efforts to replicate the research and clarify the interplay between hereditary and environmental factors in human development (Horgan 1993; Plomin 1989).

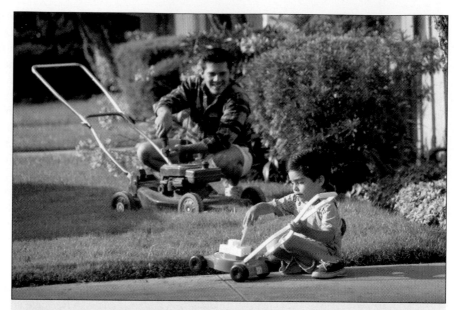

Children imitate the people around them, especially family members they continually interact with, during the *preparatory stage* described by George Herbert Mead.

THE SELF AND SOCIALIZATION

We all have various perceptions, feelings, and beliefs about who we are and what we are like. How do we come to develop these? Do they change as we age?

We were not born with these understandings. Building on the work of George Herbert Mead (1964b), sociologists recognize that we create our own designation: the self. The *self* is a distinct identity that sets us apart from others. It is not a static phenomenon but continues to develop and change throughout our lives.

Sociologists and psychologists alike have expressed interest in how the individual develops and modifies the sense of self as a result of social interaction. The work of sociologists Charles Horton Cooley and George Herbert Mead, pioneers of the interactionist approach, has

◄ p. 17 been especially useful in furthering our understanding of these important issues.

Sociological Approaches to the Self

Cooley: Looking-Glass Self

In the early 1900s, Charles Horton Cooley advanced the belief that we learn who we are by interacting with others. Our view of ourselves, then, comes not only from direct contemplation of our personal qualities but also from our impressions of how others perceive us. Cooley used the phrase *looking-glass self* to emphasize that the self is the product of our social interactions.

The process of developing a self-identity or self-concept has three phases. First, we imagine how we present ourselves to others—to relatives, friends, even strangers on the street. Then we imagine how others evaluate us (attractive, intelligent, shy, or strange). Finally, we develop some sort of feeling about ourselves, such as respect or shame, as a result of these impressions (Cooley 1902; M. Howard 1989).

A subtle but critical aspect of Cooley's looking-glass self is that the self results from an individual's "imagination" of how others view him or her. As a result, we can develop self-identities based on *incorrect* perceptions of how others see us. A student may react strongly to a teacher's criticism and decide (wrongly) that the instructor views the student as stupid. This misperception can easily be converted into a negative self-identity through the following process: (1) the teacher criticized me, (2) the teacher must think that I'm stupid, (3) I *am* stupid. Yet self-identities are also subject to change. If the student receives an A at the end of the course, he or she will probably no longer feel stupid.

Mead: Stages of the Self

George Herbert Mead continued Cooley's exploration of interactionist theory. Mead (1934, 1964a) developed a

Theory Interactionist view of the self introduced
Key Person Charles Horton Cooley
Theory Cooley's interactionist view of the looking-glass self

Key Person George Herbert Mead
Theory Mead's interactionist view of the self

useful model of the process by which the self emerges, defined by three distinct stages: the preparatory stage, the play stage, and the game stage.

The Preparatory Stage. During the *preparatory stage,* children merely imitate the people around them, especially family members with whom they continually interact. Thus, a small child will bang on a piece of wood while a parent is engaged in carpentry work, or will try to throw a ball if an older sibling is doing so nearby.

As they grow older, children become more adept at using symbols to communicate with others. *Symbols* are the gestures, objects, and words that form the basis of human communication. By interacting with relatives and friends, as well as by watching cartoons on television and looking at picture books, children in the preparatory stage begin to understand the issue of symbols. They will continue to use this form of communication throughout their lives.

Like spoken languages, symbols vary from culture to culture, and even from one subculture to another. In North America, raising one's eyebrows may communicate astonishment or doubt. In Peru, the same gesture means "money" or "pay me," and may constitute an unspoken request for a bribe. In the Pacific island nation of Tonga, raised eyebrows mean "yes" or "I agree" (Axtell 1990).

In multicultural societies, such differences in the meaning of symbols create the potential for conflict. For example, the symbolic headscarf that is worn by Muslim women recently became a major social issue in France. For years French public schools have banned overt signs of religion, such as large crosses, skullcaps, and headscarves. Muslim students who violated the informal dress code were expelled. In 2003, amid growing controversy, a government advisory panel recommended that the French Parliament strengthen the ban by writing it into law. The issue is a particularly thorny one because of the conflicting cultural meanings these symbols carry. To many of the French, the headscarf symbolizes the submission of women—an unwelcome connotation in a society that places a high value on egalitarianism. To others it represents a challenge to the French way of life. Thus, 69 percent of the French surveyed on the issue supported the ban. But to Muslims, the headscarf symbolizes modesty and respectability. Muslim schoolchildren take this symbol very seriously (*The Economist* 2004a).

The Play Stage. Mead was among the first to analyze the relationship of symbols to socialization. As children develop skill in communicating through symbols, they gradually become more aware of social relationships. As a result, during the *play stage,* they begin to pretend to be other people. Just as an actor "becomes" a character, a child becomes a doctor, parent, superhero, or ship captain.

Mead, in fact, noted that an important aspect of the play stage is role playing. *Role taking* is the process of mentally assuming the perspective of another and responding from that imagined viewpoint. For example, through this process, a young child will gradually learn when it is best to ask a parent for favors. If the parent usually comes home from work in a bad mood, the child will wait until after dinner, when the parent is more relaxed and approachable.

The Game Stage. In Mead's third stage, the *game stage,* the child of about eight or nine years old no longer just plays roles but begins to consider several actual tasks and relationships simultaneously. At this point in development, children grasp not only their own social positions but also those of others around them—just as in a football

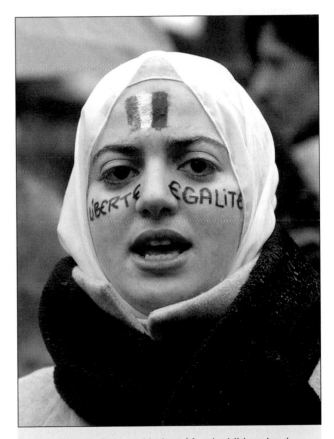

According to George Herbert Mead, children begin to communicate through symbols at an early age, and continue to use them throughout their lives. This French girl is protesting a law that forbids public school students to wear Islamic headscarves and other religious insignia. The ban against the deeply symbolic head covering has sparked considerable controversy in France.

Theory Interactionists' view of symbols and role taking
Reel Society *Reel Society* contains scenes that can be used to initiate discussion about covering and other Islamic traditions. See Intimate Relationships in the Topic Index.

Web Resource Remind students to browse through the student center in the Online Learning Center (**www.mhhe.com/schaefer6**).

game the players must understand their own and everyone else's positions. Consider a girl or boy who is part of a scout troop out on a weekend hike in the mountains. The child must understand what he or she is expected to do but also must recognize the responsibilities of other scouts as well as the leaders. This is the final stage of development under Mead's model; the child can now respond to numerous members of the social environment.

Mead uses the term ***generalized other*** to refer to the attitudes, viewpoints, and expectations of society as a whole that a child takes into account in his or her behavior. Simply put, this concept suggests that when an individual acts, he or she takes into account an entire group of people. For example, a child will not act courteously merely to please a particular parent. Rather, the child comes to understand that courtesy is a widespread social value endorsed by parents, teachers, and religious leaders.

At the game stage, children can take a more sophisticated view of people and the social environment. They now understand what specific occupations and social positions are and no longer equate Mr. Williams only with the role of "librarian" or Ms. Sanchez only with "principal." It has become clear to the child that Mr. Williams can be a librarian, a parent, and a marathon runner at the same time and that Ms. Sanchez is one of many principals in our society. Thus, the child has reached a new level of sophistication in observations of individuals and institutions.

Mead: Theory of the Self

Mead is best known for his theory of the self. According to Mead (1964b), the self begins at a privileged, central position in a person's world. Young children picture themselves as the focus of everything around them and find it difficult to consider the perspectives of others. For example, when shown a mountain scene and asked to describe what an observer on the opposite side of the mountain might see (such as a lake or hikers), young children describe only objects visible from their own vantage point. This childhood tendency to place ourselves at the center of events never entirely disappears. Many people with a fear of flying automatically assume that if any plane goes down, it will be the one they are on. And who reads the horoscope section in the paper without looking at their own horoscope first? Why else do we buy lottery tickets, if we do not imagine ourselves winning?

Nonetheless, as people mature, the self changes and begins to reflect greater concern about the reactions of others. Parents, friends, co-workers, coaches, and teachers are often among those who play a major role in shaping a person's self. The term ***significant others*** is used to refer to those individuals who are most important in the

development of the self. Many young people, for example, find themselves drawn to the same kind of work their parents engage in (Sullivan [1953] 1968).

In some instances, studies of significant others have generated controversy among researchers. For example, some researchers have contended that African American adolescents are more "peer-oriented" than their White counterparts because of presumed weaknesses in Black families. However, investigations indicate that these hasty conclusions were based on limited studies focusing on less affluent Blacks. In fact, there appears to be little difference in who African Americans and Whites from similar economic backgrounds regard as their significant others (Giordano et al. 1993; Juhasz 1989).

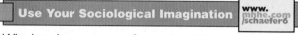

Who have been your significant others? Are you someone else's significant other?

Goffman: Presentation of the Self

How do we manage our "self"? How do we display to others who we are? Erving Goffman, a sociologist associated with the interactionist perspective, suggested that many of our daily activities involve attempts to convey impressions of who we are. His observations help us to understand the sometimes subtle yet critical ways in which we learn to present ourselves socially. They also offer concrete examples of this aspect of socialization.

Early in life, the individual learns to slant his or her presentation of the self in order to create distinctive appearances and satisfy particular audiences. Goffman (1959) referred to this altering of the presentation of the self as ***impression management.*** Box 4-1 describes an everyday example of this concept—the way students behave after receiving their exam grades. In analyzing such everyday social interactions, Goffman makes so many explicit parallels to the theater that his view has been termed the ***dramaturgical approach.*** According to this perspective, people resemble performers in action. For example, a clerk may try to appear busier than he or she actually is if a supervisor happens to be watching. A customer in a singles' bar may try to look as if he or she is waiting for a particular person to arrive.

Goffman (1959) has also drawn attention to another aspect of the self—***face-work.*** How often do you initiate some kind of face-saving behavior when you feel embarrassed or rejected? In response to a rejection at the singles' bar, a person may engage in face-work by saying, "There really isn't an interesting person in this entire crowd." We feel the need to maintain a proper image of the self if we are to continue social interaction.

Let's Discuss What characteristics do Cooley's and Mead's studies share? Do they complement one another?

Race/Ethnicity Studies of African American adolescents and whom they regard as their significant others
Key Person Erving Goffman
Theory Goffman's interactionist view of impression management
Let's Discuss In what way does Goffman's work build on the earlier work of Cooley and Mead?

When you get an exam back, you probably react differently with fellow classmates depending on the grades that you and they earned. This is all part of *impression management*, as sociologists Daniel Albas and Cheryl Albas have demonstrated. The two explored the strategies college students use to create desired appearances after receiving their grades on exams. Albas and Albas divided these encounters into three categories: those between students who have all received high grades (Ace–Ace encounters); those between students who have received high grades and those who have received low or even failing grades (Ace–Bomber encounters); and those between students who have all received low grades (Bomber–Bomber encounters).

Ace–Ace encounters occur in a rather open atmosphere, because there is comfort in sharing a high mark with another high achiever. It is even acceptable to violate the norm of modesty and brag when among other Aces, since as one student admitted, "It's much easier to admit a high mark to someone who has done better than you, or at least as well."

Ace–Bomber encounters are often sensitive. Bombers generally attempt to avoid such exchanges, because "you . . . emerge looking like the dumb one" or "feel like you are lazy or unreliable." When forced into interactions with Aces, Bombers work to appear gracious and congratulatory. For their part, Aces offer sympathy and support to the dissatisfied Bombers and even rationalize their own "lucky" high scores. To help Bombers save face, Aces may emphasize the difficulty and unfairness of the examination.

When forced into interactions with Aces, Bombers work to appear gracious and congratulatory.

Bomber–Bomber encounters tend to be closed, reflecting the group effort to wall off the feared disdain of others. Yet, within the safety of these encounters, Bombers openly share their disappointment and engage in expressions of mutual self-pity that they themselves call "pity parties." They devise face-saving excuses for their poor performances, such as "I wasn't feeling well all week" or "I had four exams and two papers due that week." If the grade distribution in a class includes particularly low scores, Bombers may blame the professor, attacking him or her as a sadist, a slave driver, or simply an incompetent.

As is evident from these descriptions, students' impression management strategies conform to society's informal norms regarding modesty and consideration for less successful peers. In classroom settings, as in the workplace and in other types of human interactions, efforts at impression management are most intense when status differentials are pronounced, as in encounters between the high-scoring Aces and the low-scoring Bombers.

Let's Discuss

1. How do you react with those who have received higher or lower grades than you? Do you engage in impression management? How would you like others to react to your grade?

2. What social norms govern students' impression management strategies?

Source: Albas and Albas 1988.

In some cultures, people engage in elaborate deceptions to avoid losing face. In Japan, for example, where lifetime employment has until recently been the norm, "company men" thrown out of work by a deep economic recession may feign employment, rising as usual in the morning, donning suit and tie, and heading for the business district. But instead of going to the office, they congregate at places such as Tokyo's Hibiya Library, where they pass the time by reading before returning home at the usual hour. Many of these men are trying to protect family members, who would be shamed if neighbors discovered the family breadwinner was unemployed. Others are deceiving their wives and families as well (French 2000).

Theory Interactionist view of students' impression management after exams

Methods The study of impression management by Albas and Albas is an example of observation research.

Goffman's work on the self represents a logical progression of sociological studies begun by Cooley and Mead on how personality is acquired through socialization and how we manage the presentation of the self to others. Cooley stressed the process by which we come to create a self; Mead focused on how the self develops as we learn to interact with others; Goffman emphasized the ways in which we consciously create images of ourselves for others.

Psychological Approaches to the Self

Psychologists have shared the interest of Cooley, Mead, and other sociologists in the development of the self. Early work in psychology, such as that of Sigmund Freud

Let's Discuss Can you think of situations in which people in the United States engage in elaborate deceptions to avoid losing face?

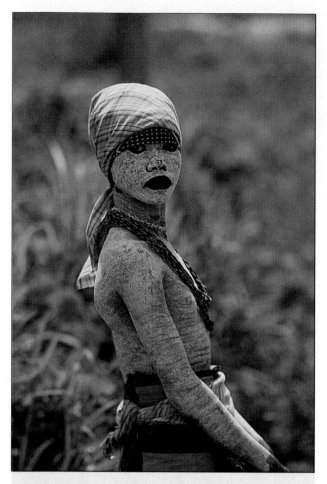

Body painting is a ritual marking the passage to puberty among young people in Liberia, in western Africa.

(1856–1939), stressed the role of inborn drives—among them the drive for sexual gratification—in channeling human behavior. More recently, psychologists such as Jean Piaget have emphasized the stages through which human beings progress as the self develops.

Like Charles Horton Cooley and George Herbert Mead, Freud believed that the self is a social product, and that aspects of one's personality are influenced by other people (especially one's parents). However, unlike Cooley and Mead, he suggested that the self has components that work in opposition to each other. According to Freud, our natural impulsive instincts are in constant conflict with societal constraints. Part of us seeks limitless pleasure, while another part favors rational behavior. By interacting with others, we learn the expectations of society and then select behavior most appropriate to our own culture. (Of course, as Freud was well aware, we sometimes distort reality and behave irrationally.)

Key Persons Sigmund Freud, Jean Piaget
Student Alert Make sure that students understand the difference between the psychological and sociological approaches to socialization.
Let's Discuss In what ways are the views of psychologists similar to and different from the views of Cooley, Mead, and Goffman?

Research on newborn babies by the Swiss child psychologist Jean Piaget (1896–1980) has underscored the importance of social interactions in developing a sense of self. Piaget found that newborns have no self in the sense of a looking-glass image. Ironically, though, they are quite self-centered; they demand that all attention be directed toward them. Newborns have not yet separated themselves from the universe of which they are a part. For these babies, the phrase "you and me" has no meaning; they understand only "me." However, as they mature, children are gradually socialized into social relationships, even within their rather self-centered world.

In his well-known *cognitive theory of development,* Piaget (1954) identified four stages in the development of children's thought processes. In the first, or *sensorimotor,* stage, young children use their senses to make discoveries. For example, through touching they discover that their hands are actually a part of themselves. During the second, or *preoperational,* stage, children begin to use words and symbols to distinguish objects and ideas. The milestone in the third, or *concrete operational,* stage is that children engage in more logical thinking. They learn that even when a formless lump of clay is shaped into a snake, it is still the same clay. Finally, in the fourth, or *formal operational,* stage, adolescents become capable of sophisticated abstract thought, and can deal with ideas and values in a logical manner.

Piaget suggested that moral development becomes an important part of socialization as children develop the ability to think more abstractly. When children learn the rules of a game such as checkers or jacks, they are learning to obey societal norms. Those under eight years old display a rather basic level of morality: rules are rules, and there is no concept of "extenuating circumstances." As they mature, children become capable of greater autonomy, and begin to experience moral dilemmas and doubts as to what constitutes proper behavior.

According to Jean Piaget, social interaction is the key to development. As they grow older, children pay increasing attention to how other people think and why they act in particular ways. In order to develop a distinct personality, each of us needs opportunities to interact with others. As we saw earlier, Isabelle was deprived of the chance for normal social interactions, and the consequences were severe (Kitchener 1991).

We have seen that a number of thinkers considered social interaction the key to the development of an individual's sense of self. As is generally true, we can best understand this topic by drawing on a variety of theory and research. Table 4-1 (page 89) summarizes the rich literature, both sociological and psychological, on the development of the self.

summingUP

Table 4-1	**Theoretical Approaches to Development of the Self**	
Scholar	**Key Concepts and Contributions**	**Major Points of Theory**
Charles Horton Cooley 1864–1929 sociologist (USA)	Looking-glass self	Stages of development not distinct; feelings toward ourselves developed through interaction with others
George Herbert Mead 1863–1931 sociologist (USA)	The self Generalized other	Three distinct stages of development; self develops as children grasp the roles of others in their lives
Erving Goffman 1922–1982 sociologist (USA)	Impression management Dramaturgical approach Face-work	Self developed through the impressions we convey to others and to groups
Sigmund Freud 1856–1939 psychotherapist (Austria)	Psychotherapy	Self influenced by parents and by inborn drives, such as the drive for sexual gratification
Jean Piaget 1896–1980 child psychologist (Switzerland)	Cognitive theory of development	Four stages of cognitive development; moral development linked to socialization

SOCIALIZATION AND THE LIFE COURSE

The Life Course

Among the Kota people of the Congo in Africa, adolescents paint themselves blue. Mexican American girls go on a daylong religious retreat before dancing the night away. Egyptian mothers step over their newborn infants seven times, and students at the Naval Academy throw their hats in the air. These are all ways of celebrating **rites of passage,** a means of dramatizing and validating changes in a person's status. The Kota rite marks the passage to adulthood. The color blue, viewed as the color of death, symbolizes the death of childhood. Hispanic girls celebrate reaching womanhood with a *quinceañera* ceremony at age 15. In the Cuban American community of Miami, the popularity of the *quinceañera* supports a network of party planners, caterers, dress designers, and the Miss Quinceañera Latina pageant. For thousands of years, Egyptian mothers have welcomed their newborns to the world in the Soboa ceremony by stepping over the

Freshman cadets at the Virginia Military Institute crawl up a muddy hill in the school's gritty indoctrination into strict military discipline, a rite of passage at the school.

Global View Adolescent males paint themselves blue in a rite of passage among the Kota people of the Congo.
Race/Ethnicity The *quinceañera* as a rite of passage for Mexican American and Cuban American girls
Classroom Tip See "Lifeline" (Class Discussion Topics).

Classroom Tip For some recent views of changes in the conceptualization of the life course, see "Rethinking the Life Course" (Additional Lecture Ideas).
Classroom Tip See "Reverse Socialization and Gender Roles" (Additional Lecture Ideas).

Table 4-2	Milestones in the Transition to Adulthood	
Life Event	**Expected Age**	**Percentage of People Who View Event as Extremely/Quite Important**
Financial independence from parents/guardians	20.9 years	80.9%
Separate residence from parents	21.1	57.2
Full-time employment	21.2	83.8
Completion of formal schooling	22.3	90.2
Capability of supporting a family	24.5	82.3
Marriage	25.7	33.2
Parenthood	26.2	29.0

Note: Based on the 2002 General Social Survey of 1,398 people.
Source: T. Smith 2003.

Think About It
Why did so few respondents consider marriage and parenthood to be important milestones? Which milestones do you think are most important?

seven-day-old infant seven times. And Naval Academy seniors celebrate their graduation from college by hurling their hats skyward (D. Cohen 1991; Garza 1993; McLane 1995; Quadagno 2002).

These specific ceremonies mark stages of development in the life course. They indicate that the process of socialization continues through all stages of the life cycle. In fact, some researchers have chosen to concentrate on socialization as a lifelong process. Sociologists and other social scientists who take such a *life course approach* look closely at the social factors that influence people throughout their lives, from birth to death. They recognize that biological changes mold but do not dictate human behavior.

In the culture of the United States, each individual has a "personal biography" that is influenced by events both in the family and in the larger society. While the completion of religious confirmations, school graduations, marriage, and parenthood can all be regarded as rites of passage in our society, people do not necessarily experience them at the same time. The timing of these events depends on such factors as one's gender, economic background, place of residence (central city, suburb, or rural area), and even time of birth.

Several life events mark the passage to adulthood. Of course, these turning points vary from one society and even one generation to the next. According to a national survey done in 2002, in the United States today the key event seems to be the completion of formal schooling (see Table 4-2). On average, Americans expect this milestone to occur by a person's 23rd birthday. Other major events in the life course, such as getting married or becoming a parent, are expected to follow three or four years later. Interestingly, comparatively few survey respondents identified marriage and parenthood as important milestones.

We encounter some of the most difficult socialization challenges (and rites of passage) in the later years of life. Assessing one's accomplishments, coping with declining physical abilities, experiencing retirement, and facing the inevitability of death may lead to painful adjustments. Old age is further complicated by the negative way that many societies, including the United States, view and treat the elderly. The common stereotypes of the elderly as helpless and dependent may well weaken an older person's self-image. However, as we will explore more fully in Chapter 11, many older people continue to lead active, productive, fulfilled lives—whether in the paid labor force or as retirees.

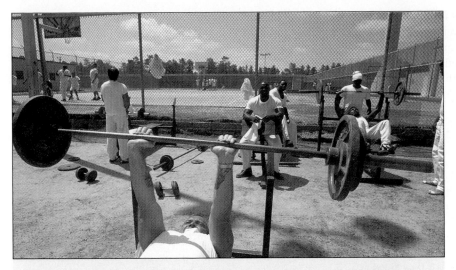

Prisons are centers of resocialization, where people are placed under pressure to discard old behavior patterns and accept new ones. These prisoners are learning to use weights to release tension and exert their strength—a socially acceptable method of handling antisocial impulses.

Use Your Sociological Imagination www.mhhe.com/schaefer6

What was the last rite of passage you participated in? Was it formal or informal?

Anticipatory Socialization and Resocialization

The development of a social self is literally a lifelong transformation that begins in the crib and continues as one prepares for death. Two types of socialization occur at many points throughout the life course: anticipatory socialization and resocialization.

Anticipatory socialization refers to the processes of socialization in which a person "rehearses" for future positions, occupations, and social relationships. A culture can function more efficiently and smoothly if members become acquainted with the norms, values, and behavior associated with a social position before actually assuming that status. Preparation for many aspects of adult life begins with anticipatory socialization during childhood and adolescence, and continues throughout our lives as we prepare for new responsibilities.

You can see the process of anticipatory socialization take place when high school students start to consider what colleges they may attend. Traditionally, this meant looking at publications received in the mail or making campus visits. However, with new technology, more and more students are using the Web to begin their college experience. Colleges are investing more time and money in developing

attractive websites through which students can take "virtual" campus walks and hear audio clips of everything from the college anthem to a sample zoology lecture.

Occasionally, assuming a new social or occupational position requires us to *unlearn* a previous orientation. **Resocialization** refers to the process of discarding former behavior patterns and accepting new ones as part of a transition in one's life. Often resocialization occurs during an explicit effort to transform an individual, as happens in reform schools, therapy groups, prisons, religious conversion settings, and political indoctrination camps. The process of resocialization typically involves considerable stress for the individual—much more so than socialization in general, or even anticipatory socialization (Gecas 1992).

Resocialization is particularly effective when it occurs within a total institution. Erving Goffman (1961) coined the term **total institution** to refer to an institution, such as a prison, the military, a mental hospital, or a convent, that regulates all aspects of a person's life under a single authority. Because the total institution is generally cut off from the rest of society, it provides for all the needs of its members. Quite literally, the crew of a merchant vessel at sea becomes part of a total institution. So elaborate are its requirements, so all-encompassing its activities, a total institution often represents a miniature society.

Goffman (1961) has identified four common traits of total institutions:

- All aspects of life are conducted in the same place under the control of a single authority.
- Any activities within the institution are conducted in the company of others in the same circumstances—for example, army recruits or novices in a convent.
- The authorities devise rules and schedule activities without consulting the participants.
- All aspects of life within a total institution are designed to fulfill the purpose of the organization. Thus, all activities in a monastery might be centered on prayer and communion with God. (Davies 1989; P. Rose et al. 1979)

People often lose their individuality within total institutions. For example, a person entering prison may

Let's Discuss Discuss anticipatory socialization for people headed to college for the first time. Does this process vary for older students who have been out of school for many years?

Classroom Tip See "The Nunnery as a Total Institution" (Class Discussion Topics).

experience the humiliation of a ***degradation ceremony*** as he or she is stripped of clothing, jewelry, and other personal possessions. From this point on, scheduled daily routines allow for little or no personal initiative. The individual becomes secondary and rather invisible in the overbearing social environment (Garfinkel 1956).

AGENTS OF SOCIALIZATION

As we have seen, the culture of the United States is defined by rather gradual movements from one stage of socialization to the next. The continuing and lifelong socialization process involves many different social forces that influence our lives and alter our self-images.

The family is the most important agent of socialization in the United States, especially for children. We'll also give particular attention in this chapter to five other agents of socialization: the school, the peer group, the mass media, the workplace, and the state. The role of religion in socializing young people into society's norms and values will be explored in Chapter 13.

Family

Children in Amish communities are raised in a highly structured and disciplined manner. But they are not immune to the temptations posed by their peers in the non-Amish world—"rebellious" acts such as dancing, drinking, and riding in cars. Still, Amish families don't get too concerned; they know the strong influence they ultimately exert over their offspring (see Box 4-2, opposite). The same is true for the family. It is tempting to say that the "peer group" or even the "media" really raise kids these days, especially when the spotlight falls on young people involved in shooting sprees and hate crimes. Almost all available research, however, shows that the role of the family in socializing a child cannot be overestimated (W. Williams 1998; for a different view see J. Harris 1998).

The lifelong process of learning begins shortly after birth. Since newborns can hear, see, smell, taste, and feel heat, cold, and pain, they are constantly orienting themselves to the surrounding world. Human beings, especially family members, constitute an important part of their social environment. People minister to the baby's needs by feeding, cleansing, carrying, and comforting the baby.

Cultural Influences

As both Charles Horton Cooley and George Herbert Mead noted, the development of the self is a critical aspect of the early years of one's life. But how children develop this sense of self can vary from one society to another. For example, most parents in the United States do not send six-year-olds to school unsupervised. But that is the norm in Japan, where parents push their children to commute to school on their own from an early age. In cities like Tokyo, first-graders must learn to negotiate buses, subways, and long walks. To ensure their safety, parents carefully lay out rules: never talk to strangers; check with a station attendant if you get off at the wrong stop; if you miss your stop stay on to the end of the line, then call; take stairs, not escalators; don't fall asleep. Some parents equip the children with cell phones or pagers. One parent acknowledges that she worries, "but after they are 6, children are supposed to start being independent from the mother. If you're still taking your child to school after the first month, everyone looks at you funny" (Tolbert 2000:17).

While we consider the family's role in socialization, we need to remember that children do not play a passive role. They are active agents, influencing and altering the families, schools, and communities of which they are a part (Corsaro 1997).

The Impact of Race and Gender

In the United States, social development includes exposure to cultural assumptions regarding gender and race.

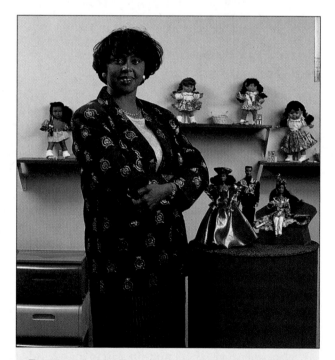

Entrepreneur Yla Eason poses with the ethnic dolls her company creates and merchandises. Because young girls learn about themselves and their social roles by playing with dolls, they benefit from exposure to dolls representing a variety of races and ethnicities.

Jacob is a typical teenager in his Amish community in Lancaster County, Pennsylvania. At 14 he is in his final year of schooling. Over the next few years he will become a full-time worker on the family farm, taking breaks only for three-hour religious services each morning. When he is a bit older, Jacob may bring a date to a community "singing" in his family's horse-drawn buggy. But he will be forbidden to date outside his own community and can marry only with the deacon's consent.

Jacob is well aware of the rather different way of life of the "English" (the Amish term for non-Amish people). One summer, late at night, he and his friends hitchhiked to a nearby town to see a movie, breaking several Amish taboos. His parents learned of his adventure, but like most Amish they are confident that their son will choose the Amish way of life. What is this way of life, and how can his parents be so sure of its appeal?

Jacob and his family live in a manner very similar to their ancestors, members of the conservative Mennonite church who migrated to North America from Europe in the 18th and 19th centuries. Schisms in the church after 1850 led to a division between those who wanted to preserve the "old order" and those who favored a "new order" with more progressive methods and organization. Today the old order Amish live in about 50 communities in the United States and Canada. Estimates put their number at about 80,000, with approximately 75 percent living in three states—Ohio, Pennsylvania, and Indiana.

The old order Amish live a simple life and reject most aspects of modernization and contemporary technology. That's why they spurn conveniences such as electricity, automobiles, radio, and television. The Amish maintain their own schools and traditions and do not want their children socialized into many norms and values of the dominant culture of the United States. Those who stray

> *The old order Amish live a "simple" life and reject most aspects of modernization and contemporary technology.*

too far from Amish mores may be excommunicated and shunned by all other members of the community—a practice of social control called *Meiding*. Sociologists sometimes use the term "secessionist minorities" to refer to groups like the Amish, who reject assimilation and coexist with the rest of society primarily on their own terms.

The socialization of Amish youths pushes them to forgo movies, radio, television, cosmetics, jewelry, musical instruments of any kind, and motorized vehicles. Yet, like Jacob did, Amish youths often test their subculture's boundaries during a period of discovery called *rumspringe*, a term that means "running around." Amish young people attend barn dances where taboos like drinking, smoking, and driving cars are commonly broken. Parents often react by looking the other way, sometimes literally. For example, when they hear radio sounds from a barn or a motorcycle entering their property in the middle of the night, they don't immediately investigate and punish their offspring. Instead, they pretend not to notice, secure in the comfort that their children almost always return to the traditions of the Amish lifestyle. Research shows that only about 20 percent of Amish youths leave the fold, generally to join a more liberal Mennonite group. Rarely does a baptized adult ever leave. The socialization of Amish youths moves them gently but firmly into becoming Amish adults.

Let's Discuss

1. What makes Amish parents so sure that their children will choose to remain in the Amish community?

2. If you lived in an Amish community, how would your life differ from the way it is now? In your opinion, what advantages and disadvantages would that lifestyle have?

Sources: Meyers 1992; Remnick 1998b; Zellner 2001.

African American parents, for example, have learned that children as young as two years old can absorb negative messages about Blacks in children's books, toys, and television shows—all of which are designed primarily for White consumers. At the same time, African American children are exposed more often than others to the inner-city youth gang culture. Because most Blacks, even those who are middle class, live near very poor neighborhoods, children such as Charisse (see the chapter-opening excerpt) are susceptible to these influences, despite their par-ents' strong family values (Linn and Poussaint 1999; Pattillo-McCoy 1999).

The term **gender roles** refers to expectations regarding the proper behavior, attitudes, and activities of males and females. For example, we traditionally think of "toughness" as masculine—and desirable only in men—while we view "tenderness" as feminine. As we will see in Chapter 11, other cultures do not necessarily assign these qualities to each gender in the way that our culture does.

Classroom Tip See "Socialization among the Amish" (Class Discussion Topics).

Classroom Tip Discuss socialization among the old-order Amish with respect to the family, schools, peers, mass media and technology, the workplace, and the state.

Classroom Tip For a discussion of child rearing quite different from that of traditional society in the United States, see "Hutterites Coming of Age" (Additional Lecture Ideas).

Race/Ethnicity Depiction of African Americans in children's books, toys, and television shows

Gender Concept of gender roles is introduced.

As the primary agents of childhood socialization, parents play a critical role in guiding children into those gender roles deemed appropriate in a society. Other adults, older siblings, the mass media, and religious and educational institutions also have a noticeable impact on a child's socialization into feminine and masculine norms. A culture or subculture may require that one sex or the other take primary responsibility for the socialization of children, economic support of the family, or religious or intellectual leadership.

Interactionists remind us that socialization concerning not only masculinity and femininity but also marriage and parenthood begins in childhood as a part of family life. Children observe their parents as they express affection, deal with finances, quarrel, complain about in-laws, and so forth. This represents an informal process of anticipatory socialization. The child develops a tentative model of what being married and being a parent are like. (We will explore socialization for marriage and parenthood more fully in Chapter 12.)

Typically, parents are thought to have a positive effect on their children's socialization. But that is not always the case. A survey of nearly 600 teens in New York, Texas, Florida, and California indicated that 20 percent had shared drugs other than alcohol with their parents, and about 5 percent were actually introduced to drugs by their mothers or fathers. Approximately 1.5 million children under the age of 18, or 2 percent of all U.S. youths, have a parent in a state or federal prison at some time during the year. Whether positive or negative, socialization within the family is a powerful process (Leinwand 2000; Mumola 2000).

School

Where did you learn the national anthem? Who taught you about the heroes of the American Revolution? Where were you first tested on your knowledge of your culture? Like the family, schools have an explicit mandate to socialize people in the United States—and especially children—into the norms and values of our culture.

As conflict theorists Samuel Bowles and Herbert Gintis (1976) have observed, schools in this country foster competition through built-in systems of reward and punishment, such as grades and evaluations by teachers. Consequently, a child who is working intently to learn a new skill can sometimes come to feel stupid and unsuccessful. However, as the self matures, children become capable of increasingly realistic assessments of their intellectual, physical, and social abilities.

Functionalists point out that schools, as agents of socialization, fulfill the function of teaching children the

values and customs of the larger society. Conflict theorists agree, but add that schools can reinforce the divisive aspects of society, especially those of social class. For example, higher education in the United States is costly despite the existence of financial aid programs. Students from affluent backgrounds have an advantage in gaining access to universities and professional training. At the same time, less affluent young people may never receive the preparation that would qualify them for the best-paying and most prestigious jobs. The contrast between the functionalist and conflict views of education will be discussed in more detail in Chapter 13.

In teaching students the values and customs of the larger society, schools in the United States have traditionally socialized children into conventional gender roles. Professors of education Myra Sadker and David Sadker (1985:54; 2000) note that "although many believe that classroom sexism disappeared in the early '70s, it hasn't." A report released by the American Association of University Women, which summarized numerous studies of girls in school, concluded that girls in U.S. schools face some special challenges.

According to this report, schools are making progress toward equitable treatment of boys and girls, but concerns remain. Girls excel in writing, foreign languages, and literature, but they lag well behind boys in technological training, which is currently much in demand in the labor force. Boys outnumber girls 3 to 1 in taking Advanced Placement tests in computer science, for example. Particularly significant, according to the report, is the fact that girls are more vulnerable than boys to sexual violence and harassment both at home and at school, which certainly threatens their success in formal schooling (American Association of University Women 1998).

In other cultures as well, schools serve socialization functions. Until the otherthrow of Saddam Hussein in 2003, the sixth-grade textbooks used in Iraqi schools concentrated almost entirely on the military and its values of loyalty, honor, and sacrifice. Children were taught that their enemies were Iran, the United States, Israel and its supporters, and NATO, the European military alliance. Within months of the regime's fall, the curriculum had been rewritten to remove indoctrination on behalf of Hussein, his army, and his Baath Socialist Party (Marr 2003).

Peer Group

Ask 13-year-olds who matters most in their lives and they are likely to answer "friends." As a child grows older, the family becomes somewhat less important in social devel-

Theory Explain the socialization process for marital roles as developed by interactionists.
Theory Bowles and Gintis's view of schooling, an example of conflict theory, is discussed more fully in Chapter 13.
Theory Functionalist and conflict views of education as an agent of socialization

Theory Conflict view of sexism in the classroom
Methods The AAUW report summarized both observation studies and surveys.
Theory Interactionist view of peer groups and their role in socialization

Table 4-3	High School Popularity		
What makes high school girls popular?		**What makes high school boys popular?**	
According to college men:	**According to college women:**	**According to college men:**	**According to college women:**
1. Physical attractiveness 2. Grades/intelligence 3. Participation in sports 4. General sociability 5. Popularity with boys	1. Grades/intelligence 2. Participation in sports 3. General sociability 4. Physical attractiveness 5. Clothes	1. Participation in sports 2. Grades/intelligence 3. Popularity with girls 4. General sociability 5. Car	1. Participation in sports 2. Grades/intelligence 3. General sociability 4. Physical attractiveness 5. School clubs/government

Note: Students at the following universities were asked in which ways adolescents in their high schools had gained prestige with their peers: Cornell University, Louisiana State University, Southeastern Louisiana University, State University of New York at Albany, State University of New York at Stony Brook, University of Georgia, and the University of New Hampshire.

Source: Suitor et al. 2001:445.

opment. Instead, peer groups increasingly assume the role of Mead's significant others. Within the peer group, young people associate with others who are approximately their own age, and who often enjoy a similar social status (Giordano 2003).

Peer groups can ease the transition to adult responsibilities. At home, parents tend to dominate; at school, the teenager must contend with teachers and administrators. But within the peer group, each member can assert himself or herself in a way that may not be possible elsewhere. Nevertheless, almost all adolescents in our culture remain economically dependent on their parents, and most are emotionally dependent as well.

Peers can be the source of harassment as well as support. This problem has received considerable attention in Japan, where bullying in school is a constant fact of life. Groups of students act together to humiliate, disgrace, or torment a specific student, a practice known in Japan as *ijime*. Most students go along with the bullying out of fear that they might be the target sometime. In some cases the *ijime* has led to a child's suicide. In 1998, the situation became so desperate that a volunteer association set up a 24-hour telephone hotline in Tokyo just for children (see the chapter-opening poster). The success of this effort convinced the government to sponsor a nationwide hotline system (Matsushita 1999; Sugimoto 1997).

Gender differences are noteworthy among adolescents. Boys and girls are socialized by their parents, peers, and the media to identify many of the same paths to popularity, but to different degrees. Table 4-3 compares male and female college students' reports of how girls and boys they knew became popular in high school. The two groups named many of the same paths to popularity but gave

them a different order of importance. While neither men nor women named sexual activity, drug use, or alcohol use as one of the top five paths, college men were much more likely than women to mention those behaviors as a means to becoming popular, for both boys and girls.

Mass Media and Technology

In the last 80 years, media innovations—radio, motion pictures, recorded music, television, and the Internet—have become important agents of socialization. Television, and increasingly the Internet, are critical forces in the socialization of children in the United States. In one national survey, 47 percent of parents reported that at least one of their children had a television in his or her bedroom. One out of four children ages two to five has a TV set in the bedroom, and 43 percent of children under age two watch television every day. Another study, whose results are shown in Figure 4-1 (page 96), indicated that a third of youths ages 10 to 17 use the Internet every day (V. Rideout et al. 2003; E. Woodard 2000).

These media, however, are not always a negative socializing influence. Television programs and even commercials can introduce young people to unfamiliar lifestyles and cultures. Not only do children in the United States learn about life in "faraway lands," but inner-city children learn about the lives of farm children, and vice versa. The same goes for children living in other countries.

Sociologists and other social scientists have also begun to consider the impact of technology on socialization, especially as it applies to family life. The Silicon Valley Cultures Project studied families in California's

Silicon Valley (a technological corridor) for 10 years, beginning in 1991. Although these families may not be typical, they represent a lifestyle that more and more households probably will approximate as time goes by. This study has found that technology in the form of e-mail, webpages, cellular phones, voice mail, digital organizers, and pagers is allowing householders to let outsiders do everything from grocery shopping to carpooling. The researchers are also finding that families are socialized into multitasking (doing more than one task at a time) as the social norm; devoting one's full attention to one task—even eating or driving—is less and less common on a typical day (Silicon Valley Cultures Project 2003).

Workplace

Learning to behave appropriately within an occupation is a fundamental aspect of human socialization. In the United States, working full-time confirms adult status; it indicates that one has passed out of adolescence. In a sense, socialization into an occupation can represent both a harsh reality ("I have to work in order to buy food and pay the rent") and the realization of an ambition ("I've always wanted to be an airline pilot") (W. Moore 1968:862).

It used to be that going to work began with the end of our formal schooling, but that is no longer the case, at least not in the United States. More and more young people work today, and not just for a parent or relative. Adolescents generally seek jobs in order to make spending money; 80 percent of high school seniors say that little or none of what they earn goes to family expenses. And these teens rarely look on their employment as a means of exploring vocational interests or getting on-the-job training.

Some observers feel that the increasing number of teenagers who are working earlier in life and for longer hours are now finding the workplace almost as important an agent of socialization as school. In fact, a number of educators complain that student time at work is adversely affecting schoolwork. The level of teenage employment in the United States is the highest among industrial countries, which may provide one explanation for why U.S. high school students lag behind those in other countries on international achievement tests.

Socialization in the workplace changes when it involves a more permanent shift from an after-school job to full-time employment. Occupational socialization can be most intense during the transition from school to job, but it continues throughout one's work history. Technological advances may alter the requirements of the position and

necessitate some degree of resocialization. Today, men and women change occupations, employers, or places of work many times during their adult years. Occupational socialization continues, then, throughout a person's years in the labor market.

FIGURE 4-1

Internet Usage, Ages 10–17

Percentage of 10–17-year-olds who go online

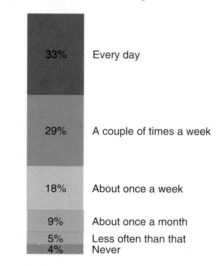

33%	Every day
29%	A couple of times a week
18%	About once a week
9%	About once a month
5%	Less often than that
4%	Never

Amount of time spend online *each week*

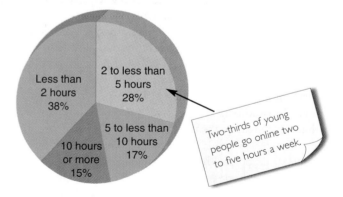

Less than 2 hours 38%

2 to less than 5 hours 28%

5 to less than 10 hours 17%

10 hours or more 15%

Two-thirds of young people go online two to five hours a week.

Notes: "Don't know" responses not included. Pie graph shows usage among the 80 percent of respondents who said they went online once a week or more. Based on a survey of 804 randomly selected youths, Silicon Valley, late 2002.

Source: Kaiser Family Foundation/*San Jose Mercury News* 2003.

Think About It
How did your use of the Internet when you were younger compare to these survey results?

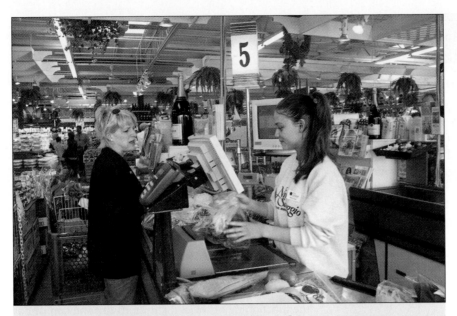

This girl's day doesn't end when school lets out. So many teenagers now work after school, the workplace has become another important agent of socialization for that age group.

College students today recognize that occupational socialization is not socialization into one lifetime occupation. They anticipate going through a number of jobs. The Bureau of Labor Statistics (2002) has found that from ages 18 to 36, the typical person holds 10 different jobs. This high rate of turnover in employment applies to both men and women, and to those with a college degree as well as those with a high school diploma.

The State

Social scientists have increasingly recognized the importance of government ("the state") as an agent of socialization because of its growing impact on the life course. Traditionally, family members have served as the primary caregivers in our culture, but in the 20th century, the fam-

ily's protective function was steadily transferred to outside agencies such as hospitals, mental health clinics, and insurance companies. The state either runs many of these agencies or licenses and regulates them (Ogburn and Tibbits 1934).

In the past, moreover, heads of households and local groups such as religious organizations influenced the life course most significantly. However, today national interests are increasingly influencing the individual as a citizen and an economic actor. For example, labor unions and political parties serve as intermediaries between the individual and the state.

The state has had a noteworthy impact on the life course by reinstituting rites of passage that had disappeared either from agricultural societies or during periods of early industrialization. For example, government regulations stipulate the ages at which a person may drive a car, drink alcohol, vote in elections, marry without parental permission, work overtime, and retire. These regulations do not constitute strict rites of passage: most 18-year-olds choose not to vote, and most people choose their age of retirement without reference to government dictates. Still, the state shapes the socialization process by regulating the life course to some degree and by influencing our views of appropriate behavior at particular ages (Mayer and Schoepflin 1989).

In the social policy section that follows, we will see that government is under pressure to become a provider of child care, which would give it a new and direct role in the socialization of infants and young children.

Let's Discuss How does socialization by the state relate to the dominant ideology discussed in Chapter 3?

Policy Pointer The role of the state as an agent of socialization and a provider of child care is discussed in the social policy section that follows.

SOCIAL POLICY and SOCIALIZATION

Child Care around the World

The Issue

The rise in single-parent families, increased job opportunities for women, and the need for additional family income have all propelled an increasing number of mothers of young children into the paid labor force of the United States. In 2002, 55 percent of women who had given birth the previous year were back in the labor force. Who, then, takes care of the children of these women during work hours?

For 35 percent of all preschoolers with employed mothers, the solution has become group child care programs. Day care centers have become the functional equivalent of the nuclear family, performing some of the nurturing and socialization functions previously handled only by family members. But how does group day care compare to care in the home? And what is the state's responsibility to assure high-quality care (Fields 2003; K. Smith 2000)?

The Setting

Few people in the United States or elsewhere can afford the luxury of having a parent stay at home, or of paying for high-quality live-in child care. For millions of mothers and fathers, finding the right kind of child care is a challenge to parenting and to the pocketbook.

Researchers have found that high-quality child care centers do not adversely affect the socialization of children; in fact, good day care benefits children. The value of preschool programs was documented in a series of studies conducted in the United States by the National Institute of Child Health and Human Development. Researchers found no significant differences in infants who had received extensive nonmaternal care compared with those who had been cared for solely by their mothers. They also reported that more and more infants in the United States are being placed in child care outside the home,

and that overall, the quality of these arrangements is better than has been found in previous studies. It is difficult, however, to generalize about child care, since there is so much variability among day care providers, and even among policies from one state to another (M. Gardner 2001; S. Loeb et al. 2004; NICHD 1998).

Sociological Insights

Studies that assess the quality of child care outside the home reflect the micro level of analysis and the interest of interactionists in the impact of face-to-face interaction. These studies also explore macro-level implications for the functioning of social institutions like the family. But some of the issues surrounding day care have also been of interest to those who take the conflict perspective.

In the United States, high-quality day care is not equally available to all families. Parents in wealthy neighborhoods have an easier time finding day care than those in poor or working-class communities. Finding *affordable* child care is also a problem. Viewed from a conflict perspective, child care costs are an especially serious burden for lower-class families. The poorest families spend 25 percent of their income for preschool

People in Sweden pay higher taxes than U.S. citizens, but they have access to excellent preschool day care at little or no cost.

Policy Pointer Child care ranges from parental care to occasional babysitters to regular nonparental care. This section concentrates on child care centers, which can be private, profit-making (private proprietary or family day care) or nonprofit (cooperatives, church-sponsored, or publicly funded).

Global View Although the section focuses on child care in the United States, it contains references to child care as a growing worldwide problem.

Theory Interactionist, functionalist, and conflict analyses of child care child care, while families who are *not* poor pay only 6 percent or less of their income for day care.

Feminists echo the concern of conflict theorists that high-quality child care receives little government support because it is regarded as "merely a way to let women work." Nearly all child care workers (97 percent) are women; many find themselves in low-status, minimum-wage jobs. Typically, food servers, messengers, and gas station attendants make more money than child care workers, most of whom earn less than $8.00 per hour. Not surprisingly, turnover among employees in child care centers runs at about 30 percent per year (Bureau of the Census 2001a:380; Clawson and Gerstel 2002).

Policy Initiatives

Policies regarding child care outside the home vary throughout the world. Most developing nations do not have the economic base to provide subsidized child care. Working mothers rely largely on relatives or take their children to work. In the comparatively wealthy industrialized countries of Western Europe, government provides child care as a basic service, at little or no expense to parents. But even those countries with tax-subsidized programs occasionally fall short of the need for high-quality child care.

When policymakers decide that child care is desirable, they must determine the degree to which taxpayers should subsidize it. In Sweden and Denmark, one-third to one-half of children under age three were in government-subsidized child care full-time in 2001. In the

United States, where government subsidies are very limited, the total cost of child care can easily run between $5,000 and $10,000 per family per year (Mencimer 2002).

We have a long way to go in making high-quality child care more affordable and accessible, not just in the United States but throughout the world. In an attempt to reduce government spending, France is considering cutting back the budgets of subsidized nurseries, even though waiting lists exist and the French public heartily disapproves of cutbacks. In Germany, reunification has reduced the options previously open to East German mothers, who had become accustomed to government-supported child care (Hank 2001; L. King 1998).

Experts in child development view such reports as a vivid reminder of the need for greater government and private-sector support for child care.

Let's Discuss

1. Were you ever in a day care program? Do you recall the experience as good or bad? In general, do you think it is desirable to expose young children to the socializing influence of day care?

2. In the view of conflict theorists, child care receives little government support because it is "merely a way to let women work." Can you think of other explanations?

3. Should the costs of day care programs be paid by government, by the private sector, or entirely by parents?

GETTING INVOLVED ──────────────────────

www.
mhhe.com
/schaefer6

To get involved in the debate over day care, visit this text's Online Learning Center, which offers links to relevant websites. Check out the Social Policy section on the Online Learning Center as well; it provides survey data on U.S. public opinion regarding this issue.

CHAPTER RESOURCES

Summary

Socialization is the process through which people learn the attitudes, values, and actions appropriate for members of a particular culture. This chapter examined the role of socialization in human development; the way in which people develop perceptions, feelings, and beliefs about themselves; the lifelong nature of the socialization process; and the important agents of socialization.

1. Socialization affects the overall cultural practices of a society; it also shapes the images that we hold of ourselves.

Theory Feminists and conflict theorists note that male-dominated governments place little priority on child care issues.
Gender The impact of child care decisions falls most heavily on women who work or wish to work.

Global View Child care issues in developing countries and around the world

2. Heredity and environmental factors interact in influencing the socialization process.

3. In the early 1900s, Charles Horton Cooley advanced the belief that we learn who we are by interacting with others, a phenomenon he called the **looking-glass self.**

4. George Herbert Mead, best known for his theory of the **self,** proposed that as people mature, their selves begin to reflect their concern about reactions from others—both **generalized others** and **significant others.**

5. Erving Goffman has shown that in many of our daily activities, we try to convey distinct impressions of who we are, a process called **impression management.**

6. Socialization proceeds throughout the life course. Some societies mark stages of development with formal **rites of passage.** In the culture of the United States, significant events such as marriage and parenthood serve to change a person's status.

7. As the primary agents of socialization, parents play a critical role in guiding children into those **gender roles** deemed appropriate in a society.

8. Like the family, schools in the United States have an explicit mandate to socialize people—especially children—into the norms and values of our culture.

9. Peer groups and the mass media, especially television, are important agents of socialization for adolescents.

10. Socialization in the workplace begins with part-time employment while we are in school and continues when we work full-time and change jobs throughout our lives.

11. The state shapes the socialization process by regulating the life course and influencing our views of appropriate behavior at particular ages.

12. As more and more mothers of young children have entered the labor market, the demand for child care has increased dramatically, posing policy questions for many nations around the world.

Critical Thinking Questions

1. Should social research be conducted on issues such as the influence of heredity and environment, even though many investigators believe that this type of analysis is potentially detrimental to large numbers of people?

2. Drawing on Erving Goffman's dramaturgical approach, discuss how the following groups engage in impression management: athletes, college instructors, parents, physicians, and politicians.

3. How would functionalists and conflict theorists differ in their analysis of socialization by the mass media?

Key Terms

Anticipatory socialization   Processes of socialization in which a person "rehearses" for future positions, occupations, and social relationships. (page 91)

Cognitive theory of development   The theory that children's thought progresses through four stages of development. (88)

Degradation ceremony   An aspect of the socialization process within some total institutions, in which people are subjected to humiliating rituals. (92)

Dramaturgical approach   A view of social interaction in which people are seen as theatrical performers. (86)

Face-work   The efforts people make to maintain the proper image and avoid public embarrassment. (86)

Gender role   Expectations regarding the proper behavior, attitudes, and activities of males and females. (93)

Generalized other   The attitudes, viewpoints, and expectations of society as a whole that a child takes into account in his or her behavior. (86)

Impression management   The altering of the presentation of the self in order to create distinctive appearances and satisfy particular audiences. (86)

Life course approach   A research orientation in which sociologists and other social scientists look closely at the social factors that influence people throughout their lives, from birth to death. (90)

Looking-glass self   A concept that emphasizes the self as the product of our social interactions. (84)

Personality   A person's typical patterns of attitudes, needs, characteristics, and behavior. (81)

Resocialization   The process of discarding former behavior patterns and accepting new ones as part of a transition in one's life. (91)

Rite of passage   A ritual marking the symbolic transition from one social position to another. (89)

Role taking   The process of mentally assuming the perspective of another and responding from that imagined viewpoint. (85)

Self A distinct identity that sets us apart from others. (84)

Significant other An individual who is most important in the development of the self, such as a parent, friend, or teacher. (86)

Socialization The lifelong process in which people learn the attitudes, values, and behaviors appropriate for members of a particular culture. (81)

Symbol A gesture, object, or word that forms the basis of human communication. (85)

Total institution An institution that regulates all aspects of a person's life under a single authority, such as a prison, the military, a mental hospital, or a convent. (91)

TECHNOLOGY RESOURCES

Internet Connection

Note: While all the URLs listed were current as of the printing of this book, these sites often change. Please check our website (www.mhhe.com/schaefer6) for updates, hyperlinks, and exercises related to these sites.

1. Parents are a key agent of socialization. The National Fatherhood Initiative (**www.fatherhood.org**) is an organization whose purpose is to educate fathers about their crucial role in socializing their children. Explore this site to learn more about the organization's efforts.

2. Toys can be an important means of socializing children into their adult roles. To see the connections between childhood play and adult roles among the Inuit, explore the online exhibit of Washington State University's Museum of Anthropology (**libarts.wsu.edu/anthro/museum/virtual%20exhibits/inuit%20toys/inuit_toys.htm**).

Online Learning Center with PowerWeb

The development of the social self is literally a lifelong transformation that begins in the crib and continues throughout one's life course. One type of socialization that can occur at some point in the life course is resocialization. *Resocialization* refers to the process of discarding former behavior patterns and accepting new ones as part of a transition in one's life. One of the Internet activities in the student center of the Online Learning Center (**www.mhhe.com/schaefer6**) gives you a glimpse into the resocialization experienced by those in concentration camps. Spend time learning about the Holocaust and life in concentration camps through the video, photographs, and stories.

Reel Society Interactive Movie CD-ROM 2.0

Reel Society 2.0 can be used to spark discussion about the following topics from this chapter:

- Agents of Socialization
- Socialization as a Life-Long Process

SOCIAL INTERACTION AND SOCIAL STRUCTURE

If this picture offends you, we apologize. If it doesn't, perhaps we should explain. Because, although this picture looks innocent enough, to the Asian market, it symbolizes death. But then, not everyone should be expected to know that.

That's where we come in. Over the last 7 years Intertrend has been guiding clients to the Asian market with some very impressive results. Clients like California Bank & Trust, Disneyland, GTE, JCPenney, Nestlé, Northwest Airlines, Sempra Energy, The Southern California Gas Company and Western Union have all profited from our knowledge of this country's fastest growing and most affluent cultural market. And their success has made us one of the largest Asian advertising agencies in the country.

We can help you as well. Give us a call or E-mail us at jych@intertrend.com. We can share some more of our trade secrets. We can also show you how we've helped our clients succeed in the Asian market. And that's something that needs no apology.

InterTrend Communications
19191 South Vermont Ave., Suite 400
Torrance, CA 90502
310.324.6313   fax 310.324.6848

OOOOPS.

In our social interactions with other cultures it is important to know what social rules apply. In Japan, for example, it is impolite to leave your chopsticks sticking up in the rice bowl—a symbol of death for the Japanese, and an insult to their dead ancestors. This poster was created by an advertising agency that promises to steer its U.S. clients clear of such gaffes.

The quiet of a summer Sunday morning in Palo Alto, California, was shattered by a screeching squad car siren as police swept through the city picking up college students in a surprise mass arrest. Each suspect was charged with a felony, warned of his constitutional rights, spread-eagled against the car, searched, handcuffed and carted off in the back seat of the squad car to the police station for booking.

After being fingerprinted and having identification forms prepared for his "jacket" (central information file), each prisoner was left isolated in a detention cell to wonder what he had done to get himself into this mess. After a while, he was blindfolded and transported to the "Stanford County Prison." Here he began the induction process of becoming a prisoner—stripped naked, skin searched, deloused, and issued a uniform, bedding, soap and towel. By late afternoon when nine such arrests had been completed, these youthful "first offenders" sat in dazed silence on the cots in their barren cells.

These men were part of a very unusual kind of prison, an experimental or mock prison, created by social psychologists for the purpose of intensively studying the effects of imprisonment upon volunteer research subjects. When we planned our two-week long simulation of prison life, we were primarily concerned about understanding the process by which people adapt to the novel and alien environment in which those called "prisoners" lose their liberty, civil rights, independence and privacy, while those called "guards" gain social power by accepting the responsibility for controlling and managing the lives of their dependent charges. . . .

Our final sample of participants (10 prisoners and 11 guards) were selected from over 75 volunteers recruited through ads in the city and campus newspapers. . . . Half were randomly assigned to role-play being guards, the others to be prisoners. Thus, there were no measurable differences between the guards and the prisoners at the start of this experiment. . . .

At the end of only six days we had to close down our mock prison because what we saw was frightening. It was no longer apparent to most of the subjects (or to us) where reality ended and their roles began. The majority had indeed become prisoners or guards, no longer able to clearly differentiate between role playing and self. There were dramatic changes in virtually every aspect of their behavior, thinking and feeling. In less than a week the experience of imprisonment undid (temporarily) a lifetime of learning; human values were suspended, self-concepts were challenged and the ugliest, most base, pathological side of human nature surfaced. We were horrified because we saw some boys (guards) treat others as if they were despicable animals, taking pleasure in cruelty, while other boys (prisoners) became servile, dehumanized robots who thought only of escape, of their own individual survival, and of their mounting hatred for the guards. *(Zimbardo et al. 1974:61, 62, 63; Zimbardo 1972:4)* ■ ◎

Additional information about this excerpt can be found on the Online Learning Center at **www.mhhe.com/schaefer6.**

In this study directed and described by social psychologist Philip Zimbardo, college students adopted the patterns of social interaction expected of guards and prisoners when they were placed in a mock prison. Sociologists use the term *social interaction* to refer to the ways in which people respond to one another, whether face to face or over the telephone or on the computer. In the mock prison, social interactions between guards and prisoners were highly impersonal. The guards addressed the prisoners by number rather than name, and they wore reflective sunglasses that made eye contact impossible.

As in many real-life prisons, the simulated prison at Stanford University had a social structure in which guards held virtually total control over prisoners. The term *social structure* refers to the way in which a society is organized into predictable relationships. The social structure of Zimbardo's mock prison influenced how the guards and prisoners interacted. Zimbardo and his colleagues (2003:546) note that it was a real prison "in the minds of the jailers and their captives." His simulated prison experiment, first conducted more than 30 years ago, has subsequently been repeated (with similar findings) both in the United States and in other countries. In fact, in 2002 the British Broadcasting Company (BBC) created a reality-based television program called *The Experiment*, in which, over the objections of Zimbardo and other scholars, producers tried to re-create the mock prison experiment. Fortunately, the presence of TV cameras mitigated the harsh treatment of prisoners.

The two concepts of social interaction and social structure are central to sociological study. They are closely related to socialization (see Chapter 4), the process through which people learn the attitudes, values, and behaviors appropriate to their culture. When the students in Zimbardo's experiment entered the mock prison, they began a process of resocialization. In that process, they adjusted to a new social structure and learned new rules for social interaction.

In this chapter we will study social structure and its effect on our social interactions. What determines a person's status in society? How do our social roles affect our social interactions? What is the place of social institutions such as the family, religion, and government in our social structure? We will begin by considering how social interactions shape the way we view the world around us. Next, we will focus on the five basic elements of social structure: statuses, social roles, groups, social networks, and social institutions. Groups are important because many of our social interactions occur in them. Social institutions such as the family, religion, and government are a fundamental aspect of social structure. As we will see, functionalists, conflict theorists, and interactionists approach these institutions quite differently. We will also compare our modern social structure with simpler forms using typologies developed by Émile Durkheim, Ferdinand Tönnies, and Gerhard Lenski. Finally, in the social policy section we will consider the AIDS crisis and its implications for social institutions throughout the world. ■

SOCIAL INTERACTION AND REALITY

When someone in a crowd shoves you, do you automatically push back? Or do you consider the circumstances of the incident and the attitude of the instigator before you react? Chances are you do the latter. According to sociologist Herbert Blumer (1969:79), the distinctive characteristic of social interaction among people is that "human beings interpret or 'define' each other's actions instead of merely reacting to each other's ac-

tions." In other words, our response to someone's behavior is based on the *meaning* we attach to his or her actions. Reality is shaped by our perceptions, evaluations, and definitions.

These meanings typically reflect the norms and values of the dominant culture and our socialization experiences within that culture. As interactionists emphasize, the meanings that we attach to people's behavior are shaped by our interactions with them and with the larger society. Social reality is literally constructed from our social interactions (Berger and Luckmann 1966).

Classroom Tip/Contemporary Culture See "Stimulating Classroom Discussions about Zimbardo's Prison Experiment" (Class Discussion Topics).
Key Person Philip Zimbardo
Methods Zimbardo's "mock prison" was an example of an experiment.
Theory Labeling theory can be applied to Zimbardo's experiment.

Classroom Tip Note the similarity between the guards' behavior in Zimbardo's experiment and the behavior of guards at the Abu Ghraib prison in Iraq in 2004.
Key Person Herbert Blumer
Theory Emphasis on interactionist perspective

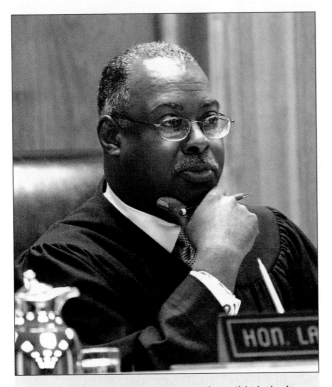

Symbols of status and power, such as this judge's robes, tend to reinforce the position of the dominant groups in society. When such symbols are associated with a member of a racial minority, they challenge prevailing racial stereotypes, changing what the interactionist William I. Thomas called "the definition of the situation."

Defining and Reconstructing Reality

How do we define our social reality? As an example, consider something as simple as how we regard tattoos. Even as recently as a few years ago, most of us in the United States considered tattoos weird or kooky. We associated them with fringe countercultural groups, such as punk rockers, bike gangs, and skinheads. Among many people, a tattoo elicited an automatic negative response. Now, however, so many people have tattoos—including society's trendsetters and major sports figures—and the ritual of getting a tattoo has become so legitimized, that mainstream culture regards tattoos differently. At this point, as a result of increased social interaction with tattooed people, tattoos look perfectly at home to us in a number of settings.

The ability to define social reality reflects a group's power within a society. In fact, one of the most crucial aspects of the relationship between dominant and subordinate groups is the ability of the dominant or majority group to define a society's values. Sociologist William I. Thomas (1923), an early critic of theories of racial and gender differences, recognized that the "definition of the situation" could mold the thinking and personality of the individual. Writing from an interactionist perspective, Thomas observed that people respond not only to the objective features of a person or situation but also to the *meaning* that person or situation has for them. For example, in Philip Zimbardo's mock prison experiment, student "guards" and "prisoners" accepted the definition of the situation (including the traditional roles and behavior associated with being a guard or prisoner) and acted accordingly.

As we have seen throughout the last 50 years—first in the civil rights movement of the 1960s and since then among such groups as women, the elderly, gays and lesbians, and people with disabilities—an important aspect of the process of social change involves redefining or reconstructing social reality. Members of subordinate groups challenge traditional definitions and begin to perceive and experience reality in a new way. For example, the world champion boxer Muhammad Ali began his career as the creation of a White male syndicate, which sponsored his early matches when he was known as Cassius Clay. Soon, however, the young boxer rebelled against those who would keep him or his race down. He broke the old stereotypes of the self-effacing Black athlete, insisting on his own political views (including refusing to serve in the Vietnam War), his own religion (Black Muslim), and his own name (Muhammad Ali). Not only did Ali change the world of sports; he also helped to alter the world of race relations (Remnick 1998a). Viewed from a sociological perspective, then, Ali was redefining social reality by rebelling against the racist thinking and terminology that restricted him and other African Americans.

Negotiated Order

As we have just seen, people can reconstruct social reality through a process of internal change, of taking a different view of everyday behavior. Yet people also reshape reality by *negotiating* changes in patterns of social interaction. The term **negotiation** refers to the attempt to reach agreement with others concerning some objective. Negotiation does not involve coercion; it goes by many names, including *bargaining, compromising, trading off, mediating, exchanging, "wheeling and dealing,"* and *collusion.* Through negotiation as a form of social interaction, society creates its social structure (A. Strauss 1977; see also Fine 1984).

Negotiation occurs in many ways. As interactionists point out, some social situations, such as buying groceries, involve no mediation, while other situations

FIGURE 5-1

Social Statuses

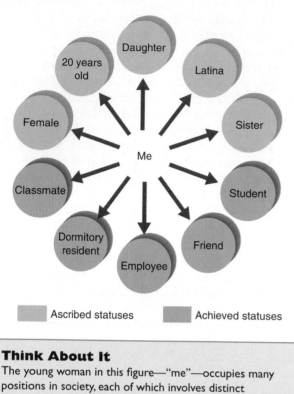

Ascribed statuses   Achieved statuses

Think About It

The young woman in this figure—"me"—occupies many positions in society, each of which involves distinct statuses. How would you define your statuses? Which have the most influence in your life?

require negotiation. For example, we may negotiate with others regarding time ("When should we arrive?"), space ("Could we meet at your house?"), or even the assignment of places in line while waiting for concert tickets. In traditional societies, impending marriage often leads to negotiations between the families of the bride and groom. For example, anthropologist Ray Abrahams (1968) has described how the Labwor people of Africa arrange for livestock to go from the groom's to the bride's family at the time of marriage. In the view of the Labwor, such bargaining over an exchange of cows and sheep culminates not only in a marriage, but more important, in the linking of two clans or families.

While such family-to-family bargaining is common in traditional cultures, negotiation can take much more elaborate forms in modern industrial societies. Consider college financial aid programs. From a sociological perspective, such programs are formal norms (reflected in established practices and procedures for granting aid to college students). Yet the programs undergo revision through negotiated outcomes involving many interests,

Theory Interactionists emphasize the importance of negotiation in everyday social behavior.
Global View Negotiation among the Labwor people of Africa
Methods Abrahams conducted observation research on the Labwor people of Africa.

including foundations, banks, the admissions office, and the faculty. On an individual level, the student applicant will mediate with representatives of the college financial aid office. Changes in the individual's situation will occur through such negotiations (Maines 1977, 1982; J. Thomas 1984).

Negotiations underlie much of our social behavior. Because most elements of social structure are not static, they are subject to change through bargaining and exchanging. Sociologists use the term *negotiated order* to underscore the fact that the social order is continually being constructed and altered through negotiation. ***Negotiated order*** refers to a social structure that derives its existence from the social interactions through which people define and redefine its character.

We can add negotiation to our list of cultural universals, because all societies provide guidelines or norms in p. 58 which negotiations take place. The recurring role of negotiation in social interaction and social structure will be apparent as we examine the major elements of social structure (A. Strauss 1977).

ELEMENTS OF SOCIAL STRUCTURE

We can examine predictable social relationships in terms of five elements: statuses, social roles, groups, social networks, and social institutions. These elements make up social structure just as a foundation, walls, and ceilings make up a building's structure. The elements of social structure are developed through the lifelong process of socialization described in Chapter 4.

Statuses

We normally think of a person's "status" as having to do with influence, wealth, and fame. However, sociologists use the term ***status*** to refer to any of the full range of socially defined positions within a large group or society, from the lowest to the highest. Within our society, a person can occupy the status of president of the United States, fruit picker, son or daughter, violinist, teenager, resident of Minneapolis, dental technician, or neighbor. A person can hold a number of statuses at the same time.

Ascribed and Achieved Status

Sociologists view some statuses as *ascribed* and others as *achieved* (see Figure 5-1). An ***ascribed status*** is assigned to a person by society without regard for the person's unique talents or characteristics. Generally, this assignment takes place at birth; thus, a person's racial back-

Classroom Tip See "Alternative Social Structure" (Class Discussion Topics).
Classroom Tip See "Social Statuses and Social Roles" (Class Discussion Topics).
Classroom Tip Can attractiveness be considered a status? See "Physical Attractiveness as a Social Status" (Class Discussion Topics).

ground, gender, and age are all considered ascribed statuses. Though these characteristics are biological in origin, they are significant mainly because of the *social* meanings they have in our culture. Conflict theorists are especially interested in ascribed statuses, since they often confer privileges or reflect a person's membership in a subordinate group. The social meanings of race and ethnicity, gender, and age will be analyzed more fully in Chapters 10–11.

In most cases, we can do little to change an ascribed status. But we can attempt to change the traditional constraints associated with such statuses. For example, the Gray Panthers—an activist political group founded in 1971 to work for the rights of older people—have tried to modify society's negative and confining stereotypes of the elderly (see Chapter 11). As a result of their work and that of other groups supporting older citizens, the ascribed status of "senior citizen" is no longer as difficult for millions of older people.

An ascribed status does not necessarily have the same social meaning in every society. In a cross-cultural study, sociologist Gary Huang (1988) confirmed the long-held view that respect for the elderly is an important cultural norm in China. In many cases, the prefix "old" is used respectfully: calling someone "old teacher" or "old person" is like calling a judge in the United States "your honor." Huang points out that positive age-seniority language distinctions are uncommon in the United States; consequently, we view the term *old man* as more of an insult than a celebration of seniority and wisdom.

Unlike ascribed statuses, an **achieved status** comes to us largely through our own efforts. Both "bank president" and "prison guard" are achieved statuses, as are "lawyer," "pianist," "sorority member," "convict," and "social worker." We must do something to acquire an achieved status—go to school, learn a skill, establish a friendship, invent a new product. But as we will see in the next section, our ascribed status heavily influences our achieved status. Being male, for example, would decrease the likelihood that we would consider child care as a career.

Master Status

Each person holds many different and sometimes conflicting statuses; some may connote higher social position and some, lower position. How, then, do others view one's overall social position? According to sociologist Everett Hughes (1945), societies deal with inconsistencies by agreeing that certain statuses are more important than others. A **master status** is a status that dominates others and thereby determines a person's general position in society. For example, Arthur Ashe, who died of AIDS in 1993, had a remarkable career as a tennis star, but at the

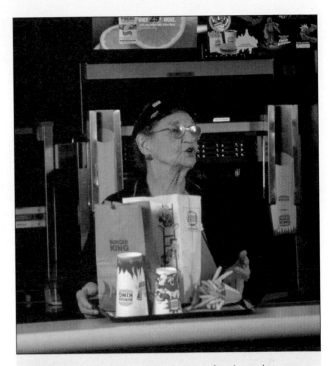

Whom do you see in this photo: a food service worker, an elderly food service worker, or an elderly woman? Our achieved and ascribed statuses determine how others see us.

end of his life, his status as a well-known personality with AIDS may have outweighed his statuses as a retired athlete, author, and political activist. Throughout the world, many people with disabilities find that their status as "disabled" receives undue weight, overshadowing their actual ability to perform successfully in meaningful employment (see Box 5-1, page 108).

Our society gives such importance to race and gender that they often dominate our lives. These ascribed statuses frequently influence our achieved status. The African American activist Malcolm X (1925–1965), an eloquent and controversial advocate of Black power and Black pride during the early 1960s, recalled that his feelings and perspectives changed dramatically while in eighth grade. When his English teacher, a White man, advised him that his goal of becoming a lawyer was "no realistic goal for a nigger" and encouraged him instead to become a carpenter, Malcolm X (1964:37) found that his position as a Black man (ascribed status) was an obstacle to his dream of becoming a lawyer (achieved status). In the United States, the ascribed statuses of race and gender can function as master statuses that have an important impact on one's potential to achieve a desired professional and social status.

Theory Conflict view of the impact of ascribed statuses
Key Person Gary Huang
Global View Respect for older people in China
Classroom Tip See "Multicultural Groups" (Additional Lecture Ideas).

Policy Pointer The social policy section at the end of the chapter will examine the AIDS crisis.

When officials in New Hampshire required a handicap access ramp for a mountain shelter, they were ridiculed for wasting taxpayers' money. Who could climb a mountain in a wheelchair? critics asked. In the summer of 2000 that challenge impelled several intrepid climbers, some in wheelchairs, to make a 12-hour trek over rocks and rough trail so that they could enter the shelter in triumph. As a result of such feats, stereotypes about the disabled are gradually falling away. But the status of "disabled" still carries a stigma.

Throughout history and around the world, people with disabilities have often been subjected to cruel and inhuman treatment. For example, in the 20th century, the disabled were frequently viewed as subhuman creatures who were a menace to society. In Japan more than 16,000 women with disabilities were involuntarily sterilized with government approval from 1945 to 1995. Sweden recently apologized for the same action taken against 62,000 of its citizens in the 1970s.

Such blatantly hostile treatment of people with disabilities has given way to a *medical model,* in which the disabled are viewed as chronic patients. Increasingly, however, people concerned with the rights of the disabled have criticized this model as well. In their view, it is the unnecessary and discriminatory barriers present in the environment—both physical and attitudinal—that stand in the way of people with disabilities, more than any biological limitations do. Applying a *civil rights model,* activists emphasize that those with disabilities face widespread prejudice, discrimination, and segregation. For example, most voting places are inaccessible to wheelchair users and fail to provide ballots that can be used by those unable to read print.

Drawing on the earlier work of Erving Goffman, contemporary sociologists have suggested that society attaches a stigma to many forms of disability, and that this stigma leads to prejudicial treatment. People with disabilities frequently observe that the nondisabled see them only as blind, wheelchair users, and so forth, rather than as complex human beings with individual strengths and weaknesses, whose blindness or use of a wheelchair is merely one aspect of their lives. A review of studies of people with disabilities disclosed that most academic

> *In Japan more than 16,000 women with disabilities were involuntarily sterilized with government approval from 1945 to 1995.*

research on the subject does not differentiate gender, thereby perpetuating the view that a disability overrides other personal characteristics. Consequently, disability serves as a master status.

Without question, people with disabilities—even the less visible ones, such as learning disabilities—occupy a subordinate position in the United States. But in 1970, a strong political movement for disability rights emerged across the nation. Women and men involved in this movement are working to challenge negative views of disabled people and to modify the social structure by reshaping laws, institutions, and environments so that people with disabilities can be fully integrated into mainstream society.

Discrimination against the disabled occurs around the world. Despite a regulation in China that universities may not reject students because of a physical disability, many universities do just that. In fact, in the last five years, the dozens of universities in Beijing alone have accepted only 236 students with any kind of disability, however minor. Bias against the disabled appears to run deep in China, where many universities use a mandate to nurture physical development as an excuse to keep out the disabled.

Kenya's constitution outlaws discrimination on the basis of many characteristics, including race, sex, tribe, place of origin, creed, and religion, but not on the basis of disability. The African nation of Botswana, on the other hand, has plans to assist its disabled, most of whom live in rural areas and need special services for mobility and economic development. In many countries, disability rights activists are targeting issues essential to overcoming this master status and becoming a full citizen, including employment, housing, education, and access to public buildings.

Let's Discuss

1. Does your campus present barriers to disabled students? If so, what kind of barriers—physical, attitudinal, or both? Describe some of them.

2. Why do you think nondisabled people see disability as the most important characteristic of a disabled person? What can be done to help people see beyond the wheelchair and the seeing-eye dog?

Sources: Albrecht et al. 2001; Goffman 1963a; D. Murphy 1997; *Newsday* 1997; E. Rosenthal 2001; Shapiro 1993; Waldrop and Stern 2003; Willet and Deegan 2000.

Student Alert Clarify the difference between the medical and the civil rights models of disability.
Let's Discuss What is the difference between referring to someone as "disabled" or as a "person with a disability"?

Key Person Erving Goffman
Classroom Tip See "China and People with Disabilities" (Additional Lecture Ideas).
Global View Treatment of people with disabilities in Kenya and Botswana

Social Roles

What Are Social Roles?

Throughout our lives, we acquire what sociologists call social roles. A *social role* is a set of expectations for people who occupy a given social position or status. Thus, in the United States, we expect that cab drivers will know how to get around a city, that receptionists will be reliable in handling phone messages, and that police officers will take action if they see a citizen being threatened. With each distinctive social status—whether ascribed or achieved—come particular role expectations. However, actual performance varies from individual to individual. One secretary may assume extensive administrative responsibilities, while another may focus on clerical duties. Similarly, in Philip Zimbardo's mock prison experiment, some students were brutal and sadistic guards; others were not.

Roles are a significant component of social structure. Viewed from a functionalist perspective, roles contribute to a society's stability by enabling members to anticipate the behavior of others and to pattern their own actions accordingly. Yet social roles can also be dysfunctional if they restrict people's interactions and relationships. If we view a person *only* as a "police officer" or "supervisor," it will be difficult to relate to him or her as a friend or neighbor.

Role Conflict

Imagine the delicate situation of a woman who has worked for a decade on an assembly line in an electrical plant, and has recently been named supervisor of her unit. How is this woman expected to relate to her longtime friends and co-workers? Should she still go out to lunch with them, as she has done almost daily for years? Is it her responsibility to recommend the firing of an old friend who cannot keep up with the demands of the assembly line?

Role conflict occurs when incompatible expectations arise from two or more social positions held by the same person. Fulfillment of the roles associated with one status may directly violate the roles linked to a second status. In the example just given, the newly promoted supervisor will most likely experience a sharp conflict between her social and occupational roles.

Such role conflicts call for important ethical choices. The new supervisor will have to make a difficult decision about how much allegiance she owes her friend and how much she owes her employers, who have given her supervisory responsibilities.

Another type of role conflict occurs when individuals move into occupations that are not common among

Police officers may face role strain when they try to develop positive community relations while maintaining an authoritative position.

people with their ascribed status. Male preschool teachers and female police officers experience this type of role conflict. In the latter case, female officers must strive to reconcile their workplace role in law enforcement with the societal view of a woman's role, which does not embrace many skills needed in police work. And while female police officers encounter sexual harassment, as women do throughout the labor force, they must also deal with the "code of silence," an informal norm that precludes their implicating fellow officers in wrongdoing (C. Fletcher 1995; S. Martin 1994).

Use Your Sociological Imagination www.mhhe.com/schaefer6

If you were a male nurse, what aspects of role conflict might you experience? Now imagine you are a professional boxer and a woman. What conflicting role expectations might that involve? In both cases, how well do you think you would handle role conflict?

Role Strain

Role conflict describes the situation of a person dealing with the challenge of occupying two social positions simultaneously. However, even a single position can cause problems. Sociologists use the term *role strain* to describe the difficulty that arises when the same social position imposes conflicting demands and expectations.

In the chapter-opening example, social psychologist Philip Zimbardo unexpectedly experienced role strain. He initially saw himself merely as a college professor directing an imaginative experiment in which students played the roles of either guard or inmate. However, he soon found that as a professor, he is also expected to look after the welfare of students, or at least not to endanger

---

Theory Functionalist view of social roles and society's stability

Classroom Tip See "Social Roles amidst Disasters" (Additional Lecture Ideas).

Gender Role conflict and gender roles for males and females

Student Alert Reinforce the difference between role conflict and role strain.

Let's Discuss See if any students in the class would like to share role conflicts or role strains they experience.

Contemporary Culture How have teenage role conflict and role strain changed since your parents were teenagers?

Reel Society Several of the *Reel Society* characters experience role conflict and role strain.

This college student in India has decorated his dorm room with photos of beautiful women and fast cars. They may signify his attempt to create a new identity, the final stage in his exit from the role of high school student living at home.

A person who is unhappy with his or her career may take a leave of absence; an unhappily married couple may begin what they see as a temporary separation.

The third stage of role exit is the *action stage* or *departure*. Ebaugh found that the vast majority of her respondents could identify a clear turning point that made them feel it was essential to take final action and leave their job, end their marriage, or engage in another type of role exit. Twenty percent of respondents saw their role exit as a gradual, evolutionary process that had no single turning point.

The last stage of role exit involves the *creation of a new identity*. Many of you participated in a role exit when you made the transition from high school to college. You left behind the role of offspring living at home and took on the role of a somewhat independent college student living with peers in a dorm. Sociologist Ira Silver (1996) has studied the central role that material objects play in this transition. The objects students choose to leave at home (like stuffed animals and dolls) are associated with their prior identities. They may remain deeply attached to those objects, but do not want them to be seen as part of their new identities at college. The objects they bring with them symbolize how they now see themselves and how they wish to be perceived. CDs and wall posters, for example, are calculated to say, "This is me."

them. Eventually he resolved the role strain by making the difficult decision to terminate the experiment. Twenty-five years later, in a television interview, he was still reflecting on the challenge of his role (CBS News 1979).

Role Exit

Often, when we think of assuming a social role, we focus on the preparation and anticipatory socialization a person undergoes for that role. Such is true if a person is about to become an attorney, a chef, a spouse, or a parent. Yet until recently, social scientists have given little attention to the adjustments involved in *leaving* social roles.

Sociologist Helen Rose Fuchs Ebaugh (1988) developed the term ***role exit*** to describe the process of disengagement from a role that is central to one's self-identity in order to establish a new role and identity. Drawing on interviews with 185 people—among them ex-convicts, divorced men and women, recovering alcoholics, ex-nuns, former doctors, retirees, and transsexuals—Ebaugh (herself a former nun) studied the process of voluntarily exiting from significant social roles.

Ebaugh has offered a four-stage model of role exit. The first stage begins with *doubt*. The person experiences frustration, burnout, or simply unhappiness with an accustomed status and the roles associated with the social position. The second stage involves a *search for alternatives*.

Groups

In sociological terms, a ***group*** is any number of people with similar norms, values, and expectations who interact with one another on a regular basis. The members of a women's basketball team, a hospital's business office, a synagogue, or a symphony orchestra constitute a group. However, the residents of a suburb would not be considered a group, since they rarely interact with one another at one time.

Every society is composed of many groups in which daily social interaction takes place. We seek out groups to establish friendships, to accomplish certain goals, and to fulfill the social roles we have acquired. In Kuwait, men gather in groups called *diwaniyas,* which means "little

Key Person Helen Rose Fuchs Ebaugh
Methods Ebaugh's study of role exit is an example of survey research.
Theory Ebaugh's study of role exit reflects an interactionist perspective.
Classroom Tip See "Role Transitions" (Additional Lecture Ideas).

Student Alert Reinforce the distinctions between a group, an aggregate, and a category.
Theory Functionalist view of the role of groups in social structure

guest house" in Arabic. Hundreds of these gatherings take place every night. *Diwaniyas* may be centered around a family, but are just as likely to be organized around a business, specific occupation, or politics. Men gather to exchange gossip or ideas in these groups, which range in size from 5 or 6 members to well over 100. Meetings can last an hour in the early evening or stretch well into the night. *Diwaniyas* have a rich history in Kuwait, going back over 200 years. Recently a handful of *diwaniyas* has begun to allow women to attend—a major departure from custom for this type of social group. We'll explore the various types of groups in which people interact in detail in Chapter 6, where we will also examine sociological investigations of group behavior (T. Marshall 2003).

Groups play a vital part in a society's social structure. Much of our social interaction takes place within groups and is influenced by their norms and sanctions. Being a teenager or a retired person takes on special meanings when we interact within groups designed for people with that particular status. The expectations associated with many social roles, including those accompanying the statuses of brother, sister, and student, become more clearly defined in the context of a group.

New technology has broadened the definition of groups to include those who interact electronically. Not all the "people" with whom we converse online are real. At some websites, *chatterbots*—fictitious correspondents created by artificial intelligence programs—respond to questions as if a human were replying. While answering product or service-related questions, the chatterbot may begin "chatting" with an online consumer about family or the weather. Ultimately, such conversations may develop into a chat group that includes other online correspondents, both real and artificial. New groups organized around old interests, such as antique collecting or bowling, have already arisen from this type of virtual reality (Van Slambrouck 1999).

For the human participant, such online exchanges offer a new opportunity to alter one's image—what Goffman (1959) refers to as impression management. How might you present yourself to an online discussion group?

The Internet has added a massive new dimension to social interaction—even though you may not be totally sure whom you are "talking to."

Social Networks and Technology

Groups do not merely serve to define other elements of the social structure, such as roles and statuses; they also link the individual with the larger society. We all belong to a number of different groups, and through our acquaintances make connections with people in different social circles. These connections are known as a ***social network***—that is, a series of social relationships that links a person directly to others, and through them indirectly to still more people. Social networks may constrain people by limiting the range of their interactions, yet networks may also empower people by making available to them vast resources (Lin 1999).

Involvement in social networks—commonly known as *networking*—is especially valuable in finding employment. Albert Einstein was successful in finding a job only when a classmate's father put him in touch with his future employer. These kinds of contacts—even those that are weak and distant—can be crucial in establishing social networks and facilitating the transmission of information.

In the workplace, networking pays off more for men than for women because of the traditional presence of men in leadership positions. One survey of executives

Why Do We Gather Together?

Around the world, people cluster at bus stops, in schools, and at houses of worship. Others gather at malls, movie theaters, and government offices. They do so for many reasons—to earn a living, get an education, or just to have fun. But there is a larger purpose to these gatherings. Humans are social creatures, with a social fabric that is knit together by the give-and-take of even the most common encounters. The people we meet with, the places where we gather, our purposes in seeking others' company—these are fundamental building blocks of our society.

Our social interactions are also defined by the social structures in which they take place. Social interactions may be relatively casual and unstructured, as they are when friends spend time hanging out together at the mall. Or they may be carefully organized, as they are when tribal musicians compete for the title of best drum circle at the powwow, or when mountain climbers attempt to reach the summit of the world's highest peak. In each case, the social interaction is defined by the larger social structure, whether it be the operators of the mall, the organizers of the intertribal competition, or the government that grants climbers permission to ascend a peak.

Base camp for a Mt. Everest expedition

Teen scene at a mall in Poughkeepsie, New York

Drum circle at an intertribal powwow

5-2 SOCIAL NETWORKS AMONG LOW-INCOME WOMEN

While sociologists have rightly paid a good deal of attention to "old-boy networks," they have been displaying growing interest in the social networks created by women. Research shows that such social networks are not limited to professional women "doing lunch" to trade inside tips or identify prospective clients. Networking is popular among women of much more modest means as well.

Sociologist Pierrette Hondagneu-Sotelo conducted observation research and interviews among Hispanic women (primarily Mexican immigrants) who live in San Francisco and are employed as domestic workers in middle- and upper-class homes. These women engage in what sociologist Mary Romero has called "job work." That is, the domestic worker has several employers and cleans each home on a weekly or biweekly basis for a flat rate of pay for the work completed (in Spanish, *por el trabajo*), as opposed to being paid an hourly rate *(por la hora)*. Job work typically involves low pay, no reimbursement for transportation costs, and no health care benefits.

At first glance, we might expect that women engaged in such job work would be isolated from each other, since they work alone. However, Hondagneu-Sotelo found that these Hispanic women have created strong social networks. Through interactions in various social settings—such as picnics, baby showers, church events, and informal gatherings at women's homes—they share such valuable information as cleaning tips, remedies for work-related physical ailments, tactics for negotiating better pay and gratuities, and advice on how to leave undesirable jobs.

Sociologists Silva Domínguez and Celeste Watkins did fieldwork among low-income women in Boston. They found that many of the younger mothers relied

> Women who were part of networks definitely had greater resources than more isolated women.

heavily on family-based social networks. The two researchers also documented the strength of friendship-based and institution-based networks. The latter included ties to social service providers, which have often been overlooked in similar studies. Ties to service providers are particularly important where family-based and friendship-based networks are unavailable or ineffective. Domínguez and Watkins found that providers offered the mothers help in the form of child care, emotional support, and small loans.

In the past, some sociologists have suspected that these low-income women's networks might help members simply to survive, rather than to improve their lives. Too often, they feared, network members would get drawn into time-consuming relationships with women who are experiencing even worse problems than their own. Yet Domínguez and Watkins found that women who were part of networks definitely had greater resources than more isolated women. Networks allowed many of the women they studied to advance both socially and economically.

Let's Discuss

1. Do you belong to an informal social network? If so, describe the members and the purpose of your network. Do the members all live near one another, or are they far-flung? How do you keep in touch? What kinds of help do you give one another?

2. Has helping a network member who is in trouble ever consumed a lot of your time and energy? If so, explain the circumstances. On balance, is your membership in the network worthwhile, despite the time and effort it requires?

Sources: Domínguez and Watkins 2003; Hondagneu-Sotelo 2001; Romero 1988.

found that 63 percent of the men used networking to find new jobs, compared to 41 percent of the women. Thirty-one percent of the women used classified advertisements to find jobs, compared to only 13 percent of the men. Still, women at all levels of the paid labor force are beginning to make effective use of social networks. A study of women who were leaving the welfare rolls to enter the paid workforce found that networking was an effective tool in their search for employment. Informal networking also helped them to locate child care and better housing—keys to successful employment. As Box 5-2 shows,

even women of modest means can make effective use of social networks (Carey and McLean 1997; Henly 1999).

With advances in technology, we can now maintain social networks electronically; we don't need face-to-face contacts. Online network-building companies emerged in 2004, offering their services free of charge at first. People log in to these sites and create a profile. Rather than remaining anonymous, as they would with an online dating service, users are identified by name and encouraged to list friends—even trusted friends of friends—who can serve as job contacts, offer advice, or simply share

Methods Observation research and interviewing used to study networking

Gender/Race/Ethnicity Networking among Hispanic women employed as domestic workers

Contemporary Culture Technology has led to the development of new communities that meet in cyberspace.

interests. One site creates "tribes" of people who share the same characteristic—a religion, hobby, music preference, or college affiliation (B. Tedeschi 2004).

Sociologist Manuel Castells (1997, 1998, 2000) views these emerging electronic social networks as fundamental to new organizations and the growth of existing businesses and associations. One such network, in particular, is changing the way people interact. *Texting* refers to the exchange of wireless e-mails over cell phones. It began first in Asia in 2000 and has now taken off in North America and Europe. Initially, texting was popular among young users, who sent shorthand messages such as "WRU" ("Where are you?") and "CU2NYT" ("See you tonight"). But now the business world has seen the advantages of transmitting e-mails via cell phones or PalmPilots. However, sociologists caution that such devices create a workday that never ends, and that increasingly people are busy checking their digital devices rather than actually conversing with those around them.

In 2003, the deployment of U.S. troops in the Middle East increased many people's reliance on e-mail. Today, digital photos and sound files accompany e-mail messages between soldiers and their families and friends. Well-established networks have developed to help those who are novices at electronic communication to connect to the Internet.

Use Your Sociological Imagination   www.mhhe.com/schaefer6

If you were deaf, what impact might instant messaging have on you?

Social Institutions

The mass media, the government, the economy, the family, and the health care system are all examples of social institutions found in our society. **Social institutions** are organized patterns of beliefs and behavior centered on basic social needs, such as replacing personnel (the family) and preserving order (the government).

A close look at social institutions gives sociologists insight into the structure of a society. Consider religion, for example. The institution of religion adapts to the segment of society that it serves. Church work has very different meanings for ministers who serve a skid row area and those who serve a suburban middle-class community. Religious leaders assigned to a skid row mission will focus on tending to the ill and providing food and shelter. In contrast, clergy in affluent suburbs will be occupied with counseling those considering marriage and divorce, arranging youth activities, and overseeing cultural events.

Functionalist View

One way to understand social institutions is to see how they fulfill essential functions. Anthropologist David F. Aberle and his colleagues (1950) and sociologists Raymond Mack and Calvin Bradford (1979) have identified five major tasks, or functional prerequisites, that a society or relatively permanent group must accomplish if it is to survive:

1. *Replacing personnel.* Any group or society must replace personnel when they die, leave, or become incapacitated. This task is accomplished through such means as immigration, annexation of neighboring groups, acquisition of slaves, or sexual reproduction. The Shakers, a religious sect that came to the United States in 1774, are a conspicuous example of a group that has *failed* to replace personnel. Their religious beliefs commit the Shakers to celibacy; to survive, the group must recruit new members. At first, the Shakers proved quite successful in attracting members, reaching a peak of about 6,000 members in the United States during the 1840s. As of 2004, however, the only Shaker community left in this country was a farm in Maine with five members—three men and two women (Sabbathday Lake 2004).

2. *Teaching new recruits.* No group or society can survive if many of its members reject the group's established behavior and responsibilities. Thus, finding or producing new members is not sufficient; the group or society must also encourage recruits to learn and accept its values and customs. Such learning can take place formally, within schools (where learning is a manifest function) or informally, through interaction and negotiation in peer groups (where instruction is a latent function).

3. *Producing and distributing goods and services.* Any relatively permanent group or society must provide and distribute desired goods and services to its members. Each society establishes a set of rules for the allocation of financial and other resources. The group must satisfy the needs of most members to some extent, or it will risk the possibility of discontent and ultimately disorder.

4. *Preserving order.* The native people of Tasmania, a large island just south of Australia, are now extinct. During the 1800s they were destroyed by the hunting parties of European conquerors, who looked upon the Tasmanians as half-human. Their annihilation underscores a critical function of every group or society—preserving order and

This memorial service for the victims of the September 11, 2001 terrorist attack incorporated many patriotic elements, all of which helped New Yorkers to maintain a sense of purpose in extremely difficult times.

protecting itself from attack. Because the Tasmanians were unable to defend themselves against the more developed European technology of warfare, an entire people was wiped out.

5. *Providing and maintaining a sense of purpose.* People must feel motivated to continue as members of a group or society in order to fulfill the first four requirements. After the September 11, 2001 attacks on New York City and Washington, D.C., memorial services and community gatherings across the nation allowed people to affirm their allegiance to their country and bind up the psychic wounds inflicted by the terrorists. Patriotism, then, assists some people in developing and maintaining a sense of purpose. For others, tribal identities, religious values, or personal moral codes are especially meaningful. Whatever the motivator, in any society there remains one common and critical reality: if an individual does not have a sense of purpose, he or she has little reason to contribute to a society's survival.

This list of functional prerequisites does not specify *how* a society and its corresponding social institutions will perform each task. For example, one society may protect itself from external attack by amassing a frightening arsenal of weaponry, while another may make determined efforts to remain neutral in world politics and to promote cooperative relationships with its neighbors. No matter what its particular strategy, any society or relatively permanent group must attempt to satisfy all these functional prerequisites for survival. If it fails on even one condition, as the Tasmanians did, the society runs the risk of extinction.

Conflict View

Conflict theorists do not concur with the functionalist approach to social institutions. Although proponents of both perspectives agree that institutions are organized to meet basic social needs, conflict theorists object to the implication that the outcome is necessarily efficient and desirable.

From a conflict perspective, the present organization of social institutions is no accident. Major institutions, such as education, help to maintain the privileges of the most powerful individuals and groups within a society, while contributing to the powerlessness of others. To give one example, public schools in the United States are financed largely through property taxes. This arrangement allows more affluent areas to provide their children with better-equipped schools and better-paid teachers than low-income areas can afford. As a result, children from prosperous communities are better prepared to compete academically than children from impoverished communities. The structure of the nation's educational system permits and even promotes such unequal treatment of schoolchildren.

Conflict theorists argue that social institutions such as education have an inherently conservative nature. Without question, it has been difficult to implement educational reforms that promote equal opportunity—whether bilingual education, school desegregation, or mainstreaming of students with disabilities. From a functionalist perspective, social change can be dysfunctional, since it often leads to instability. However, from a conflict view, why should we preserve the existing social structure if it is unfair and discriminatory?

Social institutions also operate in gendered and racist environments, as conflict theorists, as well as feminists and interactionists, have pointed out. In schools, offices, and government institutions, assumptions about what people can do reflect the sexism and racism of the larger society. For instance, many people assume that women cannot make tough decisions—even those in the top

Theory Conflict view of social institutions introduced
Gender/Race Social institutions operate in gendered and racist environments.

echelons of corporate management. Others assume that all Black students at elite colleges represent affirmative action admissions. Inequality based on gender, economic status, race, and ethnicity thrives in such an environment—to which we might add discrimination based on age, physical disability, and sexual orientation. The truth of this assertion can be seen in routine decisions by employers on how to advertise jobs, as well as whether to provide fringe benefits such as child care and parental leave.

Use Your Sociological Imagination www.mhhe.com /schaefer6

Would social networks be more important for a migrant worker in California than for someone with political and social clout? Why or why not?

Interactionist View

Social institutions affect our everyday behavior, whether we are driving down the street or waiting in a long shopping line. Sociologist Mitchell Duneier (1994a, 1994b) studied the social behavior of the word processors, all women, who work in the service center of a large Chicago law firm. Duneier was interested in the informal social norms that emerged in this work environment and the rich social network these female employees created.

The Network Center, as it is called, is merely a single, windowless room in a large office building where the law firm occupies seven floors. The center is staffed by two shifts of word processors, who work either from 4:00 P.M. to midnight or from midnight to 8:00 A.M. Each word processor works in a cubicle with just enough room for her keyboard, terminal, printer, and telephone. Work assignments for the word processors are placed in a central basket and then completed according to precise procedures.

At first glance, we might think that these women labor with little social contact, apart from limited breaks and occasional conversations with their supervisor. However, drawing on the interactionist perspective, Duneier learned that despite working in a large office, these women find private moments to talk (often in the halls or outside the washroom) and share a critical view of the law firm's attorneys and day-shift secretaries. Indeed, the word processors routinely suggest that their assignments represent work that the "lazy" secretaries should have completed during the normal workday. Duneier (1994b) tells of one word processor who resented the lawyers' superior attitude and pointedly refused to recognize or speak with any attorney who would not address her by name.

Interactionist theorists emphasize that our social behavior is conditioned by the roles and statuses we accept, the groups to which we belong, and the institutions within

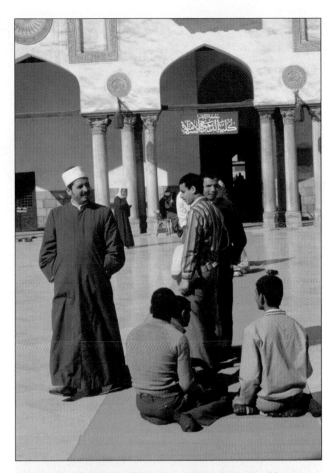

Social institutions affect the way we behave. How might the worshipers at this mosque in Egypt interact differently in school or at work?

which we function. For example, the social roles associated with being a judge occur within the larger context of the criminal justice system. The status of "judge" stands in relation to other statuses, such as attorney, plaintiff, defendant, and witness, as well as to the social institution of government. Although courts and jails have great symbolic importance, the judicial system derives its continued significance from the roles people carry out in social interactions (Berger and Luckmann 1966).

SOCIAL STRUCTURE IN GLOBAL PERSPECTIVE

Modern societies are complex, especially compared to earlier social arrangements. Sociologists Émile Durkheim, Ferdinand Tönnies, and Gerhard Lenski developed ways to contrast modern societies with simpler forms of social structure.

Theory Interactionist view of social institutions introduced
Key Person Mitchell Duneier
Gender Social behavior of women working as word processors for a large law firm
Theory Duneier drew on the interactionist perspective in studying women working as word processors.

In small communities like those of the Quechua in Peru, people maintain social control through informal means such as gossip. Tönnies referred to this type of community as a *Gemeinschaft.*

Durkheim's Mechanical and Organic Solidarity

In his *Division of Labor* ([1893] 1933), Durkheim argued that social structure depends on the division of labor in a society—in other words, on the manner in which tasks are performed. Thus, a task such as providing food can be carried out almost totally by one individual, or it can be divided among many people. The latter pattern is typical of modern societies, in which the cultivation, processing, distribution, and retailing of a single food item are performed by literally hundreds of people.

In societies in which there is minimal division of labor, a collective consciousness develops that emphasizes group solidarity. Durkheim termed this collective frame of mind *mechanical solidarity,* implying that all individuals perform the same tasks. In this type of society, no one needs to ask, "What do your parents do?" since all are engaged in similar work. Each person prepares food, hunts, makes clothing, builds homes, and so forth. Because people have few options regarding what to do with their lives, there is little concern for individual needs. Instead, the group will is the dominating force in society. Both social interaction and negotiation are based on close, intimate, face-to-face social contacts. Since there is little specialization, there are few social roles.

As societies become more advanced technologically, they rely on greater division of labor. The person who cuts down timber is not the same person who puts on your

roof. With increasing specialization, many different tasks must be performed by many different individuals—even in manufacturing a single item, such as a radio or stove. In general, social interactions become less personal than in societies characterized by mechanical solidarity. People begin relating to others on the basis of their social positions ("butcher," "nurse") rather than their distinctive human qualities. Because the overall social structure of the society continues to change, statuses and social roles are in perpetual flux.

Once society has become more complex and division of labor is greater, no individual can go it alone. Dependence on others becomes essential for group survival. In Durkheim's terms, mechanical solidarity is replaced by **organic solidarity,** a collective consciousness resting on the need a society's members have for one another. Durkheim chose the term *organic solidarity* because in his view, individuals become interdependent in much the same way as organs of the human body.

Tönnies's Gemeinschaft and Gesellschaft

Ferdinand Tönnies (1855–1936) was appalled by the rise of an industrial city in his native Germany during the late 1800s. In his view, the city marked a dramatic change from the ideal of a close-knit community, which Tönnies termed a *Gemeinschaft,* to that of an impersonal mass society, known as a *Gesellschaft* (Tönnies [1887] 1988).

The **Gemeinschaft** (pronounced guh-MINE-shoft) is typical of rural life. It is a small community in which people have similar backgrounds and life experiences. Virtually everyone knows one another, and social interactions are intimate and familiar, almost as among kinfolk. In this community there is a commitment to the larger social group and a sense of togetherness among members. People relate to others in a personal way, not just as "clerk" or "manager." With this personal interaction comes little privacy, however: we know too much about everyone.

Social control in the *Gemeinschaft* is maintained through informal means such as moral persuasion, gossip, and even gestures. These techniques work effectively because people genuinely care how others feel about them. Social change is relatively limited in the *Gemeinschaft;* the lives of members of one generation may be quite similar to those of their grandparents.

Key Person Émile Durkheim
Theory Durkheim's view of social structure is an example of functionalist analysis.

Key Person Ferdinand Tönnies
Global View Tönnies's typology of *Gemeinschaft* and *Gesellshaft* was based on his observations in Germany in the late 1800s.
Contemporary Culture Relate *Gemeinschaft* and *Gesellschaft* to reconstruction issues in Iraq.

Table 5-1	Comparison of the *Gemeinschaft* and *Gesellschaft*	
Gemeinschaft	**Gesellschaft**	
Rural life typifies this form.	Urban life typifies this form.	
People share a feeling of community that results from their similar backgrounds and life experiences.	People have little sense of commonality. Their differences appear more striking than their similarities.	
Social interactions, including negotiations, are intimate and familiar.	Social interactions, including negotiations, are likely to be impersonal and task-specific.	
People maintain a spirit of cooperation and unity of will.	Self-interest dominates.	
Tasks and personal relationships cannot be separated.	The task being performed is paramount; relationships are subordinate.	
People place little emphasis on individual privacy.	Privacy is valued.	
Informal social control predominates.	Formal social control is evident.	
People are not very tolerant of deviance.	People are more tolerant of deviance.	
Emphasis is on ascribed statuses.	Emphasis is on achieved statuses.	
Social change is relatively limited.	Social change is very evident, even within a generation.	

summingUP

Think About It
How would you classify the communities with which you are familiar? Are they more *Gemeinschaft* or *Gesellschaft*?

In contrast, the **Gesellschaft** (pronounced guh-ZELL-shoft) is an ideal community that is characteristic of modern urban life. In this community most people are strangers who feel little in common with other residents. Relationships are governed by social roles that grow out of immediate tasks, such as purchasing a product or arranging a business meeting. Self-interest dominates, and there is little consensus concerning values or commitment to the group. As a result, social control must rest on more formal techniques, such as laws and legally defined punishments. Social change is an important aspect of life in the *Gesellschaft;* it can be strikingly evident even within a single generation.

Table 5-1 summarizes the differences between the *Gemeinschaft* and the *Gesellschaft.* Sociologists have used these terms to compare social structures that stress close relationships with those that emphasize less personal ties. It is easy to view the *Gemeinschaft* with nostalgia, as a far better way of life than the "rat race" of contemporary existence. However, the more intimate relationships of the *Gemeinschaft* come at a price. The prejudice and discrimination found there can be quite confining; ascribed statuses such as family background often outweigh a person's

unique talents and achievements. In addition, the *Gemeinschaft* tends to distrust individuals who seek to be creative or just to be different.

Lenski's Sociocultural Evolution Approach

Sociologist Gerhard Lenski takes a very different view of society and social structure. Rather than distinguishing between two opposite types of society, as Tönnies did, Lenski sees human societies as undergoing a process of change characterized by a dominant pattern known as **sociocultural evolution.** This term refers to the "process of change and development in human societies that results from cumulative growth in their stores of cultural information" (Lenski et al. 2004:366).

In Lenski's view, a society's level of technology is critical to the way it is organized. Lenski defines **technology** as "cultural information about how to use the material resources of the environment to satisfy human needs and desires" (Nolan and Lenski 2004:37). The available technology does not completely define the form that a particular society and its social structure take. Nevertheless, a

"I'd like to think of you as a person, David, but it's my job to think of you as personnel."

In a *Gesellschaft,* people are likely to relate to one another in terms of their roles rather than their relationships.

low level of technology may limit the degree to which a society can depend on such things as irrigation or complex machinery. As technology advances, Lenski writes, a community evolves from a preindustrial to an industrial and finally a postindustrial society.

Preindustrial Societies

How does a preindustrial society organize its economy? If we know that, we can categorize the society. The first type of preindustrial society to emerge in human history was the **hunting-and-gathering society,** in which people simply rely on whatever foods and fibers are readily available. Technology in such societies is minimal. Organized in groups, people move constantly in search of food. There is little division of labor into specialized tasks.

Hunting-and-gathering societies are composed of small, widely dispersed groups. Each group consists almost entirely of people who are related to one another. As a result, kinship ties are the source of authority and influence, and the social institution of the family takes on a particularly important role. Tönnies would certainly view such societies as examples of the *Gemeinschaft.*

Social differentiation within the hunting-and-gathering society is based on ascribed statuses such as gender, age, and family background. Since resources are scarce, there is relatively little inequality in terms of material goods. By the close of the 20th century, hunting-and-gathering societies had virtually disappeared (Nolan and Lenski 2004).

Horticultural societies, in which people plant seeds and crops rather than merely subsist on available foods, emerged about 10,000 to 12,000 years ago. Members of horticultural societies are much less nomadic than hunters and gatherers. They place greater emphasis on the production of tools and household objects. Yet technology remains rather limited within these societies, whose members cultivate crops with the aid of digging sticks or hoes (Wilford 1997).

The last stage of preindustrial development is the **agrarian society,** which emerged about 5,000 years ago. As in horticultural societies, members of agrarian societies are engaged primarily in the production of food. However, new technological innovations such as the plow allow farmers to dramatically increase their crop yields. They can cultivate the same fields over generations, allowing the emergence of larger settlements.

The agrarian society continues to rely on the physical power of humans and animals (as opposed to mechanical power). Nevertheless, its social structure has more carefully defined roles than that of horticultural societies. Individuals focus on specialized tasks, such as the repair of fishing nets or blacksmithing. As human settlements become more established and stable, social institutions become more elaborate and property rights more important. The comparative permanence and greater surpluses of an agrarian society allow members to create artifacts such as statues, public monuments, and art objects and to pass them on from one generation to the next.

Table 5-2 on page 122 summarizes Lenski's three stages of sociocultural evolution, as well as the stages that followed, described next.

Industrial Societies

Although the industrial revolution did not topple monarchs, it produced changes every bit as significant as those resulting from political revolutions. The industrial revolution, which took place largely in England during the period 1760 to 1830, was a scientific revolution focused on the application of nonanimal (mechanical) sources of power to labor tasks. An **industrial society** is a society that depends on mechanization to produce its goods and services. Industrial societies rely on new inventions that facilitate agricultural and industrial production, and on new sources of energy, such as steam.

As the industrial revolution proceeded, a new form of social structure emerged. Many societies underwent an irrevocable shift from an agrarian-oriented economy to an industrial base. No longer did an individual or a family typically make an entire product. Instead, specialization of tasks and manufacturing of goods became increasingly common. Workers, generally men but also women and even children, left their family homesteads to work in central locations such as factories.

The process of industrialization had distinctive social consequences. Families and communities could not continue to function as self-sufficient units. Individuals, villages, and regions began to exchange goods and services and to become interdependent. As people came to rely on the labor of members of other communities, the family lost its unique position as the source of power and authority. The need for specialized knowledge led to more formalized schooling, and education emerged as a social institution distinct from the family.

Postindustrial and Postmodern Societies

When Lenski first proposed the sociocultural evolutionary approach in the 1960s, he paid relatively little attention to how maturing industrialized societies may change with the emergence of even more advanced forms of technology. More recently, he and other sociologists have studied the significant changes in the occupational structure of industrial societies as they shift from manufacturing to service economies. In the 1970s sociologist Daniel Bell wrote about the technologically advanced *postindustrial society,* whose economic system is engaged primarily in the processing and control of information. The main output of a postindustrial society is services rather than manufactured goods. Large numbers of people become involved in occupations devoted to the teaching, generation, or dissemination of ideas. Jobs in fields such as advertising, public relations, human resources, and computer information systems would be typical of a postindustrial society (D. Bell 1999).

Bell views the transition from industrial to postindustrial society as a positive development. He sees a general decline in organized working-class groups and a rise in interest groups concerned with national issues such as health, education, and the environment. Bell's outlook is functionalist, because he portrays the postindustrial society as basically consensual. As organizations and interest groups engage in an open and competitive process of decision making, Bell believes, the level of conflict between diverse groups will diminish, strengthening social stability.

Conflict theorists take issue with Bell's functionalist analysis of the postindustrial society. For example, Michael Harrington (1980), who alerted the nation to the problems of the poor in his book *The Other America,* questioned the significance that Bell attached to the

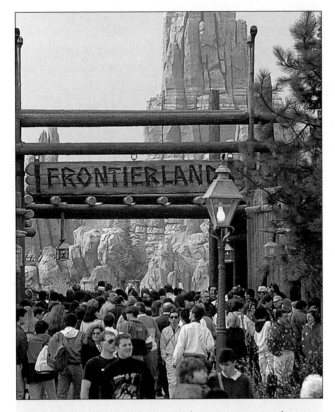

In a postmodern society, people consume goods, information, and media images en masse. In Paris, Disneyworld is popularizing U.S. media images abroad, illustrating another characteristic of postmodern societies—globalization.

growing class of white-collar workers. Harrington conceded that scientists, engineers, and economists are involved in important political and economic decisions, but he disagreed with Bell's claim that they have a free hand in decision making, independent of the interests of the rich. Harrington followed in the tradition of Marx by arguing that conflict between social classes will continue in the postindustrial society.

Sociologists have recently gone beyond discussion of the postindustrial society to the ideal of the postmodern society. A *postmodern society* is a technologically sophisticated society that is preoccupied with consumer goods and media images (Brannigan 1992). Such societies consume goods and information on a mass scale. Postmodern theorists take a global perspective, noting the ways that culture crosses national boundaries. For example, residents of the United States may listen to reggae music from Jamaica, eat sushi and other Japanese foods, and wear clogs from Sweden (Lyotard 1993).

Key Person Daniel Bell
Theory Bell's functionalist view of postindustrial societies as basically consensual

Student Alert Clarify the distinction between postindustrial and postmodern societies.
Let's Discuss How can the concept of diffusion be related to postmodernism?

Table 5-2	Stages of Sociocultural Evolution	
Societal Type	**First Appearance**	**Characteristics**
Hunting-and-gathering	Beginning of human life	Nomadic; reliance on readily available food and fibers
Horticultural	About 10,000 to 12,000 years ago	More settled; development of agriculture and limited technology
Agrarian	About 5,000 years ago	Larger, more stable settlements; improved technology, increased crop yields, and specialization of labor
Industrial	1760–1850	Reliance on mechanical power and new sources of energy; centralized workplaces; economic interdependence; formal education
Postindustrial	1960s	Reliance on services, especially the processing and control of information; expanded middle class
Postmodern	Latter 1970s	High technology; mass consumption of consumer goods and media images; cross-cultural integration

The emphasis of postmodern theorists is on observing and describing newly emerging cultural forms and patterns of social interaction. Within sociology, the postmodern view offers support for integrating the insights of various theoretical perspectives—functionalism, conflict theory, feminist theory, interactionism, and labeling theory—while incorporating other contemporary approaches. Feminist sociologists argue optimistically that with its indifference to hierarchies and distinctions, the postmodern society will discard traditional values of male dominance in favor of gender equality. Yet others contend that despite new technologies, postindustrial and postmodern societies can be expected to display the same problems of inequality that plague industrial societies (Ritzer 1995; Sale 1996; Smart 1990; B. Turner 1990; van Vucht Tijssen 1990).

Durkheim, Tönnies, and Lenski present three visions of society's social structure. While they differ, each is useful, and this textbook will draw on all three. The sociocultural evolutionary approach emphasizes a historical perspective. It does not picture different types of social structures coexisting within the same society. Consequently, one would not expect a single society to include hunters and gatherers along with a postmodern culture. In contrast, Durkheim's and Tönnies's theories allow for the existence of different types of community—such as a

Gemeinschaft and a Gesellschaft—in the same society. Thus, a rural New Hampshire community located 100 miles from Boston can be linked to the city by modern information technology. The main difference between these two theories is a matter of emphasis. While Tönnies emphasized the overriding concern in each type of community—one's own self-interest or the well-being of the larger society—Durkheim emphasized the division (or lack of division) of labor.

The work of these three thinkers reminds us that a major focus of sociology has been to identify changes in social structure and the consequences for human behavior. At the macro level, we see society shifting to more advanced forms of technology. The social structure becomes increasingly complex, and new social institutions emerge to assume some functions that once were performed by the family. On the micro level, these changes affect the nature of social interactions. Each individual takes on multiple social roles, and people come to rely more on social networks and less on kinship ties. As the social structure becomes more complex, people's relationships become more impersonal, transient, and fragmented.

In the social policy section that follows we will examine the impact of the AIDS crisis on social structure and social interaction in the United States and other nations.

Theory Conflict critique of Bell's analysis of postindustrial society
Theory Postmodernism integrates the insights of functionalism, conflict theory, interactionism, labeling theory, and feminist theory.
Theory Feminist sociologists' view of postmodernism and its possible impact on gender inequalities

Theory The work of Durkheim, Tönnies, and Lenski examines the macro and micro levels of social structure.

SOCIAL POLICY and SOCIAL STRUCTURE — The AIDS Crisis

The Issue

In his novel *The Plague*, Albert Camus (1948:34) wrote, "There have been as many plagues as wars in history, yet always plagues and wars take people equally by surprise." Regarded by many as the distinctive plague of the modern era, AIDS certainly caught major social institutions—particularly the government, the health care system, and the economy—by surprise when it was first noticed by medical practitioners in the 1970s. It has since spread around the world. While encouraging new therapies have been developed to treat AIDS, there is currently no way to eradicate the disease by medical means. Therefore, it is essential to protect people by reducing the transmission of the fatal virus. But how is that to be done, and whose responsibility is it? What is the role of social institutions in preventing the spread of AIDS?

The Setting

AIDS is the acronym for *acquired immune deficiency syndrome*. Rather than being a distinct disease, AIDS is actually a predisposition to disease that is caused by a virus, the human immunodeficiency virus (HIV). The virus gradually destroys the body's immune system, leaving the carrier vulnerable to infections such as pneumonia that those with healthy immune systems can generally resist. Transmission of the virus from one person to another appears to require either intimate sexual contact or exchange of blood or bodily fluids (whether from contaminated hypodermic needles or syringes, transfusions of infected blood, or transmission from an infected mother to her child before or during birth).

The first cases of AIDS in the United States were reported in 1981. While the numbers of new cases and deaths have recently shown some evidence of decline, an estimated 950,000 people were living with AIDS or HIV by early 2003, of whom over a fourth did not yet know they were infected. Women account for a growing proportion of new cases; racial and ethnic minorities, for 74 percent. Worldwide, AIDS is on the increase, with an estimated 40 million people infected and over 3 million dying annually (see Figure 5-2, page 124). The disease is not evenly distributed; those areas least equipped to deal with it—the developing nations of sub-Saharan Africa—face the greatest challenge (Centers for Disease Control and Prevention 2003; Maugh 2003; UNAIDS 2003).

Sociological Insights

Dramatic crises like the AIDS epidemic are likely to bring about certain transformations in a society's social structure. From a functionalist perspective, if established social institutions cannot meet a crucial need, new social networks are likely to emerge to perform that function. In the case of AIDS, self-help groups—especially in the gay communities of major cities—have organized to care for the sick, educate the healthy, and lobby for more responsive public policies.

The label of "person with AIDS" or "HIV-positive" often functions as a master status. People who have AIDS or are infected with the virus actually face a powerful dual stigma. Not only are they associated with a lethal and contagious disease, but also they have a disease that disproportionately afflicts already stigmatized groups, such as gay males and intravenous drug users. This linkage with stigmatized groups delayed recognition of the severity of the AIDS epidemic; the media took little interest in the disease until it seemed to be spreading beyond the gay community.

Viewed from a conflict perspective, policymakers were slow to respond to the AIDS crisis because those in high-risk groups—gay men and IV drug users—were comparatively powerless. Furthermore, a study done in 2002 documented the fact that female and minority groups are less likely than others to receive experimental treatments for the HIV infection (Gifford et al. 2002).

On the micro level of social interaction, observers widely forecast that AIDS would lead to a more conservative sexual climate—among both homosexuals and heterosexuals—in which people would be much more cautious about becoming involved with new partners. Yet it appears that many sexually active people in the United States have not heeded precautions about "safe sex." Data from studies conducted in the early 1990s indicated a growing complacency about AIDS, even among those most vulnerable (Centers for Disease Control and Prevention 2002; UNAIDS 2003:23–24).

Another interactionist concern is the tremendous impact that taking the appropriate medication has on one's daily routine. Tens of thousands of AIDS patients are having to reorder their lives around their medical regimens. Even infected patients without the symptoms of AIDS find the concentrated effort that is needed to fight the disease—taking 95 doses of 16 different medications every 24 hours—extremely taxing. Think for a

FIGURE 5-2

People Living with HIV/AIDS, 2003

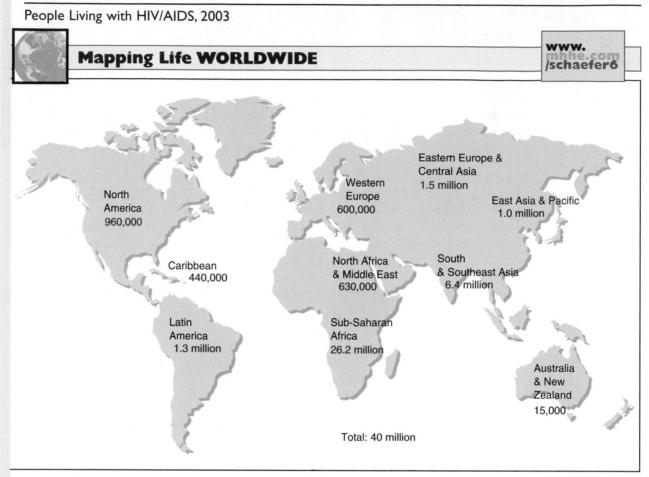

Mapping Life WORLDWIDE

www.mhhe.com/schaefer6

North America 960,000

Caribbean 440,000

Latin America 1.3 million

Western Europe 600,000

Eastern Europe & Central Asia 1.5 million

East Asia & Pacific 1.0 million

North Africa & Middle East 630,000

South & Southeast Asia 6.4 million

Sub-Saharan Africa 26.2 million

Australia & New Zealand 15,000

Total: 40 million

Note: Based on midpoint estimates; world range is 34–46 million cases.
Source: UNAIDS 2003:37.

moment about the effect such a regimen would have on your own life, from eating and sleeping to work, study, child care, and recreation.

Given the difficulty of complying with such a complicated regimen, some government officials have questioned whether drug treatments can be effective in developing countries. In 2001, the director of the U.S. Agency for International Development charged that drugs "wouldn't work" in Africa because many African patients cannot tell time. Yet recent studies of the daily lives of people with AIDS have not supported this ethnocentric claim. Surveys done in four different African countries found that in reality, African patients take about 90 percent of their AIDS medicine. That compliance rate compares well with an average of 70 percent in the United States, where homeless people

and drug users have even lower compliance rates (McNeil 2003:A5).

Policy Initiatives

AIDS has struck all societies, but not all nations can respond in the same manner. Studies done in the United States show that people with the virus and with AIDS who receive appropriate medical treatment are living longer than in the past. This advance may put additional pressure on policymakers to address the issues raised by the spread of AIDS.

In some nations, cultural practices may prevent people from dealing with the AIDS epidemic realistically. They may not be likely to take the necessary preventive measures, including open discussion of sexual-

Classroom Tip Introduce Goffman's concept of stigma in discussing HIV and AIDS as master statuses.
Theory Conflict view that policymakers were slow to respond to the AIDS crisis because high-risk groups were not powerful
Theory Interactionist view of the impact of AIDS on social and sexual behavior

Web Resource Remind students there is an interactive map for this chapter. They can view it in the student center of the Online Learning Center (www.mhhe.com/schaefer6).
Classroom Tip See "Using Humor" (Class Discussion Topics).

ity, homosexuality, and drug use. Prevention has shown signs of working among target groups, such as drug users, pregnant women, and gay men and lesbians, but preventative initiatives are few and far between in developing nations. The prescribed treatment to reduce mother-to-baby transmission of AIDS costs about $300. That amount is roughly equivalent to the average annual income in much of the world where the risk of AIDS is greatest, such as Africa, which accounts for 77 percent of the world's deaths from AIDS. The medication for adult patients with HIV is even more costly (McNeil 2003; UNAIDS 2003:5).

The high cost of drug treatment programs has generated intensive worldwide pressure on the major pharmaceutical companies to lower their prices to patients in developing nations, especially in sub-Saharan Africa. In 2001, bowing to this pressure, several of the companies agreed to make the combination therapies available at cost. Even at these much lower prices, however, in the poorest nations, less than 5 percent of those sick enough to need treatment were receiving it by mid-2004. In many nations, social institutions simply are not equipped to distribute medicine to those who need it (McNeil 2004).

Let's Discuss

1. Do the people you know take few risks sexually because of the danger of becoming infected with the AIDS virus? If not, why not?
2. Look at the map in Figure 5-2. Why do you think North Africa and the Middle East had only 630,000 people living with AIDS in 2003, while sub-Saharan Africa had 26.2 million? List as many factors as you can that might account for the disparity in numbers.
3. Aside from the obvious humanitarian reasons, why should the United States help developing countries in the fight against AIDS?

GETTING INVOLVED

To get involved in the debate over the AIDS crisis, visit this text's Online Learning Center, which offers links to relevant websites. Check out the Social Policy section on the Online Learning Center as well; it provides survey data on U.S. public opinion regarding this issue.

CHAPTER RESOURCES

Summary

Social interaction refers to the ways in which people respond to one another. *Social structure* refers to the way in which a society is organized into predictable relationships. This chapter examines the basic elements of social structure: statuses, social roles, groups, networks, and institutions.

1. People shape their social reality based on what they learn through their social interactions. Social change comes from redefining or reconstructing social reality. Sometimes change results from *negotiation.*
2. An *ascribed status* is generally assigned to a person at birth, whereas an *achieved status* is attained largely through one's own effort.
3. In the United States, ascribed statuses, such as race and gender, can function as *master statuses* that

have an important impact on one's potential to achieve a desired professional and social status.
4. With each distinctive status—whether ascribed or achieved—come particular *social roles,* the set of expectations for people who occupy that status.
5. Much of our patterned behavior takes place within *groups* and is influenced by the norms and sanctions established by groups. Groups serve as links to *social networks* and their vast resources.
6. The mass media, the government, the economy, the family, and the health care system are all examples of *social institutions.*
7. One way to understand social institutions is to ask how they fulfill essential functions, such as replacing personnel, training new recruits, and preserving order.

8. Conflict theorists argue that social institutions help to maintain the privileges of the powerful while contributing to the powerlessness of others.

9. Interactionist theorists emphasize the idea that our social behavior is conditioned by the roles and statuses we accept, the groups to which we belong, and the institutions within which we function.

10. Émile Durkheim thought that social structure depends on the division of labor in a society. According to Durkheim's theory, societies with minimal division of labor have a collective consciousness called *mechanical solidarity;* those with greater division of labor show an interdependence called *organic solidarity.*

11. Ferdinand Tönnies distinguished the close-knit community of *Gemeinschaft* from the impersonal mass society known as *Gesellschaft.*

12. Gerhard Lenski thinks that a society's social structure changes as its culture and technology become more sophisticated, a process he calls *sociocultural evolution.*

13. The AIDS crisis has changed our society's social structure, prompting the creation of new networks to care for the ill and educate the healthy. Policymakers were slow to respond to the crisis at first because the high-risk groups the disease affected were relatively powerless.

Critical Thinking Questions

1. People in certain professions seem particularly susceptible to role conflict. For example, journalists commonly experience role conflict during disasters, crimes, and other distressing situations. Should they offer assistance to the needy or cover breaking news? Select two other professions and discuss the role conflicts people in them might experience.

2. The functionalist, conflict, and interactionist perspectives can all be used in analyzing social institutions. What are the strengths and weaknesses in each perspective's analysis of these institutions?

3. In what ways does HIV serve to underscore issues of race, class, and gender in the United States today?

Key Terms

Achieved status   A social position that a person attains largely through his or her own efforts. (page 107)

Agrarian society   The most technologically advanced form of preindustrial society. Members are engaged primarily in the production of food but increase their crop yield through technological innovations such as the plow. (120)

Ascribed status   A social position assigned to a person by society without regard for the person's unique talents or characteristics. (106)

Gemeinschaft   A close-knit community, often found in rural areas, in which strong personal bonds unite members. (118)

Gesellschaft   A community, often urban, that is large and impersonal, with little commitment to the group or consensus on values. (119)

Group   Any number of people with similar norms, values, and expectations who interact with one another on a regular basis. (110)

Horticultural society   A preindustrial society in which people plant seeds and crops rather than merely subsist on available foods. (120)

Hunting-and-gathering society   A preindustrial society in which people rely on whatever foods and fibers are readily available in order to survive. (120)

Industrial society   A society that depends on mechanization to produce its goods and services. (120)

Master status   A status that dominates others and thereby determines a person's general position in society. (107)

Mechanical solidarity   A collective consciousness that emphasizes group solidarity, characteristic of societies with minimal division of labor. (118)

Negotiated order   A social structure that derives its existence from the social interactions through which people define and redefine its character. (106)

Negotiation   The attempt to reach agreement with others concerning some objective. (105)

Organic solidarity   A collective consciousness that rests on mutual interdependence, characteristic of societies with a complex division of labor. (118)

Postindustrial society   A society whose economic system is engaged primarily in the processing and control of information. (121)

Postmodern society   A technologically sophisticated society that is preoccupied with consumer goods and media images. (121)

Role conflict   The situation that occurs when incompatible expectations arise from two or more social positions held by the same person. (109)

Role exit   The process of disengagement from a role that is central to one's self-identity in order to establish a new role and identity. (110)

Role strain   The difficulty that arises when the same social position imposes conflicting demands and expectations. (109)

Social institution   An organized pattern of beliefs and behavior centered on basic social needs. (115)

Social interaction   The ways in which people respond to one another. (104)

Social network   A series of social relationships that links a person directly to others, and through them indirectly to still more people. (111)

Social role   A set of expectations for people who occupy a given social position or status. (109)

Social structure   The way in which a society is organized into predictable relationships. (104)

Sociocultural evolution   The process of change and development in human societies that results from cumulative growth in their stores of cultural information. (119)

Status   A term used by sociologists to refer to any of the full range of socially defined positions within a large group or society. (106)

Technology   Cultural information about how to use the material resources of the environment to satisfy human needs and desires. (119)

TECHNOLOGY RESOURCES

Internet Connection

*Note: While all the URLs listed were current as of the printing of this book, these sites often change. Please check our website (**www.mhhe.com/schaefer6**) for updates, hyperlinks, and exercises related to these sites.*

1. The term *sandwich generation* refers to the role conflict many people experience as they juggle the demands of caring for two different generations—their children and their parents—at once. To learn more about the challenges of this type of role conflict, visit the Sandwich Generation website (**www.thesandwichgeneration.com**).

2. How does the status of being deaf influence a person's social interactions? The National Association of the Deaf (**www.nad.org**) is an advocacy organization for the deaf and hard of hearing. Explore the "Advocacy" section of this site to learn about some social issues that are important to those who cannot hear.

Online Learning Center with PowerWeb

Try the crossword puzzle in the student center of the Online Learning Center (**www.mhhe.com/schaefer6**). Working the puzzle is a great way to test your familiarity with the important terms and concepts related to social interaction and social structure. It's also an enjoyable way to review for exams.

Reel Society Interactive Movie CD-ROM 2.0

Reel Society 2.0 can be used to spark discussion about the following topics from this chapter:

- Social Roles
- Social Roles and Expectations of Others

GROUPS AND ORGANIZATIONS

Groups come in all sizes and cover a broad array of interests. This poster is directed to a group of people interested in a marketplace featuring fashions for young men. It asks: "Are you in?"

Ray Kroc (1902–1984), the genius behind the franchising of McDonald's restaurants, was a man with big ideas and grand ambitions. But even Kroc could not have anticipated the astounding impact of his creation. McDonald's is the basis of one of the most influential developments in contemporary society. Its reverberations extend far beyond its point of origin in the United States and in the fast-food business. It has influenced a wide range of undertakings, indeed the way of life, of a significant portion of the world. And in spite of McDonald's recent and well-publicized economic difficulties, that impact is likely to expand at an accelerating rate.

However, this is *not* a book about McDonald's, or even about the fast-food business. . . . I devote all this attention to McDonald's . . . because it serves here as the major example of, and the paradigm for, a wide-ranging process I call *McDonaldization*. . . . As you will see, McDonaldization affects not only the restaurant business but also education, work, the criminal justice system, health care, travel, leisure, dieting, politics, the family, religion, and virtually every other aspect of society. McDonaldization has shown every sign of being an inexorable process, sweeping through seemingly impervious institutions and regions of the world.

Other types of business are increasingly adapting the principles of the fast-food industry to their needs. Said the vice chairman of Toys "R" Us, "We want to be thought of as a sort of McDonald's of toys." . . . Other chains with similar ambitions include Gap, Jiffy Lube, AAMCO Transmissions, Midas Muffler & Brake Shops, Great Clips, H&R Block, Pearle Vision, Bally's. . . .

Other nations have developed their own variants of this American institution. . . . Paris, a city whose love for fine cuisine might lead you to think it would prove immune to fast food, has a large number of fast-food croissanteries; the revered French bread has also been McDonaldized. India has a chain of fast-food restaurants, Nirula's, that sells mutton burgers (about 80% of Indians are Hindus, who eat no beef) as well as local Indian cuisine. Mos Burger is a Japanese chain with over fifteen hundred restaurants that in addition to the usual fare, sells Teriyaki chicken burgers, rice burgers, and "Oshiruko with brown rice cake." . . .

McDonald's is such a powerful model that many businesses have acquired nicknames beginning with Mc. Examples include "McDentists" and "McDoctors," meaning drive-in clinics designed to deal quickly and efficiently with minor dental and medical problems; "McChild" care centers, meaning child care centers such as KinderCare; "McStables," designating the nationwide race horse-training operation of Wayne Lucas; and "McPaper," describing the newspaper *USA TODAY*. (Ritzer 2004a:1–4, 10–11) ■ 🕮

GEORGE RITZER
The McDonaldization of Society
Revised New Century Edition

Additional information about this excerpt can be found on the Online Learning Center at **www.mhhe.com/schaefer6.**

In this excerpt from *The McDonaldization of Society,* sociologist George Ritzer contemplates the enormous influence of a well-known fast-food organization on modern-day culture and social life. Ritzer defines **McDonaldization** as "the process by which the principles of the fast-food restaurant are coming to dominate more and more sectors of American society as well as of the rest of the world" (Ritzer 2004a:1). In his book, he shows how the business principles on which the fast-food industry is founded—efficiency, calculability, predictability, and control—have changed not only the way Americans do business and run their organizations, but the way they live their lives. Today, busy families rely on the takeout meals served up by fast-food establishments, and McDonald's has become a regular meeting place for social groups from adolescents to senior citizens.

Despite the runaway success of McDonald's and its imitators, and the advantages these enterprises bring to millions of people around the world, Ritzer is critical of their effect on society. The waste and environmental degradation created by billions of disposable containers and the dehumanized work routines of fast-food crews are two of the disadvantages he cites in his critique. Would the modern world be a better one, Ritzer asks, if it were less McDonaldized?

This chapter considers the impact of groups and organizations on social interaction. Do we behave differently in large groups than in small ones? How do we make large organizations manageable? What effect are current social changes having on the structure of groups? We'll begin by noting the distinctions between various types of groups, with particular attention to the dynamics of small groups. We'll examine how and why formal organizations came into existence and describe Max Weber's model of the modern bureaucracy. In a case study of the loss of the space shuttle *Columbia,* we'll see how NASA's bureaucratic culture contributed to the ship's disastrous accident. Finally, we'll look at recent changes in the workplace, some of which are designed to counteract the failures of bureaucracies. The social policy section at the end of the chapter focuses on the status of organized labor today. ■

UNDERSTANDING GROUPS

Most of us use the term *group* loosely to describe any collection of individuals, whether three strangers sharing an elevator or hundreds attending a rock concert. However, in sociological terms a **group** is any number of people with similar norms, values, and expectations who interact with one another on a regular basis. College sororities and fraternities, dance companies, tenants' associations, and chess clubs are all considered examples of groups. The important point is that members of a group share some sense of belonging. This characteristic distinguishes groups from mere *aggregates* of people, such as passengers who happen to be together on an airplane flight, or from *categories* of people—those who share a common feature (such as being retired) but otherwise do not act together.

Consider the case of a college a cappella singing group. It has agreed-on values and social norms. All members want to improve their singing skills and schedule lots of performances. In addition, like many groups, the singing ensemble has both a formal and an informal structure. The members meet regularly to rehearse; they choose leaders to run the rehearsals and manage their affairs. At the same time, some group members may take on unofficial leadership roles by coaching new members in singing techniques and performing skills.

The study of groups has become an important part of sociological investigation because they play such a key role in the transmission of culture. As we interact with others, we pass on our ways of thinking and acting—from language and values to ways of dressing and leisure activities.

Types of Groups

Sociologists have made a number of useful distinctions between types of groups—primary and secondary groups, in-groups and out-groups, and reference groups.

Primary and Secondary Groups

Charles Horton Cooley (1902) coined the term **primary group** to refer to a small group characterized by intimate, face-to-face association and cooperation. The members of a street gang constitute a primary group; so do mem-

Classroom Tip/Contemporary Culture See "Stimulating Classroom Discussion about *McDonaldization*" (Class Discussion Topics).
Student Alert *Aggregate and category* are introduced not as glossary terms, but to clarify the term *group.*

Key Person Charles Horton Cooley
Student Alert See Cooley's concept of the looking-glass self in Chapter 4. Explain why *primary group* is a related concept.
Classroom Tip For analysis of primary group life in ethnic and urban communities, see "Primary Groups and Subcultures" in Topics and Sources for Student Research.

Research in Action

6-1 PIZZA DELIVERY EMPLOYEES AS A SECONDARY GROUP

What is it like to deliver pizzas for a living? Most of us give little thought to this question, but sociologists Patrick Kinkade and Michael Katovich did a scientific study of it. For 18 months, one of them worked on delivery crews at three different restaurants in Fort Worth, Texas. Taking an interactionist perspective, this participant observer explored the social relationships that developed among drivers as they worked, waited for orders, or hit the bars after work. Through observation and interview, the two researchers found that drivers formed a tight network based on shared experience—both the ordinary transactions and the occasional dangerous encounters that were part of the job.

Within their culture, the pizza delivery drivers take risks and receive minimal rewards. While attacks on them are usually publicized, they are not documented statistically. But the drivers themselves are well aware of the possible dangers and talk to one another a great deal about them. During the observation period, two drivers were robbed and eight others were "tailed," resulting in four automobile accidents.

The researchers found that the world of this secondary group is "hypermasculine," with racist and sexist overtones. The drivers uniformly characterized the dangers to their safety as coming from members of racial and ethnic communities, even when there was no evidence of their assertion. The drivers also regularly boasted of their sexual prowess, and told and retold accounts of sexual favors they received from customers.

Among the 106 drivers studied by the researchers, five types emerged:

- *The comedian.* This individual uses humor to neutralize or trivialize the anxiety of making runs into neighborhoods perceived as high-risk.
- *The adventurer.* The adventurer claims to invite problems, and actu-

> *Within their culture, the pizza delivery drivers take risks and receive minimal rewards.*

ally looks forward to testing himself in dangerous situations.
- *The denier.* This individual attempts to neutralize anxiety by suggesting that a problem does not exist or has been exaggerated.
- *The fatalist.* This person recognizes and admits the risk of danger, but simply accepts it without making any effort to neutralize it.
- *The pro.* The pro generally has had a long history in the delivery busi-

ness, having worked for several pizza services, and perhaps served as an assistant manager, if not a manager, at one of the other stores.

While on the job, members of the delivery crew may have seemed like "family" (a primary group), but their interaction was limited strictly to the job. Still, membership in the secondary group was important to the drivers. They accepted their identity as delivery persons and assumed whichever role type they felt most comfortable with. Kinkade and Katovich found that in general, crew members derived more satisfaction from their occupational camaraderie than from the job's monetary rewards. The study shows how, especially in urban environments, people use membership in secondary groups to carve out a niche in the larger social world.

Let's Discuss

1. Think about a secondary group to which you belong. Can you identify any common role types? If so, describe them.
2. If you were to do research like that of Kinkade and Katovich, what group would you choose to study? What research techniques would you use?

Source: Kinkade and Katovich 1997.

bers of a family living in the same household, as do a group of "sisters" in a college sorority.

Primary groups play a pivotal role both in the socialization process (see Chapter 4) and in the development of roles and statuses (see Chapter 5). Indeed, primary groups can be instrumental in a person's day-to-day existence. When we find ourselves identifying closely with a group, it is probably a primary group.

We also participate in many groups that are not characterized by close bonds of friendship, such as large college classes and business associations. The term *secondary group* refers to a formal, impersonal group in which there is little social intimacy or mutual understanding (see Table 6-1, page 132). The distinction between primary and secondary groups is not always clear-cut. Some social clubs may become so large and impersonal that they no longer function as primary groups.

Secondary groups often emerge in the workplace among those who share special understandings about their occupation. Almost all of us have come into contact with people who deliver pizzas. Using observation research, two sociologists have given us a new

Key Persons Patrick Kinkade, Michael Katovich
Gender/Race/Ethnicity Racist and sexist sentiments among pizza delivery employees
Methods Use of participant observation to study pizza delivery employees
Theory Use of interactionist perspective to analyze secondary groups

Let's Discuss Ask students to list the primary and secondary groups of which they are members. Discuss some of these groups.
Classroom Tip See the discussion of agents of socialization, particularly schools and peer groups, in Chapter 4.

understanding of the secondary group ties that emerge in this occupation (see Box 6-1, page 131).

In-Groups and Out-Groups

A group can hold special meaning for members because of its relationship to other groups. For example, people in one group sometimes feel antagonistic to or threatened by another group, especially if that group is perceived as being different either culturally or racially. To identify these "we" and "they" feelings, sociologists use two terms first employed by William Graham Sumner (1906): *in-group* and *out-group*.

An **in-group** can be defined as any group or category to which people feel they belong. Simply put, it comprises everyone who is regarded as "we" or "us." The in-group may be as narrow as a teenage clique or as broad as an entire society. The very existence of an in-group implies that there is an **out-group** that is viewed as "they" or "them." An out-group is a group or category to which people feel they do *not* belong.

In-group members typically feel distinct and superior, seeing themselves as better than people in the out-group. Proper behavior for the in-group is simultaneously viewed as unacceptable behavior for the out-group. This double standard enhances the sense of superiority. Sociologist Robert Merton (1968) described this process as the conversion of "in-group virtues" into "out-group vices." We can see this differential standard operating in worldwide discussions of terrorism. When a group or a nation takes aggressive actions, it usually justifies them as necessary, even if civilians are hurt and killed. Opponents are quick to label such actions with the emotion-laden

"So long, Bill. This is my club. You can't come in."

An exclusive social club is an in-group whose members consider themselves superior to others.

term of *terrorist* and appeal to the world community for condemnation. Yet these same people may themselves retaliate with actions that hurt civilians, which the first group will then condemn.

Conflict between in-groups and out-groups can turn violent on a personal as well as a political level. In 1999 two disaffected students at Columbine High School in Littleton, Colorado, launched an attack on the school that left 15 students and teachers dead, including themselves. The gunmen, members of an out-group that other students referred to as the Trenchcoat Mafia, apparently resented taunting by an in-group referred to as the Jocks. Similar episodes have occurred in schools across the nation, where rejected adolescents, overwhelmed by personal and family problems, peer group pressure, academic responsibilities, or media images of violence, have struck out against more popular classmates.

In-group members who actively provoke out-group members may have their own problems, including limited time and attention from working parents. Sociologists David Stevenson and Barbara Schneider (1999), who studied 7,000 teenagers, found that despite many opportunities for group membership, young people spend an

summingUP

Table 6-1	Comparison of Primary and Secondary Groups	
Primary Group	**Secondary Group**	
Generally small	Usually large	
Relatively long period of interaction	Relatively short duration, often temporary	
Intimate, face-to-face association	Little social intimacy or mutual understanding	
Some emotional depth in relationships	Relationships generally superficial	
Cooperative, friendly	More formal and impersonal	

Theory The "us and them" view held by in-groups increases tension (conflict approach) but can promote in-group solidarity and a sense of belonging (functionalist approach).
Key Persons William Graham Sumner, Robert Merton

Classroom Tip See "Using the Holocaust to Teach about Groups and Organizations" (Class Discussion Topics).

George Clooney in the motion picture *The Perfect Storm*. Warner Brothers changed the movie's final scene when focus groups reacted negatively to the original ending, which featured the doomed fisherman's final thoughts.

average of three and a half hours alone every day. While youths may claim they want privacy, they also crave attention, and striking out at members of an in-group or out-group, be they the wrong gender, race, or friendship group, seems to be one way to get it.

Use Your Sociological Imagination www. mhhe.com /schaefer6

Try putting yourself in the shoes of an out-group member. What does your in-group look like from that perspective?

Focus Groups

Another type of group includes people who do not interact on a regular basis. A *focus group* is composed of 10 to 15 people assembled by a researcher to discuss a predetermined topic, such as a new consumer product or community needs. Guided by a moderator, the members, who are selected to be representative of the general public, offer their own opinions on the topic and react to other members' views. Focus group members are usually paid for their participation and realize that their views are being recorded.

Focus groups were first developed by Robert Merton (1987) and his colleagues at Columbia University in the early 1940s, to evaluate the relative effectiveness of radio advertising. Today, advertisers and corporations rely heavily on this research method, which Merton called

the *focused interview*. While the corporate world has been the principal user of focus groups over the last six decades, sociologists have recently returned to the method to investigate community opinion and workplace morale. They use the information they receive from the groups to design more extensive qualitative or quantitative research.

Reference Groups

Both in-groups and primary groups can dramatically influence the way an individual thinks and behaves. Sociologists call any group that individuals use as a standard for evaluating themselves and their own behavior a *reference group*. For example, a high school student who aspires to join a social circle of hip-hop music devotees will pattern his or her behavior after that of the group. The student will begin dressing like these peers, listening to the same tapes and CDs, and hanging out at the same stores and clubs.

Reference groups have two basic purposes. They serve a normative function by setting and enforcing standards of conduct and belief. The high school student who wants the approval of the hip-hop crowd will have to follow the group's dictates at least to some extent. Reference groups also perform a comparison function by serving as a standard against which people can measure themselves and others. An actor will evaluate himself or herself against a reference group composed of others in the acting profession (Merton and Kitt 1950).

Reference groups may help the process of anticipatory socialization. For example, a college student majoring in finance may read the *Wall Street Journal*, study the annual reports of corporations, and listen to midday stock market news on the radio. Such a student is using financial experts as a reference group to which he or she aspires.

Often, two or more reference groups influence us at the same time. Our family members, neighbors, and coworkers all shape different aspects of our self-evaluation. In addition, reference group attachments change during the life cycle. A corporate executive who quits the rat race at age 45 to become a social worker will find new reference groups to use as standards for evaluation. We shift reference groups as we take on different statuses during our lives.

Classroom Tip See "Effects of the Dynamite Charge" (Class Discussion Topics).
Reel Society Relate the concepts of in-groups, out-groups, and reference groups to the problems encountered by Molly, Dave, and Gita.

Theory Functionalist view of the purposes of reference groups
Contemporary Culture Do college students today have the same reference groups as college students of a generation ago?
Classroom Tip See "Group Behavior" (Class Discussion Topics).

Groups come in all types and sizes. The members of this Manchester, Vermont, group belong to a national club of antique bicycle buffs called the Wheelmen. They take their Victorian-era bicycles out for rides and often dress in period costume from the late 1800s, as shown here.

Studying Small Groups

Sociological research done on the micro level and research done from the interactionist perspective usually focus on the study of small groups. The term *small group* refers to a group small enough for all members to interact simultaneously—that is, to talk with one another or at least be well acquainted. Certain primary groups, such as families, also may be classified as small groups. However, many small groups differ from primary groups in that they do not necessarily offer the intimate personal relationships characteristic of primary groups. For example, a manufacturer may bring together its seven-member regional sales staff twice a year for an intensive sales conference. The salespeople, who live in different cities and rarely see one another, constitute a small secondary group, not a primary group.

We may think of small groups as being informal and unpatterned; yet, as interactionist researchers have revealed, distinct and predictable processes are at work in the functioning of small groups. A long-term ethnographic study of street gangs in Chicago revealed an elaborate structure resembling that of a family business. A street gang there is composed of several geographically based units called sets, each of which possesses a leader, lower-ranking officers, and a rank-and-file membership. Besides staffing the economic network of the drug trade, gang members develop relationships with tenant leaders in public housing projects and participate in nondelinquent so-

cial activities important to the maintenance of their authority in the neighborhood (Venkatesh 2000).

Size of a Group

At what point does a collection of people become too large to be called a small group? That is not clear. In a group with more than 20 members, it is difficult for individuals to interact regularly in a direct and intimate manner. But even within a range of 2 to 20 people, group size can substantially alter the quality of social relationships. For example, as the number of group participants increases, the most active communicators become even more active relative to others. Therefore, a person who dominates a group of 3 or 4 members will be relatively more dominant in a 15-person group.

Group size also has noticeable social implications for members who do not assume leadership roles. In a larger group, each member has less time to speak, more points of view to absorb, and a more elaborate structure to function in. At the same time, an individual has greater freedom to ignore certain members or viewpoints than he or she would in a smaller group. It is harder to disregard someone in a 4-person workforce than someone in an office with 30 employees, harder to disregard someone in a string quartet than someone in a college band with 50 members.

The German sociologist Georg Simmel (1858–1918) is credited as the first sociologist to emphasize the importance of interactive processes within groups and to note how they change as the group's size changes. The simplest of all social groups or relationships is the *dyad,* or two-member group. A wife and a husband constitute a dyad, as does a business partnership or a singing duo. The dyad offers a special level of intimacy that cannot be duplicated in larger groups. However, as Simmel ([1917] 1950) noted, a dyad, unlike any other group, can be destroyed by the loss of a single member. Therefore, the threat of termination hangs over a dyadic relationship perhaps more than over any other.

Obviously, the introduction of one additional person to a dyad dramatically transforms the character of the small group. The dyad becomes a three-member group, or *triad.* The third member has many ways of interacting with and influencing the dynamics of the group. The new person may play a *unifying* role in the triad. When a mar-

Theory Analysis of small-group behavior relies on an interactionist approach.
Methods Ethnographic study of street gangs

Key Person Georg Simmel

ried couple has their first child, the baby may serve to bind the group closer together. A newcomer also may play a *mediating* role in a three-person group. If two roommates are perpetually sniping at each other, the third roommate may attempt to remain on good terms with both and to arrange compromise solutions to problems. Finally, a member of a triad can choose to employ a *divide-and-rule* strategy. Such is the case, for example, with a coach who tries to gain greater control over two assistants by making them rivals (Nixon 1979).

Coalitions

As groups grow to the size of triads or larger, coalitions begin to develop. A ***coalition*** is a temporary or permanent alliance geared toward a common goal. Coalitions can be broad-based or narrow and can take on many different objectives. Sociologist William Julius Wilson (1999b) has described community-based organizations in Texas that include Whites and Latinos, working class and affluent, who have banded together to work for improved sidewalks, better drainage systems, and comprehensive street paving. Out of this type of coalition building, Wilson hopes, will emerge better interracial understanding.

Some coalitions are intentionally short lived. Short-term coalition building is a key to success in popular TV programs like *Survivor*. In *Survivor I*, broadcast in 2000, the four members of the "Tagi alliance" banded together to vote fellow castaways off the island. The political world is also the scene of many temporary coalitions. For example, in 1997 big tobacco companies joined with anti-smoking groups to draw up a settlement for reimbursing states for tobacco-related medical costs. Soon after the settlement was announced the coalition members returned to their decades-long fight against each other (Pear 1997).

The effects of group size and coalitions on group dynamics are but two of the many aspects of the small group that sociologists have studied. Another aspect, conformity and deviance, is examined in Chapter 8. Although it is clear that small-group encounters have a considerable influence on our lives, we are also deeply affected by much larger groups of people, as we'll see in the next section.

Survivor: All-Stars featured 18 former champions of the popular reality TV series. Short-term coalition building has been one of the keys to success in the mock struggle for survival.

▮ UNDERSTANDING ORGANIZATIONS

Formal Organizations and Bureaucracies

As contemporary societies have shifted to more advanced forms of technology and their social structures have become more complex, our lives have become increasingly dominated by large secondary groups referred to as *formal organizations*. A ***formal organization*** is a group designed for a special purpose and structured for maximum efficiency. The U.S. Postal Service, McDonald's, the Boston Pops orchestra, and the college you attend are all examples of formal organizations. Though organizations vary in their size, specificity of goals, and degree of efficiency, they are all structured to facilitate the management of large-scale operations. They also have a bureaucratic form of organization, described in the next section.

In our society, formal organizations fulfill an enormous variety of personal and societal needs and shape the lives of every one of us. In fact, formal organizations have become such a dominant force that we must create organizations to supervise other organizations, such as the Securities and Exchange Commission (SEC) to regulate brokerage companies. While it sounds much more exciting to say that we live in the "computer age" than to say that ours is the "age of formal organization," the latter is probably a more accurate description of our times (Azumi and Hage 1972; Etzioni 1964).

Key Person William Julius Wilson (See Chapter 9 for Wilson's discussion of the underclass.)
Let's Discuss Have any students in the class been members of a coalition? If so, what was the common goal of the coalition members?

Classroom Tip How do sociologists study the wide range of formal organizations in the United States? See "Organizational Variables" (Additional Lecture Ideas).

Whistle-blower Colleen Rowley, an FBI agent, tried unsuccessfully to bring her superiors' attention to a French Moroccan who had signed up for pilot training at a local flight school, keen to operate a 747. The man later used his training to crash a hijacked jet into the World Trade Center. Rowley was photographed as she testified before the Senate Judiciary Committee in June 2002.

Ascribed statuses such as gender, race, and ethnicity can influence how we see ourselves within formal organizations. For example, a study of women lawyers in the nation's largest law firms found significant differences in the women's self-images, depending on the relative presence or absence of women in positions of power. In firms in which fewer than 15 percent of partners were women, the female lawyers were likely to believe that "feminine" traits were strongly devalued, and that masculinity was equated with success. As one female attorney put it, "Let's face it: this is a man's environment, and it's sort of Jock City, especially at my firm." Women in firms where female lawyers were better represented in positions of power had a stronger desire for and higher expectations of promotion (Ely 1995:619).

Characteristics of a Bureaucracy

A *bureaucracy* is a component of formal organization that uses rules and hierarchical ranking to achieve efficiency. Rows of desks staffed by seemingly faceless people, endless lines and forms, impossibly complex language, and frustrating encounters with red tape—all these unpleasant images have combined to make *bureaucracy* a dirty word and an easy target in political campaigns. As a

result, few people want to identify their occupation as "bureaucrat," despite the fact that all of us perform various bureaucratic tasks. Elements of bureaucracy enter into almost every occupation in an industrial society.

Max Weber ([1913–1922] 1947) first directed researchers to the significance of bureaucratic structure. In an important sociological advance, Weber emphasized the basic similarity of structure and process found in the otherwise dissimilar enterprises of religion, government, education, and business. Weber saw bureaucracy as a form of organization quite different from the family-run business. For analytical purposes, he developed an ideal

◀ p. 11 — type of bureaucracy that would reflect the most characteristic aspects of all human organizations. By *ideal type* Weber meant a construct or model for evaluating specific cases. In actuality, perfect bureaucracies do not exist; no real-world organization corresponds exactly to Weber's ideal type.

Weber proposed that whether the purpose is to run a church, a corporation, or an army, the ideal bureaucracy displays five basic characteristics. A discussion of those characteristics, as well as the dysfunctions of a bureau-

◀ p. 14 — cracy, follows. Table 6-2 (opposite) summarizes the discussion.

1. Division of labor. Specialized experts perform specific tasks. In your college bureaucracy, the admissions officer does not do the job of registrar; the guidance counselor doesn't see to the maintenance of buildings. By working at a specific task, people are more likely to become highly skilled and carry out a job with maximum efficiency. This emphasis on specialization is so basic a part of our lives that we may not realize that it is a fairly recent development in Western culture.

The downside of division of labor is that the fragmentation of work into smaller and smaller tasks can divide workers and remove any connection they might feel to the overall objective of the bureaucracy. In *The Communist Manifesto* (written in 1848), Karl Marx and Friedrich Engels charged that the capitalist system reduces workers to a mere "appendage of the machine" (Feuer 1989). Such a work arrangement, they wrote, produces extreme *alienation*—a condition of estrangement or dissociation from the surrounding society. According to both Marx and conflict theorists, restricting workers to very small tasks also weakens their job security, since new employees can be easily trained to replace them.

Although division of labor has certainly enhanced the performance of many complex bureaucracies, in some cases it can lead to *trained incapacity;* that is, workers become so specialized that they develop blind spots and fail to notice obvious problems. Even worse, they may not care about what is happening in the next

summingUP

| | | Negative Consequence | |
Characteristic	Positive Consequence	For the Individual	For the Organization
Division of labor	Produces efficiency in a large-scale corporation	Produces trained incapacity	Produces a narrow perspective
Hierarchy of authority	Clarifies who is in command	Deprives employees of a voice in decision making	Permits concealment of mistakes
Written rules and regulations	Let workers know what is expected of them	Stifle initiative and imagination	Lead to goal displacement
Impersonality	Reduces bias	Contributes to feelings of alienation	Discourages loyalty to company
Employment based on technical qualifications	Discourages favoritism and reduces petty rivalries	Discourages ambition to improve oneself elsewhere	Fosters Peter principle

Table 6-2   Characteristics of a Bureaucracy

department. Some observers believe that such developments have caused workers in the United States to become less productive on the job.

In some cases, the bureaucratic division of labor can have tragic results. In the wake of the coordinated attacks on the World Trade Center and the Pentagon on September 11, 2001, Americans wondered aloud how the FBI and CIA could have failed to detect the terrorists' elaborately planned operation. The problem, in part, turned out to be the division of labor between the FBI, which focuses on domestic matters, and the CIA, which operates overseas. Officials at these intelligence-gathering organizations, both of which are huge bureaucracies, are well known for jealously guarding information from one another. Subsequent investigations revealed that they knew about Osama bin Laden and his al-Qaeda terrorist network in the early 1990s. Unfortunately, five federal agencies—the CIA, FBI, National Security Agency, Defense Intelligence Agency, and National Reconnaissance Office—failed to share their leads on the network. Although the hijacking of the four commercial airliners used in the massive attacks may not have been preventable, the bureaucratic division of labor definitely hindered efforts to defend against terrorism and actually undermined U.S. national security.

2. Hierarchy of authority. Bureaucracies follow the principle of hierarchy; that is, each position is under the supervision of a higher authority. A president heads a college bureaucracy; he or she selects members of the administration, who in turn hire their own staff. In the

Roman Catholic Church, the pope is the supreme authority; under him are cardinals, bishops, and so forth.

3. Written rules and regulations. What if your sociology professor gave your classmate an A for having such a friendly smile? You might think that wasn't fair, that it was against the rules.

Rules and regulations, as we all know, are an important characteristic of bureaucracies. Ideally, through such procedures, a bureaucracy ensures uniform performance of every task. Thus your classmate cannot receive an A for a nice smile, because the rules guarantee that all students will receive essentially the same treatment.

Through written rules and regulations, bureaucracies generally offer employees clear standards for an adequate (or exceptional) performance. In addition, procedures provide a valuable sense of continuity in a bureaucracy. Individual workers will come and go, but the structure and past records of the organization give it a life of its own that outlives the services of any one bureaucrat.

Of course, rules and regulations can overshadow the larger goals of an organization to the point that they become dysfunctional. What if a hospital emergency room physician failed to treat a seriously injured person because he or she had no valid proof of U.S. citizenship? If blindly applied, rules no longer serve as a means to achieving an objective, but instead become important (and perhaps too important) in their own right. Robert Merton (1968) used the term *goal displacement* to refer to overzealous conformity to official regulations.

Let's Discuss Have working students discuss the hierarchical structure of their companies in terms of power and lines of communication. What informal chains of command exist?
Let's Discuss Analyze your college's hierarchical structure in terms of power, lines of communication, and informal chains of command.

Key Person Robert Merton
Let's Discuss Have students provide examples of *trained incapacity* and *goal displacement* at their college or places of work.

4. Impersonality. Max Weber wrote that in a bureaucracy, work is carried out *sine ira et studio,* "without hatred or passion." Bureaucratic norms dictate that officials perform their duties without giving personal consideration to people as individuals. Although this norm is intended to guarantee equal treatment for each person, it also contributes to the often cold and uncaring feeling associated with modern organizations. We typically think of big government and big business when we think of impersonal bureaucracies. In some cases, the impersonality that is associated with a bureaucracy can have tragic results, as the case study of the *Columbia* space shuttle disaster on pages 141–142 shows. More frequently, it produces frustration and disaffection. Today, even small firms screen callers with electronic menus.

5. Employment based on technical qualifications. Within the ideal bureaucracy, hiring is based on technical qualifications rather than on favoritism, and performance is measured against specific standards. Written personnel policies dictate who gets promoted, and people often have a right to appeal if they believe that particular rules have been violated. Such procedures protect bureaucrats against arbitrary dismissal, provide a measure of security, and encourage loyalty to the organization.

In this sense, the "impersonal" bureaucracy can be considered an improvement over nonbureaucratic organizations. College faculty members, for example, are ideally hired and promoted according to their professional qualifications, including degrees earned and research published, rather than because of whom they know. Once they are granted tenure, their jobs are protected against the whims of a president or dean.

Although any bureaucracy ideally will value technical and professional competence, personnel decisions do not always follow this ideal pattern. Dysfunctions within bureaucracy have become well publicized, particularly because of the work of Laurence J. Peter. According to the *Peter principle,* every employee within a hierarchy tends to rise to his or her level of incompetence (Peter and Hull 1969). This hypothesis, which has not been directly or systematically tested, reflects a possible dysfunctional outcome of advancement on the basis of merit. Talented people receive promotion after promotion, until, sadly, some of them finally achieve positions that they cannot handle with their usual competence (Blau and Meyer 1987).

The five characteristics of bureaucracy, developed by Max Weber more than 80 years ago, describe an ideal type rather than precisely defining an actual bureaucracy. Not every formal organization will possess all five of Weber's characteristics. In fact, wide variation exists among actual bureaucratic organizations.

Bureaucratization as a Process

Have you ever had to speak to 10 or 12 individuals in a corporation or government agency just to find out which official has jurisdiction over a particular problem? Ever been transferred from one department to another until you finally hung up in disgust? Sociologists have used the term **bureaucratization** to refer to the process by which a group, organization, or social movement becomes increasingly bureaucratic.

Normally, we think of bureaucratization in terms of large organizations. But bureaucratization also takes place within small-group settings. Sociologist Jennifer Bickman Mendez (1998) studied domestic houseworkers employed in central California by a nationwide franchise. She found that housekeeping tasks were minutely defined, to the point that employees had to follow 22 written steps for cleaning a bathroom. Complaints and special requests went not to the workers, but to an office-based manager.

Oligarchy: Rule by a Few

Conflict theorists have examined the bureaucratization of social movements. The German sociologist Robert Michels (1915) studied socialist parties and labor unions in Europe before World War I and found that such organizations were becoming increasingly bureaucratic. The emerging leaders of these organizations—even some of the most radical—had a vested interest in clinging to power. If they lost their leadership posts, they would have to return to full-time work as manual laborers.

Through his research, Michels originated the idea of the *iron law of oligarchy,* which describes how even a democratic organization will eventually develop into a bureaucracy ruled by a few (called an oligarchy). Why do oligarchies emerge? People who achieve leadership roles usually have the skills, knowledge, or charismatic appeal (as Weber noted) to direct, if not control, others. Michels argued that the rank and file of a movement or organization look to leaders for direction and thereby reinforce the process of rule by a few. In addition, members of an oligarchy are strongly motivated to maintain their leadership roles, privileges, and power.

Michels's insights continue to be relevant today. Contemporary labor unions in the United States and Western Europe bear little resemblance to those organized spontaneously by exploited workers. Conflict theorists have pointed to the longevity of union leaders, who are not always responsive to the needs and demands of the membership, and seem more concerned with maintaining their own positions and power. (The social policy section at the end of this chapter focuses on the status of labor unions today.)

Sociology in the Global Community

6-2 AMWAY THE CHINESE WAY

Amway began in 1959, when two young men in Michigan began a person-to-person merchandise marketing system. Today, more than 3.6 million individuals in 80 countries distribute Amway cosmetics, food supplements, and home care products. Distributors will often gather friends and neighbors at a party designed to persuade them to buy the company's products, or better yet, to become distributors themselves. Distributors' ability to line up customers who become distributors themselves, and in turn line up still more customers and distributors, has been critical to the company's success. Thus, primary group ties have become the tool of a large, bureaucratic business organization.

Amway entered China in 1995, followed closely by rival direct sellers like Avon and Mary Kay. China's more than 1 billion residents, combined with its growing acceptance of capitalistic business practices, made it an attractive market for these Western merchandisers. And Amway's emphasis on building sales networks through relatives and friends seemed a perfect fit for Chinese culture, in which personal recommendations are considered especially persuasive. After

just two years, Amway had 80,000 distributors in China. But in 1998, the Chinese government suddenly outlawed Amway's operation, accusing the company of fostering "weird cults, triads, superstitious groups, and hooliganism."

What had happened? Apparently Amway's success had produced a host of copycats, some of them con artists peddling dubious merchandise. Government officials complained, too, about the pro-

> To do business globally, Amway has successfully reinvented its business model.

motional hoopla at Amway's sales meetings, which featured songs, sloganeering, and other Western-style activities designed to encourage organizational bonding. To the Chinese, these innocuous activities suggested a cult-like fervor.

Facing the loss of their Chinese investments, Amway and other direct marketers asked the U.S. trade representative to intervene. After intense pressure, the Chinese government agreed to a partial

reversal of the ban on direct selling. Under new regulations issued in 1998, Amway, Avon, and Mary Kay are permitted to sell their products through conventional retail outlets. They can also employ salespeople to go door to door, but those salespeople cannot receive any income from signing up new distributors. Despite this handicap, China is now Amway's fourth largest market worldwide. In 2002 sales were four times what they were before the government ban on direct selling. To do business globally, Amway has successfully reinvented its business model.

Let's Discuss

1. Have you ever bought merchandise from a direct seller like Amway, perhaps at a party? If so, who introduced you to the organization? Were you comfortable with its merchandising methods? Explain.

2. Can you think of another kind of bureaucratic organization, other than a business, that exploits its members' ties to primary groups in order to grow? Analyze the organization and its operating methods from a sociological point of view.

Sources: Amway 1999, 2003; L. Chang 2003; C. Hill 2003; Wonacott 2001.

Bureaucracy and Organizational Culture

How does bureaucratization affect the average individual who works in an organization? The early theorists of formal organizations tended to neglect this question. Max Weber, for example, focused on the management personnel within bureaucracies but had little to say about workers in industry or clerks in government agencies.

According to the ***classical theory*** of formal organizations, also known as the ***scientific management approach,*** workers are motivated almost entirely by economic rewards. This theory stresses that only the physical constraints on workers limit their productivity. Therefore, workers may be treated as a resource, much like the

machines that began to replace them in the 20th century. Under the scientific management approach, management attempts to achieve maximum work efficiency through scientific planning, established performance standards, and careful supervision of workers and production. Planning involves efficiency studies but not studies of workers' attitudes or job satisfaction.

Not until workers organized unions—and forced management to recognize that they were not objects—did theorists of formal organizations begin to revise the classical approach. Along with management and administrators, social scientists became aware that informal groups of workers have an important impact on organizations (Perrow 1986). An alternative way of considering bureaucratic dynamics, the ***human relations approach,***

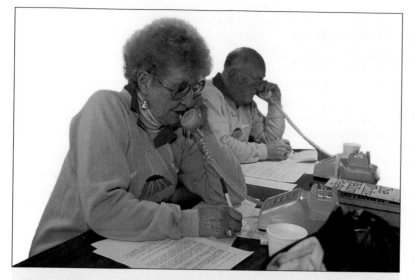

The AARP is a voluntary association of people ages 50 and older, both retired and working, that advocates for the needs of older Americans. A huge organization, it has been instrumental in maintaining Social Security benefits to retirees. Here AARP volunteers staff a phone bank in an effort to get out the vote in Des Moines, Iowa.

menter's expectations. The major focus of the Hawthorne studies, however, was the role of social factors in workers' productivity. One aspect of the research concerned the switchboard-bank wiring room, where 14 men were making parts of switches for telephone equipment. The researchers discovered that these men were producing far below their physical capabilities. The discovery was especially surprising because the men would have earned more money if they had produced more parts.

What accounted for such an unexpected restriction of output? The men feared that if they produced switch parts at a faster rate, their pay rate might be reduced, or some of them might lose their jobs. As a result, this group of workers had established their own (unofficial) norm for a proper day's work and created informal rules and sanctions to enforce it. Yet management was unaware of these practices and actually believed that the men were working as hard as they could (Roethlisberger and Dickson 1939).

Today, research on formal organizations is following new avenues. First, the proportion of women and minority group members in high-level management positions is still much lower than might be expected, given their numbers in the labor force. Researchers are now beginning to look at the impact this gender and racial/ethnic imbalance may have on managerial judgment, both formal and informal. Second, a company's power structure is only partly reflected in its formal organizational charts. In practice, core groups tend to emerge to dominate the decision-making process. Very large corporations—say, a General Electric or a Procter & Gamble—may have hundreds of interlocking core groups, each of which plays a key role in its division or region (Kleiner 2003).

emphasizes the role of people, communication, and participation in a bureaucracy. This type of analysis reflects the interest of interactionist theorists in small-group behavior. Unlike planning under the scientific management approach, planning based on the human relations perspective focuses on workers' feelings, frustrations, and emotional need for job satisfaction.

The gradual move away from a sole focus on the physical aspects of getting the job done—and toward the concerns and needs of workers—led advocates of the human relations approach to stress the less formal aspects of bureaucratic structure. Informal groups and social networks within organizations develop partly as a result of people's ability to create more direct forms of communication than under the formal structure. Charles Page (1946) used the term *bureaucracy's other face* to refer to the unofficial activities and interactions that are such a basic part of daily organizational life. As Box 6-2 (page 139) shows, some direct merchandising companies have capitalized on the existence of informal groups and social networks to build their organizations—though in China they have run into trouble with the formal government bureaucracy.

A series of classic studies illustrates the value of the human relations approach. The Hawthorne studies alerted sociologists to the fact that research subjects may p. 39 alter their behavior to match the experi-

Voluntary Associations

In the mid-19th century, the French writer Alexis de Tocqueville noted that people in the United States are "forever forming associations." By 2003, there were more than 444,000 voluntary associations in a U.S. national database. ***Voluntary associations*** are organizations established on the basis of common interest, whose members volunteer or even pay to participate. The Girl Scouts of America, the American Jewish Congress, the Kiwanis Club, and the League of Women Voters are all considered voluntary associations; so, too, are the American Associa-

Theory Interactionists emphasize the importance of informal relations within formal organizations (bureaucracy's "other face").
Methods The Hawthorne studies are an example of an experiment (introduced in Chapter 2).

Web Resource Encourage students to listen to the audio clip in the student center of the Online Learning Center **(www.mhhe.com/ schaefer6).** Richard Schaefer, the author of the text, discusses what happens when formal organizations combine, consolidate, or merge.

tion of Aardvark Aficionados, the Cats on Stamps Study Group, the Mikes of America, the New York Corset Club, and the William Shatner Fellowship (Gale Group 2003).

The categories of "formal organization" and "voluntary association" are not mutually exclusive. Large voluntary associations such as the Lions Club and the Masons have structures similar to those of profit-making corporations. At the same time, certain formal organizations, such as the Young Men's Christian Association (YMCA) and the Peace Corps, have philanthropic and educational goals usually found in voluntary associations. The Democratic Party and the United Farm Workers union are considered examples of voluntary associations. Even though membership in a political party or union can be a condition of employment and therefore not genuinely voluntary, political parties and labor unions are usually included in discussions of voluntary associations.

Participation in voluntary associations is not unique to the United States. This textbook's author attended a carnival in London featuring bungee-jumping, at which participants were expected to jump from a height of 180 feet. Skeptics were given assurances of the attraction's safety by being told that the proprietor belonged to a voluntary association: the British Elastic Rope Sports Association. An analysis of 15 industrial nations, including the United States, showed that active memberships in voluntary associations typically increased during the 1980s and 1990s. Only relatively inactive memberships in religious organizations and labor unions have showed a decline. On the whole, then, voluntary associations are fairly healthy (Baer et al. 2000).

Voluntary associations can provide support to people in preindustrial societies. During the post–World War II period, migration from rural areas of Africa to the cities was accompanied by a growth in voluntary associations, including trade unions, occupational societies, and mutual aid organizations developed along old tribal lines. As people moved from the *Gemeinschaft* of the countryside to the p. 118 *Gesellschaft* of the city, these voluntary associations provided immigrants with substitutes for the extended groups of kinfolk in their villages (Little 1988).

Voluntary associations in the United States are largely segregated by gender. Half of them are exclusively female, and one-fifth are all-male. Because the exclusively male associations tend to be larger and more heterogeneous, in terms of the background of members, all-male associations hold more promise for networking than all-female groups. Although participation varies across the population of the United States, most people belong to at least one voluntary association (see Figure 6-1), while more than one-fourth maintain three or more memberships.

The importance of voluntary associations—and especially of their unpaid workers (or volunteers)—is increasingly being recognized. Traditionally, society has devalued unpaid work, even though the skill levels, experience, and training demands are often comparable with those of wage labor. Viewed from a conflict perspective, the critical difference has been that women perform a substantial amount of volunteer work. Feminists and conflict theorists agree that like the unpaid child care and household labor of homemakers, the effort of volunteers has too often been ignored by scholars—and awarded too little respect by the larger society—because it is viewed as "women's work." Failure to recognize women's volunteerism obscures a critical contribution women make to a society's social structure (Daniels 1987, 1988).

FIGURE 6-1

Membership in Voluntary Associations in the United States

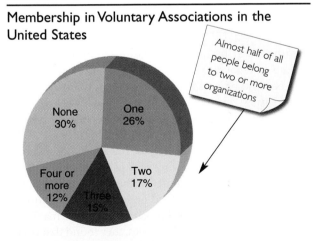

Almost half of all people belong to two or more organizations

Source: J. Davis and Smith 2001:347.

Think About It
How many voluntary associations do you belong to? What functions do they serve?

◼ CASE STUDY: BUREAUCRACY AND THE SPACE SHUTTLE *COLUMBIA*

In February 2003, the space shuttle *Columbia* disintegrated as it reentered the earth's atmosphere. Seven astronauts died in the accident, which was blamed at first on a piece of foam weighing less than two pounds that had struck the spacecraft's wing during liftoff. But by August, the *Columbia* Accident Investigation Board (2003) had identified a second cause: NASA's bureaucratic organizational culture.

The board's blistering report cited NASA's emphasis on bureaucratic rules and regulations at the expense of astronauts' safety. Though engineers had voiced safety concerns over the years, especially after the shuttle *Challenger*'s explosion in 1986, their memos rarely reached the top of NASA's hierarchy, where costs and scheduling were considered paramount. In fact, the organization's culture discouraged the expression of safety concerns (Vaughan 1996, 1999). When engineers tried to obtain special images of the *Columbia*'s wing during its last flight, so they could check for damage, managers denied their request. Aside from cost concerns, officials may have been unwilling to admit that something had gone wrong. In general, hierarchical organizations tend to encourage the concealment of mistakes.

Another part of the problem was that over the years, foam debris had fallen during liftoff in about 10 percent of NASA's launches, without disastrous results. Officials had come to expect that a shower of debris might occur, and to speak of it as an "acceptable risk." Rather than treating it as a safety issue, they labeled it a maintenance problem. Thus, bureaucratic rules and regulations that were meant to highlight such a serious risk may have had the unintended consequence of obscuring it.

Investigators had condemned the "acceptable risk" attitude following the *Challenger* explosion in 1986, but NASA's organizational culture had not changed. In a bureaucratic organization, bringing about real change can be extremely difficult. Thus, in the wake of the second disaster, members of the *Columbia* Accident Investigation Board (2003:13) predicted, "The changes we recommend will be difficult to accomplish—and will be internally resisted."

In a hangar at the Kennedy Space Center, members of the team charged with reconstructing the space shuttle *Columbia* examine what remains of the front landing gear. Damage to the ship's protective tiles, which might have been prevented by stricter adherence to safety standards, caused the disaster. Historically, insufficient attention to safety hazards has been a problem at NASA, a huge government bureaucracy with an emphasis on cost and efficiency.

THE CHANGING WORKPLACE

Weber's work on bureaucracy and Michels's thinking on oligarchy are still applicable to the organizational structure and culture of the workplace. But today's factories and offices are undergoing rapid, profound changes unanticipated a century or more ago. Besides the far-reaching impact of technological advances such as computerization, workers must cope with organizational restructuring. This section will detail the dramatic changes evident in today's workplace.

Organizational Restructuring

To some extent, individual businesses, community organizations, and government agencies are always changing, if only because of personnel turnover. But since the late 20th century, formal organizations have been experimenting with new ways of getting the job done, some of which have significantly altered the workplace.

Collective decision making, or the active involvement of employee problem-solving groups in corporate management, first became popular in the United States in the 1980s. Management gurus had noted the dazzling success of Japanese automobile and consumer products manufacturers. In studying these companies, they found that problem-solving groups were one key to success. At first, such groups concentrated on small problems at specific points in the production line. But today, these groups often cross departmental and divisional boundaries to attack problems rooted in the bureaucratic division of labor. Thus, they require significant adjustment by employees long used to working in the bureaucracy (Ouchi 1981).

Another innovation in the workplace, called *minimal hierarchy,* replaces the traditional bureaucratic hierarchy of authority with a flatter organizational structure. Minimal hierarchy offers workers greater access to those in authority, giving them an opportunity to voice concerns that might not be heard in a traditional bureaucracy. This new organizational structure is thought to minimize the potential for costly and dangerous bureaucratic oversights. Clearly, hierarchical barriers to the expression of workers' concerns contributed to the *Challenger* and *Columbia* disasters.

Finally, organizational *work teams* have become increasingly common, even in smaller organizations. There are two types of work team. *Project teams* address ongoing issues, such as safety or compliance with the Americans with Disabilities Act. *Task forces* pursue nonrecurring issues, such as a major building renovation. In both cases, team members are released to some degree from their regular duties in order to contribute to the organization-wide effort (W. Scott 2003).

The common purpose of work teams, minimal hierarchy, and collective decision making is to empower workers. For that reason, these new organizational structures can be exciting for the employees who participate in them. But these innovations rarely touch the vast numbers of workers who perform routine jobs in factories and office buildings. The 22 million part-time workers and 1 million full-time workers who earn the minimum wage or less know little about organizational restructuring (Bureau of Labor Statistics 2004b).

Telecommuting

Increasingly, in many industrial countries, workers are turning into telecommuters. *Telecommuters* are employees who work full-time or part-time at home rather than in an outside office, and who are linked to their supervisors and colleagues through computer terminals, phones, and fax machines (see Chapter 16). One national survey showed that next to on-site day care, most office workers want virtual offices that allow them to work off-site. Not surprisingly, the number of telecommuters increased

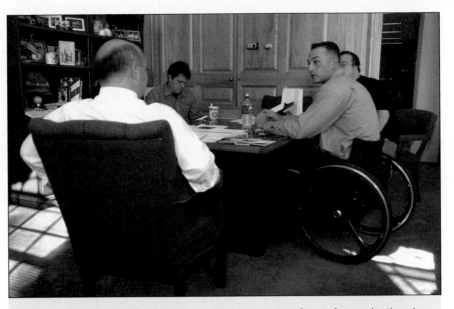

Work teams are becoming an increasingly common form of organizational restructuring. Members of this team are brainstorming ways to address the needs of the disabled.

from 8.5 million in 1995 to 28 million in 2001 (Donald B. Davis and Polonko 2001).

What are the social implications of this shift toward the virtual office? From an interactionist perspective, the workplace is a major source of friendships; restricting face-to-face social opportunities could destroy the trust that is created by "handshake agreements." Thus, telecommuting may move society further along the continuum from *Gemeinschaft* to *Gesellschaft.* On a more positive note, telecommuting may be the first social change that pulls fathers and mothers back into the home rather than pushing them out. The trend, if it continues, should also increase autonomy and job satisfaction for many employees (Castells 2001; DiMaggio et al. 2001).

Use Your Sociological Imagination www.mhhe.com/schaefer6

If your first full-time job after college involved telecommuting, what do you think would be the advantages and disadvantages of working out of a home office? Do you think you would be satisfied as a telecommuter? Why or why not?

Electronic Communication

Electronic communication in the workplace has generated some heat lately. On the one hand, e-mailing is a convenient way to push messages around, especially with the CC (carbon copy) button. It's democratic, too:

lower-status employees are more likely to participate in e-mail discussion than in face-to-face communications, giving organizations the benefit of their experience and views (DiMaggio et al. 2001).

But e-mail doesn't convey body language, which in face-to-face communication can soften insensitive phrasing and make unpleasant messages (such as a reprimand) easier to take. It also leaves a permanent record, which can be a problem if messages are written thoughtlessly. In

an antitrust case that the federal government brought against Microsoft in 1998, the prosecutors used as evidence e-mail sent to and from Microsoft's CEO Bill Gates. Finally, as will be discussed in detail in Chapter 16, companies can monitor e-mail as a means of "watching" their employees. Dartmouth professor Paul Argenti advises those who use e-mail, "Think before you write. The most important thing to know is what not to write" (Gwynne and Dickerson 1997:90).

SOCIAL POLICY and ORGANIZATIONS — The State of the Unions

The Issue

How many people do you know who belong to a labor union? Chances are you can name a lot fewer people than someone could 50 years ago. In 1954, unions represented 39 percent of workers in the private sector of the U.S. economy; in 2002 they represented only 13 percent. What has happened to diminish the importance of organized labor today? Have unions outlived their usefulness in a rapidly changing global economy that is dominated by the service sector (AFL-CIO 2001; Bureau of Labor Statistics 2004a)?

Members of the South Florida Carpenters union join together to support one another and demonstrate their strength. In recent decades economic change has eliminated many union jobs, reducing unions' membership and weakening their bargaining power.

The Setting

Labor unions consist of organized workers who share either the same skill (as in electronics) or the same employer (as in the case of postal employees). Unions began to emerge during the Industrial Revolution in England, in the 1700s. Groups of workers banded together to extract concessions from employers (e.g., safer working conditions, a shorter workweek), as well as to protect their positions. They frequently tried to protect their jobs by limiting entry to their occupation based on gender, race, ethnicity, citizenship, age, and sometimes rather arbitrary measures of skill levels. Today we see less of this protection of special interests, but individual labor unions are still the target of charges of discrimination, as are employers.

The power of labor unions varies widely from country to country. In some countries, such as Britain and Mexico, unions play a key role in the foundation of governments. In others, such as Japan and Korea, their role in politics is very limited, and even their ability to influence the private sector is relatively weak. Unions in the United States can sometimes have a significant influence on employers and elected officials, but their effect varies dramatically by type of industry and even region of the country (see Figure 6-2) (M. Wallerstein and Western 2000).

Classroom Tip When discussing the state of the unions, ask students how they feel about unions. Are any students, or their parents, members of a labor union?

Global View Role of unions in Britain, Mexico, Japan, and Korea
Policy Pointer Note that unions have historically had a great deal of political influence in the United States.

FIGURE 6-2

Union Membership in the United States

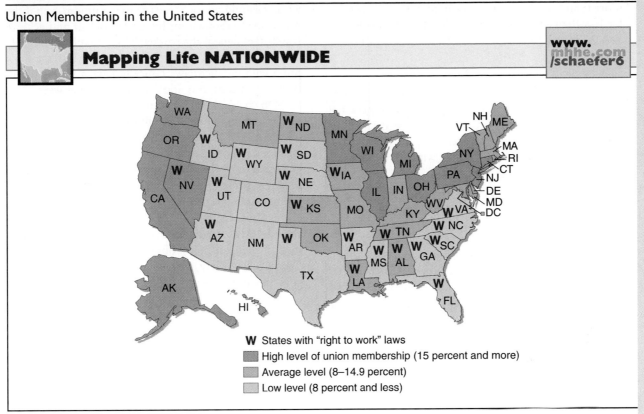

Mapping Life NATIONWIDE

www.mhhe.com/schaefer6

W States with "right to work" laws

- ▓ High level of union membership (15 percent and more)
- ▒ Average level (8–14.9 percent)
- ░ Low level (8 percent and less)

Note: Right to work means that legally, workers cannot be required to join a union or pay union dues.

Source: Developed by the author based on data from Bureau of Labor Statistics 2003; National Right to Work Legal Defense Foundation 2004.

Think About It

What is the relationship between the level of union membership in a given state and the presence of right-to-work laws?

Few people today would dispute the fact that union membership is declining. What accounts for this decline? Among the reasons offered are the following:

1. Changes in the type of industry. Manufacturing jobs, the traditional heart of the labor union, have declined, giving way to postindustrial service jobs.

2. Growth in part-time jobs. Between 1982 and 1998 the number of temporary jobs in the United States rose 577 percent, while total employment increased only 41 percent. Only in 2000 did laws governing collective bargaining allow temporary workers to join a union.

3. The legal system. The United States has not made it particularly easy for unions to organize and bargain, and some government measures have made it more difficult. A dramatic example was President Ronald Reagan's firing of 11,000 air traffic controllers in 1981, when their union threatened they would walk off the job while seeking a new contract.

4. Globalization. The threat of jobs leaving the country has undercut the ability of union leaders to organize workers at home. Some say that labor union demands for wage increases and additional benefits have themselves spurred the exodus of jobs to developing nations, where wages are significantly lower and unions are virtually nonexistent.

5. Employer offensives. Increasingly hostile employers have taken court action to block unions' efforts to represent their members.

6. Union rigidity and bureaucratization. Labor has been slow to embrace women, minorities, and immigrants. Furthermore, in some unions the election of leaders seems to dominate the organization's activity (AFL-CIO 2001; Clawson and Clawson 1999; Cornfield 1991; S. Greenhouse 2000a; *Migration News* 2001).

Perhaps as a result of all these factors, confidence in unions is low. Only 1 out of 10 persons in the United

States expresses a great deal of confidence in unions—more than for major corporations and government, but far less than for educational and religious institutions and the military (Bureau of the Census 2001a:249).

Sociological Insights

Both Marxists and functionalists would view unions as a logical response to the emergence of impersonal, large-scale, formal, and often alienating organizations. This view certainly characterized the growth of unions in major manufacturing industries with a sharp division of labor. However, as manufacturing has declined, unions have had to look elsewhere for growth (Cornfield 1991).

Today labor unions in the United States and Europe bear little resemblance to those early unions organized spontaneously by exploited workers. In line with the oligarchic model developed by Robert Michels (see page 138), unions have become increasingly bureaucratized under a self-serving leadership. Conflict theorists would point out that the longer union leaders are in office, the less responsive they are to the needs and demands of the rank and file, and the more concerned they are with maintaining their own positions and power. Yet research shows that under certain circumstances, union leadership can change significantly. Smaller unions are vulnerable to changes in leadership, as are unions whose membership shifts in composition from predominantly White to African American or Latino (Cornfield 1991; Form 1992).

Many union employees encounter role conflict. For example, they may agree to provide a needed service and then organize a strike to withhold it. Role conflict is especially apparent in the so-called helping occupa- p. 109 tions: teaching, social work, nursing, law enforcement, and firefighting. These workers may feel torn between carrying out their professional responsibilities and enduring working conditions they find unacceptable (Aronowitz and Di Fazio 1994).

Policy Initiatives

U.S. law grants workers the right to self-organize via unions. But the United States is unique among industrial democracies in allowing employers to actively oppose their employees' decision to organize (Comstock and Fox 1994).

A major barrier to union growth exists in the 21 states that have so-called right-to-work laws (see Figure 6-2, page 145). In these states, workers cannot be *required* to join or pay dues or fees to a union. The very term *right to work* reflects the anti-union view that a worker should not be forced to join a union, even if the union may negotiate on his or her behalf and achieve results that benefit the worker. This situation is unlikely to change. That is, right-to-work states will remain so; those without such laws typically have a strong union tradition or restrict union activities in other ways.

On the national level, union power is waning. In the security buildup that followed the terrorist attacks of September 11, 2001, federal officials created many new jobs and reorganized existing agencies into the Department of Homeland Security. In doing so, they specified that some 170,000 workers would not have collective bargaining rights, and that 56,000 newly federalized airport security screeners could not be unionized. Though these stipulations may or may not stand up to legal challenges, many observers see them as another sign of increasingly anti-union sentiment at all levels of government (Borosage 2003).

Yet some unions, such as the Hotel and Restaurant Employees Union, have been managing to grow by pursuing new strategies. In their recruitment efforts, these unions stress the desirability of diversity, regardless of workers' race or citizenship status. Organizers supplement their efforts to improve members' wages and working conditions by developing alliances within the broader community and by addressing social issues such as immigration (Voss and Fantasia 2004).

In Europe, labor unions tend to play a major role in political elections. (The ruling party in Great Britain, in fact, is called the Labour Party.) Although unions play a lesser political role in the United States, they have recently faced attacks for their large financial contributions to political campaigns. Debate over campaign finance reform in Congress in 2001 raised the question of whether labor unions should be able to use dues to support a particular candidate or promote a position via "issue ads" that favor one party, usually the Democrats.

Let's Discuss

1. What unions are represented on your college campus? Have you been aware of union activity? Has there been any opposition to the unions on the part of the administration?
2. Do you think nurses should be allowed to strike? Why or why not? What about teachers or police officers?
3. If a union is working on behalf of all the workers of a company, should all the employees be required to join the union and pay dues? Why or why not?

Theory Marxist and functionalist views of unions
Classroom Tip Remind students that *role conflict* is discussed in Chapter 5.

GETTING INVOLVED —————————————————————————

To get involved in the debate over the labor movement, visit this text's Online Learning Center, which offers links to relevant websites. Check out the Social Policy section on the Online Learning Center as well; it provides survey data on U.S. public opinion regarding this issue.

CHAPTER RESOURCES

Summary

Social interaction among human beings is necessary to the transmission of culture and the survival of every society. This chapter examines the social behavior of *groups, formal organizations,* and *voluntary associations.*

1. When we find ourselves identifying closely with a group, it is probably a *primary group.* A *secondary group* is more formal and impersonal.
2. People tend to see the world in terms of *in-groups* and *out-groups,* a perception often fostered by the very groups to which they belong.
3. *Reference groups* set and enforce standards of conduct and serve as a source of comparison for people's evaluations of themselves and others.
4. Interactionist researchers have noted distinct and predictable processes in the functioning of *small groups.* The simplest group is a *dyad,* composed of two members. *Triads* and larger groups increase the ways of interacting and allow for *coalitions* to form.
5. As societies have become more complex, large *formal organizations* have become more powerful and pervasive.

6. Max Weber argued that in its ideal form, every *bureaucracy* has five basic characteristics: division of labor, hierarchical authority, written rules and regulations, impersonality, and employment based on technical qualifications.
7. Bureaucracy can be understood both as a process and as a matter of degree. Thus, an organization may be more or less bureaucratic than other organizations.
8. When leaders of an organization build up their power, the result can be *oligarchy* (rule by a few).
9. The informal structure of an organization can undermine and redefine official bureaucratic policies.
10. People join *voluntary associations* for a variety of purposes—for example, to share in joint activities or to get help with personal problems.
11. Organizational restructuring and new technologies have transformed the workplace through innovations such as *collective decision making* and *telecommuting.*
12. *Labor unions* are on the decline because of major shifts in the economy.

Critical Thinking Questions

1. Think about how behavior is shaped by reference groups. What different reference groups have shaped your outlook and your goals at different periods in your life? How have they done so?
2. Are primary groups, secondary groups, in-groups, out-groups, and reference groups likely to be found within a formal organization? What functions do these groups serve for a formal organization? What dysfunctions might occur as a result of their presence?

3. Max Weber identified five basic characteristics of bureaucracy. Select an actual organization familiar to you (for example, your college, a workplace, or a religious institution or civic association you belong to) and apply Weber's five characteristics to that organization. To what degree does it correspond to Weber's ideal type of bureaucracy?

Key Terms

Alienation   A condition of estrangement or dissociation from the surrounding society. (page 136)

Bureaucracy   A component of formal organization that uses rules and hierarchical ranking to achieve efficiency. (136)

Bureaucratization   The process by which a group, organization, or social movement becomes increasingly bureaucratic. (138)

Classical theory   An approach to the study of formal organizations that views workers as being motivated almost entirely by economic rewards. (139)

Coalition   A temporary or permanent alliance geared toward a common goal. (135)

Dyad   A two-member group. (134)

Focus group   A group of 10 to 15 people assembled by a researcher to discuss a predetermined topic, guided by a moderator. (133)

Formal organization   A group designed for a special purpose and structured for maximum efficiency. (135)

Goal displacement   Overzealous conformity to official regulations of a bureaucracy. (137)

Group   Any number of people with similar norms, values, and expectations who interact with one another on a regular basis. (130)

Human relations approach   An approach to the study of formal organizations that emphasizes the role of people, communication, and participation in a bureaucracy and tends to focus on the informal structure of the organization. (139)

Ideal type   A construct or model for evaluating specific cases. (136)

In-group   Any group or category to which people feel they belong. (132)

Iron law of oligarchy   A principle of organizational life under which even democratic organizations will eventually develop into bureaucracies ruled by a few individuals. (138)

Labor union   Organized workers who share either the same skill or the same employer. (144)

McDonaldization   The process by which the principles of the fast-food restaurant are coming to dominate more and more sectors of American society as well as of the rest of the world. (130)

Out-group   A group or category to which people feel they do not belong. (132)

Peter principle   A principle of organizational life according to which every employee within a hierarchy tends to rise to his or her level of incompetence. (138)

Primary group   A small group characterized by intimate, face-to-face association and cooperation. (130)

Reference group   Any group that individuals use as a standard for evaluating themselves and their own behavior. (133)

Scientific management approach   Another name for the classical theory of formal organizations. (139)

Secondary group   A formal, impersonal group in which there is little social intimacy or mutual understanding. (131)

Small group   A group small enough for all members to interact simultaneously—that is, to talk with one another or at least be well acquainted. (134)

Telecommuter   An employee who works full-time or part-time at home rather than in an outside office, and who is linked to supervisor and colleagues through computer terminals, phone, and fax machines. (143)

Trained incapacity   The tendency of workers in a bureaucracy to become so specialized that they develop blind spots and fail to notice obvious problems. (136)

Triad   A three-member group. (134)

Voluntary association   An organization established on the basis of common interest, whose members volunteer or even pay to participate. (140)

TECHNOLOGY RESOURCES

Internet Connection

Note: While all the URLs listed were current as of the printing of this book, these sites often change. Please check our website (www.mhhe.com/schaefer6) for updates, hyperlinks, and exercises related to these sites.

1. The website of the Illinois Labor History Society (**www.kentlaw.edu/ilhs/index.html**) contains extensive information on labor unions, strikes, and disasters past and present in that state. Visit the site for an overview of labor history in Illinois.

2. The Advocacy Project (**www.advocacynet.org**) is a nonprofit organization that provides support to other organizations working for peace and human rights. Examine this site to better understand the often complex interrelationships among organizations.

Online Learning Center with PowerWeb

The focus of this chapter has been groups and organizations. Everyone is a member of an "in-group," and most people have been members of an "out-group." Visit the student center in the Online Learning Center (**www.mhhe.com/schaefer6**) and link to the first Interactive Activity, called "In-Groups, Out-Groups, and Un-words." In this activity, you will be asked to discuss your experiences as a member of an in-group and an out-group. You also can do the word scramble, which contains key words or phrases from this chapter.

Reel Society Interactive Movie CD-ROM 2.0

Reel Society 2.0 can be used to spark discussion about the following topic from this chapter:

- Understanding Groups

chapter

THE MASS MEDIA

7

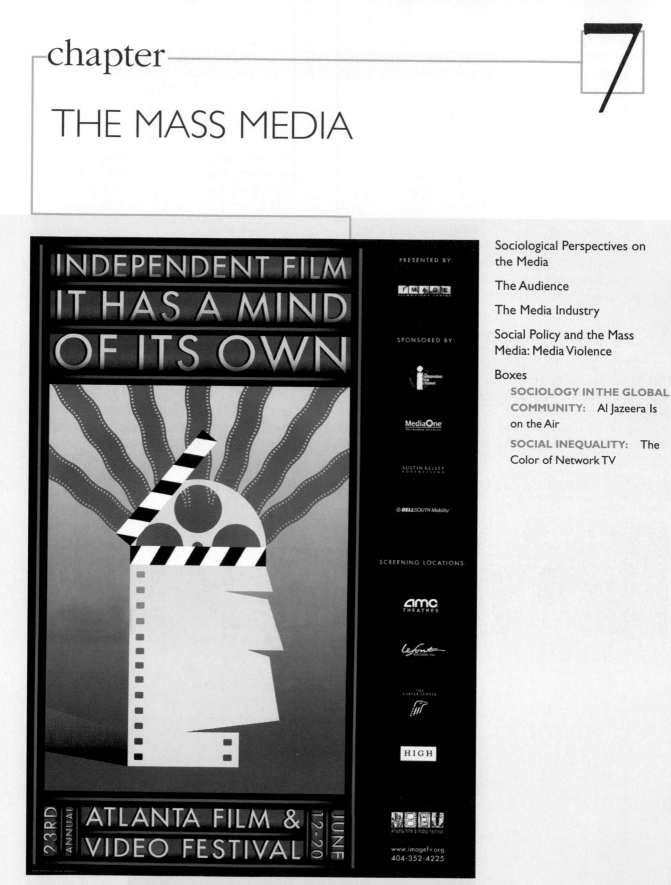

INDEPENDENT FILM
IT HAS A MIND
OF ITS OWN

PRESENTED BY:

IMAGE
FILM/VIDEO CENTER

SPONSORED BY:

Independent Film Channel

MediaOne
This is Broadband. This is the way.

AUSTIN KELLEY
ADVERTISING

BELLSOUTH Mobility

SCREENING LOCATIONS:

AMC
THEATRES

lefont
THEATRES INC.

THE
CARTER CENTER

HIGH

IMAGE
Atlanta Film & Video Festival

www.imagefv.org
404-352-4225

23RD ANNUAL ATLANTA FILM &
VIDEO FESTIVAL JUNE 12-20

Movies have long been an influential form of mass media, both reflecting and creating social mores. Sociologists are interested in the influence of other forms of mass media as well, including television, newspapers, magazines, and online content.

Sociological Perspectives on the Media

The Audience

The Media Industry

Social Policy and the Mass Media: Media Violence

Boxes
  SOCIOLOGY IN THE GLOBAL COMMUNITY: Al Jazeera Is on the Air
  SOCIAL INEQUALITY: The Color of Network TV

Everywhere, the media flow defies national boundaries. This is one of its obvious, but at the same time amazing, features. A global torrent is not, of course, the master metaphor to which we have grown accustomed. We're more accustomed to Marshall McLuhan's *global village*. Those who resort to this metaphor casually often forget that if the world is a global village, some live in mansions on the hill, others in huts. Some dispatch images and sounds around town at the touch of a button; others collect them at the touch of *their* buttons. Yet McLuhan's image reveals an indispensable half-truth. If there is a village, it speaks American. It wears jeans, drinks Coke, eats at the golden arches, walks on swooshed shoes, plays electric guitars, recognizes Mickey Mouse, James Dean, E.T., Bart Simpson, R2-D2, and Pamela Anderson. . . .

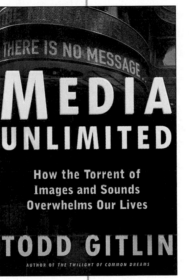

THERE IS NO MESSAGE

MEDIA UNLIMITED

How the Torrent of Images and Sounds Overwhelms Our Lives

TODD GITLIN

AUTHOR OF *THE TWILIGHT OF COMMON DREAMS*

Entertainment is one of America's top exports. In 1999, in fact, film, television, music, radio, advertising, print publishing, and computer software together were the top export, almost $80 billion worth, and while software alone accounted for $50 billion of the total, some of that category also qualifies as entertainment—video games and pornography, for example. Hardly anyone is exempt from the force of American images and sounds. . . . American popular culture is the nemesis that hundreds of millions—perhaps billions—of people love, and love to hate. The antagonism and the dependency are inseparable, for the media flood—essentially American in its origin, but virtually unlimited in its reach—represents, like it or not, a common imagination.

How shall we understand the Hong Kong T-shirt that says "I Feel Coke"? Or the little Japanese girl who asks an American visitor in all innocence, "Is there really a Disneyland in America?" (She knows the one in Tokyo.) Or the experience of a German television reporter sent to Siberia to film indigenous life, who after flying out of Moscow and then traveling for days by boat, bus, and jeep, arrives near the Arctic Sea where a tribe of Tungusians live known to ethnologists for their bear-skin rituals. In the community store sits a grandfather with his grandchild on his knee. Grandfather is dressed in traditional Tungusian clothing. Grandson has on his head a reversed baseball cap. . . .

The misleadingly easy answer to the question of how American images and sounds became omnipresent is: American imperialism. But the images are not even faintly force-fed by American corporate, political, or military power. The empire strikes from inside the spectator as well as from outside. This is a conundrum that deserves to be approached with respect if we are to grasp the fact that Mickey Mouse and Coke are everywhere recognized and often enough enjoyed. In the peculiar unification at work throughout the world, there is surely a supply side, but there is not only a supply side. Some things are true even if multinational corporations claim so: there is demand. (*Gitlin 2002:176–179*) ■ 🕸

Additional information about this excerpt can be found on the Online Learning Center at **www.mhhe.com/schaefer6.**

In his book *Media Unlimited: How the Torrent of Images and Sounds Overwhelms Our Lives,* sociologist Todd Gitlin focuses on what he calls "the obvious but hard-to-grasp truth . . . that living with the media is today one of the main things Americans and many other human beings do" (2002:5). We immerse ourselves in images and sounds. And as he noted in the opening excerpt, media entertainment is one of the top exports from the United States to the rest of the world.

By *mass media* sociologists refer to the print and electronic means of communication that carry messages to widespread audiences. Print media include newspapers, magazines, and books; electronic media include radio, television, motion pictures, and the Internet. Advertising, which falls into both categories, is also a form of mass media.

The pervasiveness of the mass media is obvious. Consider a few examples. TV dinners were invented to accommodate the millions of "couch potatoes" who can't bear to miss their favorite television programs. Today *screen time* encompasses not just television viewing but also playing video games and surfing the Internet. Candidates for political office rely on their media consultants to project a winning image both in print and in the electronic media. World leaders use all forms of media for political advantage, whether to gain territory or to bid on hosting the Olympics. In parts of Africa and Asia, AIDS education projects owe much of their success to media campaigns. During the 2003 war in Iraq, both the British and U.S. governments allowed journalists to be embedded with front-line troops as a means of "telling their story."

Few aspects of society are as central as the mass media. Through the media we expand our understanding of people and events beyond what we experience in person. The media inform us about different cultures and lifestyles and about the latest forms of technology. For sociologists, the key questions are how the mass media affect our social institutions and how they influence our social behavior.

Why are the media so influential? Who benefits from media influence and why? How do we maintain cultural and ethical standards in the face of negative media images? In this chapter we will consider the ways sociology helps us to answer these questions. First we will look at how proponents of the various sociological perspectives view the media. Then we will examine just who makes up the media's audience, as well as how the media operate, especially in their global reach. In the social policy section we will consider whether the violence shown in the media breeds violent behavior in the audience. ■

SOCIOLOGICAL PERSPECTIVES ON THE MEDIA

Over the past decade, new technologies have made new forms of mass media available to U.S. households. These new technologies have changed people's viewing and listening habits. As Figure 7-1 (opposite) shows, over the past decade, the time Americans spend watching cable TV has almost doubled, while the time they spend watching broadcast TV has declined. Americans now spend less time listening to recorded music than they did just a few years ago; they spend more time surfing the Internet. These patterns tend to vary by age group, however. Among 18- to 34-year-olds, for example, time spent watching prime-time TV—both broadcast and cable—declined by 19 percent between 1991 and 2003, as video games and the Internet took up more of their media time. What do these changes in people's viewing and listening habits signify? In the following sections we'll examine the impact of the mass media and changes in their usage patterns from the three major sociological perspectives (E. Nelson 2004).

Functionalist View

One obvious function of the mass media is to entertain. Except for clearly stated news or educational programming, we often think the explicit purpose of the mass media is to occupy our leisure time—from newspaper comics and crossword puzzles to the latest music releases on the Internet. While that is true, the media have other important functions. They also socialize us, enforce social norms, confer status, promote consumption, and keep us informed about our social environment. An important dysfunction of the mass media is that they may act as a narcotic, desensitizing us to distressing events (Lazarsfeld and Merton 1948; C. Wright 1986).

Agent of Socialization

The media increase social cohesion by presenting a common, more or less standardized view of culture through mass communication. Sociologist Robert Park (1922) studied how newspapers helped immigrants to the United States adjust to their environment by changing their customary habits and teaching them the opinions of people in their new home country. Unquestionably, the mass media play a significant role in providing a collective experience for members of a society. Think about how the mass media bring together members of a community or even a nation by broadcasting im-
◄ p. 95 portant events and ceremonies (such as inaugurations, press conferences, parades, state funerals, and the Olympics) and by covering disasters.

Which media outlets did people turn to in the aftermath of the September 11, 2001 tragedy? Television and the telephone were the primary means by which people in the United States bonded. But the Internet also played a prominent role. About half of all Internet users—more than 53 million people—received some kind of news about the attacks online. Nearly three-fourths of Internet users communicated via e-mail to show their patriotism, discuss events with their families, or reconnect with old friends. More than a third of Internet users read or posted material in online forums. In the first 30 days alone, the Library of Congress collected from one Internet site more than half a million pages having to do with the terrorist attacks. As a Library director noted, "The Internet has become for many the public commons, a place where they can come together and talk" (D. L. Miller and Darlington 2002; Mirapaul 2001:E2; Rainie 2001).

The socializing effects of the media can promote religious as well as patriotic exchanges, uniting believers from around the world. In 1995, a Hindu-language program in India showed worshipers making a symbolic offering of milk to the elephant-headed god Gamesh. Within days the global reach of cable television had broadcast the event to the world. Soon worshipers in England, Canada, and the United States

FIGURE 7-1

Number of Hours per Week Spent with Media, 1997–2008 (Projected)

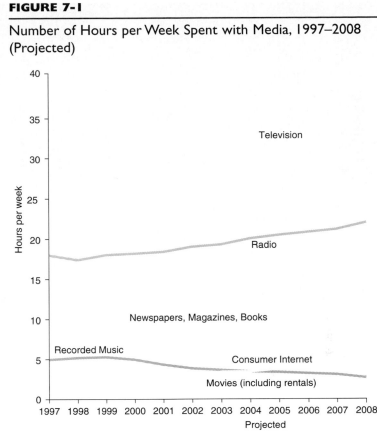

Notes: Ages varied by survey subject. Radio includes satellite radio. Recorded music excludes MP3s and Internet downloading (included in Internet).

Source: Veronis Suhler Stevenson LLC 2003:166–167 for 1997; 2004:184–185 for all other data.

were making similar sacrifices to the Hindu god (Rajagopal 2001).

Precisely because the socializing effects of the media are so powerful, media programming can easily become controversial. In January 1989, the public television network in India began broadcasting a program based on the Hindu epic *Ramayan*. The decision violated a long-standing policy to avoid religious partisanship in programming for the deeply divided country, where strife between Hindus and Muslims is common. As a result of the airing, Hindu nationalism blossomed and Indian politics became more polarized (Rajagopal 2001).

There are other problems inherent in the socialization function of the mass media. For instance, many people worry about the effect of using television as a babysitter or the impact of violent programming on viewer behavior (see the social policy section). Some people adopt a blame-the-media mentality, holding the media accountable for anything that goes wrong, especially with young people.

Key Person Robert Park
Contemporary Culture Newspapers help immigrants adjust to the United States.
Let's Discuss Ask students which media outlets they turned to in the aftermath of the September 11, 2001 tragedy.

Policy Pointer The social policy section of this chapter discusses the impact of violent programming on viewer behavior.

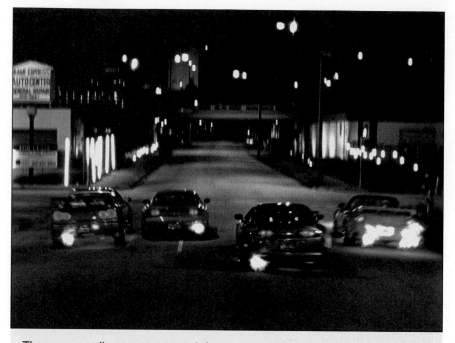

The mass media can serve to reinforce proper behavior, but they can also endorse illicit activity, such as drag racing, as shown in this scene from the movie *2 Fast 2 Furious*.

In 1997, a federal law required television networks to provide one free minute for every minute the government bought for a public service announcement with an antidrug message. The networks subsequently persuaded the government to drop the free minutes in exchange for aggressive antidrug messages embedded in their programs, such as *ER* and *The Practice*. Some people objected, saying that the networks were evading their legal responsibility in using the public airwaves, but criticism really mounted when word got out that a government agency was screening scripts in advance and even working on the story lines. Many critics felt the practice could open the way for the government to plant messages in the media on other topics as well, such as abortion or gun control (Albiniak 2000).

Enforcer of Social Norms

The media often reaffirm proper behavior by showing what happens to people who act in a way that violates societal expectations. These messages are conveyed when the bad guy gets clobbered in cartoons or is thrown in jail on *Law and Order*. Yet the media also sometimes glorify disapproved behavior, whether it is physical violence, disrespect to a teacher, or drug use.

The media play a critical role in shaping people's perceptions about the risks of substance use. Increases in substance use among youths during the 1990s were linked to a decline in warnings and antidrug messages from the media; the proliferation of pro-use messages from the entertainment industry; and high levels of tobacco and alcohol product advertising and promotion. Media content analysis shows that in the 200 most popular movie rentals of 1996 and 1997, alcohol use appeared in 93 percent, tobacco use in 89 percent, and illicit drug use in 22 percent, with marijuana and cocaine use shown most often. An analysis of the 1,000 most popular songs during the same period showed that 27 percent referred to either alcohol or illicit drugs. In 1999, 44 percent of entertainment programs aired by the four major television networks portrayed tobacco use in at least one episode (Ericson 2001; D. F. Roberts et al. 1999).

Conferral of Status

The mass media confer status on people, organizations, and public issues. Whether it is an issue such as the homeless or a celebrity such as Cameron Diaz, they single out one from thousands of other similarly placed issues or people to become significant. Table 7-1 (opposite) shows how often certain public figures are prominently featured on weekly magazine covers. Obviously, *People* magazine alone was not responsible for making Princess Diana into a worldwide figure, but collectively, all the media outlets created a notoriety that Princess Victoria of Sweden, for one, did not enjoy.

Another way the media confer celebrity status on individuals is by publishing information about the frequency of Internet searches. Some newspapers and websites carry regularly updated lists of the most heavily researched individuals and topics of the week. The means may have changed since the first issue of *Time* magazine hit the stands in 1923, but the media still confer status—often electronically.

Promotion of Consumption

Twenty-thousand commercials a year—that is the number the average child in the United States watches on television, according to the American Academy of Pediatrics.

Table 7-1		Status Conferred by Magazines			

Rank/Person	Number of Times on Cover of *Time*	Rank/Person	Number of Times on Cover of *People*	Rank/Person	Number of Times on Cover of *Ebony*
1. Richard Nixon	59	1. Princess Diana	52	1. Muhammad Ali	15
2. Ronald Reagan	36	2. Julia Roberts	29	1. Janet Jackson	15
3. Bill Clinton	30	3. Michael Jackson	15	1. Michael Jackson	15
4. Dwight Eisenhower	22	3. Elizabeth Taylor	15	4. Whitney Houston	14
4. Lyndon Johnson	22	5. Jennifer Anniston	14	5. Halle Berry	12
4. Gerald Ford	22	6. John F. Kennedy, Jr.	13	6. Diahann Carroll	11
7. George W. Bush	21	6. Madonna	13	6. Lena Horne	11
8. Jesus Christ	19	6. Jackie Onassis	13	6. Sidney Poitier	11
8. George H. W. Bush	19	6. Cher	13	9. Bill Cosby	10
8. Jimmy Carter	19	10. John Travolta	9	10. Sammy Davis, Jr.	9
		10. Princess Caroline (Monaco)	9		

Source: Author's content analysis of primary cover subject for full run of the periodicals beginning with *Time*, March 3, 1923; *People*, March 4, 1974; and *Ebony*, November 1945 through July 1, 2004. In case of ties, the more recent cover person is listed first.

Think About It
How do these magazines differ in the types of people they feature on their covers? Which type do you think enjoys the most status? Why?

Young people cannot escape commercial messages. They show up on high school scoreboards, at rock concerts, and as banners on webpages. They are even embedded in motion pictures (remember Reese's Pieces in 1982's *E.T.: The Extra-Terrestrial*?). Such *product placement* is nothing new. In 1951 *The African Queen* prominently displayed Gordon's Gin aboard the boat carrying Katherine Hepburn and Humphrey Bogart. But commercial promotion has become far more common today. Moreover, advertisers are attempting to develop brand or logo loyalty at younger and younger ages (Lasn 2003; Quart 2003).

Media advertising has several clear functions: it supports the economy, provides information about products, and underwrites the cost of media. In some cases, adver-

tising becomes part of the entertainment industry. A national survey showed that 14 percent of those who viewed the 2003 Super Bowl did so *only* for the commercials. Yet related to these functions are dysfunctions. Media advertising contributes to a consumer culture that creates "needs" and raises unrealistic expectations of what is required to be happy or satisfied. Moreover, because the media depend heavily on advertising revenue, advertisers can influence media content (FAIR 2001; Horovitz 2003).

Surveillance of the Social Environment

The *surveillance function* refers to the collection and distribution of information concerning events in the social environment. The media collect and distribute facts about

Product placement ("brand casting") is an increasingly important source of revenue for motion pictures. This scene from *Austin Powers: The Spy Who Shagged Me* (1999) doubles as a commercial for Starbucks.

a variety of events, including stock market movements and tomorrow's weather, as well as election campaigns, theater openings, sports events, and international conflicts.

But what exactly constitutes a fact? Who gets portrayed as a hero, a villain, a patriot, a terrorist? The media generally define these characters for the audience using a definition that reflects the values and orientation of their own decision makers.

> **Use Your Sociological Imagination** www.mhhe.com/schaefer6
>
> You are a news junkie. Where do you gather your facts or information—from newspapers, tabloids, magazines, TV newscasts, or the Internet? Why did you choose that medium?

Dysfunction: The Narcotizing Effect

In addition to the functions just noted, the media perform a *dysfunction*. Sociologists Paul Lazarsfeld and Robert Merton (1948) created the term *narcotizing dysfunction* to refer to the phenomenon in which the media provide such massive amounts of information that the audience becomes numb and fails to act on the information, regardless of how compelling the issue. Interested citizens may take in the information but may make no decision or take no action.

Consider how often the media initiate a great outpouring of philanthropic support in response to natural disasters or family crises. But then what happens? Research shows that as time passes, viewer fatigue sets in. The mass media audience becomes numb, desensitized to the suffering, and may even conclude that a solution to the crisis has been found (Moeller 1999).

The media's narcotizing dysfunction was identified over 50 years ago, when just a few homes had television—well before the advent of electronic media. At that time, the dysfunction went largely unnoticed, but today commentators often point out the ill effects of addiction to television or the Internet, especially among young people. Street crime, explicit sex, war, and HIV/AIDS apparently are such overwhelming topics that some in the audience may feel they have acted—or at the very least learned all they need to know—simply by watching the news.

Conflict View

Conflict theorists emphasize that the media reflect and even exacerbate many of the divisions in our society and world, including those based on gender, race, ethnicity, and social class. They point in particular to the media's ability to decide what gets transmitted through a process called gatekeeping.

Gatekeeping

What story appears on page 1 of the morning newspaper? Which motion picture plays on three screens rather than one at the local cineplex? What picture isn't released at all? Behind these decisions are powerful figures—publishers, editors, and other media moguls.

The mass media constitute a form of big business in which profits are generally more important than the quality of the programming. Within the mass media, a relatively small number of people control what eventually reaches the audience through a process known as *gatekeeping*. This term describes how material must travel through a series of checkpoints (or gates) before reaching the public. Thus, a select few decide what images to bring to a broad audience. In many countries the government plays a gatekeeping role. A study done for the World Bank found that in 97 countries, 60 percent of the top five TV stations and 72 percent of the largest radio stations are government-owned (World Bank 2001:183).

Gatekeeping prevails in all kinds of media. As sociologist C. Wright Mills ([1956] 2000b) observed, the real power of the media is that they can control what is being presented. In the recording industry, gatekeepers may reject a popular local band because it competes with a group already on their label. Even if the band gets recorded, radio programmers may reject it because it does not fit their station's "sound." Television programmers may keep a pilot for a new TV series off the air because gatekeepers believe it does not appeal to the target audience (which is sometimes determined by advertising sponsors). Similar decisions are made by gatekeepers in the publishing industry (R. Hanson 2005).

Gatekeeping is not as dominant in at least one form of mass media, the Internet. You can send virtually any message to an electronic bulletin board, create a webpage or blog (weblog) to advance any argument, including one that insists the earth is flat. The Internet is a means of quickly disseminating information (or misinformation) without going through any significant gatekeeping process.

Nevertheless, the Internet is not totally without restrictions. In many nations laws regulate content on issues such as gambling, pornography, and even politics. Popular Internet service providers will terminate accounts for offensive behavior. After the terrorist attack in 2001, eBay did not allow people to sell parts of the World Trade Center via its online auction. A World Bank study found that 17 countries place significant controls on Internet content. For example, China routinely blocks search engines like Google and AltaVista from accessing the names of groups or individuals who are critical of the government (Ni 2002; World Bank 2001:187).

Critics of the content of mass media argue that the gatekeeping process reflects a desire to maximize profits. Why else, they argue, would movie star Julia Roberts make the cover of *Time* magazine rather than Palestinian leader Yasir Arafat? Later in this chapter we will consider the role that corporate structure plays in the content and delivery of mass media. Another criticism of the gatekeeping process is that the content that makes it through the gates does not reflect the diversity of the audience.

Dominant Ideology: Constructing Reality

Conflict theorists argue that the mass media maintain the privileges of certain groups. Moreover, while protecting their own interests, powerful groups may limit the media's representation of others. The term ***dominant ideology*** describes

p. 68

a set of cultural beliefs and practices that help to maintain powerful social, economic, and political interests. The media transmit messages that virtually define what we regard as the real world, even though those images frequently vary from what the larger society experiences.

Mass media decision makers are overwhelmingly White, male, and wealthy. It may come as no surprise,

Television programmers have capitalized on the appeal of reality shows (such as *Survivor*) to young viewers. *The Bachelor* is one show that made it through the gatekeeping process. In the series, a bevy of young women seek the attention of a bachelor, who week by week eliminates candidates until only one is left.

then, that the media tend to ignore the lives and ambitions of subordinate groups, among them working-class people, African Americans, Hispanics, gays and lesbians, people with disabilities, overweight people, and older people. Worse, media content may create false images or stereotypes of these groups that become accepted as accurate portrayals of reality. ***Stereotypes*** are unreliable generalizations about all members of a group that do not recognize individual differences within the group.

Television content is a prime example of this tendency to ignore reality. How many overweight TV characters can you name? Even though in real life one out of every four women is obese (30 or more pounds over a healthy body weight), only 3 out of 100 TV characters are portrayed as obese. Heavyset television characters have fewer romances, talk less about sex, eat more often, and are more often the object of ridicule than their thin counterparts (Hellmich 2001).

Minority groups are often stereotyped in TV shows. Almost all the leading roles are cast as White, even in urban-based programs such as *Friends,* which is situated in ethnically diverse New York City. Asian Americans and Native Americans rarely appear in general roles; Blacks tend to be featured mainly in crime-based dramas; Latinos are virtually ignored. Box 7-1 (page 158) discusses the distorted picture of society presented on prime-time television programs.

Before the 2002 fall television season, executives of the major TV networks once again renewed their commitment to diversify both who is on television and who is responsible for the content. It proved to be a tough commitment to keep. Only 2 of the 26 new fall series had even one minority person in a leading role. Furthermore, a Directors Guild of America report indicated that of all 826 episodes of the 40 most popular series in 2001, 80 percent were directed by White males and 11 percent by White females. That left only 9 percent directed by Blacks, Latinos, or Asian Americans, who collectively account for more than 25 percent of television viewers.

When minority actors do appear on television and in other forms of media, their roles tend to reinforce the stereotypes associated with their ethnic or racial groups. Gifted Hispanic character actress Lupe Ontiverus has played the role of maid 150 times. Latinas are now featured as maids on *Will and Grace* (Rosario), *Dharma and Greg* (Celia), and even the animated *King of the Hill* (Lupino), to name just three television shows.

In the 1999–2000 season, the leading characters in all 26 new prime-time series were White; network gatekeepers seemed surprised by the news. Producers, writers, executives, and advertisers blamed one another for the oversight. Television pro-

> Marc Hirshfeld, an NBC executive, claims some White producers have told him they don't know how to write for Black characters.

gramming was dictated by advertisers, a former executive claimed; if advertisers said they wanted blatantly biased programming, the networks would provide it. Jery Isenberg, chairman of the Caucus for Producers, Writers & Directors, blamed the networks, saying that writers would produce a series about three-headed Martians if the networks told them to.

Beyond these excuses, real reasons can be found for the departure from the diversity exhibited in past shows and seasons. In recent years, the rise of more networks, cable TV, and the Internet has fragmented the broadcast entertainment market, siphoning viewers away from the general-audience sitcoms and dramas of the past. Both the UPN and WB networks produce situation comedies and even full evenings geared toward African American audiences. With the proliferation of cable channels such as Black Entertainment Television (BET) and the Spanish-language Telemundo and Univision, as well as websites that cater to every imaginable taste, there no longer seems to be a need for broadly popular series such as *The Cosby Show*, the tone and content of which appealed to Whites as well as Blacks in a way the newer series do not. The result of these sweeping technological changes has been a sharp divergence in viewer preferences.

Sources: Bielby and Bielby 2002; Braxton and Calvo 2001; Children Now 2002; Directors Guild of America 2002; A. Hoffman 1997; M. Navarro 2002; Poniewozik 2001; Soriano 2001; D. B. Wood 2000.

Another concern about the media, from the conflict perspective, is that television distorts the political process. Until the U.S. campaign finance system is truly reformed and the law enforced, the candidates with the most money (often backed by powerful lobbying groups) will be able to buy exposure to voters and saturate the air with commercials attacking their opponents.

When media executives seek the assistance of the powerful, the influence of the dominant ideology can be especially explicit. Filmmakers who want their motion pictures about the military to look authentic often seek assistance from Pentagon consultants. But sometimes the government refuses to cooperate, because the military is portrayed in an undesirable way. In some cases, the film industry actually *changes* the movie in order to gain access to military bases and military equipment (Robb 2001; Suid 2002).

For example, when Paramount Pictures sought military assistance for *The Sum of All Fears,* the 2002 film about nuclear terrorism, writers had to make some changes to the screenplay. The original script called for a U.S. carrier to be destroyed by cruise missiles, but Pentagon officials were troubled by the idea that an aircraft carrier could be portrayed as so vulnerable. The screenplay was revised so that the carrier remained intact while some flight operations were destroyed. This kind of exploitation in the making of war movies is mutual: the producers get authentic military hardware and technical assistance at minimal cost, while the military gets to project a positive image that attracts recruits and boosts defense budgets (Seelye 2002).

Dominant Ideology: Whose Culture?

Globalization extends the dominating reach of the U.S. media into the rest of the world. Movies produced in the United States account for 65 percent of the global box office. Magazines as diverse as *Cosmopolitan* and *Reader's*

A rare sight on television: In UPN's *The Parkers,* almost all leading roles are played by African Americans.

inner-city neighborhoods and tend to write and produce stories about people like themselves. Marc Hirshfeld, an NBC executive, claims some White producers have told him they don't know how to write for Black characters. Stephen Bochco, producer of *NYPD Blue,* is a rare exception. His series *City of Angels* featured a mostly non-White cast, like the people Bochco grew up with in an inner-city neighborhood. The series ran for 23 episodes before being canceled in 2000.

In the long run, media observers believe, the major networks will need to integrate the ranks of gatekeepers before they achieve true diversity in programming. Adonis Hoffman, director of the Corporate Policy Institute, has urged network executives to throw open their studios and boardrooms to minorities. Hoffman thinks such a move would empower Black writers and producers to present a true-to-life portrait of African Americans. There are some signs of agreement from the networks. According to Doug Herzog, president of Fox Enter-

Meanwhile, the mainstream network executives, producers, and writers remain overwhelmingly White. Most of them live far from ethnically and racially diverse

tainment, real progress means incorporating diversity from within.

Why should it matter that minority groups aren't visible on major network television, if they are well represented on other channels such as UPN, WB, BET, and Univision? The problem is that Whites as well as minorities see a distorted picture of their society every time they turn on network TV. In Hoffman's words, "African Americans, Latinos and Asians, while portrayed as such, are not merely walk-ons in our society—they are woven into the fabric of what has made this country great" (A. Hoffman 1997:M6).

Let's Discuss

1. Do you watch network TV? If so, how well do you think it represents the diversity of U.S. society?
2. Have you seen a movie or TV show recently that portrayed members of a minority group in a sensitive and realistic way—as real people rather than as stereotypes or token walk-ons? If so, describe the show.

Digest sell two issues abroad for every one they sell in the

pp. 58–59 United States. These cultural exports undermine the distinctive traditions and art forms of other societies and encourage their cultural and economic dependence on the United States. Countries throughout the world decry U.S. exports, from films to language to Bart Simpson. In the opening excerpt for this chapter, Todd Gitlin describes American popular culture as something that "people love, and love to hate" (2001:177; Farhi and Rosenfeld 1998).

The U.S. media have come to rely on the overseas market. In fact, many motion pictures have brought in more revenue abroad than at home. Through early 2004, for example, *Titanic* had earned a record-breaking $600 million in the United States and another $1.2 billion at overseas box offices. No wonder that Hollywood tailors its trailers to resonate with the local culture. For example, in the United States *Moulin Rouge* trailers showed Nicole

Kidman locked in a swirling, sensual dance with her lover. In Japan, where tragic love is considered noble and honorable, the trailers featured Kidman taking her final breath with a heartsick young man sobbing at her side. Some Hollywood movies, however, are so insensitive they cannot benefit from any amount of impression management. The James Bond movie *Die Another Day* featured a crazed North Korean colonel, a character even many *South* Koreans found unacceptable; a small boycott greeted its 2003 release in Seoul (Brooke 2003a; Eller and Muñoz 2002).

We risk being ethnocentric if we overstress U.S. dominance. For example *Survivor, Who Wants to Be a Millionaire,* and *Iron Chef*—immensely popular TV programs in the United States—came from Sweden, Britain, and Japan, respectively. The steamy telenovelas of Mexico and other Spanish-speaking countries owe very little of their origin to the soap operas on U.S. television. Unlike motion pictures, television is gradually moving away from

Global View Media cultural exports encourage economic and cultural dependence on the United States.

Global View Some immensely popular TV shows in the United States actually originated in Sweden, Britain, and Japan.
Theory Cultural domination determines which ideas and facts get transmitted.

Making movies about the military or governmental agencies is a lot easier when filmmakers can count on the government's cooperation. *Apollo 13,* which glorified NASA's space program, easily won government approval. But *G. I. Jane,* featuring Demi Moore as a Navy SEAL who bucks high-ranking military and government officials, was not approved.

U.S. domination and is more likely to be locally produced. By 2003, all the top 50 British TV shows were locally produced. *The West Wing* may appear on television in London, but it is shown late at night. Even U.S.-owned TV ventures such as Disney, MTV, and CNN have dramatically increased their locally produced programming overseas. The introduction of MTV Romania and MTV Indonesia in 2003 brought the number of local versions of the popular music channel to 38 (*The Economist* 2003b).

Nations that feel a loss of identity may try to defend against the cultural invasion from foreign countries, especially the economically dominant United States. Many developing nations have long argued for a greatly improved two-way flow of news and information between industrialized nations and developing nations. They

complain that news from the Third World is scant, and what news there is reflects unfavorably on the developing nations. For example, what do you know about South America? Most people in the United States will mention the two topics that dominate the news from countries south of the border: revolution and drugs. Most know little else about the continent. To remedy this imbalance, a resolution to monitor the news and content that cross the borders of developing nations was passed by the United Nations Educational, Scientific, and Cultural Organization (UNESCO) in the 1980s. The United States disagreed with the proposal, which became one factor in the U.S. decision to withdraw from UNESCO in the mid-1980s (Dominick 2002).

Feminist View

Feminists share the view of conflict theorists that the mass media stereotype and misrepresent social reality. According to this view, the media powerfully influence how we look at men and women, and their images of the sexes communicate unrealistic, stereotypical, and limiting perceptions. Here are three problems feminists believe arise from media coverage (J. T. Wood 1994):

1. Women are underrepresented, which suggests that men are the cultural standard and women are insignificant.

2. Men and women are portrayed in ways that reflect and perpetuate stereotypical views of gender. Women, for example, are often shown in peril, needing to be rescued by a male—rarely the reverse.

3. Depictions of male–female relationships emphasize traditional sex roles and normalize violence against women.

Educators and social scientists have long noted the stereotypical portrayal of women and men in the mass media. Women are often shown as being shallow and obsessed with beauty. They are more likely than men to be shown unclothed, in danger, or even physically victimized. Responding to the way advertising and the entertainment media objectify and even dehumanize women, Jean Kilbourne argues in her writings and film documentaries that "we [women] are the product." Feminist Vivian Gornick asserts that the portrayal of women in the media reflects "innumerable small murders of the mind and spirit [that] take place daily" (1979:ix; Cortese 1999; Goffman 1979; Kilbourne 2000a, 2000b).

A continuing, troubling issue for feminists and society as a whole is pornography. Feminists tend to be very supportive of freedom of expression and self-determination, qualities that are denied to women more often than

Let's Discuss Do students believe that the news and cultural content that cross the borders of developing nations should be monitored?

Theory Feminist analysis of mass media
Gender Media project unrealistic images of the sexes; stereotypes.
Gender Women underrepresented in the media
Gender Traditional sex roles emphasized; violence against women normalized
Key Persons Jean Kilbourne, Vivian Gornick

to men. Yet pornography presents women as sex objects and seems to make it acceptable to view women that way. But concerns about pornography are not limited to this type of objectification and imagery, as well as their implicit endorsement of violence against women. The industry that creates risqué adult images for videos, DVDs, and the Internet is largely unregulated, putting its own performers at risk. A 2002 health survey of triple-X, as the porn industry refers to itself, found that 40 percent of actors and actresses had at least one sexually transmitted disease, compared to 0.1 percent of the general population. The short career span of these women (and men) is usually about 18 months, but the profits for the industry are continuous and enormous (Huffstutter 2003).

Colorful U.S. and British flags provided a striking "photo op" for President George Bush and British Prime Minister Tony Blair in April 2003, when they were drumming up support for the war in Iraq.

As in other areas of sociology, feminist researchers caution against assuming that what holds true for men's media behavior is true for everyone. Researchers, for example, have studied the different ways that women and men approach the Internet. According to 2001 data, women's use of the Internet is increasing faster than men's. Women are also more likely to regard e-mail as a means of maintaining contact with friends and relatives. Their use of websites differs in fundamental ways from the way men use them. Women are more likely to seek health and religious information, research new jobs, and play games online. Men are more likely to use the web to get news, shop, seek financial information, and participate in online auctions (Fox and Rainie 2001; Rainie and Kohut 2000).

Interactionist View

Interactionists are especially interested in shared understandings of everyday behavior. These scholars examine the media on the micro level to see how they shape day-to-day social behavior. Researchers increasingly point to the mass media as the source of major daily activity; some argue that television serves virtually as a primary group for many individuals who share TV viewing. Other mass-media participation is not necessarily face to face. For example, we usually listen to the radio or read the newspaper as a solitary activity, although it is possible to share it with others (Cerulo et al. 1992; Waite 2000).

Friendship networks can emerge from shared viewing habits or from recollection of a cherished television series from the past. Family members and friends often gather for parties centered on the broadcasting of popular events such as the Super Bowl or the Academy Awards. And as we've noted, television often serves as a babysitter or playmate for children and even infants.

The power of the mass media encourages political leaders and entertainment figures to carefully manipulate their images through public appearances called photo opportunities, or photo ops. By embracing symbols (posing with celebrities or in front of prestigious landmarks), participants in these staged events attempt to convey self-serving definitions of social reality (M. Weinstein and Weinstein 2002).

The rise of the Internet has facilitated new forms of communication and social interaction. Grandparents can now keep up with their grandchildren via e-mail. Gay and lesbian teens have online resources for support and information. People can even find their lifetime partners through computer dating services.

Early users of the Internet established a subculture with specific norms and values. These pioneers generally resented formal rules for Internet communication, believing that access to information should be free and unlimited; they distrusted efforts to centralize control of the Internet. Their subculture developed argot terms, such as *flaming* (hurling abuse online), *chat rooms* (bulletin boards for people with common interests), and

Classroom Tip See "Stimulating Classroom Discussion about Killing Us Softly" (Classroom Discussion Topics).
Methods Research data suggest that women's use of the Internet is increasing faster than men's.
Gender Gender differences in use of websites
Theory Interactionists examine media from a micro-level approach.

Let's Discuss Does the concept of a "microprocessor generation" reinforce the possibility of competition between the young and the old?
Student Alert Review with students how they may use the Internet in their future classes. Share with them how you as an instructor have benefited from use of the Internet.
Classroom Tip The use of argot terms was discussed in Chapter 3.

hacking (using one's personal computer to break into others' electronic files).

One troubling issue has been raised about day-to-day life on the Internet. What, if anything, should be done about terrorists and other extremist groups who use the Internet to exchange messages of hatred and even bomb-making recipes? What, if anything, should be done about the issue of sexual expression on the Internet? How can children be protected from it? Should "hot chat" and X-rated film clips be censored? Or should expression be completely free? The impact of technological change on issues of privacy and censorship will be examined in Chapter 16.

While many people in the United States embrace the Internet, we should note that information is not evenly distributed throughout the population. The same people, by and large, who experience poor health and have few job opportunities also have been left off the information highway.

Finally, the interactionist perspective helps us to understand more about one important aspect of the entire mass media system—the audience. How do we actively participate in media events? How do we construct with others the meaning of media messages?

THE AUDIENCE

One night a few years ago, I was watching the Chicago Bulls make yet another bid for the NBA championship. Michael Jordan made a spectacular steal and went on to score a game-winning basket. I shouted, but what I remember most were the cheers I heard through the open window from others in Chicago. Earlier that year, my son had been watching *Beverly Hills 90210* in his college dorm room. One of the characters revealed that she was going to attend my son's university. As he and his friends screamed, they heard cheers all across the campus. In an unusual way, we had both been reminded that we are part of a larger audience.

Who Is in the Audience?

The mass media are distinguished from other social institutions by the necessary presence of an audience. It can be an identifiable, finite group, such as an audience at a jazz club or a Broadway musical, or a much larger and undefined group, such as VH-1 viewers or readers of the same issue of *USA Today*. The audience may be a secondary group gathered in a large auditorium or a primary group, such as a mother and child watching the latest Disney video at home.

We can look at the audience from the level of both *microsociology* and *macrosociology*. At the micro level, we

would consider how audience members interacting among themselves would respond to the media, or in the case of live performances, would actually influence the performers. At the macro level, we would examine broader societal consequences of the media, such as the early childhood education delivered through programming like *Sesame Street*.

Even if an audience is spread out over a wide geographic area and members don't know one another, it is still distinctive in terms of age, gender, income, political party, formal schooling, race, and ethnicity. The audience for a ballet, for example, would differ substantially from the audience for alternative music.

Use Your Sociological Imagination

Think about the last time you were part of an audience. How similar or different from yourself were the other audience members? What might account for whatever similarities or differences you noticed?

The Segmented Audience

Increasingly, the media are marketing themselves to a *particular* audience. Once a media outlet, such as a radio station or a magazine, has identified its audience, it targets that group. To some degree, this specialization is driven by advertising. Media specialists have sharpened their ability, through survey research, to identify particular target audiences. As a result, Nike would be much more likely to promote a new line of golf clubs on the Golf Cable Channel, for example, than on an episode of *SpongeBob*. The many more choices that the growing Internet and satellite broadcast channels offer audiences also foster specialization. Members of these audiences are more likely to *expect* content geared to their own interests.

The specialized targeting of audiences has led some scholars to question the "mass" in mass media. Are viewing audiences so segmented that large collective audiences are a thing of the past? That is not yet clear. Even though we seem to be living in an age of *personal* computers and *personal* digital assistants (PDAs), large formal organizations still do transmit public messages that reach a sizable, heterogeneous, and scattered audience (Dominick 2002).

Audience Behavior

Sociologists have long researched how audiences interact with one another and how they share information after a media event. The role of audience members as opinion leaders particularly intrigues social researchers. An **opinion leader** is someone who influences the opinions and

Student Alert Review the differences between micro- and macro-level approaches to social phenomena.
Theory Role of the audience from the interactionist perspective
Theory Concept of the audience presented on both a micro and macro level

Let's Discuss What are the manifest and latent functions and dysfunctions of a segmented broadcast entertainment market?
Let's Discuss Ask students to discuss the segmented broadcast entertainment market from a conflict perspective.

decisions of others through day-to-day personal contacts and communication. A movie or theater critic functions as an opinion leader. Sociologist Paul Lazarsfeld and his colleagues (1948) pioneered the study of opinion leaders in their research on voting behavior in the 1940s. They found that opinion leaders encourage their relatives, friends, and co-workers to think positively about a particular candidate, perhaps pushing them to listen to the politician's speeches or read the campaign literature.

Today, film critics often attribute the success of low-budget independent films to word of mouth. This is another way of saying that the mass media influence opinion leaders, who in turn influence others. The audience, then, is not a group of passive people but of active consumers who are often impelled to interact with others after a media event (Croteau and Hoynes 2003; C. R. Wright 1986).

Despite the role of opinion leaders, members of an audience do not all interpret media in the same way. Often their response is influenced by their social characteristics, such as occupation, race, education, and income. Take the example of the televised news coverage of the riots in Los Angeles in 1992. The riots were an angry response to the acquittal of two White police officers accused of severely beating a Black motorist. Sociologist Darnell Hunt (1997) wondered how the social composition of audience members would affect the way they interpreted the news coverage. He gathered 15 groups from the Los Angeles area, whose members were equally divided among Whites, African Americans, and Latinos. He showed each group a 17-minute clip from the televised coverage of the riots and asked members to discuss how they would describe what they had just seen to a 12-year-old. In analyzing the discussions, Hunt found that although gender and class did not cause respondents to vary their answers by much, race did.

Hunt went beyond noting simple racial differences in perceptions; he also analyzed how the differences were manifested. For example, Black viewers were much more likely than Latinos or Whites to refer to the events in terms of "us" and "them." Another difference was that Black and Latino viewers were more animated and critical than the White viewers as they watched the film clip. White viewers tended to sit quietly, still and unquestioning, suggesting that they were more comfortable with the news coverage than the Blacks or Hispanics.

▮ THE MEDIA INDUSTRY

"My Heart Will Go On," the hit song from the movie *Titanic,* was a real crowd pleaser. But how did the song come into being? That requires looking at the music industry from what researchers call the *production perspective,* which emphasizes the production process over the specific media product. The music production process requires the contribution of a songwriter, a performer, a movie soundtrack producer, a music video director, advertisers, and promoters, to name just a few participants (Croteau and Hoynes 2001, 2003).

Media Concentration

Who owns the media production process? Even though there are thousands of independent media outlets in every state, the clear trend is toward centralization. A handful of multinational corporations now dominate the publishing, broadcasting, and film industries, though they may be hard to identify, since global conglomerates manage many different product names. Walt Disney alone owns 16 television channels that reach 140 countries. Media outlets are likely to become even more concentrated if a 2003 ruling by the Federal Communications Commission (FCC) is allowed to stand. The ruling relaxes restrictions on owning more than one media outlet in the same market area (Carter and Rutenberg 2003; Rutenberg 2002).

A prime example of media concentration was the merger in 2001 of AOL and Time Warner, which created a new corporation that permeates almost every media sector. The AOL network, along with its Netscape Internet browser, operates the most popular Internet sites and boasts more than 32 million online subscribers worldwide. Time Warner is the largest U.S. magazine publisher based on advertising revenue earned. Time Warner's subsidiaries, Warner Brothers and New Line Cinema, rank among the top 10 motion picture producers. Warner Music Group artists accounted for 17 percent of all U.S. album sales in 2002. And Time Warner Cable provides many of the most popular cable channels, including HBO, TBS, CNN, TNT, Nickelodeon, and the WB network (AOL Time Warner 2003; TimeWarner 2004).

AOL Time Warner is only *one* media giant. Add to the list Walt Disney (which includes ABC, ESPN, and Lifetime networks); Rupert Murdoch's News Corporation of Australia (Fox Network Television, book publishers, numerous newspapers and magazines, and 20th Century Fox); Sony of Japan (Columbia Pictures, IMAX, CBS Records, and Columbia Records); and Viacom (Paramount, MTV, CBS, UPN, Black Entertainment Television, Simon and Schuster, and Blockbuster). This concentration of media giants fosters considerable cross-promotion. For example, the release of the Warner Brothers film *The Matrix Reloaded* in 2003 was heavily promoted by both CNN and *Time* magazine. In fact,

A 24-hour-a-day televised news network with short bulletins every hour, followed by a fast-paced montage of news clips—all broadcast globally by satellite-linked cable stations. This could be CNN but it's *Al Jazeera*, the Arabic-language television news network based in the small Persian Gulf state of Qatar. The name Al Jazeera means "island" or "peninsula," in reference to the network's home country. Founded in 1996, the channel now has 60 correspondents and an audience of about 35 million Arabs worldwide, including 150,000 Arab Americans.

Most people in the United States had never heard of Al Jazeera until October 7, 2001. That was when the channel aired the first of several videotaped messages from Osama bin Laden, the mastermind of the Al Qaeda terrorist network. U.S. news outlets also televised the messages, but stopped after the government objected to the airing of bin Laden's calls for violence against U.S. citizens.

Al Jazeera refused to acquiesce to the government request, invoking its motto,

"The Opinion, and the Other Opinion Too." Al Jazeera officials insist that they promote a forum for independent dialogue and debate, an unusual practice in the Arab world, where most media outlets are state controlled. In fact, several Arab states, including Saudi Arabia, Jordan, and Bahrain, have banned or restricted Al Jazeera because of the network's critical coverage of affairs in their

> *"You have to be a supporter of Al Jazeera, even if you have to hold your nose sometimes."*

country. Other Arab nations criticize Al Jazeera for giving too much airplay to U.S. news.

Though many media observers see Al Jazeera as biased, many viewers around the world might see CNN, ABC, and Fox News as biased. For example, in virtually all media outlets in the United States, the immorality of Palestinian suicide bombings is an unstated assumption. However,

many people in the Arab world would regard that assumption as fundamentally wrong. Similarly, most Muslims worldwide would question why CBS's respected news show *60 Minutes* would give exposure to Jerry Falwell, who called the Prophet Muhammad a terrorist. According to Kenton Keith, a former U.S. ambassador to Qatar, Al Jazeera has a slant, but no more than other news organizations. It just happens to be a slant that most Americans aren't comfortable with.

Al Jazeera does offer diverse views. On its popular talk show *The Opposing View*, two women hotly debated polygamy among Muslim men. On another popular program, *Sharia [Islamic Law] and Life*, the speaker dared to reassure Muslim women that the Koran does not force them to marry suitors designated by their parents. Ambassador Keith believes that "for the long-range importance of press freedom in the Middle East and the advantages that will ultimately have for the West, you have to be a supporter of Al Jazeera, even if you have to hold your nose sometimes" (Barr 2002:7).

Sources: Al Jazeera 2004; Barr 2002; Daniszewski 2003; Department of State 2004; MediaGuardian 2001; H. Rosenberg 2003; Rutenberg 2003; Stack 2004; Urbana 2002.

Time managed to devote its cover to the film's release in the midst of the war in Iraq.

Similar concerns have been raised about the situation in countries such as China, Cuba, Iraq, and North Korea, where the ruling party owns and controls the media. The difference, which is considerable, is that in the United States the gatekeeping process is in the hands of private individuals, who desire to maximize profits. In the other countries, the gatekeeping process belongs to political leaders, who desire to maintain control of the government.

We should note one significant exception to the centralization and concentration of the media—the Internet. Currently the web is accessible through independent outlets to millions of producers of media content. Obviously, the producer must be technologically proficient and must have access to a computer, but compared to other media outlets, the Internet is readily available.

Media conglomerates, well aware of the Internet's potential, are already delivering their material via the web. Still, for now, the Internet allows the individual to become a media entrepreneur with a potential audience of millions.

The Media's Global Reach

Has the rise of the electronic media created a "global village"? Canadian linguist Marshall McLuhan predicted it would some 40 years ago. Today, physical distance is no longer a barrier, and instant messaging is possible across the world. The mass media have indeed created a global village. Not all countries are equally connected, as Figure 7-2 (page 166) shows, but the progress is staggering, considering that voice transmission was just beginning 100 years ago (McLuhan 1964; McLuhan and Fiore 1967).

Global View Arabic-language television
Contemporary Culture Cross-cultural perspectives on controversial political issues

Web Resource Students will find the crossword puzzle in the student center of the Online Learning Center (**www.mhhe.com/schaefer6**) challenging.

Global View In China, Cuba, Iraq, and North Korea, the ruling party owns and controls the media.

An Al Jazeera staff member monitors the news at the network's headquarters in Qatar. The Al Jazeera network was featured in the 2004 documentary film *Control Room*.

pose, however, is to win over the hearts and minds of a population that is deeply suspicious of U.S. motives. Paid for as part of an $87 billion aid package for Iraq and Afghanistan, Al Hurra, whose name means "The Free One," is the latest in a series of U.S. attempts at improving public relations with the Islamic world. Knowledgeable observers view the effort with some skepticism, however. Given U.S. failure to resolve the Israeli-Palestinian conflict—a prime source of tension in the Middle East for decades—and the 2003 invasion of Iraq, they doubt the new network will have much effect.

Let's Discuss

1. Do you find news outlets in the United States biased? How would you judge?
2. What do you think of the new Al Hurra network in the Middle East? Can it win over the hearts and minds of viewers there? Should the U.S. government be using taxpayers' dollars to fund the effort?

To counter Al Jazeera's influence, in 2004 the U.S. State Department established its own satellite network, Al Hurra, in the Middle East. Based in Springfield, Virginia, and staffed by veteran Arab journalists, the new network promises balanced and objective reporting on regional issues and events. Its ultimate pur-

Sociologist Todd Gitlin considers "global torrent" a more apt metaphor for the media's reach than "global village" (see this chapter's opening essay). The media permeate all aspects of everyday life. Take advertising, for example. Consumer goods are vigorously marketed worldwide, from advertisements on airport baggage carriers to imprints on sandy beaches. Little wonder that people around the world develop loyalty to a brand and are as likely to sport a Nike, Coca-Cola, or Harley-Davidson logo as they are their favorite soccer or baseball insignia (Gitlin 2002; N. Klein 1999).

A highly visible part of the media, whether it be print or electronic, is news. Most people in the United States, however, have had little familiarity with news outlets outside their own country, with the possible exception of the British-based Reuters and BBC News. Like so many other things, that all changed after September 11, 2001, when an Arab news network took center stage (see Box 7-2).

The key to creating a truly global network that reaches directly into workplaces, schools, and homes is the introduction of the Internet. Although much of the online global transmission today is limited to print and pictures, the potential to send audio and video via the Internet will increasingly reach into every part of the world. Social interaction will then truly take place on a global scale.

The Internet has also facilitated other forms of communication. Reference materials and data banks can now be made accessible across national boundaries. Information related to international finance, marketing, trade, and manufacturing is literally just a keystroke away. We have seen the emergence of truly world news outlets and the promotion of a world music that is not clearly identifiable with any single culture. Even the most future-oriented thinker would find the growth in the reach of the mass media in postindustrial and postmodern societies

FIGURE 7-2

Media Penetration in Selected Countries

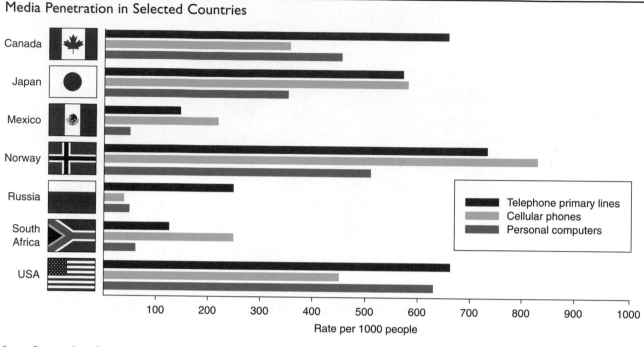

Source: Bureau of the Census 2003a:870.

Think About It
What is the economic and political significance of media penetration?

remarkable (Castells 2000, 2001; Croteau and Hoynes 2001, 2003).

The lack of one national home for the various forms of mass media raises a potential dilemma for users. People worry that unhealthy influences and even crime are taking place in today's electronic global village, and that few if any controls prevent them. For example, the leaders of Bhutan worry about the impact of newly introduced television programming on their culture and their people. Similarly, in industrial countries, including the United States, officials are concerned about everything from video poker to online pornography to the menace posed by hackers. In the social policy section that follows, we'll consider how the violence that is portrayed in the media can have an undesirable influence on society.

These Bhutanese householders are watching the *Oprah Winfrey Show* on their brand-new television set. Marshall McLuhan's global village has become a reality in their remote Asian kingdom, where rulers are concerned about the cultural impact of Western media.

Global View Media in selected countries
Reel Society See Media in the Topic Index.

Global View Impact of television on the culture and people of Bhutan

SOCIAL POLICY and the MASS MEDIA | Media Violence

The Issue

A film tells the story of 42 ninth-graders abducted to a remote island and forced to play the ultimate game of survivor: kill or be killed until only one is left. In gruesome detail, the movie portrays teachers doing away with students, young girls murdering shy admirers, and popular students dispatching rivals with hatchets and grenades, poison and machine guns. The film, *Battle Royale,* by the renowned Japanese director Kinji Fukasaku, shows a Japan that is falling apart in the early 21st century. Millions are out of work, bureaucrats have lost control, and government officials are convinced that this deadly game is the only way to teach rampaging juveniles a lesson (Magnier 1999).

What effect do this movie and hundreds of others like it have on audiences? The portrayal of violence is not limited to motion pictures but is common in television, Internet sites, and video games as well. The video game *Grand Theft Auto III (GTA3)* sold 7 million copies in 2002; it is a virtual urban war game. Companion Internet sites encourage players to run over pedestrians, shoot the paramedics who show up, and loot the bodies for spare change. The 2003 sequel, *Vice City,* set in Miami around 1986, featured gun-toting thugs perpetrating killings and hijackings with rocket launchers and Molotov cocktails (Grossman 2002).

Does violence in the media lead people, especially youths, to become more violent? This question has been raised since the early days of comic books, when POW! and SPLAT! were accompanied by vivid pictures of fights. Today the mass media show far more violent and gruesome scenes, and every year the amount of violence seems to increase. A comparison of the top-grossing movies of 2000 with those from 1998 showed that the ones made in 2000 had 6 percent more episodes of violence, even though they were more often rated PG-13. Similarly, a recent study of network television showed an increase in violence at every hour of prime-time TV—see Figure 7-3 on page 168 (Lichter et al. 2002).

The Setting

We spend a great deal of time with the media. According to a communications industry study, people spend 10 hours every day with television, videotaped movies, computer games, radio, and other media outlets. At the end of a week, the time averages more than 72 hours—far more than a full workweek (Bureau of the Census 2003a:720).

But does watching hours of mass media with violent images cause one to behave differently? This research question is exceedingly complex, since many social factors influence behavior. Some researchers use an experimental method in which participants are randomly assigned to view either violent or nonviolent media and are later assessed for aggression. Other researchers survey subjects' media habits and aggressive behavior or attitudes. The most comprehensive analysis of more than 200 studies on media violence and aggressive behavior found that exposure to violence causes short-term increases in the aggressive behavior of youths. Another more recent study found that less exposure to television and other media is related to less observed physical aggression. But these research findings also show that other factors besides the media are related to aggressive behavior. Witnessing and experiencing violence in one's own home and encouragement from others have also been shown to be related to violent behavior (G. Anderson and Bushman 2001; J. Johnson et al. 2002; Paik and Comstock 1994; Robinson et al. 2001; U.S. Surgeon General 2001).

Sociological Insights

The controversy surrounding violence and the media raises some basic questions about the function of the media. If the media's functions are to entertain, socialize, and enforce social norms, how can violence be a part of its programming, especially when the offender rarely pays any consequences?

Even if a viewer does not necessarily become more violent from watching violent images, a kind of desensitization could be taking place. Using the premise of the narcotizing dysfunction, one might suggest that extended exposure to violent imagery leads to an increased tolerance and acceptance of violence in others.

Both conflict and feminist theorists are troubled that the victims in violent scenes are often those who receive less respect than others in real life: women, children, the poor, racial minorities, citizens of foreign countries, even the physically disabled. The media routinely portray rape in a way that further devalues women. Women are often cast as prostitutes, even in well-regarded motion pictures, from Federico Fellini's *Nights of Cabiria* (1956) to Jodie Foster in *Taxi Driver* (1976), Julia Roberts in *Pretty Woman* (1990), and Elisabeth Shue in *Leaving Las Vegas* (1995).

Interactionists are especially interested in whether violence in the media may become a script for real-life behavior. Because aggression is a product of socialization, people may model themselves after the violent behavior they see, especially if the situations approximate their own lives. Battling the Green Goblin in *Spider-Man* is one thing, but what about violence that represents only a slight deviation from normal behavior? In the 1995 film *The Program*, high school football players proved their manhood by lying in the middle of a highway at night. After several deaths had occurred when young men tried to prove their own manhood by imitating the scene, Touchstone Films ordered its removal.

Policy Initiatives

Policymakers have responded to the links between media violence and real-life aggression on two levels. In public statements, politicians are quick to call for more family-oriented, less violent content, but on the legislative level, they are reluctant to engage in what could be regarded as censorship. They encourage the media to regulate themselves.

The U.S. Surgeon General's 2001 report on youth violence recommended that parents use V-chip technology to screen the television programs their children watch. Yet despite parental concerns, a 2001 national

FIGURE 7-3

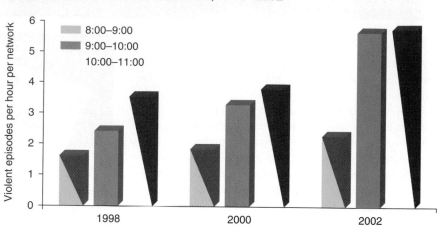

Violence on Prime-Time Television, 1998–2002

Source: Parents Television Council 2003.

Note: Content analysis of programming on ABC, CBS, NBC, FOX, UPN, and WB. Times are Eastern Standard Time.

study showed that only 17 percent of parents use the V-chip to block programs with sexual or violent content. In general, most observers agree that parents should play a stronger role in monitoring their children's media consumption (Kaiser Family Foundation 2001; U.S. Surgeon General 2001).

Often government studies are initiated by violent events we desperately wish to explain. The 2001 Surgeon General's report on youth violence came out of the 1999 Columbine High School shootings in Colorado. Canada launched a serious look at media violence following a 1989 incident at a Montreal university in which 14 young women were shot to death. A senseless beating of a five-year-old girl by three friends in Norway in 1994 led that country to look at violence in the media. In all these cases, initial calls for stiff government regulation eventually gave way to industry self-regulation and greater adult involvement in young people's viewing patterns (Bok 1998; Health Canada 1993).

Much of our knowledge of media violence comes from the study of children who watch traditional television programming. Some more recent studies have tried to assess the impact of video games. We should not lose sight of the fact that media outlets are becoming increasingly diverse, especially given the role the Internet now plays in the delivery of media content. Much of this new content holds great promise for broadening educational horizons, but unfortunately, these new outlets also offer a diet of violence (A. Alexander and Hanson 2001:44).

Theory Conflict and feminist views of violent imagery in the media
Theory Interactionist perspective on media violence as a script for real-life behavior

Methods Survey conducted by Kaiser shows that only 17 percent of parents use a V-chip.
Methods The 2001 U.S. Surgeon General's report on youth violence was a survey.
Global View Canada and Norway have studied media violence.

Let's Discuss

1. Do you know of anyone whose behavior has become more aggressive from exposure to violence in the media? How was this aggression expressed? Have you noticed any changes in your own behavior?
2. To what extent should government act as a media censor, especially in regard to violent content directed toward young people?
3. What role do you think parents should have in monitoring their children's viewing habits? Would you limit your children's access to the media outlets? What alternative activities might children be offered?

GETTING INVOLVED

To get involved in the debate over violence in the media, visit this text's Online Learning Center, which offers links to relevant websites. Check out the Social Policy section on the Online Learning Center as well; it provides survey data on U.S. public opinion regarding this issue.

www.mhhe.com/schaefer6

CHAPTER RESOURCES

Summary

The *mass media* refer to the print and electronic instruments of communication that carry messages to often widespread audiences. They pervade all social institutions, from entertainment to education to politics. This chapter examines how the mass media affect those institutions and influence our social behavior.

1. From the functionalist perspective, the media entertain, socialize, enforce social norms, confer status, promote consumption, and keep us informed (the *surveillance function*). They can be dysfunctional to the extent that they desensitize us to serious events and issues (the *narcotizing dysfunction*).
2. Conflict theorists see the media as reflecting and even deepening the divisions in society through *gatekeeping*—controlling the material that reaches the public—and the spread of the *dominant ideology,* which defines reality, overwhelming local cultures.
3. Feminist theorists point out that media images of the sexes communicate unrealistic, stereotypical, limiting, and sometimes violent perceptions of women.
4. Interactionists examine the media on the micro level to see how they shape day-to-day social behavior. They have studied shared TV viewing and staged public appearances intended to convey self-serving definitions of reality.
5. The mass media require the presence of an audience—whether it is small and well defined or large and amorphous. With increasing numbers of media outlets, there has been more and more targeting of segmented (or specialized) audiences.
6. Social researchers have studied the role of *opinion leaders* in influencing audiences.
7. The media industry is becoming more and more concentrated, creating media conglomerates. This concentration raises concerns about how innovative and independent the media can be. In some countries, governments own and control the media.
8. The Internet is the one significant exception to the trend toward centralization, allowing millions of people to produce their own media content.
9. The media have a global reach thanks to new communications technology, especially the Internet. Some people are concerned that the media's global reach will spread unhealthy influences to other cultures.
10. Sociologists are studying the ways that scenes of violence in the media may promote aggressive behavior or desensitization to violence in viewers.

Critical Thinking Questions

1. What kind of audience is targeted by the producers of televised professional wrestling? By the creators of an animated film? By a rap group? What kinds of factors determine who makes up a particular audience?

2. Trace the production process for a new television situation comedy (sitcom). Who do you imagine are the gatekeepers in the process?

3. Use the functionalist, conflict, and interactionist perspectives to assess the effects of global TV programming on developing countries.

Key Terms

Dominant ideology   A set of cultural beliefs and practices that help to maintain powerful social, economic, and political interests. (page 157)

Gatekeeping   The process by which a relatively small number of people in the media industry control what material eventually reaches the audience. (156)

Mass media   Print and electronic means of communication that carry messages to widespread audiences. (152)

Narcotizing dysfunction   The phenomenon in which the media provide such massive amounts of information that the audience becomes numb and fails to act on the information, regardless of how compelling the issue. (156)

Opinion leader   Someone who influences the opinions and decisions of others through day-to-day personal contacts and communication. (162)

Stereotype   An unreliable generalization about all members of a group that does not recognize individual differences within the group. (157)

Surveillance function   The collection and distribution of information concerning events in the social environment. (155)

TECHNOLOGY RESOURCES

www.mhhe.com/schaefer6   Internet Connection

*Note: While all the URLs listed were current as of the printing of this book, these sites often change. Please check our website (**www.mhhe.com/schaefer6**) for updates, hyperlinks, and exercises related to these sites.*

1. Numerous organizations have been formed for the purpose of providing alternatives to mainstream mass media. One of them is Paper Tiger Television (**www.papertiger.org**). Explore this site and become more aware of ways in which media gatekeeping may be challenged.

2. In China, the mass media are largely government controlled. Browse through the English version of China's leading national newspaper, the *People's Daily* (**english.peopledaily.com.cn/**), to see how government control affects the paper's news coverage.

Online Learning Center with PowerWeb

Visit the student center in the Online Learning Center at **www.mhhe.com/schaefer6** and link to "Use Your Sociological Imagination." You will be asked to become a news junkie, and to think about where you will gather your "facts" or information. Next, you will be asked to imagine yourself as part of an audience for a ballet performance, and to think about the similarities you might share with other audience members. Use your sociological imagination to answer the questions.

Reel Society Interactive Movie CD-ROM 2.0

Reel Society 2.0 can be used to spark discussion about the following topics in this chapter:

- Sociological Perspectives on the Media
- The Media Industry

DEVIANCE AND SOCIAL CONTROL

Lick it up.

After rock and rolling all night, we need nourishment. And every drop of chocolate milk has the same vitamins and minerals regular milk has. All the more reason to have a really, really long tongue.

got milk?

KISS ©1998 NATIONAL FLUID MILK PROCESSOR PROMOTION BOARD

Deviance and conformity are relative concepts that can change over time. KISS was a leading example of shock rock in the 1970s, when the band's theatrical costumes and makeup appeared deviant to some. Today, the group's well-known image is less shocking, and the milk industry has enlisted the group to promote its product to young consumers.

Wallbangin' is a gang term that means, roughly, "gangbangin' on a wall." This can be through straightforward writing or through crossing out the writing of others; either activity enforces relationships of power between gangs. Gang members in Los Angeles generally recognize this as a generic term for the activity of wall writing. . . .

Any type of cultural or artistic production forces change on an environment. Most of the time, people abide by well-established rules for culture-producing activities. They do it through consuming certain products in certain ways or by creating symbols of their identity within the scope of what is legal for the entire society. In general, people who write graffiti produce culture in a different manner. No matter what it says, the manner in which graffiti is produced defines the writer's position as an outsider and alienates that person from the rest of society. . . .

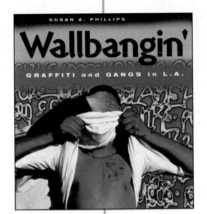

Criminal aspects of graffiti free the writers from constraints that laws would place on their creations. Writers force change on an environment, but without recourse or permission. Their marks are like advertising for groups and individuals who may themselves be outside the law already. Graffiti writers usurp public and private property for their own purposes. The graffitists have not been paid, nor do they pay for the space they use for the privilege. Viewed from the larger society's perspective, graffiti is always just wallbangin': it is cultural production through destruction. . . .

The antisocial nature of graffiti makes its analysis an inherently social endeavor. Graffiti is all about people. It's about relationships, and individuals, and motives. As a researcher, you need to get hold of a social situation on the ground in order to understand the story presented on the walls. . . .

A young man from 29th Street in South Central Los Angeles explained it like this:

It all comes down to basically politics, like everything else. . . . Graffiti . . . to us . . . what we write on the walls . . . is to mark our territory. Which you already know. A way of us marking our territory so people know. See right now we might not be here to represent our neighborhood, but they pass through this, "oh look this is where so and so kicks back." See, it does serve a purpose! That's what we use it for. But yet when we try different styles and different things. Because, believe it or not, we try to make our neighborhood look good. . . . We don't want to write on the wall and just leave it all ugly, we want to write on the wall and make it look nice. . . .

Whether in alleys, around hangouts, parks, on main drags, or on major streets, gang members write graffiti for themselves and others who understand their messages as acts of representing. Gang members use graffiti to organize the spaces in which they reside; in the process, they cover the streets with manifestations of their own identity. Like silent sentinels, the graffiti keep watch and inform onlookers of the affiliations and activities that define a certain area. *(S. A. Phillips 1999:21, 23, 134–135)* ■ 🌀

Additional information about this excerpt can be found on the Online Learning Center at **www.mhhe.com/schaefer6.**

Anthropologist Susan Phillips studied graffiti writing in Los Angeles neighborhoods over a period of six years. In her book *Wallbangin': Graffiti and Gangs in L.A.* she notes that while graffiti writing is regarded as vandalism in the eyes of the law, it actually serves important social purposes for gang members, from making political statements to identifying home turf and making the "neighborhood look good" (S. A. Phillips 1999:135).

As Phillips makes clear, what should be considered deviant is not always obvious. Wall writing, in fact, has an illustrious history. She begins her book with pages of descriptions of wall writing from such literary sources as the Bible, Mark Twain, Edgar Allan Poe, and George Orwell. Even today, Phillips points out, government authorities sometimes protect graffiti. At Los Angeles harbor, officials do not erase the writing of sailors. Along the Harlem River Parkway in New York City, a playground wall with graffiti by the late artist Keith Haring (who began as a tagger) has been preserved as a work of art.

As another example of the difficulty of determining what is and is not deviant, consider the issue of binge drinking on campus. On the one hand, we can view binge drinking as *deviant*, as violating a school's standards of conduct and endangering one's health. On the other hand, we can see it as *conforming*, or complying with peer culture. In the United States, people are socialized to have mixed feelings about both conforming and nonconforming behavior. The term *conformity* can conjure up images of mindless imitation of one's peer group—whether a circle of teenagers wearing "phat pants" or a group of business executives all dressed in gray suits. Yet the same term can also suggest that an individual is cooperative, or a "team player." What about those who do not conform? They may be respected as individualists, leaders, or creative thinkers who break new ground. Or they may be labeled as "troublemakers" and "weirdos" (Aronson 1999).

This chapter examines the relationship between conformity, deviance, and social control. When does conformity verge on deviance? And how does a society manage to control its members and convince them to conform to its rules and laws? What are the consequences of deviance? We will begin by distinguishing between conformity and obedience and then look at two experiments on conforming behavior and obedience to authority. Next we will analyze the informal and formal mechanisms societies use to encourage conformity and discourage deviance. We will pay particular attention to the legal order and how it reflects underlying social values.

The second part of the chapter focuses on theoretical explanations for deviance, including the functionalist approach employed by Émile Durkheim and Robert Merton; interactionist-based theories; labeling theory, which draws on both the interactionist and the conflict perspectives; and conflict theory.

The third part of the chapter focuses on crime, a specific type of deviant behavior. As a form of deviance that is subject to official, written norms, crime has been a special concern of policymakers and the public in general. We will look at various types of crime found in the United States, the ways crime is measured, and international crime rates. Finally, the social policy section considers the controversial topic of gun control and its relation to violent crime. ∎

SOCIAL CONTROL

As we saw in Chapter 3, each culture, subculture, and group has distinctive norms governing appropriate behavior. Laws, dress codes, bylaws of organizations, course requirements, and rules of sports and games all express social norms.

How does a society bring about acceptance of basic norms? The term **social control** refers to the techniques and strategies for preventing deviant human behavior in any society. Social control occurs on all levels of society. In the family, we are socialized to obey our parents simply because they are our parents. Peer groups introduce us to informal norms, such as dress codes, that govern the behavior of their members. Colleges establish standards they expect of students. In bureaucratic organizations, workers encounter a formal system of rules and regulations. Finally, the government of every society legislates and enforces social norms.

Classroom Tip See "Stimulating Classroom Discussions about *Wallbangin'* " (Class Discussion Topics).
Contemporary Culture Ask students to interpret some graffiti images.
Gender Binge drinking is a concern among both male and female college students.

Student Alert Take this early opportunity to note that crime and deviance are not necessarily the same.

Most of us respect and accept basic social norms and assume that others will do the same. Even without thinking, we obey the instructions of police officers, follow the day-to-day rules at our jobs, and move to the rear of elevators when people enter. Such behavior reflects an effective process of socialization to the dominant standards of a culture. At the same time, we are well aware that individuals, groups, and institutions *expect* us to act "properly." This expectation carries with it **p. 66** *sanctions,* penalties and rewards for conduct concerning a social norm. If we fail to live up to the norm, we may face punishment through informal sanctions such as fear and ridicule, or formal sanctions such as jail sentences or fines.

The challenge to effective social control is that people often receive competing messages about how to behave. While the state or government may clearly define acceptable behavior, friends or fellow employees may encourage quite different behavior patterns. Historically, legal measures aimed at blocking discrimination based on race, religion, gender, age, and sexual orientation have been difficult to implement, because many people tacitly encourage the violation of such measures.

Functionalists maintain that people must respect social norms if any group or society is to survive. In their view, societies literally could not function if massive numbers of people defied standards of appropriate conduct. In contrast, conflict theorists contend that the "successful functioning" of a society will consistently benefit the powerful and work to the disadvantage of other groups. They point out that in the United States, widespread resistance to social norms was necessary to win our independence from England, to overturn the institution of slavery, to allow women to vote, to secure civil rights, and to force an end to the war in Vietnam.

Conformity and Obedience

Techniques for social control operate on both the group level and the societal level. People we think of as peers or equals influence us to act in particular ways; the same is true of people who hold authority over us or occupy awe-inspiring positions. Stanley Milgram (1975) made a useful distinction between these two important levels of social control.

Milgram used the term *conformity* to mean going along with peers—individuals of our own status, who have no special right to direct our behavior. In contrast, *obedience* is compliance with higher authorities in a hierarchical structure. Thus, a recruit entering military service will typically *conform* to the habits and language of other recruits and *obey* the orders of superior officers. Students will *conform* to the drinking behavior of their peers and *obey* the requests of campus security officers.

Conformity to Prejudice

We often think of conformity as being rather harmless, as when members of an expensive health club all don the same costly sportswear. But researchers have found that people may conform to the attitudes and behavior of their peers even when it means expressing intolerance toward others. Fletcher Blanchard, Teri Lilly, and Leigh Ann Vaughn (1991) conducted an experiment at Smith College and found that the statements people overhear others make influence their own expressions of opinion on the issue of racism.

Social control, Finnish style. This young man is relaxing in his prison cell, not in his college dorm room. Thirty years ago Finland rejected the rigid Soviet model of imprisonment and adopted a gentler correctional system meant to shape prisoners' values and encourage moral behavior. Today, Finland's rate of imprisonment is less than half that of England's and one-fourth that of the United States.

Classroom Tip Stress the sociological position highlighted in the cultural transmission theory, that deviance is learned through socialization.
Student Alert Remind students that sanctions can also be positive (e.g., applause, promotions, rewards).
Theory Functionalist and conflict views of social norms contrasted

Methods Blanchard and his colleagues conducted an experiment on conformity to prejudice.
Race/Ethnicity Conformity to prejudice concerning racial and ethnic minorities is a measurable phenomenon.
Classroom Tip See "Group Pressure" (Class Discussion Topics).

In one of Stanley Milgram's experiments, the "learner" supposedly received an electric shock from a shock plate when he answered a question incorrectly. At the 150-volt level, the "learner" would demand to be released and would refuse to place his hand on the shock plate. The experimenter would then order the actual subject (the "teacher") to force the hand onto the plate, as shown in the photo. Though 40 percent of the true subjects stopped complying with Milgram at this point, 30 percent did force the "learner's" hand onto the shock plate, despite his pretended agony.

In the experiment, a student who was a confederate (or ally) of the researchers approached 72 White students as each was walking across campus. She said she was conducting an opinion poll for a class. At the same time, she stopped a second White student—actually another confederate working with the researchers—and asked the person to participate in the survey. The first question concerned how Smith College should respond to anonymous racist notes that were sent to four African American students in 1989. The confederate always answered first. In some cases, she condemned the notes; in others, she justified them.

Blanchard and his colleagues (1991:102–103) concluded that "hearing at least one other person express strongly antiracist opinions produced dramatically more strongly antiracist public reactions to racism than hearing others express equivocal opinions or opinions more accepting of racism." When the confederate expressed sentiments justifying racism, subjects were much less likely to express antiracist opinions than were those who

heard no such opinions. In this experiment, social control influenced people's attitudes, or at least the expression of those attitudes, through the process of conformity. In the next section, we will see that social control can alter people's behavior through the process of obedience.

Obedience to Authority

If ordered to do so, would you comply with an experimenter's instruction to administer increasingly painful electric shocks to a subject? Most people would say no; yet the research of social psychologist Stanley Milgram (1963, 1975) suggests that most of us *would* obey such orders. In Milgram's words (1975:xi), "Behavior that is unthinkable in an individual . . . acting on his own may be executed without hesitation when carried out under orders."

Milgram placed advertisements in New Haven, Connecticut, newspapers to recruit subjects for a learning experiment at Yale University. Participants included postal clerks, engineers, high school teachers, and laborers. They were told that the purpose of the research was to investigate the effects of punishment on learning. The experimenter, dressed in a gray technician's coat, explained that in each test, one subject would be randomly selected as the "learner," while another would function as the "teacher." However, the experiment was rigged so that the "real" subject would always be the teacher, while an associate of Milgram's served as the learner.

At this point, the learner's hand was strapped to an electric apparatus. The teacher was taken to an electronic "shock generator" with 30 levered switches labeled from 15 to 450 volts. Before beginning the experiment, all subjects received sample shocks of 45 volts, to convince them of the authenticity of the experiment. The experimenter then instructed the teacher to apply shocks of increasing voltage each time the learner gave an incorrect answer on a memory test. Teachers were told that "although the shocks can be extremely painful, they cause no permanent tissue damage." In reality, the learner did not receive any shocks.

In a prearranged script, the learner deliberately gave incorrect answers and expressed pain when "shocked." For example, at 150 volts, the learner would cry out, "Get me out of here!" At 270 volts, the learner would scream in agony. When the shock reached 350 volts, the learner would fall silent. If the teacher wanted to stop the experiment, the experimenter would insist that the teacher continue, using such statements as "The experiment requires that you continue" and "You have no other choice; you *must* go on" (Milgram 1975:19–23).

The results of this unusual experiment stunned and dismayed Milgram and other social scientists. A sample of psychiatrists had predicted that virtually all subjects would refuse to shock innocent victims. In their view, only a "pathological fringe" of less than 2 percent would continue administering shocks up to the maximum level. Yet almost *two-thirds* of participants fell into the category of "obedient subjects."

Why did these subjects obey? Why were they willing to inflict seemingly painful shocks on innocent victims who had never done them any harm? There is no evidence that these subjects were unusually sadistic; few seemed to enjoy administering the shocks. Instead, in Milgram's view, the key to obedience was the experimenter's social role as a "scientist" and "seeker of knowledge."

Milgram pointed out that in the modern industrial world, we are accustomed to submitting to impersonal authority figures whose status is indicated by a title (professor, lieutenant, doctor) or by a uniform (the technician's coat). Because we view the authority as larger and more important than the individual, we shift responsibility for our behavior to the authority figure. Milgram's subjects frequently stated, "If it were up to me, I would not have administered shocks." They saw themselves as merely doing their duty (Milgram 1975).

From an interactionist perspective, one important aspect of Milgram's findings is the fact that subjects in follow-up studies were less likely to inflict the supposed shocks as they were moved physically closer to their victims. Moreover, interactionists emphasize the effect of *incrementally* administering additional dosages of 15 volts. In effect, the experimenter negotiated with the teacher and convinced the teacher to continue inflicting higher levels of punishment. It is doubtful that anywhere near the two-thirds rate of obedience would have been reached had the experimenter told the teachers to administer 450 volts immediately (B. Allen 1978; Katovich 1987).

Milgram launched his experimental study of obedience to better understand the involvement of Germans in the annihilation of 6 million Jews and millions of other people during World War II. In an interview conducted long after the publication of his study, he suggested that "if a system of death camps were set up in the United States of the sort we had seen in Nazi Germany, one would be able to find sufficient personnel for those camps in any medium-sized American town" (CBS News 1979:7–8).

Use Your Sociological Imagination www.mhhe.com/schaefer6

If you were a participant in Milgram's research on conformity, how far do you think you would go in carrying out orders? Do you see any ethical problem with the experimenter's manipulation of the control subjects?

Theory Reflecting the interactionist perspective, Milgram's study found that proximity affects subjects' degree of obedience.
Classroom Tip Refer to "Obedience: Another Look" in Topics and Sources for Student Research for material on replications of Milgram's study.

Informal and Formal Social Control

The sanctions that are used to encourage conformity and obedience—and to discourage violation of social norms—are carried out through both informal and formal social control. As the term implies, people use **informal social control** casually to enforce norms. Examples include smiles, laughter, a raised eyebrow, and ridicule.

In the United States and many other cultures, adults often view spanking, slapping, or kicking children as a proper and necessary means of informal social control. Child development specialists counter that such corporal punishment is inappropriate because it teaches children to solve problems through violence. They warn that slapping and spanking can escalate into more serious forms of abuse. Yet, despite a 1998 policy statement by the American Academy of Pediatrics that corporal punishment is not effective and can indeed be harmful, 59 percent of pediatricians support the use of corporal punishment, at least in certain situations. Our culture widely accepts this form of informal social control (Wolraich et al. 1998).

Formal social control is carried out by authorized agents, such as police officers, judges, school administrators, employers, military officers, and managers of movie theaters. It can serve as a last resort when socialization and informal sanctions do not bring about desired behavior. An increasingly significant means of formal social control in the United States is to imprison people. During the course of a year, 6 to 7 million adults undergo some form of correctional supervision—jail, prison, probation, or parole. Put another way, almost 1 out of every 30 adult Americans is subject to this very formal type of social control every year (Glaze 2002).

Which behaviors are subject to formal social control, and how severe should the sanctions be? Societies vary. In the nation of Singapore, chewing gum is restricted, feeding birds can lead to fines of up to $640, and there is even a $95 fine for failing to flush the toilet. Singapore deals with serious crimes especially severely. The death penalty is mandatory for murder, drug trafficking, and crimes committed with firearms.

In the aftermath of September 11, 2001, new measures of social control became the norm in the United States. Some of them, such as stepped-up security at airports and high-rise buildings, were highly visible to the public. The federal government has also publicly urged citizens to engage in informal social control by watching for and reporting people whose actions seem suspicious. But many other measures taken by the government have increased the covert surveillance of private records and communications.

Methods Survey research on views of corporal punishment among physicians
Let's Discuss Canvas students as to whether corporal punishment was used in their elementary schools.

Sociology on Campus

8-1   BINGE DRINKING

Scott Krueger was an outstanding high school student, well liked, well rounded, and academically gifted. Courted by the best engineering schools —Penn, Cornell, Michigan, MIT—Scott chose MIT, after an overnight visit convinced him that "they weren't all geeks" there.

One night in September 1997, after Scott had been at MIT a little more than a month, he told his sister over the phone that his fraternity pledge class had a big night ahead. Collectively, they had to drink a large amount of alcohol. Several hours later Scott lay comatose in a hospital emergency room. His blood-alcohol level was 4.1—five times the drunken driving standard in Massachusetts. A few days later he died, another college-age victim of binge drinking.

Scott was not unusual in his behavior. According to a study published by the Harvard School of Public Health in 2002, 44 percent of college students indulge in binge drinking (defined as at least five drinks in a row for men and four in a row for women). For those who live in a Greek fraternity or sorority, the rates are even higher—four out of five are binge drinkers (see the figure). These numbers represent an increase from 1990s data, despite efforts on many campuses across the nation to educate students about the risks of binge drinking. The problem is not confined to the

---

44 percent of college students indulge in binge drinking.

United States—Britain, Russia, and South Africa all report regular "drink till you drop" alcoholic consumption among young people.

Binge drinking on campus presents a difficult social problem. On the one hand, it can be regarded as *deviant,* violating the standards of conduct expected of those in an academic setting. In fact, Harvard researchers consider binge drinking the most serious public health hazard facing colleges. Not only does it cause about 50 fatalities a year and hundreds of cases of alcohol poisoning; it increases the likelihood of falling behind in schoolwork, getting injured, and damaging property.

The other side of this potentially self-destructive behavior is that binge drinking represents *conformity* to the peer culture, especially in fraternities and sororities, which serve as social centers on many campuses. Most students seem to take an "everybody does it— no big deal" attitude toward the behavior. Many find that taking five drinks in a row is fairly typical. As one student at Boston University noted, "Anyone that goes to a party does that or worse. If you talk to anyone college age, it's normal."

Some colleges and universities are taking steps to make binge drinking a bit less "normal" by means of *social control*— banning kegs, closing fraternities and

Sources: Glauber 1998; Goldberg 1998; Hoover 2002; Leinwand 2003; McCormick and Kalb 1998; Wechsler et al. 2002.

Just 45 days after September 11, with virtually no debate, Congress passed the USA PATRIOT Act of 2001. (The phrase USA PATRIOT is an acronym for "Uniting and Strengthening America by Providing Appropriate Tools Required to Intercept and Obstruct Terrorism.") Sections of this sweeping legislation revoked legal checks on the power of law enforcement agencies. Without a warrant or probable cause, the Federal Bureau of Investigation (FBI) can now secretly access most private records, including medical histories, library accounts, and student registrations. In 2002, for example, the FBI searched the records of hundreds of dive shops and scuba organizations. Agents had been directed to identify every person who had taken diving lessons in the past three years because of speculation that terrorists might try to approach their targets underwater (Moss and Fessenden 2002).

Many people think this kind of social control goes too far. Civil rights advocates also worry that the government's request for information on suspicious activities may encourage negative stereotyping of Muslims and Arab Americans. We will return to this topic in the social policy section of Chapter 16, which addresses the trade-off between the benefits of new surveillance technology and the right to privacy.

The interplay between formal and informal social control can be complicated, especially if people are encouraged to violate social norms. Box 8-1 considers binge drinking among college students, who receive conflicting messages about the acceptability of the behavior from sources of formal and informal social control.

Law and Society

Some norms are so important to a society that they are formalized into laws controlling people's behavior. *Law* may be defined as governmental social control (Black 1995). Some laws, such as the prohibition against murder, are directed at all members of society. Others, such as fish-

Classroom Tip See "Field Trips" (Class Discussion Topics).
Contemporary Culture Discuss whether students support the Patriot Act.

Reel Society See Deviance in the Topic Index.

178

sororities, encouraging liquor retailers not to sell in high volume to students, and expelling students after three alcohol-related infractions. Yet many colleges still tolerate spring break organizers who promote "All you can drink" parties as part of a tour package.

Let's Discuss

1. Why do you think most college students regard binge drinking as a normal rather than a deviant behavior?
2. Which do you think would be more effective in stopping binge drinking on your campus, informal or formal social control?

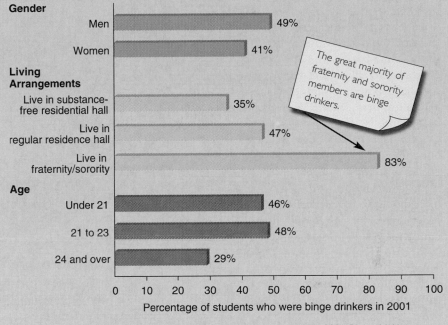

Gender
Men — 49%
Women — 41%

Living Arrangements
Live in substance-free residential hall — 35%
Live in regular residence hall — 47%
Live in fraternity/sorority — 83%

The great majority of fraternity and sorority members are binge drinkers.

Age
Under 21 — 46%
21 to 23 — 48%
24 and over — 29%

Percentage of students who were binge drinkers in 2001

Note: Based on a national survey of more than 10,000 college students in 2001. Binge drinking was defined as one drinking session of at least five drinks for men or four drinks for women during the two weeks prior to the self-administered questionnaire.

Source: Wechsler et al. 2002:208.

ing and hunting regulations, primarily affect particular categories of people. Still others govern the behavior of social institutions (for instance, corporate law and laws regarding the taxing of nonprofit enterprises).

Sociologists see the creation of laws as a social process. Because laws are passed in response to perceived needs for formal social control, sociologists have sought to explain how and why such perceptions arise. In their view, law is not merely a static body of rules handed down from generation to generation. Rather, it reflects continually changing standards of what is right and wrong, of how violations are to be determined, and of what sanctions are to be applied (Schur 1968).

Sociologists representing varying theoretical perspectives agree that the legal order reflects the values of those in a position to exercise authority. Therefore, the creation of civil and criminal law can be a most controversial matter. Should it be against the law to employ illegal immigrants in a factory (see Chapter 10), to have an abortion (see Chapter 11), to allow prayer in public schools (Chapter 13), or to smoke on an airplane? Such issues have been bitterly debated, because they require a choice among competing values. Not surprisingly, laws that are unpopular—such as the onetime prohibition of alcohol under the Eighteenth Amendment and the widespread establishment of a 55-mile-per-hour speed limit on highways—become difficult to enforce when there is no consensus supporting the norms.

One current and controversial debate over laws governing behavior is whether people should be allowed to use marijuana legally, for medical purposes. Although the majority of adults polled in national surveys support such use, state governments have been reluctant to grant the right to use marijuana for medical purposes; see Figure 8-1, page 180.

Socialization is actually the primary source of conforming and obedient behavior, including obedience to law. Generally, it is not external pressure from a peer

Let's Discuss Is binge drinking deviant behavior on a college campus? In a workplace? At home?
Global View Binge drinking is a concern in Britain, Russia, South Africa.
Gender Binge drinking is a concern among both male and female college students.

Classroom Tip See "Marijuana for Medical Use" (Additional Lecture Ideas).

group or authority figure that makes us go along with social norms. Rather, we have internalized such norms as valid and desirable and are committed to observing them. In a profound sense, we want to see ourselves (and to be seen) as loyal, cooperative, responsible, and respectful of others. In the United States and other societies around the world, people are socialized both to want to belong and to fear being viewed as different or deviant.

Control theory suggests that our connection to members of society leads us to systematically conform to society's norms. According to sociologist Travis Hirschi and other control theorists, our bonds to family members, friends, and peers induce us to follow the mores and folkways of our society. We give little conscious thought to whether we will be sanctioned if we fail to conform. Socialization develops our self-control so well that we don't need further pressure to obey social norms. While control theory does not effectively explain the rationale for every conforming act, it nevertheless reminds us that while the media may focus on crime and disorder, most members of most societies conform to and obey basic norms (Gottfredson and Hirschi 1990; Hirschi 1969).

DEVIANCE

What Is Deviance?

For sociologists, the term *deviance* does not mean perversion or depravity. **Deviance** is behavior that violates the standards of conduct or expectations of a group or society (Wickman 1991:85). In the United States, alcoholics, compulsive gamblers, and the mentally ill would all be classified as deviants. Being late for class is categorized as a deviant act; the same is true of wearing jeans to a formal wedding. On the basis of the sociological definition, we are all deviant from time to time. Each of us violates common social norms in certain situations.

FIGURE 8-1

The Status of Medical Marijuana

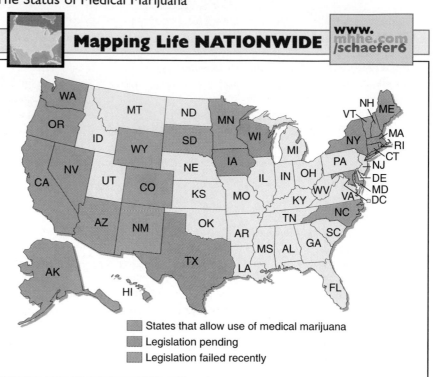

Note: Federal law confers a one-year prison sentence on those convicted of possessing a small amount of marijuana. No exception is made for medical use, even if state law allows it, as it does in California.

Source: Developed by author based on data from Americans for Medical Rights 2003.

Is being overweight an example of deviance? In the United States and many other cultures, unrealistic standards of appearance and body image place a huge strain on people—especially adult women and girls—based on how they look. Journalist Naomi Wolf (1992) has used the term *beauty myth* to refer to an exaggerated ideal of beauty, beyond the reach of all but a few females, which has unfortunate consequences. In order to shed their "deviant" image and conform to unrealistic societal norms, many women and girls become consumed with adjusting their appearances. Yet what is deviant in one culture may be celebrated in another. In Nigeria, for example, being fat is considered a mark of beauty. Part of the coming-of-age ritual calls for young girls to spend a month in a "fattening room." Among Nigerians, being thin at this point in the life course is deviant (A. Simmons 1998).

Deviance involves the violation of group norms, which may or may not be formalized into law. It is a comprehensive concept that includes not only criminal behavior but also many actions that are not subject to prosecution. The public official who takes a bribe has defied social norms, but so has the high school student who refuses to sit in an assigned seat or cuts class. Of course, deviation from norms is not always negative, let alone criminal. A member of an exclusive social club who speaks out against a traditional policy of excluding women, Blacks, and Jews from admittance is deviating from the club's norms. So is a police officer who blows the whistle on corruption or brutality within the department.

From a sociological perspective, deviance is hardly objective or set in stone. Rather, it is subject to social definition within a particular society and at a particular time. For that reason, what is considered deviant can shift from one social era to another. In most instances, those individuals and groups with the greatest status and power define what is acceptable and what is deviant. For example, despite serious medical warnings against the dangers of tobacco, made since 1964, cigarette smoking continued to be accepted for decades—in good part because of the power of tobacco farmers and cigarette manufacturers. Only after a long campaign led by public health and anticancer activists did cigarette smoking become more of a deviant activity. Today, many state and local laws limit where people can smoke.

While deviance can include relatively minor day-to-day decisions about our personal behavior, in some cases it can become part of a person's identity. This process is called *stigmatization*.

Deviance and Social Stigma

There are many ways a person can acquire a deviant identity. Because of physical or behavioral characteristics, some people are unwillingly cast in negative social roles. Once they have been assigned a deviant role, they have

`p. 86` trouble presenting a positive image to others and may even experience lowered self-esteem. Whole groups of people—for instance, "short people" or "redheads"—may be labeled in this way. The interactionist Erving Goffman coined the term **stigma** to describe the labels society uses to devalue members of certain social groups (Goffman 1963a; Heckert and Best 1997).

Prevailing expectations about beauty and body shape may prevent people who are regarded as ugly or obese from advancing as rapidly as their abilities permit. Both overweight and anorexic people are assumed to be weak in character, slaves to their appetites or to media images. Because they do not conform to the beauty myth, they may be viewed as "disfigured" or "strange" in appearance, bearers of what Goffman calls a "spoiled identity." However, what constitutes disfigurement is a matter of interpretation. Of the 1 million cosmetic procedures done every year in the United States alone, many are performed on women

who would be defined objectively as having a normal appearance. And while feminist sociologists have accurately noted that the beauty myth makes many women feel uncomfortable with themselves, men too lack confidence in their appearance. The number of males who choose to undergo cosmetic procedures has risen sharply in recent years; men now account for 20 percent of such surgeries, including liposuction (American Academy of Cosmetic Surgery 2004).

Often people are stigmatized for deviant behaviors they may no longer engage in. The labels "compulsive gambler," "ex-convict," "recovering alcoholic," and "ex–mental patient" can stick to a person for life. Goffman draws a useful distinction between a prestige symbol that draws attention to a positive aspect of one's identity, such as a wedding band or a badge, and a stigma symbol that discredits or debases one's identity, such as a conviction for child molestation. While stigma symbols may not always be obvious, they can become a matter of public knowledge. Starting in 1994, many states required convicted sex offenders to register with local police departments. Some communities publish the names and addresses, and in some instances even the pictures, of convicted sex offenders on the web.

A person need not be guilty of a crime to be stigmatized. Homeless people often have trouble getting a job, because employers are wary of applicants who cannot give a home address. Moreover, hiding one's homelessness is difficult, since agencies generally use the telephone to contact applicants about job openings. If a homeless person has access to a telephone at a shelter, the staff generally answers the phone by announcing the name of the institution—a sure way to discourage prospective employers. Even if a homeless person surmounts these obstacles and manages to get a job, she or he is often fired when the employer learns of the situation. Regardless of a person's positive attributes, employers regard the spoiled identity of homelessness as sufficient reason to dismiss an employee.

While some types of deviance will stigmatize a person, other types do not carry a significant penalty. Some good examples of socially tolerated forms of deviance can be found in the world of high technology.

Deviance and Technology

Technological innovations such as pagers and voice mail can redefine social interactions and the standards of behavior related to them. When the Internet was first made available to the general public, no norms or regulations governed its use. Because online communication offers a high degree of anonymity, uncivil behavior—speaking harshly of others or monopolizing chat

Let's Discuss Are redheads stigmatized? In what way? Are they viewed as deviant? Have students give examples of other stigmatized groups.
Key Person Erving Goffman
Theory Interactionist perspective used to examine stigma and deviance

Gender Females and males both succumb to the beauty myth.
Contemporary Culture Deviant behavior on the Internet

Who Is Deviant?

Customary greeting among residents of the mountainous kingdom of Bhutan

What if your teachers greeted you in class by extending their tongues and hands? What if your girlfriend started to elongate her neck by layering it with heavy brass coils? Wouldn't you think they were behaving in bizarre ways? Certainly by the standards of U.S. society, they would be. But not if you were living in Bhutan, where such greetings are customary, or among the Kayan tribe in northern Thailand, where females traditionally wear up to 12 pounds of coils around the neck as a mark of beauty and tribal identity. Because deviance is socially constructed, it is subject to different social interpretations over time and across cultures.

As these photos show, what is deviant in one culture could very well be celebrated in another. In Latin America, Spain, Portugal, and many other countries, bullfighting is a popular sport. But imagine how Hindus, who consider the cow sacred, would react to the dance of death in the bullring. Looking at other peoples and cultures from their point of view, as well as from our own, helps us to understand deviance as a social construction.

"Long-necked" girls of the Kayan tribe in Thailand

Matador in the bullring, Portugal

183

FIGURE 8-2

Catching Music Thieves

Investigators can track down a computer used to swap music files by using the same software used for file sharing. How the tracking process works:

1 The investigator loads a copy of the peer-to-peer network's software program, such as Grokster or Morpheus, and a software "robot" that monitors traffic on the network.

Investigator

Computer with music files

"Robot"

2 The robot takes snapshots of the files being shared and notes the cutomer's Internet Protocol (IP) address. That address can then be used to find the user's Internet service provider (ISP).

File-sharing network

File-sharing "customer"

3 The investigator subpoenas the ISP to obtain access to records that will match the IP address to a specific home, dorm room or office cubicle.

Source: Healey 2003:A21.

At the urging of the music industry, law enforcement agencies have tracked down individuals who set up Internet servers to share music illegally. College students working from computers in their residence halls have been among those prosecuted.

room "space"—quickly became common. Online bulletin boards designed to carry items of community interest became littered with commercial advertisements. Such deviant acts are beginning to provoke calls for the establishment of formal rules for online behavior. For example, policymakers have debated whether to regulate the content of websites featuring hate speech and pornography (see the social policy section of Chapter 16).

Some deviant uses of technology are criminal, though not all participants see it that way. The pirating of software, motion pictures, and music has become a big business. At conventions and swap meets, pirated copies of movies, CDs, and DVDs are sold openly. Some of the products are obviously counterfeit, but many come in sophisticated packaging, complete with warranty cards. The vendors say

they merely want to be compensated for their time and the cost of materials, or that the software they have copied is in the public domain.

Similarly, the downloading of music from the Internet, which is typically protected by copyright, is widely accepted. But file sharing, like the pirating of CDs and DVDs, has grown to the point that it is threatening the profits of copyright owners. Napster, the renegade website that allowed thousands of people to download from a wide selection of music files for free, has been shut down, the victim of a court challenge by the music industry. Nevertheless, its fleeting success has encouraged imitators, many of them college students who run file-sharing programs from their dorm rooms. The music industry is fighting back by urging law enforcement agents to track the pirates down and prosecute them (see Figure 8-2).

Though most of these black market activities are clearly illegal, many consumers and small-time pirates are proud of their behavior. They may even think themselves smart for figuring out a way to avoid the "unfair" prices charged by "big corporations." Few people see the pirating of a new software program or a first-run movie as a threat to the public good, as they would embezzling from a bank. Similarly, most businesspeople who "borrow" software from another department, even though they lack a site license, do not think they are doing anything wrong. No social stigma attaches to their illegal behavior.

Deviance, then, is a complex concept. Sometimes it is trivial, sometimes profoundly harmful. Sometimes it is accepted by society and sometimes soundly rejected. What accounts for deviant behavior and people's reaction to it? In the next section we will examine four theoretical explanations for deviance.

Explaining Deviance

Why do people violate social norms? We have seen that deviant acts are subject to both informal and formal social

Let's Discuss Is viewing pornography on the Internet deviant behavior? Should it be censored? Is viewing it in the library deviant behavior? Should it be censored?

Race/Let's Discuss The expression "black market" uses the word *black* in a negative context that stigmatizes an entire group. Cite other examples of how everyday language stigmatizes groups.

control. The nonconforming or disobedient person may face disapproval, loss of friends, fines, or even imprisonment. Why, then, does deviance occur?

Early explanations for deviance identified supernatural causes or genetic factors (such as "bad blood" or evolutionary throwbacks to primitive ancestors). By the 1800s, substantial research efforts were being made to identify biological factors that lead to deviance, and especially to criminal activity. While such research was discredited in the 20th century, contemporary studies, primarily by biochemists, have sought to isolate genetic factors that suggest a likelihood of certain personality traits. Although criminality (much less deviance) is hardly a personality characteristic, researchers have focused on traits that might lead to crime, such as aggression. Of course, aggression can also lead to success in the corporate world, in professional sports, or in other walks of life.

The contemporary study of the possible biological p. 64 roots of criminality is but one aspect of the larger debate over sociobiology. In general, sociologists reject any emphasis on the genetic roots of crime and deviance. The limitations of current knowledge, the possibility of reinforcing racist and sexist assumptions, and the disturbing implications for the rehabilitation of criminals have led sociologists to draw largely on other approaches to explain deviance (Sagarin and Sanchez 1988).

Functionalist Perspective

According to functionalists, deviance is a common part of human existence, with positive as well as negative consequences for social stability. Deviance helps to define the limits of proper behavior. Children who see one parent scold the other for belching at the dinner table learn about approved conduct. The same is true of the driver who receives a speeding ticket, the department store cashier who is fired for yelling at a customer, and the college student who is penalized for handing in papers weeks overdue.

Durkheim's Legacy Émile Durkheim ([1895] 1964) focused his sociological investigations mainly on criminal acts, yet his conclusions have implications for all types of deviant behavior. In Durkheim's view, the punishments established within a culture (including both formal and informal mechanisms of social control) help to define acceptable behavior and thus contribute to stability. If improper acts were not sanctioned, people might stretch their standards of what constitutes appropriate conduct.

Kai Erikson (1966) illustrated the boundary-maintenance function of deviance in his study of the Puritans of 17th-century New England. By today's standards, the Puritans placed tremendous emphasis on conventional

morals. Their persecution and execution of women as witches represented a continuing attempt to define and redefine the boundaries of their community. In effect, their changing social norms created "crime waves," as people whose behavior was previously acceptable suddenly faced punishment for being deviant (Abrahamson 1978; N. Davis 1975).

Durkheim ([1897] 1951) introduced the term *anomie* into sociological literature to describe the loss of direction felt in a society when social control of individual behavior has become ineffective. Anomie is a state of normlessness that typically occurs during a period of profound social change and disorder, such as a time of economic collapse. People become more aggressive or depressed, which results in higher rates of violent crime and suicide. Since there is much less agreement on what constitutes proper behavior during times of revolution, sudden prosperity, or economic depression, conformity and obedience become less significant as social forces. It also becomes much more difficult to state exactly what constitutes deviance.

Merton's Theory of Deviance What do a mugger and a teacher have in common? Each is "working" to obtain money that can then be exchanged for desired goods. As this example illustrates, behavior that violates accepted norms (such as mugging) may be performed with the same basic objectives in mind as those of people who pursue more conventional lifestyles.

On the basis of this kind of analysis, sociologist Robert Merton (1968) adapted Durkheim's notion of anomie to explain why people accept or reject the goals of a society, the socially approved means of fulfilling their aspirations, or both. Merton maintained that one important cultural goal in the United States is success, measured largely in terms of money. In addition to providing this goal for people, our society offers specific instructions on how to pursue success—go to school, work hard, do not quit, take advantage of opportunities, and so forth.

What happens to individuals in a society with a heavy emphasis on wealth as a basic symbol of success? Merton reasoned that people adapt in certain ways, either by conforming to or by deviating from such cultural expectations. His *anomie theory of deviance* posits five basic forms of adaptation (see Table 8-1, page 186).

Conformity to social norms, the most common adaptation in Merton's typology, is the opposite of deviance. It involves acceptance of both the overall societal goal ("become affluent") and the approved means ("work hard"). In Merton's view, there must be some consensus regarding accepted cultural goals and the legitimate means for attaining them. Without such a consensus, societies could

Under cover of darkness, drag racers await the start signal on a deserted Los Angeles street. Sutherland's concepts of differential association and cultural transmission would both apply to the practice of drag racing on city streets.

exist only as collectives of people rather than as unified cultures and might experience continual chaos.

The other four types of behavior represented in Table 8-1 all involve some departure from conformity. The "innovator" accepts the goals of society but pursues them with means that are regarded as improper. For instance, a safecracker may steal money to buy consumer goods and expensive vacations.

In Merton's typology, the "ritualist" has abandoned the goal of material success and become compulsively committed to the institutional means. Work becomes simply a way of life rather than a means to the goal of success. An example would be the bureaucratic official who blindly applies rules and regulations without remembering the larger goals of an organization. Certainly this would be true of a welfare caseworker who refuses to assist a homeless family because their last apartment was in another district.

The "retreatist," as described by Merton, has basically withdrawn (or retreated) from both the goals and the means of a society. In the United States, drug addicts and vagrants are typically portrayed as retreatists. Concern has been growing that adolescents who are addicted to alcohol will become retreatists at an early age.

The final adaptation identified by Merton reflects people's attempts to create a *new* social structure. The "rebel" feels alienated from the dominant means and goals, and may seek a dramatically different social order. Members of a revolutionary political organization, such as a militia group, can be categorized as rebels according to Merton's model.

Merton's theory, though popular, has had relatively few applications. Little effort has been made to determine to what extent all acts of deviance can be accounted for by his five modes. Moreover, while Merton's theory is useful in examining certain types of behavior, such as illegal gambling by disadvantaged "innovators," his formulation fails to explain key differences in crime rates. Why, for example, do some disadvantaged groups have lower rates of reported crime than others? Why do many people in adverse circumstances reject criminal activity as a viable alternative? Merton's theory of deviance does not answer such questions easily (Clinard and Miller 1998).

Still, Merton has made a key contribution to the sociological understanding of deviance by pointing out that deviants such as innovators and ritualists share a great deal with conforming people. The convicted felon may

Table 8-1	Modes of Individual Adaptation	
Mode	Institutionalized Means (Hard Work)	Societal Goal (Acquisition of Wealth)
Nondeviant		
Conformity	Accept	Accept
Deviant		
Innovation	Reject	Accept
Ritualism	Accept	Reject
Retreatism	Reject	Reject
Rebellion	Replace with new means	Replace with new goals

Source: Adapted from Merton 1968:194.

hold many of the same aspirations as people with no criminal background. The theory helps us to understand deviance as a socially created behavior rather than as the result of momentary pathological impulses.

Interactionist Perspective

The functionalist approach to deviance explains why rule violations continue to happen despite pressure to conform and obey. However, functionalists do not indicate how a given person comes to commit a deviant act, or why on some occasions crimes do or do not occur. The emphasis on everyday behavior that is the focus of the interactionist perspective offers two explanations of crime—cultural transmission and routine activities theory.

Cultural Transmission The graffiti writers described by Susan Phillips in the chapter-opening excerpt learn from one another. In fact, Phillips (1999) was surprised by how stable their focus was over time. She also noted how other ethnic groups built on the models of the African American and Chicano gangs, superimposing Cambodian, Chinese, or Vietnamese symbols.

Humans *learn* how to behave in social situations, whether properly or improperly. There is no natural, innate manner in which people interact with one another. These simple ideas are not disputed today, but such was not the case when sociologist Edwin Sutherland (1883–1950) first advanced the idea that an individual undergoes the same basic socialization process in learning conforming and deviant acts.

Sutherland's ideas have been the dominating force in criminology. He drew on the ***cultural transmission*** school, which emphasizes that one learns criminal behavior by interacting with others. Such learning includes not only the techniques of lawbreaking (for example, how to break into a car quickly and quietly) but also the motives, drives, and rationalizations of the criminal. The cultural transmission approach can also be used to explain the behavior of those who habitually abuse alcohol or drugs.

Sutherland maintained that through interactions with a primary group and significant others, people acquire definitions of proper and improper behavior. He used the term ***differential association*** to describe the process through which exposure to attitudes *favorable* to criminal acts leads to the violation of rules. Research suggests that this view of differential association also applies to noncriminal deviant acts such as smoking, truancy, and early sexual behavior (E. Jackson et al. 1986).

To what extent will a given person engage in activity that is regarded as proper or improper? For each individual, it will depend on the frequency, duration, and importance of two types of social interaction—those experiences that endorse deviant behavior and those that promote acceptance of social norms. People are more likely to engage in norm-defying behavior if they are part of a group or subculture that stresses deviant values, such as a street gang.

Sutherland offers the example of a boy who is sociable, outgoing, and athletic and who lives in an area with a high rate of delinquency. The youth is very likely to come into contact with peers who commit acts of vandalism, fail to attend school, and so forth, and may come to adopt such behavior. However, an introverted boy who lives in the same neighborhood may stay away from his peers and avoid delinquency. In another community, an outgoing and athletic boy may join a Little League baseball team or a scout troop because of his interactions with peers. Thus, Sutherland views improper behavior as the result of the types of groups to which one belongs and the kinds of friendships one has (Sutherland et al. 1992).

According to critics, however, the cultural transmission approach may explain the deviant behavior of juvenile delinquents or graffiti artists, but it fails to explain the conduct of the first-time impulsive shoplifter or the impoverished person who steals out of necessity. While it is not a precise statement of the process through which one becomes a criminal, differential association theory does direct our attention to the paramount role of social interaction in increasing a person's motivation to engage in deviant behavior (Cressey 1960; E. Jackson et al. 1986; Sutherland et al. 1992).

Routine Activities Theory Another, more recent interactionist explanation considers the requisite conditions for a crime or deviant act to occur: there must be, at the same time and in the same place, a perpetrator, a victim, and/or an object of property. ***Routine activities theory*** contends that criminal victimization increases when motivated offenders and suitable targets converge. It goes without saying that you cannot have car theft without automobiles, but the greater availability of more valuable automobiles to potential thieves *heightens* the likelihood that such a crime will occur. Campus and airport parking lots, where vehicles may be left in isolated locations for long periods, represent a new target for crime that was unknown just a generation ago. Routine activity of this nature can occur even in the home. If a parent keeps a number of liquor bottles in an easily accessible place, juveniles can siphon off the contents without attracting attention to their "crime." This theory derives its name from the fact that the elements of a criminal or deviant act come together in normal, legal, and routine activities. It is considered interactionist because of its emphasis on everyday behavior and micro-level social interactions.

Key Person Edwin Sutherland
Theory Concepts of cultural transmission and differential association introduced
Let's Discuss Are there groups or subcultures on campus that stress deviant values?

Theory *Routine activities theory* is a relatively new interactionist explanation of deviance.
Let's Discuss Ask students if they think any of the areas around the World Trade Center site became "hot spots" for crime right after the September 11, 2001 attack.

In the 1930s, the Federal Bureau of Narcotics launched a campaign to portray marijuana as a dangerous drug rather than a pleasure-inducing substance. From a conflict perspective, those in power often use such tactics to coerce others into adopting a different point of view.

Advocates of this theory see it as a powerful explanation for the rise in crime over the last 50 years. That is, routine activities have changed, making crime more likely. Homes left vacant during the day or during long vacations are more accessible as targets of crime. The greater presence of highly portable consumer goods, such as video equipment and computers, is another change that makes crime more likely (L. Cohen and Felson 1979; Felson 2002).

Some significant research supports routine activities theory. For example, studies done in the aftermath of Hurricane Andrew in Florida (1992) show that certain crimes increased as citizens and their property became more vulnerable. Studies of urban crime have documented the existence of "hot spots," such as tourist destinations and automated teller (ATM) machines, where people are more likely to be victimized because of their routine comings and goings (Cromwell et al. 1995; Sherman et al. 1989).

Labeling Theory

The Saints and Roughnecks were two groups of high school males who were continually engaged in excessive drinking, reckless driving, truancy, petty theft, and vandalism. There the similarity ended. None of the Saints was ever arrested, but every Roughneck was frequently in trouble with police and townspeople. Why the disparity in their treatment? On the basis of observation research in their high school, sociologist William Chambliss (1973) concluded that social class played an important role in the varying fortunes of the two groups.

The Saints hid behind a facade of respectability. They came from "good families," were active in school organizations, planned on attending college, and received good grades. People generally viewed their delinquent acts as a few isolated cases of sowing wild oats. The Roughnecks had no such aura of respectability. They drove around town in beat-up cars, were generally unsuccessful in school, and aroused suspicion no matter what they did.

We can understand such discrepancies by using an approach to deviance known as **labeling theory.** Unlike Sutherland's work, labeling theory does not focus on why some individuals come to commit deviant acts. Instead, it attempts to explain why certain people (such as the Roughnecks) are *viewed* as deviants, delinquents, bad kids, losers, and criminals, while others whose behavior is similar (such as the Saints) are not seen in such harsh terms. Reflecting the contribution of interactionist theorists, labeling theory emphasizes how a person comes to be labeled as deviant, or to accept that label. Sociologist Howard Becker (1963:9; 1964), who popularized this approach, summed it up with this statement: "Deviant behavior is behavior that people so label."

Labeling theory is also called the **societal-reaction approach,** reminding us that it is the *response* to an act, and not the behavior itself, that determines deviance. For example, studies have shown that some school personnel and therapists expand educational programs designed for learning-disabled students to include those with behavioral problems. Consequently, a "troublemaker" can be improperly labeled as learning-disabled and vice versa.

Traditionally, research on deviance has focused on people who violate social norms. In contrast, labeling theory focuses on police, probation officers, psychiatrists, judges, teachers, employers, school officials, and other regulators of social control. These agents, it is argued, play a significant role in creating the deviant identity by designating certain people (and not others) as deviant. An important aspect of labeling theory is the recognition that some individuals or groups have the power to *define* labels and apply them to others. This view ties into the conflict perspective's emphasis on the social significance of power.

In recent years the practice of *racial profiling,* in which people are identified as criminal suspects purely on the basis of their race, has come under public scrutiny. Studies confirm the public's suspicions that in some jurisdictions, police officers are much more likely to stop African American males than White males for routine traffic violations, in the expectation of finding drugs or guns in their cars. Civil rights activists refer to these cases sarcastically as DWB violations (Driving While Black). Beginning in 2001, profiling took a new turn as people who appeared to be Arab or Muslim came under special scrutiny.

The labeling approach does not fully explain why certain people accept a label and others manage to reject it. In fact, this perspective may exaggerate the ease with which societal judgments can alter our self-images. Labeling theorists do suggest, however, that the power one has relative to others is important in determining a person's ability to resist an undesirable label. Competing approaches (including that of Sutherland) fail to explain why some deviants continue to be viewed as conformists rather than as violators of rules. According to Howard Becker (1973), labeling theory was not conceived as the *sole* explanation for deviance; its proponents merely hoped to focus more attention on the undeniably important actions of those people who are officially in charge of defining deviance (N. Davis 1975; compare with Cullen and Cullen 1978).

The popularity of labeling theory is reflected in the emergence of a related perspective, called social constructionism. According to the ***social constructionist perspective,*** deviance is the product of the culture we live in. Social constructionists focus specifically on the decision-making process that creates the deviant identity. They point out that "child abductors," "deadbeat dads," "spree killers," and "date rapists" have always been with us, but at times have become *the* major social concern of policy makers because of intensive media coverage (Liska and Messner 1999; E. R. Wright et al. 2000).

Use Your Sociological Imagination www.mhhe.com/schaefer6

You are a teacher. What labels, freely used in educational circles, might you attach to your students?

Conflict Theory

Conflict theorists point out that people with power protect their own interests and define deviance to suit their own needs. Sociologist Richard Quinney (1974, 1979, 1980) is a leading exponent of the view that the criminal justice system serves the interests of the powerful. Crime, according to Quinney (1970), is a definition of conduct

created by authorized agents of social control—such as legislators and law enforcement officers—in a politically organized society. He and other conflict theorists argue that lawmaking is often an attempt by the powerful to coerce others into their own morality (see also Spitzer 1975).

This theory helps to explain why our society has laws against gambling, drug usage, and prostitution, many of which are violated on a massive scale (we will examine these "victimless crimes" later in the chapter). According to conflict theorists, criminal law does not represent a consistent application of societal values, but instead reflects competing values and interests. Thus, marijuana is outlawed in the United States because it is alleged to be harmful to users, yet cigarettes and alcohol are sold legally almost everywhere. Similarly, conflict theorists contend that the entire criminal justice system of the United States treats suspects differently on the basis of their racial, ethnic, or social class background (see Box 8-2, page 190).

The perspective advanced by conflict and labeling theorists forms quite a contrast to the functionalist approach to deviance. Functionalists see standards of deviant behavior as merely reflecting cultural norms; conflict and labeling theorists point out that the most powerful groups in a society can shape laws and standards and determine who is (or is not) prosecuted as a criminal. These groups would be unlikely to apply the label "deviant" to the corporate executive whose decisions lead to large-scale environmental pollution. In the opinion of conflict theorists, agents of social control and other powerful groups can impose their own self-serving definitions of deviance on the general public.

Feminist Perspective

Feminist criminologists such as Freda Adler and Meda Chesney-Lind have suggested that many of the existing approaches to deviance and crime were developed with only men in mind. For example, in the United States, for many years any husband who forced his wife to have sexual intercourse—without her consent and against her will—was not legally considered to have committed rape. The law defined rape as pertaining only to sexual relations between people who were not married to each other, reflecting the overwhelmingly male composition of state legislatures at the time.

It took repeated protests by feminist organizations to get changes in the criminal law defining rape. Beginning in 1996, husbands in all 50 states could be prosecuted under most circumstances for the rape of their wives. There remain alarming exceptions: for example, in Tennessee a husband may legally use force or coercion to rape his wife as long as no weapon is present and he has not inflicted

Classroom Tip For more on labeling theory, see "Primary and Secondary Deviance" (Additional Lecture Ideas).
Theory Labeling theorists' view of deviance ties into conflict perspective.
Classroom Tip Carefully distinguish between labeling theory, the societal reaction approach, and the social constructionist perspective.
Key Person Richard Quinney

Classroom Tip See "Controversies about Campus Crime" (Additional Lecture Ideas).
Theory Labeling and conflict views of deviance contrasted with functionalist approach.
Gender Impact of the feminist movement on laws against rape of wives by their husbands

Race matters in the criminal justice system. Conflict theorists remind us that while the basic purpose of law is to maintain stability and order, it can actually perpetuate inequality. In many cases, criminal justice officials use their *discretionary powers*—decisions made on their own discretion about whether to press charges or drop them, whether to set bail and how much, whether to offer parole or deny it—in biased ways. Researchers have found that discretionary differences in the way social control is exercised put African Americans and Latinos at a disadvantage in the justice system, both as juveniles and as adults. In this way, Richard Quinney and other conflict theorists argue, the criminal justice system keeps the poor and oppressed in their deprived positions.

How do sociologists determine whether suspects and offenders are treated dif-

---

On average, White offenders receive shorter sentences than comparable Latino and African American offenders.

---

ferently based on racial, ethnic, and social class backgrounds? One way is to look at convicted criminals and compare the sentences they receive for equivalent crimes. The task can be complicated, because researchers must take into consideration a number of factors that affect sentencing. For example, in their study of federal court data, sociologists Darrell Steffensmeier and Stephen Demuth examined the severity of the crime and the convict's prior arrest record. Even after taking these and other factors into consideration, they found that on average, White offenders receive shorter sentences than comparable Latino and African American offenders.

Race plays a crucial role in death penalty cases, as the accompanying figure shows. While White non-Hispanics make

up 71 percent of the U.S. population, they constitute only 45 percent of criminals sentenced to death. Conflict theorists point out that the overwhelming majority of prosecutors in death penalty cases are White and non-Hispanic. The victim's race matters a great deal in these cases, as well. Studies have consistently shown that a convicted criminal is much more likely to be sentenced to death if the victim is White and non-Hispanic than if the victim is non-White or Hispanic.

Let's Discuss

1. Do you know anyone who was treated leniently by the criminal justice system? If so, was the person White and non-Hispanic? Why do you think police and/or other officials used their discretionary powers to excuse the person's offense or reduce the penalties?
2. Besides race, what other factors might contribute to the disproportionately severe sentencing of Black and Hispanic defendants? Explain.

Race and the Death Penalty

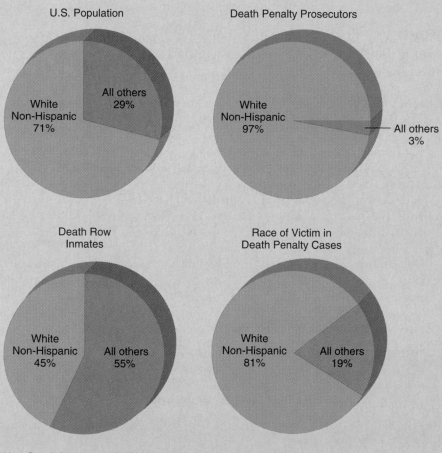

U.S. Population
White Non-Hispanic 71%
All others 29%

Death Penalty Prosecutors
White Non-Hispanic 97%
All others 3%

Death Row Inmates
White Non-Hispanic 45%
All others 55%

Race of Victim in Death Penalty Cases
White Non-Hispanic 81%
All others 19%

Note: Population data are for 2000; data on prosecutors, for 1998; data on inmates, for December 1, 2003; and data on victims, for 1977–December 1, 2003.

Sources: Based on Bureau of the Census 2003a; Death Penalty Information Center 2004.

Sources: Bushway and Piehl 2001; Dighton 2003; Hawkins et al. 2002; Liptak 2004b; Quinney 1974; Steffensmeier and Demuth 2000.

Classroom Tip Refer back to Figure 1-1.
Theory Conflict view of criminal law
Theory Conflict perspective on law and inequality
Race/Ethnicity Differential treatment of African Americans and Hispanics by the justice system
Method Steffensmeier and Demuth used survey data.

Classroom Tip See "Public Opinion on the Death Penalty" (Class Discussion Topics).
Classroom Tip See "Discretionary Justice" (Additional Lecture Ideas).
Classroom Tip See "Violent Juveniles" (Class Discussion Topics).

summingUP

Table 8-2	Approaches to Deviance		
Approach	**Perspective**	**Proponents**	**Emphasis**
Anomie	Functionalist	Émile Durkheim Robert Merton	Adaptation to societal norms
Cultural transmission/ Differential association	Interactionist	Edwin Sutherland	Patterns learned through others
Routine activities	Interactionist	Marcus Felson	Impact of the social environment
Labeling/Social constructionist	Interactionist	Howard Becker	Societal response to acts
Conflict	Conflict	Howard Quinney	Dominance by authorized agents Discretionary justice
Feminist	Conflict/Feminist	Freda Adler Meda Chesney-Lind	Role of gender Women as victims and perpetrators

"serious bodily harm." Despite such exceptions, the rise of the women's movement has unquestionably led to important changes in societal notions of criminality. For example, judges, legislators, and police officers now view wife battering and other forms of domestic violence as serious crimes (National Center on Women and Family Law 1996).

When it comes to crime and to deviance in general, society tends to treat women in a stereotypical fashion. For example, consider how women who have many and frequent sexual partners are more likely to be viewed with scorn than men who are promiscuous. Cultural views and attitudes toward women influence how they are perceived and labeled. The feminist perspective also emphasizes that deviance, including crime, tends to flow from economic relationships. Traditionally, men have had greater earning power than their wives. As a result, wives may be reluctant to report acts of abuse to the authorities, and lose what may be their primary or even sole source of income. In the workplace, men have exercised greater power than women in pricing, accounting, and product control, giving them greater opportunity to engage in such crimes as embezzlement and fraud. But as women take more active and powerful roles both in the household and in business, these gender differences in deviance and crime will undoubtedly narrow (F. Adler 1975; F. Adler et al. 2004; Chesney-Lind 1989).

In the future, feminist scholarship can be expected to grow dramatically. Particularly on topics such as white-collar crime, drinking behavior, drug abuse, and differential sentencing rates between the genders, as well as on the fundamental question of how to define deviance, feminist scholars will have much to say.

We have seen that over the past century, sociologists have taken many different approaches in studying deviance, arousing some controversy in the process. Table 8-2 summarizes the various theoretical approaches to this topic.

CRIME

Crime is a violation of criminal law for which some governmental authority applies formal penalties. It represents a deviation from formal social norms administered by the state. Laws divide crimes into various categories, depending on the severity of the offense, the age of the offender, the potential punishment, and the court that holds jurisdiction over the case.

Over 1.4 million violent crimes were reported in the United States in 2000, including more than 15,500 homicides. The key ingredients in the incidence of street crime appeared to be drug use and the widespread presence of firearms. According to the FBI, 19 percent of all reported aggravated assaults, 42 percent of reported robberies, and 67 percent of reported murders in 2002 involved a firearm. Even with a recent decline in major crime in the United States, current levels exceed levels experienced in the 1960s (Department of Justice 2002c:23, 35, 38).

Types of Crime

Rather than relying solely on legal categories, sociologists classify crimes in terms of how they are committed and how society views the offenses. In this section, we will

Theory Feminist perspective on deviance and economic relationships

Taking Sociology To Work

TIFFANY ZAPATA-MANCILLA   Victim Witness Specialist, Cook County State's Attorney's Office

Tiffany Zapata-Mancilla's typical day brings her into contact with all manner of crime victims—those who have survived murder attempts, domestic assault, child abuse, robbery, and other violent crimes—as well as family members who testify on behalf of victims. She works closely with victims who have witnessed a crime, since they are invariably called to testify in a trial. "My job is to make the courtroom experience for them as comfortable as possible," she says. That may mean offering them referral for crisis counseling, a court escort, court orientation, help with impact statements, assistance with restitution, protection services, transportation, child care, emergency financial assistance, or just a hot lunch. Her caseload of 500 cases comes from the four to eight courtrooms to which she is assigned in Chicago's Cook County.

"My sociological background helps me in all situations on a daily basis," Zapata-Mancilla says. In particular, it helps her to recognize the underlying societal issues, even in what seem to be horrendous individual acts, and to help victims to recognize those issues as well. "I do not judge those who come into the courtroom; I can only judge society," she says. According to Zapata-Mancilla, that doesn't mean that individuals have no personal responsibility for their life choices. But it helps to understand that people are conditioned by the environment and society they live in. One of her cases involved a young man who was called to testify to who killed his younger brother in a gang

shootout. At the time of the trial, two years later, he denied knowing anything about the killing, and afterward went out to eat with the defendant. It appears he might have been offered a drug job in return for not testifying. Instead of taking a judgmental attitude, Zapata-Mancilla recognized the young man's need to survive. Social problems such as poverty dictate to some degree the choices people believe they need to make.

Zapata-Mancilla majored in sociology at DePaul University after becoming hooked by her introductory course. She went on to earn her master's degree in sociology there in 2001. "I was very interested in societal issues such as poverty, crime, organized crime, and gang involvement, and how they influenced the lifestyles and psychology of individuals. Sociology, for me, offers reasons, not excuses, for why individuals act and react in certain ways," she says. She also thinks she has gained a greater understanding of herself as a Latina through her studies.

Her advice for students: "Keep an open mind and don't be judgmental of others."

Let's Discuss

1. Why do you think victim witnesses need special attention?
2. What aspect of sociological study do you think best prepared Zapata-Mancilla for her job?

examine four types of crime differentiated by sociologists: professional crime, organized crime, white-collar crime, and victimless crimes.

Professional Crime

Although the adage "Crime doesn't pay" is familiar, many people do make a career of illegal activities. A *professional criminal* (or career criminal) is a person who pursues crime as a day-to-day occupation, developing skilled techniques and enjoying a certain degree of status among other criminals. Some professional criminals specialize in burglary, safecracking, hijacking of cargo, pickpocketing, and shoplifting. Such people have acquired skills that reduce the likelihood of arrest, conviction, and imprison-

ment. As a result, they may have long careers in their chosen "professions."

Edwin Sutherland (1937) offered pioneering insights into the behavior of professional criminals by publishing an annotated account written by a professional thief. Unlike the person who engages in crime only once or twice, professional thieves make a business of stealing. They devote their entire working time to planning and executing crimes, and sometimes travel across the nation to pursue their "professional duties." Like people in regular occupations, professional thieves consult with their colleagues concerning the demands of work, becoming part of a subculture of similarly occupied individuals. They exchange information on places to burglarize, on outlets

Student Alert Distinguish between professional crime and organized crime.

Classroom Tip To learn how a hit man approaches killing as "just a job," see "Being a Hit Man" (Additional Lecture Ideas).

for unloading stolen goods, and on ways of securing bail bonds if arrested.

Organized Crime

A 1978 government report devotes three pages to defining the term *organized crime.* For our purposes, we will consider **organized crime** to be the work of a group that regulates relations among criminal enterprises involved in illegal activities, including prostitution, gambling, and the smuggling and sale of illegal drugs. Organized crime dominates the world of illegal business just as large corporations dominate the conventional business world. It allocates territory, sets prices for goods and services, and acts as an arbitrator in internal disputes. A secret, conspiratorial activity, it generally evades law enforcement. It takes over legitimate businesses, gains influence over labor unions, corrupts public officials, intimidates witnesses in criminal trials, and even "taxes" merchants in exchange for "protection" (National Advisory Commission on Criminal Justice 1976).

Organized crime serves as a means of upward mobility for groups of people struggling to escape poverty. Sociologist Daniel Bell (1953) used the term *ethnic succession* to describe the sequential passage of leadership from Irish Americans in the early part of the 20th century to Jewish Americans in the 1920s and then to Italian Americans in the early 1930s. Recently, ethnic succession has become more complex, reflecting the diversity of the nation's latest immigrants. Colombian, Mexican, Russian, Chinese, Pakistani, and Nigerian immigrants are among those who have begun to play a significant role in organized crime activities (Chin 1996; Kleinknecht 1996).

There has always been a global element in organized crime. But law enforcement officials and policymakers now acknowledge the emergence of a new form of organized crime that takes advantage of advances in electronic communications. *Transnational* organized crime includes drug and arms smuggling, money laundering, and trafficking in illegal immigrants and stolen goods, such as automobiles (Lumpe 2003; Office of Justice Programs 1999).

White-Collar and Technology-Based Crime

Income tax evasion, stock manipulation, consumer fraud, bribery and extraction of kickbacks, embezzlement, and misrepresentation in advertising—these are all examples of **white-collar crime,** illegal acts committed in the course of business activities, often by affluent, "respectable" people. Edwin Sutherland (1949, 1983) likened these crimes to organized

"BUT IF WE GO BACK TO SCHOOL AND GET A GOOD EDUCATION, THINK OF ALL THE DOORS IT'LL OPEN TO WHITE-COLLAR CRIME."

crime because they are often perpetrated through occupational roles.

A new type of white-collar crime has emerged in recent decades: computer crime. The use of high technology allows criminals to carry out embezzlement or electronic fraud, often leaving few traces, or to gain access to a company's inventory without leaving home. According to a 2002 study by the FBI and the Computer Security Institute, 90 percent of companies relying on computer systems had detected computer security breaches in the past year, but only 34 percent reported those attacks to authorities. Recently, an increasing proportion of such attacks—65 percent in 2003—has been coming from outside the United States (Cha 2003; R. Power 2002).

Sutherland (1940) coined the term *white-collar crime* in 1939 to refer to acts by individuals, but the term has been broadened more recently to include offenses by businesses and corporations as well. *Corporate crime,* or any act by a corporation that is punishable by the government, takes many forms and includes individuals, organizations, and institutions among its victims. Corporations may engage in anticompetitive behavior, environmental pollution, tax fraud, stock fraud and manipulation, accounting fraud, the production of unsafe goods, bribery and corruption, and health and safety violations (Hansen 2002; Jost 2002a).

For many years, corporate wrongdoers got off lightly in court by documenting their long history of charitable contributions and agreeing to help law enforcement officials find other white-collar criminals. In 2003, ten investment firms and two stock analysts collectively paid a $1.4 billion settlement for issuing fraudulent information to investors. While the magnitude of the fine grabbed headlines nationwide, it must be balanced against the millions of investors who were lured into buying billions of dollars' worth of shares in companies that the accused knew were either troubled or on the verge of collapse. The bottom line is that no individual served a jail sentence as part of the settlement, and no firm lost its license to do business. Prosecutors in other investigations into corporate scandals have pledged to pursue jail sentences for white-collar criminals, but to date most defendants have only been fined (Labaton 2003; J. O'Donnell and Willig 2003).

Conviction for corporate crime does not generally harm a person's reputation and career aspirations nearly so much as conviction for street crime would. Apparently, the label "white-collar criminal" does not carry the stigma of the label "felon convicted of a violent crime." Conflict theorists don't find such differential treatment surprising. They argue that the criminal justice system largely disregards the crimes of the affluent, focusing on crimes committed by the poor. Generally, if an offender holds a position of status and influence, his or her crime is treated as less serious than others' crimes, and the sanction is much more lenient.

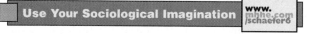
Use Your Sociological Imagination www.mhhe.com/schaefer6

As a newspaper editor, how might you treat stories on corporate crime differently from those on violent crime?

Victimless Crimes

White-collar and street crimes endanger people's economic or personal well-being against their will (or without their direct knowledge). By contrast, sociologists use the term *victimless crime* to describe the willing exchange among adults of widely desired, but illegal, goods and services, such as prostitution (Schur 1965, 1985).

Some activists are working to decriminalize many of these illegal practices. Supporters of decriminalization are troubled by the attempt to legislate a moral code for adults. In their view, prostitution, drug abuse, gambling, and other victimless crimes are impossible to prevent. The already overburdened criminal justice system should instead devote its resources to "street crimes" and other offenses with obvious victims.

Despite the wide use of the term *victimless crime,* however, many people object to the notion that there is no victim other than the offender in such crimes. Excessive drinking, compulsive gambling, and illegal drug use contribute to an enormous amount of personal and property damage. A person with a drinking problem can become abusive to a spouse or children; a compulsive gambler or drug user may steal to pursue his obsession. And feminist sociologists contend that prostitution, as well as the more disturbing aspects of pornography, reinforce the misconception that women are "toys" who can be treated as objects rather than people. According to critics of decriminalization, society must not give tacit approval to conduct that has such harmful consequences (Flavin 1998; Jolin 1994; National Advisory Commission on Criminal Justice 1976; Schur 1968, 1985).

The controversy over decriminalization reminds us of the important insights of labeling and conflict theorists presented earlier. Underlying this debate are two questions: Who has the power to define gambling, prostitution, and public drunkenness as "crimes"? and Who has the power to label such behaviors as "victimless"? The answer is generally the state legislatures, and in some cases, the police and the courts.

Again, we can see that criminal law is not simply a universal standard of behavior agreed on by all members of society. Rather, it reflects a struggle among competing individuals and groups to gain governmental support for their moral and social values. For example, organizations such as Mothers Against Drunk Driving (MADD) and Students Against Drunk Driving (SADD) have been successful in recent years in modifying public attitudes toward drunkenness. Rather than being viewed as a victimless crime, drunkenness is increasingly associated with the potential dangers of driving while under the influence of alcohol. As a result, the mass media are giving greater (and more critical) attention to people who are found guilty of drunk driving, and many states have instituted severe fines and jail terms for a wide variety of alcohol-related offenses.

Crime Statistics

Crime statistics are not as accurate as social scientists would like. However, since they deal with an issue of grave concern to the people of the United States, they are frequently cited as if they were completely reliable. Such data do serve as an indicator of police activity, as well as an approximate indication of the level of certain crimes. Yet it would be a mistake to interpret these data as an exact representation of the incidence of crime.

Understanding Crime Statistics

Reported crime is very high in the United States, and the public regards crime as a major social problem. However, there has been a significant decline in violent crime nationwide following many years of increases. A number of explanations have been offered, including:

- A booming economy and falling unemployment rates through most of the 1990s.
- Community-oriented policing and crime prevention programs.
- New gun control laws.
- A massive increase in the prison population, which at least prevents inmates from committing crimes outside prison.

It remains to be seen whether this pattern will continue, but even with current declines, reported crimes remain well above those of other nations, and exceed the reported rates in the United States of just 20 years earlier. Feminist scholars draw our attention to one significant variation: the proportion of major crimes committed by women has increased. In a recent 10-year period (1993–2002), female arrests for major reported crimes increased 14 percent, while comparable male arrests declined 6 percent (Department of Justice 2002c:232).

Sociologists have several ways of measuring crime. Historically, they have relied on police data, but underreporting has always been a problem with such measures. Because members of racial and ethnic minority groups often distrust law enforcement agencies, they may not contact the police. Feminist sociologists and others have noted that many women do not report rape or spousal abuse out of fear they will be blamed for the crime.

Partly because of these deficiencies in official statistics, the National Crime Victimization Survey was initiated in 1972. The Bureau of Justice Statistics, in compiling this annual report, seeks information from law enforcement agencies, but also interviews members of over 42,000 households and asks if they have been victims of a specific set of crimes during the preceding year. In general, those who administer *victimization surveys* question ordinary people, not police officers, to determine whether they have been victims of crime.

Unfortunately, like other crime data, victimization surveys have particular limitations. They require that victims understand what has happened to them and are willing to disclose such information to interviewers. Fraud, income tax evasion, and blackmail are examples of crimes that are unlikely to be reported in victimization studies. Nevertheless, 92 percent of all households have been willing to cooperate with investigators for the Na-

FIGURE 8-3

Victimization Rates, 1973–2002

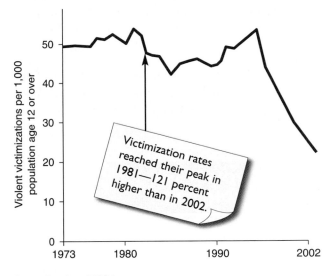

Source: Rennison 2003:1.

tional Crime Victimization Survey. As shown in Figure 8-3, data from these surveys reveal a fluctuating crime rate with significant declines in both the 1980s and 1990s (Rennison and Rand 2003).

International Crime Rates

If developing reliable crime data is difficult in the United States, making useful cross-national comparisons is even more difficult. Nevertheless, with some care, we can offer preliminary conclusions about how crime rates differ around the world.

During the 1980s and 1990s, violent crimes were much more common in the United States than in Western Europe. Murders, rapes, and robberies were reported to the police at much higher rates in the United States. Yet the incidence of certain other types of crime appears to be higher elsewhere. For example, England, Italy, Australia, and New Zealand all have higher rates of car theft than the United States. Developing nations have significant rates of reported homicide due to civil unrest and political conflict among civilians (International Crime Victim Survey 2004; World Bank 2003a).

Why are rates of violent crime so much higher in the United States than in Western Europe? Sociologist Elliot Currie (1985, 1998) has suggested that our society places greater emphasis on individual economic achievement than other societies. At the same time, many observers have noted that the culture of the United States has long tolerated, if not condoned, many forms of violence. Coupled with sharp disparities between poor and affluent

Let's Discuss Female arrests for major crimes have increased over the past 10 years, while comparable male arrests decreased 6 percent. Why do you think this pattern has emerged?
Race/Ethnicity/Gender Underreporting of crimes in ethnic and racial minority communities and among women
Methods Use of victimization surveys to gather crime statistics

Global View International crime rates
Classroom Tip See "Teaching about Sexual Assault" (Class Discussion Topics).

citizens, significant unemployment, and substantial alcohol and drug abuse, these factors combine to produce a climate conducive to crime.

However, disturbing increases in violent crime are evident in other Western societies. For example, crime has skyrocketed in Russia since the overthrow of Communist Party rule (with its strict controls on guns and criminals) in 1991. In 1998 there were fewer than 260 homicides in Moscow, but now there are more than 1,000 homicides a year. Organized crime has filled a power vacuum in Moscow since the end of communism; one result is that gangland shootouts and premeditated "contract hits" have become more common. Some prominent reformist politicians have been targeted as well. Russia is the only nation in the world that incarcerates a higher proportion of its citizens than the United States. The country imprisons 580 per 100,000 of its adults on a typical day, compared to 550 in the United States, fewer than 100 in Mexico or Britain, and only 16 in Greece (Currie 1998; Shinkai and Zvekic 1999).

SOCIAL POLICY and SOCIAL CONTROL — Gun Control

Two high school students present themselves at Kmart's national headquarters. They are not looking for jobs. Survivors of the mass murders at Columbine High School in 1999, they still have bullets lodged in their bodies—bullets their attackers bought at Kmart. In a symbolic protest, the two young people ask Kmart's representative if they may return the bullets.

This scene was shown in the Academy Award–winning documentary *Bowling for Columbine.* Producer-director Michael Moore was amazed when the day after he filmed the encounter, Kmart announced that the store would cease to sell the ammunition.

Michael Moore purchases ammunition at a Kmart store in a scene from his award-winning documentary film *Bowling for Columbine.*

The Issue

While reported crime has declined in recent years, the role of firearms in crime has remained fairly consistent. Over the past 10 years, two-thirds of all murders were committed with firearms. Although handgun owners frequently insist that they need to own firearms to protect themselves and their loved ones from violent crime, over the years, high-profile assassinations of public figures such as President John F. Kennedy, Senator Robert Kennedy, Dr. Martin Luther King Jr., and Beatle John Lennon have forced legislators to consider stricter gun control measures (Department of Justice 2002a).

In 1994 Congress passed the Brady Handgun Violence Prevention Act, named after White House press secretary Jim Brady, who was seriously wounded in the 1981 assassination attempt against President Ronald Reagan. John Hinckley, the would-be assassin, had given false information about himself at the pawnshop where he bought the gun he used to shoot Reagan and Brady. The Brady Act mandates that firearms dealers run criminal history background checks on people who wish to purchase handguns. About 2 percent of all purchases are denied as a result of the checks—roughly 370 purchases per day (Bowling et al. 2003).

Gun control supporters claim that even stricter legislation is needed, but opponents charge that the Brady Act only hampers honest people who want to buy guns, since those with criminal intent can turn to other sources. Opponents suggest, instead, strengthening and enforcing criminal penalties for the illegal use of guns.

The Setting

Guns and ammunition are big business in the United States, where the Second Amendment to the Constitution guarantees the "right of the people to keep and bear arms." Currently, 30 to 35 million people in the United States own handguns, and about 45 percent of U.S. households have some type of firearm on the premises. Informal gun clubs of both a primary- and secondary-group nature flourish across the country. On a national basis, powerful formal organizations promote gun ownership. Clearly, owning a gun is not a deviant act in our society (National Rifle Association 2004).

Sociological Insights

Since the Brady Act went into effect, support for stricter measures has actually declined. Still, national surveys show that about half of all adults in the United States favor stricter laws covering the sale of firearms; about 1 in 10 favor more lenient laws. Though support for gun control far outweighs sentiment against it, the nation's major anti–gun control lobby, the National Rifle Association (NRA), has been able to use its impressive power to block or dilute such measures (Peter Brown and Abel 2002; Gallup 2002).

Conflict theorists contend that powerful groups like the NRA can dominate the legislative process because of their ability to mobilize resources in opposition to majority will. Founded in 1871, the NRA has 3.8 million members; state rifle associations, with 4 to 5 million members, support many of the NRA's goals. In contrast, Handgun Control, a key organization in the gun control battle, has only 400,000 members. Compared to the NRA's formidable war chest, Handgun Control's resources are limited.

Policy Implications

Advocates for stricter gun control laws identify a series of measures they would like to see enacted:

- A total ban on assault weapons.
- Tight restrictions on permits to carry concealed weapons.
- Regulation of gun shows, where "private sellers" often trade in firearms unrestricted by the Brady Act.

- Increased penalties for leaving firearms where they are easily accessible to children and others who could misuse them.

Efforts to pass these measures have been made at all levels of government, since towns, states, and the federal government all have the authority to regulate the possession and sale of firearms (Brady Campaign 2003).

Proposed legal restrictions on gun ownership have met strong opposition by both the NRA and firearms manufacturers. The NRA has been particularly successful in defeating political candidates who favor stricter laws, and in backing those who seek to weaken such restrictions. Except in a handful of states, office seekers rarely risk taking an antigun position. Alarmed by the NRA's rhetoric, many voters fear that restricting the sale of firearms will hamper their ability to protect themselves, independent of law enforcement officers. Indeed, in light of growing concern over terrorism on the home front, the handgun debate has turned now to the question of allowing pilots to carry guns in the cockpit (Tumulty and Novak 2002).

The firearms issue is not limited to the United States. In the 1990s the International Committee of the Red Cross expressed concern over the global glut of firearms—one gun for every 10 people on earth. An estimated 200,000 people die from gunshots every year as a result of criminal violence, suicide, or accident. While support is gaining for regulation of transnational gun trafficking, the challenges of cross-border gun control are much more difficult to meet than the problems nations face within their own borders (Lumpe 2003).

Let's Discuss

1. Do you see guns more as weapons that could jeopardize your safety or as protection against those who would harm you? What formal or informal sources of social control may have influenced you to form this attitude?

2. Kmart changed its policy on the sale of ammunition after being visited by survivors of the Columbine High School shootings. Analyze the company's decision as a sociologist would. If retailers' policies on the sale of ammunition had been different in 1999, could the massacre at Columbine High have been prevented?

3. Did the September 11, 2001, terrorist attacks on the United States strengthen or weaken the case for stronger control of firearms? Explain your position.

GETTING INVOLVED

www.
mhhe.com
/schaefer6

To get involved in the debate over gun control, visit this text's Online Learning Center, which offers links to relevant websites. Check out the social policy section on the Online Learning Center as well; it provides survey data on U.S. public opinion regarding this issue.

CHAPTER RESOURCES

Summary

Conformity and *deviance* are two ways in which people respond to real or imagined pressure from others. In this chapter, we examined the relationship between conformity, deviance, and mechanisms of *social control.*

1. A society uses social control to encourage the acceptance of basic norms.

2. Stanley Milgram defined *conformity* as going along with one's peers; *obedience* is defined as compliance with higher authorities in a hierarchical structure.

3. Some norms are so important to a society, they are formalized into *laws.* Socialization is a primary source of conforming and obedient behavior, including obedience to law.

4. Deviant behavior violates social norms. Some forms of deviance carry a negative social *stigma,* while other forms are more or less accepted.

5. From a functionalist point of view, deviance and its consequences help to define the limits of proper behavior.

6. Some interactionists maintain that people learn criminal behavior by interacting with others (*cultural transmission*). To them, deviance results from exposure to attitudes that are favorable to criminal acts (*differential association*).

7. Other interactionists stress that for a crime to occur, there must be a convergence of motivated offenders and suitable targets of crime (*routine activities theory*).

8. An important aspect of *labeling theory* is the recognition that some people are viewed as deviant, while others who engage in the same behavior are not.

9. The conflict perspective views laws and punishments as a reflection of the interests of the powerful.

10. The feminist perspective emphasizes that cultural attitudes and differential economic relationships help to explain gender differences in deviance and crime.

11. *Crime* represents a deviation from formal social norms administered by the state.

12. Sociologists differentiate among *professional crime, organized crime, white-collar crime,* and *victimless crimes* (such as drug use and prostitution).

13. Crime statistics are among the least reliable social data, partly because so many crimes are not reported to law enforcement agencies. Rates of violent crime are higher in the United States than in other Western societies, although they have been dropping.

14. Illegal gun trafficking has become a major problem not just in the United States, but around the world. Every year, 200,000 people die from gunshot wounds sustained as a result of crime, suicide, or accident.

Critical Thinking Questions

1. What mechanisms of formal and informal social control are evident in your college classes and in day-to-day life and social interactions at your school?

2. What approach to deviance do you find most persuasive: that of functionalists, conflict theorists, interactionists, or labeling theorists? Why do you consider that approach more convincing than the other three? What are the main weaknesses of each approach?

3. Rates of violent crime in the United States are higher than they are in Western Europe, Canada, Australia, or New Zealand. Draw on as many of the theories discussed in this chapter as possible to explain why the United States is such a comparably violent society.

Key Terms

Anomie   Durkheim's term for the loss of direction felt in a society when social control of individual behavior has become ineffective. (page 185)

Anomie theory of deviance   Robert Merton's theory of deviance as an adaptation of socially prescribed goals or of the means governing their attainment, or both. (185)

Conformity   Going along with peers—individuals of our own status, who have no special right to direct our behavior. (175)

Control theory   A view of conformity and deviance that suggests that our connection to members of society leads us to systematically conform to society's norms. (180)

Crime   A violation of criminal law for which some governmental authority applies formal penalties. (191)

Cultural transmission   A school of criminology that argues that criminal behavior is learned through social interactions. (187)

Deviance   Behavior that violates the standards of conduct or expectations of a group or society. (180)

Differential association   A theory of deviance that holds that violation of rules results from exposure to attitudes favorable to criminal acts. (187)

Formal social control   Social control that is carried out by authorized agents, such as police officers, judges, school administrators, and employers. (177)

Informal social control   Social control that is carried out casually by ordinary people through such means as laughter, smiles, and ridicule. (177)

Labeling theory   An approach to deviance that attempts to explain why certain people are viewed as deviants while others engaged in the same behavior are not. (188)

Law   Governmental social control. (178)

Obedience   Compliance with higher authorities in a hierarchical structure. (175)

Organized crime   The work of a group that regulates relations among criminal enterprises involved in illegal activities, including prostitution, gambling, and the smuggling and sale of illegal drugs. (193)

Professional criminal   A person who pursues crime as a day-to-day occupation, developing skilled techniques and enjoying a certain degree of status among other criminals. (192)

Routine activities theory   The notion that criminal victimization increases when motivated offenders and suitable targets converge. (187)

Sanction   A penalty or reward for conduct concerning a social norm. (175)

Social constructionist perspective   An approach to deviance that emphasizes the role of culture in the creation of the deviant identity. (189)

Social control   The techniques and strategies for preventing deviant human behavior in any society. (174)

Societal-reaction approach   Another name for *labeling theory*. (188)

Stigma   A label used to devalue members of certain social groups. (181)

Victimization survey   A questionnaire or interview given to a sample of the population to determine whether people have been victims of crime. (195)

Victimless crime   A term used by sociologists to describe the willing exchange among adults of widely desired, but illegal, goods and services. (194)

White-collar crime   Illegal acts committed by affluent, "respectable" individuals in the course of business activities. (193)

TECHNOLOGY RESOURCES

Internet Connection

*Note: While all the URLs listed were current as of the printing of this book, these sites often change. Please check our website (**www.mhhe.com/schaefer6**) for updates, hyperlinks, and exercises related to these sites.*

1. The United Nations Office on Drugs and Crime (**www.unodc.org/unodc/crime_cicp_sitemap. html**) maintains a website that describes its anticrime programs and documents the prevalence of several types of crime worldwide. Visit the site to learn about global crime.

2. Graffiti aptly demonstrates that deviance is relative. Though spray-painting public and private property without permission is officially a crime, many people regard the practice as a beautiful and socially significant art form. For an alternative to the mainstream perspective on graffiti, explore the images on Art Crimes (**www.graffiti.org**).

Online Learning Center with PowerWeb

If you are interested in what people in the United States think about the death penalty, visit the student center of the Online Learning Center at **www.mhhe.com/ schaefer6**. Link to "How Americans Feel About. . . . " You will find colorful graphs showing what percentage of citizens favor the death penalty, what percentage do not feel it is imposed often enough, and what percentage support the death penalty even though they believe innocent people have been executed.

Reel Society Interactive Movie CD-ROM 2.0

Reel Society 2.0 can be used to spark discussion about the following topics from this chapter:

- Conformity and Obedience
- Informal and Formal Social Control
- Deviance
- Discretionary Justice

STRATIFICATION IN THE UNITED STATES AND WORLDWIDE

This UNICEF poster reminds affluent Western consumers that the brand-name jeans they wear may be produced by exploited workers in developing countries. In sweatshops throughout the developing world, nonunion garment workers—some of them still children—labor long hours for extremely low wages.

Understanding Stratification

Stratification by Social Class

Social Mobility

Stratification in the World System

Stratification within Nations: A Comparative Perspective

Case Study: Stratification in Mexico

Social Policy and Stratification: Rethinking Welfare in North America and Europe

Boxes

SOCIOLOGY IN THE GLOBAL COMMUNITY: Under Pressure: The Caste System in India

RESEARCH IN ACTION: When Jobs Disappear

201

In the early 1990s, the McDonald's Corporation launched a television ad campaign featuring a young black man named Calvin, who was portrayed sitting atop a Brooklyn stoop in his Golden Arches uniform while his friends down on the sidewalk passed by, giving him a hard time about holding down a "McJob." After brushing off their teasing with good humor, Calvin is approached furtively by one young black man who asks, *sotto voce*, whether Calvin might help him get a job too. He allows that he could use some earnings and that despite the ragging he has just given Calvin, he thinks the uniform is really pretty cool—or at least that having a job is pretty cool. . . .

Americans have always been committed to the moral maxim that work defines the person. We carry around in our heads a rough tally that tells us what kinds of jobs are worthy of respect and what kinds are to be disdained, a pyramid organized by the income a job carries, the sort of credentials it takes to secure a particular position, the qualities of an occupation's incumbents—and we use this system of stratification (ruthlessly at times) to boost the status of some and humiliate others. This penchant for ranking by occupation is more pervasive in the United States than in other societies, where there are different ways of evaluating the personal worth of individuals. In these societies, coming from a "good family" counts heavily in the calculus of social

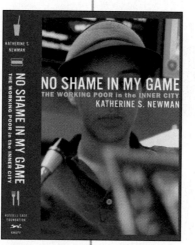

standing. Here in America, there is no other metric that matters as much as the kind of job you hold.

Given our tradition of equating moral value with employment, it stands to reason that the most profound dividing line in our culture is that separating the working person from the unemployed. Only after this canyon has been crossed do we begin to make the finer gradations that distinguish white-collar worker from blue-collar worker, CEO from secretary. We attribute a whole host of moral virtues—self-discipline, personal responsibility, maturity—to those who have found and kept a job, almost any job, and dismiss those who haven't as slothful or irresponsible.

We inhabit an unforgiving culture that is blind to the many reasons why some people cross that employment barrier and others are left behind. While we may remember, for a time, that unemployment rates are high, or that particular industries have downsized millions of workers right out of a job, or that racial barriers or negative attitudes toward teenagers make it harder to get a job at some times and for some people, in the end American culture wipes these background truths out in favor of a simpler dichotomy: the worthy and the unworthy, the working stiff and the lazy sloth. *(K. Newman 1999:86, 86–87)* ■ ◉

Additional information about this excerpt can be found on the Online Learning Center at **www.mhhe.com/schaefer6**.

I n this excerpt from her book *No Shame in My Game*, Katherine Newman, an anthropologist and professor of urban studies at Harvard University, examines the role of work in defining a person's status, especially in the United States. *No Shame in My Game* is based on Newman's research, a study of 200 fast-food workers in Harlem, New York. For a year and a half, using interviews, home and school visits, and on-site observation of the workplace, Newman tracked workers as they struggled to get a job and keep it, to balance work with school and family, to tolerate long hours and ill-mannered customers. In the course of her study, she described the workers' social hierarchy.

Newman's goal in researching fast-food work was to highlight a segment of the population often overlooked by social scientists and policymakers. The working poor—Black, White, Latino—are in fact a significant segment of the labor force, yet they are largely invisible to the better-off people who eat at the restaurants and visit the hotels where they work. Moreover, they are virtually nonexistent to the legislators who represent them. Still, as the title of Newman's book suggests, they take considerable pride in the fact that they do work. Socially, they have leapt the deep gulf that separates those who work from those who do not.

Ever since people first began to speculate about the nature of human society, their attention has been drawn to the differences between individuals and groups within a society. The term *social inequality* describes a condition in which members of a society have different amounts of wealth, prestige, or power. Some degree of social inequality characterizes every society.

When a system of social inequality is based on a hierarchy of groups, sociologists refer to it as *stratification*: a structured ranking of entire groups of people that perpetuates unequal economic rewards and power in a society. These unequal rewards are evident not only in the distribution of wealth and income, but even in the distressing mortality rates of impoverished communities. Stratification involves the ways in which one generation passes on social inequalities to the next, producing groups of people arranged in rank order from low to high.

Stratification is a crucial subject of sociological investigation because of its pervasive influence on human interactions and institutions. It inevitably results in social inequality, because certain groups of people stand higher in social rankings, control scarce resources, wield power, and receive special treatment. As we will see in this chapter, the consequences of stratification are evident in the unequal distribution of wealth and income within industrial societies. The term *income* refers to salaries and wages. In contrast, *wealth* is an inclusive term encompassing all a person's material assets, including land, stocks, and other types of property.

Is social inequality an inevitable part of society? How are wealth and income distributed, and how much opportunity does the average worker have to move up the social ladder? What economic and political conditions explain the divide between rich nations and poor? This chapter focuses on the unequal distribution of socially valued rewards and its consequences, both in the United States and around the world. We will examine four general systems of stratification and study several theoretical perspectives on stratification, with particular attention to the thinking of Karl Marx and Max Weber. We will see how sociologists define social class and examine the consequences of stratification in terms of wealth and income, health, and educational opportunities. We will confront the question of social mobility, both upward and downward. On an international level, we will examine the impact on developing countries of colonialism and neocolonialism, globalization, and the rise of multinational corporations. In a special case study, we'll look closely at social stratification in Mexico. Finally, in the social policy section, we'll address the issue of welfare reform in North America and Europe. ■

UNDERSTANDING STRATIFICATION

Systems of Stratification

Look at the four general systems of stratification examined here—slavery, castes, estates, and social classes—as ideal types useful for purposes of analysis. Any stratification system may include elements of more than one type. For example, prior to the Civil War, you could find in the southern states of the United States both social classes dividing Whites from Whites and the institutionalized enslavement of Blacks.

To understand these systems better, it may be helpful to review the distinction between *achieved status* and *ascribed status*, explained in Chapter 5. *Ascribed status* is

Jacob Lawrence's painting *Harriet Tubman* Series No. 9 graphically illustrates the torment of slavery as once practiced in the United States. Slavery is the most extreme form of legalized social inequality.

a social position assigned to a person without regard for that person's unique talents or characteristics. In contrast, *achieved status* is a social position that a person attains largely through his or her own efforts. The two are closely linked. The nation's most affluent families generally inherit wealth and status, while many members of racial and ethnic minorities inherit disadvantaged status. Age and gender, as well, are ascribed statuses that influence a person's wealth and social position.

pp. 106–107

Slavery

The most extreme form of legalized social inequality for individuals or groups is *slavery.* What distinguishes this oppressive system of stratification is that enslaved individuals are *owned* by other people, who treat these human beings as property, just as if they were household pets or appliances.

Slavery has varied in the way it has been practiced. In ancient Greece, the main source of slaves consisted of captives of war and piracy. Although succeeding generations could inherit slave status, it was not necessarily permanent. A person's status might change depending on which city-state happened to triumph in a military conflict. In effect, all citizens had the potential of becoming slaves or of being granted freedom, depending on the circumstances of history. In contrast, in the United States and Latin America, where slavery was an ascribed status, racial and legal barriers prevented the freeing of slaves.

Today, the Universal Declaration of Human Rights, which is binding on all members of the United Nations, pro-

hibits slavery in all its forms. Yet around the world, millions of people still live as slaves. In many developing countries, bonded laborers are imprisoned in virtual lifetime employment; in some countries, human beings are owned outright. But slavery also exists in Europe and the United States, where guest workers and illegal immigrants have been forced to labor for years under terrible conditions, either to pay off debts or to avoid being turned over to immigration authorities (Cockburn 2003).

Castes

Castes are hereditary ranks that are usually religiously dictated, and that tend to be fixed and immobile. The caste system is generally associated with Hinduism in India and other countries. In India there are four major castes, called *varnas.* A fifth category of outcastes, referred to as *untouchables* or the *dalit,* is considered to be so lowly and unclean as to have no place within this system of stratification. There are also many minor castes. Caste membership is an ascribed status (at birth, children automatically assume the same position as their parents). Each caste is quite sharply defined, and members are expected to marry within that caste.

In recent decades, industrialization and urbanization have weakened India's rigid caste system. Box 9-1 examines the changes that are taking place in this ancient form of stratification.

Estates

A third type of stratification system, called *estates,* was associated with feudal societies during the Middle Ages. The *estate system,* or feudalism, required peasants to work land leased to them by nobles in exchange for military protection and other services. The basis for the system was the nobles' ownership of land, which was critical to their superior and privileged status. As in systems based on slavery and caste, inheritance of one's position largely defined the estate system. The nobles inherited their titles and property, whereas the peasants were born into a subservient position within an agrarian society.

As the estate system developed, it became more differentiated. Nobles began to achieve varying degrees of authority. By the 12th century, a priesthood had emerged in most of Europe, along with classes of merchants and

Sociology in the Global Community

9-1 UNDER PRESSURE: THE CASTE SYSTEM IN INDIA

In 2001, the murder of a young Indian man in the small village of Kalvakol became the subject of international outrage. The man, an untouchable, or dalit, had been dragged into a field, tortured, and killed by upper-caste villagers. His crime: he had dared to speak his mind in a village where untouchables are not supposed to have opinions. Those arrested for the murder were defiant. Said one, "What do you expect us to do, hand over the whole village to those people?"

The murder was one sign of the tensions that have arisen from the weakening of the traditional Hindu caste system. India's constitution, adopted in 1950, formally abolished discrimination against untouchables, whose status as outcastes excluded them from temples, schools, and most forms of employment. Yet the caste system prevails today, because it is founded not in law but in religious custom. It is strongest in the rural villages, where almost 90 percent of untouchables still live. It is weakest in the fast-growing cities, where low-caste migrants from the country may blend into the crowd unrecognized in public schools, hospitals, and transportation facilities.

Historically, the caste system has not been immune to change. During the Mogul empire, many untouchables escaped their status as outcastes by converting to Islam. And when the British took over during the colonial period, imposing Western-style agriculture, industry, and bureaucracy on the country, they opened up new opportunities to caste-bound Indians. In the 20th century, government leaders tried to level the playing field for the lower castes, but with limited success. Government "reservations," a kind of quota system, set aside a certain percentage of government jobs and educational opportunities for the lower castes—a policy that has produced a sharp backlash among the upper castes. The need is greatest among the untouchables, con-

> *Urbanization and technological advances have brought more change to India's caste system than the government or politics has.*

fined to menial labor at jobs that are fast disappearing, yet barred from training for better employment. Today, these 160 million outcastes, who constitute about a quarter of India's population, have organized and are making their voices heard in electoral politics. In 1997, for the first time in India's history, the symbolic but high-status position of president went to an untouchable, K. R. Narayanan.

On the whole, urbanization and technological advances have brought more change to India's caste system than the government or politics has. Besides the anonymity of city life, which tends to blur caste boundaries, the globalization of high technology has opened up India's social order, bringing new opportunities to those who possess the skills and ability to capitalize on them. Srinivas Rao, a lower-caste Indian who started his own information technology company, is one example of the liberating effects of technological change. Though Rao still suffers in small ways because of his caste, his achievement is a remarkable sign of social change in a country where such upward mobility was unknown a generation ago.

Let's Discuss

1. If you were a government official in India, would you favor the "reservations" system that is aimed at reducing discrimination against people of lower castes? If not, what other solutions would you recommend?

2. Compare India's caste system, which is based on religious custom, to the form of slavery that was once practiced in the United States, which was based on racial differences. How would the experiences of a former slave and an untouchable differ?

Sources: Dugger 1999; Gose 2003; McGivering 2001; National Campaign on Dalit Human Rights 2003; O'Neill 2003; Overland 2004; Schmetzer 1999; Seabrook 2002.

artisans. For the first time, there were groups of people whose wealth did not depend on land ownership or agriculture. This economic change had profound social consequences as the estate system ended and a class system of stratification came into existence.

Social Classes

A *class system* is a social ranking based primarily on economic position in which achieved characteristics can influence social mobility. In contrast to slavery and caste systems, the boundaries between classes are imprecisely defined, and one can move from one stratum, or level, of society to another. Even so, class systems maintain stable stratification hierarchies and patterns of class divisions, and they, too, are marked by unequal distribution of wealth and power. Class standing, though it is achieved, is heavily dependent on family and ascribed factors, such as race and ethnicity.

Income inequality is a basic characteristic of a class system. In 2003, the median household income in the

Reel Society Several scenes in *Reel Society* address stratification. See Stratification—Gender, Stratification—Race/Ethnicity, and Stratification—Religion in the Topic Index.

Let's Discuss Can you describe the various social hierarchies that exist on your college campus? Among sororities and fraternities (if any)? In the college's administrative structure?

FIGURE 9-1

Household Income in the United States, 2003

Note: Data do not add to 100 percent due to rounding.
Source: DeNavas-Walt et al. 2004:27.

United States was $43,318. In other words, half of all households had higher incomes in that year and half had lower incomes. But this fact does not fully convey the income disparities in our society. As Figure 9-1 shows, there is a broad range around the median household income. Furthermore, considerable numbers of people fall at the extremes. In 2000, about 240,000 tax returns reported incomes in excess of $1 million. At the same time, about 20 million households reported incomes under $9,000 (Bureau of the Census 2003a:332; DeNavas-Walt et al. 2004).

Sociologist Daniel Rossides (1997) uses a five-class model to describe the class system of the United States: the upper class, the upper-middle class, the lower-middle class, the working class, and the lower class. Although the lines separating social classes in his model are not so sharp as the divisions between castes, members of the five classes differ significantly in ways other than just income level.

Rossides categorizes about 1 to 2 percent of the people of the United States as *upper class,* a group limited to the very wealthy. These people associate in exclusive clubs and social circles. In contrast, the *lower class,* consisting of approximately 20 to 25 percent of the population, dispro-

portionately consists of Blacks, Hispanics, single mothers with dependent children, and people who cannot find regular work or must make do with low-paying work. This class lacks both wealth and income and is too weak politically to exercise significant power.

Both these classes, at opposite ends of the nation's social hierarchy, reflect the importance of ascribed status and achieved status. Ascribed statuses such as race clearly influence a person's wealth and social position. Sociologist Richard Jenkins (1991) has researched how the ascribed status of being disabled marginalizes a person in the labor market of the United States. People with disabilities are particularly vulnerable to unemployment, are often poorly paid, and in many cases are on the lower rung of occupational ladders. Regardless of their actual performance on the job, the disabled are stigmatized as not earning their keep. Such are the effects of ascribed status.

Sandwiched between the upper and lower classes in this model are the upper-middle class, the lower-middle class, and the working class. The *upper-middle class,* numbering about 10 to 15 percent of the population, is composed of professionals such as doctors, lawyers, and architects. They participate extensively in politics and take leadership roles in voluntary associations. The *lower-middle class,* which accounts for approximately 30 to 35 percent of the population, includes less affluent professionals (such as elementary school teachers and nurses), owners of small businesses, and a sizable number of clerical workers. While not all members of this varied class hold degrees from a college, they share the goal of sending their children there.

Rossides describes the *working class*—about 40 to 45 percent of the population—as people who hold regular manual or blue-collar jobs. Certain members of this class, such as electricians, may have higher incomes than people in the lower-middle class. Yet even if they have achieved some degree of economic security, they tend to identify with manual workers and their long history of involvement in the labor movement of the United States. Of the five classes, the working class is declining noticeably in size. In the economy of the United States, service and technical jobs are replacing those involved in the actual manufacturing or transportation of goods.

Social class is one of the independent or explanatory variables most frequently used by social scientists to shed light on social issues. In later chapters, we will analyze the relationships between social class and divorce patterns (Chapter 12), religious behavior (Chapter 13), and formal schooling (Chapter 13), as well as other relationships in which social class is a variable.

Perspectives on Stratification

Sociologists have hotly debated stratification and social inequality and have reached varying conclusions. No theorist stressed the significance of class for society—and for social change—more strongly than Karl Marx. Marx viewed class differentiation as the crucial determinant of social, economic, and political inequality. In contrast, Max Weber questioned Marx's emphasis on the overriding importance of the economic sector, and argued that stratification should be viewed as having many dimensions.

Karl Marx's View of Class Differentiation

Karl Marx has been aptly described as both a revolutionary and a social scientist. Marx was concerned with stratification in all types of human societies, beginning with primitive agricultural tribes and continuing into feudalism. But his main focus was on the effects of economic inequality on all aspects of 19th-century Europe. The plight of the working class made him feel that it was imperative to strive for changes in the class structure of society (Beeghley 1978:1).

In Marx's view, social relations during any period of history depend on who controls the primary mode of economic production, such as land or factories. Differential access to scarce resources shapes the relationship between groups. Thus, under the feudal estate system, most production was agricultural, and the land was owned by the nobility. Peasants had little choice but to work according to terms dictated by those who owned the land.

Using this type of analysis, Marx examined social relations within *capitalism*—an economic system in which the means of production are held largely in private hands and the main incentive for economic activity is the accumulation of profits (D. H. Rosenberg 1991). Marx focused on the two classes that began to emerge as the feudal estate system declined, the bourgeoisie and the proletariat. The *bourgeoisie,* or capitalist class, owns the means of production, such as factories and machinery; the *proletariat* is the working class. In capitalist societies,

Karl Marx would identify these coal miners as members of the *proletariat,* or working class. For generations, miners were forced to spend their meager wages at "company stores," whose high prices kept them perpetually in debt. The exploitation of the working class is a core principle of Marxist theory.

the members of the bourgeoisie maximize profit in competition with other firms. In the process, they exploit workers, who must exchange their labor for subsistence wages. In Marx's view, members of each class share a distinctive culture. Marx was most interested in the culture of the proletariat, but he also examined the ideology of the bourgeoisie, through which that class justifies its dominance over workers.

According to Marx, exploitation of the proletariat will inevitably lead to the destruction of the capitalist system, because the workers will revolt. But first, the working class must develop *class consciousness*—a subjective awareness of common vested interests and the need for collective political action to bring about social change. Workers must often overcome what Marx termed *false consciousness,* or an attitude held by members of a class that does not accurately reflect their objective position. A worker with false consciousness may adopt an individualistic viewpoint toward capitalist exploitation ("*I* am being exploited by *my* boss"). In contrast, the class-conscious worker realizes that all workers are being exploited by the bourgeoisie and have a common stake in revolution.

For Marx, class consciousness is part of a collective process in which the proletariat comes to identify the bourgeoisie as the source of its oppression. Revolutionary leaders will guide the working class in its struggle. Ultimately, the proletariat will overthrow the rule of both the bourgeoisie and the government (which Marx saw as representing the interests of capitalists) and will eliminate private ownership of the means of production. In Marx's rather utopian view, classes and oppression will cease to exist in the postrevolutionary workers' state.

How accurate were Marx's predictions? He failed to anticipate the emergence of labor unions, whose power in collective bargaining weakens the stranglehold that capitalists maintain over workers. Moreover, as contemporary conflict theorists note, he did not foresee the extent to which political liberties and relative prosperity could contribute to false consciousness. Many workers have come to view themselves as individuals striving for improvement within free societies that offer substantial mobility, rather than as downtrodden members of a social class who face a collective fate. Finally, Marx did not predict that Communist Party rule would be established and later overthrown in the former Soviet Union and throughout Eastern Europe. Still, the Marxist approach to the study of class is useful in stressing the importance of stratification as a determinant of social behavior and the fundamental separation in many societies between two distinct groups, the rich and the poor.

Max Weber's View of Stratification

Unlike Karl Marx, Max Weber insisted that no single characteristic (such as class) totally defines a person's position within the stratification system. Instead, writing in 1916, he identified three distinct components of stratification: class, status, and power (Gerth and Mills 1958).

Weber used the term *class* to refer to a group of people who have a similar level of wealth and income. For example, certain workers in the United States try to support their families through minimum-wage jobs. According to Weber's definition, these wage earners constitute a class because they share the same economic position and fate. Although Weber agreed with Marx on the importance of this economic dimension of stratification, he argued that the actions of individuals and groups could not be understood *solely* in economic terms.

Weber used the term *status group* to refer to people who have the same prestige or lifestyle. An individual gains status through membership in a desirable group, such as the medical profession. But status is not the same as economic class standing. In our culture, a successful pickpocket may be in the same income class as a college professor. Yet the thief is widely regarded as a member of a low-status group, whereas the professor holds high status.

For Weber, the third major component of stratification has a political dimension. *Power* is the ability to exercise one's will over others. In the United States, power stems from membership in particularly influential groups, such as corporate boards of directors, government bodies, and interest groups. Conflict theorists generally agree that two major sources of power—big business and government—are closely interrelated (see Chapter 14). For instance, many of the heads of major corporations also hold powerful positions in the government or military.

The corporate executives who head private companies in the United States earn the highest incomes in the nation. They represent the pinnacle not just of U.S. society, but of corporate executives around the world. Figure 9-2 shows how much better heads of U.S. corporations are compensated than chief executive officers (CEOs) in other industrial countries. The compensation these CEOs receive is not necessarily linked to conventional measures of success, however. As the U.S. economy worsened in 2002, an analysis showed that the CEOs who received the highest compensation were generally those who authorized the largest layoffs (Klinger et al. 2002).

To summarize, in Weber's view, each of us has not one rank in society but three. Our position in a stratification system reflects some combination of class, status, and power. Each factor influences the other two, and in fact the rankings on these three dimensions often tend to coincide. John F. Kennedy came from an extremely wealthy family, attended exclusive preparatory schools, graduated from Harvard University, and went on to become president of the United States. Like Kennedy, many people from affluent backgrounds achieve impressive status and power.

Interactionist View

Both Karl Marx and Max Weber looked at inequality primarily from a macrosociological perspective, considering the entire society or even the global economy. Marx did suggest the importance of a more microsociological analysis, however, when he stressed the ways in which individuals develop a true class consciousness.

Interactionists, as well as economists, have long been interested in the importance of social class in shaping a person's lifestyle. The theorist Thorstein Veblen (1857–1929) noted that those at the top of the social hierarchy typically convert part of their wealth into *conspicuous consumption,* purchasing more automobiles than they can reasonably use and building houses with more rooms than they can possibly occupy. Or they may engage in *conspicuous leisure,* jetting to a remote destination and

Student Alert Emphasize that the fall of communism does not devalue Marx's insights into class differentiation and inequality.
Key Person Max Weber
Student Alert Remind students about the concept of the *ideal type,* introduced in Chapter 1.

Contemporary Culture In what specific ways do Americans engage in conspicuous consumption and conspicuous leisure?

FIGURE 9-2

Around the World: What's a CEO Worth?

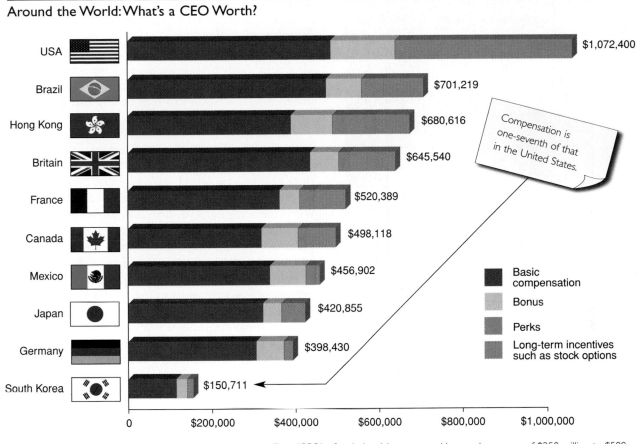

Note box: Compensation is one-seventh of that in the United States.

Country	Value
USA	$1,072,400
Brazil	$701,219
Hong Kong	$680,616
Britain	$645,540
France	$520,389
Canada	$498,118
Mexico	$456,902
Japan	$420,855
Germany	$398,430
South Korea	$150,711

Legend:
- Basic compensation
- Bonus
- Perks
- Long-term incentives such as stock options

Note: The average annual pay package of the chief executive officer (CEO) of an industrial company with annual revenues of $250 million to $500 million, in 10 countries. Figures are from April 1998 and are not weighted to compensate for different costs of living or levels of taxation.

Source: Towers Perrin in Bryant 1999:Section 4, p. 1.

Think About It
Why should CEOs in the United States be worth more than those in other countries?

staying just long enough to have dinner or view a sunset over some historic locale (Veblen [1899] 1964).

At the other end of the spectrum, behavior that is judged to be typical of the lower class is subject not only to ridicule but even to legal action. Communities have, from time to time, banned trailers from people's front yards and sofas from their front porches. In some communities, it is illegal to leave a pickup truck in front of the house overnight.

Use Your Sociological Imagination www.mhhe.com/schaefer6

Refer to the photo essay on pages 4–5. How do you think Thorstein Veblen would answer the question posed in the title? What do you think he would say about the three families pictured in the essay?

Is Stratification Universal?

Must some members of society receive greater rewards than others? Do people need to feel socially and economically superior to others? Can social life be organized without structured inequality? These questions have been debated for centuries, especially among political activists. Utopian socialists, religious minorities, and members of recent countercultures have all attempted to establish communities that to some extent or other would abolish inequality in social relationships.

Social scientists have found that inequality exists in all societies—even the simplest. For example, when anthropologist Gunnar Landtman ([1938] 1968) studied the Kiwai Papuans of New Guinea, at first he noticed little differentiation among them. Every man in the village

Methods Landtman conducted observation research among the Kiwai Papuans.
Global View Differentiation among the Kiwai Papuans of New Guinea

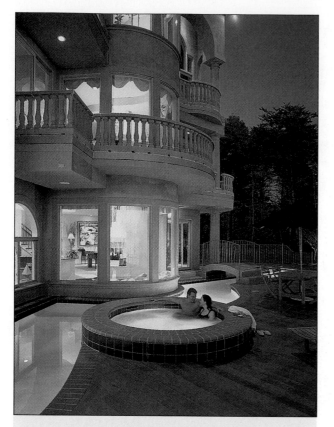

This couple's expensive lifestyle illustrates Thorstein Veblen's concept of conspicuous consumption, a spending pattern common to those at the very top of the social ladder.

did the same work and lived in similar housing. However, on closer inspection, Landtman observed that certain Papuans—men who were warriors, harpooners, and sorcerers—were described as "a little more high" than others. In contrast, villagers who were female, unemployed, or unmarried were considered "down a little bit" and were barred from owning land.

Stratification is universal in that all societies maintain some form of social inequality among members. Depending on its values, a society may assign people to distinctive ranks based on their religious knowledge, skill in hunting, beauty, trading expertise, or ability to provide health care. But why has such inequality developed in human societies? And how much differentiation among people, if any, is actually essential?

Functionalist and conflict sociologists offer contrasting explanations for the existence and necessity of social stratification. Functionalists maintain that a differential system of rewards and punishments is necessary for the efficient operation of society. Conflict theorists argue that competition for scarce resources results in significant political, economic, and social inequality.

Functionalist View

Would people go to school for many years to become physicians if they could make as much money and gain as much respect working as street cleaners? Functionalists say no, which is partly why they believe that a stratified society is universal.

In the view of Kingsley Davis and Wilbert Moore (1945), society must distribute its members among a variety of social positions. It must not only make sure that these positions are filled but also see that they are staffed by people with the appropriate talents and abilities. Rewards, including money and prestige, are based on the importance of a position and the relative scarcity of qualified personnel. Yet this assessment often devalues work performed by certain segments of society, such as women's work in the home or in occupations traditionally filled by women, or low-status work in fast-food outlets.

Davis and Moore argue that stratification is universal and that social inequality is necessary so that people will be motivated to fill functionally important positions. But critics say that unequal rewards are not the only means of encouraging people to fill critical positions and occupations. Personal pleasure, intrinsic satisfaction, and value orientations also motivate people to enter particular careers. Functionalists agree, but they note that society must use some type of reward to motivate people to enter unpleasant or dangerous jobs and professions that require a long training period. This response does not justify stratification systems in which status is largely inherited, such as slave or caste societies. Similarly, it is difficult to explain the high salaries our society offers to professional athletes or entertainers on the basis of how critical those jobs are to the survival of society. And even if stratification is inevitable, the functionalist explanation for differential rewards does not explain the wide disparity between the rich and the poor (Collins 1975; Kerbo 2003; Tumin 1953, 1985).

Conflict View

The writings of Karl Marx lie at the heart of conflict theory. p. 12 Marx viewed history as a continuous struggle between the oppressors and the oppressed, which would ultimately culminate in an egalitarian, classless society. In terms of stratification, he argued that under capitalism, the dominant class —the bourgeoisie—manipulates the economic and political systems in order to maintain control over the exploited proletariat. Marx did not believe that stratification was inevitable, but he did see inequality and oppression as inherent in capitalism (E. Wright et al. 1982).

Theory Functionalist and conflict views of the existence of stratification are contrasted.

Theory Conflict view of stratification introduced

Like Marx, contemporary conflict theorists believe that human beings are prone to conflict over scarce resources such as wealth, status, and power. However, Marx focused primarily on class conflict; more recent theorists have extended the analysis to include conflicts based on gender, race, age, and other dimensions. British sociologist Ralf Dahrendorf is one of the most influential contributors to the conflict approach.

Dahrendorf (1959) has modified Marx's analysis of capitalist society to apply to *modern* capitalist societies. For Dahrendorf, social classes are groups of people who share common interests resulting from their authority relationships. In identifying the most powerful groups in society, he includes not only the bourgeoisie—the owners of the means of production—but also the managers of industry, legislators, the judiciary, heads of the government bureaucracy, and others. In that respect, Dahrendorf has merged Marx's emphasis on class conflict with Weber's recognition that power is an important element of stratification (Cuff et al. 1990).

As popular songs and movies suggest, long-haul truck drivers take pride in their low-prestige job. According to the conflict perspective, the cultural beliefs that form a society's dominant ideology, such as the popular image of the truck driver as hero, help the wealthy to maintain their power and control at the expense of the lower classes.

Conflict theorists, including Dahrendorf, contend that the powerful of today, like the bourgeoisie of Marx's time, want society to run smoothly so that they can enjoy their privileged positions. Because the status quo suits those with wealth, status, and power, they have a clear interest in preventing, minimizing, or controlling societal conflict.

One way for the powerful to maintain the status quo is to define and disseminate the society's dominant ideology. The term *dominant ideology* describes a set of cultural beliefs and practices that helps to maintain powerful **p. 68** social, economic, and political interests. For Karl Marx, the dominant ideology in a capitalist society serves the interests of the ruling class. From a conflict perspective, the social significance of the dominant ideology is that not only do a society's most powerful groups and institutions control wealth and property; even more important, they control the means of producing beliefs about reality through religion, education, and the media (Abercrombie et al. 1980, 1990; Robertson 1988).

The powerful, such as leaders of government, also use limited social reforms to buy off the oppressed and reduce the danger of challenges to their dominance. For example,

minimum wage laws and unemployment compensation unquestionably give some valuable assistance to needy men and women. Yet these reforms also serve to pacify those who might otherwise rebel. Of course, in the view of conflict theorists, such maneuvers can never entirely eliminate conflict, since workers will continue to demand equality, and the powerful will not give up their control of society.

Conflict theorists see stratification as a major source of societal tension and conflict. They do not agree with Davis and Moore that stratification is functional for a society or that it serves as a source of stability. Rather, conflict sociologists argue that stratification will inevitably lead to instability and to social change (R. Collins 1975; L. Coser 1977).

Table 9-1 (page 212) summarizes and compares the three major perspectives on social stratification.

Lenski's Viewpoint

Let's return to the question posed earlier—Is stratification universal?—and consider the sociological response. Some form of differentiation is found in every culture, from the most primitive to the most advanced industrial societies of our time. Sociologist Gerhard Lenski, in his sociocultural evolution approach, described how economic systems change as their level of technology becomes more complex, beginning with hunting and

Key Person Ralf Dahrendorf
Theory Conflict view of the social significance of the dominant ideology
Classroom Tip See "Comparison of Perspectives on Stratification" (Additional Lecture Ideas).

Key Person Gerhard Lenski

summingUP

Table 9-1	Major Perspectives on Social Stratification		
	Functionalist	**Conflict**	**Interactionist**
Purpose of social stratification	Facilitates filling of social positions	Facilitates exploitation	Influences people's lifestyles
Attitude toward social inequality	Necessary to some extent	Excessive and growing	—
Analysis of the wealthy	Talented and skilled, creating opportunities for others	Use the dominant ideology to further their own interests	Exhibit conspicuous consumption and conspicuous leisure

gathering and culminating eventually with industrial society. In subsistence-based hunting-and-gathering societies, people focus on survival. While some inequality and [pp. 119–122] differentiation are evident, a stratification system based on social class does not emerge because there is no real wealth to be claimed.

As a society advances technologically, it becomes capable of producing a considerable surplus of goods. The emergence of surplus resources greatly expands the possibilities for inequality in status, influence, and power and allows a well-defined, rigid social class system to develop. To minimize strikes, slowdowns, and industrial sabotage, the elites may share a portion of the economic surplus with the lower classes, but not enough to reduce their own power and privilege.

As Lenski argued, the allocation of surplus goods and services controlled by those with wealth, status, and power reinforces the social inequality that accompanies stratification systems. While this reward system may once have served the overall purposes of society, as functionalists contend, the same cannot be said for the large disparities separating the haves from the have-nots in current societies. In contemporary industrial society, the degree of social and economic inequality far exceeds what is needed to provide for goods and services (Lenski 1966; Nolan and Lenski 2004).

STRATIFICATION BY SOCIAL CLASS

Measuring Social Class

We continually assess how wealthy people are by looking at the cars they drive, the houses they live in, the clothes they wear, and so on. Yet it is not so easy to locate an individual within our social hierarchies as it would be in slavery or caste systems of stratification. To determine someone's class position, sociologists generally rely on the objective method.

Objective Method

In the *objective method* of measuring social class, class is viewed largely as a statistical category. Researchers assign individuals to social classes on the basis of criteria such as occupation, education, income, and place of residence. The key to the objective method is that the *researcher*, rather than the person being classified, identifies an individual's class position.

The first step in using this method is to decide what indicators or causal factors will be measured objectively, whether wealth, income, education, or occupation. The prestige ranking of occupations has proved to be a useful indicator of a person's class position. For one thing, it is much easier to determine accurately than income or wealth. The term *prestige* refers to the respect and admiration that an occupation holds in a society. "My daughter, the physicist" connotes something very different from "my daughter, the waitress." Prestige is independent of the particular individual who occupies a job, a characteristic that distinguishes it from esteem. *Esteem* refers to the reputation that a specific person has earned within an occupation. Therefore, one can say that the position of president of the United States has high prestige, even though it has been occupied by people with varying degrees of esteem. A hairdresser may have the esteem of his clients, but he lacks the prestige of a corporate executive.

Table 9-2 ranks the prestige of a number of well-known occupations. In a series of national surveys, sociologists assigned prestige rankings to about 500 occupations, ranging from physician to newspaper vendor. The highest possible prestige score was 100; the lowest was 0. Physician, lawyer, dentist, and college professor were the most highly regarded occupations. Sociologists have used such data to assign prestige rankings to virtually all jobs and have found a stability in rankings from 1925 to the present. Similar studies in other countries have also developed useful prestige rankings of occupations (Hodge and Rossi 1964; Lin and Xie 1988; Treiman 1977).

Gender and Occupational Prestige

For many years, studies of social class tended to neglect the occupations and incomes of *women* as determinants of social rank. In an exhaustive study of 589 occupations, sociologists Mary Powers and Joan Holmberg (1978) examined the impact of women's participation in the paid labor force on occupational status. Since women tend to dominate the relatively low-paying occupations, such as bookkeeper and child care worker, their participation in the workforce has led to a general upgrading of the status of most male-dominated occupations. More recent research conducted in both the United States and Europe has noted the occupations of husbands *and* wives in determining the class positions of families (Sørensen 1994). With more than half of all married women now working outside the home (see Chapter 11), this approach seems long overdue, but it raises some questions. For example, how is class or status to be judged in dual-career families—by the occupation regarded as having greater prestige, the average, or some other combination of the two?

Sociologists—in particular, feminist sociologists in Great Britain—are drawing on new approaches to assess women's social class standing. One approach is to focus on the individual (rather than the family or household) as the basis for categorizing a woman's class position. Thus, a woman would be classified based on her own occupational status rather than that of her spouse (M. O'Donnell 1992).

Another feminist effort to measure the contribution of women to the economy reflects a more clearly political agenda. International Women Count Network, a global grassroots feminist organization, has sought to give a monetary value to women's unpaid work. Besides providing symbolic recognition of women's role in labor, this value would also be used to calculate pension and other benefits that are based on wages received. The United Nations has placed an $11 trillion price tag on unpaid labor by women, largely in child care, housework, and agriculture. Whatever the figure, the continued undercounting of many workers' contributions to a family and to an entire economy means that virtually all measures of stratification are in need of reform (United Nations Development Programme 1995; Wages for Housework Campaign 1999).

Multiple Measures

Another complication in measuring social class is that advances in statistical methods and computer technology

Table 9-2	Prestige Rankings of Occupations		
Occupation	**Score**	**Occupation**	**Score**
Physician	86	Secretary	46
Lawyer	75	Insurance agent	45
Dentist	74	Bank teller	43
College professor	74	Nurse's aide	42
Architect	73	Farmer	40
Clergy	69	Correctional officer	40
Pharmacist	68	Receptionist	39
Registered nurse	66	Barber	36
High school teacher	66	Child care worker	35
Accountant	65	Hotel clerk	32
Airline pilot	60	Bus driver	32
Police officer and detective	60	Truck driver	30
Prekindergarten teacher	55	Salesworker (shoes)	28
Librarian	54	Garbage collector	28
Firefighter	53	Waiter and waitress	28
Social worker	52	Bartender	25
Electrician	51	Farm worker	23
Funeral director	49	Janitor	22
Mail carrier	47	Newspaper vendor	19

Note: 100 is the highest and 0 the lowest possible prestige score.
Source: J. Davis et al. 2003.

FIGURE 9-3

Comparison of Distribution of Income and Wealth in the United States

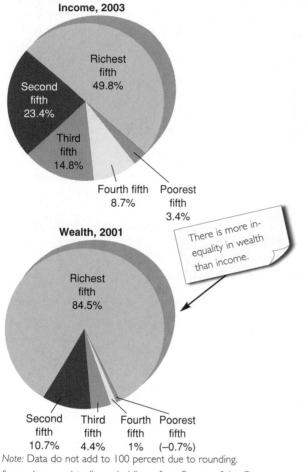

Income, 2003

Richest fifth 49.8%

Second fifth 23.4%

Third fifth 14.8%

Fourth fifth 8.7%

Poorest fifth 3.4%

Wealth, 2001

Richest fifth 84.5%

There is more inequality in wealth than income.

Second fifth 10.7%

Third fifth 4.4%

Fourth fifth 1%

Poorest fifth (−0.7%)

Note: Data do not add to 100 percent due to rounding.

Source: Income data (household) are from Bureau of the Census (DeNavas-Walt et al. 2004:4). Data on wealth are from Wolff 2002.

have multiplied the factors used to define class under the objective method. No longer are sociologists limited to annual income and education in evaluating a person's class position. Today, studies use as criteria the value of homes, sources of income, assets, years in present occupations, neighborhoods, and considerations regarding dual careers. Adding these variables will not necessarily paint a different picture of class differentiation in the United States, but it does allow sociologists to measure class in a more complex and multidimensional way.

Whatever the technique used to measure class, the sociologist is interested in real and often dramatic differences in power, privilege, and opportunity in a society. The study of stratification is a study of inequality. Nowhere is the truth of that statement more evident than in the distribution of wealth and income.

Wealth and Income

By all measures, income in the United States is distributed unevenly. Nobel Prize–winning economist Paul Samuelson has described the situation in the following words: "If we made an income pyramid out of building blocks, with each layer portraying $500 of income, the peak would be far higher than Mount Everest, but most people would be within a few feet of the ground" (P. Samuelson and Nordhaus 2001:386).

Recent data support Samuelson's analogy. As Figure 9-3 shows, in 2003, members of the richest fifth (or top 20 percent) of the nation's population earned $86,867 or more, accounting for nearly 50 percent of the nation's total income. In contrast, members of the bottom fifth of the nation's population earned just $17,984 or less, accounting for only 3 percent of the nation's total income.

The United States has seen modest redistribution of income over the past 70 years. From 1929 through 1970, the government's economic and tax policies shifted income slightly toward the poor. However, in the last three decades—especially during the 1980s—federal tax policies have favored the affluent. The Federal Reserve reported in 2003 that while a rising economic tide lifted the boats of almost all families in the late 1990s, it also sharply increased the gap in wealth between the rich and the rest of society (Aizcorbe et al. 2003).

Survey data show that only 38 percent of people in the United States believe that government should take steps to reduce the income disparity between the rich and the poor. In contrast, 80 percent of people in Italy, 66 percent in Germany, and 65 percent in Great Britain support governmental efforts to reduce income inequality. It is not surprising, then, that many European countries provide more extensive safety nets to assist and protect the disadvantaged. In contrast, the strong cultural value placed on individualism in the United States leads to greater possibilities for both economic success and failure (Lipset 1996).

Wealth in the United States is much more unevenly distributed than income. As Figure 9-3 shows, in 2001, the richest fifth of the population held 84.5 percent of the nation's wealth. Government data indicate that more than 1 out of every 100 households had assets over $2.4 million, while one-fifth of all households were in debt and therefore had a negative net worth. Researchers have also found a dramatic disparity in wealth between African Americans and Whites. This disparity is evident even when educational backgrounds are held constant: the households of college-educated Whites have about three times as much wealth as the households of college-educated Blacks (Oliver and Shapiro 1995; Wolff 2002).

Theory Conflict theorists emphasize that federal budgetary policies have favored the affluent.
Methods Use of a survey to assess dissatisfaction with income disparities in the United States
Global View Dissatisfaction with income disparities examined in the United States, Italy, Germany, and Great Britain

Poverty

Approximately one out of every nine people in the United States lives below the poverty line established by the federal government. In 2003, 35.9 million people were living in poverty. The economic boom of the 1990s passed these people by. A recent Bureau of the Census report showed that one in five households has trouble meeting basic needs—everything from paying the utility bills to buying dinner. In this section, we'll consider just how we define *poverty* and who is included in that category (Bauman 1999; DeNavas-Walt et al. 2004).

Studying Poverty

The efforts of sociologists and other social scientists to better understand poverty are complicated by the difficulty of defining it. This problem is evident even in government programs that conceive of poverty in either absolute or relative terms. ***Absolute poverty*** refers to a minimum level of subsistence that no family should be expected to live below.

Policies concerning minimum wages, housing standards, or school lunch programs for the poor imply a need to bring citizens up to some predetermined level of existence. For example, the federal minimum wage rate was last raised to $5.15 an hour in 1997. Even so, when one takes inflation into account, this standard is currently *lower* than the wage workers were guaranteed in 1950. Today, more than a million workers over the age of 25 are employed at or below the minimum wage. Yet to rise above the current poverty threshold, a single worker would need to work full-time for $7.05 per hour (Bureau of the Census 2003a:425).

One commonly used measure of absolute poverty is the federal government's *poverty line,* a money income figure that is adjusted annually to reflect the consumption requirements of families based on their size and composition. The poverty line serves as an official definition of which people are poor. In 2003, for example, any family of four (two adults and two children) with a combined income of $18,660 or less fell below the poverty line. This definition determines which individuals and families will be eligible for certain government benefits (DeNavas-Walt et al. 2004:39).

Although by absolute standards, poverty has declined in the United States, it remains higher than in many other industrial nations. As Figure 9-4 (page 216) shows, a comparatively high proportion of U.S. households are poor, meaning that they are unable to purchase basic consumer goods. If anything, this cross-national comparison understates the extent of poverty in the United States, since U.S. residents are likely to pay more for housing, health care, child care, and education than residents of other countries, where such expenses are often subsidized.

In contrast, ***relative poverty*** is a floating standard of deprivation by which people at the bottom of a society, whatever their lifestyles, are judged to be disadvantaged *in comparison with the nation as a whole.* Therefore, even if the poor of 2005 are better off in absolute terms than the poor of the 1930s or 1960s, they are still seen as deserving of special assistance.

In the 1990s, debate grew over the validity of the poverty line as a measure of poverty and a standard for allocating government benefits. Some critics charge that the poverty line is too low; they note that the federal government continues to use 20-year-old nutritional standards in assessing people's level of poverty. If the poverty line is too low, then government data will underestimate the extent of poverty in the United States, and many deserving poor citizens will fail to receive benefits.

Other observers dispute this view. They argue that the poverty line may actually overestimate the number of low-income people because it fails to consider noncash benefits (such as Medicare, Medicaid, food stamps, public housing, and health care and other fringe benefits provided by some employers). In response, the Bureau of the Census has considered several different definitions of poverty, which showed at most a 1.4 percent lower rate. That is, if the official poverty threshold places 13 percent of the population in the category of the poor, the poverty estimate including *all* these noncash benefits would account for about 11.6 percent of the population (Brady 2003; Short et al. 1999).

Who Are the Poor?

Not only does the category of the poor defy any simple definition; it counters the common stereotypes about "poor people" that Barbara Ehrenreich addressed in her book *Nickel and Dimed* (see the opening excerpt in Chapter 1). For example, many people in the United States believe that the vast majority of the poor are able to work but will not. Yet many poor adults do work outside the home, although only a small portion of them work full-time throughout the year. In 2003, about 30 percent of all poor adults worked full-time, compared to 66 percent of all adults. Of those poor adults who do not work, most are ill or disabled, or are occupied in maintaining a home (DeNavas-Walt et al. 2004).

Though many of the poor live in urban slums, a majority live outside those poverty-stricken areas. Poverty is no stranger in rural areas, from Appalachia to hard-hit farming regions to Native American reservations. Table 9-3 (page 217) provides additional statistical information regarding low-income people in the United States.

Classroom Tip See "Estimating the Poverty Level for a Family" (Class Discussion Topics); "Poverty and Wealth" (Class Discussion Topics); "Income Levels" (Class Discussion Topics); "Introducing Social Class" (Class Discussion Topics); "Social Stratification—An Active Learning Technique" (Class Discussion Topics); "Homeless Women" (Class Discussion Topics); "Understanding Income and Wealth Inequality" (Additional Lecture Ideas); "Income Differences by Gender and Race" (Additional Lecture Ideas).

Contemporary Culture What does it say about American society that a working person can still be poor?

FIGURE 9-4

Absolute Poverty in Selected Industrial Countries

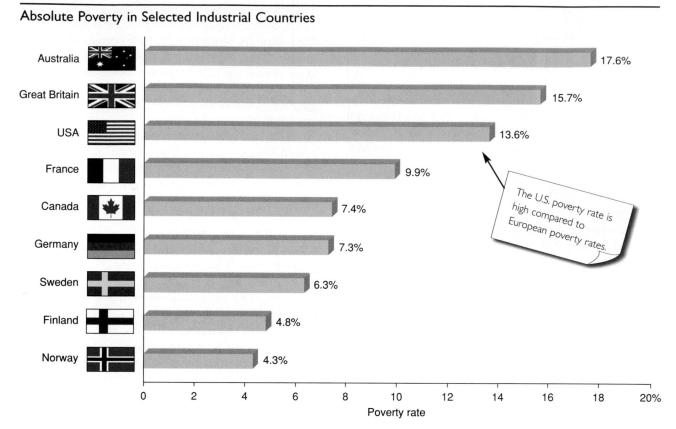

Source: Smeeding et al. 2001:51.

Since World War II, an increasing proportion of the poor people of the United States have been women, many of whom are divorced or never-married mothers. In 1959, female householders accounted for 26 percent of the nation's poor; by 2003, that figure had risen to 51 percent (see Table 9-3 on page 217). This alarming trend, known as the *feminization of poverty,* is evident not just in the United States but around the world.

About half of all women living in poverty in the United States are in transition, coping with an economic crisis caused by the departure, disability, or death of a husband. The other half tend to be economically dependent either on the welfare system or on friends and relatives living nearby. A major factor in the feminization of poverty has been the increase in families with women as single heads of the household (see Chapter 12). In 2003, 28 percent of households headed by single mothers lived in poverty, compared to 5.4 percent of married couples in the United States. Conflict theorists and other observers trace the higher rates of

◀ pp. 98–99 poverty among women to three distinct factors: the difficulty in finding affordable child care, sexual harassment, and sex discrimination in the labor market.

In 2003, 51 percent of poor people in the United States were living in central cities. These highly visible urban residents are the focus of most governmental efforts to alleviate poverty. Yet according to many observers, the plight of the urban poor is growing worse, owing to the devastating interplay of inadequate education and limited employment prospects. Traditional employment opportunities in the industrial sector are largely closed to the unskilled poor. Past and present discrimination heightens these problems for those low-income urban residents who are Black and Hispanic (DeNavas-Walt et al. 2004).

Sociologist William Julius Wilson (1980, 1987, 1989, 1996) and other social scientists have used the term **underclass** to describe the long-term poor who lack training and skills. According to an analysis of Census 2000 data, 7.9 million people live in high-poverty neighborhoods. About 30 percent of the population in these neighborhoods is Black, 29 percent Hispanic, and 24 percent White. In central cities, about 49 percent of the underclass is African American, 29 percent Hispanic, 17 percent White, and 5 percent "other" (Jargowsky 2003:4–5; O'Hare and Curry-White 1992).

Global View Absolute poverty in selected industrial countries
Gender The feminization of poverty
Global View The feminization of poverty is evident around the world.
Theory Conflict view of the feminization of poverty
Classroom Tip The ascribed status of being disabled often functions as a master status, as was disclosed in Chapter 5.

Gender Black women are particularly subject to joblessness.
Key Person William Julius Wilson

Conflict theorists, among others, have expressed alarm at the portion of the nation's population living on this lower rung of the stratification ladder, and at society's reluctance to address the lack of economic opportunities for these people. Often, portraits of the underclass seem to blame the victims for their own plight, while ignoring other factors that push people into poverty. Box 9-2 (page 218) considers Wilson's latest research into the persistence of urban poverty.

Analyses of the poor in general reveal that they are not a static social class. The overall composition of the poor changes continually, because some individuals and families near the top edge of poverty move above the poverty level after a year or two, while others slip below it. Still, hundreds of thousands of people remain in poverty for many years at a time. African Americans and Latinos are more likely than Whites to be persistently poor. Over a 21-year period, 15 percent of African Americans and 10 percent of Latinos were persistently poor, compared to only 3 percent of Whites. Both Latinos and Blacks are less likely than Whites to leave the welfare rolls as a result of welfare reform, discussed in the social policy section of this chapter (Mangum et al. 2003).

Explaining Poverty

Why is it that poverty pervades a nation of such vast wealth? Sociologist Herbert Gans (1995), who has applied functionalist analysis to the existence of poverty, argues that various segments of society actually *benefit* from the existence of the poor. Gans has identified a number of social, economic, and political functions that the poor perform for society:

- The presence of poor people means that society's dirty work—physically dirty or dangerous, dead-end and underpaid, undignified and menial jobs—will be performed at low cost.
- Poverty creates jobs for occupations and professions that serve the poor. It creates both legal employment (public health experts, welfare caseworkers) and illegal jobs (drug dealers, numbers runners).
- The identification and punishment of the poor as deviants upholds the legitimacy of conventional social norms and mainstream values regarding hard work, thrift, and honesty.
- Within a relatively hierarchical society, the existence of poor people guarantees the higher status of the more affluent. As psychologist William Ryan (1976) has noted, affluent people may justify inequality (and gain a measure of satisfaction) by blaming the victims of poverty for their disadvantaged condition.
- Because of their lack of political power, the poor often absorb the costs of social change. Under the policy of deinstitutionalization, mental patients released from long-term hospitals have been transferred primarily to low-income communities and neighborhoods. Similarly, halfway houses for rehabilitated drug abusers, rejected by more affluent communities, often end up in poorer neighborhoods.

p. 181

Table 9-3	Who Are the Poor in the United States?	
Group	Percentage of the Population of the United States	Percentage of the Poor of the United States
Under 18 years old	26%	30%
18 to 64 years old	61	54
65 years and older	13	10
Whites (non-Hispanic)	83	44
Blacks	12	25
Hispanics	11	25
Asians and Pacific Islanders	4	4
Married couples and families with male householders	82	49
Families with female householders	18	51

Note: Data are for 2003, as reported by the Bureau of the Census in 2004.
Source: DeNavas-Walt et al. 2004:10.

Theory Conflict view of the size and composition of the nation's underclass
Policy Pointer The social policy section at the end of the chapter focuses on the U.S. welfare system.
Classroom Tip See "Is There a 'Culture of Poverty'?" (Additional Lecture Ideas).

Student Alert If poverty were evenly distributed by age, race, ethnicity, and head of household, then the two columns in Table 9-3 would show identical data.
Key Person Herbert Gans
Theory Gans applied functionalist analysis to the study of poverty.

Woodlawn, an urban neighborhood on Chicago's South Side, used to boast more than 800 commercial and industrial establishments. Today, some 50 years later, there are only about 100 left: mostly barber shops, thrift stores, and small catering businesses. One Woodlawn resident described the changes on returning after many years: "I was just really appalled. . . . Those resources are just gone, completely. . . . And . . . everybody has moved, there are vacant lots everywhere" (W. J. Wilson 1996:5). Another South Side resident noted, "Jobs were plentiful in the past. You could walk out of the house and get a job. . . . Now, you can't find anything" (p. 36).

More than 35 years have passed since President Lyndon Johnson launched a series of federal programs known as the "war on poverty," yet poverty is still with us. Using surveys, interviews, and census data from 1987 to the present, sociologist and past president of the American Sociology Association William Julius Wilson has undertaken a major study of poverty, the Urban Poverty and Family Life Study (UPFLS). Increasingly, Wilson and his colleagues have noted, the jobless dominate low-income Chicago neighborhoods, some of which have poverty rates of at least 20 percent. The absence of full-time workers is especially noticeable in African American neighborhoods, which have become increasingly marginal to the

city's economic, social, and cultural life. Wilson sees this trend as a movement away from what historian Allan Spear (1967) termed the institutional ghetto, where viable social institutions served the minority community, toward a new *jobless ghetto.*

What drives the trend toward increasing poverty in urban areas? According to Wilson, it is primarily the exodus of well-paid jobs, especially in the manufacturing sector. Over the last several decades, U.S. manufacturers have relied more and more on improved technology and

> "Jobs were plentiful in the past. You could walk out of the house and get a job."

skilled workers. They no longer hire many unskilled assembly-line workers, who once enjoyed union benefits and some protection from layoffs. A generation ago, the typical ghetto resident might have worked as a machine operator or assembler; today, he is working as a waiter or janitor—if he is working at all.

In Wilson's view, the economy, not the poor, needs to be reformed. He has proposed some initiatives, such as national education standards, to upgrade the skills of youths in poverty-stricken areas. His research also shows a clear need for ex-

William Julius Wilson, a sociologist at Harvard University, specializes in the study of urban poverty.

panded child care and family support services. And he calls for metropolitan solutions that bridge the central cities and the suburbs. Wilson admits these approaches are not likely to meet with easy acceptance. There is no simple solution to reducing poverty when jobs disappear.

Let's Discuss

1. Have jobs disappeared from a community you live in or near? If so, what changes took place in your neighborhood as a result?
2. Where have the assembly-line jobs that once supported inner-city neighborhoods gone?

Sources: Small and Newman 2001; Spear 1967; W. J. Wilson 1996, 1999a, 2003a, 2003b.

In Gans's view, then, poverty and the poor actually satisfy positive functions for many nonpoor groups in the United States.

Life Chances

Max Weber saw class as being closely related to people's *life chances*—that is, their opportunities to provide themselves with material goods, positive living conditions, and favorable life experiences (Gerth and Mills

1958). Life chances are reflected in measures such as housing, education, and health. Occupying a higher position in a society improves your life chances and brings greater access to social rewards. In contrast, people in the lower social classes are forced to devote a larger proportion of their limited resources to the necessities of life.

In times of danger, the affluent and powerful have a better chance of surviving than people of ordinary means. When the supposedly unsinkable British oceanliner *Titanic* hit an iceberg in 1912, it was not carrying enough lifeboats to accommodate all passengers. Plans had been made to evacuate only first- and second-class passengers. About 62 percent of the first-class passengers survived the disaster. Despite a rule that women and children would go first, about a third of those passengers were male. In contrast, only 25 percent of the passengers in third class survived. The first attempt to alert them to the need to abandon ship came at least 45 minutes after other passengers had been notified (Butler 1998; Crouse 1999; Riding 1998).

Class position also affects people's day-to-day health. In fact, class and wealth are increasingly viewed as important predictors of health. As Figure 9-5 (page 220) shows, the poorer the social stratum, the greater the percentage of people with less than good health. The affluent avail themselves of improved health services, but such advances bypass poor people. Indeed, the chances of a child's dying during the first year of life are much higher in poor families than among the middle class. This higher infant mortality rate results in part from the inadequate nutrition received by low-income expectant mothers. Even when the poor survive infancy, they are more likely than the affluent to suffer from serious, chronic illnesses such as arthritis, bronchitis, diabetes, and heart disease. In addition, the poor are less likely to be protected from the high costs of illness by private health insurance. They may have jobs that do not offer health insurance, may work part-time and not be eligible for employee health benefits, or may simply be unable to afford the premiums (Huie et al. 2003; DeNavas-Walt et al. 2004).

Like disease, crime can be particularly devastating when it attacks the poor. According to the 2002 National Crime Victimization Survey, people in low-income families were more likely to be assaulted, raped, or robbed than were the most affluent people. Furthermore, if accused of a crime, a person with low income and status is likely to be represented by an overworked public defender. Whether innocent or guilty, the accused may sit in jail for months, unable to raise bail (Rennison and Rand 2003).

Some people have hoped that the Internet revolution would help to level the playing field by making information and markets uniformly available. Unfortunately, however, not everyone can get onto the information superhighway, so yet another aspect of social inequality has emerged—the *digital divide*. The poor, minorities, and those who live in rural communities and inner cities are not getting connected at home or at work. A recent government study found that despite falling computer prices, the Internet gap between the haves and have-nots has not narrowed. For example, while 51 percent of all households could access the Internet in 2001, about 85 percent of households with family incomes over $75,000 but fewer than 21 percent of households with family incomes

In the movie *Titanic,* the romantic fantasy of a love affair that crossed class lines obscured the real and deadly effects of the social class divide. This poster appeared in Japan.

less than $5,000 had such access. As wealthier people begin to buy high-speed Internet connections, they will be able to take advantage of even more sophisticated interactive services, and the digital divide will grow even wider (Bureau of the Census 2003a:736).

Wealth, status, and power may not ensure happiness, but they certainly provide additional ways of coping with problems and disappointments. For this reason, the opportunity for advancement—for social mobility—is of special significance to those on the bottom of society. These people want the rewards and privileges that are granted to high-ranking members of a culture.

Use Your Sociological Imagination www.mhhe.com/schaefer6

Imagine a society in which there are no social classes—no differences in people's wealth, income, and life chances. What would such a society be like? Would it be stable, or would its social structure change over time?

Let's Discuss See "Life Chances Simulations" (Class Discussion Topics).
Contemporary Culture Computers and the Internet and differential life chances
Let's Discuss Who is likely to become president of the United States first: a woman, a Black man, a Hispanic man, an Asian American man, or a Jewish man?

Methods Survey data from National Crime Victimization Survey
Web Resource Encourage students to take the true–false quiz in the student center of the Online Learning Center (www.mhhe.com/schaefer6). Remind them that the quiz gives immediate feedback for incorrect answers.

FIGURE 9-5

Health Status of the Poor and Nonpoor, 2000

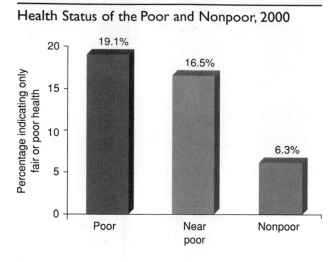

Note: Respondent-assessed in National Health Interview Survey.
Source: National Center for Health Statistics 2002:192.

SOCIAL MOBILITY

In the movie *Maid in Manhattan,* Jennifer Lopez plays the lead in a modern-day Cinderella story, rising from the lowly status of chambermaid in a big-city hotel to become a company supervisor and the girlfriend of a well-to-do politician. The ascent of a person from a poor background to a position of prestige, power, or financial reward is an example of social mobility. The term ***social mobility*** refers to the movement of individuals or groups from one position in a society's stratification system to another. But how significant—how frequent, how dramatic—is mobility in a class society such as the United States?

Open versus Closed Stratification Systems

Sociologists use the terms *open stratification system* and *closed stratification system* to indicate the degree of social mobility in a society. An ***open system*** implies that the position of each individual is influenced by his or her *achieved* status. Such a system encourages competition among members of society. The United States is moving toward this ideal type as the government attempts to reduce the barriers faced by women, racial and ethnic minorities, and people born in lower social classes.

At the other extreme of social mobility is the ***closed system,*** which allows little or no possibility of individual social mobility. The slavery and caste systems of stratifi-

cation are examples of closed systems. In such societies, social placement is based on *ascribed* statuses, such as race or family background, which cannot be changed.

Types of Social Mobility

An airline pilot who becomes a police officer moves from one social position to another of the same rank. Each occupation has the same prestige ranking: 60 on a scale ranging from a low of 0 to a high of 100 (see Table 9-2 on page 213). Sociologists call this kind of movement ***horizontal mobility.*** However, if the pilot were to become a lawyer (prestige ranking of 75), he or she would experience ***vertical mobility,*** the movement of an individual from one social position to another of a different rank. Vertical mobility can also involve moving *downward* in a society's stratification system, as would be the case if the airline pilot became a bank teller (ranking of 43). Pitirim Sorokin ([1927] 1959) was the first sociologist to distinguish between horizontal and vertical mobility. Most sociological analysis, however, focuses on vertical rather than horizontal mobility.

One way of examining vertical social mobility is to contrast intergenerational and intragenerational mobility. ***Intergenerational mobility*** involves changes in the social position of children relative to their parents. Thus, a plumber whose father was a physician provides an example of downward intergenerational mobility. A film star whose parents were both factory workers illustrates upward intergenerational mobility.

Intragenerational mobility involves changes in social position within a person's adult life. A woman who enters the paid labor force as a teacher's aide and eventually becomes superintendent of the school district experiences upward intragenerational mobility. A man who becomes a taxicab driver after his accounting firm goes bankrupt undergoes downward intragenerational mobility.

Social Mobility in the United States

The belief in upward mobility is an important value in our society. Does that mean that the United States is indeed the land of opportunity? Not unless such ascriptive characteristics as race, gender, and family background have ceased to be significant in determining one's future prospects. We can see the impact of these factors in the occupational structure.

Occupational Mobility

Two sociological studies conducted a decade apart offer insight into the degree of mobility in the nation's occupational structure (Blau and Duncan 1967; Featherman and Hauser 1978). Taken together, these investigations lead to several noteworthy conclusions. First, occupational mobility (both intergenerational and intragenerational) has been common among males. Approximately 60 to 70 percent of sons are employed in higher-ranked occupations than their fathers.

Second, although there is a great deal of mobility in the United States, much of it is minor. That is, people who reach an occupational level above or below that of their parents usually advance or fall back only one or two out of a possible eight occupational levels. Thus, the child of a laborer may become an artisan or a technician, but he or she is less likely to become a manager or professional. The odds against reaching the top are extremely high unless one begins from a relatively privileged position.

The Impact of Education

Another conclusion of both studies is that education plays a critical role in social mobility. The impact of formal schooling on adult status is even greater than that of family background (although as we have seen, family background influences the likelihood that one will receive higher education). Furthermore, education represents an important means of intergenerational mobility. Three-fourths of college-educated men in these studies achieved some upward mobility, while only 12 percent of those who received no schooling did (see also J. Davis 1982).

The impact of education on mobility has diminished somewhat in the last decade, however. An undergraduate degree—a B.A. or a B.S.—serves less as a guarantee of upward mobility now than it did in the past, simply because more and more entrants into the job market hold such a degree. Moreover, intergenerational mobility is declining, since there is no longer such a stark difference between generations. In earlier decades, many high school–educated parents successfully sent their children to college, but today's college students are increasingly likely to have college-educated parents (Hout 1988).

The Impact of Race

Sociologists have long documented the fact that the class system is more rigid for African Americans than it is for members of other racial groups. Black men who have good jobs, for example, are less likely than White men to see their adult children attain the same status. The cumulative disadvantage of discrimination plays a significant role in the disparity between the two groups' experiences. Compared to White households, the relatively modest wealth of African American households means that adult Black children are less likely than adult White children to receive financial support from their parents. Indeed, young Black couples are much more likely than

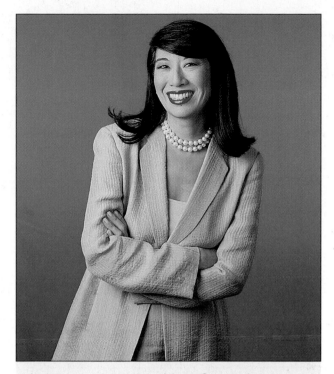

Andrea Jung, president of Avon Corporation, is one of the few women in the United States who has risen to the top of the corporate hierarchy. Despite the passage of equal opportunity laws, occupational barriers still limit women's social mobility.

young White couples to be assisting their parents—a sacrifice that hampers their social mobility.

The African American middle class has grown over the last few decades, due to economic expansion and the benefits of the civil rights movement of the 1960s. Yet many of these middle-class households have little savings, a fact that puts them in danger during times of crisis. Studies have consistently shown that downward mobility is significantly higher for Blacks than it is for Whites (Oliver and Shapiro 1995; Sernau 2001; W. J. Wilson 1996).

The Impact of Gender

Studies of mobility, even more than those of class, have traditionally ignored the significance of gender, but some research findings are now available that explore the relationship between gender and mobility.

Women's employment opportunities are much more limited than men's (as Chapter 11 will show). Moreover, according to recent research, women whose skills far exceed the jobs offered them are more likely than men to withdraw entirely from the paid labor force. Their withdrawal violates an assumption common to

Methods Secondary data were used by Blau and Duncan and by Featherman and Hauser.
Student Alert Education is often a means of intergenerational mobility. But an adult returning to school to start a new career is an example of intragenerational mobility.
Race The impact of race on mobility

Race/Ethnicity Limits on occupational mobility among African Americans
Gender Restrictions on mobility among women
Theory Conflict theorists would argue that women's mobility remains more limited than men's because of continuing prejudice and discrimination.

traditional mobility studies: that most people will aspire to upward mobility and seek to make the most of their opportunities.

In contrast to men, women have a rather large range of clerical occupations open to them. But the modest salary ranges and few prospects for advancement in many of these positions limit the possibility of upward mobility. Self-employment as shopkeepers, entrepreneurs, independent professionals, and the like—an important road to upward mobility for men—is more difficult for women, who find it harder to secure the necessary financing. Although sons commonly follow in the footsteps of their fathers, women are unlikely to move into their fathers' positions. Consequently, gender remains an important factor in shaping social mobility. Women in the United States (and in other parts of the world) are especially likely to be trapped in poverty, unable to rise out of their low-income status (Heilman 2001).

STRATIFICATION IN THE WORLD SYSTEM

Kwabena Afari is a pineapple exporter in Ghana. For years his customers had to show a great deal of ingenuity to get in touch with him. First a call had to be placed to Accra, the capital city. Someone there would call the post office in Afari's hometown; then the post office would send a messenger to his home. Afari has recently solved his problem by getting a cellular phone, but his longtime dilemma symbolizes the difficulties of the roughly 600 million people who live in sub-Saharan Africa and are being left behind by the trade and foreign investment that is transforming the global economy. As one African entrepreneur notes, "It's not that we have been left behind. It's that we haven't even started" (Buckley 1997:8).

It is true that technology, the information superhighway, and innovations in telecommunications have all made the world a smaller and more unified place. Yet while the world marketplace is gradually shrinking in communications time and tastes, business profits are not being shared equally. There remains a substantial disparity between the world's "have" and "have-not" nations. For example, in 2002, the average value of goods and services produced per citizen (per capita gross national income) in the industrialized countries of the United States, Japan, Switzerland, Belgium, and Norway was more than $25,000. In at least 13 poorer countries the value was $800 or less. In fact, the richest 1 percent of the world's population received as much income as the poorest 57 percent. Figure 9-6 illustrates these stark contrasts. Three forces discussed here are particularly responsible

for the domination of the world marketplace by a few nations: the legacy of colonialism, the advent of multinational corporations, and modernization (Haub 2003; United Nations Development Programme 2001).

The Legacy of Colonialism

Colonialism occurs when a foreign power maintains political, social, economic, and cultural domination over a people for an extended period. In simple terms, it is rule by outsiders. The long reign of the British Empire over much of North America, parts of Africa, and India is an example of colonial domination. The same can be said of French rule over Algeria, Tunisia, and other parts of North Africa. Relations between the colonial nation and colonized people are similar to those between the dominant capitalist class and the proletariat, as described by Karl Marx.

By the 1980s, colonialism had largely disappeared. Most of the nations that were colonies before World War I had achieved political independence and established their own governments. However, for many of these countries, the transition to genuine self-rule was not yet complete. Colonial domination had established patterns of economic exploitation that continued even after nationhood was achieved—in part because former colonies were unable to develop their own industry and technology. Their dependence on more industrialized nations, including their former colonial masters, for managerial and technical expertise, investment capital, and manufactured goods kept former colonies in a subservient position. Such continuing dependence and foreign domination are referred to as *neocolonialism.*

The economic and political consequences of colonialism and neocolonialism are readily apparent. Drawing on the conflict perspective, sociologist Immanuel Wallerstein (1974, 1979a, 2000) views the global economic system as being divided between nations that control wealth and nations from which resources are taken. Through his *world systems analysis,* Wallerstein has described the unequal economic and political relationships in which certain industrialized nations (among them the United States, Japan, and Germany) and their global corporations dominate the *core* of this system (see Figure 9-7, page 224). At the *semiperiphery* of the system are countries with marginal economic status, such as Israel, Ireland, and South Korea. Wallerstein suggests that the poor developing countries of Asia, Africa, and Latin America are on the *periphery* of the world economic system. The key to Wallerstein's analysis is the exploitative relationship of core nations toward noncore nations. Core nations and their corporations control and exploit

FIGURE 9-6

Gross National Income per Capita, 2002

Mapping Life WORLDWIDE

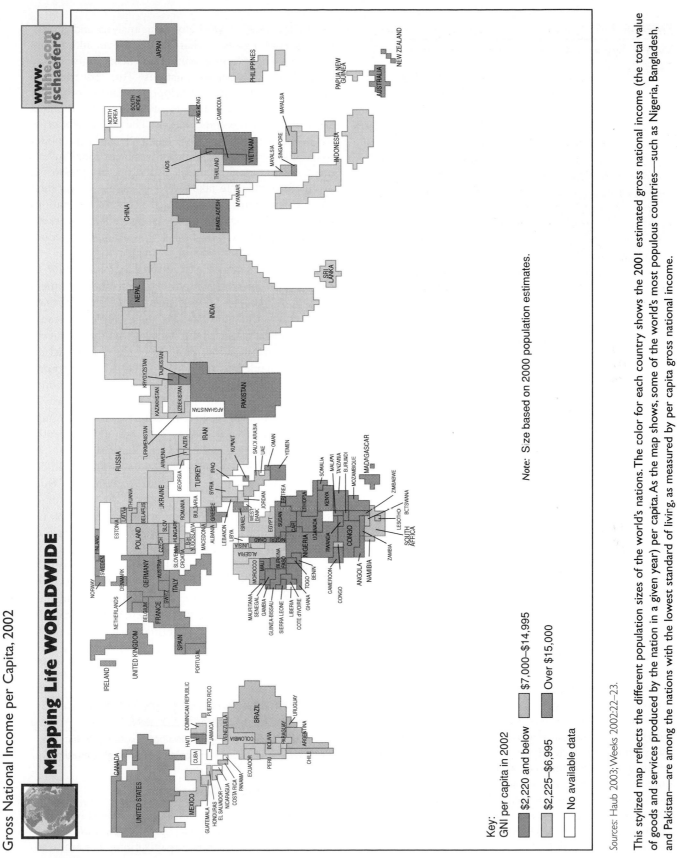

Key:
GNI per capita in 2002

- $2,220 and below
- $2,225–$6,995
- $7,000–$14,995
- Over $15,000
- No available data

Note: Size based on 2000 population estimates.

Sources: Haub 2003; Weeks 2002:22–23.

This stylized map reflects the different population sizes of the world's nations. The color for each country shows the 2001 estimated gross national income (the total value of goods and services produced by the nation in a given year) per capita. As the map shows, some of the world's most populous countries—such as Nigeria, Bangladesh, and Pakistan—are among the nations with the lowest standard of living, as measured by per capita gross national income.

Student Alert GDP is now referred to as gross national income in U.N. publications.

Web Resource Remind students that there is an interactive map for this chapter in the student center of the Online Learning Center (**www.mhhe.com/schaefer6**).

FIGURE 9-7

World Systems Analysis at the Beginning of the 21st Century

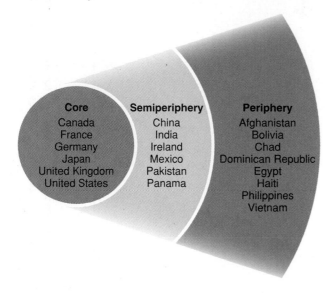

Core
Canada
France
Germany
Japan
United Kingdom
United States

Semiperiphery
China
India
Ireland
Mexico
Pakistan
Panama

Periphery
Afghanistan
Bolivia
Chad
Dominican Republic
Egypt
Haiti
Philippines
Vietnam

Note: Figure shows only a partial listing of countries.

noncore nations' economies. Unlike other nations, they are relatively independent of outside control (Chase-Dunn and Grimes 1995).

The division between core and periphery nations is significant and remarkably stable. A study by the International Monetary Fund (2000) found little change over the course of the *last 100 years* for the 42 economies that were studied. The only changes were Japan's movement up into the group of core nations and China's movement down toward the margins of the semiperiphery nations. Yet Wallerstein (2000) speculates that the world system as we currently understand it may soon undergo unpredictable changes. The world is becoming increasingly urbanized, a trend that is gradually eliminating the large pools of low-cost workers in rural areas. In the future, core nations will have to find other ways to reduce their labor costs. The exhaustion of land and water resources through clear-cutting and pollution is also driving up the costs of production.

Wallerstein's world systems analysis is the most widely used version of *dependency theory.* According to this theory, even as developing countries make economic advances, they remain weak and subservient to core nations and corporations in an increasingly intertwined global economy. This interdependency allows industrialized nations to continue to exploit developing countries for their own gain. In a sense, dependency theory applies the conflict perspective on a global scale.

Student Alert Clarify why dependency theory is similar to world systems analysis.

In the view of world systems analysis and dependency theory, a growing share of the human and natural resources of developing countries is being redistributed to the core industrialized nations. This redistribution happens in part because developing countries owe huge sums of money to industrialized nations as a result of foreign aid, loans, and trade deficits. The global debt crisis has intensified the Third World dependency begun under colonialism, neocolonialism, and multinational investment. International financial institutions are pressuring indebted countries to take severe measures to meet their interest payments. The result is that developing nations may be forced to devalue their currencies, freeze workers' wages, increase privatization of industry, and reduce government services and employment.

Closely related to these problems is *globalization,* or p. 59 the worldwide integration of government policies, cultures, social movements, and financial markets through trade and the exchange of ideas. Because world financial markets transcend governance by conventional nation states, international organizations such as the World Bank and the International Monetary Fund have emerged as major players in the global economy. The function of these institutions, which are heavily funded and influenced by core nations, is to encourage economic trade and development and to ensure the smooth operation of international financial markets. As such, they are seen as promoters of globalization and defenders primarily of the interests of core nations. Critics call attention to a variety of issues, including violations of workers' rights, the destruction of the environment, the loss of cultural identity, and discrimination against minority groups in periphery nations.

Some observers see globalization and its effects as the natural result of advances in communications technology, particularly the Internet and satellite transmission of the mass media. Others view it more critically, as a process that allows multinational corporations to expand unchecked, as we will see in the next section (Chase-Dunn et al. 2000; Feketekuty 2001; Feuer 1989; Pearlstein 2001).

Use Your Sociological Imagination www.mhhe.com/schaefer6

You are traveling through a developing country. What evidence do you see of neocolonialism and globalization?

Multinational Corporations

A key role in neocolonialism today is played by worldwide corporate giants. The term *multinational corporations* refers to commercial organizations that are head-

Theory/Student Alert Note how the global debt crisis illustrates world systems analysis, dependency theory, and conflict theory.
Theory Functional analysis of world financial markets
Classroom Tip See "Globalization and Sociology" (Class Discussion Topics).

quartered in one country but do business throughout the world. Such private trade and lending relationships are not new; merchants have conducted business abroad for hundreds of years, trading gems, spices, garments, and other goods. However, today's multinational giants are not merely buying and selling overseas; they are also *producing goods* all over the world (I. Wallerstein 1974).

Moreover, today's "global factories" (factories throughout the developing world that are run by multinational corporations) may now have the "global office" alongside them. Multinationals that are based in core countries are beginning to establish reservations services and centers for processing data and insurance claims in the periphery nations. As service industries become a more important part of the international marketplace, many companies are concluding that the low costs of overseas operations more than offset the expense of transmitting information around the world.

Do not underestimate the size of these global corporations. As Table 9-4 (page 226) shows, the total revenues of multinational businesses are on a par with the total value of goods and services exchanged in *entire nations*. Foreign sales represent an important source of profit for multinational corporations, which encourages them to expand into other countries (in many cases, the developing nations). The economy of the United States is heavily dependent on foreign commerce, much of which is conducted by multinationals. Over one-fourth of all goods and services in the United States has to do with either the export of goods to foreign countries or the import of goods from abroad (U.S. Trade Representative 2003).

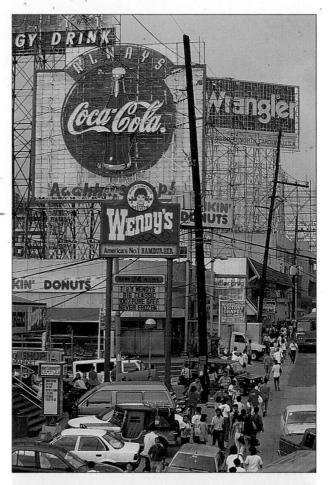

The influence of multinational corporations abroad can be seen in this street scene from Manila, capital of the Philippines.

Functionalist View

Functionalists believe that multinational corporations can actually help the developing nations of the world. They bring jobs and industry to areas where subsistence agriculture previously served as the only means of survival. Multinationals also promote rapid development through the diffusion of inventions and innovations from industrial nations. Viewed from a functionalist perspective, the combination of skilled technology and management provided by multinationals and the relatively cheap labor available in developing nations is ideal for a global enterprise. Multinationals can take maximum advantage of technology while reducing costs and boosting profits.

Through their international ties, multinational corporations also make the nations of the world more interdependent. These ties may prevent certain disputes from reaching the point of serious conflict. A country cannot afford to sever diplomatic relations or engage in warfare

with a nation that is the headquarters for its main business suppliers or a key outlet for its exports.

Conflict View

Conflict theorists challenge this favorable evaluation of the impact of multinational corporations. They emphasize that multinationals exploit local workers to maximize profits. Starbucks—the international coffee retailer based in Seattle—gets some of its coffee from farms in Guatemala. But to earn enough money to buy a pound of Starbucks coffee, a Guatemalan farmworker would have to pick 500 pounds of beans, representing five days of work (Entine and Nichols 1996).

The pool of cheap labor in the developing world prompts multinationals to move factories out of core countries. An added bonus for the multinationals is that the developing world discourages strong trade unions.

Classroom Tip Futurist Alvin Toffler (*Power Shift*, Bantam, 1990) contends that *multinational* is an obsolete term, because megafirms are nonnational. Companies from several nations are linked in global alliances.

Theory Functional and conflict analysis of multinational corporations

Table 9-4	Multinational Corporations Compared to Nations		
Corporation	**Revenues ($ millions)**	**Comparable Nation(s)**	**Gross Domestic Product ($ millions)**
1. Wal-Mart (USA)	$246,525	Switzerland	$239,800
2. General Motors (USA)	186,763	Austria	189,000
3. ExxonMobil (USA)	182,466	Venezuela plus Pakistan	182,100
4. Royal Dutch/Shell Group (Netherlands/Britain)	179,431	Egypt plus Philippines	173,400
5. BP–British Petroleum (Britain)	178,721	Saudi Arabia	173,300
6. Ford Motor (USA)	163,871	Norway	161,800
7. DaimlerChrysler (Germany)	141,421	Colombia plus Peru	134,800
8. Toyota Motor (Japan)	131,754	South Africa	125,900
9. General Electric (USA)	131,698	Finland	121,500
13. Citigroup (USA)	100,789	Ireland	93,900
16. Nippon Telephone and Telegraph (Japan)	89,644	Malaysia	89,700

Notes: Revenues are for 2002. GDP data are for 2000, based on local currencies converted to prevailing U.S. dollar equivalents. Corporations are ranked by their placement on the Fortune 500 list of global corporations.

Sources: For corporate data, *Fortune* 2003; for GDP data, United Nations Development Programme 2002:190–193.

Think About It

What happens to society when corporations grow richer than countries and spill across international borders?

In industrialized countries, organized labor insists on decent wages and humane working conditions, but governments seeking to attract or keep multinationals may develop a "climate for investment" that includes repressive antilabor laws that are restrictive of union activity and collective bargaining. If labor's demands become too threatening, the multinational firm will simply move its plant elsewhere, leaving a trail of unemployment behind. Nike, for example, moved its factories from the United States to Korea to Indonesia to Vietnam in search of the lowest labor costs. Conflict theorists conclude that on the whole, multinational corporations have a negative social impact on workers in *both* industrialized and developing nations.

Workers in the United States and other core countries are beginning to recognize that their own interests are served by helping to organize workers in developing nations. As long as multinationals can exploit cheap labor abroad, they will be in a strong position to reduce

wages and benefits in industrialized countries. With this in mind, in the 1990s, labor unions, religious organizations, campus groups, and other activists mounted public campaigns to pressure companies such as Nike, Starbucks, Reebok, Gap, and Wal-Mart to improve wages and working conditions in their overseas operations (Global Alliance for Workers and Communities 2003; Gonzalez 2003).

Several sociologists who have surveyed the effects of foreign investment by multinationals conclude that although it may initially contribute to a host nation's wealth, it eventually increases economic inequality within developing nations. This conclusion is true for both income and ownership of land. The upper and middle classes benefit most from economic expansion, whereas the lower classes are less likely to benefit. Multinationals invest in limited economic sectors and restricted regions of a nation. Although certain sectors of the host nation's economy expand, such as hotels and expensive restau-

Methods The comparison of corporate and national financial data relies on secondary analysis.
Classroom Tip See "Political Coalitions and the Poor in Developing Countries" (Additional Lecture Ideas).

Classroom Tip See "Development" (Class Discussion Topics).
Classroom Tip See "Anti-Globalism" (Class Discussion Topics).

rants, this very expansion appears to retard growth in agriculture and other economic sectors. Moreover, multinational corporations often buy out or force out local entrepreneurs and companies, thereby increasing economic and cultural dependence (Chase-Dunn and Grimes 1995; Kerbo 2003; I. Wallerstein 1979b).

STRATIFICATION WITHIN NATIONS: A COMPARATIVE PERSPECTIVE

At the same time that the gap between rich and poor nations is widening, so too is the gap between rich and poor citizens *within* nations. As discussed earlier, stratification in developing nations is closely related to their relatively weak and dependent position in the global economy. Local elites work hand in hand with multinational corporations and prosper from such alliances. At the same time, the economic system creates and perpetuates the exploitation of industrial and agricultural workers. That's why foreign investment in developing countries tends to increase economic inequality (Bornschier et al. 1978; Kerbo 2003). But inequality within a society is also evident in industrialized nations such as Japan.

Disparities in income are perhaps the best illustration of stratification within nations. In at least 24 nations around the world, the most affluent 10 percent of the population receives at least 40 percent of all income. The list includes the African nation of Namibia

(the leader, at 65 percent of all income), as well as Colombia, Mexico, Nigeria, and South Africa. Figure 9-8 (page 228) compares the distribution of income in selected industrialized and developing nations.

Women in developing countries find life especially difficult. Karuna Chanana Ahmed, an anthropologist from India who has studied women in developing nations, calls women the most exploited of oppressed people. Beginning at birth, women face sex discrimination. They are commonly fed less than male children, are denied educational opportunities, and are often hospitalized only when they are critically ill. Inside or outside the home, women's work is devalued. When economies fail, as they did in Asian countries in the late 1990s, women are the first to be laid off from work (E. Anderson and Moore 1993; Kristof 1998).

Surveys show a significant degree of *female infanticide* (the killing of baby girls) in China and rural areas of India. Only one-third of Pakistan's sexually segregated schools are for women, and one-third of those schools have no buildings. In Kenya and Tanzania, it is illegal for a woman to own a house. In Saudi Arabia, women are prohibited from driving, walking alone in public, and socializing with men outside their families (C. Murphy 1993). We will explore women's second-class status throughout the world more fully in Chapter 11.

Studies of the distribution of wealth and income within various countries and cross-cultural research consistently reveal that stratification based on class, gender, and other factors shows up within a wide range of societies. Clearly, a worldwide view of stratification must include not only the sharp contrast between wealthy and impoverished nations, but also the layers of hierarchies *within* industrialized societies and developing countries.

Use Your Sociological Imagination www.mhhe.com/schaefer6

Imagine that the United States borders a country with a much higher standard of living. In this neighboring country, the salaries of workers with a college degree start at $120,000 a year. What would life in the United States be like?

Theory From a conflict perspective, worldwide stratification is evident not only between rich and poor nations but between rich and poor citizens within nations.
Classroom Tip See "Cross-National Studies of Inequality" (Class Discussion Topics).
Classroom Tip See "Lorenz Curve" in Topics for Student Research.

FIGURE 9-8

Distribution of Income in Nine Nations

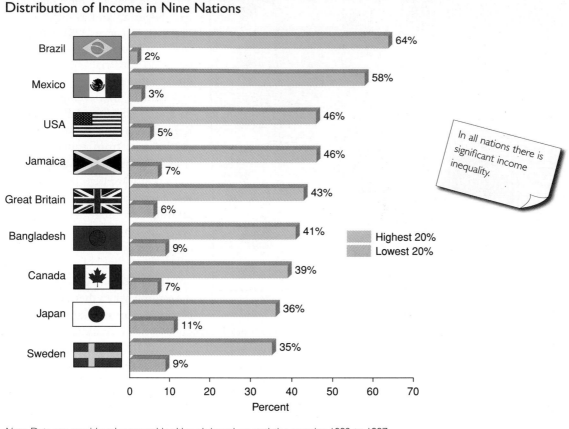

Note: Data are considered comparable although based on statistics covering 1992 to 1997.

Source: World Bank 2003b:64–66.

CASE STUDY:
STRATIFICATION IN MEXICO

In May 2003, on a stretch of highway in southern Arizona, the open doors of an abandoned tractor trailer revealed the dead bodies of 19 Mexicans. The truck had been carrying a group of illegal immigrants across the Sonoran Desert when the people hidden inside began to suffer from the intense desert heat. Their story was not unusual. In 2002, almost a hundred illegal immigrants died attempting to traverse the U.S.–Mexican border in the hot, arid corridor that connects the state of Sonora in Mexico to the state of Arizona in the United States.

Why do Mexicans risk their lives crossing the dangerous desert that lies between the two countries? The answer to this question can be found in the income disparity between the two nations—one an industrial giant and the other a partially developed country, still recovering from a history of colonialism and neocolonialism. In this

section we will look in some detail at the dynamics of stratification in Mexico, a country of 102 million people. Since the early 20th century there has been a close cultural, economic, and political relationship between Mexico and the United States, but it has clearly been a relationship in which the United States is the dominant party. According to Wallerstein's analysis, the United States is at the core while neighboring Mexico is still on the semiperiphery of the world economic system.

MEXICO'S ECONOMY

Mexico lobbied strongly for acceptance of the North American Free Trade Agreement (NAFTA), signed in 1993, which provided for the dismantling of almost all trade barriers among the United States, Canada, and Mexico. Officials hoped the country's struggling economy

Web Resource Remind students to visit the student center in the Online Learning Center (www.mhhe.com/schaefer6). Learning tools include activities, exercises, and crossword puzzles.

would receive a major boost from its favorable link to the world's largest consumer market, the United States. Indeed, in 1995, Mexico recorded its first trade surplus with the United States since 1990. Still, any benefit from NAFTA was dramatically undercut by the collapse of the peso, Mexico's unit of currency, in 1994. Since then, job competition from China and the shock to the U.S. economy of the terrorist attacks of September 11, 2001, have further undercut NAFTA's benefits. Although U.S. investment in Mexico has increased since the signing of NAFTA, implementation of the agreement has meant little in the day-to-day economic struggles of the average Mexican (Kraul 2003).

If we compare Mexico's economy to that of the United States, differences in the standard of living and in life chances are quite dramatic, even though Mexico is considered a semiperipheral nation. The gross domestic product—the value of all final goods and services produced in a country—is a commonly used measure of an average resident's economic well-being. In 2003, the gross domestic product per person in the United States came to $34,280; in Mexico, it was a mere $8,240. About 87 percent of adults in the United States have a high school education, compared to only 22 percent of those in Mexico. And only 7 of every 1,000 infants in the United States die in the first year of life, compared to about 23 in Mexico (Bureau of the Census 2003a:847, 850; Haub 2003).

Although Mexico is unquestionably a poor country, the gap between its richest and poorest citizens is one of the widest in the world (refer back to Figure 9-8). According to the World Bank, in 2003, 24 percent of the population survived on $2 per day. At the same time, the wealthiest 10 percent of Mexico's people accounted for 42 percent of the entire nation's income. According to a *Forbes* magazine portrait of the world's wealthiest individuals, Mexico had the fourth-largest number of people on the list—behind only the United States, Germany, and Japan (Castañeda 1995; World Bank 2003b:59).

Political scientist Jorge Castañeda (1995:71) calls Mexico a "polarized society with enormous gaps between rich and poor, town and country, north and south, white and brown (or *criollos* and *mestizos*)." He adds that the country is also divided along lines of class, race, religion, gender, and

A worker cleans the reflecting pool at the opulent Casa del Mar Hotel in San Jose del Cabo, Mexico. Though international tourism is a major industry in Mexico, most Mexicans have not benefited much from it. Mexican workers who are employed in the industry earn low wages, and their jobs are jeopardized by the travel industry's frequent boom and bust cycles.

age. We will next examine stratification within Mexico by focusing on race relations and the plight of Mexican Indians, the status of Mexican women, and emigration to the United States and its impact on the U.S.–Mexican borderlands.

RACE RELATIONS IN MEXICO: THE COLOR HIERARCHY

On January 1, 1994, rebels from an armed insurgent group called the Zapatista National Liberation Army seized four towns in the state of Chiapas, in southern Mexico. The rebels—who named their organization after Emiliano Zapata, a farmer and leader of the 1910 revolution against a corrupt dictatorship—were backed by 2,000 lightly armed Mayan Indians and peasants. Zapatista leaders declared that they had turned to armed insurrection to protest economic injustices and discrimination against the region's Indian population. The Mexican government mobilized the army to crush the revolt, but was forced to retreat as news organizations broadcast pictures of the confrontation around the world. Though a cease-fire was declared after only 12 days of fighting, 196 people died. Negotiations between the Mexican government and the Zapatista National Liberation Army have been shaky ever since.

In response to the crisis, the Mexican legislature enacted the Law on Indian Rights and Culture, which went into effect in 2001. The act allows 62 recognized Indian groups to apply their own customs in resolving conflicts and electing leaders. Unfortunately, state legislatures must give final approval to these arrangements, a requirement that severely limits the rights of large Indian groups whose territories span several states. Tired of waiting for state approval, many indigenous communities in Chiapas have declared self-rule without obtaining official recognition (Boudreaux 2002; J. Smith 2001).

While many factors contributed to the Zapatista revolt, the subordinate status of Mexico's Indian citizens, who account for an estimated 14 percent of the nation's population, was surely important. More than 90 percent of the indigenous population lives in houses without sewers, compared with 21 percent of the population as a whole. And whereas just 10 percent of Mexican adults are illiterate, the proportion for Mexican Indians is 44 percent (Boudreaux 2002; *The Economist* 2004c; Thompson 2001b).

The subordinate status of Mexico's Indians is but one reflection of the nation's color hierarchy, which links social class to the appearance of racial purity. At the top of this hierarchy are the *criollos,* the 10 percent of the population who are typically White, well-educated members of the business and intellectual elites with familial roots in Spain. In the middle is the large, impoverished *mestizo* majority, most of whom have brown skin and a mixed racial lineage as a result of intermarriage. At the bottom of the color hierarchy are the destitute, full-blooded Mexican Indian minority and a small number of Blacks, some descended from 200,000 African slaves brought to Mexico. This color hierarchy is an important part of day-to-day life—enough so that some Mexicans in the cities use hair dyes, skin lighteners, and blue or green contact lenses to appear more White and European. Ironically, however, nearly all Mexicans are considered part Indian because of centuries of intermarriage (Castañeda 1995; DePalma 1995a).

Many observers take note of widespread denial of prejudice and discrimination against people of color in Mexico. Schoolchildren are taught that the election of Benito Juárez, a Zapotec Indian, as president of Mexico in the 19th century proves that all Mexicans are equal. Yet there has been a marked growth in the last decade of formal or-

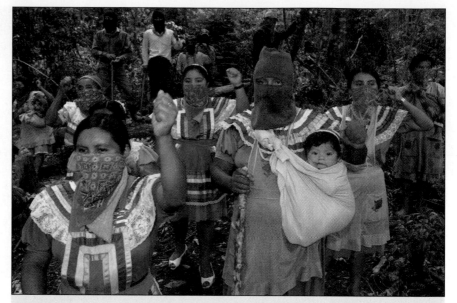

In 2000, a group of masked women demonstrated outside the Mexican Army's barracks in the state of Chiapas, demanding that the soldiers leave. The women were supporters of the Zapatista National Liberation Army, an insurgent group that protests economic injustices and discrimination against the Indian population in Chiapas.

ganizations and voluntary associations representing indigenous Indians. The Zapatista revolt in Chiapas was an even more dramatic indication that those at the bottom of Mexico's color hierarchy are weary of inequality and injustice (DePalma 1995a, 1996; Stavenhagen 1994; Utne 2003).

THE STATUS OF WOMEN IN MEXICO

In 1975, Mexico City hosted the first international conference on the status of women, convened by the United Nations. Much of the focus was on the situation of women in developing countries; in that regard, the situation is mixed. Women now constitute 42 percent of the labor force—an increase from 34 percent over the past 20 years, but still less than in industrial countries. Unfortunately, Mexican women are even more mired in the lowest-paying jobs than their counterparts in industrial nations. In the political arena, women are rarely seen in top decision-making positions, though they have increased their representation in the national legislature to 16 percent, ranking Mexico at 55th among 181 nations worldwide (Bureau of the Census 2003a:859; Inter-Parliamentary Union 2003).

Feminist sociologists emphasize that even when Mexican women work outside the home, they often are not recognized as active and productive household mem-

Race/Ethnicity Subordinate status of Mexican Indians
Let's Discuss Ask students to consider the impact of having no sewers on health and disease.
Let's Discuss What are the parallels in race relations in Mexico and the United States?

Gender The status of women in Mexico

bers, whereas men are typically viewed as heads of the household. As one consequence, women find it difficult to obtain credit and technical assistance in many parts of the country and to inherit land in rural areas. Within manufacturing and service industries, women generally receive little training and tend to work in the least-automated and least-skilled jobs—in good part because there is little expectation that women will pursue career advancement, organize for better working conditions, or become active in labor unions (Kopinak 1995; Martelo 1996; see also Young 1993).

In recent decades, Mexican women have begun to organize to address an array of economic, political, and

health issues. Since women continue to serve as the household managers for their families, even when they work outside the home, they are well aware of the consequences of the inadequate public services in lower-income urban neighborhoods. As far back as 1973, women in Monterrey—the nation's third-largest city—began protesting the continuing disruptions of the city's water supply. After individual complaints to city officials and the water authority proved fruitless, social networks of female activists began to emerge. These activists sent delegations to confront politicians, organized protest rallies, and blocked traffic as a means of getting media attention. Though their efforts brought improvements in

FIGURE 9-9

The Borderlands

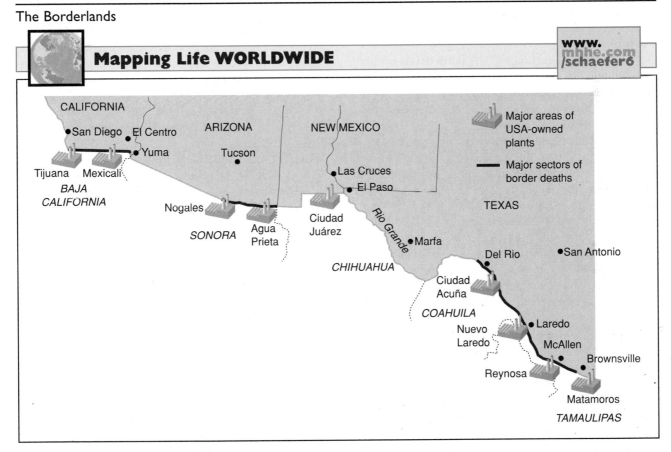

Source: Prepared by the author based on Ellingwood 2001; Thompson 2001a.

Maquiladoras located just south of the U.S.–Mexican border employ uninsured Mexican workers at wages considerably lower than those earned by U.S. workers. In search of higher wages, undocumented Mexicans often attempt to cross the border illegally, risking their lives in the process.

Think About It
How do U.S. consumers benefit from the buildup of factories along the U.S.–Mexican border?

Gender Role of Mexican women in addressing economic, political, and health issues

Monterrey's water service, the issue of reliable and safe water remains a concern in Mexico and many developing countries (Vivienne Bennett 1995).

THE BORDERLANDS

Water pollution is but one of the many ways in which the problems of Mexico and the United States intertwine. Growing recognition of the borderlands reflects the increasingly close and complex relationship between these two countries. The term **borderlands** refers to the area of common culture along the border between Mexico and the United States. Legal and illegal emigration from Mexico to the United States, day laborers crossing the border regularly to go to jobs in the United States, the implementation of the North American Free Trade Agreement, and the exchange of media across the border all make the notion of separate Mexican and U.S. cultures obsolete in the borderlands.

The economic position of the borderlands is rather complicated, as we can see in the emergence of *maquiladoras* on the Mexican side (see Figure 9-9, page 231). These are foreign-owned factories established just across the border in Mexico, where the companies that own them do not have to pay taxes or provide insurance and benefits to workers. The *maquiladoras* have attracted manufacturing jobs from other parts of North America to Mexico. As of the fall of 2002, 1.1 million people were employed in the *maquiladoras*, where the daily take-home pay for entry-level workers was $4 to $5. Since many of these firms come from the United States and sell their products to Mexico's vast domestic market, their operations deepen the impact of U.S. consumer culture on Mexico's urban and rural areas (Thompson 2001c).

The *maquiladoras* have contributed to Mexico's economic development, but not without some cost. Conflict theorists note that unregulated growth allows the owners to exploit the workers with jobs that lack security, possibilities for advancement, and decent wages. Moreover, many of the U.S.-owned factories require female job applicants to take a urine test to screen out those who are pregnant—a violation of Mexican law as well as of NAFTA, and the source of numerous cases of sexual discrimination. Social activists also complain that tens of thousands of Mexicans work on *maquiladora* assembly lines for very low wages, such as $1 an hour, raising the issue of sweatshop labor noted earlier in this chapter (Dillon 1998; Dougherty and Holthouse 1999).

Ironically, the *maquiladoras* are now experiencing the same challenge from global trade as U.S. manufacturing plants did. Beginning in 2001, some companies began shifting their operations to China. While Mexican labor costs (wages plus benefits) are just $2 to $2.50 an hour, Chinese labor costs are even lower—50 cents to $1 an hour. Of the 700,000 new *maquiladora* jobs created in NAFTA's first seven years, 43 percent were eliminated between 2000 and 2003 (*Migration News* 2002c, 2004).

When people in the United States think about the borderlands, they generally think about immigration. As we'll see in the social policy section of Chapter 10, immigration is a controversial political issue in the United States—especially immigration across the Mexican border. For its part, Mexico is concerned about the priorities and policies of its powerful northern neighbor. From the Mexican point of view, the United States too often regards Mexico simply as a reserve pool of cheap labor, encouraging Mexicans to cross the border when workers are needed but discouraging and cracking down on them when they are not. Some people, then, see immigration more as a labor market issue than a law enforcement issue. Viewed from the perspective of Immanuel Wallerstein's world systems analysis and dependency theory, it is yet another example of a core industrialized nation exploiting a developing country.

As we saw at the beginning of this case, the risks of immigration are considerable. Following September 11, 2001, when the U.S. government increased surveillance at common entry points along the border, migrants without proper documentation moved to more remote and dangerous locations. In all, several hundred illegal immigrants lose their lives every year while attempting to cross the long border, many of them from dehydration in the intense desert heat (Dellios 2002).

The social impact of emigration to the United States is felt throughout Mexico. According to sociological research, the earliest emigrants were typically married men of working age who came from the middle of the stratification system. They had enough financial resources to afford the costs and risks of emigration, yet were experiencing enough financial strain that entering the United States was attractive to them. Over time, kinship ties to migrants multiplied and emigration became less class-selective, with entire families making the trek to the United States. More recently, the occupational backgrounds of Mexican emigrants have widened further, reflecting not only changes in U.S. immigration policy but the continuing crisis in the Mexican economy (Massey 1998).

Many Mexicans who have come to the United States send some part of their earnings back across the border to family members still in Mexico. This substantial flow of money, sometimes referred to as **remittances** or *migradollars,* is estimated at a minimum of $15 billion a year, and is surpassed only by oil as a source of income. If

Theory Conflict analysis of *maquiladoras* in Mexico
Gender Gender discrimination in the *maquiladoras* in Mexico
Let's Discuss Have students explain the *maquiladoras* within the context of Wallerstein's world systems analysis.

these funds went solely into the purchase of consumer goods, they would underscore the view of dependency theory, that Mexico's economy is little more than an extension of the economy of the United States. In fact, however, some of these migradollars are used by Mexicans to establish and maintain small business enterprises, such as handicraft workshops and farms. Consequently, the transfer of migradollars does stimulate the local and national economies of Mexico (Thompson 2003).

As we have seen, social inequality is a problem not just in developing countries like Mexico, but in industrialized countries like the United States. We turn now to a

comparison of the welfare systems in the United States and Europe. We will see that in the United States, government efforts to help those at the bottom of the income scale have been complicated by the attitudes Americans hold toward people who do not work.

Use Your Sociological Imagination www.mhhe.com/schaefer6

Imagine a day when the border between the United States and Mexico is completely open. What would the two countries' economies be like? What would their societies be like?

SOCIAL POLICY and STRATIFICATION

Rethinking Welfare in North America and Europe

The Issue

- In Milwaukee, a single mother of six has just lost her job as a security guard. Once considered a success story of the welfare reform program, she has fallen victim to the economic recession that followed the boom years of the 1990s. Because she has been on welfare before, she is ineligible to receive additional assistance from the state of Wisconsin. Yet like many other workers who made the transition from welfare to work in the late 1990s, she does not qualify for unemployment benefits; food stamps are all she can count on (Pierre 2002).
- In Paris, France, Hélène Desegrais, another single mother, waited four months to place her daughter in government-subsidized day care. Now she can seek a full-time job, but she is concerned about government threats to curtail such services in order to keep taxes down (Simons 1997).

These are the faces of people living on the edge—often women with children seeking to make a go of it amid changing social policies. Governments in all parts of the world are searching for the right solution to welfare: How much subsidy should they provide? How much responsibility should fall on the shoulders of the poor?

The Setting

In the 1990s, an intense debate took place in the United States over the issue of welfare. Welfare programs were costly, and concern was widespread (however un-

founded) that welfare payments discouraged recipients from seeking jobs. Both Democrats and Republicans vowed to "end welfare as we know it."

In late 1996, in a historic shift in federal policy, Congress passed the Personal Responsibility and Work Opportunity Reconciliation Act, ending the long-standing federal guarantee of assistance to every poor family that meets eligibility requirements. The law set a lifetime limit of five years of welfare benefits, and required all able-bodied adults to work after receiving two years of benefits (although hardship exceptions were allowed). The federal government would give block grants to the states to use as they wished in assisting poor and needy residents, and it would permit states to experiment with ways to move people off welfare.

Other countries vary widely in their commitment to social service programs. But most industrialized nations devote higher proportions of their expenditures to housing, social security, welfare, health care, and unemployment compensation than the United States does. Data available in 2002 indicated that in Ireland, 76 percent of health expenditures were paid for by the government; in Switzerland, 73 percent; in Canada, 71 percent; but in the United States, only 44 percent (World Bank 2002:102–104).

Sociological Insights

Many sociologists tend to view the debate over welfare reform throughout industrialized nations from a conflict perspective: the "haves" in positions of policymaking listen to the interests of other "haves," while the cries of the "have-nots" are drowned out. Critics of welfare

Let's Discuss Is the welfare debate about absolute or relative poverty?
Theory How would conflict and functionalist theorists analyze the 1996 Personal Responsibility and Work Opportunity Reconciliation Act?

Global View Comparative expenditures for social services for the poor
Theory Conflict analysis of welfare programs in industrialized nations
Race/Ethnicity Backlash to welfare in the United States may reflect deep-seated racist hostility.
Classroom Tip See "Opinions on Welfare Linked to Racial Views" (Additional Lecture Ideas).

reform believe that the nation's economic problems are unfairly blamed on welfare spending and the poor. From a conflict perspective, this backlash against welfare recipients reflects deep fears and hostility toward the nation's urban, predominantly African American and Hispanic underclass.

Those who are critical of the backlash note that "welfare scapegoating" conveniently ignores the lucrative federal handouts that go to *affluent* individuals and families. For example, while federal housing aid to the poor was cut drastically in the 1980s, tax deductions for mortgage interest and property taxes more than doubled. The National Association of Home Builders, an ardent defender of the mortgage-interest deduction, estimates that this subsidy costs the federal government $60 billion a year in lost taxes. The deduction generally benefits affluent taxpayers who own their own homes. According to one study, more than 44 percent of the benefits from this tax break go to the 5 percent of taxpayers with the highest incomes, who together save themselves $22 billion annually (Goodgame 1993; Johnston 1996).

Those who take a conflict perspective also urge policymakers and the general public to look closely at *corporate welfare*—the tax breaks, direct payments, and grants that the government makes to corporations—rather than to focus on the comparatively small allowances being given to welfare mothers and their children. Yet any suggestion to curtail such corporate welfare brings a strong response from special-interest groups that are much more powerful than any coalition on behalf of the poor. One example of corporate welfare is the airline bailout bill that was passed in the wake of terrorist attacks on the United States in September 2001. Within 11 days the federal government had approved the bailout, whose positive impact was felt largely by airline executives and shareholders. Relatively low-paid airline employees were still laid off, and hundreds of thousands of low-wage workers in airports, hotels, and related industries received little or no assistance. Efforts to broaden unemployment assistance to help these marginally employed workers failed (Hartman and Miller 2001).

SHARING THE BURDEN

HUCK/KONOPACKI LABOR CARTOONS
WWW.SOLIDARITY.COM/HKCARTOONS - JAN 03
KONOPACKI
© 2003

Policy Initiatives

The government likes to highlight welfare reform success stories. Though many people who once depended on tax dollars are now working and paying taxes themselves, it is much too soon to see if "workfare" will be successful. The new jobs that were generated by the booming economy of the late 1990s were an unrealistic test of the system. Prospects for the hard-core jobless—those people who are difficult to train or are encumbered by drug or alcohol abuse, physical disabilities, or child care needs—have faded as the boom passed and the economy moved into recession (A. Dworsky et al. 2003).

True, fewer people remained on welfare after enactment of the welfare reform law in August 1996. By June 2003, 7.4 million people had left the system, reducing the rolls to under 5 million people. Yet research showed that most adults who had gone off welfare had taken low-wage jobs that did not offer benefits. As they moved off welfare, their Medicaid coverage ended, leaving them without health insurance. Support has also been lacking for working parents who need high-quality child care. And assistance to immigrants, even those who are legal residents, continues to be limited (Department of Health and Human Services 2004; Ehrenreich and Piven 2002).

European governments have encountered many of the same citizen demands as in North America: Keep our taxes low, even if it means reducing services to the poor. However, nations in eastern and central Europe have faced a special challenge since the end of commu-

Student Alert Remind students of earlier data on the breakdown of poor people in the United States by race and ethnicity.
Theory Conflict view of lucrative handouts to affluent individuals and families and of "corporate welfare"

Methods Survey of needs of welfare-to-work employees
Global View International demands to cut back on welfare expenditures
Policy Pointer In concluding this examination of welfare policy, it may be helpful to review Gans on the functions of poverty.

nism. Though governments in those nations had traditionally provided an impressive array of social services, they differed from capitalist systems in several important respects. First, the communist system was premised on full employment, so there was no need to provide unemployment insurance; social services focused on the old and the disabled. Second, subsidies for housing and even utilities played an important role. With new competition from the West and tight budgets, some of these countries are beginning to realize that universal coverage is no longer affordable and must be replaced with targeted programs. Even Sweden, despite its long history of social welfare programs, is feeling the pinch. Still, only modest cutbacks have been made in European social service programs, leaving them much more generous than those in the United States (J. Gornick 2001).

Both in North America and in Europe, people are beginning to turn to private means to support themselves. For instance, they are investing money for their later years rather than depending on government social security programs. But that solution works only if you have a job and can save money. Increasingly, people are seeing the gap between themselves and the affluent grow, with fewer government programs available to assist them. Solutions are frequently left to the private sector, while government policy initiatives at the national level all but disappear.

Let's Discuss

1. Do you personally know anyone who has had to depend on public assistance, such as food stamps, now or in the past? If so, what were the circumstances? Would you yourself need government assistance under such circumstances?

2. Do you think welfare recipients should be required to work? If so, what kind of support should they receive? Should any exceptions be granted to the work requirement?

3. Why do you think Western and Northern European countries have more generous welfare programs than the United States?

GETTING INVOLVED

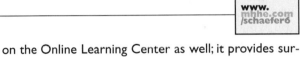

To get involved in the debate over welfare reform, visit this text's Online Learning Center, which offers links to relevant websites. Check out the social policy section on the Online Learning Center as well; it provides survey data on U.S. public opinion regarding this issue.

CHAPTER RESOURCES

Summary

Stratification is the structured ranking of entire groups of people that perpetuates unequal economic rewards and power in a society. In this chapter we examined four general systems of stratification, the explanations offered by functionalist and conflict theorists for the existence of ***social inequality,*** and the relationship between stratification and ***social mobility.*** Worldwide, stratification can be seen in the gap between rich and poor nations and the inequality that exists within countries. We studied the ways in which ***globalization*** and ***multinational corporations*** contribute to these inequalities.

1. Some degree of ***social inequality*** characterizes all cultures.
2. Systems of social stratification include ***slavery, castes,*** the ***estate system,*** and social classes.

3. Karl Marx saw that differences in access to the means of production created social, economic, and political inequality and two distinct classes, owners and laborers.
4. Max Weber identified three analytically distinct components of stratification: ***class, status group,*** and ***power.***
5. Functionalists argue that stratification is necessary to motivate people to fill society's important positions, conflict theorists see stratification as a major source of societal tension and conflict. Interactionists stress the importance of social class in determining a person's lifestyle.
6. One consequence of social class in the United States is that both ***wealth*** and ***income*** are distributed unevenly.

Classroom Tip See "Using Humor" (Class Discussion Topics).

7. The category of the poor defies any simple definition and counters common stereotypes about poor people. The long-term poor, who lack training and skills, form an *underclass.*

8. Functionalists find that the poor satisfy positive functions for many of the nonpoor in the United States.

9. One's *life chances*—opportunities for obtaining material goods, positive living conditions, and favorable life experiences—are related to one's social class. Occupying a high social position improves a person's life chances.

10. *Social mobility* is more likely to be found in an *open system* that emphasizes achieved status than in a *closed system* that focuses on ascribed characteristics. Race, gender, and family background are important factors in social mobility.

11. Worldwide, former colonized nations are kept in a subservient position, subject to foreign domination, through the process of *neocolonialism.*

12. Drawing on the conflict perspective, proponents of the *world systems analysis* of sociologist Immanuel Wallerstein view the global economic system as one divided between nations that control wealth *(core nations)* and those from which capital is taken *(periphery nations).*

13. According to *dependency theory,* even as developing countries make economic advances, they remain weak and subservient to core nations and corporations in an increasingly integrated global economy.

14. *Globalization,* or the worldwide integration of government policies, cultures, social movements, and financial markets through trade and the exchange of ideas, is a controversial trend that critics blame for contributing to the cultural domination of periphery nations by core nations.

15. *Multinational corporations* bring jobs and industry to developing nations, but they also tend to exploit workers in order to maximize profits.

16. The economic relationship between Mexico, a semiperipheral nation, and the United States, a core nation, is a good illustration of dependency theory. The establishment of U.S.-owned *maquiladoras* just across the Mexican border has not benefited Mexican workers nearly as much as it has the companies that built the factories.

17. Today, many governments are struggling with how much tax revenue to spend on welfare programs. The trend in the United States is to put welfare recipients to work.

Critical Thinking Questions

1. Sociologist Daniel Rossides has conceptualized the class system of the United States using a five-class model. According to Rossides, the upper-middle class and the lower-middle class together account for about 40 percent of the nation's population. Yet studies suggest that a higher proportion of respondents identify themselves as middle class. Drawing on the model presented by Rossides, suggest why members of both the upper class and the working class might prefer to identify themselves as middle class.

2. Sociological study of stratification is generally conducted at the macro level and draws most heavily on the functionalist and conflict perspectives. How might sociologists use the *interactionist* perspective to examine social class inequalities in a college community?

3. Imagine that you have the opportunity to spend a year in Mexico studying inequality in that nation. How would you draw on the research designs (surveys, observation, experiments, existing sources) to better understand and document stratification in Mexico?

Key Terms

Absolute poverty   A minimum level of subsistence that no family should be expected to live below. (page 215)

Achieved status   A social position that a person attains largely through his or her own efforts. (204)

Ascribed status   A social position assigned to a person by society without regard for the person's unique talents or characteristics. (203)

Borderlands   The area of common culture along the border between Mexico and the United States. (232)

Bourgeoisie   Karl Marx's term for the capitalist class, comprising the owners of the means of production. (207)

Capitalism   An economic system in which the means of production are held largely in private hands and the main incentive for economic activity is the accumulation of profits. (207)

Caste   A hereditary rank, usually religiously dictated, that tends to be fixed and immobile. (204)

Class   A group of people who have a similar level of wealth and income. (208)

Class consciousness   In Karl Marx's view, a subjective awareness held by members of a class regarding their common vested interests and need for collective political action to bring about social change. (207)

Class system   A social ranking based primarily on economic position in which achieved characteristics can influence social mobility. (205)

Closed system   A social system in which there is little or no possibility of individual social mobility. (220)

Colonialism   The maintenance of political, social, economic, and cultural dominance over a people by a foreign power for an extended period. (222)

Corporate welfare   Tax breaks, direct payments, and grants that the government makes to corporations. (234)

Dependency theory   An approach to stratification that contends that industrialized nations continue to exploit developing countries for their own gain. (224)

Dominant ideology   A set of cultural beliefs and practices that helps to maintain powerful social, economic, and political interests. (211)

Estate system   A system of stratification under which peasants were required to work land leased to them by nobles in exchange for military protection and other services. Also known as *feudalism.* (204)

Esteem   The reputation that a specific person has earned within an occupation. (212)

False consciousness   A term used by Karl Marx to describe an attitude held by members of a class that does not accurately reflect their objective position. (207)

Globalization   The worldwide integration of government policies, cultures, social movements, and financial markets through trade and the exchange of ideas. (224)

Horizontal mobility   The movement of an individual from one social position to another of the same rank. (220)

Income   Salaries and wages. (203)

Intergenerational mobility   Changes in the social position of children relative to their parents. (220)

Intragenerational mobility   Changes in social position within a person's adult life. (220)

Life chances   The opportunities people have to provide themselves with material goods, positive living conditions, and favorable life experiences. (218)

Multinational corporation   A commercial organization that is headquartered in one country but does business throughout the world. (224)

Neocolonialism   Continuing dependence of former colonies on foreign countries. (222)

Objective method   A technique for measuring social class that assigns individuals to classes on the basis of criteria such as occupation, education, income, and place of residence. (212)

Open system   A social system in which the position of each individual is influenced by his or her achieved status. (220)

Power   The ability to exercise one's will over others. (208)

Prestige   The respect and admiration that an occupation holds in a society. (212)

Proletariat   Karl Marx's term for the working class in a capitalist society. (207)

Relative poverty   A floating standard of deprivation by which people at the bottom of a society, whatever their lifestyles, are judged to be disadvantaged *in comparison with the nation as a whole.* (215)

Remittances   The monies that immigrants return to their families of origin. Also called *migradollars.* (232)

Slavery   A system of enforced servitude in which some people are owned by other people. (204)

Social inequality   A condition in which members of a society have different amounts of wealth, prestige, or power. (203)

Social mobility   Movement of individuals or groups from one position in a society's stratification system to another. (220)

Status group   People who have the same prestige or lifestyle, independent of their class positions. (208)

Stratification   A structured ranking of entire groups of people that perpetuates unequal economic rewards and power in a society. (203)

Underclass   The long-term poor who lack training and skills. (216)

Vertical mobility   The movement of an individual from one social position to another of a different rank. (220)

Wealth   An inclusive term encompassing all a person's material assets, including land, stocks, and other types of property. (203)

World systems analysis   A view of the global economic system as one divided between certain industrialized nations that control wealth and developing countries that are controlled and exploited. (222)

TECHNOLOGY RESOURCES

 ## Internet Connection

*Note: While all the URLs listed were current as of the printing of this book, these sites often change. Please check our website (**www.mhhe.com/schaefer6**) for updates, hyperlinks, and exercises related to these sites.*

1. The question of where to draw the poverty line is a controversial one in the United States. The Economic Policy Institute's website (**www.epinetorg**) offers some tools that you can use to explore the issue. Using the online calculators, find out what a budget-conscious family in your community needs to get by. Then read more about the poverty line in the issue guides.

2. Chief executive officers (CEOs) of U.S. corporations are handsomely compensated relative to CEOs in other industrialized nations. The AFL-CIO (**www.aflcio.org/corporateamerica/paywatch**) maintains an extensive database of the compensation companies offer their executives. Visit the site to find out what CEOs are making at the companies you know.

 ## Online Learning Center with PowerWeb

When you visit the student center in the Online Learning Center at **www.mhhe.com/schaefer6**, link to Audio Clips. Listen to Richard Schaefer, the author of your textbook, talk about some sociology students he taught and their prestige rankings of various occupations. These so-ciology students were all "lifers" in a maximum-security prison. Professor Schaefer defines prestige, then tells you how these students ranked the prestige of police officers, judges, lawyers, and governors.

Reel Society Interactive Movie CD-ROM 2.0

Reel Society 2.0 can be used to spark discussion about the following topics from this chapter:

- Understanding Stratification
- Stratification by Social Class
- Social Mobility

chapter

10

RACIAL AND ETHNIC INEQUALITY

This advertisement for the American Indian College Fund explodes common stereotypes about Native Americans with its photograph of Blackfeet Indian Carly Kipp, a doctoral candidate in veterinary medicine. Historically, prejudice and discrimination against members of minority groups have prevented them from reaching their full potential.

Ah so. No tickee, no washee. So sorry, so sollee.

Chinkee, Chink. Jap, Nip, zero, kamikaze. Dothead, flat face, flat nose, slant eye, slope. Slit, mamasan, dragon lady. Gook, VC, Flip, Hindoo.

By the time I was ten, I'd heard such words so many times I could feel them coming before they parted lips. I knew they were meant in the unkindest way. Still, we didn't talk about these incidents at home, we just accepted them as part of being in America, something to learn to rise above.

The most common taunting didn't even utilize words but a string of unintelligible gobbledygook that kids—and adults—would spew as they pretended to speak Chinese or some other Asian language. It was a mockery of how they imagined my parents talked to me.

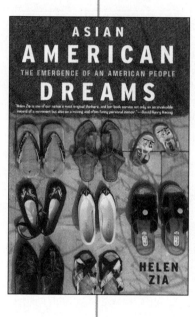

Truth was that Mom and Dad rarely spoke to us in Chinese, except to scold or call us to dinner. Worried that we might develop an accent, my father insisted that we speak English at home. This, he explained, would lessen the hardships we might encounter and make us more acceptable as Americans.

I'll never know if my father's language decision was right. On the one hand, I, like most Asian Americans, have been complimented countless times on my spoken English by people who assumed I was a foreigner. "My, you speak such good English," they'd cluck.

"No kidding, I ought to," I would think to myself, then wonder: should I thank them for assuming that English isn't my native language? Or should I correct them on the proper usage of "well" and "good"?

More often than feeling grateful for my American accent, I've wished that I could jump into a heated exchange of rapid-fire Chinese, volume high and spit flying. But with a vocabulary limited to *"Ni hao?"* (How are you?) and *"Ting bu dong"* (I hear but don't understand), meaningful exchanges are woefully impossible. I find myself smiling and nodding like a dashboard ornament. I'm envious of the many people I know who grew up speaking an Asian language yet converse in English beautifully.

Armed with standard English and my flat New Jersey "a," I still couldn't escape the name-calling. I became all too familiar with other names and faces that supposedly matched mine—Fu Manchu, Suzie Wong, Hop Sing, Madame Butterfly, Charlie Chan, Ming the Merciless—the "Asians" produced for mass consumption. Their faces filled me with shame whenever I saw them on TV or in the movies. They defined my face to the rest of the world: a sinister Fu, Suzie the whore, subservient Hop Sing, pathetic Butterfly, cunning Chan, and warlike Ming. Inscrutable Orientals all, real Americans none. *(Zia 2000)* ■ 🌀

Additional information about this excerpt can be found on the Online Learning Center at **www.mhhe.com/schaefer6.**

Helen Zia, the journalist and community activist who wrote this reminiscence from her childhood, is the successful daughter of Chinese immigrants to the United States. As her story shows, Zia experienced blatant prejudice against Chinese Americans, even though she spoke flawless English. In fact, all new immigrants and their families have faced stereotyping and hostility, whether they were White or non-White, Asian, African, or East European. In this multicultural society, those who are different from the dominant social group have never been welcome.

Today, millions of African Americans, Asian Americans, Hispanic Americans, and many other racial and ethnic minorities continue to experience the often bitter contrast between the "American dream" and the grim realities of poverty, prejudice, and discrimination. Like class, the social definitions of race and ethnicity still affect people's place and status in a stratification system, not only in this country but throughout the world. High incomes, a good command of English,

and hard-earned professional credentials do not always override racial and ethnic stereotypes or protect those who fit them from the sting of racism.

What is prejudice, and how is it institutionalized in the form of discrimination? In what ways have race and ethnicity affected the experience of immigrants from other countries? What are the fastest growing minority groups in the United States today? In this chapter we will focus on the meaning of race and ethnicity. We will begin by identifying the basic characteristics of a minority group and distinguishing between racial and ethnic groups. Then we will examine the dynamics of prejudice and discrimination. After considering the functionalist, conflict, and interactionist perspectives on race and ethnicity, we'll take a look at common patterns of intergroup relations. The following section will describe the major racial and ethnic groups in the United States. Finally, in the social policy section, we will explore issues related to global immigration. ◼

MINORITY, RACIAL, AND ETHNIC GROUPS

Sociologists frequently distinguish between racial and ethnic groups. The term *racial group* describes a group that is set apart from others because of obvious physical differences. Whites, African Americans, and Asian Americans are all considered racial groups in the United States. While race does turn on physical differences, it is the culture of a particular society that constructs and attaches social significance to those differences, as we will see later. Unlike racial groups, an *ethnic group* is set apart from others primarily because of its national origin or distinctive cultural patterns. In the United States, Puerto Ricans, Jews, and Polish Americans are all categorized as ethnic groups (see Table 10-1, page 242).

Minority Groups

A numerical minority is any group that makes up less than half of some larger population. The population of the United States includes thousands of numerical minorities, including television actors, green-eyed people, tax lawyers,

and descendants of the Pilgrims who arrived on the *Mayflower*. However, these numerical minorities are not considered to be minorities in the sociological sense; in fact, the number of people in a group does not necessarily determine its status as a social minority (or a dominant group). When sociologists define a minority group, they are concerned primarily with the economic and political power, or powerlessness, of that group. A *minority group* is a subordinate group whose members have significantly less control or power over their own lives than the members of a dominant or majority group have over theirs.

Sociologists have identified five basic properties of a minority group: unequal treatment, physical or cultural traits, ascribed status, solidarity, and in-group marriage (Wagley and Harris 1958):

1. Members of a minority group experience unequal treatment compared to members of a dominant group. For example, the management of an apartment complex may refuse to rent to African Americans, Hispanics, or Jews. Social inequality may be created or maintained by prejudice, discrimination, segregation, or even extermination.

Classroom Tip/Contemporary Culture See "Stimulating Classroom Discussion about *Asian American Dreams*" (Class Discussion Topics). **Race/Ethnicity** Given the subject matter of Chapter 10, this type of annotation will not be used throughout the chapter.

Student Alert Stress to students that a minority group is not necessarily a numerical minority; the critical factor is unequal treatment in terms of power and influence, access to resources, and life chances (see Chapter 9). **Classroom Tip** Integrate with material later in the chapter about discrimination and institutional discrimination.

had social significance in the South, enough so that White legislators established official standards about who was "Black" and who was "White."

The one-drop rule was a vivid example of the *social construction of race*—the process by which people come to define a group as a race based in part on physical characteristics, but also on historical, cultural, and economic factors. For example, in the 1800s, immigrant groups such as Italian and Irish Americans were not at first seen as being "White," but as foreigners who were not necessarily trustworthy. The social construction of race is an ongoing process that is subject to debate, especially in a diverse society such as the United States, where each year increasing numbers of children are born to parents of different racial backgrounds.

Not long ago, these children of a White mother and an African American father would automatically have assumed their father's racial identity. Today, however, some children of mixed-race families identify themselves as biracial.

In the 2000 census, nearly 7 million people in the United States (or about 2 percent of the population) reported that they were of two or more races. Half the people classified as multiracial were under age 18, suggesting that this segment of the population will grow in the years to come. People who claimed both White and American Indian ancestry were the largest group of multiracial residents (Grieco and Cassidy 2001).

This statistical finding of millions of multiracial people obscures how individuals handle their identity, however. The prevailing social construction of race pushes people to choose just one race, even if they acknowledge a broader cultural background. For example, the enrollment forms for government programs typically include only a few broad racial-ethnic categories. This approach to racial categorization is part of a long history that dictates single-race identities. Still, many individuals, especially young adults, struggle against social pressure to choose a single identity, and instead openly embrace multiple heritages. Tiger Woods, the world's best-known professional golfer, considers himself both Asian and African American.

A dominant or majority group has the power not only to define itself legally but to define a society's values. Sociologist William I. Thomas (1923), an early critic of theories of racial and gender differences, saw that the "definition of the situation" could mold the personality of the individual. To put it another way, Thomas, writing from the interactionist perspective, observed that people respond not only to the objective features of a situation or person but also to the *meaning* that situation or person has for them. Thus, we can create false images or stereotypes that become real in their consequences. *Stereotypes* are unreliable generalizations about all members of a group that do not recognize individual differences within the group.

In the last 30 years, critics have pointed out the power of the mass media to perpetuate false racial and ethnic stereotypes. Television is a prime example: Almost all the leading dramatic roles are cast as Whites, even in urban-based programs like *Friends* (see Chapter 7). Blacks tend to be featured mainly in crime-based dramas.

Use Your Sociological Imagination www.mhhe.com/schaefer6

Using a TV remote control, how quickly do you think you could find a television show in which all the characters share your own racial or ethnic background? What about a show in which all the characters share a different background from your own—how quickly could you find one?

Ethnicity

An ethnic group, unlike a racial group, is set apart from others because of its national origin or distinctive cultural patterns. Among the ethnic groups in the United States are peoples with a Spanish-speaking background, referred to collectively as *Latinos* or *Hispanics,* such as

Classroom Tip See "The Complexity of Racial and Ethnic Identity" (Additional Lecture Ideas) and "The Shared History of Blacks and Irish Americans" (Additional Lecture Ideas).
Let's Discuss Ask students to anonymously list their races. Compare the percentage of multiracial people in the class to that of the 2000 census (about 2%).

Classroom Tip See "Stereotypes—A Class Activity" (Class Discussion Topics) and "Picturing Stereotypes" (Class Discussion Topics).
Student Alert Terms used in the popular press, such as *Latinos* and Spanish surnames, are synonyms for *Hispanics*.
Classroom Tip See "Museums as a Useful Tool for Exploring Ethnic Diversity" (Class Discussion Topics).

Puerto Ricans, Mexican Americans, Cuban Americans, and other Latin Americans. Other ethnic groups in this country include Jewish, Irish, Italian, and Norwegian Americans. While these groupings are convenient, they serve to obscure differences *within* ethnic categories (as in the case of Hispanics), as well as to overlook the mixed ancestry of so many ethnic people in the United States.

The distinction between racial and ethnic minorities is not always clear-cut. Some members of racial minorities, such as Asian Americans, may have significant cultural differences from other racial groups. At the same time, certain ethnic minorities, such as Latinos, may have obvious physical differences that set them apart from other ethnic groups in the United States.

Despite categorization problems, sociologists continue to feel that the distinction between racial groups and ethnic groups is socially significant. In most societies, including the United States, physical differences tend to be more visible than ethnic differences. Partly as a result of this fact, stratification along racial lines is more resistant to change than stratification along ethnic lines. Over time, members of an ethnic minority can sometimes become indistinguishable from the majority—although the process may take generations, and may never include all members of the group. In contrast, members of a racial minority find it much more difficult to blend in with the larger society and gain acceptance from the majority.

PREJUDICE AND DISCRIMINATION

In recent years, college campuses across the United States have been the scene of bias-related incidents. Student-run newspapers and radio stations have ridiculed racial and ethnic minorities; threatening literature has been stuffed under the doors of minority students; graffiti endorsing the views of White supremacist organizations such as the Ku Klux Klan have been scrawled on university walls. In some cases, there have even been violent clashes between groups of White and Black students (Bunzel 1992; Schaefer 2004). What causes such ugly incidents?

Prejudice

Prejudice is a negative attitude toward an entire category of people, often an ethnic or racial minority. If you resent your roommate because he or she is sloppy, you are not necessarily guilty of prejudice. However, if you immediately stereotype your roommate on the basis of such characteristics as race, ethnicity, or religion, that is a form of prejudice. Prejudice tends to perpetuate false definitions of individuals and groups.

Student Alert Prejudice is the attitudinal or cognitive component; discrimination is the behavioral component.
Contemporary Culture Present some information on hate crimes in your community.

Sometimes prejudice results from *ethnocentrism*— the tendency to assume that one's own culture and way of life represent the norm or are superior to all others. Ethnocentric people judge other cultures by the standards of their own group, which leads quite easily to prejudice against cultures they view as inferior.

p. 72

One important and widespread form of prejudice is *racism,* the belief that one race is supreme and all others are innately inferior. When racism prevails in a society, members of subordinate groups generally experience prejudice, discrimination, and exploitation. In 1990, as concern mounted about racist attacks in the United States, Congress passed the Hate Crimes Statistics Act. This law directs the Department of Justice to gather data on crimes motivated by the victim's race, religion, ethnicity, or sexual orientation. In 2002 alone, more than 8,800 hate crimes were reported to authorities. Some 49 percent of those crimes against persons involved racial bias; another 19 percent, religious bias; 17 percent, sexual orientation bias; and 15 percent, ethnic bias. Most of the crimes were carried out by individuals acting alone or with a few friends (Department of Justice 2003).

A particularly horrifying hate crime made the front pages in 1998: In Jasper, Texas, three White men with possible ties to race-hate groups tied up a Black man, beat him with chains, and then dragged him behind their truck until his body was dismembered. Numerous groups in the United States have been victims of hate crimes as well as generalized prejudice. In the wake of the terrorist attacks of September 11, 2001, hate crimes against Asian Americans and Muslim Americans escalated rapidly. Box 10-1 (pages 246–247) examines prejudice against Arab Americans and Muslims who live in the United States.

As Figure 10-2 (page 248) shows, there is a disturbingly large number of hate groups in the United States. Their activity appears to be increasing, both in reality and in virtual reality. Although only a few hundred such groups may exist, thousands of websites advocate racial hatred on the Internet. Particularly troubling are sites disguised as video games for young people or as "educational sites" about crusaders against prejudice. The technology of the Internet has allowed race-hate groups to expand far beyond their traditional southern base to reach millions (*Intelligence Report* 2003; Sandberg 1999).

Discriminatory Behavior

Prejudice often leads to *discrimination,* the denial of opportunities and equal rights to individuals and groups because of prejudice or other arbitrary reasons. Say that a White corporate president with a prejudice against Asian Americans has to fill an executive position. The most

Contemporary Culture Hate crimes against Asian Americans and Muslim Americans escalated rapidly in the wake of the terrorist attacks of September 11, 2001.
Let's Discuss Why are hate crimes based on race much more common than hate crimes based on sexual orientation, ethnicity, or religion?
Contemporary Culture Racism on the Internet

10-1 PREJUDICE AGAINST ARAB AMERICANS AND MUSLIM AMERICANS

As marginal groups with little political power, Arab Americans and Muslim Americans are vulnerable to prejudice and discrimination. In the first five days after the terrorist attack on the World Trade Center in September 2001, these groups filed more than 300 reports of harassment and abuse, including one death. Six years earlier, when the bombing of a federal office building in Oklahoma City was mistakenly attributed to Middle Eastern terrorism, many Arabic and Muslim schoolchildren in the United States were blamed for the attack. One fifth-grade boy was told, "Go back where you came from!" His mother, an attorney and second-generation Syrian American, asked where her children were supposed to go. One was born in Texas, the other in Oklahoma.

Sociologists have observed two trends in the United States over the last 20 years. First, the numbers of people in the United States who are Arab or who practice the Islamic faith have increased dramatically. Second, the open expression of hostility toward Arab and Muslim people has also increased. This heightened hostility has discouraged many Arab and Muslim Americans from participating in civic life. In 2002, a year after the attack on the World Trade Center, only 70 Muslims ran for office anywhere in the United States, compared to 700 in the year 2000.

"Profiling" of potential terrorists at airports has put Arab and Muslim Americans under special surveillance. A number of airlines and law enforcement authorities use appearance and ethnic-sounding names to identify and take aside Arab Americans (or those who

---

One fifth-grade boy was told, "Go back where you came from!"

---

match the "profile") and search their belongings. After the terrorist attacks of September 2001, criticism of this practice declined as concern for the public's safety mounted.

Muslim women who choose to don head scarves or *hijab* in keeping with their tradition of dressing modestly encounter harassment from strangers in the street. Many employers insist that the women shed the covering if they wish to get a job or expect to be promoted. These women find it difficult to understand such attitudes in a nation founded on religious freedom.

Many people in the United States inaccurately lump together Arab Americans and Muslims. While these groups overlap, many Arab Americans are Christians (as is true of many Arabs living in the Middle East) and many Muslims (such as African Americans, Iranians, and Pakistanis) are non-Arabs. Currently, an estimated 870,000 Arab Americans live in the United States (see the map). Many cling to the culture of their nation of origin, which can vary considerably, from nations in North Africa to the Middle East.

At present, perhaps as many as 3 million Muslims live in the United States, of whom about 42 percent are African American, 24 percent are South Asian, 12 percent are Arab, and 22 percent are "other." Muslims are followers of Islam, the world's largest faith after Christianity. Their religion is based on the teachings found in the Koran (or Al-Qur'an), by the seventh-century prophet Mohammed. Muslims are divided into a variety of faiths and sects, such as Sunnis and Shiites, which are sometimes antagonistic to-

Sources: American Civil Liberties Union of Northern California 2002; El-Badry 1994; Henneberger 1995; Lindner 1998; Power 1998; Shaheen 1999; Tom Smith 2001; H. Weinstein et al. 2001.

qualified candidate for the job is a Vietnamese American. If the president refuses to hire this candidate and instead selects an inferior White candidate, he or she is engaging in an act of racial discrimination.

A recent study by sociologist Devah Pager (2003) documents this kind of racial discrimination. Pager sent four young men out to look for an entry-level job in Milwaukee, Wisconsin. All four were 23-year-old college students, but they presented themselves as high school graduates with similar job histories. Two of the men were Black and two were White. One Black applicant and one White applicant claimed to have served 18 months in jail for a felony conviction (possession of cocaine with intent to distribute).

As one might expect, the four men's experiences with 350 potential employers were vastly different. Predictably, the White applicant with a purported prison record received only half as many callbacks as the other White applicant (17 percent compared to 34 percent). But as dramatic as the effect of his criminal record was, the effect of his race was more significant. Despite his prison record, he received slightly more callbacks than the Black applicant *with no criminal record* (17 percent compared to 14 percent). Race, it seems, was more of a concern to potential employers than a criminal background (Pager 2003).

Prejudiced *attitudes* should not be equated with discriminatory *behavior*. Although the two are generally related, they are not identical; either condition can be

Theory Labeling theory is useful in examining stereotyping of Arabs and Muslims.
Global View Islamic faith introduced
Gender Gender discrimination directed at Muslim women

Methods Devah Pager conducted an experiment to assess the impact of race on employment.

ward one another (just as religious rivalries exist among Christians and Jews).

Today, there are more than 1,200 mosques in this country, of which 80 percent were established in the last 25 years. The largest group of Muslims in the United States, African Americans, is divided between those who follow mainstream Islamic doctrine and those who follow the teachings of the controversial Nation of Islam (headed by Minister Louis Farrakhan). The Muslim population of the United States is growing significantly, owing to high birthrates, substantial immigration rates, and conversion of non-Muslims.

Let's Discuss

1. Do you know an Arab American or Muslim American who has been the subject of ethnic profiling? If so, explain the circumstances. What was the person's reaction?

2. What can be done to promote better understanding of Arab and Muslim Americans and counter prejudice and discrimination against them?

Distribution of the Arab American Population by State, 2000

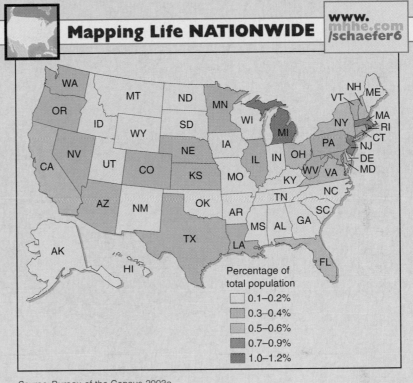

Mapping Life NATIONWIDE www.mhhe.com/schaefer6

Percentage of total population
- 0.1–0.2%
- 0.3–0.4%
- 0.5–0.6%
- 0.7–0.9%
- 1.0–1.2%

Source: Bureau of the Census 2003c.

---

present without the other. A prejudiced person does not always act on his or her biases. The White president, for example, might choose—despite his or her stereotypes—to hire the Vietnamese American. That would be prejudice without discrimination. On the other hand, a White corporate president with a completely respectful view of Vietnamese Americans might refuse to hire them for executive posts out of fear that biased clients would take their business elsewhere. In that case, the president's action would constitute discrimination without prejudice.

Discrimination persists even for the most educated and qualified minority group members from the best family backgrounds. Despite their talents and experiences, they sometimes encounter attitudinal or organizational bias that prevents them from reaching their full potential. The term *glass ceiling* refers to an invisible barrier that blocks the promotion of a qualified individual in a work environment because of the individual's gender, race, or ethnicity (R. Schaefer 2004; Yamagata et al. 1997).

In early 1995, the federal Glass Ceiling Commission issued the first comprehensive study of barriers to promotion in the United States. The commission found that glass ceilings continue to block women and minority group men from top management positions in the nation's industries. While White men constitute 45 percent of the paid labor force, they hold down a much higher proportion of top positions. Even in *Fortune* magazine's

Classroom Tip The term *concrete walls* is also used to refer to the difficulties women and racial and ethnic minorities face in getting lateral transfers to jobs in such areas as marketing, which are more likely to lead to advancement than positions in human resources or community affairs.

FIGURE 10-2

Active Hate Groups in the United States, 2002

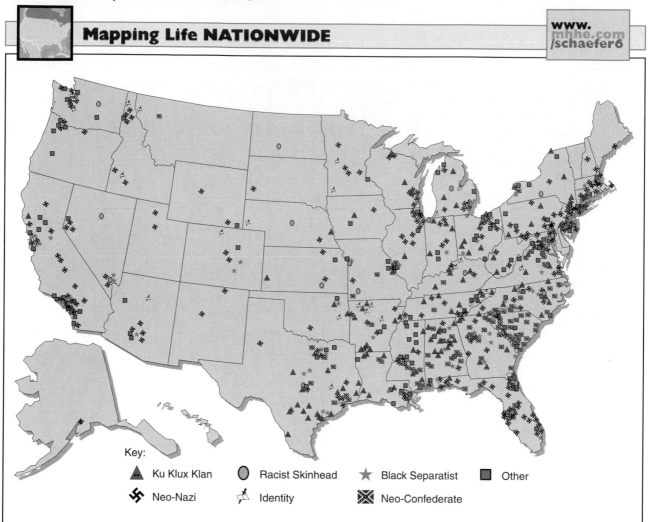

Mapping Life NATIONWIDE

www. mhhe.com /schaefer6

Key:

▲ Ku Klux Klan   ◯ Racist Skinhead   ★ Black Separatist   ■ Other

卐 Neo-Nazi   ⚑ Identity   ✕ Neo-Confederate

Source: Southern Poverty Law Center 2003.

Think About It
Why do you think state legislators enacted special hate crime laws covering acts that already were illegal?

2002 listing of the most diversified corporations, White men held more than 80 percent of both the board of directors seats and the top 50 paid positions in the firms. The existence of this glass ceiling results principally from the fears and prejudices of many middle- and upper-level White male managers, who believe that the inclusion of women and minority group men in management circles will threaten their own prospects for advancement (Bureau of the Census 2003a:385; Department of Labor 1995a, 1995b; Hickman 2002).

Classroom Tip See "Social Distance Scale" (Class Discussion Topics).

The Privileges of the Dominant

One aspect of discrimination that is often overlooked is the privileges that dominant groups enjoy at the expense of others. For instance, we tend to focus more on the difficulty women have getting ahead at work and getting a hand at home than on the ease with which men avoid household chores and manage to make their way in the world. Similarly, we concentrate more on discrimination against racial and ethnic minorities than on the advantages members of the White majority enjoy. Indeed, most White people rarely think about their "Whiteness," taking their status for granted. But sociologists and other social scientists are becoming increasingly interested in what it means to be "White," for White privilege is the other side of the proverbial coin of racial discrimination.

The feminist scholar Peggy McIntosh (1988) became interested in White privilege after noticing that most men would not acknowledge that there were privileges attached to being male—even if they would agree that being female had its disadvantages. Did White people suffer from a similar blind spot regarding their own racial privilege? she wondered. Intrigued, McIntosh began to list all the ways in which she benefited from her Whiteness. She soon realized that the list of unspoken advantages was long and significant.

McIntosh found that as a White person, she rarely needed to step out of her comfort zone, no matter where she went. If she wished to, she could spend most of her time with people of her own race. She could find a good place to live in a pleasant neighborhood, buy the foods she liked to eat from almost any grocery store, and get her hair styled in almost any salon. She could attend a public meeting without feeling that she did not belong, that she was different from everyone else.

McIntosh discovered, too, that her skin color opened doors for her. She could cash checks and use credit cards without suspicion, browse through stores without being shadowed by security guards. She could be seated without difficulty in a restaurant. If she asked to see the manager, she could assume he or she would be of her own race. If she needed help from a doctor or a lawyer, she could get it.

McIntosh also realized that her Whiteness made the job of parenting easier. She did not need to worry about protecting her children from people who didn't like them. She could be sure that their textbooks would show pictures of people who looked like them, and that their history texts would describe White people's achievements. She knew that the television programs they watched would include White characters.

Finally, McIntosh had to admit that others did not constantly evaluate her in racial terms. When she appeared in public, she didn't need to worry that her clothing or behavior might reflect poorly on White people. If she was recognized for an achievement, it was seen as her achievement, not that of an entire race. And no one ever assumed that the personal opinions she voiced should be those of all White people. Because McIntosh blended in with the people around her, she wasn't always onstage.

These are not all the privileges White people take for granted as a result of their membership in the dominant racial group in the United States. As Devah Pager's study (page 246) showed, White job seekers enjoy a tremendous advantage over equally well-qualified—even better-qualified—Blacks. Whiteness *does* carry privileges—to a much greater extent than most White people realize.

Institutional Discrimination

Discrimination is practiced not only by individuals in one-to-one encounters but also by institutions in their daily operations. Social scientists are particularly concerned with the ways in which structural factors such as employment, housing, health care, and government operations maintain the social significance of race and ethnicity. *Institutional discrimination* refers to the denial of opportunities and equal rights to individuals and groups that results from the normal operations of a society. This kind of discrimination consistently affects certain racial and ethnic groups more than others.

The Commission on Civil Rights (1981:9–10) has identified various forms of institutional discrimination:

- Rules requiring that only English be spoken at a place of work, even when it is not a business necessity to restrict the use of other languages.
- Preferences shown by law and medical schools in the admission of children of wealthy and influential alumni, nearly all of whom are White.
- Restrictive employment-leave policies, coupled with prohibitions on part-time work, that make it difficult for the heads of single-parent families (most of whom are women) to obtain and keep jobs.

A recent example of institutional discrimination occurred in the wake of the September 11, 2001, terrorist attacks on the United States. In the heat of demands to prevent terrorist takeovers of commercial airplanes, Congress passed the Aviation and Transportation Security Act, which was intended to strengthen airport screening procedures. The law stipulated that all airport screeners must be U.S. citizens. Nationally, 28 percent of all airport screeners were legal residents but not citizens of the United States; as a group, they were disproportionately Latino, Black, and Asian. Many observers noted that other airport and airline workers, including pilots, cabin attendants, and even armed National Guardsmen stationed at airports, need not be citizens. Efforts are now being made to test the constitutionality of the act. At the least, the debate over its fairness shows that even well-meant legal measures can have disastrous consequences for racial and ethnic minorities (H. Weinstein 2002).

Classroom Tip See "Discrimination on Television" (Class Discussion Topics).
Reel Society See Stratification—Race/Ethnicity in the Topic Index.

Theory Conflict view of institutional discrimination by race and ethnicity in the United States
Classroom Tip See "Institutional Discrimination" (Class Discussion Topics).

Before passage of the Civil Rights Act (1964), segregation of public accommodations was the norm throughout the South. Whites used the most up-to-date bathrooms, waiting rooms, and even drinking fountains, while Blacks ("Colored") were directed to older facilities in inferior condition. Such separate-but-unequal arrangements are a blatant example of institutional discrimination.

In some cases, even ostensibly neutral institutional standards can turn out to have discriminatory effects. African American students at a midwestern state university protested a policy under which fraternities and sororities that wished to use campus facilities for a dance were required to post $150 security deposits to cover possible damages. The Black students complained that the policy had a discriminatory impact on minority student organizations. Campus police countered that the university's policy applied to all student groups interested in using the facilities. However, since the overwhelmingly White fraternities and sororities at the school had their own houses, which they used for dances, the policy indeed affected only African American and other minority organizations.

Attempts have been made to eradicate or compensate for discrimination in the United States. The 1960s saw the passage of many pioneering civil rights laws, including the landmark 1964 Civil Rights Act (which prohibits discrimination in public accommodations and publicly owned facilities on the basis of race, color, creed, national origin, and gender). In two important rulings in 1987, the Supreme Court held that federal prohibitions against racial discrimination protect members of all ethnic minorities—including Hispanics, Jews, and Arab Americans—even though they may be considered White.

For more than 40 years, affirmative action programs have been instituted to overcome past discrimination. *Affirmative action* refers to positive efforts to recruit minority group members or women for jobs, promotions,

and educational opportunities. Many people resent these programs, arguing that advancing one group's cause merely shifts the discrimination to another group. By giving priority to African Americans in admissions, for example, schools may overlook more qualified White candidates. In many parts of the country and many sectors of the economy, affirmative action is being rolled back, even though it was never fully implemented. The social policy section in Chapter 14 will discuss affirmative action in more detail.

Discriminatory practices continue to pervade nearly all areas of life in the United States today. In part, that is because various individuals and groups actually *benefit* from racial and ethnic discrimination in terms of money, status, and influence. Discrimination permits members of the majority to enhance their wealth, power, and prestige at the expense of others. Less qualified people get jobs and promotions simply because they are members of the dominant group. Such individuals and groups will not surrender these advantages easily. We'll turn now to a closer look at this functionalist analysis, as well as the conflict and interactionist perspectives on race and ethnicity.

STUDYING RACE AND ETHNICITY

Relations among racial and ethnic groups lend themselves to analysis from the three major sociological perspectives. Viewing race from the macro level, functionalists observe that racial prejudice and discrimination serve positive functions for dominant groups. Conflict theorists see the economic structure as a central factor in the exploitation of minorities. On the micro level, interactionist researchers stress the manner in which everyday contact between people from different racial and ethnic backgrounds contributes to tolerance or hostility.

Functionalist Perspective

What possible use could racial bigotry have? Functionalist theorists, while agreeing that racial hostility is hardly to be admired, point out that it serves positive functions for those who practice discrimination.

Anthropologist Manning Nash (1962) has identified three functions that racially prejudiced beliefs have for the dominant group:

1. Racist views provide a moral justification for maintaining an unequal society that routinely deprives a minority group of its rights and privileges. Southern Whites justified slavery by believing that Africans were physically and spiritually subhuman and devoid of souls (Hoebel 1949).
2. Racist beliefs discourage the subordinate minority from attempting to question its lowly status, which would be to question the very foundations of society.
3. Racial myths suggest that any major societal change (such as an end to discrimination) would only bring greater poverty to the minority and lower the majority's standard of living. As a result, Nash suggests, racial prejudice grows when a society's value system (one underlying a colonial empire or perpetuating slavery, for example) is threatened.

Although racial prejudice and discrimination may serve the interests of the powerful, such unequal treatment also can be dysfunctional for a society and even for the dominant group. Sociologist Arnold Rose (1951) has outlined four dysfunctions associated with racism:

1. A society that practices discrimination fails to use the resources of all individuals. Discrimination limits the search for talent and leadership to the dominant group.
2. Discrimination aggravates social problems such as poverty, delinquency, and crime, and places the financial burden of alleviating those problems on the dominant group.
3. Society must invest a good deal of time and money to defend its barriers to the full participation of all members.
4. Racial prejudice and discrimination often undercut goodwill and friendly diplomatic relations between nations.

Conflict Perspective

Conflict theorists would certainly agree with Arnold Rose that racial prejudice and discrimination have many harmful consequences for society. Sociologists such as Oliver Cox (1948), Robert Blauner (1972), and Herbert M. Hunter (2000) have used the *exploitation theory* (or *Marxist class theory*) to explain the basis of racial subordination in the United States. As we saw in Chapter 9,

Karl Marx viewed the exploitation of the lower class as a basic part of the capitalist economic system. From a Marxist point of view, racism keeps minorities in low-paying jobs, thereby supplying the capitalist ruling class with a pool of cheap labor. Moreover, by forcing racial minorities to accept low wages, capitalists can restrict the wages of *all* members of the proletariat. Workers from the dominant group who demand higher wages can always be replaced by minorities who have no choice but to accept low-paying jobs.

The conflict view of race relations seems persuasive in a number of instances. Japanese Americans were the object of little prejudice until they began to enter jobs that brought them into competition with Whites. The movement to keep Chinese immigrants out of the United States became most fervent during the latter half of the 19th century, when Chinese and Whites fought over dwindling work opportunities. Both the enslavement of Blacks and the extermination and removal westward of Native Americans were, to a significant extent, economically motivated.

However, the exploitation theory is too limited to explain prejudice in its many forms. Not all minority groups have been economically exploited to the same extent. In addition, many groups (such as the Quakers and the Mormons) have been victimized by prejudice for other than economic reasons. Still, as Gordon Allport (1979:210) concludes, the exploitation theory correctly "points a sure finger at one of the factors involved in prejudice, . . . rationalized self-interest of the upper classes."

The practice of racial profiling fits both the conflict perspective and labeling theory. ***Racial profiling*** may be

p. 188 defined as any arbitrary action initiated by an authority based on race, ethnicity, or national origin rather than on a person's behavior. Generally, racial profiling occurs when law enforcement officers—customs officials, airport security personnel, and police—assume that people who fit certain descriptions are likely to be engaged in illegal activities. Skin color became a key characteristic of criminal profiles beginning in the 1980s, with the emergence of the crack cocaine market. But profiling also can involve a much more explicit use of stereotypes. For example, the federal antidrug initiative Operation Pipeline encouraged officers to look specifically for people wearing dreadlocks and for Latino men traveling together.

In 2003 President George W. Bush banned racial profiling by federal agencies but specifically exempted security personnel. Thus, immigration officials can continue to require visitors from Middle Eastern countries to register with the government, even though visitors from other countries are not required to register. Conflict

Theory Functions that racially prejudiced beliefs have for majority group members
Theory Dysfunctions of racism for society
Theory Conflict view of racial prejudice and discrimination

Classroom Tip See "Multicultural Pedagogy" (Class Discussion Topics).

PRUDENCE HANNIS Researcher and Community Activist, Quebec Native Women

Prudence Hannis is an Abenaki First Nations (Native American) woman who works with the organization Quebec Native Women, where she is responsible for the women's health portfolio. Her job entails the organizing and facilitating of various activities, such as seminars on sexual abuse in local communities and the production of a resource booklet on the subject for community members. Prudence also works for the Centre of Excellence on Women's Health, Consortium Université de Montréal, where she focuses on First Nations women's health issues such as HIV and AIDS, prostitution, poverty, sexual discrimination, drug and alcohol abuse, and family violence.

Prudence received her B.A. in sociology from the University of Quebec at Montreal. "Sociology is now, more than it has ever

been, a part of my job," she says. "The purpose of my job is to defend First Nations' women's concerns, to be their spokesperson when needed, to analyze critical situations for our sisters, and mostly, to determine ways in which women can empower themselves, their families, and their communities."

Let's Discuss

1. Explain the connection between Native Americans' ethnicity and their health.
2. In speaking of empowering First Nations women, what sociological perspective do you think Hannis is drawing on?

---

theorists point out that in all these cases, the powerful and privileged dominant majority determines who is profiled and for what purposes (D. Harris 1999; Lightblau 2003; D. Ramirez et al. 2000).

Interactionist Perspective

A Hispanic woman is transferred from a job on an assembly line to a similar position working next to a White man. At first, the White man is patronizing, assuming that she must be incompetent. She is cold and resentful; even when she needs assistance, she refuses to admit it. After a week, the growing tension between the two leads to a bitter quarrel. Yet over time, each slowly comes to appreciate the other's strengths and talents. A year after they begin working together, these two workers become respectful friends. This story is an example of what interactionists call the *contact hypothesis* in action.

The **contact hypothesis** states that in cooperative circumstances, interracial contact between people of equal status will cause them to become less prejudiced and to abandon old stereotypes. People begin to see one another as individuals and discard the broad generalizations characteristic of stereotyping. Note the phrases *equal status* and *cooperative circumstances*. In the story above, if the two workers had been competing for one vacancy as a su-

pervisor, the racial hostility between them might have worsened (Allport 1979; R. Schaefer 2004; Sigelman et al. 1996).

As Latinos and other minorities slowly gain access to better-paying and more responsible jobs, the contact hypothesis may take on even greater significance. The trend in our society is toward increasing contact between individuals from dominant and subordinate groups. That may be one way of eliminating—or at least reducing—racial and ethnic stereotyping and prejudice. Another may be the establishment of interracial coalitions, an idea suggested by sociologist William Julius Wilson (1999b). To work, such coalitions would obviously need to be built on an equal role for all members.

Contact between individuals occurs on the micro level. We turn now to a consideration of intergroup relations on the macro level.

PATTERNS OF INTERGROUP RELATIONS

Racial and ethnic groups can relate to one another in a wide variety of ways, ranging from friendships and intermarriages to hostility, from behaviors that require mutual approval to behaviors imposed by the dominant group.

One devastating pattern of intergroup relations is *genocide*—the deliberate, systematic killing of an entire people or nation. This term describes the killing of 1 million Armenians by Turkey beginning in 1915. It is most commonly applied to Nazi Germany's extermination of 6 million European Jews, as well as gays, lesbians, and the Romani people ("Gypsies"), during World War II. The term *genocide* is also appropriate in describing the United States' policies toward Native Americans in the 19th century. In 1800, the Native American (or American Indian) population of the United States was about 600,000; by 1850, it had been reduced to 250,000 through warfare with the U.S. cavalry, disease, and forced relocation to inhospitable environments.

The *expulsion* of a people is another extreme means of acting out racial or ethnic prejudice. In 1979, Vietnam expelled nearly 1 million ethnic Chinese, partly as a result of centuries of hostility between Vietnam and neighboring China. In a more recent example of expulsion (which had aspects of genocide), Serbian forces began a program of "ethnic cleansing" in 1991, in the newly independent states of Bosnia and Herzegovina. Throughout the former nation of Yugoslavia, the Serbs drove more than 1 million Croats and Muslims from their homes. Some they tortured and killed, others they abused and terrorized, in an attempt to "purify" the land for the Serbian majority. In 1999, Serbs again became the focus of worldwide condemnation as they sought to "cleanse" the province of Kosovo of ethnic Albanians.

Genocide and expulsion are extreme behaviors. More typical intergroup relations follow four identifiable patterns: (1) amalgamation, (2) assimilation, (3) segregation, and (4) pluralism. Each pattern defines the dominant group's actions and the minority group's responses. Intergroup relations are rarely restricted to only one of the four patterns, although invariably one does tend to dominate. Think of these patterns primarily as ideal types.

Amalgamation

Amalgamation happens when a majority group and a minority group combine to form a new group. Through intermarriage over several generations, various groups in society combine to form a new group. This pattern can be expressed as A + B + C → D, where A, B, and C represent different groups in a society, and D signifies the end result, a unique cultural-racial group unlike any of the initial groups (W. Newman 1973).

The belief in the United States as a "melting pot" became compelling in the first part of the 20th century, particularly since that image suggested that the nation had an almost divine mission to amalgamate various groups

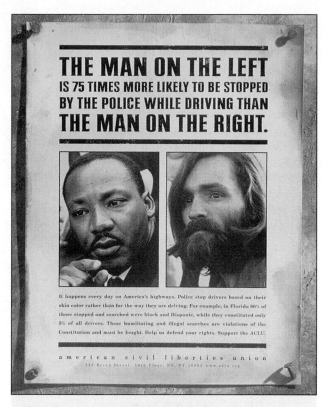

THE MAN ON THE LEFT IS 75 TIMES MORE LIKELY TO BE STOPPED BY THE POLICE WHILE DRIVING THAN **THE MAN ON THE RIGHT.**

It happens every day on America's highways. Police stop drivers based on their skin color rather than for the way they are driving. For example, in Florida 80% of those stopped and searched were black and Hispanic, while they constituted only 5% of all drivers. These humiliating and illegal searches are violations of the Constitution and must be fought. Help us defend your rights. Support the ACLU.

american civil liberties union
125 Broad Street, 18th Floor, NY, NY 10004 www.aclu.org

Too often, authorities treat individuals differently based solely on their race or ethnicity. This poster dramatizes the injustice of racial profiling, a practice in which a man who looks like the Reverend Martin Luther King Jr. (left) would be treated with more suspicion than the mass murderer Charles Manson (right).

into one people. However, in actuality, many residents were not willing to include Native Americans, Jews, African Americans, Asian Americans, and Irish Roman Catholics in the melting pot. Therefore, this pattern does not adequately describe dominant–subordinate relations in the United States.

Assimilation

Many Hindus in India complain about Indian citizens who copy the traditions and customs of the British. In Australia, Aborigines who have become part of the dominant society refuse to acknowledge their darker-skinned grandparents on the street. In the United States, some Italian Americans, Polish Americans, Hispanics, and Jews have changed their ethnic-sounding family names to names that are typically found among White Protestant families.

Assimilation is the process through which a person forsakes his or her own cultural tradition to become part

Global View Genocide committed by Turkey and Nazi Germany
Global View Expulsion in Asia and Eastern Europe
Classroom Tip Another term used by sociologists to describe amalgamation is *fusion.*

Global View Assimilation in India and Australia

of a different culture. Generally, it is practiced by a minority group member who wants to conform to the standards of the dominant group. Assimilation can be described as a pattern in which A + B + C → A. The majority, A, dominates in such a way that members of minorities B and C imitate it and attempt to become indistinguishable from it (W. Newman 1973).

Assimilation can strike at the very roots of a person's identity. Alphonso D'Abuzzo, for example, changed his name to Alan Alda. The British actress Joyce Frankenberg changed her name to Jane Seymour. Name changes, switches in religious affiliation, and dropping of native languages can obscure one's roots and heritage. However, assimilation does not necessarily bring acceptance to minority group individuals. A Chinese American such as Helen Zia (see the chapter-opening excerpt) may speak English fluently, achieve high educational standards, and become a well-respected professional or businessperson and *still* be seen as different. Other Americans may reject her as a business associate, neighbor, or marriage partner.

A policeman stops to chat with three young residents of the Langston Hughes housing project in East New York. Although the United States is a diverse society, U.S. neighborhoods are not. Public housing projects often reinforce the racial segregation in existing neighborhoods, even though the federal government has outlawed discrimination in housing.

> **Use Your Sociological Imagination** www.mhhe.com/schaefer6
>
> You have immigrated to another country with a very different culture. What steps might you take to assimilate?

Segregation

Separate schools, separate seating on buses and in restaurants, separate washrooms, even separate drinking fountains—these were all part of the lives of African Americans in the South when segregation ruled early in the 20th century. *Segregation* refers to the physical separation of two groups of people in terms of residence, workplace, and social events. Generally, a dominant group imposes this pattern on a minority group. Segregation is rarely complete, however. Intergroup contact inevitably occurs, even in the most segregated societies.

From 1948 (when it received its independence) to 1990, the Republic of South Africa severely restricted the movement of Blacks and other non-Whites by means of a wide-ranging system of segregation known as *apartheid.* Apartheid even included the creation of sep-

arate homelands where Blacks were expected to live. However, decades of local resistance to apartheid, combined with international pressure, led to marked political changes in the 1990s. In 1994, a prominent Black activist, Nelson Mandela, was elected South Africa's president in the first election in which Blacks (the majority of the nation's population) were allowed to vote. Mandela had spent almost 28 years in South African prisons for his anti-apartheid activities. His election was widely viewed as the final blow to South Africa's oppressive policy of apartheid.

Long-entrenched social patterns are difficult to change, however. In the United States today, despite federal laws that forbid housing discrimination, residential segregation is still the norm, as a recent analysis of living patterns in metropolitan areas shows. Across the nation, neighborhoods remain divided along both racial and ethnic lines. The average White person lives in an area that is at least 83 percent White, while the average African American lives in a neighborhood that is mostly Black. The typical Latino lives in an area that is 42 percent Hispanic. Overall, segregation flourishes at the community and neighborhood level, despite the increasing diversity of the nation as a whole (Lewis Mumford Center 2001).

Whatever the country, residential segregation directly limits people's economic opportunity. Sociologists Douglas Massey and Nancy Denton (1993), in a book aptly titled *American Apartheid,* noted that segregation separates poor people of color from job opportunities and isolates them from successful role models. This pattern repeats itself the world over, from South Central Los Angeles to Oldham, England, and Soweto, South Africa.

Pluralism

In a pluralistic society, a subordinate group does not have to forsake its lifestyle and traditions. *Pluralism* is based on mutual respect for one another's cultures among the various groups in a society. This pattern allows a minority group to express its own culture and still participate without prejudice in the larger society. Earlier, we described amalgamation as A + B + C → D, and assimilation as A + B + C → A. Using this same approach, we can conceive of pluralism as A + B + C → A + B + C. All the groups coexist in the same society (W. Newman 1973).

In the United States, pluralism is more of an ideal than a reality. There are distinct instances of pluralism—the ethnic neighborhoods in major cities, such as Koreatown, Little Tokyo, Andersonville (Swedish Americans), and Spanish Harlem—yet there are also limits to cultural freedom. To survive, a society must promote a certain consensus among its members regarding basic ideals, values, and beliefs. Thus, if a Romanian immigrant to the United States wants to move up the occupational ladder, he or she cannot avoid learning the English language.

Switzerland exemplifies the modern pluralistic state. There the absence of both a national language and a dominant religious faith leads to a tolerance for cultural diversity. In addition, various political devices safeguard the interests of ethnic groups in a way that has no parallel in the United States. By contrast, Great Britain has had difficulty achieving cultural pluralism in a multiracial society. East Indians, Pakistanis, and Blacks from the Caribbean and Africa experience prejudice and discrimination within the dominant White society. Some British advocate cutting off all Asian and Black immigration, and a few even call for expulsion of those non-Whites currently living in Britain.

RACE AND ETHNICITY IN THE UNITED STATES

Few societies have a more diverse population than the United States; the nation is truly a multiracial, multiethnic society. Of course, that has not always been the

case. The population of what is now the United States has changed dramatically since the arrival of European settlers in the 1600s, as Figure 10-1 (page 243) showed. Immigration, colonialism, and in the case of Blacks, slavery determined the racial and ethnic makeup of our present-day society. Figure 10-3, on page 256, shows where various racial and ethnic minorities are concentrated in the United States.

Racial Groups

The largest racial minorities in the United States are African Americans, Native Americans, and Asian Americans.

African Americans

"I am an invisible man," wrote Black author Ralph Ellison in his novel *Invisible Man* (1952:3). "I am a man of substance, of flesh and bone, fiber and liquids—and I might even be said to possess a mind. I am invisible, understand, simply because people refuse to see me."

Over five decades later, many African Americans still feel invisible. Despite their large numbers, they have long been treated as second-class citizens. Currently, by the standards of the federal government, more than 1 out of every 4 Blacks—as opposed to 1 out of every 12 Whites—is poor.

Contemporary institutional discrimination and individual prejudice against African Americans are rooted in the history of slavery in the United States. Many other subordinate groups had little wealth and income, but as sociologist W. E. B. Du Bois (1909) and others have noted, enslaved Blacks were in an even more oppressive situation, because by law, they could not own property and could not pass on the benefits of their labor to their children. Today, increasing numbers of African Americans and sympathetic Whites are calling for *slave reparations* to compensate for the injustices of forced servitude. Reparations could include official expressions of apology from governments such as the United States, ambitious programs to improve African Americans' economic status, or even direct payments to descendants of slaves (D. Williams and Collins 2004).

The end of the Civil War did not bring genuine freedom and equality for Blacks. The Southern states passed "Jim Crow" laws to enforce official segregation, and the Supreme Court upheld them as constitutional in 1896. In addition, Blacks faced the danger of lynching campaigns, often led by the Ku Klux Klan, during the late 1800s and early 1900s. From a conflict perspective, Whites maintained their dominance formally through legalized segregation and informally by means of vigilante terror and violence (Franklin and Moss 2000).

FIGURE 10-3

Census 2000: The Image of Diversity

Mapping Life NATIONWIDE

www.mhhe.com/schaefer6

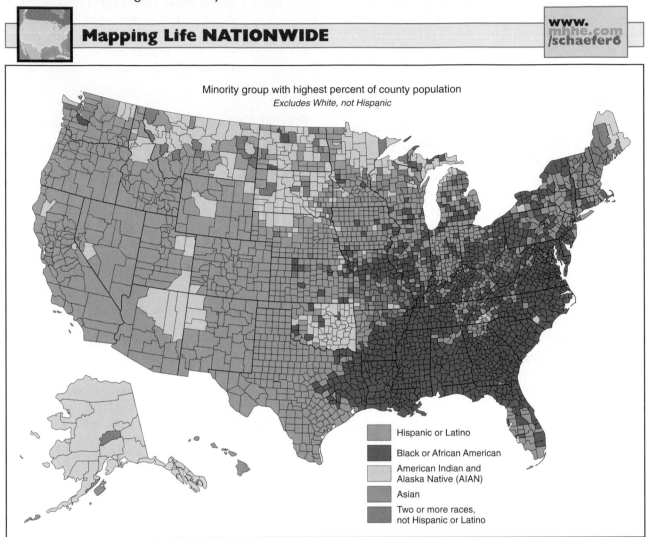

Minority group with highest percent of county population
Excludes White, not Hispanic

Hispanic or Latino

Black or African American

American Indian and
Alaska Native (AIAN)

Asian

Two or more races,
not Hispanic or Latino

Source: C. Brewer and Suchan 2001:20.

Think About It
The United States is a diverse nation. Why, in many parts of the country, can't people see that diversity in their own towns?

A turning point in the struggle for Black equality came in 1954 with the unanimous Supreme Court decision in the case of *Brown v. Board of Education of Topeka, Kansas.* The Court outlawed segregation of public school students, ruling that "separate educational facilities are inherently unequal." In the wake of the *Brown* decision, there was a surge of activism on behalf of Black civil rights, including boycotts of segregated bus companies and sit-ins at restaurants and lunch counters that refused to serve Blacks.

During the 1960s, a vast civil rights movement emerged, with many competing factions and strategies for change. The Southern Christian Leadership Conference (SCLC), founded by Dr. Martin Luther King Jr., used nonviolent civil disobedience to oppose segregation. The National Association for the Advancement of Colored People (NAACP) favored use of the courts to press for equality for African Americans. But many younger Black leaders, most notably Malcolm X, turned toward an ideology of Black power. Proponents of ***Black power*** rejected the goal of as-

Key Persons Dr. Martin Luther King Jr.; Malcolm X

Table 10-2	Relative Economic Positions of Various Racial and Ethnic Groups				
Characteristic	Whites	African Americans	Native Americans	Asian Americans	Hispanics
Four-year college education, people 25 and over (2003)	27.6%	17.3%	11.5%	49.8%	11.4%
Median household income (2003)	$46,400	$29,026	$32,116	$52,626	$33,103
Unemployment rate (2004)	4.9%	10.5%	—	5.3%	8.2%
People below the poverty line (2003)	8.0%	24.1%	25.7%	10.1%	21.8%

Notes: Data on Whites, where available, are for White non-Hispanics. On reservations, estimated median family income for Native American households is $18,063. Educational and poverty data for Native Americans are for 2000 and 1999, respectively. Unemployment rate for Asian Americans estimated by author.

Sources: Bauman and Graf 2003:5; Bishaw and Iceland 2003; Bureau of the Census 2003a:44–47; DeNavas-Walt et al. 2004:29–31, 42–44; Department of Labor 2004; McKinnon 2003; Ramirez and de la Cruz 2003; Reeves and Bennett 2003; Stoops 2004.

Think About It
Notice how much higher the rate for college education is among Asian Americans than among Whites. Yet the median income for Asian Americans is only slightly higher than it is for Whites. What might explain this disparity?

similation into White middle-class society. They defended the beauty and dignity of Black and African cultures and supported the creation of Black-controlled political and economic institutions (Ture and Hamilton 1992).

Despite numerous courageous actions to achieve Black civil rights, Black and White citizens are still separate, still unequal. From birth to death, Blacks suffer in **pp. 218–219** terms of their life chances. Life remains difficult for millions of poor Blacks, who must attempt to survive in ghetto areas shattered by high unemployment and abandoned housing. The economic position of Blacks is shown in Table 10-2. The median household income of Blacks is still only 60 percent that of Whites, and the unemployment rate among Blacks is more than twice that of Whites.

Some African Americans—especially middle-class men and women—have made economic gains over the last 50 years. For example, data compiled by the Department of Labor show that the number of African Americans in management increased nationally from 2.4 percent of the total in 1958 to 8.0 percent in 2002. Yet Blacks still represent only 5 percent or less of all physicians, engineers, scientists, lawyers, judges, and marketing managers. In another occupation important to developing role models, African Americans and Hispanics together account for less than 10 percent of all editors and

reporters in the United States (Bureau of the Census 2003a:399).

In many respects, the civil rights movement of the 1960s left institutionalized discrimination against African Americans untouched. Consequently, in the 1970s and 1980s, Black leaders worked to mobilize African American political power as a force for social change. Between 1970 and 2001, the number of African American elected officials increased sixfold. Even so, Blacks remain significantly *underrepresented*. That underrepresentation is especially distressing in view of the fact that sociologist W. E. B. Du Bois observed over 90 years ago that Blacks could not expect to achieve equal social and economic opportunities without first gaining political rights (Bureau of the Census 2003a:268; Green and Driver 1978).

Native Americans

Today, 2.5 million Native Americans represent a diverse array of cultures distinguishable by language, family organization, religion, and livelihood. The outsiders who came to the United States—European settlers and their descendants—came to know these native peoples' forefathers as "American Indians." By the time the Bureau of Indian Affairs (BIA) was organized as part of the War Department in 1824, Indian–White relations had already included three centuries of mutual misunderstanding.

Contemporary Culture Differential life chances of Blacks

Cabazon men perform a traditional dance during a tribal gathering in California. In recent years, Native Americans have used such "powwows" to revive customs that Whites once encouraged them to abandon.

During the 19th century many bloody wars wiped out a significant part of the nation's Indian population. By the end of the century, schools for Indians—operated by the BIA or by church missions—prohibited the practice of Native American cultures. Yet at the same time, such schools did little to make the children effective competitors in White society.

Today, life remains difficult for members of the 554 tribal groups in the United States, whether they live in cities or on reservations. For example, one Native American teenager in six has attempted suicide—a rate four times higher than the rate for other teenagers. Traditionally, some Native Americans have chosen to assimilate and abandon all vestiges of their tribal cultures to escape certain forms of prejudice. However, by the 1990s, an increasing number of people in the United States were openly claiming a Native American identity. Since 1960, the federal government's count of Native Americans has tripled, to an estimated 2.5 million. According to the 2000 census, the Native American population increased 26 percent during the 1990s. Demographers believe that more and more Native Americans who previously concealed their identity are no longer pretending to be White (Grieco and Cassidy 2001).

The introduction of gambling on Indian reservations threatens to become still another battleground between Native Americans and the dominant White society. About one-third of all tribes operate off-track betting, casino games such as blackjack and roulette, slot machines, high-stakes bingo, sports betting, and video gambling. The gamblers—who are overwhelmingly not Native Americans—typically travel long distances to wager money at the new casinos. While gambling on reservations generates $16.2 billion annually, the profits are not evenly spread among tribes. Much of Native America is untouched by casino windfalls. The lopsided nature of these revenues, with huge profits going to just a few tribes and non-Indian investors, is the reason the economic standing of the vast majority of Native Americans has not changed much. Some Native Americans oppose gambling on moral grounds and charge that it is being marketed in a manner incompatible with Native American culture. Yet some reservations have managed profits from gambling well and have invested them in projects for the betterment of the entire reservation. At the same time, established White gambling interests, particularly in Nevada and New Jersey, have pressured Congress to restrict Native American casinos (P. Marshall 2003; Schaefer 2004).

Use Your Sociological Imagination www.mhhe.com/schaefer6

You are a Native American whose tribe is about to open a reservation-based casino. Will the casino further the assimilation of your people into mainstream society or encourage pluralism?

Asian Americans

Asian Americans are a diverse group, one of the fastest-growing segments of the U.S. population (up 69 percent between 1990 and 2000). Among the many groups of

FIGURE 10-4

Major Asian American Groups in the United States, 2000

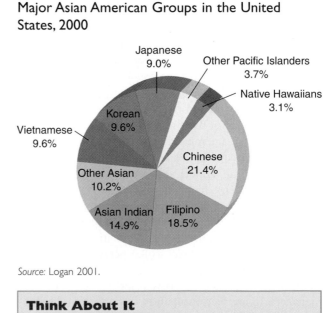

Source: Logan 2001.

Think About It
Do Asian Americans really have a common identity?

Theory Conflict view of historic mistreatment of Native Americans and their subordinate position today
Contemporary Culture Introduction of gambling on Indian reservations

Theory Conflict analysis of gambling on Indian reservations

Americans of Asian descent are Vietnamese Americans, Chinese Americans, Japanese Americans, and Korean Americans (see Figure 10-4).

Asian Americans are held up as a *model* or *ideal minority* group, supposedly because despite past suffering from prejudice and discrimination, they have succeeded economically, socially, and educationally without resorting to confrontations with Whites. The existence of a model minority seems to reaffirm the notion that anyone can get ahead in the United States with talent and hard work, and implies that those minorities that don't succeed are somehow responsible for their failures. Viewed from a conflict perspective, this attitude is yet another instance of "blaming the victims" (Hurh and Kim 1998).

The concept of a model minority ignores the diversity among Asian Americans: There are rich and poor Japanese Americans, rich and poor Filipino Americans, and so forth. In fact, Southeast Asians living in the United States have the highest rate of welfare dependency of any racial or ethnic group. As Table 10-2 (page 257) shows, Asian Americans have substantially more schooling than other ethnic groups, but their median income is only slightly higher than Whites' income, and their poverty rate is higher. In 2003, for every Asian American family with an annual income of $100,000 or more, there was another earning less than $25,000 a year. Moreover, even when Asian Americans are clustered at the higher-paying end of the stratification system, the glass ceiling may limit how far they can rise (DeNavas-Walt et al. 2003:20).

Vietnamese Americans Each Asian American group has its own history and culture. Vietnamese Americans, for instance, came to the United States primarily during and after the Vietnam War—especially after the U.S. withdrawal from the conflict in 1975. Assisted by local agencies, refugees from the communist government in Vietnam settled throughout the United States, tens of thousands of them in small towns. But over time, Vietnamese Americans have gravitated toward the larger urban areas, establishing Vietnamese restaurants and grocery stores in their ethnic enclaves there.

In 1995, the United States resumed normal diplomatic relations with Vietnam. Gradually, the *Viet Kieu,* or Vietnamese living abroad, began to return to their old country to visit, but usually not to take up permanent residence. Today, 30 years after the end of the Vietnam War, sharp differences of opinion remain among Vietnamese Americans, especially the older ones, concerning the war and the present government of Vietnam (Lamb 1997).

Chinese Americans Unlike African slaves and Native Americans, the Chinese were initially encouraged to im-

migrate to the United States. From 1850 to 1880, thousands of Chinese immigrated to this country, lured by job opportunities created by the discovery of gold. However, as employment possibilities decreased and competition for mining jobs grew, the Chinese became the target of a bitter campaign to limit their numbers and restrict their rights. Chinese laborers were exploited, then discarded.

In 1882, Congress enacted the Chinese Exclusion Act, which prevented Chinese immigration and even forbade Chinese in the United States to send for their families. As a result, the Chinese population steadily declined until after World War II. More recently, the descendants of the 19th-century immigrants have been joined by a new influx from Hong Kong and Taiwan. These groups may contrast sharply in their degree of assimilation, desire to live in Chinatowns, and feelings about this country's relations with the People's Republic of China.

Currently, about 2.7 million Chinese Americans live in the United States. Some Chinese Americans have entered lucrative occupations, yet many immigrants struggle to survive under living and working conditions that belie the model-minority stereotype. New York City's Chinatown district is filled with illegal sweatshops in which recent immigrants—many of them Chinese women—work for minimal wages. Even in legal factories in the garment industry, hours are long and rewards are limited. A seamstress typically works 11 hours per day, 6 days a week, and earns about $10,000 a year. Other workers, such as hemmers and cutters, earn only $5,000 per year (Finder 1995; Lum and Kwong 1989).

Japanese Americans Approximately 1.1 million Japanese Americans live in the United States. As a people, they are relatively recent arrivals. In 1880, only 148 Japanese lived in the United States, but by 1920 there were more than 110,000. Japanese immigrants—called the *Issei,* or first generation—were usually males seeking employment opportunities. Many Whites saw them (along with Chinese immigrants) as a "yellow peril" and subjected them to prejudice and discrimination.

In 1941, the attack on Hawaii's Pearl Harbor by Japan had severe repercussions for Japanese Americans. The federal government decreed that all Japanese Americans on the West Coast must leave their homes and report to "evacuation camps." Japanese Americans became, in effect, scapegoats for the anger that other people in the United States felt concerning Japan's role in World War II. By August 1943, in an unprecedented application of guilt by virtue of ancestry, 113,000 Japanese Americans had been forced into hastily built camps. In striking contrast, only a few German Americans and Italian Americans were sent to evacuation camps (Hosokawa 1969).

Theory Labeling Asian Americans as a "model minority" ignores their diversity, and from a conflict perspective, contributes to blaming other minorities who may have been less successful.
Let's Discuss Could the "model minority" stereotype be part of our society's dominant ideology?

Theory From a functionalist perspective, even positive stereotypes of Asian Americans as "academic stars" can be dysfunctional for those Asian Americans who are not successful.
Classroom Tip See "School Desegregation and a Hmong Community" (Additional Lecture Ideas).

This mass detention was costly for Japanese Americans. The Federal Reserve Board estimates their total income and property losses at nearly half a billion dollars. Moreover, the psychological effect on these citizens—including the humiliation of being labeled "disloyal"—was immeasurable. Eventually, children born in the United States to the *Issei*, called *Nisei*, were allowed to enlist in the Army and serve in Europe in a segregated combat unit. Others resettled in the East and Midwest to work in factories.

In 1983, a federal commission recommended government payments to all surviving Japanese Americans who had been held in detention camps. The commission reported that the detention was motivated by "race prejudice, war hysteria, and a failure of political leadership." It added that "no documented acts of espionage, sabotage, or fifth-column activity were shown to have been committed" by Japanese Americans. In 1988, President Ronald Reagan signed the Civil Liberties Act, which required the federal government to issue individual apologies for all violations of Japanese Americans' constitutional rights, and established a $1.25 billion trust fund to pay reparations to the approximately 77,500 surviving Japanese Americans who had been interned (Department of Justice 2000).

Korean Americans   At 1.2 million, the population of Korean Americans now exceeds that of Japanese Americans. Yet Korean Americans are often overshadowed by other groups from Asia.

Today's Korean American community is the result of three waves of immigration. The initial wave arrived between 1903 and 1910, when Korean laborers migrated to Hawaii. The second wave followed the end of the Korean War in 1953; most of these immigrants were wives of U.S. servicemen and war orphans. The third wave, continuing to the present, has reflected the admissions priorities set up in the 1965 Immigration Act. These well-educated immigrants arrive in the United States with professional skills. Yet because of language difficulties and discrimination, many must settle at least initially for positions of lower responsibility than those they held in Korea and must suffer through a period of disenchantment. Stress, loneliness, and family strife may accompany the pain of adjustment.

Like many other Asian American women, Korean American women commonly participate in the paid labor force, though in Korea women are expected to serve as mothers and homemakers only. While these roles carry over to the United States, Korean American women are also pressed to support their families while their husbands struggle to establish themselves financially. Many Korean American men begin small service and retail businesses and gradually involve their wives in the ventures. Making the situation even more difficult is the hostility Korean American–run businesses often encounter from their prospective customers (Hurh 1994, 1998; Kim 1999).

In the early 1990s, the apparent friction between Korean Americans and another subordinate racial group, African Americans, attracted nationwide attention. In New York City, Los Angeles, and Chicago, Korean American merchants confronted Blacks who were allegedly threatening them or robbing their stores. Black neighborhoods responded with hostility to what they perceived as the disrespect and arrogance of Korean American entrepreneurs. In South Central Los Angeles, the only shops in which to buy groceries, liquor, or gasoline were owned by Korean immigrants, who had largely replaced White businesspeople. African Americans were well aware of the dominant role that Korean Americans played in their local retail markets. During the 1992 riots in South Central Los Angeles, small businesses owned by Koreans were a particular target. More than 1,800 Korean businesses were looted or burned during the riots (Kim 1999).

Conflict between the two groups was dramatized in Spike Lee's 1989 movie *Do the Right Thing*. The situation stems from Korean Americans' position as the latest immigrant group to cater to the needs of inner-city populations abandoned by those who have moved up the economic ladder. This type of friction is not new; generations of Jewish, Italian, and Arab merchants have encountered similar hostility from what to outsiders seems an unlikely source—another oppressed minority.

Ethnic Groups

Unlike racial minorities, members of subordinate ethnic groups generally are not hindered by physical differences from assimilating into the dominant culture of the United States. However, members of ethnic minority groups still face many forms of prejudice and discrimination. Take the cases of the country's largest ethnic groups—Latinos, Jews, and White ethnics.

Latinos

Together, the various groups included under the general category *Latinos* represent the largest minority in the United States. In 2002 there were more than 37 million Hispanics in this country, including 25 million Mexican Americans, more than 3 million Puerto Ricans, and smaller numbers of Cuban Americans and people of Central and South American origin (see Figure 10-5). The latter group represents the fastest-growing and most diverse segment of the Hispanic community.

Theory From a conflict perspective, the confinement of Japanese Americans in evacuation camps was an extreme example of institutionalized discrimination based on race.

Classroom Tip See "Complexities of Race and Nationality: The Case of Peruvian Japanese" (Additional Lecture Ideas).

Theory Conflict theorists observe that amidst competition for scarce resources, rivalries and conflict develop even among subordinate groups.

According to Census Bureau data, the Latino population now outnumbers the African American population in 6 of the 10 largest cities of the United States: Los Angeles, Houston, Phoenix, San Diego, Dallas, and San Antonio. Hispanics are now the majority of residents in cities such as Miami, Florida; El Paso, Texas; and Santa Ana, California. The rise in the Hispanic population of the United States—fueled by comparatively high birthrates and levels of immigration—has intensified debates over public policy issues such as bilingualism and immigration.

The various Latino groups share a heritage of Spanish language and culture, which can cause serious problems in their assimilation. An intelligent student whose first language is Spanish may be presumed slow or even unruly by English-speaking schoolchildren, and frequently by English-speaking teachers as well. The labeling of Latino children as underachievers, as learning disabled, or emotionally disturbed can act as a self-fulfilling prophecy for some chil-

◀ p. 73 dren. Bilingual education aims at easing the educational difficulties experienced by Hispanic children and others whose first language is not English.

The educational difficulties of Latino students certainly contribute to the generally low economic status of Hispanics. In 2003 about 19 percent of all Hispanic households earned less than $15,000, compared to less than 13 percent of non-Hispanic White households. Up to the year 2000, only 11 percent of Hispanic adults had completed college, compared to 28 percent of non-Hispanic Whites. In that same year the poverty rate for people ages 18 to 64 was 18.1 percent for Hispanics, compared to only 7.5 percent for non-Hispanic Whites. Overall, Latinos are not as affluent as White non-Hispanics, but a middle class is beginning to emerge within the Latino community: see Box 10-2, page 262 (DeNavas-Walt et al. 2004:29, 31; Proctor and Dalaker 2003:29, 32).

Mexican Americans The largest Latino population is Mexican Americans, who can be further subdivided into those descended from residents of the territories annexed after the Mexican-American War of 1848 and those who have immigrated from Mexico to the United States. The opportunity for a Mexican to earn in one hour what it would take an entire day to earn in Mexico has pushed millions of legal and illegal immigrants north.

FIGURE 10-5

Major Hispanic Groups in the United States, 2002

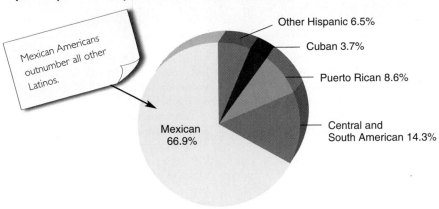

Source: R. Ramirez and de la Cruz 2003:1.

Aside from the family, the most important social organization in the Mexican American (or Chicano) community is the church, specifically the Roman Catholic church. This strong identification with the Catholic faith has reinforced the already formidable barriers between Mexican Americans and their predominantly White and Protestant neighbors in the Southwest. At the same time, the Catholic Church helps many immigrants to develop a sense of identity and assists their assimilation into the norms and values of the dominant culture of the United States. The complexity of the Mexican American community is underscored by the fact that Protestant churches—especially those that endorse expressive, open worship—have attracted increasing numbers of Mexican Americans (Herrmann 1994; Kanellos 1994).

Puerto Ricans The second-largest segment of Latinos in the United States is Puerto Ricans. Since 1917, residents of Puerto Rico have held the status of American citizens; many have migrated to New York and other eastern cities. Unfortunately, Puerto Ricans have experienced serious poverty both in the United States and on the island. Those who live in the continental United States earn barely half the family income of Whites. As a result, a reverse migration began in the 1970s, when more Puerto Ricans were leaving for the island than were coming to the mainland (Lemann 1991).

Politically, Puerto Ricans in the United States have not been as successful as Mexican Americans in organizing for their rights. For many mainland Puerto Ricans—as for many residents of the island—the paramount political issue is the destiny of Puerto Rico itself: Should it continue in its present commonwealth status,

Theory Labeling Latino children as underachievers or as learning disabled often acts as a self-fulfilling prophecy.
Contemporary Culture The poverty rate for Hispanics ages 18 to 64 was 18.1 percent in 2000.

10-2 THE LATINO MIDDLE CLASS

No racial or ethnic group belongs to just one social class. Among Latinos, as in society as a whole, there is a social class hierarchy. The recent rapid growth of the Hispanic population, which rose 58 percent in the 1990s, has focused marketers' attention on the burgeoning Latino middle class, which grew 71 percent in the same period. Latino-oriented magazines and advertising, not always published in Spanish, are one sign of this group's growing economic power. Segments of the Mexican American and Cuban American communities have begun to display the typical signs of middle-class status: moderate to high incomes, postgraduate and professional schooling, and substantial assets, including homes in middle- and upper-class neighborhoods.

Mexican Americans were among the first middle-class people in North America. In the 1660s, settlers in San Antonio enjoyed an almost aristocratic status granted by the Spanish crown. Some of these old-line families, as well as Hispanic families in other parts of the Southwest, have been able to retain their elevated status. In the 20th century, well-trained professionals who fled Cuba following the revolution created middle-class Hispanic communities in South Florida.

Among other Latinos, social mobility has created an unmistakable middle class. About one in nine Latinos now has a college degree; one in six U.S.-born Latinos is college educated. A growing number of Latinos own their own businesses—more

---

A growing number of Latinos own their own businesses—more than 1.2 million firms nationally.

---

than 1.2 million firms nationally. Latino-owned businesses account for about one-quarter of all businesses in metropolitan Los Angeles and San Diego, as well as in the state of New Mexico. Women—that is, *Latinas*—are especially prominent in these businesses, most of which are very small family-owned enterprises.

Will these newly affluent Latinos continue to ally themselves with the concerns of lower-income Hispanics? Although many still favor liberalized immigration laws and bilingual education, some affluent Latinos have begun to back more restrictive immigration policies and to question the wisdom of funding bilingual education.

The assimilated children of the Latino middle class, like all children of immigrants, are caught between two worlds. Close to half of all the children of Latino immigrants consider themselves to be primarily English speakers. By the next generation, the proportion increases to 78 percent. Consequently, some of these young adults are now studying *Español*, either to boost their careers or to become better acquainted with their roots.

Let's Discuss

1. Have you seen signs of Latino affluence on television or in magazine advertisements? What stores or brand names are pitching their wares directly to Latinos?
2. Why do you think marketers aim their promotional materials at specific racial and ethnic groups?

Sources: Bean et al. 2001; Brischetto 2001; Bureau of the Census 2001b; Campo-Flores 2000; Gonzales 1997; R. Ramirez and de la Cruz 2003; Romney 1998; Suro and Passel 2003.

petition for admission to the United States as the 51st state, or attempt to become an independent nation? This question has divided Puerto Rico for decades and remains a central issue in Puerto Rican elections. In a 1998 referendum, voters supported a "none of the above" option, effectively favoring continuing the commonwealth status over statehood or independence.

Cuban Americans Cuban immigration to the United States dates back as far as 1831, but it began in earnest following Fidel Castro's assumption of power in the Cuban revolution (1959). The first wave of 200,000 Cubans included many professionals with relatively high levels of schooling; these men and women were largely welcomed as refugees from communist tyranny. However, more recent waves of immigrants have aroused growing concern, partly because they were less likely to be skilled professionals. Throughout these waves of immigration, Cuban Americans have been encouraged to locate around the United States. Nevertheless, many continue to settle in (or return to) metropolitan Miami, Florida, with its warm climate and proximity to Cuba.

The Cuban experience in the United States has been mixed. Some detractors worry about the vehement anticommunism of Cuban Americans and the apparent growth of an organized crime syndicate that engages in the drug trade and ganglike violence. Recently, Cuban Americans in Miami have expressed concern over what they view as the indifference of the city's Roman Catholic hierarchy. Like other Hispanics, Cuban Americans are underrepresented in leadership positions within the church. Finally—despite many individual success stories—as a group, Cuban Americans in Miami remain behind "Anglos"

Contemporary Culture College education among Latinos

(Whites) in income, rate of employment, and proportion of professionals (Gonzalez-Pando 1998).

Jewish Americans

Jews constitute almost 3 percent of the population of the United States. They play a prominent role in the worldwide Jewish community, because the United States has the world's largest concentration of Jews. Like the Japanese, many Jewish immigrants came to this country and became white-collar professionals in spite of prejudice and discrimination.

Anti-Semitism—that is, anti-Jewish prejudice—has often been vicious in the United States, although rarely so widespread and never so formalized as in Europe. In many cases, Jews have been used as scapegoats for other people's failures. Not surprisingly, Jews have not achieved equality in the United States. Despite high levels of education and professional training, they are still conspicuously absent from the top management of large corporations (except for the few firms founded by Jews). Until the late 1960s, many prestigious universities maintained restrictive quotas that limited Jewish enrollment. Private social clubs and fraternal groups frequently limit membership to gentiles (non-Jews), a practice upheld by the Supreme Court in the 1964 case *Bell v. Maryland*.

The Anti-Defamation League (ADL) of B'nai B'rith funds an annual survey of reported anti-Semitic incidents. Although the number has fluctuated, the 1994 tabulation reached the highest level in the 19 years the ADL has been recording such incidents. The total reported incidents of harassment, threats, vandalism, and assaults came to 1,559 in 2002. Some incidents were inspired and carried out by neo-Nazi skinheads—groups of young people who champion racist and anti-Semitic ideologies. Such threatening behavior only intensifies the fears of many Jewish Americans, who find it difficult to forget the Holocaust—the extermination of 6 million Jews by the Nazi Third Reich during World War II (Anti-Defamation League 2003).

As is true for other minorities discussed in this chapter, Jewish Americans face the choice of maintaining ties to their long religious and cultural heritage or becoming as indistinguishable as possible from gentiles. Many Jews have tended to assimilate, as is evident from the rise in

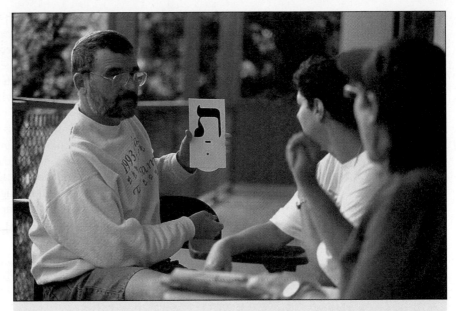

For practicing Jews, the Hebrew language is an important part of religious instruction. This teacher is showing flashcards of Hebrew alphabetic characters to deaf students.

marriages between Jews and Christians. A study released in 2003 found that 47 percent of Jews who had married in the past five years chose to marry a non-Jew. Many people in the Jewish community worry that intermarriage will lead to a rapid decline in those who identify themselves as "Jewish." Yet when asked which was the greater threat to Jewish life in the United States—intermarriage or anti-Semitism—only 41 percent of respondents replied that intermarriage was the greater threat; 50 percent selected anti-Semitism (American Jewish Committee 2001; United Jewish Communities 2003).

White Ethnics

A significant segment of the population of the United States is made up of White ethnics whose ancestors arrived from Europe within the last century. The nation's White ethnic population includes about 43 million people who claim at least partial German ancestry, 31 million Irish Americans, 16 million Italian Americans, and 9 million Polish Americans, as well as immigrants from other European nations. Some of these people continue to live in close-knit ethnic neighborhoods, while others have largely assimilated and left the "old ways" behind (Brittingham and de la Cruz 2004).

Many White ethnics today identify only sporadically with their heritage. *Symbolic ethnicity* refers to an emphasis on concerns such as ethnic food or political issues rather than on deeper ties to one's ethnic heritage. It is reflected in the occasional family trip to an ethnic bakery,

Methods Secondary analysis (a survey of data gathered by law enforcement agencies) is used in the Anti-Defamation League's study of anti-Semitic incidents.
Theory Conflict theorists would view anti-Semitic attacks in the United States as a reflection of continuing prejudice and discrimination.

Methods Survey research on intermarriage involving Jewish Americans
Classroom Tip Have an officer of a White ethnic club (such as the Sons of Norway) speak to the class on the history and functions of the organization.

the celebration of a ceremonial event such as St. Joseph's Day among Italian Americans, or concern about the future of Northern Ireland among Irish Americans. Except in cases in which new immigration reinforces old traditions, symbolic ethnicity tends to decline with each passing generation (Alba 1990; Gans 1979).

White ethnics and racial minorities have often been antagonistic to one another because of economic competition—an interpretation that agrees with the conflict approach to sociology. As Blacks, Latinos and Native Americans emerge from the lower class, they must compete with working-class Whites for jobs, housing, and educational opportunities. In times of high unemployment or inflation, any such competition can easily generate intense intergroup conflict.

In many respects, the plight of White ethnics raises the same basic issues as that of other subordinate people in the United States. How ethnic can people be—how much can they deviate from an essentially White, Anglo-Saxon, Protestant norm—before society punishes them for their willingness to be different? Our society does seem to reward people for assimilating. Yet as we have seen, assimilation is no guarantee of equality or freedom from discrimination. In the social policy section that follows, we will focus on immigrants, people who inevitably face the question of whether or not to strive for assimilation.

SOCIAL POLICY and RACE AND ETHNICITY | Global Immigration

The Issue

Worldwide, immigration is at an all-time high. Each year, about 2.3 percent of the world's population, or 146 million people, move from one country to another. A million of them enter the United States legally, to join the 12 percent of the population who are foreign born. The constantly increasing numbers of immigrants and the pressure they put on job opportunities and welfare capabilities in the countries they enter raise troubling questions for many of the world's economic powers. Who should be allowed in? At what point should immigration be curtailed (Schmidley and Robinson 2003; Stalker 2000)?

The Setting

The migration of people is not uniform across time or space. At certain times, war or famine may precipitate large movements of people, either temporarily or permanently. Temporary dislocations occur when people wait until it is safe to return to their home areas. However, more and more migrants who cannot make an adequate living in their home nations are making permanent moves to developed nations. The major migration streams flow into North America, the oil-rich areas of the Middle East, and the industrial economies of western Europe and Asia. Currently, seven of the world's wealthiest nations (including Germany, France, the United Kingdom, and the United States) shelter about one-third of the world's migrant population, but less than one-fifth of the world's total population. As long as disparities in job opportunities exist among countries, there is little reason to expect this international trend to reverse.

Countries that have long been a destination for immigrants, such as the United States, usually have policies to determine who has preference to enter. Often, clear racial and ethnic biases are built into these policies. In the 1920s, U.S. policy gave preference to people from western Europe, while making it difficult for residents of southern and eastern Europe, Asia, and Africa to enter the country. During the late 1930s and early 1940s, the federal government refused to lift or loosen restrictive immigration quotas in order to allow Jewish refugees to escape the terror of the Nazi regime. In line with this policy, the SS *St. Louis,* with more than 900 Jewish refugees on board, was denied permission to land in the United States in 1939. The ship was forced to sail back to Europe, where it is estimated that at least a few hundred of its passengers later died at the hands of the Nazis (A. Morse 1967; G. Thomas and Witts 1974).

Since the 1960s, U.S. policy has encouraged the immigration of relatives of U.S. residents as well as of people who have desirable skills. This change has significantly altered the pattern of sending nations. Previously, Europeans dominated, but for the last 40 years, immigrants have come primarily from Latin America and Asia (see Figure 10-6). Thus, an ever-growing proportion of the United States will be Asian or Hispanic (see Figure 10-7, page 266). To a large degree, fear and resentment of growing racial and ethnic diversity is a key factor in opposition to immigration. In many nations, people are concerned that the new arrivals do not reflect their own cultural and racial heritage.

Theory Conflict view of the antagonism between White ethnics and racial minorities
Classroom Tip Provide information on the number and background of immigrants in your community or state.

Let's Discuss When the U.S. government refused to let the SS *St. Louis* land, was it complicit in genocide?
Web Resource There is a true–false quiz for this chapter in the student center of the Online Learning Center (**www.mhhe.com/schaefer6**). Remind students that the quiz gives immediate feedback for incorrect answers.

FIGURE 10-6

Immigration in the United States, 1820–2000

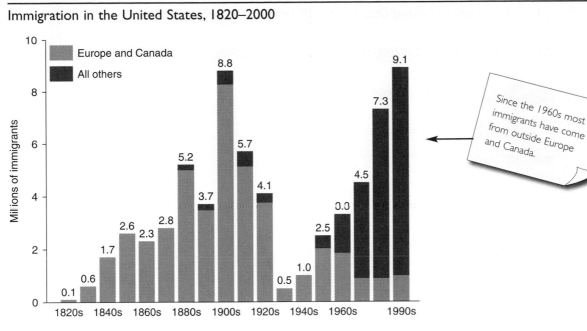

Since the 1960s most immigrants have come from outside Europe and Canada.

Sources: Bureau of the Census 2003a: 11; Immigration and Naturalization Service 1999a, 1999b.

Research suggests that immigrants adapt well to life in the United States, becoming an asset to the nation's economy. In some areas, heavy immigration may drain a local community's resources, but in other areas it revitalizes the local economy. A national survey done in 2003 showed that 9 out of 10 immigrants believe that learning English is extremely important. Eighty-eight percent judge the United States to be better than their home country at offering "more opportunity to earn a good living" (Farkas et al. 2003; Fix et al. 2001; Smith and Edmonston 1997).

Sociological Insights

Despite people's fears, immigration performs many valuable functions. For the receiving society, it alleviates labor shortages, as it does in health care and technology in the United States. In 1998, Congress debated not whether individuals with technological skills should be allowed into the country, but just how much to increase the annual quota. For the sending nation, migration can relieve an economy unable to support large numbers of people. Often overlooked is the large amount of money, called *remittances*, that immigrants send *back* to their home nations. Worldwide, immigrants send more than $80 billion a year back home to their relatives—an amount that represents a major source of income for developing nations (World Bank 2003c).

Immigration can be dysfunctional as well. Although studies generally show that it has a positive impact on the receiving nation's economy, areas that accept high concentrations of immigrants may find it difficult to meet short-term social service needs. And when migrants with skills or educational potential leave developing countries, their departure can be dysfunctional for those nations. No amount of payments sent back home can make up for the loss of valuable human resources from poor nations (P. Martin and Midgley 1999; Mosisa 2002).

Conflict theorists note how much of the debate over immigration is phrased in economic terms. But the debate intensifies when the arrivals are of a different racial and ethnic background from the host population. For example, Europeans often refer to "foreigners," but the term does not necessarily mean one of foreign birth. In Germany, "foreigners" refers to people of non-German ancestry, even if they were *born* in Germany; it does not refer to people of German ancestry born in another country, who may choose to return to their "mother country." Fear and dislike of "new" ethnic groups divides countries throughout the world.

Policy Initiatives

The long border with Mexico provides ample opportunity for illegal immigration into the United States.

FIGURE 10-7

Foreign-Born Population of the United States, from 10 Leading Countries, 2000

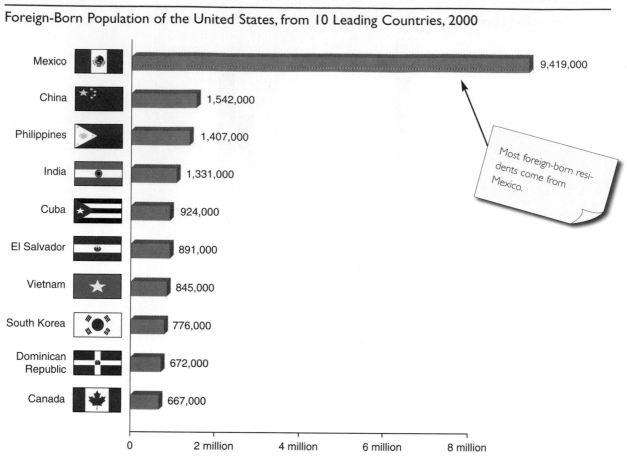

Mexico — 9,419,000

China — 1,542,000

Philippines — 1,407,000

India — 1,331,000

Cuba — 924,000

El Salvador — 891,000

Vietnam — 845,000

South Korea — 776,000

Dominican Republic — 672,000

Canada — 667,000

0   2 million   4 million   6 million   8 million

Most foreign-born residents come from Mexico.

Note: Based on annualized averages of Current Population Survey. Chinese total includes Hong Kong and Taiwan.

Sources: Schmidley and Robinson 2003:Table A-3.

Throughout the 1980s, the public perception that the United States had lost control of its borders grew. Feeling pressure for immigration control, Congress ended a decade of debate by approving the Immigration Reform and Control Act of 1986. The act marked a historic change in the nation's immigration policy. For the first time, the hiring of illegal aliens was outlawed, and employers caught violating the law became subject to fines and even prison sentences. Just as significant a change was the extension of amnesty and legal status to many illegal immigrants already living in the United States. Almost 20 years later, however, the act appears to have had mixed results. Substantial numbers of illegal immigrants continue to enter the country each year, with an estimated 8 to 9 million present at any given time (FAIR US 2003).

The entire world feels the overwhelming impact of globalization on immigration patterns. The European Union agreement of 1997 gave the governing commission authority to propose a Europewide policy on immigration. An EU policy that allows residents of one EU country to live and work in another EU country is expected to complicate efforts by sending nations, such as Turkey, to become members of the EU. Immigrants from Turkey's predominantly Muslim population are not welcome in many EU countries (Denny 2004).

In the wake of the attacks of September 11, 2001, on the World Trade Center and the Pentagon, immigration procedures were complicated by the need to detect potential terrorists. Illegal immigrants especially, but even legal immigrants, have felt increased scrutiny by government officials around the world. For would-be immigrants to many nations, the wait to receive the right to enter a country—even to join relatives—has increased substantially, as immigration officials scrutinize what were once routine applications more closely.

The intense debate over immigration reflects deep value conflicts in the cultures of many nations. One

Classroom Tip Emphasize that while national attention is largely focused on immigration from Mexico, the immigrant population of the United States is actually quite varied.
Theory Conflict analysis of the Immigration Reform and Control Act of 1986

Global View Immigration issues in Europe
Theory Conflict theorists emphasize that immigrants face harassment and discrimination.
Policy Pointer Discuss the impact of immigration into the United States on debates over multiculturalism (Chapter 3) and on the social construction of race.

strand of our culture, for example, has traditionally emphasized egalitarian principles and a desire to help people in time of need. At the same time, hostility to potential immigrants and refugees—whether the Chinese in the 1880s, European Jews in the 1930s and 1940s, or Mexicans, Haitians, and Arabs today—reflects not only racial, ethnic, and religious prejudice, but a desire to maintain the dominant culture of the in-group by keeping out those viewed as outsiders.

Let's Discuss

1. Did you or your parents or grandparents immigrate to the United States from another nation? If so, when and where did your family come from, and why?
2. Do you live, work, or study with recent immigrants to the United States? If so, are they well accepted in your community, or do they face prejudice and discrimination?
3. On balance, do the functions of immigration to the United States outweigh the dysfunctions?

GETTING INVOLVED

www. mhhe.com /schaefer6

To get involved in the debate over global immigration, visit this text's Online Learning Center, which offers links to relevant websites. Check out the Social Policy section in the Online Learning Center as well; it provides survey data on U.S. public opinion regarding this issue.

CHAPTER RESOURCES

Summary

The social dimensions of race and ethnicity are important factors in shaping people's lives in the United States and other countries. In this chapter, we examine the meaning of race and ethnicity and study the major racial and ethnic groups of the United States.

1. A *racial group* is set apart from others by obvious physical differences; an *ethnic group* is set apart primarily by national origin or cultural patterns.
2. When sociologists define a *minority group,* they are concerned primarily with the economic and political power, or powerlessness, of the group.
3. In a biological sense, there are no "pure races," and no physical traits that can be used to describe one group to the exclusion of all others.
4. The meaning people attach to the physical differences between races gives social significance to race, producing *stereotypes.*
5. *Prejudice* often leads to *discrimination,* but the two are not identical; each can be present without the other.
6. *Institutional discrimination* results from the normal operations of a society.

7. Functionalists point out that discrimination is both functional and dysfunctional for a society. Conflict theorists explain racial subordination through *exploitation theory.* Interactionists pose the *contact hypothesis* as a means of reducing prejudice and discrimination.
8. Four patterns describe typical intergroup relations in North America and elsewhere: *amalgamation, assimilation, segregation,* and *pluralism.* Pluralism remains more of an ideal than a reality.
9. Contemporary prejudice and discrimination against African Americans are rooted in the history of slavery in the United States.
10. Asian Americans are commonly viewed as a *model* or *ideal minority,* a stereotype not necessarily beneficial to members of that group.
11. The various groups included under the general term *Latinos* represent the largest ethnic minority in the United States.
12. The increase in immigration worldwide has raised questions in many nations about how to control the process.

Critical Thinking Questions

1. Why is institutional discrimination even more powerful than individual discrimination? How would functionalists, conflict theorists, and interactionists study institutional discrimination?

2. Examine the relations between dominant and subordinate racial and ethnic groups in your hometown or your college. Can the community in which you grew up or the college you attend be viewed as genuine examples of pluralism?

3. What are some of the similarities and differences in the position of African Americans and Hispanics in the United States? What are some of the similarities and differences in the position of Asian Americans and Jewish Americans?

Key Terms

Affirmative action   Positive efforts to recruit minority group members or women for jobs, promotions, and educational opportunities. (page 250)

Amalgamation   The process through which a majority group and a minority group combine to form a new group. (253)

Anti-Semitism   Anti-Jewish prejudice. (263)

Apartheid   A former policy of the South African government, designed to maintain the separation of Blacks and other non-Whites from the dominant Whites. (254)

Assimilation   The process through which a person forsakes his or her own cultural tradition to become part of a different culture. (253)

Black power   A political philosophy promoted by many younger Blacks in the 1960s that supported the creation of Black-controlled political and economic institutions. (256)

Contact hypothesis   An interactionist perspective which states that in cooperative circumstances, interracial contact between people of equal status will reduce prejudice. (252)

Discrimination   The denial of opportunities and equal rights to individuals and groups because of prejudice or other arbitrary reasons. (245)

Ethnic group   A group that is set apart from others primarily because of its national origin or distinctive cultural patterns. (241)

Ethnocentrism   The tendency to assume that one's own culture and way of life represent the norm or are superior to all others. (245)

Exploitation theory   A Marxist theory that views racial subordination in the United States as a manifestation of the class system inherent in capitalism. (251)

Genocide   The deliberate, systematic killing of an entire people or nation. (253)

Glass ceiling   An invisible barrier that blocks the promotion of a qualified individual in a work environment because of the individual's gender, race, or ethnicity. (247)

Institutional discrimination   The denial of opportunities and equal rights to individuals and groups that results from the normal operations of a society. (249)

Issei   Japanese immigrants to the United States. (259)

Minority group   A subordinate group whose members have significantly less control or power over their own lives than the members of a dominant or majority group have over theirs. (241)

Model or **ideal minority**   A minority group that despite past prejudice and discrimination, succeeds economically, socially, and educationally without resorting to confrontations with Whites. (259)

Nisei   Children born in the United States to the Issei. (260)

Pluralism   Mutual respect for one another's cultures among the various groups in a society, which allows minorities to express their own cultures without experiencing prejudice. (255)

Prejudice   A negative attitude toward an entire category of people, often an ethnic or racial minority. (245)

Racial group   A group that is set apart from others because of obvious physical differences. (241)

Racial profiling   Any arbitrary action initiated by an authority based on race, ethnicity, or national origin rather than on a person's behavior. (251)

Racism   The belief that one race is supreme and all others are innately inferior. (245)

Segregation   The physical separation of two groups of people in terms of residence, workplace, and social events; often imposed on a minority group by a dominant group. (254)

Stereotype   An unreliable generalization about all members of a group that does not recognize individual differences within the group. (244)

Symbolic ethnicity   An ethnic identity that emphasizes concerns such as ethnic food or political issues rather than deeper ties to one's ethnic heritage. (263)

TECHNOLOGY RESOURCES

Internet Connection

*Note: While all the URLs listed were current as of the printing of this book, these sites often change. Please check our website (**www.mhhe.com/schaefer6**) for updates, hyperlinks, and exercises related to these sites.*

1. Native Web (**www.nativeweb.org**) is a great resource for information on the world's indigenous (native) people. For more topic-specific links, click on "Resource Center." This part of the site also lists hundreds of indigenous groups under the heading "Nations Index."

2. How has the African American experience changed over the past 30 years? A photographic exhibit on the website for the U.S. National Archives and Records Administration chronicles daily life among African American residents of Chicago during the 1970s. Explore these images at **www.archives.gov/exhibit_hall/portrait_of_black_chicago/introduction.html**.

Online Learning Center with PowerWeb

The Civil Rights movement was a defining sociological event in modern U.S. history. To learn more about this movement, go to the Online Learning Center at **www.mhhe.com/schaefer6** and visit the student center. Link to "Internet Exercises" and scroll down to the third exercise. Through the Papers Project, Stanford University has helped to preserve the words and life of Dr. Martin Luther King Jr., leader of the Civil Rights movement.

Reel Society Interactive Movie CD-ROM 2.0

Reel Society 2.0 can be used to spark discussion about the following topics from this chapter:

- Minority Groups
- Race
- Ethnicity
- Prejudice and Discrimination

STRATIFICATION BY GENDER AND AGE

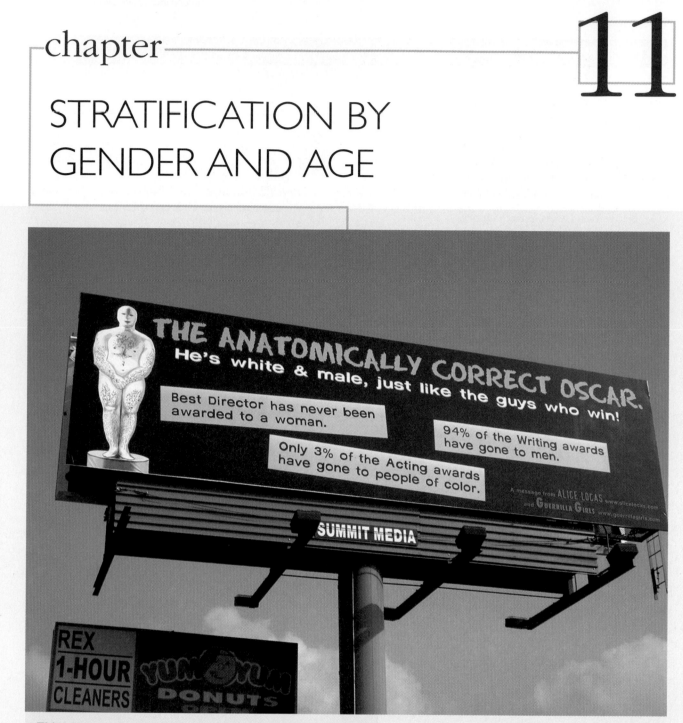

This billboard in Hollywood, California, produced by the feminist advocacy group Guerrilla Girls, points out the gender inequities in the motion picture industry.

At last, after a long silence, women took to the streets. In the two decades of radical action that followed the rebirth of feminism in the early 1970s, Western women gained legal and reproductive rights, pursued higher education, entered the trades and the professions, and overturned ancient and revered beliefs about their social role. A generation on, do women feel free?

The affluent, educated, liberated women of the First World, who can enjoy freedoms unavailable to any women ever before, do not feel as free as they want to. And they can no longer restrict to the subconscious their sense that this lack of freedom has something to do with—with apparently frivolous issues, things that really should not matter. Many are ashamed to admit that such trivial concerns—to do with physical appearance, bodies, faces, hair, clothes— matter so much. But in spite of shame, guilt, and denial, more and more women are wondering if . . . something important is indeed at stake that has to do with the relationship between female liberation and female beauty.

During the past decade, women breached the power structure; meanwhile, eating disorders rose exponentially and cosmetic surgery became the fastest-growing medical specialty. During the past five years, consumer spending doubled, pornography became the main media category, ahead of legitimate films and records combined, and thirty-three thousand American women told researchers that they would rather lose ten to fifteen pounds than achieve any other goal. More women have more money and power and scope and legal recognition than we have ever had before; but in terms of how we feel about ourselves *physically,* we may actually be worse off than our unliberated grandmothers. Recent research consistently shows that inside the majority of the West's controlled, attractive, successful working women, there is a secret "underlife" poisoning our freedom; infused with notions of beauty, it is a dark vein of self-hatred, physical obsessions, terror of aging, and dread of lost control.

It is no accident that so many potentially powerful women feel this way. We are in the midst of a violent backlash against feminism that uses images of female beauty as a political weapon against women's advancement: the beauty myth. . . .

The beauty myth tells a story: The quality called "beauty" objectively and universally exists. Women must want to embody it and men must want to possess women who embody it. This embodiment is an imperative for women and not for men, which situation is necessary and natural because it is biological, sexual, and evolutionary: Strong men battle for beautiful women, and beautiful women are more reproductively successful. Women's beauty must correlate to their fertility, and since this system is based on sexual selection, it is inevitable and changeless.

None of this is true. "Beauty" is a currency system like the gold standard. Like any economy, it is determined by politics, and in the modern age in the West it is the last, best belief system that keeps male dominance intact. *(Wolf 1992:9–10, 12)* ■ ⊚

NATIONAL BESTSELLER

THE BEAUTY MYTH

HOW IMAGES OF BEAUTY ARE USED AGAINST WOMEN

"*The Beauty Myth is a smart, angry, insightful book, and a clarion call to freedom. Every woman should read it.*"
—GLORIA STEINEM

NAOMI WOLF

Additional information about this excerpt can be found on the Online Learning Center at **www.mhhe.com/schaefer6.**

In this excerpt from Naomi Wolf's book *The Beauty Myth,* a feminist confronts the power of a false ideal of womanhood. In recent decades, American women have broken legal and institutional barriers that once limited their educational opportunities and career advancement. But psychologically, Wolf writes, they are still enslaved by unrealistic standards of appearance. The more freedom women have gained, in fact, the more obsessed they seem to have become with the ideal of the ultrathin supermodel—an ideal that few women can ever hope to attain, even if they are willing to jeopardize their health through obsessive dieting and exercise, plastic surgery, anorexia or bulimia.

Wolf asserts that the beauty myth is a societal control mechanism that is meant to keep women in their place—as subordinates to men at home and on the job. But men too are captive to unrealistic expectations regarding their physical appearance. In hopes of attaining a brawny, muscular physique, more and more men are now taking steroids or electing to undergo cosmetic surgery. Today's media bombard both men and women with the need to look good in ads hawking everything from nutrition supplements to hair color formulas to expensive exercise equipment and health club memberships. The latest manifestation of this trend is ABC Television's *Extreme Makeover,* a show that follows volunteers of both sexes as they undergo a variety of cosmetic surgeries. In screening the 7,000 people who responded to the show's initial casting call, however, producers found that the overwhelming majority were women (P. Thomas and Owens 2000).

The beauty myth is but one example of how cultural norms may lead to differentiation based on an ascribed status such as one's gender. This type of differentiation is evident in virtually every human society about which we have information. Like gender, age is a socially constructed concept that is used as a basis for differentiation. It is an ascribed status that dominates people's perceptions of others, obscuring individual differences. Rather than suggesting that a particular elderly person is no longer competent to drive, for instance, we may condemn the entire age group: "Those old codgers shouldn't be allowed on the road." Not surprisingly, many of the cosmetic procedures that Naomi Wolf writes about in *The Beauty Myth* are intended to disguise a man or woman's age.

We saw in Chapters 9 and 10 that most societies establish hierarchies based on social class, race, and ethnicity. This chapter will examine the ways in which societies stratify their members based on gender and age. Do gender roles differ from one culture to another? Are women in the United States still oppressed because of their gender, as Naomi Wolf asserts? How does ageism affect an older person's employment opportunities? And what are the social implications of the growing number of elderly in the United States? To answer these and other questions, we will look first at how various cultures, including our own, assign women and men to particular social roles. Then we will consider sociological explanations for gender stratification. Next, we will focus on the unique situation of women as an oppressed majority. In the second part of the chapter we will look at the process of aging around the world, focusing primarily on the United States. We will explore various theories of the impact of aging, paying particular attention to the effects of prejudice and discrimination. The chapter will close with a social policy section on the intense and continuing controversy over a woman's right to abortion. ▪

SOCIAL CONSTRUCTION OF GENDER

How many airline passengers do you think are startled on hearing a female captain's voice from the cockpit? What do we make of a father who announces that he will be late for work because his son has a routine medical checkup? Consciously or unconsciously, we are likely to assume that flying a commercial plane is a *man's* job and that most parental duties are, in fact, *maternal* duties. Gender is such a routine part of our everyday activities that we typically take notice only when someone deviates from conventional behavior and expectations.

Although a few people begin life with an unclear sexual identity, the overwhelming majority begin with a definite sex and quickly receive societal messages about how to behave. In fact, many societies have established social distinctions between females and males that do not inevitably result from biological differences between the sexes (such as women's reproductive capabilities).

In studying gender, sociologists are interested in the gender-role socialization that leads females and males to behave differently. In Chapter 4, **gender roles** were defined as expectations regarding the proper behavior, attitudes, and activities of males and females. The application of traditional gender roles leads to many forms of differentiation between women and men. Both sexes are physically capable of learning to cook and sew, yet most Western societies determine that women should perform these tasks. Both men and women are capable of learning to weld and fly airplanes, but those functions are generally assigned to men.

Gender roles are evident not only in our work and behavior but also in how we react to others. We are constantly "doing gender" without realizing it. If the father just discussed sits in the doctor's office with his son in the middle of a workday, he will probably receive approving glances from the receptionist and from other patients. "Isn't he a wonderful father?" runs through their minds. But if the boy's mother leaves *her* job and sits with the son in the doctor's office, she will not receive such silent applause.

We construct our behavior socially so as to create or exaggerate male–female differences. For example, men and women come in a variety of heights, sizes, and ages. Yet traditional norms regarding marriage and even casual dating tell us that in heterosexual couples, the man should be older, taller, and wiser than the woman. As we will see throughout this chapter, such social norms help to reinforce and legitimize patterns of male dominance.

In recent decades, women have increasingly entered occupations and professions previously dominated by men. Yet our society still focuses on "masculine" and "feminine" qualities, as if men and women must be evaluated in those terms. Clearly, we continue to "do gender," and our construction of gender continues to define significantly different expectations for females and males (Lorber 1994; Rosenbaum 1996; West and Zimmerman 1987).

Gender Roles in the United States

Gender-Role Socialization

Male babies get blue blankets; females get pink ones. Boys are expected to play with trucks, blocks, and toy soldiers; girls receive dolls and kitchen goods. Boys must be masculine—active, aggressive, tough, daring, and dominant—but girls must be feminine—soft, emotional, sweet, and submissive. These traditional gender-role patterns have been influential in the socialization of children in the United States.

An important element in traditional views of proper "masculine" and "feminine" behavior is ***homophobia,*** fear of and prejudice against homosexuality. Homophobia contributes significantly to rigid gender-role socialization, since many people stereotypically associate male homosexuality with femininity and lesbianism with masculinity. Consequently, men and women who deviate from traditional expectations about gender roles are often presumed to be gay. Despite the advances made by the gay liberation movement, the continuing stigma attached to homosexuality in our culture places pressure on all males (whether gay or not) to exhibit only narrow "masculine" behavior and on all females (whether lesbian or not) to exhibit only narrow "feminine" behavior (Seidman 1994; see also Lehne 1995).

It is *adults,* of course, who play a critical role in guiding children into those gender roles deemed appropriate in a society. Parents are normally the first and p. 92 most crucial agents of socialization. But other adults, older siblings, the mass media, and religious

Society often exaggerates male–female differences in appearance and behavior. In 1964, the G.I. Joe doll (left) had a realistic appearance, but by 1992 (middle) it had begun to acquire the exaggerated muscularity characteristic of professional wrestlers (right). The change intensified the contrast with ultrathin female figures, like the Barbie doll (Angier 1998).

Classroom Tip See "Gender Differences in Child Care" (Class Discussion Topics).
Theory Interactionist approach to the social construction of gender and gender-role socialization
Classroom Tip See "Gender Socialization" and "Homophobia" (Class Discussion Topics).

Let's Discuss Are G.I. Joe and other action toys boys' dolls? What is the significance of these toys for future parenting roles?
Classroom Tip See "Superhero Comic Books and Gender Analysis" (Class Discussion Topics).
Reel Society See Gender Roles in the Topic Index.

Table 11-1	An Experiment in Gender Norm Violation by College Students	
Norm Violations by Women		**Norm Violations by Men**
Send men flowers		Wear fingernail polish
Spit in public		Needlepoint in public
Use men's bathroom		Throw Tupperware party
Buy jock strap		Cry in public
Buy/chew tobacco		Have pedicure
Talk knowledgeably about cars		Apply to baby-sit
Open doors for men		Shave body hair

Source: Nielsen et al. 2000:287.

In an experiment testing gender-role stereotypes, sociology students were asked to behave in ways that might be regarded as violations of gender norms, and to keep notes on how others reacted. This is a sample of their choices of behavior over a seven-year period. Do you agree that these actions test the boundaries of conventional gender behavior?

and educational institutions also exert an important influence on gender-role socialization, in the United States and elsewhere.

It is not hard to test how rigid gender-role socialization can be. Just try transgressing some gender norm—say, by smoking a cigar in public if you are female, or by carrying a purse if you are male. That was exactly the assignment given to sociology students at the University of Colorado and Luther College in Iowa. Professors asked students to behave in ways that they thought violated norms of how a man or woman should act. The students had no trouble coming up with gender-norm transgressions (see Table 11-1), and they kept careful notes on others' reactions to their behavior, ranging from amusement to disgust (Nielsen et al. 2000).

Women's Gender Roles

How does a girl come to develop a feminine self-image, while a boy develops one that is masculine? In part, they do so by identifying with females and males in their families and neighborhoods and in the media. If a young girl regularly sees female television characters working as defense attorneys and judges, she may believe that she herself can become a lawyer. And it will not hurt if women that she knows—her mother, sister, parents' friends, or neighbors—are lawyers. In contrast, if this young girl sees women portrayed on television only as models, nurses, and secretaries, her identification and self-image will be quite different. Even if she does become a professional, she may secretly regret falling short of the media stereo-

type—a shapely, sexy young woman in a bathing suit.

Television is far from alone in stereotyping women. Studies of children's books published in the United States in the 1940s, 1950s, and 1960s found that females were significantly underrepresented in central roles and illustrations. Virtually all female characters were portrayed as helpless, passive, incompetent, and in need of a strong male caretaker. Studies of picture books published from the 1970s through the 1990s found some improvement, but males still dominated the central roles. While males were portrayed as a variety of characters, females tended to be shown mostly in traditional roles, such as mother, grandmother, or volunteer, even if they also held nontraditional roles, such as working professional (Etaugh 2003).

Social research on gender roles reveals some persistent differences between men and women in North America and Europe. Women tend to feel pressure both to marry and to become a mother. Often, marriage is viewed as their true entry into adulthood. And women are expected not only to become mothers but to *want* to be mothers. Obviously, men play a role in marriage and parenthood, but also these events do not appear to be as critical in the life course of a man. Society defines men's identities by their economic success. And even though many women today fully expect to have careers and achieve recognition in the labor force, success at work is not as important to their identity as it is for men (Doyle and Paludi 1998; Russo 1976).

Traditional gender roles have restricted females more severely than males. This chapter shows how women have been confined to subordinate roles within the political and economic institutions of the United States. Yet it is also true that gender roles have restricted males.

Men's Gender Roles

Stay-at-home fathers? Until recent decades such an idea was unthinkable. Yet in a nationwide survey done in 2002, 69 percent of respondents said that if one parent stays home with the children, it makes no difference whether that parent is the mother or the father. Only 30 percent thought that the mother should be the one to stay home. But while people's conceptions of gender roles are obviously changing, the fact is that men who stay home to

Web Resource The interactive activity in the student center of the Online Learning Center (**www.mhhe.com/schaefer6**) allows students to indicate their agreement or disagreement with the gender norm violations in Table 11-1.
Contemporary Culture How are women portrayed on MTV? On weekly television sitcoms? In the movies?

Methods Content analysis of gender stereotyping in children's books
Theory Conflict theorists note that women have been confined to subordinate roles.
Student Alert When we speak of gender roles, it is important to recognize that male gender roles are as evident as female gender roles.

care for their children are still an unusual phenomenon. In 2001, for every stay-at-home dad there were about seven married stay-at-home moms (Bureau of the Census 2002a:374; Robison 2002).

While attitudes toward parenting may be changing, studies show little change in the traditional male gender role. Men's roles are socially constructed in much the same way as women's roles are. Family, peers, and the media all influence how a boy or a man comes to view his appropriate role in society. Robert Brannon (1976) and James Doyle (1995) have identified five aspects of the male gender role:

- Antifeminine element—show no "sissy stuff," including any expression of openness or vulnerability.
- Success element—prove one's masculinity at work and sports.
- Aggressive element—use force in dealing with others.
- Sexual element—initiate and control all sexual relations.
- Self-reliant element—keep cool and unflappable.

No systematic research has established all these elements as necessarily common to all males, but specific studies have confirmed individual elements.

Males who do not conform to the socially constructed gender role face constant criticism and even humiliation, both from children when they are boys and from adults as men. It can be agonizing to be treated as a "chicken" or a "sissy" as a youth—particularly if such remarks come from one's father or brothers. And grown men who pursue nontraditional occupations, such as preschool teaching or nursing, must constantly deal with others' misgivings and strange looks. In one study, interviewers found that such men frequently had to alter their behavior in order to minimize others' negative reactions. One 35-year-old nurse reported that he had to claim he was "a carpenter or something like that" when he "went clubbing," because women weren't interested in getting to know a male nurse. The subjects made similar accommodations in casual exchanges with other men (Cross and Bagilhole 2002:215).

At the same time, boys who successfully adapt to cultural standards of masculinity may grow up to be inexpressive men who cannot share their feelings with others. They remain forceful and tough, but as a result they are also closed and isolated. In fact, a small but growing body of scholarship suggests that for men as well as women, traditional gender roles may be disadvantageous. In many communities across the nation, girls seem to outdo boys in high school, grabbing a disproportionate share of the lead-

ership positions, from valedictorian to class president to yearbook editor—everything, in short, except captain of the boys' athletic teams. Their advantage continues after high school. In the 1980s, girls in the United States became more likely than boys to go to college. By 2001, women accounted for over 57 percent of college students nationwide. And in 2002, for the first time, more women than men in the United States earned doctoral degrees (Faludi 1999; McCreary 1994; Sheehy 1999; Smallwood 2003).

Some of this discrepancy in achievment can be explained by noting that men can earn good hourly wages with less formal schooling than women. Yet by a number of measures, girls appear to take schooling more seriously than boys. In 2002, for example, female students taking the Advanced Placement (AP) tests outnumbered male students in 19 out of 33 subjects. Overall, they accounted for 54 percent of students who took the AP tests. Educational professionals need to look more closely at men's underperformance in school, not to mention their overrepresentation in reported crime and illegal drug use (Bureau of the Census 2003a:176, 183; Conlin 2003; Rollins 2003; Smallwood 2003; Sommers 2000).

In the last 40 years, inspired in good part by the contemporary feminist movement (examined later in the chapter), increasing numbers of men in the United States have criticized the restrictive aspects of the traditional male gender role. Some men have taken strong public positions in support of women's struggle for full equality, and have even organized voluntary associations such as the National Organization for Men Against Sexism (NOMAS), founded in 1975 to support positive changes for men. Nevertheless, the traditional male gender role remains well entrenched as an influential element of our culture (Messner 1997; National Organization for Men Against Sexism 2003).

Use Your Sociological Imagination www.mhhe.com/schaefer6

You are living in a society in which there are no gender roles. What is your life like?

Cross-Cultural Perspective

To what extent do actual biological differences between the sexes contribute to the cultural differences associated with gender? This question brings us back to the debate over "nature versus nurture." In assessing the alleged and real differences between men and women, it is useful to examine cross-cultural data.

pp. 81–84

The research of anthropologist Margaret Mead points to the importance of cultural conditioning—as opposed to biology—in defining the social roles of males

Cultural conditioning is important in the development of gender role differences. Among the Bororo, a semi-nomadic people of West Africa, the male gender role includes ceremonial dancing, body painting, and other forms of personal adornment.

and females. In *Sex and Temperament,* Mead ([1935] 2001; 1973) describes the typical behaviors of each sex in three different cultures in New Guinea:

> In one [the Arapesh], both men and women act as we expect women to act—in a mild parental responsive way; in the second [the Mundugumor], both act as we expect men to act—in a fierce initiating fashion; and in the third [the Tchambuli], the men act according to our stereotypes for women—are catty, wear curls, and go shopping—while the women are energetic, managerial, unadorned partners. (Preface to 1950 ed.)

If biology determined all differences between the sexes, then cross-cultural differences, such as those described by Mead, would not exist. Her findings confirm the influential role of culture and socialization in gender-role differentiation. There appears to be no innate or biological reason to designate completely different gender roles for men and women.

In any society, gender stratification requires not only individual socialization into traditional gender roles within the family, but the promotion and support of those traditional roles by other social institutions, such as religion and education. Moreover, even with all major institutions socializing the young into conventional gender roles, every society has women and men who resist and successfully oppose the stereotypes: strong women who become leaders or professionals, gentle men who care

for children, and so forth. It seems clear that differences between the sexes are not dictated by biology. Indeed, the maintenance of traditional gender roles requires constant social controls—and those controls are not always effective.

We can see the social construction of gender roles in process in societies strained by war and social upheaval. By summer 2004, a year after the war in Iraq began, young girls in Baghdad seldom ventured out to the park or swimming pool. When they did, their parents made sure they were dressed conservatively, in loose clothing and perhaps a headscarf. The overthrow of Saddam Hussein's secular regime had emboldened Islamic fundamentalists, who had begun visiting schools, urging young women to wear long sleeves and cover their heads. Though school officials resisted, many girls dropped out, some out of fear for their safety and others because of financial hardship. In the atmosphere of violence and lawlessness that followed the 2003 invasion, young women wondered what the future would hold for them, and whether they would ever have the opportunity to become educated professionals, as their mothers had (Sengupta 2004).

EXPLAINING STRATIFICATION BY GENDER

Cross-cultural studies indicate that societies dominated by men are much more common than those in which women play the decisive role. Sociologists have turned to all the major theoretical perspectives to understand how and why these social distinctions are established. Each approach focuses on culture rather than biology as the primary determinant of gender differences. Yet in other respects, advocates of these sociological perspectives disagree widely.

The Functionalist View

Functionalists maintain that gender differentiation has contributed to overall social stability. Sociologists Talcott Parsons and Robert Bales (1955) argued that to function most effectively, the family requires adults who specialize

Global View Mead's cross-cultural anthropological research in New Guinea
Methods Mead conducted observation research on three New Guinea cultures.

Theory Functionalist view of gender stratification
Key Persons Talcott Parsons, Robert Bales

in particular roles. They viewed the traditional gender roles as arising out of the need to establish a division of labor between marital partners.

Parsons and Bales contended that women take the expressive, emotionally supportive role and men the instrumental, practical role, with the two complementing each other. *Instrumentality* refers to an emphasis on tasks, a focus on more distant goals, and a concern for the external relationship between one's family and other social institutions. *Expressiveness* denotes concern for the maintenance of harmony and the internal emotional affairs of the family. According to this theory, women's interest in expressive goals frees men for instrumental tasks, and vice versa. Women become anchored in the family as wives, mothers, and household managers; men become anchored in the occupational world outside the home. Of course, Parsons and Bales offered this framework in the 1950s, when many more women were full-time homemakers than is true today. These theorists did not explicitly endorse traditional gender roles, but they implied that dividing tasks between spouses was functional for the family as a unit.

Given the typical socialization of women and men in the United States, the functionalist view is initially persuasive. However, it would lead us to expect girls and women who have no interest in children to become babysitters and mothers. Similarly, males who love spending time with children might be programmed into careers in the business world. Such differentiation might harm the individual who does not fit into prescribed roles, as well as deprive society of the contributions of many talented people who feel confined by gender stereotyping. Moreover, the functionalist approach does not convincingly explain why men should be assigned categorically to the instrumental role, and women to the expressive role.

The Conflict Response

Viewed from a conflict perspective, the functionalist approach masks the underlying power relations between men and women. Parsons and Bales never explicitly presented the expressive and instrumental roles as being of unequal value to society, yet their inequality is quite evident. Although social institutions may pay lip service to women's expressive skills, men's instrumental skills are more highly rewarded, whether in terms of money or prestige. Consequently, according to feminists and conflict theorists, any division of labor by gender into instrumental and expressive tasks is far from neutral in its impact on women.

Conflict theorists contend that the relationship between females and males has traditionally been one of

Theory Conflict critique of Parsons and Bales's functionalist approach
Theory Conflict view of gender stratification

unequal power, with men in a dominant position over women. Men may originally have become powerful in preindustrial times because their size, physical strength, and freedom from childbearing duties allowed them to dominate women physically. In contemporary societies, such considerations are not so important, yet cultural beliefs about the sexes are long established, as anthropologist Margaret Mead and feminist sociologist Helen Mayer Hacker (1951, 1974) both stressed. Such beliefs support a social structure that places males in controlling positions.

Conflict theorists, then, see gender differences as a reflection of the subjugation of one group (women) by another group (men). If we use an analogy to Marx's analysis

pp. 12, 207 of class conflict, we can say that males are like the bourgeoisie, or capitalists; they control most of the society's wealth, prestige, and power. Females are like the proletariat, or workers; they can acquire valuable resources only by following the dictates of their bosses. Men's work is uniformly valued; women's work (whether unpaid labor in the home or wage labor) is devalued.

The Feminist Perspective

A significant component of the conflict approach to gen-

p. 16 der stratification draws on feminist theory. Although use of that term is comparatively recent, the critique of women's position in society and culture goes back to some of the earliest works that have influenced sociology. Among the most important are Mary Wollstonecraft's *A Vindication of the Rights of Women* (originally published in 1792), John Stuart Mill's *The Subjection of Women* (originally published in 1869), and Friedrich Engels's *The Origin of the Family, Private Property, and the State* (originally published in 1884).

Engels, a close associate of Karl Marx, argued that women's subjugation coincided with the rise of private property during industrialization. Only when people moved beyond an agrarian economy could males enjoy the luxury of leisure and withhold rewards and privileges from women. Drawing on the work of Marx and Engels, contemporary feminist theorists often view women's subordination as part of the overall exploitation and injustice that they see as inherent in capitalist societies. Some radical feminist theorists, however, view the oppression of women as inevitable in *all* male-dominated societies, whether they are labeled capitalist, socialist, or communist (Feuer 1989; Tuchman 1992).

Feminist sociologists would find little to disagree with in the conflict theorists' perspective but are more likely to embrace a political agenda. Feminists would also argue that until recently, the very discussion of women and society, however well meant, was distorted by the exclusion of

Key Persons Mary Wollstonecraft, John Stuart Mill, Friedrich Engels
Methods Sociological studies have traditionally focused on males to the exclusion of females.

Stratification by Gender and Age 277

In April 2002, the Congressional Women's Caucus conferred with Kofi Annan, secretary general of the United Nations, at his office in New York. Despite some gains, women are still underrepresented in Congress.

The Interactionist Approach

While functionalists and conflict theorists who study gender stratification typically focus on macro-level social forces and institutions, interactionist researchers tend to examine gender stratification on the micro level of everyday behavior. As an example, studies show that men initiate up to 96 percent of all interruptions in cross-sex (male–female) conversations. Men are more likely than women to change the topic of conversation, to ignore topics chosen by members of the opposite sex, to minimize the contributions and ideas of members of the opposite sex, and to validate their own contributions. These patterns reflect the conversational (and in a sense, political) dominance of males. Moreover, even when women occupy a prestigious position, such as that of physician, they are more likely to be interrupted than their male counterparts (Ridgeway and Smith-Lovin 1999; Tannen 1990; West and Zimmerman 1983).

These findings regarding cross-sex conversations have been frequently replicated. They have striking implications when one considers the power dynamics underlying likely cross-sex interactions—employer and job seeker, college professor and student, husband and wife, to name just a few. From an interactionist perspective, these simple, day-to-day exchanges are one more battleground in the struggle for gender equality—as women try to get a word in edgewise in the midst of men's interruptions and verbal dominance (Hollander 2002; Okamoto and Smith-Lovin 2001; Tannen 1994a, 1994b).

women from academic thought, including sociology. We have noted the many accomplishments of Jane Addams pp. 13, 16 and Ida Wells-Barnett, but they generally worked outside the discipline, focusing on what we would now call applied sociology and social work. At the time their efforts, while valued as humanitarian, were seen as unrelated to the research and conclusions being reached in academic circles, which of course were male academic circles (Andersen 1997; J. Howard 1999).

Feminist theorists today (including conflict theorists) emphasize that in the United States male dominance goes far beyond the economic sphere. Throughout this textbook, we examine disturbing aspects of men's behavior toward women. The ugly realities of rape, wife battering, sexual harassment, and street harassment all illustrate and intensify women's subordinate position. Even if women reach economic parity with men, even if they win equal representation in government, genuine equality between the sexes cannot be achieved if these attacks remain as common as they are today.

Functionalist, conflict, and feminist theorists acknowledge that it is not possible to change gender roles drastically without making dramatic revisions in a culture's social structure. Functionalists perceive the potential for social disorder, or at least unknown social consequences, if all aspects of traditional gender stratification are disturbed. Yet for conflict and feminist theorists, no social structure is ultimately desirable if it is maintained by oppressing a majority of citizens. These theorists argue that gender stratification may be functional for men—who hold the power and privilege—but it is hardly in the interests of women.

WOMEN: THE OPPRESSED MAJORITY

Many people, both male and female, find it difficult to conceive of women as a subordinate and oppressed group. Yet take a look at the political structure of the United States: Women remain noticeably underrepresented. In 2003, for example, only 6 of the nation's 50 states had a female governor (Arizona, Delaware, Hawaii, Kansas, Michigan, and Montana).

Women have made slow but steady progress in certain political arenas. In 1981, out of 535 members of Congress, there were only 21 women: 19 in the House of Representatives and 2 in the Senate. In contrast, the Congress

Key Persons Jane Addams, Ida Wells-Barnett (see additional information in Chapter 1)
Classroom Tip See "Gender Stratification on the Micro Level" (Class Discussion Topics).

Theory Interactionist view of gender stratification
Classroom Tip See "Gendered Spaces" (Additional Lecture Ideas).
Methods Experiments on dominance in cross-sex conversations
Contemporary Culture Only 6 percent of the nation's 50 states had a female governor in 2003.

11-1   GENDER DIFFERENCES IN PHYSICIANS' COMMUNICATION WITH PATIENTS

When Perri Klass told her four-year-old son she would be taking him to the pediatrician, he replied, "Is she a nice doctor?" Klass, a professor of pediatrics, was struck by his innocent assumption that like his mother, all pediatricians were female. "Boys can be doctors too," she told him.

Not long ago, there would have been little potential for confusion on her son's part. Klass probably would not have been admitted to medical school, no less appointed a professor of medicine. But since the advent of the women's movement, the medical profession has been integrating women into its ranks. Now, more than two dozen studies done over the past three and a half decades indicate that not only are women competent physicians; in some respects they are more effective than their male counterparts.

The female advantage is particularly noteworthy in physician–patient communication. Female primary care physicians spend an extra two minutes talking with patients, or 10 percent more time than male primary care physicians. They also engage in more patient-centered communication, listening more, asking questions about patients' personal well-being, and counseling patients about the

> Not only are women competent physicians; in some respects they are more effective than their male counterparts.

concerns they bring to the doctor's office. Perhaps most important, female physicians tend to see their relationship with patients as an active partnership, one in which they discuss several treatment options with patients rather than recommending a single course of treatment. From a sociological point of view, these differences between female and male physicians correspond to the gender differences in communication style that interactionist researchers have noted.

In some respects, female and male physicians do not differ. Researchers noted no differences in the quality or amount of time the two groups spend on purely medical matters, or on the length of time they spend conversing socially with patients.

Let's Discuss

1. In your own experience, have you noted a gender difference in the way doctors communicate with their patients? Explain.
2. Why is the quality of a doctor's communication with patients important? What might be the benefit of female physicians' superior communication style?

Sources: Carroll 2003; Klass 2003:319; Roter et al. 2002.

that took office in January 2003 had 72 women: 59 in the House and 13 in the Senate. Yet the membership and leadership of Congress remain overwhelmingly male (Center for American Women and Politics 2003).

In October 1981, Sandra Day O'Connor was sworn in as the nation's first female Supreme Court justice. Still, no woman has ever served as president of the United States, vice president, speaker of the House of Representatives, or chief justice of the Supreme Court.

Sexism and Sex Discrimination

Just as African Americans are victimized by racism, women suffer from sexism in our society. *Sexism* is the ideology that one sex is superior to the other. The term is generally used to refer to male prejudice and discrimination against women. In Chapter 10, we noted that Blacks can suffer from both individual acts of racism and institutional discrimination. *Institutional discrimination*

was defined as the denial of opportunities and equal rights to individuals and groups that results from the normal operations of a society. In the same sense, women suffer from both individual acts of sexism (such as sexist remarks and acts of violence) and institutional sexism.

It is not simply that particular men in the United States are biased in their treatment of women. All the major institutions of our society—including the government, armed forces, large corporations, the media, universities, and the medical establishment—are controlled by men. These institutions, in their normal, day-to-day operations, often discriminate against women and perpetuate sexism. For example, if the central office of a nationwide bank sets a policy that single women are a bad risk for loans—regardless of their incomes and investments—that bank will discriminate against women in state after state. It will do so even at branches where loan officers hold no personal biases toward women, but are merely "following orders." Box 11-1 dispels the sexist myth that women cannot be

Contemporary Culture In what other traditionally male occupations might women be more effective than men? In what ways, and why?

Key Person Justice Sandra Day O'Connor
Student Alert Note that Justice O'Connor was appointed, not elected.
Theory Conflict view of institutional discrimination against women

good doctors, which medical schools used for years to justify their discriminatory admissions policies.

Our society is run by male-dominated institutions, yet with the power that flows to men come responsibility and stress. Men have higher reported rates of certain types of mental illness than women, and a greater likelihood of death due to heart attack or stroke. The pressure on men to succeed, and then to remain on top in the competitive world of work, can be especially intense. That is not to suggest that gender stratification is as damaging to men as it is to women. But it is clear that the power and privilege men enjoy are no guarantee of personal well-being.

Sexual Harassment

The courts recognize two kinds of sexual harassment. Formally defined, *sexual harassment* is behavior that occurs when work benefits are made contingent on sexual favors (as a quid pro quo), or when touching, lewd comments, or the exhibition of pornographic material creates a "hostile environment" in the workplace. In 1998, the Supreme Court ruled that harassment applies to people of the same sex as well as the opposite. The quid pro quo type of harassment is fairly easy to identify in a court of law. But the issue of hostile environment has become the subject of considerable debate both in courts and in the general public (L. Greenhouse 1998; Lewin 1998).

Sexual harassment must be understood in the context of continuing prejudice and discrimination against women. Whether it occurs in the federal bureaucracy, in the corporate world, or in universities, sexual harassment generally takes place in organizations in which White males are at the top of the hierarchy of authority, and women's work is valued less than men's. One survey of the private sector found that African American women were three times more likely than White women to experience sexual harassment. From a conflict perspective, it is not surprising that women—and especially women of color—are most likely to become victims of sexual harassment. In terms of job security, these groups are typically an organization's most vulnerable employees (J. Jones 1988).

Use Your Sociological Imagination | www.mhhe.com/schaefer6

How would Naomi Wolf (author of *The Beauty Myth*) interpret the problem of sexual harassment?

The Status of Women Worldwide

A detailed overview of the status of the world's women, issued by the United Nations in 2000, noted that women and men live in different worlds—worlds that differ in terms of access to education and work opportunities, as well as in health, personal security, and human rights. The Hindu culture of India, for example, makes life especially harsh for widows. When Hindu women marry, they join their husband's family. If the husband dies, the widow is the "property" of that family. In many cases, she ends up working as an unpaid servant; in others she is simply abandoned and left penniless. Ancient Hindu scriptures portray widows as "inauspicious" and advise that "a wise man should avoid her blessings like the poison of a snake" (Burns 1998:10). (Though Westerners tend to view Muslim societies as being similarly harsh toward women, that perception is actually an overgeneralization. Muslim countries are exceedingly varied and complex and do not often fit the stereotypes created by the Western media.)

It is estimated that women grow half the world's food, but they rarely own land. They constitute one-third of the world's paid labor force, but are generally found in the lowest-paying jobs. Single-parent households headed by women, which appear to be on the increase in many nations, are typically found in the poorest sections of the population. The feminization of poverty has become a global phenomenon. As in the United States, women around the world are underrepresented politically.

While acknowledging that much has been done to sharpen people's awareness of gender inequities, a UN report issued in 2000 identified several continuing concerns:

- Despite their advances in higher education, women still face major barriers when they attempt to use their educational achievements to advance in the workplace. For example, women rarely hold more than 1 to 2 percent of top executive positions.
- Women almost always work in occupations with lower status and pay scales than men. In both developing and developed countries, many women work as unpaid family laborers. (Figure 11-1 shows the paid labor force participation of women in seven industrialized countries.)
- Despite social norms regarding support and protection, many widows around the world receive little concrete support from extended family networks.
- In many African and a few Asian nations, traditions mandate the cutting of female genitals, typically by practitioners who fail to use sterilized instruments. This practice can lead to immediate and serious complications, from infection to long-term health problems.
- While males outnumber females as refugees, refugee women have unique needs, such as protection against physical and sexual abuse (United Nations 2000).

Classroom Tip Have an administrator come to the class to discuss the sexual harassment policy on campus.
Theory Conflict analysis of sexual harassment
Global View Analysis of the status of women worldwide

Classroom Tip See "The Head Scarf and the Veil" (Additional Lecture Ideas).
Classroom Tip See "Gender Dominance in Jobs Cross-Culturally" in Topics and Sources for Student Research.

Despite these challenges, women are not responding passively; they are mobilizing, individually and collectively. Given the significant underrepresentation of women in government offices and national legislatures, however, the task is difficult, as we shall see in Chapter 14.

What conclusions can we draw about women's inequality worldwide? First, as anthropologist Laura Nader (1986:383) has observed, even in the relatively more egalitarian nations of the West, women's subordination is "institutionally structured and culturally rationalized, exposing them to conditions of deference, dependency, powerlessness, and poverty." While the situation of women in Sweden and the United States is significantly better than that of women in Saudi Arabia and Bangladesh, women nevertheless remain in a second-class position in the world's most affluent and developed countries.

Second, there is a link between the wealth of industrialized nations and the poverty of developing countries. Viewed from a conflict perspective or through the lens of Immanuel Wallerstein's world systems analysis, the economies of developing nations are controlled and exploited by industrialized countries and multinational corporations based in those countries. Much of the exploited labor in developing nations, especially in the nonindustrial sector, is performed by women. Women workers typically toil long hours for low pay, but contribute significantly to their families' incomes (Jacobson 1993).

◀ pp. 222–226

Women in the Workforce of the United States

Almost 30 years ago, the United States Commission on Civil Rights (1976:1) concluded that the passage in the Declaration of Independence proclaiming that "all men are created equal" has been taken too literally for too long—especially with respect to women's opportunities for employment. In this section we will see how gender bias has limited women's opportunities for employment outside the home, at the same time that it forces them to carry a disproportionate burden inside the home.

Global View Second-class status of women in the United States, Sweden, Saudi Arabia, and Bangladesh
Theory From a conflict view, the subordinate status of Third World women is linked to the exploitation of developing countries by Western industrialized nations.

FIGURE 11-1

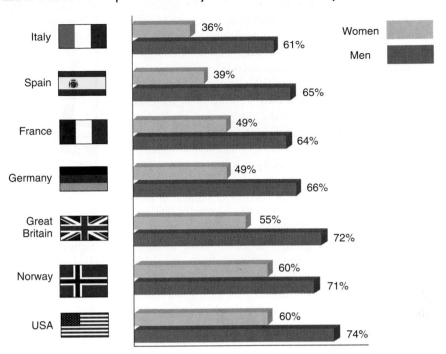

Labor Force Participation Rates by Gender and Country, 2001

	Women	Men
Italy	36%	61%
Spain	39%	65%
France	49%	64%
Germany	49%	66%
Great Britain	55%	72%
Norway	60%	71%
USA	60%	74%

Source: Department of Labor 2003b.

Think About It

In all countries, what appears to be the relationship between gender and participation in the labor force? What can be said about the relationship between country and labor force participation?

A Statistical Overview

Women's participation in the paid labor force of the United States increased steadily throughout the 20th century (see Figure 11-2, page 282). No longer is the adult woman associated solely with the role of homemaker. Instead, millions of women—married and single, with and without children—are working in the paid labor force. In 2002, 60 percent of adult women in the United States held jobs outside the home, compared with 38 percent in 1960. A majority of women are now members of the paid labor force. Among new mothers, 56 percent return to the labor force within a year of giving birth. As recently as 1975 only 29 percent went back to work (Bureau of the Census 2003a:390, 391).

Yet women entering the job market find their options restricted in important ways. Particularly damaging is occupational segregation, or confinement to sex-typed "women's jobs." For example, in 2001, women accounted for 98 percent of all secretaries and dental assistants and 86 percent of all librarians. Entering such sex-typed

Classroom Tip See "Feminization of the Banking Industry" (Additional Lecture Ideas).
Let's Discuss What proportion of your school's administrators, senior faculty, and junior faculty are women?
Theory Conflict view of occupational segregation by gender in the United States

occupations places women in "service" roles that parallel the traditional gender-role standard under which housewives "serve" their husbands.

Women are *underrepresented* in occupations historically defined as "men's jobs," which often carry much greater financial rewards and prestige than women's jobs. For example, in 2001, women accounted for approximately 47 percent of the paid labor force of the United States. Yet they constituted only 11 percent of all engineers, 19 percent of all dentists, 28 percent of all computer systems analysts, and 31 percent of all physicians (see Table 11-2).

Such occupational segregation is not unique to the United States but typical of industrial countries. In Great Britain, for example, only 29 percent of computer analysts are women, while 81 percent of cashiers and 90 percent of nurses are women (Cross and Bagilhole 2002).

Women from all groups and men from minority groups sometimes encounter attitudinal or organizational bias that prevents them from reaching their full potential. As we saw in Chapter 10, the term **glass ceiling** refers to an invisible barrier that blocks the promotion of a qualified individual in a work environment because of the individual's gender, race, or ethnicity. A study of the Fortune 1,000 largest corporations in the United States showed that less than 15 percent of the seats on their boards of directors were held by women in 2002 (G. Strauss 2002).

One response to the glass ceiling and other types of gender bias in the workplace is to start your own business and work for yourself. This route to success, traditionally taken by men from immigrant and racial minority groups, has become more common among women as

they have increasingly sought paid employment outside the home. According to the latest data, women own an impressive 5.4 million businesses in the United States. However, many of these operations are very small, self-run firms. Only 16 percent of women-owned businesses have any paid employees (Bureau of the Census 2003a:508).

The workplace patterns described here have one crucial result: women earn less money than men in the paid labor force. A study done by the General Accounting Office (2002) compared managerial salaries for women and men in the 10 industries that employ 70 percent of women workers, including entertainment, insurance, retailing, public administration, and education. Women managers came closest to matching men's salaries in education, where those who worked full time earned 91 cents for every dollar received by their male counterparts. But on average, women earned only about 78 cents for every

FIGURE 11-2

Trends in U.S. Women's Participation in the Paid Labor Force, 1890–2002

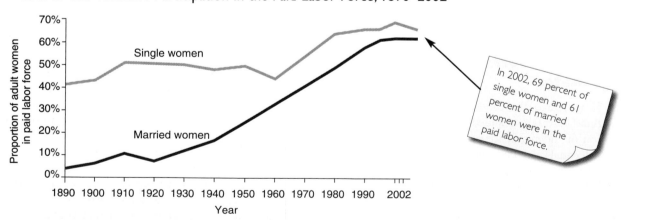

Sources: Bureau of the Census 1975; 2003a:390.

dollar earned by men. Particularly troubling was the finding that in most industries, the male–female earnings gap actually widened between 1995 and 2000. The gap remained even after researchers adjusted their findings for variables such as education, age, and marital status. The glass ceiling is very firm.

While women may well be at a disadvantage in male-dominated occupations, the same is not true for men in female-dominated occupations. Sociologist Michelle Budig (2002) examined a national database containing career information on more than 12,000 men, collected over the course of 15 years. She found that men were uniformly advantaged in female occupations. Though male nurses, grade school teachers, and librarians may experience some scorn in the larger society, they are much more likely than women to be encouraged to become administrators. Observers of the labor force have termed this advantage for men in female-dominated occupations the *glass escalator*—quite a contrast to the glass ceiling (J. Jacobs 2003; C. L. Williams 1992, 1995).

Table 11-2	U.S. Women in Selected Occupations, 2002: Women as Percentage of All Workers in the Occupation		
Underrepresented		**Overrepresented**	
Firefighters	3%	High school teachers	58%
Airline pilots	4	Social workers	74
Engineers	11	Cashiers	77
Clergy	14	File clerks	82
Police	18	Librarians	82
Dentists	19	Elementary teachers	83
Computer systems analysts	28	Registered nurses	93
Lawyers	29	Receptionists	97
Mail carriers	30	Child care workers	98
Physicians	31	Dental hygienists	98
College teachers	43	Secretaries	99

Source: Bureau of the Census 2003a:399–401.

Social Consequences of Women's Employment

Today, many women face the challenge of trying to juggle work and family. Their situation has many social consequences. For one thing, it puts pressure on child care facilities, public financing of day care, and even the fast-food industry, which provides many of the meals women used to prepare themselves. For another, it raises questions about what responsibility male wage earners have in the household.

Who does the housework when women become productive wage earners? Studies indicate that there is a clear gender gap in the performance of housework, although it has been narrowing. Still, as Figure 11-3 (page 284) shows, one study found women doing more housework and spending more time on child care than men, whether on a workday or a nonworkday. Taken together, then, a woman's workday on and off the job is much longer than a man's. Another recent development, over the last 20 years is women's involvement in elder care. According to national studies, 60 percent of these caregivers are women who typically spend around 18 hours per week caring for a parent (Department of Labor 1998; Kornblum 2004).

Sociologist Arlie Hochschild (1989, 1990) has used the phrase *second shift* to describe the double burden—work outside the home followed by child care and housework—that many women face and few men share equitably. On the basis of interviews with and observations of 52 couples over an eight-year period, Hochschild reports that the wives (and not their husbands) drive home from the office while planning domestic schedules and play dates for children—and then begin their second shift. Drawing on national studies, she concludes that women spend 15 fewer hours each week in leisure activities than their husbands. In a year, these women work an extra month of 24-hour days because of the second shift; over a dozen years, they work an extra year of 24-hour days. Hochschild found that the married couples she studied were fraying at the edges, and so were their careers and their marriages. With such reports in mind, many feminists have advocated greater governmental and corporate support for child care, more flexible family leave policies, and other reforms designed to ease the burden on the nation's families (Mattingly and Bianchi 2003).

pp. 98–99

Most studies of gender, child care, and housework focus on the time actually spent by women and men in performing these duties. However, sociologist Susan Walzer (1996) was interested in whether there are gender differences in the amount of time parents spend *thinking* about the care of their children. Drawing on interviews with 25 couples, Walzer found that mothers are much more involved than fathers in the invisible mental labor

FIGURE 11-3

Gender Differences in Child Care and Housework, 1997

Hours in child care

Workdays | MEN | WOMEN
1977 | 1.8 | 3.3
1997 | 2.3 | 3.0

Non-Workdays
1977 | 5.2 | 7.3
1997 | 6.4 | 8.3

Hours in housework

Workdays | MEN | WOMEN
1977 | 1.2 | 3.7
1997 | 2.2 | 3.1

Non-Workdays
1977 | 4.2 | 7.2
1997 | 5.1 | 6.1

Women still spend more time on child care and housework than men.

Source: Bond et al. 1998:40–41, 44–45.

associated with caring for a baby. For example, while involved in work outside the home, mothers are more likely to think about their babies, and to feel guilty if they become so consumed with the demands of their jobs that they *fail* to think about their babies.

Women: Emergence of a Collective Consciousness

The feminist movement of the United States was born in upstate New York, in a town called Seneca Falls, in the summer of 1848. On July 19, the first women's rights convention began, attended by Elizabeth Cady Stanton, Lucretia Mott, and other pioneers in the struggle for women's rights. This first wave of *feminists,* as they are currently known, battled ridicule and scorn as they fought for legal and political equality for women. They were not afraid to risk controversy on behalf of their cause; in 1872, Susan B. Anthony was arrested for attempting to vote in that year's presidential election.

Ultimately, the early feminists won many victories, among them the passage and ratification of the Nineteenth Amendment to the Constitution, which granted women the right to vote in national elections beginning in 1920. But suffrage did not lead to other reforms in women's social and economic position, and in the early and middle 20th century the women's movement became a much less powerful force for social change.

The second wave of feminism in the United States emerged in the 1960s and came into full force in the 1970s. In part, the movement was inspired by three pioneering books arguing for women's rights: Simone de Beauvoir's *The Second Sex,* Betty Friedan's *The Feminine Mystique,* and Kate Millett's *Sexual Politics.* In addition, the general political activism of the 1960s led women— many of whom were working for Black civil rights or

against the war in Vietnam—to reexamine their own powerlessness. The sexism often found within allegedly progressive and radical political circles convinced many women that they needed to establish their own move-

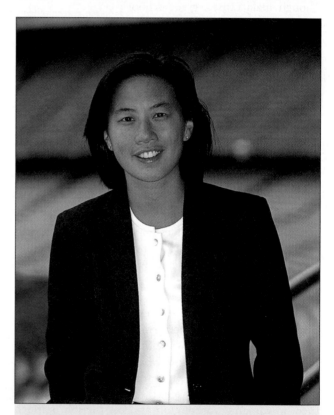

Kim Ng is vice president and assistant general manager of the Los Angeles Dodgers. In the virtually all-male world of major league baseball, she has overcome both racial-ethnic and gender bias, winning a reputation as a tough negotiator in player arbitration cases.

Key Persons Elizabeth Cady Stanton, Lucretia Mott, Susan B. Anthony
Key Persons Simone de Beauvoir, Betty Friedan, Kate Millett

ment for women's liberation (Evans 1980; S. Firestone 1970; Freeman 1973, 1975).

As more and more women became aware of sexist attitudes and practices, including attitudes they themselves had accepted through socialization into traditional gender roles, they began to challenge male dominance. A sense of sisterhood, much like the class consciousness that Marx hoped would emerge in the proletariat, became evident. Individual women identified their interests with those of the collectivity *women*. No longer were women happy in submissive, subordinate roles ("false consciousness" in Marxist terms).

National surveys done today, however, show that while women generally endorse feminist positions, they do not necessarily accept the label *feminist*. Close to 40 percent of women considered themselves feminists in 1989; the proportion dropped to about 20 percent in 1998. Feminism as a unified political cause, requiring one to accept a similar stance on everything from abortion to sexual harassment to pornography to welfare, has fallen out of favor. Both women and men prefer to express their views on these complex issues individually, rather than under a convenient umbrella like feminism. Still, feminism is very much alive in the growing acceptance of women in nontraditional roles, and even the basic acknowledgment that a married mother not only can work outside the home but perhaps *belongs* in the labor force. A majority of women say that given the choice, they would prefer to work outside the home rather than stay home and take care of a house and family, and about one-quarter of women prefer *Ms.* to *Miss* or *Mrs.* (Bellafante 1998; Geyh 1998).

The women's movement has undertaken public protests on a wide range of issues. Feminists have endorsed passage of the equal rights amendment, government subsidies for child care (see Chapter 4), affirmative action for women and minorities (see Chapter 14), federal legislation outlawing sex discrimination in education (see Chapter 13), greater representation of women in government (see Chapter 14), and the right to legal abortions (discussed in the social policy section of this chapter).

Policy Pointer Day care was discussed in the social policy section of Chapter 4, and abortion will be examined in the social policy section at the end of this chapter.
Classroom Tip See "Youth Is America's Best Last Hope" (Class Discussion Topics)

In Korea, certain birthdays are celebrated as milestones, complete with formal feast. At a 60th birthday celebration, for example, all the younger family members bow before the fortunate elder one by one, in order of their ages, and offer gifts. Later they compete with one another in composing poetry and singing songs to mark the occasion. Unfortunately, not all old people are so lucky; in many other cultures, being old is considered next to being dead.

AGING AND SOCIETY

The Sherpas—a Tibetan-speaking Buddhist people in Nepal—live in a culture that idealizes old age. Almost all elderly members of the Sherpa culture own their homes, and most are in relatively good physical condition. Typically, older Sherpas value their independence and prefer not to live with their children. Among the Fulani of Africa, however, older men and women move to the edge of the family homestead. Since that is where people are buried, the elderly sleep over their own graves, for they are viewed socially as already dead. Like gender stratification, age stratification varies from culture to culture. One society may treat older people with great reverence, while another sees them as unproductive and "difficult" (M. Goldstein and Beall 1981; Stenning 1958; Tonkinson 1978).

It is understandable that all societies have some system of age stratification that associates certain social roles with distinct periods in life. Some of this age differentiation seems inevitable; it would make little sense to send young children off to war, or to expect most older citizens to handle physically demanding tasks, such as loading freight at shipyards. However, as is the case with

Global View Aging among the Sherpas in Tibet and the Fulani of Africa stratification by gender, in the United States age stratification goes far beyond the physical constraints of human beings at different ages.

"Being old" is a master status that commonly overshadows all others in the United States. The insights of labeling theory can help us in analyzing the consequences of aging. Once people have been labeled "old," the desig- *p. 188* nation has a major impact on how others perceive them, and even on how they view themselves. Negative stereotypes of the elderly contribute to their position as a minority group subject to discrimination, as we will see later in the chapter.

The model of five basic properties of a minority or subordinate group (introduced in Chapter 10) can be applied to older people in the United States to clarify their *pp. 241–242* subordinate status:

1. The elderly experience unequal treatment in employment, and may face prejudice and discrimination.
2. The elderly share physical characteristics that distinguish them from younger people. In addition, their cultural preferences and leisure-time activities often differ from those of the rest of society.
3. Membership in this disadvantaged group is involuntary.
4. Older people have a strong sense of group solidarity, as is reflected in the growth of senior citizens' centers, retirement communities, and advocacy organizations.
5. Older people generally are married to others of comparable age.

There is one crucial difference between older people and other subordinate groups, such as racial and ethnic minorities or women: *All* of us who live long enough will eventually assume the ascribed status of an older person (Barron 1953; J. Levin and Levin 1980; Wagley and Harris 1958).

EXPLAINING THE AGING PROCESS

Aging is one important aspect of socialization—the lifelong process through which an individual learns the cultural norms and values of a particular society. There are no clear-cut definitions for different periods of the aging cycle in the United States. *Old age* has typically been regarded as beginning at 65, which corresponds to the retirement age for many workers, but not everyone in the United States accepts that definition. With the increase in life expectancy, writers are beginning to refer to people in

their 60s as the "young old," to distinguish them from those in their 80s and beyond (the "old old"). Box 11-2 considers some of the consequences of the growth of both these age groups.

The particular problems of the elderly have become the focus for a specialized field of research and inquiry known as gerontology. *Gerontology* is the scientific study of the sociological and psychological aspects of aging and the problems of the aged. It originated in the 1930s, as an increasing number of social scientists became aware of the plight of the elderly.

Gerontologists rely heavily on sociological principles and theories to explain the impact of aging on the individual and society. They also draw on psychology, anthropology, physical education, counseling, and medicine in their study of the aging process. Two influential views of aging—disengagement theory and activity theory—can be best understood in terms of the sociological perspectives of functionalism and interactionism, respectively. The conflict perspective also contributes to our sociological understanding of aging.

Use Your Sociological Imagination www.mhhe.com/schaefer6

Time has passed, and you are now in your 70s or 80s. How does old age in your generation compare with your parents' or grandparents' experience of old age?

Functionalist Approach: Disengagement Theory

After studying elderly people in good health and relatively comfortable economic circumstances, Elaine Cumming and William Henry (1961) introduced their *disengagement theory,* which implicitly suggests that society and the aging individual mutually sever many of their relationships. In keeping with the functionalist perspective, disengagement theory emphasizes that passing social roles on from one generation to another ensures social stability.

According to this theory, the approach of death forces people to drop most of their social roles—including those of worker, volunteer, spouse, hobby enthusiast, and even reader. Younger members of society then take on these functions. The aging person, it is held, withdraws into an increasing state of inactivity while preparing for death. At the same time, society withdraws from the elderly by segregating them residentially (in retirement homes and communities), educationally (in programs designed solely for senior citizens), and recreationally (in senior citizens' centers). Implicit in disengagement theory is the view that society should *help* older people to withdraw from their accustomed social roles.

Theory Labeling theorists' view of "being old" as a master status
Classroom Tip See "Stereotyping" (Class Discussion Topics).
Student Alert As with race and gender, unequal treatment is the key characteristic in viewing the elderly as a subordinate group.
Global View Treatment of the elderly in the United States
Classroom Tip See "Typology of the Elderly" (Additional Lecture Ideas).

Student Alert Chronological age is an ascribed characteristic, but we are more concerned here with the social meanings attached to age groups.
Theory Disengagement theory as a functionalist view of aging

An electric water kettle is wired so that people in another location can determine if it has been used in the previous 24 hours. This may seem a zany use of modern technology, but it symbolizes a change taking place around the globe—the growing needs of an aging population. The Japanese Welfare Network Ikebukuro Honcho has installed these wired hot pots so that volunteers can monitor whether the elderly have used the devices to prepare their morning tea. An unused pot initiates contacts to see if the older person needs help. This technological monitoring system is an indication of the tremendous growth of Japan's elderly population, and particularly significant, the increasing numbers who live *alone*.

Around the world, there are more than 442 million people aged 65 or over, representing about 7 percent of the world's population. In an important sense, the aging of the world's population represents a major success story that unfolded during the latter years of the 20th century. Through the efforts of both national governments and international agencies, many societies have drastically reduced the incidence of diseases and the rates of death. Consequently, these nations—especially the industrialized countries of Europe and North America—now have increasingly higher proportions of older members.

The overall population of Europe is older than that of any other continent. As the proportion of older people in Europe continues to rise, many governments that have long prided themselves on their

> *An unused pot initiates contacts to see if the older person needs help.*

pension programs have reduced benefits and raised the age at which retired workers can receive benefits. By 2050, Europe's population is projected to have a median age of over 52, compared to 35 in the United States.

In most developing countries, people over 60 are likely to be in poorer health than their counterparts in industrialized nations. Yet few of those countries are in a position to offer extensive financial support to the elderly. Ironically, modernization of the developing world, while bringing with it many social and economic advances, has undercut the traditionally high status of the elderly. In many cultures, the earning power of younger adults now exceeds that of older family members.

Worldwide, governments are beginning to pay attention to population aging and the permanent social transformation it represents. In 1940, of the 227 nations with a population of at least 5,000, only 33 had some form of old-age disability or survivors' program. By 2001 the number stood at 167, or 74 percent of those 227 nations.

Let's Discuss

1. For an older person, how might life in Pakistan differ from life in France?

2. Do you know an aged person who lives alone? What arrangements have been made (or should be made) for the person's care in case of emergency?

Sources: AARP 2004; Bernstein 2003; Hani 1998; Haub 2003; Kinsella and Velkoff 2001; R. Samuelson 2001.

Since it was first outlined more than four decades ago, disengagement theory has generated considerable controversy. Some gerontologists have objected to the implication that older people want to be ignored and put away—and even more to the idea that they should be encouraged to withdraw from meaningful social roles. Critics of disengagement theory insist that society *forces* the elderly into an involuntary and painful withdrawal from the paid labor force and from meaningful social relationships. Rather than voluntarily seeking to disengage, older employees find themselves pushed out of their jobs—in many instances, even before they are entitled to maximum retirement benefits (Boaz 1987).

Although functionalist in its approach, disengagement theory ignores the fact that postretirement employment has been *increasing* in recent decades. In the United States, fewer than half of all employees actually retire from their career jobs. Instead, most move into a "bridge job"—employment that bridges the period between the end of a person's career and his or her retirement. Unfortunately, the elderly can be victimized easily in such "bridge jobs." Psychologist Kathleen Christensen (1990), warning of "bridges over troubled water," emphasizes that older employees do not want to end their working days as minimum-wage jobholders engaged in activities unrelated to their career jobs (Doeringer 1990; Hayward et al. 1987).

Interactionist Approach: Activity Theory

Ask Ruth Vitow if she would like to trade her custom lampshade business in New York City for a condo in Florida, and you will get a quick response: "Deadly! I'd hate it." Vitow, in her 90s, vows to give up her business

These "silver surfers" still enjoy life to the fullest, just as they did when they were young. Staying active and socially involved has been shown to be healthy for the older population.

sulted in more regular contact with family members and friends (Klinenberg 2002; R. Schaefer 1998a).

Often seen as an opposing approach to disengagement theory, *activity theory* suggests that elderly people who remain active and socially involved will be best-adjusted. Proponents of this perspective acknowledge that a 70-year-old person may not have the ability or desire to perform various social roles that he or she had at age 40. Yet they contend that old people have essentially the same need for social interaction as any other group.

The improved health of older people—sometimes overlooked by social scientists—has strengthened the arguments of activity theorists. Illness and chronic disease are no longer quite the scourge of the elderly that they once were. The recent emphasis on fitness, the availability of better medical care, greater control of infectious diseases, and the reduction of fatal strokes and heart attacks have combined to mitigate the traumas of growing old. Accumulating medical research also points to the importance of remaining socially involved. Among those who decline in

"when it gives me up." James Russell Wiggins has been working at a weekly newspaper in Maine since 1922. At age 95 he is now the editor. Vitow and Wiggins are among the 9 percent of the men and 3 percent of the women aged 75 years or older who are still participating in the nation's labor force (Himes 2001).

How important is it for older people to stay actively involved, whether at a job or in other pursuits? A tragic disaster in Chicago in 1995 showed that it can be a matter of life and death. An intense heat wave lasting more than a week—with a heat index exceeding 115 degrees on two consecutive days—resulted in 733 heat-related deaths. About three-fourths of the deceased were 65 and older. Subsequent analysis showed that older people who lived alone had the highest risk of dying, suggesting that support networks for the elderly literally help to save lives. Older Hispanics and Asian Americans had lower death rates from the heat wave than other racial and ethnic groups. Their stronger social networks probably re-

their mental capacities later in life, deterioration is most rapid in those who withdraw from social relationships and activities. Fortunately, the aged are finding new ways to remain socially engaged, as evidenced by their increasing use of the Internet, especially to keep in touch with family and friends (Korczyk 2002).

Admittedly, many activities open to the elderly involve unpaid labor, for which younger adults may receive salaries. Unpaid elderly workers include hospital volunteers (versus aides and orderlies), drivers for charities such as the Red Cross (versus chauffeurs), tutors (as opposed to teachers), and craftspeople for charity bazaars (as opposed to carpenters and dressmakers). However, some companies have recently begun programs to hire retirees for full-time or part-time work.

Though disengagement theory suggests that older people find satisfaction in withdrawal from society, conveniently receding into the background and allowing the next generation to take over, proponents of activity theory

Methods The analysis of deaths from the Chicago heat wave drew on existing sources.
Race/Ethnicity Significance of race and ethnicity in the death rate of older people during the Chicago heat wave

Classroom Tip See "Worried Well Myth" (Additional Lecture Ideas).

Table 11-3	Theoretical Perspectives on Aging		
Sociological Perspective	**View of Aging**	**Social Roles**	**Portrayal of Elderly**
Functionalist	Disengagement	Reduced	Socially isolated
Interactionist	Activity	Changed	Involved in new networks
Conflict	Competition	Relatively unchanged	Victimized, organized to confront their victimization

view such withdrawal as harmful to both the elderly and society. Activity theorists focus on the potential contributions of older people to the maintenance of society. In their opinion, aging citizens will feel satisfied only when they can be useful and productive in society's terms—primarily by working for wages (Civic Ventures 1999; Crosnoe and Elder, Jr. 2002; Dowd 1980; Quadagno 2005).

The Conflict Approach

Conflict theorists have criticized both disengagement theorists and activity theorists for failing to consider the impact of social structure on aging patterns. Neither approach, they say, questions why social interaction must change or decrease in old age. In addition, they often ignore the impact of social class on the lives of the elderly.

The privileged upper class generally enjoys better health and vigor and less likelihood of dependency in old age. Affluence cannot forestall aging indefinitely, but it can soften the economic hardships people face in later years. Although pension plans, retirement packages, and insurance benefits may be developed to assist older people, those whose wealth allows them access to investment funds can generate the greatest income for their later years.

In contrast, the working class often faces greater health hazards and a greater risk of disability; aging is particularly difficult for those who suffer job-related injuries or illnesses. Working-class people also depend more heavily on Social Security benefits and private pension programs. During inflationary times, their relatively fixed incomes from these sources barely keep pace with the escalating costs of food, housing, utilities, and other necessities (Atchley 1985).

Conflict theorists have noted that in the developing world, the transition from agricultural economies to industrialization and capitalism has not always been beneficial to the elderly. As a society's production methods

change, the traditionally valued role of older people tends to erode. Their wisdom is no longer relevant in the new economy.

According to the conflict approach, the treatment of older people in the United States reflects the many divisions in our society. The low status of older people is seen in prejudice and discrimination against them, in age segregation, and in unfair job practices—none of which are directly addressed by either disengagement or activity theory.

In sum, the three perspectives considered here take different views of the elderly. Functionalists portray older people as socially isolated, with reduced social roles; interactionists see them as involved in new networks and changing social roles; conflict theorists see them as victimized by social structure, with their social roles relatively unchanged but devalued. Table 11-3 summarizes these perspectives.

AGE STRATIFICATION IN THE UNITED STATES

The "Graying of America"

When Lenore Schaefer, a ballroom dancer, tried to get on the *Tonight Show,* she was told she was "too young": she was in her early 90s. When she turned 101, she made it. But even at that age, Lenore is no longer unusual in our society. Today, people over 100 constitute, proportionately, the country's fastest-growing age group. They are part of the increasing proportion of the population of the United States composed of older people (Himes 2001; Rimer 1998).

As Figure 11-4 (page 290) shows, in the year 1900, men and women aged 65 and older constituted only 4.1 percent of the nation's population, but by 2005, that age group is expected to grow to 12.4 percent. According to current projections, the over-65 segment will continue to increase throughout this century, with the "old old" (people who are 85 and older) increasing in numbers at an ever-faster rate.

In 2005, 15.1 percent of non-Hispanic Whites are projected to be older than 65, compared to 8.2 percent of African Americans, 8.5 percent of Asian Americans, and 5.4 percent of Hispanics. These differences reflect the shorter life spans of the latter groups, as well as immigration patterns among Asians and Hispanics, who tend to be young when they enter the country. Yet people of color are increasing their presence among the elderly population of the United States. By 2050, 36 percent of the elderly will be non-White, compared to only 16 percent in 2000 (Bureau of the Census 2003a:19; Graham 2002).

The highest proportions of older people are found in Florida, Pennsylvania, Rhode Island, Iowa, West Virginia, and Arkansas. However, many more states are undergoing an aging trend. In 2000, Florida was the state most populated by the elderly, with 17.6 percent of the population over the age of 65. Yet as Figure 11-5 shows, in about another 20 years, more than half the states will have a greater proportion of elderly than Florida does now.

The graying of the United States is a phenomenon that can no longer be ignored, either by social scientists or by government policymakers. Advocates for the elderly have spoken out on a wide range of issues, as we will see later in the chapter. Politicians court the votes of older people, since they are the age group most likely to register and vote. In fact, in the 2000 presidential race, people 60 or older made up 22 percent of the total vote (Berke 2001).

Wealth and Income

There is significant variation in wealth and poverty among the nation's older people. Some individuals and couples find themselves poor in part because of fixed pensions and skyrocketing health care costs (see Chapter 15). Nevertheless, as a group, older people in the United States are neither homogeneous nor poor. The typical elderly person enjoys a standard of living that is much higher now than at any point in the nation's past. Class differences among the elderly remain evident, but tend to narrow somewhat: Those older people who enjoyed middle-class incomes while younger tend to remain better off after retirement, but less so than before (Denise Smith and Tillipman 2000).

To some extent, older people owe their overall improved standard of living to a greater accumulation of wealth—in the form of home ownership, private pensions, and other financial assets. But much of the improvement is due to more generous Social Security benefits. While modest when compared with other countries' pension programs, Social Security nevertheless provides 40 percent of all income received by older people in the United States. Still, about 10 percent of the nation's elderly population lives below the poverty line. At the extremes of poverty are those groups who were more likely to be poor at earlier points in the life cycle: female-headed

households and racial and ethnic minorities (AARP 2001; Saad and Carroll 2003; Denise Smith 2003).

Viewed from a conflict perspective, it is not surprising that older women experience a double burden; the same is true of elderly members of racial and ethnic minorities. For example, in 2003 the proportion of older Latinos with incomes below the poverty level (19.5 percent) was more than twice as large as the proportion of older non-Hispanic Whites (8.0 percent). Moreover, 23.5 percent of older African Americans fell below the federal government's poverty line (DeNavas-Walt et al. 2004:Table POV01).

Ageism

Physician Robert Butler (1990) became concerned 30 years ago when he learned that a housing development near his home in metropolitan Washington, D.C., barred the elderly. Butler coined the term *ageism* to refer to prejudice and discrimination based on a person's age. For example, we may choose to assume that someone cannot handle a rigorous job because he is "too old," or we may refuse to give someone a job with authority because she is "too young."

Ageism is especially difficult for the old, because at least youthful recipients of prejudice know that in time

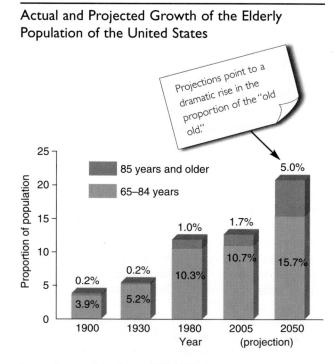

FIGURE 11-4

Actual and Projected Growth of the Elderly Population of the United States

Sources: Bureau of the Census 1975, 2003a:14.

Classroom Tip See "Age and Economic Hardship" (Class Discussion Topics).
Theory Conflict view of double burden of older women and elderly members of racial and ethnic minorities
Race/Ethnicity/Age Proportion of older Latinos and percentage of older African Americans who fell below the poverty level in 2000

Contemporary Culture How will your obligations to your parents change as they age?
Theory Conflict view of ageism
Theory Labeling theorists would be especially interested in stereotyping based on how old someone looks.

they will be "old enough." For many, old age symbolizes disease. With ageism all too common in the United States, it is hardly surprising that older people are barely visible on television. In 2002, the Senate Special Committee on Aging convened a panel on the media's portrayal of older people and sharply criticized media and marketing executives for bombarding audiences with negative images of the aged. The social consequences of such images are significant. Research shows that older people who have positive perceptions of aging live an average of 7.5 years longer than those who have negative perceptions (M. Gardner 2003; Levy et al. 2002; E. Ramirez 2002).

Use Your Sociological Imagination
www.mhhe.com/schaefer6

It is September and you are channel surfing through the new fall TV series. How likely are you to watch a television show that is based on older characters who spend a lot of time together?

Competition in the Labor Force

Participation in paid work is not typical after the age of 65. In 2001, 31 percent of men ages 65 to 69 and 20 percent of women participated in the paid labor force. While some people view these workers as experienced contributors to the labor force, others see them as "job stealers," a biased judgment similar to that directed against illegal immigrants. This mistaken belief not only intensifies age conflict but leads to age discrimination (Himes 2001).

While firing people simply because they are old violates federal law, courts have upheld the right to lay off older workers for economic reasons. Critics contend that later the same firms hire young, cheaper workers to replace experienced older workers. When economic growth began to slow in 2001 and companies cut back on their workforces, complaints of age bias grew sharply as older workers began to suspect they were bearing a disproportionate share of the layoffs. According to the Equal Employment Opportunity Commission, between 1999 and 2004, complaints of age discrimination rose more than 41 percent. However, evidence of a countertrend has emerged. Some firms have been giving larger raises to older workers, to encourage their retirement at the higher salary—a tactic that prompts younger workers to complain of age discrimination (Novelli 2004; Uchitelle 2003).

A controlled experiment conducted by the AARP confirmed that older people often face discrimination when applying for jobs. Comparable résumés for two applicants—one 57 years old and the other 32 years old— were sent to 775 large firms and employment agencies around the United States. In situations for which positions were actually available, the younger applicant received a favorable response 43 percent of the time. By contrast, the older applicant received favorable responses less than half as often (only 17 percent of the time). One Fortune 500 corporation asked the younger applicant for more information, while informing the older applicant that no appropriate positions were open (Bendick et al. 1993).

In contrast to the negative stereotypes, researchers have found that older workers can be an *asset* to employers. According to a study issued in 1991, older workers can be retrained in new technologies, have lower rates of absenteeism than younger employees, and are often more effective salespeople. The study focused on two corporations based in the United States (the hotel chain Days Inns of America and the

FIGURE 11-5

Twenty-Six Floridas by 2025

Mapping Life NATIONWIDE
www.mhhe.com/schaefer6

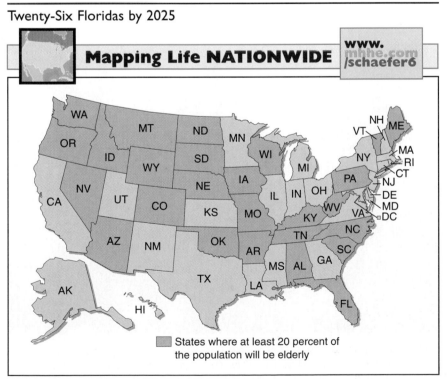

States where at least 20 percent of the population will be elderly

Source: Bureau of the Census, in Yax 1999.

About 30 percent of older workers choose to remain on the job past the usual retirement age. Research shows they can be retrained in new technologies and are more dependable than younger workers.

difficulty getting insurance because of age prejudice. Many of the AARP's services involve discounts and insurance for its 35 million members (44 percent of Americans aged 50 or older), but the organization is also a powerful lobbying group. Recognizing that many elderly are still gainfully employed, it has dropped its full name, American Association of *Retired* Persons.

The potential power of the AARP is enormous. It is the third-largest voluntary association in the United States (behind only the Roman Catholic church and the American Automobile Association), representing one out of every four registered voters in the United States. The AARP has endorsed voter registration campaigns, nursing home reforms, and pension reforms. In acknowledgment of its difficulties recruiting members of racial and ethnic minority groups, the AARP recently began a Minority Affairs Initiative. The spokeswoman for the initiative, Margaret Dixon, became the AARP's first African American president in 1996 (AARP 2003).

holding company Travelers Corporation of Hartford) and a British retail chain—all of which have long-term experience in hiring workers age 50 and over. An official of the private fund that commissioned the study concluded, "We have here the first systematic hard-nosed economic analysis showing older workers are good investments" (Telsch 1991:A16).

The Elderly: Emergence of a Collective Consciousness

During the 1960s, students at colleges and universities across the country, advocating "student power," collectively demanded a role in the governance of educational institutions. In the following decade, many older people became aware that *they* were being treated as second-class citizens and turned to collective action.

The largest organization representing the nation's elderly is the AARP, founded in 1958 by a retired school principal who was having

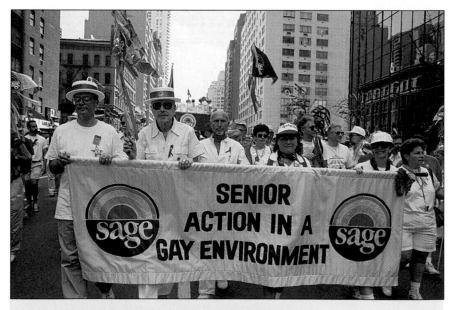

Members of SAGE, Senior Action in a Gay Environment, take part in a gay pride demonstration in New York City. This nationwide organization focuses on the special needs of gay seniors.

Let's Discuss How does Karl Marx's concept of class consciousness apply to the elderly?

Race/Ethnicity The AARP has faced criticism because its membership is overwhelmingly White.
Key Person Margaret Dixon
Gender/Race/Ethnicity For the first time, an African American woman is president of the AARP.

People grow old in many different ways. Not all the elderly face the same challenges or enjoy the same resources. While the AARP lobbies to protect the elderly in general, other groups work in more specific ways. For example, the National Committee to Preserve Social Security and Medicare, founded in 1982, successfully lobbied Congress to keep Medicare benefits for the ailing poor elderly. Other large special interest groups represent retired federal employees, retired teachers, and retired union workers (Quadagno 2005).

Still another manifestation of the new awareness of older people is the formation of organizations for elderly homosexuals. One such group, Senior Action in a Gay Environment (SAGE), was established in New York City in 1977 and now oversees a nationwide network of community groups, as well as affiliates in Canada and Germany. Like more traditional senior citizens' groups, SAGE sponsors workshops, classes, dances, and food deliveries to the homebound. At the same time, the group must deal with special concerns, such as informing gay people of their rights, supporting gay people with Alzheimer's, and advocating for gays who face eviction (Senior Action in a Gay Environment 2003).

The elderly in the United States are better off today both financially and physically than ever before. Many of them have strong financial assets and medical care packages that will take care of almost any health need. But as we have seen, a significant segment is impoverished, faced with the prospect of declining health and mounting medical bills. And some older people must now add being aged to a lifetime of disadvantage. As in all other stages of the life course, the aged constitute a diverse group in the United States and around the world.

SOCIAL POLICY and GENDER STRATIFICATION

The Battle over Abortion from a Global Perspective

The Issue

Few issues seem to stir as much intense conflict as abortion. A critical victory in the struggle for legalized abortion in the United States came in 1973 when the Supreme Court granted women the right to terminate pregnancies. This ruling, known as *Roe v. Wade*, was based on a woman's right to privacy. The Court's decision was generally applauded by pro-choice groups, which believe women should have the right to make their own decisions about their bodies and should have access to safe and legal abortions. It was bitterly condemned by those opposed to abortion. For these pro-life groups, abortion is a moral and often a religious issue. In their view, human life begins at the moment of conception, so that its termination through abortion is essentially an act of murder.

The Setting

The debate that has followed *Roe v. Wade* revolves around prohibiting abortion altogether, or at the very least, putting limits on it. In 1979, for example, Missouri required parental consent for minors wishing to obtain an abortion, and the Supreme Court upheld the law. Parental notification and consent have become especially sensitive issues in the debate. Pro-life activists argue that the parents of teenagers should have the right to be notified about—and to permit or prohibit—abortions. In their view, parental authority deserves full support at a time when the traditional nuclear family is embattled. However, pro-choice activists counter that many pregnant teenagers come from troubled families where they have been abused. These young women may have good reason to avoid discussing such explosive issues with their parents.

Changing technology has had its impact on the debate. "Day-after" pills, which have been available in some nations since 1998, are now prescribed in the United States. These pills can abort a fertilized egg the day after conception. In 2000, the U.S. government approved RU-486, an abortion-inducing pill that can be used in the first seven weeks of pregnancy. The regime requires doctor visits but no surgical procedures. In addition, doctors, guided by ultrasound, can now end a pregnancy as early as eight days after conception. Pro-life activists are concerned that the use of ultrasound technology will allow people to abort unwanted females in nations where a premium is placed on male offspring.

As of 2004, the people of the United States appeared to support their right to legal abortion, but with reservations. According to a national survey done the year before, 60 percent favor a woman's general right to have an abortion. However, only 40 percent feel abortion should be legal if a family is very poor and cannot afford a child (Graham 2003).

Methods Survey of U.S. citizens' attitudes about abortion rights

Policy Pointer Legal abortion was a priority of the feminist movement in the late 1960s and early 1970s.
Let's Discuss Parental notification and parental consent—central issues in the abortion controversy—should be of special interest to college students.

FIGURE 11-6

Restrictions on Public Funding for Abortion

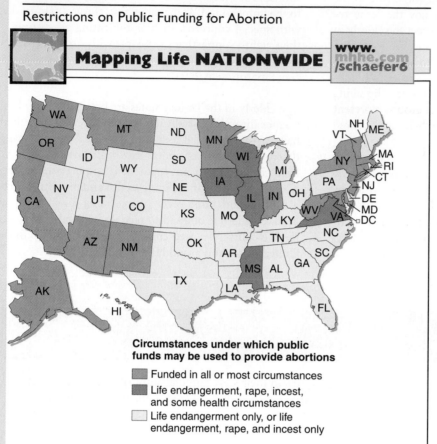

Mapping Life NATIONWIDE www.mhhe.com/schaefer6

Circumstances under which public funds may be used to provide abortions

- Funded in all or most circumstances
- Life endangerment, rape, incest, and some health circumstances
- Life endangerment only, or life endangerment, rape, and incest only

Source: NARAL Pro-Choice America 2003:xxii–xxiii.

Sociological Insights

Sociologists see gender and social class as the defining issues surrounding abortion. The intense conflict over abortion reflects broader differences over women's position in society. Sociologist Kristin Luker (1984) has studied activists in both the pro-choice and pro-life movements. Luker interviewed 212 activists in California, overwhelmingly women, who spent at least five hours a week working for one of the two movements. According to Luker, each group has a consistent, coherent view of the world. Feminists involved in defending abortion rights typically believe that men and women are essentially similar; they support women's full participation in work outside the home and oppose all forms of sex discrimination. In contrast, most antiabortion activists believe that men and women are fundamentally different. In their view, men are best suited to the public world of work, while women are best suited to the demanding and crucial task of rearing children. These activists are troubled by women's

growing participation in work outside the home, which they view as destructive to the family and ultimately to society.

In regard to social class, the first major restriction on the legal right to terminate a pregnancy affected poor people. In 1976, Congress passed the Hyde Amendment, which banned the use of Medicaid and other federal funds for abortions. The Supreme Court upheld this legislation in 1980. State laws also restrict the use of public funds for abortions (see Figure 11-6).

Another obstacle facing the poor is access to abortion providers. In the face of vocal pro-life sentiment, fewer and fewer hospitals throughout the world are allowing physicians to perform abortions, except in extreme cases. As of 2001, only about 6 percent of specialists in obstetrics and gynecology in the United States were trained and willing to perform abortions under any circumstances, and a majority of those physicians were in their 50s and 60s. To avoid controversy, many medical schools have ceased to offer training in the procedure. Moreover, some doctors who work in clinics, intimidated by death threats and actual murders, have stopped performing abortions. For poor people in rural areas, this reduction in service makes it more difficult to locate and travel to a facility that will accommodate their wishes. Viewed from a conflict perspective, this is one more financial burden that falls especially heavily on low-income women (T. Edwards 2001; Villarosa 2002).

Policy Initiatives

The Supreme Court currently supports the general right to terminate a pregnancy by a narrow 5–4 majority. Although pro-life activists continue to hope for an overruling of *Roe v. Wade,* they have focused in the interim on weakening the decision through tactics such as limiting the use of fetal tissue in medical experiments and prohibiting certain late-term abortions, which they term "partial-birth" abortions. The Supreme Court continues to hear cases involving such restrictions. In 1998,

Methods Luker interviewed pro-choice and pro-life activists (survey research).

Theory Conflict theory used to examine the abortion issue
Theory Conflict view of how the right to legal abortions has special significance for poor women
Policy Pointer The makeup of the Supreme Court is a crucial aspect of the conflict over abortion, as has been evident in the battles over recent Court nominees.

FIGURE 11-7

The Global Divide on Abortion

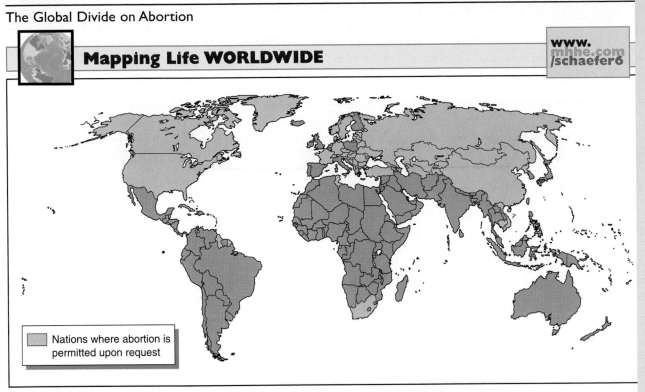

Mapping Life WORLDWIDE

www.
mhhe.com
/schaefer6

Nations where abortion is permitted upon request

Note: Data current as of June 2001.

Sources: Developed by the author based on Gonnut 2001 and United Nations Population Division 1998.

the Court gave the states the authority (32 have done so) to prohibit abortions at the point where the fetus is viable outside the mother's womb—a point that continues to be redefined by new developments in medical technology (Biskupic 2000).

What is the policy in other countries? As in the United States, many European nations responded to public opinion and liberalized abortion laws in the 1970s, although Ireland, Belgium, and Malta continue to prohibit abortion. Austria, Denmark, Greece, the Netherlands, Norway, and Sweden have laws that allow a woman to have an abortion on request. Other countries have much more restrictive legislation, especially concerning abortions in the later stages of pregnancy. Inspired by their counterparts in the United States, antiabortion activists have become more outspoken in Great Britain, France, Spain, Italy, and Germany.

The policies of the United States and developing nations are intertwined. Throughout the 1980s and 1990s, antiabortion members of Congress have often successfully blocked foreign aid to countries that might use the funds to encourage abortion. And yet those developing nations generally have the most restrictive abortion laws. As shown in Figure 11-7, it is primarily in Africa, Latin America, and parts of Asia that women are not allowed to terminate a pregnancy on request. As might be expected, illegal abortions are most common in those nations. An estimated quarter of the world's women live in countries where abortion is illegal or is permitted only if a woman's life is in jeopardy. Hence, 40 percent of abortions worldwide—about 20 million procedures each year—are performed illegally (Joynt and Ganeshananthan 2003).

Let's Discuss

1. Do you know anyone who has undergone an illegal abortion? If so, what were the circumstances? Was the woman's health endangered by the procedure?
2. Do you think teenage girls should have to get their parents' consent before having an abortion? Why?
3. Under what circumstances should abortions be allowed? Explain your reasoning.

Policy Pointer Review the most recent court rulings on abortion.
Global View Abortion policies in other countries
Global View Abortion as a controversial issue in western Europe

Let's Discuss Do students believe that abortion policies will become more or less restrictive in the United States over the next decade?
Classroom Tip See "Using Humor" (Class Discussion Topics).

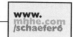

GETTING INVOLVED

To get involved in the debate over abortion, visit this text's Online Learning Center, which offers links to relevant websites. Check out the Social Policy section on the Online Learning Center as well; it provides survey data on U.S. public opinion regarding this issue.

CHAPTER RESOURCES

Summary

Gender and age are ascribed statuses that provide a basis for social differentiation. This chapter examines the social construction of gender, theories of stratification by gender, women as an oppressed majority group, theories of aging, age stratification and *ageism*, and the growing political activism of the elderly.

1. In the United States, the social construction of gender continues to define significantly different expectations for females and males.
2. *Gender roles* show up in our work and behavior and in how we react to others.
3. Though females have been more severely restricted than men by traditional gender roles, those roles have also restricted males.
4. The research of anthropologist Margaret Mead points to the importance of cultural conditioning in defining the social roles of males and females.
5. Functionalists maintain that sex differentiation contributes to overall social stability, but conflict theorists charge that the relationship between females and males is one of unequal power, with men dominating women. This dominance shows up in people's everyday interactions.
6. Women around the world suffer from *sexism, institutional discrimination,* and *sexual harassment.*
7. As women have taken on more and more hours of paid employment outside the home, they have been only partially successful in getting their husbands to take on more homemaking duties, including child care.
8. Many women agree with the positions of the feminist movement but reject the label *feminist.*
9. Like other forms of stratification, age stratification varies from culture to culture.
10. In the United States, being old is a master status that seems to overshadow all others.
11. The particular problems of the aged have become the focus for a specialized area of research and inquiry known as *gerontology.*
12. *Disengagement theory* implicitly suggests that society should help older people to withdraw from their accustomed social roles. In contrast, *activity theory* suggests that the elderly person who remains active and socially involved will be better adjusted.
13. From a conflict perspective, the low status of older people is reflected in prejudice and discrimination against them and in unfair job practices.
14. An increasing proportion of the population of the United States is composed of older people.
15. *Ageism* reflects a deep uneasiness about growing old on the part of younger people.
16. The AARP is a powerful lobbying group that backs legislation to benefit senior citizens.
17. The issue of abortion has bitterly divided the United States (as well as other nations), pitting pro-choice activists against pro-life activists.

Critical Thinking Questions

1. Imagine that you are assigned the opposite gender at birth, but that your race, ethnicity, religion, and social class background remain the same. Drawing on the information contained in this chapter, describe how your life as a member of the opposite sex might differ from your life today.
2. You have been asked to study political activism among women. How might you employ surveys,

observations, experiments, and existing sources to better understand such activism?

3. If you were hired to run a senior center where you live, how would you use what you have learned in this chapter to better the lives of your community's seniors?

Key Terms

Activity theory   An interactionist theory of aging that suggests that elderly people who remain active and socially involved will be best-adjusted. (page 288)

Ageism   Prejudice and discrimination based on a person's age. (290)

Disengagement theory   A functionalist theory of aging that implicitly suggests that society and the aging individual mutually sever many of their relationships. (286)

Expressiveness   Concern for the maintenance of harmony and the internal emotional affairs of the family. (277)

Gender role   Expectations regarding the proper behavior, attitudes, and activities of males and females. (272)

Gerontology   The scientific study of the sociological and psychological aspects of aging and the problems of the aged. (286)

Glass ceiling   An invisible barrier that blocks the promotion of a qualified individual in a work environment because of the individual's gender, race, or ethnicity. (282)

Homophobia   Fear of and prejudice against homosexuality. (273)

Institutional discrimination   The denial of opportunities and equal rights to individuals and groups that results from the normal operations of a society. (279)

Instrumentality   An emphasis on tasks, a focus on more distant goals, and a concern for the external relationship between one's family and other social institutions. (277)

Second shift   The double burden—work outside the home followed by child care and housework—that many women face and few men share equitably. (283)

Sexism   The ideology that one sex is superior to the other. (279)

Sexual harassment   Behavior that occurs when work benefits are made contingent on sexual favors (as a quid pro quo), or when touching, lewd comments, or the exhibition of pornographic material creates a "hostile environment" in the workplace. (280)

TECHNOLOGY RESOURCES

Internet Connection

www. mhhe.com /schaefer6

*Note: While all the URLs listed were current as of the printing of this book, these sites often change. Please check our website (**www.mhhe.com/schaefer6**) for updates, hyperlinks, and exercises related to these sites.*

1. In this chapter you have learned about gender inequality based mainly on social statistics compiled in the United States. To access data on stratification by gender in hundreds of other countries, go to the GenderStats page at the World Bank's website (**devdata.worldbank.org/gender stats/home.asp**). How does the status of women in the United States compare to that of women in other developed countries? To that of women in developing countries?

2. The needs of the aging population vary by racial and ethnic group, as does their access to essential resources. Organizations like the University of North Dakota's National Resource Center on Native American Aging acknowledge these facts and strive to assist the elderly in particular racial and ethnic groups. Visit the website (**http://www. med.und.nodak.edu/depts/rural//nrcnaa/**). To learn about the Center's goals and activities, click on "Site Map," and look at the list of links under "National Resource Center on Native American Aging."

Online Learning Center with PowerWeb

Few issues seem to stir as much intense conflict as abortion. To find out how Americans feel about abortion, visit the student center at the Online Learning Center (**www.mhhe.com/schaefer6**) and link to "How Americans Feel About. . . ." Read an overview of the abortion issue and then look at the colorful pie charts and graphs. These charts and graphs show what percentage of Americans surveyed consider themselves pro-choice or pro-life, how they feel about the *Roe v. Wade* decision, and how both men and women feel about the legality of abortion.

Reel Society Interactive Movie CD-ROM 2.0

Reel Society 2.0 can be used to spark discussion about the following topics from this chapter:

- Gender Roles in the United States
- Cross-Cultural Perspectives on Gender
- Sexism and Sex Discrimination
- The Status of Women Worldwide

THE FAMILY AND INTIMATE RELATIONSHIPS

WANTED: My Daddy

Genetica
DNA · LABORATORIES · INC

DNA Paternity Testing
1-800-IDENTITY

Reproductive technology is changing people's personal lives, raising questions about ethics and social policy in the process. For the first time, mothers can positively identify the fathers of their children, and parents can manipulate their children's genes—a prospect many people find disturbing.

From the time of the breakdown of my marriage to Cliff's mother in 1979 to my marriage to Elleni in 1990, I was forced to deal with a difficult but nonetheless standard set of problems. My ex-wife was awarded custody of two-year-old Cliff and then decided to move to Atlanta. I had no recourse, legal or otherwise. And yet in my struggle to build a close relationship with my son, I now had to cope with an almost impossible set of barriers. Hundreds of miles separated me from Cliff, and I had limited visitation rights—a few specified weekends during the year plus three months in the summer. Besides which, what would I do with my son during our precious time together? My bachelor homes did not provide a supportive context for a four-year-old or a nine-year-old—there were no kids on the block, no basketball hoop in the back yard. But I wrestled with these problems and over time developed a strategy that worked, albeit imperfectly.

I hit upon this great solution for the summers. I would take Cliff back to Sacramento, back to the loving, child-centered home that had been so good to me and my siblings a generation ago. It required a lot of stretching and bending of the rules, but I organized life so that I really could take two and a half months out of the year. It meant postponing book deadlines and taming an almost impossible travel schedule, but it was well worth it. Those summers in Sacramento stand out like jewels in my memory. My parents' home turned out to be a profoundly healing place in which Cliff and I could reach out to one another. It provided the deeply needed (and yet so hard to contrive) rhythms and routines of normal family life. Three meals a day; regular bedtimes; clean clothes; a bevy of cousins—Kahnie, Phillip and Phyllis, Cornel and Erika—just around the corner, on tap for casual play; bicycles and baseball gear in the garage all ready to be put to use whenever a grownup was available. And hovering in the backgrounds, loving, eagle-eyed grandparents.... The evening meal was particularly important, as all three generations gathered for a cookout in the back yard. Conversation and laughter flowed, advice was sought and help was freely offered, jokes and stories were traded, and the children, spellbound, hung on the edges, absorbing the spirit and the meaning of family life.

The rest of the year was a struggle. I maintained regular telephone contact with Cliff, calling him several times a week just to hear his voice and shoot the breeze. But in the rushed, tantalizing visits around Thanksgiving, Christmas, and Easter, it was always hard not to lapse into the role of being a "good-time dad," showering gifts on him in an attempt to make up for real time or a deeper agenda. *(Hewlett and West 1998:21–22)* ■ ✆

Additional information about this excerpt can be found on the Online Learning Center at **www.mhhe.com/schaefer6.**

In this excerpt from *The War Against Parents,* philosophy scholar Cornel West underscores how deeply family life has been altered by divorce, one of many social factors that have gradually but inevitably turned the traditional nuclear family on its head. The family of today is not what it was a century ago, or even a generation ago. New roles, new gender distinctions, new child-rearing patterns have all combined to create new forms of family life. Today, for example, more and more women are taking the breadwinner's role, whether married or as a single parent. Blended families—the result of divorce and remarriage—are almost the norm. And many people are seeking intimate relationships outside marriage, whether it be in gay partnerships or in cohabiting arrangements.

This chapter addresses family and intimate relationships in the United States as well as other parts of the world. As we will see, family patterns differ from one culture to another, and even within the same culture. Despite the differences, however, the family is universal—found in every culture. A *family* can be defined as a set of people related by blood, marriage or some other agreed-upon relationship, or adoption, who share the primary responsibility for reproduction and caring for members of society.

What are families in different parts of the world like? How do people select their mates? When a marriage fails, how does the divorce affect the children? What are the alternatives to the nuclear family, and how prevalent are they? In this chapter we will look at the family and intimate relationships from the functionalist, conflict, and interactionist points of view. We'll examine variations in marital patterns and family life, including child rearing, paying particular attention to the increasing numbers of people in dual-income and single-parent families. We'll examine divorce in the United States, and consider diverse lifestyles such as cohabitation, lesbian and gay relationships, and marriage without children. In the social policy section we will confront the controversial issue of gay marriage. ■

GLOBAL VIEW OF THE FAMILY

Among Tibetans, a woman may be simultaneously married to more than one man, usually brothers. This system allows sons to share the limited amount of good land. Among the Betsileo of Madagascar, a man has multiple wives, each one living in a different village where he cultivates rice. Wherever he has the best rice field, that wife is considered his first or senior wife. Among the Yanomami of Brazil and Venezuela, it is considered proper to have sexual relations with your opposite-sex cousins if they are the children of your mother's brother or your father's sister. But if your opposite-sex cousins are the children of your mother's sister or your father's brother, the same practice is considered to be incest (Haviland et al. 2005; Kottak 2004).

As these examples illustrate, there are many variations in the family from culture to culture. Yet the family as a social institution is present in all cultures. Moreover, certain general principles concerning its composition, kinship patterns, and authority patterns are universal.

Composition: What Is the Family?

If we were to take our information on what a family is from what we see on television, we might come up with some very strange scenarios. The media don't always present a realistic view of the family. Moreover, many people still think of the family in very narrow terms—as a married couple and their unmarried children living together, like the family in the old *Cosby Show* or *Family Ties* or even *Dawson's Creek.* However, this is but one type of family, what sociologists refer to as a **nuclear family.** The term *nuclear family* is well chosen, since this type of family serves as the nucleus, or core, on which larger family groups are built.

Most people in the United States see the nuclear family as the preferred family arrangement. Yet by 2000, only about a third of the nation's family households fit this model. The proportion of households in the United States that is composed of married couples with children at home has decreased steadily over the last 40 years, and is expected to continue shrinking. At the same time, the number of single-parent households has increased (see Figure 12-1, page 302).

A family in which relatives—such as grandparents, aunts, or uncles—live in the same home as parents and their children is known as an **extended family.** Although not common, such living arrangements do exist in the United States. The structure of the extended family offers certain advantages over that of the nuclear family. Crises such as death, divorce, and illness put less strain on family members, since more people can provide assistance and

Classroom Tip See "Stimulating Classroom Discussions about *The War Against Parents*" (Class Discussion Topics).
Classroom Tip See "Family History" and "What Is a Marriage?" (Class Discussion Topics).
Global View Family patterns among Tibetans, the Betsileo, and the Yanomami.

Classroom Tip See "Tibetan Family Life" (Additional Lecture Ideas).
Contemporary Culture/Classroom Tip See "Extraordinary Groups" (Class Discussion Topics).
Theory Functionalist view of the advantages and disadvantages of an extended family

emotional support. In addition, the extended family constitutes a larger economic unit than the nuclear family. If the family is engaged in a common enterprise—a farm or a small business—the additional family members may represent the difference between prosperity and failure.

In considering these differing family types, we have limited ourselves to the form of marriage that is characteristic of the United States—monogamy. The term *monogamy* describes a form of marriage in which one woman and one man are married only to each other. Some observers, noting the high rate of divorce in the United States, have suggested that "serial monogamy" is a more accurate description of the form that marriage takes in this country. In *serial monogamy,* a person may have several spouses in his or her lifetime, but only one spouse at a time.

Some cultures allow an individual to have several husbands or wives simultaneously. This form of marriage is known as *polygamy.* In fact, most societies throughout the world, past and present, have preferred polygamy to monogamy. Anthropologist George Murdock (1949, 1957) sampled 565 societies and found that in more than 80 percent, some type of polygamy was the preferred form. While polygamy declined steadily through most of the 20th century, in at least five countries in Africa 20 percent of men still have polygamous marriages (Population Reference Bureau 1996).

There are two basic types of polygamy. According to Murdock, the most common—endorsed by the majority of cultures he sampled—is *polygyny.* Polygyny refers to the marriage of a man to more than one woman at the same time. The wives are often sisters, who are expected to hold similar values and have already had experience sharing a household. In polygynous societies, relatively few men actually have multiple spouses. Most individuals live in monogamous families; having multiple wives is viewed as a mark of status.

The other principal variation of polygamy is *polyandry,* in which a woman may have more than one husband at the same time. Such is the case in the culture of the Todas of southern India. Polyandry, however, is exceedingly rare today. It has been accepted by some extremely poor societies that practice female infanticide (the killing of baby girls), and thus have a relatively small number of women. Like many other societies, polyandrous cultures devalue the social worth of women.

Kinship Patterns: To Whom Are We Related?

Many of us can trace our roots by looking at a family tree or by listening to elderly family members talk about their lives—and about the lives of ancestors who died long before we were born. Yet a person's lineage is more than simply a personal history; it also reflects societal patterns that govern descent. In every culture, children encounter relatives to whom they are expected to show an emotional attachment. The state of being related to others

FIGURE 12-1

U.S. Households by Family Type, 1940–2003

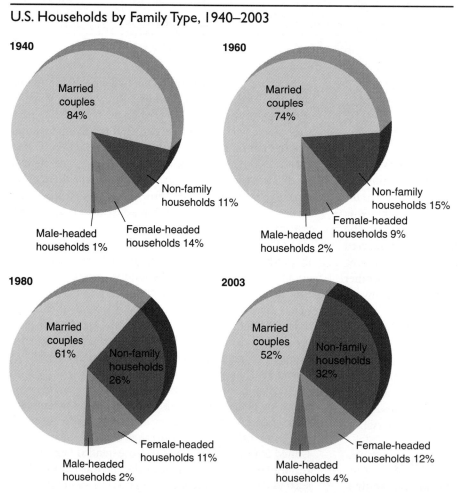

1940
Married couples 84%
Non-family households 11%
Male-headed households 1%
Female-headed households 14%

1960
Married couples 74%
Non-family households 15%
Female-headed households 9%
Male-headed households 2%

1980
Married couples 61%
Non-family households 26%
Female-headed households 11%
Male-headed households 2%

2003
Married couples 52%
Non-family households 32%
Female-headed households 12%
Male-headed households 4%

Source: Fields 2003; see also McFalls, Jr. 2003:23.

Global View Murdock's study of polygamy and monogamy in 565 societies

Methods Murdock's study drew on observation research on family life.

is called **kinship.** Kinship is culturally learned, however, and is not totally determined by biological or marital ties. For example, adoption creates a kinship tie that is legally acknowledged and socially accepted.

The family and the kin group are not necessarily one and the same. Whereas the family is a household unit, kin do not always live together or function as a collective body on a daily basis. Kin groups include aunts, uncles, cousins, in-laws, and so forth. In a society such as the United States, the kinship group may come together only rarely, for a wedding or funeral. However, kinship ties frequently create obligations and responsibilities. We may feel compelled to assist our kin, and we feel free to call upon them for many types of aid, including loans and babysitting.

How do we identify kinship groups? The principle of descent assigns people to kinship groups according to their relationship to a mother or father. There are three primary ways of determining descent. The United States follows the system of **bilateral descent,** which means that both sides of a person's family are regarded as equally important. For example, no higher value is given to the brothers of one's father than to the brothers of one's mother.

Most societies—according to George Murdock, 64 percent—give preference to one side of the family or the other in tracing descent. In **patrilineal** (from the Latin *pater,* "father") **descent,** only the father's relatives are significant in terms of property, inheritance, and emotional ties. Conversely, in societies that favor **matrilineal** (from the Latin *mater,* "mother") **descent,** only the mother's relatives are significant.

New forms of reproductive technology will necessitate a new way of looking at kinship. Today, a combination of biological and social processes can "create" a family member, requiring that more distinctions be made about who is related to whom.

Authority Patterns: Who Rules?

Imagine that you have recently married and must begin to make decisions about the future of your new family. You and your spouse face many questions. Where will you live? How will you furnish your home? Who will do the cook-

This Turkish kin group was photographed in Berlin, Germany. Though the three generations shown here probably do not all live in the same household, their support for one another undoubtedly helps them to meet the special challenges they face as immigrants.

ing, the shopping, the cleaning? Whose friends will be invited to dinner? Each time a decision must be made, an issue is raised: Who has the power to make the decision? In simple terms, who rules the family? Conflict theorists examine these questions in the context of traditional gender p. 277 stratification, under which men have held a dominant position over women.

Societies vary in the way that power is distributed within the family. A society that expects males to dominate in all family decision making is termed a **patriarchy.** In patriarchal societies, such as Iran, the eldest male often wields the greatest power, although wives are expected to be treated with respect and kindness. A woman's status in Iran is typically defined by her relationship to a male relative, usually as a wife or daughter. In many patriarchal societies, women find it more difficult to obtain a divorce than a man does. In contrast, in a **matriarchy,** women have greater authority than men. Matriarchies, which are very uncommon, emerged among Native American tribal societies and in nations in which men were absent for long periods because of warfare or food-gathering expeditions (Farr 1999).

In a third type of authority pattern, the **egalitarian family,** spouses are regarded as equals. That does not mean, however, that all decisions are shared in such families. Wives may hold authority in some spheres, husbands in others. Many sociologists believe the

Contemporary Culture The impact of reproductive technology on kinship patterns

Gender Discussion of patriarchy, matriarchy, and the egalitarian family
Global View/Gender Patriarchal family systems in Iran

egalitarian family has begun to replace the patriarchal family as the social norm in the United States.

STUDYING THE FAMILY

Do we really need the family? A century ago, Friedrich Engels ([1884] 1959), a colleague of Karl Marx, described the family as the ultimate source of social inequality because of its role in the transfer of power, property, and privilege. More recently, conflict theorists have argued that the family contributes to societal injustice, denies women opportunities that are extended to men, and limits freedom in sexual expression and mate selection. In contrast, the functionalist perspective focuses on the ways in which the family gratifies the needs of its members and contributes to social stability. The interactionist view considers the intimate, face-to-face relationships that occur in the family.

Functionalist View

The family performs six paramount functions, first outlined more than 65 years ago by sociologist William F. Ogburn (Ogburn and Tibbits 1934):

1. **Reproduction.** For a society to maintain itself, it must replace dying members. In this sense, the family contributes to human survival through its function of reproduction.
2. **Protection.** Unlike the young of other animal species, human infants need constant care and economic security. In all cultures, the family assumes the ultimate responsibility for the protection and upbringing of children.
3. **Socialization.** Parents and other kin monitor a child's behavior and transmit the norms, values, and language of their culture to the child.
4. **Regulation of sexual behavior.** Sexual norms are subject to change both over time (for instance, in the customs for dating) and across cultures (compare strict Saudi Arabia to the more permissive Denmark). However, whatever the time period or cultural values of a society, standards of sexual behavior are most clearly defined within the family circle.
5. **Affection and companionship.** Ideally, the family provides members with warm and intimate relationships, helping them to feel satisfied and secure. Of course, a family member may find such rewards outside the family—from peers, in school, at work—and may even perceive the home as an unpleasant or abusive setting. Nevertheless, we expect

our relatives to understand us, to care for us, and to be there for us when we need them.

6. **Provision of social status.** We inherit a social position because of the family background and reputation of our parents and siblings. The family presents the newborn child with an ascribed status based on race and ethnicity that helps to determine his or her place within society's stratification system. Moreover, family resources affect children's ability to pursue certain opportunities, such as higher education and special lessons.

Traditionally, the family has fulfilled a number of other functions, such as providing religious training, education, and recreational outlets. But Ogburn argued that other social institutions have gradually assumed many of those functions. Education once took place at the family fireside; now it is the responsibility of professionals working in schools and colleges. Even the family's traditional recreational function has been transferred to outside groups such as Little Leagues, athletic clubs, and Internet chat rooms.

Conflict View

Conflict theorists view the family not as a contributor to social stability, but as a reflection of the inequality in wealth and power that is found within the larger society. Feminist and conflict theorists note that the family has traditionally legitimized and perpetuated male dominance. Throughout most of human history—and in a wide range of societies—husbands have exercised overwhelming power and authority within the family. Not until the first wave of contemporary feminism in the United States, in the mid-1800s, was there a substantial challenge to the historic status of wives and children as the legal property of husbands.

While the egalitarian family has become a more common pattern in the United States in recent decades—owing in good part to the activism of feminists beginning in the late 1960s and early 1970s—male dominance within the family has hardly disappeared. Sociologists have found that women are significantly more likely to leave their jobs when their husbands find better employment opportunities than men are when their wives receive desirable job offers (Bielby and Bielby 1992). And unfortunately, many husbands reinforce their power and control over wives and children through acts of domestic violence. Box 12-1 (opposite) considers cross-cultural findings about violence within the home.

Conflict theorists also view the family as an economic unit that contributes to societal injustice. The family is the basis for transferring power, property, and privilege from one generation to the next. Although the

Sociology in the Global Community

12-1   DOMESTIC VIOLENCE

The phone rings two or three dozen times a day at the Friend of the Family Hotline in San Salvador, the capital city of El Salvador. Each time the staff receives a report of family violence, a crisis team is immediately dispatched to the caller's home. Caseworkers provide comfort to victims, as well as accumulate evidence for use in the attacker's prosecution. In the first three years of its existence, Friend of the Family handled over 28,000 cases of domestic violence.

Wife battering and other forms of domestic violence are not confined to El Salvador. Drawing on studies conducted throughout the world, we can make the following generalizations:

- Women are most at risk of violence from the men they know.
- Violence against women occurs in all socioeconomic groups.
- Family violence is at least as dangerous as assaults committed by strangers.
- Though women sometimes exhibit violent behavior toward men, the

majority of violent acts that cause injury are perpetrated by men against women.
- Violence within intimate relationships tends to escalate over time.
- Emotional and psychological abuse can be at least as debilitating as physical abuse.
- Use of alcohol exacerbates family violence but does not cause it.

The family can be a dangerous place not only for women but also for children and the elderly.

Using the conflict and feminist models, researchers have found that in relationships in which the inequality between men and women is great, the likelihood of assault on wives increases dramatically. This discovery suggests that much of the violence between intimates, even when sexual in nature, is about power rather than sex.

The family can be a dangerous place not only for women but also for children and the elderly. In 2000, public agencies in the United States received more than 3 million reports of child abuse and/or neglect. That means reports were filed on about 1 out of every 25 children. Another national study found that 1 million violent crimes a year are committed by current or former spouses, boyfriends, or girlfriends.

Let's Discuss

1. Do you know of a family that has experienced domestic violence? Did the victim(s) seek outside help, and if so, was it effective?
2. Why might the degree of equality in a relationship correlate to the likelihood of domestic violence? How might conflict theorists explain this finding?

Sources: American Bar Association 1999; Gelles and Cornell 1990; Heise et al. 1999; Rennison and Welchans 2000; Spindel et al. 2000; Valdez 1999; J. J. Wilson 2000.

pp. 220–222 United States is widely viewed as a land of opportunity, social mobility is restricted in important ways. Children inherit the privileged or less-than-privileged social and economic status of their parents (and in some cases, of earlier generations as well). As conflict theorists point out, the social class of parents significantly influences children's socialization experiences and the degree of protection they receive. This means that the socioeconomic status of a child's family will have a marked influence on his or her nutrition, health care, housing, educational opportunities, and in many respects, life chances as an adult. For this reason, conflict theorists argue that the family helps to maintain inequality.

Interactionist View

Interactionists focus on the micro level of family and other intimate relationships. They are interested in how individuals interact with one another, whether they are cohabiting partners or longtime married couples. For example, in a study of both Black and White two-parent households, researchers found that when fathers are more involved with their children (reading to them, helping them with homework, or restricting their television viewing) children have fewer behavior problems, get along better with others, and are more responsible (Mosley and Thomson 1995).

Another interactionist study might examine the role of the stepparent. The increased number of single parents who remarry has sparked an interest in those who are helping to raise other people's children. Studies have found that stepmothers are more likely than stepfathers to accept the blame for bad relations with their stepchildren. Interactionists theorize that stepfathers (like most fathers) may simply be unaccustomed to interacting directly with children when the mother isn't there (Bray and Kelly 1999; Furstenberg and Cherlin 1991).

Global View Domestic violence in San Salvador
Classroom Tip See "Steps to Prevent Domestic Violence" (Additional Lecture Ideas).
Theory Conflict and feminist views of family violence

Theory Interactionist view of the family introduced

These family patterns are changing, however, in response to changes in Latinos' social class standing, educational achievements, and occupations. Like other Americans, career-oriented Latinos in search of a mate but short on spare time are turning to Internet sites. As Latinos and other groups assimilate into the dominant culture of the United States, their family lives take on both the positive and negative characteristics associated with White households (Becerra 1999; Vega 1995).

Child-Rearing Patterns in Family Life

The Nayars of southern India acknowledge the biological role of fathers, but the mother's eldest brother is responsible for her children. In contrast, uncles play only a peripheral role in child care in the United States. Caring for children is a universal function of the family, yet the ways in which different societies assign this function to family members can vary significantly. Even within the United States, child-rearing patterns are varied. We'll take a look here at parenthood and grandparenthood, adoption, dual-income families, single-parent families, and stepfamilies.

Parenthood and Grandparenthood

The socialization of children is essential to the maintenance of any culture. Consequently, parenthood is one of the most important (and most demanding) social roles in the United States. Sociologist Alice Rossi (1968, 1984) has identified four factors that complicate the transition to parenthood and the role of socialization. First, there is lit-

◀ p. 91 tle anticipatory socialization for the social role of caregiver. The normal school curriculum gives scant attention to the subjects most relevant to successful family life, such as child care and home maintenance. Second, only limited learning occurs during the period of pregnancy itself. Third, the transition to parenthood is quite abrupt. Unlike adolescence, it is not prolonged; unlike the transition to work, the duties of caregiving cannot be taken on gradually. Finally, in Rossi's view, our society lacks clear and helpful guidelines for successful parenthood. There is little consensus on how parents can produce happy and well-adjusted offspring—or even on what it means to be well-adjusted. For these reasons, socialization for parenthood involves difficult challenges for most men and women in the United States.

One recent development in family life in the United States has been the extension of parenthood, as adult children continue to live at home or return home after college. In 2000, 56 percent of men and 43 percent of women ages 18 to 24 lived with their parents. Some of these adult children were still pursuing an education, but in many instances,

Race/Ethnicity Use of Internet sites by career-oriented Latinos in search of mates
Global View Family life among the Nayars of southern India
Student Alert Review the concept of anticipatory socialization

FIGURE 12-3

Rise of Single-Parent Families in the United States, 1970–2000

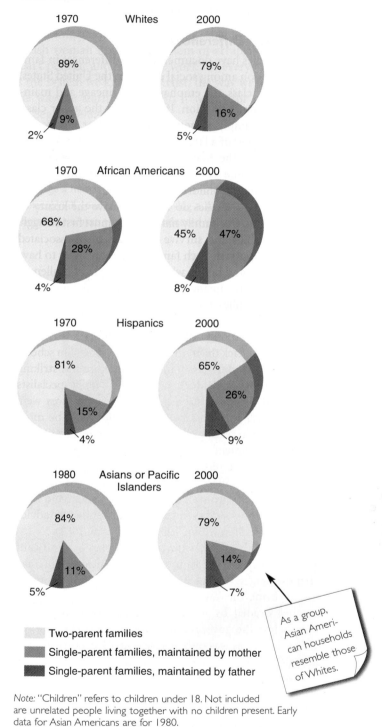

Two-parent families

Single-parent families, maintained by mother

Single-parent families, maintained by father

As a group, Asian American households resemble those of Whites.

Note: "Children" refers to children under 18. Not included are unrelated people living together with no children present. Early data for Asian Americans are for 1980.

Source: Bureau of the Census 1994:63; Fields 2001:7.

financial difficulties lay at the heart of these living arrangements. While rents and real estate prices have skyrocketed, salaries for younger workers have not kept pace, and many find themselves unable to afford their own homes. Moreover, with many marriages now ending in divorce—most commonly in the first seven years of marriage—divorced sons and daughters often return to live with their parents, sometimes with their own children (Fields 2003).

Is this living arrangement a positive development for family members? Social scientists have just begun to examine the phenomenon, sometimes called the "boomerang generation" or the "full-nest syndrome" in the popular press. One survey in Virginia seemed to show that neither the parents nor their adult children were happy about continuing to live together. The children often felt resentful and isolated, but the parents suffered too: Learning to live without children in the home is an essential stage of adult life, and may even be a significant turning point for a marriage (*Berkeley Wellness Letter* 1990; Mogelonsky 1996).

In some homes, the full nest holds grandchildren. In 2002, 5.6 million children, or 8 percent of all children in the United States, lived in a household with a grandparent. In about a third of these homes, no parent was present to assume responsibility for the youngsters. Special difficulties are inherent in such relationships, including legal custodial concerns, financial issues, and emotional problems for adults and youths alike. Little surprise that support groups such as Grandparents as Parents have emerged to provide assistance (Fields 2003).

Adoption

In a legal sense, *adoption* is a "process that allows for the transfer of the legal rights, responsibilities, and privileges of parenthood" to a new legal parent or parents (E. Cole 1985:638). In many cases, these rights are transferred from a biological parent or parents (often called birth parents) to an adoptive parent or parents.

Viewed from a functionalist perspective, government has a strong interest in encouraging adoption. Policymakers, in fact, have both a humanitarian and a financial stake in the process. In theory, adoption offers a stable family environment for children who otherwise might not receive satisfactory care. Moreover, government data show that unwed mothers who keep their babies tend to be of lower socioeconomic status, and often require public assistance to support their children. The government can lower its social welfare expenses, then, if children are transferred to economically self-sufficient families. From an interactionist perspective, however, adoption may require a child to adjust to a very different family environment and parental approach to child rearing.

About 4 percent of all people in the United States are adopted, about half of whom were adopted by persons not related to them at birth. There are two legal methods of adopting an unrelated person: the adoption may be arranged through a licensed agency, or in some states it may be arranged through a private agreement sanctioned by the courts. Adopted children may come from the United States or from abroad. In 2003 more than 21,000 children entered the United States as the adopted children of U.S. citizens (Children's Bureau 2003; Department of State 2004; Fisher 2003).

In some cases the adopters are not married. In 1995, an important court decision in New York held that a couple does not need to be married to adopt a child. Under this ruling, unmarried heterosexual couples, lesbian couples, and gay male couples can all legally adopt children in New York. Writing for the majority, Chief Justice Judith Kaye argued that by expanding the boundaries of who can be legally recognized as parents, the state may be able to assist more children in securing "the best possible home." With this ruling, New York became the third state (after Vermont and Massachusetts) to recognize the right of unmarried couples to adopt children (Dao 1995).

For every child who is adopted, many more remain the wards of state-sponsored child protective services. At any given time, over half a million children in the United States are living in foster care. These children are often moved from family to family during their childhood and adolescence. Each year about 20,000 of them reach the age of 18 and enter adulthood without the financial or emotional support of a permanent family (Children's Bureau 2002; C. J. Williams 1999).

Dual-Income Families

The idea of a family consisting of a wage-earning husband and a wife who stays at home has largely given way to the *dual-income household*. Among married people between the ages of 25 and 34, 92 percent of the men and 75 percent of the women were in the labor force in 2002.

Why has there been such a rise in the number of dual-income couples? A major factor is economic need. In 2003, the median income for households with both partners employed was 99 percent more than in households in which only one person was working outside the home ($71,496, compared with $35,977). Of course, because of such work-related costs as child care, not all of a family's second wage is genuine additional income. Other factors that have contributed to the rise of the dual-income model include the nation's declining birthrate, the increase in the proportion of women with a college education, the shift in the economy of the United States from manufacturing to service industries, and the impact

What Is a Family?

The acclaimed amateur photographer Milton Rogovin (1994) first began photographing residents of the Lower West Side, a deeply impoverished multiethnic neighborhood in Buffalo, New York, in 1972. Over the next three years he made a thousand portraits in the six-block area. Residents slowly came to trust him and look forward to his visits, as he himself became attached to them. Twice over the next two decades, Rogovin returned to the neighborhood to photograph its people and document their changing lives and families (Burghart 2003).

Rogovin's well-known series of photographs shows how families change over time. His time-lapse portraits highlight the social dynamics of the family as it forms, grows, and develops from one generation to the next. As a couple makes room for children, then watches them mature and bear children of their own, their relationship with each other and with the larger society changes along with their family.

In 1973 this couple's four children were still young. When Rogovin returned in 1986, the children had grown but were still single. Six years later, in 1992, the original six-member household had become an extended family with four grandchildren.

1973

1986

1992

313

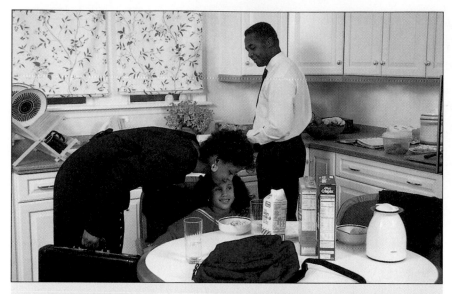

Dad takes breakfast duty while Mom rushes off to work in this dual-income family. An increasing proportion of couples in the United States reject the traditional nuclear family model of husband as breadwinner and wife as homemaker.

The lives of single parents and their children are not inevitably more difficult than life in a traditional nuclear family. It is as inaccurate to assume that a single-parent family is necessarily deprived as it is to assume that a two-parent family is always secure and happy. Nevertheless, life in a single-parent family can be extremely stressful, in both economic and emotional terms. A family headed by a single mother faces especially difficult problems when the mother is a teenager.

Why might low-income teenage women wish to have children and face the obvious financial difficulties of motherhood? Viewed from an interactionist perspective, these women tend to have low self-esteem and limited options; a child may provide a sense of motivation and purpose for a teenager whose economic worth in our society is limited at best. Given the barriers that many young women face because of their gender, race, ethnicity, and class, many teenagers may believe they have little to lose and much to gain by having a child.

of the feminist movement in changing women's consciousness (DeNavas-Walt et al. 2004:HINC-01 table).

Single-Parent Families

In the United States during the late 19th century, immigration and urbanization made it increasingly difficult to maintain *Gemeinschaft* communities, where everyone knew one another and shared the responsibility for unwed mothers and their children. In 1883, the Florence Crittenton Houses were founded in New York City—and subsequently around the nation—as refuges for prostitutes (then stigmatized as "fallen women"). Within a few years, the Crittenton homes began accepting unwed mothers as residents. By the early 1900s, sociologist W. E. B. Du Bois (1911) had noted that the institutionalization of unwed mothers was occurring in segregated facilities. At the time he was writing, there were seven homes for unwed Black mothers nationwide, as well as one Crittenton home reserved for that purpose.

In recent decades, the stigma attached to unwed mothers and other single parents has significantly diminished. *Single-parent families,* in which only one parent is present to care for the children, can hardly be viewed as a rarity in the United States. In 2000, a single parent headed about 21 percent of White families with children under 18, 35 percent of Hispanic families with children, and 55 percent of African American families with children (see Figure 12-3 on page 310).

According to a widely held stereotype, "unwed mothers" and "babies having babies" in the United States are predominantly African American. However, this view is not entirely accurate. African Americans account for a disproportionate share of births to unmarried women and teenagers, but the majority of all babies born to unmarried teenage mothers are born to White adolescents. Moreover, since 1980, birthrates among Black teenagers

SO EVEN THOUGH SHE'S FROM AN UNUSUAL FAMILY, WE STILL TREAT HEATHER WITH RESPECT.

Most households in the United States do not consist of two parents living with their unmarried children.

have declined steadily (B. Hamilton et al. 2003; J. Martin et al. 2003; Ventura et al. 2003).

Although 82 percent of single parents in the United States are mothers, the number of households headed by single fathers more than quadrupled over the period 1980 to 2000. The stereotypes of single fathers hold that they raise only boys or older children. But in 2002, about 43 percent of children living in such households were girls, and over one-third of children cared for by single fathers were preschoolers. Though single mothers often develop social networks, single fathers are typically more isolated. In addition, they must deal with schools and social service agencies that are more accustomed to women as custodial parents (Fields 2003).

Stepfamilies

Approximately 45 percent of all people in the United States will marry, divorce, and then remarry. The rising rates of divorce and remarriage have led to a noticeable increase in stepfamily relationships. In 1991, 9.4 percent of all children lived with a stepparent, but just five years later, that figure had increased to 16.5 percent (Furukawa 1994:4; Kreider and Fields 2002).

The exact nature of blended families has social significance for adults and children alike. Certainly resocialization is required when an adult becomes a stepparent or a child becomes a stepchild and stepsibling. Moreover, an important distinction must be made between first-time stepfamilies and households where there have been repeated divorces, breakups, or changes in custodial arrangements.

In evaluating the rise of stepfamilies, some observers have assumed that children would benefit from remarriage because they would be gaining a second custodial parent, and would potentially enjoy greater economic security. However, after reviewing many studies of stepfamilies, sociologist Andrew J. Cherlin (2002:476) concluded that "the well-being of children in stepfamilies is no better, on average, than the well-being of children in divorced, single-parent households."

Stepparents can play valuable and unique roles in their stepchildren's lives, but their involvement does not guarantee an improvement in family life. In fact, standards may decline. Studies suggest that children raised in families with stepmothers are likely to have less health care, education, and money spent on their food than children raised by biological mothers. The measures are also negative for children raised by stepfathers, but only half as negative as in the case of stepmothers. These results don't mean that stepmothers are "evil"—it may be that the stepmother holds back out of concern for seeming too intrusive, or relies mistakenly on the biological father to carry out parental duties (Lewin 2000).

DIVORCE

"Do you promise to love, honor, and cherish . . . until death do you part?" Every year, people of all social classes and racial and ethnic groups make this legally binding agreement. Yet an increasing number of these promises shatter in divorce.

Statistical Trends in Divorce

Just how common is divorce? Surprisingly, this is not a simple question; divorce statistics are difficult to interpret. The media frequently report that one out of every two marriages ends in divorce. But that figure is misleading, since many marriages last for decades. It is based on a comparison of all divorces that occur in a single year (regardless of when the couples were married) with the number of new marriages in the same year.

In the United States, and many other countries, divorce began to increase in the late 1960s, but then started to level off and has even declined since the late 1980s (see Figure 12-4). This trend is due partly to the aging of the baby boomer population and the corresponding decline in the proportion of people of marriageable age. But it also indicates an increase in marital stability in recent years.

FIGURE 12-4

Trends in Marriage and Divorce in the United States, 1920–2003

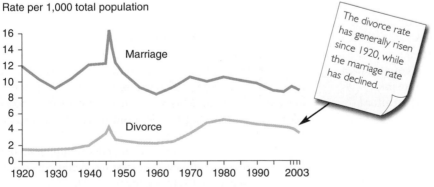

Rate per 1,000 total population

Sources: Bureau of the Census 1975:64, 2000a; National Vital Statistics Reports 2004.

Gender Stereotypes of single father shown to be incorrect
Methods Cherlin's analysis of stepfamilies utilized secondary analysis.

Student Alert Be sure students understand why it is misleading to say that one out of every two marriages ends in divorce.

Getting divorced obviously does not sour people on marriage. About 63 percent of all divorcees in the United States have remarried. Women are less likely than men to remarry because many retain custody of their children after a divorce, which complicates a new adult relationship (Bianchi and Spain 1996; Saad 2004).

Some people regard the nation's high rate of remarriage as an endorsement of the institution of marriage, but it does lead to the new challenges of a kin network composed of both current and prior marital relationships. Such networks can be particularly complex if children are involved or if an ex-spouse remarries.

Factors Associated with Divorce

Perhaps the most important factor in the increase in divorce over the last hundred years has been the greater social *acceptance* of divorce. It's no longer considered necessary to endure an unhappy marriage. More important, various religious denominations have relaxed their negative attitudes toward divorce, so that most religious leaders no longer treat it as a sin.

The growing acceptance of divorce is a worldwide phenomenon. Only a decade ago, Sunoo, South Korea's foremost matchmaking service, had no divorced clients. Few Koreans divorced; those who did felt social pressure to resign themselves to the single life. But over the last seven years, South Korea's divorce rate has doubled. Today, 15 percent of Sunoo's membership is divorced (Onishi 2003).

In the United States, several factors have contributed to the growing social acceptance of divorce:

- Most states have adopted more liberal divorce laws in the last three decades. No-fault divorce laws, which allow a couple to end their marriage without fault on either side (by specifying adultery, for instance), accounted for an initial surge in the divorce rate after they were introduced in the 1970s, but appear to have had little effect beyond that.
- Divorce has become a more practical option in newly formed families, since families tend to have fewer children now than in the past.
- A general increase in family incomes, coupled with the availability of free legal aid for some poor people, has meant that more couples can afford costly divorce proceedings.
- As society provides greater opportunities for women, more and more wives are becoming less dependent on their husbands, both economically and emotionally. They may feel more able to leave a marriage if it seems hopeless.

Impact of Divorce on Children

Divorce is traumatic for all involved, as Cornel West made clear in the excerpt that opened this chapter. But it has special meaning for the more than 1 million children whose parents divorce each year (see Box 12-2, opposite).

Of course, for some of these children, divorce signals the welcome end to a very dysfunctional relationship. A national sample conducted by sociologists Paul R. Amato and Alan Booth (1997) showed that in about a third of divorces, the children benefit from parental separation because it lessens their exposure to conflict. But in about 70 percent of divorces, the parents engaged in a low level of conflict; in those cases, the realities of divorce appeared to be harder for the children to bear than living with the marital unhappiness. Other researchers, using differing definitions of conflict, have found greater unhappiness for children living in homes with marital differences. Still, it would be simplistic to assume that children are automatically better off following the breakup of their parents' marriage. The interests of the parents do not necessarily serve children well.

> **Use Your Sociological Imagination**   www. mhhe.com /schaefer6
>
> In a society that maximizes the welfare of all family members, how easy should it be for couples to divorce? How easy should it be to get married?

DIVERSE LIFESTYLES

Marriage is no longer the presumed route from adolescence to adulthood. In fact, it has lost much of its social significance as a rite of passage. The nation's marriage rate has declined since 1960 because people are postponing marriage until later in life, and because more couples, including same-sex couples, are deciding to form partnerships without marriage.

Cohabitation

Saint Paul once wrote, "It is better to marry than to burn." However, as journalist Tom Ferrell (1979) has suggested, more people than ever "prefer combustible to connubial bliss." One of the most dramatic trends of recent years has been the tremendous increase in male–female couples who choose to live together without marrying, a practice called **cohabitation.**

About half of all *currently* married couples in the United States say that they lived together before marriage. This percentage is likely to increase. The number of unmarried-couple households in the United States rose

Theory Interactionist analysis of family networking after a divorce
Classroom Tip See "Inheriting Divorce" (Additional Lecture Ideas).
Classroom Tip See "Speakers" (Class Discussion Topics).
Global View Attitude toward divorce in South Korea

Methods Amato and Booth employed a survey to study children of divorce in the United States.
Let's Discuss How do students view divorce? How many are divorced? How many have divorced parents?
Contemporary Culture/Classroom Tip See "Good Marriages" (Class Discussion Topics).

12-2 THE LINGERING IMPACT OF DIVORCE

What happens to the children of divorce? Early research suggested that the negative effects of divorce on children were confined to the first few years following a breakup. According to these studies, most children eventually adjusted to the change in family structure and went on to live normal lives. But recent studies suggest that the effects of divorce may linger much longer than scholars at first suspected, peaking in the adult years, when grown children are attempting to establish their own marriages and families.

A foremost proponent of this view is psychologist Judith A. Wallerstein, who has been conducting qualitative research on the effects of divorce on children since 1971. Wallerstein has been following the original 131 children in her study for 30 years; her subjects are now ages 28 to 43. She is convinced that these adult children of divorce have had greater difficulty than other adults in forming and maintaining intimate relationships because they have never witnessed the daily give-and-take of a successful marital partnership.

Another researcher, sociologist Paul R. Amato, agrees that divorce can affect children into adulthood, but for a differ-

ent reason. Amato thinks that the parents' decision to end their marriage lies at the root of the higher-than-normal divorce rate among their children. In this study, based on telephone interviews, children whose parents had divorced had a 30 percent divorce rate themselves, which is 12 to 13 percent higher than the divorce rate among children whose parents had *not* divorced. Significantly, children of parents who did not divorce had

---

Recent studies suggest that the effects of divorce may linger much longer than scholars at first suspected.

---

roughly the same divorce rate regardless of whether the level of conflict in their parents' marriage was low or high. The parental example that a marriage contract can be broken—not the demonstration of poor relationship skills—is what makes an adult child more vulnerable than others to divorce, Amato thinks.

Sociologist Andrew J. Cherlin concedes that divorce can have lingering effects, but thinks the potential for harm

has been exaggerated. Cherlin, who has conducted quantitative analyses of the effects of divorce on thousands of children, finds that parental divorce does elevate children's risk of emotional problems, school withdrawal, and teen pregnancy. But most children, he emphasizes, do not develop those problems. Even Wallerstein admits that the ill effects of divorce do not apply across the board. Some children seem to be strengthened by the crisis, she observes, and go on to lead highly successful lives, both personally and professionally.

Let's Discuss

1. Do you know any adult children of divorce who have had difficulty establishing successful marriages? If so, what seems to be the problem, an inability to handle conflict or a lack of commitment to the marriage?

2. What practical conclusions should we draw from the research on children of divorce? Should couples stay together for the sake of their children?

Sources: Amato 2001; Amato and Sobolewski 2001; Bumiller 2000; Cherlin 2005; J. Wallerstein et al. 2000. For a different view, see Hetherington and Kelly 2002.

---

sixfold in the 1960s and increased another 72 percent between 1990 and 2000. Presently over 8 percent of opposite-sex couples are unmarried. Cohabitation is more common among African Americans and American Indians than among other racial and ethnic groups; it is least common among Asian Americans. Figure 12-5 (page 318) shows regional variations in cohabitation (K. Peterson 2003; T. Simmons and O'Connell 2003).

In much of Europe, cohabitation is so common that the general sentiment seems to be "Love, yes; marriage, maybe." In Iceland, 62 percent of all children are born to single mothers; in France, Great Britain, and Norway, the proportion is about 40 percent. Government policies in these countries make few legal distinctions between married and unmarried couples or households (Lyall 2002).

People commonly associate cohabitation only with college campuses or sexual experimentation. But according to a study done in Los Angeles, working couples are almost twice as likely to cohabit as college students. And census data show that in 2000, 41 percent of unmarried couples had one or more children present in the household. These cohabitants are more like spouses than dating partners. Moreover, in contrast to the common perception that people who cohabit have never been married, researchers report that about half of all people involved in cohabitation in the United States have been previously married. Cohabitation serves as a temporary or permanent alternative to matrimony for many men and women who have experienced their own or their parents' divorces (Fields 2003; Popenoe and Whitehead 1999).

Key Persons Judith A. Wallerstein, Paul Amato, Andrew Cherlin
Methods Wallerstein's research was qualitative.
Methods Amato's study was based on telephone interviews.
Methods Cherlin's study was quantitative in nature.

Methods Survey data on cohabitation in the United States and other countries
Let's Discuss Why is data on cohabitation harder to obtain than data on marriage?
Global View Cohabitation in European countries

FIGURE 12-5

Unmarried-Couple Households by State

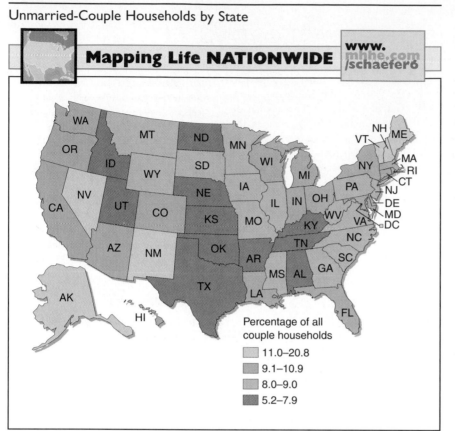

Mapping Life NATIONWIDE

www.
mhhe.com
/schaefer6

Percentage of all
couple households

- 11.0–20.8
- 9.1–10.9
- 8.0–9.0
- 5.2–7.9

Note: Data are for 2000 and include both opposite-sex and same-sex partners. U.S. average is 9.1 percent.
Source: T. Simmons and O'Connell 2003:4.

Recent research has documented significant increases in cohabitation among older people in the United States. For example, census data indicate that in 1980, 340,000 cohabiting opposite-sex couples were over the age of 45. By 1999, there were 1,108,000 such couples—three times as many. Older couples may choose cohabitation rather than marriage for many reasons: because of religious differences, to preserve the full Social Security benefits they receive as single people, out of fear of commitment, to avoid upsetting children from previous marriages, because one partner or both are not legally divorced, or because one or both have lived through a spouse's illness and death, and do not want to do so again. But some older couples simply see no need for marriage, and report being happy simply living together (Bureau of the Census 2001a:48).

Periodically, legislators attempt to bolster the desirability of a lifelong commitment to marriage. In 2002, President George W. Bush backed funding for an initiative to promote marriage among those who receive pub-

lic assistance. Under the "Healthy Marriage Initiative," married couples would receive special monthly bonuses not available to others. The proposal garnered widespread support, though it drew some opposition from defenders of single-parent families. The debate became more heated when activists succeeded in legalizing gay marriage in Massachusetts: see the social policy section at the end of this chapter (Cherlin 2003).

Remaining Single

Looking at TV programs today, you would be justified in thinking that most households are composed of singles. Although that is not the case, it is true that more and more people in the United States are *postponing* entry into first marriages. As of 2000, one out of every four households in the United States (accounting for over 28 million people) was a single-member household. Even so, fewer than 4 percent of women and men in the United States are likely to remain single throughout their lives (Bureau of the Census 2003a:60–61).

The trend toward maintaining a single lifestyle for a longer period is related to the growing economic independence of young people. This trend is especially significant for women. Freed from financial needs, women don't necessarily need to marry to enjoy a satisfying life. p. 281 Divorce, late marriage, and longevity also figure into this trend.

There are many reasons why a person may choose not to marry. Some singles do not want to limit their sexual intimacy to one lifetime partner. Some men and women do not want to become highly dependent on any one person—and do not want anyone depending heavily on them. In a society that values individuality and self-fulfillment, the single lifestyle can offer certain freedoms that married couples may not enjoy.

Remaining single represents a clear departure from societal expectations; indeed, it has been likened to "being single on Noah's Ark." A single adult must confront the inaccurate view that he or she is always lonely, is a workaholic, or is immature. These stereotypes help to sup-

Gender Greater options for women in the labor force remove financial pressures to marry.

port the traditional assumption in the United States and most other societies that to be truly happy and fulfilled, a person must get married and raise a family. To counter these societal expectations, singles have formed numerous support groups, such as Alternative to Marriage Project (www.unmarried.org).

Singlehood—living without a partner and without children—also has social implications for the broader society. According to Robert Putnam (2000) of Harvard University, people in the United States are now less active both politically and socially than they were in the 1970s, due in part to the fact that more of them are living the single life. Experts worry about a potential decline in support for local schools, as well as a probable rise in the number of elderly people needing home care (Belsie 2001).

Marriage without Children

There has been a modest increase in childlessness in the United States. According to census data, about 16 to 17 percent of women will now complete their childbearing years without having borne any children, compared to 10 percent in 1980. As many as 20 percent of women in their 30s expect to remain childless (Clausen 2002).

Childlessness within marriage has generally been viewed as a problem that can be solved through such means as adoption and artificial insemination. More and more couples today, however, choose not to have children, and regard themselves as child-free, not childless. They do not believe that having children automatically follows from marriage, nor do they feel that reproduction is the duty of all married couples. Childless couples have formed support groups (with names like No Kidding) and set up websites on the Internet (Terry 2000).

Economic considerations have contributed to this shift in attitudes; having children has become quite expensive. According to a government estimate made in 2001, the average middle-class family will spend $161,430 to feed, clothe, and shelter a child from birth to age 18. If the child attends college, that amount could double, depending on the college chosen. Aware of the financial pressures, some couples are having fewer children than they otherwise might, and others are weighing the advantages of a child-free marriage (Bureau of the Census 2003a:450).

Childless couples are beginning to question current practices in the workplace. While applauding employers' p. 98 efforts to provide child care and flexible work schedules, some nevertheless express concern about tolerance of employees who leave early to take children to doctors, ballgames, or after-school classes. As

more dual-career couples enter the paid labor force and struggle to balance career and familial responsibilities, conflicts with employees who have no children may increase (Burkett 2000).

Use Your Sociological Imagination www.mhhe.com/schaefer6

What would happen to our society if many more married couples suddenly decided not to have children? How would society change if cohabitation and/or singlehood became the norm?

Lesbian and Gay Relationships

Twenty-one-year-old Parke, a junior in college, grew up in a stable, loving family. A self-described fiscal conservative, he credits his parents with instilling in him a strong work ethic. Sound like an average child of an average family? The only break with traditional expectations in this case is that Parke is the son of a lesbian couple (P. L. Brown 2004).

The lifestyles of lesbians and gay men are varied. Some live in long-term, monogamous relationships; others live alone or with roommates. Some remain in "empty-shell" heterosexual marriages and do not publicly acknowledge their homosexuality. Others live with children from a former marriage or with adopted children. Based on election exit polls, researchers for the National Health and Social Life Survey and the Voter News Service estimate that 2 to 5 percent of the adult population identify themselves as either gay or lesbian. An analysis of the 2000 census shows a minimum of at least 600,000 gay households, and a gay and lesbian adult population approaching 10 million (Lauman et al. 1994b:293; David M. Smith and Gates 2001).

Gay and lesbian couples face discrimination on both a personal and a legal level. Their inability to marry denies them many rights that married couples take for granted, from the ability to make decisions for an incapacitated partner to the right to receive government benefits to dependents, such as Social Security payments. Though gay couples consider themselves families, just like the ones who live down the street, they are often treated as if they are not. For instance, one gay couple in Connecticut was denied a family membership at their municipal swimming pool (*New York Times* 1998).

Precisely because of such inequities, many gay and lesbian couples are now demanding the right to marry. In the social policy section that follows we will examine the highly controversial issue of gay marriage.

Theory/Classroom Tip Indicate how interactionists and functionalists would comment on the formation of support groups among singles.
Contemporary Culture Having children has become quite expensive.

Methods The NHSLS study was an example of survey research; the census findings on gay households also relied on survey research.
Methods Use of census data to determine occurrence of gay and lesbian couples in the United States
Classroom Tip See "Joint Marriage Rights" (Additional Lecture Ideas).

The Issue

In the United States, attitudes toward marriage are complex. As always, society and popular culture suggest that a young man or woman should find the perfect mate, settle down and marry, and live "happily ever after." But young people are also bombarded by messages implying the frequency of adultery and the acceptability of divorce. In this atmosphere, the idea of same-sex marriage strikes some people as only the latest of many attacks on traditional marriage. To others, it seems an overdue acknowledgment of the formal relationships that faithful, monogamous gay couples have long maintained.

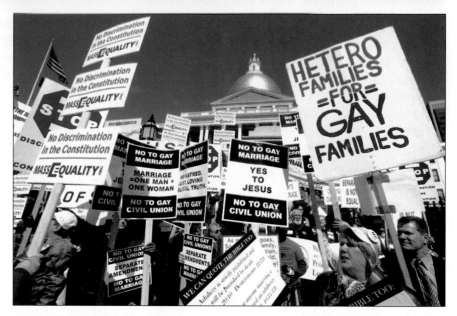

Sin or civil right? Protesters both for and against gay marriage clashed in this demonstration outside the Massachusetts State House in Boston.

The Setting

In 2004, in his State of the Union message, President George W. Bush warned "activist judges" against attempts to broaden the definition of marriage to include same-sex couples. The only recourse to such measures, he said, would be a constitutional amendment banning same-sex unions.

What made gay marriage the focus of national attention? Events in two states brought the issue to the forefront. In 1999, Vermont gave gay couples the legal benefits of marriage through civil union, but stopped short of calling the arrangement a marriage. Then, in 2003, the Massachusetts Supreme Court ruled 4–3 that under the state's constitution, gay couples have the right to marry.

Sociological Insights

Functionalists have traditionally seen marriage as a social institution that is closely tied to human reproduction. Same-sex marriage would at first appear not to fit that arrangement. But many same-sex couples are entrusted with the socialization of young children, whether or not their relationship is recognized by the state. Functionalists also wonder whether religious views toward marriage can be ignored. The courts have focused on civil marriage, but religious views are hardly

irrelevant, even in a country like the United States, which observes a separation between religion and the state. Indeed, religious teachings have led even some staunch supporters of gay rights to oppose same-sex marriage on spiritual grounds.

Conflict theorists have charged that denial of the right to marry reinforces the second-class status of gays and lesbians. Some have compared the ban against gay marriage to past policies that banned interracial marriage in 32 states (Liptak 2004b).

Interactionists generally avoid the policy question and focus instead on the nature of same-sex households. They ask many of the same questions about gay partner relations and child rearing that they raise about conventional couples. Of course, much less research has been done on same-sex households than on other families, but the studies published to date raise the same issues as those that apply to conventional married couples, plus a few more. For gay couples, the support or opposition of family, co-workers, and friends looms large (Dundas and Kaufman 2000; G. Dunne 2000).

Recently, national surveys of attitudes toward gay marriage have been showing volatile shifts in public opinion. Typically, people are more opposed to gay

FIGURE 12-6

Discriminatory Marriage and Anti–Gay Discrimination Laws

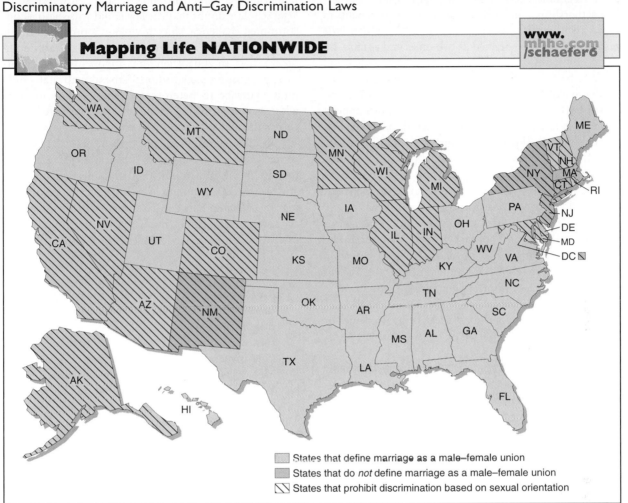

Mapping Life NATIONWIDE

www.
mhhe.com
/schaefer6

☐ States that define marriage as a male–female union
▨ States that do *not* define marriage as a male–female union
⧄ States that prohibit discrimination based on sexual orientation

Note: Vermont prohibits same-sex marriage but provides for same-sex civil union.
Source: Human Rights Campaign 2004.

marriage than to civil union: about one-third of respondents favor gay marriage, while as many as half favor civil union. Still, less than half the population endorses a constitutional amendment to ban gay marriage (ABC News/*Washington Post* 2004).

Policy Initiatives

The United States is not the first nation to consider this issue. Recognition of same-sex partnerships is not uncommon in Europe, including Denmark, the Netherlands, France, Germany, Italy, and Portugal. In 2001, the Netherlands converted its "registered same-sex partnerships" to full-fledged marriages, with provisions for divorce. As many as 8 percent of all marriages there are now same-sex. The trend is toward recognition in North America as well. In the province of Ontario, Canada, in 2003, same-sex marriages were upheld as legal, with the expectation that proposed legislation would extend the policy to the entire nation (Lyall 2004; Richburg 2003).

Many nations are strongly opposed to such measures, however. For example, when Kofi Annan, secretary general of the United Nations (UN), proposed extending the benefits that married UN employees receive to employees' same-sex partners in 2004, so many countries rose in protest that he reneged. Annan decided that such benefits would extend only to those UN employees whose member nations extend the same benefits to their citizens. Of the UN's 191 member nations, only two—Belgium and the Netherlands—extend the full benefits of marriage to same-sex couples (Farley 2004).

Methods Survey of public opinion on same-sex marriage
Global View Policies on same-sex partnerships in Europe.

In the United States, many local jurisdictions have passed legislation allowing for the registration of domestic partnerships, and have extended employee benefits to those relationships. Under such policies, a *domestic partnership* may be defined as two unrelated adults who share a mutually caring relationship, reside together, and agree to be jointly responsible for their dependents, basic living expenses, and other common necessities. Domestic partnership benefits can apply to couples' inheritance, parenting, pensions, taxation, housing, immigration, workplace fringe benefits, and health care. Even though the most passionate support for domestic partnership legislation has come from lesbian and gay male activists, the majority of those eligible for such benefits would be cohabiting heterosexual couples.

Such legislation faces strong opposition from conservative religious and political groups, however. In the view of opponents, support for domestic partnership undermines society's historic preference for the nuclear family. Advocates of domestic partnership counter that such relationships fulfill the same functions as the traditional family, both for the individuals involved and for society; they should therefore enjoy the same legal protections and benefits.

In the United States, marriage has traditionally been under the jurisdiction of state lawmakers. But recently, pressure has been mounting for national legislation. The Defense of Marriage Act, passed in 1996, provided that no state is obliged to recognize same-sex marriages performed in another state. However, some legal scholars doubt that the law could withstand a constitutional challenge, since it violates a provision in the Constitution that requires states to recognize one another's laws. In 2003, therefore, opponents of gay marriage proposed a constitutional amendment that would limit marriage to heterosexual couples. The measure was introduced in the Senate in 2004, but failed to receive sufficient support to come to a vote.

In the meantime, as Figure 12-6 (page 321) shows, some states have moved to ban same-sex marriage, though they still prohibit discrimination against gays and lesbians. And though local jurisdictions such as the mayor's office in San Francisco may perform marriage ceremonies amid great publicity, the marriage certificates they confer on gay couples are of dubious legality.

Let's Discuss

1. If marriage is good for heterosexual couples and their families, why isn't it good for homosexual couples and their families?
2. How can interactionist studies of gay couples and their families inform policymakers who are dealing with the issue of gay marriage? Give a specific example.
3. Who are the stakeholders in the debate over gay marriage, and what do they stand to gain or lose? Whose interest do you think is most important?

GETTING INVOLVED

www.
mhhe.com
/schaefer6

To get involved in the debate over gay marriage, visit this text's Online Learning Center, which offers links to relevant websites. Check out the Social Policy section in the Online Learning Center as well; it provides survey data on U.S. public opinion regarding this issue.

CHAPTER RESOURCES

Summary

The *family,* in its many varying forms, is present in all human cultures. This chapter examines the state of marriage, the family, and other intimate relationships in the United States and considers alternatives to the traditional nuclear family.

1. Families vary from culture to culture and even within the same culture.
2. The structure of the *extended family* can offer certain advantages over that of the *nuclear family.*

3. Societies determine *kinship* by descent from both parents *(bilateral descent),* from the father only *(patrilineal descent),* or from the mother only *(matrilineal descent).*
4. Sociologists do not agree on whether the *egalitarian family* has replaced the patriarchal family as the social norm in the United States.
5. William F. Ogburn outlined six basic functions of the family: reproduction, protection, socialization,

Let's Discuss How is a domestic partnership different from a marriage?
Let's Discuss How is the concept of dominant ideology relevant in examining the controversy over domestic partnerships?

regulation of sexual behavior, companionship, and the provision of social status.

6. Conflict theorists argue that male dominance of the family contributes to societal injustice and denies women opportunities that are extended to men.

7. Interactionists focus on how individuals interact in the family and in other intimate relationships.

8. Feminists stress the need to broaden research on the family. Like conflict theorists, they see the family's role in socializing children as the primary source of sexism.

9. Mates are selected in a variety of ways. Some marriages are arranged; in other societies people choose their own mates. Some societies require mates to be chosen within a certain group *(endogamy)* or outside certain groups *(exogamy)*.

10. In the United States, family life varies with social class, race, and ethnicity.

11. Currently, in the majority of all married couples in the United States, both husband and wife work outside the home.

12. *Single-parent families* account for an increasing proportion of U.S. families.

13. Among the factors that contribute to the rising divorce rate in the United States are greater social acceptance of divorce and the liberalization of divorce laws in many states.

14. More and more people are living together without marrying, a practice known as *cohabitation.* People are also staying single longer, and some married couples are deciding not to have children.

15. The gay marriage movement, which would confer equal rights on gay and lesbian couples and their dependents, is strongly opposed by conservative religious and political groups.

Critical Thinking Questions

1. In an increasing proportion of couples in the United States, both partners work outside the home. What are the advantages and disadvantages of the dual-income model for women, for men, for children, and for society as a whole?

2. Consider the foster care system in the United States. Given the fact that so many children in the United States need caring homes, why do so many couples seek to adopt foreign children? Why do state agencies often deny same-sex couples the right to adopt? What can be done to improve the foster care system?

3. Given the high rate of divorce in the United States, would it be more appropriate to view divorce as dysfunctional or as a normal part of our marriage system? What would be the implications of viewing divorce as normal rather than as dysfunctional?

Key Terms

Adoption In a legal sense, a process that allows for the transfer of the legal rights, responsibilities, and privileges of parenthood to a new legal parent or parents. (page 311)

Bilateral descent A kinship system in which both sides of a person's family are regarded as equally important. (303)

Cohabitation The practice of living together as a male–female couple without marrying. (316)

Domestic partnership Two unrelated adults who share a mutually caring relationship, reside together, and agree to be jointly responsible for their dependents, basic living expenses, and other common necessities. (322)

Egalitarian family An authority pattern in which spouses are regarded as equals. (303)

Endogamy The restriction of mate selection to people within the same group. (307)

Exogamy The requirement that people select a mate outside certain groups. (307)

Extended family A family in which relatives—such as grandparents, aunts, or uncles—live in the same home as parents and their children. (301)

Familism Pride in the extended family, expressed through the maintenance of close ties and strong obligations to kinfolk outside the immediate family. (309)

Family A set of people related by blood, marriage or some other agreed-upon relationship, or adoption, who share the primary responsibility for reproduction and caring for members of society. (301)

Incest taboo The prohibition of sexual relationships between certain culturally specified relatives. (307)

Kinship The state of being related to others. (303)

Machismo A sense of virility, personal worth, and pride in one's maleness. (309)

Matriarchy A society in which women dominate in family decision making. (303)

Matrilineal descent A kinship system in which only the relatives of the mother are significant. (303)

Monogamy A form of marriage in which one woman and one man are married only to each other. (302)

Nuclear family A married couple and their unmarried children living together. (301)

Patriarchy A society in which men dominate in family decision making. (303)

Patrilineal descent A kinship system in which only the relatives of the father are significant. (303)

Polyandry A form of polygamy in which a woman may have more than one husband at the same time. (302)

Polygamy A form of marriage in which an individual may have several husbands or wives simultaneously. (302)

Polygyny A form of polygamy in which a man may have more than one wife at the same time. (302)

Serial monogamy A form of marriage in which a person may have several spouses in his or her lifetime, but only one spouse at a time. (302)

Single-parent family A family in which only one parent is present to care for the children. (314)

TECHNOLOGY RESOURCES

Internet Connection

*Note: While all the URLs listed were current as of the printing of this book, these sites often change. Please check our website (**www.mhhe.com/schaefer6**) for updates, hyperlinks, and exercises related to these sites.*

1. More and more U.S. families include two income earners. In such households, spouses must find a way to balance their work and family obligations and accommodate each other's career needs. The Employment and Family Careers Institute at Cornell University is devoted to the study of dual-career families. Explore the institute's site (**www.lifecourse.cornell.edu/cci/default.html**) to learn more about this social trend.

2. U.S. families have undergone rapid change over the past few decades. To read about the latest trends, go to the Census Bureau's website (**www.census.gov**). Under Subjects A to Z, click on "Families/Households and Families Data" and select the most recent report titled "America's Families and Living Arrangements."

Online Learning Center with PowerWeb

Visit the student center in the Online Learning Center at **www.mhhe.com/schaefer6** and link to "Audio Clips." Listen to Richard Schaefer, the author of this text, discuss how chat rooms are playing the role that singles' bars did in the 1980s. Professor Schaefer notes that sociologists are trying to determine whether the Internet is restructuring dating behavior or merely facilitating it.

Reel Society Interactive Movie CD-ROM 2.0

Reel Society 2.0 can be used to spark discussion about the following topics from this chapter:

- Authority Patterns
- Studying the Family
- Marriage and Family
- Diverse Lifestyles

13

RELIGION AND EDUCATION

In this billboard, Volkswagen of France compares a secular event, the introduction of a new model ("Rejoice, my friends, for a new Golf is born"), to a sacred event. While such tongue-in-cheek references to religion may offend believers, they indicate the continuing relevance of religion, even in modern, industrialized societies.

Growing up in a small mixed-blood community of seven hundred on the eastern edge of the Pine Ridge Reservation in South Dakota, I uncritically accepted the idea that the old Dakota religion and Christianity were both "true" and in some mysterious way compatible with each other. There were, to be sure, Christian fundamentalists with their intolerance and the old traditional Indians who kept their practices hidden, but the vast majority of the people in the vicinity more or less assumed that a satisfactory blend had been achieved that guaranteed our happiness.

Although my father was an Episcopal priest with a large number of chapels in a loosely organized Episcopal missionary district known (to Episcopalians) as "Corn Creek," he was far from an orthodox follower of the white man's religion. I always had the feeling that within the large context of "religion," which in a border town meant the Christian milieu, there was a special area in his spiritual life in which the old Dakota beliefs and practices reigned supreme. He knew thirty-three songs; some of them social, some ancient, and several spiritual songs used in a variety of ceremonial contexts. Driving to his chapels to hold Christian services he would open the window of the car and beat the side of the door with his hand for the drum beat and sing song after song....

When I went to college I was exposed to a much larger canvas of human experience upon which various societies had left their religious mark. My first reaction was the belief that most of the religious traditions were simply wrong, that a few of them had come close

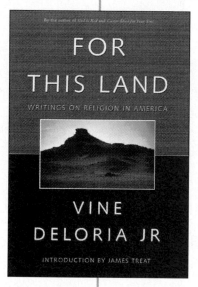

to describing religious reality, but that it would take some intensive study to determine which religious traditions would best assist human beings in succeeding in the world. It was my good fortune to have as a religion and philosophy professor a Christian mystic who was trying to prove the deepest mysteries of the faith. He also had some intense personal problems which emerged again and again in his beliefs, indicating to me that religion and the specific individual path of life were always intertwined.

Over several years and many profound conversations he was able to demonstrate to me that each religious tradition had developed a unique way to confront some problems and that they had something in common if only the search for truth and the elimination of many false paths. But his solution, after many years, became untenable for me. I saw instead religion simply as a means of organizing a society, articulating some reasonably apparent emotional truths, but ultimately becoming a staid part of social establishments that primarily sought to control human behavior and not fulfill human individual potential. It seemed as if those religions that placed strong emphasis on certain concepts failed precisely in the areas in which they claimed expertise. Thus religions of "love" could point to few examples of their efficacy; religions of "salvation" actually saved very few. The more I learned about world religions, the more respect I had for the old Dakota ways. *(Deloria 1999:273–275)* ■ ⊚

Additional information about this excerpt can be found on the Online Learning Center at **www.mhhe.com/schaefer6.**

326

In this excerpt from *For This Land,* Vine Deloria—a Standing Rock Sioux—reveals his deep personal ties to the religion of his ancestors, undiluted by the overlays of missionary Christian theology. Though his father is an Episcopal priest, Deloria is keenly aware of how tribal beliefs intrude on and color his father's religious sensibility. He is also aware of the fact that Native American rites and customs have been appropriated by a generation of non-Indians seeking a kind of New Age "magic." For Deloria, Indian spiritual beliefs are an integral part of the Native American culture and help to define that culture. Mixing those beliefs with the beliefs of other religions or systems of thought threatens to undermine the culture's strength.

Religion plays a major role in people's lives, and religious practices of some sort are evident in every society. That makes religion a *cultural universal,* along with other common practices or beliefs found in every

p. 58 culture, such as dancing, food preparation, the family, and personal names. At present, an estimated 4 billion people belong to the world's many religious faiths (see Figure 13-1, page 328).

When religion's influence on other social institutions in a society diminishes, the process of *secularization* is said to be under way. During this process, religion will survive in the private sphere of individual and family life (as in the case of many Native American families); it may even thrive on a personal level. But at the same time, other social institutions—such as the economy, politics, and education—maintain their own sets of norms, independent of religious guidance (Stark and Iannaccone 1992).

Like religion, education is a cultural universal. As such it is an important aspect of socialization—the lifelong process of learning the attitudes, values, and behavior considered appropriate to members of a particular culture. As we saw in Chapter 4, socialization can occur in the classroom or at home, through interactions with parents, teachers, friends, and even strangers. Exposure to books, films, television, and other forms of communication also promotes socialization. When learning is explicit and formalized—when some people consciously teach, while others adopt the role of learner—the process of socialization is called *education.* But students learn far more about their society at school than what is included in the curriculum.

What social purposes do education and religion serve? Does religion help to hold society together or foster social change? What is the "hidden curriculum" in U.S. schools? Do public schools offer everyone a way up the socioeconomic ladder, or do they reinforce divisions among social classes? This chapter concentrates on the formal systems of education and religion that characterize modern industrial societies. We will begin with a brief description of the sociological approach to religion, followed by an overview of the world's major religions. Next, we will explore religion's role in societal integration, social support, social change, and social control. We'll examine three important dimensions of religious behavior—belief, ritual, and experience—as well as the basic forms of religious organization, including new religious movements. Then we'll discuss three theoretical perspectives on education. We'll examine schools as formal organizations—as bureaucracies and as subcultures of teachers and students. The chapter will close with a social policy discussion of the controversy over religion in the public schools. ■

DURKHEIM AND THE SOCIOLOGICAL APPROACH TO RELIGION

If a group believes that it is being directed by a "vision from God," sociologists will not attempt to prove or disprove the revelation. Instead, they will assess the effects of the religious experience on the group. What sociologists are interested in is the social impact of religion on individuals and institutions (McGuire 2002).

Émile Durkheim was perhaps the first sociologist to recognize the critical importance of religion in human societies. He saw its appeal for the individual, but more important, he stressed the *social* impact of religion. In

p. 10 Durkheim's view, religion is a collective act that includes many forms of behavior in which people interact with others. As in his work on suicide, Durkheim was not so interested in the personalities of religious believers as he was in understanding religious behavior within a social context.

Durkheim defined *religion* as a "unified system of beliefs and practices relative to sacred things." In his view, religion involves a set of beliefs and practices that are uniquely the property of religion, as opposed to other social institutions and ways of thinking. Durkheim ([1912] 2001) argued that religious faiths distinguish between certain transcending events and the everyday world. He referred to those realms as the *sacred* and the *profane.*

Classroom Tip See "Stimulating Classroom Discussions about *For This Land*" (Class Discussion Topics).
Race/Ethnicity Native American religious beliefs
Classroom Tip Review material about assimilation and pluralism in Chapter 10.

Student Alert Sociology evaluates religion not as an element of human belief but as a part of culture, like the family and education, and a collective act.
Key Person Émile Durkheim
Theory Durkheim's functionalist analysis of religion as a collective act

FIGURE 13-1

Religions of the World

Mapping Life **WORLDWIDE**

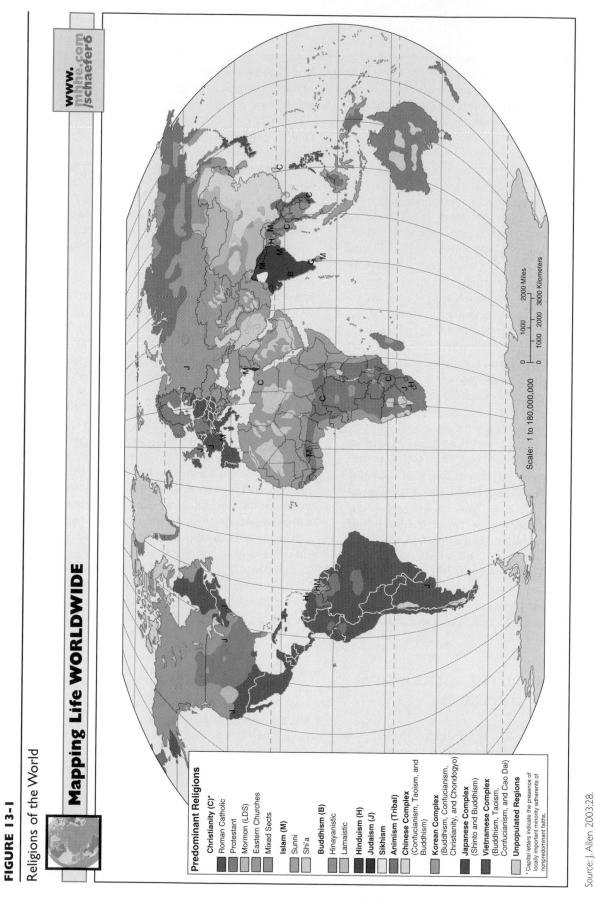

Predominant Religions

Christianity (C)*
- Roman Catholic
- Protestant
- Mormon (LDS)
- Eastern Churches
- Mixed Sects

Islam (M)
- Sunni
- Shi'a

Buddhism (B)
- Hinayanistic
- Lamaistic

Hinduism (H)

Judaism (J)

Sikhism

Animism (Tribal)

Chinese Complex
(Confucianism, Taoism, and Buddhism)

Korean Complex
(Buddhism, Confucianism, Christianity, and Chondogyo)

Japanese Complex
(Shinto and Buddhism)

Vietnamese Complex
(Buddhism, Taoism, Confucianism, and Cao Dai)

Unpopulated Regions

* Capital letters indicate the presence of locally important minority adherents of nonpredominant faiths.

Scale: 1 to 180,000,000

0   1000   2000 Miles
0   1000   2000   3000 Kilometers

Source: J. Allen 2003:28.

Web Resource Remind students this map is also an interactive map in the student center of the Online Learning Center **(www.mhhe.com/schaefer6).**

The *sacred* encompasses elements beyond everyday life that inspire awe, respect, and even fear. People become part of the sacred realm only by completing some ritual, such as prayer or sacrifice. Because believers have faith in the sacred, they accept what they cannot understand. In contrast, the *profane* includes the ordinary and commonplace. This concept can be confusing, however, because the same object can be either sacred or profane, depending on how it is viewed. A normal dining room table is profane, but becomes sacred to some Christians if it bears the elements of a communion. A candelabra becomes sacred to Jews if it is a menorah. For Confucians and Taoists, incense sticks are not mere decorative items, but highly valued offerings to the gods in religious ceremonies that mark the new and full moons.

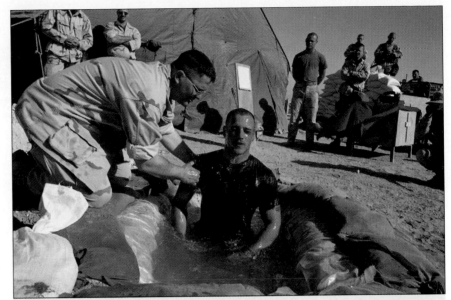

A military chaplain baptizes a U.S. Marine in the Kuwaiti desert during the 2003 war in Iraq. Chaplains turn secular space into sacred space, bringing comfort to soldiers serving far from home.

Following the direction established by Durkheim almost a century ago, contemporary sociologists view religions in two different ways. They study the norms and values of religious faiths by examining their substantive beliefs. For example, it is possible to compare the degree to which Christian faiths interpret the Bible literally, or Muslim groups follow the Qur'an (or Koran), the sacred book of Islam. At the same time, sociologists examine religions in terms of the social functions they fulfill, such as providing social support or reinforcing social norms. By exploring both the beliefs and the functions of religion, we can better understand its impact on the individual, on groups, and on society as a whole.

WORLD RELIGIONS

Tremendous diversity exists in religious beliefs and practices. Overall, about 85 percent of the world's population adheres to some religion; only about 15 percent is nonreligious. Christianity is the largest single faith; the second largest is Islam (see Table 13-1, page 330). Although news events often suggest an inherent conflict between Christians and Muslims, the two faiths are similar in many ways. Both are monotheistic (that is, based on a single deity); both include a belief in prophets, an afterlife, and a judgment day. In fact, Islam recognizes Jesus as a prophet, though not as the son of God. Both faiths impose a moral code on believers, which varies from fairly rigid proscriptions for fundamentalists to relatively relaxed guidelines for liberals (Barrett and Johnson 2004).

The followers of Islam, called *Muslims,* believe that Islam's holy scriptures were received from Allah (God) by the prophet Mohammad nearly 1,400 years ago. They see Mohammad as the last in a long line of prophets, preceded by Adam, Abraham, Moses, and Jesus. Islam is more communal in its expression than Christianity, particularly the more individualistic Protestant denominations. Consequently, in countries that are predominantly Muslim, the separation of religion and the state is not considered necessary or even desirable. In fact, Muslim governments often reinforce Islamic practices through their laws. Muslims do vary sharply in their interpretation of several traditions, some of which—such as the wearing of veils by women—are more cultural than religious in origin.

Like Christianity and Islam, Judaism is monotheistic. Jews believe that God's true nature is revealed in the Torah, which Christians know as the first five books of the Old Testament. According to these scriptures, God formed a covenant, or pact, with Abraham and Sarah, the ancestors of the tribes of Israel. Even today, Jews believe, this covenant holds them accountable to God's will. If they follow both the letter and spirit of the Torah, a long-awaited Messiah will one day bring paradise to earth. Although Judaism has a relatively small following compared

Classroom Tip See "Unitarian Universalism" (Additional Lecture Ideas).
Global View Comparison of Christianity and Islam

Contemporary Culture How have Americans' views of Islam changed since September 11, 2001?

summingUP

Table 13-1	Major World Religions			
Faith	**Current Following, in Millions (and Percent of World Population)**	**Primary Location of Followers Today**	**Founder (and Approximate Birth Date)**	**Important Texts (and Holy Sites)**
Buddhism	364 (5.9%)	Southeast Asia, Mongolia, Tibet	Gautama Siddhartha (563 B.C.)	Triptaka (areas in Nepal)
Christianity	2,039 (33%)	Europe, North America, South America	Jesus (6 B.C.)	Bible (Jerusalem, Rome)
Hinduism	828 (13.3%)	India, Indian communities overseas	No specific founder (1500 B.C.)	Sruti and Smrti texts (seven sacred cities, including Vavansi)
Islam	1,226 (19.8%)	Middle East, Central Asia, North Africa, Indonesia	Mohammad (A.D. 570)	Qur'an, or Koran (Mecca, Medina, Jerusalem)
Judaism	14 (0.2%)	Israel, United States, France, Russia	Abraham (2000 B.C.)	Torah, Talmud (Jerusalem)

to other major faiths, it forms the historical foundation for both Christianity and Islam. That is why Jews revere many of the same sacred Middle Eastern sites as Christians and Muslims.

Two other major faiths developed in a different part of the world, India. The earliest, Hinduism, originated around 1500 B.C. Hinduism differs from Judaism, Christianity, and Islam in that it embraces a number of gods and minor gods, although most worshipers are devoted primarily to a single deity, such as Shiva or Vishnu. Hinduism is also distinguished by a belief in reincarnation, or the perpetual rebirth of the soul after death. Unlike Judaism, Christianity, and Islam, which are based largely on sacred texts, Hindu beliefs have been preserved mostly through oral tradition.

A second religion, Buddhism, developed in the sixth century B.C. as a reaction against Hinduism. This faith is founded on the teachings of Siddhartha (later called Buddha, or "the enlightened one"). Through meditation, followers of Buddhism strive to overcome selfish cravings for physical or material pleasures, with the goal of reaching a state of enlightenment, or *nirvana*. Buddhists created the first monastic orders, which are thought to be the models for monastic orders in other religions, including Christianity. Though Buddhism emerged in India, its followers were eventually driven out of that country by the Hindus. It is now found primarily in other parts of Asia. (Contemporary adherents of Buddhism in India are relatively recent converts.)

Although the differences among religions are striking, they are exceeded by variations within faiths. Consider the differences within Christianity, from relatively liberal denominations such as Presbyterians or the United Church of Christ to the more conservative Mormons and Greek Orthodox Catholics. Similar divisions exist within Hinduism, Islam, and other world religions (Barrett and Johnson 2001; David Levinson 1996).

THE ROLE OF RELIGION

Since religion is a cultural universal, it is not surprising that it plays a basic role in human societies. In sociological terms, it performs both manifest and latent functions. Among its *manifest* (open and stated) functions, religion defines the spiritual world and gives meaning to the divine. It provides an explanation for events that seem difficult to understand, such as what lies beyond the grave. The *latent* functions of religion are unintended, covert, or hidden. Even though the manifest

p. 14

function of a church service is to offer a forum for religious worship, it might at the same time fulfill a latent social function as a meeting ground for unmarried members.

Functionalists and conflict theorists both evaluate religion's impact on human societies. We'll consider a functionalist view of religion's role in integrating society, providing social support, and promoting social change, and then look at religion from the conflict perspective, as a means of social control. Note that for the most part, religion's impact is best understood from a macro-level viewpoint that is oriented toward the larger society. Its social support function is an exception: it is best viewed on the micro, or individual, level.

The Integrative Function of Religion

Émile Durkheim viewed religion as an integrative force in human society—a perspective that is reflected in functionalist thought today. Durkheim sought to answer a perplexing question: "How can human societies be held together when they are generally composed of individuals and social groups with diverse interests and aspirations?" In his view, religious bonds often transcend these personal and divisive forces. Durkheim acknowledged that religion is not the only integrative force; nationalism or patriotism may serve the same end.

How does religion provide this "societal glue"? Religion, whether it be Buddhism, Islam, Christianity, or Judaism, gives meaning and purpose to people's lives. It offers certain ultimate values and ends to hold in common. Although they are subjective and not always fully accepted, these values and ends help society to function as an integrated social system. For example, funerals, weddings, bar and bat mitzvahs, and confirmations serve to integrate people into larger communities by providing shared beliefs and values about the ultimate questions of life.

Religion also serves to bind people together in times of crisis and confusion. Immediately after the terrorist attacks of September 11, 2001, on New York City and Washington, D.C., attendance at worship services in the United States increased dramatically. Muslim, Jewish, and Christian clerics made joint appearances to honor the dead and urge citizens not to retaliate against those who looked, dressed, or sounded different from others. A year later, however, attendance levels had returned to normal (D. Moore 2002).

The integrative power of religion can be seen, too, in the role that churches, synagogues, and mosques have traditionally played and continue to play for immigrant groups in the United States. For example, Roman Catholic immigrants may settle near a parish church that offers services in their native language, such as Polish or Spanish. Similarly, Korean immigrants may join a Presbyterian church that has many Korean American members and follows religious practices like those of churches in Korea. Like other religious organizations, these Roman Catholic and Presbyterian churches help to integrate immigrants into their new homeland.

In some instances, religious loyalties are *dysfunctional;* that is, they contribute to tension and even conflict between groups or nations. During the Second World War, the German Nazis attempted to exterminate the Jewish people; approximately 6 million European Jews were killed. In modern times, nations such as Lebanon (Muslims versus Christians), Israel (Jews versus Muslims, as well as Orthodox versus secular Jews), Northern Ireland (Roman Catholics versus Protestants), and India (Hindus versus Muslims, and more recently, Sikhs) have been torn by clashes that are in large part based on religion. (See the case study on page 342 for a more detailed discussion of religious conflict in India.)

Religious conflict (though on a less violent level) has been increasingly evident in the United States as well. Sociologist James Davison Hunter (1991) has referred to the "cultural war" taking place in the United States. In many communities, Christian fundamentalists, conservative Catholics, and Orthodox Jews have joined forces in a battle against liberal denominations for control of the secular culture. The battlefield is an array of familiar social issues, among them multiculturalism, child care (Chapter 4), abortion (Chapter 11), home schooling, gay rights, pp. 98, 293 media censorship, and government funding for the arts.

Religion and Social Support

Most of us find it difficult to accept the stressful events of life—the death of a loved one, serious injury, bankruptcy, divorce, and so forth. This is especially true when something "senseless" happens. How can family and friends come to terms with the death of a talented college student, not even 20 years old?

Through its emphasis on the divine and the supernatural, religion allows us to "do something" about the calamities we face. In some faiths, adherents can offer sacrifices or pray to a deity in the belief that such acts will change their earthly condition. On a more basic level, religion encourages us to view our personal misfortunes as relatively unimportant in the broader perspective of human history—or even as part of an undisclosed divine purpose. Friends and relatives of the deceased college student may see his death as being "God's will" or as having some ultimate benefit that we cannot understand now. This perspective may be much more comforting than the

Theory Functionalist view of the integrative function of religion
Contemporary Culture Worship attendance in the United States increased dramatically following the terrorist attacks on September 11, 2001 but returned to normal after a year.
Race/Ethnicity Churches, synagogues, and mosques help to integrate immigrants in the United States.

Theory Functionalist view of dysfunctions of religious loyalties
Let's Discuss How is the concept of dominant ideology relevant to the "cultural war" taking place in the United States?

Why Do Sociologists Study Religion?

Altar assistant at the Roman Catholic cathedral in Miami

ociologists find religion a fascinating subject of study because it is a cultural universal whose collective expression can be manifested in so many different ways. For example, Christians (above) worship one God and base their beliefs and values on the life and works of Jesus Christ. Muslims (next page, top) are also monotheistic, but they base their beliefs on scriptural revelations about God in the Koran. Hindus (next page, bottom left) hold many aspects of life sacred, and emphasize the importance of being good in this life in order to advance in the next. Buddhists (next page, bottom right) strive to overcome worldly desires in order to reach a state of enlightenment.

Sociologists are interested in how widely and strongly such beliefs are held, and what influences individuals to adopt religious beliefs. They study the impact of the family, schools, the state, and the predominant culture, among other factors. Also of interest to sociologists are the ways in which people express their faith. Do they do so by attending services? By meditating privately? By performing rituals? At the societal level, sociologists consider what impact religious organizations have on society, and conversely, how a particular culture affects the practice of religion.

Muslim men at prayer in Kurdistan, Iraq

Hindu holy man at the sacred River Ganges, India

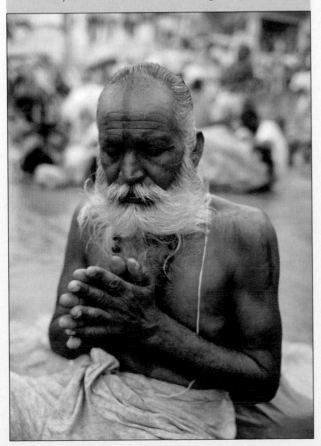

Buddhist monks receiving food, Laos

333

terrifying feeling that any of us can die senselessly at any moment—and that there is no divine answer to why one person lives a long and full life, while another dies tragically at a relatively early age.

Faith-based community organizations have taken on more and more responsibilities in the area of social assistance. In fact, President George W. Bush created the Office of Faith-Based and Community Initiatives to give socially active religious groups access to government funding. Sociologist William Julius Wilson (1999b) has singled out faith-based organizations in 40 communities from California to Massachusetts as models of social reform. These organizations identify experienced leaders and assemble them into nonsectarian coalitions that are devoted to community development.

Religion and Social Change

The Weberian Thesis

When someone seems driven to work and succeed, we often attribute the Protestant work ethic to that person. The term comes from the writings of Max Weber, who carefully examined the connection between religious allegiance and capitalist development. His findings appeared in his pioneering work *The Protestant Ethic and the Spirit of Capitalism* ([1904] 1958a).

Weber noted that in European nations with both Protestant and Catholic citizens, an overwhelming number of business leaders, owners of capital, and skilled workers were Protestant. In his view, this fact was no mere coincidence. Weber pointed out that the followers of John Calvin (1509–1564), a leader of the Protestant Reformation, emphasized a disciplined work ethic, this-worldly concerns, and a rational orientation to life that have become known as the ***Protestant ethic.*** One by-product of the Protestant ethic was a drive to accumulate savings that could be used for future investment. This "spirit of capitalism," to use Weber's phrase, contrasted with the moderate work hours, leisurely work habits, and lack of ambition that he saw as typical of the times.

Few books on the sociology of religion have aroused as much commentary and criticism as Weber's work. It has been hailed as one of the most important theoretical works in the field and an excellent example of macro-level analysis. Like Durkheim, Weber demonstrated that religion is not solely a matter of intimate personal beliefs. He stressed that the collective nature of religion has social consequences for society as a whole.

Weber provided a convincing description of the origins of European capitalism. But this economic system has now been adopted by non-Calvinists in many parts of the world. Studies done in the United States today show little or no difference in achievement orientation between Roman Catholics and Protestants. Apparently, the "spirit of capitalism" has emerged as a generalized cultural trait rather than a specific religious tenet (Greeley 1989).

Conflict theorists caution that Weber's theory—even if it is accepted—should not be regarded as an analysis of mature capitalism, as reflected in the rise of multinational corporations. Marxists would disagree with Weber not on the origins of capitalism, but on its future. Unlike Marx, Weber believed that capitalism could endure indefinitely as an economic system. He added, however, that the decline of religion as an overriding force in society opened the way for workers to express their discontent more vocally (Collins 1980).

p. 224

Liberation Theology

Sometimes the clergy can be found in the forefront of social change. Many religious activists, especially in the Roman Catholic Church in Latin America, support ***liberation theology***—the use of a church in a political effort to eliminate poverty, discrimination, and other forms of injustice from a secular society. Advocates of this religious movement sometimes sympathize with Marxism. Many believe that radical change, rather than economic development in itself, is the only acceptable solution to the desperation of the masses in impoverished developing countries. Activists associated with liberation theology believe that organized religion has a moral responsibility to take a strong public stand against the oppression of the poor, racial and ethnic minorities, and women (C. Smith 1991).

The term *liberation theology* dates back to the publication in 1973 of the English translation of *A Theology of Liberation.* The book was written by a Peruvian priest, Gustavo Gutiérrez, who lived in a slum area of Lima during the early 1960s. After years of exposure to the vast poverty around him, Gutiérrez concluded that "in order to serve the poor, one had to move into political action" (R. M. Brown 1980:23; G. Gutiérrez 1990). Eventually, politically committed Latin American theologians came under the influence of social scientists who viewed the domination of capitalism and multinational corporations as central to the hemisphere's problems. One result was a new approach to theology that built on the cultural and religious traditions of Latin America rather than on models developed in Europe and the United States.

Liberation theology may be dysfunctional, however. Some Roman Catholic worshipers have come to believe that by focusing on political and governmental injustice, the clergy are no longer addressing their personal and spiritual needs. Partly as a result of such disenchantment, some Catholics in Latin America are converting to mainstream Protestant faiths or to Mormonism.

Classroom Tip See "Goal Multiplication and Religious Organizations" (Additional Lecture Ideas).
Theory Functionalist view of religion as a source of social assistance
Key Person Max Weber
Theory Weber's view of religion as reinforcing capitalism
Key Person John Calvin

Theory Conflict theorists' critique of Weber's analysis of religion
Global View Religious activism in Latin America
Global View Church activists in Latin America who aim to eliminate poverty, discrimination, and social injustices
Theory Dysfunction of liberation theology

Social Inequality
13-1 THE STAINED GLASS CEILING

What is the role of women in organized religion? Most faiths have a long tradition of exclusively male spiritual leadership. Furthermore, most religions are patriarchal, so they tend to reinforce men's dominance in secular as well as spiritual matters. Women do play a vital role as volunteers, staff, and religious educators, but even today, decision making and leadership typically fall to the men. There are exceptions to this rule, such as the Shakers and Christian Scientists, as well as Hinduism with its long goddess heritage, but they are rare.

Nationally, women compose only about 14 percent of U.S. clergy, though they have accounted for 31 percent of students enrolled in theological institutions over the last two decades. Women clerics typically have shorter careers than men, often in related fields such as counseling, which do not involve congregational leadership. In faiths that restrict leadership positions to men, women still serve unofficially. For example, about 4 percent of Roman Catholic congrega-

> *A stained glass ceiling seems to hover over clergy women, limiting their occupational mobility.*

tions are led by women who hold nonordained pastoral positions—a necessity in a church that faces a shortage of male priests.

In the United States, congregations headed by women tend to be smaller and poorer than those headed by men. Conse-

quently, women church leaders are much less likely than men to have any paid full-time staff. They are also more likely to begin and end their careers in positions that do not lead to advancement in their denominations. A stained glass ceiling seems to hover over clergy women, limiting their occupational mobility.

Let's Discuss

1. Does a religious community in your town or city have a female leader? If so, was her calling controversial? What do you think her prospects are for career advancement?
2. From society's point of view, what are the pros and cons of admitting women to religious leadership?

Sources: Bureau of the Census 2003a:399; Chang 1997; Konieczny and Chaves 2000; van Biema 2004; Winseman 2004.

Use Your Sociological Imagination www.mhhe.com/schaefer6

The social support that religious groups provide is suddenly withdrawn from your community. How will your life or the lives of others change? What will happen if religious groups stop pushing for social change?

Religion and Social Control: A Conflict View

Liberation theology is a relatively recent phenomenon that marks a break with the traditional role of churches. It was this traditional role that Karl Marx opposed. In his view, religion *impeded* social change by encouraging oppressed people to focus on otherworldly concerns rather than on their immediate poverty or exploitation. Marx described religion as an "opiate" that was particularly harmful to oppressed peoples. He felt that religion often drugged the masses into submission by offering a consolation for their harsh lives on earth: the hope of salvation in an ideal afterlife. For example, during the period of slavery in the United States, White masters forbade Blacks to practice native African

religions, while encouraging them to adopt Christianity, which taught them that obedience would lead to salvation and eternal happiness in the hereafter. Viewed from a conflict perspective, Christianity may have pacified certain slaves and blunted the rage that often fuels rebellion.

Marx acknowledged that religion plays an important role in propping up the existing social structure. The values of religion, as already noted, tend to reinforce other social institutions and the social order as a whole. From Marx's perspective, however, religion's promotion of social stability only helps to perpetuate patterns of social inequality. According to Marx, the dominant religion reinforces the interests of those in power.

For example, contemporary Christianity reinforces traditional patterns of behavior that call for the subordination of the less powerful. The role of women in the church is an example of this uneven distribution of power. Assumptions about gender roles leave women in a subservient position both within Christian churches and at home. In fact, women find it as difficult to achieve leadership positions in many churches as they do in large corporations. Box 13-1 describes the "stained glass

Gender Women's subordinate role within organized religion
Classroom Tip See "Women in Clergy" (Additional Lecture Ideas).
Contemporary Culture Nationally, women comprise only about 14 percent of the clergy.

Key Person Karl Marx
Theory Conflict view of religion as a means of social control

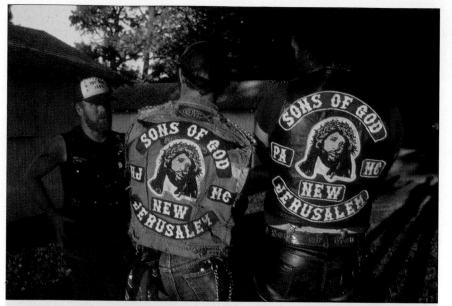

Religious expression can take many forms. This Christian motorcycle club's attire ensures that members will not be mistaken for Hell's Angels, despite their freewheeling lifestyle.

Belief

Some people believe in life after death, in supreme beings with unlimited powers, or in supernatural forces. *Religious beliefs* are statements to which members of a particular religion adhere. These views can vary dramatically from religion to religion.

The Adam and Eve account of creation found in Genesis, the first book of the Old Testament, is an example of a religious belief. Many people in the United States strongly adhere to this biblical explanation of creation, and even insist that it be taught in public schools. These people, known as *creationists,* are worried by the secularization of society, and oppose teaching that directly or indirectly questions biblical scripture. (The social policy section at the end of this chapter examines the issue of religion in the schools in depth.)

ceiling" that tends to stunt clergywomen's career development even in the most liberal denominations.

Like Marx, conflict theorists argue that to whatever extent religion actually does influence social behavior, it reinforces existing patterns of dominance and inequality. From a Marxist perspective, religion keeps people from seeing their lives and societal conditions in political terms—for example, by obscuring the overriding significance of conflicting economic interests. Marxists suggest p. 207 that by inducing a "false consciousness" among the disadvantaged, religion lessens the possibility of collective political action that can end capitalist oppression and transform society.

As Figure 13-2 shows, worldwide, the strength of religious beliefs varies dramatically. In general, spirituality is not as strong in industrialized nations as in developing nations. The United States is an exception to the trend toward secularization, in part because the government encourages religious expression (without explicitly supporting it) by allowing religious groups to claim charitable status, and even to receive federal aid for activities such as educational services. And although belief in God is relatively weak in formerly communist states such as Russia, surveys show a growth in spirituality in communist countries over the last 10 years.

RELIGIOUS BEHAVIOR

All religions have certain elements in common, yet those elements are expressed in the distinctive manner of each faith. These patterns of religious behavior, like other patterns of social behavior, are of great interest to sociologists—especially interactionists—since they underscore the relationship between religion and society.

Religious beliefs, religious rituals, and religious experience all help to define what is sacred and to differentiate the sacred from the profane. Let's examine these three dimensions of religious behavior, as seen through the eyes of interactionists.

Ritual

Religious rituals are practices required or expected of members of a faith. Rituals usually honor the divine power (or powers) worshiped by believers; they also remind adherents of their religious duties and responsibilities. Rituals and beliefs can be interdependent; rituals generally affirm beliefs, as in a public or private statement confessing a sin. Like any social institution, religion develops distinctive norms to structure people's behavior. Moreover, sanctions are attached to religious rituals, whether rewards (bar mitzvah gifts) or penalties (expulsion from a religious institution for violation of norms).

Theory Conflict view of religion as reinforcing patterns of dominance and inequality
Reel Society See Stratification—Religion in the Topic Index.

Classroom Tip A Muslim ritual unfamiliar to most people in the United States is Ramadan. See "Ramadan" (Class Discussion Topics).
Classroom Tip See "Ritual" (Class Discussion Topics).

In the United States, rituals may be very simple, such as saying grace at a meal or observing a moment of silence to commemorate someone's death. Yet certain rituals, such as the process of canonizing a saint, are quite elaborate. Most religious rituals in our culture focus on services conducted at houses of worship. Attendance at a service, silent and spoken prayers, communion, and singing of spiritual hymns and chants are common forms of ritual behavior that generally take place in group settings. From an interactionist perspective, these rituals serve as important face-to-face encounters in which people reinforce their religious beliefs and their commitment to their faith.

For Muslims, a very important ritual is the *hajj,* a pilgrimage to the Grand Mosque in Mecca, Saudi Arabia. Every Muslim who is physically and financially able is expected to make this trip at least once. Each year 2 million pilgrims go to Mecca during the one-week period indicated by the Islamic lunar calendar. Muslims from all over the world make the *hajj,* including those in the United States, where many tours are arranged to facilitate the trip.

FIGURE 13-2

Belief in God Worldwide

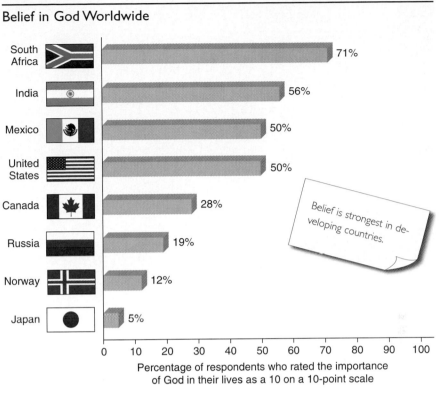

South Africa 71%
India 56%
Mexico 50%
United States 50%
Canada 28%
Russia 19%
Norway 12%
Japan 5%

Belief is strongest in developing countries.

Percentage of respondents who rated the importance of God in their lives as a 10 on a 10-point scale

Note: Data are from World Values surveys for 1995–1998, except for Canada, 1990–1991.
Source: Inglehart and Baker 2000:47.

Think About It
Canada and the United States are similar in many ways. Why would faith in God be less important to Canadians than to Americans?

Experience

In the sociological study of religion, the term ***religious experience*** refers to the feeling or perception of being in direct contact with the ultimate reality, such as a divine being, or of being overcome with religious emotion. A religious experience may be rather slight, such as the feeling of exaltation a person receives from hearing a choir sing Handel's "Hallelujah Chorus." But many religious experiences are more profound, such as a Muslim's experience on a *hajj.* In his autobiography, the late African American activist Malcolm X (1964:338) wrote of his *hajj* and how deeply moved he was by the way that Muslims in Mecca came together across race and color lines. For Malcolm X, the color blindness of the Muslim world "proved to me the power of the One God."

Another profound religious experience, for many Christians, is being "born again"—that is, at a turning point in one's life, making a personal commitment to Jesus. According to a 2003 national survey, 42 percent of people in the United States claim they have had a born-again Christian experience at some time in their lives. An earlier survey found that Southern Baptists (75 percent) were the most likely to report such experiences; in contrast, only 21 percent of Catholics and 24 percent of Episcopalians stated that they had been born again. The collective nature of religion, as emphasized by Durkheim, is evident in these statistics. The beliefs and rituals of a particular faith can create an atmosphere either friendly or indifferent to this type of religious experience. Thus, a Baptist would be encouraged to come forward and share such experiences with others, whereas an Episcopalian who claims to have been born again would receive much less interest (Newport 2004).

Table 13-2 (page 339) summarizes the three major theoretical perspectives on religion.

Methods Survey of "born-again" experiences among Christians
Let's Discuss How might religious behavior differ across Black and White congregations, and why?

Pilgrims on *hajj* to the Grand Mosque in Mecca, Saudi Arabia. Islam requires all Muslims who are able to undertake a pilgrimage to the Holy Land.

Use Your Sociological Imagination www.mhhe.com /schaefer6

Choose a religious tradition other than your own. How would your religious beliefs, rituals, and experience differ if you had been raised in that tradition?

RELIGIOUS ORGANIZATION

The collective nature of religion has led to many forms of religious association. In modern societies, religion has become increasingly formalized. Specific structures such as churches and synagogues have been constructed for religious worship; individuals have been trained for occupational roles within various fields. These developments make it possible to distinguish clearly between the sacred and secular parts of one's life—a distinction that could not be made easily in earlier times, when religion was largely a family activity carried out in the home.

Sociologists find it useful to distinguish between four basic forms of organization: the ecclesia, the denomina-

tion, the sect, and the new religious movement, or cult. We can see differences among these four forms of organization in their size, power, degree of commitment expected from members, and historical ties to other faiths.

Ecclesiae

An *ecclesia* (plural, *ecclesiae*) is a religious organization that claims to include most or all members of a society and is recognized as the national or official religion. Since virtually everyone belongs to the faith, membership is by birth rather than conscious decision. Examples of ecclesiae include Islam in Saudi Arabia and Buddhism in Thailand. However, significant differences exist within this category. In Saudi Arabia's Islamic regime, leaders of the ecclesia hold vast power over actions of the state. In contrast, the Lutheran church in contemporary Sweden holds no such power over the Riksdag (parliament) or the prime minister.

Generally, ecclesiae are conservative, in that they do not challenge the leaders of a secular government. In a society with an ecclesia, the political and religious institu-

Classroom Tip See "Market-Based Theory of Religious Growth" (Class Discussion Topics).
Classroom Tip See "Doing Religion" (Additional Lecture Ideas).

Global View Ecclesiae in various nations

Table 13-2 | **Sociological Perspectives on Religion**

summing**UP**

Theoretical Perspective	Emphasis
Functionalist	Religion as a source of social integration and unification
	Religion as a source of social support for individuals
Conflict	Religion as a potential obstacle to structural social change
	Religion as a potential source of structural social change (through Liberation Theology)
Interactionist	Individual religious expression through belief, ritual, and experience

tions often act in harmony and reinforce each other's power in their relative spheres of influence. In the modern world, ecclesiae are declining in power.

Denominations

A *denomination* is a large, organized religion that is not officially linked with the state or government. Like an ecclesia, it tends to have an explicit set of beliefs, a defined system of authority, and a generally respected position in society. Denominations claim as members large segments of a population. Generally, children accept the denomination of their parents and give little thought to membership in other faiths. Denominations also resemble ecclesiae in that they make few demands on members. However, there is a critical difference between these two forms of religious organization. Although the denomination is considered respectable and is not viewed as a challenge to the secular government, it lacks the official recognition and power held by an ecclesia (Doress and Porter 1977).

The United States is home to a large number of denominations (see Figure 13-3, page 340). In good measure, this diversity is a result of our nation's immigrant heritage. Many settlers brought with them the religious commitments native to their homelands. Some Christian denominations in the United States, such as the Roman Catholics, Episcopalians, and Lutherans, are the outgrowth of ecclesiae established in Europe. New Christian denominations also emerged, including the Mormons and Christian Scientists. Within the last generation, immigrants have increased the number of Muslims, Hindus, and Buddhists living in the United States.

Although by far the largest single denomination in the United States is Roman Catholicism, at least 23 other Christian faiths have 1 million or more members. Protestants collectively accounted for about 49 percent of the nation's adult population in 2003, compared with 24 percent for Roman Catholics and 2 percent for Jews. There are also 3 mil-

lion Muslims in the United States, and large numbers of people adhere to Eastern faiths such as Buddhism (2 million) and Hinduism (1 million) (Lindner 2004; Newport 2004).

Sects

A *sect* can be defined as a relatively small religious group that has broken away from some other religious organization to renew what it considers the original vision of the faith. Many sects, such as that led by Martin Luther during the Reformation, claim to be the "true church," because they seek to cleanse the established faith of what they regard as extraneous beliefs and rituals (Stark and Bainbridge 1985). Max Weber ([1916] 1958b:114) termed the sect a "believer's church," because affiliation is based on conscious acceptance of a specific religious dogma.

Sects are fundamentally at odds with society and do not seek to become established national religions. Unlike ecclesiae and denominations, they require intensive commitments and demonstrations of belief by members. Partly owing to their outsider status, sects frequently exhibit a higher degree of religious fervor and loyalty than more established religious groups. Recruitment focuses mainly on adults, and acceptance comes through conversion.

Sects are often short-lived. Those that are able to survive may become less antagonistic to society over time and begin to resemble denominations. In a few instances, sects have been able to endure over several generations while remaining fairly separate from society. Sociologist J. Milton Yinger (1970:226–73) uses the term *established sect* to describe a religious group that is the outgrowth of a sect, yet remains isolated from society. The Hutterites, Jehovah's Witnesses, Seventh-Day Adventists, and Amish are contemporary examples of established sects in the United States.

New Religious Movements or Cults

In 1997, 38 members of the Heaven's Gate cult were found dead in Southern California after a mass suicide timed to occur with the appearance of the Hale-Bopp comet. They believed the comet hid a spaceship on which they could catch a ride once they had broken free of their "bodily containers."

Partly as a result of the notoriety generated by such groups, the popular media have stigmatized the word *cult*, associating it with the occult and the use of intense and forceful conversion techniques. The stereotyping of

Classroom Tip See "Protestant Diversity" (Class Discussion Topics).
Race/Ethnicity The immigrant heritage of the United States has contributed to the proliferation of religious denominations.
Classroom Tip See "Student Census" (Class Discussion Topics).

Key Person Max Weber
Let's Discuss What is the relationship between sects and subcultures and countercultures (see Chapter 3)?

FIGURE 13-3

Largest Religious Groups in the United States by County, 2000

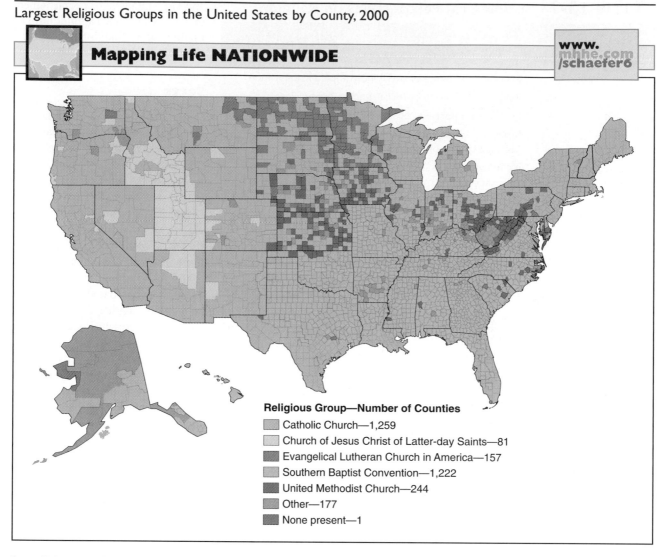

Source: D. Jones et al. 2002:592.

This map, which shows only the largest participating religious group in each county, nevertheless suggests the large variety of faiths practiced in the United States. A total of 149 religious denominations reported the numbers of their adherents for the study on which this map is based.

cults as uniformly bizarre and unethical has led sociologists to abandon the term and refer instead to a *new religious movement (NRM)*. While some NRMs exhibit strange behavior, many do not. They attract new members just like any other religion, and often follow teachings similar to those of established Christian denominations, though with less ritual.

Sects are difficult to distinguish from cults. A ***new religious movement (NRM)*** or ***cult*** is generally a small, secretive religious group that represents either a new religion or a major innovation of an existing faith. NRMs are

similar to sects in that they tend to be small and are often viewed as less respectable than more established faiths. Unlike sects, however, NRMs normally do not result from schisms or breaks with established ecclesiae or denominations. Some cults, such as those focused on UFO sightings, may be totally unrelated to existing faiths. Even when a cult does accept certain fundamental tenets of a dominant faith—such as a belief in Jesus as divine or in Mohammad as a messenger of God—it will offer new revelations or insights to justify its claim to being a more advanced religion (Stark and Bainbridge 1979, 1985).

summingUP

Table 13-3	Characteristics of Ecclesiae, Denominations, Sects, and New Religious Movements			
Characteristic	**Ecclesia**	**Denomination**	**Sect**	**New Religious Movement (or Cult)**
Size	Very large	Large	Small	Small
Wealth	Extensive	Extensive	Limited	Variable
Religious Services	Formal, little participation	Formal, little participation	Informal, emotional	Variable
Doctrines	Specific, but interpretation may be tolerated	Specific, but interpretation may be tolerated	Specific, purity of doctrine emphasized	Innovative, pathbreaking
Clergy	Well-trained, full-time	Well-trained, full-time	Trained to some degree	Unspecialized
Membership	By virtue of being a member of society	By acceptance of doctrine	By acceptance of doctrine	By an emotional commitment
Relationship to the state	Recognized, closely aligned	Tolerated	Not encouraged	Ignored or challenged

Source: Adapted from G. Vernon 1962; see also Chalfant et al. 1994.

Like sects, NRMs may be transformed over time into other types of religious organizations. An example is the Christian Science Church, which began as a new religious movement under the leadership of Mary Baker Eddy. Today, this church exhibits the characteristics of a denomination. In fact, most major religions, including Christianity, began as cults. NRMs may be in the early stages of developing into a denomination or new religion, or they may just as easily fade away through the loss of members or weak leadership (J. Richardson and van Driel 1997).

Comparing Forms of Religious Organization

How can we determine whether a particular religious group falls into the sociological category of ecclesia, denomination, sect, or NRM? As we have seen, these types of religious organizations have somewhat different relationships to society. Ecclesiae are recognized as national churches; denominations, although not officially approved by the state, are generally widely respected. In contrast, sects and NRMs are much more likely to be at odds with the larger culture.

Still, ecclesiae, denominations, and sects are best viewed as types along a continuum rather than as mutually exclusive categories. Table 13-3 summarizes some of the primary characteristics of these ideal types. Since the United States has no ecclesia, sociologists studying this country's religions have focused on the denomination and the sect. These religious forms have been pictured on either end of a continuum, with denominations accommodating to the secular world and sects protesting against established religions. While NRMs have been included in Table 13-3, they lie outside the continuum, because they generally define themselves in terms of a new view of life rather than in terms of existing religious faiths.

Advances in electronic communications have led to still another form of religious organization: the electronic church. Facilitated by cable television and satellite transmissions, *televangelists* (as they are called) direct their messages to more people—especially in the United States—than are served by all but the largest denominations. While some televangelists are affiliated with religious denominations, most give viewers the impression that they are disassociated from established faiths.

At the close of the 1990s, the electronic church had taken on yet another dimension: the Internet. In one study, researchers estimated that on a typical day in 2000, as many as 2 million people used the Internet for religious purposes. Much of the spiritual content on the Internet is tied to organized denominations. People use cyberspace to learn more about their faith, or even just the activities of their own place of worship (Larsen 2000).

Student Alert The role of Mary Baker Eddy in the Christian Science Church was unusual; in patriarchal societies, religious movements rarely emerge through the leadership of women.

Web Resource In the audio clip, Richard Schaefer, the author of the text, discusses how worship in cyberspace makes us reflect on Durkheim's notion of religion as a collective system of beliefs and practices relative to the sacred. Students can listen to the audio clip in the student center of the Online Learning Center (**www.mhhe.com/schaefer6**).

From a sociological point of view, the nation of India is large and complex enough that it might be considered a world of its own. Four hundred languages are spoken in India, 18 of which are officially recognized by the government. Besides the two major religions that originated there—Hinduism and Buddhism—several other faiths animate this society. Demographically the nation is huge, with over a billion residents. This teeming country is expected to overtake China as the most populous nation in the world in about three decades (Third World Institute 2003; United Nations Population Information Network 2003).

THE RELIGIOUS TAPESTRY IN INDIA

Hinduism and Islam, the two most important religions in India, were described on pages 329–330. Islam arrived in India in the year 1000 A.D., with the first of many Muslim invasions. It flowered there during the Mogul empire (1526–1857), the period when the Taj Mahal was built. Today, Muslims account for 11 percent of India's population; Hindus make up 83 percent.

Another religion, the Sikh faith, originated in the 15th century A.D. with a Hindu named Nanak, the first of a series of *gurus* (prophets). Sikhism shows the influence of Islam in India, in that it is monotheistic (based on a belief in one god rather than many). It resembles Buddhism in its emphasis on meditation and spiritual transcendence of the everyday world. *Sikhs* (learners) pursue their goal of spiritual enlightenment through meditation with the help of a *guru*.

Sikh men have a characteristic mode of dress that makes them easy to identify. They do not cut their beards or hair, and they wrap their heads in turbans. (Because of their distinctive dress, the 400,000 Sikhs who live in the United States are often mistaken—and discriminated against—as Muslims.) Sikhs are highly patriotic. Though their 20 million members make up just 2 percent of India's population, they account for 25 percent of India's army. Their presence in the military gives them a much larger voice in the governance of the country than might be expected, given their numbers (Fausset 2003).

Another faith that has been influential beyond its numbers in India is Jainism (pronounced *Jinism*). This religion was founded six centuries before the birth of Christ—about the same time as Buddhism—by a young Hindu named Mahavira. Offended by the Hindu caste system, the rigid social hierarchy that reduces some people to the status of outcastes based solely on their birth, and by

the numerous Hindu deities, Mahavira left his family and his wealth behind to become a beggar monk. His teachings attracted many followers, and the faith grew and flourished until the Muslim invasions of the 12th century A.D.

According to the Jain faith, there is no god; each person is responsible for his or her own spiritual well-being. By following a strict code of conduct, Jains believe they can ultimately free their souls from the endless cycle of death and rebirth and attain *nirvana* (spiritual enlightenment). Jains are required to meditate; forswear lying and stealing; limit their personal wealth; and practice self-denial, chastity, and nonviolence. Because they will not knowingly harm other living beings, including plants and animals, Jains shun meat, fish, or even vegetables whose harvest kills the entire plant, such as carrots and potatoes. They will not work in the military, in farming or fishing, or in the manufacture or sale of alcohol and drugs.

Though the Jains are a relatively small group (about 4 million), they exercise considerable influence in India through their business dealings and charitable contributions. Together with Christians and Buddhists, Jains make up 4 percent of India's population (Embree 2003).

RELIGION AND THE STATE IN INDIA

Religion was a moving force in India's drive to overturn British colonialism. The great Mohandas K. Gandhi (1869–1948) led the long struggle to regain India's sovereignty, which culminated in its independence in 1947. A proponent of nonviolent resistance, Gandhi persuaded Hindus and Muslims, ancient enemies, to join together in defying British domination. But his influence as a peacemaker could not override the Muslims' demand for a separate state of their own. Immediately after independence was granted, India was partitioned into two states, Pakistan for the Muslims and India for the Hindus. The new arrangement caused large-scale migrations of Indians, especially Muslims, from one nation to the other, and sparked boundary disputes that continue to this day. In many areas Muslims were forced to abandon places they considered sacred. In the chaotic months that followed, centuries of animosity between the two groups boiled over into riots, ending in Gandhi's assassination in January 1948.

Today, India is a secular state that is dominated by Hindus (see Figure 13-1 on page 328). Though the government is officially tolerant of the Muslim minority, tensions between Hindus and Muslims remain high in some states. Conflict also exists among various Hindu groups, from fundamentalists to more secular and ecumenical adherents (Embree 2003).

Many observers see religion as the moving force in Indian society. That certainly can be said of politics. When Indian political parties align themselves along religious lines, their actions polarize the nation's population. One party in particular, the Bharatiya Janata Party (BJP), is dominated by Hindu nationalists. The BJP, a major national party, led the coalition that controlled the Indian government from 1998 to 2004. Members of this party who manage to get elected to local office tend to tolerate anti-Muslim violence. In 2003, the BJP's electoral victories in the state of Gujarat were followed by over 2,000 deaths and the displacement of 220,000 people from their homes. Many commentators see the religious divide in India as being greater now than it has been at any time since the partition of India and Pakistan (*The Economist* 2004b).

Use Your Sociological Imagination   www.mhhe.com/schaefer6

Suppose the political landscape in the United States has changed. The two mainstream parties, which once appealed to a broad cross-section of U.S. voters, have begun to champion specific religious beliefs. As you prepare to cast your vote, what are your concerns, both personal and societal? Assuming that one of the parties supports your religious views, would you vote for its candidates on that basis? What would you do if neither party was sympathetic to your beliefs?

SOCIOLOGICAL PERSPECTIVES ON EDUCATION

Besides being a major industry in the United States, education is the social institution that formally socializes members of our society. In the last few decades, increasing proportions of people have obtained high school diplomas, college degrees, and advanced professional degrees. For example, the proportion of people 25 years of age or over with a high school diploma increased from 41 percent in 1960 to more than 84 percent in 2000. Those with a college degree rose from 8 percent in 1960 to about 28 percent in 2000 (see Figure 13-4, page 344, for international comparisons).

Throughout the world, education has become a vast and complex social institution that prepares citizens for the roles demanded by other social institutions, such as the family, government, and the economy. The functionalist, conflict, and interactionist perspectives offer distinctive views of education as a social institution.

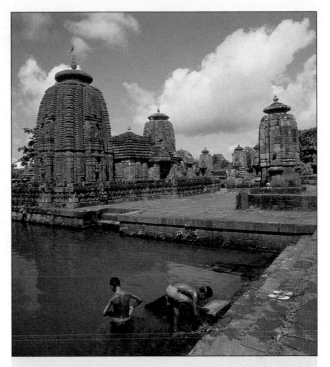

This Hindu temple in Khajuraho was built in the 11th century A.D. The Hindu faith is enormously influential in India, the country where most Hindus live.

Functionalist View

Like other social institutions, education has both manifest (open, stated) and latent (hidden) functions. The most basic *manifest* function of education is the transmission of knowledge. Schools teach students how to read, speak foreign languages, and repair automobiles. Another important manifest function is the bestowal of status. Because many believe this function is performed inequitably, we will consider it later, in the section on the conflict view of education.

In addition to these manifest functions, schools perform a number of *latent* functions: transmitting culture, promoting social and political integration, maintaining social control, and serving as an agent of change.

Transmitting Culture

As a social institution, education performs a rather conservative function—transmitting the dominant culture. Schooling exposes each generation of young people to the existing beliefs, norms, and values of their culture. In our society, we learn respect for social control and reverence for established institutions, such as religion, the family, and the presidency. Of course, this statement is

FIGURE 13-4

Percentage of Adults Ages 25 to 64 Who Have Completed Higher Education, 2000

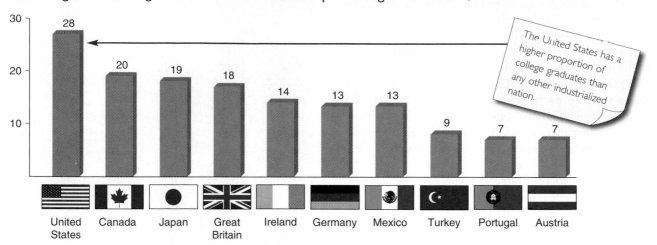

Source: Bureau of the Census 2003a:850.

true of many other cultures as well. While schoolchildren in the United States are hearing about the accomplishments of George Washington and Abraham Lincoln, British children are hearing about the distinctive contributions of Queen Elizabeth I and Winston Churchill.

In Great Britain, the transmission of the dominant culture through schools goes far beyond learning about monarchs and prime ministers. In 1996, the government's chief curriculum adviser—noting the need to fill a void left by the diminishing authority of the Church of England—proposed that British schools should socialize students into a set of core values. The list included honesty, respect for others, politeness, a sense of fair play, forgiveness, punctuality, nonviolent behavior, patience, faithfulness, and self-discipline (Charter and Sherman 1996).

Sometimes nations may reassess the ways in which they transmit culture. Recently South Koreans began to question the content of their school curriculum. South Korean schools teach traditional Confucian values, with a focus on rote memorization. The emphasis is on accumulating facts rather than on reasoning logically. Entrance to college turns on a highly competitive exam that tests students' knowledge of facts. Once in college, students have virtually no opportunity to change their educational programs, and their instruction continues to emphasize memorization. The combination of an economic crisis and growing complaints about the educational process has caused government officials to reevaluate the nation's educational structure. Moreover, growth in juvenile crime, although low by our standards, has led the government to introduce a new civic education program emphasizing honesty and discipline (Woodard 1998).

On the college level in the United States, controversy has been growing over the general education or basic curriculum requirements. Critics charge that standard academic curricula have failed to represent the important contributions of women and people of color to history, literature, and other fields of study. The underlying questions raised by this debate, still to be resolved, are: Which ideas and values are essential for instruction? Which culture should be transmitted by the schools and colleges of the United States?

Promoting Social and Political Integration

Many institutions require students in their first year or two of college to live on campus, to foster a sense of community among diverse groups. Education serves the latent function of promoting social and political integration by transforming a population composed of diverse racial, ethnic, and religious groups into a society whose members share—to some extent—a common identity. Historically, schools in the United States have played an important role in socializing the children of immigrants into the norms, values, and beliefs of the dominant culture. From a functionalist perspective, the common identity and social integration fostered by education contribute to societal stability and consensus (Touraine 1974).

In the past, the integrative function of education was most obvious in its emphasis on promoting a common language. Immigrant children were expected to learn English. In some instances, they were even forbidden to speak their native languages on school grounds. More p. 73 recently, bilingualism has been defended both for its educational value and as a means of encour-

---

Global View Transmission of the dominant culture in Great Britain and South Korea

Let's Discuss Do your students think their college classes give enough attention to the contributions of women and people of color?
Theory Functionalist view that education promotes social and political integration
Policy Pointer The debate over bilingualism in the United States

aging cultural diversity. However, critics argue that bilingualism undermines the social and political integration that education has traditionally promoted.

Maintaining Social Control

In performing the manifest function of transmitting knowledge, schools go far beyond teaching skills like reading, writing, and mathematics. Like other social institutions, such as the family and religion, education prepares young people to lead productive and orderly lives as adults by introducing them to the norms, values, and sanctions of the larger society.

Through the exercise of social control, schools teach students various skills and values essential to their future positions in the labor force. They learn punctuality, discipline, scheduling, and responsible work habits, as well as how to negotiate the complexities of a bureaucratic organization. As a social institution, education reflects the interests of both the family and another social institution, the economy. Students are trained for what is ahead, whether it be the assembly line or a physician's office. In effect, then, schools serve as a transitional agent of social control, bridging the gap between parents and employers in the life cycle of most individuals (Bowles and Gintis 1976; M. Cole 1988).

Schools direct and even restrict students' aspirations in a manner that reflects societal values and prejudices. School administrators may allocate ample funds for athletic programs but give much less support to music, art, and dance. Teachers and guidance counselors may encourage male students to pursue careers in the sciences but steer female students into careers as early childhood teachers. Such socialization into traditional gender roles can be viewed as a form of social control.

Serving as an Agent of Change

So far, we have focused on the conservative functions of education—on its role in transmitting the existing culture, promoting social and political integration, and maintaining social control. Yet education can also stimulate or bring about desired social change. Sex education classes were introduced in public schools in response to the soaring pregnancy rate among teenagers.

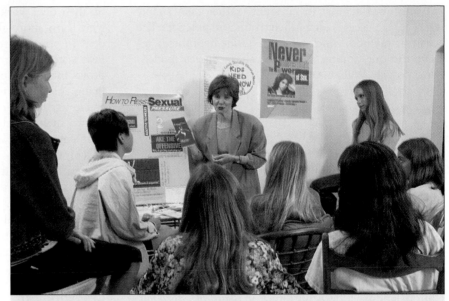

In response to a high pregnancy rate among adolescent girls, many schools now offer sex education courses that promote abstinence. When schools attempt to remedy negative social trends, they are serving as an agent of social change.

Affirmative action in admissions—giving priority to females or minorities—has been endorsed as a means of p. 250 countering racial and sexual discrimination. Project Head Start, an early childhood program that serves more than 905,000 children annually, has sought to compensate for the disadvantages in school readiness experienced by children from low-income families (Bureau of the Census 2002a:357).

Education also promotes social change by serving as a meeting ground where distinctive beliefs and traditions can be shared. In 2002, there were 582,867 foreign students in the United States, of whom 72 percent were from developing nations. Cross-cultural exchanges between these visitors and citizens of the United States ultimately broaden the perspective of both the hosts and their guests. The same is certainly true when students from the United States attend schools in Europe, Latin America, Africa, or the Far East.

Numerous sociological studies have revealed that additional years of formal schooling are associated with openness to new ideas and more liberal social and political viewpoints. Sociologist Robin Williams points out that better-educated people tend to have greater access to factual information, to hold more diverse opinions, and to possess the ability to make subtle distinctions in analysis. Formal education stresses both the importance of qualifying statements (in place of broad generalizations)

Web Resource Refer students to the "Social Policy" link for Chapter 3 in the student center of the Online Learning Center (**www.mhhe.com/schaefer6**). They can see how people feel about speaking and teaching English in school.
Gender Socialization into traditional gender roles

and the need at least to question (rather than simply [p. 29] accept) established truths and practices. The scientific method, which relies on *testing* hypotheses, reflects the questioning spirit that characterizes modern education (R. Williams et al. 1964).

Conflict View

The functionalist perspective portrays contemporary education as a basically benign institution. For example, it argues that schools rationally sort and select students for future high-status positions, thereby meeting society's need for talented and expert personnel. In contrast, the conflict perspective views education as an instrument of elite domination. Conflict theorists point out the sharp inequalities that exist in the educational opportunities available to different racial and ethnic groups. In 2004, the nation marked the 50th anniversary of the Supreme Court's landmark decision *Brown v. Board of Education*, which declared unconstitutional the segregation of public schools. Yet today, African Americans are still 11 percent less likely than Whites, and Latinos 36 percent less likely than Whites, to have completed high school. Furthermore, Black and Latino schoolchildren continue to underperform White schoolchildren on nationally standardized tests (Hurn 1985; National Center for Education Statistics 2004).

Conflict theorists also argue that the educational system socializes students into values dictated by the powerful, that schools stifle individualism and creativity in the name of maintaining order, and that the level of change they promote is relatively insignificant. From a conflict perspective, the inhibiting effects of education are particularly apparent in the "hidden curriculum" and the differential way in which status is bestowed.

The Hidden Curriculum

Schools are highly bureaucratic organizations, as we will see later. Many teachers rely on rules and regulations to maintain order. Unfortunately, the need for control and discipline can take precedence over the learning process. Teachers may focus on obedience to the rules as an end in itself, in which case students and teachers alike become victims of what Philip Jackson (1968) has called the *hidden curriculum* (see also Margolis 2001; B. Smith 2004).

The term *hidden curriculum* refers to standards of behavior that are deemed proper by society and are taught subtly in schools. According to this curriculum, children must not speak until the teacher calls on them, and must regulate their activities according to the clock or bells. In addition, they are expected to concentrate

on their own work rather than to assist other students who learn more slowly. A hidden curriculum is evident in schools around the world. For example, Japanese schools offer guidance sessions that seek to improve the classroom experience and develop healthy living skills. In effect, these sessions instill values and encourage behavior useful in the Japanese business world, such as self-discipline and openness to group problem solving and decision making (Okano and Tsuchiya 1999).

In a classroom that is overly focused on obedience, value is placed on pleasing the teacher and remaining quiet rather than on creative thought and academic learning. Habitual obedience to authority may result [p. 176] in the type of distressing behavior documented by Stanley Milgram in his classic obedience studies.

Credentialism

Fifty years ago, a high school diploma was the minimum requirement for entry into the paid labor force of the United States. Today, a college diploma is virtually the bare minimum. This change reflects the process of *credentialism*—a term used to describe an increase in the lowest level of education needed to enter a field.

In recent decades, the number of occupations that are viewed as professions has risen. Credentialism is one symptom of this trend. Employers and occupational associations typically contend that such changes are a logical response to the increasing complexity of many jobs. However, in many cases, employers raise the degree requirements for a position simply because all applicants have achieved the existing minimum credential (D. Brown 2001; Hurn 1985).

Conflict theorists observe that credentialism may reinforce social inequality. Applicants from poor and minority backgrounds are especially likely to suffer from the escalation of qualifications, since they lack the financial resources needed to obtain degree after degree. In addition, upgrading of credentials serves the self-interest of the two groups most responsible for this trend. Educational institutions profit from prolonging the investment of time and money that people make by staying in school. Moreover, as C. J. Hurn (1985) has suggested, current jobholders have a stake in raising occupational requirements, since credentialism can increase the status of an occupation and lead to demands for higher pay. Max Weber anticipated this possibility as early as 1916, concluding that the "universal clamor for the creation of educational certificates in all fields makes for the formation of a privileged stratum in businesses and in offices" (Gerth and Mills 1958:240–241).

Use Your Sociological Imagination | www.mhhe.com/schaefer6

How would you react if the job you have or plan to pursue suddenly required a higher-level degree? If suddenly the requirements were lowered?

Bestowal of Status

Both functionalist and conflict theorists agree that education performs the important function of bestowing status. As noted earlier, an increasing proportion of people in the United States are obtaining high school diplomas, college degrees, and advanced professional degrees. From a functionalist perspective, this widening bestowal of status is beneficial not only to particular recipients but to society as a whole. According to Kingsley Davis and Wilbert E. Moore (1945), society must distribute its members among a variety of social positions. Education can contribute to this process by sorting people into appropriate levels and courses of study that will prepare them for positions within the labor force.

◀ p. 210

Conflict theorists are far more critical of the *differential* way in which education bestows status. They stress that schools sort pupils according to their social class backgrounds. Although the educational system helps certain poor children to move into middle-class professional positions, it denies most disadvantaged children the same educational opportunities afforded to children of the affluent. In this way, schools tend to preserve social class inequalities in each new generation (Giroux 1988; Pinkerton 2003).

Even a single school can reinforce class differences by putting students in tracks. The term ***tracking*** refers to the practice of placing students in specific curriculum groups on the basis of their test scores and other criteria.

Studies conducted since 1987 suggest that the funding inequities between richer and poorer school districts have actually widened in recent years.

Theory Functionalist view of how widening bestowal of status is beneficial to society as a whole; conflict view that schools bestow status according to the students' social class background

Tracking begins very early, often in reading groups during first grade. Most recent research on such ability groupings raises questions about its effectiveness, especially for low-ability students. Tracks can reinforce the disadvantages that children from less affluent families may face if they haven't been exposed to reading materials, computers, and other forms of educational stimulation during their early childhood years. It is estimated that about 60 percent of elementary schools in the United States and about 80 percent of secondary schools use some form of tracking (Hallinan 2003; Sadker and Sadker 2003).

Tracking and differential access to higher education are evident in many nations around the world. Japan's educational system mandates equality in school funding and insists that all schools use the same textbooks. Nevertheless, only the more affluent Japanese families can afford to send their children to *juku,* or cram schools. These afternoon schools prepare high school students for examinations that determine admission into prestigious colleges (Efron 1997).

Conflict theorists hold that the educational inequalities produced by tracking are designed to meet the needs of modern capitalist societies. Samuel Bowles and Herbert Gintis (1976) have argued that capitalism requires a skilled, disciplined labor force, and that the educational system of the United States is structured with that objective in mind. Citing numerous studies, they offer support for what they call the ***correspondence principle.*** According to this approach, schools promote the values expected of individuals in each social class and perpetuate social class divisions from one generation to the next. Thus, working-class children, assumed to be destined for subordinate positions, are likely to be placed in high school vocational and general tracks, which emphasize close supervision and compliance with authority. In contrast, young people from more affluent families are likely to be directed to college preparatory tracks, which stress leadership and decision making—the skills they are expected to need as adults.

Treatment of Women in Education

The educational system of the United States, like many other social institutions, has long been characterized by discriminatory treatment of women. In 1833, Oberlin College became the first institution of higher learning to admit female students—some 200 years after the first men's college was established. But Oberlin believed that women should aspire to become wives and mothers, not lawyers and intellectuals. In addition to attending classes, female students washed men's clothing, cared for their rooms, and served them at meals. In the 1840s, Lucy Stone, then an

Let's Discuss What proportion of your students were tracked during high school?
Global View Cram schools in Japan

Although the Chinese government is attempting to address educational inequalities, girls continue to receive less education than boys—especially in rural areas.

cation is instrumental in preparing them for those roles. Educating women, especially young girls, yields high social returns by lowering birthrates and improving agricultural productivity through better management (I. Coleman 2004).

Interactionist View

In George Bernard Shaw's play *Pygmalion,* later adapted as the hit Broadway musical *My Fair Lady,* flower girl Eliza Doolittle is transformed into a "lady" by Professor Henry Higgins, who changes her manner of speech and teaches her the etiquette of "high society." When Eliza is introduced to society as an aristocrat, she is readily accepted. People treat her as a "lady" and she responds as one.

Oberlin undergraduate and later one of the nation's most outspoken feminist leaders, refused to write a commencement address because it would have been read to the audience by a male student.

In the 20th century, sexism in education showed up in many ways—in textbooks with negative stereotypes of women, counselors' pressure on female students to prepare for "women's work," and unequal funding for women's and men's athletic programs. But perhaps nowhere was educational discrimination more evident than in the employment of teachers. The positions of university professor and college administrator, which hold relatively high status in the United States, were generally filled by men. Public school teachers, who earn much lower salaries, were largely female.

Women have made great strides in one area: the proportion of women who continue their schooling. Women's access to graduate education and to medical, dental, and law schools has increased dramatically in the last few decades as a result of the Education Act of 1972. Box 13-2 examines the far-reaching effects of Title IX, the part of the act that concerns discrimination against women in education.

In cultures in which traditional gender roles remain the social norm, women's education suffers appreciably. Since September 11, 2001, the growing awareness of the Taliban's repression of Afghan women has dramatized the gender disparities in education in developing nations. Research has demonstrated that women are critical to economic development and good governance, and that edu-

The labeling approach suggests that if we treat people p. 187 in particular ways, they may fulfill our expectations. Children who are labeled as "troublemakers" may come to view themselves as delinquents. Similarly, a dominant group's stereotyping of racial minorities may limit their opportunities to break away from expected roles.

Can the labeling process operate in the classroom? Because of their focus on micro-level classroom dynamics, interactionist researchers have been particularly interested in this question. Howard S. Becker (1952) studied public schools in low-income and more affluent areas of Chicago. He noticed that administrators expected less of students from poor neighborhoods, and wondered if teachers accepted their view. A decade later, in *Pygmalion in the Classroom,* psychologist Robert Rosenthal and school principal Lenore Jacobson (1968) documented what they referred to as a ***teacher-expectancy effect***—the impact that a teacher's expectations about a student's performance may have on the student's actual achievements. This effect is especially evident in the lower grades (through grade three).

In this experiment, children in a San Francisco elementary school were administered a verbal and reasoning pretest. Rosenthal and Jacobson then *randomly* selected 20 percent of the sample and designated them as "spurters"—children of whom teachers could expect superior performance. On a later verbal and reasoning test, the spurters were found to score significantly higher than before. Moreover, teachers evaluated them as more interesting, more curious, and better-adjusted than their classmates. These results were striking. Apparently, teachers'

Classroom Tip See "Both Boys and Girls Have Reason to Feel Disadvantaged in School" (Additional Lecture Ideas); and "Inequality in Education" (Additional Lecture Ideas).
Gender Treatment of women in education
Theory Conflict view of sexism in education
Global View Treatment of girls in Afghanistan

Theory Interactionist view of education introduced
Methods Becker did observation research in Chicago schools.
Theory Discussion of the teacher-expectancy effect draws on interactionism and labeling theory.

Few federal policies have had such a visible effect on education over the last 30 years as Title IX, which mandates gender equity in education in federally funded schools. Congressional amendments to the Education Act of 1972, together with guidelines for their implementation developed by the Department of Health, Education, and Welfare in 1974–1975, have brought significant changes for both men and women at all levels of schooling. Title IX eliminated sex-segregated classes, prohibited sex discrimination in admissions and financial aid, and mandated that girls receive more opportunities to play sports, in proportion to their enrollment and interest.

Today, Title IX is still one of the more controversial attempts ever made by the federal government to promote equality for all citizens. Its consequences for the funding of college athletics programs are hotly debated, while its real and lasting effects on college admissions and employment are often forgotten. Critics charge that men's teams have suffered from proportional funding of women's teams and athletic scholarships, since schools with tight athletic budgets can expand women's sports only at the expense of men's sports. To a certain extent, non-revenue-producing men's sports such as wrestling and golf do appear to have suffered as women's teams have been added. But the high expense of some men's sports, particularly football,

would be beyond many schools' means even without Title IX expenditures. And the gains for women have more than made up for the losses to men. In 1971, when there were few opportunities for women athletes on college campuses, only 300,000 girls participated in high school sports. In 2003, three decades after Title IX opened up college athletics to women, the figure was 2.7 million.

For minority women, however, the results have been less satisfactory. Most of the women's sports that have benefited from increases in scholarships over the

> *Critics charge that men's teams have suffered from proportional funding of women's teams and athletic scholarships.*

last 20 years, like rowing and volleyball, traditionally have not been attractive to minority women. Twenty-five years ago, just 2 percent of female college athletes were African American. Today, the percentage is a disappointing 2.7 percent.

Sociologists note, too, that the social effects of sports on college campuses are not all positive. Michael A. Messner, professor of sociology at the University of Southern California, points to some troubling results of a survey by the Women's Sports Foundation. The study shows that teenage girls who play sports

simply for fun have more positive body images than girls who don't play sports. But those who are "highly involved" in sports are more likely than other girls to take steroids and to become binge drinkers and risk takers. "Everyone has tacitly agreed, it seems, to view men's sports as the standard to which women should strive to have equal access," Messner writes. "Missing from the debate is any recognition that men's sports have become sources of major problems on campuses: academic cheating, sexual violence, alcohol abuse, steroid use, serious injuries and other health issues, to name just a few" (Messner 2002:B9). Messner is skeptical of a system that propels a lucky few college athletes to stardom each year while leaving the majority, many of them African American, without a career or an education. Certainly that was not the kind of equal opportunity legislators envisioned when they wrote Title IX.

Let's Discuss

1. Has Title IX had an effect on you personally? If so, explain. On balance, do you think the increase in women's participation in sports has been good for society as a whole?
2. Are the negative social effects of men's sports evident on your campus? If so, what changes would you recommend to address the problem?

Sources: Federal Register, June 4, 1975; V. Gutierrez 2002; H. Mason 2003; Messner 2002.

perceptions that the students were exceptional led to noticeable improvements in their performance.

Studies in the United States have revealed that teachers wait longer for an answer from a student they believe to be a high achiever and are more likely to give such children a second chance. In one experiment, teachers' expectations were even shown to have an impact on students' athletic achievements. Teachers obtained better athletic performance—as measured in the number of sit-ups or push-ups performed—from those

students of whom they *expected* higher numbers (Babad and Taylor 1992).

Despite these findings, some researchers continue to question the accuracy of the teacher-expectancy effect. They claim it is too difficult to define and measure teacher expectancy. Further studies are needed to clarify the relationship between teacher expectations and actual student performance. Nevertheless, interactionists emphasize that ability alone may be less predictive of academic success than one might think (Brint 1998).

Methods Experiments on teacher-expectancy effect in the United States _summingUP_

Table 13-4	Sociological Perspectives on Education
Theoretical Perspective	**Emphasis**
Functionalist	Transmission of the dominant culture
	Integration of society
	Promotion of social norms, values, and sanctions
	Promotion of desirable social change
Conflict	Domination by the elite through unequal access to schooling
	Hidden curriculum
	Credentialism
	Bestowal of status
Interactionist	Teacher-expectancy effect

Table 13-4 summarizes the three major theoretical perspectives on education.

SCHOOLS AS FORMAL ORGANIZATIONS

Nineteenth-century educators would be amazed at the scale of schools in the United States in the 21st century. For example, California's public school system, the largest in the nation, currently enrolls as many children as there were in secondary schools in the entire country in 1950 (Bureau of the Census 1975:368; 2003a).

In many respects, today's schools, when viewed as an example of a formal organization, are similar to factories, hospitals, and business firms. Like these organizations, schools do not operate autonomously; they are influenced by the market of potential students. This statement is especially true of private schools, but could have broader impact if acceptance of voucher plans and other school choice programs increases. The parallels between schools and other types of formal organizations will become more apparent as we examine the bureaucratic nature of schools, teaching as an occupation, and the student subculture (K. Dougherty and Hammack 1992).

Bureaucratization of Schools

It simply is not possible for a single teacher to transmit culture and skills to children of varying ages who will enter many diverse occupations. The growing number of students being served by individual schools and school sys-

tems, as well as the greater degree of specialization required within a technologically complex society, have combined to bureaucratize schools.

Max Weber noted five basic pp. 136–138 characteristics of bureaucracy, all of which are evident in the vast majority of schools, whether at the elementary, secondary, or even college level.

1. **Division of labor.** Specialized experts teach particular age levels and specific subjects. Public elementary and secondary schools now employ instructors whose sole responsibility is to work with children with learning disabilities or physical impairments.
2. **Hierarchy of authority.** Each employee of a school system is responsible to a higher authority. Teachers must report to principals and assistant principals, and may also be supervised by department heads. Principals are answerable to a superintendent of schools, and the superintendent is hired and fired by a board of education.
3. **Written rules and regulations.** Teachers and administrators must conform to numerous rules and regulations in the performance of their duties. This bureaucratic trait can become dysfunctional; the time invested in completing required forms could instead be spent in preparing lessons or conferring with students.
4. **Impersonality.** As class sizes have swelled at schools and universities, it has become more difficult for teachers to give personal attention to each student. In fact, bureaucratic norms may actually encourage teachers to treat all students in the same way, despite the fact that students have distinctive personalities and learning needs.
5. **Employment based on technical qualifications.** At least in theory, the hiring of instructors is based on professional competence and expertise. Promotions are normally dictated by written personnel policies; people who excel may be granted lifelong job security through tenure.

Functionalists take a generally positive view of the bureaucratization of education. Teachers can master the skills needed to work with a specialized clientele, since they no longer are expected to cover a broad range of instruction. The chain of command within schools is clear.

Theory Functionalist view of the bureaucratization of education
Key Person Max Weber

Students are presumably treated in an unbiased fashion because of uniformly applied rules. Finally, security of position protects teachers from unjustified dismissal. In general, then, functionalists stress that the bureaucratization of education increases the likelihood that students, teachers, and administrators will be dealt with fairly—that is, on the basis of rational and equitable criteria.

In contrast, conflict theorists argue that the trend toward more centralized education has harmful consequences for disadvantaged people. The standardization of educational curricula, including textbooks, will generally reflect the values, interests, and lifestyles of the most powerful groups in our society, and may ignore those of racial and ethnic minorities. In addition, the disadvantaged, more so than the affluent, will find it difficult to sort through complex educational bureaucracies and to organize effective lobbying groups. Therefore, in the view of conflict theorists, low-income and minority parents will have even less influence over citywide and statewide educational administrators than they have over local school officials (Bowles and Gintis 1976; M. Katz 1971).

Sometimes schools can seem overwhelmingly bureaucratic, with the effect of stifling rather than nourishing intellectual curiosity in students. This concern has led many parents and policymakers to push for school choice programs—allowing parents to choose the school that suits their children's needs, and forcing schools to compete for their "customers."

In the United States, another significant countertrend to the bureaucratization of schools is the availability of education over the Internet. Increasingly, colleges and universities are reaching out via the web, offering entire courses and even majors to students in the comfort of their homes. Online curricula provide flexibility for working students and others who may have difficulty attending conventional classes because of distance or disability. Research on this type of learning is just beginning, so the question of whether teacher–student contact can thrive online remains to be settled. Computer-mediated instruction may also have an impact on instructors' status as employees, which we will discuss next, as well as on alternative forms of education like adult education and homeschooling.

Use Your Sociological Imagination www.mhhe.com/schaefer6

How would you make your school less bureaucratic? What would it be like?

Teachers: Employees and Instructors

Whether they serve as instructors of preschoolers or graduate students, teachers are employees of formal organiza-

Theory Conflict view of the bureaucratization of education as harmful to disadvantaged people

tions with bureaucratic structures. There is an inherent conflict in serving as a professional in a bureaucracy. The organization follows the principles of hierarchy and expects adherence to its rules, but professionalism demands the individual responsibility of the practitioner. This conflict is very real for teachers, who experience all the positive and negative consequences of working in bureaucracies (see Table 6-2 on page 137).

A teacher undergoes many perplexing stresses every day. While teachers' academic assignments have become more specialized, the demands on their time remain diverse and contradictory. There are conflicts inherent in serving as an instructor, a disciplinarian, and an employee of a school district at the same time. Burnout is one result of these stresses: 40 to 50 percent of new teachers quit the profession within five years (G. Gordon 2004).

Given these difficulties, does teaching remain an attractive profession in the United States? In 2003, 5.3 percent of first-year college students indicated that they were interested in becoming elementary school teachers, and 4.4 percent, high school teachers. These figures are dramatically lower than the 13 percent of first-year male students and 38 percent of first-year female students who held these occupational aspirations in 1968 (Astin et al. 1994; Sax et al. 2003:30).

Undoubtedly, economic considerations enter into students' feelings about the attractiveness of teaching. In 2002, the average salary for all public elementary and secondary school teachers in the United States was $44,367, placing teachers somewhere near the average of all wage earners in the nation. In most other industrial countries, teachers' salaries are higher in relation to the general standard of living (F. H. Nelson and Drown 2003).

The status of any job reflects several factors, including the level of education required, financial compensation, and the respect given the occupation within society. The teaching profession (see Table 9-2, page 213) is feeling pressure in all three of these areas. First, the amount of formal schooling required for teaching remains high, and the public has begun to call for new competency examinations. Second, the statistics just cited demonstrate that teachers' salaries are significantly lower than those of many professionals and skilled workers. Finally, the overall prestige of the teaching profession has declined in the last decade. Many teachers have become disappointed and frustrated and have left the educational world for careers in other professions.

Student Subcultures

An important latent function of education relates directly to student life: Schools provide for students' social and

Theory Interactionist view of role conflict among teachers
Contemporary Culture Forty to 50 percent of new teachers quit the profession within five years.
Classroom Tip Review the findings on the prestige of teachers in Table 9-2.
Student Alert Review the concept of subculture (Chapter 3).

recreational needs. Education helps toddlers and young children to develop interpersonal skills that are essential during adolescence and adulthood. In their high school and college years, students may meet future husbands and wives and establish lifelong friendships.

When people observe high schools, community colleges, or universities from the outside, students appear to constitute a cohesive, uniform group. However, the student subculture is actually complex and diverse. High school cliques and social groups may crop up based on race, social class, physical attractiveness, placement in courses, athletic ability, and leadership roles in the school and community. In his classic community study of "Elmtown," August B. Hollingshead (1975) found some 259 distinct cliques in a single high school. The cliques, whose average size was five, were centered on the school itself, on recreational activities, and on religious and community groups.

Amid these close-knit and often rigidly segregated cliques, gay and lesbian students are particularly vulnerable. Peer group pressure to conform is intense at this age. Although coming to terms with one's sexuality is difficult for all adolescents, it can be downright dangerous for those whose sexual orientation does not conform to societal expectations. According to a study by the Massachusetts Department of Education (2000), students who describe themselves as gay, lesbian, or bisexual are significantly more likely than others to attempt suicide, miss classes, and be threatened or injured by other students (see Figure 13-5).

Teachers and administrators are becoming more sensitized to these issues. Perhaps more important, some schools are creating gay–straight alliances (GSAs), school-sponsored support groups that bring gay teens together with sympathetic straight peers. Begun in Los Angeles in 1984, these programs numbered 1,623 nationwide in 2003; most were founded after the murder of Matthew Shepard, a gay college student, in 1998. In some districts parents have objected to these organizations, but the same court rulings that protect the right of conservative Bible groups to meet on school grounds also protect GSAs. In 2003, the gay–straight movement reached a milestone when the New York City public schools moved an in-school program for

FIGURE 13-5

Students at Risk: Gay, Lesbian, and Bisexual

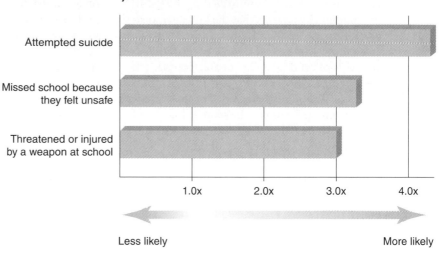

Source: Massachusetts Department of Education 2000.

Students who describe themselves as gay, lesbian, or bisexual are significantly more likely than their straight peers to attempt suicide, miss school, or be threatened or injured at school.

gays, bisexuals, and transgender students to a separate school of their own. The Harvey Milk High School was named in memory of San Francisco's first openly gay city supervisor, who was assassinated in 1978 (Gay, Lesbian and Straight Education Network 2004).

We can find a similar diversity of student groups at the college level. Burton Clark and Martin Trow (1966) and more recently, Helen Lefkowitz Horowitz (1987) have identified four distinctive subcultures among college students:

1. The *collegiate* subculture focuses on having fun and socializing. These students define what constitutes a "reasonable" amount of academic work (and what amount of work is "excessive" and leads to being labeled as a "grind"). Members of the collegiate subculture have little commitment to academic pursuits. Athletes often fit into this subculture.
2. The *academic* subculture identifies with the intellectual concerns of the faculty and values knowledge for its own sake.
3. The *vocational* subculture is primarily interested in career prospects, and views college as a means of obtaining degrees that are essential for advancement.
4. Finally, the *nonconformist* subculture is hostile to the college environment, and seeks out ideas that

Theory Latent functions of education in meeting students' social and recreational needs
Methods Hollingshead's observation research on cliques in a high school
Contemporary Culture/Gender Some schools are creating gay–straight alliances (GSAs).

Classroom Tip See "Subcultures on Campus" (Class Discussion Topics).
Methods Observation research by Clark and Trow, and by Horowitz, on college student subcultures

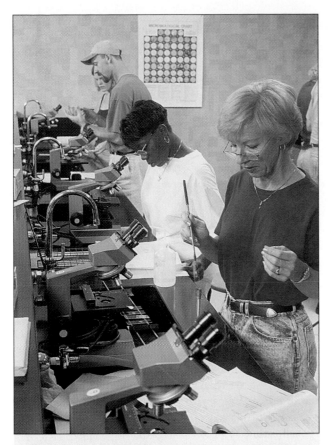

Student subcultures are more diverse today than they were in the past. Many adults are returning to college to obtain further education, advance their careers, or change their line of work.

may or may not relate to academic studies. This group may find outlets through campus publications or issue-oriented groups.

Each college student is eventually exposed to these competing subcultures and must determine which (if any) seems most in line with his or her feelings and interests.

The typology used by the researchers reminds us that school is a complex social organization—almost like a community with different neighborhoods. Of course, these four subcultures are not the only ones evident on college campuses in the United States. For example, one might find subcultures of Vietnam veterans or former full-time homemakers at community colleges and four-year commuter institutions.

Sociologist Joe R. Feagin has studied a distinctive collegiate subculture: Black students at predominantly White universities. These students must function academically and socially within universities where there are few Black faculty members or Black administrators,

where harassment of Blacks by campus police is common, and where the curricula place little emphasis on Black contributions. Feagin (1989:11) suggests that "for minority students life at a predominantly White college or university means long-term encounters with *pervasive whiteness*." In Feagin's view, African American students at such institutions experience both blatant and subtle racial discrimination, which has a cumulative impact that can seriously damage the students' confidence (see also Feagin et al. 1996).

Homeschooling

When most people think of school, they think of bricks and mortar and the teachers, administrators, and other employees who staff school buildings. But for an increasing number of students in the United States, home is the classroom and the teacher is a parent. More than 1.6 million students are now being educated at home. That is about 4 percent of the K–12 school population. For these students, the issues of bureaucratization and social structure are less significant than they are for public school students (R. Cox 2003:27).

In the 1800s, after the establishment of public schools, families that taught their children at home lived in isolated environments or held strict religious views that were at odds with the secular environment of public schools. But today, homeschooling is attracting a broader range of families not necessarily tied to organized religion. Poor academic quality, peer pressure, and school violence are motivating many parents to teach their children at home. The recent publicity given to school shooting sprees seems to have accelerated the move toward homeschooling.

While supporters of homeschooling believe children can do just as well or better in homeschools as in public schools, critics counter that because homeschooled children are isolated from the larger community, they lose an important chance to improve their socialization skills. But proponents of homeschooling claim their children benefit from contact with others besides their own age group. They also see homeschools as a good alternative for children who suffer from attention deficit disorder (ADD) and learning disorders (LDs). Such children often do better in smaller classes, which present fewer distractions to disturb their concentration (National Homeschool Association 1999).

Quality control is an issue in homeschooling. While homeschooling is legal in all 50 states, only 37 states regulate homeschools; 29 monitor students' progress through tests or evaluations. Despite the lack of uniform standards, a national study funded by the Home School Legal

Key Person Joe Feagin
Race/Ethnicity Black student subcultures at predominantly White universities
Theory Conflict view of the isolation of Black students at predominantly White universities

Classroom Tip See "Online Education" (Additional Lecture Ideas).
Contemporary Culture Discuss homeschooling and its impact on peer socialization.
Theory Functions and dysfunctions of homeschooling
Theory Interactionist view of homeschooling

Defense Association reports that homeschooled students score higher than others on standardized tests, in every subject and every grade. Almost 25 percent of the students who participated in the study were working above grade level for their age (Matthews 1999; Paulson 2000).

Who are the people who are running homeschools? In general, they tend to have higher-than-average incomes and educational levels. Most are two-parent families, and their children watch less television than average—both factors that are likely to support superior educational performance. The same students, with the same types of family and the same support from their parents, would probably do just as well in the public schools. As research has repeatedly shown, small classes are better than big classes, and strong parental and community involvement is key (R. Cox 2003:28).

SOCIAL POLICY and RELIGION — Religion in the Schools

The Issue

Should public schools be allowed to sponsor organized prayers in the classroom? How about reading Bible verses, or just a collective moment of silence? Can public school athletes offer up a group prayer in a team huddle? Should students be able to initiate voluntary prayers at school events? Each of these situations has been an object of great dissension among those who see a role for prayer in the schools and those who want to maintain strict separation of church and state.

Another controversy concerns the teaching of theories about the origin of humans and the universe. Mainstream scientific thinking holds that humans evolved over billions of years from one-celled organisms, and that the universe came into being 15 billion years ago as a result of a "big bang." These theories are challenged by people who hold to the biblical account of the creation of humans and the universe some 10,000 years ago—a viewpoint known as *creationism*. Creationists want their theory taught in the schools as the only one, or at the very least, as an alternative to the theory of evolution.

Who has the right to decide these issues, and what is the "right" decision? Religion in the schools is one of the thorniest issues in U.S. public policy today.

The Setting

The issues just described go to the heart of the First Amendment's provisions on religious freedom. On the one hand, the government must protect the right to practice one's religion; on the other hand, it cannot take any measures that would seem to "establish" one religion over another (separation of church and state).

In the key case of *Engle v. Vitale*, the Supreme Court ruled in 1962 that the use of nondenominational prayer in New York schools was "wholly inconsistent" with the First Amendment's prohibition against government establishment of religion. In finding that organized school prayer violated the Constitution—even when no student was required to participate—the Court argued, in effect, that promoting religious observance was not a legitimate function of government or education. Subsequent Court decisions have allowed *voluntary* school prayer by students, but forbid school officials to *sponsor* any prayer or religious observance at school events. Despite these rulings, many public schools still regularly lead their students in prayer recitations or Bible reading (D. Firestone 1999).

The controversy over whether the biblical account of creation should be presented in school curricula recalls the famous "monkey trial" of 1925. In that trial, high school biology teacher John T. Scopes was convicted of violating a Tennessee law making it a crime to teach the scientific theory of evolution in public schools. Today, creationists have gone beyond espousing fundamentalist religious doctrine; they are attempting to reinforce their position regarding the origins of humanity and the universe with quasi-scientific data.

In 1987, the Supreme Court ruled that states could not compel the teaching of creationism in public schools if the primary purpose was to promote a religious viewpoint. For a while, this ruling gave priority to the theory of evolution in most public school districts, but especially in the South and Midwest, creationists have been chipping away at the dominance of evolutionary theory in the classroom. Many school districts now require that teachers entertain alternative theories to evolution and the creation of the universe, and some discount evolution altogether.

Sociological Insights

Supporters of school prayer and of creationism feel that strict Court rulings have forced too great a separation between what Émile Durkheim called the *sacred* and the *profane.* They insist that the use of nondenominational prayer can in no way lead to the establishment of an ecclesia in the United States. Moreover, they believe that school prayer—and the teaching of creationism—can provide the spiritual guidance and socialization that many children today do not receive from parents or regular church attendance. Many communities also believe that schools should transmit the dominant culture of the United States by encouraging prayer.

Opponents of school prayer and creationism argue that a religious majority in a community might impose religious viewpoints specific to its faith at the expense of religious minorities. These critics question whether school prayer can remain truly voluntary. Drawing on the interactionist perspective and small-group research, they suggest that children will face enormous social pressure to conform to the beliefs and practices of a religious majority.

Policy Initiatives

School education is fundamentally a local issue, so most initiatives and lobbying have taken place at the local or state level. A significant departure from the local nature of this issue came in 2003, when President George W. Bush declared that schools whose policies prevent constitutionally protected school prayer risk losing their federal education funds. At the same time, federal courts were taking a hard line on religion in the schools. In a decision that is unlikely to be upheld, a federal appeals court ruled that reciting the phrase "under God" during the Pledge of Allegiance that opens each school day violates the U.S. Constitution (Religion News Service 2003).

GOD BLESS AMERICA

In a controversial ruling in 2003, the U.S. Ninth Circuit Court of Appeals declared that reciting the phrase "under God" in public schools during the Pledge of Allegiance violates the U.S. Constitution. The ruling, which is under appeal, may well be reversed.

The activism of religious fundamentalists in the nation's public school system raises a more general question: whose ideas and values deserve a hearing in classrooms? Critics see this campaign as one step toward sectarian religious control of public education. They worry that at some point in the future, teachers may not be able to use books or make statements that conflict with fundamentalist interpretations of the Bible. For advocates of a liberal education who are deeply committed to intellectual (and religious) diversity, this is a genuinely frightening prospect.

Let's Discuss

1. Was there any organized prayer in the school you attended? Was creationism part of the curriculum?
2. Do you think that promoting religious observance is a legitimate function of education?
3. How might a conflict theorist view the issue of organized school prayer?

GETTING INVOLVED

www.mhhe.com/schaefer6

To get involved in the debate over religion in the schools, visit this text's Online Learning Center, which offers links to relevant websites. Check out the Social Policy section on the Online Learning Center as well; it provides survey data on U.S. public opinion regarding this issue.

Student Alert Review the differences between the sacred and the profane.
Key Person Émile Durkheim
Theory Conflict view of school prayer
Theory Interactionist view of school prayer

Classroom Tip See "Using Humor" (Class Discussion Topics).
Web Resource Remind students there are flash cards containing key terms and definitions for this chapter in the student center of the Online Learning Center (www.mhhe.com/schaefer6).
Classroom Tip See "Field Trips" (Class Discussion Topics).

Summary

Religion and *education* are cultural universals found throughout the world in various forms. This chapter examines the major world religions, the functions and dimensions of religion, and the four basic types of religious organization. It considers several sociological views of education and analyzes schools as an example of formal organizations.

1. Émile Durkheim stressed the social impact of religion in attempting to understand individual religious behavior within the context of the larger society.

2. Eighty-five percent of the world's population adheres to some form of religion. Tremendous diversity exists in religious beliefs and practices, which may be heavily influenced by culture.

3. Religion helps to integrate a diverse society and provides social support in time of need.

4. Max Weber saw a connection between religious allegiance and capitalistic behavior in a religious orientation he termed the *Protestant ethic.*

5. In *liberation theology,* the teachings of Christianity become the basis for political efforts to alleviate poverty and social injustice.

6. From a Marxist point of view, religion serves to reinforce the social control of those in power. It discourages collective political action, which could end capitalist oppression and transform society.

7. Religious behavior is expressed through religious *beliefs, rituals,* and *experience.*

8. Sociologists have identified four basic types of religious organization: the *ecclesia,* the *denomination,* the *sect,* and the *new religious movement (NRM),* or *cult.*

9. Advances in communications have led to a new type of church organization, the electronic church. Tele-

vangelists now preach to more people than belong to many denominations, and roughly 2 million people a day use the Internet for religious purposes.

10. India is a secular state that is dominated by a religious majority, the Hindus. The creation of a separate nation, Pakistan, for the Muslim minority following India's independence in 1947 did not end the centuries-old strife between the two groups, which has worsened with their political polarization.

11. The transmission of knowledge and bestowal of status are manifest functions of education. Among the latent functions are transmitting culture, promoting social and political integration, maintaining social control, and serving as an agent of social change.

12. In the view of conflict theorists, education serves as an instrument of elite domination by creating standards for entry into occupations, bestowing status unequally, and subordinating the role of women.

13. Teacher expectations about a student's performance can sometimes have an impact on the student's actual achievements.

14. Today, most schools in the United States are organized in a bureaucratic fashion. Weber's five basic characteristics of bureaucracy are all evident in schools.

15. Homeschooling has become a viable alternative to traditional public and private schools. An estimated 1.6 million or more American children are now educated at home.

16. Today, the question of how much religion, if any, should be permitted in the U.S. public schools is a matter of intense debate.

Critical Thinking Questions

1. Do politics and religion mix? Explain your reasoning.

2. What are the functions and dysfunctions of tracking in schools? Viewed from an interactionist perspective, how would tracking of high school students influence the interactions between students and teachers? In what ways might tracking have positive and negative impacts on the self-concepts of various students?

3. Are the student subcultures identified in this text evident on your campus? What other student subcultures are present? Which subcultures have the highest (and the lowest) social status? How might functionalists, conflict theorists, and interactionists view the existence of student subcultures on a college campus?

Key Terms

Correspondence principle The tendency of schools to promote the values expected of individuals in each social class and to prepare students for the type of job typically held by members of their class. (page 347)

Creationism A literal interpretation of the Bible regarding the creation of humanity and the universe, used to argue that evolution should not be presented as established scientific fact. (354)

Credentialism An increase in the lowest level of education needed to enter a field. (346)

Cultural universal A common practice or belief found in every culture. (327)

Denomination A large, organized religion that is not officially linked with the state or government. (339)

Ecclesia A religious organization that claims to include most or all members of a society, and is recognized as the national or official religion. (338)

Education A formal process of learning in which some people consciously teach while others adopt the social role of learner. (327)

Established sect A religious group that is the outgrowth of a sect, yet remains isolated from society. (339)

Hidden curriculum Standards of behavior that are deemed proper by society and are taught subtly in schools. (346)

Liberation theology Use of a church, primarily Roman Catholicism, in a political effort to eliminate poverty, discrimination, and other forms of injustice from a secular society. (334)

New religious movement (NRM) or **cult** A small, secretive religious group that represents either a new religion or a major innovation of an existing faith. (340)

Profane The ordinary and commonplace elements of life, as distinguished from the sacred. (329)

Protestant ethic Max Weber's term for the disciplined work ethic, this-worldly concerns, and rational orientation to life emphasized by John Calvin and his followers. (334)

Religion A unified system of beliefs and practices relative to sacred things. (327)

Religious belief A statement to which members of a particular religion adhere. (336)

Religious experience The feeling or perception of being in direct contact with the ultimate reality, such as a divine being, or of being overcome with religious emotion. (337)

Religious ritual A practice required or expected of members of a faith. (336)

Sacred Elements beyond everyday life that inspire awe, respect, and even fear. (329)

Sect A relatively small religious group that has broken away from some other religious organization to renew what it considers the original vision of the faith. (339)

Secularization The process through which religion's influence on other social institutions diminishes. (327)

Teacher-expectancy effect The impact that a teacher's expectations about a student's performance may have on the student's actual achievements. (348)

Tracking The practice of placing students in specific curriculum groups on the basis of their test scores and other criteria. (347)

TECHNOLOGY RESOURCES

www.mhhe.com/schaefer6 Internet Connection

*Note: While all the URLs listed were current as of the printing of this book, these sites often change. Please check our website (**www.mhhe.com/schaefer6**) for updates, hyperlinks, and exercises related to these sites.*

1. In the context of religion, ordinary objects can take on extraordinary significance. The Material History of American Religion Project has catalogued dozens of interesting—and often quirky—religious objects. To view them, go to the project's website (**www.materialreligion.org**) and select "Objects."

2. Humanitarian organizations are concerned about access to education in developing countries. To find out about charitable efforts to improve basic education in the world's poorest countries, go to the Oxfam website (**www.oxfam.org.uk/what_we_do/issues/education/index.htm**) and explore the section on education.

Online Learning Center with PowerWeb

The formation of student subcultures is one of the latent functions of education. You can conduct your own "Cyber Student Organization Fair" by visiting the Online Learning Center at **www.mhhe.com/schaefer6** and linking to the student center. While you are in the student center, link to "Internet Exercises." The third exercise will direct you to sites where you can learn about organizations found on university and college campuses.

Reel Society Interactive Movie CD-ROM 2.0

Reel Society 2.0 can be used to spark discussion about the following topics from this chapter:

- Durkheim and the Sociological Approach to Religion
- The Role of Religion
- World Religions
- Religious Belief, Ritual, and Experience
- Sociological Perspectives on Education
- Trends in Contemporary Education

chapter 14

GOVERNMENT, THE ECONOMY, AND THE ENVIRONMENT

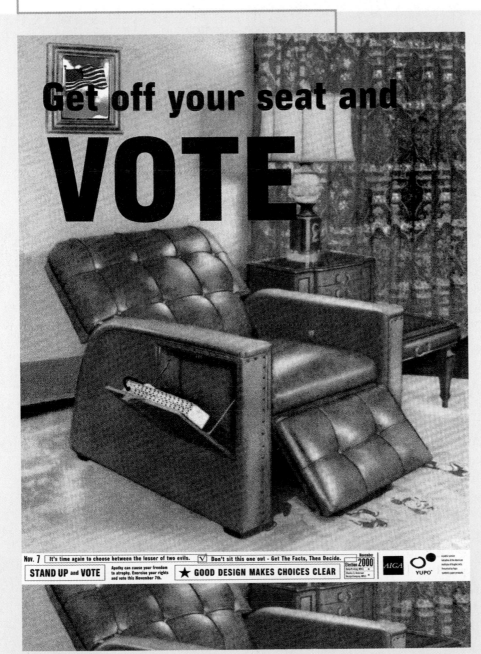

Get off your seat and VOTE

Nov. 7 | It's time again to choose between the lesser of two evils. | ☑ Don't sit this one out - Get The Facts, Then Decide.
STAND UP and VOTE | Apathy can cause your freedom to atrophy. Exercise your rights and vote this November 7th. | ★ GOOD DESIGN MAKES CHOICES CLEAR

This poster, sponsored by the American Institute of Graphic Arts, urges citizens to overcome their apathy toward politics and vote. In the United States, most eligible voters either are not registered or do not bother to vote.

The power elite and Congress are more diverse than they were before the social movements that emerged in the 1960s brought pressure to bear on corporations, politicians, and government. Although the power elite is still composed primarily of Christian white men, there are now Jews, women, blacks, Latinos, and Asian Americans on the boards of the country's largest corporations; presidential cabinets are far more diverse than was the case forty years ago; and the highest ranks of the military are no longer filled solely by white men. In the case of elected officials in Congress, the trend toward diversity is even greater for women and all of the minority groups that we have studied. . . .

Ultimately we suggest that the increase in diversity at the top contains several ironies, the most important of which is related to what is perhaps the major unresolved tension in American life, between liberal individualism and the class structure. The diversification of the power elite has been celebrated, but this celebration ignores the continuing importance of the class structure. The movements that led to diversity in the power elite have succeeded to some extent, especially for women and minorities from privileged social backgrounds, but there has been no effect on the way the power elite functions or on the class structure itself. . . .

The power elite has been strengthened because diversity has been achieved primarily by the selection of women and minorities who share the prevailing perspectives and values of those already in power. The power elite is not "multicultural" in any full sense of the concept, but only in terms of ethnic or racial origins. This process has been helped along by those who have called for the inclusion of women and minorities without any consideration of criteria other than sex, race, or ethnicity. Because the demand was strictly for a woman on the Supreme Court, President Reagan could comply by choosing a conservative upper-class corporate lawyer, Sandra Day O'Connor. When pressure mounted to have more black justices, President Bush could respond by appointing Clarence Thomas, a conservative black Republican with a law degree from Yale University. It is yet another irony that appointments like these served to undercut the liberal social movements that caused them to happen. . . .

We therefore have to conclude on the basis of our findings that the diversification of the power elite did not generate any changes in an underlying class system. . . . The values of liberal individualism embedded in the Declaration of Independence, the Bill of Rights, and the civic culture were renewed by vigorous and courageous activists, but despite their efforts the class structure remains a major obstacle to individual fulfillment for the overwhelming majority of Americans. This fact is more than an irony. It is a dilemma. It combines with the dilemma of race to create a nation that celebrates equal opportunity but is, in reality, a bastion of class privilege and conservatism. *(Zweigenhaft and Domhoff 1998:176–177, 192, 194)* ■ 🐚

Additional information about this excerpt can be found on the Online Learning Center at **www.mhhe.com/schaefer6.**

HAVE WOMEN AND MINORITIES REACHED THE TOP?

Diversity in the Power Elite

RICHARD L. ZWEIGENHAFT AND G. WILLIAM DOMHOFF

alf a century ago C. Wright Mills ([1956] 2000b), the originator of the phrase *the sociological imagination,* studied the political process in the United States and articulated the concept of the power elite—a White male group of decision makers who in effect ruled the country. Four decades later sociologist G. William Domhoff and psychologist Richard L. Zweigenhaft returned to the question of who rules the United States. As the opening excerpt from their book *Diversity in the Power Elite* (1998) shows, they found only modest changes in the nation's power structure. Today, a few privileged women occupy positions in the power elite, but the majority of the nation's decision makers are still men, and virtually all of them are White.

The power elite operates within the framework of the existing political system, be it local, state, national, or international. By **political system,** sociologists mean the social institution that is founded on a recognized set of procedures for implementing and achieving society's goals, such as the allocation of valued resources. Like religion and the family, the political system is a cultural universal: It is found in every society. In the United States, the political system holds the ultimate responsibility for addressing the social policy issues examined in this textbook: child care, the AIDS crisis, welfare reform, and so forth.

The term **economic system** refers to the social institution through which goods and services are produced, distributed, and consumed. As with social institutions such as the family, religion, and government, the economic system shapes other aspects of the social order and is in turn influenced by them. Throughout this textbook, you have been reminded of the economy's impact on social behavior—for example, individual and group behavior in factories and offices. You have studied the work of Karl Marx and Friedrich [p. 12] Engels, who emphasized that the economic system of a society can promote social inequality. And you have learned that foreign investment in [pp. 225–226] developing countries can intensify inequality among residents.

It is hard to imagine two social institutions more intertwined than government and the economy. Besides serving as the largest employer in the nation, government at all levels regulates commerce and entry into many occupations. At the same time, the economy generates the revenue to support government services. Yet this close relationship is not without conflict, for the interests of the two institutions often diverge. The competing interests of government and the economy can be seen clearly, for example, in frequent disagreements over the state of the environment. Government officials, mindful of their duty to ensure the public's well-being, have issued regulations to protect the air and water from industrial pollution. Business leaders counter that the government's strict environmental standards reduce their profits and retard economic growth.

This chapter will present a sociological analysis of government, the economy, and the environment. How does the power elite maintain its power? Is war necessary in settling international disputes? How have the trends toward deindustrialization and the outsourcing of service jobs affected our economy? What effect does economic development have on the environment? The chapter begins with a macro-level analysis of two ideal types of economic system, capitalism and socialism. This theoretical discussion is followed by a case study of China's decision to allow capitalist entrepreneurial activity within its socialist economy. Next, we'll examine some general theories of power and authority, and see how groups actually exert power in the U.S. political system. We'll discuss the costs of war and ways of promoting peace in a world that is threatened by global terrorism. In the following section we'll look at ways in which the U.S. economy is changing in response to globalization. Finally, we'll draw on the functionalist and conflict perspectives to better understand the conflicting interests of government and business in the debate over environmental issues. The chapter will close with a social policy section on the controversy over affirmative action, an equal opportunity initiative that has caused a good deal of political conflict. ■

ECONOMIC SYSTEMS

The sociocultural evolution approach developed by Gerhard Lenski [p. 120] categorizes preindustrial society according to the way in which the economy is organized. The principal types of preindustrial society, as you recall, are hunting-and-gathering societies, horticultural societies, and agrarian societies.

As noted in Chapter 5, the *industrial revolution*— [p. 120] which took place largely in England during the period 1760 to 1830—brought about changes in the social organization of the workplace. People left their homesteads and began working in central locations such

Classroom Tip/Contemporary Culture See "Stimulating Classroom Discussions about *Diversity in the Power Elite*" (Class Discussion Topics).
Gender Note Mills's exclusion of women from the power elite.

Key Person Gerhard Lenski
Reel Society See Economic Systems in the Topic Index.

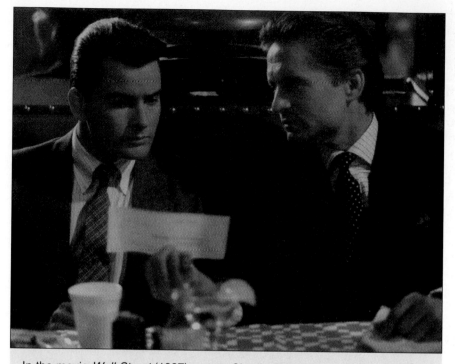

In the movie *Wall Street* (1987), actors Charlie Sheen and Michael Douglas played greedy speculators engaged in insider trading and stock price manipulation. Popular culture often presents capitalists as selfish people who profit unfairly from the labor of others—an image recent corporate scandals have reinforced.

the hope of realizing even greater profits and thereby became owners of property and business firms.

The transition to private ownership of business was accompanied by the emergence of the capitalist economic system. *Capitalism* is an economic system in which the means of production are held largely in private hands, and the main incentive for economic activity is the accumulation of profits. In practice, capitalist systems vary in the degree to which the government regulates private ownership and economic activity (D. Rosenberg 1991).

Immediately following the industrial revolution, the prevailing form of capitalism was what is termed *laissez-faire* ("let them do"). Under the principle of laissez-faire, as expounded and endorsed by British economist Adam Smith (1723–1790), people could compete freely, with minimal government intervention in the economy. Business retained the right to regulate itself and operated essentially without fear of government regulation (Smelser 1963).

Two centuries later, capitalism has taken on a somewhat different form. Private ownership and maximization of profits still remain the most significant characteristics of capitalist economic systems. However, in contrast to the era of laissez-faire, capitalism today features extensive government regulation of economic relations. Without restrictions, business firms can mislead consumers, endanger the safety of their workers, and even defraud the companies' investors—all in the pursuit of greater profits. That is why the government of a capitalist nation often monitors prices, sets safety and environmental standards for industries, protects the rights of consumers, and regulates collective bargaining between labor unions and management. Yet under capitalism as an ideal type, government rarely takes over ownership of an entire industry.

Contemporary capitalism also differs from laissez-faire in another important respect: capitalism tolerates monopolistic practices. A *monopoly* exists when a single business firm controls the market. Domination of an industry allows the firm to effectively control a commodity by dictating pricing, standards of quality, and availability. Buyers have little choice but to yield to the firm's decisions; there is no other place to purchase the product or

as factories. As the industrial revolution proceeded, a new form of social structure emerged: the *industrial society*, a society that depends on mechanization to produce its goods and services.

Two basic types of economic systems distinguish contemporary industrial societies: capitalism and socialism. As described in the following sections, capitalism and socialism serve as ideal types of economic systems. No nation precisely fits either model. Instead, the economy of each individual state represents a mixture of capitalism and socialism, although one type or the other is generally useful in describing a society's economic structure.

Capitalism

In preindustrial societies, land functioned as the source of virtually all wealth. The industrial revolution changed all that. It required that certain individuals and institutions be willing to take substantial risks in order to finance new inventions, machinery, and business enterprises. Eventually, bankers, industrialists, and other holders of large sums of money replaced landowners as the most powerful economic force. These people invested their funds in service. Monopolistic practices violate the ideal of free competition cherished by Adam Smith and other supporters of laissez-faire capitalism.

Some capitalistic nations, such as the United States, outlaw monopolies through antitrust legislation. Such laws prevent any business from taking over so much of the competition in an industry that it controls the market. The U.S. federal government allows monopolies to exist only in certain exceptional cases, such as the utility and transportation industries. Even then, regulatory agencies scrutinize these officially approved monopolies and protect the public. The protracted legal battle between the Justice Department and Microsoft, owner of the dominant operating system for personal computers, illustrates the uneasy relationship between government and private monopolies in capitalistic countries.

Conflict theorists point out that although *pure* monopolies are not a basic element of the economy of the United States, competition is much more restricted than one might expect in what is called a *free enterprise system*. In numerous industries, a few companies largely dominate the field and keep new enterprises from entering the marketplace.

As we have seen in earlier chapters, globalization and the rise of multinational corporations have spread the capitalistic pursuit of profits around the world. Especially in developing countries, governments are not always prepared to deal with the sudden influx of foreign capital and its effects on their economies. One particularly striking example of how unfettered capitalism can harm developing nations is found in the Democratic Republic of Congo (formerly Zaire). The Congo has significant deposits of the metal columbite-tantalite—coltan, for short—which is used in the production of electronic circuit boards. Until the market for cell phones, pagers, and laptop computers heated up recently, U.S. manufacturers got most of their coltan from Australia. But at the height of consumer demand, they turned to miners in the Congo to increase their supply.

Predictably, the escalating price of the metal—as much as $400 a kilogram at one point, or more than three times the average Congolese worker's yearly wages—attracted undesirable attention. Soon the neighboring countries of Rwanda, Uganda, and Burundi, at war with one another and desperate for resources to finance the conflict, were raiding the Congo's national parks, slashing and burning to expose the coltan underneath the forest floor. Indirectly, the sudden increase in the demand for coltan was financing war and the rape of the environment. U.S. manufacturers have since cut off their sources in the Congo in an effort to avoid abetting the destruction. But their action has only penalized legitimate miners in the impoverished country (Austin 2002; Delawala 2002).

Classroom Tip See "Monopoly" (Class Discussion Topics); "Marx and Marxism Analyzed" (Additional Lecture Ideas).
Theory Conflict view of the domination of industries in the United States by a few companies

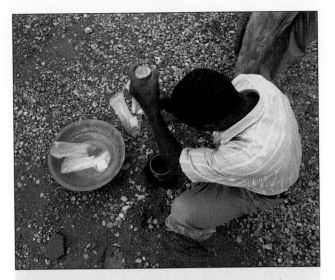

A worker mines for coltan with sweat and a stick. The sudden increase in demand for the metal by U.S. computer manufacturers caused incursions into the Congo by neighboring countries hungry for capital to finance a war. Too often, globalization can have unintended consequences for a nation's economy and social welfare.

Socialism

p. 12 Socialist theory was refined in the writings of Karl Marx and Friedrich Engels. These European radicals were disturbed by the exploitation of the working class that emerged during the industrial revolution. In their view, capitalism forced large numbers of people to exchange their labor for low wages. The owners of an industry profit p. 207 from the labor of workers primarily because they pay workers less than the value of the goods produced.

As an ideal type, a socialist economic system attempts to eliminate such economic exploitation. Under *socialism,* the means of production and distribution in a society are collectively rather than privately owned. The basic objective of the economic system is to meet people's needs rather than to maximize profits. Socialists reject the laissez-faire philosophy that free competition benefits the general public. Instead, they believe that the central government, acting as the representative of the people, should make basic economic decisions. Therefore, government ownership of all major industries—including steel production, automobile manufacturing, and agriculture—is a primary feature of socialism as an ideal type.

In practice, socialist economic systems vary in the extent to which they tolerate private ownership. For example, in Great Britain, a nation with some aspects of both a socialist and a capitalist economy, passenger airline

Key Persons Karl Marx, Friedrich Engels
Theory Conflict view of socialism as an alternative to capitalism
Global View Socialist aspects of Great Britain's economy

service is concentrated in the government-owned corporation British Airways. Yet private airlines are allowed to compete with it.

Socialist societies differ from capitalist nations in their commitment to social service programs. For example, the U.S. government provides health care and health insurance to the elderly and poor through the Medicare and Medicaid programs. But socialist countries typically offer government-financed medical care to *all* citizens. In theory, the wealth of the people as a collectivity is used to provide health care, housing, education, and other key services to each individual and family.

Marx believed that each socialist state would eventually "wither away" and evolve into a *communist* society. As an ideal type, **communism** refers to an economic system under which all property is communally owned and no social distinctions are made on the basis of people's ability to produce. In recent decades, the Soviet Union, the People's Republic of China, Vietnam, Cuba, and nations in Eastern Europe were popularly thought of as examples of communist economic systems. However, this usage represents an incorrect application of a term with sensitive political connotations. All nations known as communist in the 20th century actually fell far short of the ideal type.

By the early 1990s, Communist parties were no longer ruling the nations of Eastern Europe. The first major challenge to Communist rule came in 1980 when Poland's Solidarity movement—led by Lech Walesa and backed by many workers—questioned the injustices of that society. Though martial law forced Solidarity underground, the movement eventually negotiated the end of Communist Party rule in 1989. Over the next two years, Communist parties were overthrown by popular uprisings in the Soviet Union and throughout Eastern Europe. The former Soviet Union, Czechoslovakia, and Yugoslavia were then subdivided to accommodate ethnic, linguistic, and religious differences within these areas.

As of 2003, China, Cuba, and Vietnam remained socialist societies ruled by Communist parties. Even in those countries, however, capitalism had begun to make inroads. In China, fully 25 percent of the country's production originated in the private business sector. (See the case study Capitalism in China for a fuller discussion.)

As we have seen, capitalism and socialism serve as ideal types of economic systems. In reality, the economy of each industrial society—including the United States, the European Union, and Japan—includes certain elements of both capitalism and socialism. Whatever the differences—whether a society more closely fits the ideal type of capitalism or socialism—all industrial societies rely chiefly on mechanization in the production of goods and services.

Global View The overthrow of Communist Party rule in the former Soviet Union and Eastern Europe

Global View Capitalism was making inroads in China, Cuba, and Vietnam as of 2003.

Global View See "In Defense of Socialist Planning" (Additional Lecture Ideas).

The Informal Economy

In many countries, one aspect of the economy defies description as either capitalist or socialist. In the *informal economy,* transfers of money, goods, or services take place but are not reported to the government. Examples of the informal economy include trading services with someone—say, a haircut for a computer lesson; selling goods on the street; and engaging in illegal transactions, such as gambling or drug deals. Participants in this type of economy avoid taxes and government regulations.

In developing nations, the informal economy represents a significant and often unmeasured part of total economic activity. Yet because this sector of the economy depends to a large extent on the labor of women, work in the informal economy is undervalued or even unrecognized the world over.

Functionalists contend that bureaucratic regulations sometimes contribute to the rise of an informal economy. In the developing world, governments often set up burdensome business regulations that overworked bureaucrats must administer. When requests for licenses and permits pile up, delaying business projects, legitimate entrepreneurs find they need to "go underground" to get anything done. Despite its apparent efficiency, this type of informal economy is dysfunctional for a country's overall political and economic well-being. Since informal firms typically operate in remote locations to avoid detection, they cannot easily expand when they become profitable. And given the limited protection for their property and contractual rights, participants in the informal economy are less likely than others to save and invest their income.

Whatever functions an informal economy may serve, it is in some respects dysfunctional for workers. Working conditions in these illegal businesses are often unsafe or dangerous, and the jobs rarely provide any benefits to those who become ill or cannot continue to work. Perhaps more significant, the longer a worker remains in the informal economy, the less likely that person is to make the transition to the regular economy. No matter how efficient or productive a worker, employers expect to see experience in the formal economy on a job application. Experience as a successful street vendor or self-employed cleaning person does not carry much weight with interviewers.

Use Your Sociological Imagination www.mhhe.com/schaefer6

Some of your relatives are working full-time in the informal economy—for example, babysitting, lawn cutting, house cleaning—and are earning all their income that way. What will be the consequences for them in terms of job security and health care? Will you try to persuade them to seek formal employment, regardless of how much money they are making?

CASE STUDY:
CAPITALISM IN CHINA

Today's China is not the China of past generations. In a country where the Communist Party once dominated people's lives, few now bother to follow party proceedings. Instead, after a decade of rapid economic growth, most Chinese are more interested in acquiring the latest consumer goods. Ironically, it was party officials' decision to transform China's economy by opening it up to capitalism that reduced the once omnipotent institution's influence.

THE ROAD TO CAPITALISM

When the communists assumed leadership of China in 1949, they cast themselves as the champions of workers and peasants and the enemies of those who exploited workers, namely landlords and capitalists. Profit making was outlawed, and those who engaged in it were arrested. By the 1960s, China's economy was dominated by huge state-controlled enterprises, such as factories. Even private farms were transformed into community-owned organizations. Peasants essentially worked for the government, receiving payment in goods based on their contribution to the collective. In addition, they could receive a small plot of land on which to produce food for their families or for exchange with others. But while the centralization of production for the benefit of all seemed to make sense ideologically, it did not work well economically.

In the 1980s, the government eased restrictions against private enterprise somewhat, permitting small businesses with no more than seven employees. But business owners could not hold policymaking positions in the party, at any level. Late in the decade, party leaders began to make market-oriented reforms, revising the nation's legal structure to promote private business. For the first time, private entrepreneurs were allowed to compete with some state-controlled businesses. By the mid-1990s, impressed with the results of the experiment, party officials had begun to hand some ailing state-controlled businesses over to private entrepreneurs, in hopes they could be turned around (Lynch 2002; Pan 2002).

THE CHINESE ECONOMY TODAY

Today, the entrepreneurs who weathered government harassment during the Communist Party's early years are among the nation's wealthiest capitalists. Some even hold positions on government advisory boards. The growing free-market economy they spawned has brought significant inequality to Chinese workers, however. While wages are up for millions, the average wage bought less in 2004 than it did 10 years before, given price increases. Marxist critics have condemned China's leaders for reducing Chinese workers to the status of servants of the global economy (Kahn 2004a).

The transition from an economy dominated by state-owned companies to one in which private firms can flourish has been surprisingly rapid. By 2004, nine years after the government began turning over troubled state-owned companies to private entrepreneurs, only about 35 percent of urban workers were employed at state-owned companies. Many of the companies that were privatized turned out to be money losers, however—a challenge to even the most enterprising of managers (*The Economist* 2004d).

Chinese capitalists have also had to compete with multinational corporations, which can operate more easily in China now, thanks to government economic reforms. General Motors (GM) first became interested

A Chinese consumer shops for a television in Beijing. Though multinational corporations first moved factories to China to take advantage of the low wages there, they have discovered they can also sell their products in China.

2002—up 30 percent from the year before (Bradsher 2004; Iritani and Dickerson 2002; Kahn 2003b).

For the average worker, party membership is less important now than in the past. Instead, managerial skill and experience are much in demand. Hong Kong sociologist Xiaowei Zang (2002) surveyed 900 workers in a key industrial city and found that party members still had an advantage in government and state-owned companies, where they earned higher salaries than other workers. But in private businesses, seniority and either managerial or entrepreneurial experience were what counted. As might be expected, being male and well educated also helped.

Women have been slower to advance in the workplace than men. Traditionally, Chinese women have been relegated to subservient roles in the patriarchal family structure. Communist Party rule has allowed them to make significant gains in employment, income, and education, although not as quickly as promised. For rural women in China, the growth of a market economy has meant a choice between working in a factory or on a farm. Given recent economic changes, which have been massive, scholars are waiting to see whether Chinese women will maintain the progress they began under Communism (Bian 2002; Lu et al. 2002; Shu and Bian 2003).

in China in 1992, hoping to use the nation's low-cost labor to manufacture cars for overseas markets. But more and more, foreign-owned enterprises like GM are selling to the Chinese market. By 2003, GM's Chinese operation was producing 110,000 automobiles a year for Chinese consumers, at a profit twice as high as that in the United States (Kahn 2003a).

Those Chinese who run small family-owned businesses are prospering in the new economic climate. In a national survey of 3,000 households done in 1996, sociologist Andrew Walder (2002) found that in general, these mom-and-pop businesses brought in significantly more income than other livelihoods. But in places where workers had the chance to desert the farm for wage work in factories and businesses, they were doing just as well as local businesspeople. As China's economy continues to develop, Walder believes, competition will increase both inside and outside China, and the economic advantages of entrepreneurism will diminish.

CHINESE WORKERS IN THE NEW ECONOMY

For Chinese workers, the loosening of state control over the economy has meant a rise in occupational mobility, which was severely limited in the early days of Communist Party rule. The new markets created by private entrepreneurs are allowing ambitious workers to advance their careers by changing jobs or even cities. On the other hand, many middle-aged urban workers have lost their jobs to rural migrants seeking higher wages. Moreover, the privately owned factories that churn out lawn chairs and power tools for multinational corporations offer limited opportunities and very long hours. Wages average only $75 a month—⅙ what factory workers earn in Mexico, and 1/40 of U.S. workers' wages. In many small businesses, worker safety is not a priority. Just south of Shanghai, in the over 7,000 small, privately owned hardware factories that operate in the region, the unofficial injury rate is 2,500 serious injuries a year. Nationally, China recorded 140,000 workplace deaths in

POWER AND AUTHORITY

In any society, someone or some group makes important decisions about how to use resources and how to allocate

Web Resource Students can work a crossword puzzle containing key words and phrases from the chapter if they link to the student center in the Online Learning Center **(www.mhhe.com/schaefer6).**

goods, whether it be a tribal chief or a parliament or a dictator. A cultural universal common to all societies, then, is the exercise of power and authority. Inevitably, the struggle for power and authority involves *politics,* which political scientist Harold Lasswell (1936) tersely defined as "who gets what, when, and how." In their study of politics and government, sociologists are concerned with social interactions among individuals and groups and their impact on the larger political and economic order.

Power

p. 208 Power lies at the heart of a political system. According to Max Weber, *power* is the ability to exercise one's will over others. To put it another way, whoever can control the behavior of others is exercising power. Power relations can involve large organizations, small groups, or even people in an intimate association.

Because Weber developed his conceptualization of power in the early 1900s, he focused primarily on the nation-state and its sphere of influence. Today scholars recognize that the trend toward globalization has brought new opportunities, and with them new concentrations of power. Power as the ability to exercise one's will over others is now exercised on a global as well as a national stage, as countries and multinational corporations vie to control access to resources and manage the distribution of capital (Sernau 2001).

There are three basic sources of power within any political system: force, influence, and authority. *Force* is the actual or threatened use of coercion to impose one's will on others. When leaders imprison or even execute political dissidents, they are applying force; so, too, are terrorists when they seize or bomb an embassy or assassinate a political leader. *Influence,* on the other hand, refers to the exercise of power through a process of persuasion. A citizen may change his or her view of a Supreme Court nominee because of a newspaper editorial, the expert testimony of a law school dean before the Senate Judiciary Committee, or a stirring speech by a political activist at a rally. In each case, sociologists would view such efforts to persuade people as examples of influence. Now let's take a look at the third source of power, *authority.*

Alan Greenspan, chairman of the Board of Governors of the Federal Reserve, meeting with some of the other board members. The 12-member Board of Governors is a government body that exerts economic power by controlling key interest rates. Board meetings are held behind closed doors, adding to the influence of these elite decision makers.

Types of Authority

The term *authority* refers to institutionalized power that is recognized by the people over whom it is exercised. Sociologists commonly use the term in connection with those who hold legitimate power through elected or publicly acknowledged positions. A person's authority is often limited. Thus, a referee has the authority to decide whether a penalty should be called during a football game, but has no authority over the price of tickets to the game.

Max Weber ([1913] 1947) developed a classification system for authority that has become one of the most useful and frequently cited contributions of early sociology. He identified three ideal types of authority: traditional, legal-rational, and charismatic. Weber did not insist that only one type applies to a given society or organization. All can be present, but their relative importance will vary. Sociologists have found Weber's typology valuable in understanding different manifestations of legitimate power within a society.

Traditional Authority

Until the middle of the last century, Japan was ruled by a revered emperor whose absolute power was passed down from generation to generation. In a political system based on *traditional authority,* legitimate power is conferred by custom and accepted practice. A king or queen is accepted as ruler of a nation simply by virtue of inheriting the crown; a tribal chief rules because that is the accepted practice. The ruler may be loved or hated,

The charismatic Nelson Mandela became the first democratically elected president of South Africa. He served from 1994 to 1999.

competent or destructive; in terms of legitimacy, that does not matter. For the traditional leader, authority rests in custom, not in personal characteristics, technical competence, or even written law. People accept the ruler's authority because that is how things have always been done. Traditional authority is absolute when the ruler has the ability to determine laws and policies.

Legal-Rational Authority

The U.S. Constitution gives Congress and our president the authority to make and enforce laws and policies. Power made legitimate by law is known as **legal-rational authority.** Leaders derive their legal-rational authority from the written rules and regulations of political systems, such as a constitution. Generally, in societies based on legal-rational authority, leaders are thought to have specific areas of competence and authority but are not thought to be endowed with divine inspiration, as in certain societies with traditional forms of authority.

Charismatic Authority

Joan of Arc was a simple peasant girl in medieval France, yet she was able to rally the French people and lead them in major battles against English invaders. How was this possible? As Weber observed, power can be legitimized by the *charisma* of an individual. The term **charismatic authority** refers to power made legitimate by a leader's exceptional personal or emotional appeal to his or her followers.

Charisma lets a person lead or inspire without relying on set rules or traditions. In fact, charismatic author-

ity is derived more from the beliefs of followers than from the actual qualities of leaders. So long as people *perceive* a leader as having qualities that set him or her apart from ordinary citizens, that leader's authority will remain secure and often unquestioned.

Unlike traditional rulers, charismatic leaders often become well known by breaking with established institutions and advocating dramatic changes in the social structure and the economic system. Their strong hold over their followers makes it easier to build protest movements that challenge the dominant norms and values of a society. Thus, charismatic leaders such as Jesus, Joan of Arc, Gandhi, Malcolm X, and Martin Luther King, Jr. all used their power to press for changes in accepted social behavior. But so did Adolf Hitler, whose charismatic appeal turned people toward violent and destructive ends in Nazi Germany.

Observing from an interactionist perspective, sociologist Carl Couch (1996) points out that the growth of the electronic media has facilitated the development of charismatic authority. During the 1930s and 1940s, the heads of state of the United States, Great Britain, and Germany all used radio to issue direct appeals to citizens. In recent decades, television has allowed leaders to "visit" people's homes and communicate with them. In both Taiwan and South Korea in 1996, troubled political leaders facing reelection campaigns spoke frequently to national audiences and exaggerated military threats from neighboring China and North Korea, respectively.

As we noted earlier, Weber used traditional, legal-rational, and charismatic authority as ideal types. In reality, particular leaders and political systems combine elements of two or more of these forms. Presidents Franklin D. Roosevelt, John F. Kennedy, and Ronald Reagan wielded power largely through the legal-rational basis of their authority. At the same time, they were unusually charismatic leaders who commanded the personal loyalty of large numbers of citizens.

Use Your Sociological Imagination www.mhhe.com /schaefer6

What would our government be like if it were founded on traditional rather than legal-rational authority? What difference would it make to the average citizen?

POLITICAL BEHAVIOR IN THE UNITED STATES

Citizens of the United States take for granted many aspects of their political system. They are accustomed to living in a nation with a Bill of Rights, two major political

Let's Discuss What type of authority is exercised by parents? (traditional) By a university registrar? (legal-rational)

Global View Couch's examination of electronic media in Great Britain and Germany
Theory Couch drew on the interactionist perspective in his study of electronic media.
Reel Society See Political Power in the Topic Index.
Key Person Max Weber

parties, voting by secret ballot, an elected president, state and local governments distinct from the national government, and so forth. Yet each society has its own ways of governing itself and making decisions. Just as U.S. residents expect Democratic and Republican candidates to compete for public office, residents of Cuba and the People's Republic of China are accustomed to one-party rule by the Communist party. In this section, we will examine several aspects of political behavior within the United States.

Participation and Apathy

In theory, a representative democracy will function most effectively and fairly if an informed and active electorate communicates its views to government leaders. Unfortunately, that is hardly the case in the United States. Virtually all citizens are familiar with the basics of the political process,

Table 14-1	Political Preferences in the United States
Party Identification	**Percentage of Population**
Strong Democrat	15
Not very strong Democrat	19
Independent, close to Democrat	10
Independent	19
Independent, close to Republican	7
Not very strong Republican	17
Strong Republican	12

Note: Data are for 2002. Numbers do not add to 100 percent because around 1 percent indicated other parties.

Source: J. Davis et al. 2003.

Think About It
Why do so many U.S. voters identify themselves as independents?

and most tend to identify to some extent with a political party (see Table 14-1), but only a small minority (often members of the higher social classes) actually participate in political organizations on a local or national level. Studies reveal that only 8 percent belong to a political club or organization. Not more than one in five has *ever* contacted an official of national, state, or local government about a political issue or problem (Orum 2001).

By the 1980s, it had become clear that many people in the United States were beginning to be turned off by political parties, politicians, and big government. The most dramatic indication of this growing alienation came from voting statistics. Today, voters of all ages and races appear to be less enthusiastic than ever about elections, even presidential contests. For example, in the presidential election of 1896, almost 80 percent of eligible voters in the United States went to the polls. Yet by the 2000 election, turnout had fallen to less than 51 percent of all eligible voters. Obviously, even modestly higher voter turnout could dramatically change election outcomes, as we saw in the razor-thin margin in the 2000 presidential election.

While a few nations still command high voter turnout, it is increasingly common to hear national leaders of other countries complain of voter apathy. Japan typically enjoyed 70 percent turnout in its Upper House elections through the mid-1980s, but by 2000 turnout was closer to 59 percent. In 2001, only 58 percent of British voters participated in the general elections. More recently, just 49 percent of Swiss voters went to the polls (Peck 2002:49).

In the end, political participation makes government accountable to the voters. If participation declines,

Methods Data in Table 14-1 are from a survey by NORC.
Methods By comparison, the preferences in 1982 were Strong Democrat, 16%; Not Very Strong Democrat, 25%; Independent, Close to Democrat, 13%; Independent, 13%; Independent, Close to Republican, 10%; Not Very Strong Republican, 14%; Strong Republican, 9%.

Classroom Tip Compare students' political preferences with the national data in Table 14-1.
Global View Voter turnout in the United States compared with voter turnout in other countries
Methods Surveys of voter turnout in the U.S. and other countries

government operates with less of a sense of accountability to society. This issue is most serious for the least powerful individuals and groups in the United States. Voter turnout has been particularly low among members of racial and ethnic minorities. In postelection surveys, fewer African Americans and Hispanics than Whites report that they actually voted. Many more potential voters fail to register to vote. The poor—whose focus understandably is on survival—are traditionally underrepresented among voters as well. The low turnout found among these groups is explained, at least in part, by their common feeling of powerlessness. Yet these low statistics encourage political power brokers to continue to ignore the interests of the less affluent and the nation's minorities. The segment of the voting population that has shown the most voter apathy is the young: see Box 14-1 (Casper and Bass 1998).

Women in Politics

In the United States, women are dramatically underrepresented in the halls of government. As of mid-2004, there were only 73 women in Congress; they accounted for 59 of the 435 members of the House of Representatives and 14 of the 100 members of the Senate. Only 8 states had female governors: Arizona, Delaware, Hawaii, Kansas, Louisiana, Michigan, Montana, and Utah (Center for American Women and Politics 2004).

p. 279 Sexism has been the most serious barrier to women interested in holding office. Women were not even allowed to vote in national elections until 1920. Female candidates have had to overcome the prejudices of both men and women regarding women's fitness for leadership. Moreover, women often encounter prejudice, discrimination, and abuse *after* they are elected. Despite these problems, more women are being elected to political office, and more of them are identifying themselves as feminists.

Women politicians may be enjoying more electoral success now than in the past, but there is evidence that the media cover them differently from men. A content analysis of newspaper coverage of recent gubernatorial races showed that reporters wrote more often about a female candidate's personal life, appearance, or personality than a male candidate's, and less often about her political positions and voting record. Furthermore, when political issues were raised in newspaper articles, reporters were more likely to illustrate them with statements made by male candidates than by female candidates (Devitt 1999).

While the proportion of women in national legislatures has increased in the United States and many other nations, women still do not account for half the members of the national legislature in any country. The African Re-

public of Rwanda ranks the highest, with 48.8 percent of its legislative seats held by women. Overall, the United States ranked 57th among 135 nations in the proportion of women serving as national legislators in 2004. To remedy this situation, many countries—including the world's largest democracy, India—have reserved a minimum number of legislative seats for women.

A new dimension of women and politics emerged beginning in the 1980s. Surveys detected a growing "gender gap" in the political preferences and activities of males and females. Specifically, women were more likely to register as Democrats than as Republicans. According to political analysts, the Democratic Party's support for the right to choose a legal abortion, for family and medical leave legislation, and for governmental action to require insurers to cover a minimum two-day hospital stay for new mothers has attracted women voters.

The gender gap was still evident in the 2000 presidential election. Data from exit polls revealed that Democrat Al Gore received 54 percent of women's votes, compared to 42 percent of men's votes. The 12 percent gap between the sexes indicates that turnout of female voters is a key to Democratic victories. When women did not turn out in the 1994 congressional elections, solid support from White male voters was an important factor in Republican success (Voter News Service 2000).

Use Your Sociological Imagination www.mhhe.com/schaefer6

Imagine a world in which women, not men, held the majority of elective offices. What kind of world would it be?

MODELS OF POWER STRUCTURE IN THE UNITED STATES

Who really holds power in the United States? Do "we the people" genuinely run the country through our elected representatives? Or is it true that behind the scenes, a small elite controls both the government and the economic system? It is difficult to determine the location of power in a society as complex as the United States. In exploring this critical question, social scientists have developed two basic views of our nation's power structure: the power elite and the pluralist models.

Power Elite Models

Karl Marx believed that 19th-century representative democracy was essentially a sham. He argued that industrial societies were dominated by relatively small numbers of people who owned factories and controlled natural

---

Methods/Race/Ethnicity Postelection surveys indicate fewer African Americans and Hispanics than Whites report they actually voted.
Classroom Tip See "Gender and Politics" (Class Discussion Topics).
Global View/Gender Women are underrepresented in government.
Theory Conflict view of impact of sexism in the U.S. political system
Methods Content analysis of media coverage of candidates

Methods/Gender Gender gap in the 2000 U.S. presidential election
Classroom Tip See "Gender Assumptions in Politics" (Class Discussion Topics).
Methods Networks' exit polls are an example of survey research.
Let's Discuss Do students believe that women are likely to hold even 50 percent of elective offices during their lifetime?

All through the 1960s, young people in the United States participated actively in a range of political issues, from pushing civil rights to protesting the Vietnam War. They were especially disturbed by the fact that young men were barred from voting but were being drafted to serve in the military and were dying for their country. In response to these concerns, the 26th Amendment to the Constitution was ratified in 1971, lowering the voting age from 21 to 18.

Now, more than 30 years later, we can consider the available research and see what happened. Frankly, what is remarkable is what did *not* happen. First, young voters (those between ages 18 and 21) have not united in any particular political sentiment. We can see in how the young vote the same divisions of race, ethnicity, and gender that are apparent among older age groups.

Second, while the momentum for lowering the voting age came from college campuses, the majority of young voters are not students at all. Many are already part of the workforce and either live with their parents or have established their own households.

Third, and particularly troubling, is their low voter turnout. In the highly competitive 2000 presidential election, only 32 percent of young people cast a vote. Compared to the figure of 50 percent in the 1972 election—the first in which 18-year-olds could vote—this turnout was extremely low.

What lies behind this voter apathy among the young? The popular explanation is that people—especially young

> While the momentum for lowering the voting age came from college campuses, the majority of young voters are not students at all.

people—are alienated from the political system, turned off by the shallowness and negativity of candidates and campaigns. True, studies have documented that young voters are susceptible to cynicism and distrust, but those qualities are not necessarily associated with voter apathy. Numerous studies show that the relationship between how people perceive the candidates and issues and their likelihood

of voting is a very complex one. Young people do vote as they age. Any disaffection with the voting booth is certainly not permanent.

Other explanations for the lower turnout among the young seem more plausible. First, the United States is virtually alone in requiring citizens to vote twice, in effect. They must first *register* to vote, often at a time when issues are not on the front burner and candidates haven't even declared. Second, while citizens in the United States tend to be more active than their counterparts in other countries in politics on the community level, young people often feel unmoved by such local issues as public school financing.

Let's Discuss

1. How often do you vote? If you do not vote, what accounts for your apathy? Are you too busy to register? Are community issues uninteresting to you?
2. Do you think voter apathy is a serious social problem? What might be done to increase voter participation in your age group and community?

Sources: Alwin 2002; Clymer 2000; A. Goldstein and Morin 2002; Jamieson et al. 2002; Y. Rosenberg 2004.

---

resources. In Marx's view, government officials and military leaders were essentially servants of this capitalist class and followed their wishes. Therefore, any key decisions made by politicians inevitably reflected the interests of the dominant bourgeoisie. Like others who hold an ***elite model*** of power relations, Marx believed that society is ruled by a small group of individuals who share a common set of political and economic interests.

Mills's Model

Sociologist C. Wright Mills, referred to earlier in this chapter, took this model a step further in his pioneering work *The Power Elite* ([1956] 2000b). Mills described a small group of military, industrial, and government leaders who controlled the fate of the United States—the

power elite. Power rested in the hands of a few, both inside and outside government.

A pyramid illustrates the power structure of the United States in Mills's model (see Figure 14-1a, page 372). At the top are the corporate rich, leaders of the executive branch of government, and heads of the military (whom Mills called the "warlords"). Directly below are local opinion leaders, members of the legislative branch of government, and leaders of special-interest groups. Mills contended that these individuals and groups would basically follow the wishes of the dominant power elite. At the bottom of the pyramid are the unorganized, exploited masses.

The power elite model is, in many respects, similar to the work of Karl Marx. The most striking difference is

Classroom Tip See "Class Voting Behavior" (Class Discussion Topics).
Methods Data from the Bureau of the Census
Race/Ethnicity/Gender Young voters mimic the voting behavior of adults in their racial, ethnic, and gender groups.

Key Persons Karl Marx, C. Wright Mills
Theory Mills's power elite model reflects a conflict perspective.
Classroom Tip See "Corporate Power" (Class Discussion Topics).

FIGURE 14-1

Power Elite Models

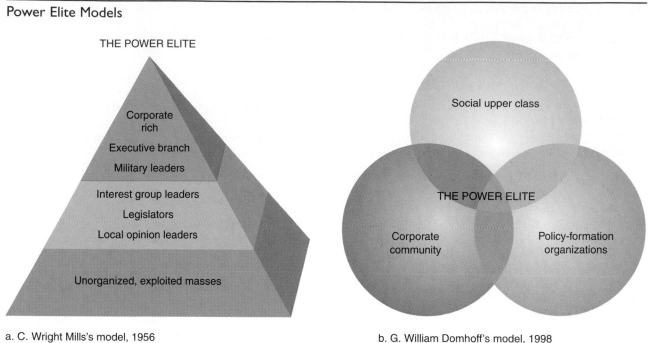

a. C. Wright Mills's model, 1956

b. G. William Domhoff's model, 1998

Source: Domhoff 2001:96.

that Mills believed that the economically powerful coordinate their maneuvers with the military and political establishments to serve their common interests. Yet, reminiscent of Marx, Mills argued that the corporate rich were perhaps the most powerful element of the power elite (first among "equals"). And the powerless masses at the bottom of Mills's power elite model certainly bring to mind Marx's portrait of the oppressed workers of the world, who have "nothing to lose but their chains."

A fundamental element in Mills's thesis is that the power elite not only includes relatively few members but also operates as a self-conscious, cohesive unit. Although not necessarily diabolical or ruthless, the elite comprises similar types of people who regularly interact with one another and have essentially the same political and economic interests. Mills's power elite is not a conspiracy but rather a community of interest and sentiment among a small number of influential people (A. Hacker 1964).

Admittedly, Mills failed to clarify when the elite opposes protests and when it tolerates them; he also failed to provide detailed case studies that would substantiate the interrelationships among members of the power elite. Nevertheless, his challenging theories forced scholars to look more critically at the democratic political system of the United States.

In commenting on the scandals that have rocked major corporations such as Enron and Arthur Andersen

over the last decade, observers have noted that members of the business elite *are* closely interrelated. In a study of the members of the boards of directors of Fortune 1,000 corporations, researchers found that each director can reach *every* other board of directors in just 3.7 steps. That is, by consulting acquaintances of acquaintances, each director can quickly reach someone who sits on each of the other 999 boards. Furthermore, the face-to-face contact directors regularly have in their board meetings makes them a highly cohesive elite. Finally, the corporate elite is not only wealthy, powerful, and cohesive; it is also overwhelmingly White and male (G. Davis 2003, 2004; Mizruchi 1996; G. Strauss 2002).

Domhoff's Model

Over the last three decades, sociologist G. William Domhoff (2001), coauthor of the chapter-opening excerpt from *Diversity in the Power Elite,* has agreed with Mills that a powerful elite runs the United States. He finds that it is still largely White, male, and upper class, as he wrote in his book with Richard L. Zweigenhaft (1998). But Domhoff stresses the role played both by elites of the corporate community and by the leaders of policy-formation organizations such as chambers of commerce and labor unions. Many of the people in both groups are also members of the social upper class.

While these groups overlap, as Figure 14-1b shows, they do not necessarily agree on specific policies. Domhoff notes that in the electoral arena, two different coalitions have exercised influence. A *corporate-conservative coalition* has played a large role in both political parties, generating support for particular candidates through direct-mail appeals. A *liberal-labor coalition* is based in unions, local environmental organizations, a segment of the minority group community, liberal churches, and the university and arts communities (Zweigenhaft and Domhoff 1998).

Pluralist Model

Several social scientists insist that power in the United States is shared more widely than the elite models indicate. In their view, a pluralist model more accurately describes the nation's political system. According to the **pluralist model,**

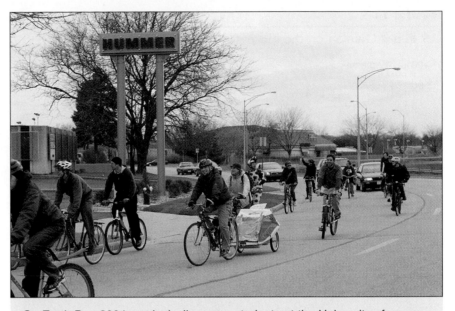

On Earth Day 2004, ecologically aware students at the University of Wisconsin, Madison, hopped on their bicycles and joined local residents at the Hummer dealership. Protesters were hoping to disrupt sales of the huge gas-guzzling vehicles by blocking traffic. When public interest groups seek to exert their power through such mass protests, they are demonstrating a belief in the pluralist model of the United States' power structure.

many conflicting groups within the community have access to government, so that no single group is dominant.

The pluralist model suggests that a variety of groups play a significant role in decision making. Typically, pluralists make use of intensive case studies or community studies based on observation research. One of the most famous—an investigation of decision making in New Haven, Connecticut—was reported by Robert Dahl (1961). Dahl found that although the number of people involved in any important decision was rather small, community power was nonetheless diffuse. Few political actors exercised decision-making power on all issues. One individual or group might be influential in a battle over urban renewal but at the same time have little impact on educational policy.

The pluralist model, however, has not escaped serious questioning. Domhoff (1978, 2001) reexamined Dahl's study of decision making in New Haven and argued that Dahl and other pluralists had failed to trace how local elites who were prominent in decision making were part of a larger national ruling class. In addition, studies of community power, such as Dahl's work in New Haven, can examine decision making only on issues that become part of the political agenda. They fail to address the possible power of elites to keep certain matters entirely out of the realm of government debate.

Dianne Pinderhughes (1987) has criticized the pluralist model for failing to account for the exclusion of African Americans from the political process. Drawing on her studies of Chicago politics, Pinderhughes points out that the residential and occupational segregation of Blacks and their long political disenfranchisement violates the logic of pluralism—which would hold that such a substantial minority should always have been influential in community decision making. This critique applies to many cities across the United States, where other large racial and ethnic minorities, among them Asian Americans, Puerto Ricans, and Mexican Americans, are relatively powerless. The problems encountered by African American voters in Florida in the 2000 election bear out this critique of the pluralist model (Berry 2001).

Historically, pluralists have stressed ways in which large numbers of people can participate in or influence governmental decision making. New communications technologies like the Internet are increasing the opportunity to be heard, not just in countries such as the United States but in developing countries the world over. One common point of the elite and pluralist perspectives stands out, however: in the political system of the United States, power is unequally distributed. All citizens may be equal in theory, yet those who are high in the nation's power structure are "more equal." New communications

Student Alert The pluralist model has certain aspects of the elite model. Pluralists see decision making as more widely shared but would agree that the disadvantaged are often excluded.
Key Person Robert Dahl

Race/Ethnicity Pinderhughes's critique of the pluralist model for failing to account for the exclusion of African Americans from the political process

FIGURE 14-2

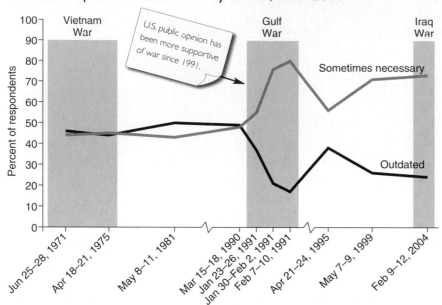

U.S. Public Opinion on the Necessity of War, 1971–2004

U.S. public opinion has been more supportive of war since 1991.

Note: Respondents replied to the following question: "Some people feel that war is an outmoded way of settling differences between nations. Others feel that wars are sometimes necessary to settle differences. With which point of view do you agree?"

Source: Arora 2004.

technology may or may not change that distribution of power.

Perhaps the ultimate test of power, no matter what a nation's power structure, is the decision to go to war. Because the rank and file of any army is generally drawn from the lower classes—the least powerful groups in society—such a decision has life-and-death consequences for people far removed from the center of power. In the long run, if the general population is not convinced that war is necessary, military action is unlikely to succeed. Thus, war is a risky way in which to address conflict between nations. In the following section we will contrast war and peace as ways of addressing societal conflict, and more recently, the threat of terrorism.

WAR AND PEACE

Conflict is a central aspect of social relations. Too often it becomes ongoing and violent, engulfing innocent bystanders as well as intentional participants. Sociologists Theodore Caplow and Louis Hicks (2002:3) have defined *war* as conflict between organizations that possess trained combat forces equipped with deadly weapons. This meaning is broader than the legal definition, which typically requires a formal declaration of hostilities.

War

Sociologists approach war in three different ways. Those who take a global view study how and why two or more nations become engaged in military conflict. Those who take a nation-state view stress the interaction of internal political, socioeconomic, and cultural forces. And those who take a micro view focus on the social impact of war on individuals and the groups they belong to (Kiser 1992).

The internal decision-making process that leads to war has been much studied. During the Vietnam War, Presidents Johnson and Nixon both misled Congress, painting a falsely optimistic picture of the likely outcome. Based on their intentional distortions, Congress appropriated the military funds the two administrations requested. But in 1971 the *New York Times* published a set of classified documents now known as "The Pentagon Papers," which revealed the real prospects for the war. Two years later—over Nixon's veto—Congress passed the War Powers Act, which requires the president to notify Congress of the reasons for committing combat troops to a hostile situation (T. Patterson 2003).

Though war is a decision that is entered into by governments, public opinion plays a significant role in its execution. By 1971, the number of U.S. soldiers killed in Vietnam had surpassed 50,000, and antiwar sentiment was strong. Surveys done at that time showed the public was split roughly equally on the question of whether war was an appropriate way to settle differences between nations (see Figure 14-2). This division in public opinion continued until the United States became involved in the Gulf War following Iraq's invasion of Kuwait in 1990. Since then, U.S. sentiment has been more supportive of war as a means of resolving disputes.

Historically, the U.S. military has not been reflective of the society it serves. During the Vietnam War, members of the lower social classes were more likely than others to be drafted. Today, however, the United States' all-volunteer army tends to be more representative of the nation's population. During the war in Iraq, which began in 2003, ap-

Global View Conflict between nations
Let's Discuss Who should have the power to declare war?
Contemporary Culture How does public sentiment about the war in Iraq compare to public sentiment about the Vietnam War?

RICHARD J. HAWK **Vice President and Financial Consultant, Smith Barney**

Richard Hawk had no idea what he wanted to do with his life when he entered DePauw University in Indiana, and no idea what sociology was about when he registered for his first course. But he soon realized that he liked the faculty in the sociology department, and he liked the perspective the subject gave him on other subjects he was studying—economics, history, and communications. In his junior year, Hawk took a course on marriage and the family that helped him to see the "trickle-down effect" of major economic decisions on individuals and communities.

Today, Hawk credits sociology with giving him "a better overall understanding of things," one he uses daily. Asked to elaborate, he replies, "You have to realize that everyone is affected one way or another" by economic and political decisions. He points to the war in Iraq: "Half of the forces are reservists. Look at the social and financial effect on the family, the economic effect on the companies these people work for domestically, not to mention the obvious effects on the Iraqi people." Hawk sees these effects play themselves out in his clients' lives, whether they are physicians or blue-collar workers facing an early retirement. In developing their financial plans, he keeps the big picture in mind.

As a financial consultant, Hawk meets with clients, confers with money managers and financial analysts, and prepares proposals for prospective clients. He applies the same analytical perspective that he uses with clients to the economy and current business issues. "The past few years have not been particularly kind to the equity markets," he observes. "We were in a technology bubble, and as a result, we have been experiencing dramatic changes in accounting methods, compensation issues, and ethics in general."

Hawk advises first-time sociology students to approach the subject with an open mind, to "be willing to look at issues from a different perspective." Doing so, he thinks, will pay off in some valuable insights.

Let's Discuss

1. Pick an economic issue or decision that has been in the news recently and show how it could affect your family.
2. Take the same issue or decision and imagine how it might affect the people you will deal with in your future career.

proximately 40 percent of U.S. troops in the combat zone were reservists or Guardsmen—so-called weekend warriors. Because these troops represented a broad spectrum of the U.S. population, the casualties they suffered may have strengthened antiwar sentiment (Caplow and Hicks 2002; Fallows 2004; T. Wilson 1995).

Another indication of the changing composition of the U.S. military is the growing presence of women. Over 212,000 women, or about 15 percent of U.S. military forces, are now in uniform, serving not just as support personnel but as an integral part of combat units. The first casualty of the war in Iraq, in fact, was Private First Class Lori Piestewa, a member of the Hopi tribe and a descendant of Mexican settlers in the Southwest (Department of Defense 2003).

From a micro point of view, war can bring out the worst as well as the best in people. In 2004, graphic images of the abuse of Iraqi prisoners by U.S. soldiers at Iraq's Abu Ghraib prison shocked the world. For social scientists, the deterioration of the guards' behavior recalled memories of Philip Zimbardo's mock prison experiment, done in 1971. Though the results of the experiment, highlighted in Chapter 5, have been applied primarily to civilian correctional facilities, Zimbardo's study was actually funded by the Office of Naval Research. In July 2004, the U.S. military began using a documentary film about the experiment to train military interrogators to avoid mistreatment of prisoners (Zarembo 2004; Zimbardo 2004).

Peace

Sociologists have considered **peace** both as the absence of war and as a proactive effort to develop cooperative relations among nations. While we will focus here on international relations, we should note that in the 1990s, 90 percent of the world's armed conflicts occurred *within* rather than between states. Often, outside powers became involved in these internal conflicts, either as supporters of

Race/Ethnicity/Gender The roles of women and minorities in the military
Let's Discuss What are some of the micro-level social impacts of the war in Iraq?

Let's Discuss To what extent should outside nations become involved in domestic conflicts?

A representative of the International Red Crescent Society delivers an aid parcel in the southern Iraqi town of Safwan. The Red Crescent delivers emergency aid to victims of war and disaster in Muslim communities. Such nongovernmental organizations (NGOs) help to bind countries together, promoting peaceful relations.

Finally, many analysts stress that nations cannot maintain their security by threatening violence. Peace, they contend, can best be maintained by developing strong mutual security agreements between potential adversaries (Etzioni 1965; Shostak 2002).

In recent years, the United States has begun to recognize that its security can be threatened not just by nation states, but by political groups that operate outside the bounds of legitimate authority. Indeed, terrorism is now considered the foremost threat to U.S. security—one the U.S. military is unaccustomed to fighting.

Terrorism

Acts of terror, whether perpetrated by a few or by many people, can be a powerful political force. Formally defined, *terrorism* is the use or threat of violence against random or symbolic targets in pursuit of political aims. For terrorists, the end justifies the means. They believe the status quo is oppressive, and desperate measures are essential to end the suffering of the deprived. Convinced that working through the formal political process will not effect the desired political change, terrorists insist that illegal actions—often directed against innocent people—are needed. Ultimately, they hope to intimidate society and thereby bring about a new political order.

An essential aspect of contemporary terrorism involves use of the media. Terrorists may wish to keep secret their individual identities, but they want their political messages and goals to receive as much publicity as possible. Drawing upon Erving Goffman's dramaturgical approach, sociologist Alfred McClung Lee has likened terrorism to the theater, where certain scenes are played out in predictable fashion. Whether through calls to the media, anonymous manifestos, or other means, terrorists typically admit responsibility for and defend their violent acts.

Since September 11, 2001, governments around the world have renewed their efforts to fight terrorism. Though the public has generally regarded increased surveillance and social control as a necessary evil, these measures have nonetheless raised governance issues. For example, some citizens in the United States and elsewhere have questioned whether measures such as the USA

particular factions or in an attempt to broker a peace accord. In at least 28 countries where such conflicts occurred—none of which would be considered core nations in world systems analysis—at least 10,000 people died (Kriesberg 1992; Dan Smith 1999).

Sociologists and other social scientists who draw on sociological theory and research have tried to identify conditions that deter war. One of their findings is that international trade acts as a deterrent to armed conflict. As countries exchange goods, people, and then cultures, they become more integrated and less likely to threaten each other's security. Viewed from this perspective, not just trade but immigration and foreign exchange programs have a beneficial effect on international relations.

Another means of fostering peace is the activity of international charities and activist groups called nongovernmental organizations (NGOs). The Red Cross and Red Crescent, Doctors Without Borders, and Amnesty International donate their services wherever they are needed, without regard to nationality. In the last decade or more, these global organizations have been expanding in number, size, and scope. By sharing news of local conditions and clarifying local issues, they often prevent conflicts from escalating into violence and war. Some NGOs have initiated cease-fires, reached settlements, and even ended warfare between former adversaries.

PATRIOT Act of 2001 threaten civil liberties. Citizens also complain about the heightened anxiety created by the vague alerts issued by the federal government from time to time. Worldwide, immigration and the processing of refugees have slowed to a crawl, separating families and preventing employers from filling job openings. As these efforts to combat political violence illustrate, the term *terrorism* is an apt one (R. Howard and Sawyer 2003; A. Lee 1983; R. Miller 1988).

THE CHANGING ECONOMY

As advocates of the power elite model point out, the trend in capitalist societies has been toward concentration of ownership by giant corporations, especially multina- p. 224 tional ones. For example, there were 7,032 mergers in 2002 alone, involving $1.2 trillion in business. The U.S. economy is changing in important ways, in part because it is increasingly intertwined with and dependent on the global economy. In 2002, foreign companies acquired 336 U.S. firms valued together at $68 billion (Bureau of the Census 2003a:571).

In the following sections, we will examine two developments in the economy that have interested sociologists: the changing face of the workforce and deindustrialization. As these trends show, any change in the economy inevitably has social and political implications that soon become a concern of policymakers.

The Changing Face of the Workforce

The workforce in the United States is constantly changing. During World War II, when men were mobilized to fight abroad, women entered the workforce in large numbers. And with the rise of the civil rights movement in the 1960s, minorities found numerous job opportunities opening to them. The active recruitment of women and minorities into the workplace, known as *affirmative action,* is the subject of this chapter's social policy section.

While predictions are not always reliable, sociologists and labor specialists foresee a workforce increasingly composed of women and racial and ethnic minorities. In 1960 there were twice as many men in the labor force as women. During the period from 1980 to 2020, three women are expected to enter the labor force for every two men. It's possible that by 2020 the female workforce may be only 3 percent smaller than the male workforce. The dynamics for minority groups in the workforce are even more dramatic. The number of Black, Latino, and Asian American workers continues to increase at a rate faster than the number of White workers, as Figure 14-3 shows (Toossi 2002:24).

More and more, the workforce reflects the diversity of the population, as ethnic minorities enter the labor force and immigrants and their children move from marginal jobs or employ- pp. 220–221 ment in the informal economy to positions of greater visibility and responsibility. The impact of this changing labor force is not merely statistical. A more diverse workforce means that relationships between workers are more likely to cross gender, racial, and ethnic lines. Interactionists note that people will find themselves supervising and being supervised by people very different from themselves. In response to these changes, 75 percent of businesses had instituted some type of cultural diversity training program as of 2000 (Melia 2000).

Deindustrialization

What happens when a company decides it is more profitable to move its operations out of a long-established community to another part of the

FIGURE 14-3

Racial and Ethnic Composition of the U.S. Labor Force, 1980 and 2020 (projection)

Source: Toossi 2002:24.

Sociology in the Global Community

14-2 OFFSHORING SERVICE JOBS

Ten thousand employees have gathered under a tent to celebrate a corporate milestone: Infosys Technologies has reached $1 billion in annual revenue. To add to the excitement, the company has announced that $23 million in bonuses will be distributed to deserving employees. The scene is not Silicon Valley, however, but the Indian city of Bangalore—the epicenter of a surge in offshore outsourcing.

U.S. firms have outsourced certain types of work for generations. For example, moderate-sized businesses such as furniture stores and commercial laundries have long contracted for, or outsourced, their delivery services to domestic carriers. The new trend toward "offshoring" carries this practice one step further, by transferring work to foreign contractors. Now, even large companies are turning to overseas firms, many of them located in developing countries. Offshoring has become the latest tactic in the time-worn business strategy of raising profits by reducing costs.

Originally, companies transferred manufacturing jobs to foreign factories, where wage rates were much lower. But the transfer of work from one country to another is no longer limited to manufacturing. Office and professional jobs are being exported, too, thanks to advanced telecommunications and the growth of skilled, English-speaking labor forces in

developing nations with relatively low wage scales. The trend includes even those jobs that require considerable training, such as accounting and financial analysis, computer programming, claims adjustment, telemarketing, and hotel and airline reservations. Today, when you call a toll-free number to reach a customer sevice representative, chances are the person who answers the phone will not be speaking from the United States.

Estimates are that by the year 2015, 3.3 million white-collar jobs worth an es-

> *Offshoring has become the latest tactic in the time-worn business strategy of raising profits by reducing costs.*

timated annual payroll of $136.4 billion will have moved overseas. Admittedly, that is only a small fraction of service-sector jobs. But more and more, increases in overseas outsourcing are being accompanied by job reductions at home. Middle-class workers *and voters* are alarmed by the trend. While moving high-tech work to India does help to lower costs, the impact on those technical and service workers who have been displaced is clearly devastating. Economists argue for assistance to laid-off workers

but against broad-based efforts to block outsourcing.

There is a downside to offshoring for foreigners as well. Though outsourcing is a significant source of employment for India's upper middle class, hundreds of millions of other Indians have seen little to no positive impact from the trend. Most households in India do not have any form of high technology: only about 1 out of 10 have a telephone, and 3 out of 1,000 a computer. Instead of improving these people's lives, the new business centers have siphoned water and electricity away from those who are most in need. Even the high-tech workers are experiencing negative consequences. Many suffer from stress disorders such as stomach problems and difficulty sleeping; more than half quit their jobs before the end of a year.

Let's Discuss

1. How might the number of foreign students who are educated in the United States contribute to the trend toward offshoring? On balance, do you think the gain from training foreign students outweighs the loss from exported jobs?
2. What do you think will be the political impact of the growing trend toward offshoring of service jobs?

Sources: Brainard and Litan 2004; Drezner 2004; Mangan 2004; Rajan 2004; Scheiber 2004; Waldman 2004a, 2004b, 2004c.

country, or out of the country altogether? People lose jobs; stores lose customers; the local government's tax base declines and it cuts services. This devastating process has occurred again and again in the last decade or so.

The term *deindustrialization* refers to the systematic, widespread withdrawal of investment in basic aspects of productivity, such as factories and plants. Giant corporations that deindustrialize are not necessarily refusing to invest in new economic opportunities. Rather, the targets and locations of investment change, and the need for labor decreases as technology continues to automate production.

First, there may be a relocation of plants from the nation's central cities to the suburbs. The next step may be relocation from suburban areas of the Northeast and Midwest to southern states, where labor laws place more restrictions on unions. Finally, a corporation may simply relocate *outside* the United States to a country with a lower rate of prevailing wages. General Motors, for example, decided to build a multibillion-dollar plant in China rather than in Kansas City or even Mexico (Lynn 2003).

Although deindustrialization often involves relocation, in some instances it takes the form of corporate

Let's Discuss Have you ever dialed a customer service number and realized that you were connected to a foreign country?
Contemporary Culture Expansion in jobs outsourced to non-U.S. countries.
378 Let's Discuss Are there limits to the types of jobs that can be outsourced?

Theory Conflict theorists would see deindustrialization as only widening the divide between the haves and the have-nots.
Let's Discuss How can world systems analysis be applied in examining deindustrialization?
Classroom Tip See "Division of Labor" (Class Discussion Topics).

restructuring, as companies seek to reduce costs in the face of growing worldwide competition. When such restructuring occurs, the impact on the bureaucratic hierarchy of formal organizations can be significant. A large corporation may choose to sell off or entirely abandon less productive divisions and to eliminate layers of management viewed as unnecessary. Wages and salaries may be frozen and fringe benefits cut—all in the name of restructuring. Increasing reliance on automation also spells the end of work as we have known it.

The term *downsizing* was introduced in 1987 to refer to reductions taken in a company's workforce as part of deindustrialization. Viewed from a conflict perspective, the unprecedented attention given to downsizing in the mid-1990s reflected the continuing importance of social class in the United States. Conflict theorists note that job loss has long been a feature of deindustrialization among blue-collar workers. But when large numbers of middle-class managers and other white-collar employees with substantial incomes began to be laid off, suddenly the media began expressing great concern over downsizing. Box 14-2 highlights the latest version of this issue, the outsourcing of service jobs at U.S. companies to workers in foreign countries (Richtel 2000; Safire 1996; R. Samuelson 1996a, 1996b).

The social costs of deindustrialization and downsizing cannot be overemphasized. Plant closings lead to substantial unemployment in a community, which can have a devastating impact on both the micro and macro levels. On the micro level, the unemployed person and his or her family must adjust to a loss of spending power. Painting or re-siding the house, buying health insurance or saving for retirement, even thinking about having another child must be put aside. Both marital happiness and family cohesion may suffer as a result. Although many dismissed workers eventually reenter the paid labor force, they must often accept less desirable positions with lower salaries and fewer benefits (DePalma 2002). Unemployment and underemployment are tied to many of the social problems discussed throughout this textbook, among them the need for child care, the controversy over welfare, and pp. 98, 233, 264 immigration issues.

THE ENVIRONMENT

Decisions made in the economic and political spheres often have environmental consequences. We can see signs of despoliation almost everywhere. Our air, our water, and our land are being polluted, whether we live in St. Louis, Mexico City, or Lagos, Nigeria. In North America, each summer brings power failures or brownouts to sweltering cities as the consumption of electricity exceeds the supply. In the following section, we will survey these problems and see what sociologists have to say about them.

Environmental Problems: An Overview

In recent decades, the world has witnessed serious environmental disasters. For example, Love Canal, near Niagara Falls in New York State, was declared a disaster area in 1978 because of chemical contamination. In the 1940s and 1950s, a chemical company had disposed of waste products on the site where a housing development and a school were later built. The metal drums that held the chemical wastes eventually rusted out, and toxic chemicals with noxious odors began seeping into the residents' yards and basements. Subsequent investigations revealed that the chemical company knew as early as 1958 that toxic chemicals were seeping into homes and a school playground. After repeated protests in the late 1970s, 239 families living in Love Canal had to be relocated.

In 1986, a series of explosions set off a catastrophic nuclear reactor accident at Chernobyl, a part of Ukraine (in what was then the Soviet Union). The accident killed at least 32,000 people. Some 300,000 residents had to be evacuated, and the area became uninhabitable for 19 miles in any direction. High levels of radiation were found as far as 30 miles from the reactor site, and radioactivity levels were well above normal as far away as Sweden and Japan. According to one estimate, the Chernobyl accident and the resulting nuclear fallout may ultimately result in 100,000 excess cases of cancer worldwide (Shcherbak 1996).

While Love Canal, Chernobyl, and other environmental disasters understandably grab headlines, it is the silent, day-to-day deterioration of the environment that ultimately poses a devastating threat to humanity. Examining all our environmental problems in detail would be impossible, but three broad areas of concern stand out: air pollution, water pollution, and contamination of land.

Air Pollution

More than 1 billion people on the planet are exposed to potentially health-damaging levels of air pollution. Unfortunately, in cities around the world, residents have come to accept smog and polluted air as normal. Air pollution in urban areas is caused primarily by emissions from automobiles and secondarily by emissions from electric power plants and heavy industries. Urban smog not only limits visibility; it can lead to health problems as uncomfortable as eye irritation and as deadly as lung cancer. Such problems are especially severe in developing countries. The World Health Organization estimates that

Theory Conflict view of why attention has recently been given to downsizing
Classroom Tip See "Alienation among Workers" (Class Discussion Topics).
Theory Interactionist view of the impact of unemployment on the micro level

Global View Environmental issues are a worldwide concern.
Classroom Tip See "Class Project—Learning More about Environmental Problems" (Class Discussion Topics).

up to 700,000 premature deaths *per year* could be prevented if pollutants were brought down to safer levels (Carty 1999; World Resources Institute 1998).

People are capable of changing their behavior, but they are also unwilling to make such changes permanent. For example, during the 1984 Olympics in Los Angeles, residents were asked to carpool and stagger their work hours to relieve traffic congestion and improve the quality of the air athletes would breathe. These changes resulted in a remarkable 12 percent drop in ozone levels. However, when the Olympians left, people reverted to their normal behavior and the ozone levels climbed back up (McCright and Dunlap 2003; Nussbaum 1998).

Water Pollution

Throughout the United States, dumping of waste materials by both industries and local governments has polluted streams, rivers, and lakes. Consequently, many bodies of water have become unsafe for drinking, fishing, and swimming. Around the world, the pollution of the oceans is an issue of growing concern. Such pollution results regularly from waste dumping and is made worse by fuel leaks from shipping and occasional oil spills. In a dramatic accident in 1989, the oil tanker *Exxon Valdez* ran aground in Prince William Sound, Alaska. The tanker's cargo of 11 million gallons of crude oil spilled into the sound and washed onto the shore, contaminating 1,285 miles of shoreline. About 11,000 people joined in a cleanup effort that cost over $2 billion. As we saw in ◀ p. 43 Chapter 2, ExxonMobil continues to fight court-ordered settlements that would partially cover the cost of the cleanup.

Less dramatic than large-scale accidents or disasters, but more common in many parts of the world, are problems with the basic water supply. Worldwide, over 1 billion people lack safe and adequate drinking water, and 2.4 billion have no acceptable means of sanitation—a problem that further threatens the quality of water supplies. The health costs of unsafe water are enormous (United Nations 2003).

What are the basic causes of our growing environmental problems? Some observers, such as Paul Ehrlich and Anne Ehrlich, see the pressure of world population growth as the central factor in environmental deterioration. They argue that population control is essential in preventing widespread starvation and environmental decay. Barry Commoner, a biologist, counters that the primary cause of environmental ills is the increasing use of technological innovations that are destructive to the world's environment—among them plastics, detergents, synthetic fibers, pesticides, herbicides, and chemical fertilizers. In the following sections, we will contrast the functionalist and conflict approaches to the study of environmental issues (Commoner 1971, 1990; Ehrlich 1968; Ehrlich and Ehrlich 1990; Ehrlich and Ellison 2002).

Functionalism and Human Ecology

Human ecology is an area of study concerned with interrelationships between people and their environment. Environmentalist Barry Commoner (1971:39) has stated that "everything is connected to everything else." Human ecologists focus on how the physical environment shapes people's lives and on how people influence the surrounding environment.

In an application of the human ecological perspective, sociologist Riley Dunlap and his colleagues (2002) have suggested that the natural environment performs three basic functions for humans, as it does for the many animal species:

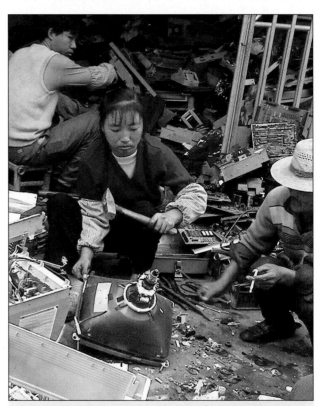

In a makeshift recycling center, a Chinese woman uses a hammer to open an old cathode ray tube. She wants the copper that is inside, but in the process she will release several pounds of lead into the soil and groundwater. Scientists have found alarmingly high levels of toxic heavy metals in the rivers that flow by such rural recycling operations.

Web Resource Students can link to the Greenpeace website through the Internet exercises in the student center of the Online Learning Center (**www.mhhe.com/schaefer6**). The Greenpeace site allows students to take a virtual tour of the organization's worldwide environmental efforts.
Reel Society See Environmental Problems in the Topic Index.

Key Persons Paul Ehrlich, Anne Ehrlich, Barry Commoner
Theory Functionalist view of environmental issues introduced
Key Person Riley Dunlap

1. **The environment provides the resources essential for life.** These include air, water, and materials used to create shelter, transportation, and needed products. If human societies exhaust these resources—for example, by polluting the water supply or cutting down rain forests—the consequences can be dire.

2. **The environment serves as a waste repository.** More so than other living species, humans produce a huge quantity and variety of waste products—bottles, boxes, papers, sewage, garbage, and so on. Various types of pollution have become more common because human societies are generating more wastes than the environment can safely absorb.

3. **The environment "houses" our species.** It is our home, our living space, the place where we reside, work, and play. At times we take this truism for granted, but not when day-to-day living conditions become unpleasant and difficult. If our air is "heavy," if our tap water turns brown, if toxic chemicals seep into our neighborhood, we remember why it is vital to live in a healthful environment.

Dunlap points out that these three functions of the environment actually compete with one another. Human use of the environment for one of these functions will often strain its ability to fulfill the other two. For example, with world population continuing to rise, we have an increasing need to raze forests or farmland and build housing developments. But each time we do so, we are reducing the amount of land that provides food, lumber, or habitat for wildlife.

The tension between the three essential functions of the environment brings us back to the human ecologists' view that "everything is connected to everything else." In facing the environmental challenges of the twenty-first century, government policymakers and environmentalists must determine how they can fulfill human societies' pressing needs (for example, for food, clothing, and shelter) while at the same time preserving the environment as a source of resources, a waste repository, and our home.

Conflict View of Environmental Issues

In Chapter 9, we drew on world systems analysis to show how a growing share of the human and natural resources of developing countries is being redistributed to the core industrialized nations. This process only intensifies the destruction of natural resources in poorer regions of the world. From a conflict perspective, less affluent nations are being forced to exploit their mineral deposits, forests, and fisheries in order to meet their debt obligations. The poor turn to the only means of survival available to them: They plow mountain slopes, burn plots in tropical forests, and overgraze grasslands (Livernash and Rodenburg 1998).

Brazil exemplifies this interplay between economic troubles and environmental destruction. Each year more than 5.7 million acres of forest are cleared for crops and livestock. The elimination of the rain forest affects worldwide weather patterns, heightening the gradual warming of the earth. These socioeconomic patterns, with harmful environmental consequences, are evident not only in Latin America but in many regions of Africa and Asia (*National Geographic* 2002).

Conflict theorists are well aware of the environmental implications of land use policies in the Third World, but they contend that such a focus on the developing countries can contain an element of ethnocentrism. Who, they ask, is more to blame for environmental deterioration: the poverty-stricken and

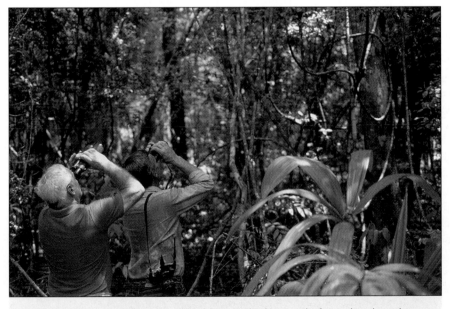

Vacation in an unspoiled paradise! Increasingly, people from developed countries are turning to ecotourism as an environmentally friendly way to see the world. The new trend bridges the interests of environmentalists and businesspeople, especially in developing countries. These birdwatchers are vacationing in Belize.

Theory Conflict view of environmental issues introduced

"food-hungry" populations of the world or the "energy-hungry" industrialized nations? These theorists point out that the industrialized nations of North America and Europe account for only 12 percent of the world's population but are responsible for 60 percent of worldwide consumption. The money their residents spend on ocean cruises each year could provide clean drinking water for everyone on the planet. Ice cream expenditures in Europe alone could be used to immunize every child in the world. Thus, conflict theorists charge, the most serious threat to the environment comes from the global consumer class (G. Gardner et al. 2004).

Allan Schnaiberg (1994) further refines this analysis by criticizing the focus on affluent consumers as the cause of environmental troubles. In his view, a capitalist system creates a "treadmill of production" because of its inherent need to build ever-expanding profits. This treadmill necessitates creating an increasing demand for products, obtaining natural resources at minimal cost, and manufacturing products as quickly and cheaply as possible—no matter what the long-term environmental consequences.

Environmental Justice

In a stretch of land along the lower Mississippi River in Louisiana, one factory after another pours its industrial waste into the water, raising pollution counts to dangerous levels. It is no accident that the people who live nearby are African American. Poor and lacking in political clout, the communities that border these industrial sites are no match for the powerful business interests that built them (Bullard 1993).

Observations like this one have given rise to *environmental justice,* a legal strategy based on claims that racial minorities are subjected disproportionately to environmental hazards. The approach has had some success. In 1998 a chemical company called Shintech dropped plans to build a plastics plant in a poor black community in Mississippi after opponents filed a civil rights complaint with the Environmental Protection Agency (EPA). EPA administrator Carol Browner praised the company's decision: "The principles applied to achieve this solution should be incorporated into any blueprint for dealing

with environmental justice issues in communities across the nation" (Associated Press 1998:18).

Following reports from the EPA and other organizations documenting the discriminatory location of hazardous waste sites, President Bill Clinton issued an executive order in 1994 that requires all federal agencies to ensure that low-income and minority communities have access to better information about their environment, and an opportunity to participate in shaping government policies that affect their health. Initial efforts to implement the policy have aroused widespread opposition because of the delays it imposes in establishing new industrial sites. Some observers question the wisdom of an order that slows economic development in areas that are in dire need of employment opportunities. Others point out that such businesses employ few unskilled or less skilled workers, and only make the environment less livable for those left behind (Pellow 2002).

To date, most sociological studies of the problem of industrial waste have focused on the discriminatory nature of the siting process. A new study suggests that not only do these facilities tend to locate near poor minority communities; over time, they tend to increase segregation in the area. The study, done in Hillsborough County, Florida, found that between 1987 and 1999, the student bodies of grade schools located close to hazardous waste sites became more and more heavily Black and Latino. Other schools located farther from the waste sites became more heavily White. A combination of poverty and institutional discrimination may prevent minority group members from moving away from the sites, as Whites might be expected to do. The authors of the study concluded that while the siting of hazardous waste dumps is an important public policy issue, the racial and ethnic segregation that follows may be just as important, if not more so (Stretesky and Lynch 2002).

Use Your Sociological Imagination www.mhhe.com/schaefer6

Your community has been designated as a site for burial of toxic waste. How will you react? Will you organize a protest? Or will you make sure the authorities carry the project out safely? How can such sites be chosen fairly?

Key Person Allan Schnaiberg
Theory Schnaiberg's critique foreshadows the conflict perspective on environmental issues.

Race/Ethnicity Challenges being made to "environmental justice"
Classroom Tip See "Environmental Racism in Albany" (Additional Lecture Ideas).

The Issue

Jessie Sherrod began picking cotton in the fields of Mississippi when she was eight years old, earning $1.67 for a 12-hour day. Today she is a Harvard-educated pediatrician who specializes in infectious diseases. But the road from the cotton fields to the medical profession was hardly an easy one. "You can't make up for 400 years of slavery and mistreatment and unequal opportunity in 20 years," she says angrily. "We had to ride the school bus for five miles . . . and pass by a white school to get to our black elementary school. Our books were used books. Our instructors were not as good. We didn't have the proper equipment. How do you make up for that?" (Stolberg 1995:A14). Some people think it should be done through affirmative action programs.

The term *affirmative action* first appeared in an executive order issued by President John F. Kennedy in 1961. That order called for contractors to "take affirmative action to ensure that applicants are employed, and that employees are treated during employment, without regard to their race, creed, color, or national origin." In 1967, the order was amended by President Lyndon Johnson to prohibit discrimination on the basis of sex as well, but affirmative action remained a vague concept. Currently, **affirmative action** refers to positive efforts to recruit minority group members or women for jobs, promotions, and educational opportunities. But many people think that affirmative action programs constitute reverse discrimination against qualified Whites and males. Does government have a responsibility to make up for past discrimination? If so, how far should it go?

The Setting

A variety of court decisions and executive branch statements have outlawed certain forms of job discrimination based on race, sex, or both, including (1) word-of-mouth recruitment among all-White or all-male workforces, (2) recruitment exclusively in schools or colleges that are limited to one sex or are predominantly White, (3) discrimination against married women or forced retirement of pregnant women, (4) advertising in male and female "help wanted" columns when gender is not a legitimate occupational qualification, and (5) job qualifications and tests that are not substantially related to the job. In addition, the lack of minority (African American, Asian, Native American, or Hispanic) or female employees may in itself represent evidence of unlawful exclusion (Commission on Civil Rights 1981).

In the late 1970s, a number of bitterly debated cases on affirmative action reached the Supreme Court. In 1978, in the *Bakke* case, by a narrow 5–4 vote, the Supreme Court ordered the medical school of the University of California at Davis to admit Allen Bakke, a White engineer who originally had been denied admission. The justices ruled that the school had violated Bakke's constitutional rights by establishing a fixed quota system for minority students. The Court added, however, that it was constitutional for universities to adopt flexible admissions programs that include race as one factor in decision making.

Sociological Insights

Sociologists—and especially conflict theorists—view affirmative action as a legislative attempt to reduce the inequality embedded in the social structure by increasing the opportunities of groups that have been deprived in the past, such as women and African Americans. The gap in earning power between White males and other groups (see Figure 14-4, page 384) is one indication of the inequality that needs to be addressed. But even acknowledging the disparity in earnings between White males and others, many people in the United States doubt that everything done in the name of affirmative action is desirable. In a 2004 national survey, 60 percent of respondents favored affirmative action in college admissions programs. There were clear racial and gender differences in the responses. Among Blacks, 87 percent favored affirmative action; among Hispanics, the rate was 77 percent. While 60 percent of White women approved of the programs, only 49 percent of White men did (Pew Research Center 2004).

Some conflict theorists contend that the present emphasis on racial and gender disparities in college admissions is too narrow. These critics argue that the lack of diversity on four-year college campuses extends to the relative absence of students from low-income families, whatever their race or gender. Studies show that students from less affluent households are as likely as other students to graduate from college, but first they must be admitted and assemble the necessary financial support. Increasingly, low-income students are having difficulty finding a way to pay for college (Kahlenberg 2004; Schmidt 2004).

Gender/Race/Ethnicity The issue of affirmative action has particular relevance for women and for racial and ethnic minorities.
Classroom Tip May want to reintroduce the concept of the glass ceiling discussed in Chapters 10 and 11.

Policy Pointer The term *affirmative action* implies positive steps to ensure equality; civil rights legislation implies it is enough to stop discriminating.
Policy Pointer Affirmative action is intended to remedy past institutional discrimination, discussed in Chapters 10 and 11.
Theory From a conflict perspective, affirmative action emerged as a result of social inequality based on gender, race, and ethnicity.

Much less documented than racial and economic inequality are the social consequences of affirmative action policies on everyday life. Interactionists focus on situations in which some women and minorities in underrepresented professions and schools are often mistakenly viewed as products of affirmative action. Fellow students and workers may stereotype them as less qualified, seeing them as beneficiaries of preference over more qualified White males. Obviously, that is not necessarily the case, but such labeling may well affect social relationships. Sociologist Orlando Patterson (1998) has noted that the workplace isolation experienced by minority workers inhibits their advancement up the corporate ladder; yet if efforts to increase their representation are scaled back, their problems in advancement will persist.

FIGURE 14-4

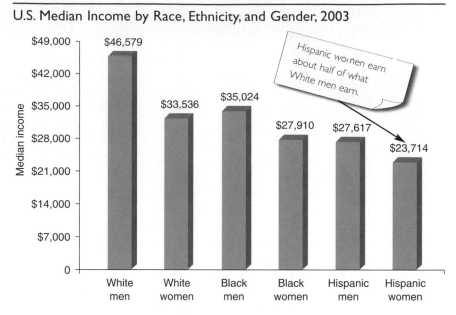

U.S. Median Income by Race, Ethnicity, and Gender, 2003

Hispanic women earn about half of what White men earn.

Note: Median income includes all financial sources and is limited to year-round, full-time workers over 25 years of age. "White" refers to non-Hispanic.

Source: DeNavas-Walt et al. 2004.

Policy Initiatives

By the early 1990s, affirmative action had emerged as an increasingly important issue in state and national political campaigns. Generally, discussion focused on the use of quotas (or the "Q word," as it came to be known) in hiring practices. Supporters of affirmative action argue that hiring goals (or targets) establish floors for minority inclusion but do not exclude truly

GOSH, IT WORKS! SINCE WE ENDED AFFIRMATIVE ACTION HERE ON CAMPUS, I NEVER NOTICE ANYONE'S SKIN COLOR ANYMORE!

qualified candidates from any group. Opponents insist that these "targets" are, in fact, quotas that lead to reverse discrimination. However, affirmative action has caused very few legal claims of reverse discrimination by White people.

In the 1996 elections, California's voters approved by a 54 to 46 percent margin the California Civil Rights Initiative, also known as Proposition 209. This measure amends the state constitution to *prohibit* any program that gives preference to women and minorities in college admissions, hiring, promotion, or government contracts. In other words, it aims to abolish affirmative action programs. The courts have since upheld the measure. In 1998, voters in Washington state passed a similar anti-affirmative action measure.

In 2003, focusing specifically on college admissions in a pair of decisions involving policies at the University of Michigan, the Supreme Court ruled that colleges may consider race and ethnicity as one factor in their admissions decisions. However, they cannot assign a specific value to being a minority candidate in such a way that race becomes the overriding factor in a decision. The ruling allowed many colleges and universities to continue their existing affirmative action policies. But critics complained that it permits blatant favoritism toward the children of alumni, who are more likely than others to be White, while subjecting programs that favor disadvantaged minority candidates to much greater scrutiny (University of Michigan 2003).

The United States is not alone in its struggle to find acceptable ways of compensating for generations of inequality between racial groups. After dismantling the system of apartheid that favored Whites economically and socially, the Republic of South Africa is now trying to level the playing field by giving Blacks preference in managerial positions. The Malaysian constitution gives preference to Malays to counteract the legacy of colonialism, under which the British gave special protection to the Chinese. And in Brazil, public universities are expected to meet admission quotas for Blacks—a policy that may be extended to government employment. The specifics may be different from one country to the next, but the social concerns are familiar (*The Economist* 2003a; Rohter 2003a; Schaefer 2004).

Let's Discuss

1. Would a conflict theorist support the policy of affirmative action? Why or why not?
2. Do you think claims of reverse discrimination have any validity? If so, what should be done about them?
3. If you were to draft legislation either supporting or abolishing affirmative action, what provisions would it include?

GETTING INVOLVED

To get involved in the debate over affirmative action, visit this text's Online Learning Center, which offers links to relevant websites. Check out the Social Policy section on the Online Learning Center as well; it provides survey data on U.S. public opinion regarding this issue.

CHAPTER RESOURCES

Summary

Every society must have both an *economic system* and a *political system* that provide recognized procedures for the allocation of valued resources. These two closely intertwined systems have an important influence on social behavior and social institutions, as well as on our general well-being. One example of their far-reaching effects is the impact of political and economic decisions on the state of our environment.

1. With the industrial revolution, a new form of social structure emerged: the *industrial society.*
2. Systems of *capitalism* vary in the degree to which the government regulates private ownership and economic activity, but all emphasize the profit motive.
3. The basic objective of *socialism* is to eliminate economic exploitation and meet people's needs.
4. Marx believed that *communism* would evolve naturally out of socialism.
5. China, once a strictly socialist economy, has begun to turn over some of its state-controlled industries to private enterprise.
6. There are three basic sources of *power* within any political system: *force, influence,* and *authority.*
7. Max Weber identified three ideal types of authority: *traditional, legal-rational,* and *charismatic.*
8. Women are still underrepresented in politics, but are becoming more successful at winning election to public office.
9. Advocates of the *elite model* of the U.S. power structure see the nation as being ruled by a small group of individuals who share common political and economic interests *(a power elite),* whereas advocates of a *pluralist model* believe that power is shared more widely among conflicting groups.
10. *War* may be defined as conflict between organizations that possess trained combat forces equipped with deadly weapons—a definition that includes conflict with terrorist organizations.
11. The nature of the U.S. economy is changing. Sociologists are interested in the changing face of the workforce and the effects of *deindustrialization.*
12. Three broad areas of environmental concern include air and water pollution and land contamination.

13. Using the human ecological perspective, sociologist Riley Dunlap suggests that the natural environment serves three basic functions: It provides essential resources, serves as a waste repository, and houses our species.

14. Conflict theorists charge that the most serious threat to the environment comes from Western industrialized nations.

15. *Environmental justice* addresses the disproportionate subjection of minorities to environmental hazards.

16. Despite numerous **affirmative action** programs, White males continue to hold the overwhelming majority of prestigious, high-paying jobs in the United States.

Critical Thinking Questions

1. The United States has long been put forward as the model of a capitalist society. Drawing on material in earlier chapters of this textbook, discuss the values and beliefs that have led people in the United States to cherish a laissez-faire, capitalist economy. To what degree have those values and beliefs changed over the past hundred years? What aspects of socialism are now evident in the nation's economy? Have our values and beliefs changed to support certain principles traditionally associated with socialist societies?

2. Who really holds power in the college or university you attend? Describe the distribution of power at your school, drawing on the elite and pluralist models where relevant.

3. Imagine that you have been asked to study the issue of air pollution in the largest city in your state. How might you draw on surveys, observation research, experiments, and existing sources to study the issue?

Key Terms

Affirmative action   Positive efforts to recruit minority group members or women for jobs, promotions, and educational opportunities. (page 383)

Authority   Institutionalized power that is recognized by the people over whom it is exercised. (367)

Capitalism   An economic system in which the means of production are held largely in private hands, and the main incentive for economic activity is the accumulation of profits. (362)

Charismatic authority   Power made legitimate by a leader's exceptional personal or emotional appeal to his or her followers. (368)

Communism   As an ideal type, an economic system under which all property is communally owned and no social distinctions are made on the basis of people's ability to produce. (364)

Deindustrialization   The systematic, widespread withdrawal of investment in basic aspects of productivity, such as factories and plants. (378)

Downsizing   Reductions taken in a company's workforce as part of deindustrialization. (379)

Economic system   The social institution through which goods and services are produced, distributed, and consumed. (361)

Elite model   A view of society as being ruled by a small group of individuals who share a common set of political and economic interests. (371)

Environmental justice   A legal strategy based on claims that racial minorities are subjected disproportionately to environmental hazards. (382)

Force   The actual or threatened use of coercion to impose one's will on others. (367)

Human ecology   An area of study concerned with the interrelationships between people and their environment. (380)

Industrial society   A society that depends on mechanization to produce its goods and services. (362)

Influence   The exercise of power through a process of persuasion. (367)

Informal economy   Transfers of money, goods, or services that are not reported to the government. (364)

Laissez-faire   A form of capitalism under which people compete freely, with minimal government intervention in the economy. (362)

Legal-rational authority   Power made legitimate by law. (368)

Monopoly   Control of a market by a single business firm. (362)

Peace   The absence of war, or more broadly, a proactive effort to develop cooperative relations among nations. (375)

Pluralist model   A view of society in which many competing groups within the community have access to government, so that no single group is dominant. (373)

Political system   The social institution that is founded on a recognized set of procedures for implementing and achieving society's goals. (361)

Politics   In Harold Lasswell's words, "who gets what, when, and how." (367)

Power   The ability to exercise one's will over others. (367)

Power elite   A small group of military, industrial, and government leaders who control the fate of the United States. (371)

Socialism   An economic system under which the means of production and distribution are collectively owned. (363)

Terrorism   The use or threat of violence against random or symbolic targets in pursuit of political aims. (376)

Traditional authority   Legitimate power conferred by custom and accepted practice. (367)

War   Conflict between organizations that possess trained combat forces equipped with deadly weapons. (374)

TECHNOLOGY RESOURCES

Internet Connection

*Note: While all the URLs listed were current as of the printing of this book, these sites often change. Please check our website (**www.mhhe.com/schaefer6**) for updates, hyperlinks, and exercises related to these sites.*

1. The Center for American Women and Politics at Rutgers University is an excellent source of information on women's political participation, both nationally and on the state level. To learn about topics such as the gender gap in voter turnout, party identification, and attitudes on public policy issues, visit the center's website (**www.rci.rutgers.edu/~cawp**) and click on "Facts and Findings" at the top of the page.

2. The Earthwatch Institute strives to protect the environment by organizing volunteers to participate in environmental research. To learn about the issues that concern this group, go to its website (**www.earthwatch.org**) and choose "Get Involved" at the top of the page. Click on "Join an Expedition" and read through some of the volunteer opportunities.

Online Learning Center with PowerWeb

If you are interested in how people feel about the environment, you will want to visit the student center at the Online Learning Center at **www.mhhe.com/schaefer6**. Link to "How Americans Feel About. . . ." You will read about three alternative approaches to protecting the environment and view colorful graphs and pie charts showing whether the people surveyed thought the environment would be better, worse, or the same in four years. You will also find out what people your age thought about the long-term future of the environment.

Reel Society Interactive Movie CD-ROM 2.0

Reel Society 2.0 can be used to spark discussion about the following topics from this chapter:

- Power and Authority
- Economic Systems
- The Changing Economy
- The Environment

chapter

15

POPULATION, COMMUNITIES, AND HEALTH

WELCOME TO AMERICA

the only industrialized country besides South Africa without national healthcare

This billboard protests the lack of a national health care program in the United States. The reference to South Africa was especially pointed when the poster first appeared in 1989, because of the racist apartheid regime that held sway there.

Demography: The Study of Population

World Population Patterns

Fertility Patterns in the United States

How Did Communities Originate?

Urbanization

Types of Communities

Sociological Perspectives on Health and Illness

Social Epidemiology and Health

Social Policy and Health: Financing Health Care Worldwide

Boxes

SOCIOLOGY IN THE GLOBAL COMMUNITY: Population Policy in China

RESEARCH IN ACTION: Store Wars

TAKING SOCIOLOGY TO WORK: Kelsie Lenor Wilson-Dorsett, Deputy Director, Department of Statistics, Government of Bahamas

It is not hard to understand why Hakim Hasan came to see himself as a public character. Early one July morning, a deliveryman pulled his truck up to the curb behind Hakim's vending table on Greenwich Avenue off the corner of Sixth Avenue [in lower Manhattan] and carried a large box of flowers over to him.

"Can you hold these until the flower shop opens up?" the deliveryman asked.

"No problem," responded Hakim as he continued to set up the books on his table. "Put them right under there."

When the store opened for business, he brought them inside and gave them to the owner.

"Why did that man trust you with the flowers?" I later asked.

"People like me are the eyes and ears of this street," he explained, echoing [sociologist] Jane Jacobs again. "Yes, I could take those flowers and sell them for a few hundred dollars. But that deliveryman sees me here every day. I'm as dependable as any store-owner." . . .

Another day, I was present at the table when a traffic officer walked by to give out parking tickets.

"Are any of these your cars?" she asked Hakim.

"Yes, that one, and that one," said Hakim, pointing.

"What is that all about?" I asked.

"The day I met her, we got into an argument," he explained. "She was getting ready to give the guy across the street a ticket. I say, 'You can't do this!' She said, 'Why not?' I say, "Cause I'm getting ready to put a quarter in.' She said, 'You can't do that.' I guess that, because of the way I made my argument, she didn't give out the ticket, and from that point onward we became friends. And when she comes on the block, she asks me, for every car on the block that has a violation sign, 'Is that your car?' Meaning, 'Is it someone you know?' And depending on whether I say yes or no, that's it—they get a ticket." . . .

"Are these things part of your job description as a vendor?" I asked him once.

"Let me put it to you this way, Mitch," he replied. "I kind of see what I loosely call my work on the sidewalk as going far, far beyond just trying to make a living selling books. That sometimes even seems secondary. Over time, when people see you on the sidewalk, there is a kind of trust that starts. They've seen you so long that they walk up to you. There have been occasions when I've had to have directions translated out of Spanish into French to get somebody to go someplace!"

It is not only directions and assistance that I have seen Hakim give out. He also tells people a great deal about books—so much so that he once told me he was thinking of charging tuition to the people who stand in his space on the sidewalk. *(Duneier 1999:17–18)* ■ 🐛

Additional information about this excerpt can be found on the Online Learning Center at **www.mhhe.com/schaefer6.**

SIDEWALK

MITCHELL DUNEIER

WITH PHOTOGRAPHS BY OVIE CARTER

389

This excerpt from *Sidewalk*, by the sociologist Mitchell Duneier, describes the social position of Hakim Hasan, a sidewalk book vendor in New York City's Greenwich Village. The author, who for two years lived just around the corner from Hasan's table, was so fascinated by street life in the Village that he decided to do observation research on it. As Duneier explains in his book, street vendors like Hasan are just as much a part of the neighborhood as the shopkeepers who occupy the storefronts behind them—even if they don't have a mailing address. In fact, their presence on the street, day in and day out, contributes to the neighborhood's safety and stability (Duneier 1999).

Duneier's work emphasizes the importance of community in our lives. In sociological terms, a **community** may be defined as a spatial or political unit of social organization that gives people a sense of belonging. That sense of belonging can be based either on shared residence in a particular city or neighborhood, such as Greenwich Village, or on a common identity, such as that of street vendors, homeless people, or gays and lesbians. Whatever the members have in common, communities give people the feeling that they are part of something larger than themselves (Dotson 1991; see also Hillery 1955).

Communities are deeply affected by two other topics of this chapter: health and population patterns. Population patterns determine which communities will grow and prosper and which will wither and die. They can also promote or undermine the health of those who live in communities. How is the world's population changing, and what effects will those changes have on our communities? Throughout the world, why have large communities grown at the expense of small villages? How do a population's health and well-being vary from one community to another, and from one part of the world to another?

Sociologist Mitchell Duneier *(right)* did participant observation as he worked the tables of sidewalk vendors in Greenwich Village.

In this chapter we will take a sociological overview of the world's population and its effects on our communities and health. We will begin with Thomas Robert Malthus's controversial analysis of population trends and Karl Marx's critical response. A brief overview of world population patterns follows, with particular emphasis on the current problem of overpopulation. Next, we will trace the development of communities from their ancient origins in small bands of seminomadic peoples to the birth of the modern megalopolis. We'll consider two different views of urbanization, one stressing its functions and the other its dysfunctions. Finally, we'll see how functionalists, conflict theorists, interactionists, and labeling theorists study health issues. We'll discover that the distribution of disease in a population varies with social class, race and ethnicity, gender, and age. In the social policy section that closes the chapter we'll explore the issue of how to finance health care worldwide. ■

DEMOGRAPHY: THE STUDY OF POPULATION

The study of population issues engages the attention of both natural and social scientists. The biologist explores the nature of reproduction and casts light on factors that affect *fertility,* the level of reproduction in a society. The medical pathologist examines and analyzes trends in the causes of death. Geographers, historians, and psychologists also have distinctive contributions to make to our understanding of population. Sociologists, more than these other researchers, focus on the *social* factors that influence population rates and trends.

In their study of population issues, sociologists are aware that the norms, values, and social patterns of a society profoundly affect various elements of population, such as fertility, *mortality* (the amount of death), and migration. Fertility is influenced by people's age of entry into sexual unions and by their use of contraception—both of which, in turn, reflect the social and religious values that guide a particular culture. Mortality is shaped by a nation's level of nutrition, acceptance of immunization, and provisions for sanitation, as well as its general commitment to health care and health education. Migration from one country to another can depend on marital and kinship ties, the relative degree of racial and religious tolerance in various societies, and people's evaluations of employment opportunities.

Demography is the scientific study of population. It draws on several components of population, including size, composition, and territorial distribution, to understand the social consequences of population change. Demographers study geographical variations and historical trends in their effort to develop population forecasts. They also analyze the structure of a population—the age, gender, race, and ethnicity of its members. A key figure in this analysis was Thomas Malthus.

Malthus's Thesis and Marx's Response

The Reverend Thomas Robert Malthus (1766–1834), who was educated at Cambridge University, spent his life teaching history and political economy. He strongly criticized two major institutions of his time—the church and slavery—yet his most significant legacy for contemporary scholars is his still-controversial *Essays on the Principle of Population*, published in 1798.

Essentially, Malthus held that the world's population was growing more rapidly than the available food supply. Malthus argued that food supply increases in arithmetic progression (1, 2, 3, 4, and so on), whereas population expands by geometric progression (1, 2, 4, 8, and so on). According to his analysis, the gap between food supply and population will continue to grow over time. Even though the food supply will increase, it will not increase nearly enough to meet the needs of an expanding world population.

Malthus advocated population control to close the gap between rising population and food supply, yet he explicitly denounced artificial means of birth control because they were not sanctioned by religion. For Malthus, one appropriate way to control population was to postpone marriage. He argued that couples must take responsibility for the number of children they choose to bear; without such restraint, the world would face widespread hunger, poverty, and misery (Malthus et al. [1824] 1960; Petersen 1979).

As early as the late 1700s, the Reverend Thomas Robert Malthus suggested that the world's population was growing more rapidly than the available food supply.

Karl Marx strongly criticized Malthus's views on population. Marx pointed to the nature of economic relations in Europe's industrial societies as the central problem. He could not accept the Malthusian notion that rising world population, rather than capitalism, was the cause of social ills. In Marx's opinion, there was no special relationship between world population and the supply of resources (including food). If society were well ordered, increases in population would lead to greater wealth, not to hunger and misery.

Of course, Marx did not believe that capitalism operated under these ideal conditions. He maintained that capitalism devoted its resources to the financing of buildings and tools rather than to the equitable distribution of food, housing, and other necessities of life. Marx's work is important to the study of population because he linked overpopulation to the unequal distribution of resources—a topic that will be taken up again later in this chapter. His concern with the writings of Malthus also testifies to the importance of population in political and economic affairs.

Key Person Reverend Thomas Robert Malthus
Contemporary Culture What are the ethical boundaries of population control?

Key Person Karl Marx
Theory Marx's conflict view that capitalism thwarts equitable distribution of food and housing

KELSIE LENOR WILSON-DORSETT **Deputy Director, Department of Statistics, Government of Bahamas**

Kelsie Wilson-Dorsett was born in the Bahamas, where she received her primary and secondary education. She graduated from McMaster University in Hamilton, Ontario, with a combined honors degree in sociology and political science. In studying for her master's degree in sociology at the University of Western Ontario in London, she specialized in demography.

Currently, Wilson-Dorsett holds the positions of Deputy Director, Department of Statistics and Head of the Social Statistics Division, Government of Bahamas, where she oversees the country's census, vital statistics, and other surveys. In this position, she is responsible for the execution of the Bahamas' first Living Conditions Survey (BLCS) which, when completed, will enable the government to establish a poverty line and to measure the incidence and extent of poverty in that country.

Wilson-Dorsett's study of sociology is directly related to her current job. She states, "The study of sociology has enabled me

to put meaning to the figures which come into my office and has provided me with avenues to interpret these figures and determine the direction of future data collection. The analysis of census data, for instance, allows me to see where my country was several years ago, where it is now, and where it is likely to be in the years ahead."

Let's Discuss

1. What challenges do you think Wilson-Dorsett might encounter as she oversees a national census in a country like the Bahamas?

2. What other areas of specialization in sociology would be helpful to someone interpreting the results of a project such as the Living Conditions Survey (BLCS)?

The insights of Malthus and Marx regarding population issues have come together in what is termed the *neo-Malthusian view,* best exemplified by the work of Paul Ehrlich (1968; Ehrlich and Ehrlich 1990), author of *The Population Bomb.* Neo-Malthusians agree with Malthus that world population growth is outstretching natural resources. However, in contrast to the British theorist, they insist that birth control measures are needed to regulate population increases. Showing a Marxist bent, neo-Malthusians condemn developed nations, which despite their low birthrates, consume a disproportionately large share of world resources. While rather pessimistic about the future, these theorists stress that birth control and sensible use of resources are essential responses to rising world population (J. Tierney 1990; Weeks 2002).

Studying Population Today

The relative balance of births and deaths is no less important today than it was during the lifetime of Malthus and Marx. The suffering that Malthus spoke of is certainly a reality for many people of the world who are

hungry and poor. Malnutrition remains the largest contributing factor to illness and death among children in developing countries. Almost 18 percent of these children will die before age five—a rate over 11 times higher than in developed nations. Warfare and large-scale migration intensify problems of population and food supply. For example, recent strife in Afghanistan, the Congo, and Iraq has caused maldistribution of food supplies, leading to regional concerns about health. Combating world hunger may require reducing human births, dramatically increasing the world's food supply, or perhaps both at the same time. The study of population-related issues, then, seems to be essential today.

In the United States and most other countries, the census is the primary mechanism for collecting population information. A *census* is an enumeration, or counting, of a population. The Constitution of the United States requires that a census be held every 10 years to determine congressional representation. This periodic investigation is supplemented by *vital statistics,* or records of births, deaths, marriages, and divorces that are gathered through a registration system maintained by governmental units. In addition, other government surveys provide up-to-date information on commercial developments, educational trends, industrial expansion, agricultural practices, and the status of groups such as children, the elderly, racial minorities, and single parents.

In administering a nationwide census and conducting other types of research, demographers employ many of the skills and techniques described in Chapter 2, including questionnaires, interviews, and sampling. The precision of population projections depends on the accuracy of a series of estimates that demographers must make. First, they must determine past population trends and establish a current base population. Next, birthrates and death rates must be determined, along with estimates of future fluctuations. In making projections for a nation's population trends, demographers must consider migration as well, since a significant number of individuals may enter and leave a country.

Elements of Demography

Demographers communicate population facts with a language derived from the basic elements of human life—birth and death. The *birthrate* (or more specifically, the *crude birthrate*) is the number of live births per 1,000 population in a given year. In 2002, for example, there were 14 live births per 1,000 people in the United States. The birthrate provides information on the actual reproductive patterns of a society.

One way demographers can project future growth in a society is to make use of the *total fertility rate (TFR)*. The TFR is the average number of children born alive to any woman, assuming that she conforms to current fertility rates. The TFR reported for the United States in 2002 was 2.0 live births per woman, compared to over 8 births per woman in a developing country such as Niger (Hamilton 2004).

Mortality, like fertility, is measured in several different ways. The *death rate* (also known as the *crude death rate*) is the number of deaths per 1,000 population in a given year. In 2002, the United States had a death rate of 8.5 per 1,000 population. The *infant mortality rate* is the number of deaths of infants under one year old per 1,000 live births in a given year. This particular measure serves as an important indicator of a society's level of health care; it reflects prenatal nutrition, delivery procedures, and infant screening measures. The infant mortality rate also functions as a useful indicator of future population growth, since those infants who survive to adulthood will contribute to further population increases.

A general measure of health used by demographers is *life expectancy,* the median number of years a person can be expected to live under current mortality conditions. Usually the figure is reported as life expectancy *at birth*. At present, Japan reports a life expectancy at birth of 81 years—slightly higher than the United States' figure of 77 years. In contrast, life expectancy at birth is less than 45 in several developing nations, including Zambia.

The *growth rate* of a society is the difference between births and deaths, plus the difference between *immigrants* (those who enter a country to establish permanent residence) and *emigrants* (those who leave a country permanently) per 1,000 population. For the world as a whole, the growth rate is simply the difference between births and deaths per 1,000 population, since worldwide immigration and emigration must of necessity be equal. In 2001, the United States had a growth rate of 0.6 percent, compared to an estimated 1.3 percent for the entire world (Haub 2003).

WORLD POPULATION PATTERNS

One important aspect of demographic work involves a study of the history of population. But how is that possible? After all, official national censuses were relatively rare before 1850. Researchers interested in early population must turn to archeological remains, burial sites, baptismal and tax records, and oral history sources. In the next section we will see what such detective work has told us about changes in population over time.

Demographic Transition

On October 13, 1999, in a maternity clinic in Sarajevo, Bosnia-Herzegovina, Helac Fatina gave birth to a son who has been designated the 6 billionth person on this planet. Until modern times, relatively few humans lived in the world. One estimate places the world population of a million years ago at only 125,000 people. As Table 15-1 (page 394) indicates, in the last 200 years the population has exploded (World Health Organization 2000:3).

The phenomenal growth of world population in recent times can be accounted for by changing patterns in births and deaths. Beginning in the late 1700s—and continuing until the mid-1900s—death rates in northern and western Europe gradually decreased. People were beginning to live longer because of advances in food production, sanitation, nutrition, and public health care. But while death rates fell, birthrates remained high; as a result, this period of European history brought unprecedented population growth. By the late 1800s, however, the birthrates of many European countries had begun to decline, and the rate of population growth had also decreased.

Table 15-1	Estimated Time for Each Successive Increase of 1 Billion People in World Population		
Population Level	**Time Taken to Reach New Population Level**	**Year of Attainment**	
First billion	Human history before 1800	1804
Second billion	123 years	1927
Third billion	32 years	1959
Fourth billion	14 years	1973
Fifth billion	14 years	1987
Sixth billion	12 years	1999
Seventh billion	13 years	2012
Eighth billion	16 years	2028
Ninth billion	21 years	2049

Source: Bureau of the Census 2004d.

The changes in birthrates and death rates in 19th century Europe serve as an example of *demographic transition.* Demographers use the term **demographic transition** to describe changes in birthrates and death rates that occur during a nation's development, resulting in new patterns of vital statistics. In many nations today, we are seeing a demographic transition from high birthrates and death rates to low birthrates and death rates. As Figure 15-1 shows, this process typically takes place in three stages:

1. Pretransition stage: high birthrates and death rates with little population growth.
2. Transition stage: declining death rates—primarily the result of reductions in infant deaths—along with high to medium fertility, resulting in significant population growth.
3. Posttransition stage: low birthrates and death rates with little population growth.

The demographic transition should be regarded not as a "law of population growth," but rather as a generalization of the population history of industrial nations. This concept helps us to understand world population problems better. About two-thirds of the world's nations have yet to pass fully through the second stage of the demographic transition. Even if such nations make dramatic advances in fertility control, their populations will nevertheless increase greatly because of the large base of people already at prime childbearing age.

The pattern of demographic transition varies from nation to nation. One particularly useful distinction is the

contrast between the rapid transition now occurring in developing nations—which include about two-thirds of the world's population—and that which occurred over the course of almost a century in more industrialized countries. In developing nations, the demographic transition has involved a rapid decline in death rates without adjustments in birthrates.

Specifically, in the post–World War II period, the death rates of developing nations began a sharp decline. This revolution in "death control" was triggered by antibiotics, immunization, insecticides (such as DDT, used to strike at malaria-bearing mosquitoes), and largely successful campaigns against such fatal diseases as smallpox. Substantial medical and public health technology was imported almost overnight from more developed

FIGURE 15-1

Demographic Transition

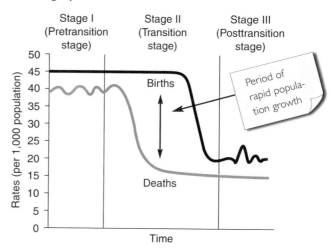

Demographers use the concept of *demographic transition* to describe changes in birthrates and death rates that occur during a nation's development. This graph shows the pattern that took place in presently developed nations. In the first stage, both birthrates and death rates were high, so that there was little population growth. In the second stage, the birthrate remained high while the death rate declined sharply, which led to rapid population growth. By the last stage, which many developing countries have yet to enter, the birthrate had declined as well, reducing population growth.

nations. As a result, the drop in death rates that had taken a century in Europe was telescoped into two decades in many developing countries.

Birthrates had little time to adjust. Cultural beliefs about the proper size of families could not possibly change as quickly as the falling death rates. For centuries, couples had given birth to as many as eight or more children, knowing that perhaps only two or three would survive to adulthood. Families were more willing to accept technological advances that prolonged life than to abandon fertility patterns that reflected time-honored tradition and religious training. The result was an astronomical "population explosion" that was well under way by the middle 1900s. By the middle 1970s, however, demographers had observed a slight decline in the growth rate of many developing nations, as family planning efforts began to take hold (Crenshaw et al. 2000; McFalls 1998).

The Population Explosion

Apart from war, rapid population growth has been perhaps the dominant international social problem of the past 40 years. Often this issue is referred to in emotional terms as the "population bomb" or the "population explosion." Such striking language is not surprising, given the staggering increases in world population recorded during the 20th century (refer to Table 15-1). The population of our planet rose from 1 billion around the year 1800 to 6.4 billion by 2004.

Beginning in the 1960s, governments in certain developing nations sponsored or supported campaigns to encourage family planning. In good part as the result of government-sponsored birth control campaigns, Thailand's total fertility rate fell from 6.1 births per woman in 1970 to only 1.7 in 2002. In China, the government's strict one-child policy actually produced a negative growth rate in some urban areas (see Box 15-1, page 396). Yet even if

family planning efforts are successful in reducing fertility rates, the momentum toward growing world population is well established. Developing nations face the prospect of continued population growth, since a substantial proportion of their population is approaching the childbearing years (see the top half of Figure 15-2).

A *population pyramid* is a special type of bar chart that shows the distribution of a population by gender and age; it is generally used to illustrate the population structure of a society. As Figure 15-2 shows, a substantial portion of the population of Afghanistan consists of children

FIGURE 15-2

Population Structure of Afghanistan and the United States, 2005

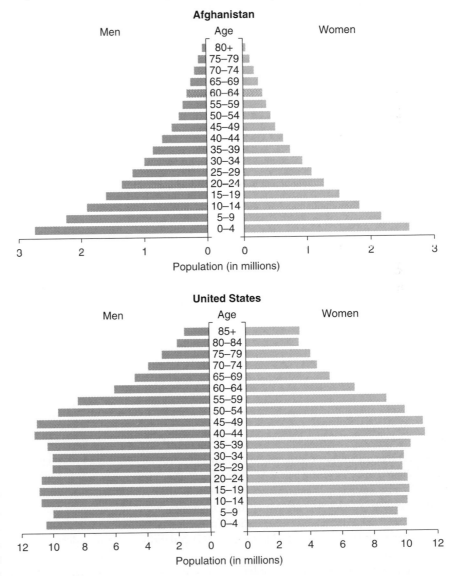

Source: Projections from Bureau of the Census 2004c.

Student Alert Population pyramids are not necessarily pyramidal in shape.
Classroom Tip See "Population Pyramid" (Class Discussion Topics).
Classroom Tip Note the relationship between demographic changes and economic problems.

In a residential district in Shanghai, a member of the local family planning committee knocks on the door of a childless couple. Why, she inquires, have they not started a family?

Such a question would have been unthinkable in 1979, when family planning officials, in an attempt to avoid a looming population explosion, began resorting to sterilization to enforce the government rule of one child per family. Since then, the government has quietly begun to grant exceptions to the one-child policy to adults who are only children themselves. In 2002 it extended the privilege to all families, but at a price. A new family planning law imposes "social compensation fees" to cover the cost to society of an additional child. The fee, which is substantial, is equivalent to 20 years' worth of a rural farm family's income.

Chinese families are beset, too, by the unforeseen results of their attempts to circumvent the one-child policy. In the past, in an effort to ensure that their one child would be a male capable of perpetuating the family line, many couples chose to abort female fetuses, or quietly allowed female infants to die of neglect. As a result,

among children one to four years old, China's sex ratio (the ratio of males to females) is now about 121 to 100—well above the normal rate at birth of 106 to 100. The difference in birthrates translates into 1.7 million fewer female births per year than normal—and down the line, to many fewer childbearers than normal.

Chinese women have borne the brunt not just of the government's population policy, but of the economic dislocation caused by recent market reforms and the

> *A new family planning law imposes "social compensation fees" equivalent to 20 years' income.*

redistribution of rural farmland. On rural farms, they struggle to cope without their husbands, many of whom have gone to work in city factories. The female suicide rate in rural China is now the highest in the world. Experts think this alarming statistic reflects a fundamental lack of self-esteem among rural Chinese women. The social patterns of centuries, unlike birthrates, cannot be changed in a generation.

Finally, the one-child policy has caused a shortage not just of rural workers, but of caretakers for the elderly. Coupled with improvements in longevity, the generation-long decline in births has greatly increased the ratio of dependent elders to able-bodied children. The migration of young adults to other parts of China has further compromised their ability to care for their elders. To compound the crisis, barely one in four of China's elders receives any pension at all. No other country in the world faces the prospect of caring for such a large population of seniors with so little available social support.

Let's Discuss

1. Does any government, no matter how overpopulated a country is, have a right to sterilize people who do not voluntarily limit the size of their families? Why or why not?
2. What do you think was the most dramatic consequence of the one-child policy?

Sources: Glenn 2004; Kahn 2004b; *Migration News* 2002b; N. Riley 2004.

under age 15, whose childbearing years are still to come. Thus, the built-in momentum for population growth is much greater in Afghanistan (and in many other developing countries in other parts of the world) than in western Europe or the United States.

Consider the population data for India, which in 2000 surpassed 1 billion residents. Sometime between the years 2040 and 2050 India's population will exceed China's. The substantial momentum for growth that is built into India's age structure means that the nation will face a staggering increase in population in the coming decades, even if its birthrate declines sharply (Population Reference Bureau 2004).

Population growth is not a problem in all nations. Today, a handful of countries are even adopting policies that

encourage growth. One such country is Japan, where the total fertility rate has fallen sharply. Nevertheless, a global perspective underscores the serious consequences that could result from continued population growth overall.

Sadly, in the last 15 years, the spread of the once unknown disease of AIDS has begun to restrict population growth. p. 123 Worldwide, the HIV/AIDS epidemic killed more than 3 million people in 2003 alone; that same year, an estimated 5 million more acquired the virus. About 80 percent of all AIDS cases are concentrated in sub-Saharan Africa and Southeast Asia. In the most deeply affected African nations, life expectancy is projected to drop 10 years over the next couple of decades, and to fall below age 40 in at least eight of them (Population Reference Bureau 2004; UNAIDS 2003).

AIDS has had a dramatic impact on the death rates in many developing countries, particularly in Africa.

Use Your Sociological Imagination www.mnhe.com/jschaefer6

You are living in a country that is so heavily populated, basic resources such as food, water, and living space are running short. What will you do? How will you respond to the crisis if you are a government social planner? A politician?

FERTILITY PATTERNS IN THE UNITED STATES

During the last four decades, the United States and other industrial nations have passed through two different patterns of population growth—the first marked by high fertility and rapid growth (stage II in the theory of demographic transition), the second marked by declining fertility and little growth (stage III). Sociologists are keenly aware of the social impact of these fertility patterns.

The Baby Boom

The most recent period of high fertility in the United States has often been referred to as the *baby boom*. During World War II, large numbers of military personnel were separated from their spouses. When they returned, the annual number of births began to rise dramatically. Still, the baby boom was not a return to the large families common in the 1800s. In fact, there was only a slight increase in the proportion of couples having three or more children. Instead, the boom resulted from a striking decrease in the number of childless marriages and one-child families. Although a peak was reached in 1957, the nation maintained a relatively high birthrate of over 20 live births per 1,000 population until 1964. By 2002, the birthrate had fallen to 15 live births per 1,000 population—30 percent lower than in 1964 (Bureau of the Census 1975; Haub 2003).

It would be a mistake to attribute the baby boom solely to the return home of large numbers of soldiers. High wages and general prosperity during the postwar period encouraged many married couples to have children and purchase homes. In addition, several sociologists—as well as feminist author Betty Friedan (1963)—have noted the strong societal pressures on women during the 1950s to marry and become mothers and homemakers (Bouvier 1980).

Stable Population Growth

Although the total fertility rate of the United States has remained low over the last two decades, the nation continues to grow in size because of two factors: the momentum built into our age structure by the postwar population boom and the continued high rates of immigration. Because of the upsurge of births beginning in the 1950s, there are now many more people in their childbearing years than there are in older age groups (in which most deaths occur). This growth of population represents a "demographic echo" of the baby boom generation, many of whom are now parents. Consequently, the number of people born each year in the United States continues to exceed the number who die. In addition, the nation allows a large number of immigrants to enter each year; these immigrants currently account for between one-fourth and one-third of annual growth.

Despite these trends, some analysts in the 1980s and early 1990s projected relatively low fertility levels and moderate net migration over the coming decades. As a result, it seemed possible that the United States might reach **zero population growth (ZPG).** ZPG is the state of a population in which the number of births plus immigrants equals the number of deaths plus emigrants. In the recent past, although some nations have achieved ZPG, it has been relatively short-lived. Yet 65 countries, 40 of them in Europe, are today actually showing a *decline* in population (Haub 2003; Longman 2004).

Gender Pressures on women in the United States in the 1950s to marry and become mothers and homemakers

What would a society with stable population growth be like? In demographic terms, it would be quite different from the United States of the 1990s. There would be relatively equal numbers of people in each age group, and the median age of the population might perhaps be as high as 38 (compared to 35 in 2000). As a result, the population pyramid of the United States (as shown in Figure 15-2) would look more like a rectangle (Bureau of the Census 2003a:14–15).

There would also be a much larger proportion of older people, especially age 75 and over. These citizens would place a greater demand on the nation's social service programs and health care institutions. On a more positive note, the economy would be less volatile under ZPG, since the number of entrants into the paid labor force would remain stable. ZPG would also lead to changes in family life. With fertility rates declining, women would devote fewer years to child rearing and to the social roles of motherhood; the proportion of married women entering the labor force would continue to rise (Spengler 1978; Weeks 2002).

We have seen how population patterns tend to vary over time with a society's level of economic development. In the next few sections, we will study the effect of economic and technological advances on the communities people live in. We'll see that not just a society's birth and death rates, but its entire way of life changes as its ability to use technology develops.

HOW DID COMMUNITIES ORIGINATE?

As we noted in the chapter opening, a *community* is a spatial or political unit of social organization that gives people a sense of belonging. The nature of community has changed greatly over the course of history—from early hunting-and-gathering societies to highly modernized postindustrial cities.

Early Communities

For most of human history, people used very basic tools and knowledge to survive. They satisfied their need for an adequate food supply through hunting, foraging for fruits or vegetables, fishing, and herding. In comparison with later industrial societies, early civilizations were much more dependent on the physical environment and much less able to alter that environment to their advantage.

p. 120

The emergence of horticultural societies, in which people cultivated food rather than merely gathering fruits

and vegetables, led to many dramatic changes in human social organization. It was no longer necessary to move from place to place in search of food. Because people had to remain in specific locations to cultivate crops, more stable and enduring communities began to develop. As agricultural techniques became more and more sophisticated, a cooperative division of labor involving both family members and others developed. People gradually began to produce more food than they actually needed for themselves. They could provide food, perhaps as part of an exchange, to others who might be involved in nonagricultural labor. This transition from subsistence to surplus represented a critical step in the emergence of cities.

Eventually, people produced enough goods to cover both their own needs and those of people not engaged in agricultural tasks. At first the surplus was limited to agricultural products, but gradually it evolved to include all types of goods and services. Residents of a city came to rely on community members who provided craft products and means of transportation, gathered information, and so forth (Nolan and Lenski 2004).

With these social changes came an even more elaborate division of labor, as well as greater opportunity for differential rewards and privileges. So long as everyone had been engaged in the same tasks, stratification had been limited to such factors as gender, age, and perhaps the ability to perform some task (a skillful hunter could win unusual respect from the community). But the surplus allowed for the expansion of goods and services, leading to greater differentiation, a hierarchy of occupations, and social inequality. Thus the surplus was a precondition not only for the establishment of cities but for the division of members of a community into social classes (see Chapter 9). The ability to produce goods for other communities marked a fundamental shift in human social organization.

Preindustrial Cities

It is estimated that beginning about 10,000 B.C., permanent settlements free from dependence on crop cultivation emerged. Yet by today's standards, these early communities would barely qualify as cities. The **preindustrial city,** as it is termed, generally had only a few thousand people living within its borders, and was characterized by a relatively closed class system and limited mobility. In these early cities status was usually based on ascribed characteristics such as family background, and education was limited to members of the elite. All the residents relied on perhaps 100,000 farmers and their own part-time farming to provide the needed agricultural surplus. The Mesopotamian city of Ur had a population of about

Theory Conflict view of how surplus contributes to social inequality

10,000 and was limited to roughly 220 acres of land, including the canals, the temple, and the harbor.

Why were these early cities so small and relatively few in number? Several key factors restricted urbanization:

- **Reliance on animal power (both humans and beasts of burden) as a source of energy for economic production.** This factor limited the ability of humans to make use of and alter the physical environment.
- **Modest levels of surplus produced by the agricultural sector.** Between 50 and 90 farmers may have been required to support one city resident (K. Davis [1949] 1995).
- **Problems in transportation and the storage of food and other goods.** Even an excellent crop could easily be lost as a result of such difficulties.
- **Hardships of migration to the city.** For many peasants, migration was both physically and economically impossible. A few weeks of travel was out of the question without more sophisticated food storage techniques.
- **Dangers of city life.** Concentrating a society's population in a small area left it open to attack from outsiders, as well as more susceptible to extreme damage from plagues and fires.

Gideon Sjoberg (1960) examined the available information on early urban settlements in medieval Europe, India, and China. He identified three preconditions of city life: advanced technology in both agricultural and nonagricultural areas, a favorable physical environment, and a well-developed social organization.

For Sjoberg, the criteria for defining a "favorable" physical environment were variable. Proximity to coal and iron helps only if a society knows how to *use* those natural resources. Similarly, proximity to a river is particularly beneficial only if a culture has the means to transport water efficiently to the fields for irrigation and to the cities for consumption.

A sophisticated social organization is also an essential precondition for urban existence. Specialized social roles bring people together in new ways through the exchange of goods and services. A well-developed social organization ensures that these relationships are clearly defined and generally acceptable to all parties. Admittedly, Sjoberg's view of city life is an ideal type, since inequality did not vanish with the emergence of urban communities.

Industrial and Postindustrial Cities

Imagine how harnessing the energy of air, water, and other natural resources could change a society. Advances in agri-

cultural technology led to dramatic changes in community life, but so did the process of industrialization. The *industrial revolution,* which began in the middle of the 18th century, focused on the application of nonanimal sources of power to labor tasks. Industrialization had a wide range of effects on people's lifestyles, as well as on the structure of communities. Emerging urban settlements became centers not only of industry but also of banking, finance, and industrial management.

The factory system that developed during the industrial revolution led to a much more refined division of labor than was evident in preindustrial cities. The many new occupations that were created produced a complex set of relationships among workers. Thus, the *industrial city* was not merely more populous than its predecessors; it was based on very different principles of social organization. Sjoberg outlined the contrasts between preindustrial and industrial cities; see Table 15-2, page 400.

In comparison with preindustrial cities, industrial cities have a more open class system and more social mobility. After initiatives in industrial cities by women's rights groups, labor unions, and other political activists, formal education gradually became available to many children from poor and working-class families. While ascribed characteristics such as gender, race, and ethnicity remained important, a talented or skilled individual had greater opportunity to better his or her social position. In these and other respects, the industrial city was genuinely a different world from the preindustrial urban community.

In the latter part of the 20th century, a new type of urban community emerged. The *postindustrial city* is a city in which global finance and the electronic flow of information dominate the economy. Production is decentralized and often takes place outside of urban centers, but control is centralized in multinational corporations whose influence transcends urban and even national boundaries. Social change is a constant feature of the postindustrial city. Economic restructuring and spatial change seem to occur each decade, if not more frequently. In the postindustrial world, cities are forced into increasing competition for economic opportunities, which deepens the plight of the urban poor (E. Phillips 1996; D. A. Smith and Timberlake 1993).

Sociologist Louis Wirth (1928, 1938) argued that a relatively large and permanent settlement leads to distinctive patterns of behavior, which he called **urbanism.** He identified three critical factors that contribute to urbanism: the size of the population, population density, and the heterogeneity (variety) of the population. A frequent result of urbanism, according to Wirth, is that we become insensitive to events around us and restrict our attention to the primary groups to which we are emotionally attached.

Global View Preindustrial cities worldwide
Theory Sjoberg's functionalist view of sophisticated social organization as a precondition of urban life

Student Alert May need to review the concept of postindustrial society introduced in Chapter 5
Key Person Louis Wirth

summingUP

Table 15-2	Comparing Types of Cities	
Preindustrial Cities (through 18th century)	**Industrial Cities (18th through mid-20th century)**	**Postindustrial Cities (beginning late 20th century)**
Closed class system—pervasive influence of social class at birth	Open class system—mobility based on achieved characteristics	Wealth based on ability to obtain and use information
Economic realm controlled by guilds and a few families	Relatively open competition	Corporate power dominates
Beginnings of division of labor in the creation of goods	Elaborate specialization in manufacturing of goods	Sense of place fades, transnational networks emerge
Pervasive influence of religion on social norms	Influence of religion limited as society becomes more secularized	Religion becomes more fragmented; greater openness to new religious faiths
Little standardization of prices, weights, and measures	Standardization enforced by custom and law	Conflicting views of prevailing standards
Population largely illiterate, communication by word of mouth	Emergence of communication through posters, bulletins, and newspapers	Emergence of extended electronic networks
Schools limited to elites and designed to perpetuate their privileged status	Formal schooling open to the masses and viewed as a means of advancing the social order	Professional, scientific, and technical personnel become increasingly important

Sources: Based on E. Phillips 1996:132–135; Sjoberg 1960:323–328.

Table 15-2 summarizes the differences among preindustrial, industrial, and postindustrial cities.

Use Your Sociological Imagination www.mhhe.com/schaefer6

What would the ideal city of the future look like? Describe its architecture, public transportation, neighborhoods, schools, and workplaces. What kinds of people would live and work there?

URBANIZATION

The 1990 census was the first to demonstrate that more than half the population of the United States lived in urban areas of 1 million or more residents. In only three states (Mississippi, Vermont, and West Virginia) do more than half the residents live in rural areas. Clearly, urbanization has become a central aspect of life in the United States (Bureau of the Census 1991).

Urbanization can be seen throughout the rest of the world, too. In 1900, only 10 percent of the world's people lived in urban areas, but by 2000, that proportion had risen to around 50 percent. By the year 2025, the number of city dwellers could reach 5 billion. During the 19th and early 20th centuries, rapid urbanization occurred primarily in

European and North American cities. Since World War II, however, there has been an urban explosion in the world's developing countries (Koolhaas et al. 2001:3).

Some metropolitan areas have spread so far that they have connected with other urban centers. Such a densely populated area, containing two or more cities and their suburbs, has become known as a *megalopolis.* An example is the 500-mile corridor stretching from Boston south to Washington, D.C., which includes New York City, Philadelphia, and Baltimore and accounts for one-sixth of the total population of the United States. Even when the megalopolis is divided into autonomous political jurisdictions, it can be viewed as a single economic entity. The megalopolis is also evident in Great Britain, Germany, Italy, Egypt, India, Japan, and China.

Functionalist View: Urban Ecology

As we saw in Chapter 14, *human ecology* is concerned with the interrelationships between people and their environment. Human ecologists have long been interested in how the physical environment shapes people's lives (for example, how rivers can serve as a barrier to residential expansion) and in how people influence the surrounding environment (for example, how air-conditioning has accelerated the growth of major metro-

Classroom Tip See "Systemic Model" (Additional Lecture Ideas).
Classroom Tip See "Community Theory and Simulation" (Class Discussion Topics) and "Land-Use Map" (Class Discussion Topics).
Global View By the year 2025, the number of city dwellers worldwide could reach 5 billion.

Classroom Tip See "Human Ecology: Housing in Japan" (Additional Lecture Ideas).

politan areas in the Southwest). *Urban ecology* focuses on such relationships as they emerge in urban areas. Although the urban ecological approach focuses on social change in cities, it is nevertheless functionalist in orientation because it emphasizes how different elements in urban areas contribute to social stability.

Early urban ecologists such as Robert Park (1916, 1936) and Ernest Burgess (1925) concentrated on city life but drew on the approaches used by ecologists who study plant and animal communities. With few exceptions, urban ecologists trace their work back to the **concentric-zone theory** devised in the 1920s by Burgess (see Figure 15-3a). Using Chicago as an example, Burgess proposed a theory for describing land use in industrial cities. At the center, or nucleus, of such a city is the central business district. Large department stores, hotels, theaters, and financial institutions occupy this highly valued land. Surrounding this urban center are zones devoted to other types of land use that illustrate the growth of the urban area over time.

Note that the creation of zones is a *social* process, not the result of nature alone. Families and business firms compete for the most valuable land; those who possess the most wealth and power are generally the winners. The concentric-zone theory proposed by Burgess represented a dynamic model of urban growth. As urban growth proceeded, each zone would move even farther from the central business district.

Because of its functionalist orientation and its emphasis on stability, the concentric-zone theory tended to understate or ignore certain tensions that were apparent in metropolitan areas. For example, the growing use by the affluent of land in a city's peripheral areas was uncritically approved, while the arrival of African Americans in White neighborhoods in the 1930s was described by some sociologists in terms such as *invasion* and *succession*. Moreover, the urban ecological perspective gave little thought to gender inequities, such as the establishment of men's softball and golf leagues in city parks, without any programs for women's sports. Consequently, the urban ecological approach has been criticized for its failure to address issues of gender, race, and class.

By the middle of the 20th century, urban populations had spilled beyond traditional city limits. No longer could urban ecologists focus exclusively on *growth* in the central city, for large numbers of urban residents were abandoning the cities to live in suburban areas. As a response to the emergence of more than one focal point in some metropolitan areas, Chauncy D. Harris and Edward Ullman (1945) presented the **multiple-nuclei theory** (see Figure 15-3b). In their view, all urban growth does not radiate outward from a central business district. Instead, a metropolitan area may have many centers of development, each of which reflects a particular urban need or activity. Thus, a city may have a financial district, a manufacturing zone, a waterfront area, an entertainment center, and so forth. Certain types of business firms and certain types of housing will naturally cluster around each distinctive nucleus (Squires 2002).

The rise of suburban shopping malls is a vivid example of the phenomenon of multiple nuclei within metropolitan areas. Initially, all major retailing in urban areas

FIGURE 15-3

Ecological Theories of Urban Growth

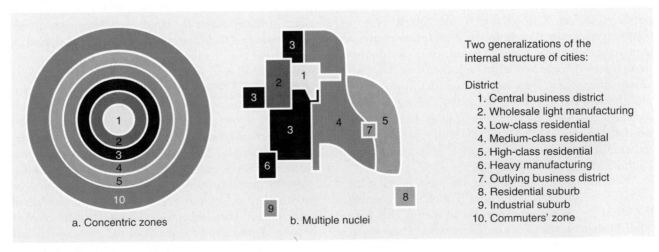

a. Concentric zones

b. Multiple nuclei

Two generalizations of the internal structure of cities:

District
1. Central business district
2. Wholesale light manufacturing
3. Low-class residential
4. Medium-class residential
5. High-class residential
6. Heavy manufacturing
7. Outlying business district
8. Residential suburb
9. Industrial suburb
10. Commuters' zone

Source: C. Harris and Ullmann 1945:13.

Theory Urban ecology is functionalist in orientation.
Key Persons Robert Park, Ernest Burgess
Theory Concentric zone theory has a functionalist orientation and an emphasis on stability.

Race/Ethnicity The use of terms such as *invasion* and *succession* by sociologists to describe the arrival of African Americans in White neighborhoods in the 1930s
Theory Viewed from a conflict perspective, the urban ecological approach has failed to address the issues of gender, race, and class.

was located in the central business district. Each residential neighborhood had its own grocers, bakers, and butchers, but people traveled to the center of the city to make major purchases at department stores. However, as metropolitan areas expanded and the suburbs became more populous, increasing numbers of people began to shop nearer their homes. Today, the suburban mall is a significant retailing and social center in communities across the United States.

In a refinement of the multiple-nuclei theory, contemporary urban ecologists have begun to study what journalist Joel Garreau (1991) has called "edge cities." These communities, which have grown up on the outskirts of major metropolitan areas, are economic and social centers with identities of their own. By any standard of measurement—height of buildings, amount of office space, presence of medical facilities, presence of leisure-time facilities, or of course, population—edge cities qualify as independent cities rather than as large suburbs.

Whether metropolitan areas include edge cities or multiple nuclei, more and more of them are characterized by spread-out development and unchecked growth. In recent years, Las Vegas has been the most dramatic example. With a new house built every 20 minutes, by 2004 the city had mushroomed from 38 to 235 square miles. The social consequences of such rapid growth are equally dramatic, from a shortage of affordable housing and an inadequate number of food pantries to an overstretched water supply, poor health care delivery, and impossible traffic. Today's cities are very different from the preindustrial cities of a thousand years ago (D. Murphy 2004).

Conflict View: New Urban Sociology

Contemporary sociologists point out that metropolitan growth is not governed by waterways and rail lines, as a purely ecological interpretation might suggest. From a conflict perspective, communities are human creations that reflect people's needs, choices, and decisions—though some people have more influence over those decisions than others. Drawing on conflict theory, an approach that has come to be called the **new urban sociology** considers the interplay of local, national, and worldwide forces and their effect on local space, with special emphasis on the impact of global economic activity (Gottdiener and Hutchison 2000).

New urban sociologists note that proponents of the ecological approaches have typically avoided examining the social forces, largely economic in nature, that have guided urban growth. For example, central business districts may be upgraded or abandoned, depending on whether urban policymakers grant substantial tax ex-

emptions to developers. The suburban boom in the post–World War II era was fueled by highway construction and federal housing policies that channeled investment capital into the construction of single-family homes rather than affordable rental housing in the cities. Similarly, while some observers suggest that the growth of sun-belt cities is due to a "good business climate," new urban sociologists counter that the term is actually a euphemism for hefty state and local government subsidies and antilabor policies intended to draw manufacturers (Gottdiener and Feagin 1988; M. Smith 1988).

The new urban sociology draws generally on the conflict perspective, and more specifically on sociologist Immanuel Wallerstein's **world systems analysis.** Wallerstein argues that certain industrialized nations (among them the United States, Japan, and Germany) hold a dominant position at the *core* of the global economic system. At the same time, the poor developing countries of Asia, Africa, and Latin America lie on the *periphery* of the global economy, controlled and exploited by core industrialized nations. Using world systems analysis, new urban sociologists consider urbanization from a global perspective. They view cities not as independent and autonomous entities, but as the outcome of decision-making processes directed or influenced by a society's dominant classes and by core industrialized nations. New urban sociologists note that the rapidly growing cities of the world's developing countries were shaped first by colonialism and then by a global economy controlled by core nations and multinational corporations. The outcome has not been beneficial to the poorest citizens. An unmistakable feature of many cities in developing countries is the existence of large squatter settlements just outside city limits (Gottdiener and Feagin 1988; D. A. Smith 1995).

The urban ecologists of the 1920s and 1930s were aware of the role that the larger economy played in urbanization, but their theories emphasized the impact of local rather than national or global forces. In contrast, through their broad, global emphasis on social inequality and conflict, new urban sociologists concentrate on such topics as the existence of an underclass, the power of multinational corporations, deindustrialization, homelessness, and residential segregation.

For example, developers, builders, and investment bankers are not especially interested in urban growth when it means providing housing for middle- or low-income people. Their lack of interest contributes to the problem of homelessness. These urban elites counter that the nation's housing shortage and the plight of the homeless are not their fault, and insist that they do not have the capital needed to construct and support such housing. But afflu-

p. 222

pp. 216, 224, 378

Let's Discuss Are there urban centers or edge cities near your school?
Contemporary Culture Overall, 8 out of every 10 U.S. cities extended over a much greater geographical area in 2000 than they did in 1990.

Theory The new urban sociology draws on the conflict perspective.
Key Person Immanuel Wallerstein
Global View Wallerstein's world systems analysis

ent people *are* interested in growth, and they *can* somehow find capital to build new shopping centers, office towers, and ballparks. Why, then, can't they provide the capital for affordable housing, ask new urban sociologists?

Part of the answer is that developers, bankers, and other powerful real estate interests view housing in quite a different manner from tenants and most homeowners. For a tenant, an apartment is shelter, housing, a home. But for developers and investors—many of them large (and sometimes multinational) corporations—an apartment is simply a housing investment. These financiers and owners are concerned primarily with maximizing profit, not with solving social problems (Feagin 1983; Gottdiener and Hutchison 2000).

As we have seen throughout this textbook, in studying such varied issues as deviance, race and ethnicity, and aging, no single theoretical approach necessarily offers the only valuable perspective. As Table 15-3 shows, urban ecology and the new urban sociology offer significantly different ways of viewing urbanization, both of which enrich our understanding of this complex phenomenon.

TYPES OF COMMUNITIES

Communities vary substantially in the degree to which their members feel connected and share a common iden-

◀ p. 118 tity. Ferdinand Tönnies ([1887]1988) used the term *Gemeinschaft* to describe a close-knit community where social interaction among people is intimate and familiar. This is the kind of place where people in a coffee shop will stop talking whenever anyone enters, because they are sure to know whoever walks through the door. A shopper at the small grocery store in this town would expect to know every employee, and probably every other customer as well. In contrast, the ideal type of the *Gesellschaft* describes modern urban life, in which

people have little in common with others. Social relationships often result from interactions focused on immediate tasks, such as purchasing a product. In the United States, contemporary city life generally resembles a *Gesellschaft*.

The following sections will examine different types of communities found in the United States, focusing on the distinctive characteristics and problems of central cities, suburbs, and rural communities.

Central Cities

In terms of both land and population, the United States is the fourth-largest nation in the world. Yet three-quarters of the population is concentrated in a mere 1.5 percent of the nation's land area. In 2000 some 226 million people—accounting for 79 percent of the nation's population—lived in metropolitan areas. Even those who live outside central cities, such as residents of suburban and rural communities, find that urban centers heavily influence their lifestyles (Bureau of the Census 2003a:34).

Urban Dwellers

Many urban residents are the descendants of European immigrants—Irish, Italians, Jews, Poles, and others—who came to the United States in the 19th and early 20th centuries. The cities socialized these newcomers to the norms, values, and language of their new homeland and gave them an opportunity to work their way up the economic ladder. In addition, a substantial number of low-income African Americans and Whites came to the cities from rural areas in the period following World War II.

Even today, cities in the United States are the destinations of immigrants from around the world—including Mexico, Ireland, Cuba, Vietnam, and Haiti—as well as

Table 15-3	Major Perspectives on Urbanization	
	Urban Ecology	**New Urban Sociology**
Theoretical perspective	Functionalist	Conflict
Primary focus	Relationship of urban areas to their spatial setting and physical environment	Relationship of urban areas to global, national, and local forces
Key source of change	Technological innovations such as new methods of transportation	Economic competition and monopolization of power
Initiator of actions	Individuals, neighborhoods, communities	Real estate developers, banks and other financial institutions, multinational corporations
Allied disciplines	Geography, architecture	Political science, economics

summingUP

Key Person Ferdinand Tönnies

Classroom Tip See "Apathy in the City?" (Additional Lecture Ideas).
Race/Ethnicity Immigration to the urban centers of the United States

of migrants from the U.S. commonwealth of Puerto Rico. Yet unlike those who came to this country 100 years ago, current immigrants are arriving at a time of growing urban decay. Thus they have more difficulty finding employment and decent housing.

Urban life is noteworthy for its diversity, so it would be a serious mistake to see all city residents as being alike. Sociologist Herbert J. Gans (1991) has distinguished five types of people found in cities:

1. **Cosmopolites.** These residents remain in cities to take advantage of unique cultural and intellectual benefits. Writers, artists, and scholars fall into this category.
2. **Unmarried and childless people.** Such people choose to live in cities because of the active nightlife and varied recreational opportunities.
3. **Ethnic villagers.** These urban residents prefer to live in their own tight-knit communities. Typically, immigrant groups isolate themselves in such neighborhoods to avoid resentment from well-established urban dwellers.
4. **The deprived.** Very poor people and families have little choice but to live in low-rent, and often run-down, urban neighborhoods.
5. **The trapped.** Some city residents wish to leave urban centers but cannot because of their limited economic resources and prospects. Gans includes the "downward mobiles" in this category—people who once held higher social positions, but who are forced to live in less prestigious neighborhoods owing to loss of a job, death of a wage earner, or old age. Both elderly individuals living alone and families may feel trapped in part because they resent changes in their communities. Their desire to live elsewhere may reflect their uneasiness with unfamiliar immigrant groups who have become their neighbors.

These categories remind us that the city represents a choice (even a dream) for certain people and a nightmare for others.

Gans's work underscores the importance of neighborhoods in contemporary urban life. Ernest Burgess, in his study of life in Chicago in the 1920s, gave special attention to the ethnic neighborhoods of that city. Many decades later, residents in such districts as Chinatowns or Greektowns continue to feel attached to their own ethnic communities rather than to the larger unit of a city. Even outside ethnic enclaves, a special sense of belonging can take hold in a neighborhood.

In a more recent study in Chicago, Gerald Suttles (1972) coined the term **defended neighborhood** to refer to people's definitions of their community boundaries. Neighborhoods acquire unique identities because residents view them as geographically separate—and socially different—from adjacent areas. The defended neighborhood, in effect, becomes a sentimental union of similar people. Neighborhood phone directories, community newspapers, school and parish boundaries, and business advertisements all serve to define an area and distinguish it from nearby communities.

Issues Facing Cities

People and neighborhoods vary greatly within any city in the United States. Yet all residents of a central city—regardless of social class, racial, and ethnic differences—face certain common problems. Crime, air pollution, noise, unemployment, overcrowded schools, inadequate public transportation—these unpleasant realities and many more are an increasingly common feature of contemporary urban life.

Perhaps the single most dramatic reflection of the nation's urban ills has been the apparent death of entire neighborhoods. In some urban districts, business activity seems virtually nonexistent. Visitors can walk for blocks and find little more than deteriorated, boarded-up, abandoned, and burned-out buildings. Vacant factories mark the sites of businesses that relocated a generation ago. Such urban devastation has greatly contributed to the growing problem of homelessness.

Residential segregation has also been a persistent problem in cities across the United States. Segregation has resulted from the policies of financial institutions, the business practices of real estate agents, the actions of home sellers, and even urban planning initiatives (for example, decisions about where to locate public housing). Sociologists Douglas Massey and Nancy Denton (1993) have used the term *American apartheid* to refer to such residential patterns. In their view, we no longer perceive segregation as a problem, but rather accept it as a feature of the urban landscape. For subordinate minority groups, segregation means not only limited housing opportunities but reduced access to employment, retail outlets, and medical services.

Another critical problem for the cities has been mass transportation. Since 1950, the number of cars in the United States has multiplied twice as fast as the number of people. Growing traffic congestion in metropolitan areas has led many cities to recognize a need for safe, efficient, and inexpensive mass transit systems. However, the federal government has traditionally given much more assistance to highway programs than to public transportation. Conflict theorists note that such a bias favors the relatively affluent (automobile owners) as well as corporations such as auto manufacturers, tire makers, and oil companies. Meanwhile, low-income residents of metropolitan areas, who are much less likely to own cars than members of the middle and upper classes, face higher fares on public transit along with deteriorating service (J. W. Mason 1998).

Asset-Based Community Development

For many people, the words *South Bronx, South Central Los Angeles,* or even *public housing* call forth a variety of negative stereotypes and stigmas. How do communities—whether neighborhoods or cities—that have been labeled as ghettos address the challenges they face? Typically, policymakers have identified an area's problems, needs, or deficiencies and then tried to find solutions. But in the last decade, community leaders, policymakers, and applied sociologists have begun to advocate an approach called **asset-based community development (ABCD),** in which they first identify a community's strengths and then seek to mobilize those assets.

In a distressed community, the ABCD approach helps people to recognize human resources they might otherwise overlook. A community's assets may include its residents' skills; the power of local associations; its institutional resources, whether public, private, or nonprofit;

and any physical and economic resources it has. By identifying these assets, planners can help to counter negative images and rebuild even the most devastated communities. The anticipated result is to strengthen the community's capacity to help itself and diminish its need to rely on outside organizations or providers. In fact, one consequence of this approach is to direct assistance to agencies within the community rather than to outside service providers (Asset-Based Community Development Institute 2001; Kretzmann and McKnight 1993; McKnight and Kretzmann 1996).

Tragically, the events of September 11, 2001, have caused many communities both large and small to recognize the ways in which neighbors can depend on one another. Middletown, New Jersey, a suburban community that lost 36 residents in the terrorist attack on the World Trade Center, is one example. In response to the catastrophe, a group of townspeople founded Friends Assisting Victims of Terror (FAVOR) and began canvassing every homeowner and business in the community on behalf of the bereaved families, most of whom had lost a breadwinner. At the end of the first year, the group had collected more than $700,000, along with donations of goods and services ranging from plumbing, car repair, and tree removal to haircuts, karate lessons, and chiropractor's appointments. The town also set up a scholarship fund for the three dozen children who had lost their fathers or mothers. In taking care of their own, the people of Middletown discovered the richness and variety of their resources (A. Jacobs 2001a, 2001b, 2002; Sheehy 2003).

Suburbs

The term *suburb* derives from the Latin *sub urbe,* meaning "under the city." Until recent times, most suburbs were just that—tiny communities totally dependent on urban centers for jobs, recreation, and even water.

Today, the term **suburb** defies simple definition. The term generally refers to any community near a large city—or as the Census Bureau would say, any territory within a metropolitan area that is not included in the central city. By that definition, more than 138 million people, or about 51 percent of the population of the United States, live in the suburbs (Kleniewski 2002).

C stands for "congestion." In 2003, to alleviate gridlock, officials of the city of London began to charge vehicles about $10 a day to enter designated congestion zones. Traffic reductions of 30 percent resulted, leading city planners around the world to consider adopting the idea.

Theory Conflict view of the bias toward the relatively affluent (automobile owners) as well as auto manufacturers and oil companies
Contemporary Culture Asset-based community development (ABCD) identifies a community's strengths and seeks to mobilize those assets.
Classroom Tip See "Urban Problems" (Class Discussion Topics).

Classroom Tip See "The Continuing Move to the Suburbs: Chicago" (Additional Lecture Topics).
Classroom Tip See "Neighborhood Stabilization" (Class Discussion Topics).

Urban parishioners gather after a church service. Religious organizations are one of the many resources that form the foundation of asset-based community development.

Three social factors differentiate suburbs from cities. First, suburbs are generally less dense than cities; in the newest suburbs, no more than two dwellings may occupy an acre of land. Second, the suburbs consist almost exclusively of private space. For the most part, private ornamental lawns replace common park areas. Third, suburbs have more exacting building design codes than cities, and those codes have become increasingly precise in the last decade. While the suburbs may be diverse in population, their design standards give the impression of uniformity.

Distinguishing between suburbs and rural areas can also be difficult. Certain criteria generally define suburbs: Most people work at urban (as opposed to rural) jobs, and local governments provide services such as water supply, sewage disposal, and fire protection. In rural areas, these services are less common, and a greater proportion of residents is employed in farming and related activities.

Suburban Expansion

Whatever the precise definition of a suburb, it is clear that suburbs have expanded. In fact, suburbanization was the most dramatic population trend in the United States throughout the 20th century. Suburban areas grew at first along railroad lines, then at the termini of streetcar tracks, and by the 1950s along the nation's growing systems of freeways and expressways. The suburban boom has been especially evident since World War II.

Proponents of the new urban sociology contend that initially, industries moved their factories from central cities to suburbs to reduce the power of labor unions. Subsequently, many suburban communities induced businesses to relocate there by offering them subsidies and tax incentives. As sociologist William Julius Wilson (1996) has observed, federal housing policies contributed to the suburban boom by withholding mortgage capital from inner-city neighborhoods, by offering favorable mortgages to military veterans, and by assisting the rapid development of massive amounts of affordable tract housing in the suburbs. Moreover, federal highway and transportation policies provided substantial funding for expressway systems (which made commuting to the cities much easier), while undermining urban communities by building freeway networks through the heart of cities.

All these factors contributed to the movement of the (predominantly White) middle class out of the central cities, and as we shall see, out of the suburbs as well. From the perspective of new urban sociology, suburban expansion is far from a natural ecological process; rather, it reflects the distinct priorities of powerful economic and political interests.

Diversity in the Suburbs

In the United States, race and ethnicity remain the most important factors that distinguish cities from suburbs. Nevertheless, the common assumption that suburbia includes only prosperous Whites is far from correct. The last 20 years have witnessed the diversification of suburbs in terms of race and ethnicity. For example, by 2000, 34 percent of Blacks in the United States, 46 percent of Latinos, and 53 percent of Asians lived in the suburbs. Like the rest of the nation, members of racial and ethnic minorities are becoming suburban dwellers (El Nasser 2001; Frey 2001).

But are the suburban areas re-creating the racial segregation of the central cities? A definite pattern of clustering, if not outright segregation, is emerging. A study of suburban residential patterns in 11 metropolitan areas found that Asian Americans and Hispanics tend to reside in equivalent socioeconomic areas with Whites—that is, affluent Hispanics live alongside affluent Whites, poor Asians near poor Whites, and so on. However, the case for African Americans

Key Person William Julius Wilson: See discussion of the underclass in Chapter 9.
Theory The critical view of suburban expansion offered by proponents of new urban sociology draws on the conflict perspective.
Race/Ethnicity African Americans, Hispanics, and Asian Americans in the suburbs

is quite distinct. Suburban Blacks live in poorer suburbs than Whites, even after taking into account differences in individuals' income, education, and homeownership.

Again, in contrast to prevailing stereotypes, the suburbs include a significant number of low-income people from all backgrounds—White, Black, and Hispanic. Poverty is not conventionally associated with the suburbs, partly because the suburban poor tend to be scattered among more affluent people. In some instances, suburban communities intentionally hide social problems such as homelessness so they can maintain a "respectable image." Soaring housing costs have contributed to suburban poverty, which is rising at a faster rate than urban poverty (Jargowsky 2003).

In Brandon, Florida, cattle graze in front of a new apartment complex. Throughout the United States, suburban sprawl is rapidly engulfing small farms and open fields.

Rural Communities

As we have seen, the people of the United States live mainly in urban areas. Yet according to the 2000 census, 59 million Americans, or 21 percent of the population, live in rural areas. There is quite a range in the number of rural residents from state to state: In California, fewer than 6 percent of residents live in rural areas; in Vermont, more than 60 percent. As is true of the suburbs, it would be a mistake to view these rural communities as fitting one set image. Turkey farms, coal-mining towns, cattle ranches, and gas stations along interstate highways are all part of the rural landscape in the United States (Bureau of the Census 2003a:34).

Today, many rural areas are facing problems that were first associated with the central cities, and are now evident in the suburbs. Overdevelopment, gang warfare, and drug trafficking can be found on the policymaking agenda far outside major metropolitan areas. While the magnitude of the problems may not be as great as in the central cities, rural resources cannot begin to match those that city mayors can marshall in an attempt to address social ills (Graham 2004; Osgood and Chambers 2003).

The postindustrial revolution has been far from kind to the rural communities of the United States. Of the fewer than 3 million farm and ranch operators nationwide, little more than a third consider agriculture their principal occupation. Farm residents now represent less than 1 percent of the nation's population, compared to 95 percent in 1790. The depopulation of farming areas has been especially hard on the youngest residents. It is not uncommon for rural children to travel 90 minutes each way to school, compared to a nationwide one-way commute of less than 25 minutes for urban workers (Department of Agriculture 2004; Dillon 2004).

In desperation, residents of depressed rural areas have begun to encourage prison construction, which they once discouraged, to bring in badly needed economic development. Ironically, in regions where the prison population has declined, communities have been hurt yet again by their dependence on a single industry (Kilborn 2001).

The construction of large businesses can create its own problems, as small communities that have experienced the arrival of large discount stores, such as Wal-Mart, Target, Home Depot, or Costco, have discovered. Although many residents welcome the new employment opportunities and the convenience of one-stop shopping, local merchants see their longtime family businesses endangered by formidable 200,000-square-foot competitors with a national reputation. Even when such discount stores provide a boost to a town's economy (and they do not always do so), they can undermine the town's sense of community and identity. Box 15-2 (page 408) chronicles the "store wars" that often ensue.

Policy Pointer Suburban communities intentionally hide the homeless to maintain a "respectable" image.
Theory The efforts of suburban communities to keep the homeless out of sight can be viewed as impression management.
Contemporary Culture Is it acceptable to hide the homeless?

Web Resource Encourage students to link to the Use Your Sociological Imagination component of the student center in the Online Learning Center (www.mhhe.com/schaefer6).

No organization exists in a vacuum, especially not a corporate giant. Executives of Wal-Mart know that. The epitome of the superstore, Wal-Mart has become the center of controversy in towns and cities across the United States, despite the familiar smiley-face logo and its red, white, and blue corporate image. The reason: A new Wal-Mart can have powerfully negative effects on the surrounding community.

Wal-Mart was founded in 1962 by Sam Walton, whose strategy was to locate new stores in rural communities, where competition from other retailers was weak and unions were not organized. Over the years, as the enormously successful discount chain expanded to become the world's largest corporation, Wal-Mart began to move into the fringes of metropolitan areas as well. But the residents of the communities Wal-Mart moved into did not always welcome their new neighbor.

In Ashland, Virginia, a community of 7,200 people, residents worried that Wal-Mart would destroy the small-town atmosphere they treasured. Would their cozy grocery store, known for its personal service, survive the discount giant's competition? Would their quaint and charming Main Street fall into decline? Would full-time jobs with full benefits give way to part-time employment? (Studies have shown that superstores ultimately *reduce* employment.) Ashland's grassroots opposition to Wal-Mart, chronicled in the PBS documentary *Store Wars*, ultimately lost its battle because of Wal-Mart's promised low prices and increased tax revenues. But citizens in many other communities have won, at least temporarily.

On the urban fringes, too, residents have mobilized to stop new superstores. In Bangor, Maine, environmentalists raised an alarm over a proposed Wal-Mart superstore, to be located next to a marsh that sheltered endangered wildlife. Activists in Riverside, California, also challenged Wal-Mart, again on environmental grounds.

In Ashland, Virginia, residents worried that Wal-Mart would destroy the small-town atmosphere they treasured.

But the issue is more complicated in these areas, because communities on the urban fringe are hardly untouched by economic development. Wal-Mart's proposed site in Bangor, for instance, is not far from the Bangor mall. And the huge new houses that dot the suburbs surrounding new stores, built on lots carved out of farmland or forest, have had an environmental impact themselves. In fact, the trend toward the superstore seems to parallel the emergence of the megalopolis, whose boundaries push further and further outward, eating up open space in the process. Recognizing the drawbacks of urban sprawl, some planners are beginning to advocate "smart growth"—restoring the central city and its older suburbs rather than abandoning them for the outer rings.

Not all communities reject superstores. In countries like Mexico, where the economic outlook has been poor recently, people have welcomed Wal-Mart. From Tijuana to Cancún, in fact, public reaction to the U.S. chain's arrival has been almost universally positive. Mexican shoppers appreciate Wal-Mart's wide selection and low prices.

Wal-Mart executives are unapologetic about the chain's rapid expansion. They argue that their aggressive competition has lowered prices and raised working people's standard of living. And they say they have given back to the communities where their stores are located by donating money to educational institutions and local agencies.

Let's Discuss

1. Is there a Wal-Mart, Home Depot, or some other superstore near you? If so, was its opening a matter of controversy in your community?
2. What do you think of the "smart growth" movement? Should communities attempt to redirect business and residential development, or should developers be free to build wherever and whatever they choose?

Sources: Leaf 2003; *Maine Times* 2001; PBS 2001; Saporito 2003; Smart Growth 2001; Wal-Mart 2001; Wal-Mart Watch 2003; Weiner 2003.

Rural communities that do survive may feel threatened by other changes intended to provide jobs, income, and financial security. For example, the town of Postville, Iowa—with a population of only 1,478—was dying in 1987 when an entrepreneur from New York City bought a run-down meat processing plant. The plant was subsequently transformed into a kosher slaughtering house, and today 150 Postville residents are devout Hasidic Jews from the Lubavitcher sect. The new residents occupy key managerial positions in the slaughtering house, while Lubavitcher rabbis supervise the kosher processing of the meat to ensure that it is acceptable under Jewish dietary laws. Initially, longtime residents of Postville distrusted their new neighbors, but gradually each group came to realize that it needed the other (Bloom 2000; Mihalopoulos 2003; Simon 2001).

Contemporary Culture Wal-Mart, the epitome of the superstore, has become the center of controversy in towns and cities across the United States.

Theory Conflict analysis of the effects of a new Wal-Mart on the surrounding community

Global View In Mexico, economically depressed communities are welcoming Wal-Mart.

Race/Ethnicity Interaction between Hasidic Jews and longtime residents of Postville, Iowa

On a more positive note, advances in electronic communication have allowed some people in the United States to work wherever they wish. For those who are concerned about quality-of-life issues, working at home in a rural area that has access to the latest high-tech services is the perfect arrangement. No matter where people make their homes—whether in the city, the suburbs, or a country village—economic and technological change will have an impact on their quality of life.

Use Your Sociological Imagination   www.mhhe.com/schaefer6

You have fast-forwarded to a future in which there are no central cities—just sprawling suburbs and isolated rural communities. What are the economic and social effects of the disappearance of the downtown area?

SOCIOLOGICAL PERSPECTIVES ON HEALTH AND ILLNESS

The communities people live in have an impact on their health. In many rural areas, for example, residents must travel many miles to see a doctor. The nearest hospital may be hundreds of miles away. On the other hand, people who live in the country escape many of the stresses and strains that plague people who live in cities.

Observant Jews pray in the locker room at a kosher meat processing plant near Postville, Iowa. When the plant first opened, the rural Christians hired to work there were unfamiliar with Jewish culture and faith, but members of the two groups soon learned to work together.

Culture, too, contributes to differences in medical care, and even in how health is defined. In Japan, for instance, organ transplants are rare. The Japanese do not generally favor harvesting organs from brain-dead donors. Researchers have shown that diseases themselves are rooted in the shared meanings of particular cultures.

If social factors contribute to the evaluation of a person as "healthy" or "sick," how can we define health? We can imagine a continuum with health on one end and death on the other. In the preamble to its 1946 constitution, the World Health Organization defined **health** as a "state of complete physical, mental, and social well-being, and not merely the absence of disease and infirmity" (Leavell and Clark 1965:14).

In this definition, the "healthy" end of the continuum represents an ideal rather than a precise condition. Along the continuum, people define themselves as healthy or sick on the basis of criteria established by each individual, relatives, friends, co-workers, and medical practitioners. Because health is relative, we can view it in a social context and consider how it varies in different situations or cultures.

Why is it that you may consider yourself sick or well when others do not agree? Who controls definitions of health and illness in our society, and for what ends? What are the consequences of viewing yourself (or of being viewed) as ill or disabled? Drawing on four sociological perspectives—functionalism, conflict theory, interactionism, and labeling theory—we can gain greater insight into the social context that shapes definitions of health and the treatment of illness.

Functionalist Approach

Illness entails breaks in our social interactions, both at work and at home. From a functionalist perspective, then, being sick must be controlled, so that not too many people are released from their societal responsibilities at any one time. Functionalists contend that an overly broad definition of illness would disrupt the workings of a society.

Sickness requires that one take on a social role, even if temporarily. The **sick role** refers to societal expectations about the attitudes and behavior of a person viewed as being ill. Sociologist Talcott Parsons (1951,

---

Contemporary Culture Electronic information technology and changes in urban areas and rural communities
Web Resource Remind students that there are flash cards with key terms and definitions for this chapter. They can link to the flash cards through the student center in the Online Learning Center **(www.mhhe.com/schaefer6).**

Theory Labeling view of how people define themselves as "healthy" or "sick"
Theory Functionalist approach to health and illness introduced
Key Person Talcott Parsons
Theory Parsons's functionalist view of the "sick role"
Classroom Tip See "Disability—An Exercise" (Class Discussion Topics).

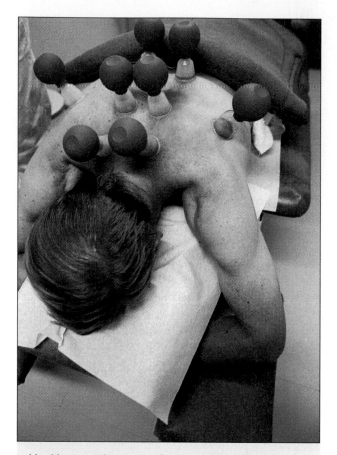

Health care takes many forms around the world. Cupping—a traditional practice used in ancient China, India, Egypt, and Greece—survives in modern Finland. Physiotherapists there use suction cups to draw out blood in order to lower patients' blood pressure, improve their circulation, and relieve muscular pain.

pp. 14–15 1975), well known for his contributions to functionalist theory, outlined the behavior required of people who are considered sick. They are exempted from their normal, day-to-day responsibilities and generally do not suffer blame for their condition. Yet they are obligated to try to get well, which may include seeking competent professional care. Attempting to get well is particularly important in the world's developing countries. Modern automated industrial societies can absorb a greater degree of illness or disability than horticultural or agrarian societies, in which the availability of workers is far more critical (Conrad 2000).

According to Parsons's theory, physicians function as "gatekeepers" for the sick role. They either verify a patient's condition as "illness" or designate the patient as "recovered." The ill person becomes dependent on the physician, because the latter can control valued rewards (not only treatment of illness, but also excused absences from work and school). Parsons suggests that the physician–patient relationship is somewhat like that between parent and child. Like a parent, the physician helps the patient to enter society as a full and functioning adult (A. Segall 1976).

The concept of the sick role is not without criticism. First, patients' judgments regarding their own state of health may be related to their gender, age, social class, and ethnic group. For example, younger people may fail to detect warning signs of a dangerous illness, while the elderly may focus too much on the slightest physical malady. Second, the sick role may be more applicable to people experiencing short-term illnesses than to those with recurring, long-term illnesses. Finally, even simple factors, such as whether a person is employed, seem to affect one's willingness to assume the sick role—as does the impact of socialization into a particular occupation or activity. For example, beginning in childhood, athletes learn to define certain ailments as "sports injuries" and therefore do not regard themselves as "sick." Nonetheless, sociologists continue to rely on Parsons's model for functionalist analysis of the relationship between illness and societal expectations of the sick (Curry 1993).

Conflict Approach

Conflict theorists observe that the medical profession has assumed a preeminence that extends well beyond whether to excuse a student from school or an employee from work. Sociologist Eliot Freidson (1970:5) has likened the position of medicine today to that of state religions yesterday—it has an officially approved monopoly of the right to define health and illness and to treat illness. Conflict theorists use the term *medicalization of society* to refer to the growing role of medicine as a major institution of social control (Conrad and Schneider 1992; McKinlay and McKinlay 1977; Zola 1972, 1983).

The Medicalization of Society

Social control involves techniques and strategies for regulating behavior in order to enforce the distinctive norms
p. 174 and values of a culture. Typically, we think of informal social control as occurring within families and peer groups, and formal social control as being carried out by authorized agents such as police officers, judges, school administrators, and employers. However, viewed from a conflict perspective, medicine is not simply a "healing profession"; it is a regulating mechanism as well.

How does medicine manifest its social control? First, medicine has greatly expanded its domain of expertise in recent decades. Physicians now examine a wide range of

Theory Conflict view of health and medicine introduced
Theory Conflict view of medicine as a mechanism of social control

issues, among them sexuality, old age, anxiety, obesity, child development, alcoholism, and drug addiction. Society tolerates such expansion of the boundaries of medicine because we hope that these experts can bring new "miracle cures" to complex human problems, as they have to the control of certain infectious diseases.

The social significance of this expanding medicalization is that once a problem is viewed using a *medical model*—once medical experts become influential in proposing and assessing relevant public policies—it becomes more difficult for common people to join the discussion and exert influence on decision making. It also becomes more difficult to view these issues as being shaped by social, cultural, or psychological factors, rather than simply by physical or medical factors (Caplan 1989; Conrad and Schneider 1992; Starr 1982).

Second, medicine serves as an agent of social control by retaining absolute jurisdiction over many health care procedures. It has even attempted to guard its jurisdiction by placing health care professionals such as chiropractors and nurse-midwives outside the realm of acceptable medicine. Despite the fact that midwives first brought professionalism to child delivery, they have been portrayed as having invaded the "legitimate" field of obstetrics, both in the United States and Mexico. Nurse-midwives have sought licensing as a way to achieve professional respectability, but physicians continue to exert power to ensure that midwifery remains a subordinate occupation (Friedland 2000).

Inequities in Health Care

The medicalization of society is but one concern of conflict theorists as they assess the workings of health care institutions. As we have seen throughout this textbook, in analyzing any issue, conflict theorists seek to determine who benefits, who suffers, and who dominates at the expense of others. Viewed from a conflict perspective, glaring inequities exist in health care delivery in the United States. For example, poor areas tend to be underserved because medical services concentrate where people are wealthy.

Similarly, from a global perspective, there are obvious inequities in health care delivery. Today, the United States has about 25 physicians per 1,000 people, while African nations have fewer than 1 per 1,000. This situation is only worsened by the **brain drain**—the immigration to the United States and other industrialized nations of skilled workers, professionals, and technicians who are desperately needed in their home countries. As part of this brain drain, physicians, nurses, and other health care professionals have come to the United States from developing countries such as India, Pakistan, and various African states. Conflict theorists view such emigration

The trend toward the medicalization of society now encompasses obesity, especially among youths. In China, the government has established "fat reduction hospitals" to treat overweight youths like this one, about to have his weight checked. Physicians are concerned about obesity because it is a precursor to heart disease and diabetes.

out of the Third World as yet another way in which the world's core industrialized nations enhance their quality of life at the expense of developing countries. One way the developing countries suffer is in lower life expectancy. In Africa and much of Latin America and Asia, life expectancy is far lower than in industrialized nations (World Bank 2003b:112–113).

Conflict theorists emphasize that inequities in health care have clear life-and-death consequences. From a conflict perspective, the dramatic differences in infant mortality rates around the world (see Figure 15-4, page 412) reflect, at least in part, unequal distribution of health care resources based on the wealth or poverty of various communities and nations. Still, despite the wealth of the United States, at least 31 nations have *lower* infant mortality rates, among them Canada, Great Britain, and Japan. Conflict theorists point out that unlike the United

Let's Discuss How does the medical model shed light on the concept of disability as a master status?
Theory Conflict view of the medical profession's opposition to chiropractors and midwives
Classroom Tip See "Professional Marginality: Chiropractors" (Additional Lecture Ideas).

Global View The "brain drain" out of Third World countries
Classroom Tip Note how U.S. immigration policy has affected health care not only in the United States but especially in the Third World.
Global View Lower life expectancy in Africa, Latin America, and Asia than in industrialized nations
Global View Infant mortality rates around the world

FIGURE 15-4

Infant Mortality Rates, 2002

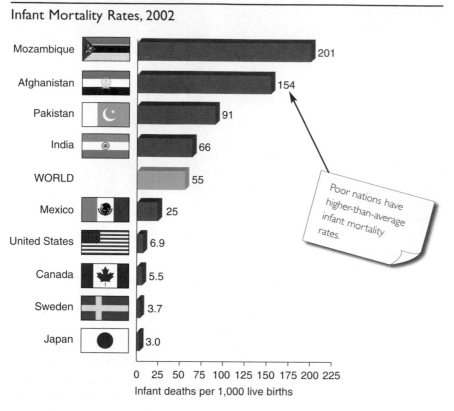

Mozambique 201
Afghanistan 154
Pakistan 91
India 66
WORLD 55
Mexico 25
United States 6.9
Canada 5.5
Sweden 3.7
Japan 3.0

Poor nations have higher-than-average infant mortality rates.

0   25   50   75   100 125 150 175 200 225
Infant deaths per 1,000 live births

Source: Haub 2003.

States, these countries offer some form of government-supported health care for all citizens, which typically leads to greater availability and use of prenatal care.

Interactionist Approach

From an interactionist point of view, patients are not passive; often, they actively seek the services of a health care practitioner. In examining health, illness, and medicine as a social institution, then, interactionists engage in micro-level study of the roles played by health care professionals and patients. Interactionists are particularly interested in how physicians learn to play their occupational role. According to Brenda L. Beagan (2001), the technical language students learn in medical school becomes the basis for the script they follow as novice physicians. The familiar white coat is their costume—one that helps them to appear confident and professional at the same time that it identifies them as doctors to patients and other staff members. Beagan found that many medical students struggle to project the appearance of competence they think their role demands.

Sometimes patients play an active role in health care by *failing* to follow a physician's advice. For example, some patients stop taking medications long before they should. Some take an incorrect dosage on purpose, and others never even fill their prescriptions. Such noncompliance results in part from the prevalence of self-medication in our society; many people are accustomed to self-diagnosis and self-treatment. On the other hand, patients' active involvement in their health care can sometimes have very *positive* consequences. Some patients read books about preventive health care techniques, attempt to maintain a healthful and nutritious diet, carefully monitor any side effects of medication, and adjust the dosage based on perceived side effects. Finally, physicians may *change* their approach to a patient based on the patient's wishes.

Labeling Approach

Labeling theory helps us to understand why certain p. 187 stand why certain people are *viewed* as deviants, "bad kids," or criminals, whereas others whose behavior is similar are not. Labeling theorists also suggest that the designation "healthy" or "ill" generally involves social definition by others. Just as police officers, judges, and other regulators of social control have the power to define certain people as criminals, health care professionals (especially physicians) have the power to define certain people as sick. Moreover, like labels that suggest nonconformity or criminality, labels that are associated with illness commonly reshape how others treat us and how we see ourselves. Our society attaches serious consequences to labels that suggest less-than-perfect physical or mental health (Becker 1963; C. Clark 1983; Schwartz 1987).

A historical example illustrates perhaps the ultimate extreme in labeling social behavior as a sickness. As enslavement of Africans in the United States came under increasing attack in the 19th century, medical authorities provided new rationalizations for the oppressive practice. Noted physicians published articles stating that the skin color of Africans deviated from "healthy" white skin coloring because Africans suffered from congenital leprosy. Moreover, the continuing efforts of enslaved Africans to escape from their White masters were classified as an ex-

Theory Conflict view of the impact of government-supported health care on infant mortality rates
Theory Interactionist view of health and illness introduced

ample of the "disease" of drapetomania (or "crazy runaways"). The prestigious *New Orleans Medical and Surgical Journal* suggested that the remedy for this "disease" was to treat slaves kindly, as one might treat children. Apparently, these medical authorities would not entertain the view that it was healthy and sane to flee slavery or join in a slave revolt (Szasz 1971).

By the late 1980s, the power of one particular label— "person with AIDS"—had become quite evident. As we saw **◀ p. 107** in our discussion of the late Arthur Ashe, this label often functions as a master status that overshadows all other aspects of a person's life. Once someone is told that he or she has tested positive for HIV, the virus associated with AIDS, that person is forced to confront immediate and difficult questions: Should I tell my family members, my sexual partner(s), my friends, my co-workers, my employer? How will these people respond? People's intense fear of the disease has led to prejudice and discrimination—even social ostracism—against those who have (or are suspected of having) AIDS. A person who has AIDS must deal not only with the serious medical consequences of the disease, but **◀ p. 123** with the distressing social consequences associated with the label.

According to labeling theorists, we can view a variety of life experiences as illnesses or not. Recently, premenstrual syndrome, posttraumatic disorders, and hyperactivity have been labeled medically recognized disorders. In addition, disagreement continues in the medical community over whether chronic fatigue syndrome constitutes a medical illness.

Probably the most noteworthy medical example of labeling is the case of homosexuality. For years, psychiatrists classified being gay or lesbian not as a lifestyle but as a mental disorder subject to treatment. This official sanction by the psychiatry profession became an early target of the growing gay and lesbian rights movement in the United States. In 1974, members of the American Psychiatric Association voted to drop homosexuality from the standard manual on mental disorders (Adam 1995; Monteiro 1998).

The four sociological approaches described here share certain common themes. First, any person's health or illness is more than an organic condition, since it is subject to the interpretation of others. The impact of culture, family and friends, and the medical profession mean that health and illness are not purely biological occurrences, but sociological occurrences as well. Second, since members of a society (especially industrial societies) share the same health care delivery system, health is a group and societal concern. Although health may be defined as the complete well-being of an individual, it is also the result of his or her social environment, as the next section will show (Cockerham 1998).

In South Africa, the children's television program *Sesame Street* features an HIV-positive Muppet named Kami, created to foster a culture of acceptance for people living with AIDS. Around the world, people who suffer from AIDs must deal with the prejudice, discrimination, and even social ostracism that result from the negative label "person with AIDS."

■ SOCIAL EPIDEMIOLOGY AND HEALTH

Social epidemiology is the study of the distribution of disease, impairment, and general health status across a population. Epidemiology initially concentrated on the scientific study of epidemics, focusing on how they started and spread. Contemporary social epidemiology is much broader in scope, concerned not only with epidemics but also with nonepidemic diseases, injuries, drug addiction and alcoholism, suicide, and mental illness. Recently, epidemiologists took on the new role of tracking bioterrorism. In 2001 they mobilized to trace the anthrax outbreak and prepare for any terrorist use of smallpox or other lethal microbes. Epidemiologists draw on the work of a wide variety of scientists and researchers, among them physicians, sociologists, public health officials, biologists, veterinarians, demographers, anthropologists, psychologists, and meteorologists.

Researchers in social epidemiology commonly use two concepts: *incidence* and *prevalence. Incidence* refers

Race/Ethnicity Prejudiced views of the health and well-being of enslaved African Americans
Theory Impact of the label "person with AIDS"
Policy Pointer The AIDS crisis was examined in the social policy section of Chapter 5.
Theory Labeling life experiences as illness

Reel Society See Health and Epidemiology in the Topic Index.

FIGURE 15-5

Percentage of People without Health Insurance, 2003

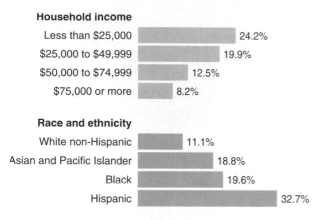

Household income

Less than $25,000 — 24.2%

$25,000 to $49,999 — 19.9%

$50,000 to $74,999 — 12.5%

$75,000 or more — 8.2%

Race and ethnicity

White non-Hispanic — 11.1%

Asian and Pacific Islander — 18.8%

Black — 19.6%

Hispanic — 32.7%

Source: DeNavas-Walt et al. 2004:15.

to the number of new cases of a specific disorder occurring within a given population during a stated period, usually a year. For example, the incidence of AIDS in the United States in 2001 was 43,158 cases. In contrast, *prevalence* refers to the total number of cases of a specific disorder that exist at a given time. The prevalence of AIDS in the United States through December 2002 was about 385,000 cases (Bureau of the Census 2003a:132; Centers for Disease Control and Prevention 2003).

When disease incidence figures are presented as rates, or as the number of reports per 100,000 people, they are called **morbidity rates.** (The term **mortality rate** refers to the incidence of *death* in a given population.) Sociologists find morbidity rates useful because they reveal that a specific disease occurs more frequently among one segment of a population than another. As we shall see, social class, race, ethnicity, gender, and age can all affect a population's morbidity rates. In 1999, the U.S. Department of Health and Human Services, recognizing the inequality inherent in U.S. morbidity and mortality rates, launched the Campaign for 100% Access and Zero Health Disparities, an ambitious undertaking (Bureau of Primary Health Care 1999).

Social Class

Social class is clearly associated with differences in morbidity and mortality rates. Studies in the United States and other countries have consistently shown that people in the lower classes have higher rates of mortality and disability than others. One study concluded that Americans whose family incomes were less than $10,000 could expect to die seven years sooner than those with incomes of at least $25,000 (Pamuk et al. 1998).

Why is class linked to health? Crowded living conditions, substandard housing, poor diet, and stress all contribute to the ill health of many low-income people in the United States. In certain instances, poor education may lead to a lack of awareness of measures necessary to maintain good health. Financial strains are certainly a major factor in the health problems of less affluent people in the United States.

Another reason for the link between class and health is that the poor—many of whom belong to racial and ethnic minorities—are less able than others to afford quality medical care. As Figure 15-5 shows, the affluent are more likely to have health insurance, either because they can afford it or because they have jobs that provide it.

Another factor in the link between class and health is evident at the workplace: The occupations of people in the working and lower classes of the United States tend to be more dangerous than those of more affluent citizens. Miners, for example, risk injury or death from explosions and cave-ins; they are also vulnerable to respiratory diseases such as black lung. Workers in textile mills who are exposed to toxic substances may contract a variety of illnesses, including one commonly known as *brown lung disease.* In recent years, the nation has learned of the perils of asbestos poisoning, a particular worry for construction workers (Hall 1982).

In the view of Karl Marx and contemporary conflict theorists, capitalist societies such as the United States care more about maximizing profits than they do about the health and safety of industrial workers. As a result, government agencies do not take forceful action to regulate conditions in the workplace, and workers suffer many preventable job-related injuries and illnesses. Research also shows that the lower classes are more vulnerable to environmental pollution than the affluent, not only where they work but also where they live (see Chapter 14).

Race and Ethnicity

The health profiles of many racial and ethnic minorities reflect the social inequality evident in the United States. The poor economic and environmental conditions of groups such as African Americans, Hispanics, and Native Americans are manifested in high morbidity and mortality rates for these groups. It is true that some afflictions, such as sickle-cell anemia among Blacks, have a clear genetic basis. But in most instances, environmental factors contribute to the differential rates of disease and death.

In many respects, the mortality rates for African Americans are distressing. Compared with Whites, Blacks have higher death rates from heart disease, pneumonia, diabetes, and cancer. The death rate from stroke is twice as high among African Americans. Such epidemiological findings reflect in part the fact that a high proportion of Blacks are found among the nation's lower classes. According to the National Center for Health Statistics, Whites can expect to live 77.7 years. In contrast, life expectancy for Blacks is 72.2 years (Arias 2004).

As noted earlier, infant mortality is regarded as a primary indicator of health care. There is a significant gap in the United States between the infant mortality rates of African Americans and Whites. Generally, the rate of infant deaths is more than twice as high among Blacks. African Americans account for 15 percent of all live births in the nation but 30 percent of infant deaths. Puerto Ricans and Native Americans have infant mortality rates that are lower than African Americans' but higher than Whites' (Mathews et al. 2002).

A Mexican folk healer, or *curandero,* massages a patient's feet. About 20 percent of Hispanics rely on the home remedies folk healers offer.

The medical establishment is not exempt from racism. The media often focus on obvious forms of racism, such as hate crimes, while overlooking more insidious forms in social institutions like the medical establishment. One review of more than 100 studies conducted over the last decade concluded that minorities receive inferior care even when they are insured. Despite having access to care, Blacks, Latinos, and American Indians are treated unequally as a result of racial prejudice and differences in the quality of various health care plans. Furthermore, national clinical studies have shown that even allowing for differences in income and insurance coverage, racial and ethnic minorities are less likely than other groups to receive both standard health care and life-saving treatment for conditions such as HIV infection (Budrys 2003; Caesar and Williams 2002; Smedley et al. 2002).

Drawing on the conflict perspective, sociologist Howard Waitzkin (1986) suggests that racial tensions also contribute to the medical problems of Blacks. In his view, the stress resulting from racial prejudice and discrimination helps to explain the higher rates of hypertension found among African Americans (and Hispanics) compared to Whites. Hypertension—twice as common in Blacks as in Whites—is believed to be a critical factor in Blacks' high mortality rates from heart disease, kidney disease, and stroke (Morehouse Medical Treatment and Effectiveness Center 1999).

Some Mexican Americans as well as many other Latinos adhere to cultural beliefs that make them less likely to use the established medical system. They may interpret their illnesses according to traditional Latino folk medicine, or **curanderismo**—a form of holistic health care and healing. *Curanderismo* influences how one approaches health care and even how one defines illness. Most Hispanics probably use folk healers, or *curanderos,* infrequently, but perhaps 20 percent rely on home remedies. Some define such illnesses as *susto* (fright sickness) and *atague* (or fighting attack) according to folk beliefs. Because these complaints often have biological bases, sensitive medical practitioners need to deal with them carefully and diagnose and treat illnesses accurately (Council on Scientific Affairs 1999; Trotter and Chavira 1997).

Gender

A large body of research indicates that in comparison with men, women experience a higher prevalence of many illnesses, though they tend to live longer. There are variations—for example, men are more likely to have parasitic diseases, whereas women are more likely to become diabetic—but as a group, women appear to be in poorer health than men.

The apparent inconsistency between the ill health of women and their greater longevity deserves an explanation, and researchers have advanced a theory. Women's lower rate of cigarette smoking (reducing their risk of heart disease, lung cancer, and emphysema), lower consumption of alcohol (reducing the risk of auto accidents and cirrhosis of the liver), and lower rate of employment in dangerous occupations explain about one-third of their greater longevity than men. Moreover, some clinical studies suggest that the differences in morbidity may actually be less pronounced than the data show. Researchers argue that women are much more likely than men to seek treatment, to be diagnosed as having a disease, and thus to have their illnesses reflected in the data examined by epidemiologists.

From a conflict perspective, women have been particularly vulnerable to the medicalization of society, with everything from birth to beauty being treated in an increasingly medical context. Such medicalization may contribute to women's higher morbidity rates compared to those of men. Ironically, even though women have been especially affected by medicalization, medical researchers have often excluded women from clinical studies. Female physicians and researchers charge that sexism lies at the heart of such research practices, and insist there is a desperate need for studies of female subjects (Bates 1999; McDonald 1999; Vidaver et al. 2000).

Age

Health is the overriding concern of the elderly. Most older people in the United States report having at least one chronic illness, but only some of those conditions are potentially life threatening or require medical care. At the same time, health problems can affect the quality of life of older people in important ways. Almost half of older people in the United States are troubled by arthritis, and many have visual or hearing impairments that can interfere with the performance of everyday tasks.

Older people are also especially vulnerable to certain types of mental health problems. Alzheimer's disease, the leading cause of dementia in the United States, afflicts an estimated 4 million older people. While some individuals with Alzheimer's exhibit only mild symptoms, the risk of severe problems resulting from this disease rises substantially with age (Alzheimer's Association 1999).

Not surprisingly, older people in the United States (ages 75 and older) are three times more likely to use health services and to be hospitalized than younger people (ages 15–24). The disproportionate use of the U.S. health care system by older people is a critical factor in all discussions about the cost of health care and possible reforms of the health care system (Bureau of the Census 2002a).

In sum, to achieve the goal of 100 percent access and zero health disparities, federal health officials must overcome inequities that are rooted not just in age, but in social class, race and ethnicity, and gender. If that were not enough, they must also deal with a geographical disparity in health care resources. Dramatic differences in the availability of physicians, hospitals, and nursing homes exist between urban and rural areas.

SOCIAL POLICY and HEALTH

Financing Health Care Worldwide

The Issue

Though modern medicine can save and extend lives that would have been lost just a few decades ago, its miracles come at a high price. In the United States, employers pick up much of the bill through the group health insurance plans they sponsor. Until recently, they have been able to pass on the cost to customers in the form of price increases. Employee health insurance adds a hefty amount to the price tag of U.S.-made products and services. About $1,300 of the cost of a midsize car, for example, goes to pay for workers' health insurance.

This "privatized" approach to funding health care has been strained by the globalization of manufacturing and services, however. In some foreign countries, mainly the industrialized ones, the government provides health insurance. In developing countries, workers typically receive no health benefits, either from the government or from employers. When U.S. manufacturers attempt to sell their products in these countries, the cost of health insurance for workers back home becomes a handicap. U.S.-made products simply cost more than foreign-made products, in large part because of the generous benefits employees are accustomed to receiving. To reduce this competitive disadvantage, U.S. companies have been moving their production lines abroad and offshoring their service jobs. Needless to say, this strategy reduces employment at home—as well as the number of U.S. workers who have health insurance (Clinton 2004).

Meanwhile, in many developing nations, governments struggle to meet the much more basic needs of primary care. The goals established at the UN's World Health Assembly in 1981 were modest by North American standards: safe water in the home or within 15 min-

Theory Conflict view of women's vulnerability to the medicalization of society
Gender Exclusion of women from clinical studies because of sexism

Age Use of health services by older people in the United States
Gender/Race/Ethnicity/Age Inequities in provision of health care based on gender, race, ethnicity, and age
Classroom Tip Health care issues in developing countries

utes' walking distance; immunization against major infectious diseases; availability of essential drugs within an hour's walk or travel; and the assistance of trained personnel for pregnancy and childbirth. While some areas have made significant progress in meeting these goals, many developing countries have seen little improvement; in some places, health care has deteriorated (World Bank 1997).

The focus of this social policy section, however, is on those industrialized (or developed) nations where the *availability* of health care is not an issue. The question is more one of accessibility and affordability. What steps are being taken to make the available services reachable and affordable?

The Setting

The United States is now the only Western industrial democracy that does not treat health care as a basic right. According to the Bureau of the Census, in 2003, some 45 million people in the United States had no health insurance the entire year. The uninsured typically include self-employed people with limited incomes, illegal immigrants, and single and divorced mothers who are the sole providers for their families. As we saw in Figure 15-5 earlier, African Americans, Asian Americans, and Hispanics are less likely than Whites to carry private health insurance. Substantial numbers of people at all income levels; but especially poorer people, go without coverage for some or most of any given year (DeNavas-Walt et al. 2004:15).

National health insurance is a general term for legislative proposals that focus on ways to provide the entire population with health care services. First discussed by government officials in the United States in the 1930s, it has come to mean many different things, ranging from narrow health insurance coverage with minimal federal subsidies to broad coverage with large-scale federal funding.

Opponents of national health insurance insist that it would be extremely costly and would lead to significant tax increases. Defenders counter, however, that countries such as Great Britain and Sweden have maintained broad governmental health coverage for decades. Ironically, while these countries offer extensive health coverage for all citizens, the United States has higher health care costs than any other nation: an average annual cost of $4,499 per person, compared to $2,058 in Canada and only $1,747 in Great Britain. As Figure 15-6 (page 418) shows, most industrial nations finance a substantially larger share of health care costs through government than the United States does (World Bank 2003a:92–94).

Sociological Insights

As conflict theorists suggest, the health care system, like other social institutions, resists basic change. In general, those who receive substantial wealth and power through the workings of an existing institution will have a strong incentive to keep things as they are. In this case, private insurance companies are benefiting financially from the current system, and have a clear interest in opposing certain forms of national health insurance. In addition, the American Medical Association (AMA), one of Washington's most powerful lobbying groups, has been successfully fighting national health insurance since the 1930s.

The health care system is unquestionably undergoing "corporatization," as for-profit health care companies (often linking insurers, hospitals, and groups of physicians) are achieving increasing dominance. Conflict theorists have long argued that an underlying and disturbing aspect of capitalism in the United States is that illness may be exploited for profit. Critics of the corporatization of health care worry that the growing pressures on physicians and other health care providers to make cost-effective decisions may lead to inadequate and even life-threatening patient care (Sherrill 1995).

Race/Ethnicity African Americans, Asian Americans, and Hispanics are less likely than Whites to carry private health insurance.
Global View Health care in Great Britain, Sweden, and Canada

Theory Conflict view of resistance to change in the health care system
Theory Conflict view of illness as a source of profit in capitalist societies

FIGURE 15-6

Government Expenditures for Health Care, Selected Countries

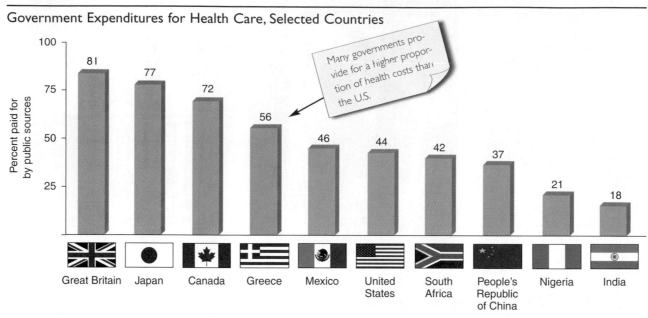

Source: World Bank 2003a:92–94.

Policy Initiatives

Early in the 1990s, the U.S. Congress dismissed the idea of any sort of national health insurance. Although virtually everyone agreed that the existing fee-for-service system was too costly, a major move to centralize financing, and hence control, of health care was deemed unacceptable. Yet even without legislative reform, major changes have been occurring.

Today, more and more people are enrolled in managed care plans, which limit patients' choice of physicians and treatments but cover most medical costs. ***Health maintenance organizations (HMOs),*** which provide comprehensive medical services for a preestablished fee, are playing a prominent role in managed care.

Concern is growing about the quality of care people receive through managed care plans such as HMOs—especially the elderly and minorities, who are less likely to be able to afford private insurance plans. According to a national survey, people in managed care feel they spend less time with physicians, find it more difficult to see specialists, and generally sense that the overall quality of health care has deteriorated (Brubaker 2001).

Many industrial countries are paying greater attention than the United States to unequal health care delivery. Addressing this problem, however, often creates difficulties. Great Britain, for example, closed facilities in

London and other metropolitan areas in an attempt to reassign medical staff to underserved rural areas. In addition to these concerns about the quality and availability of medical care, Britain's National Health Service remains underfunded (Christie 2001).

Medical services have in the past been delivered according to the ability to pay for services and the availability of facilities and personnel. As governments throughout the world take greater responsibility for health care, and as care becomes increasingly expensive, governments can be expected to pay more and more attention to controlling expenditures. Although the U.S. federal government has not been as heavily involved as other nations, the widespread introduction of managed care plans has created a degree of control previously unknown in the United States.

Let's Discuss

1. Are you and your family covered by a health insurance plan? If not, why aren't you covered? Has anyone in your family ever required a medical procedure he or she couldn't pay for?

2. Have you ever belonged to a health maintenance organization? If so, how satisfied were you with the care you received? Were you ever denied a specific treatment because it was too costly?

3. Should health care be a basic right of all Americans?

Global View Unequal health care delivery in Great Britain
Classroom Tip See "Using Humor" (Class Discussion Topics).

GETTING INVOLVED

To get involved in the debate over how to finance health care, visit this text's Online Learning Center, which offers links to relevant websites. Check out the Social Policy section on the Online Learning Center as well; it provides survey data on U.S. public opinion regarding this issue.

CHAPTER RESOURCES

Summary

The size, composition, and distribution of the population have an important influence on the **communities** people live in, as well as on people's **health** and well-being. This chapter examines the current problem of overpopulation and the possibility of **zero population growth,** the process of urbanization and its effects on communities both urban and rural, and several sociological perspectives on health. It closes with a discussion of the challenges of financing health care.

1. Thomas Robert Malthus suggested that the world's population was growing more rapidly than the available food supply, and that the gap would increase over time. However, Karl Marx saw capitalism, rather than rising world population, as the real cause of social ills.

2. The primary mechanism for obtaining population information in the United States and most other countries is the *census.*

3. Roughly two-thirds of the world's nations have yet to pass fully through the second stage of *demographic transition.* Thus they continue to experience significant population growth.

4. Developing nations face the prospect of continued population growth because a substantial portion of their population is approaching childbearing age. Some developed nations, however, have begun to stabilize their population growth.

5. Stable **communities** began to develop when people stayed in one place to cultivate crops; surplus production enabled cities to emerge.

6. Gideon Sjoberg identified three preconditions of city life: advanced technology, a favorable physical environment, and a well-developed social organization.

7. Over time, cities changed and developed with their economies. In the industrial revolution, the *preindustrial city* of agricultural societies gave way to the *industrial city;* the advent of the information age brought with it the *postindustrial city.*

8. Urbanization is evident not only in the United States but throughout the world; by 2000, 50 percent of the world's population lived in urban areas.

9. The *urban ecological* approach is functionalist because it emphasizes how different elements in urban areas contribute to social stability. *New urban sociology* emphasizes the interplay of a community's political and economic interests, as well as the impact of the global economy on communities in the United States and other countries.

10. In the last three decades, cities have confronted an overwhelming array of economic and social problems, including crime, unemployment, and the deterioration of schools and public transit systems.

11. *Asset-based community development (ABCD)* is a new approach to the revitalization of distressed neighborhoods in which planners first identify an area's resources and then mobilize them, channeling assistance to local agencies based in the community.

12. Suburbanization was the most dramatic population trend in the United States throughout the 20th century. In recent decades, *suburbs* have become more racially and ethnically diverse.

13. The effect of culture on **health** can be seen in cultural differences in medical care and in the *incidence* and *prevalence* of certain diseases.

14. According to Talcott Parsons's functionalist perspective, physicians function as "gatekeepers" for the *sick role,* either verifying a person's condition as "ill" or designating the person as "recovered."

15. Conflict theorists use the term *medicalization of society* to refer to medicine's growing role as a major institution of social control.

16. Labeling theorists suggest that the designation of a person as "healthy" or "ill" generally involves social definition by others. These definitions affect how others see us and how we view ourselves.

17. Contemporary *social epidemiology* is concerned not only with epidemics but with nonepidemic diseases, injuries, drug addiction and alcoholism, suicide, mental illness, and bioterrorism.

18. Studies have consistently shown that people in the lower classes have higher disability and **mortality rates** than others. Racial and ethnic minorities have higher mortality and **morbidity rates** than Whites. Women tend to have poorer health than men but live longer. Older people are especially vulnerable to mental health problems, such as Alzheimer's disease.

19. In the developed world, an aging population and technological breakthroughs have made health care both more extensive and more costly. At the same time, developing nations struggle to provide primary care for a burgeoning population.

Critical Thinking Questions

1. Some European nations are experiencing population declines. Their death rates are low and their birthrates are even lower than in stage III of the demographic transition model. Does this pattern suggest that there is a fourth stage in the demographic transition? What are the implications of negative population growth for an industrialized nation in the 21st century?

2. How has your home community (your city, town, or neighborhood) changed over the years you have lived there? Have there been significant changes in the community's economic base or its racial and ethnic profile? Have the community's social problems intensified or lessened? Is unemployment currently a major problem? What are the community's future prospects?

Key Terms

Asset-based community development (ABCD)   An approach to community development in which planners first identify a community's strengths and then seek to mobilize those assets. (page 405)

Birthrate   The number of live births per 1,000 population in a given year. Also known as the *crude birthrate*. (393)

Brain drain   The immigration to the United States and other industrialized nations of skilled workers, professionals, and technicians who are desperately needed in their home countries. (411)

Census   An enumeration, or counting, of a population. (392)

Community   A spatial or political unit of social organization that gives people a sense of belonging, based either on shared residence in a particular place or on a common identity. (390)

Concentric-zone theory   A theory of urban growth devised by Ernest Burgess that sees growth in terms of a series of rings radiating from the central business district. (401)

Curanderismo   Latino folk medicine, a form of holistic health care and healing. (415)

Death rate   The number of deaths per 1,000 population in a given year. Also known as the *crude death rate*. (393)

Defended neighborhood   A neighborhood that residents identify through defined community borders and a perception that adjacent areas are geographically separate and socially different. (404)

Demographic transition   A term used to describe the change from high birthrates and death rates to low birthrates and death rates that occurs during a nation's development. (394)

Demography   The scientific study of population. (391)

Fertility   The level of reproduction in a society. (390

Growth rate   The difference between births and deaths, plus the difference between immigrants and emigrants, per 1,000 population. (393)

Health   As defined by the World Health Organization, a state of complete physical, mental, and social well-being, and not merely the absence of disease and infirmity. (409)

Health maintenance organization (HMO)   An organization that provides comprehensive medical services for a preestablished fee. (418)

Human ecology   An area of study concerned with the interrelationships between people and their environment. (400)

Incidence   The number of new cases of a specific disorder occurring within a given population during a stated period. (413)

Industrial city   A relatively large city characterized by open competition, an open class system, and elaborate specialization in the manufacturing of goods. (399)

Infant mortality rate   The number of deaths of infants under one year old per 1,000 live births in a given year. (393)

Life expectancy   The median number of years a person can be expected to live under current mortality conditions. (393)

Megalopolis   A densely populated area containing two or more cities and their surrounding suburbs. (400)

Morbidity rate   The incidence of disease in a given population. (414)

Mortality rate   The incidence of death in a given population. (414)

Multiple-nuclei theory   A theory of urban growth developed by Harris and Ullman that views growth as emerging from many centers of development, each of which reflects a particular urban need or activity. (401)

New urban sociology   An approach to urbanization that considers the interplay of local, national, and worldwide forces and their effect on local space, with special emphasis on the impact of global economic activity. (402)

Population pyramid   A special type of bar chart that shows the distribution of a population by gender and age. (395)

Postindustrial city   A city in which global finance and the electronic flow of information dominate the economy. (399)

Preindustrial city   A city of only a few thousand people that is characterized by a relatively closed class system and limited mobility. (398)

Prevalence   The total number of cases of a specific disorder that exist at a given time. (414)

Sick role   Societal expectations about the attitudes and behavior of a person viewed as being ill. (409)

Social epidemiology   The study of the distribution of disease, impairment, and general health status across a population. (413)

Suburb   According to the Census Bureau, any territory within a metropolitan area that is not included in the central city. (405)

Total fertility rate (TFR)   The average number of children born alive to any woman, assuming that she conforms to current fertility rates. (393)

Urban ecology   An area of study that focuses on the interrelationships between people and their environment in urban areas. (401)

Urbanism   A term used by Louis Wirth to describe distinctive patterns of social behavior evident among city residents. (399)

Vital statistics   Records of births, deaths, marriages, and divorces that are gathered through a registration system maintained by governmental units. (392)

World systems analysis   Immanuel Wallerstein's view of the global economic system as one divided between certain industrialized nations that control wealth and developing countries that are controlled and exploited. (402)

Zero population growth (ZPG)   The state of a population in which the number of births plus immigrants equals the number of deaths plus emigrants. (397)

TECHNOLOGY RESOURCES

| www. mhhe.com /schaefer6 | **Internet Connection** |

*Note: While all the URLs listed were current as of the printing of this book, these sites often change. Please check our website (**www.mhhe.com/schaefer6**) for updates, hyperlinks, and exercises related to these sites.*

1. The Population Reference Bureau is an organization that provides information about the connection between demographics and social issues. To explore this topic, visit their very informative site (**www.prb.org**) and choose the DataFinder link.

2. The University of Michigan is the home of a research institute whose focus is health inequalities. To view some enlightening figures that illustrate the connections among race, class, and health, visit the Michigan Center for the Study of Health Inequalities (**www.sph.umich.edu/miih/ index2.html**) and link to "Facts."

Online Learning Center with PowerWeb

Chicago is one of the largest urban areas in the United States. Learn more about Chicago by visiting the student center in the Online Learning Center at **www.mhhe.com/schaefer6** and linking to "Internet Exercises." Exercise 2 links you to Don Brown's Chicago Daily Picture Page, which presents interesting photos of life in the Windy City. For contrast, link to the Kentucky Photo File.

Reel Society Interactive Movie CD-ROM 2.0

Reel Society 2.0 can be used to spark discussion about the following topics from this chapter:

- Demography: The Study of Population
- Social Epidemiology and Health

chapter 16

SOCIAL MOVEMENTS, SOCIAL CHANGE, AND TECHNOLOGY

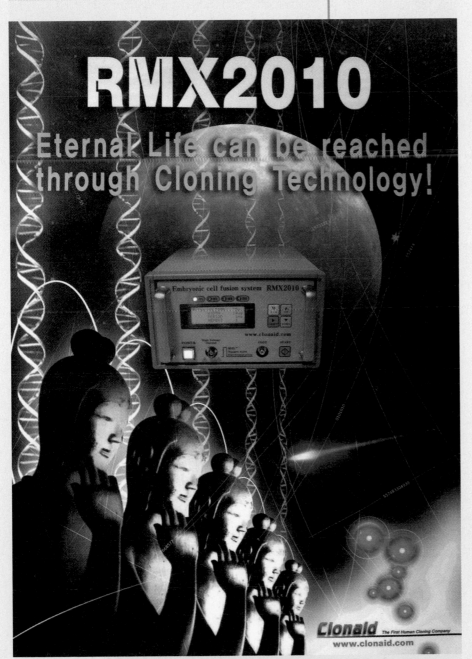

Social Movements

Theories of Social Change

Resistance to Social Change

Technology and the Future

Technology and Society

Social Policy and Technology: Privacy and Censorship in a Global Village

Boxes

RESEARCH IN ACTION: The Human Genome Project

SOCIOLOGY ON CAMPUS: Antiwar Protests

Technological change poses ethical challenges to society. This poster was commissioned by Clonaid, a biotech company that claims to have cloned humans. Though scientists doubt the truth of the company's claim, most find the idea that someone might attempt to clone humans profoundly disturbing.

423

On January 20, 2001, President Joseph Estrada of the Philippines became the first head of state in history to lose power to a smart mob. More than 1 million Manila residents, mobilized and coordinated by waves of text messages, assembled at the site of the 1986 "People Power" peaceful demonstrations that had toppled the Marcos regime. Tens of thousands of Filipinos converged on Epifanio de los Santas Avenue, known as "Edsa," within an hour of the first text message volleys: "Go 2EDSA, Wear blck." Over four days, more than a million citizens showed up, mostly dressed in black. Estrada fell. The legend of "Generation Txt" was born.

Bringing down a government without firing a shot was a momentous early eruption of smart mob behavior. It wasn't, however, the only one.

- On November 30, 1999, autonomous but internetworked squads of demonstrators protesting the meeting of the World Trade Organization used "swarming" tactics, mobile phones, Web sites, laptops, and handheld computers to win the "Battle of Seattle."

- In September 2000, thousands of citizens in Britain, outraged by a sudden rise in gasoline prices, used mobile phones, SMS, email from laptop PCs, and CB radios in taxicabs to coordinate dispersed groups that blocked fuel delivery at selected service stations in a wildcat political protest....

- Since 1992, thousands of bicycle activists have assembled monthly for "Critical Mass" moving demonstrations, weaving through San Francisco streets en masse. Critical Mass operates through loosely linked networks, alerted by mobile phone and email trees, and breaks up into smaller, telecoordinated groups when appropriate....

Location-sensing wireless organizers, wireless networks, and community supercomputing collectives all have one thing in common: *They enable people to act together in new ways and in situations where collective action was not possible before....*

As indicated by their name, smart mobs are not always beneficial. Lynch mobs and mobocracies continue to engender atrocities. The same convergence of technologies that opens new vistas of cooperation also makes possible a universal surveillance economy and empowers the bloodthirsty as well as the altruistic. Like every previous leap in technological power, the new convergence of wireless computation and social communication will enable people to improve life and liberty in some ways and to degrade it in others. The same technology has the potential to be used as both a weapon of social control and a means of resistance. Even the beneficial effects will have side effects. *(Rheingold 2003:157–158, viii).* ■ 🖲

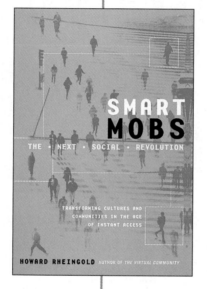

SMART MOBS

THE ・ NEXT ・ SOCIAL ・ REVOLUTION

TRANSFORMING CULTURES AND COMMUNITIES IN THE AGE OF INSTANT ACCESS

HOWARD RHEINGOLD AUTHOR OF *THE VIRTUAL COMMUNITY*

Additional information about this excerpt can be found on the Online Learning Center at **www.mhhe.com/schaefer6.**

I n this excerpt from *Smart Mobs,* Howard Rheingold (2003) describes a new phenomenon in which strangers linked by mobile communications devices converge spontaneously to achieve some common goal. Rheingold, an acknowledged authority on the social implications of new technologies, has identified an emergent social behavior. Such unforeseen effects are to be expected. As a rule, new technologies cannot help but change the way people live their lives, and by extension, the evolution of their culture and society. The invention of the personal computer and its integration into people's day-to-day lives is another example of the social change that often follows the introduction of a new technology.

Social change has been defined as significant alteration over time in behavior patterns and culture, including norms and values (W. Moore 1967). But what constitutes a "significant" alteration? Certainly the dramatic rise in formal education documented in Chapter 13 represents a change that has had profound social consequences. Other social changes that have had long-term and important consequences include the emergence of slavery as a system of stratification (see Chapter 9), the industrial revolution (Chapters 5 and 14), the increased participation of women in the paid labor forces of the United States and Europe (Chapter 11), and the worldwide population explosion (Chapter 15). As we will see in this chapter, social movements have played an important role in promoting social change.

How does social change happen? Is the process unpredictable, or can we make certain generalizations about it? Why do some people resist social change? What changes are likely to follow the technologies of the future? And what have been the negative effects of the sweeping technological changes of the last century? In this chapter we will examine the process of social change, with special emphasis on the impact of technological advances. We will begin with social movements—collective efforts to bring about deliberate social change. Then we will turn to the unanticipated social change that occurs when innovations such as new technologies sweep through society. Efforts to explain such long-term social change have led to the development of theories of change; we will consider the evolutionary, functionalist, and conflict approaches to change. We will see how vested interests attempt to block changes that they view as threatening. We'll also look at various aspects of our technological future, such as the Internet and biotechnology. We will examine the effects of technological advances on culture and social interaction, social control, and social stratification and inequality. Taken together, the impact of these technological changes may be approaching a level of magnitude comparable to that of the industrial revolution. Finally, in the social policy section we will discuss the ways in which technological advances have intensified concerns over privacy and censorship. ■

SOCIAL MOVEMENTS

Although such factors as physical environment, population, technology, and social inequality serve as sources of change, it is the *collective* effort of individuals organized in social movements that ultimately leads to change. Sociologists use the term **social movement** to refer to organized collective activities to bring about or resist fundamental change in an existing group or society (Benford 1992). Herbert Blumer (1955:19) recognized the special importance of social movements when he defined them as "collective enterprises to establish a new order of life."

In many nations, including the United States, social movements have had a dramatic impact on the course of

history and the evolution of the social structure. Consider the actions of abolitionists, suffragists, civil rights workers, and activists opposed to the war in Vietnam. Members of each social movement stepped outside traditional channels for bringing about social change, yet had a noticeable influence on public policy. Equally dramatic collective efforts in Eastern Europe helped to topple Communist regimes in a largely peaceful manner, in nations that many observers had thought were "immune" to such social change (Ramet 1991).

Though social movements imply the existence of conflict, we can also analyze their activities from a functionalist perspective. Even when they are unsuccessful, social movements contribute to the formation of public

Classroom Tip See "Stimulating Classroom Discussions about *Smart Mobs*" (Class Discussion Topics).
Classroom Tip See "Social Movement Speaker" (Class Discussion Topics).
Reel Society See Social Change in the Topic Index.

Contemporary Culture About which issues do today's Americans feel strongly enough to form a social movement?
Web Resource The interactive activity asks students to discuss a social movement that has affected society in their lifetime. Students can link to the activity through the student center in the Online Learning Center (**www.mhhe.com/schaefer6**).

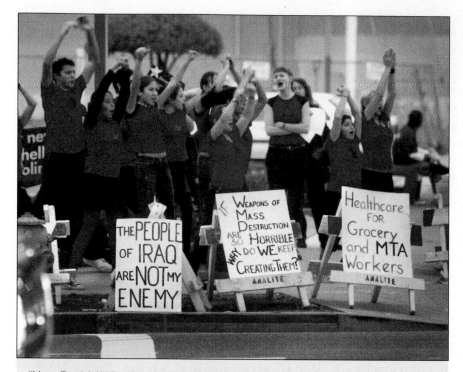

"Hey, Bush! / Who fights your wars? / Just minorities and the poor!" Los Angeles high school students protest the war in Iraq while demonstrating in support of striking supermarket workers in Eagle Rock, California. In their stand against war and for fair labor practices, the group, called the Radical Teen Cheerleaders, illustrates the relative deprivation theory of social movements.

opinion. Initially, people thought the ideas of Margaret Sanger and other early advocates of birth control were radical, yet contraceptives are now widely available in the United States. Moreover, functionalists view social movements as training grounds for leaders of the political establishment. Such heads of state as Cuba's Fidel Castro and South Africa's Nelson Mandela came to power after serving as leaders of revolutionary movements. Poland's Lech Walesa, Russia's Boris Yeltsin, and the Czech playwright Vaclav Havel all led protest movements against Communist rule and later became leaders of their countries' governments.

How and why do social movements emerge? Obviously, people are often discontented with the way things are. But what causes them to organize at a particular moment in a collective effort to effect change? Sociologists rely on two explanations for why people mobilize: the relative-deprivation and resource-mobilization approaches.

Relative Deprivation

Those members of a society who feel most frustrated and disgruntled by social and economic conditions are not necessarily worst off in an objective sense. Social scientists have long recognized that what is most significant is how people *perceive* their situation. As Karl Marx pointed out, although the misery of the workers was important to their perception of their oppressed state, so was their position *relative* to the capitalist ruling class (Marx and Engels [1847] 1955).

The term ***relative deprivation*** is defined as the conscious feeling of a negative discrepancy between legitimate expectations and present actualities (John Wilson 1973). In other words, things aren't as good as you hoped they would be. Such a state may be characterized by scarcity rather than a complete lack of necessities (as we saw in the distinction between absolute and relative poverty in Chapter 9). A relatively deprived person is dissatisfied because he or she feels downtrodden relative to some appropriate reference group. Thus, blue-collar workers who live in two-family houses on small plots of land—though hardly at the bottom of the economic ladder—may nevertheless feel deprived in comparison to corporate managers and professionals who live in lavish homes in exclusive suburbs.

In addition to the feeling of relative deprivation, two other elements must be present before discontent will be channeled into a social movement. People must feel that they have a *right* to their goals, that they deserve better p. 222 than what they have. For example, the struggle against European colonialism in Africa intensified when growing numbers of Africans decided that it was legitimate for them to have political and economic independence. At the same time, the disadvantaged group must perceive that it cannot attain its goals through conventional means. This belief may or may not be correct. Whichever is the case, the group will not mobilize into a social movement unless there is a shared perception that members can end their relative deprivation only through collective action (Morrison 1971).

Critics of this approach have noted that people don't need to feel deprived to be moved to act. In addition, this approach fails to explain why certain feelings of deprivation are transformed into social movements, whereas in other similar situations, no collective effort is made to re-

Gender Early advocates of birth control were viewed as radical.
Theory Functionalist view of social movements as a training ground for leaders of the establishment
Classroom Tip See "Why Do People Join Social Movements?" (Additional Lecture Ideas).

Theory The relative deprivation approach draws on the conflict perspective.
Key Person Karl Marx

shape society. Consequently, in recent years, sociologists have paid increasing attention to the forces needed to bring about the emergence of social movements (Alain 1985; Finkel and Rule 1987; Orum 1989).

Resource Mobilization

It takes more than desire to start a social movement. It helps to have money, political influence, access to the media, and personnel. The term **resource mobilization** refers to the ways in which a social movement utilizes such resources. The success of a movement for change will depend in good part on what resources it has and how effectively it mobilizes them (see also Gamson 1989; Staggenborg 1989a, 1989b).

Sociologist Anthony Oberschall (1973:199) has argued that to sustain social protest or resistance, there must be an "organizational base and continuity of leadership." As people become part of a social movement, norms develop to guide their behavior. Members of the movement may be expected to attend regular meetings of organizations, pay dues, recruit new adherents, and boycott "enemy" products or speakers. An emerging social movement may give rise to special language or new words for familiar terms. In recent years, social movements have been responsible for such new terms of self-reference as *Blacks* and *African Americans* (used to replace *Negroes*), *senior citizens* (used to replace *old folks*), *gays* (used to replace *homosexuals*), and *people with disabilities* (used to replace *the handicapped*).

Leadership is a central factor in the mobilization of the discontented into social movements. Often, a movement will be led by a charismatic figure, such as Dr. Martin Luther King Jr. As Max Weber described it in 1904,

◀ p. 368   *charisma* is that quality of an individual that sets him or her apart from ordinary people. Of course, charisma can fade abruptly, which helps to account for the fragility of certain social movements (A. Morris 2000).

Yet many social movements do persist over long periods because their leadership is well organized and ongoing. Ironically, as Robert Michels (1915) noted, political movements that are fighting for social change eventually take on some of the aspects of bureaucracy that they were organized to protest. Leaders tend to dominate the decision-making process without directly consulting followers. The bureaucratization of social movements is not inevitable, however. More radical movements that advocate major structural change in society and embrace mass actions tend not to be hierarchical or bureaucratic (Fitzgerald and Rodgers 2000).

Why do certain individuals join a social movement while others who are in similar situations do not? Some

of them are recruited to join. Karl Marx recognized the

◀ p. 207   importance of recruitment when he called on workers to become *aware* of their oppressed status and to develop a class consciousness. Like theorists of the resource-mobilization approach, Marx held that a social movement (specifically, the revolt of the proletariat) would require leaders to sharpen the awareness of the oppressed. They would need to help workers to overcome feelings of **false consciousness,** or attitudes that do not reflect workers' objective position, in order to organize a revolutionary movement. Similarly, one of the challenges faced by women's liberation activists of the late 1960s and early 1970s was to convince women that they were being deprived of their rights and of socially valued resources.

Even in movements that arise virtually overnight in response to events such as an unpopular war, recruiters play a part. During the 2003 war in Iraq, outside organizers helped to galvanize student protests (see Box 16-1, page 428).

Gender and Social Movements

Sociologists point out that gender is an important element in understanding social movements. In our male-dominated society, women find it more difficult than men to assume leadership positions in social movement organizations. While women often serve disproportionately as volunteers in these movements, their work is not always recognized, nor are their voices as easily heard as men's. Moreover, gender bias causes the real extent of women's influence to be overlooked. Traditional examination of the sociopolitical system tends to focus on such male-dominated corridors of power as legislatures and corporate boardrooms, to the neglect of more female-dominated domains such as households, community-based groups, and faith-based networks. But efforts to influence family values, child rearing, relationships between parents and schools, and spiritual values are clearly significant to a culture and society (Ferree and Merrill 2000; Noonan 1995).

Scholars of social movements now realize that gender can affect even the way we view organized efforts to bring about or resist change. For example, an emphasis on using rationality and cold logic to achieve goals helps to obscure the importance of passion and emotion in successful social movements. It would be difficult to find any movement—from labor battles to voting rights to animal rights—in which passion was not part of the consensus-building force. Yet calls for a more serious study of the role of emotion are frequently seen as applying only to the women's movement, because emotion is traditionally thought of as being feminine (Ferree and Merrill 2000; Taylor 1995).

Theory Labeling theorists would be especially interested in how social movements choose new terms of self-reference.
Key Person Martin Luther King Jr.
Key Person Robert Michels

Theory Marx's conflict view of false consciousness

aped to the sidewalks and the walls outside classrooms, flyers urged students to join the protest. Soon large groups had gathered at the appointed place, shouting their anger at the government as campus police eyed them nervously. The 1960s? It could have been, but it was 2004. On hundreds of campuses around the United States, students were voicing their opposition to the war in Iraq.

On most campuses, such student activism was a relatively recent development. In the 1990s, observers had noted student apathy toward politics, except for highly local issues such as campus housing policy or financial aid requirements. But gradually, student sentiment had manifested itself in protests against the sweatshop labor used to make the shirts and caps that bore school logos. When U.S. diplomats began to put together a coalition of nations willing to invade Iraq, students organized to question the basis for the action.

Student protests weren't as numerous as those that had occurred during the war in Vietnam, nor as long-lasting. And unlike the protests in the 1960s, these protests did not necessarily originate with students. Instead, calls to demonstrate and speak out came first from off-campus peace activists. To aging 60s activists, the speed with which the demonstrations were organized was striking. Using e-mail, students both for and against war could coalesce in a matter of hours—not the days or weeks their predecessors had needed. And regardless of their views, they could quickly locate like-minded students online.

Most significant, the recent protests featured some unprecedented role reversals. Many faculty who had been shaped

---

Using e-mail, students both for and against war could coalesce in a matter of hours.

---

as students by the movement against war in Vietnam took a strong public stand against war in Iraq. Their students, still traumatized by the terrorist attacks of September 11, 2001, and not subject themselves to the draft as an earlier generation had been, were less apt to protest. So on campuses such as Brandeis and Yale, some demonstrations were pro-war.

Another difference from the 1960s protests was the reaction of campus officials. In the 1980s, many universities had created "free-speech zones" to contain political demonstrations and prevent them from interrupting classes. In effect, these zones had limited the constitutional right to free speech to a few small areas on campus, banning students from speaking out everywhere else. But as student protesters began to gear up in 2003, many colleges dropped the hated restrictions, allowing demonstrations to proceed unhampered by police. Administrators too, it seemed, had learned some lessons from the war in Vietnam.

Let's Discuss

1. Have you ever witnessed a student-led protest in your high school or college? If so, what issues sparked the protest, and how did school administrators respond?
2. Suppose that in 2004 college administrators had attempted to prohibit students from organizing and speaking out against the war. As a practical matter (not a legal one), could such a policy have been easily enforced? What circumstances might make present-day protest movements harder to contain than protest movements of the past?

Sources: Blandy 2004; Colapinto 2003; Frost 2003; Sharp 2002; Zernike 2003.

New Social Movements

Beginning in the late 1960s, European social scientists observed a change in both the composition and the targets of emerging social movements. Previously, traditional social movements had focused on economic issues, often led by labor unions or by people who shared the same occupation. However, many social movements that have become active in recent decades—including the contemporary women's movement, the peace movement, and the environmental movement—do not have the social class roots typical of the labor protests in the United States and Europe over the past century (Tilly 1993).

The term *new social movements* refers to organized collective activities that address values and social identities, as well as improvements in the quality of life. These movements may be involved in developing collective identities. Many have complex agendas that go beyond a single issue, and even cross national boundaries. Educated, middle-class people are significantly represented in some of these new social movements, such as the women's movement and the movement for lesbian and gay rights.

New social movements generally do not view government as their ally in the struggle for a better society. While they typically do not seek to overthrow the government,

Classroom Tip See "The Social Movement for Prostitutes' Rights" (Additional Lecture Ideas).

Classroom Tip See "Student Social Movements in Beijing" (Class Discussion Topics).
Classroom Tip See "Colleges and Social Change" (Class Discussion Topics).

they may criticize, protest, or harass public officials. Researchers have found that members of new social movements show little inclination to accept established authority, even scientific or technical authority. This characteristic is especially evident in the environmental and anti–nuclear power movements, whose activists present their own experts to counter those of government or big business (Garner 1996; Polletta and Jasper 2001; A. Scott 1990).

The environmental movement is one of many new movements with a worldwide focus. In their efforts to reduce air and water pollution, curtail global warming, and protect endangered animal species, environmental activists have realized that strong regulatory measures within a single country are not sufficient. Similarly, labor union leaders and human rights advocates cannot adequately address exploitative sweatshop conditions in a developing country if a multinational corporation can simply move the factory to another country, where workers earn even less. Whereas traditional views of social movements tended to emphasize resource mobilization on a local level, new social movement theory offers a broader, global perspective on social and political activism.

Table 16-1 summarizes the sociological approaches that have contributed to social movement theory. Each approach has added to our understanding of the development of social movements.

THEORIES OF SOCIAL CHANGE

A new millennium provides the occasion to offer explanations of *social change,* which we have defined as significant alteration over time in behavior patterns and cul-

Table 16-1 | Contributions to Social Movement Theory

Approach	Emphasis
Relative deprivation approach	Social movements are especially likely to arise when rising expectations are frustrated.
Resource mobilization approach	The success of social movements depends on which resources are available and how effectively they are used.
New social movement theory	Social movements arise when people are motivated by value issues and social identity questions.

summingUP

ture. Such explanations are clearly a challenge in the diverse and complex world we inhabit today. Nevertheless, theorists from several disciplines have sought to analyze social change. In some instances, they have examined historical events to arrive at a better understanding of contemporary changes. We will review three theoretical approaches to change—evolutionary, functionalist, and conflict theory—and then take a look at global change.

Evolutionary Theory

The pioneering work of Charles Darwin (1809–1882) in biological evolution contributed to 19th-century theories of social change. Darwin's approach stresses a continuing progression of successive life forms. For example, human beings came at a later stage of evolution than reptiles and represent a more complex form of life. Social theorists seeking an analogy to this biological model originated *evolutionary theory,* in which society is viewed as moving in a definite direction. Early evolutionary theorists generally agreed that society was progressing inevitably to a higher state. As might be expected, they concluded in ethnocentric fashion that their own behavior and culture were more advanced than those of earlier civilizations.

p. 9   August Comte (1798–1857), a founder of sociology, was an evolutionary theorist of change. He saw human societies as moving forward in their thinking from mythology to the scientific method. Similarly, Émile Durkheim ([1893]1933) maintained that society progressed from simple to more complex forms of social organization.

The writings of Comte and Durkheim are examples of *unilinear evolutionary theory.* This approach contends that all societies pass through the same successive stages of evolution and inevitably reach the same end. English sociologist Herbert Spencer (1820–1903) used a p. 10 similar approach: Spencer likened society to a living body whose interrelated parts were moving toward a common destiny. However, contemporary evolutionary theorists such as Gerhard Lenski are more likely to see social change as being multilinear than to rely on the more limited unilinear perspective. *Multilinear evolutionary theory* holds that change can occur in several ways, and does not inevitably lead in the same direction (Haines 1988; J. Turner 1985).

Multilinear theorists recognize that human culture has evolved along a number of lines. For example, the theory of demographic transition graphically demonstrates that population change in developing nations has not necessarily followed the model evident in industrialized nations. Sociologists today hold that events do not necessarily follow in a single or even several straight lines, but instead are subject to disruptions—a topic we will consider later, in our discussion of global social change.

Functionalist Theory

Because functionalist sociologists focus on what *maintains* a system, not on what changes it, they might seem to offer little to the study of social change. Yet as the work of sociologist Talcott Parsons demonstrates, functionalists have made a distinctive contribution to this area of sociological investigation.

Parsons (1902–1979), a leading proponent of functionalist theory, viewed society as being in a natural state [p. 14] of equilibrium. By "equilibrium," he meant that society tends toward a state of stability or balance. Parsons would view even prolonged labor strikes or civilian riots as temporary disruptions in the status quo rather than as significant alterations in social structure. Therefore, according to his **equilibrium model,** as changes occur in one part of society, adjustments must be made in other parts. If not, society's equilibrium will be threatened and strains will occur.

Reflecting the evolutionary approach, Parsons (1966) maintained that four processes of social change are inevitable. The first, *differentiation,* refers to the increasing complexity of social organization. A transition from "medicine man" to physician, nurse, and pharmacist is an illustration of differentiation in the field of health. This process is accompanied by *adaptive upgrading,* in which social institutions become more specialized in their purposes. The division of physicians into obstetricians, internists, surgeons, and so forth is an example of adaptive upgrading.

The third process Parsons identified is the *inclusion* of groups that were previously excluded because of their gender, race, ethnicity, and social class background. Medical schools have practiced inclusion by admitting increasing numbers of women and African Americans. Finally, Parsons contends that societies experience *value generalization,* the development of new values that tolerate and legitimate a greater range of activities. The acceptance of preventive and alternative medicine is an example of value generalization: society has broadened its view of health care. All four processes identified by Parsons stress consensus—societal agreement on the nature of social organization and values (B. Johnson 1975; Wallace and Wolf 1980).

Though Parsons's approach explicitly incorporates the evolutionary notion of continuing progress, the dominant theme in his model is balance and stability. Society

may change, but it remains stable through new forms of integration. For example, in place of the kinship ties that provided social cohesion in the past, people develop laws, judicial processes, and new values and belief systems.

Functionalists assume that social institutions would not persist unless they continued to contribute to society. This assumption leads them to conclude that drastically altering institutions will threaten societal equilibrium. Critics note that the functionalist approach virtually disregards the use of coercion by the powerful to maintain the illusion of a stable, well-integrated society (Gouldner 1960).

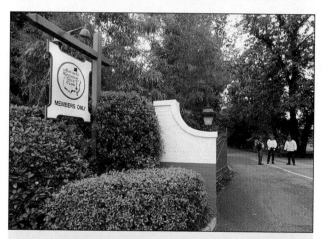

Since 1990, African American golfers like Tiger Woods have been welcome at the most exclusive private golf courses. Their acceptance in previously all-White enclaves like the Augusta National Golf Club, home of the Masters Tournament, illustrates the process of *inclusion* described by Talcott Parsons. Yet the process is far from complete. Women are still barred from joining the Augusta National and other elite clubs, no matter how wealthy or accomplished they are.

Conflict Theory

The functionalist perspective minimizes the importance of change. It emphasizes the persistence of social life, and sees change as a means of maintaining the equilibrium (or balance) of a society. In contrast, conflict theorists contend that social institutions and practices persist because powerful groups have the ability to maintain the status quo. Change has crucial significance, since it is needed to correct social injustices and inequalities.

Karl Marx accepted the evolutionary argument that societies develop along a particular path. However, unlike Comte and Spencer, he did not view each successive stage as an inevitable improvement over the previous one. History, according to Marx, proceeds through a series of stages, each of which exploits a class of people. Ancient society exploited slaves; the estate system of feudalism exploited serfs; modern capitalist society exploits the working class. Ultimately, through a socialist revolution led by the proletariat, human society will move toward the final stage of development: a classless communist society, or "community of free individuals," as Marx described it in *Das Kapital* in 1867 (see Bottomore and Rubel 1956:250).

As we have seen, Marx had an important influence

p. 12 on the development of sociology. His thinking offered insights into such institutions as the economy, the family, religion, and government. The Marxist view of social change is appealing because it does not restrict people to a passive role in responding to inevitable cycles or changes in material culture. Rather, Marxist theory offers a tool for those who wish to seize control of the historical process and gain their freedom from injustice. In contrast to functionalists' emphasis on stability, Marx argues that conflict is a normal and desirable aspect of social change. In fact, change must be encouraged as a means of eliminating social inequality (Lauer 1982).

One conflict theorist, Ralf Dahrendorf (1958), has noted that the contrast between the functionalist perspective's emphasis on stability and the conflict perspective's focus on change reflects the contradictory nature of society. Human societies are stable and long-lasting, yet they also experience serious conflict. Dahrendorf found that the functionalist approach and the conflict approach were ultimately compatible, despite their many points of disagreement. Indeed, Parsons spoke of new functions that result from social change, and Marx recognized the need for change so that societies could function more equitably.

Global Social Change

We are at a truly dramatic time in history to consider global social change. Maureen Hallinan (1997), in her

presidential address to the American Sociological Association, asked those present to consider just a few of the recent political events: the collapse of communism; terrorism in various parts of the world, including the United States; major regime changes and severe economic disruptions in Africa, the Middle East, and Eastern Europe; the spread of AIDS; and the computer revolution. Just a few months after her remarks came the first verification of the cloning of a complex animal, Dolly the sheep.

In this era of massive social, political, and economic change on a global scale, is it possible to predict change? Some technological changes seem obvious, but the collapse of communist governments in the former Soviet Union and Eastern Europe in the early 1990s took people by surprise. Yet prior to the Soviet collapse, sociologist Randall Collins (1986, 1995), a conflict theorist, had observed a crucial sequence of events that most observers had missed.

In seminars as far back as 1980, and in a book published in 1986, Collins had argued that Soviet expansionism had resulted in an overextension of resources, including disproportionate spending on military forces. Such an overextension will strain a regime's stability. Moreover, geopolitical theory suggests that nations in the middle of a geographic region, such as the Soviet Union, tend to fragment into smaller units over time. Collins predicted that the coincidence of social crises on several frontiers would precipitate the collapse of the Soviet Union.

And that is just what happened. In 1979, the success of the Iranian revolution had led to an upsurge of Islamic fundamentalism in nearby Afghanistan, as well as in Soviet republics with substantial Muslim populations. At the same time, resistance to Communist rule was growing both throughout Eastern Europe and within the Soviet Union itself. Collins had predicted that the rise of a dissident form of communism within the Soviet Union might facilitate the breakdown of the regime. Beginning in the late 1980s, Soviet leader Mikhail Gorbachev chose not to use military power and other types of repression to crush dissidents in Eastern Europe. Instead, he offered plans for democratization and social reform of Soviet society, and seemed willing to reshape the Soviet Union into a loose federation of somewhat autonomous states. But in 1991, six republics on the western periphery declared their independence, and within months the entire Soviet Union had formally disintegrated into Russia and a number of other independent nations.

In her address, Hallinan (1997) cautioned that we need to move beyond the restrictive models of social change—the linear view of evolutionary theory and the assumptions about equilibrium in functionalist theory. She and other sociologists have looked to the "chaos theory" advanced by mathematicians to understand erratic events as a part of

Theory Conflict view of social change introduced
Key Person Karl Marx
Classroom Tip See "Modern Industrial Society: A Recent Development" (Class Discussion Topics).
Key Person Ralf Dahrendorf
Key Person Maureen Hallinan

Key Person Randall Collins
Classroom Tip See "Assessing Social Change Through Reality TV" (Additional Lecture Ideas).
Global View Success of the Iranian revolution
Theory Conflict theorists would tie the end of the Soviet Union to competing interests fighting over limited resources.

The toppling of Saddam Hussein's totalitarian rule over Iraq in 2003 was one of several regime changes that occurred at the beginning of the 21st century. In a global society, such changes affect people throughout the world, not just those in one nation.

change. Hallinan noted that upheavals and major chaotic shifts do occur, and that sociologists must learn to predict their occurrence, as Collins did with the Soviet Union. For example, imagine the dramatic nonlinear social change that will result from major innovations in communications and biotechnology—topics we will discuss later in the chapter.

RESISTANCE TO SOCIAL CHANGE

Efforts to promote social change are likely to meet with resistance. In the midst of rapid scientific and technological innovations, many people are frightened by the demands of an ever-changing society. Moreover, certain individuals and groups have a stake in maintaining the existing state of affairs.

Social economist Thorstein Veblen (1857–1929) coined the term **vested interests** to refer to those people or groups who will suffer in the event of social change. For example, the American Medical Association (AMA) has taken strong stands against national health insurance [p. 411] and the professionalization of midwifery. National health insurance could lead to limits on physicians' income, and a rise in the status of midwives could threaten the preeminent position of doctors as deliverers of babies. In general, those with a disproportionate share

of society's wealth, status, and power, such as members of the American Medical Association, have a vested interest in preserving the status quo (Starr 1982; Veblen 1919).

Economic and Cultural Factors

Economic factors play an important role in resistance to social change. For example, it can be expensive for manufacturers to meet high standards for the safety of products and workers, and for the protection of the environment. Conflict theorists argue that in a capitalist economic system, many firms are not willing to pay the price of meeting strict safety and environmental standards. They may resist social change by cutting corners or by pressuring the government to ease regulations.

Communities, too, protect their vested interests, often in the name of "protecting property values." The abbreviation *NIMBY* stands for "not in my backyard," a cry often heard when people protest landfills, prisons, nuclear power facilities, and even bike trails and group homes for people with developmental disabilities. The targeted community may not challenge the need for the facility, but may simply insist that it be located elsewhere. The "not in my backyard" attitude has become so common that it is almost impossible for policymakers to find acceptable locations for facilities such as hazardous waste dumps (Jasper 1997).

Like economic factors, cultural factors frequently shape resistance to change. William F. Ogburn (1922) distinguished between material and nonmaterial aspects of culture. *Material culture* includes inventions, artifacts, and [p. 61] technology; *nonmaterial culture* encompasses ideas, norms, communications, and social organization. Ogburn pointed out that one cannot devise methods for controlling and utilizing new technology before the introduction of a technique. Thus, nonmaterial culture typically must respond to changes in material culture. Ogburn introduced the term **culture lag** to refer to the period of maladjustment when the nonmaterial culture is still struggling to adapt to new material conditions. One example is the Internet. Its rapid uncontrolled growth raises questions about whether to regulate it, and if so, how much (see the social policy section at the end of this chapter).

In certain cases, changes in material culture can strain the relationships between social institutions. For example, new means of birth control have been developed in recent decades. Large families are no longer economically necessary, nor are they commonly endorsed by social norms. But certain religious faiths, among them Roman Catholicism, continue to extol large families and to disapprove methods of limiting family size, such as contraception and abortion. This issue represents a lag between aspects of material culture (technology) and nonmaterial culture (religious beliefs). Conflicts may also emerge between religion and other social institutions, such as government and the educational system, over the dissemination of birth control and family-planning information (M. Riley et al. 1994a, 1994b).

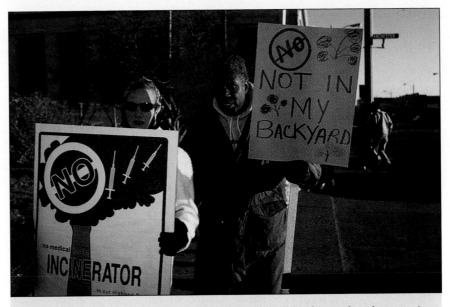

"Not in my backyard!" say these demonstrators, objecting to the placement of a new incinerator in a Highland Park, Michigan, neighborhood. The NIMBY phenomenon has become so common that it is almost impossible for policymakers to find acceptable locations for incinerators, landfills, and hazardous waste dumps.

Resistance to Technology

Technological innovations are examples of changes in

`p. 120` material culture that often provoke resistance. The *industrial revolution,* which took place largely in England during the period 1760 to 1830, was a scientific revolution focused on the application of nonanimal sources of power to labor tasks. As this revolution proceeded, societies came to rely on new inventions that facilitated agricultural and industrial production, and on new sources of energy such as steam. In some industries, the introduction of power-driven machinery reduced the need for factory workers and made it easier for factory owners to cut wages.

Strong resistance to the industrial revolution emerged in some countries. In England, beginning in 1811, masked craft workers took extreme measures: They mounted nighttime raids on factories and destroyed some of the new machinery. The government hunted these rebels, known as **Luddites,** and ultimately banished or hung them. In a similar effort in France, angry workers threw their wooden shoes (*sabots*) into factory machinery to destroy it, giving rise to the term *sabotage*. While the resistance of the Luddites and the French workers was short-lived and unsuccessful, they have come to symbolize resistance to technology.

Are we now in the midst of a second industrial revolution, with a contemporary group of Luddites engaged in resisting? Many sociologists believe that we are living

`p. 121` in a *postindustrial society*. It is difficult to pinpoint exactly when this era began. Generally, it is viewed as having begun in the 1950s, when for the first time the majority of workers in industrial societies became involved in services rather than in the actual manufacturing of goods (D. Bell 1999; Fiala 1992).

Just as the Luddites resisted the industrial revolution, people in many countries have resisted postindustrial technological changes. The term *neo-Luddites* refers to those who are wary of technological innovations, and who question the incessant expansion of industrialization, the increasing destruction of the natural and agrarian world, and the "throw it away" mentality of contemporary capitalism, with its resulting pollution of the environment. Neo-Luddites insist that whatever the presumed benefits of industrial and postindustrial technology, such technology has distinctive social costs, and may represent a danger to both the future of the human species and our planet (Bauerlein 1996; Rifkin 1995b; Sale 1996; Snyder 1996).

These concerns are worth remembering as we turn to our technological future and its possible impact on social change.

In London, a cell phone subscriber walks past a line of outmoded phone booths recycled as environmental art. Around the world, technological change has toppled once established communications channels, altering people's day-to-day social interactions in the process.

TECHNOLOGY AND THE FUTURE

Technology is information about how to use the material resources of the environment to satisfy human needs and desires. Technological advances—the airplane, the automobile, the television, the atomic bomb, and more recently, the computer, the fax machine, and the cellular phone—have brought striking changes to our cultures, our patterns of socialization, our social institutions, and our day-to-day social interactions. Technological innovations are, in fact, emerging and being accepted with remarkable speed.

In the following sections, we will examine various aspects of our technological future and consider their impact on social change, including the social strain they will cause. We will focus in particular on recent developments in computer technology and biotechnology.

Computer Technology

The last decade has witnessed an explosion of computer technology in the United States and around the world. Its effects are particularly noteworthy with regard to the Internet, the world's largest computer network. Estimates are that by 2005, the Internet will reach 1.1 billion computer users, compared to just 50 million in 1996 (Global Reach 2004).

The Internet evolved from a computer system built in 1962 by the U.S. Defense Department, to enable scholars and military researchers to continue their government work even if part of the nation's communications system were destroyed by a nuclear attack. Until recently, it was difficult to gain access to the Internet without holding a position at a university or a government research laboratory. Today, however, virtually anyone can reach the Internet with a phone line, a computer, and a modem. People buy and sell cars, trade stocks, auction off items, research new medical remedies, vote, and track down long-lost friends online—to mention just a few of the thousands of possibilities (Reddick and King 2000).

Unfortunately, not everyone can get onto the information highway, especially not the less affluent. Moreover, this pattern of inequality is global. The core nations that Immanuel Wallerstein described in his *world systems analysis* have a virtual monopoly on information technology; the peripheral nations of Asia, Africa, and Latin America depend on them both for technology and for the information it provides. For example, North America, Europe, and a few industrialized nations in other regions possess almost all the world's *Internet hosts*—computers that are connected directly to the worldwide network. The same is true for newspapers, telephones, televisions, and even radios. Low-income peripheral nations have an average of only 30 telephone lines per 1,000 people, compared to 593 per 1,000 in high-income nations. The disparity is even greater for cell phones: low-income nations have an average of 10 cell phones per 1,000 people, compared to 609 per 1,000 in high-income nations (World Bank 2003b).

Biotechnology

Sex selection of fetuses, genetically engineered organisms, cloning of sheep and cows—these have been among the significant yet controversial scientific advances in the field of biotechnology in recent years. George Ritzer's concept of McDonaldization applies to the entire area of biotechnology. Just as the fast-food concept has permeated society, no phase of life now seems exempt from therapeutic or medical intervention. In fact, sociologists view many aspects of biotechnology as an extension of the trend toward the medicalization of society, discussed in Chapter 15. Through genetic manipulation, the medical profession is expanding its turf still further (Clarke et al. 2003).

p. 119

p. 222

p. 59

Classroom Tip See "Virtual Reality" (Additional Lecture Ideas).
Classroom Tip See "Futurists" (Additional Lecture Ideas).
Let's Discuss Ask for a show of hands. How many students have color televisions, VCRs, CD players, computers, and fax machines?
Classroom Tip See "The Next Hundred Years" (Class Discussion Topics).

Global View Core nations have a virtual monopoly on information technology, and they control the Internet.
Student Alert Review with students how they may use the Internet in all their future classes. Share with them how you as an instructor have benefited from use of the Internet.

Today's biotechnology holds itself out as totally beneficial to human beings, but it is in constant need of monitoring. As we will see in the following sections, biotechnological advances have raised many difficult ethical and political questions (D. Weinstein and Weinstein 1999).

Sex Selection

Advances in reproductive and screening technology have effectively become techniques for sex selection. In the United States, the prenatal test called amniocentesis has been used for more than 25 years to ascertain the presence of certain defects that require medical attention prior to birth. Such tests can also identify the sex of the fetus, as can ultrasound scans. This outcome has had profound social implications.

In many societies, young couples planning to have only one child will want to ensure that the child is a boy, because their culture places a premium on a male heir. In such instances, advances in fetal testing may lead to abortion if the fetus is found to be female. Fetal testing clinics in Canada currently advertise that they can tell parents the sex of a fetus. Such advertising is targeted particularly at Asian Indian communities in both Canada and the United States. But in the United States, the preference for a male child is hardly limited to people from India. In one study, when asked what sex they would prefer for an only child, 86 percent of men and 59 percent of women said they wanted a boy. Moreover, through fetal testing, couples today routinely learn the sex of their child (M. Hall 1993; Sohoni 1994).

Sex selection is also possible in connection with a procedure called *in vitro fertilization.* In this procedure, which is intended to help infertile couples conceive a child, an egg is fertilized in a test tube and then implanted in the mother's womb. Couples who use this expensive procedure can now obtain a genetic analysis of the embryo before it is implanted. While the purpose of the analysis is to confirm that an embryo will be free from genetic defects, the results can also be used to select an embryo of the desired sex (Gezari 2002).

From a functionalist perspective, we can view sex selection as an adaptation of the basic family function of regulating reproduction. However, conflict theorists emphasize that sex selection may intensify the male dominance of our society and undermine the advances women have made in entering careers formerly restricted to men.

Genetic Engineering

Even more grandiose than sex selection—and not necessarily improbable—is the possibility of altering human behavior through genetic engineering. Fish and plant genes have already been mixed to create frost-resistant potato and tomato crops; more recently, human genes have been implanted in pigs to provide humanlike kidneys for organ transplants.

One of the latest developments in genetic engineering is gene therapy. Geneticists working with mouse fetuses have managed to disable genes that carry an undesirable trait and replace them with genes carrying a desirable trait. Such advances raise staggering possibilities for altering animal and human life forms. Still, gene therapy remains highly experimental, and must be considered a long, long shot (Kolata 1999).

The debate on genetic engineering escalated in 1997 when scientists in Scotland announced that they had cloned a sheep. After many unsuccessful attempts, they had

In Spain, Greenpeace members protest the European Union's proposed approval of a strain of genetically modified corn. The insect-resistant sweet corn produces a substance that is toxic to corn borers and earworms but not to humans. Nevertheless, opponents of this type of biotechnology have raised questions about its potential health effects. Their vocal opposition has disrupted international trade and caused friction between the United States and Europe.

Gender Preferences for male heirs
Global View Practices of fetal testing in Canada

Theory Functionalist and conflict views of sex selection
Student Alert Review the seemingly simple but genuinely complex issue of "nature versus nurture." (See Chapter 4.)

A Hazardous Materials worker bags dust samples taken from the Associated Press mailroom in October 2001, after letters containing deadly anthrax bacteria were sent to newsrooms in Florida and New York. The threat of bioterrorism has become a matter of increasing concern to governments and organizations throughout the world.

passed. However, state legislatures have grappled with the issue. As of mid-2003, only California specifically allowed human cloning, while Iowa and South Dakota explicitly banned it (Brainard 2003).

William F. Ogburn probably could not have anticipated such scientific developments when he wrote of culture lag 70 years earlier. However, the successful cloning of sheep illustrates again how quickly material culture can change, and how nonmaterial culture moves more slowly in absorbing such changes.

While cloning grabs the headlines, controversy has been growing concerning genetically modified (GM) food. This issue arose in Europe but has since spread to other parts of the world, including the United States. The idea behind the technology is to increase food production and make agriculture more economical. But critics use the term *Frankenfood* (as in "Frankenstein") to refer to everything from breakfast cereals made from genetically engineered grains to "fresh" GM tomatoes. They object to tampering with nature, and are concerned about the possible health effects of GM food. Supporters of genetically modified food include not just biotech companies, but those who see the technology as a way to help feed the burgeoning populations of Africa and Asia (Golden 1999).

Another form of biotechnology with a potentially wide-ranging impact is the Human Genome Project. This effort involves teams of scientists around the world in sequencing and mapping all the 30,000 to 40,000 human genes in existence, which are collectively known as the *human genome*. Supporters say that the resulting knowledge could revolutionize doctors' ability to treat and even prevent disease. But sociologists worry about the ethical implications of such research. Box 16-2 provides an overview of the many issues the project has raised.

Bioterrorism

Because biotechnology has generally been seen as a benefit to society, critics have been concerned mostly with the possibility of unintended negative consequences. Yet scientists have long recognized that chemical and biological agents can be used intentionally as weapons of mass destruction. Combatants in World War I used mustard gas, and nerve gas was used shortly thereafter. Today as many as 26 nations appear to have stockpiled chemical weapons, and another 10 have developed biological weapons programs.

More disturbing still is the prospect that terrorists might develop their own biological or chemical weapons, which are not difficult or expensive to make. The deaths that occurred as a result of anthrax contamination of the U.S. mails in 2001, shortly after the attacks on the

finally been able to replace the genetic material of a sheep's egg with DNA from an adult sheep, creating a lamb that was a clone of the adult. The very next year, Japanese researchers successfully cloned cows. These developments raised the possibility that in the near future, scientists may be able to clone human beings.

In 1997, President Bill Clinton banned any federal support for human cloning and urged private laboratories to abide by a voluntary moratorium until the ethical issues could be carefully considered. Six years later, no federal law on human cloning had been drafted, no less

Together with geneticists, pathologists, and microbiologists, sociologist Troy Duster of New York University has been grappling with the ethical, legal, and social issues raised by the Human Genome Project since 1989. An original member of the oversight committee appointed to deal with such matters, he does not expect that his work will be done anytime in the near future.

Duster, who is also president of the American Sociological Association, has been asked to explain why his committee is taking so long to conclude its work. In reply, he lists the many issues raised by the massive project. First, he is concerned that the medical breakthroughs made possible by the project will not benefit all people equally. He notes that biotechnology firms have used the project's data to develop a test for cystic fibrosis in White Americans, but not for the same syndrome in Zuni Indians. Biotechnology companies are profit-making ventures, not humanitarian organizations. So while the scientists involved in the Human Genome Project hope to map the genes of all the peoples of the world, not everyone may benefit from the project in practical ways.

Duster's committee has also struggled with the question of informed consent—making sure that everyone who donates genes to the project will do so voluntarily, after being informed of the risks and benefits. In Western societies, scientists commonly obtain such consent from the individuals who participate in their research. But according to Duster, many non-Western societies do not acknowledge the individual's right to make such decisions. Instead, a leader makes the decision for the group as a whole. "When Western-trained researchers descend upon a village," Duster asks, "who should they turn to for consent?" (Duster 2002:69) And what if the answer is no?

Race, too, is a knotty problem for Duster's committee. DNA analysis shows conclusively that there is no genetic dif-

A group's economic and political power help to determine which diseases scientists study.

ference between the races. Given that analysis, geneticists do not want to invest more time and effort in research on racial differences. As a sociologist, Duster knows that race is socially constructed. Yet he also knows that for millions of people around the world, race has a significant effect on their health and well-being. More to the point, he knows that a group's economic and political power help to determine which diseases scientists study. "We may be 99.9 percent alike at the level of DNA," Duster writes, "but if that were the end of the story, we could all pack up and go home" (Duster 2002:70).

Troy Duster, a sociologist at NYU, also teaches and directs the American Cultures Center at the University of California, Berkeley.

Let's Discuss

1. What other criteria besides the power of a racial or ethnic group could be used to determine how much research is done on diseases that affect the group?

2. What should a researcher do if a tribal leader refuses to allow members of the tribe to participate in a research project?

Source: Duster 2002.

Pentagon and World Trade Center, underscored the relative ease with which biotechnology can be used for hostile purposes. In fact, between 1975 and August 2000, terrorists created 342 incidents involving biological or chemical agents. Only about a third of those events were real attacks, and most caused few injuries and even fewer deaths. Yet because chemical and biological weapons are easy to use, these agents, which have come to be known as the poor person's nuclear bomb, are a source of increasing concern to governments the world over (Henry L. Stimson Center 2001; J. Miller et al. 2001; Mullins 2001; White 2002).

Use Your Sociological Imagination   www.mhhe.com/schaeferb

Try to imagine the world 100 years from now. On balance, is it a world in which technology contributes to or threatens people's well-being? In what ways?

Let's Discuss Are students concerned about biological warfare?

TECHNOLOGY AND SOCIETY

An automated teller machine (ATM) that identifies a person by his or her facial structure; a small device that sorts through hundreds of odors to ensure the safety of a chemical plant; a cell phone that recognizes its owner's voice—these are real-life examples of technologies that were science fiction a few decades ago. Today's computer chip cannot simply think, but can see, smell, and hear, too (Salkever 1999).

Such technological advances can dramatically transform the material culture. The word processor, pocket calculator, photocopying machine, and compact disc player have largely eliminated the typewriter, adding machine, mimeograph, and turntable—all of which were once technological advances themselves.

Moreover, technological change can also reshape *nonmaterial* culture. In the following sections, we will examine the effects of technological advances on culture and social interaction, social control, and stratification and inequality.

Culture and Social Interaction

In Chapter 3, we emphasized that language is the foundation of every culture. From a functionalist perspective, language can bring members of a society together and promote cultural integration. However, from a conflict perspective, the use of language can intensify divisions between groups and societies—just look at the battles over language in the United States, Canada, and many other societies.

How will social interaction be transformed by the growing availability of electronic forms of communication? Will people turn to e-mail, websites, and faxes rather than to telephone conversations and face-to-face meetings? Certainly, the technological shift to the telephone reduced letter writing as a means of maintaining kinship and friendship ties. For this reason, some people worry that computers and other forms of electronic communication may be socially isolating. Sociologist Sherry Turkle (1999) has warned that some individuals may become so gratified by their online lives that they may lose touch with their families, friends, and work responsibilities.

Yet Turkle (1995, 1999) has found positive effects from Internet usage as well. Over a 10-year period, she made anonymous visits to chat rooms and multiuser domains (MUDs), which allow people to assume new identities in role-playing games. She also conducted face-to-face interviews with more than 1,000 people who communicate by e-mail and participate actively in MUDs.

Distinguishing between users' on-screen personae and their real identities, Turkle concluded that many MUD users' lives were enhanced by the opportunity to engage in role playing and "become someone else." A new sense of self had emerged, she wrote, that was "decentered and multiple." In making this observation, Turkle was expanding on George Herbert Mead's notion of self (Nass and Moon 2000).

One obvious form of online role playing is gender switching. In a 1999 study, researchers found that 40 percent of their subjects had presented themselves online as a member of the opposite sex. Yet gender switching does not appear to dominate online communication. Even among the gender-switched, the majority of subjects in this study spent only about 10 percent of their time online disguised as the opposite sex (L. Roberts and Parks 1999).

If electronic communication can facilitate social interaction within a community—if it can create ties among people in different communities or even countries who "meet" in chat rooms or MUDs—then has it created a new interactive world known as cyberspace? The term *cyberspace* was introduced in 1984 by William Gibson, a Canadian science fiction writer. He came up with the term after he walked by a video arcade and noticed the intensity of the players hunched over their screens. Gibson felt that video game enthusiasts "develop a belief that there's some kind of actual space behind the screen. Some place that you can't see but you know is there" (Elmer-DeWitt 1995:4; Turkle 2004).

The emergence of cyberspace can be viewed as yet another step away from Ferdinand Tönnies's concept of the familiar, intimate *Gemeinschaft* and toward the comparatively impersonal *Gesellschaft*—yet another way in which social cohesion is being eroded in contemporary society. Critics of electronic communication question whether nonverbal communication, voice inflections, and other forms of interpersonal interaction will be lost as people turn to e-mail and chat rooms (P. Schaefer 1995; Schellenberg 1996).

But while some people think that by opening up the world to cyberspace interaction, we may have reduced face-to-face interaction, others have reached a different conclusion. Researchers surveyed more than 2,000 households nationwide to assess the impact of the Internet on the everyday lives of its users. Parents reported that they often surfed the web together with their children, and that the Internet had had little effect on their children's interactions with friends. Researchers concluded that about two-thirds of the people in the United States are using the Internet more than ever, without sacrificing their social lives (Cha 2000; P. Howard et al. 2001; Nie 2001).

Y

Social Control

A data entry employee pauses to say hello to a colleague. A checker at the supermarket takes a moment to banter with a customer. A telephone representative takes too much time helping callers. Each of these situations is subject to computer surveillance. Given the absence of strong protective legislation, employees in the United States are subject to increasing and pervasive supervision by computer.

Supervisors have always scrutinized the performance of workers, but with so much work now being handled electronically, the possibilities for surveillance have risen dramatically. According to a 2001 study, one-third of the online workforce is under continuous electronic surveillance. With Big Brother watching and listening in more and more, the danger is that electronic monitoring will become a substitute for effective management, or worse, lead to perceptions of unfairness and intrusiveness (T. Levin et al. 2002; Schulman 2001).

In recent years, a new type of corporate surveillance has emerged. A number of Internet sites have been highly critical of the operations of various corporations. On McSpotlight, one could find attacks on nutritional practices at McDonald's; on Up Against the Wal, one could study advice on how to fight the opening of a new Wal-Mart store. The Internet sites of such "anticorporate vigilantes" are generally protected by the First Amendment, but powerful corporations are carefully monitoring them in an attempt to counteract their activities (Neuborne 1996).

Technological advances have also created the possibility of a new type of white-collar crime: computer crime. It is now possible to gain access to a computer without leaving home, and to carry out embezzlement or electronic fraud without leaving a trace. One report released in 2000 put cybercrime losses by big businesses at $10 billion in the United States alone. Typically, discussions of computer crime focus on computer theft and on problems caused by "hackers," but widespread use of computers has facilitated many new ways of participating in deviant behavior. Consequently, greatly expanded police resources may be needed to deal with online child molesters, prostitution rings, software pirates, con artists, and other types of computer criminal. There

"Keystroke! ... Keystroke! ... Keystroke!"

is now a Computer Crime and Intellectual Property section of the Justice Department. The consensus of the heads of the section is that these cases are increasing and becoming more difficult to solve (Piller 2000).

Not all the technological advances relevant to social control have been electronic in nature. DNA data banks have given police a powerful new weapon for solving crimes; they have also opened the way to freeing wrongfully convicted citizens. From 1993 through May 2004, 15 death row inmates were released on the basis of DNA evidence. Efforts are under way to make such testing and other forms of DNA evidence as easily available as fingerprinting. While appropriate safeguards must be devised, the creation of DNA data banks has the potential to revolutionize law enforcement in the United States—especially in the prosecution of sex crimes, for which biological evidence is telling (Death Penalty Information Center 2004b).

Another connection between technology and social control is the use of computer databases and electronic verification of documents to reduce illegal immigration to the United States, especially from Muslim nations. While they are concerned about the issue of illegal entry, many Arab Americans, Hispanics, and Asian Americans nevertheless believe that *their* privacy, rather than that of Whites, is most likely to be infringed by government authorities. In the next section we will consider more fully how technological changes can intensify stratification and inequality based on race, ethnicity, and other factors.

Methods A study revealed that one-third of the online workforce is under continuous electronic surveillance.
Classroom Tip Computer crime and other forms of white-collar crime were examined in Chapter 8.

Let's Discuss We have seen that crimes such as rape and domestic violence are underreported. Is there reason to suspect that computer crime may also be underreported?
Web Resource Remind students there is a crossword puzzle for this chapter. They can link to the puzzle through the student center of the Online Learning Center (www.mhhe.com/schaefer6).

FIGURE 16-1

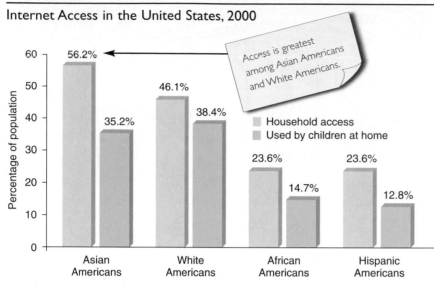

Internet Access in the United States, 2000

Source: Newburger 2001:3–4.

Stratification and Inequality

"Today we stand at the brink of becoming two societies, one largely white and plugged in and the other black and unplugged." This is how Black historian Henry Lewis Gates, Jr., starkly describes today's "digital divide" (Gates 1999:A15). Stratification is a continuing theme in sociology. Thus far, there is little evidence to suggest that technology will reduce inequality; in fact, it may only intensify it. Technology is costly, so it is generally impossible to introduce it to everyone simultaneously. Who gets access first? Conflict theorists contend that as we travel further and further along the electronic frontier, through advances such as telecommuting and the Internet, the disenfranchised poor may become isolated from mainstream society in an "information ghetto," just as racial and ethnic minorities have traditionally been subjected to residential segregation (DiMaggio et al. 2001).

Available data show clear differences in the use of computers based on class, race, and ethnicity. A national study released in 2001 estimated that only 14 percent of households earning less than $15,000 had access to the Internet, compared to 79 percent of those with incomes of $75,000 or more. Moreover, 56 percent of Asian American households and 46 percent of White households used the Internet, compared with 24 percent of Hispanic and African American households (see Figure 16-1).

This issue goes beyond individual interest or lack of interest in computers. Accessibility is a major concern. According to a study by the Consumer Federation of America and the National Association for the Advancement of Colored People (NAACP), accessibility to computer networks through fiber-optic corridors (the "information superhighway") may bypass poor neighborhoods and minority populations. The researchers concluded that regional telephone companies' plans for these advanced communications networks target affluent areas and may lead to an exclusionary "electronic redlining" that resembles discrimination in fields such as banking, real estate, and insurance (Lieberman 1999; Lohr 1994).

Industry executives counter that they have repeatedly stated their intention to deploy the information superhighway to *all* areas. Congress has proposed regulatory legislation to ensure equal access to the information superhighway by mandating the wiring of schools, libraries, and hospitals. And several communities, such as Manchester, New Hampshire, and Oakland, California, have recently arranged for computer hookups in publicly built low-income housing.

The issue of technology and inequality is especially sensitive when viewed in cross-cultural perspective. Although industrialization has dramatically improved many workers' standard of living, it has allowed elites to amass untold wealth. Moreover, the activities of multinational corporations have increased the inequality between industrialized core nations such as the United States, Germany, and Japan and peripheral developing countries.

Use Your Sociological Imagination www.mhhe.com/schaefer6

One hundred years from now, how might society have changed? Will people be as free as they are today? Will the differences among social classes be more or less pronounced than they are now? What about the differences among nations, races, religions, and ethnic groups?

The Issue

According to BBC News, the average city dweller is seen on closed-circuit TV about 300 times a day. Preposterous, you say? Look around you. In train stations and lobbies, on street corners and in elevators, the electronic eye is watching you. In some places, digital cameras may be snapping your picture and sending it to a computer that compares it to the photos of known criminals. You may not want to know about it, but your phone calls, e-mails, credit card purchases, and other forms of electronic communication are all being monitored in some way or other (Rheingold 2003).

Not all these means of surveillance are used for crime prevention. Much of the data organizations gather about you is used for marketing purposes, or compiled for resale to other organizations or individuals. While many people consider such activities an invasion of privacy, at this point in the United States, privacy laws have so many loopholes, it is often difficult to distinguish between legally and illegally gathered data. The other side of this coin is censorship—the fear that in an attempt to protect citizens' privacy, government will restrict the flow of electronic information too much. Not everyone is worried about censorship, however; many people think the government should be allowed to ban pornography on the Internet.

The Setting

The typical consumer in the United States is included in dozens of marketing databases. These lists may seem innocent enough at first. Does it really matter if companies can buy lists of our names, addresses, and telephone numbers? Part of the problem is that computer technology has made it increasingly easy for any individual, business firm, or government agency to retrieve and store more and more information about any of us.

For the average U.S. citizen, the question of how much free expression should be permitted on the Internet relates to the issue of pornography. Pornographic websites have proliferated, especially since the Supreme Court struck down federal legislation to regulate "indecent" words and images in 1997. Some of the X-rated material is perfectly legal, if inappropriate for children. Some sites are clearly illegal, such as those that serve the needs of pedophiles who prey on young children. Others are morally and legally ambiguous, such as the sites that post images taken by cameras aimed up the skirts of unsuspecting women in public places.

In other countries, censorship of the Internet is the major issue. For instance, the People's Republic of China bans independent reporting in online discussion groups that are not approved by the government. Also prohibited are discussion of sensitive issues, such as economic failures, and Web postings that challenge the Communist party (Magnier 2004).

Sociological Insights

In this technological age, the complex issue of privacy versus censorship can be considered an illustration of culture lag. As usual, the material culture (technology) is changing faster than the nonmaterial culture (norms for controlling the use of technology).

Functionalists point to the Internet's manifest function of facilitating communication. They identify its latent function as providing a way for groups with few resources to communicate with tens of millions of people. In this arena, poorly financed groups ranging from hate organizations to special interest groups can vie with powerful, wealthy interests. Thus, functionalists would see technology as fostering communication. The issue of censorship depends on how one views the content of the message; the issue of privacy, on how information is used.

Viewed from a conflict perspective, however, there is an ever-present danger that a society's most powerful groups will use technological advances to invade the privacy of the less powerful. In the past, totalitarian governments have routinely done so, in an effort to stifle dissent and maintain political and social control. Civil liberties advocates remind us that the same abuses can occur in the United States if citizens are not vigilant in protecting their right to privacy.

If anything, however, people seem to be less vigilant today about maintaining their privacy than they were before the information age. Young people who have grown up browsing the Internet seem to accept the existence of the "cookies" and "spyware" they may pick up while surfing. They have become accustomed to adult surveillance of their conversation in electronic chatrooms. Many see no risk in providing personal information about themselves to the strangers they meet online. Little wonder that college professors find their students do not appreciate the political significance of their right to privacy (Turkle 2004).

Let's Discuss Does your college have provisions to protect the privacy of e-mail communications?
Classroom Tip See "Identity Theft in Cyberspace" (Class Discussion Topics).

Student Alert Review William F. Ogburn's concepts of culture lag, material culture, and nonmaterial culture in Chapter 3.
Theory Functionalist and conflict views of the Internet
Theory From a conflict view, there is danger that technological advances will be used to invade the privacy of the less powerful and will intensify injustice.

Interactionists view the debate over privacy and censorship as one that parallels the concerns people have in any social interaction. Just as we may disapprove of some associations that relatives or friends have with other people, we express concern over controversial websites. We may attempt to monitor both. Obviously, the Internet facilitates interactions with a broad range of people, with minimal likelihood of detection compared to face-to-face interactions. Moreover, one can easily move a website from one country to another, avoiding not only detection but also prosecution.

Policy Initiatives

In 1986, the federal government passed the Electronic Communications Privacy Act. Wire communications—defined as use of the human voice in telephone and cordless calls—are highly protected. They cannot be subjected to surveillance unless a prosecutor obtains authorization from both the U.S. attorney general and a federal judge. In contrast, telegrams, faxes, and e-mail can be monitored with the approval of a judge (Eckenwiler 1995).

In 1996, the Communications Decency Act made it a federal crime to transmit "indecent" or "patently offensive" material over the Internet without maintaining safeguards to ensure that children cannot see it. Private e-mail and online chat room communications with anyone under the age of 18 were subjected to the same standard (Fernández 1996; Lappin 1996).

Civil liberties advocates insisted that such governmental action infringes on private communications between consenting adults and inevitably limits freedom of speech. Organizations such as the American Civil Liberties Union (ACLU), the American Library Association, the American Society of Newspaper Editors, and the National Writers Union supported lawsuits challenging the constitutionality of the Communications Decency Act. In 1997, the Supreme Court declared major parts of the act unconstitutional. The Court called government attempts to regulate content on the Internet an attack on the First Amendment guarantee of freedom of speech (Fernández 1996; Harmon 1998).

One month after the terrorist attacks of September 11, 2001, however, Congress passed the USA PATRIOT Act, which empowered authorities to move quickly against terrorist threats. As a result, legal checks on surveillance by law enforcement officers have been relaxed. Federal agencies are now freer to gather data electronically, including the credit card receipts and banking records of both citizens and foreign residents.

Both at home and abroad, the U.S. government has been developing a reputation for opposing efforts to protect people's privacy. For example, in 1998 the Center for

Public Integrity, a nonpartisan research organization, issued a report that criticized the government for failing to pass legislation protecting the confidentiality of medical records. In another case, a U.S. Navy investigator persuaded America Online to reveal the identity of a sailor who had described himself online as gay. In 1998, both the Navy and America Online were forced to reach settlements for violating the sailor's privacy. At the same time, the United States has been vocal in opposing efforts by the European Union to implement a tough new law designed to protect citizens from computer-age privacy invasions. The U.S. technology industry does not want access to information blocked, since information is vital to global commerce. While a compromise is likely, this case

The 1974 motion picture *The Conversation,* in which Gene Hackman eavesdropped on other characters' conversations in their homes and in the park, raised an alarm among viewers concerned about their privacy. A generation later, citizens wonder how much of their electronic communication is monitored, and for what purposes.

Theory Interactionist view of the Internet
Policy Pointer How is each major social institution of our society affected by the privacy and censorship issues raised in this policy section?

illustrates the fine line between safeguarding privacy and stifling the electronic flow of information (Center for Public Integrity 1998; Locy 2004; Shenon 1998).

The conflict over privacy and censorship is far from over. As technology continues to advance in the twenty-first century, new battles are sure to be fought.

Let's Discuss

1. What are some of the ways that people can obtain information about you? Are you aware of any databases that contain information about your personal life?

2. Do you think corporations and employers have a right to monitor employees' e-mail and phone calls? Why or why not?

3. Are you more concerned about government censorship of electronic communication or about unauthorized invasion of your privacy? As a policymaker, how would you balance these concerns?

GETTING INVOLVED

To get involved in the debate over privacy and censorship, visit this text's Online Learning Center, which offers links to relevant websites. Check out the Social Policy section on the Online Learning Center as well; it provides survey data on U.S. public opinion regarding this issue.

CHAPTER RESOURCES

Summary

Social change is significant alteration over time in behavior patterns and culture, including norms and values. Sometimes social change is promoted by *social movements,* but more often it is the unintended effect of technological progress. This chapter examines sociological theories of social change and social movements, resistance to change, and the impact of *technology* on the future of society.

1. A group will not mobilize into a **social movement** unless there is a shared perception that its *relative deprivation* can be ended only through collective action.
2. The success of a social movement depends in good part on effective *resource mobilization.*
3. *New social movements* tend to focus on more than just economic issues, and often cross national boundaries.
4. Early advocates of the *evolutionary theory* of social change believed that society was progressing inevitably toward a higher state.
5. Talcott Parsons, a leading advocate of functionalist theory, viewed society as being in a natural state of equilibrium, or balance.
6. Conflict theorists see change as having crucial significance, since it is needed to correct social injustices and inequalities.

7. In general, those with a disproportionate share of society's wealth, status, and power have a *vested interest* in preserving the status quo, and will resist change.
8. The period of maladjustment when a nonmaterial culture is still struggling to adapt to new material conditions is known as *culture lag.*
9. The core industrialized nations have a virtual monopoly on information technology, making the peripheral nations dependent on them both for technology and for the information it provides.
10. Advances in biotechnology have raised difficult ethical questions about genetic engineering and the sex selection of fetuses.
11. Computer and video technology have facilitated supervision, control, and even domination of workers and citizens by employers and the government.
12. Conflict theorists fear that the disenfranchised poor may become isolated from mainstream society in an "information ghetto," just as racial and ethnic minorities have been subjected to residential segregation.
13. Computer technology has made it increasingly easy for any individual, business firm, or government agency to retrieve more and more

information about any of us, thereby infringing on our privacy. How much government should re-

strict access to electronic information is an important public policy issue.

Critical Thinking Questions

1. Select one social movement that is currently working for change in the United States. Analyze that movement, drawing on the concepts of relative deprivation, resource mobilization, and false consciousness.

2. In the last few years we have witnessed phenomenal growth in the use of cellular phones around the world. Analyze this form of material culture in terms of culture lag. Consider usage, government regulation, and privacy issues.

3. Consider one of the technological advances discussed in the section on technology and the future. Analyze this new technology, focusing on whether it is likely to increase or reduce inequality in the coming decades. Whenever possible, address issues of gender, race, ethnicity, and class, as well as inequality between nations.

Key Terms

Culture lag   A period of maladjustment when the nonmaterial culture is still struggling to adapt to new material conditions. (page 432)

Equilibrium model   The functionalist view that society tends toward a state of stability or balance. (430)

Evolutionary theory   A theory of social change that holds that society is moving in a definite direction. (429)

False consciousness   A term used by Karl Marx to describe an attitude held by members of a class that does not accurately reflect their objective position. (427)

Luddites   Rebellious craft workers in 19th-century England who destroyed new factory machinery as part of their resistance to the industrial revolution. (433)

Multilinear evolutionary theory   A theory of social change that holds that change can occur in several ways and does not inevitably lead in the same direction. (429)

New social movement   An organized collective activity that addresses values and social identities, as well as improvements in the quality of life. (428)

Relative deprivation   The conscious feeling of a negative discrepancy between legitimate expectations and present actualities. (426)

Resource mobilization   The ways in which a social movement utilizes such resources as money, political influence, access to the media, and personnel. (427)

Social change   Significant alteration over time in behavior patterns and culture, including norms and values. (425)

Social movement   An organized collective activity to bring about or resist fundamental change in an existing group or society. (425)

Technology   Information about how to use the material resources of the environment to satisfy human needs and desires. (434)

Unilinear evolutionary theory   A theory of social change that holds that all societies pass through the same successive stages of evolution and inevitably reach the same end. (429)

Vested interests   Those people or groups who will suffer in the event of social change, and who have a stake in maintaining the status quo. (432)

TECHNOLOGY RESOURCES

Internet Connection

*Note: While all the URLs listed were current as of the printing of this book, these sites often change. Please check our website (**www.mhhe.com/schaefer6**) for updates, hyperlinks, and exercises related to these sites.*

1. Some people feel overwhelmed by our culture's emphasis on consumerism. The Center for a New American Dream is a social movement whose goal—among others—is to help Americans reduce the role of consumerism in their lives. To see how members of this movement aim to change society, visit the center's website (**www.newdream.org**).

2. Life in the United States has changed a great deal over the past century. To get a feel for some of the changes, visit the website of the Library of Congress (**lcweb2.loc.gov/wpaintro/wpahome. html**) and go to the American Life Histories section. There you can page through life-history interviews with hundreds of Americans, all collected in the 1930s as part of the WPA Federal Writers' Project.

Online Learning Center with PowerWeb

If you need to review for a test, visit the student center in the Online Learning Center at **www.mhhe.com/ schaefer6** and link to the True/False Quiz. It will test your knowledge and give you immediate feedback on incorrect answers.

Reel Society Interactive Movie CD-ROM 2.0

Reel Society 2.0 can be used to spark discussion about the following topic from this chapter:

• Theories of Social Change

Glossary

Numbers following the definitions indicate pages where the terms were identified. Consult the index for further page references.

Absolute poverty A minimum level of subsistence that no family should be expected to live below. (215)

Achieved status A social position that a person attains largely through his or her own efforts. (107, 204)

Activity theory An interactionist theory of aging that suggests that elderly people who remain active and socially involved will be best-adjusted. (288)

Adoption In a legal sense, a process that allows for the transfer of the legal rights, responsibilities, and privileges of parenthood to a new legal parent or parents. (311)

Affirmative action Positive efforts to recruit minority group members or women for jobs, promotions, and educational opportunities. (250, 383)

Ageism A term coined by Robert N. Butler to refer to prejudice and discrimination based on a person's age. (290)

Agrarian society The most technologically advanced form of preindustrial society. Members are engaged primarily in the production of food, but increase their crop yield through such innovations as the plow. (120)

Alienation The condition of estrangement or dissociation from the surrounding society. (136)

Amalgamation The process through which a majority group and a minority group combine to form a new group. (253)

Anomie Durkheim's term for the loss of direction felt in a society when social control of individual behavior has become ineffective. (10, 185)

Anomie theory of deviance Robert Merton's theory of deviance as an adaptation of socially prescribed goals or of the means governing their attainment, or both. (185)

Anticipatory socialization Processes of socialization in which a person "rehearses" for future positions, occupations, and social relationships. (91)

Anti-Semitism Anti-Jewish prejudice. (263)

Apartheid The former policy of the South African government designed to maintain the separation of Blacks and other non-Whites from the dominant Whites. (254)

Argot Specialized language used by members of a group or subculture. (69)

Ascribed status A social position assigned to a person by society without regard for the person's unique talents or characteristics. (106, 203)

Asset-based community development (ABCD) An approach to community development in which planners first identify a community's strengths and then seek to mobilize those assets. (405)

Assimilation The process through which a person forsakes his or her own cultural tradition to become part of a different culture. (253)

Authority Institutionalized power that is recognized by the people over whom it is exercised. (367)

Bilateral descent A kinship system in which both sides of a person's family are regarded as equally important. (303)

Bilingualism The use of two or more languages in a particular setting, such as the workplace or schoolroom, treating each language as equally legitimate. (73)

Birthrate The number of live births per 1,000 population in a given year. Also known as the *crude birthrate*. (393)

Black power A political philosophy promoted by many younger Blacks in the 1960s that supported the creation of Black-controlled political and economic institutions. (256)

Borderlands The area of common culture along the border between Mexico and the United States. (231)

Bourgeoisie Karl Marx's term for the capitalist class, comprising the owners of the means of production. (207)

Brain drain The immigration to the United States and other industrialized nations of skilled workers, professionals, and technicians who are desperately needed in their home countries. (411)

Bureaucracy A component of formal organization that uses rules and hierarchical ranking to achieve efficiency. (136)

Bureaucratization The process by which a group, organization, or social movement becomes increasingly bureaucratic. (138)

Capitalism An economic system in which the means of production are held largely in private hands and the main incentive for economic activity is the accumulation of profits. (207, 362)

Caste A hereditary rank, usually religiously dictated, that tends to be fixed and immobile. (204)

Causal logic The relationship between a condition or variable and a particular consequence, with one event leading to the other. (31)

Census An enumeration, or counting, of a population. (392)

Charismatic authority Max Weber's term for power made legitimate by a leader's exceptional personal or emotional appeal to his or her followers. (368)

Class A group of people who have a similar level of wealth and income. (208)

Class consciousness In Karl Marx's view, a subjective awareness held by members of a class regarding their common vested interests and need for collective political action to bring about social change. (207)

Classical theory An approach to the study of formal organizations that views workers as being motivated almost entirely by economic rewards. (139)

Class system A social ranking based primarily on economic position in which achieved characteristics can influence social mobility. (205)

Closed system A social system in which there is little or no possibility of individual social mobility. (220)

Coalition A temporary or permanent alliance geared toward a common goal. (135)

Code of ethics The standards of acceptable behavior developed by and for members of a profession. (41)

Cognitive theory of development Jean Piaget's theory that children's thought progresses through four stages of development. (88)

Cohabitation The practice of living together as a male–female couple without marrying. (316)

Colonialism The maintenance of political, social, economic, and cultural dominance over a people by a foreign power for an extended period. (222)

Communism As an ideal type, an economic system under which all property is communally owned and no social distinctions are made on the basis of people's ability to produce. (364)

Community A spatial or political unit of social organization that gives people a sense of belonging, based either on shared residence in a particular place or on a common identity. (390)

Concentric-zone theory A theory of urban growth devised by Ernest Burgess that sees growth in terms of a series of rings radiating from the central business district. (401)

Conflict perspective A sociological approach that assumes that social behavior is best understood in terms of conflict or tension between competing groups. (15)

Conformity Going along with peers—individuals of our own status, who have no special right to direct our behavior. (175)

Contact hypothesis An interactionist perspective stating that in cooperative circumstances, interracial contact between people of equal status will reduce prejudice. (252)

Content analysis The systematic coding and objective recording of data, guided by some rationale. (40)

Control group The subjects in an experiment who are not introduced to the independent variable by the researcher. (39)

Control theory A view of conformity and deviance that suggests that our connection to members of society leads us to systematically conform to society's norms. (180)

Control variable A factor that is held constant to test the relative impact of an independent variable. (34)

Corporate welfare Tax breaks, direct payments, and grants that the government makes to corporations. (234)

Correlation A relationship between two variables in which a change in one coincides with a change in the other. (31)

Correspondence principle A term used by Bowles and Gintis to refer to the tendency of schools to promote the values expected of individuals in each social class and to prepare students for the type of job typically held by members of their class. (347)

Counterculture A subculture that deliberately opposes certain aspects of the larger culture. (71)

Creationism A literal interpretation of the Bible regarding the creation of humanity and the universe, used to argue that evolution should not be presented as established scientific fact. (354)

Credentialism An increase in the lowest level of education needed to enter a field. (346)

Crime A violation of criminal law for which some governmental authority applies formal penalties. (191)

Cult Due to stereotyping, this term has been abandoned by sociologists in favor of *new religious movement*. (340)

Cultural relativism The viewing of people's behavior from the perspective of their own culture. (72)

Cultural transmission A school of criminology that argues that criminal behavior is learned through social interactions. (187)

Cultural universal A common practice or belief found in every culture. (58, 327)

Culture The totality of learned, socially transmitted customs, knowledge, material objects, and behavior. (55)

Culture lag Ogburn's term for a period of maladjustment when the nonmaterial culture is still struggling to adapt to new material conditions. (61, 432)

Culture shock The feeling of surprise and disorientation that people experience when they encounter cultural practices that are different from their own. (71)

Curanderismo Latino folk medicine, a form of holistic health care and healing. (415)

Death rate The number of deaths per 1,000 population in a given year. Also known as the *crude death rate.* (393)

Defended neighborhood A neighborhood that residents identify through defined community borders and a perception that adjacent areas are geographically separate and socially different. (404)

Degradation ceremony An aspect of the socialization process within some total institutions, in which people are subjected to humiliating rituals. (92)

Deindustrialization The systematic, widespread withdrawal of investment in basic aspects of productivity, such as factories and plants. (378)

Demographic transition A term used to describe the change from high birthrates and death rates to low birthrates and death rates that occurs during a nation's development. (394)

Demography The scientific study of population. (391)

Denomination A large, organized religion that is not officially linked with the state or government. (339)

Dependency theory An approach to stratification that contends that industrialized nations continue to exploit developing countries for their own gain. (224)

Dependent variable The variable in a causal relationship that is subject to the influence of another variable. (31)

Deviance Behavior that violates the standards of conduct or expectations of a group or society. (180)

Differential association A theory of deviance proposed by Edwin Sutherland that holds that violation of rules results from exposure to attitudes favorable to criminal acts. (187)

Diffusion The process by which a cultural item spreads from group to group or society to society. (59)

Discovery The process of making known or sharing the existence of an aspect of reality. (58)

Discrimination The denial of opportunities and equal rights to individuals and groups because of prejudice or other arbitrary reasons. (245)

Disengagement theory A functionalist theory of aging introduced by Cumming and Henry that implicitly suggests that society and the aging individual mutually sever many of their relationships. (286)

Domestic partnership Two unrelated adults who share a mutually caring relationship, reside together, and agree to be jointly responsible for their dependents, basic living expenses, and other common necessities. (322)

Dominant ideology A set of cultural beliefs and practices that helps to maintain powerful social, economic, and political interests. (68, 157, 211)

Downsizing Reductions taken in a company's workforce as part of deindustrialization. (379)

Dramaturgical approach A view of social interaction, popularized by Erving Goffman, in which people are seen as theatrical performers. (18, 86)

Dyad A two-member group. (134)

Dysfunction An element or process of a society that may disrupt the social system or reduce its stability. (14)

Ecclesia A religious organization that claims to include most or all members of a society, and is recognized as the national or official religion. (338)

Economic system The social institution through which goods and services are produced, distributed, and consumed. (361)

Education A formal process of learning in which some people consciously teach while others adopt the social role of learner. (327)

Egalitarian family An authority pattern in which spouses are regarded as equals. (303)

Elite model A view of society as being ruled by a small group of individuals who share a common set of political and economic interests. (371)

Endogamy The restriction of mate selection to people within the same group. (307)

Environmental justice A legal strategy based on claims that racial minorities are subjected disproportionately to environmental hazards. (382)

Equilibrium model Talcott Parsons's functionalist view that society tends toward a state of stability or balance. (430)

Established sect A religious group that is the outgrowth of a sect, yet remains isolated from society. (339)

Estate system A system of stratification under which peasants were required to work land leased to them by nobles in exchange for military protection and other services. Also known as *feudalism.* (204)

Esteem The reputation that a specific person has earned within an occupation. (212)

Ethnic group A group that is set apart from others primarily because of its national origin or distinctive cultural patterns. (241)

Ethnocentrism The tendency to assume that one's own culture and way of life represent the norm or are superior to all others. (72, 245)

Ethnography The study of an entire social setting through extended systematic observation. (38)

Evolutionary theory A theory of social change that holds that society is moving in a definite direction. (429)

Exogamy The requirement that people select a mate outside certain groups. (307)

Experiment An artificially created situation that allows a researcher to manipulate variables. (39)

Experimental group The subjects in an experiment who are exposed to an independent variable introduced by a researcher. (39)

Exploitation theory A Marxist theory that views racial subordination in the United States as a manifestation of the class system inherent in capitalism. (251)

Expressiveness A term used by Parsons and Bales to refer to concern for the maintenance of harmony and the internal emotional affairs of the family. (277)

Extended family A family in which relatives—such as grandparents, aunts, or uncles—live in the same home as parents and their children. (301)

Face-work A term used by Erving Goffman to refer to the efforts people make to maintain the proper image and avoid public embarrassment. (86)

False consciousness A term used by Karl Marx to describe an attitude held by members of a class that does not accurately reflect their objective position. (207, 427)

Familism Pride in the extended family, expressed through the maintenance of close ties and strong obligations to kinfolk outside the immediate family. (309)

Family A set of people related by blood, marriage or some other agreed-upon relationship, or adoption, who share the primary responsibility for reproduction and caring for members of society. (301)

Feminist view A sociological approach that views inequity in gender as central to all behavior and organization. (16)

Fertility The level of reproduction in a society. (390)

Focus group A group of 10 to 15 people assembled by a researcher to discuss a predetermined topic, guided by a moderator. (133)

Folkway A norm governing everyday behavior whose violation raises comparatively little concern. (65)

Force The actual or threatened use of coercion to impose one's will on others. (367)

Formal norm A norm that has been written down and that specifies strict punishments for violators. (65)

Formal organization A group designed for a special purpose and structured for maximum efficiency. (135)

Formal social control Social control that is carried out by authorized agents, such as police officers, judges, school administrators, and employers. (177)

Functionalist perspective A sociological approach that emphasizes the way in which the parts of a society are structured to maintain its stability. (14)

Gatekeeping The process by which a relatively small number of people in the media industry control what material eventually reaches the audience. (156)

Gemeinschaft A term used by Ferdinand Tönnies to describe a close-knit community, often found in rural areas, in which strong personal bonds unite members. (118)

Gender roles Expectations regarding the proper behavior, attitudes, and activities of males and females. (93, 272)

Generalized other A term used by George Herbert Mead to refer to the attitudes, viewpoints, and expectations of society as a whole that a child takes into account in his or her behavior. (86)

Genocide The deliberate, systematic killing of an entire people or nation. (253)

Gerontology The scientific study of the sociological and psychological aspects of aging and the problems of the aged. (286)

Gesellschaft A term used by Ferdinand Tönnies to describe a community, often urban, that is large and impersonal, with little commitment to the group or consensus on values. (119)

Glass ceiling An invisible barrier that blocks the promotion of a qualified individual in a work environment because of the individual's gender, race, or ethnicity. (247, 282)

Globalization The worldwide integration of government policies, cultures, social movements, and financial markets through trade and the exchange of ideas. (59, 224)

Goal displacement Overzealous conformity to official regulations of a bureaucracy. (137)

Group Any number of people with similar norms, values, and expectations who interact with one another on a regular basis. (110, 130)

Growth rate The difference between births and deaths, plus the difference between immigrants and emigrants, per 1,000 population. (393)

Hawthorne effect The unintended influence that observers of experiments can have on their subjects. (39)

Health As defined by the World Health Organization, a state of complete physical, mental, and social well-being, and not merely the absence of disease and infirmity. (409)

Health maintenance organization An organization that provides comprehensive medical services for a preestablished fee. (418)

Hidden curriculum Standards of behavior that are deemed proper by society and are taught subtly in schools. (346)

Homophobia Fear of and prejudice against homosexuality. (273)

Horizontal mobility The movement of an individual from one social position to another of the same rank. (220)

Horticultural society A preindustrial society in which people plant seeds and crops rather than merely subsist on available foods. (120)

Human ecology An area of study concerned with the interrelationships between people and their environment. (380, 400)

Human relations approach An approach to the study of formal organizations that emphasizes the role of people, communication, and participation in a bureaucracy and tends to focus on the informal structure of the organization. (139)

Hunting-and-gathering society A preindustrial society in which people rely on whatever foods and fibers are readily available in order to survive. (120)

Hypothesis A speculative statement about the relationship between two or more variables. (31)

Ideal type A construct or model for evaluating specific cases. (11, 136)

Impression management A term used by Erving Goffman to refer to the altering of the presentation of the self in order to create distinctive appearances and satisfy particular audiences. (86)

Incest taboo The prohibition of sexual relationships between certain culturally specified relatives. (307)

Incidence The number of new cases of a specific disorder occurring within a given population during a stated period. (413)

Income Salaries and wages. (203)

Independent variable The variable in a causal relationship that causes or influences a change in a second variable. (31)

Industrial city A relatively large city characterized by open competition, an open class system, and elaborate specialization in the manufacturing of goods. (399)

Industrial society A society that depends on mechanization to produce its goods and services. (120, 362)

Infant mortality rate The number of deaths of infants under one year old per 1,000 live births in a given year. (393)

Influence The exercise of power through a process of persuasion. (367)

Informal economy Transfers of money, goods, or services that are not reported to the government. (364)

Informal norm A norm that is generally understood but not precisely recorded. (65)

Informal social control Social control that is carried out casually by ordinary people through such means as laughter, smiles, and ridicule. (177)

In-group Any group or category to which people feel they belong. (132)

Innovation The process of introducing a new idea or object to a culture through discovery or invention. (58)

Institutional discrimination The denial of opportunities and equal rights to individuals and groups that results from the normal operations of a society. (249, 279)

Instrumentality An emphasis on tasks, a focus on more distant goals, and a concern for the external relationship between one's family and other social institutions. (277)

Interactionist perspective A sociological approach that generalizes about everyday forms of social interaction in order to explain society as a whole. (17)

Intergenerational mobility Changes in the social position of children relative to their parents. (220)

Interview A face-to-face or telephone questioning of a respondent to obtain desired information. (36)

Intragenerational mobility Changes in social position within a person's adult life. (220)

Invention The combination of existing cultural items into a form that did not exist before. (58)

Iron law of oligarchy A principle of organizational life developed by Robert

Michels under which even democratic organizations will eventually develop into bureaucracies ruled by a few individuals. (138)

Issei Japanese immigrants to the United States. (259)

Kinship The state of being related to others. (303)

Labeling theory An approach to deviance that attempts to explain why certain people are viewed as deviants while others engaged in the same behavior are not. (188)

Labor union Organized workers who share either the same skill or the same employer. (144)

Laissez-faire A form of capitalism under which people compete freely, with minimal government intervention in the economy. (362)

Language An abstract system of word meanings and symbols for all aspects of culture; includes gestures and other nonverbal communication. (62)

Latent function An unconscious or unintended function that may reflect hidden purposes. (14)

Law Governmental social control. (65, 178)

Legal-rational authority Max Weber's term for power made legitimate by law. (368)

Liberation theology Use of a church, primarily Roman Catholicism, in a political effort to eliminate poverty, discrimination, and other forms of injustice from a secular society. (334)

Life chances Max Weber's term for people's opportunities to provide themselves with material goods, positive living conditions, and favorable life experiences. (218)

Life-course approach A research orientation in which sociologists and other social scientists look closely at the social factors that influence people throughout their lives, from birth to death. (90)

Life expectancy The median number of years a person can be expected to live under current mortality conditions. (393)

Looking-glass self A concept used by Charles Horton Cooley that emphasizes the self as the product of our social interactions. (84)

Luddites Rebellious craft workers in 19th-century England who destroyed new factory machinery as part of their resistance to the industrial revolution. (433)

Machismo A sense of virility, personal worth, and pride in one's maleness. (309)

Macrosociology Sociological investigation that concentrates on large-scale phenomena or entire civilizations. (13)

Manifest function An open, stated, and conscious function. (14)

Mass media Print and electronic means of communication that carry messages to widespread audiences. (152)

Master status A status that dominates others and thereby determines a person's general position in society. (107)

Material culture The physical or technological aspects of our daily lives. (61)

Matriarchy A society in which women dominate in family decision making. (303)

Matrilineal descent A kinship system in which only the relatives of the mother are significant. (303)

McDonaldization The process by which the principles of the fast-food restaurant are coming to dominate more and more sectors of American society as well as of the rest of the world. (130)

Mechanical solidarity A collective consciousness that emphasizes group solidarity, characteristic of societies with minimal division of labor. (118)

Megalopolis A densely populated area containing two or more cities and their surrounding suburbs. (400)

Microsociology Sociological investigation that stresses the study of small groups, often through experimental means. (13)

Minority group A subordinate group whose members have significantly less control or power over their own lives than the members of a dominant or majority group have over theirs. (241)

Model or **ideal minority** A group that despite past prejudice and discrimination, succeeds economically, socially, and educationally without resorting to confrontations with Whites. (259)

Monogamy A form of marriage in which one woman and one man are married only to each other. (302)

Monopoly Control of a market by a single business firm. (362)

Morbidity rate The incidence of disease in a given population. (414)

Mores Norms deemed highly necessary to the welfare of a society. (65)

Mortality rate The incidence of death in a given population. (414)

Multilinear evolutionary theory A theory of social change that holds that change can occur in several ways, and does not inevitably lead in the same direction. (429)

Multinational corporation A commercial organization that is headquartered in one country but does business throughout the world. (224)

Multiple-nuclei theory A theory of urban growth developed by Harris and Ullman that views growth as emerging from many centers of development, each of which reflects a particular urban need or activity. (401)

Narcotizing dysfunction The phenomenon in which the media provide such massive amounts of information that the audience becomes numb and fails to act on the information, regardless of how compelling the issue. (156)

Natural science The study of the physical features of nature and the ways in which they interact and change. (6)

Negotiated order A social structure that derives its existence from the social interactions through which people define and redefine its character. (106)

Negotiation The attempt to reach agreement with others concerning some objective. (105)

Neocolonialism Continuing dependence of former colonies on foreign countries. (222)

New religious movement (NRM) or **cult** A small, secretive religious group that represents either a new religion or a major innovation of an existing faith. (340)

New social movement An organized collective activity that addresses values and social identities, as well as improvements in the quality of life. (428)

New urban sociology An approach to urbanization that considers the interplay of local, national, and worldwide forces and their effect on local space, with special emphasis on the impact of global economic activity. (402)

Nisei Children born in the United States to the Issei. (260)

Nonmaterial culture Ways of using material objects, as well as customs, beliefs, philosophies, governments, and patterns of communication. (61)

Nonverbal communication The sending of messages through the use of gestures, facial expressions, and postures. (17)

Norm An established standard of behavior maintained by a society. (64)

Nuclear family A married couple and their unmarried children living together. (301)

Obedience Compliance with higher authorities in a hierarchical structure. (175)

Objective method A technique for measuring social class that assigns individuals to classes on the basis of criteria such as occupation, education, income, and place of residence. (212)

Observation A research technique in which an investigator collects information through direct participation and/or by closely watching a group or community. (38)

Open system A social system in which the position of each individual is influenced by his or her achieved status. (220)

Operational definition An explanation of an abstract concept that is specific enough to allow a researcher to assess the concept. (30)

Opinion leader Someone who influences the opinions and decisions of others through day-to-day personal contacts and communication. (162)

Organic solidarity A collective consciousness that rests on mutual interdependence, characteristic of societies with a complex division of labor. (118)

Organized crime The work of a group that regulates relations among criminal enterprises involved in illegal activities, including prostitution, gambling, and the smuggling and sale of illegal drugs. (192)

Out-group A group or category to which people feel they do not belong. (132)

Patriarchy A society in which men dominate in family decision making. (303)

Patrilineal descent A kinship system in which only the relatives of the father are significant. (303)

Peace The absence of war, or more broadly, a proactive effort to develop cooperative relations among nations. (375)

Personality A person's typical patterns of attitudes, needs, characteristics, and behavior. (81)

Peter principle A principle of organizational life, originated by Laurence J. Peter, according to which every employee within a hierarchy tends to rise to his or her level of incompetence. (138)

Pluralism Mutual respect for one another's cultures among the various groups in a society, which allows minorities to express their own cultures without experiencing prejudice. (255)

Pluralist model A view of society in which many competing groups within the community have access to government so that no single group is dominant. (373)

Political system The social institution that is founded on a recognized set of procedures for implementing and achieving society's goals. (361)

Politics In Harold Lasswell's words, "who gets what, when, and how." (367)

Polyandry A form of polygamy in which a woman may have more than one husband at the same time. (302)

Polygamy A form of marriage in which an individual may have several husbands or wives simultaneously. (302)

Polygyny A form of polygamy in which a man may have more than one wife at the same time. (302)

Population pyramid A special type of bar chart that shows the distribution of the population by gender and age. (395)

Postindustrial city A city in which global finance and the electronic flow of information dominate the economy. (399)

Postindustrial society A society whose economic system is engaged primarily in the processing and control of information. (121)

Postmodern society A technologically sophisticated society that is preoccupied with consumer goods and media images. (121)

Power The ability to exercise one's will over others. (208, 367)

Power elite A term used by C. Wright Mills for a small group of military, industrial, and government leaders who control the fate of the United States. (371)

Preindustrial city A city of only a few thousand people that is characterized by a relatively closed class system and limited mobility. (398)

Prejudice A negative attitude toward an entire category of people, often an ethnic or racial minority. (245)

Prestige The respect and admiration that an occupation holds in a society. (212)

Prevalence The total number of cases of a specific disorder that exist at a given time. (414)

Primary group A small group characterized by intimate, face-to-face association and cooperation. (130)

Profane The ordinary and commonplace elements of life, as distinguished from the sacred. (329)

Professional criminal A person who pursues crime as a day-to-day occupation, developing skilled techniques and enjoying a certain degree of status among other criminals. (191)

Proletariat Karl Marx's term for the working class in a capitalist society. (207)

Protestant ethic Max Weber's term for the disciplined work ethic, this-worldly concerns, and rational orientation to life emphasized by John Calvin and his followers. (334)

Qualitative research Research that relies on what is seen in the field or naturalistic settings more than on statistical data. (36)

Quantitative research Research that collects and reports data primarily in numerical form. (36)

Questionnaire A printed or written form used to obtain information from a respondent. (36)

Racial group A group that is set apart from others because of obvious physical differences. (241)

Racial profiling Any arbitrary action initiated by an authority based on race, ethnicity, or national origin rather than on a person's behavior. (251)

Racism The belief that one race is supreme and all others are innately inferior. (245)

Random sample A sample for which every member of an entire population has the same chance of being selected. (33)

Reference group Any group that individuals use as a standard for evaluating themselves and their own behavior. (133)

Relative deprivation The conscious feeling of a negative discrepancy between legitimate expectations and present actualities. (426)

Relative poverty A floating standard of deprivation by which people at the bottom of a society, whatever their lifestyles, are judged to be disadvantaged *in comparison with the nation as a whole.* (215)

Reliability The extent to which a measure produces consistent results. (34)

Religion According to Émile Durkheim, a unified system of beliefs and practices relative to sacred things. (327)

Religious belief A statement to which members of a particular religion adhere. (336)

Religious experience The feeling or perception of being in direct contact with the ultimate reality, such as a divine being, or of being overcome with religious emotion. (337)

Religious ritual A practice required or expected of members of a faith. (336)

Remittances The monies that immigrants return to their families of origin. Also called *migradollars.* (232)

Research design A detailed plan or method for obtaining data scientifically. (36)

Resocialization The process of discarding former behavior patterns and accepting new ones as part of a transition in one's life. (91)

Resource mobilization The ways in which a social movement utilizes such resources as money, political influence, access to the media, and personnel. (427)

Rite of passage A ritual marking the symbolic transition from one social position to another. (89)

Role conflict The situation that occurs when incompatible expectations arise from two or more social positions held by the same person. (109)

Role exit The process of disengagement from a role that is central to one's self-identity in order to establish a new role and identity. (110)

Role strain The difficulty that arises when the same social position imposes conflicting demands and expectations. (109)

Role taking The process of mentally assuming the perspective of another and responding from that imagined viewpoint. (85)

Routine activities theory The notion that criminal victimization increases when motivated offenders and suitable targets converge. (187)

Sacred Elements beyond everyday life that inspire awe, respect, and even fear. (329)

Sample A selection from a larger population that is statistically representative of that population. (31)

Sanction A penalty or reward for conduct concerning a social norm. (66, 175)

Sapir-Whorf hypothesis A hypothesis concerning the role of language in shaping our interpretation of reality. It holds that language is culturally determined. (62)

Science The body of knowledge obtained by methods based on systematic observation. (6)

Scientific management approach Another name for the *classical theory* of formal organizations. (139)

Scientific method A systematic, organized series of steps that ensures maximum objectivity and consistency in researching a problem. (29)

Secondary analysis A variety of research techniques that make use of previously collected and publicly accessible information and data. (40)

Secondary group A formal, impersonal group in which there is little social intimacy or mutual understanding. (131)

Second shift The double burden—work outside the home followed by child care and housework—that many women face and few men share equitably. (283)

Sect A relatively small religious group that has broken away from some other religious organization to renew what it considers the original vision of the faith. (339)

Secularization The process through which religion's influence on other social institutions diminishes. (327)

Segregation The physical separation of two groups of people in terms of residence, workplace, and social events; often imposed on a minority group by a dominant group. (254)

Self A distinct identity that sets us apart from others. (84)

Serial monogamy A form of marriage in which a person may have several spouses in his or her lifetime, but only one spouse at a time. (302)

Sexism The ideology that one sex is superior to the other. (279)

Sexual harassment Behavior that occurs when work benefits are made contingent on sexual favors (as a quid pro quo), or when touching, lewd comments, or the exhibition of pornographic material creates a "hostile environment" in the workplace. (280)

Sick role Societal expectations about the attitudes and behavior of a person viewed as being ill. (409)

Significant other A term used by George Herbert Mead to refer to an individual who is most important in the development of the self, such as a parent, friend, or teacher. (86)

Single-parent family A family in which only one parent is present to care for children. (314)

Slavery A system of enforced servitude in which some people are owned by other people. (204)

Small group A group small enough for all members to interact simultaneously—that is, to talk with one another or at least be well acquainted. (134)

Social change Significant alteration over time in behavior patterns and culture, including norms and values. (425)

Social constructionist perspective An approach to deviance that emphasizes the role of culture in the creation of the deviant identity. (189)

Social control The techniques and strategies for preventing deviant human behavior in any society. (174)

Social epidemiology The study of the distribution of disease, impairment, and general health status across a population. (413)

Social inequality A condition in which members of a society have different amounts of wealth, prestige, or power. (20, 203)

Social institution An organized pattern of beliefs and behavior centered on basic social needs. (115)

Social interaction The ways in which people respond to one another. (104)

Socialism An economic system under which the means of production and distribution are collectively owned. (363)

Socialization The lifelong process in which people learn the attitudes, values, and behaviors appropriate for members of a particular culture. (81)

Social mobility Movement of individuals or groups from one position in a society's stratification system to another. (220)

Social movement An organized collective activity to bring about or resist fundamental change in an existing group or society. (425)

Social network A series of social relationships that links a person directly to others, and through them indirectly to still more people. (111)

Social role A set of expectations for people who occupy a given social position or status. (109)

Social science The study of the social features of humans and the ways in which they interact and change. (6)

Social structure The way in which a society is organized into predictable relationships. (104)

Societal-reaction approach Another name for *labeling theory*. (188)

Society A fairly large number of people who live in the same territory, are relatively independent of people outside it, and participate in a common culture. (58)

Sociobiology The systematic study of how biology affects human social behavior. (61)

Sociocultural evolution The process of change and development in human societies that results from cumulative growth in their stores of cultural information. (119)

Sociological imagination An awareness of the relationship between an individual and the wider society. (3)

Sociology The systematic study of social behavior and human groups. (3)

Status A term used by sociologists to refer to any of the full range of socially defined positions within a large group or society. (106)

Status group A term used by Max Weber to refer to people who have the same prestige or lifestyle, independent of their class positions. (208)

Stereotype An unreliable generalization about all members of a group that does not recognize individual differences within the group. (157, 244)

Stigma A label used to devalue members of certain social groups. (181)

Stratification A structured ranking of entire groups of people that perpetuates unequal economic rewards and power in a society. (203)

Subculture A segment of society that shares a distinctive pattern of mores, folkways, and values that differs from the pattern of the larger society. (68)

Suburb According to the Census Bureau, any territory within a metropolitan area that is not included in the central city. (405)

Surveillance function The collection and distribution of information concerning events in the social environment. (155)

Survey A study, generally in the form of an interview or questionnaire, that provides researchers with information about how people think and act. (36)

Symbolic ethnicity An ethnic identity that emphasizes concerns such as ethnic food or political issues rather than deeper ties to one's ethnic heritage. (263)

Symbol A gesture, object, or word that forms the basis of human communication. (85)

Teacher-expectancy effect The impact that a teacher's expectations about a student's performance may have on the student's actual achievements. (348)

Technology Information about how to use the material resources of the environment to satisfy human needs and desires. (61, 119, 434)

Telecommuter An employee who works full-time or part-time at home rather than in an outside office, and who is linked to supervisor and colleagues through computer terminals, phones, and fax machines. (143)

Terrorism The use or threat of violence against random or symbolic targets in pursuit of political aims. (376)

Theory In sociology, a set of statements that seeks to explain problems, actions, or behavior. (8)

Total fertility rate (TFR) The average number of children born alive to any woman, assuming that she conforms to current fertility rates. (393)

Total institution A term coined by Erving Goffman to refer to an institution that regulates all aspects of a person's life under a single authority, such as a prison, the military, a mental hospital, or a convent. (91)

Tracking The practice of placing students in specific curriculum groups on the basis of their test scores and other criteria. (347)

Traditional authority Legitimate power conferred by custom and accepted practice. (367)

Trained incapacity The tendency of workers in a bureaucracy to become so specialized that they develop blind spots and fail to notice obvious problems. (136)

Triad A three-member group. (134)

Underclass The long-term poor who lack training and skills. (216)

Unilinear evolutionary theory A theory of social change that holds that all societies pass through the same successive stages of evolution and inevitably reach the same end. (429)

Urban ecology An area of study that focuses on the interrelationships between people and their environment in urban areas. (401)

Urbanism A term used by Louis Wirth to describe distinctive patterns of social behavior evident among city residents. (399)

Validity The degree to which a measure or scale truly reflects the phenomenon under study. (34)

Value A collective conception of what is considered good, desirable, and proper—or bad, undesirable, and improper—in a culture. (66)

Value neutrality Max Weber's term for objectivity of sociologists in the interpretation of data. (44)

Variable A measurable trait or characteristic that is subject to change under different conditions. (31)

Verstehen The German word for "understanding" or "insight"; used by Max Weber to stress the need for sociologists to take into account the subjective meanings people attach to their actions. (11)

Vertical mobility The movement of an individual from one social position to another of a different rank. (220)

Vested interests Veblen's term for those people or groups who will suffer in the event of social change, and who have a stake in maintaining the status quo. (432)

Victimization survey A questionnaire or interview given to a sample of the population to determine whether people have been victims of crime. (195)

Victimless crime A term used by sociologists to describe the willing exchange among adults of widely desired, but illegal, goods and services. (194)

Vital statistics Records of births, deaths, marriages, and divorces that are gathered through a registration system maintained by governmental units. (392)

Voluntary association An organization established on the basis of common interest, whose members volunteer or even pay to participate. (140)

War Conflict between organizations that possess trained combat forces equipped with deadly weapons. (374)

Wealth An inclusive term encompassing all a person's material assets, including land, stocks, and other types of property. (203)

White-collar crime Illegal acts committed by affluent, "respectable" individuals in the course of business activities. (193)

World systems analysis Immanuel Wallerstein's view of the global economic system as one divided between certain industrialized nations that control wealth and developing countries that are controlled and exploited. (222, 402)

Xenocentrism The belief that the products, styles, or ideas of one's society are inferior to those that originate elsewhere. (72)

Zero population growth (ZPG) The state of a population in which the number of births plus immigrants equals the number of deaths plus emigrants. (397)

References

AARP. 2001. *Beyond 50—A Report to the Nation on Economic Security.* Washington, DC: AARP.

———. 2003. Home page. Accessed May 12 (www.aarp.org).

———. 2004. *Global Report on Aging.* Washington, DC: AARP.

ABC News/*Washington Post.* 2004. "Same-Sex Marriage Opponents More Apt to Call It a Voting Issue." March 10, 2004. Accessed March 30 (abcnews.go.com/sections/us/PollVault/PollVault.html).

Abercrombie, Nicholas, Bryan S. Turner, and Stephen Hill, eds. 1990. *Dominant Ideologies.* Cambridge, MA: Unwin Hyman.

———, Stephen Hill, and Bryan S. Turner. 1980. *The Dominant Ideology Thesis.* London: George Allen and Unwin.

Aberle, David E., A. K. Cohen, A. K. Davis, M. J. Leng, Jr., and F. N. Sutton. 1950. "The Functional Prerequisites of a Society." *Ethics* 60 (January):100–111.

Abrahams, Ray G. 1968. "Reaching an Agreement over Bridewealth in Labwor, Northern Uganda: A Case Study." Pp. 202–215 in *Councils in Action,* edited by Audrey Richards and Adam Kuer. Cambridge: Cambridge University Press.

Abrahamson, Mark. 1978. *Functionalism.* Englewood Cliffs, NJ: Prentice Hall.

Acosta, R. Vivian, and Linda Jean Carpenter. 2001. "Women in Intercollegiate Sport: A Longitudinal Study: 1977–1998." Pp. 302–308 in *Sport in Contemporary Society: An Anthology.* 6th ed., edited by D. Stanley Eitzen. New York: Worth.

Adam, Barry D. 1995. *The Rise of a Gay and Lesbian Movement.* Rev. ed. New York: Twayne.

Addams, Jane. 1910. *Twenty Years at Hull-House.* New York: Macmillan.

———. 1930. *The Second Twenty Years at Hull-House.* New York: Macmillan.

Adler, Freda. 1975. *Sisters in Crime: The Rise of the New Female Criminal.* New York: McGraw-Hill.

———, Gerhard O. W. Mueller, and William S. Laufer. 2004. *Criminology and the Criminal Justice System.* 5th ed. New York: McGraw-Hill.

Adler, Patricia, and Peter Adler. 2003. "The Promise and Pitfalls of Going into the Field." *Contexts* (Spring):41–47.

———, Peter Adler, and John M. Johnson. 1992. "Street Corner Society Revisited." *Journal of Contemporary Ethnography* 21 (April):3–10.

AFL-CIO. 2001. *More Workers Are Choosing a Voice at Work.* Accessed April 18 (www.aflcio.org/voiceatwork/morejoin/htm).

Aizcorbe, Ana M., Arthur B. Kennickell, and Kevin B. Moore. 2003. "Recent Changes in U.S. Family Finances: Evidence from the 1998 and 2001 Survey of Consumer Finances." *Federal Reserve Bulletin* (January):1–32.

Alain, Michel. 1985. "An Empirical Validation of Relative Deprivation." *Human Relations* 38 (8):739–749.

Alba, Richard D. 1990. *Ethnic Identity: The Transformation of White America.* New Haven, CT: Yale University Press.

Albas, Daniel, and Cheryl Albas. 1988. "Aces and Bombers: The Post-Exam Impression Management Strategies of Students." *Symbolic Interaction* 11 (Fall):289–302.

Albiniak, P. 2000. "TV's Drug Deal." *Broadcasting and Cable,* January 17, pp. 3, 148.

Albrecht, Gary L., Katerine D. Steelman, and Michael Bury. 2001. *Handbook of Disabilities Study.* Thousand Oaks, CA: Sage.

Alexander, Alison, and Janice Hanson, eds. 2001. *Taking Sides: Mass Media and Society.* 6th ed. New York: McGraw-Hill/Dushkin.

Alfino, Mark, John S. Caputo, and Robin Wynyard. 1998. *McDonaldization Revisited: Critical Essays on Consumer Culture.* Westport, CT: Praeger.

Al Jazeera. 2004. "Political Disconnect Hinders US PR." News release, January 13. Accessed February 2 (http:english.aljazeera.net).

Allen, Bern P. 1978. *Social Behavior: Fact and Falsehood.* Chicago: Nelson-Hall.

Allen, John L. 2003. *Student Atlas of World Geography.* 3rd ed. New York: McGraw-Hill.

Allport, Gordon W. 1979. *The Nature of Prejudice.* 25th anniversary ed. Reading, MA: Addison-Wesley.

Alwin, Duane F. 2002. "Generations X, Y, and Z: Are They Changing America?" *Contexts* (Fall/Winter):42–51.

Alzheimer's Association. 1999. "Statistics/Prevalence." Accessed January 10, 2000 (www.alz.org/facts/stats.htm).

Amato, Paul, and Alan Booth. 1997. *A Generation at Risk.* Cambridge, MA: Harvard University Press.

Amato, Paul R. 2001. "What Children Learn from Divorce." *Population Today,* January, pp. 1, 4.

———, and Juliana M. Sobolewski. 2001. "The Effects of Divorce and Marital Discord on Adult Children's Psychological Well-Being." *American Sociological Review* 66 (December): 900–921.

American Academy of Cosmetic Surgery. 2004. "2003 Estimates Total Number of Patients Treated by All U.S.-Based AACS Members." Accessed February 21 (www.cosmeticsurgery.org/media_center/stats/statistics.html).

American Association of University Women. 1998. *Gender Gaps: Where Schools Still Fail Our Children.* Washington, DC: AAUW.

American Bar Association. 1999. "Commission on Domestic Violence." Accessed July 20 (www.abanet.org/domviol/stats.html).

American Civil Liberties Union. 2000. "State and Local Laws Protecting Lesbians and Gay Men against Workplace Discrimination." Accessed January 19 (www.aclu.org/issues/gay/gaylaws.html).

American Civil Liberties Union of Northern California. 2002. *Caught in the Backlash: Stories from Northern California.* San Francisco: ACLU of Northern California.

American Jewish Committee. 2001. "2000 Annual Survey of American Jewish Opinion." Accessed October 25 (www.ajc.org/pre/survey2000.htm).

American Lung Association. 2003. "Scenesmoking." Accessed December 19 (www.scenesmoking.org).

Americans for Medical Rights. 2003. *The State of Medipot.* Washington: Marijuana Policy Project.

American Sociological Association. 1993. *The Sociology Major as Preparation for Careers in Business and Organizations.* Washington, DC: American Sociological Association.

———. 1995. *The Sociological Advantage.* Washington, DC: American Sociological Association.

———. 1997. *Code of Ethics.* Washington, DC: American Sociological Association. Available (www.asanet.org/members/ecoderev.html).

———. 2001. *Data Brief: Profile of ASA Membership.* Washington, DC: American Sociological Association.

———. 2002. *Careers in Sociology.* 6th ed. Washington, DC: American Sociological Association.

———. 2004. *Guide to Graduate Departments of Sociology, 2004.* Washington, DC: American Sociological Association.

Amway. 1999. "Amway Asia Pacific Applauds China Commitment to Remove All Restrictions on Direct Selling." News release, April 9. Accessed March 4, 2003 (www.amway.com).

———. 2003. *Our Story.* Accessed March 4 (www.amway.org).

Andersen, Margaret. 1997. *Thinking about Women: Sociological Perspectives on Sex and Gender.* 4th ed. Boston: Allyn and Bacon.

Anderson, Craig A., and Brad J. Bushman. 2001. "Effects of Violent Video Games on Aggressive Behavior, Aggressive Cognition, Aggressive Affect, Physiological Arousal, and Prosocial Behavior: A Meta-Analytic Review of Scientific Literature." *Psychological Science* 12, (5):353–359.

Anderson, Elijah. 1978. *A Place on the Corner.* Chicago: University of Chicago Press.

———. 1990. *Streetwise: Race, Class, and Change in an Urban Community.* Chicago: University of Chicago Press.

———. 1999. *Code of the Streets.* New York: Norton.

———, and Molly Moore. 1993. "The Burden of Womanhood." *Washington Post National Weekly Edition* 10 (March 22–28):6–7.

Angier, Natalie. 1998. "Drugs, Sports, Body Image and G.I. Joe." *New York Times,* December 22, section D. pp. 1, 3.

Anti-Defamation League. 2003. *ADL Audit of Anti-Semitic Incidents, 1982–2002 (National).* (www.adl.org).

AOL Time Warner. 2003. *Factbook.* New York: AOL Time Warner.

Argetsinger, Amy, and Jonathan Krim. 2002. "Stopping the Music." *Washington Post National Weekly Edition* 20 (December 2), p. 20.

Arias, Elizabeth. 2004. "United States Life Tables, 2001." *National Vital Statistics Report,* February 18.

Armer, J. Michael, and John Katsillis. 1992. "Modernization Theory." Pp. 1299–1304 in *Encyclopedia of Sociology,* Vol. 4, edited by Edgar F. Borgatta and Marie L. Borgatta. New York: Macmillan.

Aronowitz, Stanley, and William Di Fazio. 1994. *The Jobless Future: Sci-Tech and Dogma of Work.* Minneapolis: University of Minneapolis.

Aronson, Elliot. 1999. *The Social Animal.* 8th ed. New York: Worth.

Arora, Raksha. 2004. "Is War Still Necessary in the 21st Century?" Gallup Poll Tuesday Briefing May 11 (www.gallup.com).

Asset-Based Community Development Institute. 2001. *Our Mission.* Accessed September 21 (www.northwestern.edu/IPR/abcd. html).

Associated Press. 1998. "Environmental Test Case Averted." *Christian Science Monitor,* September 21, p. 18.

———. 2001. "Member of the Dwindling Shaker Sect." *Chicago Tribune,* June 20, p. 11.

———. 2003. "House Rejects Attempt to Block Sex-Study Grants." *Seattle Post-Intelligencer,* July 11, p. A13.

Astin, Alexander, Sarah A. Parrott, William S. Korn, and Linda J. Sax. 1994. *The American Freshman: Thirty Year Trends.* Los Angeles: Higher Education Research Institute.

Atchley, Robert C. 1985. *The Social Forces in Later Life: An Introduction to Social Gerontology.* 4th ed. Belmont, CA: Wadsworth.

Austin, April. 2002. "Cellphones and Strife in Congo." *Christian Science Monitor* (December 5):11.

Axtell, Roger E. 1990. *Do's and Taboos around the World.* 2d ed. New York: John Wiley and Sons.

Azumi, Koya, and Jerald Hage. 1972. *Organizational Systems.* Lexington, MA: Heath.

Babad, Elisha Y., and P. J. Taylor. 1992. "Transparency of Teacher Expectancies Across Language, Cultural Boundaries." *Journal of Educational Research* 86:120–125.

Baer, Douglas, James Curtis, and Edward Grabb. 2000. *Has Voluntary Association Activity Declined? A Cross-National Perspective.* Paper presented at the annual meeting of the American Sociological Association, Washington, DC.

Bainbridge, William Sims. 1999. "Cyberspace: Sociology's Natural Domain." *Contemporary Sociology* 28 (November):664–667.

Baker, Therese L. 1999. *Doing Social Research.* 3d ed. New York: McGraw-Hill.

Barr, Cameron W. 2002. "Top Arab TV Network to Hit US Market." *Christian Science Monitor* (December 26):1, 7.

Barrett, David B., and Todd M. Johnson. 2001. "Worldwide Adherents of Selected Religions by Six Continental Areas, Mid-2000." In *Britannica Book of the Year 2001,* p. 302. Chicago: Encyclopedia Britannica.

———. 2004. "Worldwide Adherents of All Religions by Six Continental Areas, Mid-2003." P. 280 In *Britannica Book of the Year 2004,* p. 280. Chicago, IL: Encyclopedia Britannica.

Barron, Milton L. 1953. "Minority Group Characteristics of the Aged in American Society." *Journal of Gerontology* 8:477–482.

Bassiouni, M. Cherif. 2002. "Sexual Slavery Crosses Moral and National Boundaries." *Chicago Tribune,* February 17, sec. 2, pp. 1, 5.

Basso, Keith H. 1972. "Ice and Travel among the Fort Norman Slave: Folk Taxonomies and Cultural Rules." *Language in Society* 1 (March):31–49.

Bates, Colleen Dunn. 1999. "Medicine's Gender Gap." *Shape,* October.

Bauerlein, Monika. 1996. "The Luddites Are Back." *Utne Reader* (March/April):24, 26.

Bauman, Kurt J. 1999. "Extended Measures of Well-Being: Meeting Basic Needs." *Current Population Reports,* Ser. p. 70, No. 67. Washington, DC: U.S. Government Printing Office.

———, and Nikki L. Graf. 2003. "Education Attainment: 2000." *Census 2000 Brief,* no.

C2KBR-24. Washington, DC: U.S. Government Printing Office.

Beagan, Brenda L. 2001. "'Even If I Don't Know What I'm Doing I Can Make It Look Like I Know What I'm Doing': Becoming a Doctor in the 1990s." *Canadian Review of Sociology and Anthropology* 38:275–292.

Bean, Frank, Steven Trejo, Randy Capps, and Michael Tyler. 2001. *The Latino Middle Class: Myth, Reality and Potential.* Claremont, CA: The Thomás Rivera Policy Institute.

Becerra, Rosina M. 1999. "The Mexican-American Family." Pp. 153–171 in *Ethnic Families in America: Patterns and Variations,* 4th ed., edited by Charles H. Mindel, Robert W. Habenstein, and Roosevelt Wright, Jr. Upper Saddle River, NJ: Prentice Hall.

Becker, Howard S. 1952. "Social Class Variations in the Teacher-Pupil Relationship." *Journal of Educational Sociology* 25 (April):451–465.

———. 1963. *The Outsiders: Studies in the Sociology of Deviance.* New York: Free Press.

———, ed. 1964. *The Other Side: Perspectives on Deviance.* New York: Free Press.

———. 1973. *The Outsiders: Studies in the Sociology of Deviance.* Rev. ed. New York: Free Press.

Beeghley, Leonard. 1978. *Social Stratification in America: A Critical Analysis of Theory and Research.* Santa Monica, CA: Goodyear Publishing.

Bell, Daniel. 1953. "Crime as an American Way of Life." *Antioch Review* 13 (Summer):131–154.

———. 1999. *The Coming of Post-Industrial Society: A Venture in Social Forecasting.* With new foreword. New York: Basic Books.

Bell, Wendell. 1981. "Modernization." Pp. 186–187 in *Encyclopedia of Sociology.* Guilford, CT: DPG Publishing.

Bellafante, Ginia. 1998. "Feminism: It's All about Me!" *Time* 151 (June 20):54–62.

Belsie, Laurent. 2000. "Strange Webfellows." *Christian Science Monitor,* March 2, pp. 15–16.

———. 2001. "Rise of 'Home Alone' Crowd May Alter US Civic Life." *Christian Science Monitor,* May 24, pp. 1, 2.

Bendick, Marc, Jr., Charles W. Jackson, and J. Horacio Romero. 1993. *Employment Discrimination against Older Workers: An Experimental Study of Hiring Practices.* Washington, DC: Fair Employment Council of Greater Washington.

Bendix, B. Reinhard. 1968. "Max Weber." Pp. 493–502 in *International Encyclopedia of the Social Sciences,* edited by David L. Sills. New York: Macmillan.

Benford, Robert D. 1992. "Social Movements." Pp. 1880–1887 in *Encyclopedia of Sociology,* vol. 4, edited by Edgar F. Borgatta and Marie Borgatta. New York: Macmillan.

Benner, Richard S., and Susan Tyler Hitchcock. 1986. *Life after Liberal Arts.* Charlottesville: Office of Career Planning and Placement, University of Virginia.

Bennett, Vivienne. 1995. "Gender, Class, and Water: Women and the Politics of Water Service in Monterrey, Mexico." *Latin American Perspectives* 22 (September), pp. 76–99.

Berger, Peter, and Thomas Luckmann. 1966. *The Social Construction of Reality.* New York: Doubleday.

Berke, Richard L. 2001. "An Older Electorate, Potent and Unpredictable." *New York Times,* March 21, p. D8.

Berkeley Wellness Letter. 1990. "The Nest Refilled." 6 (February):1–2.

Berlin, Brent, and Paul Kay. 1991. *Basic Color Terms: Their Universality and Evolution.* Berkeley, CA: University of California Press.

Bernstein Richard. 2003. "An Aging Europe May Find Itself on the Sidelines." *New York Times,* June 29, p. 3.

Berry, Mary Frances. 2001. "Status Report on Probe of Election Practices in Florida During the 2000 Presidential Election." *Black Scholar* 31 (No. 2), pp. 2–5.

Bian, Yanjie. 2002. "Chinese Social Stratification and Social Mobility." Pp. 91–116 in *Annual Review of Sociology,* edited by Karen S. Cook and John Hagan. Palo Alto, CA: Annual Reviews.

Bianchi, Suzanne M., and Daphne Spain. 1996. "Women, Work, and Family in America." *Population Bulletin* 51 (December).

Bielby, Denise D., and William T. Bielby. 2002. "Hollywood Dreams, Harsh Realities: Writing for Film and Television." *Contexts* 1 (Fall/Winter):21–25.

Bielby, William T., and Denise D. Bielby. 1992. "I Will Follow Him: Family Ties, Gender-Role Beliefs, and Reluctance to Relocate for a Better Job." *American Journal of Sociology* 97 (March):1241–1267.

Billson, Janet Mancini, and Bettina J. Huber. 1993. *Embarking upon a Career with an Undergraduate Degree in Sociology.* 2d ed. Washington, DC: American Sociological Association.

Bishaw, Alemayehu, and John Iceland. 2003. "Poverty: 1999." *Census 2000 Brief* C2KBR-19. Washington, DC: U.S. Government Printing Office.

Biskupic, Joan. 2000. "Abortion Debate Will Continue to Rage." *USA Today,* June 29, p. 9A.

Black, Donald. 1995. "The Epistemology of Pure Sociology." *Law and Social Inquiry* 20 (Summer):829–870.

Blanchard, Fletcher A., Teri Lilly, and Leigh Ann Vaughan. 1991. "Reducing the Expression of Racial Prejudice." *Psychological Science* 2 (March):101–105.

Blandy, Richard. 2004. "300 Join Anti-War Protests." *The Sentinel,* Carlisle, PA, March 21.

Blau, Peter M., and Otis Dudley Duncan. 1967. *The American Occupational Structure.* New York: Wiley.

———, and Marshall W. Meyer. 1987. *Bureaucracy in Modern Society.* 3d ed. New York: Random House.

Blauner, Robert. 1972. *Racial Oppression in America.* New York: Harper and Row.

Bloom, Stephen G. 2000. *Postville: A Clash of Cultures in Heartland America.* San Diego, CA: Harcourt Brace.

Blumer, Herbert. 1955. "Collective Behavior." Pp. 165–198 in *Principles of Sociology,* 2d ed., edited by Alfred McClung Lee. New York: Barnes and Noble.

———. 1969. *Symbolic Interactionism: Perspective and Method.* Englewood Cliffs, NJ: Prentice Hall.

Boaz, Rachel Floersheim. 1987. "Early Withdrawal from the Labor Force." *Research on Aging* 9 (December):530–547.

Bok, Sissela. 1998. *Mayhem: Violence as Public Entertainment.* Reading, MA: Addison-Wesley.

Bond, James T., Ellen Galinsky, and Jennifer E. Swanberg. 1998. *The 1997 National Study of the Changing Work Force.* New York: Families and Work Institute.

Booth, William. 2000. "Has Our Can-Do Attitude Peaked?" *Washington Post National Weekly Edition* 17 (February 7):29.

Bornschier, Volker, Christopher Chase-Dunn, and Richard Rubinson. 1978. "Cross-National Evidence of the Effects of Foreign Investment and Aid on Economic Growth and Inequality: A Survey of Findings and a Reanalysis." *American Journal of Sociology* 84 (November):651–683.

Borosage, Robert L. 2003. "Class Welfare: Bush Style." *American Prospect* 14 (March):15–18.

Bottomore, Tom, and Maximilien Rubel, ed. 1956. *Karl Marx: Selected Writings in Sociology and Social Philosophy.* New York: McGraw-Hill.

Boudreaux, Richard. 2002. "Indian Rights Law Is Upheld in Mexico." *Los Angeles Times,* September 7, p. A3.

Bouvier, Leon F. 1980. "America's Baby Boom Generation: The Fateful Bulge." *Population Bulletin* 35 (April).

Bowles, Samuel, and Herbert Gintis. 1976. *Schooling in Capitalistic America: Educational Reforms and the Contradictions of Economic Life.* New York: Basic Books.

Bowling, Michael, Gene Lauver, Matthew J. Hickman, and Devon B. Adams. 2003. "Background Checks for Firearm Transfers, 2003." *Bureau of Justice Statistics Bulleton* September.

Bradsher, Keith. 2004. "Like Japan in the 1980's, China Poses Big Economic Challenge." *New York Times,* March 2, pp. A1, C2.

Brady Campaign. 2003. *Brady Campaign—Issue Briefs.* Accessed March 11 (www.bradycampaign.org).

Brady, David. 2003. "Rethinking the Sociological Measurement of Poverty." *Social Forces* 81 (March):715–752.

Brainard, Jeffrey. 2003. "Cloning Debate Moves to the States." *Chronicle of Higher Education* 49 (March 28):A22–A23.

Brainard, Lael, and Robert E. Litan. 2004. "'Offshoring' Service Jobs: Bane or Boom—and What to Do?" *Brookings Institute* Policy Brief (April), pp. 1–8.

Brannigan, Augustine. 1992. "Postmodernism." Pp. 1522–1525 in *Encyclopedia of Sociology,* vol. 3, edited by Edgar F. Borgatta and Marie L. Borgatta. New York: Macmillan.

Brannon, Robert. 1976. "Ideology, Myth, and Reality: Sex Equality in Israel." *Sex Roles* 6:403–419.

Braverman, Amy. 2002. "Open Door Sexuality." *University of Chicago Magazine* 95 (October): 20–21.

Braxton, Greg, and Dana Calvo. 2002. "Networks Come Under the Gun as Watchdogs Aim for Diversity." *Chicago Tribune,* June 4, sec. 5, p. 2.

Bray, James H., and John Kelly. 1999. *Stepfamilies: Love, Marriage, and Parenting in the First Decade.* New York: Broadway Books.

Brewer, Cynthia A., and Trudy A. Suchan. 2001. *Mapping Census 2000: The Geography of U.S. Diversity.* Washington, DC: U.S. Government Printing Office.

Brint, Steven. 1998. *Schools and Societies.* Thousand Oaks, CA: Pine Forge Press.

Brischetto, Robert R. 2001. "The Hispanic Middle Class Comes of Age." *Hispanic Business* 23 (December):21–22, 26.

Brittingham, Angela, and G. Patricia de la Cruz. 2004. *Ancestry: 2000. Census Brief* C2KBR-35. Washington, DC: U.S. Government Printing Office.

Brooke, James. 2003a. "The Power of Film: A Bond That Unites Koreans." *New York Times,* January 2.

Brown, David K. 2001. "The Social Sources of Educational Credentialism: Status Cultures, Labor Markets, and Organizations." *Sociology of Education.* 74 (Extra Issue):19–34.

Brown, Patricia Leigh. 2004. "For Children of Gays, Marriage Brings Joy." *New York Times,* March 19, p. A13.

Brown, Peter Harry, and Daniel G. Abel. 2002. *Outgunned: Up Against the NRA.* New York: The Free Press.

Brown, Robert McAfee. 1980. *Gustavo Gutierrez.* Atlanta: John Knox.

Brubaker, Bill. 2001. "A So-So Diagnosis." *Washington Post National Weekly Edition.* September 10, p. 34.

Bryant, Adam. 1999. "American Pay Rattles Foreign Partners." *New York Times,* January 17, sec. 6, pp. 1, 4.

Buckley, Stephen. 1997. "Left behind Prosperity's Door." *Washington Post National Weekly Edition,* March 24, pp. 8–9.

Budig, Michelle J. 2002. "Male Advantage and the Gender Composition of Jobs: Who Rides the Glass Escalator?" *Social Problems* 49 (2): 258–277.

Budrys, Grace. 2003. *Unequal Health: How Inequality Contributes to Health and Illness.* Lanham, MD: Rowman and Littlefield.

Bullard, Robert, D. 1993. *Dumping in Dixie: Race, Class, and Environmentalist Quality.* 2nd ed. Boulder, CO: Westin Press.

Bulle, Wolfgang F. 1987. *Crossing Cultures? Southeast Asian Mainland.* Atlanta: Centers for Disease Control.

Bumiller, Elisabeth. 2000. "Resolute Adversary of Divorce." *New York Times,* December 16, pp. A17, A19.

Bunzel, John H. 1992. *Race Relations on Campus: Stanford Students Speak.* Stanford, CA: Portable Stanford.

Bureau of Labor Statistics. 2002. "Number of Jobs Held Labor Market Activity, and Earnings Growth Among Young Baby Boomers." News release of August 27. (www.bls.gov/nls).

———. 2004a. "Union Affiliation of Employed Wage and Salary Workers by Occupation and Industry." Accessed January 26 (www.bls.gov/cps/home.htm#annual).

———. 2004b. "Current Labor Statistics." Accessed January 28 (www.bls.gov/opub/mlr/mlrhome.htm).

———. 2003. *Union Members in 2002.* Accessed February 28 (www.bls.gov).

Bureau of Primary Health Care. 1999. Home page. Accessed January 18, 2000 (www.bphc.hrsa.gov/bphcfactsheet.htm).

Bureau of the Census. 1975. *Historical Statistics of the United States, Colonial Times to 1970.* Washington, DC: U.S. Government Printing Office.

———. 1991. "Half of the Nation's Population Lives in Large Metropolitan Areas." Press release, February 21.

———. 1994. *Statistical Abstract of the United States, 1994.* Washington, DC: U.S. Government Printing Office.

———. 1998. "Race of Wife by Race of Husband." Internet release of June 10.

———. 2000a. *Statistical Abstract of the United States, 2000.* Washington, DC: U.S. Government Printing Office.

———. 2000b. "National Population Projections." Internet release of January 13. Accessed May 11 (www.census.gov/population/www/projection/natsum-T3html).

———. 2001a. *Statistical Abstract of the United States, 2001.* Washington, DC: U.S. Government Printing Office.

———. 2001b. *Hispanic 1997 Economic Census Survey of Minority-Owned Enterprises.* Series BC97CS-4. Washington, DC: U.S. Government Printing Office.

———. 2001c. *1997 Revenues for Women-Owned Businesses Show Continued Growth.* News release of April 4. Washington, DC: U.S. Government Printing Office.

———. 2002. *Statistical Abstract of the United States, 2002.* Washington, DC: U.S. Government Printing Office.

———. 2003a. *Statistical Abstract of the United States, 2003.* Washington, DC: U.S. Government Printing Office.

———. 2003b. *Census 2000.* Summary File 4 (www.factfinder.census.gov).

———. 2003c. *TM-PCT023 Percent of Persons of Arab Ancestry 2000.* Accessed March 4, 2004 (http://factfinder.census.gov).

———. 2003d. *Summary Tables on Language Use and English Ability, 2000* (PHC-T-20). Accessed January 14, 2004. (www.census.gov/population/www/cen2000/phc-t20.html).

———. 2003e. *Poverty in the United States: 2002.* Accessed May 5, 2004. (www.census.gov).

———. 2004a. *Statistical Abstract of the United States, 2003.* Washington, DC: U.S. Government Printing Office.

———. 2004b. *Interim Projections Consistent with Census 2000.* Released March 2004. Accessed March 21 (www.census.gov).

———. 2004c. "International Database Pyramids." Updates April 30 (www.census.gov/ipc/www/idbpyr.html).

———. 2004d. "Total Midyear Population for the World: 1950–2050." Updated April 30 (www.census.gov/ipc/www/worldpop.html.)

Burgess, Ernest W. 1925. "The Growth of the City." Pp. 47–62 in *The City,* edited by Robert E. Park, Ernest W. Burgess, and Roderick D. McKenzie. Chicago: University of Chicago Press.

Burghart, Tara. 2003. "Rogovin remembers the 'forgotten ones.'" *Chicago Tribune* (July 30), sect. 5, p. 6.

Burkett, Elinor. 2000. *The Baby Boom: How Family Friendly America Cheats the Childless.* New York: Free Press.

Burns, John R. 1998. "Once Widowed in India, Twice Scorned." *New York Times,* March 29, p. A1.

Bushway, Shawn D., and Anne Mourison Piehl. 2001. "Judging Judicial Discretion Legal Factors and Racial Discrimination Legal Factors and Racial Discrimination in Sentencing." *Law and Society Review* 35 (4):733–764.

Butler, Daniel Allen. 1998. *"Unsinkable": The Full Story.* Mechanicsburg, PA: Stackpole Books.

Butler, Robert N. 1990. "A Disease Called Ageism." *Journal of American Geriatrics Society* 38 (February):178–180.

Caesar, Lena G., and David R. Williams. 2002. *The ASHA Leader Online: Socioculture and the Delivery of Health Care: Who Gets What and Why.* Accessed December 1 (www.asha.org).

Campo-Flores, Arian. 2000. "Brown against Brown." *Newsweek* 136 (September 18): 49–51.

Camus, Albert. 1948. *The Plague.* New York: Random House.

Caplan, Ronald L. 1989. "The Commodification of American Health Care." *Social Science and Medicine* 28 (11):1139–1148.

Caplow, Theodore, and Louis Hicks. 2002. *Systems of War and Peace.* 2nd ed. Lanham, MD: University Press of America.

Carey, Anne R., and Elys A. McLean. 1997. "Heard It Through the Grapevine?" *USA Today,* September 15, p. B1.

Carroll, John. 2003. "The Good Doctor." *American Way* (July 15):26–31.

Carter, Bill, and Jim Rutenberg. 2003. "Shows' Creators Say Television Will Suffer in New Climate." *New York Times,* June 3, pp. C1, C8.

Carty, Win. 1999. "Greater Dependence on Cars Leads to More Pollution in World's Cities." *Population Today* 27 (December):1–2.

Casper, Lynne M., and Loretta E. Bass. 1998. "Voting and Registration in the Election of November 1996." *Current Population Reports,* ser. P-20, no. 504. Washington, DC: U.S. Government Printing Office.

Castañeda, Jorge G. 1995. "Ferocious Differences." *Atlantic Monthly* 276 (July):68–69, 71–76.

Castells, Manuel. 1997. *The Power of Identity.* Vol. 1 of *The Information Age: Economy, Society and Culture.* London: Blackwell.

———. 1998. *End of Millennium.* Vol. 3 of *The Information Age: Economy, Society and Culture.* London: Blackwell.

———. 2000. *The Information Age: Economy, Society and Culture* (3 vols.). 2d ed. Oxford and Malden, MA: Blackwell.

———. 2001. *The Internet Galaxy: Reflections on the Internet, Business, and Society.* New York: Oxford University Press.

CBS News. 1979. Transcript of *Sixty Minutes* segment, "I Was Only Following Orders." March 31, pp. 2–8.

Center for Academic Integrity. 2004. *CAI Research.* Accessed January 14 (www.academicintegrity.org).

Center for American Women and Politics. 2004. *Fact Sheet: Women in the U.S. Congress 2004 and Statewide Elective Women 2004.* Rutgers, NJ: CAWP.

Center for Public Integrity. 1998. *Nothing Sacred: The Politics of Privacy.* Washington, DC: CPI.

Centers for Disease Control and Prevention. 2002. "Need For Sustained HIV Prevention Among Men Who Have Sex With Men." Accessed January 23, 2004 (www.cdc.gov/hiv/pubs/facts/msm.htm).

———. 2003a. "Divisions of HIV/AIDS Prevention: Basic Statistics." Accessed May 17, 2004 (www.cdc.gov/hiv/stats/htm).

———. 2003b. *A Glance at the HIV Epidemic.* Accessed February 25 (www.cdc.gov).

Cerulo, Karen A., Janet M. Ruane, and Mary Chagko. 1992. "Technological Ties that Bind: Media Generated Primary Groups." *Communication Research* 19:109–129.

Cha, Ariena Eunjung. 2000. "Painting a Portrait of Dot-Camaraderie." *The Washington Post,* October 26, pp. E1, E10.

———. 2003. "Wanted, but Safe In Russia." *Washington Post National Weekly Edition* 20 (June 16):9–10.

Chalfant, H. Paul, Robert E. Beckley, and C. Eddie Palmer. 1994. *Religion in Contemporary Society.* 3d ed. Itasca, IL: F. E. Peacock.

Chambliss, William. 1973. "The Saints and the Roughnecks." *Society* 11 (November/December): 24–31.

Chang, Leslie. 2003. "Amway in China: Once Banned, Now Booming." *Wall Street Journal,* March 12, pp. B1, B5.

Chang, Patricia M. Y. 1997. "Female Clergy in the Contemporary Protestant Church: A Current Assessment." *Journal for the Scientific Study of Religion* 36 (December): 564–573.

Charter, David, and Jill Sherman. 1996. "Schools Must Teach New Code of Values." *London Times,* January 15, p. 1.

Chase-Dunn, Christopher, and Peter Grimes. 1995. "World-Systems Analysis." Pp. 387–417 in *Annual Review of Sociology, 1995,* edited by John Hagan. Palo Alto, CA: Annual Reviews.

———, Yukio Kawano, and Benjamin D. Brewer. 2000. "Trade Globalization Since 1795: Waves of Integration in the World System." *American Sociological Review* 65 (February):77–95.

Cheng, Wei-yuan, and Lung-li Liao. 1994. "Women Managers in Taiwan." Pp. 143–159 in *Competitive Frontiers: Women Managers in a Global Economy,* edited by Nancy J. Adler and Dafna N. Izraeli. Cambridge, MA: Blackwell Business.

Cherlin, Andrew J. 2003. "Should the Government Promote Marriage?" *Contexts* 2 (Fall): 22–29.

———. 2005. *Public and Private Families: An Introduction.* 4th ed. New York: McGraw-Hill.

Chesney-Lind, Meda. 1989. "Girls' Crime and Woman's Place: Toward a Feminist Model of Female Delinquency." *Crime and Delinquency* 35:5–29.

———., and Noelie Rodriguez. 1993. "Women under Lock and Key." *Prison Journal* 63:47–65.

Children Now. 2001. *The Local Television News Media's Picture of Children.* Oakland, CA: Children Now.

Children's Bureau. 2002. *FY 1998, FY 1999, and FY 2000 Foster Care: Entries, Exits and In Care on the Last Day.* Accessed May 19, 2003 (www.acf.dhhs.gov/programs/cb/dis/tables/entry exit.htm).

———. 2003. "The AFCARS Report." Accessed March 26, 2004 (www.acf.hhs.gov/progress/ob/dis/afcars/publications/afcars.htm).

Chin, Ko-lin. 1996. *Chinatown Gangs: Extortion, Enterprise, and Ethnicity.* New York: Oxford University Press.

Christensen, Kathleen. 1990. "Bridges over Troubled Water: How Older Workers View the Labor Market." Pp. 175–207 in *Bridges to Retirement,* edited by Peter B. Doeringer. Ithaca, NY: IRL Press.

Christie, Brigan. 2001. "Sociological Medicine's Aches and Pains." Pp. 222–223 in *Encyclopedia Britannica Yearbook 2001.* Chicago: Encyclopedia Britannica.

Civic Ventures. 1999. *The New Face of Retirement: Older Americans, Civic Engagement, and the Longevity Revolution.* Washington, DC: Peter D. Hart Research Associates.

Clark, Burton, and Martin Trow. 1966. "The Organizational Context." Pp. 17–70 in *The Study of College Peer Groups,* edited by Theodore M. Newcomb and Everett K. Wilson. Chicago: Aldine.

Clark, Candace. 1983. "Sickness and Social Control." Pp. 346–365 in *Social Interaction: Readings in Sociology,* 2d ed., edited by Howard Robboy and Candace Clark. New York: St. Martin's.

Clarke, Adele E., Janet K. Shim, Laura Maro, Jennifer Ruth Fusket, and Jennifer R. Fishman. 2003. "Bio Medicalization: Technoscientific Transformations of Health, Illness, and U.S. Biomedicine." *American Sociological Review* 68 (April):161–194.

Clarke, Lee. 1999. *Mission Improbable: Using Fantasy Documents to Tame Disaster.* Chicago: University of Chicago Press.

Clausen, Christopher. 2002. "To Have . . . or Not to Have." *Utne Reader* (July–August): 66–70.

Clawson, Dan, and Mary Ann Clawson. 1999. "What Has Happened to the U.S. Labor Movement? Union Decline and Renewal." Pp. 95–119 in *Annual Review of Sociology 1999,* edited by Karen S. Cook and John Hagan. Palo Alto, CA: Annual Reviews.

Clawson, Dan, and Naomi Gerstel. 2002. "Caring for Our Young: Child Care in Europe and the United States." *Contexts* 1 (Fall/Winter):23–35.

Clinard, Marshall B., and Robert F. Miller. 1998. *Sociology of Deviant Behavior.* 10th ed. Fort Worth: Harcourt Brace.

Clinton, Hillary Rodham. 2004. "Now Can We Talk About Health Care?" *New York Times Magazine,* April 18, pp. 26–31, 56.

Clymer, Adam. 2000. "College Students Not Drawn to Voting or Politics, Poll Shows." *New York Times.* January 2, p. A14.

Cockburn, Andrew. 2003. "21st Century Slaves." *National Geographic* 203 (September):2–29.

Cockerham, William C. 1998. *Medical Sociology.* 7th ed. Upper Saddle River, NJ: Prentice Hall.

Cohen, David, ed. 1991. *The Circle of Life: Ritual from the Human Family Album.* San Francisco: Harper.

Cohen, Lawrence E., and Marcus Felson. 1979. "Social Change and Crime Rate Trends: A Routine Activities Approach." *American Sociological Review* 44:588–608.

Colapinto, John. 2003. "The Young Hipublicans." *New York Times Magazine* (May 25):30–35, 58–59.

Cole, Elizabeth S. 1985. "Adoption, History, Policy, and Program." Pp. 638–666 in *A Handbook of Child Welfare,* edited by John Laird and Ann Hartman. New York: Free Press.

Cole, Mike. 1988. *Bowles and Gintis Revisited: Correspondence and Contradiction in Educational Theory.* Philadelphia: Falmer.

Coleman, Isobel. 2004. "The Payoff from Women's Rights." *Foreign Affairs* 83 (May/June):80–95.

Collins, Randall. 1975. *Conflict Sociology: Toward an Explanatory Sociology.* New York: Academic.

———. 1980. "Weber's Last Theory of Capitalism: A Systematization." *American Sociological Review* 45 (December):925–942.

———. 1986. *Weberian Sociological Theory.* New York: Cambridge University Press.

———. 1995. "Prediction in Macrosociology: The Case of the Soviet Collapse." *American Journal of Sociology* 100 (May):1552–1593.

Columbia Accident Investigation Board. 2003. "*Columbia* Accident Investigation Report Board Report: Volume I." Washington DC: CAIB, NASA.

Commission on Civil Rights. 1976. *A Guide to Federal Laws and Regulations Prohibiting Sex Discrimination.* Washington, DC: U.S. Government Printing Office.

———. 1981. *Affirmative Action in the 1980s: Dismantling the Process of Discrimination.* Washington DC: U.S. Government Printing Office.

Commoner, Barry. 1971. *The Closing Circle.* New York: Knopf.

———. 1990. *Making Peace with the Planet.* New York: Pantheon.

Comstock, P., and M. B. Fox. 1994. "Employer Tactics and Labor Law Reform." Pp. 90–109 in *Restoring the Promise of American Labor Law,* edited by S. Friedman, R. W. Hurd, R. A. Oswald, and R. L. Seeber. Ithaca, NY: ILR Press.

Conlin, Michelle. 2003. "The New Gender Gap." *Business Week,* May 26, p. 74.

Conrad, Peter, ed. 2000. *The Sociology of Health and Illness: Cultural Perspectives,* 6th ed. New York: Worth.

———, and Joseph W. Schneider. 1992. *Deviance and Medicalization: From Badness to Sickness.* Expanded ed. Philadelphia: Temple University Press.

"Control Room." 2004. A Magnolia Picture Release (www.controlroommovie.com).

Cooley, Charles. H. 1902. *Human Nature and the Social Order.* New York: Scribner.

Cornfield, Daniel B. 1991. "The US Labor Movement: Its Development and Impact on Social Inequality and Politics." In Scott, W. Richard, and Blake, Judith, eds. *Annual Review of Sociology 1991.* Palo Alto, CA: Annual Reviews.

Corsaro, William A. 1997. *The Sociology of Childhood.* Thousand Oaks, CA: Pine Forge Press.

Cortese, Anthony J. 1999. *Provocateur: Images of Women and Minorities in Advertising.* Lanham, MD: Rowman and Littlefield.

Coser, Lewis A. 1956. *The Functions of Social Conflict.* New York: Free Press.

———. 1977. *Masters of Sociological Thought: Ideas in Historical and Social Context.* 2d ed. New York: Harcourt, Brace and Jovanovich.

Couch, Carl J. 1996. *Information Technologies and Social Orders.* Edited with an introduction by David R. Maines and Shing-Ling Chien. New York: Aldine de Gruyter.

Council on Scientific Affairs. 1999. "Hispanic Health in the United States." *Journal of the American Medical Association* 265 (January 9):248–252.

Cox, Oliver C. 1948. *Caste, Class, and Race: A Study in Social Dynamics.* Detroit: Wayne State University Press.

Cox, Rachel S. 2003. "Home Schooling Debate." *CQ Researcher* 13 (January 17):25–48.

Crenshaw, Edward M., Matthew Christenson, and Doyle Ray Oakey. 2000. "Demographic Transition in Ecological Focus." *American Sociological Review* 65 (June):371–391.

Cressey, Donald R. 1960. "Epidemiology and Individual Contact: A Case from Criminology." *Pacific Sociological Review* 3 (Fall):47–58.

Cromwell, Paul F., James N. Olson, and D'Aunn Wester Avarey. 1995. *Breaking and Entering: An Ethnographic Analysis of Burglary.* Newbury Park, CA: Sage.

Crosnoe, Robert, and Glen H. Elder Jr. 2002. "Successful Adaptation in the Later Years: A Life Course Approach to Aging." *Social Psychology Quarterly* (No. 4), pp. 309–328.

Cross, Simon, and Barbara Bagilhole. 2002. "Girls' Jobs for the Boys? Men, Masculinity and Non-Traditional Occupations." *Gender, Work, and Organization* 9 (April):204–226.

Croteau, David, and William Hoynes. 2001. *The Business of the Media: Corporate Media and the Public Interest.* Thousand Oaks, CA: Pine Forge.

———. 2003. *Media/Society: Industries, Images, and Audiences.* 3d ed. Thousand Oaks, CA: Pine Forge.

Crouse, Kelly. 1999. "Sociology of the Titanic." *Teaching Sociology Listserv.* May 24.

Cuff, E. C., W. W. Sharrock, and D. W. Francis, eds. 1990. *Perspectives in Sociology.* 3d ed. Boston: Unwin Hyman.

Cullen, Francis T., Jr., and John B. Cullen. 1978. *Toward a Paradigm of Labeling Theory,* ser. 58. Lincoln: University of Nebraska Studies.

Cumming, Elaine, and William E. Henry. 1961. *Growing Old: The Process of Disengagement.* New York: Basic Books.

Currie, Elliot. 1985. *Confronting Crime: An American Challenge.* New York: Pantheon.

————. 1998. *Crime and Punishment in America.* New York: Metropolitan Books.

Curry, Timothy Jon. 1993. "A Little Pain Never Hurt Anyone: Athletic Career Socialization and the Normalization of Sports Injury." *Symbolic Interaction* 26 (Fall):273–290.

Dahl, Robert A. 1961. *Who Governs?* New Haven, CT: Yale University Press.

Dahrendorf, Ralf. 1958. "Toward a Theory of Social Conflict." *Journal of Conflict Resolution* 2 (June):170–183.

————. 1959. *Class and Class Conflict in Industrial Sociology.* Stanford, CA: Stanford University Press.

Dalla, Rochelle L., and Wendy C. Gamble. 2001. "Teenage Mothering and the Navajo Reservation: An Examination of Intergovernmental Perceptions and Beliefs." *American Indian Culture and Research Journal* 25 (1):1–19.

Daniels, Arlene Kaplan. 1987. "Invisible Work." *Social Problems* 34 (December):403–415.

————. 1988. *Invisible Careers.* Chicago: University of Chicago Press.

Daniszewski, John. 2003. "Al-Jazeera TV Draws Flak Outside—and Inside—the Arab World." *Los Angeles Times,* January 5, pp. A1, A5.

Dao, James. 1995. "New York's Highest Court Rules Unmarried Couples Can Adopt." *New York Times,* November 3, pp. A1, B2.

Darwin, Charles. 1859. *On the Origin of Species.* London: John Murray.

Davies, Christie. 1989. "Goffman's Concept of the Total Institution: Criticisms and Revisions." *Human Studies* 12 (June):77–95.

Davis, Darren W. 1997. "The Direction of Race of Interviewer Effects Among African-Americans: Donning the Black Mask." *American Journal of Political Science* 41 (January): 309–322.

Davis, Donald B., and Karen A. Polonko. 2001. *Telework America 2001 Summary.* Accessed March 3, 2003 (www.workingfrom anywhere.org/telework/twa2001.htm).

Davis, Gerald. 2003. *America's Corporate Banks Are Separated by Just Four Handshakes.* Accessed March 7 (www.bus.umich.edu/ research/davis.html).

————. 2004. "American Cronyism: How Executive Networks Inflated the Corporate Bubble." *Contexts* (Summer):34–40.

Davis, James A. 1982. "Up and Down Opportunity's Ladder." *Public Opinion* 5 (June/July): 11–15, 48–51.

————, and Tom W. Smith. 2001. *General Social Surveys, 1972–2000.* Storrs, CT: The Roper Center.

————, Tom W. Smith, and Peter V. Marsden. 2003. *General Social Surveys, 1972–2002: Cumulative Codebook.* Chicago: National Opinion Research Center.

Davis, Kingsley. 1937. "The Sociology of Prostitution." *American Sociological Review* 2 (October):744–755.

————. 1940. "Extreme Social Isolation of a Child." *American Journal of Sociology* 45 (January):554–565.

————. 1947. "A Final Note on a Case of Extreme Isolation." *American Journal of Sociology* 52 (March):432–437.

————. [1949] 1995. *Human Society.* Reprint, New York: Macmillan.

————, and Wilbert E. Moore. 1945. "Some Principles of Stratification." *American Sociological Review* 10 (April):242–249.

Davis, Nanette J. 1975. *Sociological Constructions of Deviance: Perspectives and Issues in the Field.* Dubuque, IA: Wm. C. Brown.

Death Penalty Information Center. 2003. *Black Defendant/White Victim.* Accessed December 19 (www.deathpenaltyinfo.org).

————. 2004a. "Facts About the Death Penalty, January 30, 2004." Washington, DC: DPIC.

————. 2004b. "Cases of Innocence 1973–Present." Accessed May 31 (www.deathpenalty info.org/article.php?scid=6&did=109).

Deegan, Mary Jo, ed. 1991. *Women in Sociology: A Bio-Biographical Sourcebook.* Westport, CT: Greenwood.

————. 2003. "Textbooks the History of Sociology, and the Sociological Stock of Knowledge." *Sociological Theory* 21 (November): 298–305.

Delawala, Imtyaz. 2002. "What Is Coltran?" January 21, 2002 (www.abcnews.com).

Dellios, Hugh. 2002. "Desperate Migrants Accept Risks." *New York Times,* October 20, pp. 1, 7.

Deloria, Vine, Jr. 1999. *For This Land: Writings on Religion in America.* New York: Routledge.

DeNavas-Walt, Carmen, and Robert W. Cleveland. 2002. "Money Income in the United States: 2001." *Current Population Reports,* ser. P-60, no. 218. Washington, DC.

————, Bernadette P. Proctor, and Robert J. Mills. 2004. "Income, Poverty, and Health Insurance Coverage in the United States: 2003." *Current Population Reports,* ser. P-60, no. 226. Washington, DC: U.S. Government Printing Office.

Denny, Charlotte. 2004. "Migration Myths Hold No Fears." *Guardian Weekly* (February 26):12.

DePalma, Anthony. 1995a. "Racism? Mexico's in Denial." *New York Times,* June 11, p. E4.

————. 1996. "For Mexico Indians, New Voice but Few Gains." *New York Times,* January 13, pp. B1, B2.

————. 2002. "White-Collar Layoffs, Downsized Dreams." *New York Times,* December 5, pp. A1, A38.

Department of Agriculture. 2004. *2002 Census of Agriculture: Preliminary Report AC-02-A-PR.* Washington, DC: U.S. Government Printing Office.

Department of Defense. 2003. "Selected Manpower Statistics Fiscal Year 2002." Washington, DC: Department of Defense.

Department of Health and Human Services. 2004. "Percent Change in AFDC/TANF Families and Receipts" Accessed February 22, 2004 (www.acfhhs.gov).

Department of Justice. 2000. *The Civil Liberties Act of 1988: Redress for Japanese Americans.* Accessed June 29 (http://www.usdoj.gov/crt/ ora/main.html).

————. 2001. *Crime in the United States 2000. Uniform Crime Reports.* Washington, DC: U.S. Government Printing Office.

————. 2002a. *Firearms and Crime Statistics.* Accessed December 9 (www.ojp.usdoj.gov/bjs/ guns.htm).

Department of Justice. 2002b. *Crime in the United States 2002.* Washington, DC: U.S. Government Printing Office.

Department of Labor. 1995a. *Good for Business: Making Full Use of the Nation's Capital.* Washington, DC: U.S. Government Printing Office.

————. 1995b. *A Solid Investment: Making Full Use of the Nation's Human Capital.* Washington, DC: U.S. Government Printing Office.

————. 1998. "Work and Elder Care: Facts for Caregivers and Their Employers." Accessed November 20 (www.dol.gov/dol/wb/public/ wb_pubs/elderc.htm).

————. 2003a. "Labor Force Statistics from the Current Population Survey." Accessed August 3 (http://data.bls.gov/cgi-bin/surveymost).

Department of Justice. 2003. "Hate Crime Statistics." 2002. Washington, DC: U.S. Government.

————. 2003b. *A Chartbook of International Labor Comparisons: United States, Europe, and Asia.* Washington, DC: U.S. Government Printing Office.

Department of Labor. 2004. "Employment Statistics of the Civilian Population by Race, Sex, and Age. Accessed March 1 (www.bls.gov).

Department of State. 2004a. "US Prepares to Beam Arabic Satellite TV Channel to Mideast." News release of January 29. Accessed February 2 (www.usinfo.state.gov).

————. 2004b. "Immigrant Visas Issued to Orphans Coming to the U.S." Accessed March 24 (www.travel.state.gov/orphan_numbers.html).

Derry, Charlotte. 2004. "Migration Myths Should Hold No Fears." *Guardian Weekly,* February 26, p. 12.

Devine, Don. 1972. *Political Culture of the United States: The Influence of Member Values on Regime Maintenance.* Boston: Little, Brown.

Devitt, James. 1999. *Framing Gender on the Campaign Trail: Women's Executive Leadership and the Press.* New York: Women's Leadership Conference.

Dighton, Daniel. 2003. "Minority Overrepresentation in the Criminal and Juvenile Justice Systems." *The Compiler* (Summer):1, 3–6.

Dillon, Sam. 1998. "Sex Bias at Border Plants in Mexico Reported by U.S." *New York Times,* January 13, p. A6.

————. 2004. "Education Can Be Long, Hard Haul for Nations Rural Kids." *Chicago Tribune,* May 28, p. 13.

DiMaggio, Paul, Eszter Hargittai, W. Russell Neuman, and John P. Robinson. 2001. "Social Implications of the Internet." Pp. 307–336 in *Annual Review of Sociology, 2001,* edited by

Karen S. Cook and John Hogan. Palo Alto, CA: Annual Reviews.

Directors Guild of America. 2002. *Diversity Hiring Special Report.* Los Angeles: DGA.

Dodds, Klaus. 2000. *Geopolitics in a Changing World.* Harlow, England: Pearson Education.

Doeringer, Peter B., ed. 1990. *Bridges to Retirement: Older Workers in a Changing Labor Market.* Ithaca, NY: ILR Press.

Domhoff, G. William. 1978. *Who Really Rules? New Haven and Community Power Reexamined.* New Brunswick, NJ: Transaction.

———. 2001. *Who Rules America?* 4th ed. New York: McGraw-Hill.

Dominguez, Silvia, and Celeste Watkins. 2003. "Creating Networks for Survival and Mobility: Social Capital Among African-American and Latin-American Low-Income Mothers." *Social Problems* 50 (February):111–135.

Dominick, Joseph R. 2002. *The Dynamics of Mass Communication: Media in the Digital Age.* 7th ed. New York: McGraw-Hill.

Doress, Irwin, and Jack Nusan Porter. 1977. *Kids in Cults: Why They Join. Why They Stay, Why They Leave.* Brookline, MA: Reconciliation Associates.

Dotson, Floyd. 1991. "Community." p. 55 in *Encyclopedic Dictionary of Sociology.* 4th ed. Guilford, CT: Dushkin.

Dougherty, John, and David Holthouse. 1999. "Bordering on Exploitation." Accessed March 5 (www.phoenixnewtime.com/issies/1998-07-09/feature.html).

Dougherty, Kevin, and Floyd M. Hammack. 1992. "Education Organization." Pp. 535–541 in *Encyclopedia of Sociology,* vol. 2, edited by Edgar F. Borgatta and Marie L. Borgatta. New York: Macmillan.

Dowd, James J. 1980. *Stratification among the Aged.* Monterey, CA: Brooks/Cole.

Downie, Andrew. 2000. "Brazilian Girls Turn to a Doll More Like Them." *Christian Science Monitor,* January 20. Accessed January 20 (www.csmonitor.com/durable/2000/01/20/fpls3-csm.shtml).

Doyle, James A. 1995. *The Male Experience.* 3d ed. Dubuque, IA: Brown & Benchmark.

———, and Michele A. Paludi. 1998. *Sex and Gender: The Human Experience.* 4th ed. New York: McGraw-Hill.

Drezner, Daniel W. 2004. "The Outsourcing Bogeyman." *Foreign Affairs* 3 (May/June):22–34.

Du Bois, W. E. B. 1909. *The Negro American Family.* Atlanta University. Reprinted 1970. Cambridge, MA: M.I.T. Press.

———. 1911. "The Girl Nobody Loved." *Social News* 2 (November):3.

———. [1940] 1968. *Dusk of Dawn.* New York: Harcourt, Brace. Reprinted New York: Schocken Books.

Dugger, Celia W. 1999. "Massacres of Low-Born Touch Off a Crisis in India." *New York Times,* March 15, p. A3.

Dundas, Susan, and Miriam Kaufman. 2000. "The Toronto Lesbian Family Study." *Journal of Homosexuality* 40 (20):65–79.

Duneier, Mitchell. 1994a. "On the Job, but Behind the Scenes." *Chicago Tribune,* December 26, pp. 1, 24.

———. 1994b. "Battling for Control." *Chicago Tribune,* December 28, pp. 1, 8.

———. 1999. *Sidewalk.* New York: Farrar, Straus and Giroux.

Dunlap, Riley E., William Michelson, and Glenn Stalker. 2002. "Environmental Sociology: An Introduction." Pp. 1–32 in *Handbook of Environmental Sociology,* edited by Riley E. Dunlap and William Michelson. Westport, CT: Greenwood Press.

Dunne, Gillian A. 2000. "Opting Into Motherhood: Lesbians Blurring the Boundaries and Transforming the Meaning of Parenthood and Kinship." *Gender and Society* 14 (February):11–35.

Durkheim, Émile. [1912] 2001. *The Elementary Forms of Religious Life.* A new translation by Carol Cosman. New York: Oxford University Press.

———. [1893] 1933. *Division of Labor in Society.* Translated by George Simpson. Reprint, New York: Free Press.

———. [1897] 1951. *Suicide.* Translated by John A. Spaulding and George Simpson. Reprint, New York: Free Press.

———. [1895] 1964. *The Rules of Sociological Method.* Translated by Sarah A. Solovay and John H. Mueller. Reprint, New York: Free Press.

Duster, Troy. 2002. "Sociological Stranger in the Land of the Human Genome Project." *Contexts* 1 (Fall):69–70.

———. 2003. *Backdoor to Eugenics.* 2d ed. New York: Routledge.

Dworsky, Amy, Mark Courtney, Irving Pitauin. 2003. *What Happens to Families Under W-2 in Milwaukee County, Wisconsin?* Chicago: Chapin Hall Center for Children, University of Chicago.

Ebaugh, Helen Rose Fuchs. 1988. *Becoming an Ex: The Process of Role Exit.* Chicago: University of Chicago Press.

Eckenwiler, Mark. 1995. "In the Eyes of the Law." *Internet World* (August):74, 76–77.

The Economist. 2003a. "Race in Brazil: Out of Eden." *The Economist* (July 5):31–32.

———. 2003b. "The One Where Pooh Goes to Sweden." *The Economist* (April 5):59.

———. 2004a. "Veil of Tears." *The Economist* (January 15):00–00.

———. 2004b. "Indigenous People in South America: A Political Awakening." *The Economist* (February 21):35–37.

———. 2004c. "Battle on the Home Front." *The Economist* (February 21):8–10.

———. 2004d. "We Are the Champions." *The Economist* (March 20):13–15.

Edwards, Harry. 1973. *Sociology of Sport.* Homewood, IL: Dorsey Press.

Edwards, Tamala M. 2001. "How Med Students Put Abortion Back in the Classroom." *Time* 157 (May 7):59–60.

Efron, Sonni. 1997. "In Japan, Even Tots Must Make the Grade." *Los Angeles Times,* February 16, pp. A1, A17.

Ehrenreich, Barbara. 2001. *Nickel and Dimed: On (Not) Getting By in America.* New York: Metropolitan.

———, and Frances Fox Piven. 2002. "Without a Safety Net." *Mother Jones* 27 (May/June):34–41.

Ehrlich, Paul R. 1968. *The Population Bomb.* New York: Ballantine.

———, and Anne H. Ehrlich. 1990. *The Population Explosion.* New York: Simon and Schuster.

———, and Katherine Ellison. 2002. "A Looming Threat We Won't Face." *Los Angeles Times.* January 20, p. M6.

Eitzen, D. Stanley. 2003. *Fair and Foul: Beyond the Myths and Paradoxes of Sport.* 2d ed. Lanham, MD: Rowman and Littlefield.

El-Badry, Samira. 1994. "The Arab-American Market." *American Demographics* 16 (January):21–31.

Eller, Claudia, and Lorenza Muñoz. 2002. "The Plots Thicken in Foreign Markets." *Los Angeles Times,* October 6, pp. A1, A26, A27.

Ellingwood, Ken. 2001. "Results of Crackdown and Border Called Mixed." *Los Angeles Times,* August 4, p. B9.

Ellison, Ralph. 1952. *Invisible Man.* New York: Random House.

Elmer-DeWitt, Philip. 1995. "Welcome to Cyberspace." *Time* 145 (Special Issue, Spring):4–11.

El Nasser, Haya. 2001. "Minorities Reshape Suburbs." *USA Today,* July 9, p. 1A.

Ely, Robin J. 1995. "The Power of Demography: Women's Social Construction of Gender Identity at Work." *Academy of Management Journal* 38 (3):589–634.

Embree, Ainslie. 2003. "Religion." Pp. 101–220 in *Understanding Contemporary India,* edited by Sumit Ganguly and Neil DeVotta. Boulder, CO: Lynne Rienner.

Engels, Friedrich [1884] 1959. "The Origin of the Family, Private Property, and the State." Pp. 392–394, excerpted in *Marx and Engels: Basic Writings on Politics and Philosophy,* edited by Lewis Feuer. Garden City, NY: Anchor.

England, Paula. 1999. "The Impact of Feminist Thought on Sociology." *Contemporary Sociology* 28 (May):263–268.

English-Lueck, J. A. 2002. *Cultures@SiliconValley.* Stanford, CA: Stanford University Press.

Entine, Jon, and Martha Nichols. 1996. "Blowing the Whistle on Meaningless 'Good Intentions.'" *Chicago Tribune,* June 20, Sec. 1, p. 21.

Ericson, Nels. 2001. "Substance Abuse: The Nation's Number One Health Problem." *OJJDP Fact Sheet* 17 (May):1–2.

Erikson, Kai. 1966. *Wayward Puritans: A Study in the Sociology of Deviance.* New York: Wiley.

———. 1994. *A New Species of Trouble: The Human Experience of Modern Disasters.* New York: Norton.

Etaugh, Claire. 2003. "Witches, Mothers and Others: Females in Children's Books." *Hilltopics* (Winter):10–13.

Etzioni, Amitai. 1964. *Modern Organization.* Englewood Cliffs, NJ: Prentice Hall.

———. 1965. *Political Unification.* New York: Holt, Rinehart, and Winston.

Evans, Sara. 1980. *Personal Politics: The Roots of Women's Liberation in the Civil Rights Movement and the New Left.* New York: Vintage.

FAIR. 2001. "Fear and Favor 2000." Accessed December 29, 2001 (www.FAIR.org).

FAIR US. 2003. "Issue Brief." Accessed August 24 (www.fairus.org/html/newsroom/html).

Fallows, James. 2004. "The Hollow Army: James Fallows Reports." *The Atlantic Monthly* (June):26.

Faludi, Susan. 1999. *Stiffed: The Betrayal of the American Man.* New York: William Morrow.

Farhi, Paul, and Megan Rosenfeld. 1998. "Exporting America." *Washington Post National Weekly Edition* 16 (November 30):6–7.

Farkas, Steve, Ann Duffett, and Jean Johnson. 2003. *Now That I'm Here: What America's Immigrants Have to Say About Life in the U.S. Today.* New York: Public Agenda.

Farley, Maggie. 1998. "Indonesia's Chinese Fearful of Backlash." *Los Angeles Times,* January 31, pp. A1, A8–A9.

———. 2004. "U.N. Gay Policy is Assailed." *Los Angeles Times,* April 9, p. A3.

Farr, Grant M. 1999. *Modern Iran.* New York: McGraw-Hill.

Fausset, Richard. 2003. "Sikhs Mark New Year, Fight Post-September 11 Bias." *Los Angeles Times,* April 14, pp. B1, B7.

Feagin, Joe R. 1983. *The Urban Real Estate Game: Playing Monopoly with Real Money.* Englewood Cliffs, NJ: Prentice Hall.

———. 1989. *Minority Group Issues in Higher Education: Learning from Qualitative Research.* Norman, OK: Center for Research on Minority Education, University of Oklahoma.

———. 2001. "Social Justice and Sociology: Agenda for the Twenty-First Century." *American Sociological Review* 66 (February):1–20.

———, Harnán Vera, and Nikitah Imani. 1996. *The Agony of Education: Black Students at White Colleges and Universities.* New York: Routledge.

Featherman, David L., and Robert M. Hauser. 1978. *Opportunity and Change.* New York: Aeodus.

Federal Register, June 4, 1975.

Feketekuty, Geza. 2001. "Globalization—Why All the Fuss?" p. 191 in *2001 Britannica Book of the Year.* Chicago: Encyclopedia Britannica.

Felson, Marcus. 2002. *Crime and Everyday Life.* 3d ed. Thousand Oaks, CA: Pine Forge Press.

Fernández, Sandy. 1996. "The Cyber Cops." *Ms.* 6 (May/June):22–23.

Ferree, Myra Marx, and David A. Merrill. 2000. "Hot Movements, Cold Cognition: Thinking about Social Movements in Gendered Frames." *Contemporary Society* 29 (May):454–462.

Ferrell, Tom. 1979 "More Choose to Live outside Marriage." *New York Times,* July 1, p. E7.

Feuer, Lewis S. 1989. *Marx and Engels: Basic Writings on Politics and Philosophy.* New York: Anchor Books.

Fiala, Robert. 1992. "Postindustrial Society." Pp. 1512–1522 in *Encyclopedia of Sociology,* vol. 3, edited by Edgar F. Borgatta and Marie L. Borgatta. New York: Macmillan.

Fields, Jason. 2001. "America's Families and Living Arrangements." *Current Population Reports,* ser. P-20, no. 537. Washington, DC: U.S. Government Printing Office.

———. 2003. "Children's Living Arrangements and Characteristics: March 2002." *Current Population Reports,* ser. P-20, no. 547. Washington, DC: U.S. Government Printing Office.

Finder, Alan. 1995. "Despite Tough Laws, Sweatshops Flourish." *New York Times,* January 6, pp. A1, B4.

Fine, Gary Alan. 1984. "Negotiated Orders and Organizational Cultures." Pp. 239–262 in *Annual Review of Sociology, 1984,* edited by Ralph Turner. Palo Alto, CA: Annual Reviews.

———. 1987. *With the Boys: Little League Baseball and Preadolescent Culture.* Chicago: University of Chicago Press.

Finkel, Steven E., and James B. Rule. 1987. "Relative Deprivation and Related Psychological Theories of Civil Violence: A Critical Review." *Research in Social Movements* 9:47–69.

Firestone, David. 1999. "School Prayer Is Revived as an Issue in Alabama." *New York Times,* July 15, p. A14.

Firestone, Shulamith. 1970. *The Dialectic of Sex: The Case for Feminist Revolution.* New York: Bantam.

Fisher, Allen P. 2003. "Still 'Not Quite as Good as Having Your Own' Toward a Sociology of Adoption." Pp. 335–361 in *Annual Review of Sociology 2003,* edited by Karen S. Cook and John Hogan. Palo Alto, CA: Annual Review.

Fitzgerald, Kathleen J., and Diane M. Rodgers. 2000. "Radical Social Movement Organization: A Theoretical Model." *The Sociological Quarterly* 41 (4):573–592.

Fix, Michael, Wendy Zimmerman, and Jeffrey S. Passel. 2001. *The Integration of Immigrant Families in the United States.* Washington, DC: The Urban Institute.

Flacks, Richard. 1971. *Youth and Social Change.* Chicago: Markham.

Flavin, Jeanne. 1998. "Razing the Wall: A Feminist Critique of Sentencing Theory, Research, and Policy." Pp. 145–164 in *Cutting the Edge,* edited by Jeffrey Ross. Westport, CT: Praeger.

Fletcher, Connie. 1995. "On the Line: Women Cops Speak Out." *Chicago Tribune Magazine,* February 19, pp. 14–19.

Foreman, Judy. 2002. "The Evidence Speaks Well of Bilingualism's Effect on Kids." *Los Angeles Times,* October 7, pp. 51, 56.

Form, William. 1992. "Labor Movements and Unions." Pp. 1054–1060 in *Encyclopedia of Sociology,* vol. 3., edited by Edgar F. Borgatta and Marie L. Borgatta. New York: Macmillan.

Fortune. 2003. "Fortune Global 500." *Fortune* 148 (July 21):97–126.

Fox, Susannah and Lee Rainie. 2001. *Time Online: Why Some People Use the Internet More Than Before and Why Some Use It Less.* Washington, DC: Pew Internet and American Life Project.

Franklin, John Hope, and Alfred A. Moss. 2000. *From Slavery to Freedom: A History of African Americans.* 8th ed. Upper Saddle River, NJ: Prentice Hall.

Freeman, Jo. 1973. "The Origins of the Women's Liberation Movement." *American Journal of Sociology* 78 (January):792–811.

———. 1975. *The Politics of Women's Liberation.* New York: McKay.

Freidson, Eliot. 1970. *Profession of Medicine.* New York: Dodd, Mead.

French, Howard W. 2000. "The Pretenders." *New York Times Magazine,* December 3, pp. 86–88.

Frey, William H. 2001. *Melting Pot Suburbs: A Census 2000 Study of Suburban Diversity.* Washington, DC: The Brookings Institution.

Fridlund, Alan. J., Paul Erkman, and Harriet Oster. 1987. "Facial Expressions of Emotion; Review of Literature 1970–1983." Pp. 143–224 in *Nonverbal Behavior and Communication,* 2d ed., edited by Aron W. Seigman and Stanley Feldstein. Hillsdale, NJ: Lawrence Erlbaum Associates.

Friedan, Betty. 1963. *The Feminine Mystique.* New York: Dell.

Friedland, Jonathon. 2000. "An American in Mexico Champions Midwifery as a Worthy Profession." *Wall Street Monitor,* February 15, pp. A1, A12.

Frost, Greg. 2003. "U.S. Anti-War Movement Breaks Ranks with the 60's." *Washington Post,* March 31.

Furstenberg, Frank, and Andrew Cherlin. 1991. *Divided Families: What Happens to Children When Parents Part.* Cambridge, MA: Harvard University Press.

Furukawa, Stacy. 1994. "The Diverse Living Arrangements of Children: Summer 1991." *Current Population Reports,* ser. P-70., no. 38. Washington, DC: U.S. Government Printing Office.

Gale Group. 2003. *Associations Unlimited.* Accessed March 3 (www.galegroup.com).

Gallup. 2002. "Poll Topics and Trends: Death Penalty." Accessed June 7 (www.gallup.com).

———. 2003. "The Gallup Poll of Baghdad." Accessed November 25 (www.gallup.com).

Gamson, Joshua. 1989. "Silence, Death, and the Invisible Enemy: AIDS Activism and Social Movement 'Newness.'" *Social Problems* 36 (October):351–367.

Gans, Herbert J. 1979. "Symbolic Ethnicity: The Future of Ethnic Groups and Cultures in America." *Ethnic and Racial Studies.* 2 (January): 1–20.

———. 1991. *People, Plans, and Policies: Essays on Poverty, Racism, and Other National Urban Problems.* New York: Columbia University Press and Russell Sage Foundation.

———. 1995. *The War against the Poor: The Underclass and Antipoverty Policy.* New York: Basic Books.

Gardner, Carol Brooks. 1989. "Analyzing Gender in Public Places: Rethinking Goffman's Vision of Everyday Life." *American Sociologist* 20 (Spring):42–56.

———. 1990. "Safe Conduct: Women, Crime, and Self in Public Places." *Social Problems* 37 (August):311–328.

———. 1995. *Passing By: Gender and Public Harassment.* Berkeley: University of California Press.

Gardner, Gary, Erik Assadourian, and Radhika Sarin. 2004. "The State of Consumption

Today." Pp. 3–21 in *State of the World 2004*, edited by Brian Halweil and Lisa Mastny. New York: W. W. Norton.

Gardner, Marilyn. 2001. "Media's Eye on Moms." *Christian Science Monitor*, May 30, pp. 12–13.

———. 2003. "This View of Seniors Just Doesn't 'Ad' Up." *Christian Science Monitor*, January 15, p. 15.

Garfinkel, Harold. 1956. "Conditions of Successful Degradation Ceremonies." *American Journal of Sociology* 61 (March):420–424.

Garner, Roberta. 1996. *Contemporary Movements and Ideologies*. New York: McGraw-Hill.

Garreau, Joel. 1991. *Edge City: Life on the New Frontier*. New York: Doubleday.

Garza, Melita Marie. 1993. "The Cordi-Marian Annual Cotillion." *Chicago Tribune*, May 7, sec. C, pp. 1, 5.

Gates, Henry Louis, Jr. 1999. "One Internet, Two Nations." *New York Times*, October 31, p. A15.

Gay, Lesbian and Straight Education Network. 2004. "About GLSEN." Accessed May 3 (www.glsen.org).

Gearty, Robert. 1996. "Beware of Pickpockets." *Chicago Daily News*, November 19, p. 5.

Gecas, Viktor. 1982. "Socialization." Pp. 1863–1872 in *Encyclopedia of Sociology*, Vol. 4, edited by Edgar F. Borgatta and Marie L. Borgatta. New York: Macmillan.

Gelles, Richard J., and Claire Pedrick Cornell. 1990. *Intimate Violence in Families*. 2d ed. Newbury Park, CA: Sage.

General Accounting Office. 2002. *A New Look Through the Glass Ceiling: Where Are the Women?* Washington, DC: General Accounting Office.

Gerth, H. H., and C. Wright Mills. 1958. *From Max Weber: Essays in Sociology*. New York: Galaxy.

Geyh, Paul. 1998. "Feminism Fatale?" *Chicago Tribune*, July 26, Sec. 13, pp. 1, 6.

Gezari, Vanessa. 2002. "Sex Testing Used to Call Girls." *Chicago Tribune*, November 10, p. 4.

Giddens, Anthony. 1991. *Modernity and Self-Identity: Self and Society in the Late Modern Age*. Cambridge, UK: Polity.

Gifford, Allen L., et al. 2002. "Participation in Research and Access to Experimental Treatments by HIV-Infected Patients." *New England Journal of Medicine* 346 (May):1400–1402.

Giordano, Peggy C. 2003. "Relationships in Adolescence." Pp. 257–281 in *Annual Review of Sociology, 2003*, edited by Karen S. Cook and John Hogan. Palo Alto, CA: Annual Reviews.

———, Stephen A. Cernkovich, and Alfred DeMaris. 1993. "The Family and Peer Relations of Black Adolescents." *Journal of Marriage and Family* 55 (May): 277–287.

Giroux, Henry A. 1988. *Schooling and the Struggle for Public Life: Critical Pedagogy in the Modern Age*. Minneapolis: University of Minnesota Press.

Gitlin, Todd. 2002. *Media Unlimited: How the Torrent of Images and Sounds Overwhelms Our Lives*. New York: Henry Holt and Company.

Glauber, Bill. 1998. "Youth Binge Drinking Varies Around World." *St. Louis Post-Dispatch*, February 9, p. E4.

Glaze, Lauren. 2002. "Probation and Parole in the United States, 2001." *Bureau of Justice Statistics Bulletin* (August).

Glenn, David. 2004. "A Dangerous Surplus of Sons?" *Chronicle of Higher Education* 50 (April 30):A14–A16, A18.

Global Alliance for Workers and Communities. 2003. *About Us*. Accessed April 28 (www.theglobalalliance.org).

Global Reach. 2004. *Global Internet Statistics (by Language)*. Accessed May 31 (www.global-reach.biz/globstats/erol.html).

Goffman, Erving. 1959. *The Presentation of Self in Everyday Life*. New York: Doubleday.

———. 1961. *Asylums: Essays on the Social Situation of Mental Patients and Other Inmates*. Garden City, NY: Doubleday.

———. 1963a. *Stigma: Notes on Management of Spoiled Identity*. Englewood Cliffs, NJ: Prentice Hall.

———. 1963b. *Behavior in Public Places*. New York: Free Press.

———. 1971. *Relations in Public*. New York: Basic Books.

———. 1979. *Gender Advertisements*. Cambridge. MA: Harvard University Press.

Goldberg, Carey. 1998. "Little Drop in College Binge Drinking." *New York Times*, August 11, p. A14.

Golden, Frederic. 1999. "Who's Afraid of Frankenfood?" *Time*, November 29, pp. 49–50.

Goldstein, Amy, and Richard Morin. 2002. "The Squeaky Wheel Gets the Grease." *Washington Post National Weekly Edition* 20, October 28, p. 34.

Goldstein, Melvyn C., and Cynthia M. Beall. 1981. "Modernization and Aging in the Third and Fourth World: Views from the Rural Hinterland in Nepal." *Human Organization* 40 (Spring):48–55.

Goleman, Daniel, 1991. "New Ways to Battle Bias: Fight Acts, Not Feelings." *New York Times*, July 16, pp. C1, C8.

Gonnut, Jean Pierre. 2001. Interview. June 18, 2001.

Gonzales, John M. 1997. "Relearning a Lost Language." *Los Angeles Times*, May 26, p. A1.

Gonzalez, David. 2003. "Latin Sweatshops Pressed by U.S. Campus Power." *New York Times*, April 4, p. A3.

Gonzalez-Pando, Miguel. 1998. *The Cuban Americans*. Westport, CT: Greenwood Press.

Goodgame, Dan. 1993. "Welfare for the Well-Off." *Time* 141 (February 22):36–38.

Gordon, Daniel T., ed. 2002. *Minority Achievement*. Harvard Education Letter Focus Series, no. 7. Cambridge, MA: Harvard Graduate School of Education.

Gordon, Gary. 2004. "Teacher Retention Statistics with Great Principals." *Gallup Poll Tuesday Briefing*, February 17. Accessed March 18 (www.gallup.com).

Gornick, Janet C. 2001. "Cancel the Funeral." *Dissent* (Summer):13–18.

Gornick, Vivian. 1979. "Introduction" to *Gender Advertisements*. Cambridge, MA: Harvard University Press.

Gottdiener, Mark, and Joe R. Feagin. 1988. "The Paradigm Shift in Urban Sociology." *Urban Affairs Quarterly* 24 (December):163–187.

———, and Ray Hutchison. 2000. *The New Urban Sociology*. 2d ed. New York: McGraw-Hill.

Gottfredson, Michael, and Travis Hirschi. 1990. *A General Theory of Crime*. Palo Alto, CA: Stanford University Press.

Gouldner, Alvin. 1960. "The Norm of Reciprocity." *American Sociological Review* 25 (April):161–177.

———. 1970. *The Coming Crisis of Western Sociology*. New York: Basic Books.

Graham, Judith. 2002. "Agencies Adapt to a Less-White Elderly." *Chicago Tribune*, April 11, pp. 1, 16.

———. 2003. "Most Perceive Shades of Gray in Abortion." *Chicago Tribune*, June 20, pp. 1, 18.

———. 2004. "Kids of Addicts Bear Scars as Meth Sweeps Rural Areas." *Chicago Tribune*, March 7, pp. 1, 14.

Gramsci, Antonio. 1929. *Selections from the Prison Notebooks*. Antonio Gramsci. Edited and translated by Quintin Hoare and Geoffrey Nowell Smith. London: Lawrence and Wishort.

Greeley, Andrew M. 1989. "Protestant and Catholic: Is the Analogical Imagination Extinct?" *American Sociological Review* 54 (August):485–502.

Green, Dan S., and Edwin D. Driver. 1978. "Introduction." Pp. 1–60 in *W. E. B. DuBois on Sociology and the Black Community*, edited by Dan S. Green and Edwin D. Driver. Chicago: University of Chicago Press.

Greene, Jay P. 1998. "A Meta-Analysis of the Effectiveness of Bilingual Education." Sponsored by the Toms River Policy Initiative. Accessed July 1 (http://data.Fas.harvard.edu/pepg/biling.htm).

Greenhouse, Linda. 1998. "High Court Ruling Says Harassment Includes Same Sex." *New York Times*, March 5, pp. A1, A17.

Greenhouse, Steven. 2000a. "Report Faults Laws for Slowing Growth of Unions." *New York Times*, October 24, p. A14.

Grieco, Elizabeth M., and Rachel C. Cassidy. 2001. "Overview of Race and Hispanic Origin." *Current Population Reports Series* CENBR/01–1. Washington, DC: U.S. Government Printing Office.

Grossman, Lew. 2002. "Busjocking for Grownups." *Time*, November 4, p. 80.

Groza, Victor, Daniela F. Ileana, and Ivor Irwin. 1999. *A Peacock or a Crow: Stories, Interviews, and Commentaries on Romanian Adoptions*. Euclid, OH: Williams Custom Publishing.

Guterman, Lila. 2000. "Why the 25-Year-Old Battle over Sociology Is More than Just 'An Academic Sideshow.'" *Chronicle of Higher Education*, July 7, pp. A17–A18.

Gutiérrez, Gustavo. 1990. "Theology and the Social Sciences," in Paul E. Sigmund, *Liberation Theology at the Crossroads: Democracy or Revolution?* New York: Oxford University Press, pp. 214–225.

Gutierrez, Valerie. 2002. "Minority Women Get Left Behind by Title IX." *Los Angeles Times*, June 23, pp. D1, D12.

Gwynne, S. C., and John E. Dickerson. 1997. "Lost in the E-Mail." *Time* 149 (April 21): 88–90.

Hacker, Andrew. 1964. "Power to Do What?" Pp. 134–146 in *The New Sociology,* edited by Irving Louis Horowitz. New York: Oxford University Press.

Hacker, Helen Mayer. 1951. "Women as a Minority Group." *Social Forces* 30 (October):60–69.

———. 1974. "Women as a Minority Group, Twenty Years Later." Pp. 124–134 in *Who Discriminates against Women?* edited by Florence Denmark. Beverly Hills, CA: Sage.

Haines, Valerie A. 1988. "Is Spencer's Theory an Evolutionary Theory?" *American Journal of Sociology* 93 (March):1200–1223.

Hall, Kay. 1999. "Work from Here." *Computer User* 18 (November):32.

Hall, Mimi. 1993. "Genetic-Sex-Testing a Medical Mine Field." *USA Today,* December 20, p. 6A.

Hall, Robert H. 1982. "The Truth about Brown Lung." *Business and Society Review* 40 (Winter 1981–82):15–20.

Hallinan, Maureen T. 1997. "The Sociological Study of Social Change." *American Sociological Review* 62 (February):1–11.

———. 2003. "Ability Grouping and Student Learning." Pp. 95–140 in *Brookings Papers on Education Policy,* edited by Diane Ravitch. Washington, DC: Brookings Institute Press.

Hamilton, Brady E. 2004. "Reproduction Rates for 1990–2002 and Intrinsic Rates for 2000–2001." *United States National Vital Statistics Reports* 52 (March 18).

———, Paul D. Sutton, Stephanie J. Ventura. 2003. "Revised Birth and Fertility Rates for the 1990s and New Rates for Hispanic Populations, 2000 and 2001: United States." *National Vital Statistics Reports* 51 (August 4).

Hani, Yoko. 1998. "Hot Pots Wired to Help the Elderly." *Japan Times Weekly International Edition,* April 13, p. 16.

Hank, Karsten. 2001. "Changes in Child Care Could Reduce Job Options for Eastern German Mothers." *Population Today* 29 (April):3, 6.

Hansen, Brian. 2001. "Globalization Backlash." *CQ Researcher* 11 (September 28): 761–784.

———. 2002. "Cyber-Crime." *CQ Researcher* 12 (April 12).

Hanson, Ralph E. 2005. *Mass Communication: Living in a Media World.* New York: McGraw Hill.

Harlow, Harry F. 1971. *Learning to Love.* New York: Ballantine.

Harmon, Amy. 1998. "The Law Where There Is No Land." *New York Times,* March 16, pp. C1, C9.

———. 2003. "Online Dating Sheds Its Stigma as Losers.com." *New York Times,* June 29, pp. A1, A21.

Harrington, Michael. 1980. "The New Class and the Left." Pp. 123–138 in *The New Class,* edited by B. Bruce Briggs. Brunswick, NJ: Transaction.

Harris, Chauncy D., and Edward Ullman. 1945. "The Nature of Cities." *Annals of the American Academy of Political and Social Science* 242 (November):7–17.

Harris, David A. 1999. *Driving While Black: Racial Profiling on Our Nation's Highways.* New York: American Civil Liberties Union.

Harris, Judith Rich. 1998. *The Nurture Assumption: Why Children Turn Out the Way They Do.* New York: Free Press.

Hartman, Chris, and Jake Miller. 2001. *Bail Outs That Work for Everyone.* Boston: United for a Fair Economy.

Haub, Carl. 2003. *World Population Data Sheet, 2003.* Washington, DC: Population Reference Bureau.

Haviland, William A. 2002. *Cultural Anthropology.* 10th ed. Belmont, CA: Wadsworth.

———, Harald E. L. Prins, Dana Walrath, and Bunny McBride. 2005. *Cultural Anthropology—The Human Challenge.* New York: McGraw-Hill.

Hawkins, Darnell F., et al. 2000. "Race, Ethnicity, and Serious and Violent Juvenile Offending." *Juvenile Justice Bulletin* (June):107.

Hayward, Mark D., William R. Grady, and Steven D. McLaughlin. 1987. "Changes in the Retirement Process." *Demography* 25 (August): 371–386.

Healey, Jon. 2003. "Music Industry Tries Fear as a Tactic to Stop Online Piracy." *Los Angeles Times,* April 23, pp. A1, A21.

Health Canada. 1993. *Gender and Violence in the Mass Media.* Ottawa, Canada: Health Canada.

Heckert, Druann, and Amy Best. 1997. "Ugly Duckling to Swan: Labeling Theory and the Stigmatization of Red Hair." *Symbolic Interaction* 20 (4):365–384.

Hedley, R. Alan. 1992. "Industrialization in Less Developed Countries." Pp. 914–920 in *Encyclopedia of Sociology,* vol. 2, edited by Edgar F. Borgatta and Marie L. Borgatta. New York: Macmillan.

Heilman, Madeline E. 2001. "Description and Prescription: How Gender Stereotypes Prevent Women's Ascent up the Organizational Ladder." *Journal of Social Issues* 57 (4):657–674.

Heise, Lori, M. Ellsberg, and M. Gottemuelle. 1999. "Ending Violence Against Women." *Population Reports,* ser. L, no. 11. Baltimore: Johns Hopkins University School of Public Health.

Hellmich, Nanci. 2001. "TV's Reality: No Vast American Waistlines." *USA Today,* October 8, p. 7D.

Henly, Julia R. 1999. "Challenges to Finding and Keeping Jobs in the Low-Skilled Labor Market." *Poverty Research News* 3 (1):3–5.

Henneberger, Melinda. 1995. "Muslims Continue to Feel Apprehensive." *New York Times,* April 14, p. B10.

Henry L. Stimson Center. 2001. "Frequently Asked Questions: Likelihood of Terrorists Acquiring and Using Chemical or Biological Weapons." Accessed December 28, 2001 (www.stimson.org/cwc/acquse.htm#seek).

Herrmann, Andrew. 1994. "Survey Shows Increase in Hispanic Catholics." *Chicago Sun-Times,* March 10, p. 4.

Herskovits, Melville J. 1930. *The Anthropometry of the American Negro.* New York: Columbia University Press.

Hetherington, E. Mavis, and John Kelly. 2002. *For Better or For Worse.* New York: Norton.

Hewlett, Sylvia Ann, and Cornel West. 1998. *The War Against Parents.* Boston: Houghton Mifflin.

Hickman, Jonathan. 2002. "America's 50 Best Corporations for Minorities." *Fortune* 146 (July 8):110–120.

Hill, Charles W. L. 2003. *International Business: Competing in the Global Marketplace.* 4th ed. New York: McGraw-Hill/Irwin.

Hill, Michael R., and Susan Hoecker-Drysdale, eds. 2001. *Harriet Martineau: Theoretical and Methodological Perspectives.* New York: Routledge.

Hillery, George A. 1955. "Definitions of Community: Areas of Agreement." *Rural Sociology* (2):111–123.

Himes, Vristine L. 2001. "Elderly Americans." *Population Bulletin* 56 (December).

Hirschi, Travis. 1969. *Causes of Delinquency.* Berkeley: University of California Press.

Hirst, Paul, and Grahame Thompson. 1996. *Globalization in Question: The International Economy and the Possibilities of Governance.* Cambridge, UK: Polity Press.

Hochschild, Arlie Russell. 1990. "The Second Shift: Employed Women Are Putting in Another Day of Work at Home." *Utne Reader* 38 (March/April):66–73.

———, with Anne Machung. 1989. *The Second Shift: Working Parents and the Revolution at Home.* New York: Viking Penguin.

Hodge, Robert W., and Peter H. Rossi. 1964. "Occupational Prestige in the United States, 1925–1963." *American Journal of Sociology* 70 (November):286–302.

Hoebel, E. Adamson. 1949. *Man in the Primitive World: An Introduction to Anthropology.* New York: McGraw-Hill.

Hoffman, Adonis. 1997. "Through an Accurate Prism." *Los Angeles Times,* August 8, p. M1.

Hoffman, Lois Wladis. 1985. "The Changing Genetics/Socialization Balance." *Journal of Social Issues* 41 (Spring):127–148.

Holden, Constance. 1980. "Identical Twins Reared Apart." *Science* 207 (March 21): 1323–1328.

———. 1987. "The Genetics of Personality." *Science* 257 (August 7):598–601.

Hollander, Jocelyn A. 2002. "Resisting Vulnerability: The Social Reconstruction of Gender in Interaction." *Social Problems* 49 (4):474–496.

Hollingshead, August B. 1975. *Elmtown's Youth and Elmtown Revisited.* New York: Wiley.

Homans, George C. 1979. "Nature versus Nurture: A False Dichotomy." *Contemporary Sociology* 8 (May):345–348.

Hondagneu-Sotelo, Pierette. 2001. *Domestica: Immigrant Workers Cleaning and Caring in the Shadows of Affluence.* Berkeley: University of California Press.

Hoover, Eric. 2002. "Binge Thinking." *Chronicle of Higher Education* 49 (November 8):A34–A37.

Horgan, John. 1993. "Eugenics Revisited." *Scientific American* 268 (June):122–128, 130–133.

Horovitz, Bruce. 2003. "Smile! You're the Stars of the Super Ad Bowl." *USA Today,* January 24, pp. B1, B2.

Horowitz, Helen Lefkowitz. 1987. *Campus Life.* Chicago: University of Chicago Press.

Hosokawa, William K. 1969. Nisei: *The Quiet Americans.* New York: Morrow.

Hout, Michael. 1988. "More Universalism, Less Structural Mobility: The American Occupational Structure in the 1980s." *American Journal of Sociology* 91 (May):1358–1400.

Howard, Judith A. 1999. "Border Crossings between Women's Studies and Sociology." *Contemporary Sociology* 28 (September):525–528.

Howard, Michael C. 1989. *Contemporary Cultural Anthropology.* 3d ed. Glenview, IL: Scott, Foresman.

Howard, Philip E., Lee Rainie, and Steve Jones. 2001. "Days and Nights on the Internet." *American Behavioral Scientist* 45 (November): 383–404.

Howard, Russell D., and Reid L. Sawyer. 2003. *Terrorism and Counterterrorism: Understanding the New Security Environment.* Guilford, CT: McGraw-Hill/Dushkin.

Huang, Gary. 1988. "Daily Addressing Ritual: A Cross-Cultural Study." Presented at the annual meeting of the American Sociological Association, Atlanta.

Huber, Bettina J. 1985. *Employment Patterns in Sociology: Recent Trends and Future Prospects.* Washington, DC: American Sociological Association.

Huddy, Leonie, Joshua Billig, John Bracciodieta, Lois Hoeffler, Patrick J. Moynihan, and Patricia Pugliani. 1997. "The Effect of Interviewer Gender on the Survey Response." *Political Behavior* 19 (September):197–220.

Huffstutter, P. J. 2003. "See No Evil." *Los Angeles Times,* January 12, pp. 12–15, 43–45.

Hughes, Everett. 1945. "Dilemmas and Contradictions of Status." *American Journal of Sociology* 50 (March):353–359.

Huie, Stephanie A. Bond, Patrick M. Krueger, Richard G. Rogers, and Robert A. Hummer. 2003. "Wealth, Race, and Morality." *Social Science Quarterly* 84 (September):667–684.

Human Rights Campaign. 2004. "Statewide Anti-Discrimination Laws and Policies." and "Statewide Discriminatory Marriage Laws." Accessed March 24 (www.hrc.org).

Hunt, Darnell. 1997. *Screening the Los Angeles "Riots": Race, Seeing, and Resistance.* New York: Cambridge University Press.

Hunter, Herbert M., ed. 2000. *The Sociology of Oliver C. Cox: New Perspectives: Research in Race and Ethnic Relations,* vol. 2. Stamford, CT: JAI Press.

Hunter, James Davison. 1991. *Culture Wars: The Struggle to Define America.* New York: Basic Books.

Hurh, Won Moo. 1994. *Korean Immigrants in America: A Structural Analysis of Ethnic Confinement and Adhesive Adaptation.* Rutherford, NJ: Fairleigh Dickinson University Press.

———. 1998. *The Korean Americans.* Westport, CT: Greenwood Press.

———, and Kwang Chung Kim. 1998. "The 'Success' Image of Asian Americans: Its Validity, and Its Practical and Theoretical Implications." *Ethnic and Racial Studies* 12 (October): 512–538.

Hurn, Christopher J. 1985. *The Limits and Possibilities of Schooling,* 2d ed. Boston: Allyn and Bacon.

Immigration and Naturalization Service. 1999a. *Legal Immigration, Fiscal Year 1998.* Washington, DC: U.S. Government Printing Office.

———. 1999b. *1997 Statistical Yearbook of the Immigration and Naturalization Service.* Washington, DC: U.S. Government Printing Office.

Inglehart, Ronald, and Wayne E. Baker. 2000. "Modernization, Cultural Change, and the Persistence of Traditional Values." *American Sociological Review* 65 (February):19–51.

Institute of International Education. 2004. *Open Doors: Foreign Student 2002/2003 and American Students Study Abroad.* Accessed April 5 (www.opendoors.iienetwork.org).

Intelligence Report. 2003. "Hate Web Site List." *Intelligence Report* (Spring):42–47.

International Crime Victim Survey. 2004. *Nationwide Surveys in the Industrialized Countries.* Accessed February 20 (www.ruljis.leidenuniv.nl/group/jfcr/www/icvs).

International Monetary Fund. 2000. *World Economic Outlook: Asset Prices and the Business Cycle.* Washington, DC: International Monetary Fund.

Inter-Parliamentary Union. 2003. *Women in National Parliaments.* May 31. Accessed August 6 (www.ipu.org).

Iritani, Evelyn, and Marla Dickerson. 2002. "People's Republic of Products." *Los Angeles Times,* October 20, pp. A1, A10.

Jackson, Elton F., Charles R. Tittle, and Mary Jean Burke. 1986. "Offense-Specific Models of the Differential Association Process." *Social Problems* 33 (April):335–356.

Jackson, Philip W. 1968. *Life in Classrooms.* New York: Holt.

Jackson, Shelly, Lynette Feder, David R. Forde, Robert C. Davis, Christopher D. Maxwell, and Bruce G. Taylor. 2003. *Batterer Intervention Programs. Where Do We Go From Here?* Washington, D.C.: National Institute of Justice.

Jacobs, Andrew. 2001a. "A Nation Challenged: Neighbors, Town, Shed Its Anonymity to Confront the Bereaved." *New York Times.* October 14.

———. 2001b. "A Suburb Pulls Together for Its Grieving Families." *New York Times.* November 13, p. B1.

———. 2002. "Emerging from a Cocoon of Grief." *New York Times,* September 9, p. A23.

Jacobs, Jerry. 2003. "Detours on the Road to Equality: Women, Work and Higher Education." *Contexts* (Winter):32-41.

Jacobson, Jodi. 1993. "Closing the Gender Gap in Development." Pp. 61–79 in *State of the World,* edited by Lester R. Brown. New York: Norton.

Jamieson, Arnie, Hyon B. Shin, and Jennifer Day. 2002. "Voting and Registration in the Election of November 2000." *Current Population Reports,* ser. P-20, no. 542. Washington, DC: U.S. Government Printing Office.

Jargowsky, Paul A. 2003. *Stunning Progress, Hidden Problems: The Dramatic Decline of Concentrated Poverty in the 1990s.* Washington, DC: Brookings Institute.

Jasper, James M. 1997. *The Art of Moral Protest: Culture, Biography, and Creativity in Social Movements.* Chicago: University of Chicago Press.

Jenkins, Richard. 1991. "Disability and Social Stratification." *British Journal of Sociology* 42 (December):557–580.

Jobtrak.com. 2000. "79% of College Students Find the Quality of an Employer's Website Important in Deciding Whether or Not to Apply for a Job." Accessed on June 29 (http://static.jobtrak.com/mediacenter/press_polls/polls_061200.html).

Johnson, Anne M., Jane Wadsworth, Kaye Wellings, and Julie Field. 1994. *Sexual Attitudes and Lifestyles.* Oxford: Blackwell Scientific.

Johnson, Benton. 1975. *Functionalism in Modern Sociology: Understanding Talcott Parsons.* Morristown, NJ: General Learning.

Johnson, Dirk. 1996. "Rural Life Gains New Appeal, Turning Back a Long Decline." *New York Times,* September 23, pp. A1, B6.

Johnson, Jeffrey, et al. 2002. "Television Viewing and Aggressive Behavior During Adolescence and Adulthood." *Science* 295 (March 29): 2468–2471.

Johnston, David Cay. 1996. "The Divine Write-Off." *New York Times,* January 12, pp. D1, D6.

Jolin, Annette. 1994. "On the Backs of Working Prostitutes: Feminist Theory and Prostitution Policy." *Crime and Delinquency* 40 (2):69–83.

Jones, Dale E., Dherri Doty, James E. Horsch, Richard Houseal, Mac Lynn, John P. Marcum, Kenneth M. Sanchagrin, and Richard H. Taylor. 2002. *Religious Congregations and Membership in the United States 2000: An Enumeration by Religion, State and Country Based on Data Reported by 149 Religious Bodies.* Nashville, TN: Glenmary Research Center.

Jones, James T., IV. 1988. "Harassment Is Too Often Part of the Job." *USA Today,* August 8, p. 5D.

Jones, Stephen R. G. 1992. "Was There a Hawthorne Effect?" *American Journal of Sociology* 98 (November):451–568.

Jost, Kenneth. 2002a. "Corporate Crime." *CQ Researcher* 12 (October 11).

———. 2002b. "School Vouchers Showdown." *CQ Researcher* 12 (February 15): 121-144.

Joynt, Jen, and Vasugi Ganeshananthan. 2003. "Abortion Decisions." *Atlantic Monthly* 291 (April):38–39.

Juhasz, Anne McCreary. 1989. "Black Adolescents' Significant Others." *Social Behavior and Personality* 17 (2):211–214.

Kahlenberg, Richard D., ed. 2004. *America's Untapped Resource: Low-Income Students in Higher Education.* New York: Century Fund.

Kahn, Joseph. 2003a. "Made in China, Bought in China." *New York Times,* January 5, sec. 3, pp. 1, 10.

———. 2003b. "China's Workers Risk Limbs in Export Drive." *New York Times,* April 7, p. A3.

———. 2004a. "China's Leaders Manage Class Conflict Carefully." *New York Times,* January 25, Sect. WK, p. 5.

———. 2004b. "The Most Populous Nation Faces a Population Crisis." *New York Times,* May 30, Sect. 4, p. 1

Kaiser Family Foundation. 2001. *Few Parents Use V-Chip to Block TV Sex and Violence.* Menlo Park: Kaiser Family Foundation.

———. 2003. *Sex on TV: 2003.* Santa Barbara, CA: Kaiser Family Foundation.

Kaiser Family Foundation/*The San Jose Mercury News.* 2003. *Growing Up Wired: Survey on Youth and the Internet in Silicon Valley.* Accessed January 14, 2004 (www.KFF.org).

Kanellos, Nicholas. 1994. *The Hispanic Almanac: From Columbus to Corporate America.* Detroit: Visible Ink Press.

Katovich, Michael A. 1987. Correspondence. June 1.

Katz, Michael. 1971. *Class, Bureaucracy, and the Schools: The Illusion of Educational Change in America.* New York: Praeger.

Kerbo, Harold R. 2003. *Social Stratification and Inequality: Class Conflict in Historical, Comparative, and Global Perspective.* 5th ed. New York: McGraw-Hill.

Kilborn, Peter T. 2001. "Rural Towns Turn to Prisons to Reignite Their Economies." *New York Times,* August 1, pp. A1, A11.

Kilbourne, Jean. 2000a. *Can't Buy My Love: How Advertising Changes the Way We Think and Feel.* New York: Touchstone Book, Simon and Schuster.

———. 2000b. *Killing Us Softly* 3. Videorecording. Northampton, MA: Media Education Foundation (Cambridge Documentary Films).

Kim, Kwang Chung. 1999. *Koreans in the Hood: Conflict with African Americans.* Baltimore: Johns Hopkins University Press.

King, Leslie. 1998. "France Needs Children: Pronatalism, Nationalism, and Women's Equity." *Sociological Quarterly* 39 (Winter): 33–52.

Kinkade, Patrick T., and Michael A. Katovich. 1997. "The Driver Adaptations and Identities in the Urban Worlds of Pizza Delivery Employees." *Journal of Contemporary Ethnography* 25 (January):421–448.

Kinsella, Kevin, and Victoria A. Velkoff. 2001. "An Aging World: 2001." *Current Population Reports,* ser. 95, no. 01-1. Washington, DC: U.S. Government Printing Office.

Kinsey, Alfred C., Wardell B. Pomeroy, and Clyde E. Martin. 1948. *Sexual Behavior in the Human Male.* Philadelphia: Saunders.

———, Wardell B. Pomeroy, and Paul H. Gebhard. 1953. *Sexual Behavior in the Human Female.* Philadelphia: Saunders.

Kiser, Edgar. 1992. "War." Pp. 2243–2247 in *Encyclopedia of Sociology,* edited by Edgar F. Borgatta and Marie L. Borgatta. New York: Macmillan.

Kitchener, Richard F. 1991. "Jean Piaget: The Unknown Sociologist." *British Journal of Sociology* 42 (September):421–442.

Klass, Perri. 2003. "This Side of Medicine." In *This Side of Doctoring: Reflection for Women in Medicine* by Eliza Lo Chin (ed.). P. 319 New York: Oxford University Press.

Klein, Naomi. 1999. *No Logo: Money, Marketing, and the Growing Anti-Corporate Movement.* New York: Picador (St. Martin's Press).

Kleiner, Art. 2003. "Are You In with the In Crowd?" *Harvard Business Review* 81 (July):86–92.

Kleinknecht, William. 1996. *The New Ethnic Mobs: The Changing Face of Organized Crime in America.* New York: Free Press.

Kleniewski, Nancy. 2002. *Cities, Change, and Conflict: A Political Economy of Urban Life.* 2d ed. Belmont, CA: Wadsworth.

Klinenberg, Eric. 2002. *Heat Wave: A Social Autopsy of Disaster in Chicago.* Chicago: University of Chicago Press.

Klinger, Scott et al. 2002. *Executive Excess 2002: CEOs Cook the Books, Skewer the Rest of Us.* Boston, MA: United for a Fair Economy.

Kohn, Melvin L. 1970. "The Effects of Social Class on Parental Values and Practices." Pp. 45–68 in *The American Family: Dying or Developing,* edited by David Reiss and H. A. Hoffman. New York: Plenum.

Kolata, Gina. 1999. *Clone: The Road to Dolly and the Path Beyond.* New York: William Morrow.

Komarovsky, Mirra. 1991. "Some Reflections on the Feminist Scholarship in Sociology." Pp. 1–25 in *Annual Review of Sociology,* edited by W. Richard Scott and Judith Blake. Palo Alto, CA: Annual Reviews.

Konieczny, May Ellen, and Mark Chaves. 2000. "Resources, Race, and Female-Headed Congregations in the United States." *Journal for the Scientific Study of Religion* 39 (September): 261–271.

Koolhaas, Rem, et al. 2001. *Mutations.* Barcelona, Spain: Actar.

Kopinak, Kathryn. 1995. "Gender as a Vehicle for the Subordination of Women Maquiladora Workers in Mexico." *Latin American Perspectives* 22 (Winter):30–48.

Korczyk, Sophie M. 2002. *Back to Which Future: The U.S. Aging Crisis Revisited.* Washington, DC: AARP.

Kornblum, Janet. 2004. "Sons, Daughters and Caregivers." *USA Today,* February 17, pp. 1D, 4D.

Kottak, Conrad. 2004. *Anthropology: The Explanation of Human Diversity.* New York: McGraw-Hill.

Kraul, Chris. 2003. "After Initial Boom, Mexico's Economy Goes Bust." *Los Angeles Times.* January 2, pp. A71, A36, A37.

Krauss, Clifford. 2003. "Quebec Seeking to End Its Old Cultural Divide." *New York Times,* April 13, p. A12.

Kreider, Rose M., and Jason M. Fields. 2002. "Number, Timing, and Duration of Marriages and Divorces: 1996." *Current Population Reports,* ser. P-70, no. 80. Washington, DC: U.S. Government Printing Office.

Kretzmann, John P., and John L. McKnight. 1993. *Building Communities from the Inside Out: A Path Toward Finding and Mobilizing a Communities Assets.* Evanston, IL: Institute for Policy Research.

Kriesberg, Louis. 1992. "Peace." Pp. 1432–1436 in *Encyclopedia of Sociology,* edited by Edgar F. Borgatta and Marie L. Borgatta. New York: Macmillan.

Kristof, Nicholas D. 1998. "As Asian Economies Shrink, Women Are Squeezed Out." *New York Times,* June 11, pp. A1, A12.

Labaton, Stephan. 2003. "10 Wall St. Firms Settle with U.S. in Analyst Inquiry." *New York Times,* April 29, pp. A1, C4.

Ladner, Joyce. 1973. *The Death of White Sociology.* New York: Random Books.

Lamb, David. 1997. "Viet Kieu: A Bridge Between Two Worlds." *Los Angeles Times,* November 4, pp. A1, A8.

Landtman, Gunnar. [1938] 1968. *The Origin of Inequality of the Social Class.* New York: Greenwood (original edition 1938, Chicago: University of Chicago Press).

Lang, Eric. 1992. "Hawthorne Effect." Pp. 793–794 in *Encyclopedia of Sociology,* vol. 2, edited by Edgar F. Borgatta and Marie L. Borgatta. New York: Macmillan.

Lappin, Todd. 1996. "Aux Armes, Netizens!" *The Nation* 262 (February 26):6–7.

Larsen, Elena. 2000. *Wired Churches, Wired Temples: Taking Congregations and Missions into Cyberspace.* Washington, DC: Pew Internet and American Life Project.

Lasn, Kalle. 2003. "Ad Spending Predicted for Steady Decline." *Adbusters* (January/February).

Lasswell, Harold D. 1936. *Politics: Who Gets What, When, How.* New York: McGraw-Hill.

Lauer, Robert H. 1982. *Perspectives on Social Change.* 3d ed. Boston: Allyn and Bacon.

Laumann, Edward O., John H. Gagnon, and Robert T. Michael. 1994a. "A Political History of the National Sex Survey of Adults." *Family Planning Perspectives* 26 (February):34–38.

———, John H. Gagnon, Robert T. Michael, and Stuart Michaels. 1994b. *The Social Organization of Sexuality: Sexual Practices in the United States.* Chicago: University of Chicago Press.

Lazarsfeld, Paul, Bernard Beretson, and H. Gaudet. 1948. *The People's Choice.* New York: Columbia University Press.

———, and Robert K. Merton. 1948. "Mass Communication, Popular Taste, and Organized Social Action." Pp. 95–118 in *The Communication of Ideas,* edited by Lymon Bryson. New York: Harper and Brothers.

Leaf, Nathan. 2003. "Wal-topia." *The Capital Times* (Madison, WI), May 3, pp. 1A, 4A.

Leavell, Hugh R., and E. Gurney Clark. 1965. *Preventive Medicine for the Doctor in His Community: An Epidemiologic Approach.* 3d ed. New York: McGraw-Hill.

Lee, Alfred McClung. 1983. *Terrorism in Northern Ireland.* Bayside, NY: General Hall.

Legrain, Philippe. 2003. "Cultural Globalization Is Not Americanization." *Chronicle of Higher Education* 49 (May 9):B7–B10.

Lehne, Gregory K. 1995. "Homophobia among Men: Supporting and Defining the Male Role." Pp. 325–336 in *Men's Lives,* edited by Michael S. Kimmel and Michael S. Messner. Boston: Allyn and Bacon.

Leinwand, Donna. 2000. "20% Say They Used Drugs with Their Mom and Dad." *USA Today,* August 24, pp. 1A, 2A.

———. 2003. "Alcohol-Soaked Spring Break Lures Students Abroad." *USA Today,* January 6, pp. A1, A2.

Lemann, Nicholas. 1991. "The Other Underclass." *Atlantic Monthly* 268 (December):96–102, 104, 107–108, 110.

Lengermann, Patricia Madoo, and Jill Niebrugge-Brantley. 1998. *The Women Founders: Sociology and Social Theory, 1830–1930.* Boston: McGraw-Hill.

Lenski, Gerhard. 1966. *Power and Privilege: A Theory of Social Stratification.* New York: McGraw-Hill.

———, Jean Lenski, and Patrick Nolan. 1995. *Human Societies: An Introduction to Macrosociology.* 7th ed. New York: McGraw-Hill.

Levin, Jack, and William C. Levin. 1980. *Ageism.* Belmont, CA: Wadsworth.

Levin, Thomas Y., Ursula Frohne, and Peter Weibel, eds. 2002. *Ctrl Space: Rhetorics of Surveillance from Bentham to Big Brother.* Cambridge: MIT Press.

Levinson, David. 1996. *Religion: A Cross-Cultural Encyclopedia.* New York: Oxford University Press.

Levy, Becca R., Martin D. Slade, Suzanne R. Kunkel, and Stanislav V. Kasl. 2002. "Longevity Increased by Positive Self-Perceptions of Aging." *Journal of Personality and Social Psychology* 83 (2):261–270.

Lewin, Tamar. 1998. "Debate Centers on Definition of Harassment." *New York Times,* March 22, pp. A1, A20.

———. 2000. "Differences Found in Care with Stepmothers." *New York Times,* August 17, p. A16.

Lewis, David Levering. 1994. *W. E. B. DuBois: Biography of a Race, 1868–1919.* New York: Holt.

———. 2000. *W. E. B. DuBois: The Fight for Equality and the American Century, 1919–1963.* New York: Holt.

Lewis Mumford Center. 2001. *Ethnic Diversity Grows, Neighborhood Integration Is at a Standstill.* Albany, NY: Lewis Mumford Center.

Lichter, Robert S., Linda S. Lichter, Daniel R. Amundson, and Trevor Buterworth. 2002. *Hollywood Cleans Up Its Act: Changing Rates of Sex and Violence in Entertainment Media.* Washington DC: Center for Media and Public Affairs.

Lieberman, David. 1999. "On the Wrong Side of the Wires." *USA Today,* October 11, pp. B1, B2.

Lightblau, Eric. 2003. "Bush Issues Racial Profiling Ban but Exempts Security Awareness." *New York Times,* June 18, pp. A1, A14.

Lin, Nan. 1999. "Social Networks and Status Attainment." Pp. 467–487 in *Annual Review of Sociology 1999,* edited by Karen S. Cook and John Hagen. Palo Alto, CA: Annual Reviews.

———, and Wen Xie. 1988. "Occupational Prestige in Urban China." *American Journal of Sociology* 93 (January):793–832.

Lindner, Eileen, ed. 1998. *Yearbook of American and Canadian Churches, 1998.* Nashville: Abingdon Press.

———, ed. 2004. *Yearbook of American and Canadian Churches 2004.* Nashville: Abingden Press.

Linn, Susan, and Alvin F. Poussaint. 1999. "Watching Television: What Are Children Learning About Race and Ethnicity?" *Child Care Information Exchange* 128 (July):50–52.

Lipset, Seymour Martin. 1996. *American Exceptionalism: A Double-Edged Sword.* New York: Norton.

Lipson, Karen. 1994. "'Nell' Not Alone in the Wilds." *Los Angeles Times,* December 19, pp. F1, F6.

Liptak, Adam. 2004a. "Bans on Interracial Unions Offer Perspective on Gay Ones." *New York Times,* March 17, p. A16.

———. 2004b. "Study Revises Texas's Standing as a Death Penalty Leader." *New York Times,* February 14, p. A8.

Liska, Allen E., and Steven F. Messner. 1999. *Perspectives on Crime and Deviance.* 3d ed. Upper Saddle River, NJ: Prentice Hall.

Little, Kenneth. 1988. "The Role of Voluntary Associations in West African Urbanization." Pp. 211–230 in *Anthropology for the Nineties: Introductory Readings,* edited by Johnnetta B. Cole. New York: Free Press.

Livernash, Robert, and Eric Rodenburg. 1998. "Population Change, Resources, and the Environment." *Population Bulletin* 53 (March).

Locy, Toni. 2004. "Patriot Act Blurred in the Public Mind." *USA Today,* February 26, p. 5A.

Lofland, Lyn H. 1975. "The 'Thereness' of Women: A Selective Review of Urban Sociology." Pp. 144–170 in *Another Voice,* edited by M. Millman and R. M. Kanter. New York: Anchor/Doubleday.

Logan, John R. 2001. "From Many Shores: Asians in Census 2000." Accessed November 29 (http://mumford1.dyndns:org/cen2000/Asianpop).

Lohr, Steve. 1994. "Data Highway Ignoring Poor, Study Charges." *New York Times,* May 24, pp. A1, D3.

Longman, Phillip, 2004. "The Global Baby Bust." *Foreign Affairs* 83 (May/June):64–79.

Lorber, Judith. 1994. *Paradoxes of Gender.* New Haven, CT: Yale University Press.

Lu, Ming, Jianyong Fan, Shejan Liu, and Yan Yan. 2002. "Employment Restructuring During China's Economic Transition." *Monthly Labor Review* (August):25–31.

Lukacs, Georg. 1923. *History and Class Consciousness.* London: Merlin.

Luker, Kristin. 1984. *Abortion and the Politics of Motherhood.* Berkeley: University of California Press.

Lum, Joann, and Peter Kwong. 1989. "Surviving in America: The Trials of a Chinese Immigrant Woman." *Village Voice* 34 (October 31):39–41.

Lumpe, Lora. 2003. "Taking Aim at the Global Gun Trade." *Amnesty Now* (Winter):10–13.

Luster, Tom, Kelly Rhoades, and Bruce Haas. 1989. "The Relation between Parental Values and Parenting Behavior: A Test of the Kohn Hypothesis." *Journal of Marriage and the Family* 51 (February):139–147.

Lyall, Sarah. 2002. "For Europeans, Love, Yes; Marriage, Maybe." *New York Times,* March 24, pp. 1–8.

———. 2004. "In Europe, Lovers New Purpose: Marry Me, a Little." *New York Times,* February 15, p. 3.

Lynch, David J. 2002. "China's New Attitude Toward Capitalists Too Late for Some." *USA Today,* December 9, pp. B1, B2.

Lynn, Barry C. 2003. "Trading with a Low-Wage Tiger." *The American Prospect* 14 (February):10–12.

Lyotard, Jean François. 1993. *The Postmodern Explained: Correspondence, 1982–1985.* Minneapolis: University of Minnesota Press.

Mack, Raymond W., and Calvin P. Bradford. 1979. *Transforming America: Patterns of Social Change.* 2d ed. New York: Random House.

Magnier, Mark. 1999. "Equality Evolving in Japan." *Los Angeles Times,* August 30, pp. A1, A12.

———. 2004. "China Clamps Down on Web News Discussion." *Los Angeles Times,* February 26, p. A4.

Maguire, Brendan, and Polly F. Radosh. 1999. *Introduction to Criminology.* Belmont, CA: Wadsworth/Thomson Learning.

Maine Times. 2001. Article on Wal-Mart's Plan to Build Near the Penja. January 4, 2001.

Maines, David R. 1977. "Social Organization and Social Structure in Symbolic Interactionist Thought." Pp. 235–259 in *Annual Review of Sociology, 1977,* edited by Alex Inkles. Palo Alto, CA: Annual Reviews.

———. 1982. "In Search of Mesostructure: Studies in the Negotiated Order." *Urban Life* 11 (July):267–279.

Malcolm X, with Alex Haley. 1964. The *Autobiography of Malcolm X.* New York: Grove.

Malthus, Thomas Robert. [1798] 1965. *Essays on the Principle of Population.* New York: Augustus Kelly, Bookseller.

———, Julian Huxley, and Frederick Osborn. [1824] 1960. *Three Essays on Population.* Reprint. New York: New American Library.

Mangan, Katherine S. 2004. "This Political Hot Potato Is a Course in Demand." *Chronicles of Higher Education* 50 (May 14):A12–A13.

Mangum, Garth L., Stephen L. Magnum, and Andrew M. Sum. 2003. *The Persistence of Poverty in the United States.* Baltimore: Johns Hopkins University Press.

Margolis, Eric, ed. 2001. *The Hidden Curriculum in Higher Education.* New York: Routledge.

Marquand, Robert. 2002. "Yule Trees on Buddhist Temples and Handle's Messiah in Beijing." *Christian Science Monitor,* December 23, pp. 1, 10.

Marr, Phebe. 2003. "Civics 101, Taught by Saddam Hussein: First, Join the Paramilitary." *New York Times,* April 20.

Marshall, Patrick. 2003. "Gambling in America." *CQ Researcher* 13 (March 7):201–224.

Marshall, Tyler. 2003. "Kuwait's Klatch of the Titans." *Los Angeles Times,* February 12, pp. A1, A5.

Martelo, Emma Zapata. 1996. "Modernization, Adjustment, and Peasant Production." *Latin American Perspectives* 23 (Winter):118–130.

Martin, Joyce A., Brady E. Hamilton, Paul D. Sutton, Stephanie J. Ventura, Fay Menacker, and Martha L. Munson. 2003. "Births: Final Data for 2002." *National Vital Statistics Report* 52 (December 17).

Martin, Philip, and Elizabeth Midgley. 1999. "Immigrants to the United States." *Population Bulletin* 54 (June):1–42.

Martin, Susan E. 1994. "Outsider Within the Station House: The Impact of Race and Gender on Black Women Politics." *Social Problems* 41 (August):383–400.

Martineau, Harriet. [1837] 1962. *Society in America.* Edited, abridged, with an introductory essay by Seymour Martin Lipset. Reprint. Garden City, NY: Doubleday.

———. [1838] 1989. *How to Observe Morals and Manners.* Philadelphia: Leal and Blanchard. Sesquentennial edition, edited by M. R. Hill, Transaction Books.

Marx, Karl, and Friedrich Engels. [1847] 1955. *Selected Work in Two Volumes.* Reprint, Moscow: Foreign Languages Publishing House.

Mason, Heather. 2003. "What Do American's See in Title IX's Future?" *Gallup Poll Tuesday Briefing.* Accessed on January 28, 2003 at www.gallup.com.

Mason, J. W. 1998. "The Buses Don't Stop Here Anymore." *American Prospect* 37 (March): 56–62.

Massachusetts Department of Education. 2000. *Learning Support Service Progress: Safe Schools Program for Gay and Lesbian Students.* Accessed July 19, 2001 (www.doe.mass.edu/lss/program/ ssch.html).

Massey, Douglas S. 1998. "March of Folly: U.S. Immigration Policy After NAFTA." *The American Prospect* (March/April):22–23.

———, and Nancy A. Denton. 1993. *American Apartheid: Segregation and the Making of the Underclass.* Cambridge, MA: Harvard University Press.

Mathews, T. J., Marian F. MacDorman, and Fay Menacker. 2002. "Infant Mortality Statistics from the 1999 Period Linked Birth/Infant Death Data Set." *National Vital Statistics Reports* 50 (January 30).

Matsushita, Yoshiko. 1999. "Japanese Kids Call for a Sympathetic Ear." *Christian Science Monitor,* January 20, p. 15.

Matthews, Jay. 1999. "A Home Run for Home Schooling." *Washington Post National Weekly Edition* 16 (March 29):34.

Mattingly, Marybeth J., and Suzanne M. Bianchi. 2003. "Gender Differences in the Quantity and Quality of Free Time: The U.S. Experience." *Social Forces* 81 (March):999–1031.

Maugh, Thomas H., II. 2003. "Number of AIDS Diagnoses on the Rise Again in the United States." *Los Angeles Times,* February 12, p. A36.

Mayer, Karl Ulrich, and Urs Schoepflin. 1989. "The State and the Life Course." Pp. 187–209 in *Annual Review of Sociology, 1989,* edited by W. Richard Scott and Judith Blake. Palo Alto, CA: Annual Reviews.

McCormick, John, and Claudia Kalb. 1998. "Dying for a Drink." *Newsweek,* June 15, pp. 30–34.

McCreary, D. 1994. "The Male Role and Avoiding Femininity." *Sex Roles* 31:517–531.

McCright, Aaron M., and Riley E. Dunlap. 2003. "Defeating Kyoto: The Conservative Movement's Impact on U.S. Climate Change Policy." *Social Problems* 50 (No. 3):348–373.

McDonald, Kim A. 1999. "Studies of Women's Health Produce a Wealth of Knowledge on the Biology of Gender Differences." *Chronicle of Higher Education* 45 (June 25):A19, A22.

McFalls, Joseph A., Jr. 1998. "Population: A Lively Introduction." *Population Bulletin* 53 (September).

———. 2003. "Population: A Lively Introduction." 4e, *Population Bulletin* 58. (December).

McGivering, Jill. 2001. *Activists Urge Caste Debate.* August 28. Accessed April 15, 2003 (www.news.bbc.co.uk).

McGue, Matt, and Thomas J. Bouchard, Jr. 1998. "Genetic and Environmental Influence on Human Behavioral Differences." Pp. 1–24 in *Annual Review of Neurosciences.* Palo Alto, CA: Annual Reviews.

McGuire, Meredith B. 2002. *Religion: The Social Context.* 5th ed. Belmont, CA: Wadsworth.

McIntosh, Peggy. 1988. "White Privilege and Male Privilege: A Personal Account of Coming to See Correspondence Through Work and Women's Studies." Working Paper No. 189, Wellesley College Center for Research on Women, Wellesley, MA.

McKinlay, John B., and Sonja M. McKinlay. 1977. "The Questionable Contribution of Medical Measures to the Decline of Mortality in the United States in the Twentieth Century." *Milbank Memorial Fund Quarterly* 55 (Summer):405–428.

McKinley, James C., Jr. 1999. "In Cuba's New Dual Economy, Have-Nots Far Exceed Haves." *New York Times,* February 11, pp. A1, A6.

McKinnon, Jesse. 2003. "The Black Population in the United States: March 2002." *Current Population Reports,* ser. P-20, no. 541. Washington, DC: U.S. Government Printing Office.

McKnight, John L., and John P. Kretzmann. 1996. *Mapping Community Capacity.* Evanston, IL: Institute for Policy Research.

McLane, Daisann. 1995. "The Cuban-American Princess." *New York Times Magazine,* February 26, pp. 42–43.

McLuhan, Marshall. 1964. *Understanding Media: The Extensions of Man.* New York: New American Library.

———, and Quentin Fiore. 1967. *The Medium Is the Message: An Inventory of Effects.* New York: Bantam Books.

McNeil, Jr., Donald G. 2002. "W.H.O. Moves to Make AIDS Drugs More Accessible to Poor Worldwide." *New York Times,* August 23, p. D7.

———. 2003. "Africans Outdo U.S. Patients in Following AIDS Therapy." *New York Times,* September 3, pp. A1, A5.

Mead, George H. 1934. In *Mind, Self and Society,* edited by Charles W. Morris. Chicago: University of Chicago Press.

———. 1964a. In *On Social Psychology,* edited by Anselm Strauss. Chicago: University of Chicago Press.

———. 1964b. "The Genesis of the Self and Social Control." Pp. 267–293 in *Selected Writings: George Herbert Mead,* edited by Andrew J. Reck. Indianapolis: Bobbs-Merrill.

Mead, Margaret. 1973. "Does the World Belong to Men—Or to Women?" *Redbook* 141(October):46–52.

———. [1935] 2001. *Sex and Temperament in Three Primitive Societies.* New York: Perennial, HarperCollins.

MediaGuardian. 2001. "Censorship of News in Wartime Is Still Censorship." October 15. Accessed January 25, 2003 (http://media.guardian. co.uk/attack/story/0,1301,57445,00.html).

Melia, Marilyn Kennedy. 2000. "Changing Times." *Chicago Tribune,* January 2, Sec. 17, pp. 12–15.

Mencimer, Stephanie. 2002. "Children Left Behind." *The American Prospect,* December 30, pp. 29–31.

Mendez, Jennifer Bickman. 1998. "Of Mops and Maids: Contradictions and Continuities in Bureaucratized Domestic Work." *Social Problems* 45 (February):114–135.

Menzel, Peter. 1994. *Material World.* Berkeley: University of California Press.

Merton, Robert. 1948. "The Bearing of Empirical Research upon the Development of Social Theory." *American Sociological Review* 13 (October):505–515.

———. 1968. *Social Theory and Social Structure.* New York Free Press.

———. 1987. "The Focused Interview and Focus Groups." *Public Opinion Quarterly* 51:550–566.

———, and Alice S. Kitt. 1950. "Contributions to the Theory of Reference Group Behavior." Pp. 40–105 in *Continuities in Social Research: Studies in the Scope and Methods of the American Soldier,* edited by Robert K. Merton and Paul L. Lazarsfeld. New York: Free Press.

Messner, Michael A. 1997. *Politics of Masculinities: Men in Movements.* Thousand Oaks, CA: Sage.

———. 2002. "Gender Equity in College Sports: 6 Views." *Chronicle of Higher Education.* 49 (December 6):B9–B10.

Metropolitan Community Churches. 2004. "Fact Sheet." Accessed May 1 (www.mccchurch. org).

Meyers, Thomas J. 1992. "Factors Affecting the Decision to Leave the Old Order Amish." Presented at the annual meeting of the American Sociological Association, Pittsburgh.

Michels, Robert. 1915. *Political Parties.* Glencoe, IL: Free Press (reprinted 1949).

Migration News. 2001. "Labor Unions." 8 (April). Accessed March 20 (http://migration. ucdavis.edu).

———. 2002a. "China: Migrants, One-Child, Water." (September). Accessible online at (http://migration.ucdavis.edu).

———. 2002b. "Mexico: Bush, IDs, Remittances." (December). Accessible online at (http://migration.ucdavis.edu).

———. 2003b. "China: Economy, Migrants." (January). Accessible online at (http://migration.ucdavis.edu).

———. 2004. "NAFTA at 10." *Migration News* 11 (January). Accessible online at (http://migration.ucdavis.edu).

Mihalopoulos, Dan. 2004. "Melting Pot Often Heated." *Chicago Tribune,* December 26, p. 33.

Milgram, Stanley. 1963. "Behavioral Study of Obedience." *Journal of Abnormal and Social Psychology* 67 (October):371–378.

———. 1975. *Obedience to Authority: An Experimental View.* New York: Harper and Row.

Miller, D. W. 2000. "Sociology, Not Engineering May Explain Our Vulnerability to Technological Disaster." *Chronicle of Higher Education* (October 15):A19–A20.

Miller, David L., and JoAnne DeRoven Darlington. 2002. *Fearing for the Safety of Others: Disasters and the Small World Problem.* Paper presented at Midwest Sociological Society, Milwaukee, WI.

Miller, Judith, Stephen Engelberg, and William J. Broad. 2001. *Germs: Biological Weapons and America's Secret War.* New York: Simon and Schuster.

Miller, Reuben. 1988. "The Literature of Terrorism." *Terrorism* 11 (1):63–87.

Mills, C. Wright. [1959] 2000a. *The Sociological Imagination. 40th Anniversary Edition: New Afterword by Todd Gitlin.* New York: Oxford University Press.

———. [1956] 2000b. *The Power Elite.* A New Edition. Afterword by Alan Wolfe. New York: Oxford University Press.

Mills, Robert J. 2002. "Health Insurance Coverage: 2001." *Current Population Reports,* ser. P-60, no. 220. Washington, DC: U.S. Government Printing Office.

Mills, Robert J., and Shailesh Bhandari. 2003. "Health Insurance Coverage in the United States: 2002." *Current Population Reports,* ser. P-60, no. 223. Washington, DC: U.S. Government Printing Office.

Minnesota Twin Family Study. 2004. *What's Special About Twins to Science?* Accessed January 17 (www.psych.umn.edu/psylabs/mtgs/special.htm).

Mirapaul, Matthew. 2001. "How the Net Is Documenting a Watershed Moment." *New York Times,* October 15, p. E2.

Mizruchi, Mark S. 1996. "What Do Interlocks Do? An Analysis, Critique, and Assessment of Research on Interlocking Directorates." Pp. 271–298 in *Annual Review of Sociology, 1996,* edited by John Hagan and Karen Cook. Palo Alto, CA: Annual Reviews.

Moeller, Susan D. 1999. *Compassion Fatigue.* London: Routledge.

Mogelonsky, Marcia. 1996. "The Rocky Road to Adulthood." *American Demographics* 18 (May):26–29, 32–35, 56.

Monaghan, Peter. 1993. "Sociologist Jailed Because He 'Wouldn't Snitch' Ponders the Way Research Ought to Be Done." *Chronicle of Higher Education* 40 (September 1):A8, A9.

Monteiro, Lois A. 1998. "Ill-Defined Illnesses and Medically Unexplained Symptoms Syndrome." *Footnotes* 26 (February):3, 6.

Moore, David W. 2002. "Americans' View of Influence of Religion Settling Back to Pre-September 11 Levels." *Gallup Poll Tuesday Briefing.* December 31.

Moore, Wilbert E. 1967. *Order and Change: Essays in Comparative Sociology.* New York: Wiley.

———. 1968. "Occupational Socialization." Pp. 861–883 in *Handbook of Socialization Theory and Research,* edited by David A. Goslin. Chicago: Rand McNally.

Morehouse Medical Treatment and Effectiveness Center. 1999. *A Synthesis of the Literature: Racial and Ethnic Differences in Acccess to Medical Care.* Menlo Park, CA: Henry J. Kaiser Family Foundation.

Morin, Richard. 2000. "Will Traditional Polls Go the Way of the Dinosaur?" *Washington Post National Weekly Edition* 17 (May 15):34.

Morris, Aldon. 2000. "Reflections on Social Movement Theory: Criticisms and Proposals." *Contemporary Sociology* 29 (May): 445–454.

Morris, Bonnie Rothman. 1999. "You've Got Romance! Seeking Love on Line." *New York Times,* August 26, p. D1.

Morrison, Denton E. 1971. "Some Notes toward Theory on Relative Deprivation, Social Movements, and Social Change." *American Behavioral Scientist* 14 (May/June):675–690.

Morse, Arthur D. 1967. *While Six Million Died: A Chronicle of American Apathy.* New York: Ace.

Mosisa, Abraham T. 2002. "The Role of Foreign-Born Workers in the U.S. Economy." *Monthly Labor Review* (May):3–14.

Mosley, J., and E. Thomson. 1995. Pp. 148–165 in *Fatherhood: Contemporary Theory, Research and Social Policy,* edited by W. Marsiglo. Thousand Oaks, CA: Sage.

Moss, Michael, and Ford Fessenden. 2002. "New Tools for Domestic Spying, and Qualms." *New York Times,* December 10, pp. A1, A18.

Mullins, Marcy E. 2001. "Bioterrorism Impacts Few." *USA Today,* October 18, p. 16A.

Mumola, Christopher J. 2000. *Incarcerated Parents and Their Children.* Washington, DC: U.S. Government Printing Office.

Murdock, George P. 1945. "The Common Denominator of Cultures." Pp. 123–142 in *The Science of Man in the World Crisis,* edited by Ralph Linton. New York: Columbia University Press.

———. 1949. *Social Structure.* New York: Macmillan.

———. 1957. "World Ethnographic Sample." *American Anthropologist* 59 (August): 664–687.

Murphy, Caryle. 1993. "Putting Aside the Veil." *Washington Post National Weekly Edition* 10 (April 12–18):10–11.

Murphy, Dean E. 1997. "A Victim of Sweden's Pursuit of Perfection." *Los Angeles Times,* September 2, pp. A1, A8.

———. 2004. "Desert's Promised Land: Long Odds for Las Vegas Newcomers." *New York Times,* May 30, pp. A1, A16.

Murray, Velma McBride, Amanda Willert, and Diane P. Stephens. 2001. "The Half-Full Glass: Resilient African American Single Mothers and Their Children." *Family Focus,* June, pp. F4–F5.

Nader, Laura. 1986. "The Subordination of Women in Comparative Perspective." *Urban Anthropology* 15 (Fall/Winter): 377–397.

NARAL Pro-Choice America. 2003. *Who Decides? A State-by-State Review of Abortion and Reproductive Rights.* Washington, DC: NARAL Pro-Choice America and NARAL Pro-Choice America Foundation.

Nash, Manning. 1962. "Race and the Ideology of Race." *Current Anthropology* 3 (June): 285–288.

Nass, Clifford, and Youngme Moon. 2000. "Machines and Mindlessness: Social Responses to Computers." *Journal of Social Issues* 56 (1):81–103.

National Advisory Commission on Criminal Justice. 1976. *Organized Crime.* Washington, DC: U.S. Government Printing Office.

National Campaign on Dalit Human Rights. 2003. *Who Are Dalits?* Accessed April 28 (www.dalits.org).

National Center for Education Statistics. 2004. *The Condition of Education 2004.* Washington, DC: U.S. Government Printing Office.

National Center for Health Statistics. 2002. *Health, United States, 2002.* Washington, DC: U.S. Government Printing Office.

National Center on Women and Family Law. 1996. *Status of Marital Rape Exemption Statutes in the United States.* New York: National Center on Women and Family Law.

National Geographic. 2002. "A World Transformed." *National Geographic* (September): map.

National Homeschool Association. 1999. *Homeschooling Families: Ready for the Next Decade.* Accessed November 19, 2000 (www.n-h-a.org/decade.htm).

National Organization for Men Against Sexism. 2003. Home page. Accessed May 11 (www.nomas.org).

National Rifle Association. 2004. "NRAILA 2004 Firearms Facts." Accessed February 21 (www.NRAILA.org).

National Right to Work Legal Defense Foundation. 2004. *Right to Work States.* Accessed February 28 (www.nrtw.org/rtws.htm).

National Vital Statistics Reports. 2004. "Births, Marriages, Divorces, and Deaths: Provisional Data for September 2003." *National Vital Statistics Reports* 52 (February 13).

Navarro, Mireya. 2002. "Trying to Get Beyond the Role of the Maid." *New York Times,* May 16, pp. E1, E4.

Nelson, Emily. 2004. "Goodbye, 'Friends'; Hello, New Reality." *Wall Street Journal,* February 9, pp. B6, B10.

Nelson, F. Howard, and Rachel Drown. 2003. *Survey and Analysis of Teacher Salary Trends 2002.* Washington, DC: American Federation of Teachers.

Nelson, Jack. 1995. "The Internet, the Virtual Community, and Those with Disabilities." *Disability Studies Quarterly* 15 (Spring):15–20.

Neuborne, Ellen. 1996. "Vigilantes Stir Firms' Ire with Cyber-antics." *USA Today,* February 28, pp. A1, A2.

New York Times. 1998. "2 Gay Men Fight Town Hall for a Family Pool Pass Discount." July 14, p. B2.

Newburger, Eric C. 2001. "Home Computers and Internet Use in the United States: August 2000." *Current Population Reports,* ser. P-23, no. 207. Washington, DC: U.S. Government Printing Office.

Newman, Katherine S. 1999. *No Shame in My Game: The Working Poor in the Inner City.* New York: Alfred A. Knopf and Russell Sage Foundation.

Newman, William M. 1973. *American Pluralism: A Study of Minority Groups and Social Theory.* New York: Harper and Row.

Newport, Frank. 2004. "A Look at Americans and Religion." Accessed April 14 (www.gallup.com).

Newsday. 1997. "Japan Sterilized 16,000 Women." September 18, p. A19.

Ni, Ching-Ching. 2002. "Chinese Web Surfers Still Face a Backwash." *Los Angeles Times,* September 13, p. A4.

NICHD. 1998. *Early Childhood Care.* Accessed October 19, 2000 (www.nichd.nih.gov/publications/pubs/ early_child_care.htm).

Nie, Norman H. 2001. "Sociability, Interpersonal Relations, and the Internet." *American Behavioral Scientist* 45 (November): 420–435.

Nielsen, Joyce McCarl, Glenda Walden, and Charlotte A. Kunkel. 2000. "Gendered Heteronormativity: Empirical Illustrations in Everyday Life." *Sociological Quarterly* 41(2): 283–296.

Nixon, Howard L., II. 1979. *The Small Group.* Englewood Cliffs, NJ: Prentice Hall.

Nolan, Patrick, and Gerhard Lenski. 2004. *Human Societies: An Introduction to Macrosociology.* 9th ed. Boulder, CO: Paradigm Publishers.

Noonan, Rita K. 1995. "Women Against the State: Political Opportunities and Collective Action Frames in Chile's Transition to Democracy." *Sociological Forum* 10:81–111.

Novelli, William D. 2004. "Common Sense: The Case for Age Discrimination Law." *Global Report on Aging,* pp. 4, 7. Washington, DC: AARP.

Nussbaum, Daniel. 1998. "Bad Air Days." *Los Angeles Times Magazine,* July 19, pp. 20–21.

Oberschall, Anthony. 1973. *Social Conflict and Social Movements.* Englewood Cliffs, NJ: Prentice Hall.

O'Donnell, Jayne, and Richard Willing. 2003. "Prison Time Gets Harder for White-Collar Crooks." *USA Today,* May 12, pp. A1, A2.

O'Donnell, Mike. 1992. *A New Introduction to Sociology.* Walton-on-Thames, United Kingdom: Thomas Nelson and Sons.

Office of Justice Programs. 1999. "Transnational Organized Crime." *NCJRS Catalog* 49 (November/December):21.

Ogburn, William F. 1922. *Social Change with Respect to Culture and Original Nature.* New York: Huebsch (reprinted 1966, New York: Dell).

———, and Clark Tibbits. 1934. "The Family and Its Functions." Pp. 661–708 in *Recent Social Trends in the United States,* edited by Research Committee on Social Trends. New York: McGraw-Hill.

O'Hare, William P., and Brenda Curry White. 1992. "Is There a Rural Underclass?" *Population Today* 20 (March):6–8.

Okamoto, Dina G., and Lynn Smith-Lovin. 2001. "Changing the Subject: Gender, Status, and the Dynamics of Topic Change." *American Sociological Review* 66 (December):852–873.

Okano, Kaori, and Motonori Tsuchiya. 1999. *Education in Contemporary Japan: Inequality and Diversity.* Cambridge: Cambridge University Press.

Oliver, Melvin L., and Thomas M. Shapiro. 1995. *Black Wealth/White Wealth: New Perspectives on Racial Inequality.* New York: Routledge.

O'Neill, Tom. 2004. "Untouchable." *National Geographic* 203 (June): 2–31.

Onishi, Norimitso. 2003. "Divorce in South Korea: Striking a New Attitude." *New York Times,* September 21, p. 19.

Orum, Anthony M. 1989. *Introduction to Political Sociology: The Social Anatomy of the Body Politic.* 3d ed. Englewood Cliffs, NJ: Prentice Hall.

———. 2001. *Introduction to Political Sociology.* 4th ed. Upper Saddle River, NJ: Prentice Hall.

Osgood, D. Wayne, and Jeff M. Chambers. 2003. "Community Correlates of Rural Youth Violence." *Juvenile Justice Bulletin* (May):1–9.

Ouchi, William, 1981. *Theory Z: How American Businesses Can Meet the Japanese Challenge.* Reading, MA: Addison-Wesley.

Overland, Martha Ann. 2004. "In India, Almost Everyone Wants to be Special." *Chronicle of Higher Education* (February 13), pp. A40–A42.

Page, Charles H. 1946. "Bureaucracy's Other Face." *Social Forces* 25 (October):89–94.

Pager, Devah. 2003. "The Mark of a Criminal Record." *American Journal of Sociology* 108 (March):937–975.

Paik, Haejung, and George Comstock. 1994. "The Effects of Television Violence on Anti-social Behavior: A Meta-analysis." *Communication Research* 21:516–546.

Pamuk, E., D. Makui, K. Heck, C. Reuban, and K. Lochren. 1998. *Health, United States 1998 with Socioeconomic Status and Health Chartbook.* Hyattsville, MD: National Center for Health Statistics.

Pan, Philip P. 2002. "When the Employee-Owner Doesn't Work." *Washington Post National Weekly Edition* 20, December 9, pp. 16–17.

Parents Television Council. 2003. *TV Bloodbath: Violence on Prime Time Broadcast TV.* Los Angeles: PTC.

Park, Robert E. 1916. "The City: Suggestions for the Investigation of Human Behavior in the Urban Environment." *American Journal of Sociology* 20 (March):577–612.

———. 1922. *The Immigrant Press and Its Control.* New York: Harper.

———. 1936. "Succession, an Ecological Concept." *American Sociological Review* 1 (April):171–179.

Parsons, Talcott. 1951. *The Social System.* New York: Free Press.

———. 1966. Societies: *Evolutionary and Comparative Perspectives.* Englewood Cliffs, NJ: Prentice Hall.

———. 1975. "The Sick Role and the Role of the Physician Reconsidered." *Milbank Medical Fund Quarterly Health and Society* 53 (Summer):257–278.

———, and Robert Bales. 1955. *Family: Socialization, and Interaction Process.* Glencoe, IL: Free Press.

Passero, Kathy. 2002. "Global Travel Expert Roger Axtell Explains Why." *Biography.* July, pp. 70–73, 97–98.

Patterson, Orlando. 1998. "Affirmative Action." *Brookings Review* 16 (Spring):17–23.

Patterson, Thomas E. 2003. *We the People,* 5th ed. New York: McGraw-Hill.

Pattillo-McCoy, Mary. 1999. *Black Picket Fences: Privilege and Peril among the Black Middle Class.* Chicago: University of Chicago Press.

Paulson, Amanda. 2000. "Where the School Is Home." *Christian Science Monitor,* October 10, pp. 18–21.

PBS. 2001. "Store Wars: When Wal-Mart Comes to Town." Accessed August 24, 2001 (www.pbs.org).

Pear, Robert. 1997. "Now, the Archenemies Need Each Other." *New York Times,* June 22, Sec. 4, pp. 1, 4.

Pearlstein, Steven. 2001. "Coming Soon (Maybe): Worldwide Recession." *Washington Post National Weekly Edition* 19 (November 12):18.

Peck, Don. 2002. "The Shrinking Electorate." *The Atlantic Monthly* (November):48–49.

Pellow, David Naguib. 2002. *Garbage Wars: The Struggle for Environmental Justice in Chicago.* Cambridge, MA: MIT Press.

Pelton, Tom. 1994. "Hawthorne Works' Glory Now Just So Much Rubble." *Chicago Tribune,* April 18, pp. 1, 6.

Perrow, Charles. 1986. *Complex Organizations.* 3d ed. New York: Random House.

———. 1999. *Normal Accidents: Living with High Risk Technologies.* Updated edition. New Brunswick, NJ: Rutgers University Press.

Peter, Laurence J., and Raymond Hull. 1969. *The Peter Principle.* New York: Morrow.

Petersen, William. 1979. *Malthus.* Cambridge, MA: Harvard University Press.

Peterson, Karen. S. 2003. "Unmarried with Children: For Better or Worse." *USA Today,* August 18, pp. 1A, 8A.

Pew Research Center. 2004. "Conflicted Views of Affirmative Action." News release, May 14, 2004. Washington, DC: Pew Research Center.

Phillips, E. Barbara. 1996. *City Lights: Urban— Suburban Life in the Global Society.* New York: Oxford University Press.

Phillips, Susan A. 1999. *Wallbangin': Graffiti and Gangs in L.A.* Chicago: University of Chicago Press.

Pholktales. 2004. *You Know You're a Phishhead When . . .* Accessed January 14 (www.pholktales.com).

Piaget, Jean. 1954. *The Construction of Reality in the Child.* Translated by Margaret Cook. New York: Basic Books.

Pierre, Robert E. 2002. "When Welfare Reform Stops Working." *Washington Post National Weekly Edition,* January 13, pp. 29–30.

Piller, Charles. 2000. "Cyber-Crime Loss at Firms Doubles to $10 Billion." *Los Angeles Times,* May 22, pp. C1, C4.

Pinderhughes, Dianne. 1987. *Race and Ethnicity in Chicago Politics: A Reexamination of Pluralist Theory.* Urbana: University of Illinois Press.

Pinkerton, James P. 2003. "Education: A Grand Compromise." *Atlantic Monthly* 291 (January/February):115–116.

Plomin, Robert. 1989. "Determinants of Behavior." *American Psychologist* 44 (February): 105–111.

Pollak, Michael. 2000. "World's Dying Languages, Alive on the Web." *New York Times,* October 19, p. D13.

Polletta, Francesca, and James M. Jasper. 2001. "Collective Identity and Social Movements." Pp. 283–305 in *Annual Review of Sociology, 2001,* edited by Karen S. Cook and Leslie Hogan. Palo Alto, CA: Annual Review of Sociology.

Poniewozik. 2001. "What's Wrong with This Picture?" *Time* 157 (May 28):80–81.

Popenoe, David, and Barbara Dafoe Whitehead. 1999. *Should We Live Together? What Young Adults Need to Know About Cohabitation Before Marriage.* Rutgers, NJ: The National Marriage Project.

Population Reference Bureau. 1996. "Speaking Graphically." *Population Today* 24 (June/July):b.

Population Reference Bureau. 2004. "Transitions in World Population." *Population Bulletin* 59 (March).

Power, Carla. 1998. "The New Islam." *Newsweek* 131(March 16):34–37.

Power, Richard. 2002. *2002 CSI/FBI Computer Crime and Security Survey.* San Francisco, CA: Computer Security Institute.

Powers, Mary G., and Joan J. Holmberg. 1978. "Occupational Status Scores: Changes Introduced by the Inclusion of Women." *Demography* 15 (May):183–204.

Proctor, Bernadette D., and Joseph Dalaker. 2002. "Poverty in the United States: 2001." *Current Population Reports* Series P-60, no. 219. Washington, DC: U.S. Government Printing Office.

———. 2003. "Poverty in the United States: 2002." *Current Population Reports,* ser. P-60, no. 222. Washington, DC: U.S. Government Printing Office.

Putnam, Robert D. 2000. *Bowling Alone: The Collapse and Revival of American Community.* New York: Simon and Schuster.

Pyle, Amy. 1998. "Opinions Vary on Studies That Back Bilingual Classes." *Los Angeles Times,* March 2, pp. B1, B3.

Quadagno, Jill. 2005. *Aging and the Life Course: An Introduction to Social Gerontology,* 3d ed. New York: McGraw-Hill.

Quart, Alissa. 2003. *Branded: The Buying and Selling of Teenagers.* New York: Perseus.

Quinney, Richard. 1970. *The Social Reality of Crime.* Boston: Little, Brown.

———. 1974. *Criminal Justice in America.* Boston: Little, Brown.

———. 1979. *Criminology.* 2d ed. Boston: Little, Brown.

———. 1980. *Class, State and Crime.* 2d ed. New York: Longman.

Rainie, Lee. 2001. The *Commons of the Tragedy.* Washington, DC: Pew Internet and American Life Project.

———, and Andrew Kohut. 2000. *Tracking Online Life: How Women Use the Internet to Cultivate Relationships with Family and Friends.* Washington, DC: Pew Internet and American Life League.

Rajagopal, Aruind. 2001. *Politics After Television: Hindu Nationalism and the Reshaping of the Public in India.* Cambridge, England: Oxford University Press.

Rajan, Sara. 2004. "Prosperity and Its Perils." *Time* 163 (March 1):34.

Ramet, Sabrina. 1991. *Social Currents in Eastern Europe: The Source and Meaning of the Great Transformation.* Durham, NC: Duke University Press.

Ramirez, Deborah, Jack McDevitt, and Amy Farrell. 2000. *A Resource Guide on Racial Profiling Data Collection Systems. Promising Practices and Lessons Learned.* Washington, DC: U.S. Government Printing Office.

Ramirez, Eddy. 2002. "Ageism in the Media Is Seen as Harmful to Health of the Elderly." *Los Angeles Times,* September 5, p. A20.

Ramirez, Roberta R., and G. Patricia de la Cruz. 2003. "The Hispanic Population in the Current United States: March 2002." *Current Population Reports,* ser. P-20, no. 545. Washington, DC: U.S. Government Printing Office.

Rau, William, and Ann Durand. 2000. "The Academic Ethic and College Grades: Does Hard Work Help Students to 'Make the Grade'?" *Sociology of Education* 73 (January):19–38.

Reddick, Randy, and Elliot King. 2000. *The Online Student: Making the Grade on the Internet.* Fort Worth: Harcourt Brace.

Reeves, Terrance, and Claudette Bennett. 2003. "The Asian and Pacific Islander Population in the United States: March 2002." *Current Population Reports,* ser. P-20, no. 540. Washington DC: U.S. Government Printing Office.

Reinharz, Shulamit. 1992. *Feminist Methods in Social Research.* New York: Oxford University Press.

Religion News Service. 2003. "New U.S. Guidelines on Prayer in Schools Get Mixed Reaction." *Los Angeles Times,* February 15, p. B24.

Remnick, David. 1998a. *King of the World: Muhammed Ali and the Rise of an American Hero.* New York: Random House.

———. 1998b. "Bad Seeds." *New Yorker* 74 (July 20):28–33.

Rennison, Callie Marie, and Michael R. Rand. 2003. "Criminal Victimization, 2002." Washington, DC: Bureau of Justice Statistics.

———, and Sarah Welchans. 2000. *Intimate Partner Violence.* Washington, DC: U.S. Government Printing Office.

Rheingold, Howard. 2003. *Smart Mobs: The Next Social Revolution.* Cambridge, MA: Perseus.

Richardson, James T., and Barend van Driel. 1997. "Journalists' Attitudes toward New Religious Movements." *Review of Religious Research* 39 (December):116–136.

Richardson, Laurel, Verta Taylor, and Nancy Whittier, eds. 2004. *Feminist Frontiers.* 6th ed. New York: McGraw-Hill.

Richburg, Keith B. 2003. "Gay Marriage Now Routine for Dutch." *Chicago Tribune,* September 24, p. 6.

Richtel, Matt. 2000. "www.layoffs.com." *New York Times,* June 22, pp. C1, C12.

Ridgeway, Cecilia L., and Lynn Smith-Lovin. 1999. "The Gender System and Interaction." Pp. 191–216 in *The Annual Review of Sociology 1999,* edited by Karen Cook and John Hagan. Palo Alto, CA: Annual Review.

Riding, Alan. 1998. "Why 'Titanic' Conquered the World." *New York Times,* April 26, sec. 2, pp. 1, 28, 29.

———. 2002. "Espousing a New View of Accidents." *New York Times,* December 26, Arts Section, pp. 1–2.

Rifkin, Jeremy. 1995. "Afterwork." *Utne Reader* (May/June):52–62.

Riley, Matilda White, Robert L. Kahn, and Anne Foner. 1994a. *Age and Structural Lag.* New York: Wiley InterScience.

———, Robert L. Kahn, and Anne Foner, in association with Karin A. Mock. 1994b. "Introduction: The Mismatch between People and Structures." Pp. 1–36 in *Age and Structural Lag,* edited by Matilda White Riley, Robert L. Kahn, and Ann Foner. New York: Wiley InterScience.

Riley, Nancy E. 2004. "China's Population: New Trends and Challenges." *Population Bulletin* 59 (June).

Rimer, Sara. 1998. "As Centenarians Thrive, 'Old' Is Redefined." *New York Times,* June 22, pp. A1, A14.

Ritzer, George. 1995. *Modern Sociological Theory.* 4th ed. New York: McGraw-Hill.

———. 2002. *McDonaldization: The Reader.* Thousand Oaks, CA: Pine Forge Press.

———. 2004a. *The McDonaldization of Society.* Revised New Century Edition. Thousand Oaks, CA: Pine Forge Press.

———. 2004b. *The Globalization of Nothing.* Thousand Oaks, CA: Pine Forge Press.

Robb, David. 2001. "Hollywood Wars." *Brill's Content* (Fall):134–151.

Roberson, Debi, Ian Davies, and Jules Davidoff. 2000. "Color Categories Are Not Universal: Replications and New Evidence From Stone Age Culture." *Journal of Experimental Psychology* 129 (3):369–398.

Roberts, D. F. 1975. "The Dynamics of Racial Intermixture in the American Negro—Some

Anthropological Considerations." *American Journal of Human Genetics* 7 (December): 361–367.

———, Lisa Henriksen, Peter G. Christiansson, and Marcy Kelly. 1999. "Substance Abuse in Popular Movies and Music." Accessible online (www.whitehousedrugpolicy.gov/news/press/042899.html). Washington, DC: Office of Juvenile Justice.

Roberts, Lynne D., and Malcolm R. Parks. 1999. "The Social Geography of Gender-Switching in Virtual Environments on the Internet." *Information, Communication and Society* 2 (Winter).

Robertson, Roland. 1988. "The Sociological Significance of Culture: Some General Considerations." *Theory, Culture, and Society* 5 (February):3–23.

Robinson, Thomas N., Marta L. Wilde, Lisa C. Navracruz, K. Farish Haydel, and Ann Varady. 2001. "Effects of Reducing Children's Television and Video Game Use on Aggressive Behavior." *Archives of Pediatric Adolescent Medicine* 155 (January):17–23.

Robison, Jennifer. 2002. "Should Mothers Work?" *Gallup Poll Tuesday Briefing*, Accessed August 17 (www.gallup.com).

Roethlisberger, Fritz J., and W. J. Dickson. 1939. *Management and the Worker*. Cambridge, MA: Harvard University Press.

Rogovin, Milton. 1994. *Triptychs: Buffalo's Lower West Side Revisited*. New York: W. W. Norton and Co.

Rohter, Larry. 2003a. "Racial Quotas in Brazil Touch Off Fierce Debate." *New York Times*, April 5, p. A5.

Rollins, Karina. 2003. "Boys Under Attack." *The American Enterprise* 14 (September), pp. 44–45.

Romero, Mary. 1988. "Chicanas Modernize Domestic Service." *Qualitative Sociology* 11:319–334.

Romney, Lee. 1998. "Latinos Get Down to Business." *Los Angeles Times*, November 11, pp. A1, A20.

Roosevelt, Margot. 2001. "A Setback for Medipot." *Time* 157 (May 28), p. 50.

Rose, Arnold. 1951. *The Roots of Prejudice*. Paris: UNESCO.

Rose, Peter I., Myron Glazer, and Penina Migdal Glazer. 1979. "In Controlled Environments: Four Cases of Intense Resocialization." Pp. 320–338 in *Socialization and the Life Cycle*, edited by Peter I. Rose. New York: St. Martin's.

Rosenbaum, Lynn. 1996. "Gynocentric Feminism: An Affirmation of Women's Values and Experiences Leading Us toward Radical Social Change." *SSSP Newsletter* 27 (1):4–7.

Rosenberg, Douglas H. 1991. "Capitalism." Pp. 33–34 in *Encyclopedic Dictionary of Sociology*, 4th ed., edited by Dushkin Publishing Group. Guilford, CT: Dushkin.

Rosenberg, Howard. 2003. "Snippets of the 'Unique' Al Jazeera." *Los Angeles Times*, April 4, pp. E1, E37.

Rosenberg, Yuval. 2004. "Lost Youth." *American Demographics* (March):18–19.

Rosenthal, Elizabeth. 2001. "College Entrance in China: 'No' to the Handicapped." *New York Times*, May 23, p. A3.

Rosenthal, Robert, and Lenore Jacobson. 1968. *Pygmalion in the Classroom*. New York: Holt.

Rosman, Abraham, and Paula G. Rubel. 1994. *The Tapestry of Culture: An Introduction to Cultural Anthropology*. 5th ed. Chapter 1, Map. p. 35. New York: McGraw-Hill.

Rossi, Alice S. 1968. "Transition to Parenthood." *Journal of Marriage and the Family* 30 (February):26–39.

———. 1984. "Gender and Parenthood." *American Sociological Review* 49 (February):1–19.

Rossi, Peter H. 1987. "No Good Applied Social Research Goes Unpunished." *Society* 25 (November/December):73–79.

Rossides, Daniel W. 1997. *Social Stratification: The Interplay of Class, Race, and Gender*. 2d ed. Upper Saddle River, NJ: Prentice Hall.

Roszak, Theodore. 1969. *The Making of a Counterculture*. Garden City, NY: Doubleday.

Roter, Debra L., Judith A. Hall, and Yutaka Aoki. 2002. "Physician Gender Effects in Medical Communication: A Meta-analytic Review." *Journal of the American Medical Association* 288 (August 14):756–764.

Rubin, Alissa J. 2003. "Pat-Down on the Way to Prayer." *Los Angeles Times*, November 25, pp. A1, A5.

Russo, Nancy Felipe. 1976. "The Motherhood Mandate." *Journal of Social Issues* 32:143–153.

Rutenberg, Jim. 2002. "Fewer Media Owners, More Media Choices." *New York Times*, December 2, pp. C1, C11.

———. 2003. "Coming Soon to Arab TV's: U.S. Answer to Al Jazeera, Production Values and All." *New York Times*, December 17, p. A22.

Ryan, William. 1976. *Blaming the Victim*. Rev. ed. New York: Random House.

Saad, Lydia. 2003. "What Form of Government for Iraq?" Accessed September 26 (www.gallup.com).

———. 2004. "Divorce Doesn't Last." *Gallup Poll Tuesday Briefing*, March 30 (www.gallup.com).

———, and Joe Carroll. 2003. "How Are Retirees Faring Financially?" *Gallup Poll Tuesday Briefing* (May 13) at www.gallup.com.

"Sabbathday Lake." 2004. Interview by author with Sabbathday Lake Shaker Village. July 28.

Sadker, Myra Pollack, and David Miller Sadker. 1985. "Sexism in the Schoolroom of the '80s." *Psychology Today* 19 (March): 54–57.

———. 2000. *Teachers, Schools, and Sociology*. 6th ed. New York: McGraw-Hill.

———. 2003. *Teachers, Schools and Society*, 6th ed. New York: McGraw-Hill.

Safire, William. 1996. "Downsized." *New York Times Magazine*, May 26, pp. 12, 14.

Sagarin, Edward, and Jose Sanchez. 1988. "Ideology and Deviance: The Case of the Debate over the Biological Factor." *Deviant Behavior* 9 (1):87–99.

Sale, Kirkpatrick. 1996. *Rebels against the Future: The Luddites and Their War on the Industrial Revolution* (with a new preface by the author). Reading, MA: Addison-Wesley.

Salem, Richard, and Stanislaus Grabarek. 1986. "Sociology B.A.s in a Corporate Setting: How Can They Get There and of What Value Are They?" *Teaching Sociology* 14 (October): 273–275.

Salkever, Alex. 1999. "Making Machines More Like Us." *Christian Science Monitor*, December 20, electronic edition.

Samuelson, Paul A., and William D. Nordhaus. 2001. *Economics*. 17th ed. New York: McGraw-Hill.

Samuelson, Robert J. 1996a. "Are Workers Disposable?" *Newsweek* 127, February 12, p. 47.

———. 1996b. "Fashionable Statements." *Washington Post National Weekly Edition* 13 (March 18):5.

———. 2001. "The Specter of Global Aging." *Washington Post National Weekly Edition* 18 (March 11):27.

Sandberg, Jared. 1999. "Spinning a Web of Hate." *Newsweek* 134 (July 19):28–29.

Saporito, Bill. 2003. "Can Wal-Mart Get Any Bigger?" *Time*, January 13, pp. 38–43.

Sax, Linda J., Alexander W. Astin, Jennifer A. Lindholm, William S. Korn, Victor B. Saenz, and Kathryn M. Mahoney. 2003. *The American Freshman: National Norms for Fall 2003*. Los Angeles: Higher Education Research Institute, University of California.

———, Jennifer A. Lindholm, Alexander W. Astin, William S. Korn, and Kathryn M. Mahoney. 2002. *The American Freshman: National Norms for Fall 2002*. Los Angeles: Higher Education Research Institute, UCLA.

Scarce, Rik. 1994. "(No) Trial (But) Tribulations: When Courts and Ethnography Conflict." *Journal of Contemporary Ethnography* 23 (July):123–149.

———. 1995. "Scholarly Ethics and Courtroom Antics: Where Researchers Stand in the Eyes of the Law." *American Sociologist* 26 (Spring): 87–112.

Schaefer, Peter. 1995. "Destroy Your Future." *Daily Northwestern*, November 3, p. 8.

Schaefer, Richard T. 1998a. "Differential Racial Mortality and the 1995 Chicago Heat Wave." Presentation at the annual meeting of the American Sociological Association, August, San Francisco.

———. 1998b. *Alumni Survey*. Chicago, IL: Department of Sociology, DePaul University.

———. 2004. *Racial and Ethnic Relations*. 9th ed. Upper Saddle River, NJ: Prentice Hall.

Scharnberg, Kirsten. 2002. "Tattoo Unites WTC's Laborers." *Chicago Tribune*, July 22, pp. 1, 18.

Scheiber, Noam. 2004. "As a Center for Outsourcing India Could Be Losing Its Edge." *New York Times*, May 9, Sect. BW, p. 3.

Schellenberg, Kathryn, ed. 1996. *Computers in Society*. 6th ed. Guilford, CT: Dushkin.

Schmetzer, Uli. 1999. "Modern India Remains Shackled to Caste System." *Chicago Tribune*, December 25, p. 23.

Schmidley, A. Dianne. 2002. "The Foreign-Born Population in the United States: March 2002." *Current Population Reports*, ser. P-20, no. 539. Washington, DC: U.S. Government Printing Office.

———, and J. Gregory Robinson. 2003. *Measuring the Foreign-Born Population in the United*

States with the Current Population Survey: 1994–2002. Washington, DC: Population Division, Bureau of the Census.

Schmidt, Peter. 2004. "Noted Higher-Education Research Urges Admissions Preference for the Poor." *Chronicle of Higher Education* (April 16):A26.

Schnaiberg, Allan. 1994. *Environment and Society: The Enduring Conflict.* New York: St. Martin's.

Schulman, Andrew. 2001. *The Extent of Systematic Monitoring of Employee E-mail and Internet Users.* Denver, CO: Workplace Surveillance Project, Privacy Foundation.

Schur, Edwin M. 1965. *Crimes without Victims: Deviant Behavior and Public Policy.* Englewood Cliffs, NJ: Prentice Hall.

———. 1968. *Law and Society: A Sociological View.* New York: Random House.

———. 1985. "'Crimes without Victims': A 20 Year Reassessment." Paper presented at the annual meeting of the Society for the Study of Social Problems.

Schwartz, Howard D., ed. 1987. *Dominant Issues in Medical Sociology.* 2d ed. New York: Random House.

Scott, Alan. 1990. *Ideology and the New Social Movements.* London: Unwin Hyman.

Scott, Gregory. 2001. "Broken Windows behind Bars: Eradicating Prison Gangs through Ecological Hardening and Symbolic Cleansing." *Corrections Management Quarterly* 5 (Winter):23–36.

Scott, Richard W. 2003. *Organizations: Rational, Natural, and Open Systems.* 5th ed. Upper Saddle River, NJ: Prentice Hall.

Seabrook, Jeremy. 2002. *Class, Caste and Hierarchies.* Oxford, England: New Internationalist Publications.

Seelye, Katharine Q. 2002. "When Hollywood's Big Guns Come Right from Source." *New York Times,* June 10, pp. A1, A22.

Segall, Alexander. 1976. "The Sick Role Concept: Understanding Illness Behavior." *Journal of Health and Social Behavior* 17 (June): 163–170.

Segall, Rebecca. 1998. "Sikh and Ye Shall Find." *Village Voice* 43 (December 15):46–48, 53.

Segerstråle, Ullica. 2000. *Defense of the Truth: The Battle for Science in the Sociobiology Debate and Beyond.* New York: Oxford University Press.

Seidman, Steven. 1994. "Heterosexism in America: Prejudice against Gay Men and Lesbians." Pp. 578–593 in *Introduction to Social Problems,* edited by Craig Calhoun and George Ritzer. New York: McGraw-Hill.

Sengupta, Somini. 2004. "For Iraqi Girls, Changing Land Narrows Lines." *New York Times* (June 27), pp. A1, A11.

Senior Action in a Gay Environment (SAGE). 2003. Home page. Accessed May 11 (www.sageusa.org).

Sernau, Scott. 2001. *Worlds Apart: Social Inequalities in a New Century.* Thousand Oaks, CA: Pine Forge Press.

Shaheen, Jack G. 1999. "Image and Identity: Screen Arabs and Muslims." In *Cultural Diversity: Curriculum, Classrooms, and Climate Issues,* edited by J. Q. Adams and Janice R. Welsch.

Macomb, IL: Illinois Staff and Curriculum Development Association.

Shapiro, Joseph P. 1993. *No Pity: People with Disabilities Forging a New Civil Rights Movement.* New York: Times Books.

Sharp, Deborah. 2002. "Peace Groups to Test National Clout." *USA Today,* December 10, p. 3A.

Shcherbak, Yuri M. 1996. "Ten Years of the Chernobyl Era." *Scientific American* 274 (April): 44–49.

Sheehy, Gail. 1999. *Understanding Men's Passages: Discovering the New Map of Men's Lives.* New York: Ballantine Books.

———. 2003. *Middletown America: One Town's Passage from Trauma to Hope.* New York: Random House.

Shenon, Philip. 1995. "New Zealand Seeks Causes of Suicides by Young." *New York Times,* July 15, p. 3.

———. 1998. "Sailor Victorious in Gay Case on Internet Privacy." *New York Times,* June 12, pp. A1, A14.

Sherman, Lawrence W., Patrick R. Gartin, and Michael D. Buerger. 1989. "Hot Spots of Predatory Crime: Routine Activities and the Criminology of Place." *Criminology* 27:27–56.

Sherrill, Robert. 1995. "The Madness of the Market." *The Nation* 260 (January 9–16):45–72.

Shin, Hyon B., and Rosalind Bruno. 2003. "Language Use and English-Speaking Ability: 2000." *Census 2000 Brief,* C2KBR-29. Washington, DC: U.S. Government Printing Office.

Shinkai, Hiroguki, and Ugljea Zvekic. 1999. "Punishment." Pp. 89–120 in *Global Report on Crime and Justice,* edited by Graeme Newman. New York: Oxford University Press.

Short, Kathleen, Thesia Garner, David Johnson, and Patricia Doyle. 1999. "Experimental Poverty Measures: 1990 to 1997." *Current Population Reports,* ser. P-60, no. 205. Washington, DC: U.S. Government Printing Office.

Shostak, Arthur B. 2002. "Clinical Sociology and the Art of Peace Promotion: Earning a World Without War." Pp. 325–345 in *Using Sociology: An Introduction from the Applied and Clinical Perspectives,* edited by Roger A. Straus. Lanham, MD: Rowman and Littlefield.

Shu, Xialing, and Yanjie Bian. 2003. "Marketing Transition and Gender Gap in Earnings in Urban China." *Social Forces* 81 (4):1107–1145.

Shupe, Anson D., and David G. Bromley. 1980. "Walking a Tightrope." *Qualitative Sociology* 2:8–21.

Sigelman, Lee, Timothy Bledsoe, Susan Welch, and Michael W. Combs. 1996. "Making Contact? Black-White Social Interaction in an Urban Setting." *American Journal of Sociology* 5 (March):1306–1332.

Silicon Valley Cultures Project. 2003. The Silicon Valley Cultures Project Website. Accessed September 8, 2003 (www2.sjsu.edu/depts/anthropology/svcp).

Silver, Ira. 1996. "Role Transitions, Objects, and Identity." *Symbolic Interaction* 10 (1):1–20.

Simmel, Georg. 1950. *Sociology of Georg Simmel.* Translated by K. Wolff. Glencoe, IL: Free Press (originally written in 1902–1917).

Simmons, Ann M. 1998. "Where Fat Is a Mark of Beauty." *Los Angeles Times,* September 30, pp. A1, A12.

Simmons, Tavia, and Martin O'Connell. 2003. "Married-Couple and Unmarried-Partner Households: 2000." *Census 2000 Special Reports CENBR-5.* Washington, DC: U.S. Government Printing Office.

Simon, Bernard. 2001. "Canada Warms to Wal-Mart." *New York Times* (November 1), pp. B1, B3.

Simons, Marlise. 1997. "Child Care Sacred as France Cuts Back the Welfare State." *New York Times,* December 31, pp. A1, A6.

Sjoberg, Gideon. 1960. *The Preindustrial City: Past and Present.* Glencoe, IL: Free Press.

Small, Macio Luis, and Katherine Newman. 2001. "Urban Poverty after 'The Truly Disadvantaged': The Rediscovery of the Family, the Neighborhood, and Culture." Pp. 23–45 in *Annual Review of Sociology 2001.* Palo Alto, CA: Annual Reviews.

Smallwood, Scott. 2003 "American Women Surpass Men in Earning Doctorates." *Chronicle of Higher Education* (December 12):A10.

Smart, Barry. 1990. "Modernity, Postmodernity, and the Present." Pp. 14–30 in *Theories of Modernity and Postmodernity,* edited by Bryan S. Turner. Newbury Park, CA: Sage.

Smart Growth. 2001. "About Smart Growth." Accessed August 24, 2001 (www. smartgrowth.org.).

Smedley, Brian D., Adrienne Y. Stith, and Alan R. Nelson, eds. 2002. *Unequal Treatment: Confronting Racial and Ethnic Disparities in Health Care.* Washington, DC: Institutional Medicine.

Smeeding, Timothy, Lee Rainwater, and Gary Burtless. 2001. "United States Poverty in a Cross-National Context." *Focus* 21 (Spring): 50–54.

Smelser, Neil. 1963. *The Sociology of Economic Life.* Englewood Cliffs, NJ: Prentice Hall.

———. 1981. *Sociology.* Englewood Cliffs, NJ: Prentice Hall.

Smith, Buffy. 2004. "Leave No College Student Behind." *Multicultural Education* (Spring): 48–49.

Smith, Christian. 1991. *The Emergence of Liberation Theology: Radical Religion and Social Movement Theory.* Chicago: University of Chicago Press.

Smith, Dan. 1999. *The State of the World Atlas.* 6th ed. London: Penguin.

Smith, David A. 1995. "The New Urban Sociology Meets the Old: Rereading Some Classical Human Ecology." *Urban Affairs Review* 20 (January):432–457.

———, and Michael Timberlake. 1993. "World Cities: A Political Economy/Global Network Approach." Pp. 181–207 in *Urban Sociology in Transition,* edited by Ray Hutchison. Greenwich, CT: JAI Press.

Smith, David M. and Gary J. Gates. 2001. *Gay and Lesbian Families in the United States: Same-Sex Unmarried Partner Households.* Washington, D.C.: Human Rights Campaign.

Smith, Denise. 2003. "The Older Population in the United States: March 2002." *Current Population Reports,* ser. P-20, no. 546. Washington, DC: U.S. Government Printing Office.

———, and Hava Tillipman. 2000. "The Older Population in the United States." *Current Population Reports,* ser. P-20, no. 532. Washington, DC: U.S. Government Printing Office.

Smith, James F. 2001. "Mexico's Forgotten Find Cause for New Hope." *Los Angeles Times,* February 23, pp. A1, A12, A13.

Smith, James P,. and Barry Edmonston, eds. 1997. *The New Americas: Economic, Dempgraphic, and Fiscal Effects of Immigration.* Washington, DC: National Academy Press.

Smith, Kristin. 2000. "Who's Minding the Kids? Child Care Arrangements." *Current Population Reports,* ser. P-70, no. 70. Washington, DC: U.S. Government Printing Office.

Smith, Michael Peter. 1988. *City, State, and Market.* New York: Basil Blackwell.

Smith, Tom. 2001. *Estimating the Muslim Population in the United States.* New York: American Jewish Committee.

———. 2003. Coming of Age in 21st Century America: Public Attitudes Toward the Importance and Timing of Transition to Adulthood. Chicago: National Opinion Research Center.

Snyder, Thomas D. 1996. *Digest of Education Statistics 1996.* Washington, DC: U.S. Government Printing Office.

Sohoni, Neera Kuckreja. 1994. "Where Are the Girls?" *Ms.* 5 (July/August):96.

Sommers, Christina Hoff. 2000. *The War Against Boys.* New York: Touchstone.

Sorensen, Annemette. 1994. "Women, Family and Class." Pp. 27–47 in *Annual Review of Sociology, 1994,* edited by John Hagan and Karen S. Cook. Palo Alto, CA: Annual Reviews.

Soriano, Cesar G. 2001. "Latino TV Roles Shrank in 2000, Report Finds." *USA Today,* August 26, p. 3D.

Sorokin, Pitirim A. [1927] 1959. *Social and Cultural Mobility.* New York: Free Press.

Southern Poverty Law Center. 2003. "Active Hate Groups in the United States in the Year 2002." *Southern Poverty Law Center* (Spring):36–37.

Spalter-Roth, Roberta M., and Sunhwa Lee. 2000. "Gender in the Early Stages of the Sociological Career." *Research Brief* (American Sociological Association) 1 (2):1–11.

———, Jan Thomas, and Felice J. Levine. 2000. "New Doctorates in Sociology: Professions Inside and Outside the Academy." *Research Brief* (American Sociological Association) 1 (1):1–9.

Spear, Allan. 1967. *Black Chicago: The Making of a Negro Ghetto.* Chicago, IL: University of Chicago Press.

Spengler, Joseph J. 1978. *Facing Zero Population Growth: Reactions and Interpretations, Past and Present.* Durham, NC: Duke University Press.

Spindel, Cheywa, Elisa Levy, and Melissa Connor. 2000. *With an End in Sight.* New York: United Nations Development Fund for Women.

Spitzer, Steven. 1975. "Toward a Marxian Theory of Deviance." *Social Problems* 22 (June):641–651.

Squires, Gregory D., ed. 2002. *Urban Sprawl: Causes, Consequences and Policy Responses.* Washington: Urban Institute.

Stack, Megan K. 2004. "For Arabs, It's Not Yet Must-see TV." *Los Angeles Times* (March 24), p. A4.

Staggenborg, Suzanne. 1989a. "Stability and Innovation in the Women's Movement: A Comparison of Two Movement Organizations." *Social Problems* 36 (February):75–92.

———. 1989b. "Organizational and Environmental Influences on the Development of the Pro-Choice Movement," *Social Forces* 36 (September):204–240.

Stalker, Peter. 2000. *Workers Without Frontiers.* Boulder, CO: Lynne Reinner.

Stark, Rodney, and William Sims Bainbridge. 1979. "Of Churches, Sects, and Cults: Preliminary Concepts for a Theory of Religious Movements." *Journal for the Scientific Study of Religion* 18 (June):117–131.

———. 1985. *The Future of Religion.* Berkeley: University of California Press.

———, and Laurence R. Iannaccone. 1992. "Sociology of Religion." Pp. 2029–2037 in *Encyclopedia of Sociology,* vol. 4, edited by Edgar F. Borgatta and Marie L. Borgatta. New York: Macmillan.

Starr, Paul. 1982. *The Social Transformation of American Medicine.* New York: Basic Books.

Stavenhagen, Rodolfo. 1994. "The Indian Resurgence in Mexico." *Cultural Survival Quarterly,* Summer/Fall, pp. 77–80.

Steffensmeier, Darrell, and Stephen Demuth. 2000. "Ethnicity and Sentencing Outcomes in U.S. Federal Courts: Who Is Punished More Harshly?" *American Sociological Review* 65 (October):705–729.

Steinberg, Jacques. 2000. "Test Scores Rise, Surprising Critics of Bilingual Ban." *New York Times,* August 20, pp. 1, 16.

Stenning, Derrick J. 1958. "Household Viability among the Pastoral Fulani." Pp. 92–119 in *The Developmental Cycle in Domestic Groups,* edited by John R. Goody. Cambridge, England: Cambridge University Press.

Stevenson, David, and Barbara L. Schneider. 1999. *The Ambitious Generation: America's Teenagers, Motivated but Directionless.* New Haven: Yale University Press.

Stolberg, Sheryl. 1995. "Affirmative Action Gains Often Come at a High Cost." *Los Angeles Times,* March 29, pp. A1, A13–A16.

Stoops, Nicole. 2004. "Educational Attainment in the United States." 2003. *Population Reports* p. 20 No. 550. Washington, D.C.: U.S. Government Printing Office.

Strauss, Anselm. 1977. *Negotiations: Varieties, Contexts, Processes, and Social Order.* San Francisco: Jossey Bass.

Strauss, Gary. 2002. "'Good Old Boys' Network Still Rules Corporate Boards." *USA Today,* November 1, pp. B1, B2.

Stretesky, Paul B. and Michael J. Lynch. 2002. "Environmental Hazards and School Segregation in Hillsborough County, Florida, 1987–1999." *Sociological Quarterly* 43 (No. 4): 553–573.

Sugimoto, Yoshio. 1997. *An Introduction to Japanese Society.* Cambridge, England: Cambridge University Press.

Suid, Lawrence H. 2002. *Guts and Glory: The Making of the American Military Image in Film.* Lexington, KY: University of Kentucky Press.

Suitor, J. Jill, Staci A. Minyard, and Rebecca S. Carter. 2001. "'Did You See What I Saw?' Gender Differences in Perceptions of Avenues to Prestige Among Adolescents." *Sociological Inquiry* 71 (Fall):437–454.

Sullivan, Harry Stack. [1953] 1968. *The Interpersonal Theory of Psychiatry.* Edited by Helen Swick Perry and Mary Ladd Gawel. New York: W.W. Norton.

Sumner, William G. 1906. *Folkways.* New York: Ginn.

Sunstein, Cass R., Reid Hastie, John W. Payne, David A. Schkade, W. Kip Viscusi, and George L. Priest, eds. 2003. *Punitive Damages: How Juries Decide.* Chicago: University of Chicago Press.

Suro, Roberto, and Jeffery S. Passel. 2003. *The Rise of the Second Generation: Changing Patterns in Hispanic Population Growth.* Washington, DC: Urban Institute.

Sutherland, Edwin H. 1937. *The Professional Thief.* Chicago: University of Chicago Press.

———. 1940. "White-Collar Criminality." *American Sociological Review* 5 (February):1–11.

———. 1949. *White Collar Crime.* New York: Dryden.

———. 1983. *White Collar Crime: The Uncut Version.* New Haven, CT: Yale University Press.

———, Donald R. Cressey, and David F. Luckenbill. 1992. *Principles of Criminology.* 11th ed. New York: Rowman and Littlefield.

Suttles, Gerald D. 1972. *The Social Construction of Communities.* Chicago: University of Chicago Press.

Swanson, Stevenson, and Jim Kirk. 1998. "Satellite Outage Felt by Millions." *Chicago Tribune,* May 21, pp. 1, 26.

Sweet, Kimberly. 2001. "Sex Sells a Second Time." *Chicago Journal* 93 (April):12–13.

Szasz, Thomas S. 1971. "The Same Slave: An Historical Note on the Use of Medical Diagnosis as Justificatory Rhetoric." *American Journal of Psychotherapy* 25 (April):228–239.

Talbot, Margaret. 1998. "Attachment Theory: The Ultimate Experiment." *New York Times Magazine,* May 24, pp. 4–30, 38, 46, 50, 54.

Tannen, Deborah. 1990. *You Just Don't Understand: Women and Men in Conversation.* New York: Ballantine.

———. 1994a. *Talking from 9 to 5.* New York: William Morris.

———. 1994b. *Gender and Discourse.* New York: Oxford University Press.

Taylor, Verta. 1995. "Watching for Vibes: Bringing Emotions into the Study of Feminist Organizations." Pp. 223–233 in *Feminist Organizations: Harvest of the New Women's Movement,* edited by Myra Marx Ferree and Patricia Yancy Martin. Philadelphia: Temple University Press.

Telsch, Kathleen. 1991. "New Study of Older Workers Finds They Can Become Good Investments." *New York Times,* May 21, p. A16.

Terkel, Studs. 1974. *Working.* New York: Pantheon.

Terry, Sara. 2000. "Whose Family? The Revolt of the Child-Free." *Christian Science Monitor,* August 29, pp. 1, 4.

Therrien, Melissa, and Roberto R. Ramirez. 2001. "The Hispanic Population in the United States, March 2000." *Current Population Report,* ser. P-20, no. 535. Washington, DC: U.S. Government Printing Office.

Third World Institute. 2003. *The World Guide 2003–2004.* Oxford, England. New Internationalist Publishers.

Thomas, Gordon, and Max Morgan Witts. 1974. *Voyage of the Damned.* Greenwich, CT: Fawcett Crest.

Thomas, Jim. 1984. "Some Aspects of Negotiating Order: Loose Coupling and Mesostructure in Maximum Security Prisons." *Symbolic Interaction* 7 (Fall):213–231.

Thomas, Pattie, and Erica A. Owens. 2000. "Age Care!: The Business of Passing." Presented at the annual meeting of the American Sociological Association, Washington, DC.

Thomas, R. Murray. 2003. "New Frontiers in Cheating." In *Encyclopedia Britannica 2003 Book of the Year.* Chicago: Encyclopedia Britannica.

Thomas, William I. 1923. *The Unadjusted Girl.* Boston: Little, Brown.

Thompson, Ginger. 2001a. "Chasing Mexico's Dream into Squalor." *New York Times,* February 11, pp. 1, 6.

———. 2001b. "Why Peace Eludes Mexico's Indians." *New York Times,* March 11, Sect. WK, p. 16.

———. 2001c. "Mexican Rebels' Hopes Meet Hard Indian Reality." *New York Times,* March 3, p. A4.

———. 2003. "Money Sent Home by Mexicans Is Booming." *New York Times,* October 28, p. A12.

Thornton, Russell. 1987. *American Indians Holocaust and Survival: A Population History Since 1492.* Norman: University of Oklahoma Press.

Tierney, John. 1990. "Betting the Planet." *New York Times Magazine,* December 2, pp. 52–53, 71, 74, 76, 78, 80–81.

———. 2003. "Iraqi Family Ties Complicate American Efforts for Change." *New York Times,* September 28, pp. A1, A22.

Tilly, Charles. 1993. *Popular Contention in Great Britain 1758–1834.* Cambridge, MA: Harvard University Press.

Time Warner. 2004. "America Online and AOL International: Who We Are." Accessed February 6 (www.timewarner.com).

Tolbert, Kathryn. 2000. "In Japan, Traveling Alone Begins at Age 6." *Washington Post National Weekly Edition* 17 (May 15):17.

Tonkinson, Robert. 1978. *The Mardudjara Aborigines.* New York: Holt.

Tönnies, Ferdinand. [1887] 1988. *Community and Society.* Rutgers, NJ: Transaction.

Toossi, Mitra. 2002. "A Century of Change: The U.S. Labor Force, 1050–2050." *Monthly Labor Review* (May):15–28.

Touraine, Alain. 1974. *The Academic System in American Society.* New York: McGraw-Hill.

Treiman, Donald J. 1977. *Occupational Prestige in Comparative Perspective.* New York: Academic Press.

Trotter III, Robert T., and Juan Antonio Chavira. 1997. *Curanderismo: Mexican American Folk Healing.* Athens, GA: University of Georgia Press.

Tuchman, Gaye. 1992. "Feminist Theory." Pp. 695–704 in *Encyclopedia of Sociology,* vol. 2, edited by Edgar F. Borgatta and Marie L. Borgatta. New York: Macmillan.

Tumin, Melvin M. 1953. "Some Principles of Stratification: A Critical Analysis." *American Sociological Review* 18 (August):387–394.

———. 1985. *Social Stratification.* 2d ed. Englewood Cliffs, NJ: Prentice Hall.

Tumulty, Karen, and Viveca Novak. 2002. "Dodging the Bullet." *Newsweek* 160, November 4, p. 45.

Ture, Kwame, and Charles Hamilton. 1992. *Black Power: The Politics of Liberation.* Rev. ed. New York: Vintage Books.

Turkle, Sherry. 1995. *Life on the Screen: Identity in the Age of the Internet.* New York: Simon and Schuster.

———. 1999. "Looking Toward Cyberspace: Beyond Grounded Sociology." *Contemporary Sociology* 28 (November):643–654.

———. 2004. "How Computers Change the Way We Think." *Chronicle of Higher Education* 50 (January 30):B26–B28.

Turner, Bryan S., ed. 1990. *Theories of Modernity and Postmodernity.* Newbury Park, CA: Sage.

Turner, J. H. 1985. *Herbert Spencer: A Renewed Application.* Beverly Hills, CA: Sage.

Tyre, Peg, and Daniel McGinn. 2003. "She Works, He Doesn't." *Newsweek* 141, May 12, pp. 45–52.

Uchitelle, Louis. 2003. "Older Workers Are Thriving Despite Recent Hard Times." *New York Times,* September 8, pp. A1, A13.

UNAIDS. 2003. *AIDS Epidemic Update,* December. Geneva, Switzerland: UNAIDS.

United Jewish Communities. 2003. *The National Jewish Population Survey 2000–2001.* New York : UJC.

United Nations. 2000. *The World's Women 2000: Trends and Statistics.* New York: United Nations.

———. 2003. *Water For People, Water for Life: Executive Summary.* New York: United Nations World Water Assessment Programme.

United Nations Development Programme. 1995. *Human Development Report 1995.* New York: Oxford University Press.

———. 2001. *Human Development Report 2001. Making New Technologies Work for Human Development.* New York: UNDP.

———. 2002. *Human Development Report 2002: Deepening Democracy in a Fragmented World.* New York: Oxford University Press.

United Nations Population Division. 1998. *World Abortion Policies.* New York: Department of Economic and Social Affairs, UNPD.

———. 2001a. *World Marriage Patterns 2000.* Accessed September 13, 2002 (www.undp.org/popin/wdtrends/worldmarriage.patters2000.pdf).

United Nations Population Information Network. 2003. *World Population Prospects: The 2003 Revision.* Accessed May 20 (www.un.org/popin.data.html).

University of Michigan. 2003. *Information on Admissions Lawsuits.* Accessed August 8 (www.umich.edu/~urel/admissions).

Urbina, Ian. 2002. "Al Jazeera: Hits, Misses and Ricochets." *Asia Times,* December 25.

U.S. English. 2004. *Official English: States with Official English Laws.* Accessed January 14, 2002 (www.us-english.org/inc/official/states.asp).

U.S. Surgeon General. 2001. *Youth Violence: A Report of the Surgeon General.* Washington, DC: U.S. Government Printing Office.

U.S. Trade Representative. 2003. *2002 Annual Report.* Washington, DC: U.S. Government Printing Office.

Utne, Leif. 2003. "We Are All Zapatistas." *Utne Reader* (November–December):36–37.

Valdez, Enrique. 1999. "Using Hotlines to Deal with Domestic Violence: El Salvador." Pp. 139–142 in *Too Close to Home,* edited by Andrew R. Morrison and Maria Loreto Biehl. Washington, DC: Inter-American Development Bank.

Van Biema, David. 2004. "Rising above the stain-Glassed Ceiling" *Time* 163 (June 28), pp. 58–61.

van den Berghe, Pierre. 1978. *Race and Racism: A Comparative Perspective.* 2d ed. New York: Wiley.

Van Slambrouck, Paul. 1999. "Netting a New Sense of Connection." *Christian Science Monitor,* May 4, pp. 1, 4.

van Vucht Tijssen, Lieteke. 1990. "Women between Modernity and Postmodernity." Pp. 147–163 in *Theories of Modernity and Postmodernity,* edited by Bryan S. Turner. London: Sage.

Vaughan, Diane. 1996. *The Challenger Launch Decision: Risky Technology, Culture, and Deviance at NASA.* Chicago: University of Chicago Press.

———. 1999. "The Dark Side of Organizations: Mistake, Misconduct, and Disaster." Pp. 271–305 in *Annual Review of Sociology,* edited by Karen J. Cook and John Hagen. Palo Alto, CA: Annual Reviews.

Veblen, Thorstein. [1899] 1964. *Theory of the Leisure Class.* New York: Macmillan. New York: Penguin.

———. 1919. *The Vested Interests and the State of the Industrial Arts.* New York: Huebsch.

Vega, William A. 1995. "The Study of Latino Families: A Point of Departure." Pp. 3–17 in *Understanding Latino Families: Scholarship, Policy, and Practice,* edited by Ruth E. Zambrana. Thousand Oaks, CA: Sage.

Venkatesh, Sudhir Alladi. 2000. *American Project: The Rise and Fall of a Modern Ghetto.* Cambridge, MA: Harvard University Press.

Ventura, Stephanie J., Joyce C. Abma, William D. Musher, and Stanley Henshaw. 2003. "Revised Programming Rates, 1990–97, and New Rates for 1998–99: United States." *National Vital Statistics Reports* 52 (October 31).

Vernon, Glenn. 1962. *Sociology and Religion.* New York: McGraw-Hill.

Veronis Suhler Stevenson Communication. 2003. Veronis Suhler Stevenson Communication Industry Forecast and Report: 2003 edition. New York: Veronis Suhler Stevenson Communications.

Veronis Suhler Stevenson Communication. 2004. Veronis Suhler Stevenson Communication Industry Forecast and Report: 2004 edition. New York: Veronis Suhler Stevenson Communications.

Vidaver, R. M. et al. 2000. "Women Subjects in NIH-Funded Clinical Research Literature: Lack of Progress in Both Representation and Analysis by Sex." *Journal of Women's Health Gender-Based Medicine* 9 (June):495–504.

Villarosa, Linda. 2002. "New Skill for Future Ob-Gyns: Abortion Training." *New York Times,* June 11, p. D6.

Voter News Service. 2000. "Breaking Down the Electorate." *Time* 156 (November 20):74.

Wages for Housework Campaign. 1999. *Wages for Housework Campaign.* Circular. Los Angeles.

Wagley, Charles, and Marvin Harris. 1958. *Minorities in the New World: Six Case Studies.* New York: Columbia University Press.

Waite, Linda. 2000. "The Family as a Social Organization: Key Ideas for the Twentieth Century." *Contemporary Sociology* 29 (May):463–469.

Waitzkin, Howard. 1986. *The Second Sickness: Contradictions of Capitalist Health Care.* Chicago: University of Chicago Press.

Walder, Andrew G. 2002. "Markets and Income Inequality in Rural China: Political Advantage in an Expanding Economy." *American Sociological Review* 67 (April):231–253.

Waldman, Amy. 2004a. "India Takes Economic Spotlight, and Critics and Unkind." *New York Times,* March 7, p. 3.

———. 2004b. "Low-Tech or High, Jobs Are Scarce in India's Boon." *New York Times,* May 6, p. A3.

———. 2004c. "What India's Upset Vote Reveals: The High Tech Is Skin Deep." *New York Times,* May 15, p. A5.

Waldrop, Judith, and Sharon M. Stern. 2003. *Disability Status: 2000.* Census 2000 Brief C2KBR-17. Washington, DC: U.S. Government Printing Office.

Wallace, Ruth A., and Alison Wolf. 1980. *Contemporary Sociological Theory.* Englewood Cliffs, NJ: Prentice Hall.

Wallerstein, Immanuel. 1974. *The Modern World System.* New York: Academic Press.

———. 1979a. *Capitalist World Economy.* Cambridge, England: Cambridge University Press.

———. 1979b. *The End of the World As We Know It: Social Science for the Twenty-First Century.* Minneapolis: University of Minnesota Press.

———. 2000. *The Essential Wallerstein.* New York: The New Press.

Wallerstein, Judith S., Judith M. Lewis, and Sandra Blakeslee. 2000. *The Unexpected Legacy of Deviance.* New York: Hyperion.

Wallerstein, Michael, and Bruce Western. 2000. "Unions in Decline? What Has Changed and Why." Pp. 355–377 in *Annual Review of Political Science* edited by Nelson Polsby. Palo Alto, CA: Annual Reviews.

Wal-Mart. 2001. "Wal-Mart News: Our Commitment to Communities." Accessed August 24, 2001 (www.walmartstores.com).

Wal-Mart Watch. 2003. *Wal-Mart Watch: Breaking News.* Accessed June 14 (www.walmartwatch.com).

Walsh, Mary Williams. 2001. "Reversing Decades-Long Trend, Americans Retiring Later in Life." *New York Times,* November 16, pp. A1, A13.

Walzer, Susan. 1996. "Thinking about the Baby: Gender and Divisions of Infant Care." *Social Problems* 43 (May):219–234.

Waxman, Henry A. 2003. "Politics and Science." Accessed January 8, 2004. (www.house.gov/reform/min/politicsandscience).

Weber, Max. [1913–1922] 1947. *The Theory of Social and Economic Organization.* Translated by A. Henderson and T. Parsons. New York: Free Press.

———. [1904] 1949. *Methodology of the Social Sciences.* Translated by Edward A. Shils and Henry A. Finch. Glencoe, IL: Free Press.

———. [1904] 1958a. *The Protestant Ethic and the Spirit of Capitalism.* Translated by Talcott Parsons. New York: Scribner.

———. [1916] 1958b. *The Religion of India: The Sociology of Hinduism and Buddhism.* New York: Free Press.

Wechsler, Henry, J. E. Lee, M. Kuo, M. Seibring, T. F. Nelson, and H. Lee. 2002. "Trends in College Binge Drinking During a Period of Increased Prevention Efforts: Findings from Four Harvard School of Public Health College Alcohol Surveys: 1993–2001." *Journal of American College Health* 50 (5):203–217.

Weeks, John R. 2002. *Population: An Introduction to Concepts and Issues.* 8th ed. Belmont, CA: Wadsworth.

Weiner, Tim 2003. "Wal-Mart Invades, and Mexico Gladly Surrenders." *New York Times,* December 6, pp. A1, A9.

Weinstein, Deena, and Michael A. Weinstein. 1999. "McDonaldization Enframed." Pp. 57–69 in *Resisting McDonaldization,* edited by Barry Smart. London: Sage.

Weinstein, Henry. 2002. "Airport Screener Curb Is Regretful." *Los Angeles Times,* November 16, pp. B1, B14.

———, Michael Finnegan, and Teresa Watanabe. 2001. "Racial Profiling Gains Support as Search Tactic." *Los Angeles Times,* September 24, pp. A1, M9.

Weinstein, Michael A., and Deena Weinstein. 2002. "Hail to the Shrub." *American Behavioral Scientist* 46 (December):566–580.

Wells-Barnett, Ida B. 1970. *Crusade for Justice: The Autobiography of Ida B. Wells.* Edited by Alfreda M. Duster. Chicago: University of Chicago Press.

West, Candace, and Don H. Zimmerman. 1983. "Small Insults: A Study of Interruptions in Cross Sex Conversations between Unacquainted Persons." Pp. 86–111 in *Language, Gender, and Society,* edited by Barrie Thorne, Cheris Kramarae, and Nancy Henley. Rowley, MA: Newbury House.

———. 1987. "Doing Gender." *Gender and Society* 1 (June):125–151.

White, Jonathan R. 2002. *Terrorism: An Introduction.* Belmont, CA: Wadsworth.

Whyte, William Foote. 1981. *Street Corner Society: Social Structure of an Italian Slum.* 3d ed. Chicago: University of Chicago Press.

Wickman, Peter M. 1991. "Deviance." Pp. 85–87 in *Encyclopedic Dictionary of Sociology,* 4th ed., edited by Dushkin Publishing Group. Guilford, CT: Dushkin.

Wilford, John Noble. 1997. "New Clues Show Where People Made the Great Leap to Agriculture." *New York Times,* November 18, pp. B9, B12.

Willet, Jeffrey G., and Mary Jo Deegan. 2000. "Liminality? and Disability: The Symbolic Rite of Passage of Individuals with Disabilities." Presented at the annual meeting of the American Sociological Association, Washington, DC.

Williams, Carol J. 1995. "Taking an Eager Step Back." *Los Angeles Times,* June 3, pp. A1, A14.

———. 1999. *Statement on Meet the Needs of Older Youth in Foster Care by Carol W. Williams.* Accessed May 5, 2004 (www.hhs.gov/asl/testify/t990309a.html).

Williams, Christine L. 1992. "The Glass Escalator: Hidden Advantages for Men in the 'Female' Professions." *Social Problems* 39 (3):253–267.

———. 1995. *Still a Man's World: Men Who Do Women's Work.* Berkeley: University of California Press.

Williams, David R., and Chiquita Collins. 2004. "Reparations." *American Behavioral Scientist* 47 (March):977–1000.

Williams, Robin M., Jr. 1970. *American Society.* 3d ed. New York: Knopf.

———, with John P. Dean and Edward A. Suchman. 1964. *Strangers Next Door: Ethnic Relations in American Communities.* Englewood Cliffs, NJ: Prentice Hall.

Williams, Wendy M. 1998. "Do Parents Matter? Scholars Need to Explain What Research Really Shows." *Chronicle of Higher Education* 45 (December 11):B6–B7.

Willie, Charles Vert, and Reinhard J. Reddick. 2003. *A New Look at Black Families,* 5th ed. Walnut Creek, CA: Alta Mira.

Wilson, Edward O. 1975. *Sociobiology: The New Synthesis.* Cambridge, MA: Harvard University Press.

———. 1978. *On Human Nature.* Cambridge, MA: Harvard University Press.

———. 2000. *Sociobiology: The New Synthesis.* Cambridge, MA: Belknap Press, Harvard University Press.

Wilson, John. 1973. *Introduction to Social Movements.* New York: Basic Books.

Wilson, Jolin J. 2000. *Children as Victims.* Washington, DC: U.S. Government Printing Office.

Wilson, Thomas C. 1995. "Vietnam-Era Military Service: A Test of the Class-Bias Thesis." *Armed Forces and Society* 21 (Spring):461–471.

Wilson, Warner, Larry Dennis, and Allen P. Wadsworth, Jr. 1976. "Authoritarianism Left and Right." *Bulletin of the Psychonomic Society* 7 (March):271–274.

Wilson, William Julius. 1980. *The Declining Significance of Race: Blacks and Changing American Institutions.* 2d ed. Chicago: University of Chicago Press.

———. 1987. *The Truly Disadvantaged: The Inner City, the Underclass and Public Policy* Chicago: University of Chicago Press.

———, ed. 1989. *The Ghetto Underclass: Social Science Perspectives.* Newbury Park, CA: Sage.

———. 1996. *When Work Disappears: The World of the New Urban Poor.* New York: Knopf.

———. 1999a. "Towards a Just and Livable City: The Issues of Race and Class." Address at the Social Science Centennial Conference, April 23. Chicago, IL: DePaul University.

———. 1999b. *The Bridge over the Racial Divide: Rising Inequality and Coalition Politics.* Berkeley: University of California Press.

———. 2003a. "Introduction to the 2003 Edition." In *Tally's Corner* by Elliot Liebow. Lanham, MD: Rowman and Littlefield.

———. 2003b. "There Goes the Neighborhood." *New York Times,* June 16, p. A23.

Winseman, Albert L. 2004. "Women in the Clergy: Perceptions and Reality." *GPTB Commentary.* Accessed April 14 (www.gallup.com).

Wirth, Louis. 1928. *The Ghetto.* Chicago: University of Chicago Press.

———. 1931. "Clinical Sociology." *American Journal of Sociology* 37 (July):49–60.

———. 1938. "Urbanism as a Way of Life." *American Journal of Sociology* 44 (July):1–24.

Wolf, Naomi. 1992. *The Beauty Myth: How Images of Beauty Are Used Against Women.* New York: Anchor.

Wolff, Edward N. 2002. *Top Heavy.* Updated ed. New York: New Press.

Wolraich, M., et al. 1998. "Guidance for Effective Discipline." *Pediatrics* 101 (April):723–728.

Wonacott, Peter. 2001. "China Examines Retailers in Fight Against Scams." *Wall Street Journal,* December 12, p. A10.

Wood, Daniel B. 2000. "Minorities Hope TV Deals Don't Just Lead to 'Tokenism.'" *Christian Science Monitor,* January 19.

Wood, Julia T. 1994. *Gendered Lives: Communication, Gender and Culture.* Belmont, CA: Wadsworth.

Woodard, Colin. 1998. "When Rote Learning Fails against the Test of Global Economy." *Christian Science Monitor,* April 15, p. 7.

Woodard, Emory H. 2000. *Media in the Home.* Philadelphia, PA: Amnesty Public Policy Center of the University of Pennsylvania.

World Bank. 1997. *World Development Report 1997: The State in a Changing World.* New York: Oxford University Press.

———. 2001. *World Development Report 2002. Building Instructions for Markets.* New York: Oxford University Press.

———. 2002. *World Development Indicators 2002.* Washington, DC: World Bank.

———. 2003a. *World Development Report 2003: Sustainable Development in a Dynamic World.* Washington, DC: World Bank.

———. 2003b. *Development Indicators 2003.* Washington, DC: World Bank.

———. 2003c. "Foreign Investment, Remittances Outpace Debt as Sources of Finance for Developing Countries: World Bank—Middle East and North Africa." News release, April 2. Accessed August 3 (www.worldbank.org).

World Development Forum. 1990. "The Danger of Television." 8 (July 15):4.

World Health Organization. 2000. *The World Health Report 2000. Health Systems: Improving Performance.* Geneva, Switzerland: WHO.

———. 2002. *Global Report on Health and Violence.* Geneva: WHO.

World Resources Institute. 1998. *1998–1999 World Resources: A Guide to the Global Environment.* New York: Oxford University Press.

Wright, Charles R. 1986. *Mass Communication: A Sociological Perspective.* 3d ed. New York: Random House.

Wright, Eric R., William P. Gronfein, and Timothy J. Owens. 2000. "Deinstitutionalization, Social Rejection, and the Self-Esteem of Former Mental Patients." *Journal of Health and Social Behavior* (March).

Wright, Erik Olin, David Hachen, Cynthia Costello, and Joy Sprague. 1982. "The American Class Structure." *American Sociological Review* 47 (December):709–726.

Yamagata, Hisashi, Kuang S. Yeh, Shelby Stewman, and Hiroko Dodge. 1997. "Sex Segregation and Glass Ceilings: A Comparative Statistics Model of Women's Career Opportunities in the Federal Government over a Quarter Century." *American Journal of Sociology* 103 (November):566–632.

Yax, Laura K. 1999. "National Population Projections." Accessed October 30, 1999 (www.census.gov/population/www/projections/natprog.html).

Yinger, J. Milton. 1970. *The Scientific Study of Religion.* New York: Macmillan.

Young, Alford A., Jr., and Donald R. Deskins, Jr. 2001. "Early Traditions of African-American Sociological Thought." Pp. 445–477 in *Annual Review of Sociology, 2001,* edited by Karen S. Cook and John Hagan. Palo Alto, CA: Annual Reviews.

Young, Gay. 1993. "Gender Inequality and Industrial Development: The Household Connection." *Journal of Comparative Family Studies* 124 (Spring):3–20.

Zang, Xiaowei. 2002. "Labor Market Segmentation and Income Inequality in Urban China." *Sociological Quarterly* 43 (1):27–44.

Zarembo, Alan. 2003. "Funding Studies to Suit Need." *Los Angeles Times,* December 7, pp. A1, A20.

———. 2004 "A Theater of Inquiry and Evil." *Los Angeles Times* (July 15), pp. A1, A24, A25.

Zelizer, Gerald L. 1999. "Internet Offers Only Fuzzy Cyberfaith, Not True Religious Expression." *USA Today,* August 19, p. 13A.

Zellner, William M. 1995. *Counter Cultures: A Sociological Analysis.* New York: St. Martin's Press.

———. 2001. *Extraordinary Groups: An Examination of Unconventional Lifestyles.* 7th ed. New York: Worth.

Zernike, Kate. 2002. "With Student Cheating on the Rise, More Colleges Are Turning to Honor Codes." *New York Times,* November 2, p. A10.

———. 2003. "Professors Protest as Students Debate." *New York Times,* April 4.

Zia, Helen. 2000. *Asian American Dreams: The Emergence of an American People.* New York: Farrar, Straus, and Giroux.

Zimbardo, Philip G. 1972. "Pathology of Imprisonment." *Society* 9 (April):4, 6, 8.

———. 2004. "Power turns good soldiers into 'bad apples.'" Boston Globe (May 9). Also available at www.prisonexp.org.

———, Craig Haney, W. Curtis Banks, and David Jaffe. 1974. "The Psychology of Imprisonments: Privation, Power, and Pathology." In *Doing Unto Others: Joining, Molding, Conforming, Helping, and Loving,* edited by Zick Rubin. Englewood Cliffs, NJ: Prentice Hall.

———, Ann L. Weber, and Robert Johnson. 2003. *Psychology: Core Concepts.* 4e. Boston: Allyn and Bacon.

Zola, Irving K. 1972. "Medicine as an Institution of Social Control." *Sociological Review* 20 (November):487–504.

———. 1983. *Socio-Medical Inquiries.* Philadelphia: Temple University Press.

Zweigenhaft, Richard L., and G. William Domhoff. 1998. *Diversity in the Power Elite: Have Women and Minorities Reached the Top?* New Haven, CT: Yale University Press.

Acknowledgments

Chapter 1

P. 2: Quotation from Barbara Ehrenreich. 2001. *Nickel and Dimed: On (Not) Getting By in America:* 197–198. © 2001 by Barbara Ehrenreich. Reprinted by permission of Henry Holt and Company, LLC.

P. 7: Figure 1-1 NAACP Legal Defense Fund. 2004. *Death Row USA*, January 2004. Used by permission of NAACP Legal Defense and Education Fund, Inc.

P. 21: Quotation from Carol Brooks Gardner. 1989. "Analyzing Gender in Public Places," *American Sociologist* 20 (Spring): 42–56. Copyright © 1989 by Transaction Publishers. Reprinted by permission of the publisher.

Chapter 2

P. 28: Quotation from Elijah Anderson. 1990. *Streetwise: Race, Class, and Change in an Urban Community:* 208, 220–221. Copyright 1990. Reprinted by permission of University of Chicago Press.

P. 33: Cartoon © The New Yorker Collection 1980 James Stevenson from www.cartoonbank.com. All rights reserved.

P. 34: Table 2-1 Author's analysis of General Social Survey 2002 in J. A. Davis et al. 2003. Used by permission of National Opinion Research Center.

P. 35: Figure 2-4 Author's analysis of General Social Survey 2002 in J. A. Davis et al. 2003. Used by permission of National Opinion Research Center.

P. 35: Cartoon, DOONESBURY © 1989 G. B. Trudeau. Reprinted with permission of UNIVERSAL PRESS SYNDICATE. All rights reserved.

P. 42: Figure in Box 2-2 from William Rau and Ann Durrand. 2000. "The Academic Ethic and College Grades: Does Hard Work Help Students to 'Make the Grade'?" *Sociology of Education* 2000, 73 (January): 26. Used by permission of the American Sociological Association and the authors.

P. 47: Figure 2-5 from Henry J. Kaiser Family Foundation. February 2003. Executive Summary of Sex on TV 3: 38, 40; a Biennial Report of the Kaiser Family Foundation (#3324). This information was reprinted with permission from the Henry J. Kaiser Family Foundation. The Kaiser Family Foundation, based in Menlo Park, CA, is a nonprofit, independent national health care philanthropy and is not associated with Kaiser Permanente or Kaiser Industries.

Chapter 3

P. 54: Excerpts from J. A. English-Lueck. 2002. *cultures@siliconvalley*. Copyright © 2002 by the Board of Trustees of the Leland Stanford Jr. University. All rights reserved. Used with the permission of Stanford University Press, www.sup.org.

P. 63: Figure 3-1 from John L. Allen. 2003. *Student Atlas of World Geography*, 3rd edition. Copyright © 2003 by The McGraw-Hill Companies, Inc. All rights reserved. Reprinted by permission of McGraw-Hill/Dushkin Publishing.

P. 67: Figure 3-1 as reported in Astin et al. 1994; Sax et al. 2003: 27. From UCLA Higher Education Research Institute. 2003. *The American Freshman: National Norms for Fall '01*. Reprinted by permission of UCLA.

P. 70: Figure 3-3 illustration by Jim Willis. 1996. "The Argot of Pickpockets," *New York Daily News* (No-

vember 19): 5. © New York Daily News, LP. Reprinted by permission.

P. 71: Cartoon by Sidney Harris. © 2004 by Sidney Harris. Used by permission.

P. 75: Figure 3-4 from U. S. English website www.us-english.org. Copyright, U. S. English, Inc. Used by permission.

Chapter 4

P. 80: Quotation from Mary Pattillo-McCoy. 1999. *Black Picket Fences: Privilege and Peril among the Black Middle Class:* 100–102. Copyright 1999. Reprinted by permission of University of Chicago Press.

P. 87: Quotation from Daniel Albas and Cheryl Albas. 1988. "Aces and Bombers: The Post-Exam Impression Management Strategies of Students." *Symbolic Interaction* 11 (Fall): 289–302. © 1988 by JAI Press. Reprinted by permission of University of CA Press and the authors. UC Press Journals, 2000 Center St., Suite 303, Berkeley, CA 94704-1223, (510) 642-6188.

P. 90: Table 4-2 from Tom Smith, 2003. "Coming of Age in 21st Century America: Public Attitudes Towards the Importance and Timing of Transition to Adulthood." Based on the 2002 General Social Survey of 1,398 people. Used by permission of National Opinion Research Center.

P. 95: Table 4-3 adapted from Jill Suitor, Staci A. Minyard, and Rebecca S. Carter, "Did You See What I Saw? Gender Difference in Perceptions of Avenues to Prestige Among Adolescents" *Sociological Inquiry* 71 (Fall 2001): 445, Table 2. University of Texas Press. Reprinted by permission of Blackwell Publishing Ltd.

P. 96: Figure 4-1 from "Growing up Wired: Survey on Youth and the Internet in the Silicon Valley." (#3340), The Henry J. Kaiser Family Foundation and the *San Jose Mercury News,* May 2003. This information was reprinted with permission from the Henry J. Kaiser Family Foundation. The Kaiser Family Foundation, based in Menlo Park, CA, is a nonprofit, independent national health care philanthropy and is not associated with Kaiser Permanente or Kaiser Industries.

Chapter 5

P. 103: Quotation from Philip G. Zimbardo. 1972. "Pathology of Imprisonment," *Society,* 9 (April): 4. Copyright © 1972 by Transaction Publishers. Reprinted by permission of Transaction Publishers. And Quotation from Philip G. Zimbardo, C. Haney, W. C. Banks, & D. Jaffe. 1974. "The Psychology of Imprisonment: Privation, Power, and Pathology." In Z. Rubin (Ed.), *Doing Unto Others: Explorations in Social Behavior:* 61–63. Used by permission of P. G. Zimbardo, Inc.

P. 111: Cartoon by TOLES © The Buffalo News. Reprinted with permission of UNIVERSAL PRESS SYNDICATE. All rights reserved.

P. 120: Cartoon © The New Yorker Collection 1986 Dean Vietor from www.cartoonbank.com. All rights reserved.

P. 124: Figure 5-2 from UNAIDS. 2003. *AIDS Epidemic Update,* December 2003: 37. Reprinted with permission from UNAIDS, World Health Organization, Geneva, Switzerland.

Chapter 6

P. 129, 130: Quotations from George Ritzer. 2004. *The McDonaldization of Society,* Revised New Century Edition. 2004a: 1–4, 10–11. Copyright © 2004. Reprinted by permission of Pine Forge Press, a Division of Sage Publications, Inc.

P. 132: Cartoon © The New Yorker Collection 1979 Robert Weber from www.cartoonbank.com. All rights reserved.

P. 141: Figure 6-1 from James Allan Davis and Tom W. Smith. 2001. *General Social Surveys 2001:* 347. Published by the Roper Center, Storrs, CT. Reprinted by permission of National Opinion Research Center.

Chapter 7

P. 151, 152: Quotations from Todd Gitlin. 2002. *Media Unlimited: How the Torrent of Images and Sounds Overwhelms Our Lives:* 5, 176–179. © 2002 by Todd Gitlin. Reprinted by permission of Henry Holt and Company, LLC.

P. 153: Figure 7-1 *The 2004 Communications Industry Forecast & Report*, Veronis Suhler Stevenson LLC. Used by permission.

P. 159: Quotation from Todd Gitlin. 2002. *Media Unlimited: How the Torrent of Images and Sounds Overwhelms Our Lives: 176–179.* © 2002 by Todd Gitlin. Reprinted by permission of Henry Holt and Company, LLC.

P. 167: Cartoon by Kirk Anderson. Used by permission of Kirk Anderson www.kirktoons.com.

P. 168: Figure 7-3 based on data from the Statistical Appendix of "TV Bloodbath Violence on Prime Time Broadcast TV" released 12/10/03. Used by permission of the Parents Television Council, Alexandria, VA.

Chapter 8

P. 173: Quotation from Susan A. Phillips. 1999. *Wallbangin': Graffiti and Gangs in L.A.:* 21, 23, 134–35. Copyright 1999. Used by permission of University of Chicago Press.

P. 179: Figure from Henry Wechsler et al. 2002. "Trends in College Binge Drinking During a Period of Increased Prevention Efforts," *Journal of American College Health,* 2002: 208. Copyright © 2002. Reprinted with permission of the Helen Dwight Reid Educational Foundation. Published by Heldref Publications, 1319 18th St. NW, Washington, DC 20036-1802.

P. 184: Figure 8-2 from "How Stuff Works, American Registry for Internet Numbers, Times Research." *Los Angeles Times,* April 30, 2003: A21. Copyright 2003, Los Angeles Times. All rights reserved. Reprinted with permission.

P. 186: Table 8-1 from Robert K. Merton. 1968. *Social Theory and Social Structure:* 194. Copyright © 1967, 1968 by Robert K. Merton; copyright renewed 1997 by Robert K. Merton. Adapted by permission of The Free Press, a division of Simon & Schuster Adult Publishing Group. All rights reserved.

P. 190: Figure based on data from Bureau of the Census 2003a, and data from the Death Penalty Information Center, "Facts About the Death Penalty" accessed 1/30/04 at www.deathpenaltyinfo.org. Used by permission.

P. 193: Cartoon by Sidney Harris. © 2004 by Sidney Harris. Used by permission.

P. 197: Cartoon by Dan Wasserman. Copyright, Tribune Media Services, Inc. All rights reserved. Reprinted with permission.

Chapter 9

P. 202: Quotation from Katherine S. Newman. 1999. *No Shame in My Game* 1999: 86-87. Knopf Publishing Group. Copyright © 1999 by Russell Sage Foundation. Used by permission of Alfred A. Knopf, a division of Random House, Inc.

P. 209: Figure 9-2 from Towers Perrin in Adam Bryant. 1999: Section 4, p.1. "American Pay Rattles Foreign Partners," *New York Times* (January 17): D1. The New York Times Graphics. Copyright © 1999. Reprinted by permission.

P. 213: Table 9-2 from James A. Davis et al. 2003. *General Social Surveys, 1972–2002.* Chicago: National Opinion Research Center. Used by permission of National Opinion Research Center.

P. 214: Figure 9-3 Data on Income 2003 from Carmen DeNavas-Walt, Bernadette D. Proctor, and Robert J. Mills. 2004. *Income, Poverty, and Health Insurance Coverage in the United States: 2003.* Washington, DC: U.S. Government Printing Office. Data on wealth from Edward N. Wolff. 2002. "Recent Trends in the Distribution of Household Wealth Ownership." In *Back to Shared Prosperity: The Growing Inequality of Wealth and Income in America,* ed. Ray Marshall. New York: M.E. Sharpe. Reprinted by permission of the author.

P. 216: Figure 9-4 from Timothy Smeeding, Lee Rainwater, and Gary Burtless. 2001. "United States Poverty in a Cross-National Context." *Focus,* newsletter of the Institute for Research on Poverty, 21 (Spring): 51. Used by permission of Institute for Research on Poverty.

P. 223: Figure 9-6 adapted in part from John R. Weeks. *Population: An Introduction to Concepts and Issues,* with InfoTrac 8th ed.: 22–23. Belmont, CA: Wadsworth. © 2002. Reprinted with permission of Wadsworth, a division of Thomson Learning, www.thomsonrights.com. Fax (800) 730-2215. And adapted in part from Carl Haub. 2003. *World Population Data Sheet 2003.* Used by permission of Population Reference Bureau.

P. 226: Table 9-4 adapted in part from *Fortune.* 2003. "Fortune's Global 500" Fortune, July 21. © 2003 Time Inc. All rights reserved. And adapted in part from United Nations Development Programme. 2002. *Human Development Report 2002: Deepening Democracy in a Fragmented World:* 190–193. Copyright © 2002 by the United Nations Development Programme. Used by permission of Oxford University Press, Inc.

P. 227: Cartoon by Joel Pett. © Joel Pett, Lexington Herald-Leader. All rights reserved. Used by permission.

P. 228: Figure 9-8 based on data from World Bank. 2003a. *2003 World Development Indicators:* 64–66; Table 2-8. © World Bank 2003. International Bank for Reconstruction and Development/The World Bank. Used by permission.

P. 234: Cartoon by Mike Konopacki, Huck/Konopacki Labor Cartoons. Used with permission.

Chapter 10

P. 240: Quotation from Helen Zia. 2000. *Asian American Dreams: The Emergence of an American People.* Copyright © 2000 by Helen Zia. Reprinted by permission of Farrar, Straus & Giroux, LLC.

P. 248: Figure 10-2 from Southern Poverty Law Center. 2003. "Active Hate Groups in the United States," *2003 Intelligence Report* (Spring): 34–35. Used by permission of Southern Poverty Law Center.

P. 258: Figure 10-4 from John R. Logan. 2001. *From Many Shores: Asians in Census 2000.* Accessed November 29, 2001 at http://mumford1.dyndns.org/cen2000/AsianPop. Used by permission of Lewis Mumford Center for Comparative Urban and Regional Research, SUNY at Albany, NY (www.albany.edu/mumford).

Chapter 11

P. 271: Quotation from Naomi Wolf. *The Beauty Myth.* 1992: 9–10, 12. Used by permission of Abner Stein Literary Agency for Naomi Wolf.

P. 274: Table 11-1 from Joyce McCarl Nielsen, et al. 2000. "Gendered Heteronormativity: Empirical Illustrations in Everyday Life," *Sociological Quarterly* 41 (No. 2): 287. © 2000 by the Midwest Sociological Society. Reprinted by permission of the author and UC Press Journals, 2000 Center St., Suite 303, Berkeley, CA 94704-1223, (510) 642-6188.

P. 282: Cartoon by Ed Stein. Reprinted by permission of Rocky Mountain News.

P. 284: Figure 11-3 from James T. Bond et al. 1998. *The 1997 National Study of the Changing Work Force.* New York: Families and Work Institute: 40–41, 44–45. Copyright Families and Work Institute (www.familiesandwork.org). Reprinted by permission.

P. 294: Figure 11-6 from National Abortion and Reproductive Rights Action League Foundation. 2001. *Who Decides? A State-by-State Review of Abortion and Reproductive Rights,* 10th ed.: 268. Washington, DC: NARAL Foundation. Used by permission of NARAL.

Chapter 12

P. 300: Quotation from Cornel West and Sylvia Ann Hewlett. 1998. *The War against Parents: 21–22.* Copyright © 1998 by Sylvia Ann Hewlett and Cornel West. Reprinted by permission of Houghton Mifflin Company. All rights reserved.

P. 302: Figure 12-1 in part from Joseph A. McFalls, Jr. 2003. "Population: A Lively Introduction." 4e, *Population Bulletin* 58 (December): 23. Used by permission of the Population Reference Bureau.

P. 308: Quotation from Rebecca Segall. 1998. "Sikh and Ye Shall Find," *Village Voice* 43 (December 15): 48; 53. Used by permission of Rebecca Segall.

P. 308: Figure 12-2 from United Nations Population Division. 2001a. *World Marriage Patterns 2000.* Accessed September 13, 2002 at www.undp.org/popin/wdtrends/worldmarriage.patterns2000.pdf. Used by permission of United Nations Population Division, New York.

P. 314: Cartoon by Signe Wilkinson. Used by permission of Signe Wilkinson, Cartoonists & Writers Syndicate/www.cartoonweb.com.

P. 321: Figure 12-6 from Human Rights Campaign accessed at www.hrc.org, "Statewide Anti-Discrimination Laws and Policies" and "Statewide Discriminatory Marriage Laws." Used with permission.

Chapter 13

P. 326: Quotation from Vine Deloria, Jr. 1999. *For This Land: Writings on Religion in America: 273–275, 281.* Copyright © 1998. Reproduced by permission of Routledge/Taylor & Francis Group Inc. and the author.

P. 328: Figure 13-1 from John L. Allen. 2003. *Student Atlas of World Geography,* 3rd edition. Copyright © 2003 by The McGraw-Hill Companies, Inc. All rights reserved. Reprinted by permission of McGraw-Hill/Dushkin Publishing.

P. 337: Figure 13-2 from Ronald Inglehart and Wayne Baker. 2000. "Modernization, Cultural Change, and the Persistence of Traditional Values," *American Sociological Review* 65 (February): 19–51; Table 7, p. 47. Used by permission of the American Sociological Association and the authors.

P. 340: Figure 13-2 from D. Jones et al. 2002. Reprinted with permission from *Religious Congregations and Membership in the United States: 2000.* (Nashville: Glenmary Research Center, 2002). © Association of Statisticians of American Religious Bodies. All rights reserved.

P. 347: Cartoon by Kirk Anderson. Used by permission of Kirk Anderson www.kirktoons.com.

P. 355: Cartoon by Steve Breen. Used by permission of Copley News Service.

Chapter 14

P. 360: Quotation from Richard L. Zweigenhaft and G. William Domhoff. 1998. *Diversity in the Power Elite:* 176–77, 192, 194. Yale University Press. Copyright Richard L. Zweigenhaft. Reprinted by permission of the author.

P. 365: Cartoon by Tony Auth. © 2002 The Philadelphia Inquirer. Reprinted with permission of UNIVERSAL PRESS SYNDICATE. All rights reserved.

P. 369: Cartoon by Gary Varvel. Used by permission of Creators Syndicate.

P. 369: Table 14-1 from James Allan Davis and Tom W. Smith. 2003. *General Social Surveys, 1972–2002.* Storrs, CT: The Roper Center. Reprinted by permission of National Opinion Research Center.

P. 372: Figure 14-1 from G. William Domhoff. 2001. *Who Rules America,* 4th ed.: 96. © 2001 by The McGraw-Hill Companies, Inc. Reproduced by permission of the publisher.

P. 374: Figure 14-2 from 1971–2004 The Gallup Pole. All rights reserved. Reprinted with permission from The Gallup Organization.

P. 383: Quotation from Sheryl Stolberg. 1995. "Affirmative Action Gains Often Come at a High Cost," *Los Angeles Times* (March 29): A14. Copyright 1995 Los Angeles Times. Reprinted by permission.

P. 384: Cartoon by Mike Peters. © Reprinted with special permission of King Features Syndicate.

Chapter 15

P. 389: Quotation from Mitchell Duneier. 1999. *Sidewalk.* Copyright © 1999 by Mitchell Deneier. Reprinted by permission of Farrar, Straus & Giroux, LLC.

P. 397: Cartoon by Signe Wilkinson/Philadelphia Daily News. Used by permission of Cartoonists & Writers Syndicate.

P. 400: Table 15-2 based on Gideon Sjoberg. 1960. *The Preindustrial City: Past and Present: 323–328.* Copyright © 1960 by The Free Press; copyright renewed 1968 by Gideon Sjoberg. Adapted with permission of The Free Press, a division of Simon & Schuster Adult Publishing Group. All rights reserved. And based on E. Barbara Phillips. 1996. *City Lights: Urban-Suburban Life in the Global Society,* 2/e: 132–135. Copyright © 1981 by E. Barbara Phillips and Richard T. LeGates, 1996 by E. Barbara Phillips. Used by permission of Oxford University Press, Inc.

P. 401: Figure 15-3 from Chauncy Harris and Edward Ullmann. 1945. "The Nature of Cities," *Annals of the American Academy of Political and Social Science,* 242 (November): 13. Reprinted by permission of American Academy of Political and Social Science, Philadelphia.

P. 412: Figure 15-4 from Carl Haub. 2003. *World Population Data Sheet 2003.* Used by permission of Population Reference Bureau.

P. 417: Cartoon by Jim Borgman. © Reprinted with special permission of King Features Syndicate.

P. 418: Figure 15-6 from World Bank. 2003. *World Development Indicators 2003.* Published by the World Bank. Used by permission.

Chapter 16

P. 424: Quotation from Howard Rheingold. 2003. *Smart Mobs, The Next Social Revolution: Transforming Cultures and Communities in the Age of Instant Access:* 157, 158, viii. © 2003 Howard Rheingold. Reprinted by permission of Perseus Books Publishers, a member of Perseus Books LLC.

P. 439: Cartoon © 1985 Carol * Simpson. Reprinted by permission of Carol * Simpson Productions.

Photo Credits

Chapter 16

p. 423: Stuart Isett/Polaris; p. 426: Los Angeles Times Photo by Lawrence K. Ho; p. 430 top: Reuters/Corbis; p. 430 bottom: AP/Wide World Photos; p. 432: Getty Images; p. 433: Jim West; p. 434: AP/Wide World Photos; p. 436: AP/Wide World Photos; p. 437: Troy Duster

Table of Contents

Chapter 1: Spencer Ainsley/The Image Works
Chapter 2: 2003 The Gallup Poll
Chapter 3: @2004 Peter Menzel/Material World
Chapter 4: AP/Wide World Photos
Chapter 5: AP/Wide World Photos
Chapter 6: AP/Wide World Photos
Chapter 7: Stevens Frederic/SIPA Press
Chapter 8: AP/Wide World Photos

Chapter 9: AP/Wide World Photos
Chapter 10: Courtesy of American Indian College Fund
Chapter 11: Jerry Alexander/Getty Images
Chapter 12: Mark Richards/PhotoEdit, Inc.
Chapter 13: Lindsay Hebberd/Corbis
Chapter 14: Basel Action Network
Chapter 15: Jeff Greenberg/The Image Works
Chapter 16: AP/Wide World Photos

Name Index

Page numbers followed by f refer to figures
Page numbers followed by t refer to tables

Subject Index

Alienation, 136, 148, 446
All My Children (soap opera), 61
Allah, 329
AltaVista (search engine), 157
Alzheimer's Association, 416
Amalgamation, of racial groups, 253, 268, 446
America Online (AOL), 442
American Academy of Pediatrics, 95, 154, 155, 177
American apartheid, 404
American Apartheid (Denton and Massey), 254–255
American Association of Aardvark Aficionados, 140–141
American Association of Retired Persons (AARP), 292–293
American Association of University Women, 94
American Bar Association, 305
American Civil Liberties Union (ACLU), 246, 442
American Indian College Fund, 239
American Indians. *See* Native Americans
American Institute of Graphic Arts, 359
American Jewish Committee, 263
American Jewish Congress, 140
American Library Association, 442
American Lung Association, 41
American Medical Association (AMA), 417, 432
American Psychiatric Association (APA), 413
American Society of Newspaper Editors, 442
American Sociological Association, 21, 25, 26, 218, 431, 437
    Code of Ethics, 41, 43, 48
American Sociological Society, 13
Americans with Disabilities Act, 143
Amish, 92, 93, 339
Amnesty International, 376
Amway corporation, 139
Angola, iii,
    gross national income, per capita, 223f
Animals, and social deprivaton, 82–83
Animism, tribal, 328f
Anomie, 10, 23, 185, 198
Anomie theory of deviance, 185–186, 198, 446
    modes of individual adaptation, 185
Anthrax, 436, 437
Anthropology, study of, 6
Anti-Defamaton League (ADL), 263
Anti-Semitism, 263, 268, 446
Anticipatory socialization, 91–92, 100, 446
Antiwar protests, 426, 427, 428
AOL Time Warner, 163
Apartheid, 254–255, 268, 446
    American, 404
Apollo 13 (film), 160
Appearance, physical, and gender, 180, 181
Arabic language, 62
Arabs, Arab Americans, 6
    discrimination, 439
    racial profiling, 178, 188
    stereotyping, after September 11, 2001, 246, 247
    U. S. population, by state, 247
Arapesh people, 276
Argot, 69, 70, 76, 446
Arizona, 278, 370
    abortion funding, 294f
    Arab American population, 247

bilingual education in, 75
cohabitation in, 318f
educational level, 32
elderly population, projected, 291f
household income, 32
medical use of marijuana, 178f
Arkansas
    cohabitation in, 318f
    educational level, 32
    elderly population, projected, 291f
    gay marriage laws, 321f
    household income, 32
    medical use of marijuana, 178f
Arranged marriage, 307, 308
Artifacts, cultural, 55, 61, 432–433
Arunta (Australian tribe), 10
Ascribed status, 106–107, 126, 136, 203–204, 446
    and social class, 205, 206
Asia. *See also* under individual countries
    abortion rights in, 295
    AIDS in, 124f, 396
    environmental issues, 380, 381
Asian American Dreams (Zia), 240–241
Asian Americans, 240–241, 258–260, 289
    Chinese, 243, 258f, 259
    cohabitation, 317
    as crime victims, 245
    elderly, 288, 290
    family relationships, 309
    Internet access, 440f
    Japanese, 258f, 259–260
    in the media, 157, 158
    as percentage of workforce, 377f
    percentage without health insurance, 414f
    relative economic position, 257t
    single-parent families, increase over time, 310f
    in U. S. population, 242t, 243
        projected, 243f
Asset-based community development (ABCD), 405, 406, 420, 446
Asset-Basted Community Development Institute, 405
Assimilation, 73–74, 253–254, 268, 446
Associated Press, 49, 382, 436
ATMs (automated teller machines), 438
Attention deficit disorder (ADD), 353
Audience, media, 162–163
Augusta National Golf Club, 430
Austin Powers: The Spy Who Shagged Me (film), 156
Australia, iii
    absolute poverty, 216t
    AIDS in, 124f
    crime rate, 195
    culture, 64
    percentage of people ever married, ages 20-24, 308f
Austria, iii
    abortion rights in, 295
    culture, 61
    gross national income, per capita, 223f
    percentage of college graduates, 344f
Authority, 386, 446
    obedience to, 176–177
    types of, 367–368

Baath Socialist Party, 94
Baby boom, 397
Bachelor, The (TV show), 157
Bahamas, 392
Bakke case, Supreme Court, 383
Bali, cockfights in, 6
Bangalore, India, 378
Bangladesh, iii
    gross national income, per capita, 223f
    income distribution, 228f
Barbie doll, 60
Bart Simpson, 360–361
Battle Royale (film), 167
BBC News, 165, 441
Beauty myth, 180
Beauty Myth, The (Wolf), 271–272
Belarus, gross national income, per capita, 223f
Belgium, iii
    abortion rights in, 295
    gross national income, per capita, 223f
    same-sex partnerships, 321
Belize, iii, 381
Bell v. Maryland, 263
Berkeley Wellness Letter, 311
Betsileo people, of Madagascar, 301
Beverly Hills 90210, 162
Bharatiya Janata Party, 343
Bhutan, iii, 166, 183
Bible, The, 174, 329, 354
Bilateral descent, 303, 323, 446
Bilingual education, 73, 261
    laws, by state, 75
Bilingualism, 73–76, 261, 446
Bill of Rights, 368
Binge drinking, 179
Biological weapons, 436
Biology, and social behavior, 61–62
    theories of deviance, 184
Biotechnology, 434–435
Bioterrorism, 436, 436–437
Biracial people, 243–244
Birth control, 391, 426
    and "day after" pill, 293
    in developing countries, 395
    and social change, 433
Birthrate, 393, 420, 446
Black Entertainment Television (BET), 158, 163
Black Picket Fences (Pattillo-McCoy), 80–81
Black power, 256–257, 268, 446
Black separatist hate groups, in United States, 248f
Blockbuster stores, 163
Blogs, 157
Bolivia, iii
    place in global economy, 224f
Borderlands, between U. S. and Mexico, 231–232, 236, 446
Bororo people, West Africa, 276
Bosnia-Herzegovina, iii, 393
Botswana, iii
    disabled in, 108
    gross national income, per capita, 223f
Bourgeosie, 207, 236, 446
Bowling for Columbine (film), 196
BP-British Petroleum, 226t
Brady Hand Gun Violence Protection Act, 196

Occupational prestige, and gender, 213
Occupations, ranked by prestige, 213t
Office of Justice Programs, 193
Office of Naval Research, 375
Offshoring service jobs, 378, 416
Ohio
    Arab American population, 247
    bilingual education in, 75
    cohabitation in, 318f
    educational level, 32
    elderly population, projected, 291f
    gay marriage laws, 321f
    household income, 32
    medical use of marijuana, 178f
Oil spill, Exxon Valdez, 43–44, 380
Oklahoma
    abortion funding, 294f
    Arab American population, 247
    bilingual education in, 75
    cohabitation in, 318f
    educational level, 32
    elderly population, projected, 291f
    gay marriage laws, 321f
    household income, 32
    medical use of marijuana, 178f
Old age, as master status, 286
Oligarchy, 138
    and labor unions, 146
Olin Center for Law, Harvard University, 43
Olympic Games, Los Angeles, 1984, 380
Oman, iii
    gross national income, per capita, 223f
On the Origin of Species (Darwin), 10
One-drop rule, 243–244
open system, 220, 450
Operation Pipeline, 251
Operational definition, 30, 51, 450
Opinion leaders, 162–163, 170, 450
Oprah Winfrey Show, 166
Oral History Society, 51
Oregon
    abortion funding, 294f
    Arab American population, 247
    bilingual education in, 75
    cohabitation in, 318f
    educational level, 32
    elderly population, projected, 291f
    gay marriage laws, 321f
    household income, 32
    medical use of marijuana, 178f
Organ transplantation, 409
Organic solidarity, 118, 126, 450
Organizational culture, 139–144
    at NASA, 141–142
Organizational restructuring, 142–144
Organizations, formal, 135–144
    definition, 135
Organized crime, 192–193, 199, 450
Origin of the Family, Private Property, and the State (Engels), 277
Other America, The (Harrington), 121
Out-groups, and in-groups, 132–133, 148, 450
Outsourcing, of jobs, 378, 416
Overweight people, as deviant, 180

P

Pacific Islanders
    percentage without health insurance, 414f
    single-parent families, increase over time, 310f
Pakistan, iii
    gross national income, per capita, 223f
    infant mortality rate, 412f
    place in global economy, 224f
    women in, 227
Pan Arab Research Center, 37
Panama, ii
    gross national income, per capita, 223f
    place in global economy, 224f
Papua New Guinea, ii
    gross national income, per capita, 223f
Paramount Pictures, 163
Parent, role of, 310–311
Partial-birth abortions, 294–295
Participant observation, 2–3, 28, 29, 38
Passion of The Christ, The (film), 7
Paternity testing, 299
Patriarchy, 303, 324, 450
Patrilineal descent, 303, 324, 450
Patriot Act, 68, 178, 376–377, 442
PDAs (personal digital assistants), 162
Peace, 375–376, 386, 450
Peace Corps, 141
Pearl Harbor attacked, 259
Peer groups, as agents of socialization, 174
Pennsylvania
    abortion funding, 294f
    Arab American population, 247
    bilingual education in, 75
    educational level, 32
    elderly population, 290
    elderly population, projected, 291f
    gay marriage laws, 321f
    household income, 32
    medical use of marijuana, 178f
"Pentagon Papers, The" (New York Times), 374
People magazine, 154, 155t
People's Republic of China. *See* China
Periphery nations, and core nations. *See* World systems analysis
Personal Responsibility and Work Opportunity Reconciliation Act, 233
Personality, 81, 100, 450
Peru, ii
    gross national income, per capita, 223f
Peter principle, 138, 148, 450
Pew Research Center, 383
Philippines, ii
    gross national income, per capita, 223f
    multinational corporations in, 225
    number of U. S. immigrants from, 266f
    place in global economy, 224f
    social movements, 424
Phish (band), 70
Physicians, as gatekeepers, 410
Piracy, Internet, 69, 181, 184, 439
Pizza delivery workers, 131
Place on the Corner, A (Anderson), 29
Plagiarism. *See* Cheating, academic
Plague, The (Camus), 123
Plastic surgery, 181
Play stage, of socialization, 85

Pledge of Allegiance, 355
Pluralism, racial and ethnic, 255, 268, 450
Pluralist model, of power relations, 373–374, 386, 450
Poland, iii
    gross national income, per capita, 223f
    percentage of people ever married, ages 20-24, 308f
    Solidarity movement, 364
Policemen, inn labor unions, 146
Polish Americans, 263, 403
Political behavior, 368–370
Political systems, 361, 387, 451
Politics, 387, 451
    definition, 367
    and the media, 152, 158
Polls, 33, 36
    in Baghdad, Iraq, 37
Pollution, 379–380
Polyandry, 301, 302, 324, 451
Polygamy, 302, 324, 451
Polygyny, 302, 324, 451
Polytheism, 330
Poor people. *See also* Poverty
    and abortion rights, 294
    in the suburbs, 406–407
    working, 203
Popularity, in adolescence, 95
Population Bomb, The (Ehrlich and Ehrlich), 392
Population growth, 380, 391, 393–394
    in developing countries, 394–395
    over time, 394t
Population patterns, worldwide, 393–394
Population pyramid, 395, 396, 421, 451
Population Reference Bureau, 396
Population, stable, in U. S., 397, 398
Population, study of, 390–391
Pornography, 160–161
    Internet, 441
Portugal, iii
    gross national income, per capita, 223f
    percentage of college graduates, 344f
    same-sex partnerships, 321
Postindustrial cities, 399, 400t, 421, 451
Postindustrial societies, 121–122, 122t, 126, 433, 451
    and labor unions, 144–146
Postmodern societies, 121–122, 122t, 127, 451
    and communication, 165–166
    and labor unions, 144–146
Poverty, 215–219
    absolute vs. relative, 215
    and the elderly, 290, 293
    explaining, 217, 218–220
        conflict perspective, 217
        functionalist perspective, 217–218
        Weber's view, 218–219
    feminization of, 215, 280–281, 309
    and health and illness, 414
    and healthcare, 219
    and internet access, 219
    and life chances, 218–219
    minorities in, 216–217
    and race, 233, 255
    and unemployment, 218
Power, 367, 387, 451
Power elite, 360–361, 371, 387, 451

Applications of Sociology's Major Theoretical Approaches

Sociology provides comprehensive coverage of the major sociological perspectives. The summary table below includes a sample of the topics in this text that have been explored using these approaches. The numbers in parentheses indicate the pertinent chapters.

FUNCTIONALIST PERSPECTIVE

Defined and explained (1)
Adoption (12)
AIDS and social networks (5)
Anomie theory of deviance (8)
Bilingualism (3)
Bureaucratization of schools (13)
Culture (3, 13)
Davis and Moore's view of stratification (9)
Disengagement theory of aging (11)
Dominant ideology (3)
Durkheim's view of deviance (8)
Dysfunctions of racism (10)
Electronic surveillance (16)
Ethnocentrism (3)
Family (12)
Formal organizations (6)
Gans's functions of poverty (9)
Gay marriage (12)
Gender stratification (11)
Health and illness (15)
Human ecology (14)
Immigration (10)
In-groups and out-groups (6)
Integrative function of religion (13)
Internet (16)
Media and social norms (7)
Media and socialization (7)
Media and status conferral (7)
Media promotion of consumption (7)
Multinational corporations (9)
Narcotizing effect of the media (7)
Racial prejudice and discrimination (10)
Social change (13, 16)
Social control (8, 13)
Social institutions (5)
Social networks (5)
Socialization in schools (4, 13)
Sports (1)
Subcultures (3)
Urban ecology (15)
Value neutrality (2)

CONFLICT PERSPECTIVE

Defined and explained (1)
Abortion (11)
Access to health care (15)
Access to technology (16)
Adoption (12)

Affirmative action (14)
Age stratification (11)
AIDS crisis (5)
Bilingualism (3)
Bureaucratization of schools (13)
Capitalism (13, 14)
Corporate welfare (9)
Correspondence principle (13)
Credentialism (13)
Culture (3)
Day care funding (4)
Deviance (8)
Disability as a master status (5)
Domestic violence (12)
Dominant ideology (3, 7, 9)
Downsizing (14)
Elite model of the U.S. power structure (14)
Environmental issues (14)
Ethnocentrism (3)
Exploitation theory of racial subordination (10)
Family (12)
Gay marriage (12)
Gender stratification (11)
Gender equity in education (13)
Gun control (8)
Hidden curriculum (13)
Immigration (10)
Iron Law of Oligarchy (6)
Labor unions (6)
Marx's view of stratification (9)
Media gatekeeping (7)
Media stereotypes (7)
Media violence (7)
Medicalization of society (15)
Model minority (10)
Multinational corporations (9)
New urban sociology (15)
Poverty (9)
Privacy and technology (16)
Racial profiling (10)
Racism and health (15)
Religion and social control (13)
Social change (16)
Social control (8)
Social institutions (5)
Sports (1)
Subcultures (3)
Tracking (13)
Victimless crimes (8)
White-collar crime (8)
World systems analysis (9, 15)

INTERACTIONIST PERSPECTIVE

Defined and explained (1)
Activity theory of aging (11)

Affirmative action (14)
AIDS and its impact (5)
Charismatic authority (14)
Conspicuous consumption (9)
Contact hypothesis (10)
Differential association (8)
Dramaturgical approach (4, 14)
Electronic communication (7, 16)
Family (12)
Gay marriage (12)
Gender stratification (11)
Health and illness (15)
Human relations approach (6)
Media violence (7)
Negotiated order (5)
Privacy and technology (7, 16)
Racial stereotyping (10)
Routine activities theory (8)
School prayer (13)
Small groups (6)
Social institutions (5)
Sports (1)
Tattoo symbols of 9/11 (1)
Teacher-expectancy effect (13)
Teenage pregnancy (12)
Unions (6)

FEMINIST PERSPECTIVE

Defined and explained (1)
Day care funding (4)
Domestic violence (12)
Dominant ideology (3)
Ethnographic research (2)
Family (12)
Gender stratification (11)
Language (3)
Media stereotypes (7)
Media violence (7)
Pornography (7)
Rape (8)
Sports (1)
Victimless crimes (8)
Women in public (1)

LABELING THEORY

Defined and explained (8)
AIDS and labeling (5, 15)
Disabilities and labeling (5)
Health and illness (15)
Presentation of the self (4)
Racial profiling (10)
Societal reaction approach (8)
Teacher-expectancy effect (13)
Victimless crimes (8)